Formed by a consortium of four famous British shipping lines in August 1965 to modernise their traditional cargo liner trading interests Overseas Containers Limited is today among the world's foremost container through transport operators.

OCL's initial service between Europe and Australia commenced in March 1969. Today the Group's trade-route network links four continents. OCL container services operate between Europe/Australia and New Zealand, Europe/the Far East and Europe/Southern Africa while, through Overseas Containers (Pacific) Limited, the Group has a major interest in four container services operating in the Pacific Basin Region.

The OCL Group currently operates a fleet of 17 modern containerships, employs over 40,000 containers and transports nearly a quarter of a million container loads of cargo annually. OCL's massive and continuing investment in the hardware and systems required to realise the concepts of efficient world-wide distribution is instrumental in maintaining Britain's traditional role among the leading maritime trading nations.

With Compliments

Overseas Containers Limited

Beagle House,
Braham Street,
London E1 8EP.
Telephone 01-488 1313
Telex 883947

Addresses

UK

Head Office	Overseas Containers Limited, Beagle House, Braham St., London E1 8EP Tel 01-488 1313 Telex 883947
South East Region	Box Lane, Barking, Essex IG11 0SG Tel 01-593 8181 Telex 897388
South West Region	Dukes Keep, Marsh Lane, Southampton SO9 4DA Tel 0703 35200 Telex 47384
South Wales	Agents for OCL, Couch-Burgess Ltd, 6 & 6a Wind St., Swansea SA1 10B Tel 0792 53926 Telex 48236
Midland Region	College Road, Perry Barr, Birmingham B44 8DR Tel 021-356 6933 Telex 338082
NE Region Leeds	Valley Farm Way, Wakefield Rd., Stourton, Leeds LS10 1SE Tel 0532 712255 Telex 557332
Newcastle	3rd Floor, Archbold House, Archbold Terrace, Jesmond, Newcastle-on-Tyne NE2 1DR Tel 0632 810261
Liverpool Region	14th Floor, Silkhouse Court, Tithebarn St., Liverpool L2 2LZ Tel 051-236 9911 Telex 628154
Cargo & Movements	Orrell Lane, Bootle, Lancs L20 6NT Tel 051-521 1011 Telex 627006
Manchester Region	Tanners Bridge House, Fountain St., Manchester M2 2AH Tel 061-228 6373 Telex 666414
Cargo & Movements	Barton Dock Rd., Barton Dock Estate (West) Urmston, Manchester M31 2LP Tel 061-747 7000 Telex 668422
Scottish Region	Gartsherrie Road, Coatbridge, Lanarkshire ML5 2DY Scotland Tel 0236 24922 Telex 778577
OCL EUROPEAN OFFICE	Westzeedijk 487, Rotterdam, Holland Tel 76 98 11 Telex 25210

IRELAND

Belfast	W.E. Williames & Co. Ltd, 35/39 Middlepath St., Belfast BT5 4BG Tel 55411 Telex 747166
Dublin	George Bell (Liner Agencies) Ltd, Bell House, Montague St., Dublin 2 Tel 783200 Telex 30381

AUSTRALIA

Head Office	Overseas Containers Australia Pty. Ltd, 38 Bridge Street, Sydney NSW 2000 Tel 20-575 Telex 21258

Australian Marketing Addresses

Sydney	Overseas Containers Australia Pty. Ltd, 220 George Street, Sydney NSW 2000 Tel 20-589 Telex 21766
Melbourne	Overseas Containers Australia Pty. Ltd, 29 Market Street, Melbourne 3000 Tel 62-7721 Telex 31449
Brisbane	Overseas Containers Australia Pty. Ltd, 190 Edward Street, Brisbane 4001 Tel 299-1022 Telex 40126
Adelaide	Overseas Containers Australia Pty. Ltd, 3 Santo Parade, Port Adelaide SA 5015 Tel 47-1922 Telex 82726
Fremantle	Overseas Containers Australia Pty. Ltd, 41 Cliff Street, Fremantle WA 6160 Tel 335-3811 Telex 93451
Canberra	Overseas Containers Australia Pty. Ltd, Industry House, Cnr National Circuit & Brisbane Barton ACT 2600, Canberra Tel 73-2511

Agents

Hobart	Associated Shipping Agency Pty. Ltd, 115 Collins Street, Hobart TAS 7000 Tel 232-744 Telex 58086
Townsville	Associated Shipping Agency Pty. Ltd, 17 Archer Street, Townsville OLD 4810 Tel 71-6188 Telex 47100

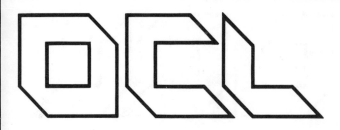

Europe/Far East Trade

CONTINENT *Agents*

Germany
M. & O. Container Transport GmbH
Postfach, 1046, Ansgaritrankpforte 1,
D-2800 Bremen 1, Germany.
Tel 31731 Telex 245928

Holland
General Steam Transport Company,
Westzeedijk 487, Rotterdam.
Tel 769711 Telex 21481

Belgium
NV General Steam (Belgium) SA,
St. Paulusstraat 23, Antwerp 2000.
Tel 327946 Telex 31365

Switzerland
Jacky Maeder Ltd.,
Wallstrasse 8, CH-4002, Basle.
Tel 236688 Telex 63659

France
Hernu Peron,
15 Rue de Nancy, 75-Paris 10, France.
Tel 203 99 60 Telex 680871

Austria
Enrico Sperco & Sohn AG,
1 Karntnerstrasse 23, 1015 Wien, Austria.
Tel 52 46 56 Telex 11834

Finland
OY Finnlines Ltd.,
Korkeavuorenkatu 32,
PO Box 218 00131 Helsinki-13.
Tel 64 98 11 Telex 12462

Sweden – Stockholm
Emil R. Boman A/B,
Box 2054, S-103, 12 Stockholm 2, Sweden
Tel (08)-249500 Telex 19348 Bomans S

Sweden – Malmo
Frostenson & Larsson A/B,
PO Box 147, S-201 21, Malmo 1, Sweden.
Tel 727 40 Telex 32338

Sweden – Gothenburg
Emil R. Boman A/B,
Box 99, 401 21 Gothenburg.
Tel 540100 Telex 21380

Norway
Linjeagenturer AS,
Torvgaten 18, N-Oslo 1, Norway.
Tel 42-07-80 Telex 11112

Denmark
Hecksher & Son Succsrs,
63 Bredgade, DK 1260 Copenhagen K,
Denmark.
Tel 11-38-30 Telex 19690

FAR EAST

Tokyo
Swire Shipping,
CPO Box 703, Tokyo 100-91, Japan.
Tel 230 9100 Telex 22248

Hong Kong
Swire Shipping (Agencies) Ltd.,
PO Box 1, General Post Office,
Hong Kong.
Tel (5) 264311 Telex 86000

Singapore & S E Asia
Mansfield Container Services Pte Ltd.,
PO Box 398, Ocean Building,
Collyer Quay, Singapore.
Tel 76061 Telex 24301

Philippines
Soriamont Steamship Agencies,
PO Box 2039, Manila D-406, Philippines.
Tel 50-18-31 Telex RCA 7227694

Taiwan
Jardine Matheson & Co. Ltd.,
PO Box 81, Taipei, Taiwan.
Tel 393 1177 Telex 11391

Thailand
Borneo Services Ltd.,
231/2 Sathorn Tai Road, Yanawa District,
Bangkok 12.
Tel 234 1622 Telex 2743

Peninsular Malaysia
Container Agencies Sendirian Berhad,
PO Box 1059, Kuala Lumpur,
Peninsular Malaysia.
Tel 290432 Telex MA 30499

S Korea
Young Chang Shipping Co. Ltd.,
CPO Box 3268, Seoul.
Tel 23-0450/9 Telex K27264

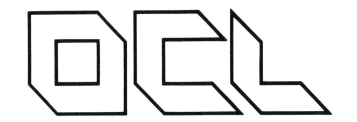

world atlas of shipping

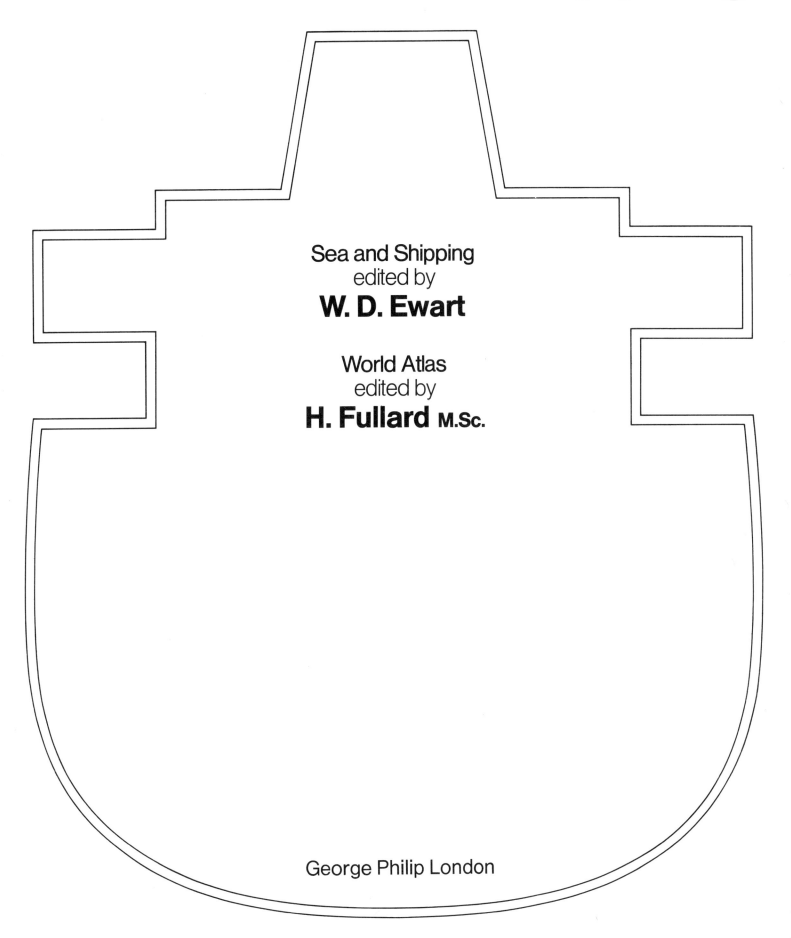

Sea and Shipping
edited by
W. D. Ewart

World Atlas
edited by
H. Fullard M.Sc.

George Philip London

Editorial Consultants and Advisors

W. E. Astle
Toplis and Harding Marine

British Chamber of Shipping

Gervase Frais
Editor, Tanker and Bulk Carrier

Dr J. David George
Natural History Museum

Dr Ronald Hope O.B.E.
Director, Seafarers Education Service

Juanita Kalerghi
Editor, Hovering Craft and Hydrofoil

Herbert Mansfield
formerly Technical Director, Mullion and Co (Shipping)

D. W. McKee
Technical Services Division,
Peninsular and Oriental Steam Navigation Company

Anthony Preston
Ships Department, National Maritime Museum

Bill Reid
Editor, Dock and Harbour Authority

Alan Stimson
Navigation Historian

Norman Tilsley
Editor, Freight Management

Text Editor: Ian Ridpath
Art Editors: Jon Lord and Garry Shewring
Cartographic Editor: Harold Fullard

George Philip and Son Limited
12-14 Long Acre London WC2E 9LP
First Published 1972
©1973 George Philip and Son Limited
ISBN 0 540 05266 3
Printed in Great Britain by
George Philip Printers Limited London

contents

contents

Circulation of world ocean currents, showing warm water
(red) and cold water (blue), centred on the Antarctic Ocean.

Water is the commonest substance on Earth.
Most of the Earth's water is contained in the
oceans. The oceans cover 139 million square
miles – 71 per cent of the Earth's surface.
Water is a compound of two parts of hydrogen
and one part of oxygen. Normally, these two
elements are found in the form of thin gas.
But when they combine, they give rise to a
liquid with remarkable properties. One of these
properties is the ability to dissolve other substances. There are large amounts of salt dis-
solved in sea water, for instance. The average
concentration of salt in the oceans is about one
part to 30 parts of water. Other substances,
although thinly concentrated, are still present
in enormous amounts. It is estimated that one
cubic mile of sea water contains about 40lb of
gold. The oceans are the world's richest mine.
They would provide more raw materials than
the Earth's crust if we knew how to process
them efficiently.

All the five named oceans are interconnected
to form one continuous body of water – the
world ocean. The ocean is spread round the
Earth like the petals of a flower with its centre
in the Antarctic. The largest petal of all is the
Pacific. There are also the stubby Indian Ocean
petal and the long, thin petal through the
Atlantic to the Arctic.

How was the watery surface of the Earth
formed? Scientists think that the continents
grew by repeated eruptions from inside the
Earth. Vast amounts of gas are given out by
volcanoes, and this gas formed the first atmosphere of the Earth. But volcanic gases are over
90 per cent water vapour – steam. As the
vapour cooled there came a steady rain and the
oceans began to fill. This process was probably
complete by 3000 million years ago. The oceans
are therefore about three quarters the age of
the Earth itself.

What the sea is made of

Seawater contains a great deal of sodium chloride – common
salt. Evaporating seawater gives both a source of fresh water
and salt. If the salt of the sea could be dried out and laid
around the globe, it would form a layer 150ft thick. About
one-third of the world's salt is now obtained from the ocean.
The sea also provides about two-thirds of the world's
bromine and magnesium metal. These requirements are
produced by just two or three extraction plants. Studies for
a more efficient plant which might also be able to extract the
rare metals present in seawater have shown that it would
make itself uneconomical by sheer overproduction of salt,
bromine and magnesium. Among valuable elements that it
may be possible to extract from the sea are uranium (14 tons
per cubic mile), silver (1.2 tons per cubic mile), tin (12 tons
per cubic mile), titanium (4.2 tons per cubic mile) and gold.

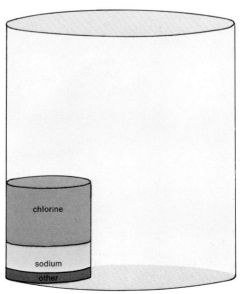

The active oceans
currents and waves

Currents

The sea is never still. It is whipped by winds, stirred by currents and pumped by the tides. Even in the calmest waters, a sluggish current may be running somewhere beneath the surface. The largest oceans are stirred by floods of moving water that flow along the surface at speeds of a few miles an hour. These surface currents circle round the oceans. They carry warm water away from the equator towards the poles, and bring back cool water to be warmed again by the tropical sun. The continual exchange of equatorial and polar water serves to moderate the Earth's climate. Each current carries millions upon millions of tons of water every second, many times the flow of all the rivers on land.

Perhaps the most famous of these gyrating patterns of water flow is that in the North Atlantic. The northbound stream of this, flowing from the Gulf of Mexico across to Europe and North Africa, is called the Gulf Stream. Within this great eddy in the North Atlantic lies the oceanic desert called the Sargasso Sea. The waters of the Sargasso Sea contain relatively little marine life, plus occasional rafts of seaweed which have drifted into the still waters. The legendary banks of clinging weeds were the product of the lively imaginations of ancient mariners.

The waters of the Sargasso Sea are a clear blue. Each of the major oceans has its clear blue eye like the Sargasso Sea. Their waters are warm and float placidly on the colder waters underneath. Like oildrops, the warmer waters rise a few feet above the average sea level. In the northern hemisphere this water is on the right of the main surface currents. The opposite is true in the southern hemisphere. However, the main currents have many branches and eddies which confuse the general pattern.

The currents pick up energy from the trade winds of the equatorial region before moving north or south. The pole-bound currents on the western sides of oceans are stronger and better-defined than the returning currents on the east sides of the oceans. Currents flow at a small fraction of the speed of the winds. The rate and extent of a current varies with the seasonal change in winds.

A certain circulation of water would occur even on a windless Earth. The warming of the water at the equator is one reason for its outward flow to the poles. At the poles, some water cools, gets denser, and sinks. Where water freezes to form polar ice caps, the salt is left behind, making it denser still. So a cold, salty current creeps back to the equator along the ocean bed. The bottom water from the Antarctic actually flows on north of the equator. Water sinking at the poles may not return to the surface for 1000 years or more.

Flowing out of the Mediterranean is a deep current made of the salty water left behind by evaporation. Surface currents of fresher water flow into the Mediterranean to replace the water lost. Currents below the surface are only poorly understood. Below the main surface currents, however, there appear to be reverse currents of similar volume flowing in the opposite direction.

Blue eye of the Atlantic: the Sargasso Sea outlined by the circulating currents of the North Atlantic.

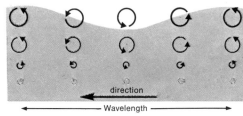

Wave-making circular motion of water particles decreases rapidly with depth

Waves

Winds whip the sea surface into waves. But waves are not all they seem. For, although they move through the sea, the sea does not move forward with them. And in any part of the world, waves are always breaking on the shore.

A wave is a form of energy – energy which has been gained from the wind. As the wave energy runs through the sea, the water particles gyrate, but end up about where they started. Waves disturb only the surface of the sea. The circular wave motion of water particles fades out a few feet below the surface.

The Ekman spiral

Direction of wind-induced water flow is shown by this spiral. At about 300 ft depth there is a small current flowing against the wind direction. Average water flow is at 90° to the wind.

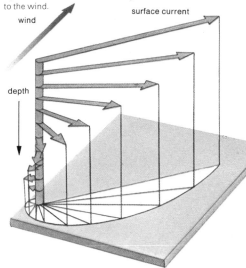

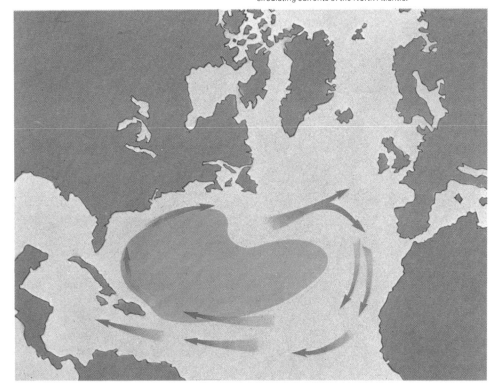

An area of choppy water whipped up by winds is called a *sea*. Compared to a single simple wave, a sea is like the sound of an orchestra compared to a single note. Outside the area of formation the waves smooth out into a gentle surge called a *swell*. The breakers that crash on a beach can be caused by swell that has travelled from a storm area thousands of miles across the ocean.

Near shore, the rising seabed interferes with the circular pumping of the water particles. Like a runner with his feet dragged back, a wave leans forward and eventually crashes down when it reaches shallow water. Its wind-given energy is released, and acts as a grinding mortar on the seashore. Thus, even a storm far out at sea helps to wear down the land.

Tides

Tides are like two giant waves that sweep over the rotating Earth every day. The tides are caused by the gravitational attractions of the Sun and Moon. Although the Sun is much bigger than the Moon, the Moon is much closer. As a result, the Moon has over twice the tidal effect of the Sun.

Tides are raised on land as well as the sea. Land tides amount to only a few inches, but water can run round the Earth to pile up at the point where attraction is strongest. This point is on the side facing the Moon. But on the opposite side of the Earth a similar, but not equally high, tide is formed. This is because the Moon is attracting the Earth slightly more strongly than the sea, and the net result is that the water runs away from the Moon.

The pattern of tides is complicated both by the presence of the continents and by the fact that the Moon and Sun do not orbit in the plane of the Earth's equator. Tides are raised at an angle to the equator and consequently two successive tides are seldom of the same height. At times of new and full Moon the gravitational attractions of the Sun and Moon add up to provide an extra-high tide called a *spring tide*. At the times of half Moon the two gravitational pulls cancel out to give more nearly equal *neap tides*. The Moon's orbit is not quite circular, and

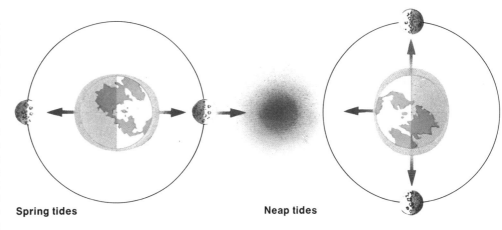

Spring tides

Neap tides

so its distance and tide-forming capacity continually vary.

The actual height of a tide at any one place depends on its location. In the deep ocean, tides measure only a few feet. Tides are highest in shallow inlets and rivers where the waters of the ocean are piled up into a confined space. In the Bay of Fundy in southeast Canada the tidal range is as much as 50 ft. Without the Moon's pull, tides would only be low and many ports would be unreachable by today's deep-draught ships. The friction of the tides on the seabed

slows the rotation of the Earth by about 1.6 seconds in 100,000 years. If there were no Moon to brake its spin, the Earth would rotate once in about 12 hours.

The continual rise and fall of the tides is a potential source of energy. In 1966 the world's first tidal power station came into operation on the Rance river, near St Malo in France. The plant produces almost 550 million kilowatts of electricity a year. A similar station was set up on the Barents Sea coast of the Soviet Union.

The progress of a wave

Floating beachball is tossed in a circular path as a wave moves through the sea, travelling from right of the diagram to left. The height of a wave depends on the diameter of the orbit of water particles.

Wave break up

When water depth (1) becomes less than half the distance between wave crests, water piles up and waves increase in height (2). The seabed restricts the movement of water particles, causing the wave to break (3, 4) and forming a surge of water (5).

depth equals half wave length

The colour of the sea

Sea water appears blue because blue light is scattered more by water than red light. The sky appears blue because blue light is scattered by the air. The bluest waters are the cleanest. However, sea water is often made green by organic material. The small plant plankton add a greenness to many waters. In other places they may give it a brownish tinge. The Red Sea takes its name from the fact that small red organisms sometimes colour its waters.

Solar radiation (red) forces up millions of gallons of sea water into the atmosphere as evaporation (blue).

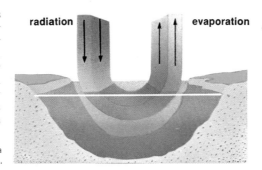

radiation   evaporation

Where the water is

The world's water weighs 1.6 million million million tons – one four thousandth the total weight of the Earth. Most of this is contained in the sea. But there is enough water in the polar caps to raise sea level by 200 ft.

The temperature of the sea

Three quarters of the ocean is colder than 10°C. Some seas have a skin of warm water extending down for over 30 ft. The heat from the Sun is radiated back into space or escapes as water evaporates into the atmosphere. Evaporation can be enormous. About 100 000 tons of water evaporate from the Mediterranean every second. If the oceans retained all the heat they get from the Sun they would be boiling within 300 years.

The temperature of water varies with its location. The surface temperature of Arctic seas is only a couple of degrees above freezing. In the North Sea temperatures can range from chilly (a few degrees) to room temperature (16–20°C). Tropical seas can be very warm. In the Persian Gulf, temperatures of over 30°C are regularly recorded. But in all waters the general pattern is that temperature drops with depth. Even in tropical seas the water is near freezing point at depths of many thousands of feet.

Fortunately, unlike most other substances, water actually gets less dense when it freezes solid. Therefore, ice rises to the surface where it can easily be melted back into water. Without this fortunate property of water, most ocean depths would be solid with ice.

Weather at sea
wind circulation

Our planet is swept and watered by a tireless attendant – the atmosphere. Like the ocean, the 5600 million million tons of the atmosphere is always on the move, sometimes at speeds of several hundred miles an hour. As the air moves it picks up moisture from the sea. There is enough water vapour in the air at any one time to provide an inch of rainfall over the entire globe. On average, a water particle stays in the atmosphere for only about 10 days at a time. During its stay it may be blown for several hundred miles. By contrast, water particles stay in the ocean for several thousand years. During that time they may pass right round the globe.

Water is slow to heat up and slow to cool down, so that the ocean acts as a flywheel on world climate. This is why the coldest and hottest months occur some time after the Sun's heat has reached its minimum or maximum. Land heats up during the day and cools again rapidly during the night. There is no such daily temperature difference in the sea. Winds sweep onto land when it is warmer than the sea. Winds sweep away from land when it is cooler than the sea. This can create coastal breezes or, in the case of giant continents such as Asia, it creates monsoon winds that blow in one direction for six months at a time.

Of course, rain or snow that falls on land is water that has evaporated from the sea. Via rivers and other water courses it flows back to the ocean's global reservoir. But 90 per cent of the world's rain falls out at sea, and goes straight back whence it came.

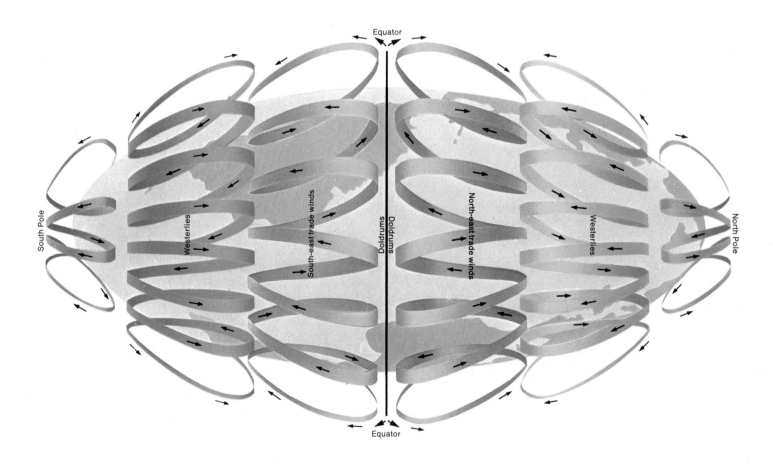

The circulation of the world's winds is bafflingly complex in detail, although simple in general outline. Around the equator, where the world gets warmed most, great columns of hot, moist air ascend into the sky. As on a hot summer's day there is little breeze. We are in the low-pressure region of the doldrums. The rising air cools and the water condenses like steam from a kettle. Great billowing clouds are formed and rainstorms lash the Earth's tropical areas below. Pushed on by more ascending air, the convection cells start to move away from the equator. At about latitude 30° the air splits. Some of the air carries on towards the pole, and the rest sinks to the surface. This is the high-pressure region of the horse latitudes, where sailing ships were often becalmed.

In the horse latitudes the descending air divides. Some moves off over the surface towards the pole, driving the depressions that create the spanking gales of the westerlies. The rest swings back towards the equator, forming the following breezes of the trade winds and picking up more moisture from the sea to erupt as another drenching tropical storm.

But the trade winds do not blow directly north-south. They converge at the equator, blowing from the east. This is because, at the equator, the Earth spins eastwards at 1000 mile/h – but the poles stand still. As air moves towards the poles it finds itself moving progressively quicker than the Earth below it. So pole-bound air or water moves east. But by the time it turns to flow back again, the wind (or the current) has taken up the slower spin of higher latitudes. Thus it falls behind the Earth as it moves into the equatorial region. This is called the Coriolis effect. It is responsible for the angled flow of winds and the gyrating flow of ocean currents.

Weather is fairly simple in the tropical trade wind region. But in temperate latitudes there is a continual clash between warm air from the tropics and cold air from the poles. The air masses meet in a *front* – a decisive-sounding word that actually describes an area of mixing air several miles across.

Because, according to the Coriolis effect, winds are deflected to the right in the northern hemisphere, the meeting warm and cold air masses are drawn into an anti-clockwise vortex called a *cyclone*, centred on a region of low pressure (a depression). As the air masses spiral into the low pressure area the cold air tries to

shut out the warm air. At the leading front, warm air rises over the cold air, forming cloud and causing rainfall. The sign of an approaching depression is high cloud and steady drizzle.

As the front passes, the air becomes warm. Behind the warm air, cooler air tries to wedge itself underneath. There is often a 'clearing shower' as the warm air passes. When the cool air finally manages to lever its way under the warm, an *occluded* front is formed. As the warm air disperses in the high atmosphere, a little eddy of cooler air is usually left at the surface.

When a front passes, the wind *veers* (changes direction clockwise), perhaps moving from

southwest to northwest. When a wind *backs*, it moves counterclockwise, as from northwest to southwest. Winds, unlike currents, are named for the direction they blow from – not the direction they blow to.

A cyclone measures perhaps a thousand miles across. Cyclones move west to east at speeds of 10 to 15 miles/h, and they last for a few days before dying out. Occasionally depressions form, for reasons not fully understood, in the trade wind areas. These can have winds of 75 mile/h or more, and are known as hurricanes or typhoons.

Beaufort scale

Wind speeds are measured on a coded scale named after the English mariner Sir Francis Beaufort. He invented the scale in 1805 and meant it to apply to the sea winds encountered by a man-of-war. Beaufort gave wind speed numbers between 0 (dead calm) and 12 (too strong for canvas to bear). Meteorologists have since modified and extended the scale to apply to all winds on Earth.

Weather symbols

clear sky		rain		cumulus	
sky 1/8 covered		drizzle		stratus	
sky 2/8 covered		snow		cirrus	
sky 3/8 covered		rain and snow		cirro-cumulus	
sky 4/8 covered		hail		alto-cumulus	
sky 5/8 covered		shower		strato-cumulus	
sky 6/8 covered		thunderstorm		nimbo-stratus	
sky 7/8 covered		fog		cirro-stratus	
sky 8/8 covered		mist		cumulo-nimbus	
sky obscured		warm front			
missing or doubtful data		cold front			
		occluded front			

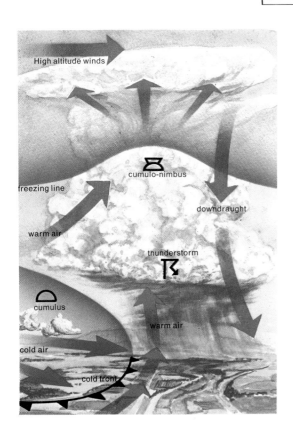

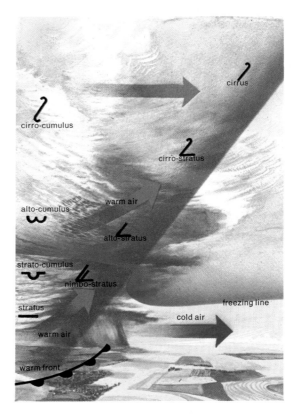

Cold front (left)
Thundercloud forms as cold air, shown advancing from left, displaces warm air. Cold front pushes warm air upwards, causing it to expand and cool, forming a towering cumulo-nimbus cloud containing violent convection currents. These can give rise to thunder and heavy rain. Above the freezing line (blue), the water freezes into ice crystals, forming an anvil-shaped cloud which is smeared out by high-altitude winds.

Warm front (right)
Warm front advancing rises above cold air. At the leading edge of the front, above the freezing line (blue), high cirrus clouds of ice crystals are formed. Lower down, condensing air forms thicker clouds which give rise to rain. The rain ceases as the front passes. Symbols describe types of cloud and weather formations, as explained in the key above.

Life in the sea
plankton, nekton and benthos

Scientists believe that life arose in the ocean. Without water, there would probably have been no life on Earth. All forms of life contain large amounts of water. Every human body is two-thirds water by weight, and many sea creatures are more than nine-tenths water. There is still a greater diversity of life in the oceans than on land.

There are three main types of life in the ocean. The tiniest is called *plankton*. These microscopic bodies float with the current in the topmost layer of the sea. There are two kinds of plankton. *Phytoplankton* are tiny plants. Like land plants, they use sunlight to grow. *Zooplankton* are small animals. They feed on the plant plankton or on each other. Larger sea creatures feed on both. If the plankton suddenly vanished, all forms of sea life would die.

The most familiar form of sea life is the *nekton*. These are animals that can swim freely and are found at all depths. They include all sorts of fish, as well as whales and octopuses. Fish are the most advanced of the creatures that developed in the sea. Some have a bony skeleton, such as the cod, bonito and mackerel. They are rivalled in mobility by sharks and rays, which have skeletons of cartilage, and by octopuses and squids, which have developed mobility despite their lack of a skeleton. Whales and porpoises are land mammals that have returned to the sea.

Animals and plants that live on the sea bottom are called *benthos*. The benthos are most numerous on the shallow continental shelves, where light penetrates to the sea bed. They include the beautiful sponges, starfish and sea anemones, forms of life that have scarcely changed in millions of years, as well as seaweed. But the richness of benthic life ends where the continental slope plunges to the abyss. In the darkness, plants cannot live. Here the nekton live on the carcasses of dead organic matter that fall from the layers above, or they cannibalize each other. Only very specialized animals, such as the mis-named sea cucumber, can scavenge a living on the deep sea bed.

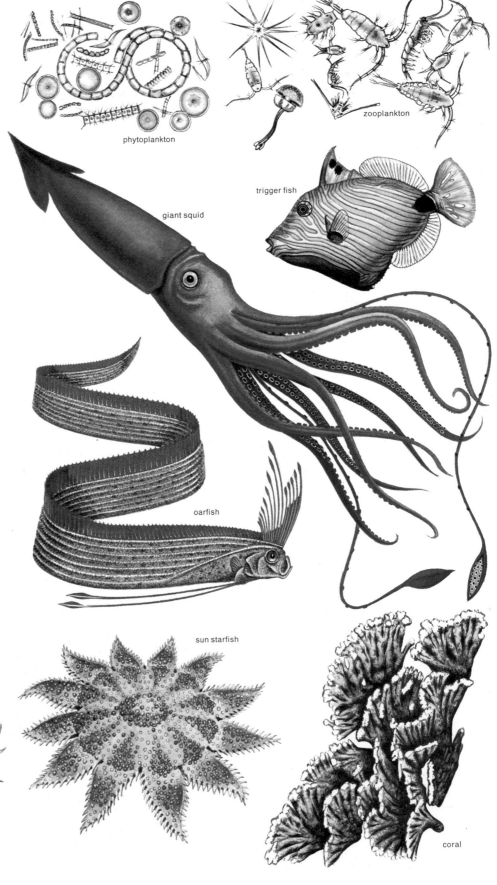

phytoplankton

zooplankton

trigger fish

giant squid

oarfish

sun starfish

banded anemone

coral

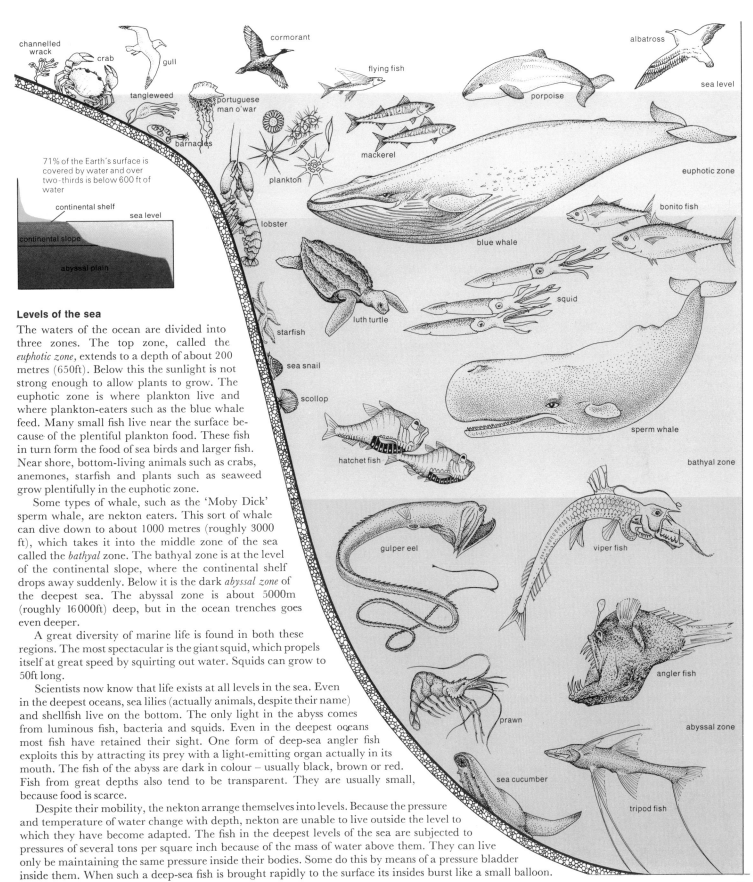

71% of the Earth's surface is covered by water and over two-thirds is below 600 ft of water

continental shelf

sea level

continental slope

abyssal plain

Levels of the sea

The waters of the ocean are divided into three zones. The top zone, called the *euphotic zone*, extends to a depth of about 200 metres (650ft). Below this the sunlight is not strong enough to allow plants to grow. The euphotic zone is where plankton live and where plankton-eaters such as the blue whale feed. Many small fish live near the surface because of the plentiful plankton food. These fish in turn form the food of sea birds and larger fish. Near shore, bottom-living animals such as crabs, anemones, starfish and plants such as seaweed grow plentifully in the euphotic zone.

Some types of whale, such as the 'Moby Dick' sperm whale, are nekton eaters. This sort of whale can dive down to about 1000 metres (roughly 3000 ft), which takes it into the middle zone of the sea called the *bathyal* zone. The bathyal zone is at the level of the continental slope, where the continental shelf drops away suddenly. Below it is the dark *abyssal zone* of the deepest sea. The abyssal zone is about 5000m (roughly 16000ft) deep, but in the ocean trenches goes even deeper.

A great diversity of marine life is found in both these regions. The most spectacular is the giant squid, which propels itself at great speed by squirting out water. Squids can grow to 50ft long.

Scientists now know that life exists at all levels in the sea. Even in the deepest oceans, sea lilies (actually animals, despite their name) and shellfish live on the bottom. The only light in the abyss comes from luminous fish, bacteria and squids. Even in the deepest oceans most fish have retained their sight. One form of deep-sea angler fish exploits this by attracting its prey with a light-emitting organ actually in its mouth. The fish of the abyss are dark in colour – usually black, brown or red. Fish from great depths also tend to be transparent. They are usually small, because food is scarce.

Despite their mobility, the nekton arrange themselves into levels. Because the pressure and temperature of water change with depth, nekton are unable to live outside the level to which they have become adapted. The fish in the deepest levels of the sea are subjected to pressures of several tons per square inch because of the mass of water above them. They can live only be maintaining the same pressure inside their bodies. Some do this by means of a pressure bladder inside them. When such a deep-sea fish is brought rapidly to the surface its insides burst like a small balloon.

The Atlantic Ocean
a spreading sea

Every year the Atlantic widens by about an inch. This slow process has been going on since the continents of America and Europe split apart 200 million years ago (top left). Before then, most of the continents we know today were fixed together in two main masses of land. South America split from Africa about 100 million years ago (above), and 50 million years ago India was on a collision course with Asia (left). The Atlantic is spreading because new material from inside the Earth is welling up along the mid-Atlantic ridge.

The Atlantic Ocean is the world's second largest body of water. Its area is about 31½ million square miles, and its average depth is 14 000 feet. The Atlantic has a long ridge running down the centre. This is the point at which new material is being added to the Atlantic seabed from inside the Earth. Iceland, which lies exactly on the ridge, is formed entirely of volcanic lava that has erupted from inside the Earth. In other places, seabed is being destroyed as it slips back into the Earth again. Where this happens, deep ocean-floor trenches are formed.

The deepest of these trenches are found on the floor of the Pacific Ocean. Over millions of years, the face of the Earth is being altered as new seas open and old ones close. Geologists use the term *plate movement* to describe the motions of the fragments of Earth's crust.

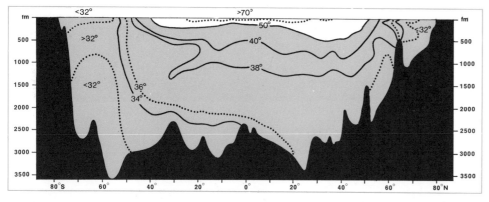

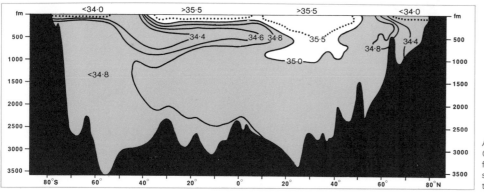

Above: South-to-north cross-section of the Atlantic Ocean showing temperature in °F from surface to 3500 fathoms (21000 feet). Below: South-to-north cross-section of the Atlantic Ocean showing salinity in parts per thousand from surface to 3500 fathoms.

NORTH AMERICA

LABRADOR BASIN

Greenland

Iceland

NEWFOUNDLAND BASIN

NORTH AMERICAN

BASIN

Ireland

United Kingdom

WEST EUROPEAN BASIN

France

EUROPE

Spain

CANARY

BASIN

Canary Is

Indies

AN

MID ATLANTIC RIDGE

CAPE VERDE BASIN

Cape Verde Is

GUIANA BASIN

Continental Shelf

SIERRA LEONE

BASIN

Continental Slope

AFRICA

GUINEA BASIN

GULF OF GUINEA

Guinea Rise

BRAZIL BASIN

MID ATLANTIC RIDGE

ANGOLA

BASIN

Rio Grande Rise

RGENTINE BASIN

Walvis Ridge

CAPE BASIN

The Pacific Ocean
a volcano-studded sea

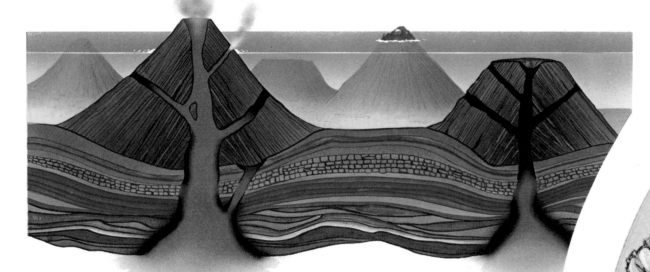

The Pacific Ocean is the world's largest and deepest ocean. It covers over a third of the Earth's surface – nearly 64 million square miles. It contains the Mariana Trench, the deepest known spot on Earth, nearly seven miles below the sea's surface. As the Atlantic widens, the Pacific closes at roughly the same rate. Volcanoes occur in arcs around the Pacific where parts of the Earth's crust are slipping under the continents. They also occur in chains in the centre of the Pacific. Where the volcanoes break the surface they cause islands, such as the Hawaiian chain. Where they fail to break surface they are called seamounts. Where they have sunk and been levelled off by water action they are called guyots.

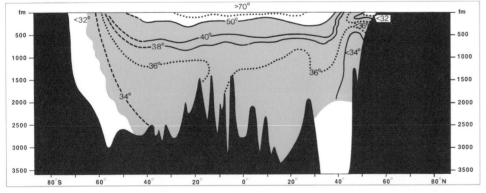

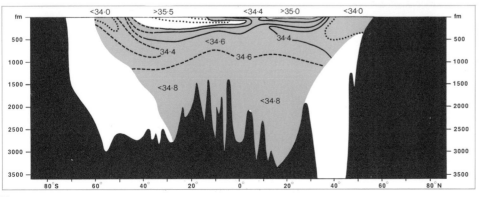

Above: South-to-north cross-section of the Pacific Ocean showing temperature in °F from surface to 3500 fathoms (21000 feet). Below: South-to-north cross-section of the Pacific Ocean showing salinity in parts per thousand from surface to 3500 fathoms.

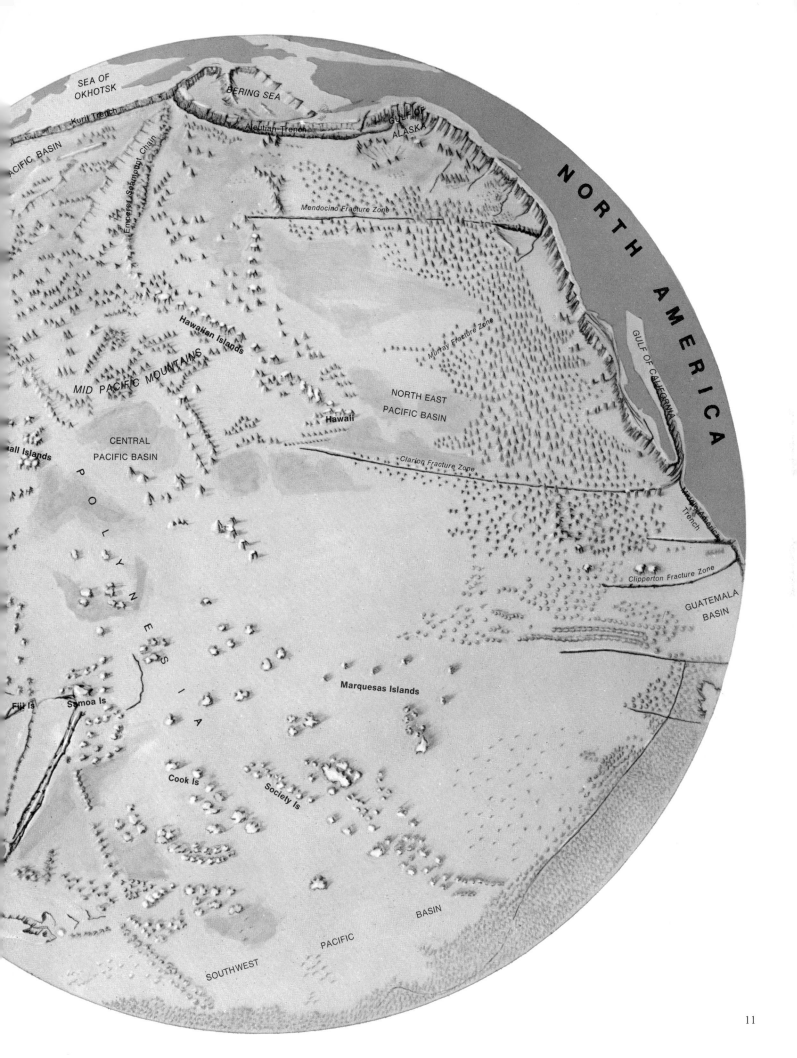

SEA OF OKHOTSK

BERING SEA

GULF OF ALASKA

NORTH AMERICA

Kuril Trench

Aleutian Trench

PACIFIC BASIN

Emperor Seamount Chain

Mendocino Fracture Zone

Murray Fracture Zone

GULF OF CALIFORNIA

Hawaiian Islands

MID PACIFIC MOUNTAINS

Hawaii

NORTH EAST PACIFIC BASIN

CENTRAL PACIFIC BASIN

Clarion Fracture Zone

Middle America Trench

all Islands

P O L Y N E S I A

Clipperton Fracture Zone

GUATEMALA BASIN

Marquesas Islands

Fiji Is

Samoa Is

Cook Is

Society Is

PACIFIC

SOUTHWEST

BASIN

11

The Indian Ocean
a sediment-lined sea

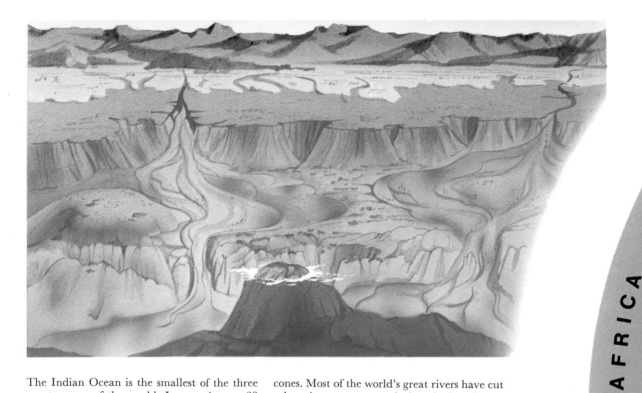

The Indian Ocean is the smallest of the three great oceans of the world. Its area is over 28 million square miles, and its average depth is 13000 feet. Sediments carried by the Ganges and Indus rivers flow over the continental shelf around India into the deep abyssal plain. The sediments flow through prominent submarine canyons cut into the continental shelf, and then fan out in deposits called abyssal cones. Most of the world's great rivers have cut submarine canyons and deposited sediment from the land in the sea, but the abyssal cone of the Ganges is by far the world's largest. It is 1500 miles long and has a volume of about 1 million cubic miles. The Ganges and Indus cones are sediment from the Himalayas, which are themselves a former seabed that was pushed up by the collision of India with Asia.

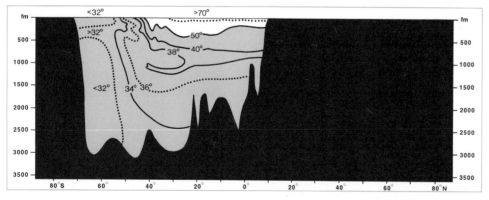

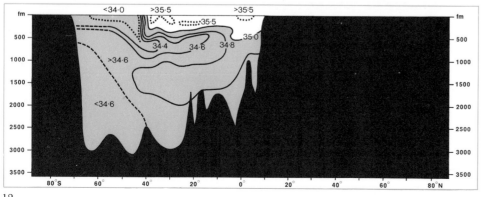

Above: South-to-north cross-section of the Indian Ocean showing temperature in °F from surface to 3500 fathoms (21000 feet). Below: South-to-north cross-section of the Indian Ocean showing salinity in parts per thousand from surface to 3500 fathoms.

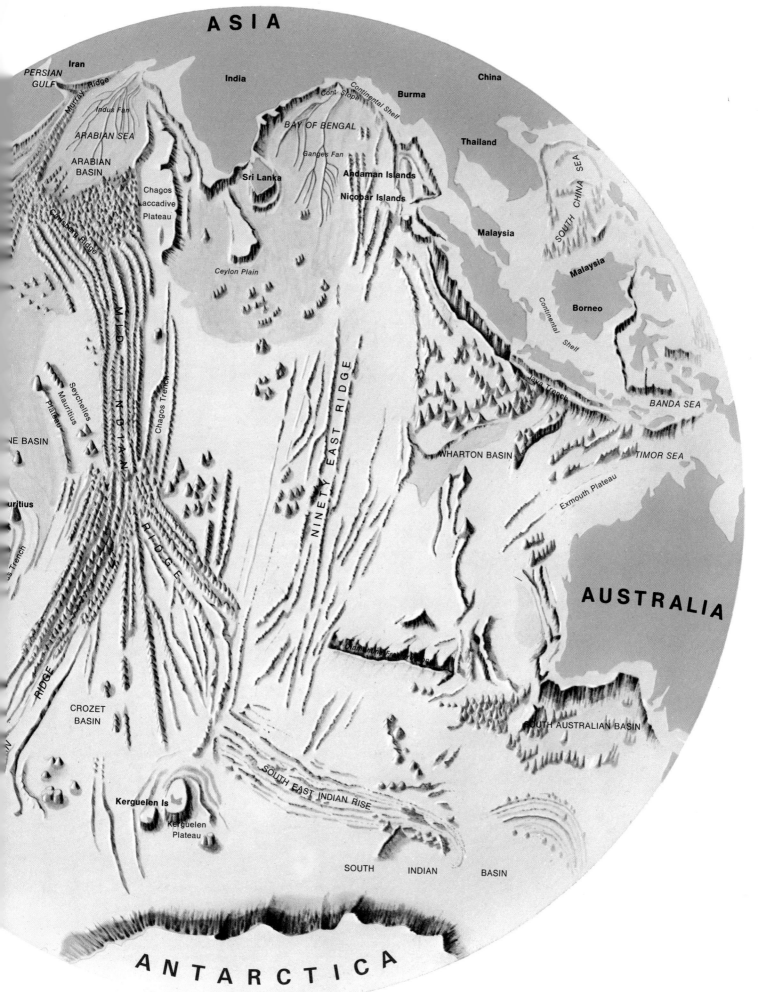

ASIA

Iran

PERSIAN
GULF

Murray Ridge

Indus Fan

India

Cont. Continental Shelf
Slope

Continental Shelf

China

Burma

ARABIAN SEA

ARABIAN
BASIN

BAY OF BENGAL

Thailand

Ganges Fan

Sri Lanka

Chagos
Laccadive
Plateau

Andaman Islands

Nicobar Islands

Malaysia

SOUTH CHINA SEA

Carlsberg Ridge

Ceylon Plain

Malaysia

Continental Shelf

Borneo

Seychelles

Mauritius
Plateau

NE BASIN

M I D - I N D I A N

Chagos Trench

NINETY EAST RIDGE

Java Trench

BANDA SEA

Mauritius

s Trench

R I D G E

WHARTON BASIN

TIMOR SEA

Exmouth Plateau

AUSTRALIA

Diamantina Fracture Zone

RIDGE

CROZET
BASIN

SOUTH EAST INDIAN RISE

SOUTH AUSTRALIAN BASIN

Kerguelen Is

Kerguelen
Plateau

SOUTH   INDIAN   BASIN

ANTARCTICA

13

Shipping
signal flags

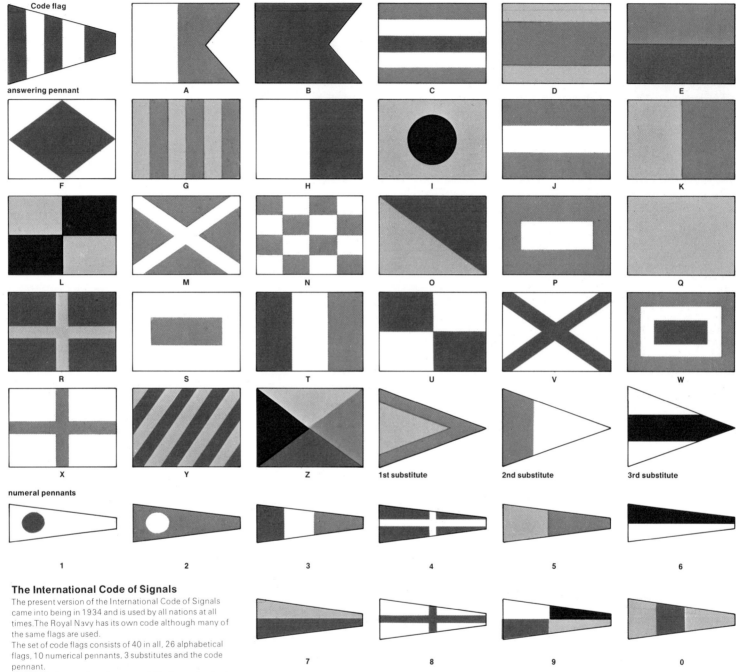

Code flag

answering pennant

A B C D E

F G H I J K

L M N O P Q

R S T U V W

X Y Z 1st substitute 2nd substitute 3rd substitute

numeral pennants

1 2 3 4 5 6

7 8 9 0

The International Code of Signals

The present version of the International Code of Signals came into being in 1934 and is used by all nations at all times. The Royal Navy has its own code although many of the same flags are used.

The set of code flags consists of 40 in all, 26 alphabetical flags, 10 numerical pennants, 3 substitutes and the code pennant.

Besides the letter values shown, each flag has a signal value. Single-letter signals are either for emergencies or in everyday use.

Every ship and even many small yachts, have a four-letter identification signal. British ships have either G or M as the first letter.

Every phrase likely to be used at sea is represented by a group of code letters. Each ship carries the official International Code books which contain these signals. To economise in flags substitute flags are used; for instance in the three letter signal ECE the first flag (or letter) is indicated by the 1st substitute. If the signal was AJJO and the 2nd flag is to be repeated, the second substitute is used.

Single letter signals

A I have a diver down
B I am taking in/discharging/carrying dangerous goods
C Yes
D Keep clear of me – I am manoeuvring with difficulty
E I am altering my course to starboard

F I am disabled – communicate with me
G I require a pilot. *By fishing vessels* – I am hauling nets
H I have a pilot on board
I I am altering my course to port
J I am on fire and have dangerous cargo – keep well clear
K I wish to communicate with you
L Stop your vessel instantly
M My vessel is stopped
N No
O Man overboard
P Blue Peter – *in harbour* (flown at foremast) : All persons should report on board as the vessel is about to sail. *At sea* (by fishing vessels) : My nets have come fast
Q My vessel is healthy – I request a free pratique (a vessel arriving in British waters from abroad must declare whether she is 'healthy' or 'suspect' If there is a case of infectious disease on board, the signal **QQ** is hoisted, signifying 'My ship is suspect'.)
R (Has not been allocated a meaning as yet)
S My engines are going astern

T Keep clear of me
U You are running into danger
V I require assistance
W I require medical assistance
X Stop carrying out your intentions and watch for my signals
Y I am dragging my anchor
Z I require a tug *By fishing vessels* – I am shooting nets

Selection of two-letter signals

AM Accident has occurred, I require a doctor
NC I am in distress and require immediate assistance
SC What is the name of your vessel ?

Selection of three-letter signals

ECE What course are you steering ?
PYV Good voyage

A four-letter signal

AJJO Liverpool

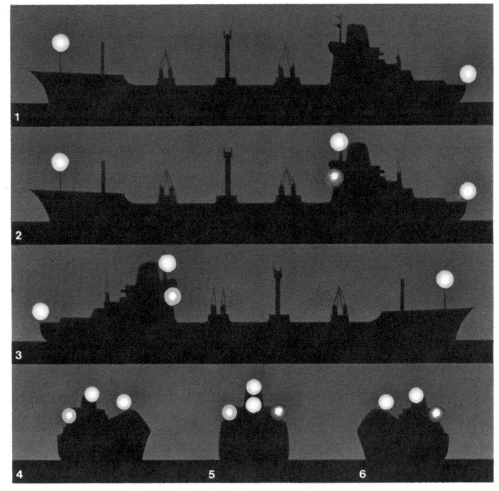

Shipping is the cheapest way to transfer goods. The cost per mile of water-borne cargo is half the cost of any other form of long-distance transport. Currently, there are around 60000 ships totalling 250 million gross tons plying the merchant routes of the world.

The success of the ship is due to the properties of water: it holds a ship up, but lets it pass through. A ship floats because its average density is less than that of water. A solid block of metal would sink straight away. But if that same block of metal were hammered into a can shape it would float easily – and it could be used to carry small loads. A ship is mostly air, and so its average density is much less than that of water. The water therefore exerts an up-thrust on it and keeps it afloat. The ship can even be loaded with cargo until it reaches a certain average density. It is fortunate indeed that oil is less dense than water, or tankers would have to sail only part-full to keep afloat.

A floating ship displaces its own weight of water. When loaded, it settles deeper to displace more water. When it gets heavier than the weight of water it is capable of displacing, a ship sinks.

A warship's weight is often referred to as its displacement. But most ships are built to carry cargo; tankers are all cargo space. The term deadweight tonnage is used to signify the total load that a ship can carry. It shows the cargo capacity of a ship, but ignores the weight of the ship itself (the *lightweight*). Gross tonnage refers to the volume of enclosed space on a ship. It is measured in cubic feet and turned into tonnage on the assumption that 100 cu. ft. equals one ton. Passenger ships are usually measured in gross tons. Net tonnage is calculated in the same way as gross tonnage, but refers only to the actual cargo-carrying volume of the ship. The net tonnage is usually the figure on which port and canal charges are calculated.

Navigation lights for vessels over 150ft in length

Anchor or riding lights: An all-round white light on the forestay 20-40ft above the hull and at the stern a similar white light 15ft lower than the forward light.
Under way: A white light on the foremast 20-40ft above the hull visible ahead and two points (22½°) abaft either beam; a similar white light on the mainmast at least 15ft higher than the forward light.
Side or bow lights: Placed lower than the white lights and visible right ahead and two points abaft the beam, red on the port side and green on the starboard side. The side lights

are fitted with inboard screens to prevent them from being seen across the bows.
Stern light: A white light visible astern and six points (67½°) right aft either beam
1 ship at anchor
2 ship underway : on the port beam white-red-white
3 ship under way : on the starboard beam white-green-white
4 from starboard bow
5 right ahead
6 from port bow

illustrations in this section are not necessarily to scale

Tonnage

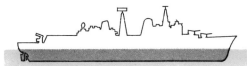

tons weight displacement
volume of water displaced: 35 cu ft = 1 ton

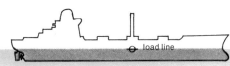

tons weight deadweight
cargo, fuel and stores

load line

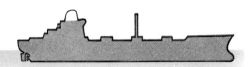

tons measurement gross register
100 cubic feet = 1 ton

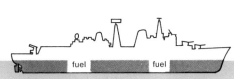

tons weight standard displacement

fuel   fuel

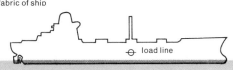

tons weight lightweight
fabric of ship

load line

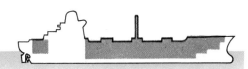

tons measurement net register

Evolution of the ship
galleys to galleons

Man has always used boats for transport and pleasure. The origins of the boat and the sail are lost in the mists of pre-history. But it was several thousand years before man learned to use sailing boats most efficiently. In early boats, sails were usually auxiliary to oars, and usable only when the wind was blowing from behind. It was well into recorded time when man discovered how to sail into the wind by tacking. This discovery opened up the ocean to wind-driven vessels. But the advent of mechanical power finally outdated sail just as it reached its peak of efficiency. The great age of sail in fact lasted a mere four centuries, from the end of the 15th century to the end of the 19th century.

The first forms of boat were probably no more than floating logs, which could be paddled along streams. Later, the logs were hollowed out to make canoes. Planks began to be used for construction and the 'open boat' evolved – still vital today as a lifeboat for abandoning more advanced ships in distress. Although man soon found he could catch the wind in a sail, the variability of wind power made it unreliable for propelling large craft over long distances. So the early ships, which had only one sail, still had a crew of oarsmen to propel them when the wind was unfavourable. One such craft was the Viking longship. Even with their relatively primitive seamanship, the Vikings in their longships reached America centuries before Columbus.

For reliability and speed, warships used as many as three banks of oars, as in the Greek trireme. Man-powered galleys dominated sea warfare in the Mediterranean for 2000 years, from the time of the Greek victory over the Persians at Salamis in 480 BC down to the Turkish defeat by the Spaniards and Italians at Lepanto in AD 1571.

But galleys were not very seaworthy, and oarsmen filled most of the available space. For carrying cargo, deeper and rounder sailing ships were used. The Romans introduced an extra sail, strung from a raking mast at the bow. This made their vessels more manageable under sail alone, and these ships plied regular trade routes in the Mediterranean. However, the Roman ship was still square rigged – the sail was set at right angles to the length of the ship. In about the 7th century the *lateen sail* was introduced. This triangular sail took its name from the word *latine*, or Latin, because it was thought to have originated in the Mediterranean. Its long edge gave better propulsion into the wind than the square sail, and allowed craft to tack. The lateen is also called the fore-and-aft sail, because it can be swung into line with the ship. Fore-and-aft rigging has now completely replaced square rigging for yachting purposes. But for many years both types had their own applications.

Early ships were steered by large paddles at the stern. The Vikings used one paddle only on the right, and this side became known as *steerboard* – the origin of our modern word starboard. But around the 12th century in northern waters the stern rudder was introduced. Northern ships also became built up with castle-like structures at the bow and stern. A couple of centuries later, after the Crusades, ship design leaped forward when northern and Mediterranean ship styles were combined. Larger, three-masted ships were built and sails were divided into convenient sizes. Fore-and-aft rigging was often combined with square rigging. Ships with such an arrangement came to be termed *full rigged*.

These developments ushered in the great age of exploration in the 15th century. Columbus crossed the Atlantic, da Gama pioneered the sea route to India, and Magellan forced his way round Cape Horn to the Pacific.

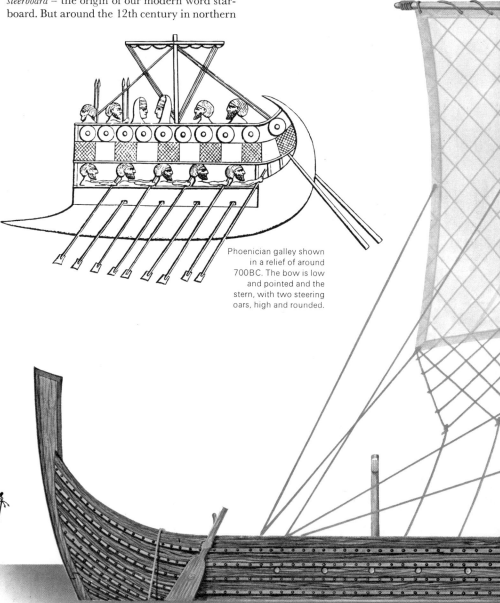

Phoenician galley shown in a relief of around 700BC. The bow is low and pointed and the stern, with two steering oars, high and rounded.

English ship, known as a *cog*, of around AD1426. The vessel has fore and after castles, and a stern rudder.

Note: Illustrations are not to the same scale

Evolution of the ship
galleons to barques

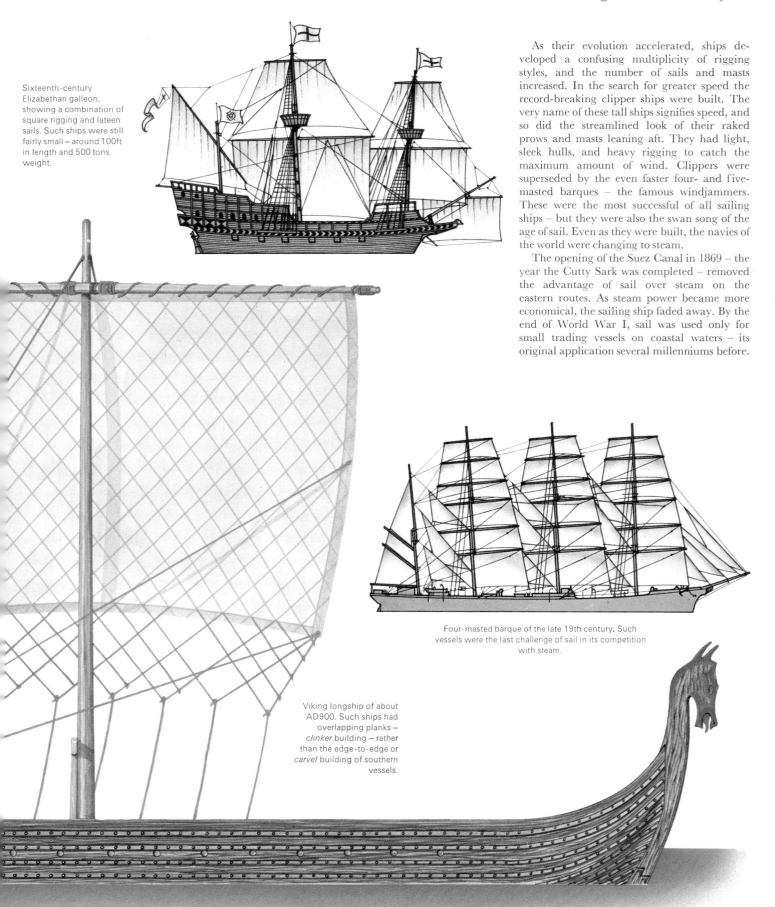

Sixteenth-century
Elizabethan galleon,
showing a combination of
square rigging and lateen
sails. Such ships were still
fairly small – around 100ft
in length and 500 tons
weight.

As their evolution accelerated, ships developed a confusing multiplicity of rigging styles, and the number of sails and masts increased. In the search for greater speed the record-breaking clipper ships were built. The very name of these tall ships signifies speed, and so did the streamlined look of their raked prows and masts leaning aft. They had light, sleek hulls, and heavy rigging to catch the maximum amount of wind. Clippers were superseded by the even faster four- and five-masted barques – the famous windjammers. These were the most successful of all sailing ships – but they were also the swan song of the age of sail. Even as they were built, the navies of the world were changing to steam.

The opening of the Suez Canal in 1869 – the year the Cutty Sark was completed – removed the advantage of sail over steam on the eastern routes. As steam power became more economical, the sailing ship faded away. By the end of World War I, sail was used only for small trading vessels on coastal waters – its original application several millenniums before.

Four-masted barque of the late 19th century. Such
vessels were the last challenge of sail in its competition
with steam.

Viking longship of about
AD900. Such ships had
overlapping planks –
clinker building – rather
than the edge-to-edge or
carvel building of southern
vessels.

The age of steam
the first steamers

Steam was first used to supplement sail in the same way that sail had originally supplemented oars. As with sail, it came to replace its predecessor for most commercial purposes – but in a much shorter time. However, the triumph of mechanical power over wind power has not been complete. There are still parts of the world where sailing vessels are more economical.

The first steps of infant steamships were as faltering as those of any child. Early steamships were unreliable, unprofitable and often slower than wind-driven ships. At its introduction, steam was ahead of its time. The world tonnage of steam vessels never exceeded that of sailing ships until 1893. The 700-foot *Great Eastern*, launched in 1858, was too large for the available passengers, cargo and docks. She was not equalled in size for 30 years. Such giant ships have become commonplace only because of the past century's growth in world trade – a growth which the improved performance of steamships themselves helped to generate.

No single person invented the steamship. The idea was proposed by many, and in the early 18th century some patents were taken out. But the first successful steamships seem to have been tried in France around 1775, a few years after the appearance of James Watt's first steam engine on land. In 1783 the French Marquis Claude de Jouffroy d'Abbans sailed a 180-ton paddlewheel steamboat on the river Saone near Lyons. Paddlewheels had been known for many centuries, but had always been worked by man or animal power. Most steamships continued to use paddlewheels (except for some attempts to mechanize ordinary

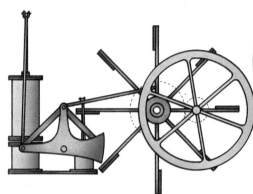

All early steamers were driven by paddlewheels. Below: Paddlewheel of Robert Fulton's steamer *Clermont*, driven by a beam engine. Right: Early paddlewheel design with foot-like paddles geared to stand upright and give maximum thrust while under water.

paddles) until the introduction of the screw in the 1830s.

Probably the most efficient early steamboat was the *Charlotte Dundas* of 1802, built by the Scotsman William Symington. The American Robert Fulton was impressed by this steam tugboat, and in 1807 built the famous ferryboat *Clermont* which, with various modifications, made regular journeys along the Hudson river for seven years. The *Clermont* inspired other Americans to build steamships, and they took the initiative in steamship development from the Europeans.

In 1819 the American sailing ship *Savannah* crossed the Atlantic to Liverpool in 29½ days, using steam power for 80 hours of the voyage. Her arrival off Ireland created reports that a

sailing ship was on fire. She consumed almost a ton of coal an hour, and had run out of fuel when she arrived. The *Savannah's* engine was removed in disappointment, and she returned to sail. Only in 1838 did the 700-ton British ship *Sirius* make the first fully steam-powered Atlantic crossing. *Sirius* was chased across the Atlantic by the 1300-ton *Great Western*, which arrived at New York only hours after *Sirius*, despite having left Britain three days later. This was the start of the rivalry in speed on the North Atlantic that came to be called the Blue Riband.

As with most ships of her time, the *Great Western* had a wooden hull and side paddlewheels. Isambard Kingdom Brunel, the *Great Western's* designer, helped change the face of shipbuilding with his next vessel, the remarkable *Great Britain*, launched in 1843. She was a 3300-ton iron ship with a propeller – although Brunel had originally intended her as a paddle steamer. The *Great Britain* crossed the Atlantic with an average speed of nearly 10 knots. She was stuck on the rocks off Ireland for nearly a year in 1846-47, but proved the superior strength of her iron hull by remaining in service until 1882, when converted into a sailing vessel. The *Great Britian* was beached in the Falkland Islands in 1886, and remained there until brought back to her building dock at Bristol in 1970.

Brunel went on to build the lavish 19000-ton *Great Eastern*. This ship was unique in having both paddlewheels and a propeller. Yet, like the *Great Britain*, she retained six masts against the possibility of a mechanical disaster. The *Great Eastern* was the only liner ever built with

Left: Isambard Kingdom Brunel's SS *Great Britain* of 1843 was the first screw-propelled iron vessel to cross the Atlantic. She is shown here as she looked after modifications made in 1845–46, when the rigging of the masts was changed and a four-bladed propeller was fitted in place of the original six-bladed one, which broke on the maiden voyage.

The age of steam
new forms of power

five funnels. Smokestacks thereafter became a status symbol, and later shipbuilders often added dummy funnels to their ships to impress passengers. The average speed of the *Great Eastern* in service was 14 knots, and she had the capacity for 4000 passengers.

But even as this iron monster slid sideways into the Thames, shipbuilders were experimenting with a new metal – steel. The lightness and added strength of steel, plus the improvements in steam engine design, allowed faster and less costly ships to be built. In 1897 the English engineer Charles Parsons introduced his steam turbine powered ship *Turbinia* to the world. She raced her 44-ton bulk at a speed of 34½ knots.

So impressive was this display that the Cunard steamship company installed steam turbines on their new ships the *Lusitania* and *Mauretania*. The 800-foot-long *Mauretania*, a four-screw ship, proved her worth shortly after her maiden voyage in 1907 by setting up a new record for the Atlantic crossing – an average speed of 25 knots. The 32000-ton *Mauretania* held the Blue Riband for 22 years.

Remaining in the forefront of developments, the *Mauretania* switched to oil from coal-burning after World War I. But by then the internal combustion engine had gone to sea, in the shape of the Diesel engine. The 5000-ton cargo vessel *Selandia* of 1911 was the first ocean-going motor ship, and she sailed successfully until 1942. Her design was entirely functional. The engine she used required no funnel – and so none was fitted. Diesel engines were eventually introduced into passenger ships in the 1920s, and proved to be more efficient in fuel consumption.

However, the most efficient fuel user of all is

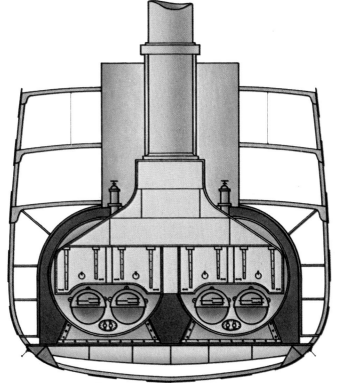

Cross section of a steamship of the late 19th century, showing boiler room located deep in the ship. Each boiler room was surrounded by coal bunkers and surmounted by a large smoke uptake leading to a funnel. Virtually the entire midship section of a steam vessel could thus be given over to the propulsion machinery. The bridge and officers' quarters were situated above.

the nuclear-powered ship. The American cargo ship *Savannah* used 120 lb of uranium fuel for 330000 miles of steaming. But the *Savannah* was not a commercial success. Two thousand tons of her weight went in shielding the nuclear power plant. And despite her low consumption, each pound of fuel costs about £3000.

Nuclear power becomes economical for ships requiring more than 100000 horsepower, and nuclear-powered container ships may be a practical proposition for the 1980s. However, the safety problems that would arise if such a

ship were grounded are dreadful to contemplate. The success of the gas turbine in powering large warships may result in its extension to merchant ships as a light, powerful propulsion system. But the natural conservatism of shipowners is shown by the fact that some new steamships still contain the old-style reciprocating steam engine. Even if a revolutionary new method of propulsion is discovered overnight, diesel engines and steam turbines are likely to remain the major movers of the world's shipping into the 1990s.

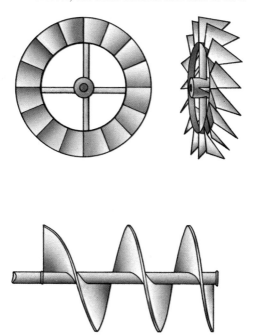

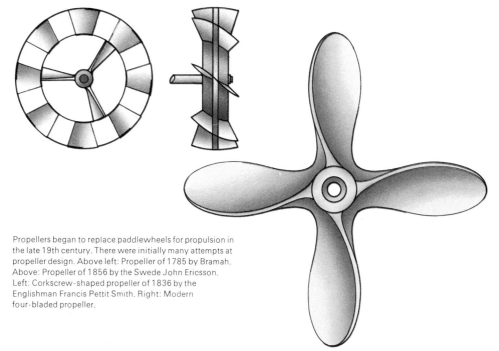

Propellers began to replace paddlewheels for propulsion in the late 19th century. There were initially many attempts at propeller design. Above left: Propeller of 1785 by Bramah. Above: Propeller of 1856 by the Swede John Ericsson. Left: Corkscrew-shaped propeller of 1836 by the Englishman Francis Pettit Smith. Right: Modern four-bladed propeller.

Ship design
the shape of ships

Ships change in shape as a result of technical advances and changing fashions in design. But until recently the conservatism of shipowners was such that technical advances did not automatically lead to outstanding changes in design. An example of this attitude came with the introduction of the marine diesel engine. Strictly, such an engine requires only an exhaust pipe, like a diesel truck, and the early diesel ship *Selandia* had no funnels at all. But shipowners preferred the more confident look of a funnel – or a row of them. Several passenger steamships have had dummy funnels added, and funnels have often been made unnecessarily high, squat or raked depending on the style then in vogue. However, tall funnels were necessary to create an up draught to keep the fires burning until the introduction of fans to either force or draw air through the boilers.

The reduction in the number of boilers, and the changeover to diesels, has reduced the need for funnels, and no one is any longer impressed by a row of smokestacks. In the case of motor ships, there have been many interesting methods of streamlining the exhausts while retaining the traditional look of a ship. Even the recent nuclear-powered ships which have no exhaust at all still retain the vestige of a funnel in their design. Such a dummy stack can serve the purpose of a mast and carry lights and flags. On some passenger ships, dummy funnels have been fitted out as lounge bars.

The early steamships had the so-called 'three-island' profile: a long forecastle, a central bridge and a raised poop at the stern. The

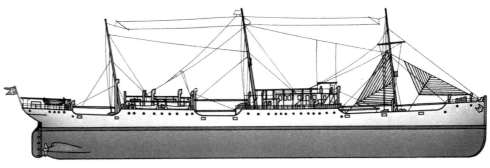

Selandia of 1911, an early diesel-propelled cargo vessel, had no funnels

introduction of tankers made it desirable to move the power plant to the stern, out of the way of the inflammable cargo.

This trend has been followed by virtually all classes of ship. The move leaves the wide midship section free for cargo or passengers.

Bow shapes are another aspect of ship design only loosely connected with actual technical advances. The bold, straight stem of ships of 50 years ago gave way to the flared and raked bows of more modern ships. The initial trend was for purely artistic reasons – a raked, clipper-like bow gave a ship a sense of speed. But later, raked bows became associated with the need to put a flare at the front to throw water clear of the decks and prevent the ship sliding straight into seas as she pitched. Another style point is a ship's stern. The old style of overhanging or *counter* stern arose in the days of slow ships that could be caught by a following sea. As ships got faster, it was found that a *cruiser* stern helped increase speed. Nowadays, the bluff *transom* stern is very common. It gives greater deck area aft, which can be used to increase the ship's carrying capacity.

The most startling design change in recent years has been the introduction of the incongruous-looking bulbous bow. This strange appendage reduces the resistance of ships

travelling at high speed. It works by changing the pressure distribution around the fore end of a ship, reducing the size of the bow wave and cutting the wave-making resistance on a ship. For the same horsepower a ship will therefore go slightly faster with a bulbous bow – perhaps as much as half a knot. Bulbous bows are fitted to a large proportion of modern container ships, tankers and bulk carriers.

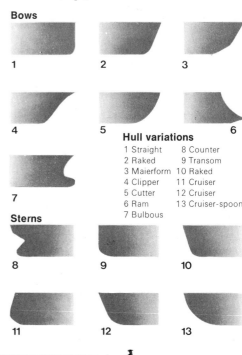

Bows

1   2   3

4   5   6

Hull variations

1 Straight	8 Counter
2 Raked	9 Transom
3 Maierform	10 Raked
4 Clipper	11 Cruiser
5 Cutter	12 Cruiser
6 Ram	13 Cruiser-spoon
7 Bulbous	

7

Sterns

8   9   10

11   12   13

Changing ship outlines: Above, three-island. Below, engines aft

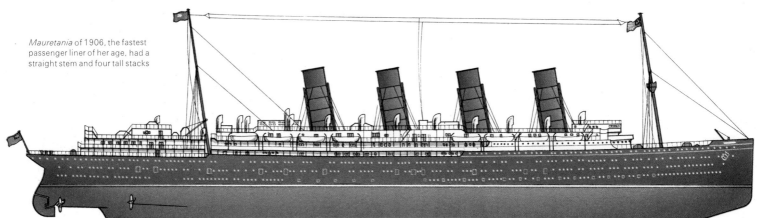

Mauretania of 1906, the fastest passenger liner of her age, had a straight stem and four tall stacks

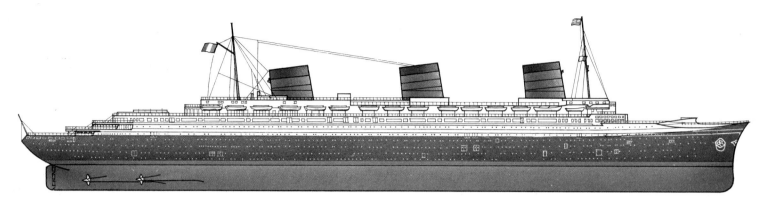

Normandie of 1935 looked like an artist's impression of a ship of the 1970s

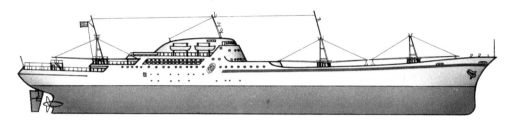

Savannah of 1962, first nuclear-powered merchant ship, signifies the shape of ships to come

Stability

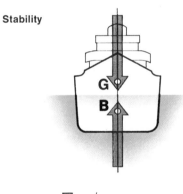

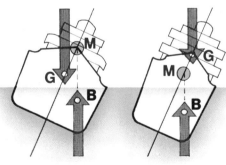

The most important safety aspect of any ship is *stability* – the capacity of keeping an even keel. The first requirement is that weight in the ship be symmetrically distributed. At sea, under the force of wind and wave, it is important that the ship is not 'top heavy'. Technically, this means that when the ship rolls, her *centre of gravity* – the point through which gravity acts on the ship – should always be on the ship-board side of the *centre of buoyancy* – the point through which the supporting force of the water acts. The centre of buoyancy shifts as the ship rolls, but the centre of gravity remains fixed. Naval architects use a point called the *metacentre* when calculating the stability of a ship. The metacentre is the point where the centre of buoyancy intersects the centre line of the ship (diagram 1). The naval architect must ensure that the centre of gravity is an acceptable distance below the metacentre (diagram 2), so that the forces of gravity and buoyancy act to upright a rolling ship. If the centre of gravity is too high, the forces of gravity and buoyancy may act to capsize the ship (diagram 3).

Planning a ship

A good ship, from an owner's point of view, is one that earns more than it costs to build and run. The shipowner tries to ensure that this requirement is met by issuing a specification to his builder. This detailed document sets out the carrying capacity of the projected ship, the speed required, maximum dimensions to ensure that she can navigate available waterways, and many other economically vital points affecting the design and operation of the ship.

The owner arrives at these specifications from a shrewd examination of the available supply and likely demand of the commodity he is shipping, plus competition from other shippers on the same route. One important factor is the prediction of future trade, for a too-small ship on an expanding route can be as much a disadvantage as a too-large ship on a route that is declining. The trick, in fact, is to produce the cheapest ship that will do the job. Some shipyards have helped in the search for economy by producing standardized general designs which can be modified in detail to meet the shipowner's demands.

The naval architect is the man who turns the owner's requirements into an actual design for a ship. Wherever possible, the naval architect uses a similar ship already in existence as a guide to the weight and dimensions of the new vessel. The dimensions affect both the carrying capacity of the ship, its stability and its structural strength, as well as the power required to propel it. Very long ships can have problems of berthing and manoeuvring in restricted waterways, and bend easily as waves pass underneath them. Consequently, tankers and bulk carriers are now made deep and wide for a given length; their beam is about one sixth their length. But for fast ships, extra width introduces more drag. Modern cargo vessels are therefore built seven or eight times longer than they are wide.

The actual lines of the ship's hull are drawn up on a series of plans. The final shape of the hull, and the exact engine power needed to propel it at the required speed, are decided by tank testing an accurate scale model. Every ship has to work against the friction of water along its hull. The more this can be reduced by reducing the underwater area of the hull, the less power is needed. Another problem is the amount of energy lost in simply pushing water aside – the so-called wave-making resistance. The higher the speed, the more energy that is lost in wave making.

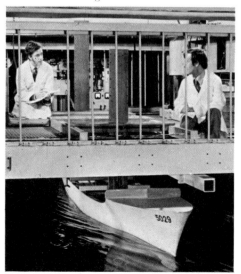

Technicians check the performance of a ship model being towed through artificial waves in a testing tank. Results of such studies aid ship designers in producing faster, more economical ships

21

Ship building
shipyard systems

Shipbuilding is a costly business. As much as £15 million has been paid for a giant tanker, and £1½ million is typical for an average-sized cargo vessel. Accordingly, in recent years shipbuilders have turned increasingly to mass production methods to keep prices down and cut delivery times. Wherever possible, men have been replaced by machines and ships are built from standard prefabricated parts. The time taken to assemble a ship can be halved. Whereas assembly of a giant tanker might have taken a year or more by traditional methods, modern shipyards are bringing this time down to about six months.

The capital outlay involved in shipyards is enormous – many millions of pounds. This money goes to install the latest techniques, which provide a continuous throughput of steel from incoming plates to outgoing ship sections. Complete sections are built in pre-fabrication sheds and lifted into position. In some large shipyards, bridge structures weighing several hundred tons can be finished down to the carpentry and plumbing before being swung out of the construction shop and onto the ship's deck by giant (and expensive) cranes.

Ships are built on land, and getting the larger vessels into their proper environment – the sea – presents a growing problem. For these ships, running down a slipway can present the most hazardous journey they will ever face. Not only is there the danger of grounding if the shipyard is on the shore of a narrow river, but stresses are set up as the stern is buoyed up by the water while the bow remains on solid land.

One solution is to build the ship in a large dry dock. This has the advantage that the vessel can be constructed on the level and is

then floated out by flooding the dock. But actually excavating such a dock costs millions of pounds, and if the shipbuilder underestimates the size of future ships he may be stuck with an expensive, and ultimately useless hole in the ground. Such has been the case in Japan, for one, where the early tanker builders failed to look far enough ahead and constructed dry docks only large enough for ships of around 100000 tons deadweight. Harland and Wolf in Belfast have built a dry dock capable of holding a million-ton tanker – which may really be the upper limit. This dock can be partitioned to build several smaller ships at a time. But the dock cost around £15 million to complete.

A cheaper approach is being pioneered by some shipyards. They build ships in large sections which are launched separately and then welded together in the water. A quarter-million-ton tanker can be constructed in two halves, while several portions could be joined up to make larger vessels. The joining operation is accomplished by accurately lining up the sections, clamping them together and placing around the join an air-filled collar large enough for workmen to operate in.

Although most ships are now made of welded steel plates, it is only since World War II that this method has become generally accepted. Shippers initially distrusted welding because they believed it produced weaker joints than riveting. Indeed, some of the standardized vessels built to short order during the last war had welded joints that failed. But riveting, which is akin to nailing together pieces of timber, was less efficient – and more costly – than welding. The overlap of plates, increases the total weight of steel in the hull

Large welded sections of a ship, seen in the foreground wait to be lifted into place by the giant crane capable of handling loads of over 800 tons.

and more power is needed to drive a riveted lapped-plate hull through the water than a flush-welded hull. Once the technical problems of welding had been sorted out, it was economically inevitable that the riveter should be forced out of business.

How is a new ship designed? The largest companies have their own designers, and in the United States there are large design consultants who prepare plans for a shipowner. In Europe and Japan, however, the shipyard often designs the ship to the owner's specification. The more standardized these designs can become, the cheaper and easier it is for the shipbuilder to construct the vessel. In Sweden the Arendal shipyard actually restricts its order to tankers and bulk carriers, preferably in series of identical sister ships.

Once the design is outlined, the shipbuilder will have a wax model tested in a water tank.

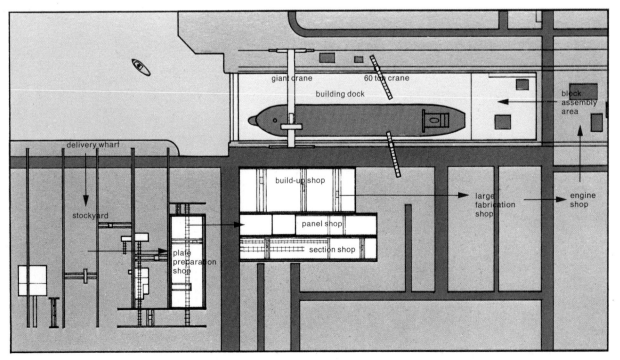

Plan view of a modern large shipbuilding works. Giant vessels are constructed in the dry dock from prefabricated parts made in the prefabrication sheds (lower centre). These sections are stored at the end of the dock, ready for lifting into position by the travelling gantry crane. Steel plates arrive and are stored in the plate yard (far left). Magnetic cranes running on overhead rails pick them up when wanted. They are cleaned and painted in adjacent sheds.

These tests were first devised around 1870 by the English naval architect William Froude, who discovered that a scale model of a ship can be used to accurately predict the behaviour of a full-sized craft. Modern testing tanks have helped discover the most efficient hull forms, and their measurements ensure that the power plant of the ship is adequately matched to the owner's requirements. Under-powered or over-powered ships can be equally wasteful.

The naval architect has to take into account the forces acting upon a ship at sea. As waves lift or strike the ship they try to bend it, crush it or throw it out of square. Forces acting at various points on a ship in different sea conditions can be measured in test tanks. It is also becoming possible to mathematically predict the performance of a given ship design, but at present designers prefer to rely on actual experiments in tanks rather than depend entirely on numerical predictions.

In the steel-plate-handling section of modern shipyards a mechanization revolution has reduced the number of men required. Incoming steel plates are cleaned by shot-blasting and then coated with a matt primer paint to

Steel plates are lifted magnetically from their piles in the plate yard and fed into shot blasting and priming shops

Prefabricated bridge structure, weighing several hundred tons, is lowered into place.

Hull of a 250 000-ton deadweight tanker takes shape in a shipyard building dock

prevent corrosion. The plates are cut by gas torches which either follow an optically projected plan or, more likely, are controlled by a series of co-ordinates in a computer which specify the exact path that the cutting torch is to follow. The old-fashioned mould loft, in which the plates were marked up from full-size templates like dress patterns, has gone for ever. Modern methods are quicker, cheaper and more accurate. Increasing mechanization means that even the curved plates required for stern and bow sections can now be shaped automatically by machine. Automatic welding of the flat, square plates that make up a ship's sides is another advance.

A completed ship goes for sea trials before its final acceptance by the shipowner. Trials, which last a few days, involve testing all equipment on board and confirming that the vessel performs as she was meant to. Only then will the shipowner take delivery of her.

Shipbuilding in the future, although it is unlikely to change as radically as in the past

20 years, will most likely emphasize the change to efficient mechanization and the further reduction of human labour. In the late 1960s shipowners, perhaps miscalculating market trends, over-ordered on new shipping. This has resulted in a depression in the shipbuilding industry during the early 1970s. But because world trade is continually growing, shipbuilding seems certain to expand again.

Production-line method of shipbuilding pioneered in Sweden is shown right. The ship is constructed under cover, starting with the stern, and pushed out of the construction shed through an adjustable door into a dry dock. Fitting out of the bridge is completed while the bow section is being built. The finished ship is launched by flooding the dock.

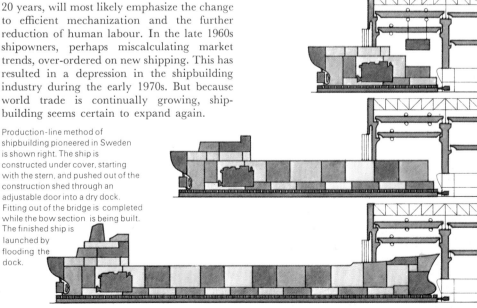

Marine engines
diesel

Marine engines come in four main types: the diesel engine, the steam turbine, the gas turbine and the marine nuclear plant. Each type has its own particular application.

The diesel engine is a form of internal combustion engine with pistons, similar to the engine in a motor vehicle. A diesel-propelled vessel is usually called a *motor ship*. Its power is expressed as *brake horsepower* – the power actually put out by the engine. *Effective horsepower* is the power developed by the piston in the cylinder, but some of this is lost by friction within the engine. Turbines, on the other hand, are large cylindrical rotors fitted with blades. As the rotors are only supported at each end the friction losses are small and the power is referred to as *shaft horsepower*. There is, however, a power loss through the gearing that is needed to reduce the turbine speed of 3000 to 5000 revolutions per minute down to the propeller speed of 80–100rpm. A propeller is more efficient the larger it is and the slower it turns.

The power output of diesel engines has risen from an average of 10000 brake horsepower in the 1940's to 40000 bhp today. By comparison, the engine of a small family car has an output of 80 bhp. Modern large diesel engines have cylinders nearly 3 ft in diameter, developing nearly 4000 bhp. The engines turn at the relatively slow speed of about 108 rpm, which

Main components for different propulsion machinery

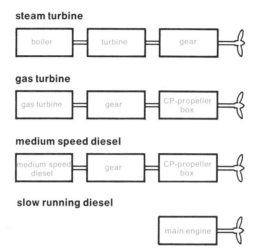

steam turbine

boiler — turbine — gear

gas turbine

gas turbine — gear — CP-propeller box

medium speed diesel

medium speed diesel — gear — CP-propeller box

slow running diesel

main engine

means that they can be directly connected to the propeller without gearing – the so-called direct-drive arrangement. Higher power could be produced by higher revolutions, but this would reduce the efficiency of the propeller. Two small 20000 bhp medium-speed diesel engines turning at 400 rpm could replace the single large slow-speed engine, but gearing would be required to obtain the correct

Four engine-room arrangements, shown left, underline the simplicity of powering a ship by slow-speed diesel. Turbines need a large reduction gearing to step down their high revolutions. Gas turbines and medium-speed diesels require controllable-pitch (CP) propellers. Changing the pitch of propeller blades gives speed adjustments which greatly increase the vessel's manoeuvrability. Reversing the pitch reverses the vessel. Steam turbines and slow-speed diesels can be reversed easily and so do not need a CP box. However, a steam turbine is open to failure from a number of sources, including the boiler. A slow-speed diesel still delivers power even if several cylinders are out of order. Only a broken propeller drive or propeller shaft would prevent the ship from proceeding under its own power.

propeller speed. An important result of the high power output of modern diesels has been that engine weight for a given power has been reduced by half in the past 20 years. Despite this, a 40000 bhp diesel engine weighs all of 1000 tons.

The large slow-speed diesel engine has a bright future because of the trend towards larger merchant ship types, particularly tankers and bulk carriers. These two predominant merchant ship types will by the 1980's have average deadweights of 200000 tons and 100000 tons respectively. At these sizes the powerful large-bore diesel engine can meet all power requirements.

There was once a trend in very large vessels towards twin screws for better manoeuvrability and improved safety at slow speeds. But the introduction of powerful bow thrusters and new steering techniques is changing this line of thought. The new large-bore diesel engines can operate quite reliably. The designs are tested extensively by computer programmes which simulate operating conditions before the machines are even built. This is far safer, more exacting and less time consuming than a series of engine tests spread over several months.

In the 1980's about half the tankers of 200000 tons will be fitted with large-bore, direct-drive diesel engines, and the same type will be fitted to approximately 75 per cent of the 100000-ton bulk carriers. The main reason for this is the low fuel consumption of this type of engine.

Work is now in progress to enable the diesel engine to operate on methane. The results indicate that they will be able to run on the gas that boils off naturally from a cargo of liquefied methane. Liquefied methane carriers have been ordered equivalent in size to tankers of 120000 to 130000 tons deadweight. For these, the large-bore diesel engines would be very suitable.

If current growth continues, in the 1980's nearly 20 per cent of the world's merchant vessels over 1000 tons gross will be powered by medium-speed diesel engines. These are so-called because they operate between 150 and 450 rpm, and are geared to the propeller. This

Cutaway of a large marine diesel, giving an indication of the size of the piston and piston stroke (which can be 6ft long or more)

Marine engines
gas turbine

type of engine was once restricted to smaller cargo ships, short-sea traders, coasters, ferries and harbour craft. But today medium-speed diesel engines are to be found in fast cargo liners of the 12000 to 15000 tons d.w. class as well as in tankers and bulk carriers. This type of machinery costs less than the slow-speed diesel engine, and its smaller size and weight can result in a smaller, cheaper ship.

The power output of medium-speed diesels ranges from 2000 to 20000 bhp. Some ships have been fitted with four such engines, giving a total power of 80000 bhp. Medium-speed engines weigh approximately 30 to 35 lb per bhp, but this will soon drop to 15 to 20 lb per bhp because of increased power output per cylinder.

In a turbine, the shaft is attached to blades or vanes which are turned by the passage of steam. A windmill is a simple form of turbine, turned by the wind. Waterwheels are also turbines.

Turbines have always signified speed at sea because in the early days gearing was not available and their fast-spinning shafts were directly coupled to the propeller. They were much used in fast passenger vessels and naval ships. Turbines used coal, and later oil, to fire boilers which turned water into steam. The fuel consumption of steam turbine plants has steadily fallen from about 0.58 lb per shp-hour in the early 1940's to 0.36 lb per shp-hour in the early 1970's. The large diesel engine uses about 0.33 lb per bhp-hour.

Now that powers of 30000 shp and upwards are becoming common, the steam turbine, operating under fully automatic control and with gearing providing the optimum propeller speed, is an attractive choice for main propulsion units. It is 50 per cent lighter than the diesel, and on very large tankers some of the steam can be used to drive the large cargo oil pumps. Turbines are nearly always the choice for container ships, which operate at high speeds, but because of their draught must use smaller propellers operating at 130 rpm.

In the mid 1950's the gas turbine was tested in two types of merchant ship, but for economical as well as technical reasons the projects failed to attract sufficient interest in the shipping industry. Gas turbines differ from steam turbines in that gas rather than steam is used to turn the shaft. The initial difficulties were due to the unavailability of metals to withstand the high temperatures of the gas, and low efficiency of operation.

Today, interest in gas turbines is increasing. Many naval vessels are powered by gas turbines, and four 30-knot, 40000 ton d.w. container ships have each been fitted with two 32000 shp gas turbines. Several other vessel types are also being fitted with this type of engine. The gas turbine is very light, easily removed for maintenance and suitable for complete automation. Gas turbines are being used to drive the cargo pumps of very large

tankers and they are also proving popular as standby electric-generating plants.

Nuclear power is technically feasible as the main propulsion source for ships, but until the recent upsurge in power requirements there was no economic justification for such machinery. The nuclear-powered ship differs from a conventional steam turbine ship in that it uses the energy released by the decay of radioactive fuel to boil water. The steam is used to turn a shaft via a turbine in the conventional way.

Now that powers of from 50000 to 120000 shp are being demanded for fast container ships the interest in the nuclear power unit has increased. Design studies indicate that a fleet of fast container ships could be operated at a profit with nuclear engines – and further price increases in oil fuels would make the nuclear plant even more attractive.

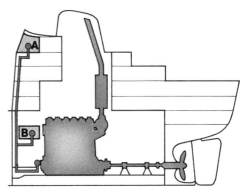

Slow-speed diesel engine shown in position on a ship, directly coupled to the propeller. Operation of the engine can be controlled from the bridge (A) or from the engine room (B)

12-cylinder marine diesel engine, capable of delivering 31 400 bhp, seen on the test bed

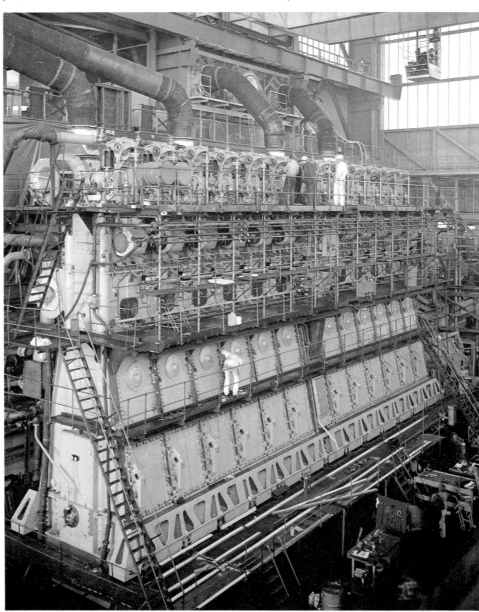

Automation in shipping
on-board information

The bridge of a ship is becoming as complex as the flight deck of an aircraft. The modern ship's master has before him an array of panels giving information on the running of the on-board machinery, and a number of controls which allow him to remotely operate the ship – everything from opening hatches to starting the engines. This is automation – the co-ordination of all the processes on a ship. Properly applied automation allows shipowners to operate their ships and machinery with the maximum efficiency.

Ships today are so expensive, and their machinery so complex and powerful that shipowners are investing in equipment to continuously monitor important circuits. An example is the control of the temperature of the lubricating oil in a diesel engine. A sensing element continually signals the oil temperature, and this figure is automatically compared with the fixed upper and lower limits of the system. If necessary, control action is taken by increasing or decreasing the flow of cooling water to the lubricating oil system. At the same time, if the oil temperature is outside the prescribed limits an alarm is sounded and a record is automatically made of the condition, with the time it occurred.

Nearly 90 per cent of the new ships coming into service are fitted with either complete or partial automation. The cost of such installations ranges from £3000 to £100000. In the case of a 250000-ton tanker costing at least £16 million the investment of £100000 in complete automation is justifiable, particularly considering the high value of the cargo.

Automation also provides new opportunities for better social conditions on board ship, relieving staff of many tedious and repetitive tasks. However, experienced engineers are still needed in case of emergencies. In many instances engine rooms can be left unmanned for periods of up to 16 hours. Special programmes are designed so that by pressing a button on the control panel on the bridge, all the auxiliary systems connected with the main engine are operated and the engine is started. Faced with a giant control panel on his bridge, the captain of at least one large ship has described his function, with an intended pun, as 'chairman of the board'.

A completely integrated ship's management system combines the functions of engine room control and monitoring, collision avoidance, docking and manoeuvring, navigation and administration. Full automation can be applied to either motor-driven or steam-turbine-driven vessels. In the latter case the control of the turbines which drive the propeller must be linked with the control of the boilers which produce the steam for the turbines.

The control centre of the engine room is air conditioned and sound proofed. This makes a much better environment for both the engine-room staff and the complex electronic equipment. Automation has brought a new

Control panel of the ISIS 300, an automatic system for monitoring the condition of ship's engines and cargo. Faults are flashed up on control panel alarms (centre of picture) and a written record is printed by the teletype machine (far left). Sensors are wired into all the systems – such as engine oil temperature – that are to be monitored. The central processor unit accepts signals from all these sensors and compares them with pre-set limits. It sounds the alarm and indicates the fault if the sensor readings stray from acceptable values. Such equipment eliminates routine watchkeeping and allows engine rooms to be left unmanned.

manning philosophy in which the engine-room department is divided into two sections, one comprising watchkeepers who are located in the control room and service engineers who are thus free to concentrate on machinery maintenance.

Automation has the advantages of making maintenance or repair periods less frequent, increasing the efficiency of machinery operation, steering a straighter course by use of the automatic helmsman, and presenting the most important information to the ship operator in order to simplify decision making. The situation is similar to that in an airliner, where the automatic equipment keeps the pilot fully informed of all the principal and many of the auxiliary systems.

Automation is not restricted to shipboard use, and many shipping companies have computer programmes which can rapidly select the best ships for a particular route. The computers can also analyse performance data of the ships, and gauge when they need taking out of service for propeller repair or bottom cleaning.

Several ships are now in service with shipboard computers which can carry out many operations, such as navigation calculations, the loading and discharging tank sequence on tankers, calculations of stresses within a ship's structure, and the operation of machinery. Some shipowners consider that a shipboard computer will be essential in the mid-1970's, particularly linked to ship's radar to give advance warning of possible collision situations.

Computers will be particularly helpful in aiding approach through river estuaries with restricted room, and also docking manoeuvres. With docking speeds down to imperceptible levels – a few feet per minute – a pilot cannot judge his closing speed and, with large tankers cannot see the ship touching its fender. Ships moving side-on can also swing lengthwise, and this is not always detectable visually. To prevent giant ships flattening their moorings, therefore, a pilot requires a ship-to-shore radar link which can compute for him the marginal alterations to speed and angle of approach that he must make to achieve a successful docking.

With a computer already on board to aid the handling of a ship, its use can be extended to include navigation by satellite. Ship control engineers speak jokingly of the imaginary *SS Keymatic* – a reference to the washing machine controlled by a simple pre-coded key. But automatic operation of a ship, particularly cargo discharge, according to a series of cards fed into its machinery is already possible. In fact, all the functions that it has traditionally required men to perform will eventually be automated. The idea of an unmanned ship sailing the seas automatically may never come to fruition – no one is likely to trust a machine that much. But just as surely as a space probe can be sent out to automatically voyage among the planets, so a fully automated ship will become possible.

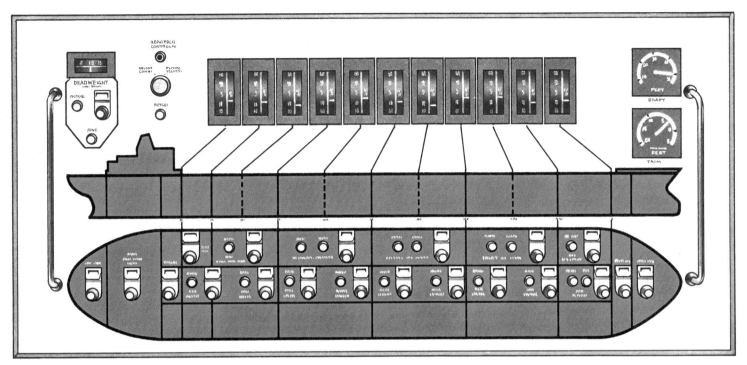

To avoid unallowable bending and shear stresses in a hull, cargo is placed according to a carefully precalculated plan. Standard plans are usually produced by a digital computer – but cannot, however, cover every distribution problem. The use of a computer on-board ship is able to overcome these problems. The computer (above) calculates correct cargo distribution in tankers and bulk carriers. Appropriate load distribution can always be determined immediately. This avoids dangerous stresses in the hull structure being set up.

The computer continuously presents deadweight, mean draught, trim and either shear forces or, by the flick of a switch, bending moments simultaneously for all read-out points.

It is important that certain types of vessel are loaded in the correct manner in order to avoid setting up high stresses in the hull structure. Very large tankers and ore carriers come into this category and so do container ships where a distortion in the hull might cause a container to stick in the guide rails which run down to the bottom of the container hold.

Several designs of cargo loading control systems are available which permit the rapid and accurate calculation of the most suitable cargo distribution in the hull. The main instrument is usually located in the bridge, each instrument being designed to incorporate certain naval architectural features of the ship.

Machinery oriented automation includes engine control, engine monitoring, auxiliary machinery control, auxiliary machinery monitoring and cargo handling. The bridge systems are concerned with collision avoidance, navigation, docking administration and communications.

While there are the two clearly separate basic systems, machinery and bridge, the latter can be represented on the bridge by a small group of instruments each representing a number of units in the machinery space. The two basic displays on the bridge are designated machinery and bridge and by a combination of the two, the officer in charge has all the information required for any decision in an emergency.

The application of modern computer technology to the marine industry is a recent development but many shipowners acknowledge the need to automate such functions as collision avoidance, navigation, control of engines and sub-systems and cargo handling.

Digital displays are fitted in the engineer's office which is within the accommodation and using closed circuit television it is possible to view the machinery data on display at any desired area in the ship.

From the bridge the opening and closing of the hatch covers is controlled and it is now possible to control the raising and lowering of the ship's anchor. Closed circuit television can be used to keep the area under the vessel's bows under close observation.

Mooring lines are attached to automatic tensioning winches so that once the mooring has been connected the tension will always be maintained whatever the state of the tide and the vessel's position at a cargo fitting.

The arbitrary barriers have been removed from between a ship's main departments, deck, engine and catering and today there are many vessels at sea with general purpose crews where each crew member can undertake a variety of tasks during moments of peak load. General purpose crews are the answer to the problems facing an owner with a greatly reduced crew due to automation within the various departments.

The 477 000-ton d.w. tanker put into service in 1973 has a crew of 38, including the captain – only 10 men more than a vessel less than half the size.

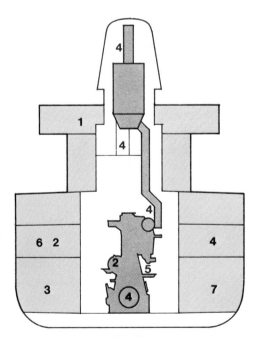

A ship owner can now be offered integrated automation packages designed to suit his particular requirements. This can cover:-
1 communication and navigational aids
2 main engine control and instrumentation
3 motor drives for auxiliaries
4 control and monitoring of pressures, levels and temperatures
5 medium speed diesel or diesel-electric propulsion
6 switchboards
7 generators

Passenger ships
old-fashioned splendour

Passenger liners have always been the glamour vessels of shipping: metal cities haring across the oceans of the world at speeds over three times those of racing yachts. But, in the past 20 years, passenger shipping has changed in the face of competition from airlines. At the peak of their popularity in 1957, liners made 2000 crossings of the North Atlantic in a year; now it's one-tenth that amount. Many routes have disappeared completely, such as the line from England to India. In 1970, after 128 years of service, this scheduled route finally became uneconomic. Lower air fares mean that ships have lost even their financial edge. The run-down in passenger sea routes is near-complete the world over.

This would be a gloomy picture indeed were it not for the booming cruise market, which has actually led to the construction of new and improved passenger ships. The *Queen Elizabeth II* is an example of how ships have had to alter. Her predecessors, the *Queen Mary* and *Queen Elizabeth*, were forced off the North Atlantic run by falling demand. They could not be switched to the tropical cruise routes because their decks had been built enclosed against the rough Atlantic weather. The *QEII* is a smaller ship, with open decks that allow her to be used as a cruise vessel when demand on the North Atlantic route declines in winter.

Passengers and cargo were once of almost equal importance to shipowners. Some passenger routes were able to operate profitably because of lucrative mail contracts from governments. It was such a contract that set up Samuel Cunard on the North Atlantic route. Up until about 50 years ago, many owners allowed passengers and cargo an equal share of space on

the same ship. But it became inconvenient to provide the necessary facilities for passengers, and shipping lines began to specialize, segregating cargo and people. The passenger-carrying cargo liner, once very popular with people but not with shipping companies, has now all but disappeared. Now that aeroplanes carry most of the passenger traffic between continents, the relative importance of cargo shipping has grown still further. The world's largest passenger-ship operators, the British P & O group, run only 13 passenger vessels out of a total fleet of 182 ships.

Modern liners are built with light, aluminium superstructure, to keep weight down and save on power requirements. In response to changing social attitudes, new passenger ships have no class structure: every passenger is given the run of the vessel. According to policy statements by the major shipping companies, one-class ships are here to stay.

The *QEII* and the French liner *France*, the only major passenger ships now operating on the North Atlantic run, are the last of a magnificent breed of ships – the superliners. Their era began just before World War I when the first passenger ships of more than 50 000 tons were built. These German liners, the *Imperator*, *Vaterland* and the *Bismarck*, were built for size rather than speed. They were not intended to outpace the record-holding British ships *Lusitania* and *Mauretania*, but rather to take advantage of the million-passenger-a-year migration from Europe to North America – and the less-publicized half-million passengers a year returning to their home countries. But this trio of German giants had no chance to establish itself before war broke out. After hostilities ceased they were transferred as war reparations to British and American lines.

In 1921 the United States began to limit immigration, and the North Atlantic passenger boom faltered. But the prosperity of postwar America pushed passenger numbers up to the million mark again by 1927, and sparked off

Air-conditioned luxury passenger cabin in the modern liner *Queen Elizabeth II* gives a view of the sea

another bout of Blue Riband fever – the race for the fastest Atlantic crossing.

The Germans, once more desperate for prestige, broke the *Mauretania's* hold on the Blue Riband in 1929 with the *Bremen*, which maintained an average speed of virtually 28 knots. In 1933 the Italian liner *Rex* went a knot above this, a performance that coincided with the introduction of the first actual trophy for the North Atlantic speed record, presented by Mr R. K. Hales.

In 1935 the 80 000-ton *Normandie* of the French Line, considered to be one of the most beautiful ships ever built, became the first liner to put up an average speed of over 30 knots across the North Atlantic. Fittingly, she was also the first liner over 1000 feet long. But the next year the *Queen Mary* appeared on the scene, and in 1938 decisively wrested the Blue Riband with a 31.7 knot crossing.

The great depression saw passenger travel diminishing during the 1930's, and a trend towards low-cost travel. A number of liners

Queen Elizabeth II from the air, showing open deck space and two outside swimming pools. The single funnel has a wind scoop to drive fumes clear of the decks. Her forward mast, topped by a satellite navigation aerial, also acts as a duct for clearing waste air from the kitchen

were taken off scheduled routes and sent cruising. Despite this the Cunard Line, determined to set up a two-ship express service, went ahead with the building of the largest-ever passenger liner, the *Queen Elizabeth*. This 83 700-ton liner was launched shortly before World War II broke out, and her first voyages were as a troop ship. She never held the Blue Riband. And if the German government had had its way she would have been dwarfed by a 90 000-ton liner they planned to call the *Viktoria*.

In 1952 the last Blue Riband holder, the 53 000-ton United States, set up a record average speed of 35 knots. As with many superliners, she was heavily subsidized by her owners' government. The US government contributed over half her £30 million cost, because the *United States* was in fact a naval auxiliary adapted for the luxury liner trade. Her turbines generated 220 000 shaft horsepower, and she was reputed to touch 40 knots flat out.

In the 1950's the number of passengers carried across the North Atlantic by liners climbed once again to the magical million-a-year mark. But at the same time the number of passengers carried by the airlines rose to the same figure. After 1957, the airline share rose and that of passenger ships declined. Currently, only 250 000 people cross the Atlantic by liner. The airlines' share has grown to well over 10 million.

In 1962 the 66 000-ton French superliner *France* completed her maiden voyage. Seven years later, she was followed by the fractionally smaller *Queen Elizabeth II*. These liners, adapted for winter cruising, co-operate on the transatlantic route during the summer season. They are the last of the superliners. By the end of the 1960's, the two original *Queens* were sold and the *United States* laid up. No one expects that such highly specialized giant liners will be built again.

Many of the ships now in full-time operation as cruise vessels were built originally for scheduled passenger transportation. They have gross tonnages of about 30 000 or 40 000 tons, and carry up to 2000 passengers. As these vessels are phased out, a new generation of ships in the 10 000 to 20 000-ton class is being built, specifically for short cruise holidays. These ships are designed around their accommodation and entertainment facilities, the accommodation being of modern hotel standard. They carry about 800 passengers.

The future of cruise ships such as these looks bright. Market research has shown that demand for holidays at sea is sure to grow. With the pleasure spots of the world becoming rapidly more developed, going to sea may be the only sure way to get away from it all.

Right: Yacht-like lines of the 14 000-ton *Cunard Adventurer*, one of the new generation of passenger ships built exclusively for cruising. Below: French Lines' *France*, 66 000-ton liner on regular summer transatlantic service with *Queen Elizabeth II*

Modern cargo ships
container

Cargo comes in all shapes and sizes. Each item of cargo must be individually arranged, counted, handled and put into a ship according to a detailed cargo plan. This takes time and manpower, and is costly. It is quicker and cheaper to have cargo of a standard shape and size which is easy to handle and stack. Such a cargo type is termed a 'unit load' – which in transportation usually means a container.

The so-called container revolution has come about only during the past decade, in response to the cost-cutting and time-saving requirements of modern trade. But the idea of containerization is not new. In fact, the use of containers for railways was proposed in 1846. A container system was introduced on the British railway network in the 1920s. In 1921 tea was carried by rail and road in metal containers made by a British firm that is still engaged in container manufacture.

What *is* new is the complete integration of road, rail, sea and handling facilities around the container. Once the cargo is packed into the container, it is not handled until it reaches its destination. This system was introduced in 1949 when John Woollam sent a box of sports goods across the Irish Sea. Woollam later founded a container shipping company, which introduced probably the world's first fully integrated container service in 1955. The White Pass and Yukon Route (originally a railway) introduced deep-sea container traffic from Canada in 1955, and had the advantage of running its own rail and road connections. In the United States, Malcolm McClean founded a container shipping service in 1956. This group came to be called Sea-Land Service, and is currently the world's largest container operator.

Part of hull in cross-section

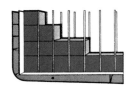

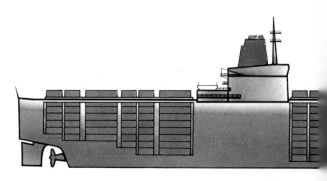

Principal dimensions

Length	950' 0"	289.55m
Beam	106' 0"	32.30m
Depth	80' 8"	24.60m
Draught	42' 8"	13.00m
Deadweight	47 800 t	
Gross tonnage	59 000 t	
Engine power	80 000 shp	
Bow thrusters	2 000 shp	
Service speed	26 knots	

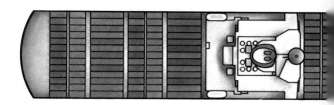

Container ships are split into vertical cells. The containers slip into position in each cell down guide rails. The containers sit on top of each other in the ship's hold. In a large ship, the containers may lie six deep and ten wide. Another three layers of containers can be stacked on the deck. The upper containers must be securely fastened for safety; in isolated cases, entire containers have been lost overboard. Other containers have been damaged by heavy seas. Container ships are now designed with distinctive, concave bow shapes to keep waves clear of the decks.

A container ship can do the work of four conventional cargo ships. Cargo vessels spend half their time tied up at a dock, loading or unloading. Charges incurred at a port could exceed the cost of an ocean journey. With containerization, the turn-round time of a large vessel has been slashed from weeks to days. The biggest container ships at present weigh 59000 tons gross (48000 tons deadweight) and have a capacity of 2200 containers. But, as with giant tankers, the sizes are sure to grow.

Containerization has involved many shipping companies in their greatest-ever single outlay. Whole fleets of container ships have been designed and built in a few years. To help share the cost and rationalize services, companies have joined into consortia. The British OCL group spent £50 million on a container programme in the late 1960s. Containerization elsewhere has been as complete. The United States Lines sold its conventional cargo vessels when its new fleet of container ships was ready. This confidence is justified by the fact that, on major routes such as the North Atlantic run, three-quarters of the cargo previously handled by cargo liners now goes to sea in a container. A container is simply a box. It is no more complex than a truck body, a railway freight van, or a ship's hold. Its advantage is that it performs all three roles.

Containers are made of aluminium, steel, plywood or fibreglass for lightness, with steel frames to give strength. The standard sizes for containers are 40, 20 or 10 feet long, 8 ft wide and 8ft high. However, some companies use their own sizes of container. The American Sea-Land Service, for instance, uses containers 35 ft long.

Most containers are completely enclosed, with locked doors at one end. But some have open tops or sides for loading special cargo. Liquids are carried in boiler-shaped tanks

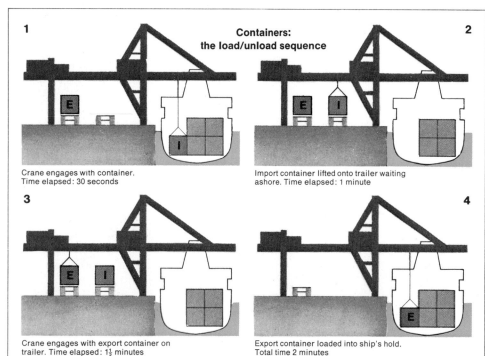

1 Crane engages with container. Time elapsed: 30 seconds

Containers: the load/unload sequence

2 Import container lifted onto trailer waiting ashore. Time elapsed: 1 minute

3 Crane engages with export container on trailer. Time elapsed: 1½ minutes

4 Export container loaded into ship's hold. Total time 2 minutes

Side view and plan of a typical fully cellular container ship capable of carrying over 2000 20 ft standard containers. This ship is powered by two steam turbines, each of 40,000 shaft horsepower, and can sail non-stop from Europe to the Far East.

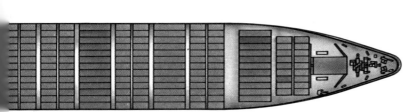

The big lift:
LASH lighter is floated out to waiting ship by a tug. At the ship's stern the on-board crane picks up the lighter and stacks it aboard. To unload a lighter, the sequence is reversed.

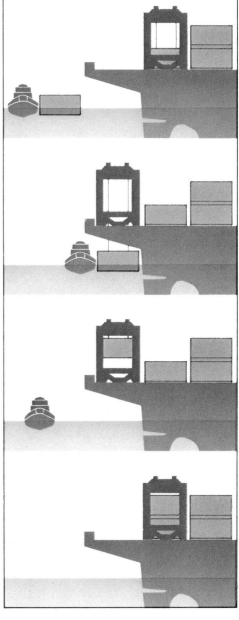

surrounded by a rectangular framework. Other containers are insulated or refrigerated. Containers are constructed according to international standards and are inspected by insurance companies. Early containers were inclined to disintegrate with wear, or the walls could distort from pressure of cargo or wave impact.

Containers carry varied cargoes. Machine parts, partially assembled aircraft, motor cars, spirits, fruit and livestock have all made up container cargo. Each cargo must be secured and padded to prevent it shifting within the container – a technique known as stuffing – but this can be done by the user before dispatch. Because the cargo is constantly protected, containerization has slashed the value of claims for damaged cargo by 90 per cent.

A typical container journey may begin at an inland factory. The container is loaded on a special container chassis, and driven to a rail terminal. Here the container is transferred to a container wagon. Along with dozens of other containers it is pulled to the container port, where special handling equipment loads it into a container ship. Across an ocean, the procedure is reversed. The container remains sealed until it reaches its destination.

A modified version of containerization arose in 1968. It is known as lighter aboard ship – LASH for short – and is patented. In the LASH system, lighters are loaded on the shore or up river and floated out to the ship waiting offshore. The ship hauls the lighters on board with its own gantry crane, and stacks them three high like containers. At the port of arrival, the lighters are unloaded and floated to shore. This saves both port costs and cuts time spent waiting for an empty berth (which can amount to days or weeks at some ports). An added advantage is that cargo can be dispatched or received in areas where there are no proper docking facilities or deep water.

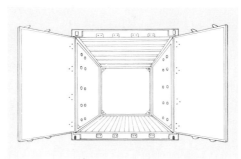

The open door:
looking inside a general cargo container

The LASH lighter is much larger than a conventional container, measuring about 61 ft long, 31 ft wide and 14 ft deep. LASH ships can load 4 lighters or 20 containers in an hour. But because of the extra capacity of a lighter, this amounts to about 1500 tons loaded by lighter per hour, as against 600 tons of cargo in containers.

LASH vessel, showing the moveable crane amidships

Conventional cargo ships
general-purpose vessels

Conventional cargo ships are not being swept from the seas by containerization. Only on certain busy routes, such as the North Atlantic run, has the switch to containers been near-complete. Elsewhere, the conventional cargo ship has maintained its hold, and is likely to do so for decades to come. It does not make economic sense for a small port, handling a few thousand tons of cargo a week, to install a container berth, handling equipment, and road and rail connections. Such a port is still best served by a general-purpose cargo ship, a judgement supported by the world's ship-owners who currently have orders for over 1000 ships, totalling something like 10 million tons deadweight.

Conventional cargo ships are helped by the fact that not all cargoes will economically containerize. Such cargoes are usually large (logs, for instance) or heavy (steel plates). Another disadvantage with containers is that, for every box at sea, another three are needed on land: one at the port of departure, one at the port of arrival, and one being repaired. Container ships themselves are expensive: they cost £240 per deadweight ton to build compared with £145 per ton for a conventional ship of the same size.

Trade data shows that the conventional cargo ship is still profitable, and many owners understandably prefer to continue using them. However, many cargo ship owners are hedging their bets by making their vessels dual purpose. Such a cargo vessel has capacity for ordinary cargo, and will in addition carry perhaps half its total load in containers. This method of hybridization is becoming a feature of modern cargo ships. Some can carry several hundred containers – more than many fully containerized vessels.

Barges being loaded onto the deck of a general-purpose cargo vessel. The barges are lifted from the water by giant Stulcken heavy-lift derricks. Those shown here are capable of lifting loads of 60 tons. The ability to load different types of cargo at speed is responsible for the wide variety of

derrick shapes seen on ships. Demand for heavier loads have led to derricks capable of lifting several hundred tons. Cranes are also being used instead of derricks, as they allow more accurate placing of cargo in hatches.

A modern cargo liner
Key

1 Swimming Pool	5 Crew Accommodation
2 Sliding Steel Hatch Covers	6 Store
	7 Refrigerated Store
3 Crane on Thwartship Track	8 Deep Tank for Liquid Cargo
4 Tween Deck Cargo Space	9 Engine Room

10 Engineers' Workshop	16 Deep Tank
11 Engine Control Room	17 Winch Control Cabin
12 Wing Fuel Tank	18 Stulcken Masts
13 Lower Hold	19 Heavy Lift Derrick
14 Water Ballast Tank	20 Radar Scanner
15 Cofferdam	

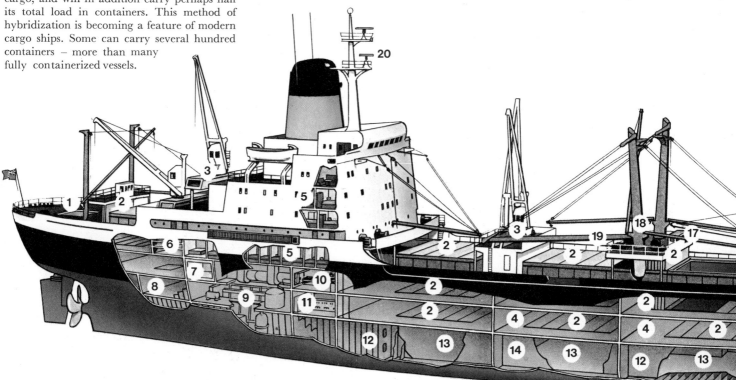

General-purpose cargo ships carry goods as various as those found in a general store: foodstuffs, textiles, machinery, consumer goods and small amounts of raw materials. These vessels fall into two main categories: the *liner,* and the dowdily named *tramp* – although the latter title no longer signifies an old and inefficient ship. The cargo liner operates to a strict schedule, arriving and departing on fixed dates and keeping to set routes. The tramp ship, unless chartered by a liner company, does not operate on fixed schedules but visits ports as and when cargoes are available.

Modern cargo liners have two or three decks, are from 10000 to 20000 tons deadweight and move at between 16 and 24 knots. They handle the so-called *break-bulk* and *bag-bulk* cargoes. These terms describe packages and loose cargo (tyres, drums and coiled wire, for instance), or cargo which is in bags such as coffee, potatoes and fertilizer. High-density cargoes such as ore and certain chemicals are only carried in small quantities, if at all. The tramp ship has one or two decks, is from 12000 to 20000 tons deadweight, and is propelled at about 15 knots. Tramp cargoes include bulk, break-bulk, bagged and high-density goods such as scrap metal. Diesel engines are used almost exclusively for all forms of cargo ship because they are more economical on fuel.

Although these ships are holding their own against containerization, there has still been a sudden move to improve general cargo ships. Side hatches have now been provided for loading of cargo by fork-lift trucks. Deck hatches have been enlarged, and derricks are being improved or replaced by heavy-duty cranes to aid loading. The modern cargo liner is also becoming a veritable express, with top speeds reaching 26 knots.

Modern general-purpose cargo liner, 521ft long, 30ft draught, 12 000 tons gross and service speed 21 knots.

One major change has been the general introduction of chilled or refrigerated compartments on cargo ships. These keep temperatures as low as −25°C for the transport of perishable goods such as meat and fish; fruit is kept chilled to prevent premature ripening but is not actually frozen. Temperatures are kept low by air coolers, which provide a continual exchange of air and thus also ventilate the cargo compartments. Some specialist cargo ships are exclusively refrigerated, and are termed *reefers.*

In recent years, the biggest development in cargo handling on conventional cargo ships is the use of *pallets.* These are boards of standard sizes – perhaps 4ft square, or as much as 16ft by 4ft – on which up to 10 or 12 tons of cargo can be loaded. Pallets can be easily lifted and stacked by fork lift trucks. They were the forerunners of containers.

In some cases, two sets of doors have been inserted on ships so that fork-lift trucks can load palletized cargo at the stern and drive off at the forward end with unloaded cargo on pallets. The after-end of some ships is now given over to vehicles which can drive in through stern doors and drive out again at their destination. This is the *roll on/roll off* system, as used in ferries.

Cargo ships have perhaps two decks, called 'tween decks, between the ship's bottom and its upper deck. These allow sections of cargo to be unloaded at intermediate ports. The enlargement of hatches means that cranes can now load cargo directly into place on these decks. Such arrangements help reduce the turn-round time of cargo ships. But in some forms of cargo ship, the 'tween decks can be folded back on hinges to the ship's walls or raised to the deck head. Movable decks add greatly to the operational scope of any general cargo ship, but are particularly suitable for car-carrying ships which need very small deck heights – only 5 or 6 feet. Such variations have enabled car exporters to ship up to 2000 cars in one direction with the decks in place and then move the decks out of the way to operate the ship as a small bulk carrier for grain or ore on the return voyage.

In the future, general cargo ships will become slightly larger, and there will eventually be much fewer of them. Shipping companies who go over to containerization tend to do so exclusively, and sell their conventional ships in order to finance their new venture. General cargo ships continue because only they can navigate in the restricted depth of water at so many of the smaller ports, and because the predominance of labour in many ports does not welcome containerization and its consequent reduction in dockside employment.

Many owners are still prepared to have ships built and to offer them for charter to shippers who have need for extra tonnage from time to time. The charter market is very common with cargo ships and tankers. The usual arrangements are *time charter* or *voyage charter*. In the first, a shipper operates an owner's ship for a given period of time. The vessel is then handed back and becomes available to another shipper who may need it. In voyage charter, the ship is taken for a specific voyage from one port to another. There is also *bareboat charter,* in which the owner hands his ship over completely for operation by the charterer for a given period. The charterer pays a rate for having the ship completely at his disposal, but he has to meet all expenditure in connection with its operation. This therefore relieves the owner of any outgoings.

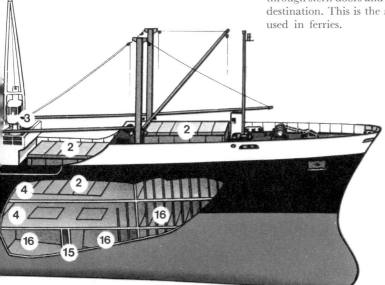

Bulk carriers

oil, bulk, ore

Underlying all developments in shipping is the need to reduce the cost of carriage, and it was for this reason that bulk carriers became popular. Once bulk carriers were used just for coal, iron ore or steel, but this cheap form of carriage is used today for numerous cargoes, including fertilizer, grain, sugar, salt, and many raw chemicals such as sulphur and phosphorus, as well as certain non-ferrous metals, for instance bauxite and alumina.

The conventional bulk carrier looks like a tanker: no cargo-handling gear, the bridge aft, and a limited number of hatches. Even its speed is the same, at between 14 and 16 knots. Bulk carriers cover the range 20 000–160 000 tons d.w. The world tonnage of ships used purely for dry-bulk carriage has risen in 10 years from 2 million to 50 million deadweight tons.

A few years ago, when shipowners realized the economies to be made by combining the role of the oil tanker with that of the bulk carrier, the oil-and-bulk carrier came into being. These vessels carry oil in large side and bottom tanks, but bulk cargo – usually iron ore – in the large centre hold. These vessels reduce the owner's dependence on the freight rate for oil, and eliminate much unprofitable time spent in ballast.

One of the modern breed of multi-purpose carriers is the so-called *OBO* ship, standing for oil-bulk-ore. These tanker-like vessels can carry more varied cargoes than the oil-ore ships. Their holds are wider because they have no wing tanks, but when carrying ore alternate holds have to be left empty to maintain stability.

The weight of the cargo is a special problem with ore-carrying ships. For one thing, a ship cannot sail brim-full with any cargo denser than water. Colliers and ore carriers sink to their load lines when only partially full. Oilmen are therefore fortunate to have a low-density cargo. The weight of ore also causes great stress on the ship's structure. A dense cargo carried low in the hold affects the ship's motion, causing what is known as a 'stiff' condition. A 'stiff' ship is not properly balanced, and will snap sharply

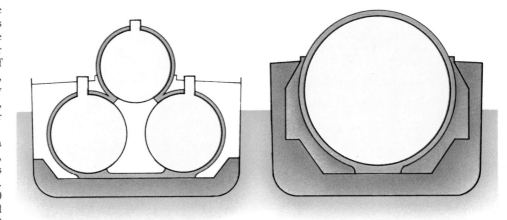

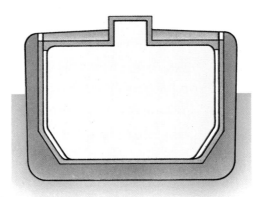

Cross-sections of cargo tanks for carrying liquefied gas. Liquid petroleum gas (such as propane and butane used for cigarette lighters and portable stoves) is carried in ships with a number of cylindrical tanks (above left). The gas is usually stored under pressure and at a low temperature. The tanks are insulated, and the ship carries water ballast in a small bottom hold. Liquefied natural gas (methane) is carried at low temperatures in spherical tanks (above right) or prismatic-shaped tanks (left). These tanks are covered with insulation and surrounded by an inert gas to prevent build up of inflammable pockets from leakage. The ship carries water ballast in wrap-around tanks

upright from a roll, causing discomfort and danger to passengers, cargo and the ship's structure. Ore carriers are built with deep false bottoms to raise the vessel's centre of gravity. The ore-carrying holds are narrow, and are flanked by wing tanks which hold water ballast.

As with tankers, bulk carriers have been getting bigger. The largest are about 1000ft long and have a draught of nearly 60ft. Bulk carriers now account for 30 per cent of total world shipping trade. This percentage is sure to grow, and the percentage of the oil tankers sure to fall, as the demand for grain and ore increases and the reserves of oil dwindle.

However, there is now an increasing demand for the transportation of natural gas. This is found underground, and is mostly made of methane. The gas is carried in liquid form – hence the name liquefied natural gas (LNG)

carriers for this type of ship. Initially the vessels for the carriage of methane were of moderate size, about 12 000 tons d.w. They carried the gas in stainless steel tanks carefully mounted and insulated, often by balsa wood, from the main steel structure of the ship's hull. It is estimated that by 1975 there will be nearly 90 vessels on order or in service designed to carry liquefied natural gas, the average cargo being about 170 000 cubic yards – equivalent in size to a 90 000 ton d.w. oil tanker. A vessel of this type and size would cost nearly £35 million, compared with about £10 million for an oil tanker of the same size. A complete project comprising the necessary shore facilities, the handling equipment, the vessels and the distribution system could approach the £200 million mark.

Giant tanker bends at sea: As waves pass a 1000-ft-long vessel it alternately bends upwards then is deflected downwards. These movements are called hogging (diagram 1) and sagging (diagram 3). Diagrams 2 and 4 show intermediate conditions. The arrows show directions of deflection, greatly exaggerated. Naval architects have to take such bending effects into account when designing large vessels

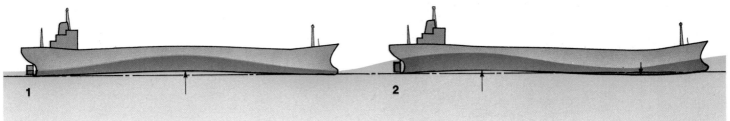

1   2

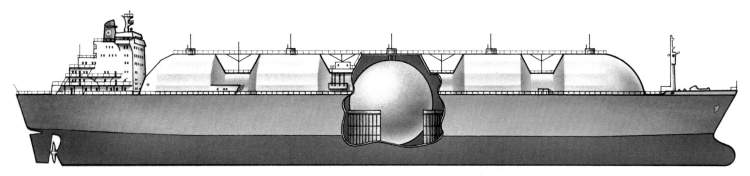

Liquefied natural gas, a fuel of growing importance, is carried in insulated tanks in vessels such as this

The natural gas is liquefied on shore by chilling to below its boiling point of −162°C. This reduces its volume 600 times and makes it much more economical to carry. The gas is not refrigerated on board ship, but prevented from absorbing heat by the insulation. Fast passages are therefore desirable. The large amount of insulation has the advantage that it effectively prevents gas escapes in the event of an accident to the liquid gas tanks.

During a voyage a certain amount of the cargo evaporates or 'boils off'. About 0.4 per cent of the liquefied gas boils off per day, and this vapour is captured and used as fuel for the boilers of a steam turbine ship or in a diesel engine which can run on either oil or gas.

Liquefied natural gas is now being sought by drilling on land and on the sea bed in order to supplement the world's reserves of fuel. Japan requires vast quantities of fuel for steel-making, and has six 150000-cubic yard LNG ships operating for the next 15 years from the gas fields at Brunei to Japan.

There are more than 200 gas carriers in service but only a few of these have been designed to carry liquefied natural gas. There are other gases associated with petroleum, such as propane and butane, which these ships (called liquefied petroleum gas, or LPG, carriers) take in liquid form under pressure, like the gas in a gas lighter refill.

In addition to liquefied natural gas, there are about 350 different chemicals requiring transport under a variety of conditions. These are usually taken by special-products carriers. In many cases only small quantities of cargo are involved, in 500 to 5000-ton lots called parcels. Such vessels are therefore often referred to as parcel tankers. They carry refined petroleum products, chemicals and vegetable oils includ-ing molasses. Some chemicals, such as phos-phorus, have a high melting point, and to keep these in a liquid state hot water at 80°C is pumped around the tanks. Other tanks may be refrigerated or pressurized. Such vessels can present something of a safety hazard with their parcels of sometimes explosive and often highly reactive chemicals.

Special-products carriers are generally in the 20000–30000 tons d.w. size range, and are diesel powered to a speed of about 16 knots. Several owners have built these vessels for time chartering to the large oil companies and many more are on order to meet the growth in the market for chemicals transport.

In 25 years the carrying capacity of the world's merchant fleet rose explosively from the 1945 total of 100 million tons d.w., valued at some £3000 million, to more than 400 million tons d.w. valued at £15000 million. This figure is certain to grow still more during the 1970's with the current increase in world trade, and the aggressive building programme of nations such as the Soviet Union and Japan, as well as the developing countries. It is the dry and liquid bulk carriers which, along with tankers and container ships, will continue to resist the competition of air freight and assure a prosperous future for cargo shipping.

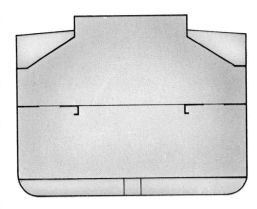

Flexibility of modern bulk carriers is shown by two different ways of loading the same ship (right). In the top diagram, the hold is full of grain cargo. Below, hatch covers are put in place on the 'tween decks to support vehicles and containers over a bulk cargo in the lower hold. More containers are piled on deck. Blue areas are ballast tanks. Different combinations of cargo can be loaded into different holds according to a loading plan, designed to maintain buoyancy and stability of the ship. Movable hatch covers allow different shapes and sizes of cargo to be carried with maximum use of space.

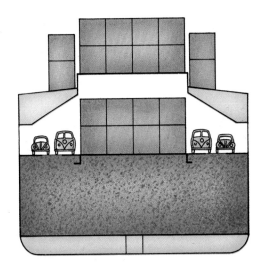

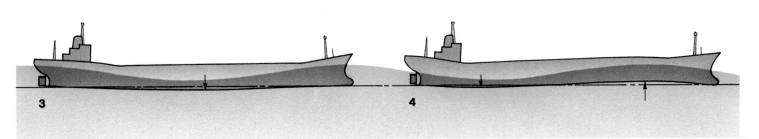

The giant tankers
oil tankers

Half the world's water-borne cargo tonnage is oil taken by tanker. A giant tanker is little more than a floating block of oil – an 'oilberg'. A so-called supertanker of 20 years ago would fit several times over into one of the current giants. Half-a-million-ton tankers are taking to the sea, and there is no technical reason why the first million-ton tanker should not follow.

The only limitation on tanker size is the depth of the ocean. The largest tankers have draughts of about 80 ft. In many waters, such as the Malacca Straight off southeast Asia, there is hardly room to stand a man in between a tanker's bottom and the seabed – even in still water. But a ship pitches in moving sea, and 'squats' under the thrust of its engines. Such effects can combine to increase the real draught of a tanker by one quarter. Add to this the fact that sand waves up to 40 ft high can form on the seabed, and it is not surprising that tankers occasionally touch bottom.

Ton for ton, tankers are the cheapest ships to build and man. They consist mostly of empty space surrounded by metal walls. The crew required for a tanker of hundreds of thousands of tons is hardly any bigger than for a tanker one tenth the size. A country such as Britain imports 100 million tons of oil a year to keep its industry running. Because oil is so valuable freight rates can go very high, and only a handful of fully laden voyages may be needed before a tanker pays back its building costs.

The first oil tanker was built in 1886. She was a German ship called *Glückauf (Good Luck)*, 300 ft long and 3000 deadweight tons. The *Glückauf* set the style for all later tankers: engines aft, with the hull acting as a compartmented tank. By 1900 there were over 100 tankers afloat. They averaged 5000 deadweight tons and made 9 knots. American tanker building in World War I raised total tonnage to 7 million tons by 1921. The standard size was 12000 tons, but the largest tankers were over 20000 tons. The need for oil during World War II provided another boost to tanker construction. Ships were made larger and faster. After the war came the supertanker, a vessel that rivalled and eventually exceeded the largest passenger liners in size. In the mid 1950s, 50000-ton tankers took to the seas. This trend was accelerated in 1956 when the Suez canal was closed for the first time. Since Suez became a battlefront and was again closed in 1967, oil producers have gone for tankers in the 200000-ton range and upwards. Speeds are settling in at around 16 knots.

The cost of tanker transportation does not drop in direct proportion to a tanker's size. For instance, the transportation costs of a 100000-ton tanker are 50 per cent less than those of a 25000-ton tanker. But the costs fall less dramatically with the largest tankers. Because of high building and insurance costs, the one-million-ton tanker may represent the practical limit of tanker construction.

Some tankers have been increased in size by inserting new cargo tanks in between the old bow and stern. This technique, called jumbo-izing, is of value because oil leaves a corrosive deposit which can halve the life of a tanker's hull. Unfortunately, early attempts at jumbo-izing produced weakened ships which split while carrying oil. Tankers have other dangers. Because of their enormous bulk, they need several miles to stop or turn, and can take an appreciable fraction of an hour doing so. When coming in to dock, these sea monsters have to be slowed to a crawling pace lest an accidental impact should flatten their moorings.

Tankers do not spell continual profits. They may spend half their life in ballast, because after unloading they must return to pick up more crude oil. Some tankers have been adapted to carry cargoes of ore on their return voyages.

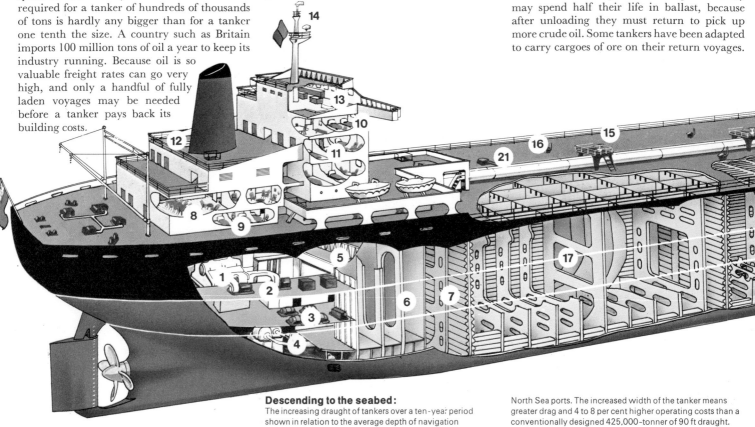

Descending to the seabed:

The increasing draught of tankers over a ten-year period shown in relation to the average depth of navigation channels in the North Sea. The last outline is a design for a tanker of restricted draught capable of a safe passage to North Sea ports. The increased width of the tanker means greater drag and 4 to 8 per cent higher operating costs than a conventionally designed 425,000-tonner of 90 ft draught. But such a conventional tanker's cargo would have to be transhipped to reach a shallow-water port.

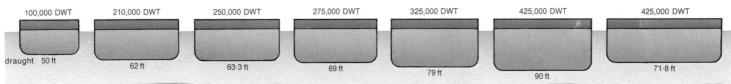

100,000 DWT	210,000 DWT	250,000 DWT	275,000 DWT	325,000 DWT	425,000 DWT	425,000 DWT
draught 50 ft	62 ft	63·3 ft	69 ft	79 ft	90 ft	71·8 ft

The giant tankers
general purpose tankers

Increased sizes of tankers also means larger, and more expensive, shore facilities. Before the advent of deep-water ports or the dredging of deeper channels into existing ports, large tankers had to discharge part of their cargo into smaller tankers. To keep dockside costs to a minimum, the capacity of pumping facilities has risen tenfold, from a few hundred tons per hour after World War II to several thousands of tons per hour. To save expensive dredging, long jetties now stretch from the shore into deep water. At Kuwait, an artificial island has been constructed 10 miles off shore, where the water is nearly 100 feet deep. Crude oil is piped to tankers in a 48-inch diameter submarine pipeline.

But the largest tankers now carry more oil than can be stored in a refinery. To save expensive reconstruction, Gulf Oil in 1968 opened a European 'oilfield' – a million ton transhipment terminal at Bantry Bay, Ireland. Here, the largest of tankers can moor in 100 ft of water and discharge their cargo into storagetanks. Smaller tankers – up to about 100000 tons – load up at their convenience and ply to smaller-capacity refineries and ports via the relatively shallow waters around northern Europe. Even with the cost of transhipment, a 300000-ton-plus tanker can bring oil around the Cape of Good Hope at half the cost per barrel of a 50000-ton tanker sailing through Suez.

Although over 90 per cent of tanker cargoes are oil, there is a growing tendency to send other liquids to sea in tankers. Wine, chemicals, molasses and even liquefied gas are now conveyed in tankers. World trade in chemicals is increasing about 40 per cent faster than ordinary trade. The capacity of chemical tankers has doubled in the past few years to 1½ million tons. Chemical tankers usually have a number of isolated compartments in which various liquid cargoes (including oil) can be stored. Some specially equipped ships carry liquid sulphur, which is maintained at temperatures above boiling point. The Guinness company operates a three-ship fleet of 1200-ton tankers to convey beer between Ireland and England. Methane (natural gas) is carried in tankers. The gas is carried in liquid form, at a temperature of −258°F (−161°C).

A modern oil tanker
Key

1 Boiler	8 Crew Mess
2 Force-Draught Fan	9 Crew Accommodation
3 Auxiliary Machinery	10 Master's Accommodation
4 Water Inlet Pipe	11 Officer's Accommodation
5 Control Room	12 Swimming Pool
6 Oil Fuel Bunker	13 Navigating Bridge
7 Permanent Ballast Tank	14 Radar Scanner
15 Fire Hydrant	19 Structural Arrangement –Wing Cargo Tank
16 Cargo Hatch and Stand Pipe	20 Hose and Cargo Derrick
17 Structural Arrangement –Centre Cargo Tank	21 Breakwater
18 Structural Arrangement –Wing Cargo Tank	22 Loading/Discharge Pipelines
	23 Bulbous Bow

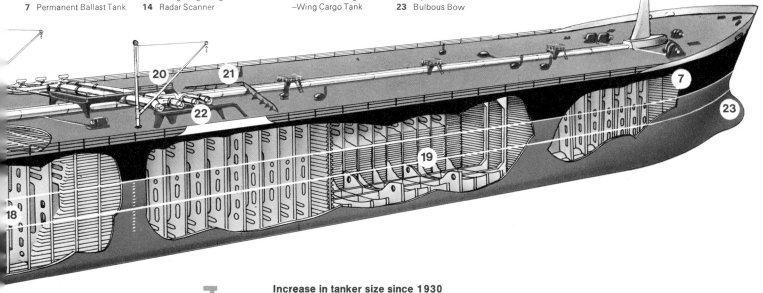

Increase in tanker size since 1930

1930	10,000 tons
1950	16,000 tons
1956	47,750 tons
1960	100,000 tons
1967	200,000 tons
planned 1973	477,000 tons

Special duty ships

survey and fishing

More than 160 types of marine craft ply the seas of the world. Eighty per cent of the world's deadweight tonnage is made up of tankers, bulk carriers, container ships, cargo liners, ferries and passenger liners – the big and spectacular ships that catch the eye. But there are many smaller, simpler forms of craft that are equally vital. Some, such as tugs and dredgers, make it possible for the larger vessels to get safely in and out of port. Other craft have duties that directly affect us all.

Trawlers, for example, are used all over the world to gain food from the sea. The increasing demand for food means new methods of trawling and new designs of craft. Some countries favour larger trawlers, about 1500 tons d.w., which can stay at sea for three or four weeks and freeze fish as they are caught. The trawl net is let out over the stern. Such stern trawlers have a much greater freeboard (height of deck above the waterline) than the old form of side trawler, and are less likely to be swamped in heavy seas.

All the work of sorting, gutting and freezing the fish is carried out in the covered area below deck. When all the fish cargo space is full the trawler returns to port and the frozen fish is unloaded into a cold store to await distribution. An alternative method used by the Russians and Japanese is to send fleets of small trawlers to sea with a fish factory ship in attendance. The catches from the trawlers are collected by the factory ship, which is often as large as 40000 tons d.w. and accommodates reserve crews for the trawlers.

Despite the advent of communication satellites, more messages are still transmitted by cable laid on the ocean bed. There are currently cables capable of carrying more than 1000 telephone circuits, and new links across the North Atlantic will use cables with four times this capacity. The earliest cable ships, such as the *Great Eastern* which laid the first transatlantic cable in 1858, were ordinary ships that had been converted. Today, specialized cable-laying vessels are built at a cost of millions of pounds.

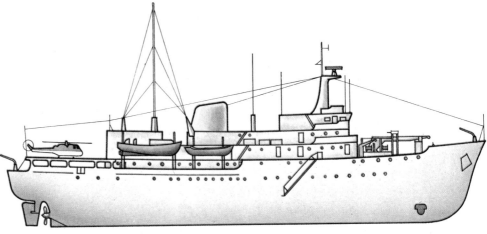

Oceanographic survey vessel also capable of undertaking hydrographic work. The main vessel studies the deep ocean and the Earth's crust beneath it (oceanography), while small boats are dispatched for survey work (hydrography) in inshore waters. The vessel can also carry a helicopter for quick travel to shore.

A new development is loading cable into the ships in containers, like loading a spool of film into a camera. This technique – called pan loading – replaces the time-consuming procedure of winding lengths of cable into cable tanks on board the vessel. It can cut the ship's turn-round time from days to hours, and will allow cable vessels to quickly deliver new lengths of cable for repairing breaks.

Cable ships have a capacity of 1000 miles or more of cable. The cable is paid out through a stern chute or through a special split bow. The ships are made particularly manoeuvrable to keep station accurately while paying out cable. The tension of the cable is constantly regulated to prevent overstraining. Cable ships must be able to grapple for broken or damaged cables and raise them for repair.

Cable repair work has been simplified by the introduction of small submarines which can operate at depths of more than 600ft. Divers can leave the submersible to carry out repair work. This is a development of techniques used in salvage work.

Salvage vessels are specially constructed for raising wrecks by the use of heavy-lift derricks and inflatable pontoons which are strapped to the sides of the wreck. Before a wreck can be raised, divers carry out a great deal of work to seal the hull so that the compressed air does not leak out.

A new type of ship which has been introduced in recent years is the off-shore supply vessel which services the rigs that search for undersea oil and gas. These small vessels of about 500 to 900 tons are strongly built and driven by powerful engines to let them stay at sea in bad weather. They are a development of the ocean-going tug or salvage tug but can carry the special equipment such as pipes and drilling bits required by the rigs.

Ocean-going tugs are among the most powerful vessels in the world for their size. A 1000-ton tug may have engines of 15000 bhp and can tow a disabled 200000 - ton tanker to port. Such tugs have a pull of more than 40 tons. Two tugs working together can make pulls up to 6000 miles.

Many ocean-going ships are strengthened for operation in ice, although they do not actually make a passage through ice. This tough work is done by the icebreaker, an extremely powerful vessel which either butts through the ice or rides up onto the ice floe until it cracks under the ship's weight. Icebreakers are used in harbours and waterways where ice forms during the winter. The St Lawrence Seaway in North America is troubled by ice in winter, and icebreakers are used to keep the waterway between the Atlantic to the Great Lakes open as long as possible.

Most ships require a pilot when entering and leaving port. The pilot is transferred from shore to ship by a pilot cutter, a small craft about 80ft long and capable of 20 knots. The direct shipment of pilots from the shore is a recent development. Previously, a pilot cutter with several pilots on board would lie at anchor two to five miles off shore, and transfer pilots to a ship by a small boat. This was tedious, and the pilot cutter presented a navigation hazard in fog and bad weather.

Side and top views of a proposed fish-meal factory mother ship. The mother ship carries a number of smaller vessels which are dispatched to actually catch fish. This design is on the lines of the Soviet *Vostok* mother ship and floating factory of 40000 tons, which carries 14 catching vessels, each of 70 tons. Such deep-sea fishing vessels of high efficiency will help to double the world catch of fish over the next 20 years.

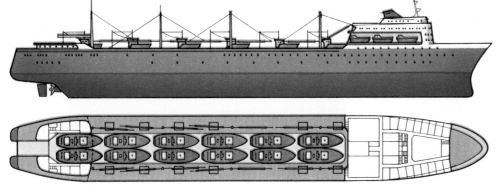

Special duty ships
cable-laying

To keep pace with the deeper channels required by today's large ships, dredgers have become as large as 12 000 tons d.w. In rivers and estuaries, where silt has to be removed, the bucket type of dredger is common. There are also screw-cutting dredgers which bore into the seabed, loosen the rocky or stony bottom and suck the aggregate up into the hopper-like holds. Dredgers are used to reclaim land by pumping ashore the material from the seabed, so that while a channel is deepened the land area may also be extended.

Certain traditional types of special-duty ship are now becoming scarce. An example is the lightship, which is being replaced in most cases by unmanned lightbuoys using an atomic power source. The whale factory ship is another ship type that is now rare, since whales have been decimated in numbers by over-hunting. Today only Russia and Japan keep large whaling fleets, with factory ships of more than 20 000 tons d.w. and 20-knot whale catchers for locating and killing the whales. Once killed, the whale is marked with a small transmitting set which sends out a signal to be picked up by the factory ship. The whale is taken on board the factory ship and cut into small pieces for freeze storage or reduction into oil and valuable greases. None of the whale is wasted.

However, other types of ship are becoming increasingly important. Examples are the oceanographic and fishery research vessels, which study the sea and its life, and hydrographic survey ships which produce accurate charts to aid the safe passage of other vessels. Worldwide awareness of the need to reduce pollution of coastal waters has led to the development of special ships built to take chemical waste to sea and burn it, leaving a harmless residue which is diluted in the ocean. Previously, sewage disposal ships dumped their cargo directly into deep water.

Dutch firefighting tug *Maasbank* of Rotterdam plays foam onto a burning tanker which was set ablaze after a collision. Firefighting tugs are necessary in harbours and rivers to douse fires in ships or in the often cramped dockside wharves.

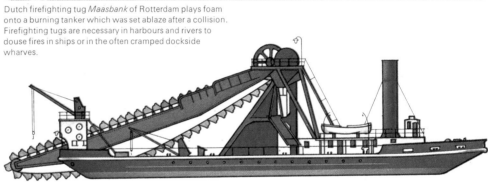

Traditional dredger of the bucket-ladder variety. Such dredgers have no propulsion machinery, but are pushed around harbours and estuaries by tugs. They tip the spoil into a hopper barge alongside (foreground of picture).

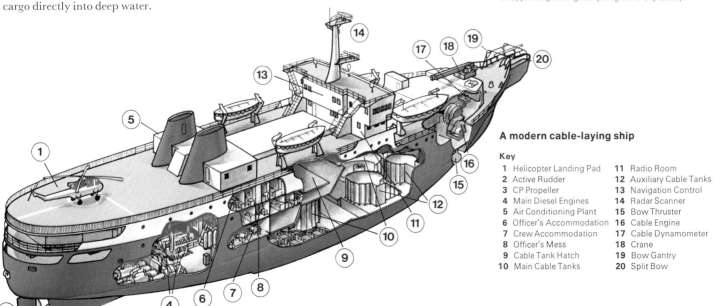

A modern cable-laying ship

Key

1	Helicopter Landing Pad	11	Radio Room
2	Active Rudder	12	Auxiliary Cable Tanks
3	CP Propeller	13	Navigation Control
4	Main Diesel Engines	14	Radar Scanner
5	Air Conditioning Plant	15	Bow Thruster
6	Officer's Accommodation	16	Cable Engine
7	Crew Accommodation	17	Cable Dynamometer
8	Officer's Mess	18	Crane
9	Cable Tank Hatch	19	Bow Gantry
10	Main Cable Tanks	20	Split Bow

Hovercraft and Hydrofoils

hovercraft

Hovercraft and hydrofoils were both developed to avoid the dragging effect of the sea which slows the passage of normal ships. Water is over 800 times as dense as air. It is a buoyant, fluid substance that supports the weight of a ship while allowing it to move. But a ship has to push water aside to move. The faster the ship goes, the greater is the resistance to its passage. Even for the most powerful and streamlined of ships and submarines, the practical limit on speed is between 40 and 50 knots. By lifting themselves above the water surface, hovercraft and hydrofoils can outpace the quickest ships – and can give a smoother ride.

A hovercraft is like a vertical take-off aircraft that flies at a few feet altitude. A hydrofoil actually flies in the water. Consequently there are problems of classification with both types of craft. Although everyone seems agreed that hydrofoils are ships, some countries have classified hovercraft as aeroplanes. Hovercraft can be made amphibious and travel over all types of terrain. But many hovercraft have been developed expressly for use at sea, for instance in ferry duties. These might be regarded as ships, particularly since large hovercraft are built around buoyancy tanks. Amphibious hovercraft should be separately classified as an entirely new type of vehicle.

Unfortunately the term hovercraft reflects the engineers' misuse of the English language. The word hover means to remain poised over one spot. But, at up to 100 mile/h, hovercraft are the fastest things at sea. The term ACV (air-cushion vehicle) is a frequently used alternative.

The first ACV was proposed in 1716 by the Swedish philosopher Emanuel Swedenborg. Others had similar ideas at various times, and several working models were built. An English engineer, John Thorneycroft, even took out an

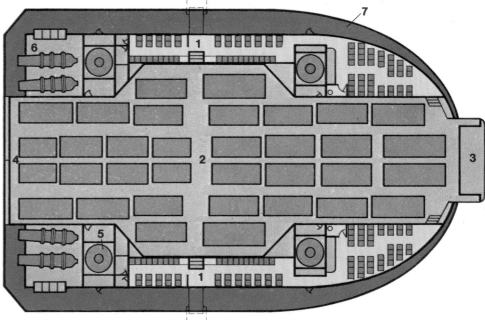

1	Passenger cabin	5	Lifting fan
2	Car deck	6	Gas turbine
3	Unloading ramp	7	Buoyancy tank
4	Rear doors	8	Passenger ramp

Internal layout of a large hovercraft, the SRN4, showing accommodation for 174 passengers and 34 vehicles. The craft is driven by four propellers, each powered by a Rolls Royce Marine Proteus gas turbine.

1877 patent on a ship that travelled on an air cushion. In the 1950s the United States actually foresaw military applications for ACVs. They have in fact been used for patrols in Vietnam.

But the man who turned the ACV into a practical proposition was the British engineer Christopher Cockerell. He demonstrated his idea to the British government in 1956, and in 1959 the first major hovercraft journey was undertaken when the SRN1 crossed the English Channel.

The first ACVs had a ground clearance of only a few inches. They could therefore be halted by small solid obstacles. At sea, even the slightest waves would cause the craft to pitch, although it could run smoothly over a long swell. The addition of a flexible skirt allows an ACV to travel over irregular surfaces. The skirt holds in the cushion of air on which the vehicle rides and, because it is flexible, acts like a suspension system to smooth the ACV's path over irregularities. For example, an ACV with a skirt 6 ft deep can travel level over waves of almost the same height. For stability, the depth of a skirt can only be about one-sixth the ACV's width. Therefore, the surface clearance of a skirted ACV goes up directly with its size. Unfortunately, the skirts can be easily damaged – and the low freeboard of an ACV makes its lightweight superstructure liable to wave damage.

The first hovercraft came into commercial service across the river Dee, between Wales and Cheshire, in 1962. It was rapidly followed by a hovercraft ferry to the Isle of Wight off the south coast of England. Hovercraft services were also introduced in North America, and by 1968 the SRN4 hovercraft type was ferrying 250 passengers and 30 cars across the English Channel to France at speeds approaching 80 mile/h.

An extension of the skirt idea for hovercraft is provided in the sidewall type of ACV. These craft have solid walls extending into the water on either side, and are intended for purely marine travel. These fixed sidewall craft are also known as CAB (captured air bubble) ships. They have flexible skirts at the front and rear to allow waves to pass under. The solid walls help seal

How a hovercraft hovers

The first hovercraft designs were based on the so-called *plenum chamber* concept (1) In this, a single large chamber beneath the craft was kept pumped with air under pressure. The system needed a great deal of power to maintain pressure. In the *peripheral jet* concept (2), a jet of air is injected around the edge of the craft. The peripheral jet keeps up the pressure under the vehicle with much less power than the plenum chamber arrangement. But both designs provide surface clearance of only a few inches. By adding a flexible skirt (3), the hover height is greatly increased. It was this modification which made ACVs useful in practice. The fixed sidewall or captured air bubble craft (4) is a further development, meant for purely marine use.

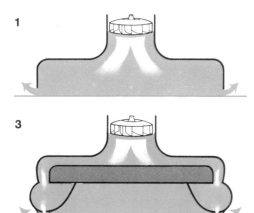
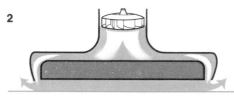
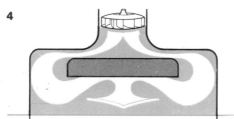

Hovercraft and Hydrofoils

hydrofoils

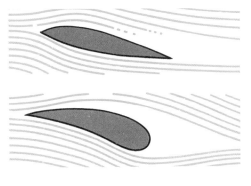

The problem with hydrofoils:
As with an aeroplane wing, fluid flow around a foil produces low pressure on one side and high pressure on the other (top). This pressure difference is the lift. Up to about 70 mile/h this effect works well. But at higher speeds small bubbles form on the low-pressure side of the foil. These bubbles, called *cavities*, collapse with a force like a small explosion; there are sometimes even small flashes of light. The cavities in the water stream cause a loss of lift, and the buffeting effect of the explosions can swiftly erode the foils. The answer seems to be to build a supercavitating foil (above). Such a foil has a sharp edge which creates a large bubble – a super cavity – on its upper edge. This clears the troublesome bubbles from the foil, and allows hydrofoil craft to be driven at speeds approaching 100 mile/h.

successfully in London in 1861. In 1906 a hydrofoil craft built by Professor Enrico Forlanini reached 45 mile/h on Lake Maggiore. In 1918 Alexander Graham Bell set up a speed record of over 70 mile/h with his five-ton hydrofoil, *Hydrodrome*. Hans von Schertel built several hydrofoil craft in Germany during World War II, and in 1953 one of his craft began the world's first commercial hydrofoil service, again on Lake Maggiore, between Italy and Switzerland.

Hydrofoils are more common in service than hovercraft. Over 500 hydrofoils were in regular ferry operation by the early 1970s, and this number is expected to double by 1980. The Russians became interested in hydrofoils after seeing the German designs, and they now use such craft extensively on the many lakes and rivers of the Soviet Union. They are the world's greatest users of hydrofoils. Most western hydrofoils follow designs by von Schertel. The largest commercial hydrofoil is the 170-ton *Expressan*, in service between Denmark and Sweden, which has a capacity of 150 passengers and 8 cars, and can move at up to 45 mile/h.

Hydrofoils have the advantage of being swift and smooth in operation. Because they are lifted above the waves, hydrofoil craft with fully submerged foils are less bothered by rough weather than small hovercraft. But they do require great power to drive them through the water at high speeds, and their future may not be so spectacular as that envisaged for ACVs. In the foreseeable future, hydrofoils will probably grow to about 1000 tons. Because of its higher speed such a craft can do the work of a 5000-ton ship. Some specialists have predicted that on coastal and inland routes the hydrofoil could oust small conventional ships. Ocean-going hydrofoils are becoming a possibility with developments in foil technology that keep them flying straight and level over the largest waves.

the air cushion beneath the craft, and they also provide extra stability.

Whereas ordinary ACVs are powered by propellers in the air, CABs can have underwater screws mounted in their sidewalls. In fact, some designs envisage CABs built almost like catamarans, with power plant and cargo carried in two streamlined sidewalls linked by a giant air bubble. The ship of tomorrow may actually be a CAB vessel of several thousand tons, skimming across the Atlantic at 100 mile/h. This will mean a revolution in shipbuilding with the introduction of low-weight, high-strength frames similar to those used in the aircraft industry. Although the development costs will be great, the chance of delivering a shipload of goods from Europe to the United States in 24 hours may be too good to miss.

Unlike hovercraft, hydrofoils have been a practical proposition for some decades. The first hydrofoil craft were tested before the first aeroplanes flew. In fact, some aviation pioneers such as the Wright brothers worked first on hydrofoils. Hydrofoil boats are lifted clear of the water by exactly the same principles that govern an aeroplane's flight. Because of the greater density of water than air, foils need only be small to generate the same lift as a large aeroplane wing. But they are subject to much greater stresses, and are usually made from solid pieces of metal.

The first known hydrofoil boat was tested

Smoothing out the waves:
One means of flattening out a hydrofoil's ride through a rough sea is called *air stabilization*. This works on the fact that air introduced into the water flow round a foil reduces its lift. Air is fed to the foils down their supporting struts and released through holes to the foil's surface, as shown in the diagram below. Sensors in the craft measure its movement and control the flow of air to the foils to counteract this. Such an arrangement can cut both pitch and roll of a hydrofoil, and compensate for any uneven loading of the craft.

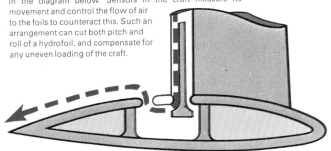

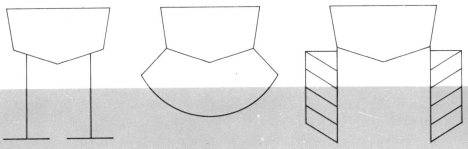

How a hydrofoil flies:
As with early aeroplanes, hydrofoils at first sprouted a large number of ladder-like foils in search of the greatest possible lift (above right). But the trend today is towards a single foil of high efficiency. There are two main types: the surface-piercing foil (above centre), and the fully submerged foil (above left). The surface-piercing variety are extremely stable and are used extensively for calm-water ferryboats. But the surface-piercing foil is very sensitive to waves and is generally unusable for ocean travel. The fully submerged type of foil can be used to give a virtually flat ride. Although it is easy to use in smooth water, a deep-water system for rough weather is difficult to develop. Stability is a problem, because the legs need to be deep enough to reach down through even the largest waves.

Charting the seas

portolans

For thousands of years, since the time of the ancient Greeks, men are known to have mapped the Earth. These maps mostly showed the land areas around the Mediterranean. The early navigators, if they used a chart at all, would only have had versions of these on which to plot their landfall. But the first appearance of a chart specifically for navigators dates from the 13th century, shortly after the invention of the compass. The first reference to a chart is in 1270, when King Louis IX of France, after six days of storm in the Mediterranean, asked the ship's position and was shown it on a chart. A chart differs from a map in that it shows information mostly of interest to seamen, and includes just enough of the land to aid navigation. A map is primarily concerned with features on land.

The earliest surviving navigation chart dates from around 1275. It is of the type known as a *portolan* (or portulan), from the Italian meaning 'sailing direction'. A portolan shows coastal outlines, usually of the Mediterranean area for that was where such charts originated. The coast is lined with names of towns and ports, leaving the sea area of the map clear. A network of so-called *rhumb lines* crosses the chart, radiating from one or two 'mother' compasses.

The rhumb lines indicate the 32 points of the compass, and from these the sailor could pick off the magnetic heading needed to reach his destination. Portolans were based on knowledge of the Mediterranean derived from compass bearings and distance estimates. It was doubtless this type of chart that King Louis was shown, and it indicates that charts were an established part of a navigator's equipment at that time.

The improvements of seamanship and navigation in the Mediterranean area resulted about 1290 in the introduction of winter as well as summer sea trading. Previously, trading ships had been laid up from October to March. The growth of trade among the developing European nations in the 14th century resulted in the extension of charts to include part of the shores of the Atlantic, including the British Isles. However, the sailor still relied on his compass, a distance estimate and depth soundings with a lead to tell him where he was. But as men started to explore new lands, this was no longer good enough. There were no sailing directions to advise him, and the deviation of the compass from true north became troublesome.

In the 15th century, as the Portuguese explored down the west coast of Africa, they kept track of their progress by comparing the changing altitude of the pole star. Later this developed into readings of latitude and largely through Portuguese work the *plane chart* was developed, showing parallels of latitude deduced from the altitude of the pole star or the Sun. From about 1530 the deviation of the magnetic compass from true north was taken into account on charts, and the Mediterranean, whose axis had previously been shown 11° out of true, was swung into its correct position.

But the plane chart still had one major flaw: It did not take into account the curvature of the Earth. Near the poles, the meridians of longitude converge. This resulted in grave distortions of coastlines in high latitudes and made it impossible to lay off accurate courses on plane charts that covered large areas. The Flemish mathematician Gerhardus Mercator solved the problem in 1569 when he published a map that held the meridians of longitude parallel, but with the latitude scale elongated accordingly. The latitude scale was marked in minutes of arc, and one minute of arc on a meridian became one nautical mile.

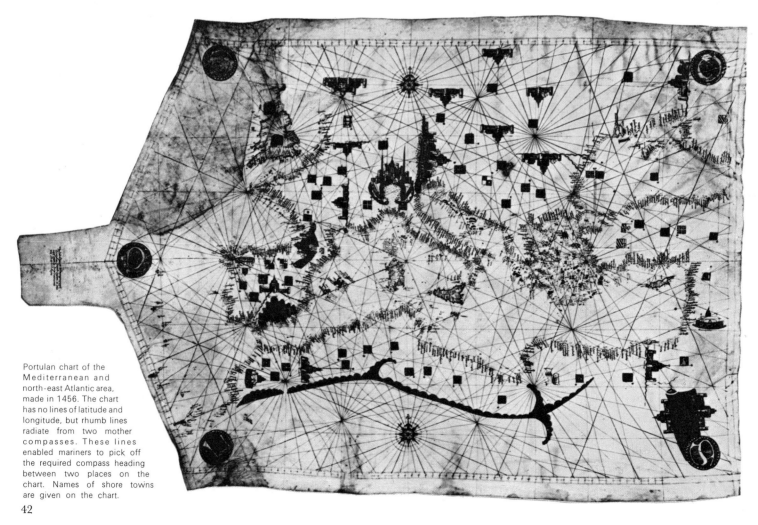

Portulan chart of the Mediterranean and north-east Atlantic area, made in 1456. The chart has no lines of latitude and longitude, but rhumb lines radiate from two mother compasses. These lines enabled mariners to pick off the required compass heading between two places on the chart. Names of shore towns are given on the chart.

On such a chart a constant course is shown as a straight line, which is a great advantage for navigators. The Mercator projection is now used for charts of most areas except those near the poles where the change in latitude scale is so rapid that it becomes unsuitable. However, the changeover to Mercator charts was slow and some plane charts remained in use until the 18th century.

The main inaccuracies on early Mercator charts were the placings of land in longitude, and the accurate finding of longitude was an important key to the progress of chart making. In 1676 the French decided to embark on a programme of accurate surveying using observations of the satellites of Jupiter as a time standard to help find longitude. The results transformed geography. The longitude of some places changed by as much as 20°, and the coastline of France was significantly altered. The French King Louis XIV complained that he had lost more land in this new survey than he had lost in any war with Britain.

Charts improved by the application of surveying techniques which had been developed ashore. The famous Captain James Cook, who did so much to advance chart making, learned much of his surveying from army officers in North America while surveying the St Lawrence river, and applied the methods to his painstaking surveys in Australasia. The main advance that Cook made was in his scientific attitude to charting, which was combined with the availability of accurate new methods of longitude finding. The portable observatories that Cook had with him on his voyages from 1768 to 1779 enabled him to pinpoint the position of the land to a fraction of a degree – within a few miles of its actual position.

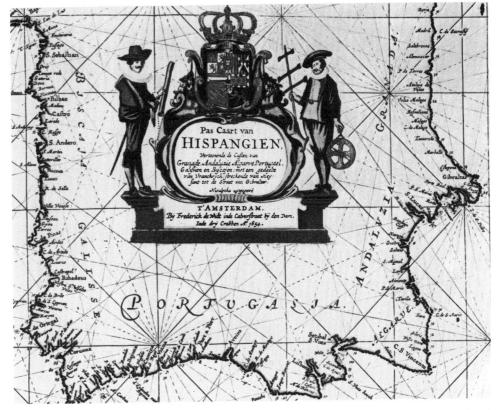

To make his charts, Cook took bearings of the coastline as he sailed past, and related these observations to the positions he had measured accurately on shore. The modern hydrographic chart, of which Cook's surveys were a forerunner, shows not simply coastlines but gives depths of water, tides, currents, dangerous shoals, safe navigation channels and navigation aids such as buoys and lighthouses. Land profiles are often included as an aid to identifying stretches of coast. A chart is vital to a navigator because all this detail is visible at a glance. The chart allows him to plot his course in advance and decide the direction in which to steer.

To make a modern chart, a system of control points is established on the shore. Their latitude and longitude is accurately known, and echo soundings made from the survey ship at sea are plotted in relation to these control points. The position of the ship is compared with the controls either optically, when near land, or by radio.

The work of a survey ship is never done. The changing position of shoals, the modification of the coastline by works of man, and the requirements of deep-draught ships make it necessary to re-survey areas once considered adequately charted. All hydrographic survey results are exchanged internationally, to help ships of all countries as they ply the waters of the world.

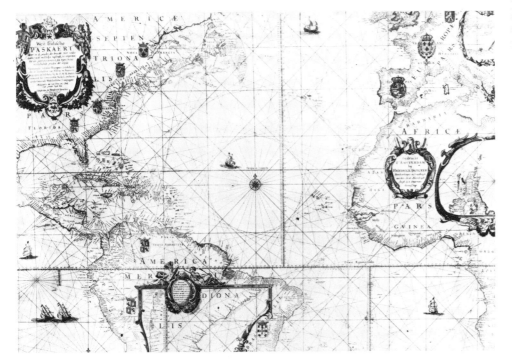

Above: Spanish sea atlas of 1654, with a design showing a mariner holding a cross staff and an astrolabe. Left: Mercator chart of c. 1660 by Hendrick Doncker, printed on vellum. The chart shows possessions and stations of the West India Company. Being on the Mercator projection the chart shows lines of latitude and longitude. Before 1840, the zero line of longitude was not standardized, and longitude readings were often referred to the mariner's own country. Only in 1840 did Greenwich become the internationally accepted zero line of longitude.

Development of navigation
compass, sand glass and log

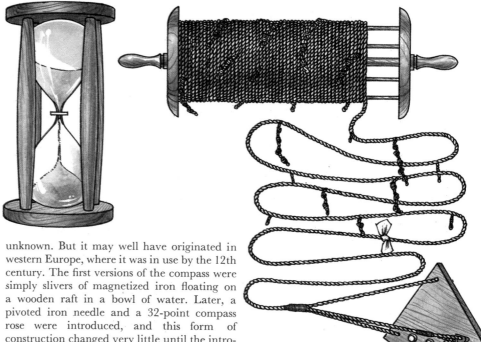

Men have steered by the stars for thousands of years. The Mediterranean peoples who came north to Britain, or the Scandinavians who went west across the Atlantic, all took bearings from the Sun and stars. Courageous mariners in search of new lands followed favourable winds, strong currents or the flight of birds. But they needed the evidence of the sky to prove where they were. They realized that as they went north or south the altitude of the noontime Sun and the pole star changed, but that the distance of these objects above the horizon remained constant as they sailed east or west. The significance of this was not missed, and civilizations centuries before Christ realized the Earth is curved. The Greek scientist Eratosthenes calculated in 200 BC that the Earth is 25000 miles in circumference – a figure we confirm today. It is surprising that 1700 years later the experienced navigator Christopher Columbus should have believed the Earth to be only half its actual size.

The first instruments used at sea may have been some form of sighting device to measure the approximate altitude of Sun or stars. But the earliest instruments for navigators that we know of definitely are the depth pole and the weighted line. Such simple devices could tell

Mariner's compass, above, was marked with 32 points to signify directions. Compass bearings are now given in degrees from north, rather than in the old terms such as north-by-northwest.

the mariner what sort of water he was getting into, and help him estimate his distance from shore. Depth lines were used several centuries before Christ, and water as deep as 1000 fathoms (6000 feet) was plumbed in this way.

In the second century AD the Greek scientist Ptolemy introduced the idea of a grid of approximate latitude and longitude lines, which he placed over his map of the known world. But no real progress in position-finding at sea was made until the long-distance voyages of exploration in the Middle Ages made it vital. By then, the mysterious north-seeking properties of the lodestone were known. The origin of the compass, perhaps the greatest direction-finding aid of all time, is

unknown. But it may well have originated in western Europe, where it was in use by the 12th century. The first versions of the compass were simply slivers of magnetized iron floating on a wooden raft in a bowl of water. Later, a pivoted iron needle and a 32-point compass rose were introduced, and this form of construction changed very little until the introduction of iron ships.

So the mariner knew in which direction he was going – but how fast? To find his speed, a mariner threw a block of wood overboard attached to a knotted line. A sand-glass ran off the time as the block (or 'log') was strung out. With the resulting estimate of distance sailed in a known direction, the navigator could roughly indicate his position from 'dead' (deduced) reckoning.

In the early 15th century the Portuguese explorers began to use celestial navigation seriously as they progressed south in latitude down the west coast of Africa. To find their latitude the explorers used a development of the *astrolabe*, a star-sighting device known for centuries on land. The astrolabe is a distant ancestor of the modern sextant, and it gave a reading of the noon Sun's altitude from which latitude could be calculated.

Hand-line and lead, for depth sounding, is one of the oldest tools of the navigator. The depth of water sounded, and the character of the mud from the sea bottom that stuck to the lead, indicated to the mariner his distance from shore and the region he was approaching. The line had various markers tied to it to show different depths. These markers took the form of strips of leather, or pieces of different-coloured cloth.

Development of navigation

A more popular device for position-finding was the *cross-staff*, which is simplicity itself. An observer held a yard-long stick to his eye, and adjusted the position of a cross-piece until its ends just seemed to stretch from the Pole Star to the horizon. The distance of the cross-piece along the staff was an indication of the Pole's altitude, and thus the observer's latitude. The cross-staff was unsuitable for sighting the Sun because of its dazzling brilliance. This disadvantage was remedied with the *back-staff*, invented around 1590 by the English mariner John Davis. To use the back-staff a mariner turned his back on the Sun and threw the shadow of a vane onto a marker that coincided with the horizon. Under ideal conditions this could give a more accurate value for the Sun's altitude, and provided latitude readings correct to a quarter of a degree.

Davis Backstaff:
At the back of the large arc is an additional scale for the sun's declination and right ascension. This Backstaff was made by Beni Macy in 1720 for a Mr. James Austin.

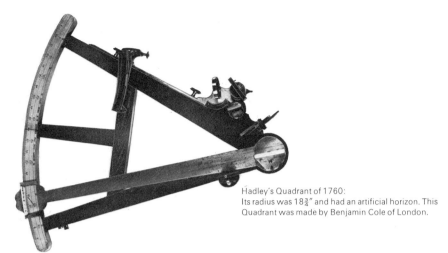

Hadley's Quadrant of 1760:
Its radius was 18¾" and had an artificial horizon. This Quadrant was made by Benjamin Cole of London.

In 1731 the Englishman John Hadley turned navigators towards the Sun again when he developed an instrument on the style of the modern sextant. The sextant uses mirrors to align the Sun's image with the horizon line, and it is still the instrument that most people associate with the word navigation.

However, although latitude was easy enough to find within a few degrees, longitude proved a very different problem. To get to a place of known latitude meant heading in a northerly or southerly direction, and then turning east or west along the line of latitude until the destination was reached. As more and more ships were wrecked because of faulty longitude determinations, the need for a solution became pressing. The Spanish and later the Dutch offered grand prizes for a solution, but the offer that aroused most interest was that put forward in 1714 by the British government. Their top prize was the princely sum of £20000.

From several suggestions of finding longitude, two stood out: the method of lunar distances (measuring the angle from the Moon to the Sun or a Star); and the clock method, which entailed knowing the difference in local time between a reference point and the mariner's actual position. The first method was originally the most favoured, and the Royal Observatory at Greenwich was set up in 1675 to accurately measure positions of the Moon and stars. In 1767 the *Nautical Almanac* was first published, containing tables to aid seamen in their calculations of longitude. James Cook used 'lunars' on his first voyage, but later supplemented this method with his 'trusty friend the watch', as he put it.

For by the mid 18th century the Yorkshireman John Harrison had revolutionised navigation with the first really accurate marine timekeepers. Harrison's chronometers were later simplified and improved by other watchmakers; but to Harrison goes the credit for first perfecting such accurate timepieces. Tested on a six-week voyage to the West Indies in 1761, a Harrison chronometer was in error by 5.1 seconds, giving a position accurate to about one mile. This was a hundred times better than the accuracy seamen were used to, and the British government eventually awarded Harrison their full £20000 prize.

With an accurate timekeeper on board,

navigators could find their longitude more easily. The principle of the clock method of longitude finding rests on the fact that the Earth rotates through 15° in one hour. Therefore a ship 15° west of Greenwich would see the Sun or a star due south one hour after it had been due south of Greenwich. Because of the British superiority in chart making and the wide usage of British time standards, Greenwich was internationally accepted as the zero line of longitude.

In 1837 the American mariner Thomas Sumner stumbled upon a discovery that made it unnecessary to take separate latitude and longitude readings. He realized that the Sun or a star would appear to have the same altitude when seen from a series of positions on Earth. These positions formed a circle around the point at which the object appeared overhead. By making three or four sightings of different stars a short time apart, the navigator could fix his location by finding where his 'lines of position' crossed.

Traditional methods of navigation have now been supplemented, but not supplanted by radio methods. However, one form of navigation that has not changed is the technique of *pilotage*, or steering by eye from reference points. All voyages start and end with piloting, the technique first used by the ancient sailors before they strayed out of sight of land.

Marine Chronometer by Larcum Kendall (1721-1790):
A direct copy of Harrison's No. 4 chronometer, completed in 1769 and went to sea with Captain Cook on his second and third voyages where it performed reliably.

Navigation in the electronic age
radio and echo sounding

From its beginnings as a primitive means of travelling between two points on the Earth's surface, navigation has become the most important factor in the operation of a ship. The mariner today must be able to navigate in all weather, particularly at terminals, harbour entrances and restricted waterways where several vessels are moving in a confined space. The development first of radio, then radar and now sophisticated electronic devices have all been of paramount importance in ensuring that a ship reaches its destination – and does it safely.

The largest vessels have such a great draught that they must be kept accurately in position in deep-water channels. To assist the navigator in such a situation there are three important devices: the echo sounder, harbour radar and some form of radio navigation equipment.

The echo sounder sends a radio signal from below the ship to the seabed, where it is reflected back. The time taken to receive the reflected signal is a measure of the depth of water under the ship. The radio pulse may be as short as 1 millisecond (thousandth of a second) and the frequency between 10 and 50 kiloHertz (thousands of cycles a second). The received pulse is displayed on a chart by a pen recorder so that the navigator can see the outline of the bottom over which the vessel is passing. A similar device of increasing importance is the sonar system, which uses high-frequency sound signals. In Sonar the sound signal can be sent ahead or sideways. The time for the echo to be sent back from an object, such as an underwater body of rock, is a measure of the object's distance from the ship. The sound waves have a frequency of about 50 kiloHertz. The sonar system can also be used to measure the speed of the vessel over the seabed, and is particularly valuable in aiding docking approaches when speeds need to be monitored closely.

Harbour radar shows shore personnel a picture on a radar screen of vessels in their area. In fog, ships can be warned when they are moving into dangerous areas or are on collision courses. The situation here is similar to that of air traffic control.

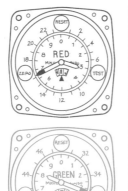

Decca navigator allows position finding by reference to signals transmitted from shore. There is a *master* station and three so-called *slave* stations. Each of the slave stations is colour coded red, green or purple. The difference in time between signals received from the master and the slave stations depends on the ship's position. The time difference defines a number of curved lines of position. On-board equipment automatically calculates the ship's position from the received signals. The position is displayed on dials and can be plotted on a chart which displays the area covered by the transmitting stations. In this diagram, only the red and green slave stations are shown. The purple slave station would be needed in areas where the red and green lines do not intersect.

It is now common for all ships – even trawlers, tugs and ferries – to be fitted with radar of their own to help maintain position when near land or in channels or waterways. But radar is only an aid to navigation. It is the correct interpretation of the picture on the circular radar screen which ensures the safe passage of the ship and the avoidance of collision with another vessel.

A radar set's screen is a cathode ray tube on which one's own ship is shown in the centre, with nearby ships shown in relation to it. In the latest designs of radar, moving objects leave a short trail to indicate their direction and speed of movement. New equipment has been developed which provides an alarm when one's own vessel is on a collision course. This eliminates the need to constantly plot the position of other targets or vessels on the radar screen to find if they are a danger. Screens have been devised which show the area of possible collision by a shading, and indicate safe changes of speed or direction by arrows.

Nearly all seagoing vessels are fitted with radio for transmitting and receiving signals, and one of the most common methods of checking a vessel's position is the radio direction finder (RDF). RDF is a simple system in which the operator finds the direction of two homing beacons. The system is prone to errors of several miles, particularly when far from the transmitting stations and in times when disturbances in the Earth's ionosphere affect the reflection of radio waves.

Equipment such as the Decca Navigator, the Omega Navigator or Loran uses synchronized signals received from specific shore stations to establish position. This may be done either by comparing the time of arrival of a certain signal from three or more stations, or by comparing the difference in phase of radio waves. There are several refinements of this idea, but all work on the same basic principle. Signals received from a pair of stations place you on one curved line of position. Anywhere along this line the received signals from the two stations would seem the same. Signals received from another pair of stations define a second line of position. Where the two lines of position cross is your actual location.

The lines of position are given on a chart of the area covered by the transmitter stations, and they form a series of 'lanes'. The lanes are often colour coded; the receiving equipment

Echo sounder reveals details of the seabed
Left: Fore-and-aft echo sounders show varying depth clearance over the length of the ship. When backing or at anchor it is necessary to know exact depth clearance fore and aft. Changing the trim of the ship often causes big differences in draught fore and aft. Right: Starboard-and-port echo sounders. With the large beam of modern giant vessels it is imperative to know the depth clearance on both sides when docking or sailing in narrow waters.

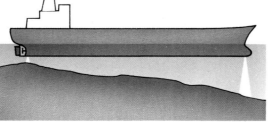

Navigation in the electronic age

steering by satellite

tells you which lanes you are in. Plotting equipment can even be supplied which locates the position automatically. The accuracy of such a system is usually around ½ mile, and in exceptional cases can be as good as a few yards.

Since the late 1960's, it has been possible to navigate by satellite. Satellites launched into a circular orbit provide a means of establishing a ship's position. Signals are received by a dish-shaped aerial on the ship. As the satellite approaches or recedes from the ship the character of the signal received from it is changed by the so-called doppler effect. This change depends on where the ship is in relation to the orbiting satellite. Since the position of the satellite is known with high accuracy, the ship's position can be fixed also. Such a system provides an accuracy of better than one-tenth of a mile in all weathers, all over the world.

The introduction of satellites can lead to the use of fully automatic navigation in the open sea. Modern liners such as the *Queen Elizabeth II* have this system, as do military vessels. But this development is some years away for merchant vessels. The only form of automation for them is the automatic helmsman which can be

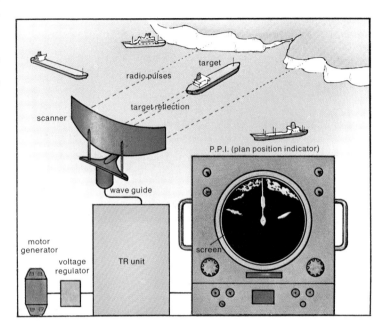

Ship's radar show up nearby vessels and coastlines. As it rotates, the radar scanner on a ship sends and receives high-frequency radio beams all round the vessel. In this case, the radar screen shows a ship directly ahead and approaching an inlet, two ships to port and another to starboard. The sending and receiving vessel is at the centre of the radar screen. The radar is driven by a generator and transformer (lower left) which feeds the transmitting and receiving unit (centre).

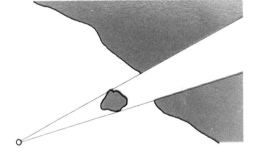

Shading effect of land may give an incomplete radar picture. In pictures at left, the bay shown on a chart does not appear on the radar screen. Equally, a mountainous island in front of shore may shade radar waves (right). Ships also throw shadows which may prevent some details from showing up on a radar screen.

switched on to keep a vessel on a specific course, with built-in allowances for sea conditions, wind force and current.

The ultimate in navigation may eventually be a dual arrangement combining satellites with inertial navigation. In inertial navigation, sensors measure the ship's speed and direction, and compute the changing position from these readings. The system is used in spacecraft. Inertial navigation is entirely internal and independent of any external references such as landmarks, the Sun, stars, radio or radar transmission. All that the equipment needs to know is the exact location of the starting point.

For naval purposes inertial navigation is essential but expensive. It may, however, also become essential for merchant ships for safety reasons – the system is capable of extreme accuracy. Using inertial navigation, a ship can be set on a course and maintained on it despite current, winds and alterations in engine power. Inertial navigation can lend itself to guidance systems controlled from shore-based offices. It may ultimately take the place of radio navigation systems.

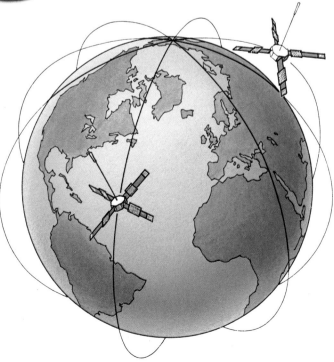

Four navigation satellites in orbit around the Earth will provide a global system of satellite navigation. The orbits are circular and pass over the poles of the Earth. Tracking stations on Earth continually monitor the positions of the satellites, and broadcast to them data which describes their orbits for a short time ahead. New information must be passed up to the satellite continually because slight air friction and irregularities in the Earth's gravitational field modify the satellites orbits over a period of time. Orbital information is re-broadcast by the satellite every two minutes, and is available to be picked up by any vessel with suitable equipment.

A career in shipping
the increase in responsibility

Conrad, Kipling, Masefield and the older writers of sea stories described an industry of which unskilled labour formed the backbone. With the exception of a few senior officers, sailors had no formal training at all. Going to sea in sail meant many years of hard, extended and ill-rewarded effort often ending in death on storm-tossed seas. By contrast, the seaman of today is a well trained, highly skilled professional.

In the days of sail, the young seafarer who intended sailing as a career became known as a cadet. He lived, worked and ate with the crew, and for this privilege his family would sometimes pay a premium or fee. If he survived the early rigours of his sea life and managed to master the arts of navigation and seamanship, the cadet eventually became a ship's officer and finally the master of his own ship. Only in exceptional cases was it also possible for ordinary crew members to qualify.

With the introduction of steam power for ships came the need to enlist engineers whose early training was acquired in shore engineering establishments. In the early 19th century,

steamships burned coal and this was handled by stokers, with greasers looking after the oiling of the then monstrous steam engines. The engineers, stokers (or firemen) and the greasers formed a new department in the ship in which discipline was as strict as in the deck department.

In every maritime nation the training of officers and crews for the national fleets has been treated more seriously as world fleets increase in size (tonnage) and as their equipment becomes more complex. Some countries, such as the USA, Japan, Spain, Germany, France and Belgium, have formed maritime academies where marine training is regarded as a major qualification and successful students are awarded a degree. The pattern is for students to follow a general course of education until the age of 13 or 14. The emphasis is then placed on marine subjects and a further division occurs at a later date between navigating and engineering officers.

Kings Point Academy in the USA is the merchant navy equivalent in terms of discipline and training to the US Navy's famous

Annapolis Academy. In the United Kingdom formal training for officers is largely the responsibility of the major shipowning companies, with the government playing a minor role. But whatever the system, the officers and men who crew the giant tankers and bulk carriers, the fast container ships and cargo liners, as well as the huge fleet of coastal and short-sea vessels, all receive a formal training of which a considerable portion takes place on land.

Seamen are taught to operate hatches, to work the cranes and derricks, and to man and operate the lifeboats all by using shore-based equipment. Deck officers are taught how to use radar and how to manoeuvre their ships. They learn on electronically operated simulators which are programmed to reproduce a wide variety of problems, including those encountered when navigating at night. The equipment is similar to that used to train airline pilots and although expensive to install it ultimately saves lives, time and money.

Many shipping companies, particularly British ones, have long operated cadet schemes for deck officers and a few have introduced sea

Deck ratings, under the supervision of the bosun, are the practical sailors of every ship. They handle the maintenance, steering, rigging and winches.

training schemes for engineer officers. For a time, one company ran a ship as a school vessel with accommodation for 70 cadets, evenly selected between deck and engine room. The cadets could combine practical with theoretical exercises. Such projects are, however, very costly. Other schemes have now been introduced which enable a young man with a reasonable standard of education to join a shipping company and combine his sea and shore training. Courses ashore are alternated with periods of service at sea.

All maritime countries share the problem of keeping men happy at sea. Good accommodation, better pay and special recreation facilities are provided, but it is impossible to reproduce shore conditions and to satisfy the natural desire for a normal family life. To compensate for the loss of social comforts many companies have introduced longer periods of regular leave and provided facilities for officers and petty officers to have their wives on board on certain voyages.

An allied problem is wastage – the resignation of employees. The growth of so many shore industries with good pay for men and women with the right qualifications is a constant attraction to the more highly qualified officer or crew member. Therefore, while the shipping company spends money training and helping the development of the young officer, he or she may soon leave the sea in favour of a good position ashore. One solution is to have smaller crews, highly automated ships and well-qualified staff who will find in the complexity of the vessel's machinery the challenge they need to keep their interest.

Another solution is the use of 'general purpose' crews. These are trained in several occupations so that a deck hand can also work in the engine room or galley, and the engine mechanic can assist in mooring the ship. The vessel is run as a land-based operation with a managing director (the captain) and two departmental heads, one responsible for watch keeping and the other in charge of daily maintenance work. When required, both departments can combine to meet an emergency or during periods of bad weather or the critical times of entering and leaving port.

For most young men and women, life at sea offers travel (and some adventure), self reliance, responsibility and leadership under good conditions of pay and accommodation. It may not be their final career but it is a rewarding one which can lead to a shore-based occupation.

Degree courses are now available in marine subjects at six universities and polytechnics in the United Kingdom, excluding the facilities for marine engineering and other engineering degrees. There are several excellent training establishments for deck officer cadets, and embryo engineer officers can now enter the merchant service through special training schemes which did not exist two decades ago.

Major shipping companies such as Ocean

Above: Midshipmen on bridge with training officer. Navigating officers on a ship play a crucial role in ensuring that the vessel is running smoothly. They provide a support team for the ship's master, and are responsible not only for route planning but also cargo loading and crew welfare.

Below: Young steward serves at the officers' table. Catering ratings play a central part in the morale of a ship – good food, and plenty of it, is essential for all ranks. The catering department prepares and serves food and drink, and looks after all the accommodation on board.

Fleets, P & O and J. and J. Denholm in the UK, and companies in Hong Kong, Japan, Spain, the USA, Norway and Sweden have introduced special training schemes. These are costly in terms of money and administrative effort, but are necessary if the fleets are to be manned by well-trained officers and crew.

As in all industries, safety is of paramount importance. The shipping companies of all nations participating in the international maritime safety conventions take special care to see that the crews are trained to meet dangers when they arise and to prevent accidents. Safety training reaches very high standards in the operation of tankers and vessels carrying chemical cargoes where one careless mistake can result in loss of the ship, crew and cargo.

More automation and smaller crews means more leisure time and fewer companions. This in itself can create social problems. However, leisure time can be used to advantage. Organizations such as the College of the Sea in the UK operate correspondence courses in a wide variety of subjects. Success in these can lead the seaman to academic qualifications.

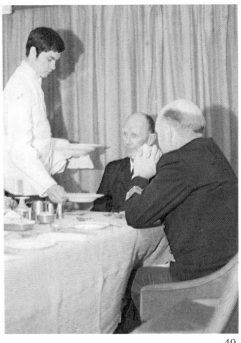

Management in shipping
subsidized fleets

The history of many nations has been influenced by the sea. More than 300 years ago merchants owned or hired craft to carry their goods across the seas. In later years, the sea carried the craft which ferried pioneers to found colonies in new lands. As man has learned to manage his affairs more efficiently, the influence of the sea on trade and national development has grown. Because of the growth of world trade, countries are now more dependent on the sea than ever before.

Early in the last century, merchant companies were formed which built up fleets of sailing vessels. Their management rested largely with their captains – who were often also the owners. But by the end of the 19th century the management of vessels became centralized in company offices on shore. Managers began to regulate the operation of ships to meet the demands of world markets. This situation lasted almost until the end of the 1930's when companies began to join forces and share various markets. On the regular trade routes, with established traditions, merchants made a point of using certain shipping companies; competition for their custom was vigorous but there were few major shipping companies and the choice of vessels was comparatively limited.

Today, shipping has changed radically. From a slow-moving industry with vessels spending months at sea and long periods in port it has become a fast-operating industry which is an integral part of the overall transport chain from a town in America to a city in Australia.

Governments have taken a hand by introducing national fleets. The traditional shipowner therefore has to operate against nationally subsidized fleets, such as those of the USA in which owners are paid a subsidy to cover their operating losses. Some governments such as Liberia offer special tax concessions for owners who register under the Liberian flag. In Greece, owners are encouraged to register and operate their vessels under the Greek flag. The most important change in shipping since the turn of the century has been this growing influence of government policies.

All these handicaps must be overcome by the shipowner operating the open market. In addition to ordering, manning and operating his fleet, the owner must resist the competition from subsidized fleets and the rules of certain nations which ensure that a certain amount of their own produce is carried in their own ships. Shipping companies have had to adopt the strategies of land-based companies to meet the demands of an industry which now demands top-class executive ability and a knowledge of international maritime affairs. Because shipping is international and subject to the policies of many governments it is not always easy for a shipping company to achieve an adequate return on its investment.

The cost of building and operating new tonnage means that the operation of a modern fleet must be highly efficient. Each route must therefore have the right design of ship in terms of size, speed and carrying capacity. In the past, shipowners used their personal knowledge of a particular route and trade when ordering new tonnage. However, the current highly competitive conditions in shipping mean that the owner must undertake intensive market research and examination of customer requirements and port facilities on the routes involved.

There are three basic categories of shipowner: those who build vessels for hiring to others whose capital is employed at such high rates of return as to make it unprofitable to venture into shipowning; the owner with vessels in the regular cargo liner trades, operating regular schedules and calling at specified ports (this category also includes the large oil companies with their fleets on regular routes); and the shipping consortia in which several owners have pooled their resources.

Effective and efficient shipowning demands the use of modern company strategy. This involves examination of new projects – not necessarily directly concerned with shipping – and the correct utilization of computer-based analyses of route and cargo requirements. This evens out the sometimes violent freight market fluctuations due to war, famine or even a warm winter.

World shipping launched annually

The graphs (right) show clearly the increase in building of oil tankers and bulk carriers. In 1971 Japan led the world with over 11 million tons of shipping launched, Sweden, West Germany and the UK maintained their 1970 levels and France launched more than a million tons for the first time. General cargo production however dropped below its 1971 level.

The increase in the number of large vessels coming into service raises the question of the adequacy of dry docking space by 1975.

The backlog of orders for tankers and bulk carriers is so vast that there is practically no berth space available to build them before the end of 1975. Gas carriers on order total more than 2.5 million tons and many shipyards have received orders for large ferries required for the tourist industry. Tonnage for delivery in 1973 is fairly evenly balanced despite the trend towards tankers and away from dry-cargo ships.

In recent years the Comecon countries have emerged as exporters. Since 1965 Russian yards have built some 100 ships totalling 650 000 gross tons for countries in Europe, the Middle East, Asia, the Orient, Africa and Latin America. (source: Lloyd's Register of Shipping).

Propulsion analysis of world tonnage

The block chart (below) shows the steady increase of motor driven ships over steamships. The percentage of steamships is still high but this is directly related to countries with old fleets. For example 52% of the USA shipping fleet is over 25 years old and 8% is over 30 years old (approximately 9.75 million gross tons).

million tons gross

- steamships burning coal
- steamships burning oil
- motorships

1920 1930 1939 1950 1960 1971

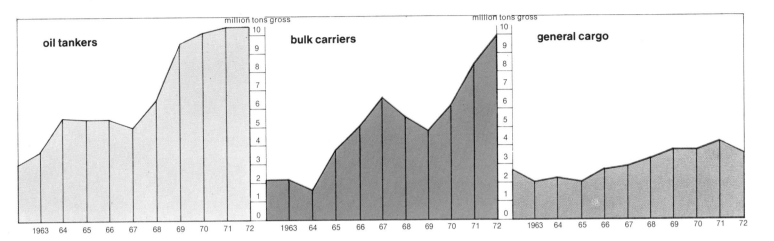

oil tankers / bulk carriers / general cargo

million tons gross

Most of the smaller companies are split into shore-based and seagoing departments. It is becoming more common for shipowners to involve their senior seagoing staff in company policy by bringing them ashore at regular intervals. During this time they learn more about management problems and contribute their experience of ship manning and efficiency of operation.

The new major developments in shipping such as container ships, giant bulk carriers, roll-on roll-off craft, and gas-carrying vessels all require high capital investment. This means a degree of financial expertise in which economics are closely linked with ship design. Small companies may not be able to afford the vast sums of money required. However, there are organizations which can provide the required economic analysis of possible projects, and there are financial houses who, depending on the results of the economic study, are willing to become involved in such projects.

A small but select band of companies specialize in ship management. For a fee, these will look after, man and maintain vessels for shipowners who do not wish to be involved in the actual business of ship operation. These management companies are in a position to expand by becoming experienced in the operation of several ship types, ranging from conventional cargo ships to gas-turbine-powered container ships and 200 000-ton tankers. One of the largest management groups operates thirty ships for six owners.

The operation of a ship management company is geared to the solving of problems and the handling of new types of vessel – and this means that the company's technical staff spends much time learning techniques for the new ships. The result is a team of highly versatile and adaptable officers afloat and an equally versatile staff ashore.

Management in shipping is not solely concerned with individual fleets of vessels. It is also involved in the successful operation of international associations and conference systems. There is, for example, an association known as the Committee of European National Shipowners' Associations which has members from 12 countries. Its main object is to ensure that its members can continue to serve world trade as cheaply and efficiently as possible.

There are 150 shipping conferences, covering the world. They are formed by international shipowners who agree to place a certain number of ships on specified routes and to call at specific ports. Minimum freight rates are agreed in order to reduce undercutting and prevent 'price wars' such as occur in other competitive businesses.

Total tonnage of tankers and dry cargo laid up

The final months of 1971 revealed depressed freight rates and the highest end-of-year figure of tonnage laid up since 1962. 1971 October figures showed that 60 tankers and 233 dry cargo vessels totalling 3 620 600 tons d.w. were laid up. By April 1972 tanker figures had increased to 79 while dry cargo vessels had reduced slightly to 229 with tonnage increasing to 4 440 000 tons d.w.

Scrap prices have fallen and some shipowners are finding it more economical to lay up in the hope of improved business prospects than to scrap their older ships at very low prices. By 1980 there will be 100 million gross tons of shipping over 20 years old and the world's shipbreaking industry will have to dispose of much of this tonnage, but the scrap industry in the past has never disposed of more than 4.3 million tons in any one year.

In the late 60's tankers of 200 000 tons d.w. were introduced and it is still unknown whether their life expectancy is as much as 20 years.

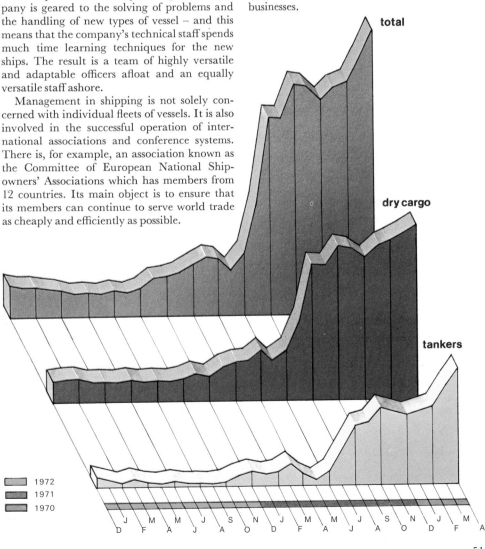

total / dry cargo / tankers

1972
1971
1970

The law of the sea
international rules

No one owns the sea. However, all maritime nations lay claim to parts of it around their shores – the so-called *territorial waters* of that nation. There is no territorial limit laid down in law. The three-mile limit so often referred to is accepted by international agreement. But it is up to any nation to pass a law claiming rights to any amount of water around its coast. In one case, this extends to 200 miles off shore.

The question of territorial waters is important in connection with fishing rights, particularly where a nation depends on its catches for the development of its trade with other countries. States are declaring rights over waters extending many miles in excess of the once-common three-mile limit. Having declared their rights, the nations prevent vessels of foreign states fishing within those areas. There is still much to be done in solving this problem with internationally agreed legislation.

Apart from territorial waters, the remainder of the sea is free for all to sail upon. However, this does not mean that everyone can act as they wish at sea. There are international laws, agreed by seafaring nations, aimed at suppressing piracy or any acts of lawlessness that might interfere with the traditional freedom of the seas. Pirates are treated as outlaws. They may be destroyed by ships of any nation, and if captured are punished under their captors' national law. The basic principle of the law of the high seas is that there shall be freedom to navigate upon those waters without fear or favour.

Safe navigation is one of the most important matters in the use of the sea. International conventions have laid down a set of rules for preventing collisions at sea. Ships of all nations must be navigated upon the high seas in accordance with these rules. There are rules specifying the display of navigation lights and the sounding of signals by vessels to notify their intention to other ships. The only exemptions from these rules are small powered or sailing vessels and rowing boats.

There are very detailed regulations for the prevention of collisions. For example, when two power-driven vessels are approaching head on, each must alter course to starboard (right) so as to pass clear of each other's port (left) side. When two power-driven vessels are crossing, with the possibility that they might collide, the vessel that has the other on her starboard side must keep out of the other's way. Power-driven vessels must keep out of the way of sailing vessels, but this does not give the sailing vessel the right to hamper a power-driven vessel in a restricted channel.

Fog is the greatest menace to safe navigation. The international rules state that in fog a ship must proceed at a moderate speed, depending on the visibility, and must stop when the position of another vessel is in doubt. Collisions at sea in fog are usually caused by the failure of one or both vessels to observe the international collision regulations.

Safety at sea is one of the major issues of international legal concern. An international conference on safety of life at sea was held in 1960, attended by all governments of seafaring nations, who undertook to act according to the decisions of the conference. The rules agreed at the convention cover all aspects of safety, from the inspection and survey of the vessel and her maintenance in a proper state of seaworthiness, life-saving equipment, and prevention and detection of fire.

For example, before a ship is put into service there will be a complete inspection of the structure of the vessel, the machinery and the equipment. Thereafter the vessel will be subjected to periodic surveys. Similarly, the vessel's life-saving appliances and fire extinguishing equipment will be periodically checked.

Many nations demand more than the rules agreed at the Safety of Life at Sea convention. Others do not demand that the ships registered with them should adhere to the international regulations of manning and safety. These ships, for example, may carry fewer and less well-qualified men than another nation might consider desirable. Vessels registered with such nations are said to be flying so-called 'flags of convenience'.

Another international law of the sea concerns a vessel's load lines. This stems from the original markings, called *Plimsoll lines*, introduced in the 19th century by the English politician Samuel Plimsoll, who was determined to cut down the loss of ships at sea caused by overloading. Ships over 24 metres (65 feet) long became known as *load line ships*. Such vessels must be marked with a load line disc through which run horizontal lines marking the maximum depth to which the vessel may be loaded. There are different lines for summer, winter or tropical sailing, as well as for salt or fresh water. These lines are governed by the different weather conditions found in various parts of the world and at various times of the year. Also, the buoyancy of salt water is greater than that of fresh water. At the bow and stern of a vessel are marked figures to show the distance between the waterline and the keel. These so-called *draught marks* allow the ship's actual draught to be found in feet and inches, or metres.

More recently, a set of international rules has been laid down to prevent pollution of the sea by oil. Under these rules, ships are prohibited from discharging persistent oils (oils that do not break up and disperse, such as crude oil) or oily mixtures at sea except in areas well away from coastlines. Individual countries have rules about the discharge of oil around their coasts and in their waterways. Anyone breaking these rules is liable to a heavy fine, plus the responsibility of cleaning up and making good any loss or damage caused.

The carriage of goods at sea is covered by the Hague Rules, originally laid down in Brussels in 1923 but since revised. These rules render the shipowner or carrier responsible should goods be damaged or lost because of the fault or neglect of himself or his agents or servants.

The United Nations conference on trade and development is responsible for reviewing this and other aspects of marine law. For instance, while the shipowner or carrier is responsible for his own or his agents' neglect resulting in damage to goods, international law does not at present make the shipowner or carrier similarly responsible for injury to any passenger being carried. The carrier may therefore operate under any terms he pleases, unless national laws at the ports of departure or arrival provide otherwise. Most nations do not provide otherwise, although the United States is a notable exception. She demands the highest degree of

Loadline disc or Plimsoll mark

The letters LR denote the classifying society, Lloyd's Register.

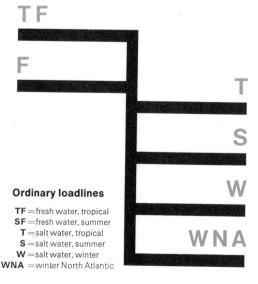

Ordinary loadlines

TF = fresh water, tropical
SF = fresh water, summer
T = salt water, tropical
S = salt water, summer
W = salt water, winter
WNA = winter North Atlantic

care for passengers carried to and from American ports. Hopefully, international law will soon extend these provisions to other countries.

Insurance and ship registration

A shipowner is not obliged to insure his ship. Nor is a merchant compelled to insure his cargo. But neither would be able to operate without insurance cover because a major disaster, such as the loss of a vessel with her cargo, could involve the shipowner in an otherwise ruinous loss of millions of pounds.

Insurance requests are usually placed with a broker who specializes in marine insurance. He will advise on the type of insurance required and then place the insurance with either underwriters at a corporation such as Lloyd's, or with a marine insurance company, or both. In the case of a high-value insurance, such as a ship, the risk is spread among many underwriters and companies. The loss of a ship and her cargo therefore does not fall heavily upon one insurer but upon many, according to the amount of the risk underwritten by the individual underwriters and companies concerned.

Shipowners in international and national trade have their vessels registered, normally in the country of their ownership which will have its own laws of registration. But there are also vessels flying what is commonly termed 'flags of convenience'. In such a case the vessel is registered in another country, perhaps because the demands of seaworthiness and manning are far less stringent in the country of registration than in the country of ownership.

In the United Kingdom it has been compulsory to register British ships since 1660. Registration brings with it the protection and privileges of the country whose flag is flown. Prior to British registry a ship must be surveyed and measured for tonnage. After registry the ship is required to be permanently marked with the name on each bow, the name and port of registry on the stern, and the official number and registered tonnage must be cut in on the main beam.

The burning hulk of the tanker *Pacific Glory* after a collision in the English Channel. 13 seamen died and the South coast of England was threatened by the danger of 80000 tons of crude oil polluting the shores.

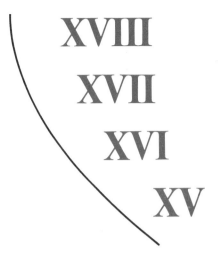

Draught marks on a vessel's bow measure the distance in feet from the ship's keel to its water line. Similar marks on the stern show the depth aft. A ship's draught is the average of bow and stern draughts. The roman numerals are six inches high and are spaced six inches apart.

Danger at sea
casualties

Sea disasters

Every day, somewhere in the world, a ship sinks at sea. Of vessels above 1000 tons, one ship in 500 is lost every year. Some of these losses are due to mechanical failure or fire on the ship. But a large percentage is due to grounding or collision – usually the failure to understand or observe light signals or collision regulations. Every year, $7\frac{1}{2}$ per cent of world ships are involved in collisions – a greater cause of ship casualties than anything else, including breakdown of propulsion machinery.

The casualties that have arisen through failure to observe the collision regulations would fill a volume. Legal experts still talk of the celebrated case in 1956 in which the passenger vessels *Stockholm* and *Andrea Doria* collided outside New York harbour. The collision took place in fog, with both vessels navigating by radar. The *Andrea Doria* deduced that the *Stockholm* would pass slightly to starboard, and moved to port to increase the passing distance. The *Stockholm* struck the *Andrea Doria* in the starboard beam, and the Italian ship sank with tremendous loss of life. The false sense of security that the unwitting misreading of a radar picture gives also leads to recklessly high speeds in poor visibility, and it was the high speed of the collision that made it such a disaster.

The Swedish *Stockholm* claimed that the *Andrea Doria* had turned across her bow and would otherwise have passed to port. This claim and counter-claim illustrates the difficulty of deciding between conflicting evidence in cases of sea collisions. The irony is that, without radar, both ships may have passed quite safely. This is an example of what is termed a *radar-assisted collision*.

Vessels may be stranded due to negligent navigation, and when they are carrying liquid cargo this can produce a terrifying pollution problem. The 100 000-ton tanker *Torrey Canyon* became a disastrous example of this in 1967 after she stranded and ruptured her tanks, allowing her cargo of heavy crude oil to be let loose along the coasts of the English Channel. Such situations are a constant nightmare with the increasingly dangerous chemical cargoes that are now going to sea. The hazard is increased by the fact that most potential danger spots, such as the English Channel, are close to populated land.

In such restricted waterways, lane systems have been introduced. However, unlike on the roads, there is as yet no compulsion to keep in lane, even though the potential disaster is many times worse than a road crash.

Leaking tankers seeking shelter in harbours are being refused entry by an increasing number of authorities because of the pollution they bring. A leaking ship can be towed from port to port until help is offered or she finally has to off load her cargo into another tanker, or is taken into deep water and scuttled.

Several tankers have burned or set other

The Greek ferryboat *Heleanna* is hosed down following the fire which raged through the vessel whilst on a regular passage from Greece to Italy. The ship was severely damaged and several passengers lost their lives.

ships on fire after colliding with them. In 1964, the tankers *Fabiola* and *Bonifaz* collided in broad daylight. The speed of the vessels was so great that the round stem of the *Bonifaz* rode up onto the deck of the *Fabiola*. One of the *Fabiola*'s tanks was ruptured and burning oil flowed out onto the sea. This ignited gas in the *Bonifaz*'s tanks, and part of the ship exploded. One ship was lost, another severely damaged, and 25 people were killed – all the result of negligent navigation.

One of the largest damage claims in maritime history concerns the 200 000-ton tanker *Aquarius* which caught fire after a collision off the Persian Gulf. She was towed to Japan, the location of the nearest dry dock that could take her, but was refused entry as a pollution hazard. Her cargo was discharged in deep waters before she finally headed back to Japan, seven months and 13 000 nautical miles after the initial accident. She needed three tugs to haul her, and even then broke clear for several days, the entire towage cost coming to over £600 000.

Fire is the hazard most feared by seamen. Nowadays, fire extinguishers at sea use substances such as foam or carbon dioxide gas to do their work. Regulations demand the use of fire-resistant materials, and smoke and heat sensors are now common on many ships.

The 24 350 ton d.w. Norwegian tanker *Sitakund* off Eastbourne after an explosion during tank cleaning.

Sea salvage

Salvage companies have millions of pounds' worth of equipment permanently standing by in case of casualty to a ship. A salvage operation requires toughness, resourcefulness and enormous financial outlay. It is worth all this because the rewards can be great: a salvor may be paid hundreds of thousands of pounds for saving one ship. But the risks are also enormous. Apart from salvors who have been contracted by an owner to attend to his ship, salvage operates on a no cure – no pay basis.

Salvage tugs are fast and powerful. They must be capable of towing off ships that are stuck aground, and their speed is essential because the benefits of salvage usually go to the first salvor on the scene. An abandoned ship is fair game for any salvor, but a manned ship can choose which salvor's offer it accepts. A ship's owner may, for instance, contract with a particular salvor to provide service.

When a vessel runs aground, attempts to refloat it involve removing cargo, ballast and fuel to restore buoyancy. Leaking holes are plugged, and compressed air is blown in to expel water from flooded compartments. Vessels stuck on mud or sand are usually refloated at the first attempt. But a ship stuck on rocks may be impossible to salvage, particularly if she has been wedged fast by heavy seas and a high tide.

It is a costly and dangerous job to raise a sunken vessel, and this has to be balanced against the value of the vessel when salved. Often only the cargo may be worth rescuing, as in the case of the P & O ship *Egypt* which sank in 1922 with £1 million worth of gold and

Massive air tanks support the crippled French submarine *Galatee* following its collision at sea with the South African submarine *Maria Van Riebeeck*

silver aboard. The salvors in this case got half the cargo they brought to the surface. But in the deepest water it is technically impossible to salvage a ship.

Capsized vessels have first to be righted, usually by hauling or by pumping compressed air into one side only. Large vessels are raised by attaching lifting gear to them, or by sinking cylindrical pontoons which are then filled with air and raise the ship with their buoyancy. More recently, salvors have successfully raised ships by pumping them full of expanded polystyrene, a material of extremely low density.

Perhaps the most complex salvage operation of all was the attempt by the United States to recover a nuclear bomb lost in 1966 off the coast of Palomares, Spain. The seabed was scoured at various depths by frogmen, suited divers, mine sweepers, sonar vessels, underwater TV and small submersibles. The bomb was finally located at a depth of 2500ft, and gingerly raised by an underwater vessel. The need for salvage at increasing depths was shown by the loss of the nuclear submarine *Thresher*,

which disappeared in deep water in 1963. The remains of the submarine and her crew lie on the seabed at a depth of 8400ft. However, automatic submersibles for deep-water salvage are being developed.

The SS Great Britain

Above middle : At rest in Sparrow Cove in the Falkland Islands before de-masting. Above : Close up shows the iron hull. The wooden sheathing was added in 1882 when she was converted into a sailing ship. Below : The Great Britain makes its 7000 mile journey back to Avonmouth in Bristol from the Falkland Islands on the 250ft pontoon *Mulus III* towed by the 724 ton converted stern trawler *Varius II*

Modern port developments
new deep-water docks

Since the first Suez crisis in 1956, ships have been outgrowing and outnumbering the available berths. The trend is now towards much larger, more mechanized docks built at river mouths in search of extra space or even jutting out several miles from the shore into deeper water. Recent years have seen the advent of barge-carrying craft, such as LASH vessels, and the prospect of airships which can lift 500 tons – many times the capacity of even the largest aircraft – from place to place without the need for any intermediate form of transport. These provide the traditional port with rivals which threaten to remove some of its traffic altogether.

At the time of the first Suez crisis the largest tankers coming to Europe were in the 28 000 to 32 000 ton deadweight range, and the typical dry-cargo ship carried about 10 000 tons. Up to that stage the shipowner could only use a port where existing facilities were able to accomodate his ship. This stagnation was reflected in ships' sizes, which had until then shown little change from one generation to another.

The closure of the canal, although for only four months, meant that ships were forced to take the longer and slower journey round the Cape of Good Hope. To maintain the same rate of delivery as before, each ship needed to carry more goods. This sparked off an increase in the size of ships, particularly of bulk carriers and tankers. With the closure of Suez again in 1967, this time apparently for good, the trend to much larger ships has been accelerated.

The increase in the size of ships, and the introduction of unit load systems such as containerization, meant that port authorities had to go out of their way to provide tailor-made facilities for ships. Container vessels have moderate draughts – 40 or 45ft at the most – and therefore do not require deep-water ports or extensively dredged channels. However, for a container port a large land area is required for the marshalling of containers. At the largest docks, this can amount to over 200 acres. Such enormous expanses are unavailable in city centres, the traditional sites of docks. Container terminals are therefore springing up in the more open spaces on coasts and estuaries.

The exceptionally deep water required by the largest tankers has resulted in oil refineries or transhipment terminals migrating even farther from traditional dock areas. In an increasing number of cases, offshore mooring buoys or jetties are being set up, sometimes several miles from the shore. The concept of such terminals at sea is given a further boost by the increasing size of bulk carriers. Ore is the second most abundant commodity carried by ship, and the increasing demand for raw materials has opened up new, and more distant, sources of supply. An Australian mining company has predicted that 500 000-ton ore carriers will be in operation by the 1980s, and they have begun to study the operation of such a ship. It would certainly require the provision of offshore terminal facilities.

Examples of the new type of offshore port facilities are found all over the world. Port Latta lies 6000ft off the coast of Tasmania, and can load 3500 tons of ore per hour into bulk carriers of up to 120 000 tons deadweight. There are two automatic loaders which can each tip cargo into several holds to ensure uninterrupted

loading without moving the ship. The increasing sophistication of loading and unloading devices at such terminals plays a major part in ensuring their efficiency. The faster a ship can be turned round at a dock the better it is for the dock authority and the shipper. This, of course, means increased mechanization instead of manpower.

A proposed offshore terminal for the salt industry of Brazil shows how investment in mechanization can benefit both producer and consumer by increased productivity. Salt has in the past been carried by small river craft to coastal vessels which must anchor eight miles offshore because of the region's shallow waters. Large bulk carriers would be uneconomical because of the slow loading rate. Consequently, the delivered price of salt is high. In the proposed system, small river craft operate a twice-daily shuttle service to an artificial island eight miles offshore. On the island, the salt is stockpiled by grades and automatically loaded into large carriers. Such a system could cut the delivered cost of salt by half.

The system of small ships stockpiling goods for collection by large vessels is already used for other substances such as ore. It is also used in reverse, allowing large tankers to unload their giant cargo for distribution by smaller tanker shuttle services. One such transhipment terminal is envisaged in plans for a three-acre oil 'island', a concrete pen for millions of tons of oil, built up from the bed of the North Sea.

Containers stacked on the dockside at a container port, awaiting loading onto a ship by the giant travelling dock crane. Containers are taken to and from the marshalling area behind the dock by special stacking trucks.

Modern port developments
tailor-made facilities

Left: Aerial view of a coal and ore terminal in a large modern port, showing piles of bulk cargo unloaded by conveyer belt. Large ports may keep stocks of such commodities for shipping to smaller docks by feeder vessels. Right: Giant bulk carrier alongside an unloading berth. Cargo may be taken from the ship's hold by grabs or by vacuum sucking techniques.

The whole concept of port development has changed with the need to accomodate giant and specialized vessels. Shippers now join with harbour authorities to build specific facilities for their ships, and often they are arranged to feed straight into industrial complexes on land. The prototype of these was Europoort, built at the mouth of the Rhine upriver from Rotterdam. The planning of Europoort began shortly after World War II, and many other countries, particularly in Europe, have followed the example with similar plans of their own. The port of Fos, near Marseilles, is being developed as the Mediterranean equivalent of Europoort, and the port of Hamburg has planned a deepwater port-and-industry complex at the mouth of the Elbe.

Europoort and other large ports are much used as transhipment terminals. In the future more large, open-sea complexes will probably be built in strategic coastal positions to act as main supply depots, with small feeder craft ferrying goods to and from local ports. The whole system is similar to that of a railway, where main line stations feed suburban lines. Such a system allows small countries with limited dock facilities to take advantage of raw materials brought by giant carriers from countries on the other side of the world. This arrangement is already developing in Europe, and plans for new dock facilities on or off the northeast coast of the United States indicate that similar trends can be expected there.

Below: Grain silos fed directly with cargo from bulk carriers. Right: Container ship alongside at a terminal, with export containers being loaded by gantry crane while import containers are rolled out by lorry.

Waterways
Panama

Passing through the 50-mile-long Panama Canal takes a ship about 8 hours. Every mile of the journey represents hundreds of lives lost in its construction and £3 million in building costs. The canal runs from north-west to south-east across the isthmus of Panama, and a ship voyaging from the Atlantic to the Pacific actually ends up 27 miles east of where it started.

Building the Panama Canal required making what was at that time the world's largest dam, across the Chagres river. The result was the 163-square-mile Gatun lake, then the largest man-made body of water in the world. Fifty-two million gallons of water flow out to sea from Gatun lake every time a ship passes through the canal. The land not flooded by the lake had to be laboriously dug out. The Gaillard cut now passes where a mountain once stood, and much of the 240 million cubic yards of earth and rock dug out to make the original canal were removed from this region. Three sets of locks raise and lower ships through the 85-ft height of the canal. The locks are in pairs so that ships can pass in both directions at once. Each lock is about 1000ft long, 110ft wide and 70ft deep, which prevents the largest ships from using the Panama Canal.

The canal lies in the 10-mile-wide Panama Canal Zone, leased permanently to the United States. In the 19th century both Britain and the United States considered a canal through Nicaragua. But a French company headed by the Suez Canal builder Ferdinand de Lesseps obtained rights to build through Panama. Work began in 1882 on a sea-level canal, but this plan was abandoned in 1886 in favour of a design with locks. Mismanagement and bad financing bankrupted the French company in 1889. The United States government took over construction of the canal in 1904, and they completed it 10 years later. The first trip through the canal was made on August 15 1914, although a landslide delayed the official opening until 1920.

Excavation in the Culebra Cut

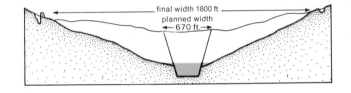

Above: A ship passes through the Gaillard Cut, 8 miles long, 500ft wide and 42ft deep, at the south-east end of Gatun Lake. Right: The Culebra Cut was originally planned to be 670ft wide. But because of landslides the final width became 1800ft.

final width 1800 ft
planned width
670 ft.

The canal has since been improved. In 1970 work was completed on widening the Gaillard cut from 300ft to 500 feet. Because of landslides, up to one million cubic yards of soil have to be dredged yearly from this cut. The Panama Canal is expected to reach its maximum capacity by about 1980. In 1964, the American President Lyndon Johnson proposed building a new sea-level canal.

Construction of the Panama Canal shortened sea routes from the Atlantic to the Pacific by as much as 8000 miles. It is now the most important artificial waterway in the world. About 40 ships pass through the canal each day, carrying a yearly total of 120 million tons of cargo. Something like £16 million a year is collected in tolls. An average toll is about £2750. The highest tolls so far paid are around £13 000 for a single ship.

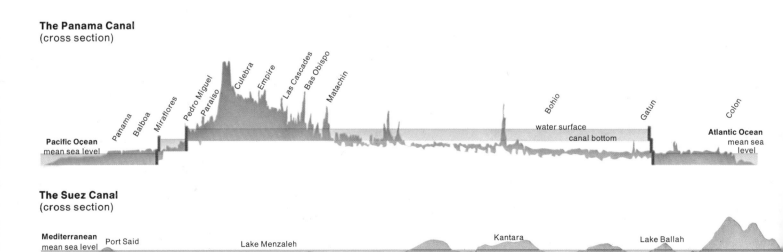

The Panama Canal
(cross section)

Pacific Ocean mean sea level — Panama — Balboa — Miraflores — Pedro Miguel — Paraiso — Culebra — Empire — Las Cascadas — Bas Obispo — Matachin — Bohio — water surface — canal bottom — Gatun — Colon — Atlantic Ocean mean sea level

The Suez Canal
(cross section)

Mediterranean mean sea level — Port Said — Lake Menzaleh — Kantara — Lake Ballah
26 ft
bottom of canal

Mediterranean entrance to the Suez Canal: ships passing through the outer harbour of Port Said before the closure of the canal forced all Europe-to-Asia shipping to go round Africa.

The narrow neck of land that joins Africa and Asia is the site of the oldest artificial waterway in history. At least four thousand years ago the Egyptians built a canal between the Nile and the Red Sea. This canal was sporadically abandoned and re-excavated until AD 800 when it finally fell into disrepair.

At the end of the 18th century Napoleon Bonaparte saw the advantages of a canal directly linking the Mediterranean and the Red Sea. But his plan was stopped by engineers who believed that the Red Sea was 30ft higher than the Mediterranean, and feared an uncontrollable flood if the two were joined.

The engineers were wrong, and 70 years later Ferdinand de Lesseps got permission from the Egyptians to drive a canal from Suez to the Mediterranean. Construction started in 1859. To bring drinking water to the construction workers, the Ismailia canal, the ancient waterway of the Egyptians, was reopened. Half a million Egyptians moved into the newly irrigated desert region as it began to flower.

After ten years' work, the Suez canal was opened on November 17 1869. It was 105 miles long, and a brand new port – Port Said – stood at its Mediterranean end. Although twice as long as the Panama canal, Suez cost less than half the amount – £38 million. This is because Suez was built through flat, easily dug sand. No expensive locks were required – it is a sea-level canal from end to end.

The canal took thousands of miles off of voyages to Asia and the South Seas. It reduced the distance between England and Hong Kong by one third. In the 15 years after the opening

Excavation of the southern end of the Suez Canal, passing through the plateau of Chalouf el Terraba.

of Suez, the cost of Oriental goods dropped by 30 per cent in New York. The canal also hastened the end of sailing ships, for they were hampered by the lack of winds on the Suez route and could not use it as efficiently as steam ships. The Suez Canal Company, owners and operators of the canal, had reduced the tolls to a quarter their original value by 1956. Between the canal's opening and its nationalization by the Egyptians, canal traffic rose from 486 to 17500 ships a year. The average time for a passage was 15 hours.

The canal was originally 200ft wide at the surface and 26ft deep. It was scarcely large enough to allow two ships to pass. By 1956 its width had been increased to as much as 500ft, and its depth to 36ft. In 1951 the 7-mile Ballah bypass was opened, where ships gathered in convoy to pass those going the other way. The improvements cost over three times as much as the original canal.

In 1957 the canal was reopened and by 1964 the depth increased to 38ft. Further development was delayed by closure from 1967 to 1975. Work has now commenced to increase the depth to 53ft, to accommodate fully loaded 150000 ton tankers by 1979.

The Bitter Lakes   Suez   **Red Sea** mean sea level

bottom of canal

World shipping lanes
passenger and cargo

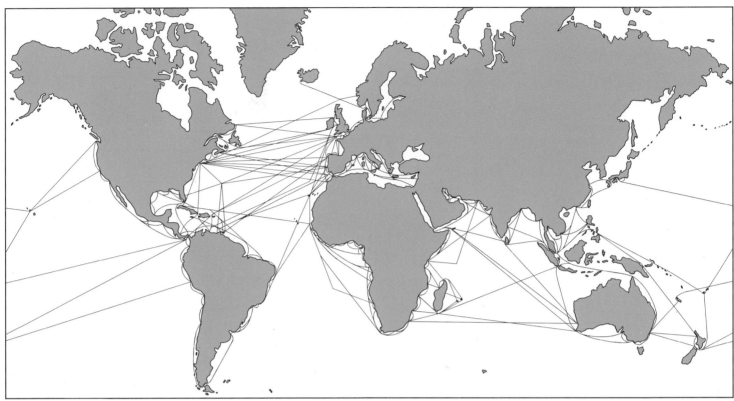

Passenger and Cargo

Containers RoRo

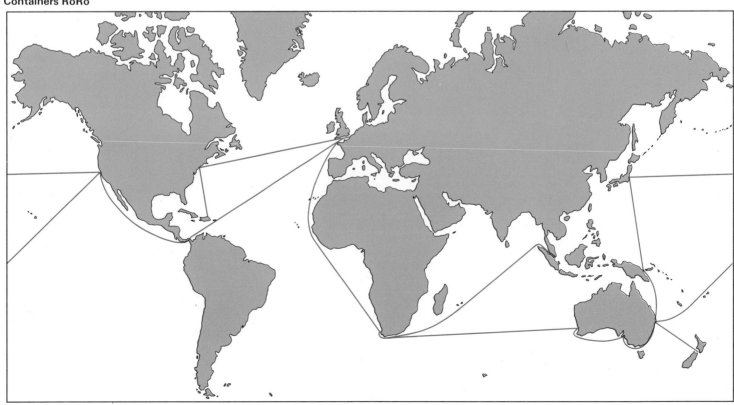

World shipping lanes
oil, iron ore and coal

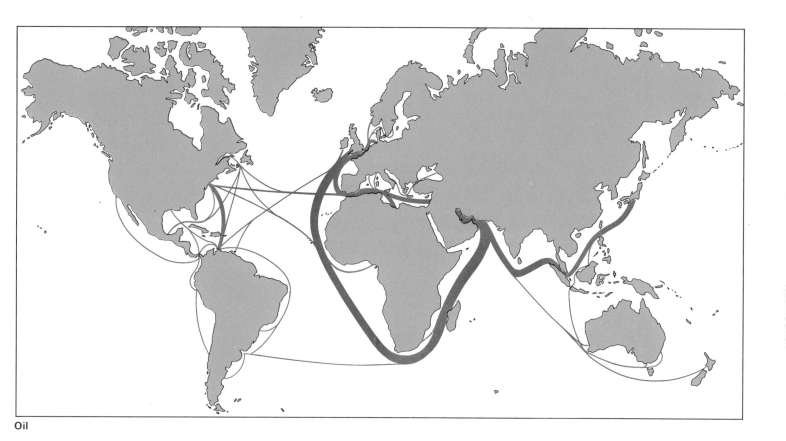

Oil

Iron Ore and Coal

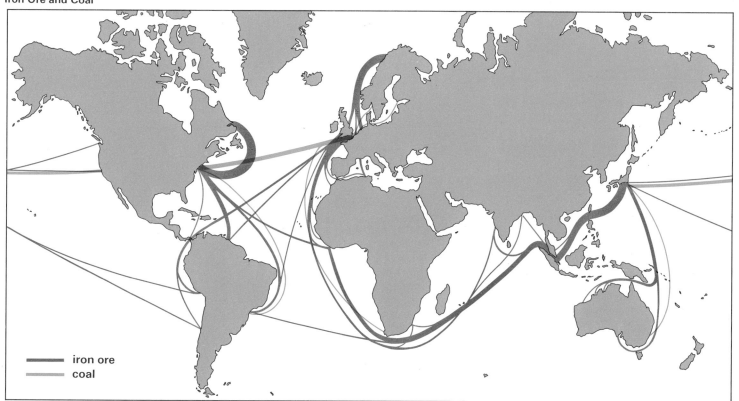

▬▬▬	iron ore
▬▬▬	coal

Future developments
submarines and twin-hulled craft

Ships have a future under the sea as well as on and above it. When the first submarine to sink an enemy ship proved her worth over 150 years ago, she started a trend that led to the fearsome nuclear-powered military submarines of today – and may some day lead to submarine merchant carriers.

At high speeds submarines need less power per knot than conventional ships. This is because displaced water can flow past the submarine on all sides, and less energy is lost in wave making. Another advantage is that at a depth of only a few hundred feet the craft avoids the disturbing effects of waves and water turbulence, which are concentrated at the ocean's surface.

The use of nuclear power means that fast underwater vessels are now feasible. Various countries have undertaken design studies of submarine oil tankers. The projected deadweight of these designs ranges from 20000 to 250000 tons, and the length envisaged in one case exceeds 1000ft. The value of a submarine tanker became particularly apparent when the discovery of oil in Alaska raised the problem of shipping the produce through ice-bound seas. In this specialized case at least, a submarine tanker could operate competitively with, and far more reliably than, an ice-breaking surface tanker. However, the point at which submarines normally have the advantage is well above the present economic speed.

Whether such giant submarine carriers become a reality or not, small submersibles most certainly have a future – either in purely scientific marine exploration or more commercial applications such as inspecting pipelines and ship's bottoms or aiding drilling programmes for oil and gas. Such vessels are now being accepted and certified by the registration societies, as with normal ships.

Another type of vessel more familiar in non-merchant applications is the catamaran or twin-hulled craft. The Englishman William Petty did some research into catamarans and built one as long ago as 1662. The high speed of this early vessel, a result of the long, narrow shape of her hulls, enabled her to win races against conventional yachts. Petty's double-bodied ship, as he called it, seems to have been invented independently of the much older catamarans of the Pacific.

The ease with which catamarans sail, and the large deck area afforded by the bridge between the two hulls, has attracted much interest. Double-hulled designs became quite popular in the days of paddle-wheel propulsion. However, the apparent advantages of catamaran-type ships are deceptive. At low speeds they in fact have greater drag than mono-hull ships, and although their deck area is large it has no depth. In limited fields, such as the carriage of bulky, low-density goods (cars, for instance) or in areas where draught is limited, catamarans have advantages over mono-hull ships. The stability of catamaran craft is an asset used in some drilling applications, where the gap between the hulls is used to sink the drill. Another suggestion for use of this gap is to place detachable cargo units in it. Barges would be floated into place between the hulls like trains entering a station, and be held by clamps. The result would be a kind of bottom-loading container ship. However, marine experts do not see catamaran vessels displacing standard-shaped ships in most commercial applications.

Twin-hulled ships shown in two different forms. Below left, and centre: End-on view and plan of a vessel in which barges are carried locked in place between the two hulls. According to one design study, four barges, each over 100ft long and with a capacity of 137500 cubic feet, would be carried in this way. Right and bottom: Compound end-on view, showing midships and stern section, and plan of container-carrying catamaran. Containers can be loaded on deck and in the body of the hulls. They are lifted by a gantry crane which can move the length of the ship. According to one design study, such a vessel would be over 600ft long and carry about 1000 containers.

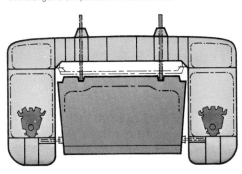

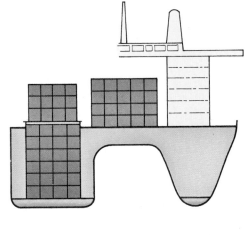

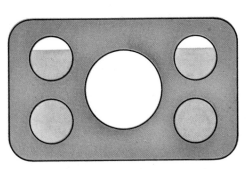

Cross section through the hull of a projected submarine tanker. Oil fills most of the tanker's body. There is a central pressure hull for crew and machinery. Four pressure tanks running longitudinally compensate for the difference between the density of sea water and oil. The main oil-filled body of the submarine tanker is not pressurized.

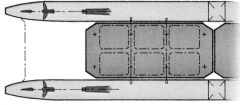

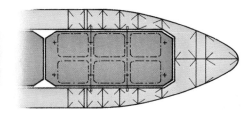

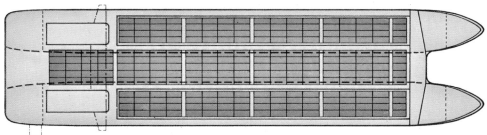

Many technical advances are sure to come to shipping, and by their very nature they are unpredictable. As with aircraft, there will doubtless be a continuing trend towards strong yet light materials for shipbuilding – the use of aluminium instead of steel for superstructures is an example of this. Some naval vessels have now been built with plastic hulls, which makes them exceptionally light and, because plastic isn't corroded by seawater, reduces the need for protective coats of paint. An advantage of plastic for military operations is that it is non-magnetic, and therefore less susceptible to mines, and it does not reflect radar waves. Scientists have also found that introducing minute amounts of polymer (a 'slippery' substance) into the water along a ship's hull reduces skin friction considerably. However, this is not yet a practical or economic proposition for merchant ships.

Hull design and structure is one of the areas of greatest research. Although current ships are very efficiently made – relative to its overall size, the thickness of a ship's hull is one-tenth that of an eggshell – there is no reason to believe that structure cannot be improved by a better understanding of the stresses endured by a ship at sea. The actual shape of hulls is still changing in response to technical advances and changing requirements. Ton for ton, a modern ship needs 30 per cent less power to drive it at the same speed as a ship of 50 years ago. Perhaps we can expect similar improvements in the future.

Most projections of future shipping see a steady evolution of current ship types, rather than a revolution. Ships are now being designed for specific purposes, and the dominant types are the tanker, bulk carrier and container vessel. Their average sizes – and their total number – will continue to grow steadily. One way they may grow is in the form of the compound or articulated ship. In this arrangement, a ship pushes a 'barge' – perhaps actually of 50 000 tons deadweight – or chain of barges, which are linked by couplings. The couplings allow the compound vessel to bend as waves pass under, and enable the total load to be distributed in sections to various wharves at the port of arrival. Although many novel types of craft, including hovercraft and hydrofoils, will undoubtedly be built in the coming decades, they will still represent only a small proportion of the total world fleet.

Looking even further ahead, one definite change that must come in the next 100 years is the eventual demise of the tanker and a changeover from oil to some other form of fuel. The reason for this is simply that the world's supply of fossil fuel is certain to run out – possibly by the year 2000. What happens then, and what power source we turn to instead, is not just of interest to the world of shipping. It concerns everybody.

Below: Tug for pushing a barge unit. The so-called tug is really a detachable engine and bridge unit, which fits into a barge to become the after end of a ship. 'Barges' of 35000 tons d.w. are in operation. The tug and barge are shaped to fit smoothly together and create a rigid ship. Other systems have been designed with articulated tug-barge linkages.

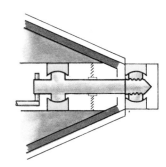

Below: Locking system for joining tug and barge. The device is located on the tug's centre line. A geared shaft in the tug (left) is screwed through a thread in the barge (right). The attaching or detaching operation takes about 15 minutes.

Below: Tug (left) approaches barge, with bollards engaging in restraining links.

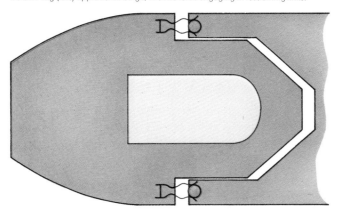

To plug the two parts of the tug-and-barge system together, the tug is ballasted to the correct draught and then moves gently into the recess at the stern of the barge. Bollards on the barge are clamped into restraining links on the tug to hold the two sections while they are bolted firmly together.

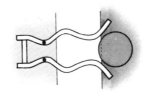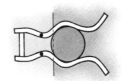

Deck restraining links to assist plugging in of barge and tug. Far left: Tug approaching barge. Left: Tug and barge union completed.

Below: Tug-barge system complete. The engine and bridge section is plugged into the cargo-carrying barge section to form a rigid 30000-ton d.w. vessel.

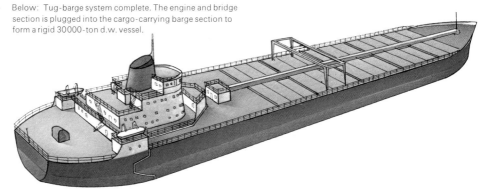

acknowledgements

Specialist sources, information and photographs:
American Bureau of Shipping
Associated Press
Athel Line
Barnaby's Picture Library
British Rail Shipping
Burmeister and Wain
Central Gulf Lines
Chamber of Shipping of the UK
Cunard
Decca Radar
English Electric-AEI
Esso
Fairplay
George Philip & Son
Gulf Oil
Harland and Wolff
Hellenic Shipping International
Hoverlloyd
Kelvin Hughes
Keystone Press Agency
Kockums
Lloyd's Register
Meteorological Office
Mobil
National Maritime Museum, London
National Physical Laboratory
Natural History Museum
North Atlantic Conference
Ocean Management Services
Overseas Containers Limited
P & O
Port of Amsterdam
Radio Times Hulton Picture Library
Royal Institution of Naval Architects
Science Museum
Shell
Shipbuilders and Repairers National Association
Sulzer

Illustrators:
Laurence Dunn
Robert Abrahams
Anthony Payne
David Watson

GENERAL REFERENCE

Abbreviations of measures used — ft Feet; mm { Millimetres / Millimeters } ; cm { Centimetres / Centimeters } ; m { Metres / Meters } ; Km { Kilometres / Kilometers } ; mb Millibars

3386 — Principal Shipping Routes
(Distances in Nautical Miles)

City and Town symbols in order of size

Sites of Archæological or Historical Importance

Principal Railways

Perennial Streams

International Boundaries

Other Railways

Seasonal Streams

International Boundaries (Undemarcated or Undefined)

Railways under construction

Seasonal Lakes, Salt Flats

Internal Boundaries

Railway Tunnels

Swamps, Marshes

Principal Roads

Principal Canals

Wells in Desert

Tracks, Seasonal and other Roads

Principal Oil Pipelines

Permanent Ice

Road Tunnels

Principal Air Routes

Passes

Principal Airports

▲ 8848 Height above sea-level
▼ 8050 Depth below sea-level
1134 Height of lake-level
} in metres

CONVERSION SCALE

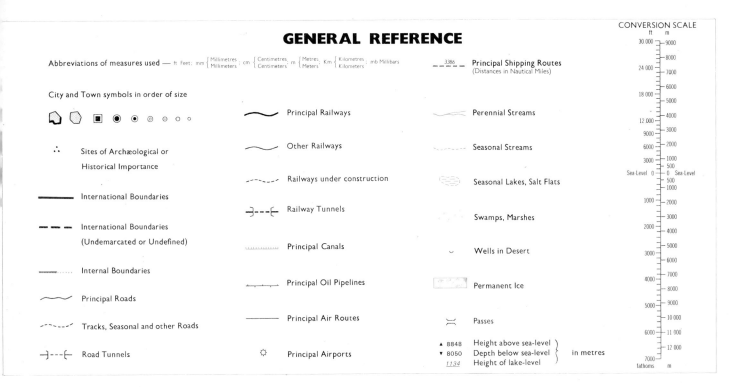

THE WORLD
Physical
1:150 000 000

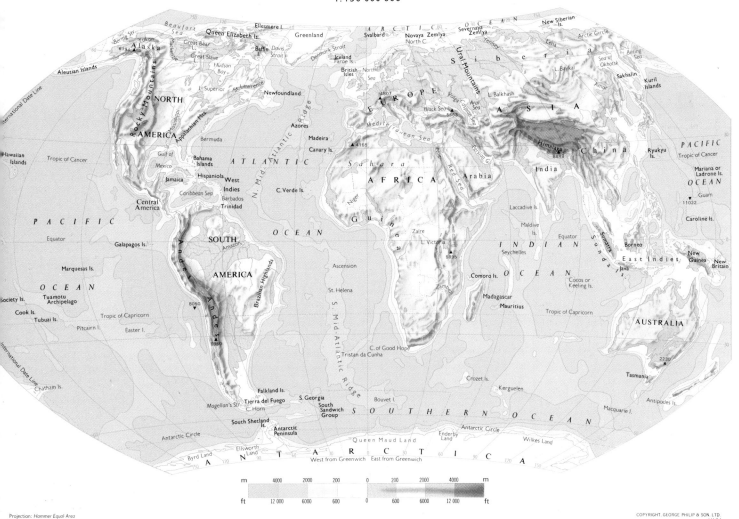

Projection: Hammer Equal Area

Projection: Hammer Equal.Area

 A R C T I C   O C E A N

Franz Joseph Ld.
Novaya Zemlya
Severnaya Zemlya
Kotelny New Siberian Is.
Kara Sea
Bolshevik Chelyuskin
East Siberian Sea
Laptev Sea
Taymyr Pen.
Khatanga
Barents Sea
Hammerfest
North C.
Tromsø
Kolguyev I.
Narvik
Murmansk
Gof Ob
Novvy Port
Igarka
Tiksi
Nizhne-Kolymsk
Kolyma
Arctic Circle
Anadyr

Bodø
White Sea
Arkhangelsk
S Dvina
Kotlas
Vorkuta
Lower Tunguska
Yokutsk
Oympiakon
Okhotsk
Bering Sea
Komandorskiye Is.
Near Is.

FINLAND
Oulu
UNION   OF   SOVIET   SOCIALIST   REPUBLICS
S i b e r i a
Stony Tunguska
Yakutsk REPUBLIC
Petropavlovsk-Kamchatskiy
Rat Is.

Stockholm
Helsinki
Leningrad
Ladoga
Onega
RUSSIAN   SOVIET   FEDERAL   SOCIALIST
Yenisey
Angara
Krasnoyarsk
Kirensk
Blagoveshchensk
Komsomolsk
Sea of Okhotsk
Nikolayevsk
Sakhalin
C. Lopatka
Kamchatka
Kuril Islands

Baltic Sea
Riga
Moskva
Gorkiy
Kazan
Sverdlovsk
Novosibirsk
Tomsk
L. Baykal
Ulan Ude
Chita
Amur
Khabarovsk

POLAND
Warszawa
Minsk
Kiyev
Voronezh
Kuybyshev
Ufa
Chelyabinsk
Omsk
Barnaul
Yenisey Irkutsk
Selenga
Ulaanbaatar
Tsitsihar
Vladivostok
Sapporo

Berlin
Wroclaw
Kharkov
Donetsk
Saratov
Orenburg
Magnitogorsk
Semipalatinsk
Novokuznetsk
MONGOLIA
Harbin
Changchun
Shenyang
Hakodate
Sea of Japan
Ryöngyang

Praha
Kraków
Lvov
Odessa
Rostov
Volga
Volgograd
KAZAKHSTAN
Karaganda
Ishim
Irtysh
Wulumuchi
Peiping
Tientsin
Lu-ta
Ryöngyang
Söul
Pusan
Kobe

Milano
Budapest
RUMANIA
Krasnodar
Astrakhan
Aral Sea
Syr Darya
L. Balkhash
CHINA
Taiyuan
Tsinan
Tsingtao
Kitakyüshü
Kyöto
Nagoya

Wien
CZECH.
YUGOSLAVIA
Beograd
BULGARIA
Black Sea
Tbilisi
Baku
UZBEKISTAN
Samarkand
Tarim
(Yarkand)
Lanchow
Sian
Nanking
Shanghai
JAPAN
Tökyö
Yokohama

Roma
Napoli
Sofiya
Bucuresti
Istanbul
Ankara
Yerevan
KIRGIZIA
Tashkent
Dushanbe
Sache
Chengtu
Wuhan
East China Sea
Osaka

Sardinia
GREECE
Athinai
Izmir
TURKEY
Georg.
TURKMENISTAN
Ashabad
Mashhad
AFGHANISTAN
Kabul
Tibet
Lhasa
Chungking
Changsha
Foochow
PACIFIC

Sicily
Crete
CYPRUS
Bayrüt
SYRIA
Baghdad
Tehran
IRAN
(PERSIA)
Kondahar
Srinagar
KASHMIR Indus
Rawalpindi
Brahmaputra
Kunming
Hainan
Taipei
TAIWAN
Ogasawareguntö
Tropic of Cancer

Tunis
MALTA
Tel Aviv-Yafo
Amman
IRAQ
Esfahan
Abādān
Shiräz
Yazd
Lahore
Delhi
NEPAL
Lucknow
Varanasi
Dacca
Kwangchow
Hong Kong
Honoi
VIET-
South China Sea
Ryukyu Is.

Mediterranean Sea
Ṭarābulus
El Iskandariya
Jerusalem
KUWAIT
Kuwait
Ar Riyād
QATAR
U.A.E.
Quetta
PAKISTAN
Agra
Kanpur
INDIA
Calcutta
BURMA
Mandalay
NAM
Hué
Manila

Banghāzī
El Qāhira
Asyūṭ
Bahrain
Bür Sa'id
Masqat
OMAN
Karachi
Ahmadabad
Nagpur
Bay of Bengal
Rangoon
THAILAND
(SIAM)
Bangkok
Quezon City
PHILIPPINES
Cebu

LIBYA
Libyan Desert
Bur Sūdān
Nejd
SAUDI
ARABIA
Arabian Sea
Bombay
Pune
Hyderabad
Madras
Andaman Is.
Phnom
Penh
CAMBODIA
Saigon
G. of Siam

Aswān
El Khartūm
Atbara
YEMEN
SOUTH YEMEN
Kuria Muria Is.
Bangalore
Madras
Tiruchirappalli (India)
Marshall Is.

NIGER
CHAD
SUDAN
El Obeid
Omdurmän
Asmera
Aden
Socotra (South Yemen)
Lakshadweep Is.
(India)
SRI LANKA
(CEYLON)
Nicobar Is.
(India)

Kano
L. Chad
Ndjamena
Addis Abeba
Djibouti
Berbera
Ras Asir
SOMALI
REP.
Colombo
Dondra Hd.
Pinang
MALAYSIA

NIGERIA
Ibadan
Benue
CENTRAL AFRICA
Bangui
UGANDA
KENYA
Mogadishu
Maldive Is.
Medan
Kuala Lumpur
MALAYA
SABAH
BRUNEI
Kuching

Douala
CAMEROON
Yaoundé
ZAIRE
(CONGO)
Kisangani
Kampala
Victoria
Nairobi
Kismayu
Equator
Sumatra
Singapore
Borneo
Irian
Jaya

GABON
CONGO
Brazzaville
Kinshasa
Kasai
RWANDA
BURUNDI
Kigoma
Seychelles
I N D I A N
Palembang
INDONESIA
Bandjarmasin
Sulawesi
New
Guinea
PAPUA
NEW
GUINEA
New
Ireland
Rabaul

Libreville
Kananga
Kisangani
Tanganyika
Dar es Salaam
Zanzibar
TANZANIA
Amirante
Is.
Chagos
Arch. (Br.)
Diego Garcia
(Br.)
O C E A N
Djakarta
Java
Ujung Pandang
Surabaja
Madang
New
Britain
Solomon Is.

Luanda
ANGOLA
Lubumbashi
Mombasa
Aldabra
Comoro
Is.
Bandung
Sunda
Islands
Port
Moresby
C. York
Tuvalu
(Ellice Is.)

Benguela
ZAMBIA
Lusaka
Malawi
MADAGASCAR
Tomatove
Cargados
Garajos (Br.)
Cocos
(Keeling) Is.
(Australia)
Timor
Timor Sea
Darwin
Arafura Sea
Torres Str.
Louisiade
Arch.
Santa Cruz
Is. (Br.)
Rotuma

Moçâmedes
RHODESIA
Salisbury
Beira
MOZAMBIQUE
Mozambique Chan.
Tananarive
Rodriguez
Christmas I.
(Australia)
NORTHERN
TERRITORY
Cairns
New
Hebrides
New
(Br.-Fr.)
Fiji Is.

C. Fria
Bulawayo
Réunion
(Fr.)
MAURITIUS
Tropic of Capricorn
P. Hedland
Dampier
North West C.
C. Preston
Mt. Isa
Townsville
WESTERN
Alice Springs
QUEENSLAND
New
Caledonia
(Fr.)
Nouméa
Vanua Levu
Vit. Levu
Suva

SOUTH WEST
AFRICA
(NAMIBIA)
Windhoek
BOTSWANA
Kalahari
Gaborone
Pretoria
Amsterdam
(Fr.)
St. Paul
(Fr.)
Geraldton
AUSTRALIA
SOUTH
AUSTRALIA
L. Eyre
AUSTRALIA
Rockhampton
Brisbane

Walvisbaai
Johannesburg
SWAZI.
Maputo
(Lourenço Marques)
Perth
Fremantle
Kalgoorlie
NEW SOUTH
WALES
Newcastle
Lord Howe I.
(Australia)
Norfolk I.
(Australia)
North C.

SOUTH AFRICA
Orange
LESO.
Durban
C. Leeuwin
Great
Australian
Bight
Adelaide
Murray
Sydney
Canberra
VICTORIA
C. Howe
Auckland
NEW
ZEALAND
North I.

Cape Town
C. of Good Hope
C. Agulhas
East London
Port Elizabeth
Albany
Melbourne
Bass Str.
TASMANIA
Tasman
Sea
Wellington

Pr. Edward Is
(South Africa)
Crozet Is.
(Fr.)
Kerguelen
(Fr.)
McDonald I.
(Australia)
Heard I.
(Australia)
Hobart
Christchurch
South I.
Dunedin
Stewart I.

Bouvet I.
(Norway)
S O U T H E R N   O C E A N
Antipodes Is.
(N.Z.)
Auckland I.
(N.Z.)

Königg Haakon VII Sea
Antarctic Circle
Enderby Land
Wilkes Land
S. Magnetic Pole 1965
Ballenny Is.
Campbell I.
(Australia)
Macquarie I.
(Australia)

Coats Land
DEPENDENCY
AUSTRALIAN DEPENDENCY
TERRE ADELIE
Ross Sea

20   40   60   80   100   120
East from Greenwich

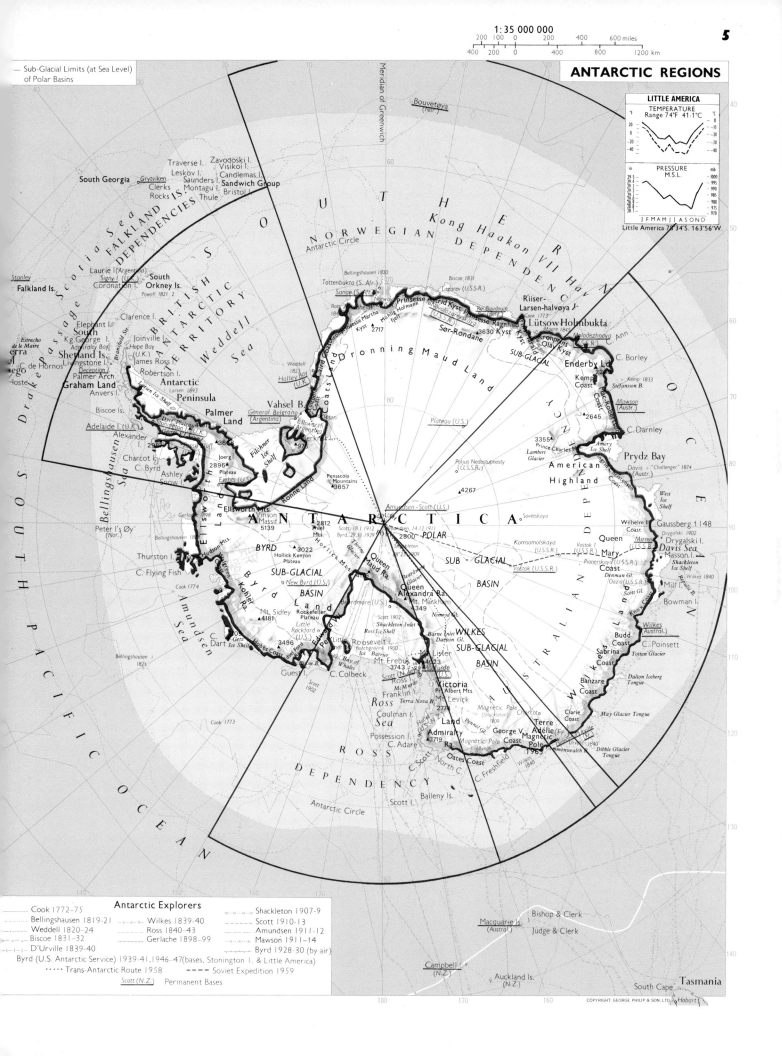

1:35 000 000

200 100 0 200 400 600 miles

400 200 0 400 800 1200 km

— Sub-Glacial Limits (at Sea Level) of Polar Basins

LITTLE AMERICA

TEMPERATURE
Range 74°F 41.1°C

PRESSURE
M.S.L.

J F M A M J J A S O N D

Little America 78°34'S. 163°56'W.

S O U T H E R N

Meridian of Greenwich

Bouvetøya (Nor.)

Antarctic Circle

Traverse I. Zavodovski I.
Visikoi I.
Leskov I. Candlemas I.
South Georgia Grytviken Saunders I. Sandwich Group
Clerks Montagu I.
Rocks Bristol I. Thule

NORWEGIAN DEPENDENCY

Kong Haakon VII Hav

Bellingshausen 1820

Biscoe 1831

Tottenbukta (S. Afr.)

Sanae (S. Afr.) Lazarev (U.S.S.R.)

Norway Novolazarevskaya Roi Baudouin (Belg.)
Fimbulheimen (U.S.S.R.)

Prinsesse Astrid Kyst Prinsesse
Ragnhild

Cook 1773

Lützow Holmbukta

Riiser-
Larsen-halvøya

Kronprins
Olav Kyst

C. Ann

Maudheim 1949

Melodezhnaya (U.S.S.R.)

Inverse Martha Kyst Mühlig Hofmann Sør-Rondane 3630 Kyst
2717 Fjell

SUB-GLACIAL

Enderby Ld

C. Borley

S O U T H

Scotia Sea

FALKLAND
DEPENDENCIES

Laurie I. (Argentina)
Signy I. (U.K.) **South
Orkney Is.**
Coronation I.
Powell 1821, 2

Clarence I.

BRITISH
ANTARCTIC
TERRITORY

Weddell
Sea

Dronning Maud Land

Kemp
Coast

Kemp 1833

Stefansson B.

Stanley
Falkland Is.

Elephant I.
**South
Kg. George I.**
Shetland Is.
Livingstone I.
Deception I.
Palmer Arch.
Graham Land
Anvers I.

Joinville
I.
Hope Bay
(U.K.)
James Ross I.
Robertson I.

Larsen Ice Shelf

Halley Bay
(U.K.)

Weddell
1823

Larsen 1893

Coats Land

Plateau (U.S.)

Mawson
(Austr.)

▲2645

C. Darnley

Mac.Robertson Coast

Estrecho
de le Maire
C. de Hornos
Hoste I.

Antarctic
Peninsula

Biscoe Is.

**Palmer
Land**

Vahsel B.

General Belgrano
(Argentina)

Ellsworth
(U.S.)

3355▲
Prince Charles Mts
Lambert Glacier

Amery
Ice Shelf

Prydz Bay

Davis "Challenger" 1874
(Austr.)

Adelaide I. (U.K.)

Stonington I.
(U.K.)

Joerg
Plateau

Filchner
Ice Shelf

Berkner I.

Pensacola
Mountains
▲3657

Pojus Nedostupnosty
(U.S.S.R.)

**American
Highland**

West
Ice
Shelf

Alexander I.

Charcot I.
C. Byrd

2896▲
Eights
Coast

Ronne Land

▲4267

Amundsen-Scott (U.S.)

Sovetskaya

**Wilhelm II
Coast**

Gaussberg 1,148

Ashley
Snow I.

Bellingshausen 181

Ellsworth Mts.
**Vinson
Massif
5139**

Scott, 18.1.1912
Byrd, 29.11.1929

Amundsen, 14.12.1911

POLAR

Komsomolskaya
(U.S.S.R.)

Queen
Mary
Coast

Mirny
(U.S.S.R.)

Drygalski I. 1902

Davis Sea

Masson I.

Peter I's Øy
(Nor.)

Thurston I.

Gerlache 1898

Thiel
Mts.

A N T A R C T I C A

2800

Vostok 1
(U.S.S.R.)

SUB-GLACIAL

Vostok (U.S.S.R.)

Pionerskaya (U.S.S.R.)

Shackleton
Ice Shelf

S O U T H

BYRD
▲3022
Hollick Kenyon
Plateau

Byrd Land

Hudson Mts.

C. Flying Fish

Cook 1774

Ellsworth Land

Shackleton 27.12.1909

SUB-GLACIAL

New Byrd (U.S.)

BASIN

Queen
Maud Ra.

Beardmore (U.S.)

BASIN

Denman Gl.
Oazis (U.S.S.R.)

Scott Gl.

Bowman I.

Mill I.

Amundsen
Sea

Kohler Ra.

Byrd Ra.

Mt. Sidley
▲4181

Rockefeller
Plateau

Little
Rockford
(U.S.)

Queen
Alexandra Ra.
Mt. Markham
▲4349

Nimrod Gl.

WILKES

Wilkes
(Austral.)

Budd
Coast

C. Poinsett

C. Dart

Getz
Ice Shelf

Hobbs Coast

3496▲

Edsel Ford

Pen.

Bay of
Whales

Borchgrevink 1900

Little
America

Little Roosevelt I.

Scott 1902

Shackleton Inlet

Ross Ice Shelf

Barne Inlet
Darwin Gl.

**SUB-GLACIAL
BASIN**

Sabrina
Coast

Totten Glacier

Banzare
Coast

Dalton Iceberg
Tongue

Bellingshausen
1821

Guest I.

Scott
1902

C. Colbeck

Ross
Sea

Mt. Erebus
▲3743
McMurdo
Scott (U.S.)
Ross I.

Mt. Lister
▲4023

Victoria
Franklin
I.

Pr. Albert Mts.

Mt. Levick
2774▲

Magnetic Pole
(Shackleton)
1909

George V
Coast

Clarie
Coast

May Glacier Tongue

Terre
Adélie (Fr.)
**Magnetic
Pole
1965**

Commonwealth B.

D'Urville 1840

Dibble Glacier
Tongue

R O S S

Land

Coulman I.

**Admiralty
Ra.**

C. Adare

Possession I.

▲3719

Magnetic Pole
1909

Terra Nova B.

D E P E N D E N C Y

C. North

C. Hallett

Oates Coast

Wilkes 1840

DRAKE PASSAGE

SOUTH PACIFIC OCEAN

Antarctic Circle

Scott I.

Balleny Is.

Antarctic Circle

Scott I.

COPYRIGHT, GEORGE PHILIP & SON, LTD.

Bishop & Clerk

Macquarie Is.
(Austral.)

Judge & Clerk

Campbell I.
(N.Z.)

Auckland Is.
(N.Z.)

Tasmania

South Cape

Hobart

Antarctic Explorers

—— Cook 1772–75	∘—∘ Shackleton 1907–9
---- Bellingshausen 1819–21	-·-· Wilkes 1839–40	----- Scott 1910–13
····· Weddell 1820–24	—·— Ross 1840–43	----- Amundsen 1911–12
—··— Biscoe 1831–32	···· Gerlache 1898–99	⁓⁓ Mawson 1911–14
–··–··– D'Urville 1839–40		+–+–+ Byrd 1928–30 (by air)

Byrd (U.S. Antarctic Service) 1939–41, 1946–47 (bases, Stonington I. & Little America)

····· Trans-Antarctic Route 1958   ---- Soviet Expedition 1959

Scott (N.Z.)   Permanent Bases

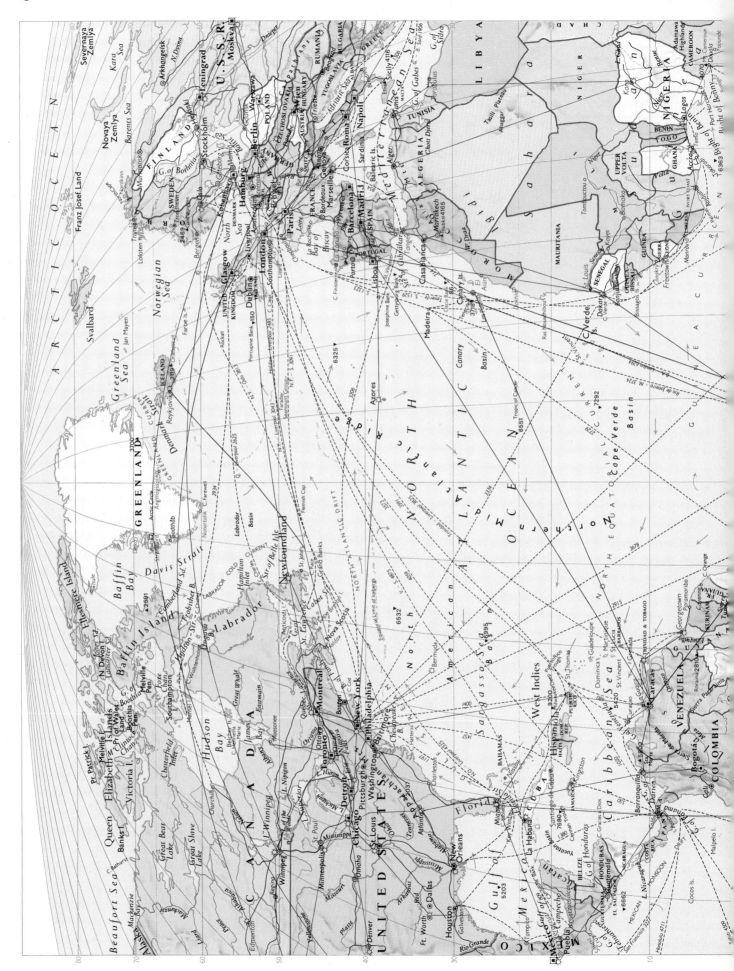

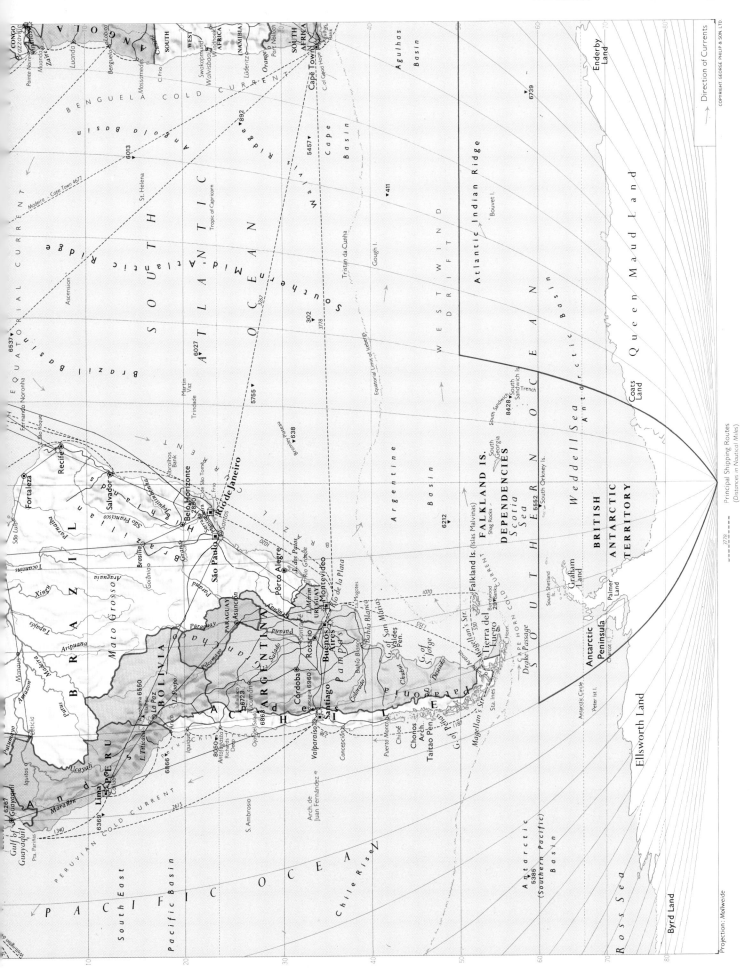

Direction of Currents

Principal Shipping Routes
(Distances in Nautical Miles)

3778

Projection: Mollweide

PACIFIC OCEAN

SOUTH ATLANTIC OCEAN

SOUTHERN OCEAN

BRAZIL

BOLIVIA

PERU

CHILE

ARGENTINA

PARAGUAY

URUGUAY

Buenos Aires

Montevideo

Rio de Janeiro

São Paulo

Santiago

Córdoba

Lima

ANGOLA

SOUTH WEST AFRICA (NAMIBIA)

SOUTH AFRICA

Cape Town

BENGUELA COLD CURRENT

PERUVIAN COLD CURRENT

EQUATORIAL CURRENT

WEST WIND DRIFT

CAPE HORN COLD CURRENT

Mid-Atlantic Ridge

Atlantic Indian Ridge

Queen Maud Land

Enderby Land

FALKLAND IS. DEPENDENCIES

BRITISH ANTARCTIC TERRITORY

Weddell Sea

Ross Sea

Byrd Land

Ellsworth Land

Coats Land

Antarctic Peninsula

Graham Land

Palmer Land

Drake Passage

Tierra del Fuego

Magellan's Str.

Falkland Is. (Islas Malvinas)

South Georgia

South Sandwich Is.

South Orkney Is.

South Shetland Is.

Tristan da Cunha

Gough I.

Bouvet I.

St. Helena

Ascension

Tropic of Capricorn

Antarctic Circle

Scotia Sea

Argentine Basin

Cape Basin

Agulhas Basin

Angola Basin

Brazil Basin

Antarctic (Southern Pacific) Basin

Chile Rise

South East Pacific Basin

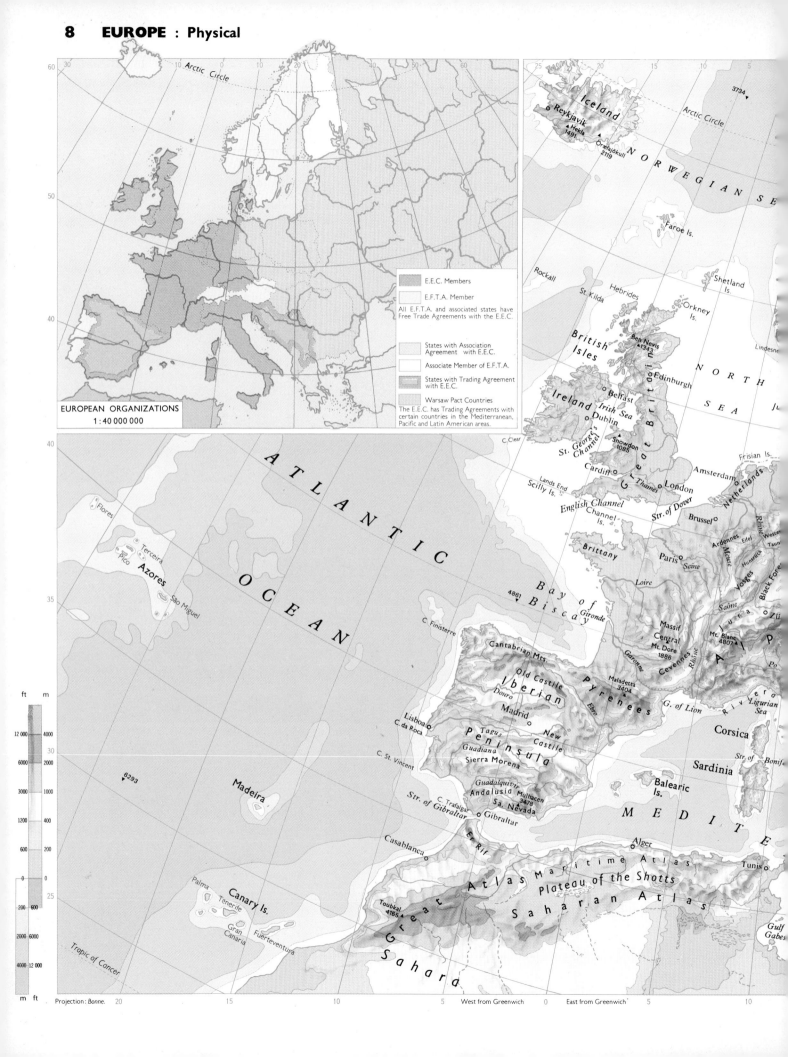

EUROPEAN ORGANIZATIONS
1:40 000 000

E.E.C. Members

E.F.T.A. Member

All E.F.T.A. and associated states have Free Trade Agreements with the E.E.C.

States with Association Agreement with E.E.C.

Associate Member of E.F.T.A.

States with Trading Agreement with E.E.C.

Warsaw Pact Countries

The E.E.C. has Trading Agreements with certain countries in the Mediterranean, Pacific and Latin American areas.

ATLANTIC OCEAN

Flores

Terceira
Pico
Azores
São Miguel

Madeira

6293

Palma
Tenerife
Canary Is.
Gran Canaria
Fuerteventura

Tropic of Cancer

Projection: Bonne.

West from Greenwich   East from Greenwich

NORWEGIAN SEA

Iceland
Reykjavík
Hekla 1491
Öræfajökull 2119
3734

Arctic Circle

Faroe Is.

Rockall

Shetland Is.

St. Kilda   Orkney Is.
Hebrides

NORTH SEA

Lindesne

British Isles
Ben Nevis 1343
Edinburgh

Ju

Ireland   Belfast
Irish Sea
Dublin
Snowdon 1085
St. George's Channel
Cardiff   Great Britain
Thames   London
Lands End   English Channel
Scilly Is.   Channel Is.   Str. of Dover
Frisian Is.
Amsterdam
Netherlands
Brussel
Ardennes   Eifel   Rhine   Weser   Taun
Meuse   Hunsruck   Black Fore
Paris   Seine   Vosges

C. Clear

Bay of Biscay
4861
Gironde

C. Finisterre

Brittany

Loire

Saône   Jura   Zü

Cantabrian Mts.
Old Castile
Douro   Iberian
Madrid
Lisboa
C. da Roca   New Castile
Tagus
Peninsula
Guadiana
Sierra Morena
Guadalquivir   Mulhacen
Andalusia   3478
C. Trafalgar   Sa. Nevada
Str. of Gibraltar   Gibraltar

Pyrenees
Maladetta 3404
Ebro
G. of Lion

Massif Central
Mt. Dore 1886
Cevennes
Garonne
Rhône
Mt. Blanc 4807
A
P
Po
era
Riviera
Ligurian Sea
Corsica
Str. of Bonif
Sardinia
Balearic Is.
MEDITE

C. St. Vincent

Casablanca
Er Rif
Great Atlas   Maritime Atlas
Toubkal 4165
Plateau of the Shotts
Saharan Atlas
Alger   Tunis
E
Gulf Gabes

Sahara

1:17 500 000

100   0   100   200   300   400   500 miles

100   0   200   400   600   800 km

Nordkapp   Nordkinn

Lofoten

L. Inari

Kola Peninsula

Kanin Peninsula

Pechora

Tundra

Ural Mountains

Narodnaya 1894

West Siberian Plain

Ob

Kebnekaise 2123

Lappland

White Sea

Mezen

Telpos Iz. 1617

Irtysh

Tobol

Scandinavia

Indalsälven

Ume älv

Finland

N. Dvina

Onega

L. Onega

Lake Ladoga

Svir

European Plain

Volga Heights

Obshchi Syrt

Kama

Ural

Kirgiz Steppe

Åland Is.

Helsinki

Neva

Leningrad

L. Chudskoye

Valdai Hills

Rybinsk Res.

Gorkiy

Volga

Oka

Oslo

Stockholm

Mälaren

Gulf of Bothnia

Gulf of Finland

Central Russian Uplands

Moskva

Volga

Vänern

Vättern

Gotland

BALTIC SEA

Dvina

Berlin

Oder

Vistula

Warszawa

Neman

Pripet

Pripet Marshes

Kiyev

Dnieper

Tsimlyansk Res.

Volga

Ust Urt Plateau

København

Katte gat

Ukraine

Mts. Praha

Sudeten

Moravian Hts.

Bohemian Forest

Danube

Tatra 2655

Carpathians

Dniester

Bug

Prut

Don

Karagiye Depression -132

Kara Bogaz

Wien

Budapest

Bakony Forest

Plain of Hungary

Mureş

Tisza

Odessa

Dnieper

Sea of Azov

Kuban

Caucasus

Elbrus 5633

Terek

Caspian Sea

Drava

Sava

Transylvanian Alps

Bucureşti

Crimea

Mouths of the Danube

Strait of Kerch

Transcaucasia

Kura

Baku

Dinaric Alps

Beograd

Wallachia

Morava

Danube

Black Sea

2211

Pontine Mts.

Ararat 5165

Araks

Gran Sasso 2914

Dalmatia

Sofiya

Balkans

Rhodope

Istanbul

Bosporus

Kuban

L. Van

L. Urmia

Elbutz Mts.

Tehrān

Adriatic Sea

Balkan Peninsula

Pindus

Sea of Marmara

Ankara

Kizil

Anatolia

Kurdistan

Apennines

Ionian Is.

Morea

Athínai

Dardanelles

Aegean Sea

L. Tuz

Erciyas 3770

Taurus Mts.

Mesopotamia

Str. of Otranto

Calabria

3263

C. Spartivento

Ionian Sea

5121

C. Matapan

Rhodes

Halab

Euphrates

Tigris

Baghdad

Sicily

Malta

Crete

Cyprus

Bayrūt

Levant

Syrian Desert

Persian Gulf

Tripoli

Gulf of Sidra

Nile Delta

Tel Aviv-Yafo

Dead Sea -395

MEDITERRANEAN SEA

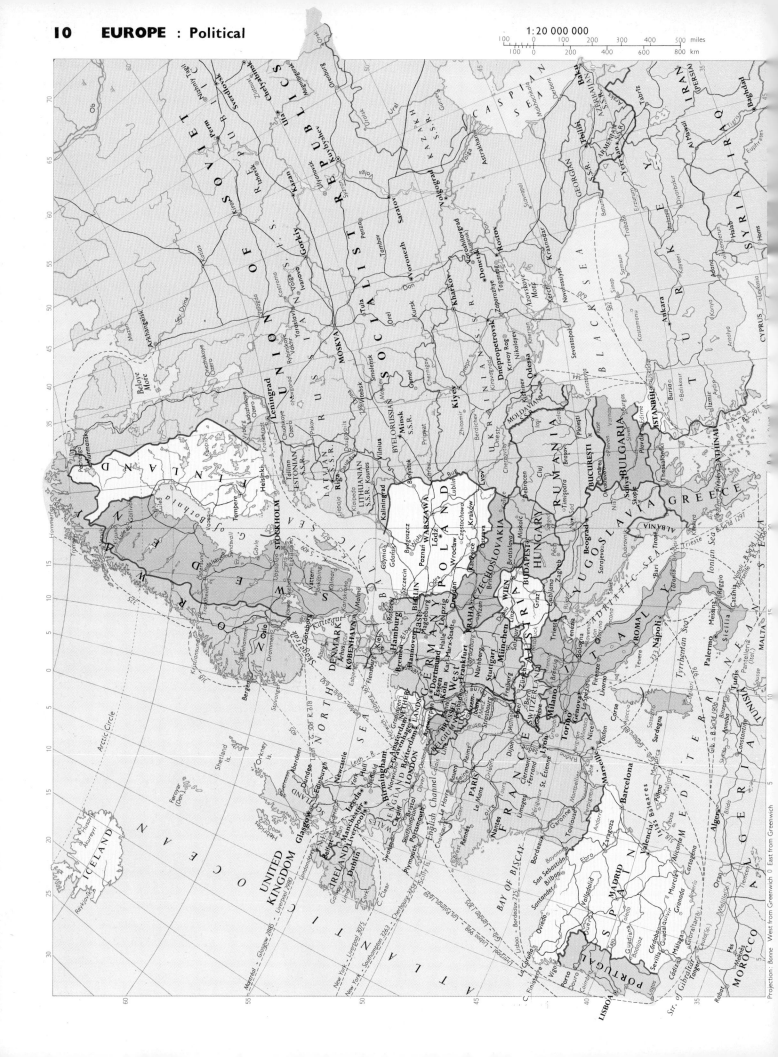

1 : 20 000 000

1 : 4 000 000

Counties : **BRITISH ISLES**

The DISTRICTS of Northern Ireland have been numbered
and can be identified by reference to this table.

1	Londonderry	14	Craigavon
2	Limavady	15	Armagh
3	Coleraine	16	Newry & Mourne
4	Ballymoney	17	Banbridge
5	Moyle	18	Down
6	Larne	19	Lisburn
7	Ballymena	20	Antrim
8	Magherafelt	21	Newtownabbey
9	Cookstown	22	Carrickfergus
10	Strabane	23	North Down
11	Omagh	24	Ards
12	Fermanagh	25	Castlereagh
13	Dungannon	26	Belfast

1 Merseyside
2 Greater Manchester
3 West Yorkshire
4 South Yorkshire
5 West Glamorgan
6 Mid Glamorgan
7 South Glamorgan

Projection : Conical with two standard parallels

West from Greenwich   East from Greenwich

COPYRIGHT. GEORGE PHILIP & SON, LTD.

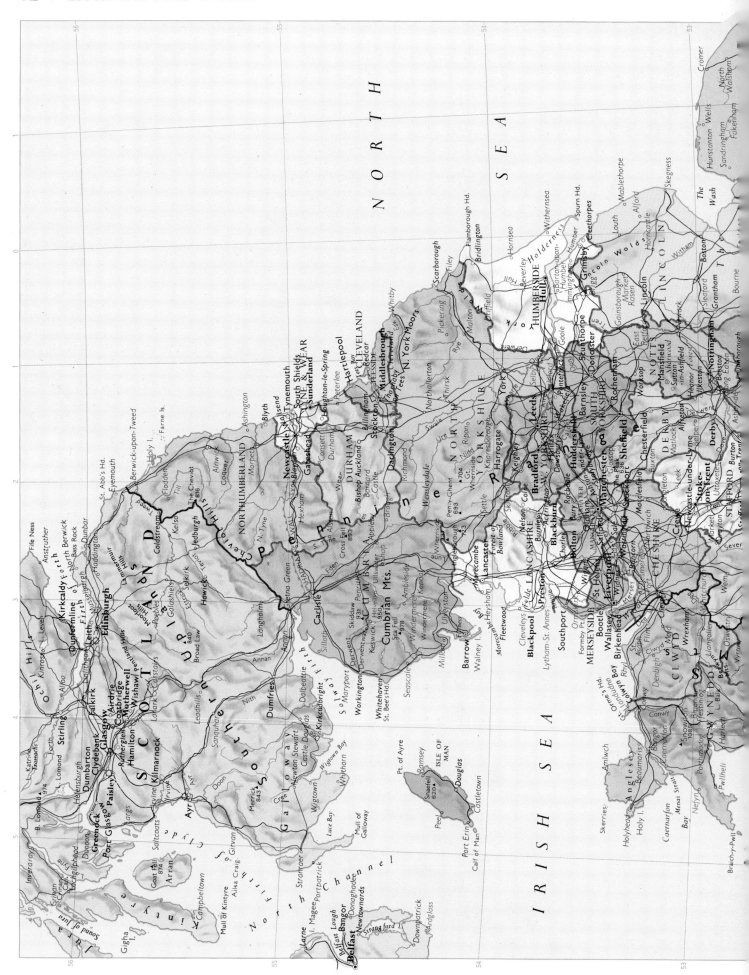

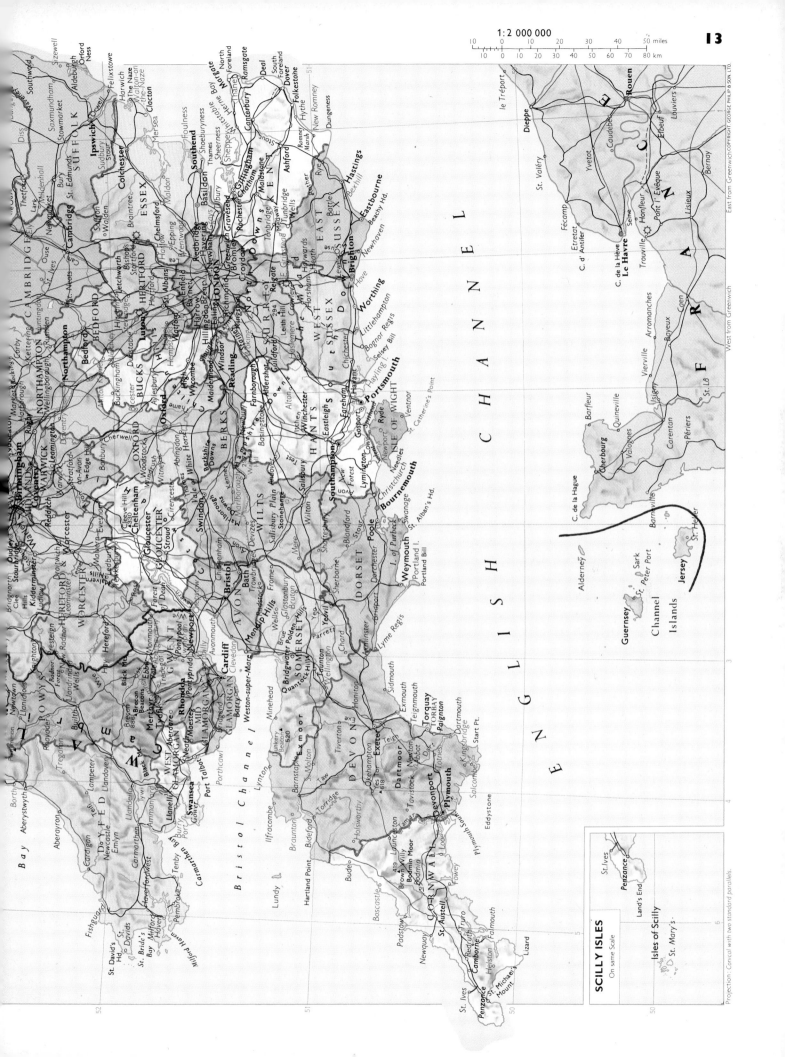

1:2 000 000

10   0   10   20   30   40   50 miles
10   0   10   20   30   40   50   60   70   80 km

ORKNEY IS.
On same scale

Orkney Is.
Hoy · Scapa Flow · South Ronaldsay
North Ronaldsay
Westray · Eday · Sanday
Rousay · Stronsay
Stromness · Mainland · Shapinsay · ORKNEY
Kirkwall · Scapa Flow
Hoy · South Ronaldsay
Pentland Firth
Dunnet Hd. · John O'Groats

SHETLAND IS.
On same scale

Unst
Fetlar
Yell
Yell Sound
Whalsay
SHETLAND · Mainland · Bressay
Scalloway · Lerwick
Foula
Sumburgh Hd.

WESTERN ISLES
Flannan Is.
Butt of Lewis
L. Roag · Stornoway · Broad Bay · Eye Pen.
Lewis · L. Seaforth
Tarbert · Harris
North Uist · Lochmaddy
Monach Is.
Benbecula
South Uist · Ben More · Lochboisdale
Barra · Sound of Barra
Barra Hd.

OUTER HEBRIDES
North Minch
Little Minch
INNER HEBRIDES

C. Wrath · Durness · Strathy Pt.
Cape Wrath · Tongue · Halladale
L. Laxford · Reay Forest · Ben Hope ▲927
Lochinver · Eddrachillis Bay
Enard Bay · B. More Assynt · Loch Shin
L. Assynt · Lairg
Ullapool · L. Broom · Oykell
B. Dearg 1081 · Invergordon
L. Fannich · Ben Wyvis 1045 · Strathpeffer · Cromarty
The Aird · Gairloch · L. Maree · Dingwall · Conon · Fortrose · Nairn · Forres · Elgin · Lossiemouth
L. Torridon · Glen Affric · Beauly · Culloden Moor · Findhorn
Trotternish · Raasay · INVERNESS · Grantown-on-Spey
Portree · Scalpay · Stromeferry · HIGHLAND · Aviemore · Monadhliath Mts. · Cairn Gorm
Cuillin Hills · Kyle of Lochalsh · Dornie · Fort Augustus · Kingussie · Cairngorm Mts. · Cairn Toul 1292 · Ben Macdhui 1311
Canna · Cuillin Sound · Glen Garry · Newtonmore · Lochnagar 1154
Rhum · L. Arkaig · Badenoch · Forest of Atholl · Braes of Angus
Eigg · Mallaig · Arisaig · Glen Spean · GRAMPIAN HIGHLANDS · Blair Atholl · Brechin
Muck · L. Moidart · Fort William · Ben Nevis 1343 · Garry · L. Tummel · Pass of Killiecrankie · Montrose
Ardnamurchan Pt. · Ardgour · L. Rannoch · Pitlochry · Kirriemuir · Forfar
Coll · Morvern · Ballachulish · Rannoch Moor · Ben Lawers 1214 · Aberfeldy · Blairgowrie · Alyth · Arbroath
Tobermory · Ben Cruachan 1124 · Killin · Breadalbane · Dunkeld · Scone · Dundee · Broughty Ferry
Tiree · Staffa · Mull · Ben More 966 · Oban · Ben More 1174 · Crieff · Perth · St. Andrews · TAYSIDE · NORTH SEA
Iona · B. Vorlich 983 · Callander · Cupar · Fife Ness · Anstruther
Colonsay · Inveraray · L. Katrine · Trossachs · CENTRAL · Ochil Hills · Kinross · FIFE · Buckhaven
Crinan · L. Awe · Ben Lomond · Stirling · Bannockburn · Dunfermline · Kirkcaldy
ATLANTIC OCEAN · Lochgilphead · Helensburgh · Dumbarton · Grangemouth · Linlithgow · Rosyth · Firth of Forth · North Berwick · Dunbar · Bass Rock
Rubh a' Mhail · Dunoon · Clydebank · Falkirk · EDINBURGH · Haddington · St. Abbs Hd.
Greenock · Port Glasgow · GLASGOW · Airdrie · Musselburgh · Dalkeith · Eymouth
Jura · Tarbert · Rothesay · Bute · Paisley · Rutherglen · Coatbridge · Motherwell · Wishaw · Pentland Hills · Penicuik · Berwick on Tweed
Islay · Largs · Kilbride · Hamilton · Carstairs · Peebles · Moorfoot Hills · Lammermuir Hills · Duns · Holy I.
Bowmore · Gigha · Ardrossan · Irvine · Kilmarnock · Lanark · Biggar · Tweed · Galashiels · Coldstream · Kelso
Port Ellen · Saltcoats · Troon · Prestwick · SOUTHERN UPLANDS · Melrose · Selkirk · Rodden
Goat Fell 874 · Arran · Brodick · Ayr · Cumnock · Leadhills · Broad Law 840 · BORDERS · Hawick · Jedburgh · The Cheviot 816
Campbeltown · Doon · Sanquhar · Moffat · Ettrick · CHEVIOT HILLS · Coquet
Rathlin · Fair Hd. · Ailsa Craig · Girvan · Dalmellington · Nith · DUMFRIES AND GALLOWAY · Langholm · Lockerbie · ENGLAND
Ballycastle · Mull of Kintyre · Merrick 843 · Ken · Dumfries · Gretna Green · N. Tyne · Hexham
NORTHERN IRELAND · Ballymena · Larne · Stranraer · Newton Stewart · Castle Douglas · Dalbeattie · Annan · Carlisle · Alston · Wear
Ballymena · Portpatrick · Galloway · Gatehouse of Fleet · Kirkcudbright · Solway Firth · Cross Fell 893 · Tees
Belfast · Bangor · Newtownards · Wigtown · Wigtown Bay · Workington · Skiddaw 931 · Penrith · Ullswater · Barnard Castle
Belfast Lough · Whithorn · Luce Bay · Mull of Galloway · CUMBRIAN MTS.
North Channel · Firth of Clyde · STRATHCLYDE · HADRIAN'S WALL

Firth of Lorn · Sound of Mull · Loch Linnhe · Glen More · Strath Spey · GRAMPIAN
Buchan · Fraserburgh · Rattray Head · Peterhead · Buchan Ness
Banff · Macduff · Cullen · Portsoy · Kinnaird's Head
Keith · Huntly · Turriff · Ellon
Rothes · Dufftown · Tomintoul · Inverurie · Alford · Don · ABERDEEN · Girdle Ness
Ballater · Aboyne · Dee · Banchory · Stonehaven
Balmoral · Braemar · Laurencekirk · Inverbervie
Forest of Atholl · Tilt · Isla · S. Esk · N. Esk

Projection: Conical with two standard parallels.   West from Greenwich   COPYRIGHT. GEORGE PHILIP & SON. LTD.

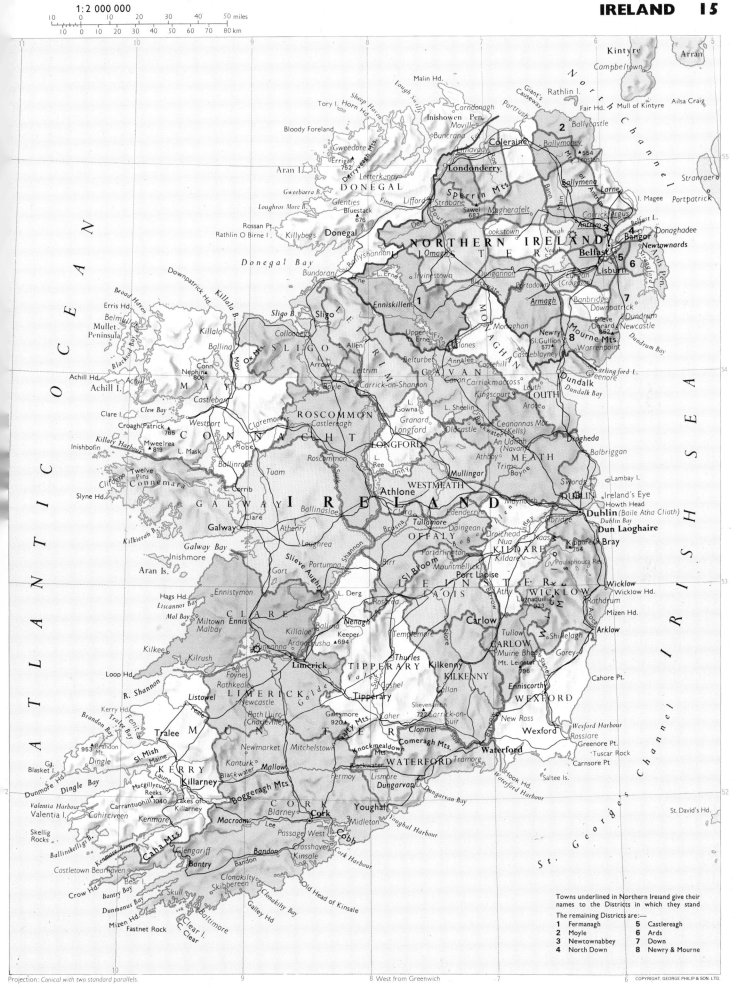

1 : 2 000 000

10   0   10   20   30   40   50 miles
10   0   10   20   30   40   50   60   70   80 km

Projection: Conical with two standard parallels.

8 West from Greenwich

COPYRIGHT. GEORGE PHILIP & SON. LTD.

Towns underlined in Northern Ireland give their
names to the Districts in which they stand
The remaining Districts are:—

1	Fermanagh	5	Castlereagh
2	Moyle	6	Ards
3	Newtownabbey	7	Down
4	North Down	8	Newry & Mourne

1:2 500 000

10   0   10   20   30   40   50 miles
10 0 10 20 30 40 50 60 70 80 km

NORTH SEA

ENGLAND

NETHERLANDS

BELGIUM

FRANCE

LUXEMBOURG

GERMANY

Dover

Great Yarmouth
Lowestoft
North Walsham
Caister
Beccles
Southwold
Aldeburgh
Orford Ness

OSTFRIESISCHE INSELN
Wangerooge Scharhörn
Spiekeroog Neuwerk
Langeoog Baltrum
Norderney Juist
Norddeich Norden
Wilhelmshaven Bremerhaven
Nordenham
Oldenburg
Emden
Leer
Papenburg
Cloppenburg
Meppen
Lingen
Nordhorn
Osnabrück
Münster

WADDEN EILANDEN
Terschelling Ameland Schiermonnikoog Rottumeroog Borkum
Vlieland
Texel
Den Burg
Den Helder

Groningen
Leeuwarden
Harlingen
Franeker
Dokkum
FRIESLAND
Heerenveen
Drachten
Assen
DRENTHE
Emmen
Hoogeveen
Coevorden
Hardenberg

Den Oever
Hoorn
Enkhuizen
Medemblik
Bergen
Alkmaar
Zaandam
AMSTERDAM
Haarlem
Heemstede
Zandvoort
Beverwijk
IJmuiden
Velsen
Hilversum
Bussum
Utrecht
Amersfoort
Apeldoorn
Deventer
Zutphen
Zwolle
Kampen
Lelystad
Noordoost Polder
IJsselmeer

Katwijk-aan-Zee
Noordwijk
Leiden
Scheveningen
's-GRAVENHAGE (The Hague)
Voorburg
Rijswijk
Delft
Hoek van Holland
Vlaardingen
Schiedam
ROTTERDAM
Dordrecht
Gouda
Arnhem
Nijmegen
Enschede
Hengelo
Almelo
Winterswijk

Middelburg
Vlissingen
Walcheren
Goes
Bergen-op-Zoom
Roosendaal
Breda
Tilburg
's-Hertogenbosch
Eindhoven
Helmond
Venlo
Oosterhout
Oss

Oostende (Ostend)
Nieuwpoort
Veurne
Brugge (Bruges)
Knokke
Zeebrugge
Blankenberge
Gent (Gand)
Sint Niklaas
ANTWERPEN
Mechelen
BRUSSEL (Bruxelles)
Leuven
Hasselt
Genk
Maastricht
Aachen
Liège
Namur
Charleroi
Mons
Tournai
Roubaix
Lille
Tourcoing
Kortrijk

Calais
Dunkerque
Gravelines
St. Omer
Boulogne-sur-Mer
Montreuil
Étaples
Berck
Abbeville
Amiens
Arras
Douai
Valenciennes
Cambrai
St. Quentin
Maubeuge

Dinant
Philippeville
Charleville-Mézières
Vervins
Laon
Soissons
Reims
Épernay
Châlons-sur-Marne

ARDENNES
Bastogne
LUXEMBURG
Luxembourg
Esch
Thionville
Metz
Nancy
Lunéville
Verdun
Saarbrücken
SAARLAND
Trier
Koblenz
Bonn
KÖLN (Cologne)
DÜSSELDORF
ESSEN
DORTMUND
DUISBURG
Mülheim
Oberhausen
Gelsenkirchen
Bochum
Krefeld
Wuppertal
Solingen
Remscheid
Mönchengladbach
Neuss
Leverkusen
Wiesbaden
Mainz

PARIS
St. Germain
Versailles
Strasbourg

Projection: Conical with two standard parallels   East from Greenwich   COPYRIGHT. GEORGE PHILIP & SON. LTD.

1:5 000 000

20 10 0 20 40 60 80 100 Statute Miles
40 20 0 40 80 120 160 Km

FRENCH DEPARTMENTS

Ai.	01	Ain
Ai.	02	Aisne
Al.	03	Allier
H.A.P.	04	Alpes-de-Haute-Provence
H.-Alpes	05	Hautes-Alpes
A.M.	06	Alpes-Maritimes
Ar.	07	Ardèche
Ardennes	08	Ardennes
Ar.	09	Ariège
Aub.	10	Aube
Aud.	11	Aude
Av.	12	Aveyron
B.R.	13	Bouches-du-Rhône
C.	14	Calvados
C.	15	Cantal
Ch.	16	Charente
Ch.M.	17	Charente-Maritime
C.O.	21	Côte-d'Or
C.N.	22	Côtes-du-Nord
Cr.	23	Creuse
Do.	25	Doubs
Dr.	26	Drôme
E.L.	28	Eure-et-Loir
F.	29	Finistère (Nord et Sud)
G.	30	Gard
H.G.	31	Haute-Garonne
Gi.	33	Gironde
H.	34	Hérault
I.V.	35	Ille-et-Vilaine
In.	36	Indre
I.L.	37	Indre-et-Loire
Is.	38	Isère
Ju.	39	Jura
La.	40	Landes
L.-et-C.	41	Loir-et-Cher
Lo.	42	Loire
H.L.	43	Haute-Loire
L.A.	44	Loire-Atlantique
Loi.	45	Loiret
Lot	46	Lot
L.G.	47	Lot-et-Garonne
Lo.	48	Lozère
M.L.	49	Maine-et-Loire
Ma.	50	Manche
Marne	51	Marne
H.M.	52	Haute-Marne
May.	53	Mayenne
M.M.	54	Meurthe-et-Moselle
Me.	55	Meuse
Mo.	56	Morbihan
Mos.	57	Moselle
Ni.	58	Nièvre
Nord	59	Nord
O.	60	Oise
Or.	61	Orne
P.C.	62	Pas-de-Calais
P.D.	63	Puy-de-Dôme
P.A.	64	Pyrénées Atlantiques
H.P.	65	Hautes Pyrénées
P.O.	66	Pyrénées (Orientales)
B.R.	67	Bas Rhin
H.R.	68	Haut Rhin
Rh.	69	Rhône
H.S.	70	Haute Saône
Sa.	71	Saône-et-Loire
Sa.	72	Sarthe
H.Sa.	73	Haute-Savoie
Sa.	74	Savoie
Paris	75	Paris
S.Me.	76	Seine-Maritime
S.M.	77	Seine-et-Marne
Y.	78	Yvelines
D.S.	79	Deux-Sèvres
So.	80	Somme
T.	81	Tarn
T.G.	82	Tarn-et-Garonne
V.	83	Var
Va.	84	Vaucluse
Ve.	85	Vendée
Vi.	86	Vienne
H.V.	87	Haute Vienne
Vo.	88	Vosges
Y.	89	Yonne
B.	90	Belfort
Es.	91	Essonne
H.Se.	92	Hauts-de-Seine
S.S.D.	93	Seine-St-Denis
V.M.	94	Val-de-Marne
V.O.	95	Val-d'Oise

CORSICA
On same scale

Corse, Bastia, Haute-Corse, Mt. Rotondo 2625, Mt. Cinto 2710, Calvi, Porto, Corse du Sud, Porto Vecchio, Corse, Bonifacio, Ajaccio, Bouches de Bonifacio

COPYRIGHT GEORGE PHILIP & SON LTD.

Projection Conical with two standard parallels

(Map of France with place names including Paris, Brest, Bordeaux, Toulouse, Marseille, Lyon, Nice, Strasbourg, Nancy, Rennes, Nantes, Le Havre, Rouen, Lille, Reims, Dijon, Limoges, Clermont Ferrand, St. Étienne, Grenoble, Toulon; neighbouring countries Belgium, Germany, Switzerland, Italy, Spain; water bodies English Channel, Bay of Biscay, Mediterranean Sea.)

ENGLAND

English Channel

CHANNEL
Guernsey
St. Peter Port
ISLANDS

Jersey
St. Helier

Golfe de
St. Malo

Baie de la
Seine

Le Havre

NORMANDIE

CALVADOS

Caen

BRETAGNE

Rennes

MANCHE

MAINE

Le Mans

BAY OF

BISCAY

Baie de Bourgneuf
Île de Noirmoutier

Nantes

Île d'Yeu

ANJOU

Angers

Cholet

VENDÉE

La Roche-
sur-Yon

DEUX
SÈVRES

Poitiers

VIENNE

Châtellerault

POITOU

Les Sables-
d'Olonne

La Rochelle

Niort

AUNIS

Île de Ré
Pertuis Breton

Pertuis d'Antioche

Île d'Oléron

Rochefort

CHARENTE
MARITIME

CHARENTE

ANGOUMOIS

Angoulême

LIMO

Projection: Conical with two standard parallels   3   2   1   West from Greenwich   0   East from Greenwich   1

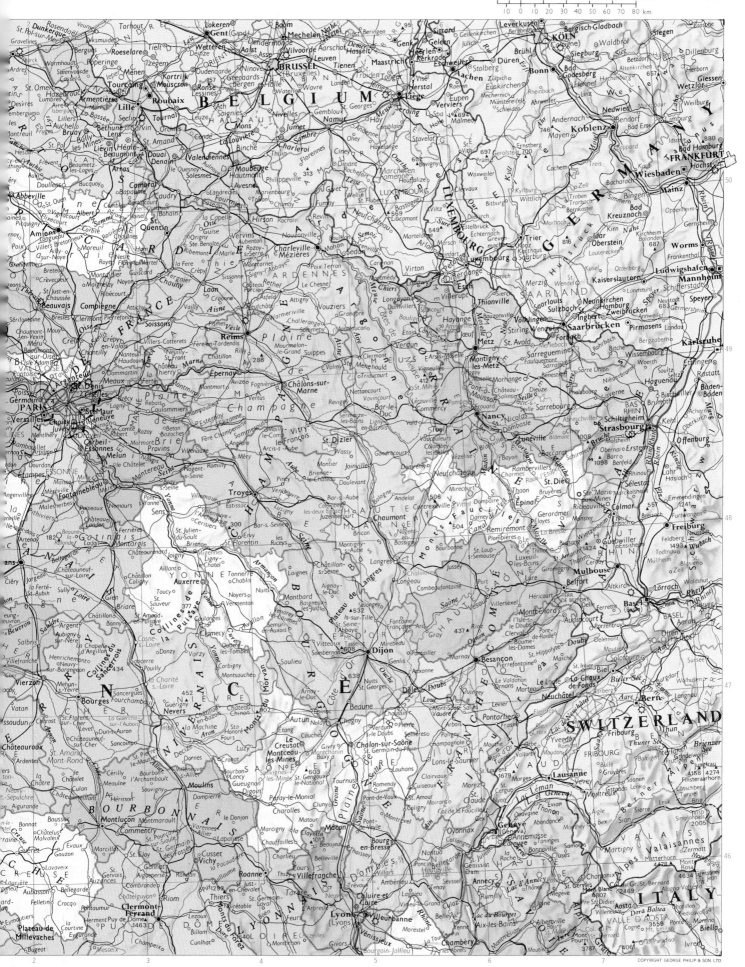

1 : 2 500 000

10   0   10   20   30   40   50 miles

10 0 10 20 30 40 50 60 70 80 km

SWITZERLAND

ITALY

CORSICA

LIGURIAN SEA

Golfo di Génova

MEDITERRANEAN SEA

Lion

COPYRIGHT. GEORGE PHILIP & SON, LTD.

NORTH SEA

BALTIC

NETHERLANDS
BELGIUM
LUX.
FRANCE
WEST GERMANY
EAST GERMANY
CZECHOS
ÖSTERREICH (AUSTRIA)
SWITZERLAND
ITALY
ADRIATIC SEA

Flensburg SCHLESWIG Schleswig Lolland Falster
Helgoland Kieler Bucht Fehmarn Belt Gedser
Kiel Neumünster Mecklenburger Bucht Rügen Sassnitz Darłowo
HOLSTEIN Lübeck Stralsund Usedom Świnoujście Kołobrzeg Koszalin
Ost-Nordernev Deutsche Bucht Brunsbüttel Elbe Wismar Rostock Güstrow Neu Brandenburg Szczecin (Stettin) Szczecinek
friesische Inseln Cuxhaven Altona Hamburg Schwerin Müritz See Goleniów Stargard
Wilhelmshaven Harburg Lüneburg Parchim Neustrelitz Prenzlau Eberswalde Gorzów Nowy Tomyśl
Bremerhaven Bremen Verden Celle Uelzen Stendal Rathenow Havel Spandau Berlin Poznań
Leeuwarden Groningen Oldenburg NIEDERSACHSEN Nienburg Braunschweig Magdeburg Brandenburg Potsdam Charlottenburg Frankfurt
Amsterdam Hannover Hildesheim Salzgitter Halberstadt Dessau Halle Leipzig Cottbus Zielona Góra Głogów
'␣s-Gravenhage Utrecht Osnabrück Herford Bielefeld Hameln Goslar Nordhausen Merseburg Erfurt Dresden Görlitz Legnica
Rotterdam Arnhem Nijmegen Münster NORDRHEIN Detmold Paderborn Kassel Mühlhausen Naumburg Jena Gera Karl-Marx-Stadt (Chemnitz) Ústí nad Labem Liberec
Dordrecht Breda Duisburg Essen Dortmund Hagen WESTFALEN Marburg Eisenach Gotha Weimar Zwickau Plauen Plzeň (Pilsen) Hradec Králové
Antwerpen Eindhoven Mönchengladbach Düsseldorf Wuppertal Remscheid Siegen Giessen Fulda Coburg Bayreuth Praha (Prague) Pardubice
Gent Brugge Aachen Köln (Cologne) Bonn Westerwald Wetzlar Vogelsberg Schweinfurt Erlangen Amberg Regensburg CZECHOS
Brussel (Bruxelles) Leuven Maastricht Liège Koblenz Taunus Frankfurt Hanau Würzburg Bamberg Fürth Nürnberg Ceskomoravská Brno (Brünn)
Lille Tournai Namur RHEINLAND Wiesbaden Mainz Offenbach Darmstadt Ansbach Böhmerwald Ceske Budejovice Znojmo
Charleroi Trier PFALZ Worms Ludwigshafen Mannheim Heidelberg Donauwörth Ingolstadt Deggendorf Passau OBER- ÖSTERREICH Wien (Vienna)
Reims Luxembourg Kaiserslautern SAARLAND Speyer Karlsruhe Heilbronn BADEN Ulm Augsburg Freising Linz NIEDER- Stockerau
Metz Saarbrücken Pforzheim Stuttgart Esslingen Donau (Danube) München (Munich) Ried St. Pölten Melk
Nancy Strasbourg Baden-Baden WÜRTTEMBERG Tübingen Reutlingen Schwäbische Alb Memmingen Rosenheim Salzburg ÖSTERREICH
LORRAINE Colmar Freiburg Schwarzwald Rottweil Tuttlingen Ravensburg Kempten Bad Ischl Steyr Wiener Neustadt
Mulhouse Belfort Schaffhausen Konstanz Friedrichshafen Bregenz Innsbruck Kufstein Gmunden Enns Baden
Besançon Basel Winterthur St. Gallen VORARLBERG TIROL Brenner Gr. Glockner SALZBURG Mürzzuschlag Semmering
Dijon Montbéliard Zürich Feldkirch Landeck Ötztal Arlberg Bad Gastein STEIERMARK Bruck Leoben Kapfenberg
Besançon Biel Aarau Luzern Schwyz LIECHTENSTEIN Chur Davos Inn Merano Lienz Drave Klagenfurt Graz
SWITZERLAND Neuchâtel Bern Interlaken Gotthard St. Moritz Engadin Ortles Bolzano KÄRNTEN Villach Maribor
Lausanne Montreux Sion Splügenpass Bernina ALTO-ADIGE TRENTINO Bressanone Karnische Alpen Bleiburg Varaždin
Genève Matterhorn Mte. Rosa Locarno Bellinzona Stelvio Adamello Trento Dolomiti Marmolada FRIULI-VENEZIA-GIULIA Celje Zagreb
Lyon Villeurbanne Mt. Blanc D'AOSTA Domodossola Lago Maggiore Lugano Como Bergamo Rovereto Bassano Vittorio Veneto Udine Trieste Ljubljana
St. Étienne Chambéry Gran Paradiso Biella Novara LOMBARDIA Lecco Lago di Garda VENETO Treviso Gorizia Koper HRV
Grenoble Briançon Torino (Turin) Vercelli Milano (Milan) Treviglio Brescia Vicenza Verona Padova (Padua) Venezia (Venice) Istra Rijeka
DAUPHINÉ PIEMONTE Asti Pavia Cremona Mantova (Mantua) Rovigo Chioggia Golfo di Venezia Krk
Mt. Pelvoux Pinerolo Alessandria Piacenza Po Adige Pula Karlovac
Mt. Viso Cúneo Savona Parma Reggio Ferrara Comácchio Lošinj Zadar
Digne Alpes Maritimes Col di Tenda Mondovi EMILIA Modena Bologna ROMAGNA Ravenna DINARIC HER
Nîmes Avignon Arles Aix Genova (Genoa) Golfo di Génova La Spézia Carrara Cesena Rímini Pésaro Dugi Otok
PROVENCE Marseille San Remo Impéria Nice Monaco Cannes Pisa Prato Firenze (Florence) Lucca San Marino

Projection: Conical with two standard parallels

East from Greenwich

1 : 5 000 000

50   0   50   100 miles
50   0   50   100 150 km

A Zatoka Gdańska
Gdynia Sopot
Zelenogradsk Kaliningrad (Königsberg) Prége Chernyakhovsk
LITHUANIAN
Vilnius
Molodechno Borisov Gorki
Gdańsk (Danzig) Elbląg Braniewo R.S.F.S.R. Gusev S.S.R. Mogilev Krichev
Starogard Malbork Lyna Gizycko Suwałki Alitus Minsk Kricher
Sgora Chełmża Kwidzyń Pojezierze Mazurskie ▲309 Augustów Varena Lida Novogrudok B Y E L O R U S S I A N Berezina
Grudziądz Olsztyn Ostróda Kętrzyn Mosty Neman Baranovichi S.S.R. Bobruysk
Chełmno Mława Ciechanów Sokółka ▲238 Grodno Volkovysk Slonim Ptich Drut
Toruń Rypin Ostrów Łomża Białystok Slucha Luninets Kalinkovichi Gomel
Lipno Mazowiecka Brańsk Hajnówka Bereza Pripyat
Włocławek Płock Wkra Ostrołęka Czeremcha Zhabinka Pripyat P o l e s y e
Gniezno Kutno Wisła (Vistula) Pułtusk Bug Brest Dubrovitsa Sarny Uzh Desna
września Koło Warszawa (Warsaw) Mińsk Mazowiecki Siedlce Biała Podlaska ▲316 Korosten
Konin Łęczyca Łowicz Pruszków Żyrardów Otwock Łuków Międzyrzec Podlaski Kovel Styr Goryn Słucz Radomyshl Kiyev Borispol
Turek L A N D Skierniewice Grójec Włodawa Vladimir Volynskiy Lutsk Rovno Korets Novograd- Volynskiy Tetérev Belaya Tserkov
Kalisz Zduńska Wola Łódź Pilica Radom Kozienice Puławy Chełm Sokal Dubno Ostrog Shepetovka Zhitomir Fastov
Ostrów Wielkopolski Tomaszów Mazowiecki Kielce Ostrowiec Świętokrzyski Kraśnik Lublin Zamość Radekhov Brody Kremenets Berdichev Kazatin Kiev
Wieluń Warta Piotrków Trybunalski Końskie Sandomierz ▲390 Przeworsk Kamenka Bugskaya Starokonstantinov Vinnitsa ▲384
Opole Radomsko Jędrzejów Zawiercie Pińczów Tarnobrzeg San Jarosław Gorodok Lvov Zolochev Khmelnitskiy U.S.S.R.
Tarnowskie Góry Zabrze Bytom Dąbrowa Tarnowska Wisła (Vistula) Rzeszów Przemyśl ▲471 Ternopol U K R A I N I A N Vinnitsa
Raciborz Gliwice Sosnowiec Kraków Tarnów Nowy Sącz Jasło Sanok Sambor Dnestr Drogobych Borislav Buchach Chortkov Zaleshchiki Kamenets-Podolskiy S. S. R. Uman
Ostrava Chorzów Katowice Wieliczka Bielsko- Biała Cieszyn Krosno Dukelský Pr. Turka Stryi Mogilev-Podolskiy Pervomaisk
Frýdek Mistek C ▲1725 Nowy Targ Krynica ▲502 Ivano-Frankovsk Snyatyn Khotin Yedintsy Sorokl Kotovsk
Tablunkovský Pr. 550 Zapadné Beskydy Vysoké Tatry Východné Beskydy ▲480 K a r p Nadvornaya ▲1881 Per Yablonitse Chernovtsy Storozhinets Dorohoi Beltsy S. S. R.
Žilina VAKIA ▲2655 Ružomberok Nízke Tatry Prešov Košice Uzhgorod Mukachevo 931 Khust a t ▲2061 Storozhinets Botoşani ▲429 Kishinev Bendery M O L D A V I A N
Gottwaldov N. Zámky Kremnica Banská Bystrica Slovenské Rudohorie Sátoraljaújhely Beregovo Satu Mare Sighet Radauti Vatra-Dornei h Suceava Iaşi Dnestr Bendery
Váh Nitra Banská Štiavnica Zvolen Lučenec Miskolc Hernád Sajó Tokaj Carei Baia Mare Pietrosul ▲2305 Piatra Neamţ Roman i a Vaslui Bělgorod- Dnestrovskiy
Komárno Esztergom Gyöngyös Eger Mezőkövesd Nyíregyháza Hajdúböszörmény Dej Bistriţa Pietrosul ▲2102 Bistriţa Vslaui Kotovsk
Győr Tatabánya Hegyeg Vác Karcag Szolnok Somes Cluj Tîrgu Mureş Praido Bacău Bîrlad Tecuci Odessa
Székesfehérvár Újpest BUDAPEST Cegléd Nagykőrös Mezőtúr Oradea Turda Sighişoara Odorhei Miercurea Ciuc Sfântu Gheorghe Bretcu Focşani Galaţi Reni Ismail BLACK
Dunaújváros U N G A R Y Kecskemét Kiskunfélegyháza Salonta Aiud Mţii Bihor ▲1848 Alba-Iulia Mediaş Vatra Câmpulung Rîmnicu Sărat Brăila ▲467 Tulcea Sulina
Dunaföldvár Kalocsa Kiskőrös Szentes Békéscsaba Gyula Crişul Abrud T r a n s i l v a n i a Odorhei Braşov Cîmpina Buzău Dunărea (Danube)
Székszárd Kiskunhalas Szeged Makó Arad Crişul Alb Brad Simeria Sibiu ▲2535 Fägäraş ▲2507 Rîmnicu Cîmpina Ploieşti Galaţi Ozero Sasyk Kiliya
Pécs Szekszárd Subotica Timişoara R U M A N I A Lugoj Hunedoara Deva Carpaţii Meridionali ▲2518 Vf. Negoiu Vf. Omul Cîmpulung Tîrgovişte Ialomiţa Călăraşi Constanţa
Mohács Senta Kikinda B a n a t Caransebeş Peleaga Petroşeni 350 Parîngul-Mare Rîmnicu Vîlcea Piteşti Argeş Dâmboviţa BUCUREŞTI (Bucharest) Cernavodă
Osijek Novi Sad Zrenjanin Petrovgrad Porta Orientalis Reşiţa ▲2509 Jiu W a l l a c h i a Slatina Oltenita Silistra
Vinkovci Petrovaradin Vršac Bela Crkva Mehadia Portile de Fier Tîrgu-Jiu Tîrgovişte Ploieşti Mangalia SEA
Brod Odžak Sremska Mitrovica Zemun Pančevo Smederevo Orsova Turnu- Severin Craiova Vedea Ozero Tolbukhin
Tuzla Bijeljina Beograd (Belgrade) Požarevac Negotin Slatina Caracal Turnu Măgurele Giurgiu Ruse (Ruschuk)
Han Pijesak ▲1346 G O S L A V I A Titovo Užice Čačak Kragujevac Morava Bor Timok Zaječar Vidin Lom Dunăre (Danube) Corabia Zimnicea BULGARIA

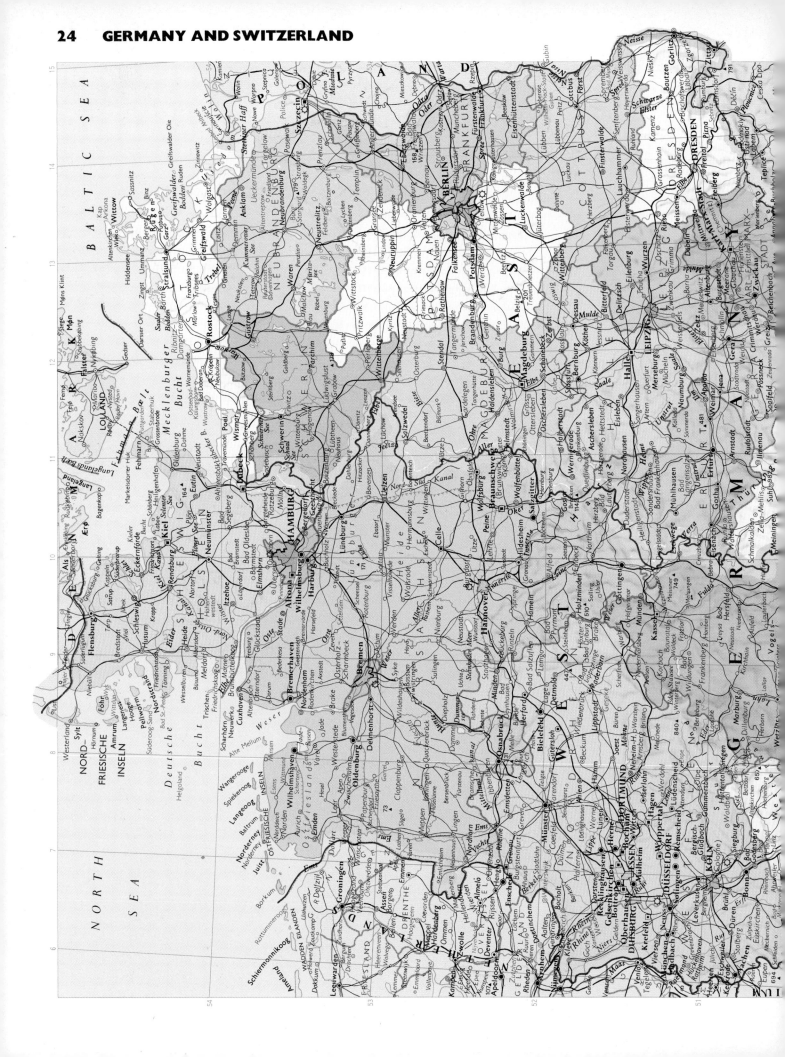

1:2 500 000

1:2 500 000

10   0   10   20   30   40   50 miles

10   0   10   20   30   40   50   60   70   80 km

East from Greenwich

COPYRIGHT. GEORGE PHILIP & SON. LTD.

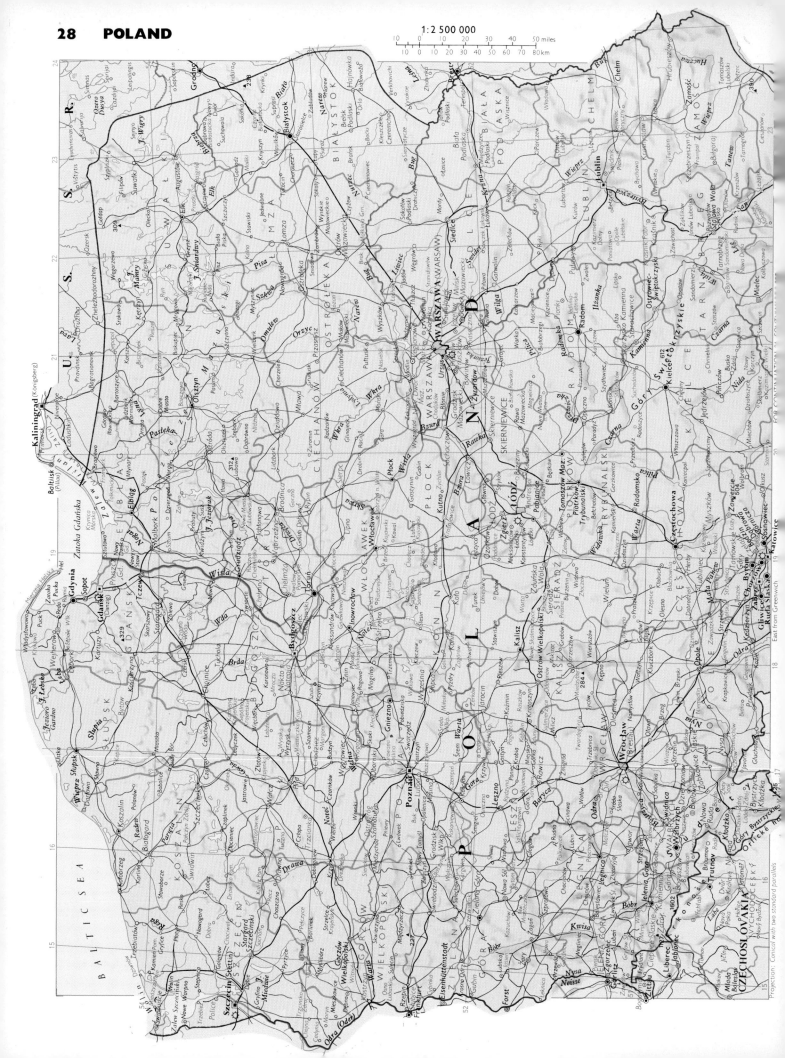

1:5 000 000

50 0 50 100 miles
50 0 50 100 150 km

East from Greenwich

West from Greenwich

Projection: Conical with two standard parallels

FRANCE

ANDORRA

PORTUGAL

SPAIN

ALGERIA

MOROCCO

GALICIA · ASTURIAS · NAVARRA · ARAGON · CATALUÑA · CASTILLA LA VIEJA · CASTILLA LA NUEVA · MURCIA · ANDALUCIA · ESTREMADURA

Madrid · Barcelona · Valencia · Sevilla · Málaga · Bilbao · Zaragoza · Lisboa · Porto · Oviedo · Gijón · La Coruña · Santiago de Compostela · Pontevedra · Vigo · Orense · Lugo · León · Palencia · Burgos · Valladolid · Salamanca · Zamora · Avila · Segovia · Soria · Logroño · Pamplona · San Sebastián · Vitoria · Huesca · Lérida · Gerona · Tarragona · Tarrasa · Sabadell · Badalona · Hospitalet · Castellón de la Plana · Teruel · Cuenca · Guadalajara · Toledo · Ciudad Real · Albacete · Alicante · Elche · Murcia · Cartagena · Lorca · Almería · Granada · Jaén · Córdoba · Linares · Jerez · Cádiz · Huelva · Badajoz · Cáceres · Mérida · Évora · Coimbra · Braga · Setúbal

Baleares · Mallorca · Menorca · Ibiza · Formentera · Cabrera · Palma

Gibraltar (Br.) · Ceuta (Sp.) · Tánger · Tetouan · Alger · Oran · Mostaganem · Blida

Golfe du Lion · Golfo de Rosas · Golfo de San Jorge · Golfo de Valencia · Mar Menor · Golfo de Cádiz · Bay of Biscay · Strait of Gibraltar · Estrecho de Gibraltar

ATLANTIC OCEAN · MEDITERRANEAN SEA

Pyrénées · Cordillera Cantábrica · Sierra de la Demanda · Sierra de Guadarrama · Sierra de Gredos · Montes de Toledo · Sierra Morena · Sierra Nevada · Sierra de Gata

Ebro · Duero · Tajo · Guadiana · Guadalquivir · Júcar · Segura · Turia

3404 · 3353 · 2224 · 2850 · 2926 · 2648 · 2762 · 2019 · 2381 · 3478 · 2592 · 2430 · 1443 · 1985 · 902

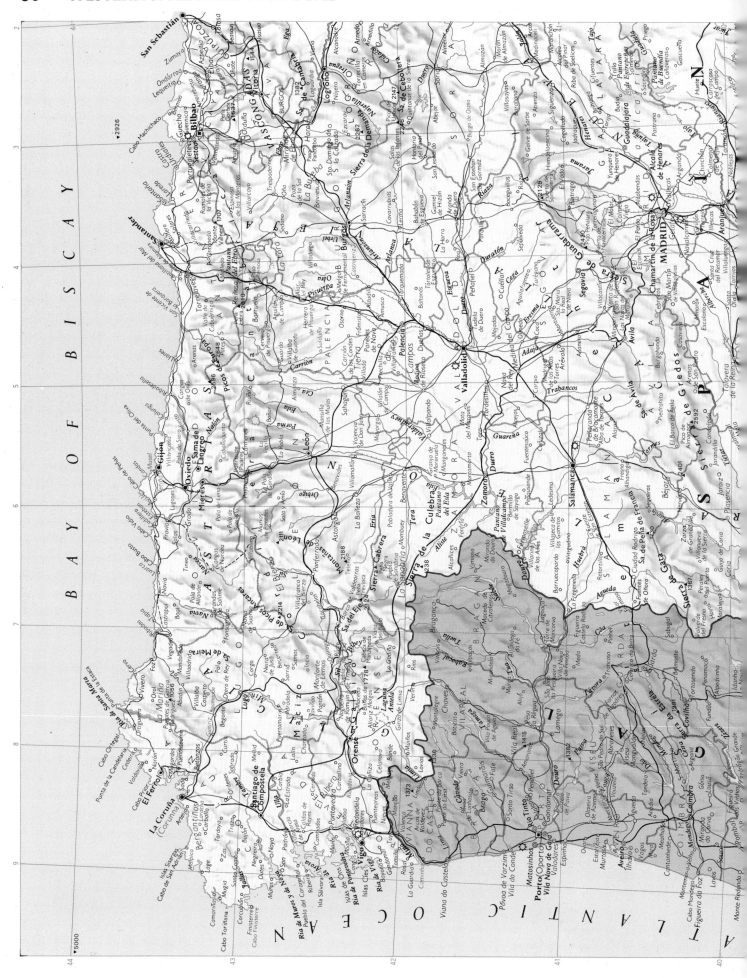

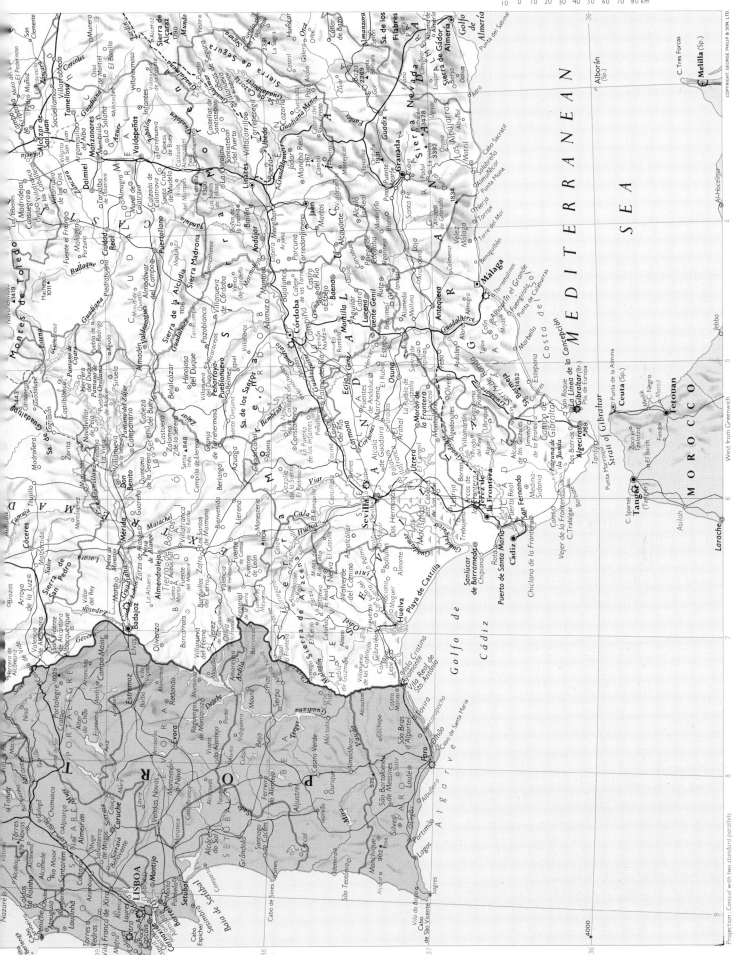

1:2 500 000

50 miles

80 km

S E A

M E D I T E R R A N E A N

Golfo de
Almería

Golfo de
Cádiz

Strait of Gibraltar

M O R O C C O

West from Greenwich

Projection: Conical with two standard parallels

COPYRIGHT GEORGE PHILIP & SON LTD.

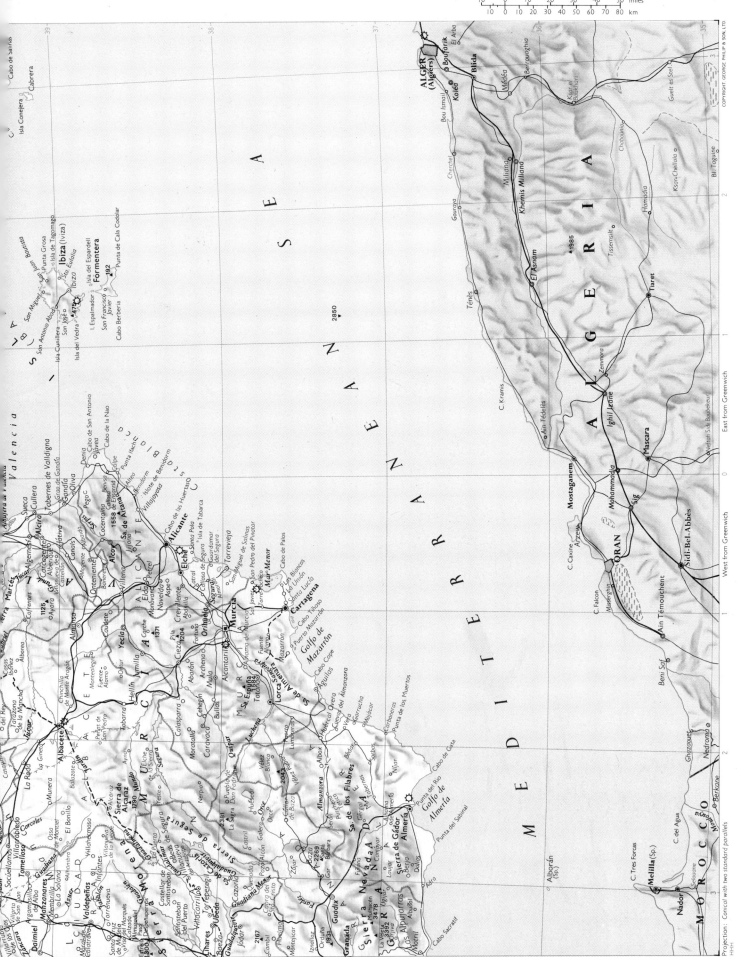

1:10 000 000

50   50   100   150   200 miles
50   0   50   100   200   300 km

POLAND
Poznań   Płock
Łódź   Warszawa
Wrocław   Radom   Brest
Chorzów   Kielce   Lublin
Ostrava   Kraków   Tarnów   Przemyśl
CZECHOSLOVAKIA
Bratislava   Miskolc   Debrecen
HUNGARY   Oradea
Budapest   Cluj
Kecskemét   Szeged   Arad   RUMANIA
Pécs   Timişoara   Sibiu
Novi Sad   Petrovaradin   Braşov
Beograd   Orasul Stalin
BOSNA   Craiova   Ploieşti
Sarajevo   Bucureşti
YUGOSLAVIA   BULGARIA   Constanţa
Niš   Sofiya   Plovdiv
Skopje   Edirne
Tirana   Bitola   İstanbul
ALBANIA   Thessaloniki   Bursa
GREECE   Ankara
Athínai   Izmir   TURKEY
Piraievs   Konya   Adana
Pelopónnisos   Antalya
CYPRUS
Kríti   Levkosía

BLACK SEA

U.   S.   S.   R.
Kiyev   Kharkov   Volgograd
Zhitomir   Poltava
Vinnitsa   UKRAINIAN   Dnepropetrovsk   Rostov
Kishinev   MOLDAVIAN   S.S.R.
Odessa   Sea of Azov
Simferopol   Krasnodar
Sevastopol   Novorossiysk

MEDITERRANEAN SEA

Benghāzi   El Iskandarîya   Bûr Saîd
Barqa   EGYPT   EL QÂHIRA
LIBYA   Es Sînā'

SYRIA
Halab
Tarabulus   Hamā'
Bayrût   Homs
LEBANON   Dimashq
Haifa   ISRAEL
Tel Aviv-Yafo   JORDAN
Jerusalem   Ammān
Gaza

COPYRIGHT. GEORGE PHILIP & SON. LTD.

SWITZERLAND

AUSTRIA

Brenner

Maribor

Klagenfurt

Bleiburg

Villach

Karawanken

Zagreb

FRIULI VENEZIA GIULIA

Ljubljana

Trieste

Rijeka

Istra

Geneve

Lyona

Villeurbanne

Grenoble

DAUPHINE

Torino (Turin)

PIEMONTE

LOMBARDIA

Milano (Milan)

Brescia

Bergamo

Como

Novara

Pavia

Cremona

Piacenza

VENETO

Verona

Vicenza

Padova (Padua)

Treviso

Venezia (Venice)

Golfo di Venezia

Pula (Pola)

ADRIATIC

Parma

Reggio

Modena

Ferrara

Bologna

EMILIA ROMAGNA

Ravenna

Forli

Cesena

Rimini

Ancona

MARCHE

Pesaro

Genova (Genoa)

La Spezia

Carrara

Pistoia

Pisa

Lucca

Firenze (Florence)

Prato

TOSCANA

Siena

Arezzo

Perugia

UMBRIA

San Marino

Ascoli Piceno

Pescara

Marseille

Nice

Cannes

Monaco

LIGURIAN SEA

CORSE (CORSICA) (Fr.)

Ajaccio

Mt. Cinto 2710

Bastia

Elba

Grosseto

Orbetello

Viterbo

Terni

ABRUZZI

L'Aquila

Teramo

Gran Sasso 2914

Mt. Amaro 2795

Sardegna (Sardinia)

Asinara

Sassari

Oristano

Nuoro

Cagliari

CORSE

ROMA (Rome)

LAZIO

Ostia

Anzio

Latina

Frosinone

CAMPANIA

Caserta

Napoli (Naples)

Salerno

Avellino

Benevento

MOLISE

Campobasso

Foggia

Cerignola

Barletta

Andria

Trani

Molfetta

BASILICATA

Potenza

Matera

Taranto

TYRRHENIAN SEA

MALTA 1:1 000 000

Valletta

Cosenza

CALABRIA

Catanzaro

Palermo

Trapani

Marsala

Caltanissetta

Enna

Catania

Siracusa (Syracuse)

Ragusa

Etna 3340

Messina

Reggio

Str. di Messina

Isole Eolie o Lipari

Stromboli

SKIKDA

Annaba

Constantine

ALGERIA

TUNISIA

Binzert (Bizerte)

Tunis

Béja

Kairouan

Sousse

Pantelleria (Ital.)

Lampedusa (Ital.)

MEDIT

MALTA

Valletta

Gozo

Comino

50   50   100 miles
50   0   50   100   150   km

COPYRIGHT. GEORGE PHILIP & SON. LTD.

1:2 500 000

10 0 10 20 30 40 50 miles
10 0 10 20 30 40 50 60 70 80 km

HUNGARY

SOMOGY

SLOVENIA

Ljubljana

YUGOSLAVIA

Zagreb

BOSNA

HERCEGOVINA

DINARA Planina

DALMACIJA

A D R I A T I C

S E A

Golfo di Venézia

VENETO

FRIULI-VENEZIA GIULIA

Trieste

PÁDOVA (Padua)

Venézia (Venice)

Ferrara

Ravenna

SAN MARINO

Ancona

MARCHE

UMBRIA

Perúgia

L. Trasimeno

ROMA (ROME)

LAZIO

ABRUZZI

Pescara

MOLISE

Monte Sant'Ángelo

FOR CONTINUATION SEE PAGE 42

CORSE

CORSICA

Îles Sanguinaires
G. d'Ajaccio
C.di Muro
G. de Valinco
Sartène
Propriano
Porto-Vecchio
Îles Cerbicales
Bonifacio
Î. de Cavallo
Bouches de Bonifacio
Maddalena
Santa Teresa Gallura
La Maddalena
Caprera

Petreto
Zonza
2136
Levie
Favone
Solenzara

Tavignano

CORSE-DU-SUD

ROMA (Rome)
Vatican City
Tivoli
Subiaco
Con del Fu
Fregene
Palestrina
Tenuta
Montmontone
Lido di Óstia (Lido di Roma)
Anguillara
Albano Laziale
Frascati
Marino
Ferentino
Alatri
Véroli
Sor

Prática di Mare
Cisterna di Latina
Anzio
Nettuno
Cori
Ceccano
Cassi
Frosinone

Latina
Priverno
Sonnino
Arpi
Sto
Sabáudia
Monte Circeo
541
Pontinia
Fondi
1533
Fórmia
Terracina
Minturno
Mondr

Zannone
Palmarola
Ponza
Ísole Ponziane
1283

Golfo di Gaeta
Vo

Ventotene

Ísch

Punta dello Scorno
Asinara
Golfo dell' Asinara
Coghinas
Tempio Pausania
Ággius
Calangiánus
1362
M. Limbara
G. di Ólbia
Golfo Aranci
Ólbia
Tavolara
Costa Smeralda
Pto. Cervo
Arzachena

Porto Tórres
C. della Nurra
Stintino
Sorso
Sássari
Óssi
Óschiri
Tananella
Posada
 Íttiri
L. di Coghinas
Ozieri
Pattada
Buddusò
Siniscola
Ferràdo
Álghero
1259
Bitti
C. Comino
Villanova Monteleone
Bonorva
1150
Orune
Bósa
Temo
Macomer
Núoro
Oliena
Dorgali
Golfo di Orosei
C. di Monte Santu

SARDEGNA

Ghilarza
L. del Tirso
Fonni
Sorgono
Cédrino
Bauen
Monti del Gennargentu
1834
Cúglieri
Oristano
SARDEGNA
M. Arci
812
Láconi
Arbatax
Tórtoli
Lanusei

Golfo di Oristano
Arborea
Santu Lussúrgiu
Nurri
Siérzu
SARDINIA

Ábbasanta
Samúgheo
Mándas
Mánnu
C. Pécora
S. Gavino Monreale
1236
Gonnosfanàdiga
Villacidro
Sanluri
Senórbi
Flumendosa
S. Vito
Villaputzu
Fluminimaggiore
M. Línas
Serramanna
Dolianova
Muravera
Gúspini
Arbus
Iglésias
Cíxerri
Asémini
Sestu
Sinnai
1069
pta. Serpedda
C. Ferrato
Portoscuso
Carloforte
Gonnesa
Siliqua
Sélargius
Quartu Sant'Elena
San Pietro
Sant'Antioco
Carbónia
1116
Cagliari
Santadi
Golfo di Cágliari
Sant' Antíoco
Porto Botte
Teulada
Pula
Serpentara
C. Carbonara
G. di Pálmas
G. di Pálmas
C. Spartivento

TYRRHENIAN
SEA
3719
3589

C. Mannu

Ústica

Íles de la
Galite

T U N I S I A

C. Serrat
Bizerte (Binzert)
C. Blanc
Cani
Plane
Zembra
Golfe de Tunis
C. Bon

El Kala
ALGÉRIA
Tabarka
Mateur
Menzel-Bourguiba
Tébourba
TUNIS
Halq el Oued (La Goulette)
Kelibia
Menzel Temime

Bou Salem
Béja
Medjerda
Soliman
Nabeul
Hammamet

Mellègue
Téboursouk
Zaghouan

PALERMO
C. San Vito
G. del Golfo
Terrasini
C. Gallo
Favarotta
Castellammare
Bagheria
Levanzo
Trápani
1110
Erice
Monreale
Partinico
Misilmeri
Íle
Alcamo
S. Giuseppe Jato
Maréttimo
Ísole Égadi
Paceco
Calatafimi
Campofelice
Marineo
Belsito
Favignana
Salemi
1613
Carleone
Lercara
Leo
Marsala
Gibellina
Bisacquino
Prizzi
Alia
Castelvetrano
Partanna
Sambuca di Sicilia
SIC
Mazara del Vallo
Menfi
Mussomeli
Castelt
Campobello di Mazara
Bélice
Sciacca
Burgio
Castel
San Cat
Campobello
Sicilian Channel
Ribera
Platani
Racalmuto
Cattólica Eraclea
Siculiana
Naro
Agrigento
Porto Empédocle
Raffadali
Favara
Palma di Montechiaro
Campobello
Car

MEDITE

Pantelleria
Pantelleria (It.)
836
1319
Mo

1:2 500 000

10 0 10 20 30 40 50 miles

10 0 10 20 30 40 50 60 70 80 km

ADRIATIC

SEA

G. di Manfredónia

Testa del Gargano

Monte Sant'Ángelo

ALBANIA

Drini

Durrës
(Durazzo)

Tirana
(Tiranë)

Shkumbini

Bari

Brindisi

Strait of Otranto

Vlorë (Valona)

Lecce

BASILICATA

Golfo di
Táranto

Táranto

Laguna e Nartës

Gjiri i Vlorës

Kérkira
(Corfu)

Kérkira

G. di
Salerno

G. di
Policastro

Monte Pollino
2271

CALABRIA

Cosenza

La Sila

1929

Crotone

G. di
Salerno

I O N I A N

3065

Isole Eólie o Lípari (Æolian Is.)

Strómboli
926

962 Salina

602 Lípari

499 Vulcano

Golfo di
Sant'Eufémia

Golfo di Squillace

Catanzaro

Vibo Valéntia

G. di Gióia

1423

Messina

Réggio
di Cálabra

1956

3340

Str. di Messina

Mi. Peloritani

Nébrodi

1847

Monti

SEA

Etna
3340

Catánia

Golfo di
Catánia

Augusta

Siracusa

Ragusa

C. Passero

R A N E A N   S E A

4116

COPYRIGHT, GEORGE PHILIP & SON LTD.

Projection: Conical with two standard parallels

East from Greenwich

1:2 500 000

10   0   10   20   30   40   50 miles

10   0   10   20 30 40 50 60 70 80 km

TRANSILVANIA

HARGHITA

MUREŞ

SIBIU

COVASNA

VRANCEA

VASLUI

U.S.S.R.

IZMAIL

UKRAINIAN S.S.R.

Ozero Kitai

Ozero Sasyk

Bratul Chilia

Bratul Sulina

Ostrov Sfîntu

Sulina

ROMANIA

Muntii Fågåraş

Meridionali

PRAHOVA

BRAILA

DOBRUGEA

Galaţi   Dunav (Danube)

Braila

Măcin

Tulcea

Bratul Sfîntu Gheorghe

Lacul Razelm

Gura Portiţei

Lacul Sinoe

VALACHIA
WALACHIA

DÎMBOVIŢA

Ploieşti

BUCUREŞTI
(Bucharest)

ILFOV

IALOMIŢA

Cernavodă

Siut Ghiol

Constanţa

OLT

Craiova

TELEORMAN

Dunărea (Danube)

Călăraşi

DOBRUDJA

Mamaia

Eforie Sud

Alexandria

Giurgiu   Ruse
(Ruschuk)

Mangalia

Tolbukhin
(Dobrich Bazargic)

Kavarna (Cavarna)

Nos Kaliakra

Zlatni Pyassatsi

Varna

BLACK

SEA

BULGARIA

Sofiya (Sofia)

Pleven

Razgrad

Türgovishte

Sredna Gora

Preslavska Planina

Kotlenska Pl.

Aytoska Pl.

Obzor

Nos Emine

Nesebûr

Pomorie (Ankhialo)

Burgaski Zaliv

Burgas

Stara Zagora

Plovdiv

Nova Zagora

Yambol

Sozopol

Maslen Nos

Primorsko

Michurin
(Tsarevo)

Ahtopol

Veleka

Rezovo

Malko Tûrnovo

Ayastafanos

Karadeniz Boğazı
(Bosporus)

Edirne
(Adrianople)

TURKEY

KIRKLARELI

Istranca Dağları

İSTANBUL

Üsküdar

GREECE

DRÁMA

XÁNTHI

TEKİRDAĞ

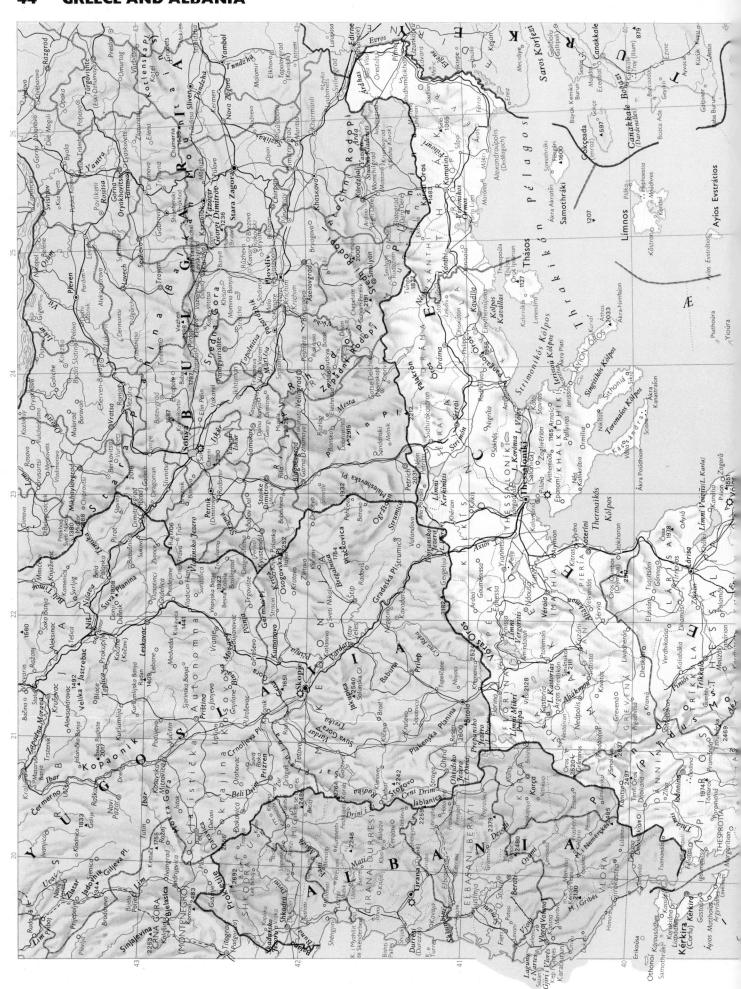

1:2 500 000

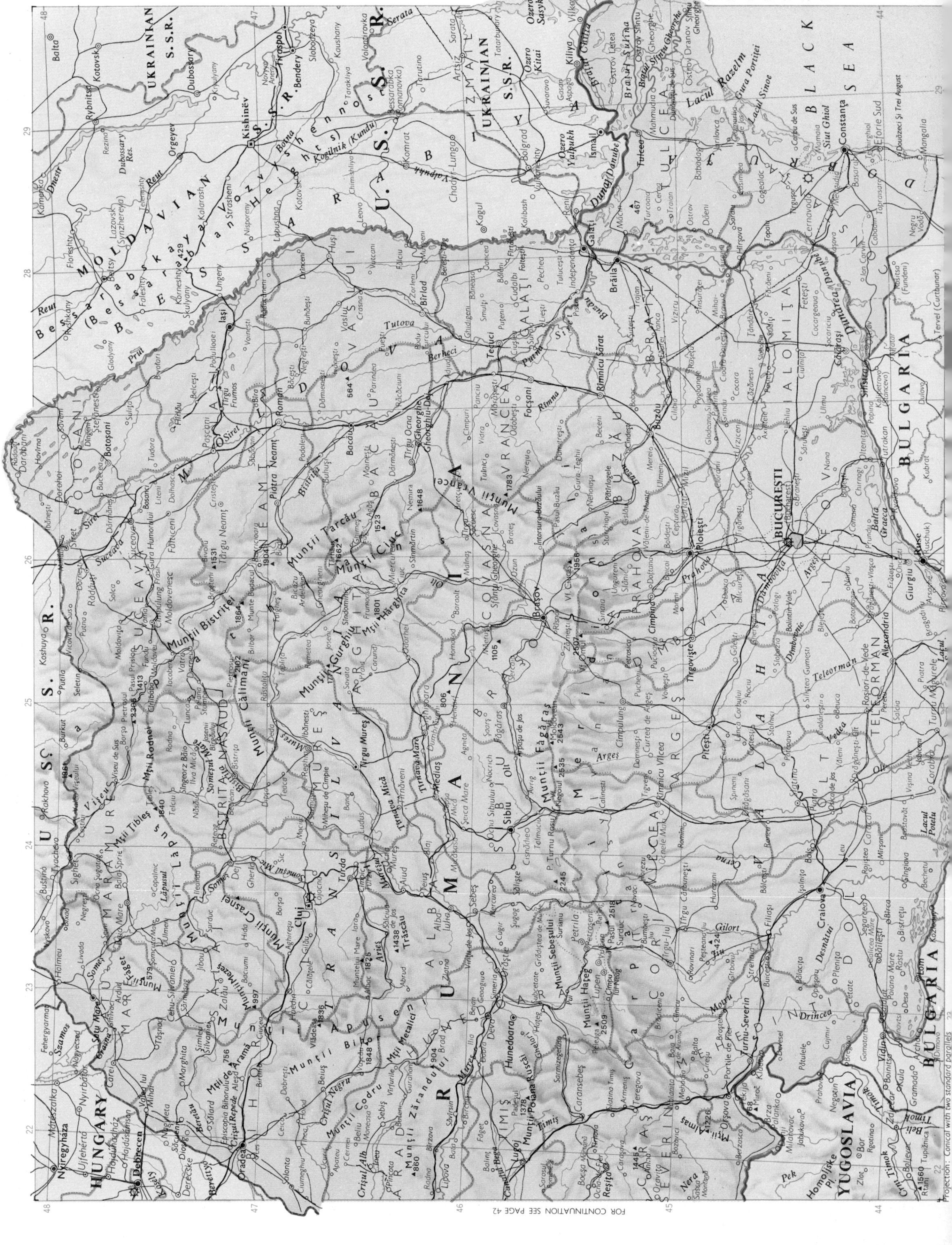

10 0 10 20 30 40 50 miles
10 0 10 20 30 40 50 60 70 80 km

U K R A I N I A N   S. S. R.

U. S. S. R.

M O L D A V I A N   S. S. R.

B E S S A R A B I A

BLACK SEA

HUNGARY

YUGOSLAVIA

BULGARIA

BUCUREŞTI

Constanţa

Galaţi

Braşov

Cluj

Sibiu

Craiova

Ploieşti

Iaşi

Debrecen

Dunărea / Dunav (Danube)

T R A N S Y L V A N I A

M U N Ţ I I   C A R P A Ţ I

Projection: Conical with two standard parallels

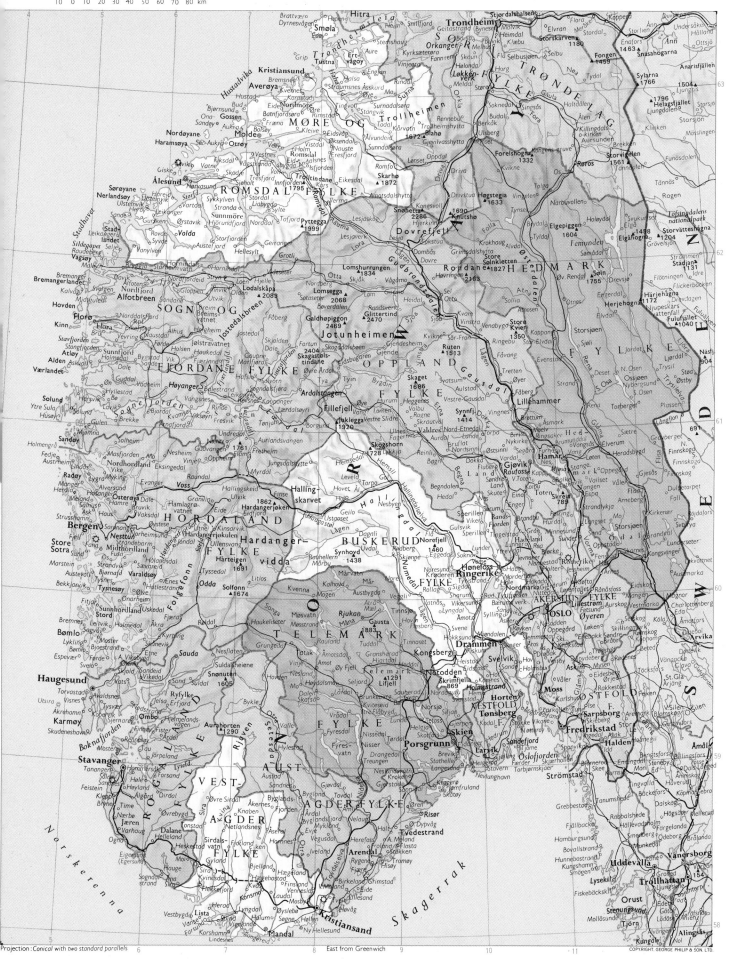

1:2 500 000

Projection: Conical with two standard parallels

East from Greenwich

COPYRIGHT. GEORGE PHILIP & SON. LTD.

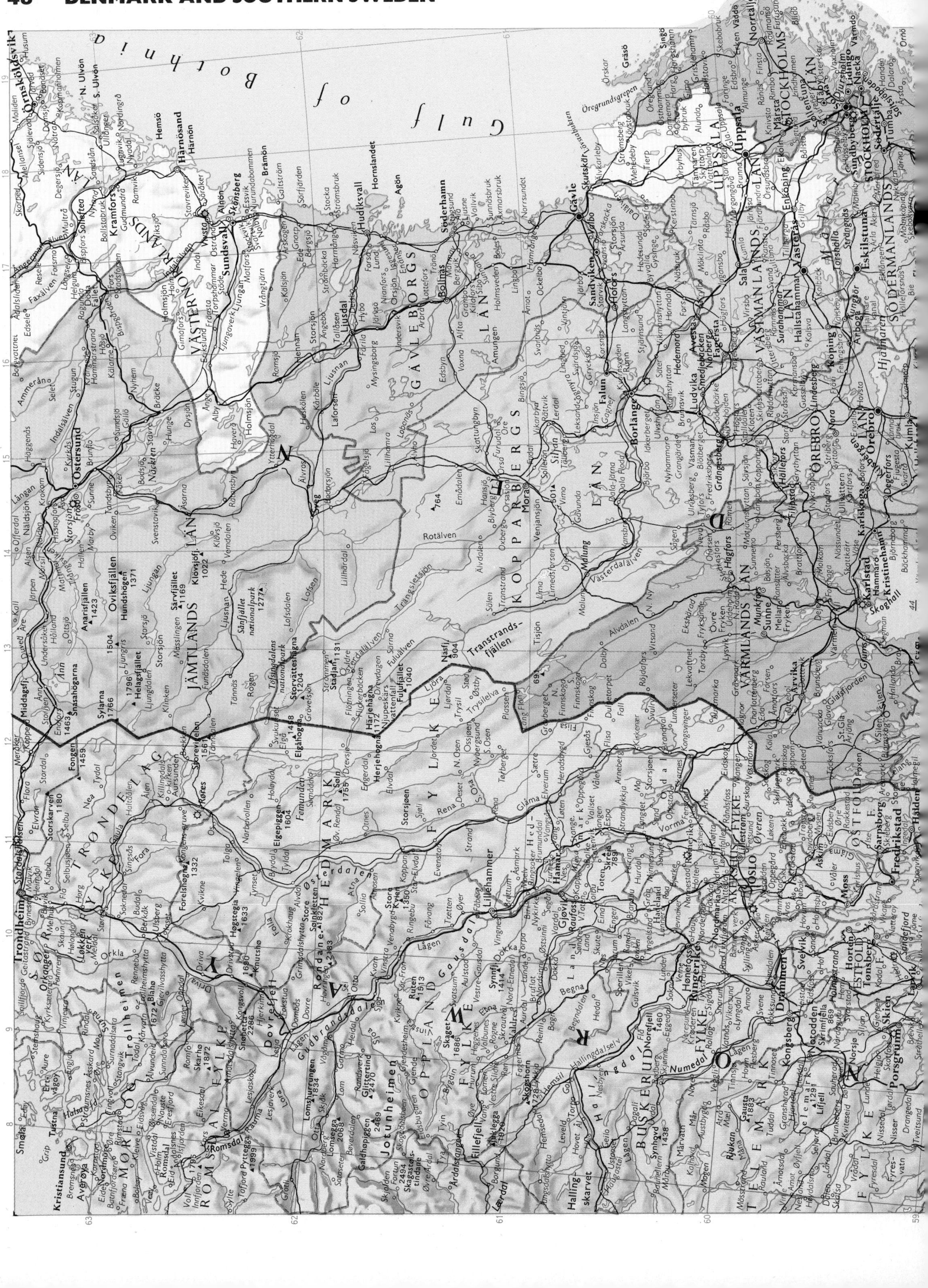

Gulf of Bothnia

STOCKHOLM

UPPSALA

Gävle

Östersund

Sundsvall

Härnösand

Örnsköldsvik

Hudiksvall

Söderhamn

Bollnäs

Ljusdal

Falun

Borlänge

ÖREBRO

Örebro

Eskilstuna

Köping

Västerås

Karlstad

Sunne

Trondheim

Lillehammer

Hamar

Drammen

Sarpsborg

Fredrikstad

Kongsberg

Notodden

Porsgrunn

Skien

Kristiansund

Åndalsnes

VÄSTERNORRLANDS LÄN

JÄMTLANDS LÄN

GÄVLEBORGS LÄN

KOPPARBERGS LÄN

VÄRMLANDS LÄN

VÄSTMANLANDS LÄN

SÖDERMANLANDS LÄN

STOCKHOLMS LÄN

UPPSALA LÄN

SØR-TRØNDELAG FYLKE

MØRE OG ROMSDAL FYLKE

OPPLAND FYLKE

HEDMARK FYLKE

BUSKERUD FYLKE

TELEMARK FYLKE

ØSTFOLD FYLKE

AKERSHUS FYLKE

VESTFOLD FYLKE

Jotunheimen

Dovrefjell

Rondane

Mora

Siljan

Ljusnan

1:2 500 000

10 0 10 20 30 40 50 miles

10 0 10 20 30 40 50 60 70 80 km

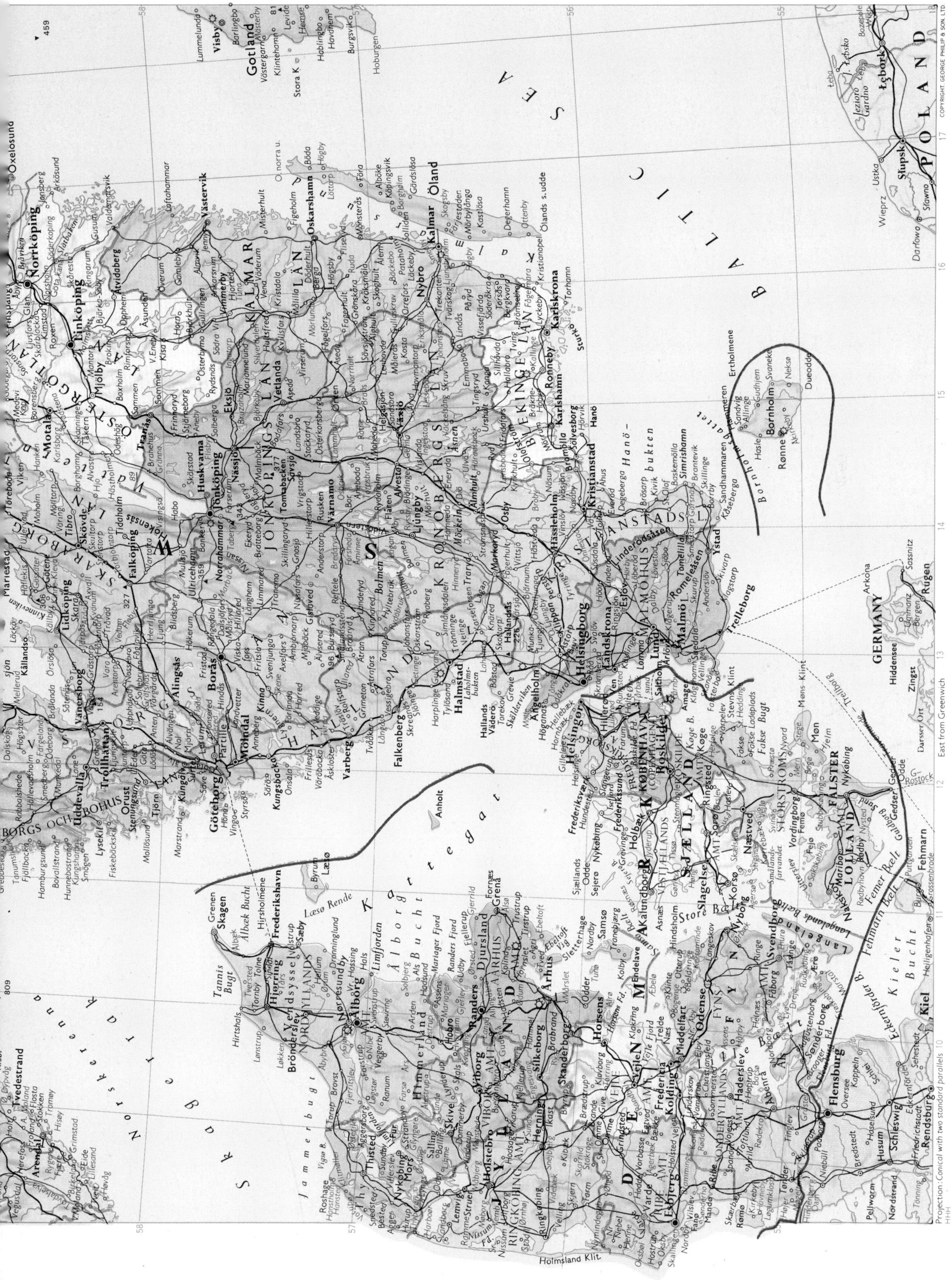

ICELAND
on the same scale
as general map

NORWEGIAN SEA

1:5 000 000

Scale markings: 20 0 20 40 60 80 100 miles / 40 20 0 40 80 120 160 km

Projection: Conical with two standard parallels

East from Greenwich

BALTIC SEA

Countries and regions: FINLAND, ESTONIAN S.S.R., LATVIA, LITHUANIAN S.S.R., R.S.F.S.R., POLAND, GERMANY, DENMARK, SWEDEN, NORWAY

Selected place names:
HELSINKI (Helsingfors), Turku (Åbo), Hangö (Hanko), Tallinn, Rakvere, Pärnu, Haapsalu, Kingisepp, Saaremaa (Ösel), Hiiumaa (Dagö), Riga, Gulf of Riga (Rigas Jūras Licis), Valmiera, Cēsis, Jelgava, Bauska, Liepaja, Klaipėda, Kaliningrad, Chernyakhovsk, Kaunas, Vilnius, Grodno, Białystok, Łomża, Ostroleka, Elbląg, Gdańsk, Gdynia, Zatoka Gdańska, Toruń, Bydgoszcz, Szczecin (Stettin), Gotland, Visby, Fårö, Öland, Kalmar, Karlskrona, Karlshamn, Kristianstad, Bornholm, Rønne, Rügen, Rostock, Stralsund, Greifswald, Lübeck, Hamburg, Kiel, Flensburg, Bremen, Bremerhaven, Wilhelmshaven, Oldenburg, Groningen, Esbjerg, Ribe, Kolding, Fredericia, Vejle, Horsens, Århus, Randers, Ålborg, Hjørring, Thisted, Viborg, Herning, Silkeborg, Odense, Svendborg, Sjælland, Roskilde, KØBENHAVN, Helsingør, Malmö, Helsingborg, Landskrona, Trelleborg, Ystad, Halmstad, Falkenberg, Varberg, Göteborg (GÖTEBORG OCH BOHUS), Borås, Uddevalla, Frederikshavn, Skagerrak, Kattegat, Oslo, Drammen, Hamar, Lillehammer, Gjøvik, Kongsvinger, Kristiansand, Arendal, Grimstad, Lillesand, Stavanger, Haugesund, Bergen, Hardangerfjord, Stockholm, Uppsala, Västerås, Eskilstuna, Södertälje, Nyköping, Norrköping, Linköping, Motala, Jönköping, Växjö, Nässjö, Örebro, Karlstad, Karlskoga, Falun, Borlänge, Gävle, Söderhamn, Sandviken, Hudiksvall, Ljusdal, Västervik, Oskarshamn, Nybro, Ronneby

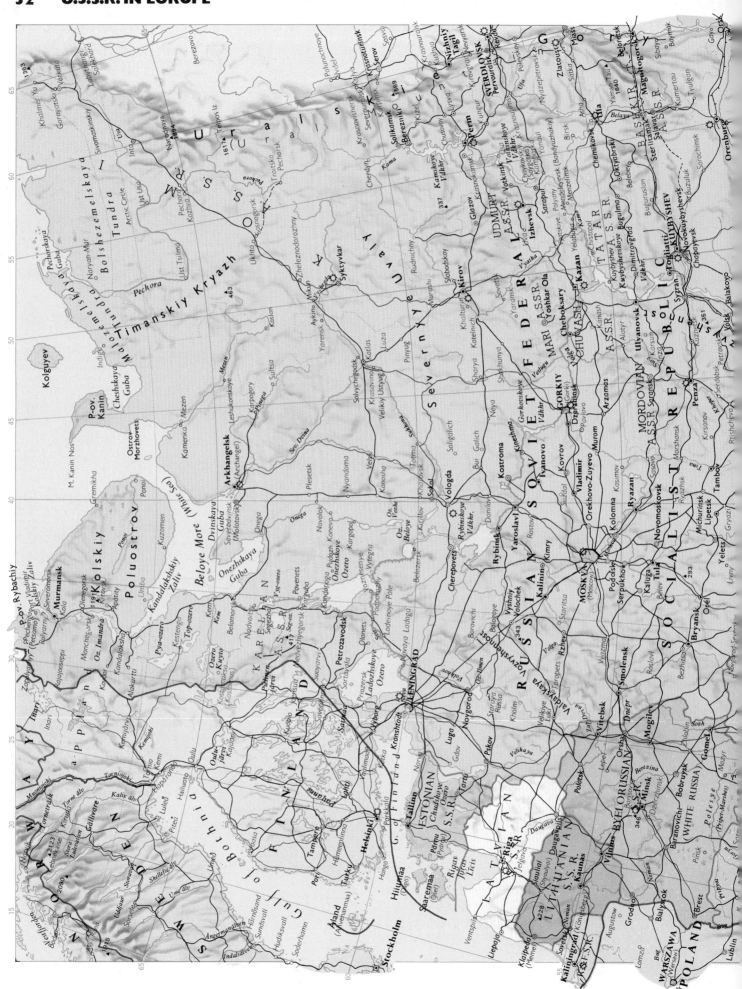

1:10 000 000

100   50   0   50   100   150   200 miles
100   50   0   100   200   300 km

Kabardino-Balkar A.S.S.R.
North Ossetian A.S.S.R. (Azer.)
Nakhichevan A.S.S.R. (Azer.)
Checheno-Ingush A.S.S.R.
Karagiye Depression

East from Greenwich

Projection: Conical with two standard parallels

East from Greenwi

1:5,000,000

50   50   100 miles
50 0 50 100 150 km

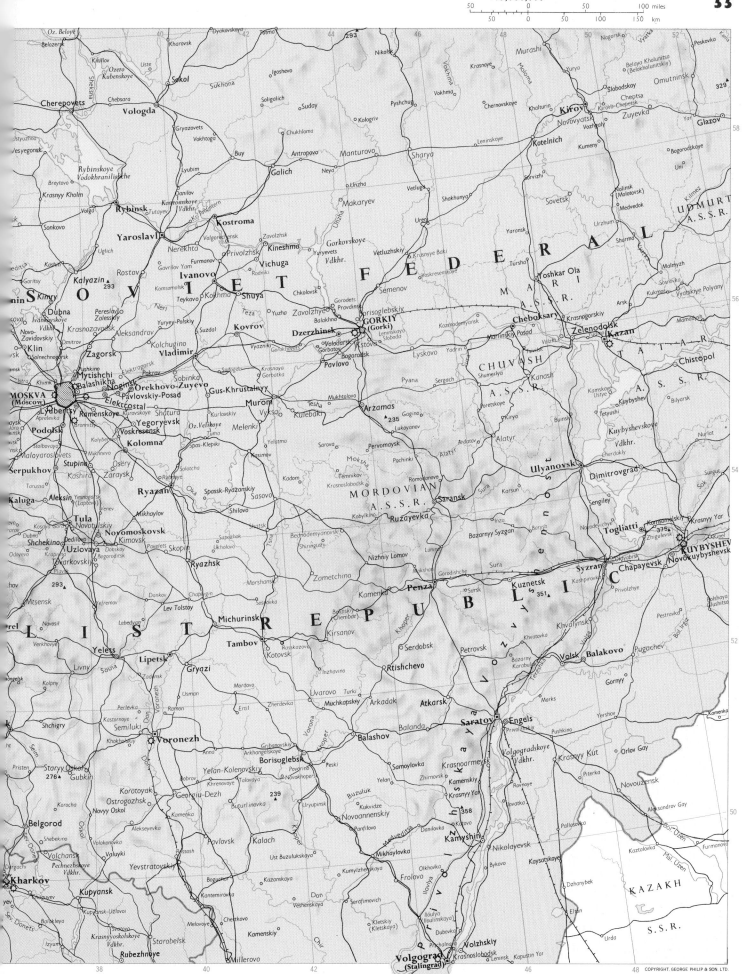

Oz. Beloye
Belozersk
Kirillov
Ozero
Kubenskoye
Uste
Sheksna
Sukhona
Dyakovskaya
Totma
Kharovsk
Nagorsk
Peskovka
Murashi
Krasnoye
Yurya
Vyatka
Cherepovets
Chebsara
Sokol
Sukhona
Pyshchug
Vokhma
Vokhma
Chernovskoye
Khalturin
Slobodskoy
Kirovo-Chepetsk
Omutninsk
Belaya Kholunitsa
(Belokholunitskiy)
Vologda
Gryazovets
Suday
Soligalich
Igoshevo
Nikolsk
Kologriv
Krasnaye
Novovyatsk
Kirov
Kotelnich
Zuyevka
329

Ustyuzhna
Vesyegonsk
Breytovo
Krasnyy Kholm
Buy
Antropovo
Manturovo
Sharya
Leninskoye
Kumeny
Zuyevka
Bogorodskaye
Glazov
58

Rybinskoye
Vodokhranilishche
Danilov
Lyubim
Galich
Neya
Vetluga
Shakhunya
Uren
Yaransk
Shurma
Malmyzh
UDMURT
A.S.S.R.

Sonkovo
Goritsy
Kashin
Kalyazin
293
Rybinsk
Tutayev
Kostromskoye
Vdkhr.
Kostroma
Privolzhsk
Kineshma
Gorkovskoye
Vdkhr.
Krasnyye Baki
Voskresenskoye
Tursha
Yoshkar Ola
Sovetsk
Nolinsk
(Molotovsk)
Medvedok
Urzhum
Arsk
Kukmor
56

SOVIET
FEDERAL

Skimry
Kalyazin
293
Uglich
Nerekhta
Volgorechensk
Zavolzhsk
Vichuga
Rodniki
Yuryevets
Gorokhovets
Semenov
Yadrin
Kozmodemyansk
MARI
A.S.S.R.
Cheboksary
Zelenodolsk
Krasnogorskiy
Malmyzh
Sosnovka
Vyatskiye Polyany
Bolshoye

Ivankovo
Vdkhr.
Dubna
Pereslavl
Zalesskiy
Rostov
Gavrilov Yam
Ivanovo
Shuya
Chkalovsk
Gorodets
Pravdinsk
Borisoglebskiy
Zavolzhye
Kstovo
Lyskovo
Yadrin
CHUVASH
A.S.S.R.
Kanash
Kazan
T A T A R
Chistopol

Novo-
Zavidovskiy
Klin
Solnechnogorsk
Dmitrov
Krasnozavodsk
Zagorsk
Aleksandrov
Yuryev-Polskiy
Kolchugino
Suzdal
Kovrov
Vyazniki
Volodarsk
GORKIY
(Gorki)
Dzerzhinsk
Bogorodsk
Pavlovo
Kozmodemyansk
Shumerlya
Alatyr
Kamskoye
Ustye
Kuybyshev
Bilyarsk
54

Istra
Khimki
Mytishchi
Balashikha
Noginsk
Elektrogorsk
Pokrov
Sobinka
Gorbatov
Vladimir
Kstovo
Pyana
Sergach
Kirya
Kuybyshevskoye
Vdkhr.
Nurlat

MOSKVA
(Moscow)
Lyubertsy
Ramenskoye
Bronnitsy
Pavlovskiy-Posad
Orekhovo-Zuyevo
Gus-Khrustalnyy
Murom
Vyksa
Kulebaki
Arzamas
235
Gagino
Lukoyanov
Ardatov
Alatyr
Sura
Cherdakly
Dimitrovgrad
Surgut

Podolsk
Aprelevka
Yegoryevsk
Shatura
Kurovskoye
Kolomna
Oz. Velikoye
Tuma
Melenki
Yelatma
Pervomaysk
Sarova
Pachinki
Romodanovo
Ulyanovsk
54

Serpukhov
Maloyaroslavets
Mikhnevo
Stupino
Kashira
Zaraysk
Ryazan
Spas-Klepiki
Kasimov
Solotcha
Kadom
Temnikov
Krasnoslobodsk
Moksha
MORDOVIAN
A.S.S.R.
Saransk
Sura
Karsun
Sengiley
Novodevichye
Togliatti
375
Zhigulevsk
Komsomolsk
Krasnyy Yar

Tarusa
Kaluga
Aleksin
Yesenogorsk
(Laptevo)
Venev
Mikhaylov
Rybnoye
Oka
Spassk-Ryazanskiy
Sasovo
Shilovo
Kobylkino
Ruzayevka
Inza
Barysh
Syzran
Chapayevsk
Novokuybyshevsk
KUYBYSHEV
Kinel

Dubna
Shchekino
Dedilovo
Tula
Novotulskiy
Novomoskovsk
Kimovsk
Pavelets
Skopin
Shatsk
Sapozhok
Ukholovo
Bednodemyanovsk
Shiringushi
Nizhniy Lomov
Lunino
Bazarnyy Syzgan
Syzran
Kashpirovka
Privolzhye
Balakhna

Odoyevo
Toxarkovskiy
Uzlovaya
Donskoy
Bogoroditsk
Ryazhsk
Morshansk
Zametchino
Gorodishche
Penza
Kuznetsk
351
Khvalynsk
Balshaya
Glushitsa
Pestravka

293
Yefremov
Lev Tolstoy
Dankov
Chaplygin
Sosnovka
Kamenka
Penza
Sursk
Serdobsk
Petrovsk
Bazarnyy
Karabulak
Pugachev

Mtsensk
Novosil
Verkhovye
Yelets
Livny
Lebedyan
Michurinsk
Kirsanov
Khoper
Rasskazovo
Inzhavino
Rtishchevo
Volsk
Balakovo
52

L I S T   R E P U B L I C

Orel
Kolpny
Lipetsk
Gryazi
Zadonsk
Tambov
Kotovsk
Mordovo
Uvarovo
Turki
Arkadak
Atkarsk
Marks
Balanda
Saratov
Engels
Gornyy

Shchigry
Semiluki
Kastornoye
Usman
Anna
Zhsdevka
Ertil
Muchkapskiy
Samoylovka
Balashov
Volgogradskoye
Vdkhr.
Krasnyy Kut
Orlov Gay

Pristen
Staryy Oskol
Gubkin
276
Bobrov
Khokholskiy
Voronezh
Yelan-Kolenovskiy
Borisoglebsk
Peski
Povorino
Novokhopersk
Yelan
Zhirnovsk
Kamenskiy
Rovnoye
Piterka
Novouzensk

Belgorod
Shebekino
Korotoyak
Ostrogozhsk
Novyy Oskol
Georgiu-Dezh
Kamenka
Buturlinovka
Uryupinsk
239
Buzuluk
Kukvidze
Novoannenskiy
Panfilovo
Danilovka
358
Kamyshin
Lovatka
Nikolayevsk
Kaztalovka
Mal Uzen
Furmanova
50

Oskol
Alekseyevka
Vplokhnovka
Valuyki
Rossosh
Pavlovsk
Kalach
Ust Buzulukskaya
Mikhaylovka
Kumylzhenskaya
Frolovo
Olkhovka
Bykovo
Kaysatskoye
Dzhanybek
KAZAKH

Kharkov
Kupyansk
Yevstratovskiy
Boguchar
Kantemirovka
Kazanskaya
Serafimovich
Don
Vyoshenskaya
Ilovlya
Dubovka
Urda
S.S.R.

Balakleya
Kupyansk-Uzlovaya
Starobelsk
Millerovo
Chettkovo
Kamenskiy
Kletskiy
(Kletskaya)
Iloulya
(Ilovlinskaya)
Elton

Izyum
Krasnyy Liman
Rubezhnoye
Chir
Volzhskiy
Volgograd
(Stalingrad)
Krasnoslobodsk
Leninsk
Kapustin Yar

38   40   42   46   48   COPYRIGHT. GEORGE PHILIP & SON. LTD.

Projection: Conical with two standard parallels

Scale 1:5 000 000

50 0 50 100 miles

50 0 50 100 150 km

Volgograd
(Stalingrad)
Volzhskiy
Krasnoslobodsk
Krasnoarmeysk
Kamyshin
Nikolayevsk
Frolovo
Privolzhskaya
Vozvyshennost
Volgogradskoye
Vdkhr.
Krasnyy Kut
Novouzensk
Pallasovka
Elton
Dzhanybek
Shungay
Verkhniy Baskunchak
Akhtubinsk
(Petropavlovskiy)
Novoannenskiy
Uryupinsk
Buzuluk
Kalach
Pavlovsk
Rossosh
Millerovo
Voroshilovgrad
(Lugansk)
Kamensk-Shakhtinskiy
Morozovsk
Krasnodon
Krasnyy Luch
Sverdlovsk
Gukovo
Belaya Kalitva
Tsimlyanskoye
Vdkhr.
Tsimlyansk
Volgodonsk
Kotelnikovo
Shakhty
Novocherkassk
Rostov
Azov
Bataysk
Veselovskoye
Vdkhr.
Zernograd
Proletarskaya
Salsk
Oz. Manych-
Gudilo
Elista
(Stepnoi)
Ergeni Vozvyshennost
K A L M Y K
A. S. S. R.
Astrakhan
Prikaspiyskaya Nizmennost
K A Z A K H
S. S. R.
Guryev
Makhambet
(Yamankhalinka)
Zelënyy
Kulsary
Mangyshlakskiy
Zaliv
Fort Shevchenko
P-ov.
Mangyshlak
Shevchenko
Kultay
C A S P I A N
S E A
Tikhoretsk
Kropotkin
Krasnodar
Armavir
Stavropol
Svetlograd
(Petrovskoye)
Blagodarnoye
Nevinnomyssk
Maykop
Cherkessk
Mineralnyye Vody
Pyatigorsk
Yessentuki
Kislovodsk
Karachayevsk
Nalchik
KABARDINO-
BALKAR
A.S.S.R.
Prikumsk
Zelenokumsk
(Vorontsovo-Aleksandrovskoye)
Kizlyar
Mozdok
CHECHENO-
INGUSH
A.S.S.R.
Grozny
Gudermes
Ordzhonikidze
Makhachkala
Kaspiysk
Buynaksk
Derbent
DAGESTAN
A.S.S.R.
Bolshoy Kavkaz
(Caucasus Mountains)
Sochi
Adler
Gagra
ABKHAZ
A.S.S.R.
Sukhumi
Ochamchire
Elbrus
5633
Kutaisi
Poti
Batumi
ADZHAR
A.S.S.R.
GEORGIA
S. S. R.
Tskhinvali
Tbilisi
Rustavi
Kazbek
5047
Bazar Dyuzi
4486
Mingechaurskoye
Vdkhr.
Kirovabad
Kirovakan
Leninakan
Aragats
4090
ARMENIAN
S.S.R.
Yerevan
Ozero
Sevan
AZERBAIJAN
S.S.R.
Sumgait
BAKU
Kazi Magomed
Trabzon
Rize
Kars
Ardahan
Sarikamis
Bayburt
Kaçkar
3937

East from Greenwich

COPYRIGHT GEORGE PHILIP & SON. LTD.

R.S.F.S.R.
1. Daghestan A.S.S.R.
2. Kabardino–Balkar A.S.S.R.
3. Mari A.S.S.R.
4. Mordovian A.S.S.R.
5. North Ossetian A.S.S.R.
6. Tatar A.S.S.R.
7. Udmurt A.S.S.R.
8. Chuvash A.S.S.R.
9. Checheno–Ingush A.S.S.R.
AZERBAIJAN
10. Nakhichevan A.S.S.R.
GEORGIA
11. Abkhaz A.S.S.R.
12. Adzhar A.S.S.R.

Projection: Conical Orthomorphic with two standard parallels

East from Greenwich

1:50 000 000

250 0 250 500 750 1000 miles

250 0 500 1000 1500 km

ARCTIC OCEAN

PACIFIC OCEAN

INDIAN OCEAN

Bering Str.
C. Dezhneva
Aleutian Is.
Kamchatka Peninsula
Klyuchevskaya 4750
Sea of Okhotsk
Bering Sea
Gydan Ra. (Kolyma)
Kolyma
Indigirka
New Siberian Is.
Wrangel I.
Verkhoyansk Range
Stanovoy Ra.
Aldan
Lena
Sakhalin
La Perouse Str.
Kuril Is.
Hokkaido 2290
Honshu
Japan
Sea of Japan
Sikhote Alin Ra.
Amur
Yablonovy Ra.
Sayan Mts.
Central Siberian Plateau
Lower Tunguska
Angara
Selenga
Plateau of Mongolia
Great Khingan Mts.
Manchurian Plain
Korea
Korea Str.
Kyushu
Yellow Sea
East China Sea
Ryukyu Is.
Formosa
Fossa Volcano
Bonin Is.
Iwo-jima
Tropic of Cancer
Guam
Caroline Is.
Pelew Is.
Philippine Is.
Luzon
Mindanao
Clube Johnson Deep 10,497
New Guinea
Australia
Halmahera
Moluccas
Celebes
Ceram
Banda Sea
Celebes Sea
Molucca
Makasar Strait
Timor
Flores
Arafura Sea
Java Sea
East Indies
Bali
Java
Sunda Is.
Borneo
Kinabalu 4101
Sulu Sea
Palawan
Hainan
G. of Tonkin
Si-kiang
Hong Kong
Mekong
Sumatra
Str. of Malacca
Menam
G. of Siam
Malay Peninsula
Salween
Irrawaddy
Andaman Is.
Nicobar Is.
Bay of Bengal
Ceylon
Polk Strait
C. Comorin
Equator
Maldive Is.
Laccadive Is.
Chagos Arch.
Amirantes
Seychelles
Socotra
Ras Asir (C. Guardafui)
G. of Aden
Somali Peninsula
Red Sea
Lake Victoria
Libyan Desert
Nile
Sinai Pen.
Suez Canal
Dead Sea
Syrian Desert
Mediterranean Sea
Cyprus
Anatolia
Taurus Mts.
Bosporus
Black Sea
Caucasus Elbruz 5633
Ararat 5165
Tigris
Euphrates
Mesopotamia
Persian Gulf
G. of Oman
Arabian Sea
Arabia
Ar Rub' al Khali
G. of Oman
Elburz Mts. Demavend 5604
Great Salt Desert
Plateau of Iran
Zagros
Hamun
Helmand
Indus
Salt Ra.
Sulaiman Range
Thar
Narmada
Godavari
Krishna
Western Ghats
Eastern Ghats
Deccan
Ganga
Kistna
Brahmaputra
Tsangpo
Everest 8883
Himalaya
Plateau of Tibet
Kunlun Shan
Koko Nor
Hwang
Great Plain of China
Po Hai
China
Yangtze
Karakoram Ra. 8611
Hindu Kush
Pamirs
Communism Pk. 7495
Tarim
Takla Makan
Tarim Basin
Turfan Basin
Gobi
Altai
Tien Shan
Belukha 4506
Aral Sea
Amu Darya
Syr Darya
Turan Plain
L. Balkhash
Chu
Ili
Irtysh
Tobol
16640
Narodnaya 1894
Ob
Ural Mountains
Ural
Volga
Don
Dnepr
Caspian Sea
Steppe
West Siberian Plain
Yenisei
Taimyr Peninsula
Khatanga
Chelyuskin
Kotuy
Severnaya Zemlya
Kara Sea
Novaya Zemlya
Barents Sea
Kola Pen.
White Sea
North Cape
Kolguyev
N. Dvina
Finland
Scandinavia
Baltic Sea
North European Plain
Central Russian Uplands
Vistula
Oder
Elbe
Rhine
Danube
Carpathians
Adriatic Sea
British Isles
North Sea
Iceland
Greenland
Svalbard
Arctic Circle

m 6000 4000 2000 1000 400 200 0 200
ft 18 000 12 000 6000 3000 1200 600 0 600
m 2000 4000 6000 8000
ft 6000 12 000 18 000 24 000

Projection: Bonne
East from Greenwich

1:50 000 000

250   0   250   500   750   1000 miles
250   0   500   1000   1500   km

Projection: Bonne

East from Greenwich

Oceans and Seas

ARCTIC OCEAN
PACIFIC OCEAN
INDIAN OCEAN
Bering Sea
Sea of Okhotsk
Japan Sea
Yellow Sea
East China Sea
South China Sea
Philippine Sea
Celebes Sea
Banda Sea
Java Sea
Sulu Sea
Arabian Sea
Bay of Bengal
Laptev Sea
Kara Sea
Barents Sea
Baltic Sea
North Sea
Black Sea
Caspian Sea
Mediterranean Sea
Red Sea
Persian Gulf
G. of Oman
G. of Aden
G. of Siam
G. of Tongking

Countries and regions

U. S. S. R.
CHINESE REPUBLIC
MONGOLIA
INNER MONGOLIA
MANCHURIA
SINKIANG UIGUR
TIBET
KOREA
JAPAN
INDIA
PAKISTAN
AFGHANISTAN
NEPAL
BHUTAN
BANGLADESH
KASHMIR
SRI LANKA (CEYLON)
BURMA
THAILAND (SIAM)
VIETNAM
LAOS
CAMBODIA
MALAYA
MALAYSIA
INDONESIA
PHILIPPINES
BRUNEI
IRAN (PERSIA)
IRAQ
SYRIA
TURKEY
LEBANON
ISRAEL
JORDAN
SAUDI ARABIA
KUWAIT
BAHRAIN
QATAR
UNITED ARAB EMIRATES
OMAN
YEMEN
SOUTH YEMEN
EGYPT
LIBYA
SUDAN
ETHIOPIA
SOMALI REP
KENYA
UGANDA
TANZANIA
ZAIRE
ZAMBIA
MALAWI
RWANDA
BURUNDI
EUROPE
UNITED KINGDOM
ICELAND
AUSTRALIA
NEW GUINEA

Cities

Tokyo, Kyoto, Osaka, Nagoya, Yokohama, Sapporo, Hakodate, Kitakyushu, Nagasaki, Hiroshima, Kobe
Seoul, Pusan, Pyongyang
Peiping, Tientsin, Shanghai, Nanking, Wuhan, Canton, Foochow, Soochow, Chungking, Chengtu, Lanchow, Sian, Tsingtao, Changchun, Shenyang, Harbin, Lu-ta, Siangtan
Hong Kong, Macau
Manila, Davao, Zamboanga
Hanoi, Saigon, Bangkok, Rangoon, Mandalay, Vientiane
Kuala Lumpur, Singapore, Kuching, Djakarta, Surabaja
Calcutta, Bombay, Madras, Delhi, Hyderabad, Ahmadabad, Bangalore, Kanpur, Lucknow, Allahabad, Varanasi, Agra, Lahore, Karachi, Colombo, Pondicherry
Kabul, Peshawar, Kandahar, Quetta, Herat, Mashhad, Gwadar
Tehrān, Esfahān, Shiraz, Tabriz, Baghdad, Al Basrah, Bandar e Bushehr
Ankara, Istanbul, Izmir, Bursa, Erzurum
Dimashq, Halab, Bayrūt, Al Quds, Amman, Makkah, Al Madinah, Aden, Muscat
El Qâhira, El Iskandarîya, Aswân, El Khartûm, El Obeid, Port Sudan, Suakin, Massawa, Addis Abeba, Mogadishu, Obbia, Nairobi, Mombasa, Dar es Salaam, Kampala, Entebbe
Berlin, Wien, Warszawa, Beograd, Roma, Athínai, Thessaloníki, Odessa, London, Paris
Moskva, Leningrad, Murmansk, Arkhangelsk, Rostov, Volgograd, Astrakhan, Baku, Tbilisi, Yerevan, Batumi
Sverdlovsk, Chelyabinsk, Magnitogorsk, Orenburg, Omsk, Novosibirsk, Tomsk, Barnaul, Semipalatinsk, Alma Ata, Tashkent, Samarkand, Bukhara, Ashkhabad, Khiva, Krasnovodsk, Mary
Krasnoyarsk, Kemerovo, Irkutsk, Chita, Ulan Bator (Ulaanbaatar), Hovd
Vladivostok, Khabarovsk, Nikolayevsk, Okhotsk, Yakutsk, Petropavlovsk
Ul-Ta, Wulumuchi (Urumuchi), Kashgar, Kaxgar, Soche, Ining, Yarkand, Hotan, Lhasa

Rivers and physical features

Lena, Amur, Ob, Irtysh, Yenisey, Angara, Aldan, Tunguska, Indigirka, Kolyma, Vilyuy, Tobol
Volga, Don, Dnepr, Danube, Rhine, Ural, Syr Darya, Amu Darya, Tigris, Euphrates, Nile
Yangtze (Chang), Hwang Ho, Mekong, Irrawaddy, Salween, Brahmaputra, Ganges, Indus, Narmada, Godavari
Lake Baikal (Ozero Baykal), Ozero Balkhash, Aral'skoye More (Aral Sea), Tsaidam

Tropic of Cancer
Equator
Arctic Circle
Limit of ice (Spring)

Aleutian Is.
Kuril Is.
Hokkaido
Honshu
Kyushu
Shikoku
Sakhalin
Novaya Zemlya
Severnaya Zemlya
Svalbard
Formosa (Taiwan)
Hainan
Luzon
Mindanao
Mindoro
Palawan
Sulawesi
Borneo
Sumatera
Java (Djawa)
Irian
Timor
New Guinea
Andaman Is. (India)
Nicobar Is. (India)
Maldive Is.
Lakshadweep Is. (India)
Socotra
Seychelles
Amirantes
Caroline Is.
Guam
Palau Is.
Ryūkyū-rettō
Moluccas (Maluku)
Ceram
Flores
Sulu Arch.
Sea of Japan

Str. of Malacca (George Town)
Sunda Str. (Selat Sunda)
Makasar Str. (Selat Makasar)
Str. of Hormuz

1 : 1 000 000

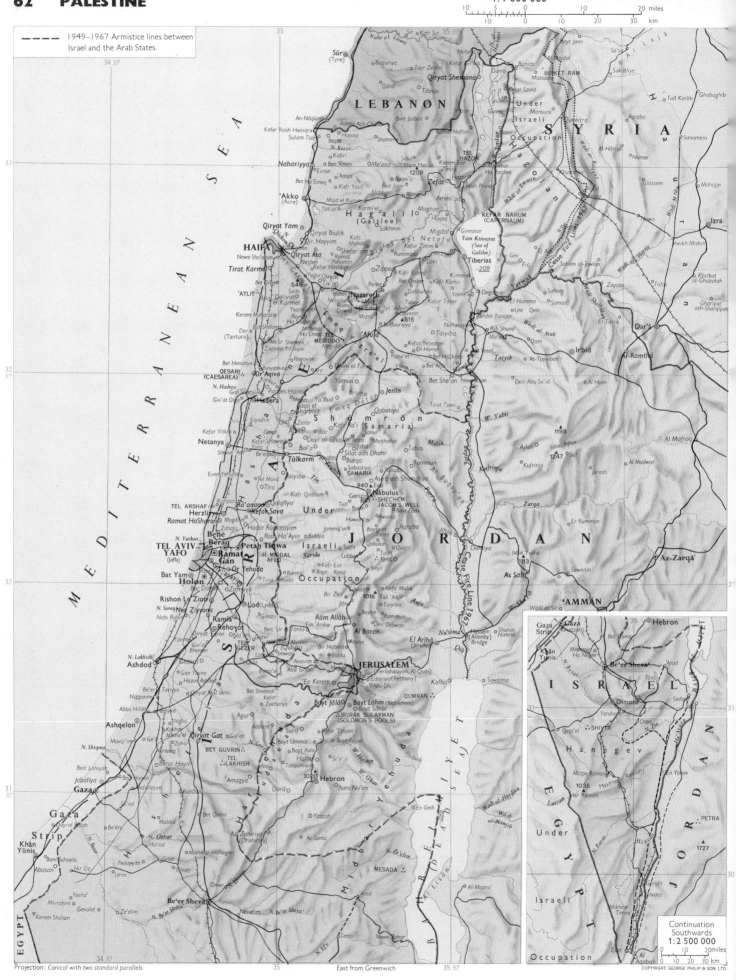

1949–1967 Armistice lines between Israel and the Arab States.

LEBANON

SYRIA

MEDITERRANEAN SEA

HAIFA

Hagalil (Galilee)

Yam Kinneret (Sea of Galilee)

Nazareth

Tiberias
−209

KEFAR NAHUM (CAPERNAUM)

MEGIDDO

Jenin

Shomron (Samaria)

Netanya

Tülkarm

SAMARIA

Nabulus

SHECHEM
JACOB'S WELL

Under

TEL AVIV-YAFO (Jaffa)

Israeli

JORDAN

Ramat Gan

Holon

Bat Yam

Rishon Le Zion

Lod (Lydda)

Ramla

Rehovot

Occupation

AMMAN

Az-Zarqa'

Ashdod

JERUSALEM (Yerüshalayim, Al Quds)

Bayt Lahm (Bethlehem)

BURAK SULAYMAN (SOLOMON'S POOLS)

Ashqelon

Qiryat Gat

BET GUVRIN
TEL LAKHISH

Hebron

Gaza

Gaza Strip

Khān Yünis

DEAD SEA

Be'er Sheva

MESADA

EGYPT

ISRAEL

Gaza Strip

Gaza

Hebron

Khān Yunis

Be'er Sheva

Dimona

H a   N e g e v

SHIVTA

JORDAN

Under

EGYPT

PETRA

Israeli

Occupation

Continuation Southwards
1 : 2 500 000

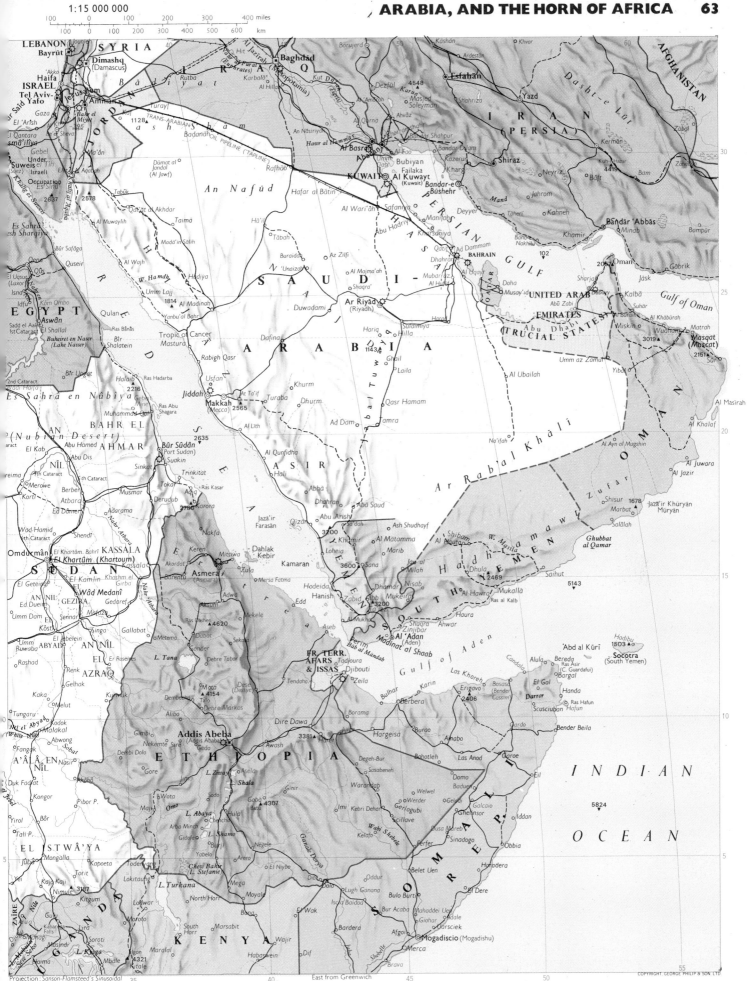

1:15 000 000

100   0   200   300   400 miles
100   0   100   200   300   400   500   600 km

LEBANON
Bayrūt
Haifa
ISRAEL
Tel Aviv-
Yafo
Gaza
El 'Arīsh
Qantara
Suweis
(Suez)
Under
Israeli
Occupation

SYRIA
Dimashq
(Damascus)

Jerusalem
Ammān

IRAQ
Baghdād
Karbalā'
An Najaf

Mosul
Kirkūk

AFGHANISTAN

Bādiyat   ash   Shām

JORDAN

An Nafūd

KUWAIT
Al Kuwayt
(Kuwait)

IRAN
(PERSIA)

Eşfahān
Yazd

Shīrāz

Bandar-e
Büshehr

PERSIAN   GULF

BAHRAIN
Ad Dammām
Dhahrān

Doha
QATAR

UNITED ARAB
EMIRATES
(TRUCIAL STATES)
Abu Dhabi

Bāndar 'Abbās

Gulf of Oman

OMAN

Masqaţ
(Muscat)

EGYPT

Aswān

RED   SEA

Jiddah
Makkah
(Mecca)

SAUDI-

Ar Riyāḍ
(Riyadh)

ARABIA

Ar   Rab   al   Khālī

SUDAN
El Khartûm (Khartoum)
Omdurmân
KASSALA

GEZIRA

Asmera
(Asmara)

ETHIOPIA
Addis Abeba
(Addis Ababa)

L. Tana

FR. TERR.
AFARS
& ISSAS
Djibouti

YEMEN
Sana
Hodeida

SOUTH   YEMEN

Al 'Adan
(Aden)

Gulf of Aden

Socotra
(South Yemen)

SOMALI   REP.

INDIAN

OCEAN

Mogadiscio (Mogadishu)

KENYA

UGANDA

ZAIRE

Projection: Sanson-Flamsteed's Sinusoidal

East from Greenwich

COPYRIGHT GEORGE PHILIP & SON, LTD

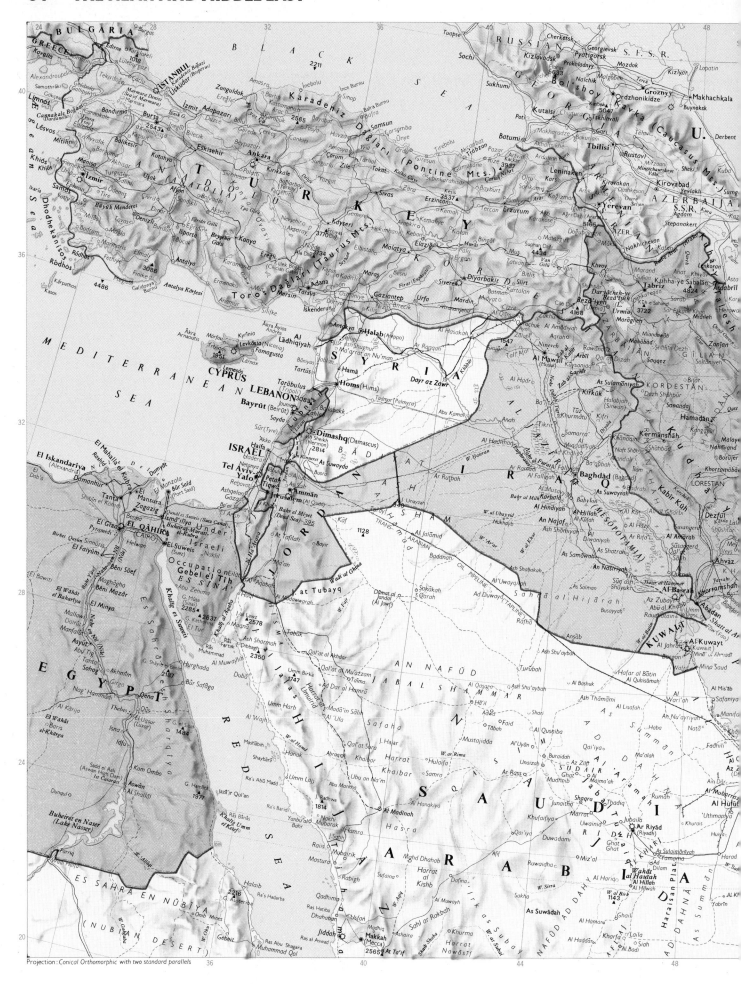

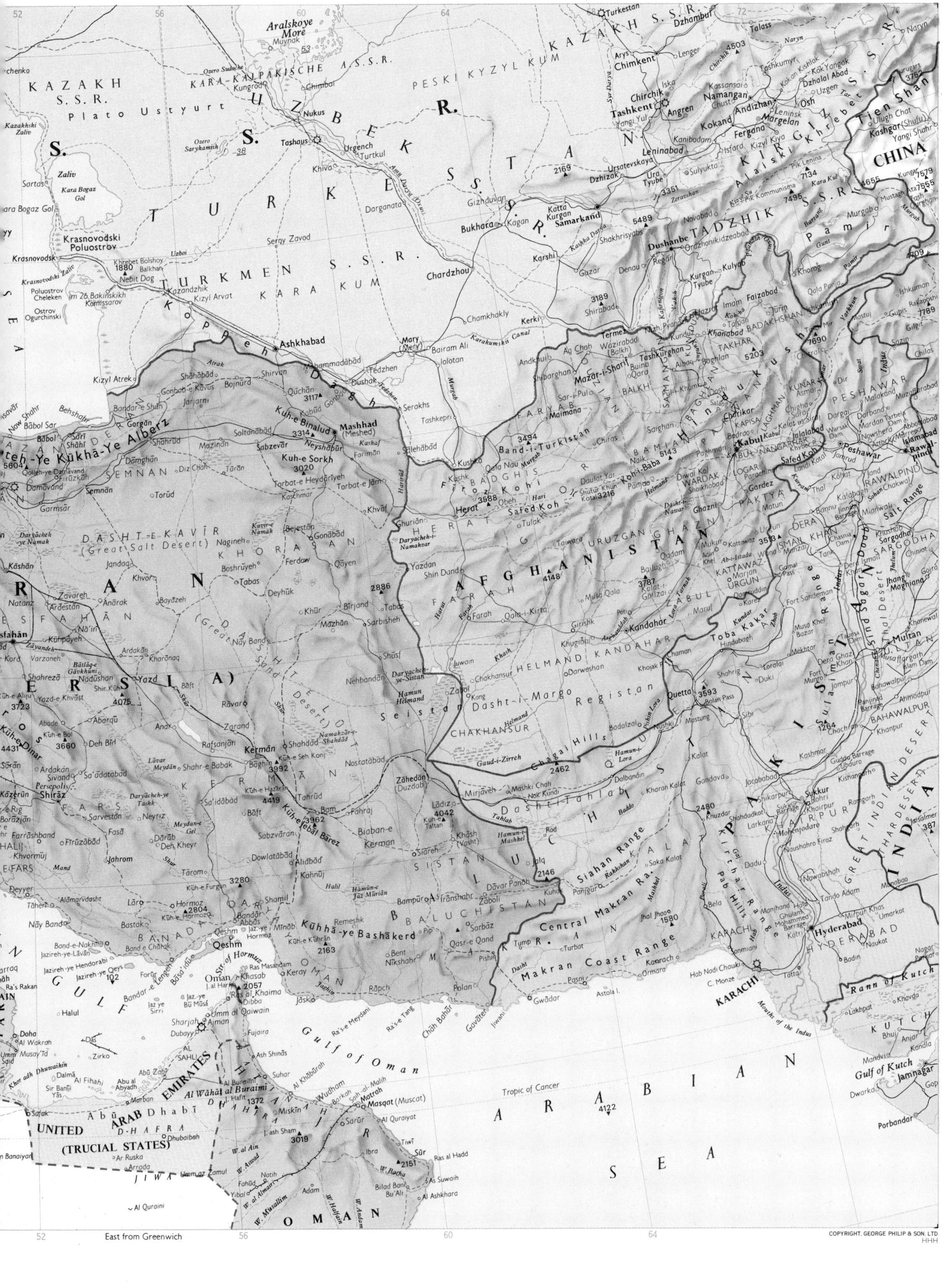

1:10 000 000

100   100   200   300 miles
100   0   100   200   300   400   500 km

KAZAKH S.S.R.

UZBEK S.S.R.

TURKMEN S.S.R.

TADZHIK S.S.R.

KIRGIZ S.S.R.

CHINA

IRAN (PERSIA)

AFGHANISTAN

PAKISTAN

INDIA

OMAN

UNITED ARAB EMIRATES (TRUCIAL STATES)

Tashkent • Samarkand • Dushanbe • Bukhara • Ashkhabad • Mashhad (Meshed) • Herat • Kabul • Peshawar • Rawalpindi • Islamabad • Kandahar • Quetta • Kerman • Shiraz • Zahedan • Multan • Hyderabad • KARACHI • Muscat (Masqat) • Abu Dhabi • Doha

Aralskoye More

Kara Kum

DASHT-E-KAVIR (Great Salt Desert)

DASHT-E-LUT (Great Desert)

Registan

Dasht-i-Margo

GULF

Gulf of Oman

ARABIAN SEA

Gulf of Kutch

Rann of Kutch

GREAT INDIAN DESERT

Tropic of Cancer

U.S.S.R.

AFGHANISTAN

HINDU KUSH

IRAN

PAKISTAN

BALUCHISTAN

ARABIAN SEA

KARACHI

HYDERABAD

Mouths of the Indus

JAMMU AND KASHMIR

KARAKORAM

PESHAWAR

Srinagar

Islamabad
Rawalpindi

LAHORE
Lahore
Amritsar

HIMACHAL PRADESH

PUNJAB

Simla
Ludhiana
Chandigarh
Ambala

DELHI

Dehra Dun

HARYANA

Meerut
Moradabad

RAJASTHAN

Indian Desert
(Thar Desert)

Bikaner
Jodhpur
Ajmer
Jaipur
Agra
Gwalior

Jhansi

Rann of Kutch

GUJARAT

Ahmadabad

Ujjain
Indore

MADHYA PRADESH

Bhopal

Rajkot
Vadodara
(Baroda)

Surat

BOMBAY

Poona (Pune)

MAHARASHTRA

Nagpur

Aurangabad

Sholapur

Hyderabad

ANDHRA PRADESH

Gulbarga

Kolhapur

Belgaum

GOA

KARNATAKA

Hubli

Bangalore

Mysore

TAMIL NADU

Madras

Salem
Coimbatore
Tiruchchirappalli
Madurai

Trivandrum

Cape Comorin

Palk Strait

Gulf of Mannar

SRI LANKA
(CEYLON)

Colombo
Kandy
Moratuwa

Galle

Dondra Head

Continuation Southwards
on same scale

Projection: Conical with two standard parallels

Tropic of Cancer

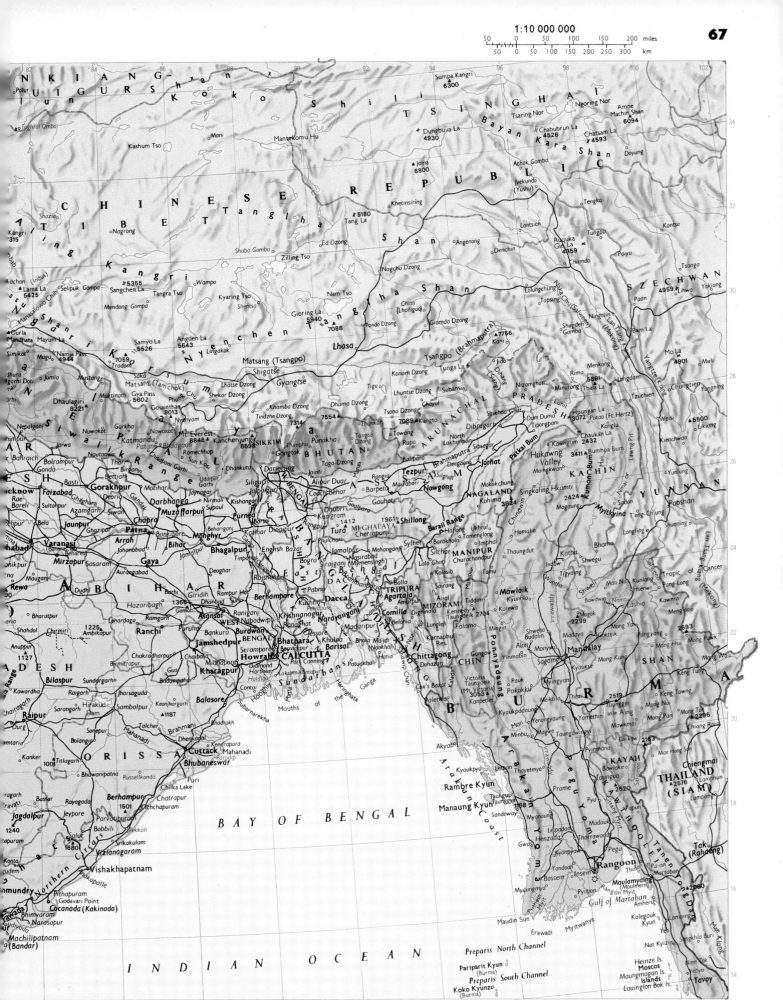

1:10 000 000

50   0   50   100   150   200 miles
50 0   50 100 150 200 250 300 km

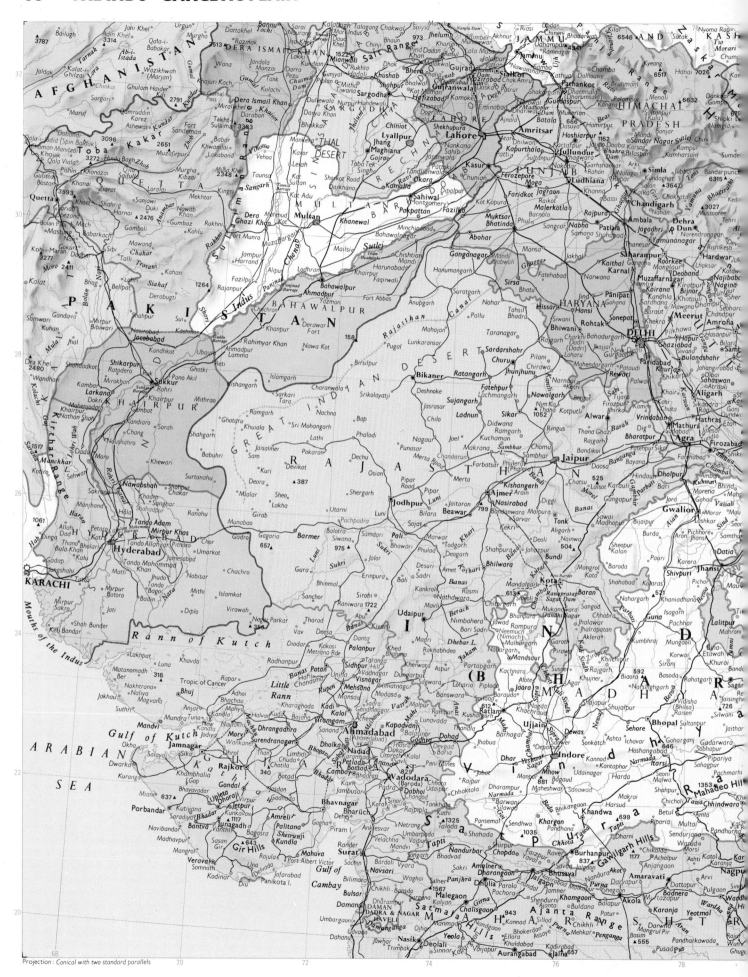

1:6 000 000

50　　0　　50　　100　　150 miles
50　0　50　100　150　200　250 km

SOUTHERN ASIA
POLITICAL
1:40 000 000

CHINESE REPUBLIC

TIBET

AFGHANISTAN
PAKISTAN
INDIA
NEPAL
BHUTAN
BANGLA-DESH
BURMA
SRI LANKA

Tropic of Cancer

BAY OF BENGAL

Mouths of the Ganga

The Sandheads

CALCUTTA
DACCA
BANGLADESH
BHUTAN
SIKKIM
MEGHALAYA
ASSAM
TRIPURA
ORISSA
BIHAR
PRADESH

Mt. Everest 8848
Kanchenjunga
Dhaulagiri 8172
Annapurna 8078
Manaslu 8156

Lucknow
Allahabad
Varanasi
Patna
Gorakhpur
Gaya
Ranchi
Jamshedpur
Bhilainagar
Raipur
Jabalpur
Bilaspur
Cuttack
Bhubaneswar
Puri
Durgapur
Khulna
Raurkela

East from Greenwich

COPYRIGHT GEORGE PHILIP & SON. LTD

1:6 000 000

50   0   50   100   150 miles
50   0   50   100   150   200   250 km

Major labels

MAHARASHTRA
MADHYA PRADESH
ANDHRA PRADESH
KARNATAKA
TAMIL NADU
GOA
KERALA

BOMBAY
Pune (Poona)
Nasik
Aurangabad
Ahmadnagar
Sholapur
Kolhapur
Sangli
Bijapur
Gulbarga
HYDERABAD
Secunderabad
Warangal
Nizamabad
Karimnagar
Nalgonda
Vijayawada
Guntur
Tenali
Machilipatnam (Bandar)
Rajahmundry
Kakinada (Cocanada)
Eluru (Ellore)
Visakhapatnam
Vizianagaram
Nellore
Cuddapah
Kurnool
Anantapur
Bellary
Hospet
Raichur
Hubli-Dharwar
Belgaum
BANGALORE
Mysore
Kolar Gold Fields
Vellore
MADRAS
Pondicherry
Cuddalore
Salem
Coimbatore
Tiruchchirappalli
Thanjavur (Tanjore)
Madurai
Tuticorin
Tirunelveli
Trivandrum
Quilon
Cochin
Ernakulam
Alleppey
Kottayam
Calicut (Kozhikode)
Mangalore
Trichur
C. Comorin

ARABIAN SEA
BAY OF BENGAL
Gulf of Mannar
Palk Strait
Palk Bay
Coromandel Coast
Cormandel Coast

SRI LANKA (inset)
SRI LANKA On same scale

SRI LANKA (CEYLON)
Colombo
Dehiwala
Moratuwa
Jaffna
Kandy
Trincomalee
Galle
Matara
Negombo
Anuradhapura
Batticaloa
Puttalam
Point Pedro
Adam's Bridge
Adam's Peak 2243
Pidurutalagala 2524

Projection: Conical with two standard parallels
East from Greenwich
COPYRIGHT. GEORGE PHILIP & SON. LTD.

1:10 000 000

50 0 50 100 150 200 miles
50 0 100 200 300 km

INDIA

BANGLADESH

CHIN

BURMA

Mandalay

Mong Wa

CHINA

Nanning

Pakhoi

Hanoi
Haiphong

Gulf of
Tongking

Hainan

VIETNAM

Luang Prabang

LAOS

Vientiane

THAILAND
(SIAM)

Hué

Da Nang (Tourane)

Khorat

Phanom Dang Raek

CAMBODIA

Nakhon
Ratchasima
(Khorat)

Angkor
Siem Reap

Tonlé Sap

Battambang

Phnom Penh

Krung Thep
(Bangkok)
Thonburi

Saigon
(Phanh Bho Ho Chi Minh)

ANDAMAN
SEA

Andaman
(India)
Islands

North
Andaman

Middle
Andaman

South
Andaman

Little
Andaman

Myeik Kyunzu
(Mergui)

Archipelago)

Gulf of Siam

Phu Quoc

Kho Khot Kra
Chumphon
(Isthmus of Kra)

Ko Samui

Surat Thani

Nakhon Si Thammarat

Phuket

SOUTH CHINA SEA

George Town,
Pulau
Pinang

WESTERN

MALAYSIA

MALAYA

Kuala Lumpur
Kelang
Seremban

SUMATERA

INDONESIA

Johor Baharu
SINGAPORE

Kepulauan
Natuna Besar

Kepulauan
Anambas

Kepulauan
Natuna Selatan

MALAYA AND SINGAPORE

1:6 000 000

50 0 50 miles
50 0 50 km

THAILAND
(SIAM)

Kota Baharu

Alor Setar

KEDAH

George Town
Butterworth
Bukit Mertajam
PINANG

Taiping

KELANTAN

PERAK

Ipoh

Kuala
Terengganu

TERENGGANU

MALAYA

Telok
Anson

PAHANG

Kuantan

SELANGOR

Kuala Lumpur
Petaling Jaya

NEGERI
SEMBILAN

Seremban

MELAKA

Melaka

JOHOR

Keluang

Bandar Maharani
(Muar)

Bandar Penggaram
(Batu Pahat)

SUMATERA

INDONESIA

Johor Baharu
SINGAPORE

Straits of Singapore

East from Greenwich

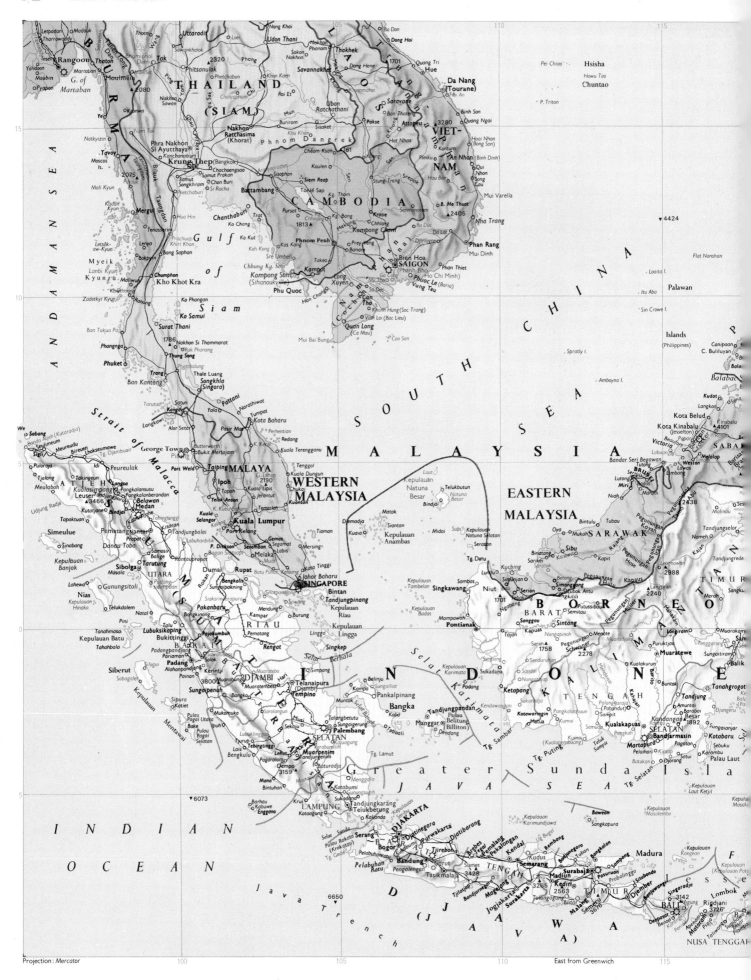

East from Greenwich

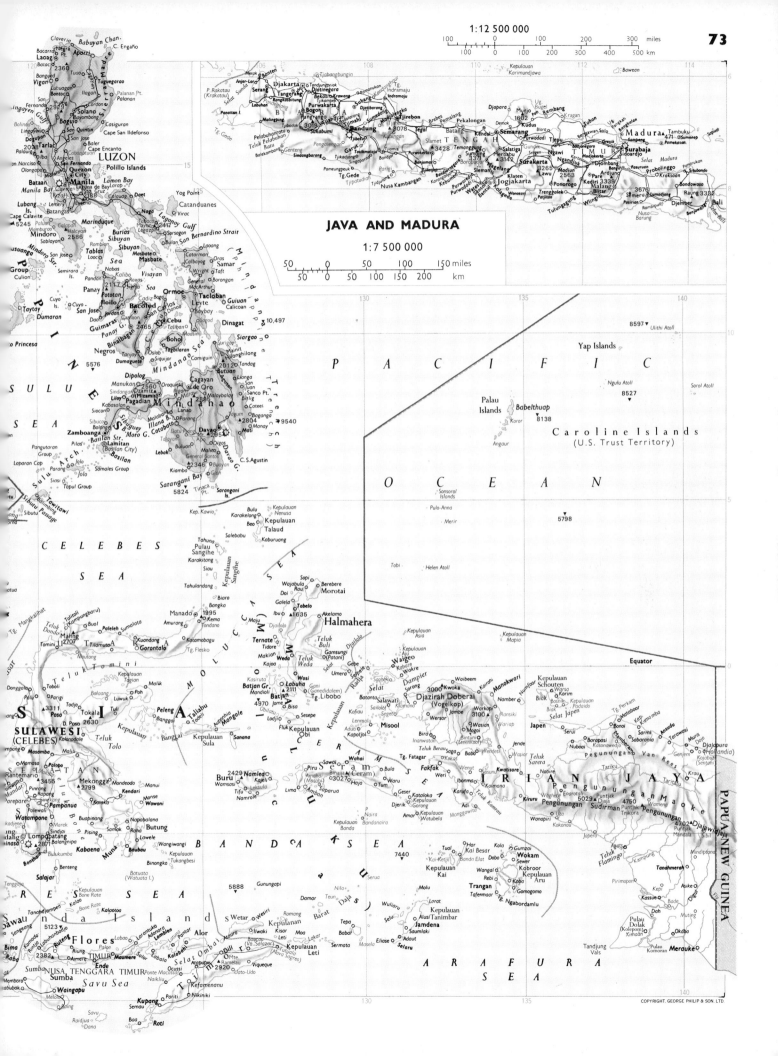

1:12 500 000

100   100   200   300 miles
100   0   100   200   300   400   500 km

JAVA AND MADURA

1:7 500 000

50   0   50   100   150 miles
50   0   50   100   150   200 km

PACIFIC

OCEAN

Caroline Islands
(U.S. Trust Territory)

Yap Islands

Palau
Islands

Babelthuap

CELEBES

SEA

MOLUCCA SEA

Halmahera

Equator

SULAWESI
(CELEBES)

IRIAN JAYA

SERAM SEA

BANDA SEA

ARAFURA
SEA

PAPUA NEW GUINEA

Flores

NUSA TENGGARA TIMUR

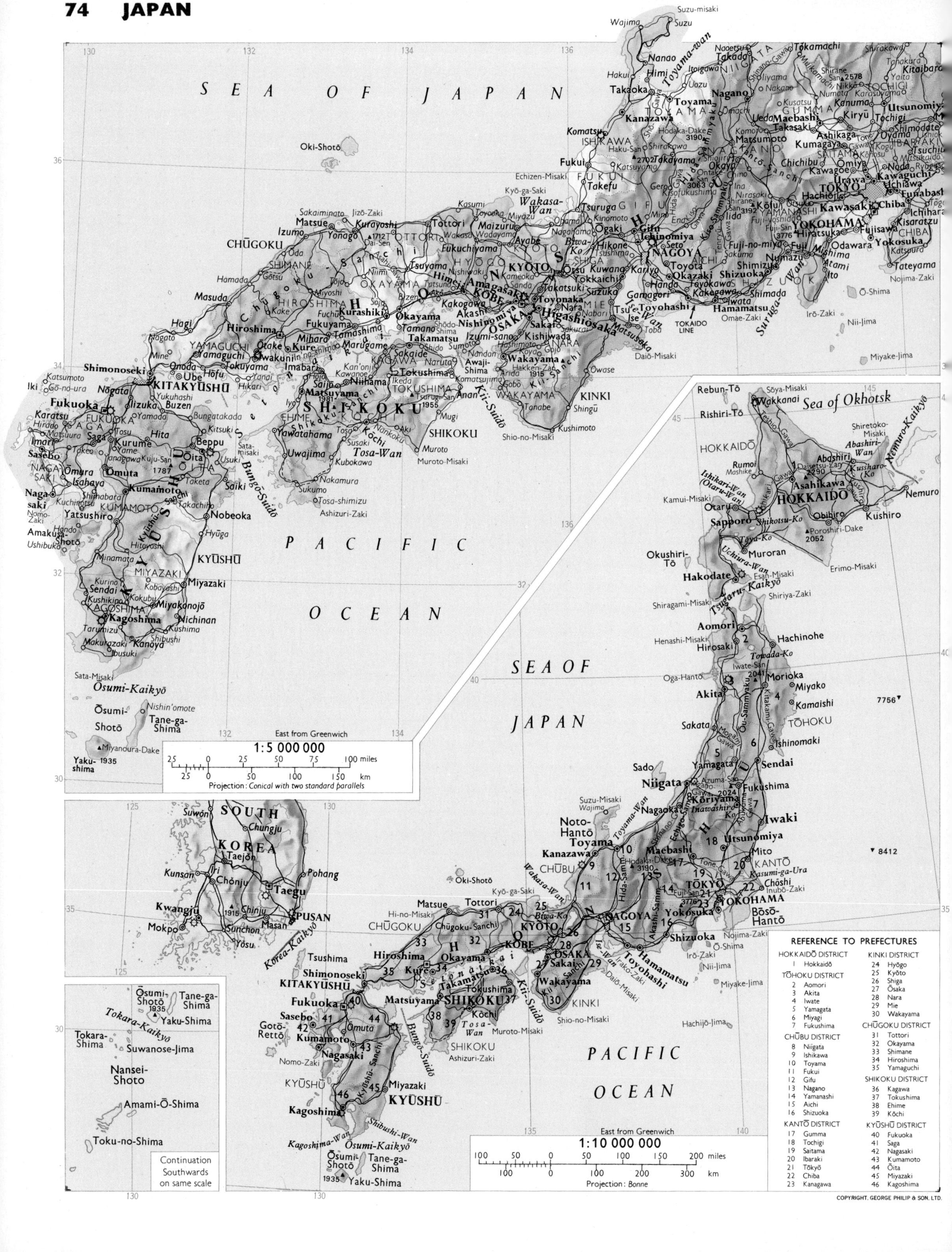

SEA OF JAPAN

CHŪGOKU

PACIFIC OCEAN

SEA OF JAPAN

SOUTH KOREA

HOKKAIDŌ

TŌHOKU

CHŪBU

KANTŌ

KINKI

SHIKOKU

KYŪSHŪ

Sea of Okhotsk

East from Greenwich

1:5 000 000

| 25 | 0 | 25 | 50 | 75 | 100 miles |

| 25 | 0 | 50 | 100 | 150 | km |

Projection: Conical with two standard parallels

East from Greenwich

1:10 000 000

| 100 | 50 | 0 | 50 | 100 | 150 | 200 miles |

| 100 | 0 | 100 | 200 | 300 | km |

Projection: Bonne

Continuation Southwards on same scale

Ōsumi-Shotō 1935 — Tane-ga-Shima

Tokara-Kaikyō

Tokara-Shima — Yaku-Shima

Suwanose-Jima

Nansei-Shoto

Amami-Ō-Shima

Toku-no-Shima

REFERENCE TO PREFECTURES

HOKKAIDŌ DISTRICT	KINKI DISTRICT
1 Hokkaidō	24 Hyōgo
TŌHOKU DISTRICT	25 Kyōto
2 Aomori	26 Shiga
3 Akita	27 Ōsaka
4 Iwate	28 Nara
5 Yamagata	29 Mie
6 Miyagi	30 Wakayama
7 Fukushima	**CHŪGOKU DISTRICT**
CHŪBU DISTRICT	31 Tottori
8 Niigata	32 Okayama
9 Ishikawa	33 Shimane
10 Toyama	34 Hiroshima
11 Fukui	35 Yamaguchi
12 Gifu	**SHIKOKU DISTRICT**
13 Nagano	36 Kagawa
14 Yamanashi	37 Tokushima
15 Aichi	38 Ehime
16 Shizuoka	39 Kōchi
KANTŌ DISTRICT	**KYŪSHŪ DISTRICT**
17 Gumma	40 Fukuoka
18 Tochigi	41 Saga
19 Saitama	42 Nagasaki
20 Ibaraki	43 Kumamoto
21 Tōkyō	44 Ōita
22 Chiba	45 Miyazaki
23 Kanagawa	46 Kagoshima

1:20 000 000

100 0 100 200 300 400 miles
100 0 100 200 300 400 500 600 km

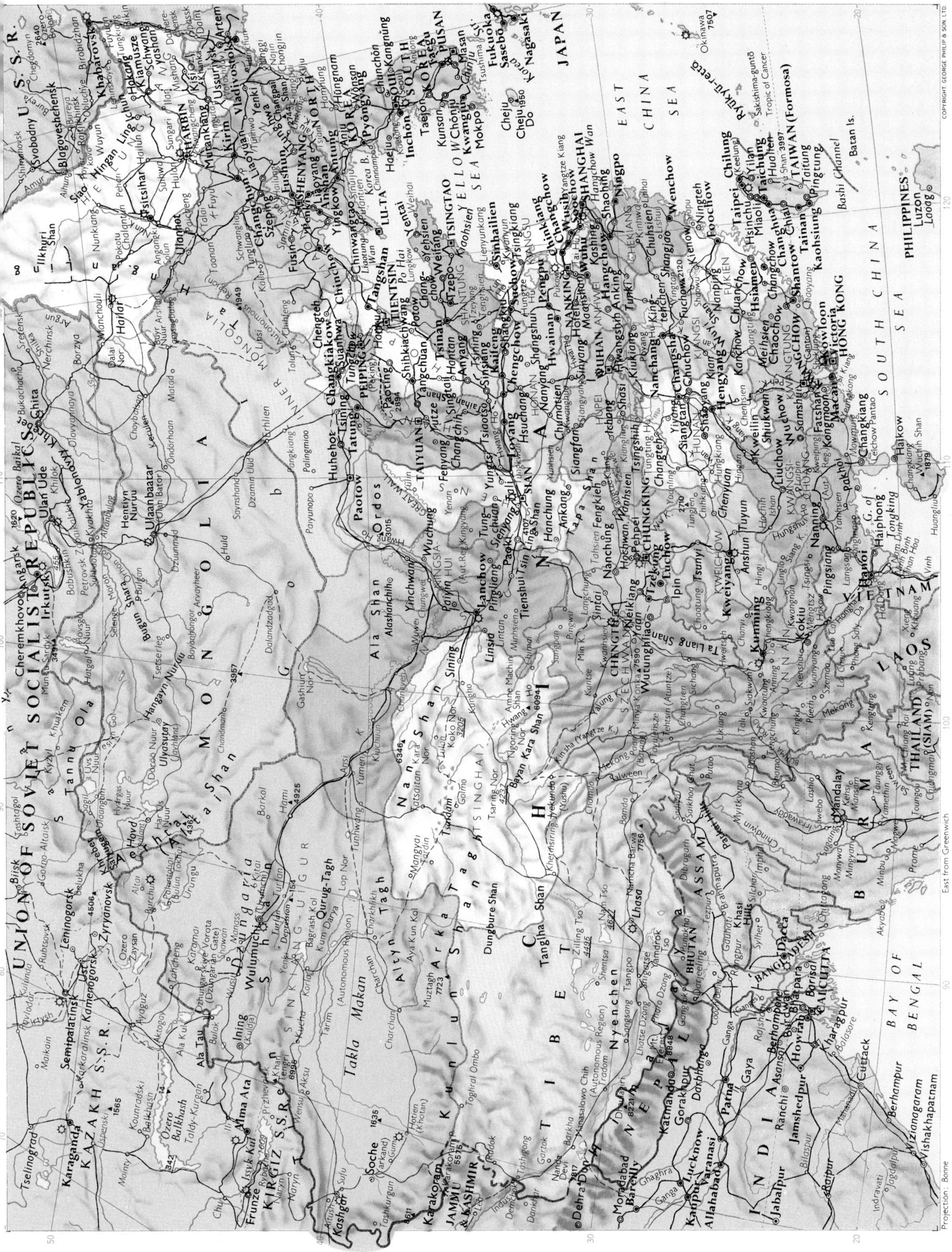

U. S. S. R.

UNION OF SOVIET SOCIALIST REPUBLICS

M O N G O L I A

INNER MONGOLIA

KAZAKH S.S.R.

KIRGIZ S.S.R.

SINKIANG-UIGUR

Takla Makan

Tarim

Kunlun Shan

Nan Shan

Tsinghai

T I B E T

Koko Nor

C H I N A

NEPAL

BHUTAN

ASSAM

I N D I A

BANGLADESH

BURMA

THAILAND (SIAM)

LAOS

VIETNAM

NORTH KOREA

SOUTH KOREA

JAPAN

TAIWAN (Formosa)

PHILIPPINES

HONG KONG

MACAO

YELLOW SEA

EAST CHINA SEA

SOUTH CHINA SEA

BAY OF BENGAL

G.of Tongking

RYUKYU-retto

Tropic of Cancer

HARBIN
SHENYANG
PEIPING
TIENTSIN
TSINGTAO
SHANGHAI
NANKING
WUHAN
CHUNGKING
CHENGTU
KUNMING
KWEIYANG
CANTON
FOOCHOW
HANGCHOW
TAIYUAN
LANCHOW
SINING
LHASA
CALCUTTA
DACCA
MANDALAY
HANOI
Haiphong
PUSAN
Pyongyang
TAIPEI

SHANTUNG
HONAN
SHANSI
SHENSI
HUPEI
ANHWEI
KIANGSU
CHEKIANG
KIANGSI
HUNAN
FUKIEN
KWANGTUNG
KWANGSI
KWEICHOW
SZECHWAN
YUNNAN
NINGSIA HUI
KANSU

GREAT WALL

Hwang Ho

Yangtze Kiang

Mekong

Salween

Projection: Bonne

East from Greenwich

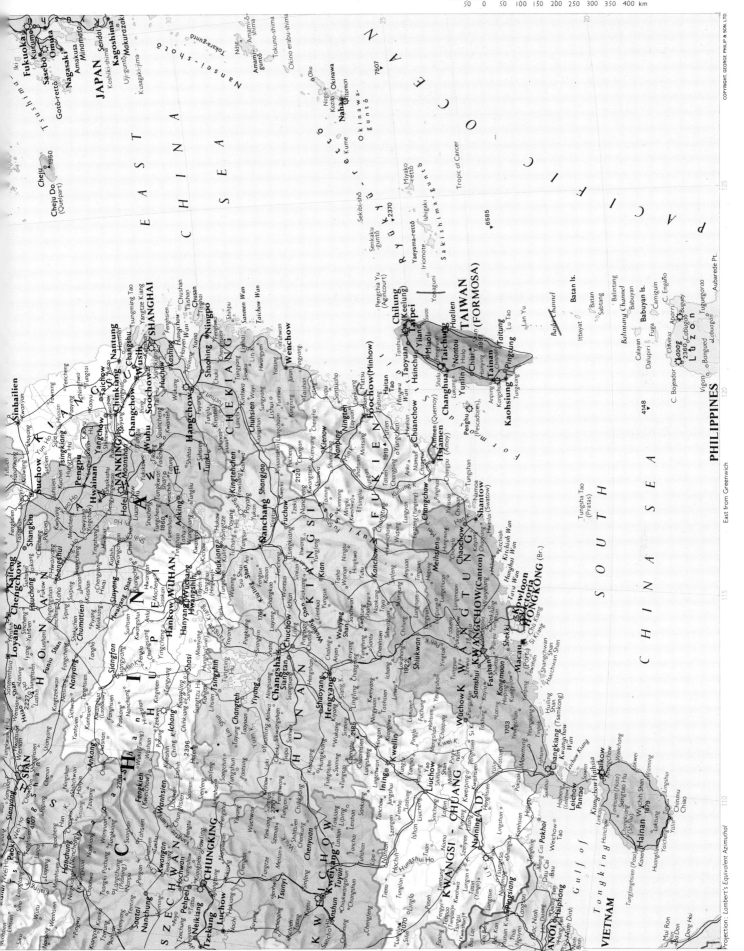

1:10 000 000

50   0   50   100   150   200   250 miles
50   0   50 100 150 200 250 300 350 400 km

JAPAN

Fukuoka
Kurume
Omuta
Sasebo Sendai
Nagasaki Kagoshima
Amakusa Makurazaki
Minamoto
Goto-retto
Koshiki-shima Uji-gunto
Kusagaki-jima

Cheju Do
(Quelpart)

Tsushima

Tokara-shoto

Nansei-shoto

Amami-gunto
Amami-o-shima
Tokuno-shima
Oku
Okino erabu-shima

EAST CHINA SEA

Nago
Kozio Okinawa
Naha Okinawa-gunto
Kume

7507

Tropic of Cancer

Senkaku gunto
2370
Sekibi-sho
Miyako Miyako-gunto
Ishigaki
Iriomote Yaeyama-retto
Yonaguni Sakishima-gunto

6585

RYUKYU ISLANDS

PACIFIC OCEAN

Batan Is.
Balintang Babuyan
Sabtang Babuyan Channel
Itbayat Babuyan Is.
Calayan Fuga
Dalupiri Camiguin
C. Engaño
Aparri

Bashi Channel

Luzon

PHILIPPINES

Pengchia Yu
(Agincourt)

Chilung
Keelung
Taipei
Tamsui Yilan
Tomshui Hualien
Taoyuan Su-o
Miaoli Hsiln
Hsinchu 3931
Nantou Taitung
Taichung
Changhua Chiai
Yunlin Shou
Tainan Anping
Pingtung
Kaohsiung Kongshan
Tungkong

TAIWAN (FORMOSA)

Lu Tao
Lan Yu

4148

SHANGHAI

CHEKIANG
KIANGSU
ANHWEI

Nantung
Changsha
Wusih Soochow
Chinkiang
Changchow
Wuhu Hangchow
Nanking Yangchow

FUKIEN

Foochow (Minhow)
Chuanchow
Amoy Hsiamen
Kinmen (Quemoy)

KWANGTUNG

Swatow Shantou
Chaochow

HONGKONG
Kowloon Victoria
Macau
HONG KONG (Br.)

KWANGCHOW (Canton)

SOUTH CHINA SEA

Tungsha Tao
(Pratas)

Gulf of Tongking

HAINAN
Hoihow Haikow

VIETNAM

HANOI
Haiphong

KIANGSI
Nanchang
Kingtehchen

HUPEH
WUHAN
Hankow Wuchang
Hanyang

HUNAN
Changsha
Hengyang
Shaoyang

KWEICHOW
Kweiyang

KWANGSI-CHUANG
Nanning
Liuchow

SZECHWAN
CHUNGKING

SHENSI

HONAN
Loyang Chengchow
Kaifeng

Shanghai

East from Greenwich

Projection: Lambert's Equivalent Azimuthal

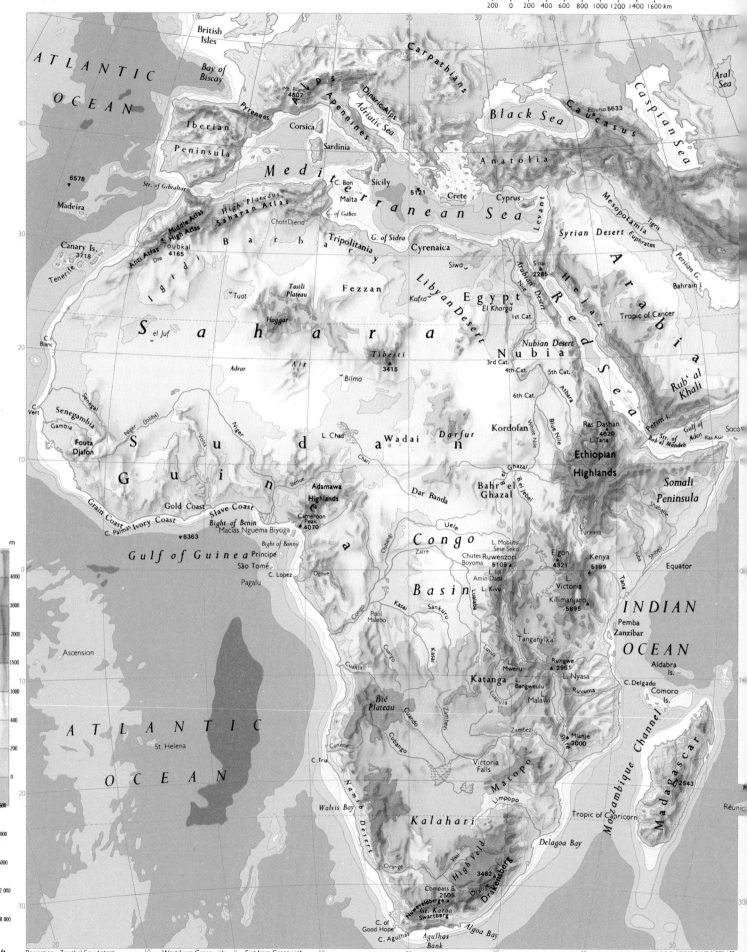

1:40 000 000

200 0 200 400 600 800 1000 miles

200 0 200 400 600 800 1000 1200 1400 1600 km

ATLANTIC OCEAN

British Isles

Bay of Biscay

Carpathians

Black Sea

Caucasus Elburus 5633

Caspian Sea

Aral Sea

Mt. Blanc 4807 Alps

Apennines

Dinaric Alps Adriatic Sea

Pyrenees

Corsica

Iberian Peninsula

Sardinia

Mediterranean Sea

Anatolia

Cyprus

Crete

Malta

C. Bon Sicily 5121

6578

Str. of Gibraltar

Madeira

Middle Atlas High Plateaus Saharan Atlas

High Atlas

B a r b a r y

Tripolitania

Cyrenaica

G. of Sidra

G. of Gabes

Chott Djerid

Mesopotamia Tigris Euphrates

Syrian Desert

Levant

Persian G.

Bahrain I.

Canary Is. 3718

Anti Atlas Toubkal 4165

Dra

Tenerife

I g i d i

Tuat

Tasili Plateau

Fezzan

Siwa

Kufra

Egypt

Libyan Desert

El Kharga 1st Cat.

Nile

Arabian Desert

Sinai 2285

Hejaz

Red Sea

A r a b i a

Tropic of Cancer

Rub' al Khali

C. Blanc

S. el Juf

S a h a r a

Hoggar

Adrar

Air

Tibesti 3415

Bilma

Nubian Desert

N u b i a

3rd Cat.

4th Cat.

5th Cat.

6th Cat.

Atbara

Ras Dashan 4620 L. Tana

Perim I.

Gulf of Aden

Ras Asir

Soco

C. Vert

Senegal

Senegambia

Gambia

Fouta Djalon

Niger (Joliba)

Niger

Volta

L. Chad

Chari

Wadai

Darfur

Kordofan

White Nile

Blue Nile

Str. of Bab el Mandeb

S u d a n

Benue

Adamawa Highlands

Dar Banda

Bahr el Ghazal

Bahr el Ghazal el Jebel

Ethiopian Highlands

Somali Peninsula

Shabelle

S u G u i n e a

Grain Coast

Gold Coast

Ivory Coast Slave Coast

C. Palmas

Bight of Benin

Macias Nguema Biyoga

Cameroon Peak 4070

6363

Bight of Bonny

Gulf of Guinea

Principe

São Tomé

C. Lopez

Pagalu

Ogoue

Uele

Oubangi

Zaire

Congo Basin

Congo

Kasai

Sankuru

Kasai

Lualaba

L. Mobutu Sese Seko

Chutes Boyoma Ruwenzori 5109

L. Idi Amin Dada

L. Kivu

L. Victoria

Elgon 4321

Kenya 5199

Kilimanjaro 5895

Equator

INDIAN OCEAN

Pemba

Zanzibar

Turkana

Juba

Shibeli

Tana

Ascension

ATLANTIC OCEAN

St. Helena

Cuanza

Kwango

Cuango

Cuanza

Pool Malebo

Bié Plateau

L. Tanganyika

Katanga

L. Mweru

Bangweulu

Luapula

Rungwe 2961

L. Nyasa

Ruvuma

Malawi

Aldabra Is.

C. Delgado

Comoro Is.

Mozambique Channel

Cunene

C. Fria

Namib Desert

Walvis Bay

Cubango

Cuando

Zambezi

Victoria Falls

Matopo

Mlanje 3000

Shire

Madagascar 2643

Réunic

Kalahari

Limpopo

Vaal

High Veld

Orange

3482

Compass B 2505

Nuweveldberge Gr. Karoo Swartberg

Drakensberg

Delagoa Bay

Tropic of Capricorn

C. of Good Hope

C. Agulhas

Agulhas Bank

Algoa Bay

ft m

12 000 4000

9000 3000

6000 2000

4500 1500

3000 1000

1200 400

600 200

0 0

200 600

1000 3000

2000 6000

4000 12 000

6000 18 000

m ft

COPYRIGHT. GEORGE PHILIP & SON LTD.

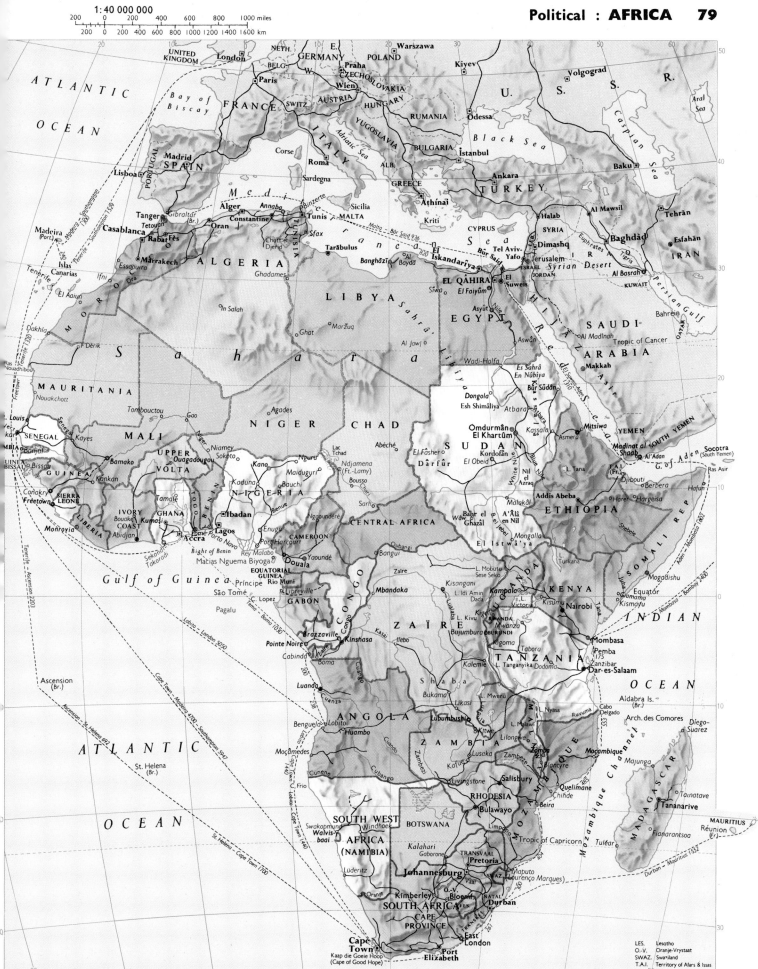

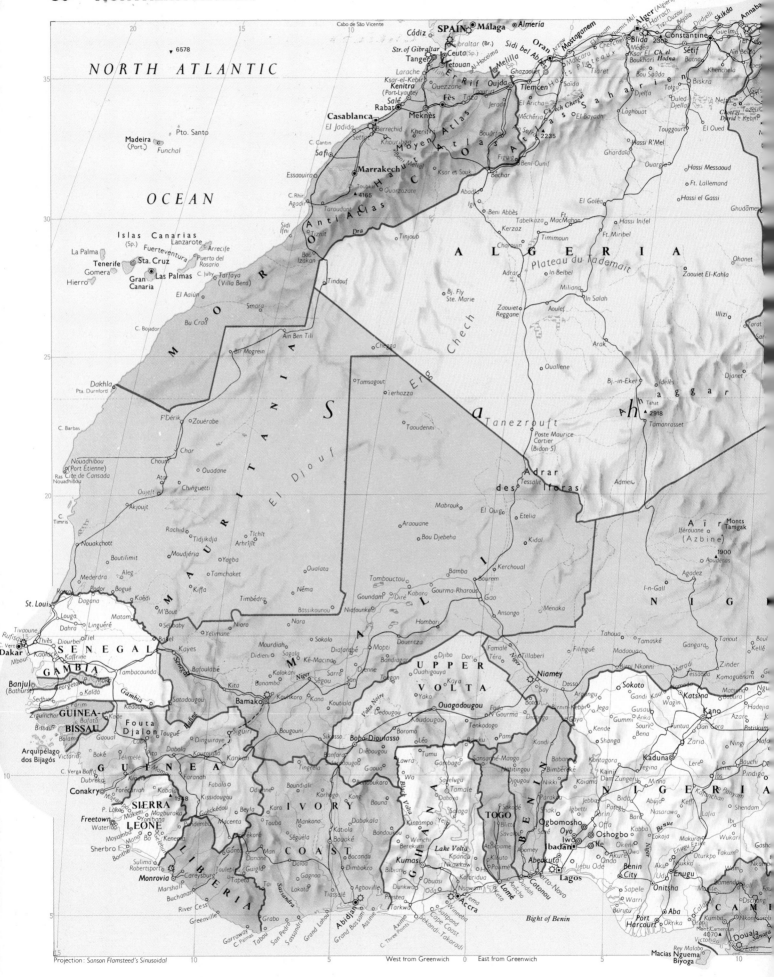

NORTH ATLANTIC

OCEAN

SPAIN

MOROCCO

ALGERIA

MAURITANIA

MALI

NIGER

SENEGAL

GAMBIA

GUINEA-BISSAU

GUINEA

SIERRA LEONE

LIBERIA

IVORY COAST

UPPER VOLTA

GHANA

TOGO

BENIN

NIGERIA

Islas Canarias (Sp.)

Madeira (Port.)

Projection: Sanson Flamsteed's Sinusoidal

West from Greenwich   East from Greenwich

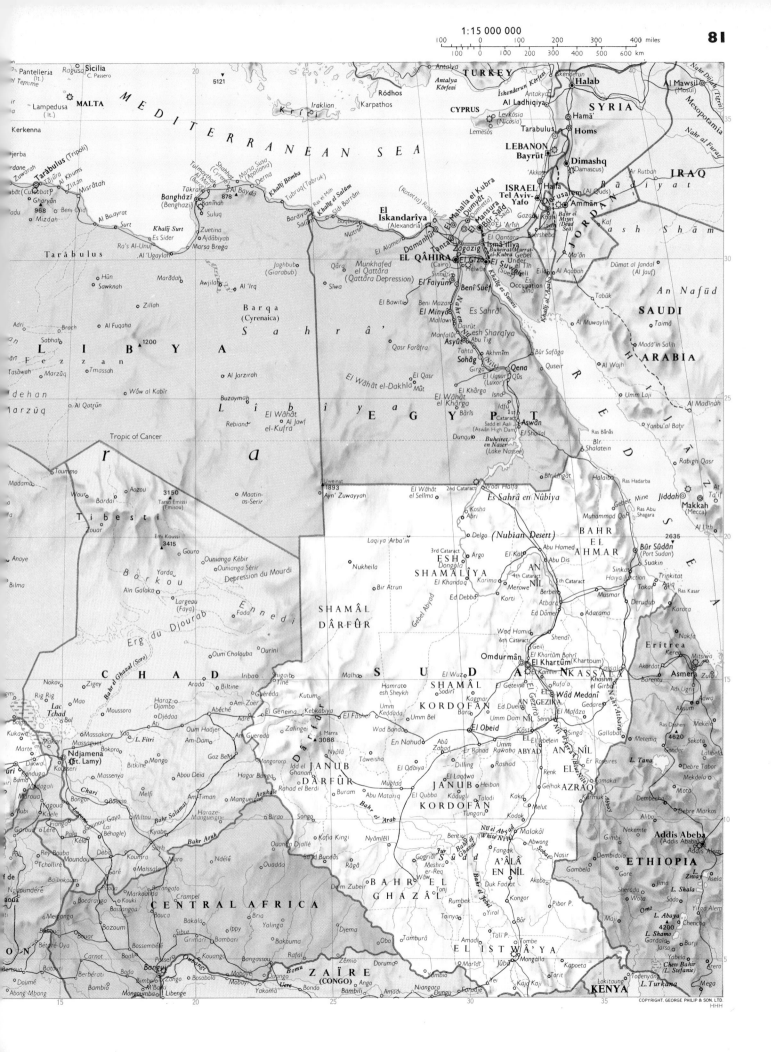

1:15 000 000

100   0   100   200   300   400 miles
100   0   100   200   300   400   500   600 km

MEDITERRANEAN SEA

Pantelleria (It.)
Sicilia
C. Passero
el Temme
Ragusa
Lampedusa
MALTA
Kerkenna
Jerba
Zuwārah
Tarābulus (Tripoli)
Tājūra
Al Khums
Zlitan
Misrātah
Gharyān
968
Beni Ulid
Al Bu'ayrat
Surt
Es Sider
Ra's Al-Unuf
Ajdābiyah
Marsa Brega
Al 'Uqaylah
Tarābulus
Hūn
Sawknah
Marādah
Awjilah
Al 'Irq
LIBYA
Barqa
(Cyrenaica)
Sahrā'

TURKEY
Antalya
Antalya Körfezi
Ródhos
Karpathos
Kriti
Iraklion
CYPRUS
Levkôsia (Nicosia)
Lemesós
SYRIA
İskenderun
Halab
Al Mawsil (Mosul)
Al Ladhiqiya
Hamā'
Homs
Tarabulus
LEBANON
Bayrūt
Dimashq (Damascus)
İskenderun Körfezi
Antakya
Ar Rutbah
IRAQ
Bādiyat
Mesopotamia
Nahr Dijlah (Tigris)
Nahr al Furay
ISRAEL
Tel Aviv-Yafo
Haifa
'Akko
Jerusalem (Al Quds)
Amman
JORDAN
Ma'ān
Al 'Aqabah
Tabūk
Dūmat al Jandal (Al Jauf)
ash Shām
An Nafūd
SAUDI
ARABIA
Tulmaythah (Ptolemais)
Shahhāt (Cyrene)
Marsa Susa (Apollonia)
Derna
Tūkrah
878
Al Baydā
Banghāzī (Benghazi)
Banīnah
Suluq
Khalīj Bomba
Tubruq (Tobruk)
Ras el Milh
Khalīj as Salūm
Bardiyah
Sīdi Barrāni
Bûqbûq
Matrûh
El 'Alamein
Ed Daba
Damanhûr
Rosetta Rashid
El Iskandarîya (Alexandria)
Dumyât
Bûr Sa'îd
El Mahalla el Kubra
El Mansura
Tanta
Zagazig
Ismâ'îlîya
Buheirat Murrat el Kubra
El Qantara
El 'Arish
Gaza
Khân Yûnis
Khalîj el Suweis
Rafah
Beersheba
Bahr el Miyet (Dead Sea)
Kaf
Qarâ
Munkhafed el Qattâra (Qattâra Depression)
Siwa
El Qâhira (Cairo)
El Gîza
El Suweis (Suez)
Helwân
Sinnûris
Gebel et Tih
Under Occupation
Es Suweis
El Faiyûm
Khalîg es Suweis
Beni Suêf
Beni Mazar
El Bawiti
El Minyâ
Mallawi
El Wâhât el-Dakhla
Qasr Farâfra
Es Sahrâ'
Esh Sharqîya
Manfalût
Asyût
Tahta
Abu Tig
Akhmîm
Sohâg
Girga
Qena
El Uqsur (Luxor)
Qûs
Qasr
Mût
El Qasr
El Khârga
El Wâhât el Khârga
Idfû
1st Cataract
Bârîs
Aswân
Sadd el Aali (Aswân High Dam)
El Shallal
Dunqul
Buheiret en Naser (Lake Nasser)
Tropic of Cancer

RED SEA
HIJAZ
Bûr Safâga
Quseir
Ras Banâs
Bîr Shalatein
Bîr Ungat
Halaib
Ras Hadarba
Umm Laji
Al Wajh
Al Madînah
Al Muwaylih
Mada'in Salih
Taimā
Yanbu'al Bahr
Rabigh Qasr
Jiddah
Makkah (Mecca)
Ta'if
At
2635

Fezzan
Tasâwah
Marzūq
dehan
Marzûq
Al Qatrûn
Al Fuqaha
Zillah
1200
Brach
Sabhah
Adri
Al Jarzirah
Buzaymah
Rebiana
El Wâhât el-Kufra
El Wâhât el Jawf
Lî   b   î   y   e   g   y   p   t
1893
Uweinat
Ayn' Zuwayyah
El Wâhât el Selîma
Wâdi Halfa
2nd Cataract
Es Sahrâ en Nûbiya
Gebel Oweinat
Gabgaba
Gemai Mine
Muhammad Qol
Ras Abu Shagara
Sinkat
Derudub
Haiya Junction
Trinkitat
Tokar
Agig
Ras Kasar
BAHR
EL
AHMAR
Bûr Sûdân (Port Sudan)
Suakin
Karora
Nakfa
Eritrea
Keren
Mitsiwa
Akordat
Asmera
Zula

Tibesti
Zouar
Aozou
Tarso Emissi (Emisou)
3150
Emi Koussi
3415
Gouro
Bardai
Woûr
Madama
Anaye
Toummo
Bilma
Borkou
Yarda
Ennedi
Erg du Djourab
Fada
Ounianga Kébir
Ounianga Sérir
Depression du Mourdi
Aïn Galaka
Largeau (Faya)
CHAD
Nokou
Zigey
Rig Rig
Mao
Lac Tchad
Bol
Massakory
Ndjamena (Ft. Lamy)
Kousseri
Maroua
Mubi
Mora
Kaélé
Lère
Pala
Chari
Bongor
Bénoué
Garoua
Rey Bouba
Tcholliré
Ngaoundéré
Meiganga
Baïbokoum
Bénoué
CENTRAL AFRICA
Bétaré-Oya
Doumé
Abong Mbang
Batouri
Berbérati
Gamboula
Carnot
Bouar
Bozoum
Bossangoa
Bocaranga
Paoua
Bossembélé
Bangui
ZAIRE (CONGO)
Zongo
Libenge
Gemena

Nukheila
Laqiya Arba'in
Bir Atrun
Delgo
Kosha
Abri
Argo
Dongola
3rd Cataract
El Kab
4th Cataract
Abu Hamed
Abu Dis
ESH
SHAMALIYA
El Khandaq
Karima
Merowe
5th Cataract
AN
NIL
El Debba
Korti
Atbara
Ed Dâmer
SHAMÂL
DÂRFÛR
Gebel Abyad
6th Cataract
Wad Hamid
Shendi
Geili
El Khartûm Bahrî
Omdurmân
El Khartûm
Khartoum
El Kamlin
El Geteina
KASSALA
Kassala
Khashm el Girba
Gedaref
Gallabat
Metema
4620
Gonder
L. Tana
Debre Tabor
Gerar
Er Roseires
Singa
El Mafâza
Gedaref
Sennâr
Wâd Medanî
Rufa'a
AN
NIL EL
AZRAQ
EL
GEZIRA
Ed Dueim
El Obeid
El Eilefun
Kôsti
Dilling
Rashad
Renk
Blue Nile
Abbay
Mekdela
Dembecha
Debre Markos
Alibo
Nekemte
ETHIOPIA
Addis Abeba (Addis Ababa)
Addis Alem
Malha
SUDAN
Iribaa
Tiné
Kutum
Hamrato esh Sheykh
Sodiri
Umm Keddada
Umm Bel
En Nahud
Abû Zabad
El Fasher
J. Marra
3088
Dârfûr
Nyâlâ
Idd el Ghanam
JANUB
DÂRFÛR
Hagar Banga
Kebkabiya
El Geneina
Adré
Am-Zoer
Abéché
Goz Beïda
Am Dam
Am Guereda
Biltine
Guéréda
Iriba
Arada
Oum Hadjer
Ati
Djédaa
Moussoro
Haraz-Djombo
Mongo
Bitkine
Bokoro
Massaguet
Massenya
Melfi
Am Timan
Bahr Salamat
Miltou
Sarh
Kyabé
Moïssala
Haraze-Mangueigne
Aoukalé
Birao
Ndélé
Songo
Ouanda Djallé
Ouadda
Mangueigne
Bahr Aouk
Maro
Koumra
Moundou
Doba
Goré
Bébédja
Kélo
Lai
Béhagle
Gounou-Gaya
Lac Iro
Kyabé
Rahad el Berdi
Buram
Abu Matariq
El Qubba
Kâdugli
Talodi
Tungaru
Kaka
Kodok
Melut
JANUB
KORDOFAN
Muglad
Nyâmlêll
Kafia Kingi
Dîm Zubeir
Râga
Sûd
Bahr el 'Arab
Bentiu
Nû el Abyad (White Nile)
Malakâl
Abwong
Sobat
Nasir
Gimbi
Dembidolo
Gore
Gambela
Gimma
L. Abaya
4200
L. Zwai
Asela
Sherada
Wota
Yigga Alem
Chencha
Maji
L. Shamo
Gardula
Burji
Yabelo
Bako
Omo
Mega
Chew Bahir (L. Stefanie)
L. Turkana
ESH
SHAMÂL
KORDOFAN
Kagmar
Bora
En Nahud
Umm Dam
El Lagowa
Er Rahad
Rawaba
ABYAD
AN
NIL
EL
ABYAD
Heiban
Gelhak
Meshra er-Req
Wâw
Tonj
Rumbek
Yirol
Bôr
Tali P.
Amadi
Tombe
Yombio
BAHR
EL
GHAZÂL
Gogrial
Jur
Bahr el Jebel
A'ÂLA
AN
NÎL
Akobo
Pibor P.
Kongor
Duk Fadiat
Fangak
Tainya
EL ISTWÂ'YA
Jûba
Mongalla
Torit
Kapoeta
Lokitaung
Todenyang
KENYA
Yei
Maridi
Nzara
Tambura
Ezo
Zêmio
Doruma
Yambio
Dungu
Aba
Faradje
Nagero

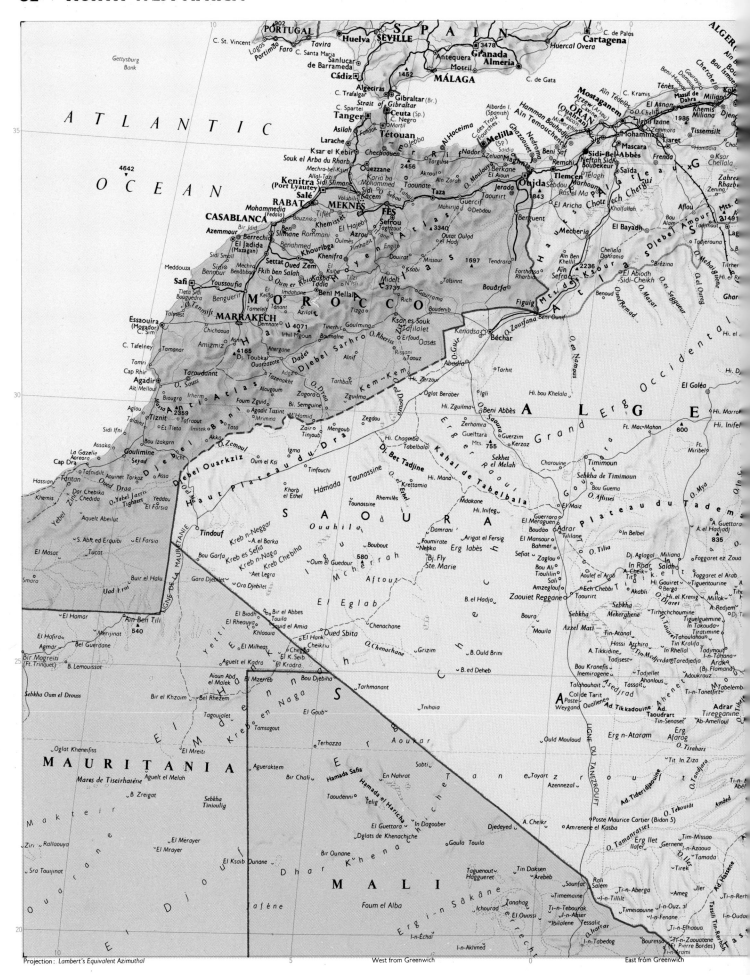

1:8 000 000

50   0   50   100   150   200 miles
50 0 50 100 150 200 250 300 km

MEDITERRANEAN SEA

SICILY
Etna 3340
Marsala
CATANIA
Agrigento Caltanissetta Siracusa
Ragusa
C. Passero
C. Spartivento

Pantelleria (Italian)

Gozo Valletta
MALTA
Linosa I. (Italian)
Lampione I. (Italian)
Lampedusa (Italian)

TUNISIA

Bejaia Djidjelli Skikda Annaba Galite Is. Menzel-Bourguiba Bizerte (Binzert)
El Kseur Collo El Milia Chetaibi Blanc Mateur Coni I.
CONSTANTINE Guelma Tabarka Béja Halq el Oued Golfe de Tunis C. Bon Zembra I.
Sétif Aïn M'lila Souk Ahras El Kef Medjerda TUNIS Soliman Kelibia
Batna Oum-el-Bouaghi Aïn Beïda Tébessa Maktar Nabeul Hammamet G. de Hammamet
Biskra Khenchela Aurès Thala Kairouan Kalaa-Kebira Sousse Monastir Moknine
Chott Melrhir Gafsa Sbeïtla Msaken Mahdia Djerba Rass Kaboudia
El Meghaier Nefta Tozeur Chott Djerid Gabès Djerba I. El Kantara
El Oued Djamâa Kebili Hamma Zorzis
Touggourt Douz Médenine Bahiret el Bibane
Ouargla Tataouine Ben Gardane **Tarābulus (Tripoli)** Al Khums
Zuwārah Al'Azīzīyah Zlītan **Misrātah (Misurata)**
Ghudāmis Nālūt Jabal Nafūsah Gharyān Bani Walīd Tāwurghā' **Banghāzī (Benghazi)**
Ghadāmis Az Zintān Mizdah Sabkhat Tāwurghā' **Khalij Surt (Gulf of Sidra)** Zueitina
AL JABAL AL GHARB Ash Shwayrif Surt Ajdabiyah Marsa Brega
AL HAMMĀDAH AL ḤAMRĀ' **MISRĀTAH**
Bi'r al Ghaylānīyah **AS SABHĀ** **AL HARUJ AL ASWAD**
Jabal as Sawdā' 840 Al Jufrah Hūn Zillah
Brach Wādī ash Shāṭi' Sabhah (Sebha) 1200
LIBYA
Awbārī Marzūq Murzuq
Idehan Marzūq Al Qaṭrūn
Ghāt Djanet Tropic of Cancer
ALGERIA Tassili n'Ajjer Hoggar Ahaggar Tamanrasset
NIGER **CHAD**
Tibesti Emi Koussi 3415

COPYRIGHT, GEORGE PHILIP & SON, LTD.

Projection: Lambert's Equivalent Azimuthal

West from Gre

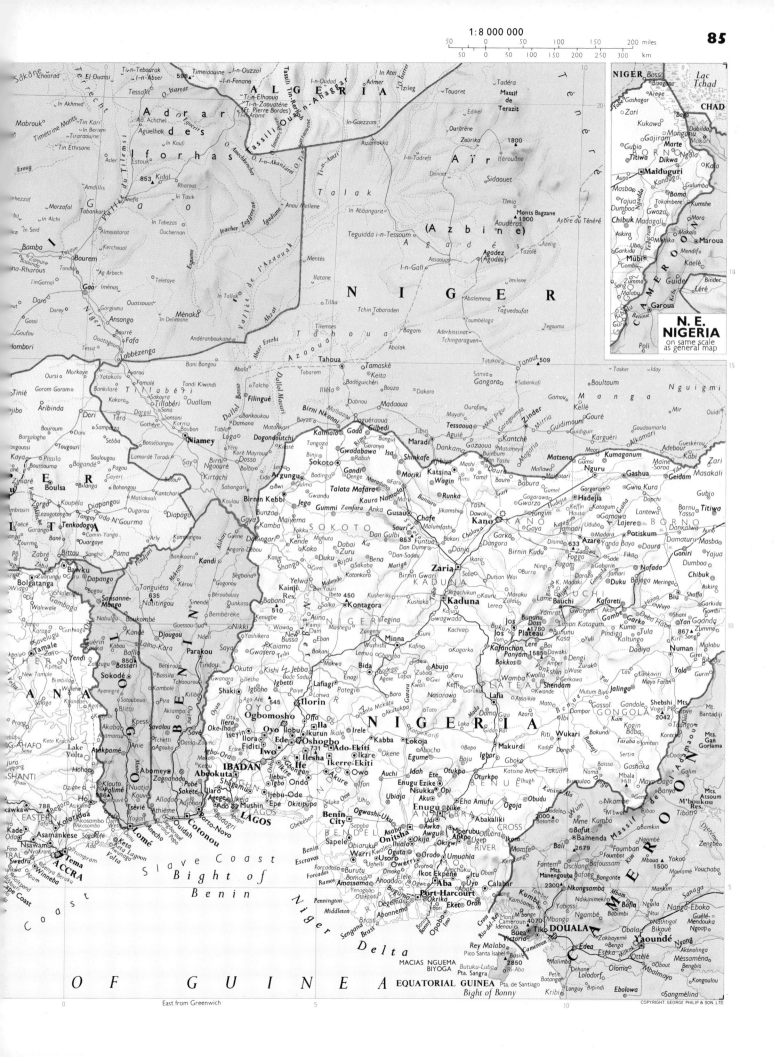

THE NILE DELTA
1:4 000 000

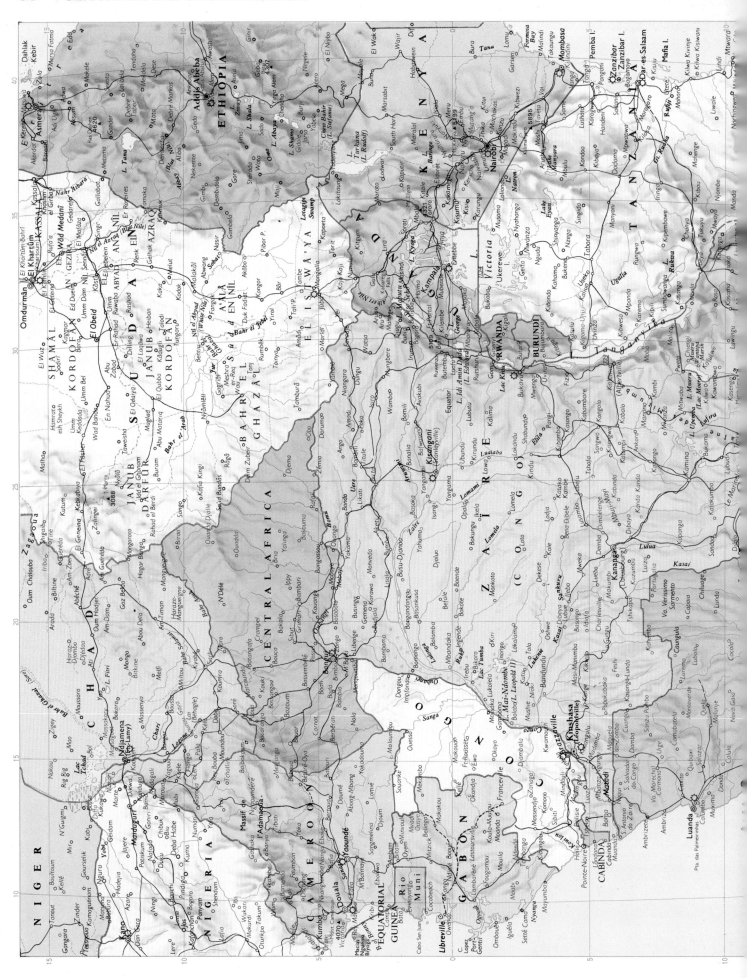

1:15 000 000

100   100   200   300   400 miles
100   0   100   200   300   400   500   600 km

INDIAN

OCEAN

MADAGASCAR

On same scale as General Map

COPYRIGHT GEORGE PHILIP & SON LTD.

Tropic of Capricorn

INDIAN

OCEAN

Bassas da India

Île Europa (Réunion)

Îles Glorieuses (Réunion)

C. St. Sebastien   C. d'Ambre

Diégo-Suárez

Vohémar

Sambava

Antalaha

5349

Montagne d'Ambre 2876

Nosy Mitsio
Nosy Bé
Hell-Ville

Ambilobe

Andapa
Antsohihy

Maroantsetra

Île Ste. Marie

Fénérive

B. de Narinda

Sofia

Analalava

Port-Bergé
Mitsinjo

Mandritsara
Mananara

Mahanoro

Mananjary

B. de la Mahajamba

Mojunga

Soalala

Marovoay

Andriba

Maevatanana

2643

Antananarive (Tananarive)

Brickaville

Tamatave

2658

Ambositra
Antsirabe

Fianarantsoa

Betafo

Mahanoro

Chesterfield

Belo sur Tsiribihina

Besalampy

Juan de Nova (Réunion)

Morafenobe

Maintirano

Malaimbandy

Mahabo

Ankazoabo

Ambalavao

Ihosy

Betroka

Vohipeno
Manakara

Farafangana

Vangaindrano

Morondava

Belo

Manja

Bekodoka

Ranohira

Tuléar

C. St. Vincent
N Morombe

Betioky

Ampanihy

Behara

Androka

Ihombe

N Morombé

Sivary

Fort-Dauphin

C. Ste. Marie

ZAMBIA

Pemba
Memba
Mossuril

Montepuez
Nampula
Mecuburi

Moçambique
Monapo

Nacala
Quinga
Angoche

Marrupa
Ribáuè
Namapa
Macaué

Meconta

Mandimba
Cuamba
Alto Molócuè
Metil

Vila Coutinho
Entre Rios
 Va. da Mogovas
Moma

Vila Cabral (Metangula)
Lichinga

Nametil
Angoche

Lago Niassa (Malawi)

Lilongwe

Zumbo
Furancungo
Muembe

Vila Fontes
Namacurra
Quelimane

Mlanje
3000
Blantyre

Shire

Chiromo
Chinde

Villa Velha

Chemba
Senga

Beira

Tete
Moatize

Nova Sofala

Va. da Barra Falsa

Salisbury

RHODESIA

Cabora Bassa Dam (Zambezi)

Fingoè

Mt. Darwin
Bindura
Gatooma
Marandellas

Umtali
Manica

Chimoio

I. do Bazaruto

Pta. Sao Sebastiao

Massinga

Nova Mambone

Morrumbene

Inhambane

Massangena
Vilanculos

Changane

Chicualacuala

Mabote

Chinhanguanine
Mapinhane

Mavue

Mau-e-ele

Pafuri

Mabalane

Guija

Limpopo

TRANSVAAL

Pretoria
Johannesburg

Maputo (Lourenço Marques)

Bela Vista

SWAZILAND

Nelspruit
Barberton

L. St. Lucia

Richards B.

Pietermaritzburg

NATAL

Durban

LESOTHO

ORANJE-VRYSTAAT (O.F.S.)

Bloemfontein
Kimberley

3482

Port Shepstone

Port St. Johns

TRANSKEI

East London

King William's Town

Port Alfred

CAPE PROVINCE

Great Karoo

Port Elizabeth

C. St. Francis

BOTSWANA

Kalahari

Okavango Swamps

Ngami Depression

Maun

Serowe

Gaborone

Lobatse

Kalahari

Upington

Orange

SOUTH WEST AFRICA (NAMIBIA)

Windhoek

2283

Rehoboth

Keetmanshoop

Lüderitz

Conception B.

Hollams Bird I.

Walvisbaai
Swakopmund

Namib Desert

Damaraland

Namaland

Cape Town (Kaapstad)

Kaap die Goeie Hoop (C. of Good Hope)

Kaap Agulhas

St. Helenabaai

Saldanha

SOUTH AFRICA

ATLANTIC

OCEAN

5283

Tropic of Capricorn

Benguela

Porto Alexandre

Cape Frio

2619

Robert Williams

Cubango

Cuando

Cuito

Owambo

Ondangua

East from Greenwich

Projection: Sanson Flamsteed's Sinusoidal

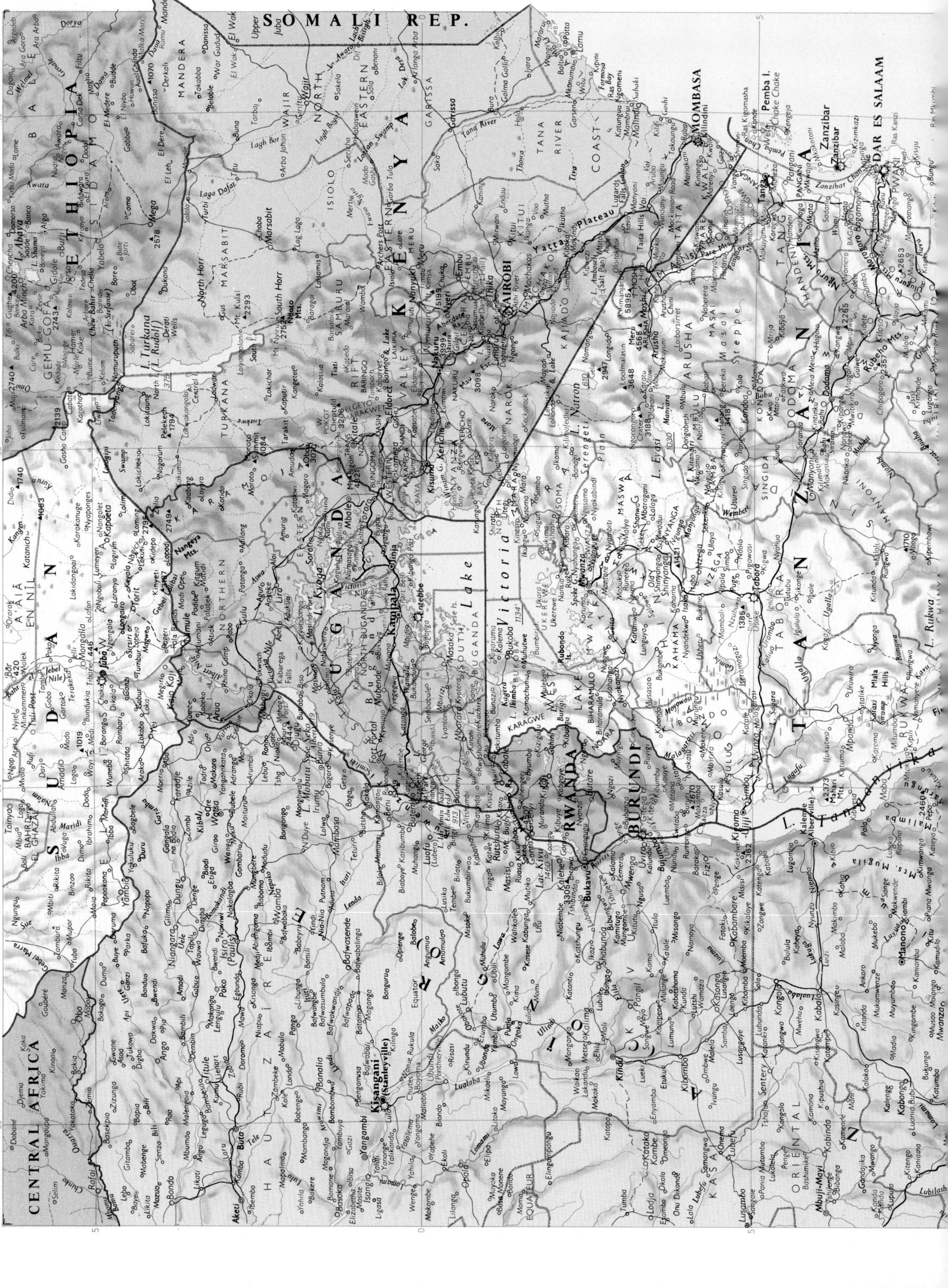

SOMALI REP.
ETHIOPIA
KENYA
UGANDA
TANZANIA
RWANDA
BURUNDI
SUDAN
ZAIRE
CENTRAL AFRICA
MOMBASA
NAIROBI
DAR ES SALAAM
Zanzibar
Pemba I.
Kisangani (Stanleyville)
Kampala
Entebbe
Lake Victoria
L. Turkana (L. Rudolf)
L. Tanganyika
L. Rukwa
L. Kyoga
L. Natron
L. Eyasi
L. Manyara
L. Kivu
Tabora
Kigoma
Bukavu
Kindu
Juba
Moshi
Arusha
Nakuru
Kisumu
Tanga
Marsabit
Garissa
Wajir
Mandera
Lamu
Malindi
Dodoma
Manono
Kabalo
Kalemie (Albertville)
Kongolo
Buta
Aketi
Isiro (Paulis)
Masai Steppe
Serengeti Plain
Tana River
Yatta Plateau

1:8,000,000

50　　　　100　　150　　200 miles
50　0　　100　　200　　300 km

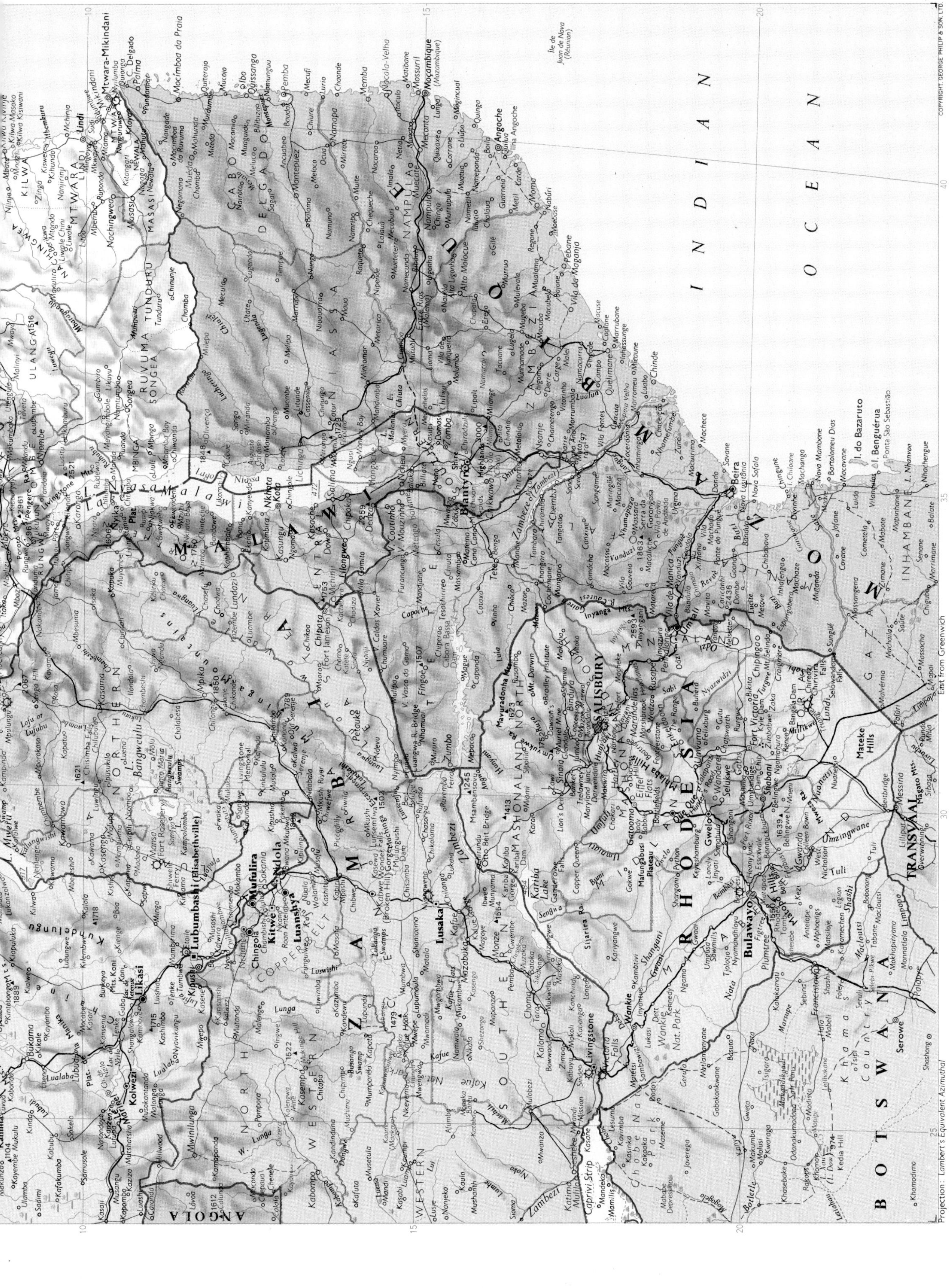

INDIAN OCEAN

MALAWI

ZAMBIA

MOÇAMBIQUE

RHODESIA

BOTSWANA

ANGOLA

TRANSVAAL

TANZANIA

Lake Malawi (Lago Niassa)

Lusaka

Salisbury

Blantyre

Bulawayo

Beira

Lubumbashi (Elisabethville)

Kitwe

Ndola

Livingstone

Kariba Lake

Zambezi

Caprivi Strip

Serowe

Victoria Falls

Wankie

COPPER BELT

Projection: Lambert's Equivalent Azimuthal

COPYRIGHT. GEORGE PHILIP & SON, LTD.

East from Greenwich

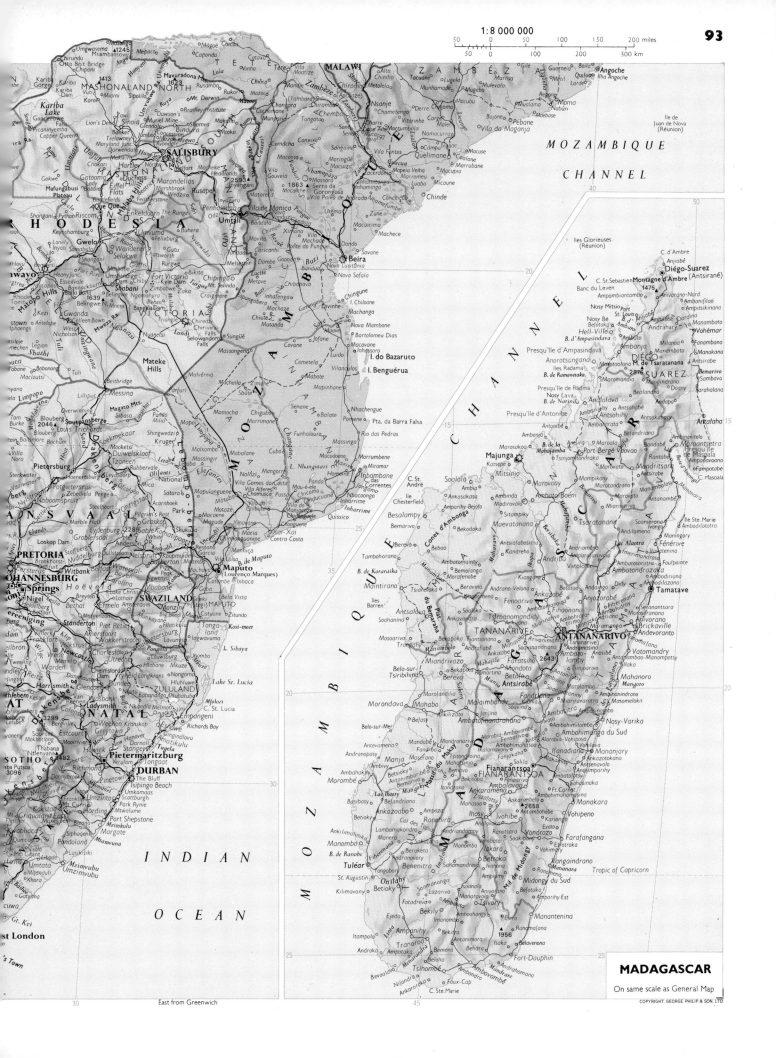

1:8 000 000

50   0   50   100   150   200 miles
50   0   100   200   300 km

MALAWI
ZAMBÉZIA
MOZAMBIQUE

MOZAMBIQUE

CHANNEL

Ile de
Juan de Nova
(Réunion)

MASHONALAND NORTH
Kariba
Lake

SALISBURY
MASHONALAND SOUTH

RHODESIA
Gwelo

VICTORIA
Beira
Nova Sofala

Mateke
Hills
I. do Bazaruto
I. Benguérua

Messina

TRANSVAAL
PRETORIA
JOHANNESBURG
Springs
Maputo
(Lourenço Marques)
SWAZILAND
Manzini

Pietersburg

NATAL
Pietermaritzburg
DURBAN
The Bluff

INDIAN

OCEAN

East London

Iles Glorieuses
(Réunion)

C. d'Ambre
Anjiabé
Diégo-Suarez
Montagne d'Ambre (Antsiranè)
1475

Nosy Mitsio
Nosy Bé
Hell-Ville
DIEGO-
SUAREZ
2876

Majunga

M

A

D

A

G

A

S

C

A

R

Ile Ste. Marie

TANANARIVE
ANTANANARIVO
(Tananarive)
2643
Antsirabé
Tamatave
Brickaville

FIANARANTSOA
Fianarantsoa

Tuléar

Tropic of Capricorn

1956

Fort-Dauphin
C. Ste. Marie

MOZAMBIQUE CHANNEL

30   East from Greenwich   45

MADAGASCAR

On same scale as General Map

COPYRIGHT. GEORGE PHILIP & SON. LTD.

Leningrad
Moskva
Sverdlovsk
Omsk
Tomsk
Okhotsk
Sea of Okhotsk
Kamchatka
Komandorskie Is. (U.S.S.R.)
Petropavlovsk
Near I. 7822
Aleutian Is.
Aleutian Trench

Novosibirsk
Barnaul
Yenisey
Irkutsk
Ozero Baykal
Chita
Ulan Ude
Blagoveshchensk
Amur
Khabarovsk
Sakhalin
Kuril Is.
10,542
Kuril Trench
Yokohama
Vancouver 4280
Emperor Seamount Chain
3389

Volga
Semipalatinsk
Karaganda
L. Balkhash
Hovd
Ulyasutay
Ulanbaatar
MONGOLIA
Manchuria
Harbin
Changchun
Vladivostok
Hakodate
La Perouse Strait
OYA SIWO
Kuril Trench
KURO SIWO
7168

Aral Sea
Alma Ata
Wulumuchi
SINKIANG-UIGUR
Lop Nor
Shenyang
Antung
KOREA
Sendai
JAPAN
TOKYO
8411
Midway Is. (U.S.)

Tashkent
Samarkand
Peiping
Tientsin
Lu-ta
Tsinan
Seoul S.
Pusan
Kyoto
Yokohama
Fuji-san 3776
Nagoya
Japan Trench
10,554

AFGHANISTAN
Srinagar
Kabul
Lahore
PAKISTAN
TIBET
Lanchow
Sian
CHINA
Tsingtao
Yellow Sea
Nanking
Kitakyushu
Nagasaki
SHANGHAI
Kyushu
Shikoku
South Honshu Ridge
Bonin Is.
Volcano Is.
6603

Mt. Everest 8848
Lhasa
Chungking
Wuhan
Hangchow
1066
Wenchow
East China Sea
Ryukyu Is.
KURO SIWO
Marcus I.

Delhi
Agra
NEPAL
Kanpur
Varanasi
Brahmaputra
Myitkyina
Kunming
Changsha
Foochow
Hsiamen
Taipei
Mariana Is. U.S. Trust Terr.
Wake I. (U.S.)
Necker Rid

INDIA
Calcutta
BANGLA-DESH
Chittagong
Mandalay
BURMA
Kwangchow
MACAU (Port.)
HONG KONG
Taiwan (Formosa)
Mariana Trench
Guam (U.S.)
NORTH
EQUATO
P A

Hyderabad
Cuttack
Bay of Bengal
Hanoi
Hainan
C. Engano
11,022
Mi
Bikini Atoll
Marshall Is. U.S. Trust Terr.

Madras
THAILAND (SIAM)
Bangkok
Rangoon
Manila
PHILIPPINES
Samar
10,497
Yap
Eniwetok Atoll
cr
o
n
e
s
i
a

Andaman Is.
Mergui Arch.
CAMBODIA
Mindoro
Palawan
Mindanao Trench
Palau Is.
Truk
Ponape
EQUATORIAL
Makin
Jaluit

SRI LANKA
Colombo
Nicobar Is.
1567
Isthmus of Kra
Gulf of Siam
Phnom Penh
Saigon
South China Sea
Sulu Sea
Kinabalu
SABAH
Mindanao
Caroline Islands
U.S. Trust Territory of the Pacific Islands
Me
l
a
n
e
s
Gilbert Is. (U.K.)

Colombo Fremantle 3120
George Town
Kuala Lumpur
MALAYA
Melaka
Natuna
BRUNEI
Labuan
SARAWAK
Celebes Sea
4101
Halmahera
Dampier Strait
Admiralty Is.
Bismarck Arch.
New Ireland
Nauru Is.
Ocean I. (U.K.)
Baker (U.

SINGAPORE
MALAYSIA
Nias
Sunda
Bangka
Palembang
INDONESIA
Borneo
Celebes
Buru
Ceram
5029
Irian Jaya
PAPUA New
Madang
Rabaul
9103
New Britain
Nauru
O

1840
Sumatra
Java Sea
Djakarta
Flores Sea
Banda Sea
Amboina
7440
Aru Is.
NEW GUINEA
Lae
Solomon Islands (U.K.)
TUVALU (Ellice Is.)
SOUTH

Christmas (Austral.)
Cocos (Keeling) Is. (Austral.)
Semarang
Surabaja
Java
Bali
Lombok
Sumbawa
Flores
Timor
Tanimbar Is.
Sumba
Arafura Sea
Torres Strait
Thursday
C. Arnhem
Port Moresby
Honiara
Guadalcanal
9165
Sta. Cruz I. (U.K.)
Rotuma
Funafuti
Wallis Arch.
Futuna (Fr.)
Tok

7450
Java Trench
1772
INDIAN
C. York
Louisiade Arch. (Austral.)
New Hebrides (U.K. & Fr.)
FIJI
Vanua Levu
Viti Levu
Suva
Tong Tren

Darwin
Ashmore Is.
Lacrimah
Wyndham
Cairns
NORTHERN TERRITORY
Newcastle Waters
G. of Carpentaria
Townsville
3772
Coral Sea
Chesterfield Is. (Fr.)
7570
New Caledonia (Fr.)
Loyalty Is. (Fr.)
Noumea
Norfolk I. (Aust.)
Niue (S. (N.Z.)

OCEAN
N.W. Cape
Onslow
AUSTRALIA
Mt. Isa
Alice Springs
Longreach
QUEENSLAND
Rockhampton
Maryborough
Brisbane
Ipswich
TONGA Friendly Is.
10,82

Shark Bay
WESTERN AUSTRALIA
Oodnadatta
L. Eyre
SOUTH AUSTRALIA
Darling
NEW SOUTH WALES
Lord Howe I. (Aust.)
Kermadec Is. (N.Z.)

Geraldton
Kalgoorlie
Perth
Fremantle
Cape Town - Fremantle 5615
Geographe Bay
Great Australian Bight
F. - A. 1353
Adelaide
Katoomba
Sydney
Newcastle
Wollongong
Tasman Sea
Norfolk I.
S - A 1274
Kermadec Trench
10,047

Amsterdam I. (Fr.)
St. Paul I. (Fr.)
Mid Oceanic Ridge
East Indian Rise
Albany
K. George Sd.
VICTORIA
Canberra
Mt. Kosciusko 2230
Ballarat
Geelong
Melbourne
Murray
Encounter Bay
Bass Strait
Launceston
TASMANIA
Hobart
W. 1293
Auckland
Hamilton
NEW ZEALAND
Palmerston N.
Cook Strait
Wellington

Crozet Is. (Fr.)
Mid Indian Ridge
Cape Town - Melbourne 5814
Cape Town - Hobart 5838
Indian Rise
Indian Ridge
Nelson
Mt. Cook 3764
Christchurch
Chatha
Oamaru
Dunedin
Pac

Kerguelen (Fr.)
Indian-Antarctic Ridge
Invercargill
Stewart
Bounty Is. (N
Antipodes Is. (N.

Heard Is. (Aust.)
Auckland Is. (N.Z.)
Macquarie Is. (Austral.)
Campbell I. (N.Z.)

5615 Principal Shipping Routes (Distances in Nautical Miles)

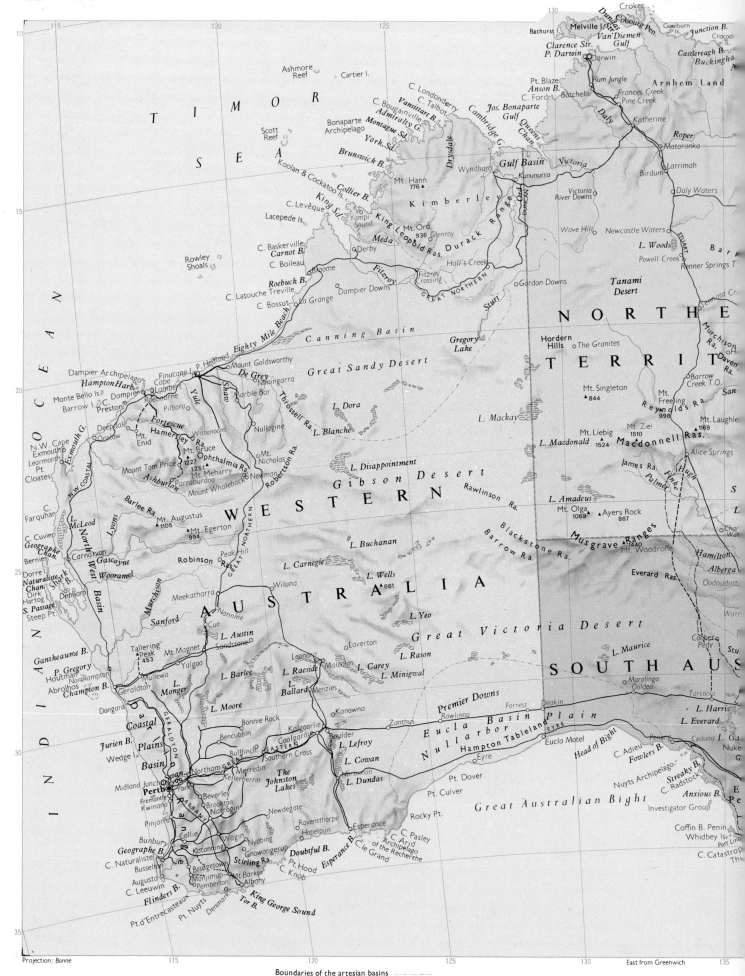

10

TIMOR SEA

Ashmore Reef   · Cartier I.

Scott Reef

Rowley Shoals

15

INDIAN OCEAN

Dampier Archipelago
Monte Bello Is.
Barrow I.
N.W. Cape
Exmouth G.
Learmonth
Pt. Cloates

20

C. Farquhar

C. Cuvier
Geographe Chan.
Bernier
Dorre I.
Naturaliste Chan.
Dirk Hartog
S. Passage
Steep Pt.

25

Gantheaume B.
P. Gregory
Houtman
Abrolhos
Champion B.

Dongara

Jurien B.
Wedge I.

30

Bunbury
Geographe B.
C. Naturaliste
Busselton
Augusta
C. Leeuwin
Flinders B.
Pt. d'Entrecasteaux   Pt. Nuyts   Denmark

35

C. Londonderry   C. Talbot
Vansittart B.
Bonaparte   Montague Sd.
Archipelago   Admiralty G.
York Sd.
Brunswick B.
Koolan & Cockatoo Is.
Collier B.
King Sd.
C. Lévêque
Lacepede Is.
C. Baskerville
Carnot B.
C. Boileau
Roebuck B.   Broome
C. Latouche Treville
C. Bossut   La Grange
Eighty Mile Beach

Cambridge G.
Jos. Bonaparte Gulf
Wyndham
Mt. Hann 776
Kimberley
Mt. Ord 936 Glenroy
King Leopold Ras.   Durack Range
Meda
Derby
Hall's Creek
Fitzroy Crossing
Dampier Downs
GREAT NORTHERN
Fitzroy   Sturt
Gordon Downs

Croker
Bathurst I.
Melville I.
Clarence Str.
P. Darwin   Darwin
Pt. Blaze
Anson B.
C. Ford
Rum Jungle
Cobourg Pen.
Goulburn Is.
Junction B.
Van Diemen Gulf
Castlereagh B.
Buckingha
Arnhem Land
Frances Creek
Pine Creek
Batchelor
Katherine
Roper
Mataranka
Larrimah
Birdum
Daly Waters
Victoria River Downs
Kununurra
Wave Hill   Newcastle Waters
L. Woods
Powell Creek   Renner Springs
Tanami Desert
NORTHE
TERRIT
Murchison Ra.   Daven Ra.
Barrow Creek T.O.   San
Tennant Cr

P. Hedland   Mount Goldsworthy
Finucane I.
Cape Lambert
Dampier   Roebourne
Hampton Harb.
Preston
De Grey
Nimingarra
Marble Bar
Yule   Shaw
Pilbara
Throssell Ra.   L. Blanche
Nullagine
Mt. Nicholas
Robertson Ra.
L. Dora

Great Sandy Desert

Canning Basin

Gregory Lake

Hordern Hills   The Granites

Mt. Singleton 844
Mt. Freeling 998
Reynolds Ra.
Mt. Laughle

Deepdale   Onslow
Fortescue
Hamersley Ra.
Mt. Enid
Wittenoom
Mount Tom Price 1227
Ophthalmia Ra.
1251   Mt. Bruce
Ashburton   Parraburdoo
Mt. Meharry
Mount Whaleback   Newman

L. Disappointment

L. Mackay

Mt. Liebig 1510
Mt. Ziel 1524   Macdonnell Ras.
L. Macdonald
James Ra.
Hugh   Alice Springs
Finke
Palmer
Char
Wat

Barlee Ra.
Mt. Augustus 1105
L. McLeod
North West Basin
Carnarvon
Gascoyne
Wooramel
Shark Basin
Denham

WESTERN

Gibson Desert

Rawlinson Ra.
L. Amadeus
Mt. Olga 1069   Ayers Rock 867
Blackstone Ra.
Barrow Ra.
Musgrave Ranges
Mt. Woodroffe 1440
Everard Ras.
Hamilton
Alberga
Oodnadatta
Warr

Mt. Egerton 994
Robinson
Peak Hill
Ras.   GREAT NORTHERN
L. Buchanan
L. Carnegie
L. Wells 661
L. Yeo
Great Victoria Desert

Coober Pedy
L. Maurice

SOUTH AUS

Murchison
Meekatharra
Sanford
Nannine
Cue
L. Austin
Sandstone
Wiluna
Laverton
L. Rason
L. Mingwal
Maralinga
Ooldea
Tarcoola
L. Harris
L. Everard

AUSTRALIA

Tallering Peak 453
Mt. Magnet
Yalgoo
Mullewa
Geraldton
L. Monger
L. Barlee
Leonora
Malcolm
Menzies
L. Raeside
L. Ballard
L. Carey

Premier Downs
Forrest
Rawlinna
Deakin

Coastal Plains Basin

Bonnie Rock
L. Moore
Kanowna
Kalgoorlie
Coolgardie
Boulder
Zanthus
Eucla Basin
Nullarbor Plain
Hampton Tableland
Eyre
Eucla Motel
Penong
Ceduna
Nuke
L. Ga

Perth
Fremantle
Kwinana
Midland Junction
Swan
Northam   York
Merredin
Kellerberrin
Beverley
Brookton
Narrogin
Bencubbin
Bullfinch
Southern Cross
The Johnston Lakes
Norseman
L. Cowan
L. Lefroy
L. Dundas

Pt. Dover
Pt. Culver
Rocky Pt.
Head of Bight
C. Adieu   Fowlers B.
Nuyts Archipelago
C. Radstock
Anxious B.
Pe

Pinjarra
Collie
Wagin
Nyabing
Newdegate
Ravensthorpe
Hopetoun
Esperance
C. Pasley
C. Arid
Archipelago of the Recherche
C. le Grand
Great Australian Bight
Investigator Group
Coffin B. Penin
Whidbey Is.
Port Lin
C. Catastrop

Bridgetown
Katanning
Gnowangerup
Pt. Hood
Doubtful B.
Esperance B.
C. le Grand

Manjimup   Pemberton
Mt. Barker
Stirling Ra.
C. Knob

Albany
King George Sound   Tor B.

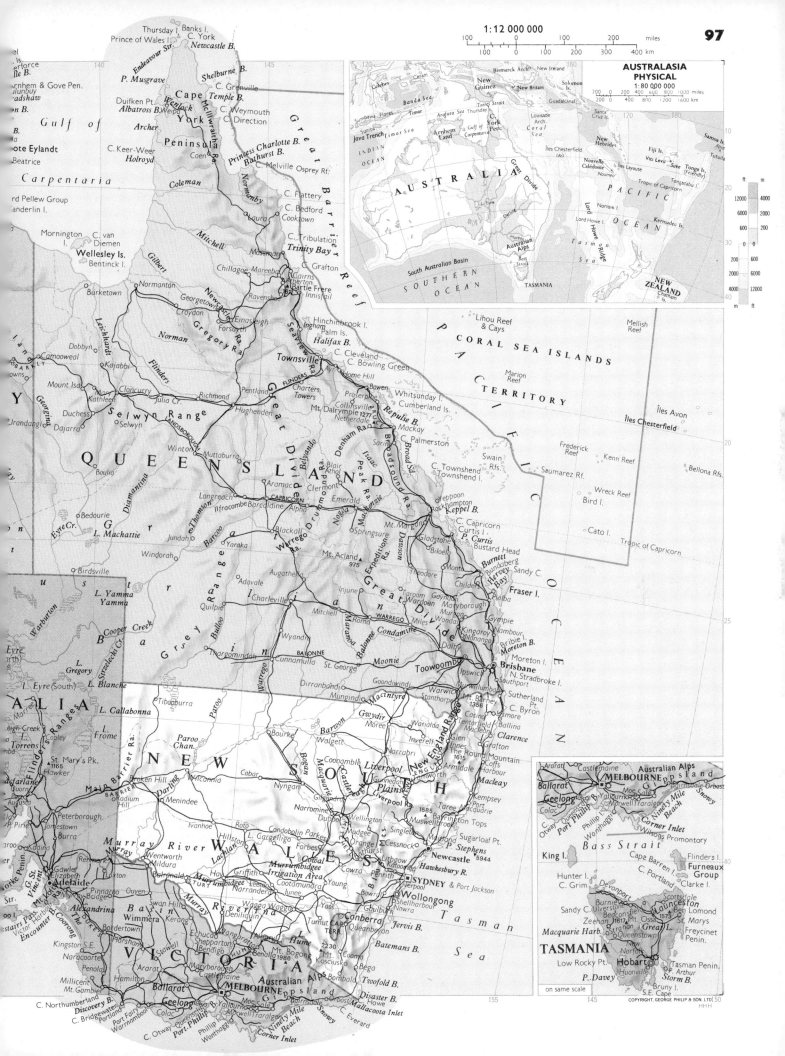

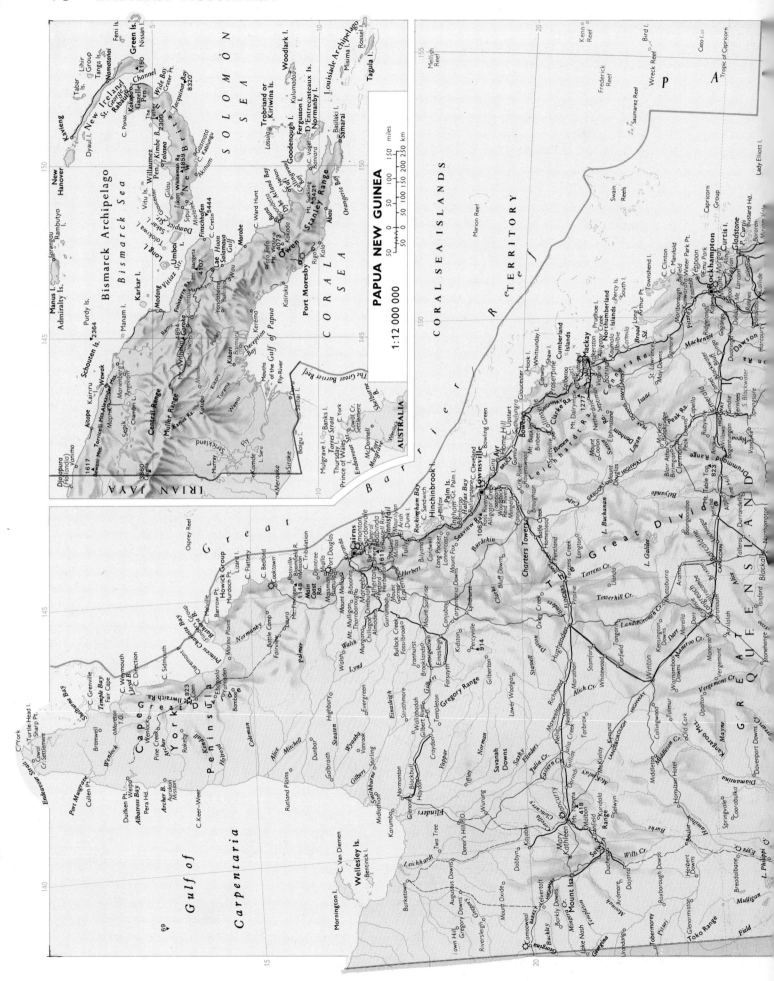

PAPUA NEW GUINEA
1:12 000 000

miles
50   100   150
0
50   100   150   200   250 km

1:7 500 000

50   0   50   100   150   200 miles
50   0   50   100   150   200   250   300 km

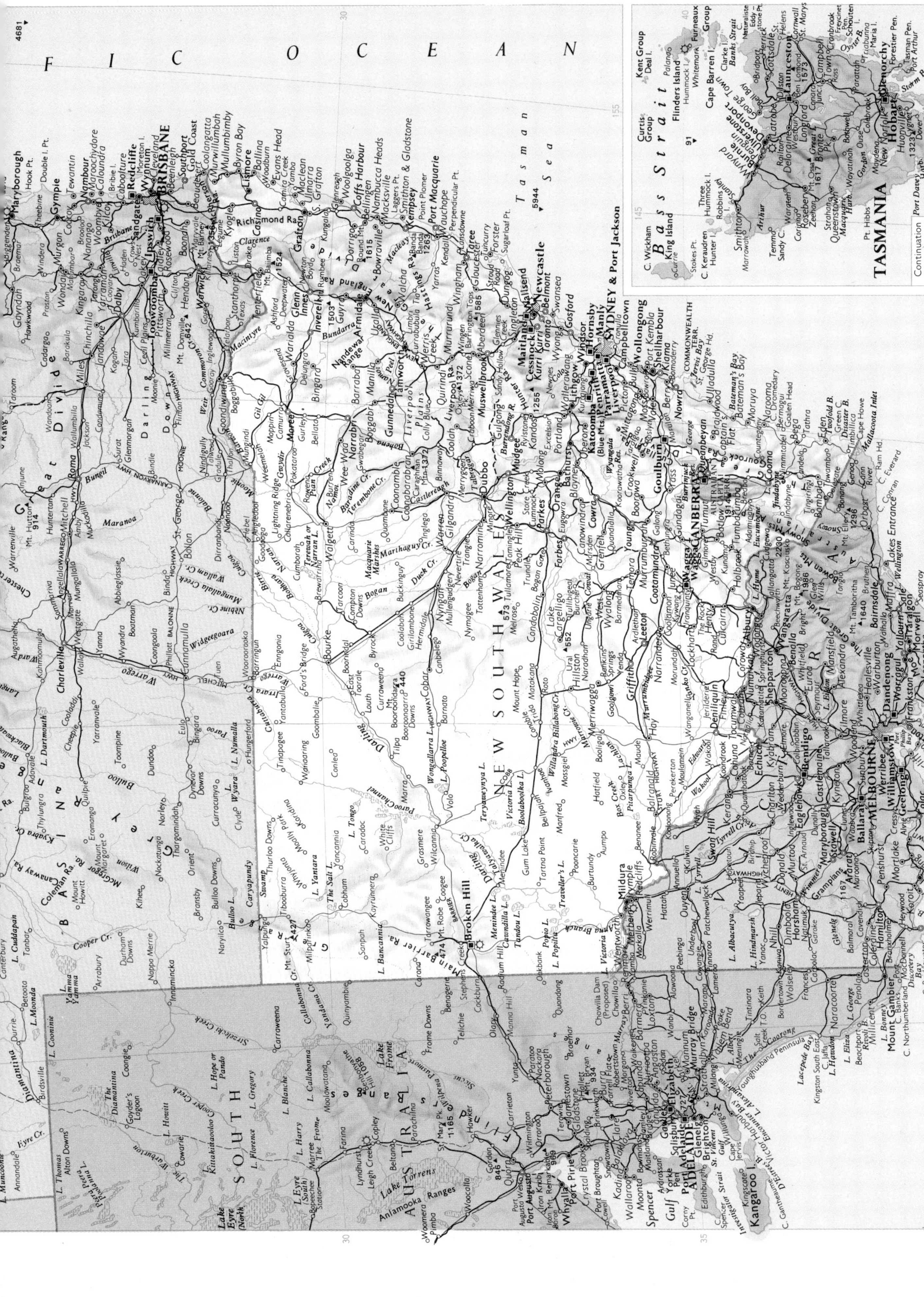

PACIFIC OCEAN

TASMANIA

Continuation
Southwards

Bass Strait

Kent Group
Flinders Island
King Island

Launceston
Devonport
Burnie
Hobart

QUEENSLAND

Maryborough
Gympie
Nambour
Redcliffe
BRISBANE
Ipswich
Toowoomba
Warwick
Southport
Gold Coast

Roma
Charleville
Cunnamulla

NEW SOUTH WALES

Lismore
Grafton
Coffs Harbour
Armidale
Tamworth
Port Macquarie
Taree
Newcastle
Maitland
Cessnock
Gosford
SYDNEY & Port Jackson
Wollongong
Katoomba
Blue Mts.
Lithgow
Bathurst
Orange
Parkes
Dubbo
Forbes
Goulburn
CANBERRA
Bourke
Broken Hill
Cobar
Griffith
Wagga Wagga
Albury
Cooma

SOUTH AUSTRALIA

Port Augusta
Port Pirie
Whyalla
ADELAIDE
Murray Bridge
Mount Gambier
Kangaroo I.
Lake Eyre
Lake Torrens
Lake Frome
Flinders Ranges
Spencer Gulf
Gulf St. Vincent

VICTORIA

Mildura
Swan Hill
Echuca
Bendigo
Ballarat
Geelong
MELBOURNE
Dandenong
Warrnambool
Hamilton
Horsham
Shepparton
Wangaratta
Wodonga
Bairnsdale
Sale
Morwell
Wilsons Promontory

Darling R.
Murray R.
Murrumbidgee R.
Lachlan R.
Macquarie R.
Great Dividing Range

Tasman Sea

Projection: Bonne

COPYRIGHT. GEORGE PHILIP & SON, LTD.

East from Greenwich

1:4 500 000

20   0   20   40   60   80   100 miles
20   0   40   80   120   160 km

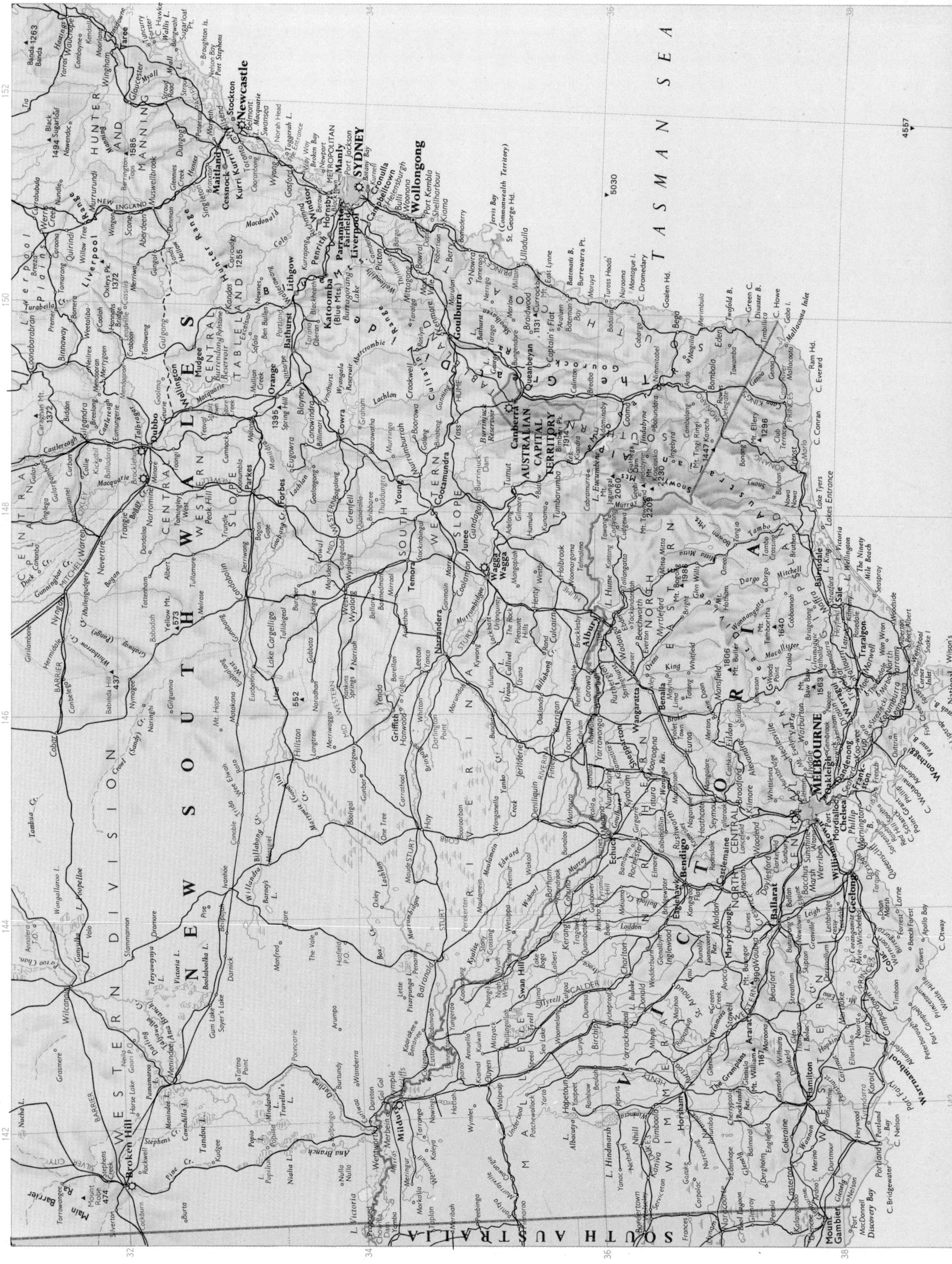

T A S M A N   S E A

SYDNEY
Newcastle
Wollongong
Canberra
MELBOURNE

NEW SOUTH WALES

VICTORIA

SOUTH AUSTRALIA

AUSTRALIAN CAPITAL TERRITORY

WESTERN DIVISION

CENTRAL DIVISION

HUNTER AND MANNING

NEW ENGLAND

CENTRAL TABLELAND

WESTERN SLOPE

SOUTH WESTERN SLOPE

RIVERINA

Projection: Albers' Equal Area with two standard parallels

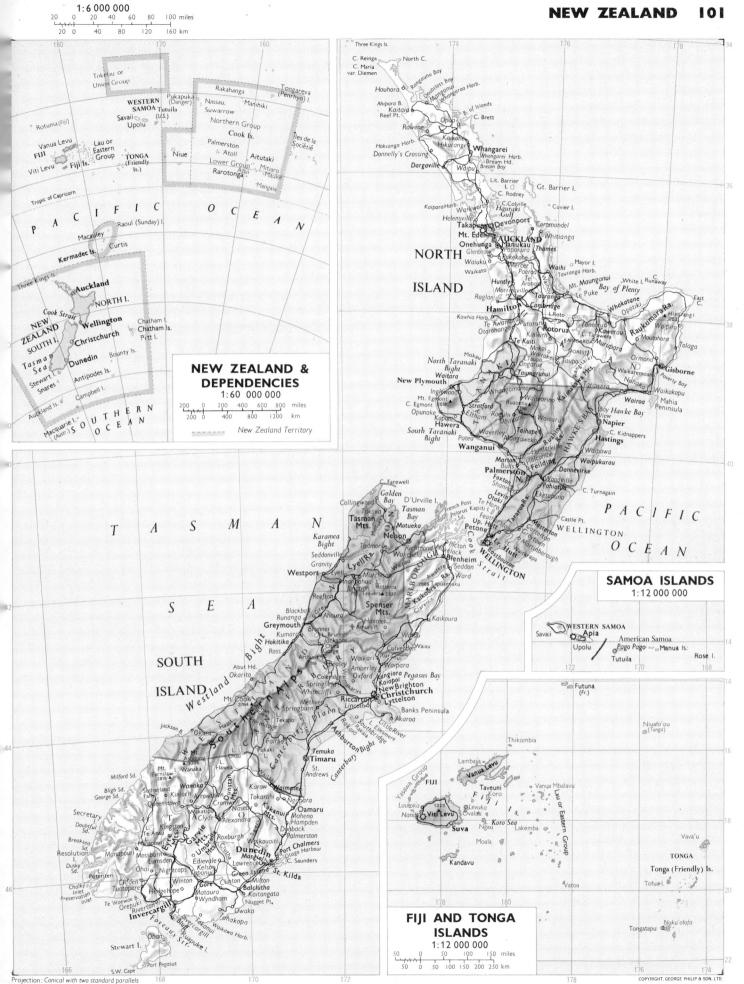

Tropic of Cancer

Bahama Islands

Milwaukee 9200
Puerto Rico
Hispaniola
Port-au-Prince
Venezuelan Basin
G. of Venezuela
Orinoco
Purus
Juruá
Bolivian Plateau
Nevado Ancohuma 6550
L. Titicaca
La Paz

Florida Strait
Cuba
Jamaica
Greater Antilles
Antilles Sea
Colombian Basin
Caribbean
Sierra de Mérida
Maracaibo
Bogotá
Cordillera Oriental
Cordillera Central
Cordillera Occidental
Napo
Putumayo
Marañón
Ucayali

La Habana
C. Sable
Yucatán Strait
Yucatán Basin
Trough
Cayman Trough 7680
C. Gracias a Dios
Cosa
S. de 5800
Sa. Nevada de Sta. Marta
G. of Darién
G. of Panamá
Panamá Canal
Panamá

A   n   d   e   s
Trench
Peru Trench
Chile
Chincha Is.
Pta. Parinas
Pta. Aguja
Lobos Is.
Lima
Quito Cotopaxi 5897
Chimborazo 6267
C. de San Francisco
G. de Guayaquil

Gulf of Mexico
M   e   x   i   c   o
C. Catoche
Yucatán Peninsula
Gulf of Campeche
Gulf of Honduras
Guatemala
3837
Guatemala Trench 6662
Isthmus of Tehuantepec
G. of Tehuantepec

Delta
Rio Grande del Norte
Monterrey
Eastern Sierra Madre
México Orizaba 5700
Puebla
Popocatépetl 5452
Guadalajara
Mexican Plateau
stern Sierra Madre
Santos
C. Corrientes

Galapagos

Gulf of California
California
C. San Lucas
Revilla Gigedo Is.

O   C   E   A   N

Clarion Fracture Zone

Tropic of Capricorn

ARCTIC OCEAN

GREENLAND
(Denmark)

Denmark Str.
Davis Strait
Baffin Island
Ellesmere I.
Queen Elizabeth Islands
Parry Is.
Lancaster Sd.
Banks I.
Victoria I.
Melville I.
Prince of Wales I.
Hudson Strait

Iceland
Liverpool 2956
Labrador

ATLANTIC
Tropic of Cancer
Bermuda (Br.)
Hatteras 1972

C   A   N   A   D   A
Hudson Bay
Churchill
Nelson
Gt. Slave L.
Gt. Bear L.
Mackenzie
Athabasca L.
Edmonton
Calgary
Lethbridge
Medicine Hat
Regina
Winnipeg
Moose Jaw
Saskatoon
St. Paul
Minneapolis
Milwaukee
Chicago
Cincinnati
Detroit
Pittsburgh
Buffalo
Toronto
Ottawa
Montréal
Québec
St. John's
Halifax
Boston
New York
Philadelphia
Baltimore
Washington

U   N   I   T   E   D   S   T   A   T   E   S
Memphis
Atlanta
New Orleans
Florida
Miami
Gulf of Mexico
Galveston
Houston
Dallas
Red
Kansas City
St. Louis
Denver
Platte
Omaha
Missouri
Snake
Salt Lake City
Gt. Salt L.
El Paso
San Francisco
Oakland
Los Angeles
Baja California

ALASKA
(U.S.)
Anchorage
Skagway
Dawson
Yukon
Fraser
Victoria
Vancouver
Seattle
Spokane
Portland
Prince Rupert
Queen Charlotte Is.

Bering Sea
Aleutian Is. (U.S.)

Honolulu 2088
Yokohama 4710

CUBA
La Habana
BAHAMAS
HAITI REP.
PUERTO RICO (U.S.)
JAMAICA
Kingston
Caribbean Sea
BELIZE
GUATEMALA
HONDURAS
EL SALVADOR
NICARAGUA
COSTA RICA
PANAMÁ
CENTRAL AMERICA

M   E   X   I   C   O
Monterrey
México
Guadalajara 5138
Acapulco
Veracruz
Tampico
Mérida
Yucatán Strait
Revilla Gigedo (Mex.)

SOUTH AMERICA
VENEZUELA
COLOMBIA
Caracas
Maracaibo
Cartagena
Barranquilla
Bogotá
Guadeloupe
Martinique (Fr.)
TRINIDAD & TOBAGO
Valparaíso 5138

West from 90 Greenwich

P   A   C   I   F   I   C   O   C   E   A   N

m ft
4000 12 000
3000 9000
2000 6000
1500 4500
1000 3000
400 1200
200 600
0
600 2000
1200 4000
2000 6000
4000 12 000
6000 18 000
8000 24 000
ft m

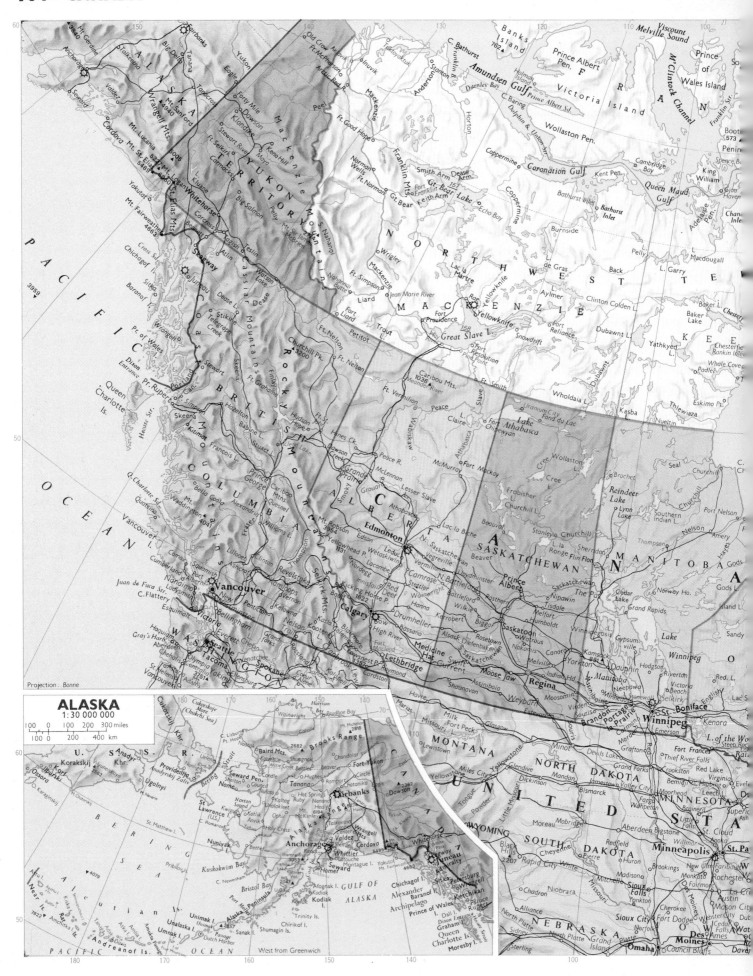

Projection: Bonne

ALASKA
1:30 000 000

100 0   100 200   300 miles
100 0   200   400 km

West from Greenwich

1:15 000 000

100 50 0 100 200 300 400 miles
100 0 100 200 300 400 500 600 km

Baffin Bay

ncaster Sound
on Island
deur
nsula
Arctic Bay
1890
Bylot I.
Pond Inlet
Pond Inlet
Milne
Inlet
Scott I.
Clyde
C. Hewett
2136

Svartenhuk
Halvø
Disko
Disko
B.
Christianshåb
Holsteinsborg
Søndre Strømfjord
Angmagssalik

GREENLAND
Kong Frederik VI's Kyst
2850
Sukkertoppen
Godthåb
Frederikshåb
Ivigtut
Frederiksdal
Juliánehåb
Nanortalik
Kap Farvel

ATLANTIC
OCEAN

Home B.
Broughton
Island
Padloping Island
C. Dyer
Cape
Dyer
Cumberland
Peninsula
Pangnirtung
Hoare B.
C. Mercy
Cumberland Sd.

Davis Strait

Igloolik
Island
Fury & Hecla Str.
Hall
Lake
Melville
Peninsula
Prince
Charles
I.
2591

Committee B.
Foxe
Basin
Nettilling
L.

ORIES
TIN

Frobisher
Bay
Amadjuak
Cape Dorset
L. Harbour
Frobisher Bay
Resolution I.

Wager
W.
B.
Repulse
Bay
oBay
Foxe
Channel
C. Dorchester
Foxe
Penin.
Amadjuak
L.

Isthmus
Southampton
I.
Coral Harbour
Ross Welcome Sd.
Digges Is.
Ivugivik
(Notre-Dame
d'Ivugivic)
Sagiouc
(Sugluk)
Koartac
(Notre Dame
de Koartac)
Maricourt
(Wakeham
Bay)
Bellin
Payne Bay)
Payne
C. Chidley
3809

Hudson Strait

Coats
I.
Mansel
I.
Akpatok
I.
Ungava Bay
Port Nouveau-Québec
(George R.)
1676
Hebron
Nutak

udson
Ottawa Is.
257
Ungava
Peninsula
Payne L.
Leaf
Koksoak
Ft. Chimo
George
Whale
Nain

Bay

Portland
Promontory
Inoucdjouac
(Port Harrison)
L. Minto
Larch
Kaniapiskau
Hopedale
C. Harrison
Indian Harbour
Rigolet
L. Melville
Cartwright

Sleeper Is.
King
George Is.
Lower Seal L.
NEWFOUND
LABRADOR
Michikamau
L.
Goose
Bay
North West
R.
Battle Harb.
Belle Isle

King George Is.
Baker's
Dozen
Clearwater
Scheffervile
Petitsikapau
L.
Lobstick
L.
Churchill
Falls
Churchill
Notre Dame B.
Twillingate
Gander
Bonavista
Trinity B.

Belcher
Is.
C. Henrietta
Maria
Gr.Whale
Poste de
la Baleine
(Great Whale River)
Fort George
Lac Bienville
Ashuanipi
L.
Wabush City
Notashquan
St. Augustin
Romaine
Lewisporte
Carbonear
Bell I.
St. John's

Winisk
D
C. Jones
Ft. George
Fort George
1128
Gagnon
Mingan
Anticosti
I.
Millertown
814
Grand
Falls
Harbour Grace
Placentia
Trepassey

Severn
ARIO
Akimiski
I.
Nouveau Comptoir
(Paint Hills)
East Main
Eastmain
L. Albanel
Moisie
Sept Îles
NEWFOUNDLAND
Corner Brook's
Ch. aux Basques
Placentia B.
C. Race

Big
rout L.
Attawapiskat
James Bay
Charlton I.
Fort Rupert
(Rupert
House)
Rupert R.
Mistassini
Moisie
Port Cartier

Joseph
Ft. Albany
Albany
Nottaway
L. Albanel
Chibougamau
Peribonca
Baie Comeau
Betsiamites
C. Gaspé
Gulf of
St. Lawrence
Magdalen Is.
Cabot St.
C. Breton I.
ST. PIERRE
et MIQUELON
(Fr.)

any
Moosonee
Missinaibi
Dolbeau
St. John
Saguenay
Matane
Gaspé
Gaspé Pen.
Campbellton
PR. EDWARD I.
C. North
Sydney
Port Hawkesbury
Sable I.
(Nova Scotia)

Nakina
Kenogami
Cochrane
L. Abitibi
Gouin
Reservoir
Senneterre
Doucet
Roberval
Jonquière
Chicoutimi
1150
Tadoussac
Rimouski
Rivière
du Loup
Summerside
Charlottetown
Northumberland Str.
New Glasgow
6309

Thunder Bay
(Pt. Arthur)
Longlac
Heron Bay
Oba
Timmins
Norand
Rouyn
Weymont
La Tuque
St. Léonard
Newcastle
Chatham
Bathurst
Pictou
C. Canso

Franz
Haileybury
Timiskaming
Kirkland
Lake
Val d'Or
Shawinigan
Québec
Lévis
Thetford Mines
Edmundston
NEW
BRUNSWICK
Moncton
Amherst
Springhill
NOVA
Truro
Windsor
Dartmouth

Michipicoten
Cobalt
Cabonga
Reservoir
Trois Rivières
Sorel
St. Hyacinthe
Woodstock
Fredericton
Kentville
Halifax

Calumet
Keweenaw
Bay
Sault Ste. Marie
Sudbury
Copper Cliff
North
Bay
Ottawa
Hull
Joliette
MONTRÉAL
Lachine
Sherbrooke
MAINE
Saint
John
B. of Fundy
Digby
Bridgewater

Sault Ste. Marie
North Chan.
Parry
Sound
Pembroke
Arnprior
Ottawa
Cornwall
L. Champlain
1917
Bangor
Liverpool
C. Sable

Manistique
Georgian
Bay
Belleville
Kingston
Burlington
VERMONT
NEW
HAMPSHIRE
Portland
Lewiston
Shelburne
Yarmouth

Cheboygan
Owen Sound
Orillia
Watertown
Glens Falls
Concord
Manchester
C. Sable

Traverse
City
Lake
Huron
Oshawa
Cobourg
L. Ontario
Rochester
Utica
Albany
Lowell
Boston
C. Cod

Cadillac
Saginaw
Green
TORONTO
Guelph
Niagara
Falls
Syracuse
Worcester
Springfield
Providence

Ludington
Manitowoc
Muskegon
Kitchener
Brantford
Buffalo
NEW YORK
Elmira
Binghamton
Waterbury
New Haven

Milwaukee
Racine
Grand
Rapids
London
Hamilton
Jamestown
Williamsport
Scranton
Newark
NEW YORK

Kenosha
Kalamazoo
Windsor
Erie
PENNSYLVANIA
Allentown
Reading
Trenton
NEW JERSEY

CHICAGO
Gary
Evanston
DETROIT
Toledo
Cleveland
Akron
Youngstown
Sey City

NOIS
INDIANA
South Bend
OHIO

West from Greenwich
COPYRIGHT. GEORGE PHILIP & SON. LTD.

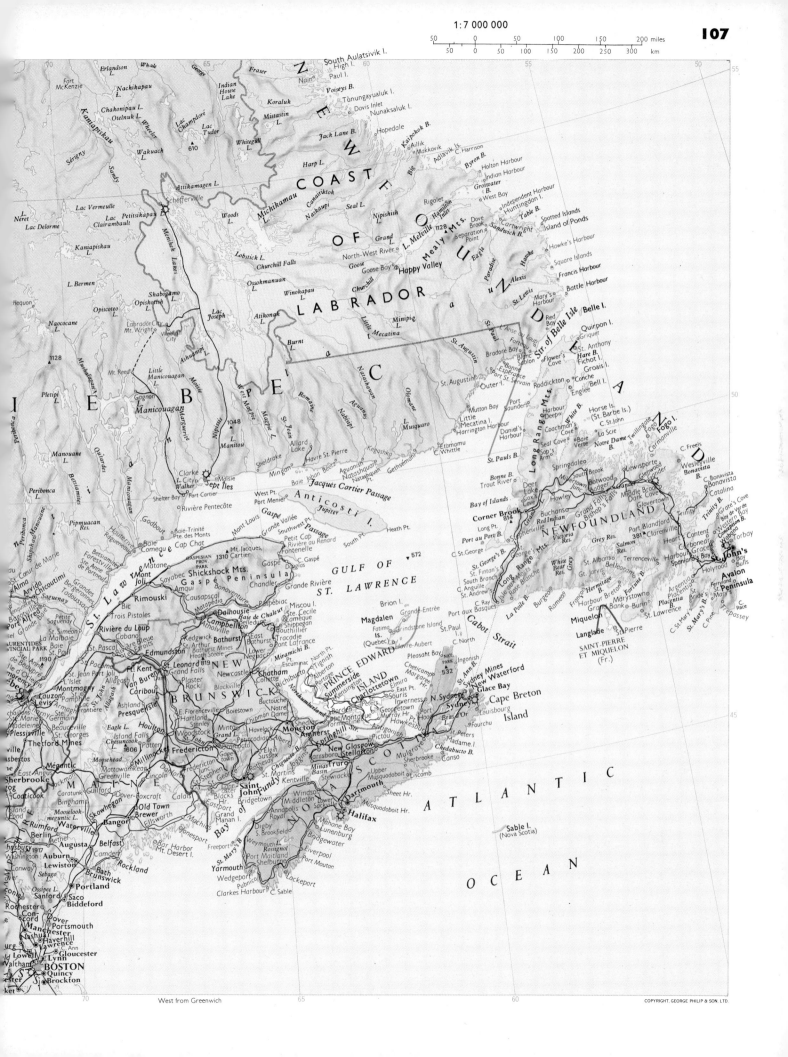

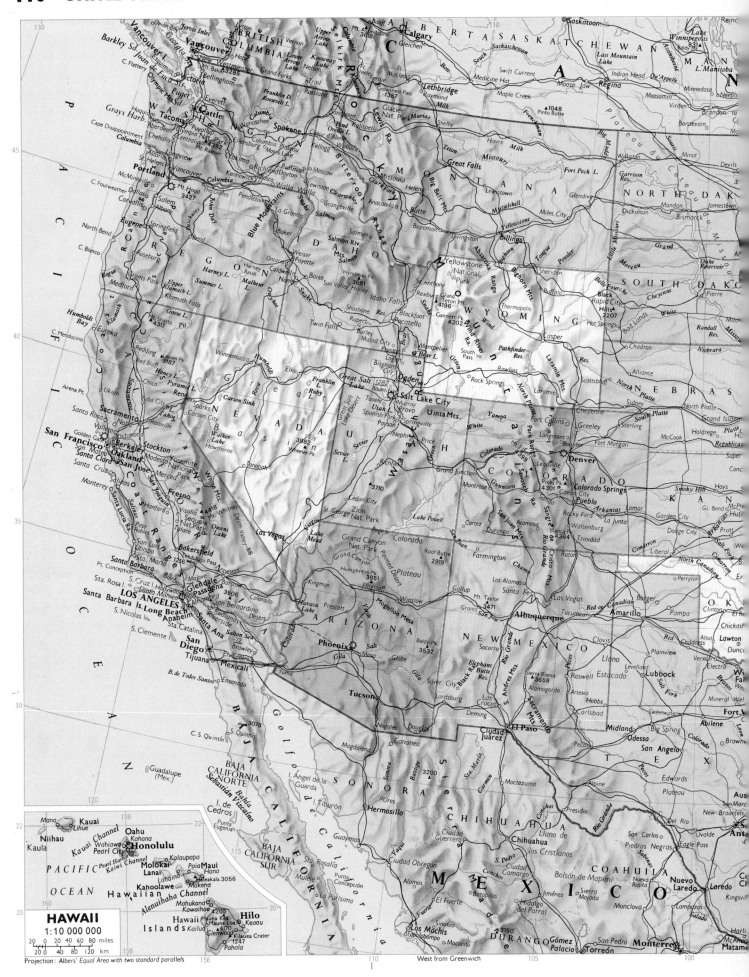

HAWAII
1:10 000 000
20 0 20 40 60 80 miles
20 0 20 40 60 80 120 km

Projection : Albers' Equal Area with two standard parallels

West from Greenwich

C A N A D A

QUEBEC

MAINE

NEW BRUNSWICK

MONTREAL

Ottawa

TORONTO

Lake Superior

MINNESOTA

Duluth

WISCONSIN

Minneapolis · St. Paul

Milwaukee

CHICAGO

DETROIT

Lake Michigan · Lake Huron · Lake Erie · Lake Ontario

IOWA

Des Moines

ILLINOIS

INDIANA

OHIO

Cleveland · Akron

PENNSYLVANIA

Pittsburgh

NEW YORK

Buffalo

Boston

MASS.

NEW YORK

PHILADELPHIA

NEW JERSEY

Baltimore

Washington D.C.

MISSOURI

Kansas City

St. Louis

KENTUCKY

WEST VIRGINIA

Richmond

VIRGINIA

Norfolk

Cincinnati

Louisville

Indianapolis

TENNESSEE

Nashville · Knoxville

NORTH CAROLINA

Charlotte · Raleigh

OKLAHOMA

Tulsa

ARKANSAS

Little Rock

Memphis

Atlanta

ALABAMA · MISSISSIPPI

GEORGIA

SOUTH CAROLINA

Charleston

Birmingham · Montgomery

Savannah

Jacksonville

LOUISIANA

Shreveport · Baton Rouge

New Orleans

Houston · Galveston

Mobile · Pensacola

FLORIDA

Tampa · Orlando

Miami

GULF OF MEXICO

BAHAMAS

ATLANTIC OCEAN

Florida Keys · Key West

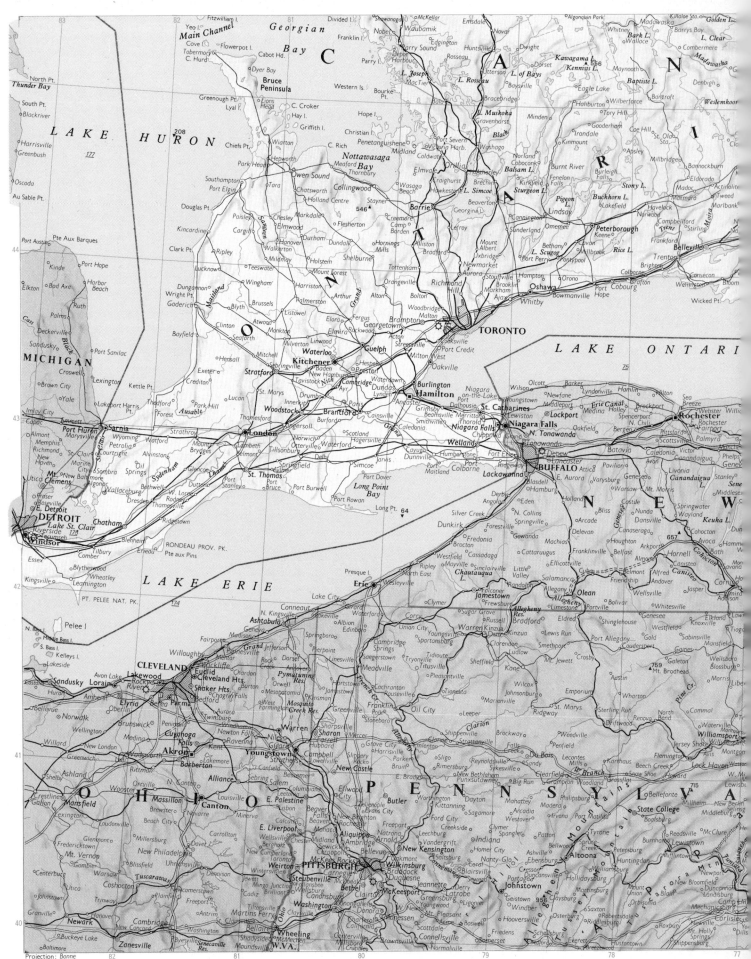

===== Interstate Highways (U.S.A.), Superhighways (Canada)

==== Interstate Highways and Superhighways under Construction

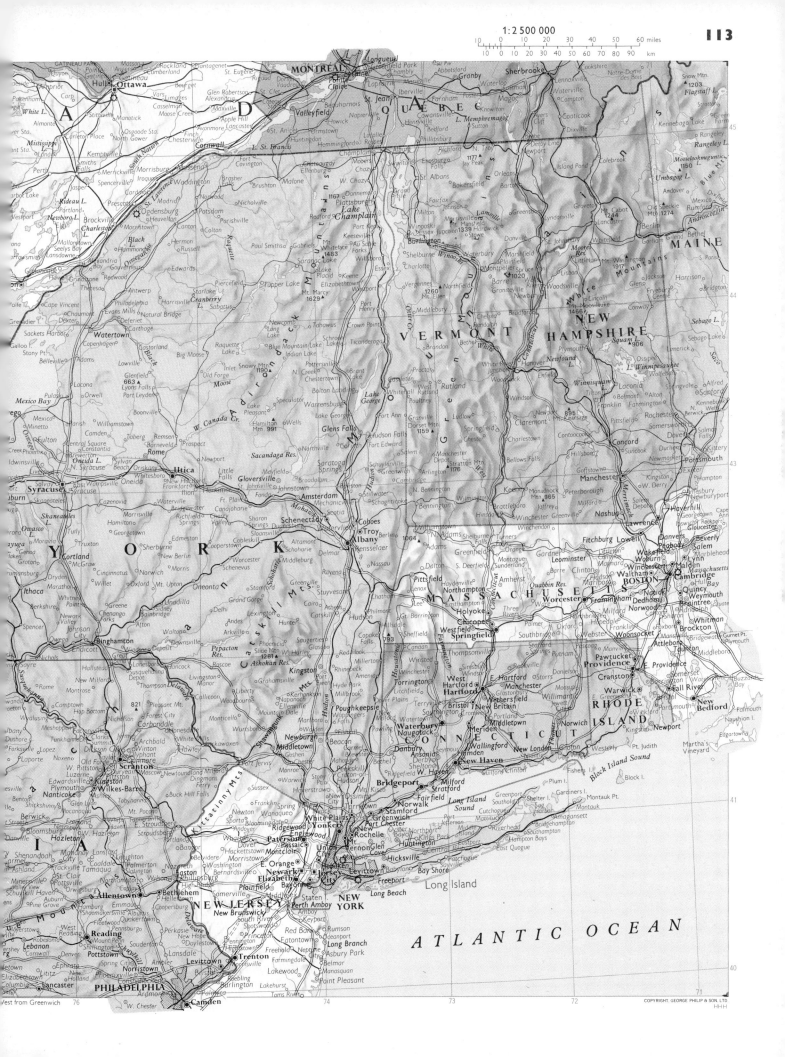

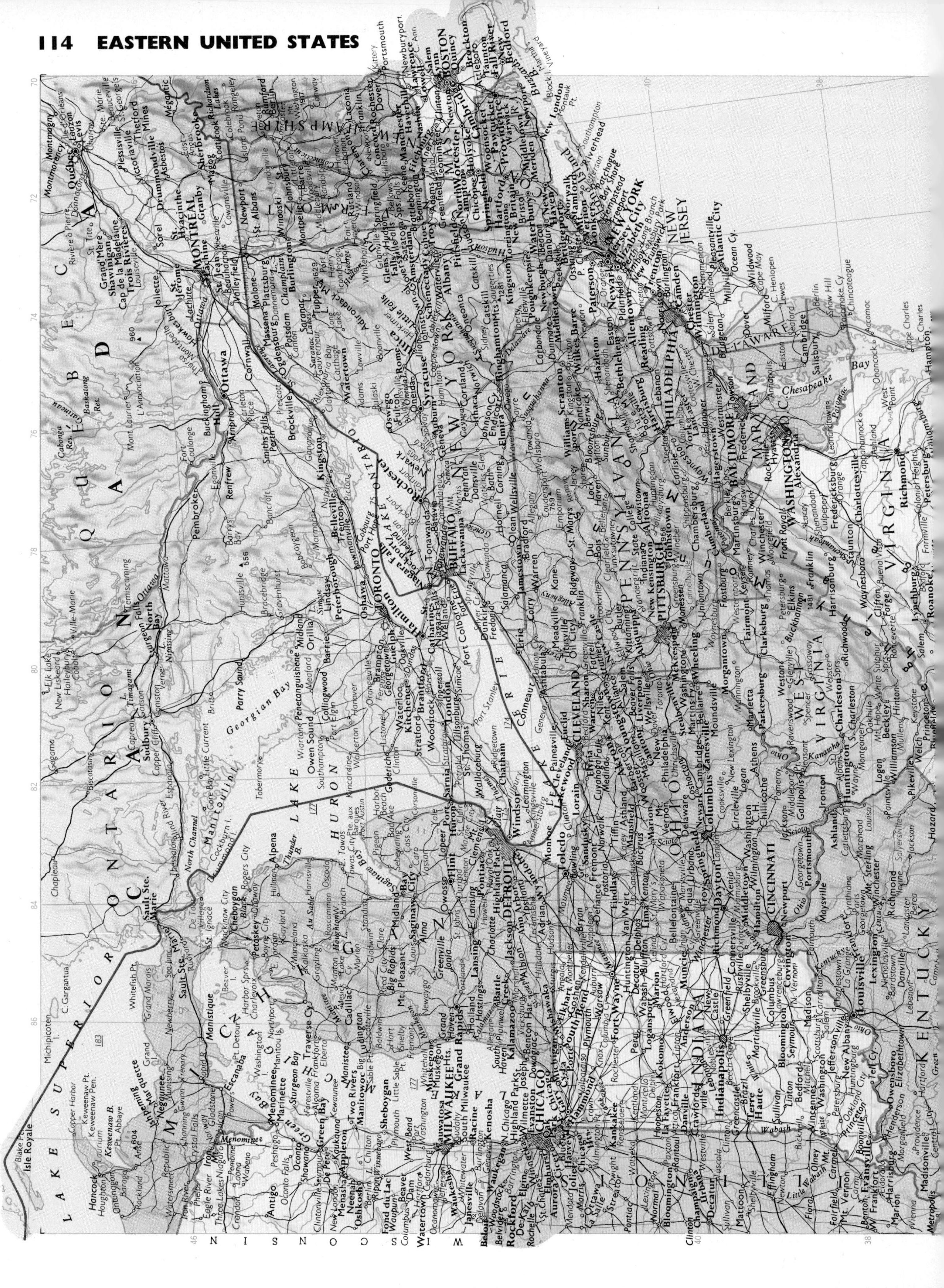
LAKE SUPERIOR
LAKE HURON
LAKE ONTARIO
LAKE ERIE
Georgian Bay
ONTARIO
QUEBEC
NEW YORK
PENNSYLVANIA
OHIO
INDIANA
MICHIGAN
WISCONSIN
WEST VIRGINIA
VIRGINIA
KENTUCKY
MARYLAND
NEW JERSEY
CHICAGO
MILWAUKEE
DETROIT
CLEVELAND
PITTSBURGH
PHILADELPHIA
BOSTON
MONTREAL
TORONTO
BUFFALO
BALTIMORE
WASHINGTON
CINCINNATI

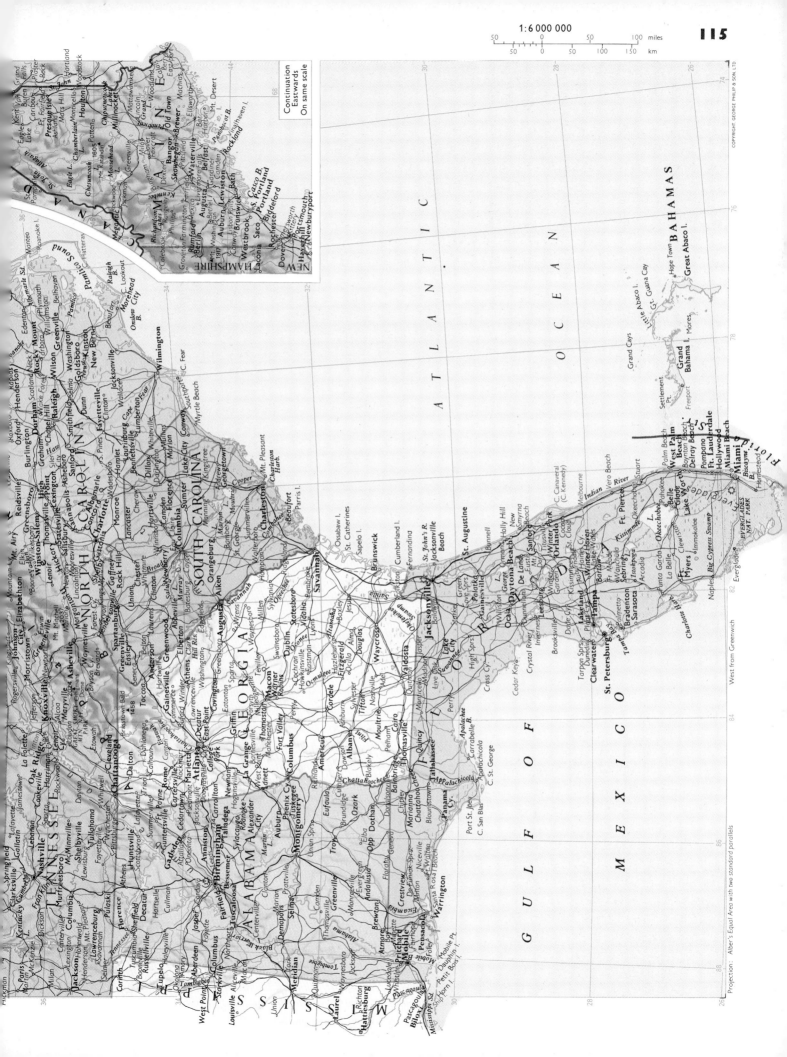

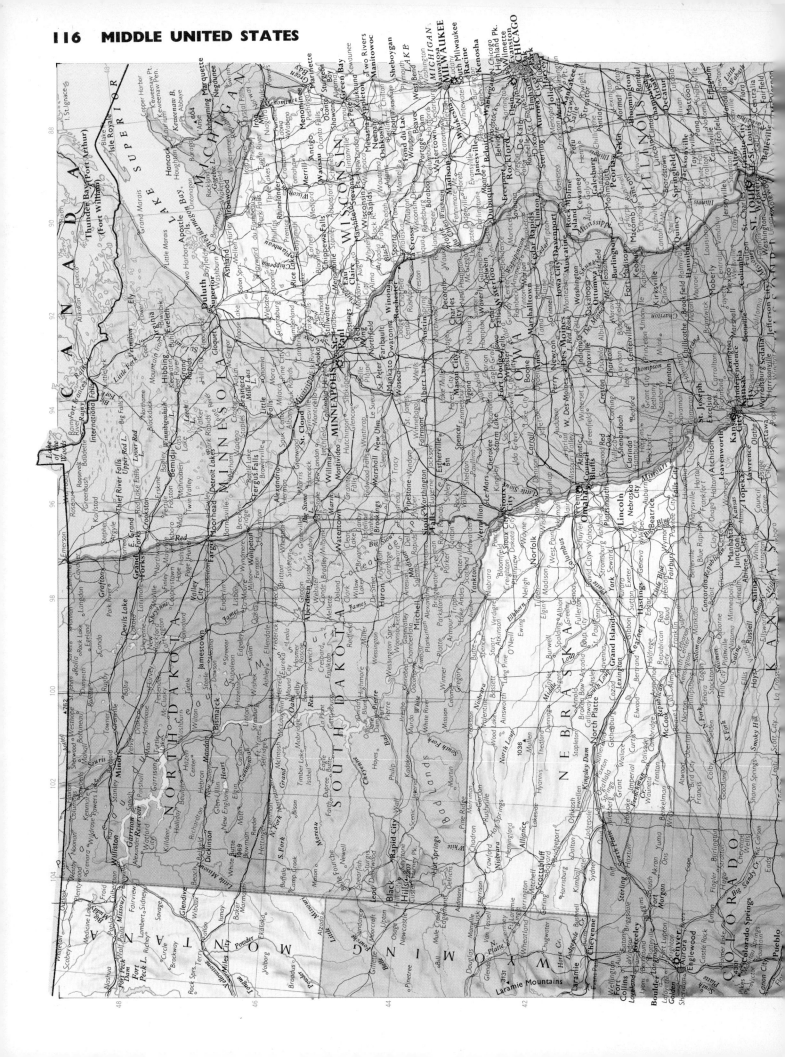

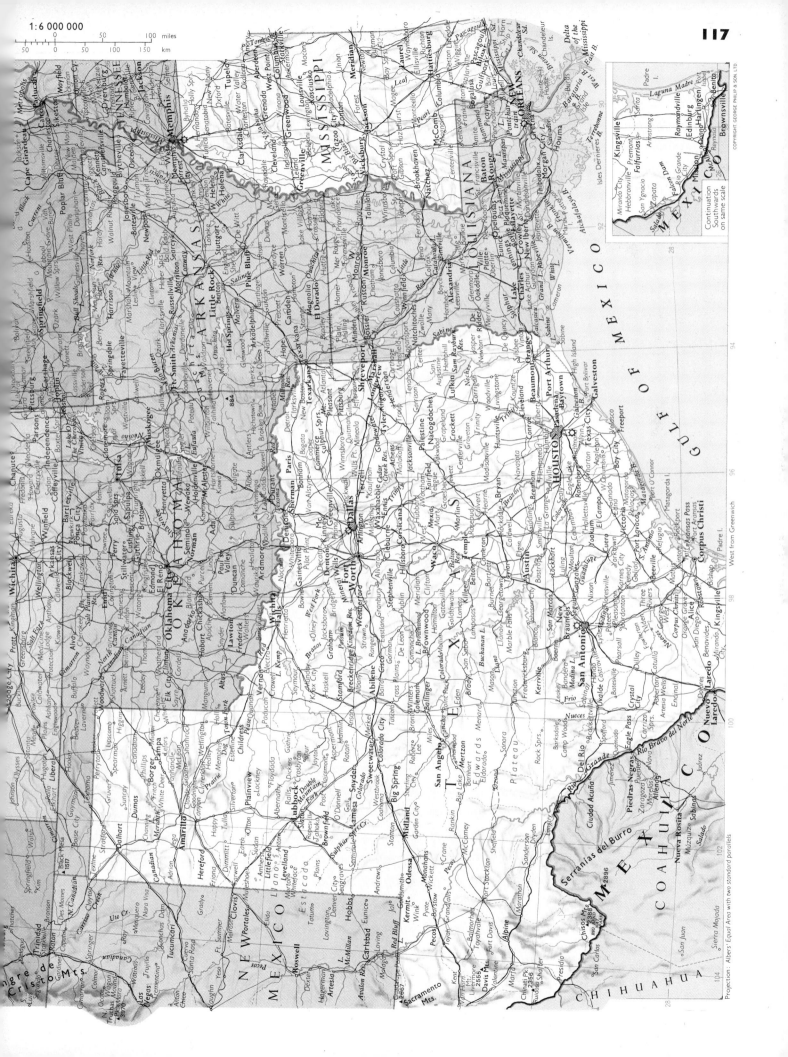

1:6 000 000

50   0   50   100 miles
50   0   50   100   150 km

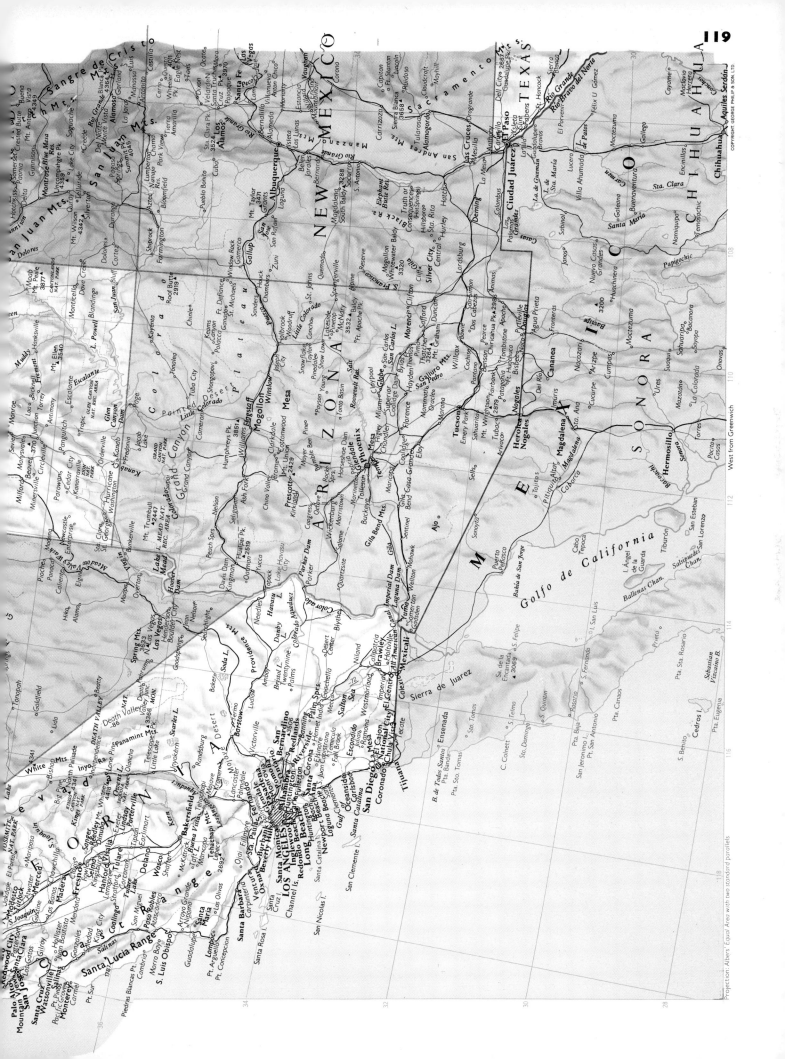

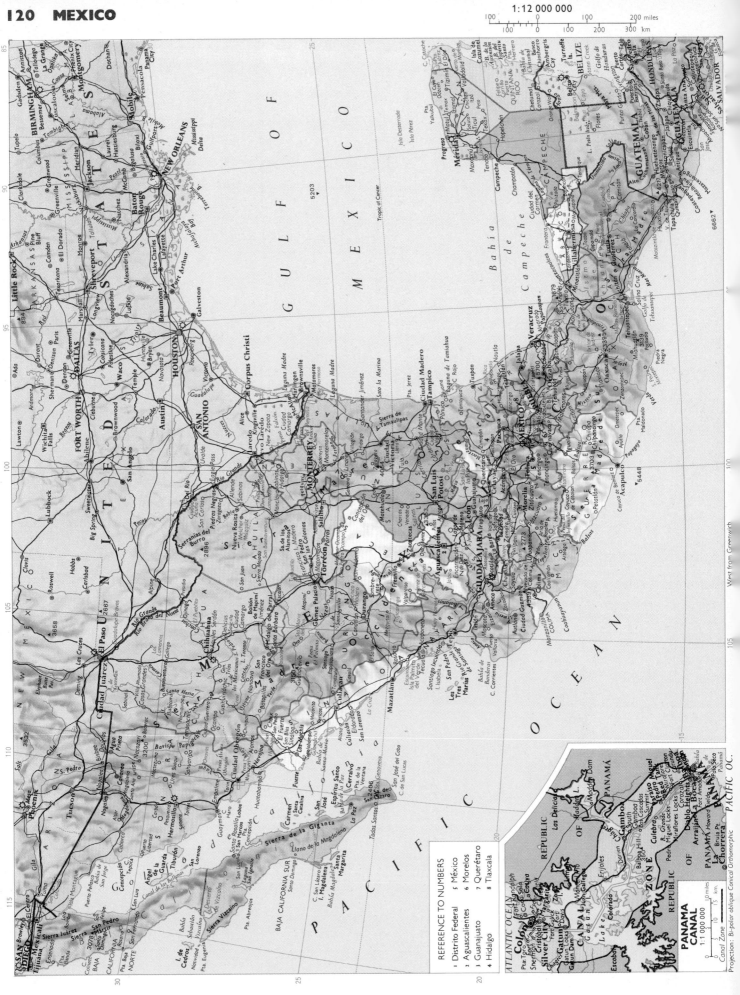

1:12 000 000

REFERENCE TO NUMBERS

1 Distrito Federal   5 México
2 Aguascalientes   6 Morelos
3 Guanajuato   7 Querétaro
4 Hidalgo   8 Tlaxcala

PANAMA CANAL
1:1 000 000

Projection: Bi-polar oblique Conical Orthomorphic

1:12 000 000

100   0   100   200 miles
100   0   100   200   300 km

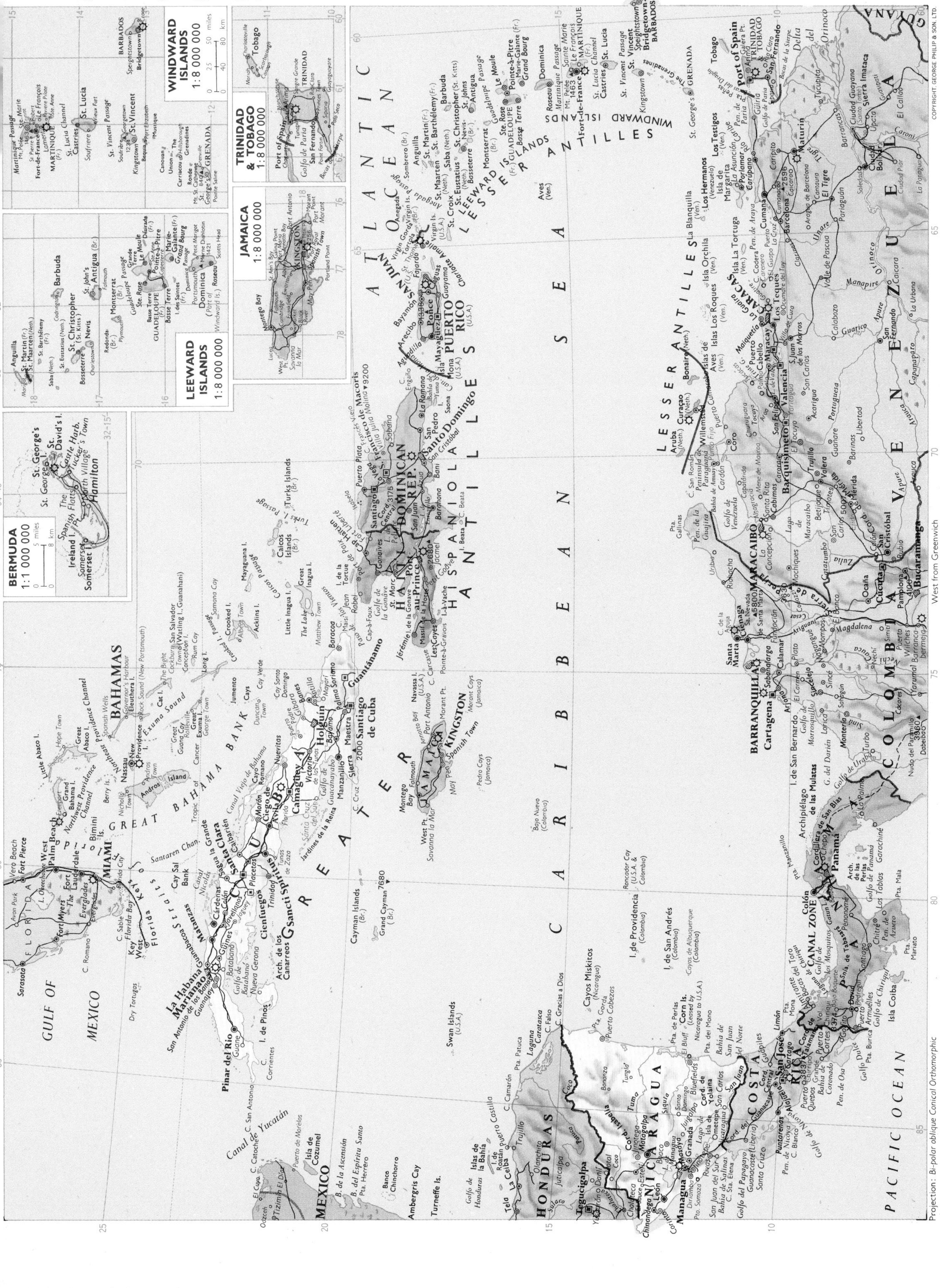

WINDWARD ISLANDS
1:8 000 000

TRINIDAD & TOBAGO
1:8 000 000

JAMAICA
1:8 000 000

LEEWARD ISLANDS
1:8 000 000

BERMUDA
1:1 000 000

GULF OF MEXICO

MEXICO

FLORIDA

MIAMI

BAHAMAS

GREAT BAHAMA BANK

CUBA

La Habana

JAMAICA

KINGSTON

Santiago de Cuba

HAITI

DOMINICAN REP.

Santo Domingo

PUERTO RICO (U.S.A.)

HISPANIOLA

ATLANTIC OCEAN

CARIBBEAN SEA

GREATER ANTILLES

LESSER ANTILLES

WINDWARD ISLANDS

LEEWARD ISLANDS

HONDURAS

NICARAGUA

Managua

COSTA RICA

PANAMA

CANAL ZONE

COLOMBIA

VENEZUELA

CARACAS

Maracaibo

Barranquilla

Cartagena

GUIANA

PACIFIC OCEAN

Port of Spain

TRINIDAD & TOBAGO

BARBADOS

GRENADA

ST. VINCENT

ST. LUCIA

MARTINIQUE

DOMINICA

GUADELOUPE

Orinoco

COPYRIGHT GEORGE PHILIP & SON, LTD.

West from Greenwich

Projection: Bi-polar oblique Conical Orthomorphic

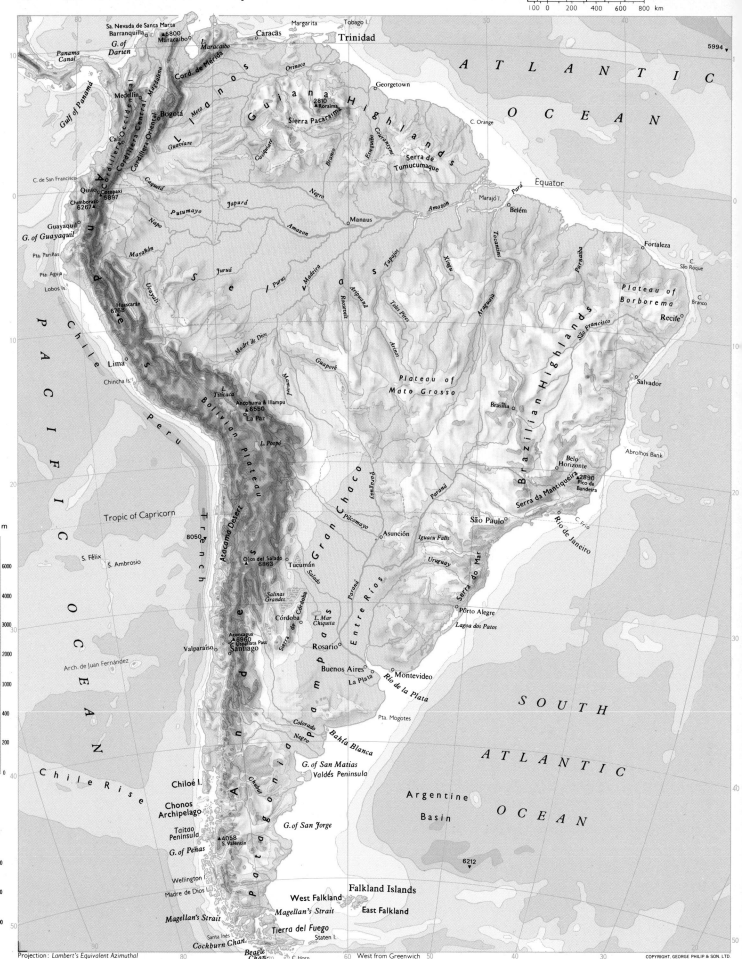

1 : 30 000 000

100 0 100 200 300 400 500 miles
100 0   200   400   600   800 km

Sa. Nevada de Santa Marta
Barranquilla
▲5800
Maracaibo
L. Maracaibo
G. of Darién
Panama Canal
Margarita
Tobago I.
Caracas
Trinidad
5994▾

Panama Canal

ATLANTIC

OCEAN

G. of Darién

Medellín
Cali
Cordillera Occidental
Cordillera Central
Cordillera Oriental
Bogotá
Magdalena
Llanos
Orinoco
Guaviare
Meta
Casiquiare
Guiana Highlands
Sierra Pacaraima
2810 ▲Roraima
Serra de Tumucumaque
Georgetown
Courantyne
Essequibo
C. Orange

Equator

C. de San Francisco
Quito
Cotopaxi 5897
Chimborazo 6267▲
Guayaquil
G. of Guayaquil
Pta. Pariñas
Pta. Aguja
Lobos Is.
Andes
Napo
Marañón
Ucayali
Putumayo
Japurá
Caquetá
Negro
Amazon
Juruá
Purus
Selvas
Madeira
Roosevelt
Aripuaná
Tapajós
Tales Pires
Xingu
Araguaia
Tocantins
Manaus
Marajó I.
Pará
Belém
Amazon
São Roque
Fortaleza
C. Branco
Plateau of Borborema
Recife

Huascarán 6768▲
Lima
Chincha Is.
L. Titicaca
Ancohuma & Illampu 6550
La Paz
L. Poopó
Bolivian Plateau
Peru
Chile
Madre de Dios
Mamoré
Guaporé
Plateau of Mato Grosso
Paraguay
São Francisco
Brazilian Highlands
Brasília
Salvador
Abrolhos Bank

Tropic of Capricorn
8050
Atacama Desert
Ojos del Salado 6863
Trench
Tucumán
Salado
Gran Chaco
Pilcomayo
Paraná
Asunción
Iguacu Falls
Uruguay
São Paulo
Belo Horizonte
2890 ▲Pico da Bandeira
Serra da Mantiqueira
Rio de Janeiro
C. Frio
Serra do Mar

S. Félix
S. Ambrosio
Arch. de Juan Fernández
Salinas Grandes
Córdoba
Sierra de Córdoba
Aconcagua 6960
Uspallata Pass
Valparaíso
Santiago
L. Mar Chiquita
Rosario
Entre Rios
Paraná
Pôrto Alegre
Lagoa dos Patos
Buenos Aires
La Plata
Montevideo
Río de la Plata
Pta. Mogotes

Chile Rise
Colorado
Negro
Bahía Blanca
Pampas

SOUTH

ATLANTIC

OCEAN

Chiloé I.
Chonos Archipelago
Taitao Peninsula
G. of Peñas
4058 ▲S. Valentin
Wellington I.
Madre de Dios I.
Patagonia
Chubut
G. of San Matias
Valdés Peninsula
G. of San Jorge
Argentine Basin
6212▾

Magellan's Strait
Santa Inés I.
Cockburn Chan.
West Falkland
Magellan's Strait
East Falkland
Falkland Islands
Tierra del Fuego
Staten I.
C. Horn
Beagle Chan.

PACIFIC

OCEAN

ft   m
18 000 6000
12 000 4000
9000   3000
6000   2000
3000   1000
1200   400
600   200
0   0
-200   600
2000   6000
4000 12 000
6000 18 000
8000 24 000
m   ft

Projection: Lambert's Equivalent Azimuthal

West from Greenwich

COPYRIGHT. GEORGE PHILIP & SON. LTD

1:30 000 000

100 0 100 200 300 400 500 miles
100 0 200 400 600 800 km

NORTH ATLANTIC OCEAN

COSTA RICA
CANAL ZONE
San José
PANAMA
Golfo de Panamá
S.F. 3277
Honolulu 4683

Barranquilla
Cartagena
Ciénaga
Maracaibo
Cabimas
Barquisimeto
Valencia
Caracas
Cumaná
Port of Spain
TRINIDAD AND TOBAGO
Trinidad
Punta Fijo
Isla de Margarita
Maturín

Golfo de Darién
Montería
San Cristóbal
Mérida
Orinoco
San Fernando
Ciudad Guayana
Ciudad Bolívar
Maracaibo

Medellín
Manizales
Pereira
Ibagué
Bogotá
Buenaventura
Cali
Popayán
Pasto
COLOMBIA
Cúcuta
Bucaramanga

VENEZUELA
Pto. Ayacucho
Ornoco

Georgetown
New Amsterdam
Paramaribo
Cayenne
C. Orange
GUYANA
SURINAM
FRENCH GUIANA

C. de San Francisco
Quito
ECUADOR
Guayaquil
Cuenca
Riobamba
Honolulu 4834
G. de Guayaquil
Pta. Aguja

Caquetá
Putumayo
Napo
Iquitos
Marañón
Negro
Japurá

Equator

Macapá
Ilha de Marajó
Belém (Pará)
Amazonas (Amazon)
Manaus
Santarem
São Luís
Bacabal
Teresina
Fortaleza (Ceara)
C. de São Roque
Natal
João Pessoa (Paraíba)
Recife (Pernambuco)

Chiclayo
Trujillo
Pucallpa
Cruzeiro do Sul
PERU
Lima
Callao
Huancayo
Ayacucho
Cuzco
Islas de Chincha

Benjamim Constant
Juruá
Purus
Madeira
Manicoré
Tapajós
Arpuana
Xingu
Tocantins
Araguaia
Parnaíba
Juazeiro do Norte
São Francisco
Maceió
Aracaju

B R A Z I L

Rio Branco
Guajará-Mirim
Madre de Dios
Guaporé
Mamoré
Pôrto Velho

Arequipa
La Paz
Mollendo
Oruro
Tacna
Cochabamba
Sucre
Arica
Iquique
Uyuni
Tarija
BOLIVIA
Santa Cruz
Titicaca
Juliaca

Cuiabá
Corumbá
Campo Grande
PARAGUAY
Asunción
Pedra Juan Caballero
Paraná

Brasília
Goiânia
Jataí
Montes Claros
Gov. Valadares
Uberaba
Ribeirão Prêto
Belo Horizonte
Vitória
Campos
Juiz de Fora
Campinas
SÃO PAULO
Santos
RIO DE JANEIRO
Niterói
Curitiba
Londrina
Bauru
Pres. Prudente
Ponta Grossa

Salvador (Bahia)

Antofagasta
Salta
San Miguel de Tucumán
Resistencia
Corrientes
Santiago del Estero
Salado
Córdoba
ARGENTINA
Coquimbo
Mendoza
Santa Fe
Paraná
Rosario
URUGUAY
Pôrto Alegre
Pelotas
Lagoa dos Patos
Santa Maria
Uruguaiana
Florianópolis
Montevideo

CHILE
Valparaíso
Santiago
San Rafael
Mercedes
BUENOS AIRES
La Plata
Río de la Plata
Montevideo
Mar del Plata
Concepción
Talca
Santa Rosa
Bahía Blanca
Tandil
Colorado
Negro
Valdivia
Viedma

Puerto Montt
San Carlos de Bariloche
Isla de Chiloé
Península Valdés
Trelew
Chubut
Archipiélago de los Chonos
Golfo Comodoro Rivadavia
San Jorge
G. de Penas
I. Wellington
Santa Cruz
Río Gallegos
Estrecho de Magallanes
Punta Arenas
Cabo de Hornos (Cape Horn)
Strait of Magellan
Isla Grande de Tierra del Fuego

FALKLAND ISLANDS (ISLAS MALVINAS) (U.K.)
West Falkland
Stanley
East Falkland

SOUTH ATLANTIC OCEAN

PACIFIC OCEAN

Isla San Félix (Chile)
Isla San Ambrosio (Chile)
Arch de Juan Fernández (Chile)

Tropic of Capricorn

West from Greenwich

Projection: Lambert's Equivalent Azimuthal

COPYRIGHT. GEORGE PHILIP & SON. LTD.

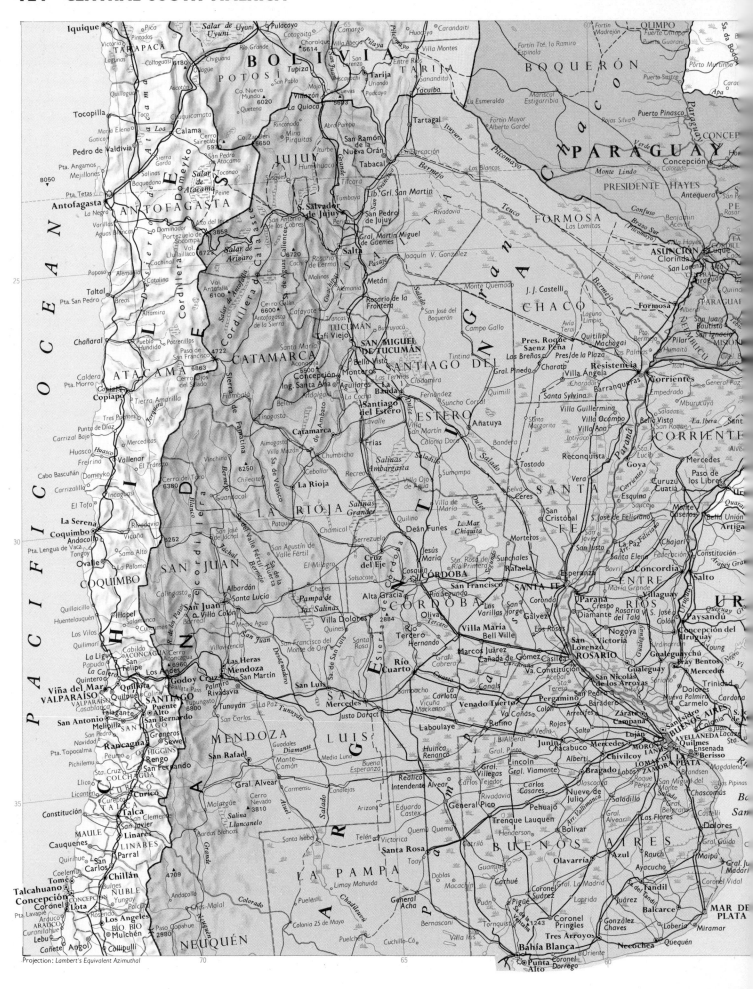

Projection: Lambert's Equivalent Azimuthal

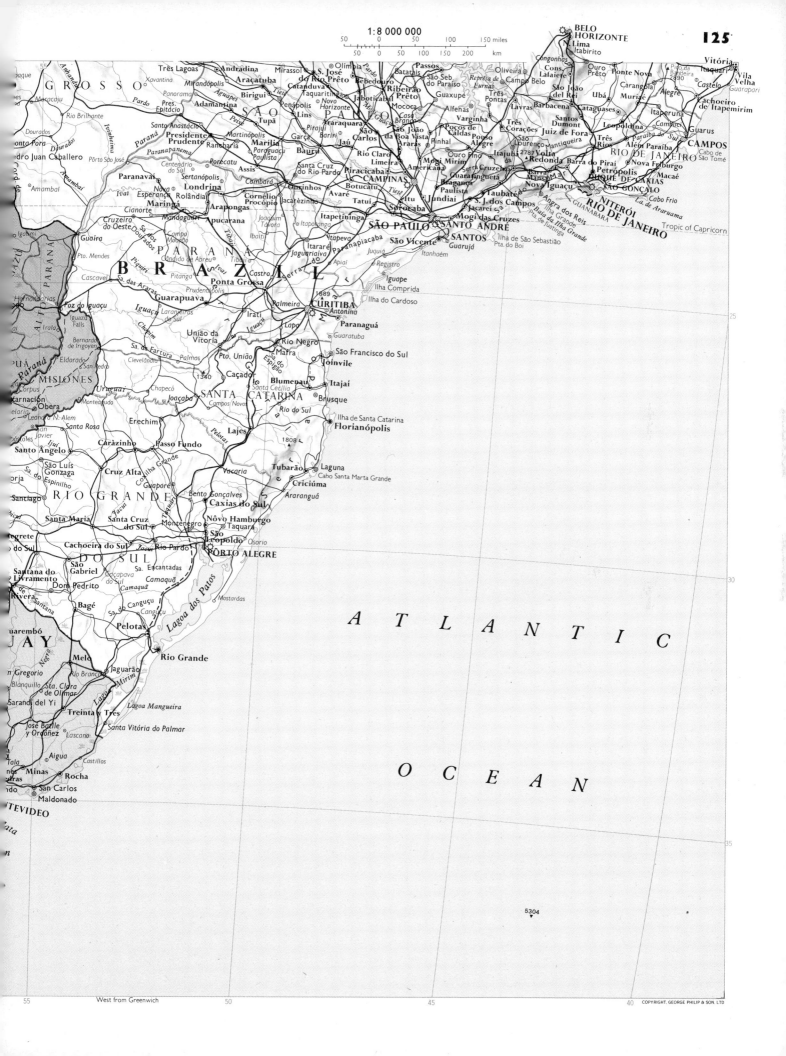

1:16 000 000

100   0   100   200   300   400   500 miles
100   0   100 200 300 400 500 600 700 800 km

A T L A N T I C

Paramaribo
Nieuw Amsterdam
Moengo
Mana
Iracoubo
Sinnamary
Kourou
Albina
St. Laurent
St. Georges
Cayenne
Kaw
Approuague

FR.
GUIANA
C. Orange
Oiapoque

AM

Tumucumaque

AMAPÁ
C. do Norte

Meruma
Araguari
Serra
do Navio
Sta. Grande
Macapá
Amapá
Ilha de Maracá

Estuario do
Rio Amazonas
Ilha Caviana
Ilha Mexiana

Equator

E Q U A T O R

Jari
Mazagão
Afuá
Chaves
Souré
Curuçá
Salinópolis
Bragança

I. Grande
de Gurupá
Ilha de
Marajó

Monte Alegre
Prainha
Almeirim
Breves
Muaná
Vigia
Igarapé-Açu

Óbidos
Porto de Móz
Gurupá
Abaetetuba
Belém (Pará)
Acará

A M A Z O N A S

Santarém (Amazon)
Belterra
Altamira
Baião
Turiaçu
Guimarães
Alcântara

B. de São Marcos
São Luís (Maranhão)
Barreirinhas

A T L A N T I C

Brasília Legal
Itaituba
Tapajóz

Souzel
Baido
Cametá
Rosário
Viana
Itapecuru-Mirim

Tutóia
Luís Correia
Camocim

St. Paul's Rocks

Fernando de Noronha
(Braz.)

P A R Á

Iriri
Xingu
Curuá

Marabá
Sa. dos Carajás
Tocantins

MARANHÃO
Bacabal
Coroatá
Caxias
Teresina

Parnaíba
Piracuruca
Miguel de Piriri
Barras
Campo Maior
União

Sobral
Maranguape
Granja

Fortaleza (Ceará)

Caucia

Rocas

O C E A N

Rondon
Conceição do Araguaia
Araguacema

Imperatriz
Grajaú
Porto Franco
Carolina
Riachão

Barra do Corda
Grajaú
Colinas
Floriano
Loreto
Novalorque

Amarante
Valença do Piauí

Oeiras

C E A R Á

Crateús
Iguatú
Oros

Baturité
Ipu
Quixadá
Russas
Senador Pompeu
Areia Branca
Macau
Mossoró
Ceará Mirim
C. de São Roque

Aracati

Cajazeiras

RIO GRANDE
DO NORTE
Natal
Nova Cruz

Marabá
Tocantinópolis

PIAUI
Uruçuí
São João do Piauí
Sta. Filomena
Chap. do Araripe
Juazeiro do Norte

Crato
Cedro
Sousa
Pombal
Patos

Caicó
Currais Novos
Cangaretama

Conguaretama

Araguacema

Pedro Afonso

Sa. do Estrondo

Caracol
Dois Irmãos
Remanso

Petrolina
Casa Nova
Juàzeiro

Paulistana
Curuci

PARAÍBA
Campina Grande
Arcoverde
Sertânia

Itabaiana
Limoeira
Cabedelo
João Pessoa
(Paraiba)

B R A Z I L

Niquelândia
1678

Porto Nacional
Natividade

Barra
Xique-Xique
Parnaguá

Campo Formoso
Senhor do Bonfim

Queimadas
Vaza-Barris

Garanhuns
Palmares
Pesqueira
Caruaru
RECIFE
(Pernambuco)

PERNAMBUCO

São Francisco
Paulo Afonso

Petrolandia
Qelmira
Pal dos Indios
Gouveia

Viçosa
Barreiros
Rio Largo

A r c o r e s

Sta. Isabel
Ilha do Bananal

GOIÁS

Manuel Alves
Peixe
Taguatinga

Campos Belos
São Domingos

Barreiras
Ibotirama

B A H I A
Jacobina
Serrinha

Feira de Santana
Santo Amaro

ALAGOAS
Maceió

Propriá
SERGIPE
Penedo

Aracajú

GROSSO

Planalto do

Mato Grosso

Rondonópolis
Baliza
Aruanã
Uruaca

1678

Sa. Dourada
Campos Belos
Parané
Palma
São Domingos

Sta. Maria
da Vitória
1850
Itaberaba
Ituaçú

Paratinga
Bom Jesus
da Lapa

Amargosa
Sincará
Valença
Nazaré

Castro Alves
Cachoeira
Santo Amaro

São Cristóvão
Estância

Alagoinhas

Santo Amaro
Salvador (Bahia)

B. de Todos os Santos

Jequié
Brumado
Coités

Jaguaribe

Vitória da
Conquista

Ubaitaba
Itacaré
Itabuna
Ilhéus

Anápolis
Luziânia
Vianópolis

DIST.
FED.
Brasília
Formoso
Corumbá

Caldas

Januária
Monte Azul

Condeúba
Gavião

Itambé

Pedra Azul

Canavieiras

Belmonte
Porto Seguro

Goiânia

Catalão

Corumbaíba
São Francisco
Salinas
Jequitinhonha
Jequitaí

Montes
Claros

Araçuaí

P l a n a l t o

Prado
Caravelas
Banka
Abrolhos
Mucuri

Piraporá
Paracatú
Botaiuva
Riacho

Teófilo Otoni
Diamantina

Nanuque

Campo Grande
Agua Clara
Três Lagoas
Alto Araguaia

Verde
Morrinhos
Rio Verde

Jataí
Baus
Aporé

Coxim

Uberlândia
Araguari
Ituiutaba
1340

MINAS GERAIS

Patos de Minas
Patrocínio

Curvelo

Gov. Valadares
Aimorés

Conceição da Barra
São Mateus

Dourados

Ribas do Rio Pardo
Nova Andradina
Pres. Epitácio
Panorama

Uberaba
Frutal

Bom Despacho
Lagoas
Sete
Lagoas
Belo Horizonte
Ouro Preto 2890

Caratinga
Muriaé

Nova
Venecia
Doce

Vitória
Cachoeiro de Itapemirim

Trindade
(Braz.)

Ponta Pora

Paranaíba
Ituiutaba
Nova Colombia
S. José do Rio Prêto

Franca
Oliveira
Lavras
Barbacena
Juiz de Fora

Campos

Pres. Prudente
Araçatuba
Lins
Jaú
São Carlos
Mogi Mirim

SÃO
PAULO
Bauru
Piracicaba
Limeira
Campinas

Três Rios
Nova Friburgo
Petrópolis
RIO DE JANEIRO
Niterói

Marília
Botucatu

GUANABARA

1:16 000 000

100 50 0   100   200   300 miles
100   0   100 200 300 400 km

PARAGUAY

Asunción

PARANÁ

RIO DE JANEIRO

SÃO PAULO

Curitiba

SANTA CATARINA

Florianópolis

RIO GRANDE DO SUL

Pôrto Alegre

Chaco Boreal

Chaco Central

Chaco Austral

Antofagasta

Tropic of Capricorn

Salta

San Miguel de Tucumán

Catamarca

La Rioja

Córdoba

Santa Fe

Paraná

Rosario

URUGUAY

MONTEVIDEO

La Serena
Coquimbo

San Juan

Mendoza

Viña del Mar
Valparaíso
SANTIAGO

Buenos Aires
La Plata
Avellaneda

Mar del Plata

Bahía Blanca

Neuquén

Talcahuano
Concepción

Valdivia

Osorno
Puerto Montt

I. de Chiloé

Archipiélago de los Chonos

Carmen de Patagones
Viedma

Golfo San Matías

Península Valdés

Trelew

Golfo San Jorge

Comodoro Rivadavia

SOUTH ATLANTIC OCEAN

I. Wellington

Río Gallegos

Estrecho de Magallanes
(Magellan's Str.)

Arch. Reina Adelaida

Punta Arenas

Tierra del Fuego

FALKLAND ISLANDS
(ISLAS MALVINAS)
(Br.)
West Falkland   Stanley
East Falkland

South Georgia
(Br.)

Cabo de Hornos (C. Horn)

Projection: Sanson-Flamsteed's Sinusoidal

West from Greenwich

COPYRIGHT GEORGE PHILIP & SON, LTD.

Index

The number which precedes each entry in the index is the page of the atlas where that particular feature can be found. The geographical co-ordinates which follow the entry are primarily intended as a guide to locating the feature on the map and in some cases are only approximate.

Where the same name refers to places in different countries, these place-names are followed by the country name and are arranged according to the alphabetical order of the country. If the same name occurs a number of times within one country the names are followed by the name of the administrative subdivision in which they are found, and are arranged in the alphabetical order of the subdivision name.

If the same name occurs a number of times town names are given first followed by the names referring to other geographical features.

The symbol ■ indicates the name of a country and is always first in a list of identical place-names. The symbol ♦ indicates the name of an administrative subdivision of a country and these names are always last in a list of identical place-names.

Names beginning with M', Mc, M'c and Mac are all listed under Mac.

Former names of certain towns are referenced to the names in current use; Stalingrad=Volgograd. English conventional name forms for certain towns are referenced to the local spelling of that town name; Florence=Firenze.

The following is a list of abbreviations used in the index.

The Trucial States became fully independent in December 1971 and adopted the name—United Arab Emirates.
Papua and North East New Guinea both became independent in December 1973 and are now known together as Papua New Guinea.

Following the Local Government Acts, 1972, a number of the county boundaries and names in England and Wales, Scotland and Northern Ireland have changed. There is a list of the new county, region and district names on the last page of the Index.

Afghan. – *Afghanistan*
Afr. – *Africa, African*
Ala. – *Alabama*
Alas. – *Alaska*
Alb. – *Albania*
Alg. – *Algeria*
Alta. – *Alberta*
Amaz. – *Amazonas*
Amer. – *America*
And. P. – *Andhra Pradesh*
Ang. – *Angola*
Ant. – *Antarctica*
Arab. – *Arabia*
Arch. – *Archipelago*
Arg. – *Argentina*
Ariz. – *Arizona*
Ark. – *Arkansas*
A.S.S.R. – *Autonomous Soviet Socialist Republic*
Aust. – *Austria*
Austral. – *Australia*
B. – *Bay, Bight, (Baie, Bahia, Baia)*
B.C. – *British Columbia*
Bangla. – *Bangladesh*
Bav. – *Bavaria (Bayern)*
Beds. – *Bedfordshire*
Belg. – *Belgium*
Beng. – *Bengal*
Berks. – *Berkshire*
Bg. – *Berg.*
Bk. – *Bank*
Bol. – *Bolivia*
Bots. – *Botswana*
Br., Brit. – *British, Britain*
Braz. – *Brazil*
Bucks. – *Buckinghamshire*
Bulg. – *Bulgaria*
C. – *Cape (Cabo), Coast*
Calif. – *California*
Cam. – *Cameroon*
Cambod. – *Cambodia*
Cambs. – *Cambridgeshire & Isle of Ely*
Can. – *Canada, Canal*
Can. Is. – *Canary Islands*
Cant. – *Canton*
Cap. – *Capital*
Cards. – *Cardiganshire*
Cas. – *Castle*
Cent. – *Central*
Cey. – *Ceylon*
Chan. – *Channel*
Ches. – *Cheshire*
Co. – *County*
Col. – *Colombia, Columbia, Colony*
Colo. – *Colorado*
Conn. – *Connecticut*

Cont. – *Continent*
C. Prov. – *Cape Province*
Cr. – *Creek*
C. Rica – *Costa Rica*
Cumb. – *Cumberland*
Cz. – *Czechoslovakia*
D.C. – *District of Columbia*
Del. – *Delaware*
Den. – *Denmark*
Dépt. – *Département, Department*
Des. – *Desert*
Dist. – *District*
Div. – *Division*
Dj. – *Djebel*
Dom. Rep. – *Dominican Republic*
Dun. – *Dunbarton*
E. – *East*
Ec. – *Ecuador*
Eg. – *Egypt*
Eng. – *England*
Equat. – *Equatorial*
Est. – *Estuary*
Eth. – *Ethiopia*
Eur. – *Europe*
Falk. Is. – *Falkland Islands*
Fd. – *Fiord, Fjord*
Fed. – *Federal, Federation*
Fin. – *Finland*
Fla. – *Florida*
For. – *Forest*
Fr. – *France, French*
Fr. Gui. – *French Guiana*
Fs. – *Falls*
F.T.A.I. – *Fr. Terr. of the Afars and Issas*
Ft. – *Fort*
G. – *Gulf, Gebel*
Ga. – *Georgia*
Gam. – *Gambia*
Ger. – *Germany*
Gl. – *Glacier*
Glos. – *Gloucestershire*
Gr. – *Greece*
Green. – *Greenland*
Grn. – *Green*
Grp. – *Group*
Gt. – *Great*
Guat. – *Guatemala*
Guin. – *Guinea*
Guy. – *Guyana*
Hants. – *Hampshire*
Hr., Harb. – *Harbor, Harbour*
Hd. – *Head*
Here. – *Herefordshire*
Herts. – *Hertfordshire*
Him. P. – *Himachal Pradesh*
Ho. – *House*
Hond. – *Honduras*

Hs. – *Hills*
Hts. – *Heights*
Hung. – *Hungary*
Hunt. – *Huntingdon & Peterborough*
I.(s) – *Island(s) (Isle, Ile)*
Ice. – *Iceland*
Ill. – *Illinois*
Ind. – *Indiana, Indian*
Indon. – *Indonesia*
I. of M. – *Isle of Man*
I. of W. – *Isle of Wight*
Ire. – *Ireland*
Isr. – *Israel*
Isth. – *Isthmus*
It. – *Italy*
J. – *Jebel, Jabal*
Jam. – *Jamaica*
Jap. – *Japan*
Jc., Junc. – *Junction*
Kans. – *Kansas*
Kg. (Malay) – *Kampong (Village)*
King. – *Kingdom*
Ky. – *Kentucky*
L. – *Lake, Lough, Loch, Lago*
La. – *Louisiana*
Lab. – *Labrador*
Lag. – *Lagoon, Laguna, Lagôa*
Lancs. – *Lancashire*
Ld. – *Land*
Leics. – *Leicestershire*
Les. – *Lesotho*
Lib. – *Liberia*
Lim. – *Limerick*
Lincs. – *Lincolnshire*
Lit. – *Little*
Lr. – *Lower*
Lt. Ho. – *Lighthouse*
Lux. – *Luxembourg*
Mad. – *Madras*
Mad. P. – *Madhya Pradesh*
Mal. – *Malawi*
Malag. – *Malagasy Republic*
Malay. – *Malaysia*
Man. – *Manitoba*
Mass. – *Massachusetts*
Maur. – *Mauritania*
Md. – *Maryland*
Me. – *Maine*
Medit. – *Mediterranean*
Mex. – *Mexico*
M. Grosso – *Mato Grosso*
Mich. (U.S.A.) – *Michigan*
Mich. (Mexico) – *Michoacan*
Mid. – *Middle*
Min. Ger. – *Minas Gerais*
Minn. – *Minnesota*
Miss. – *Mississippi*

Mo. – *Missouri*
Mon. – *Monmouthshire*
Mong. – *Mongolia*
Mont. – *Montana*
Mor. – *Morocco*
Mozam. – *Mozambique*
Mt. – *Mountain, Mount*
Mte. – *Monte*
Mth. – *Mouth*
Mti. – *Monti*
Mţii (Rum.) – *Munţii (Mts.)*
Mts. – *Mountains, Monts.*
Mys. – *Mysore*
N. – *North, Northern*
Nat. – *Natal, National*
N.B. – *New Brunswick*
N.C. – *North Carolina*
N.D. – *North Dakota*
Neb. – *Nebraska*
Neth. – *Netherlands*
Nev. – *Nevada*
Newf. – *Newfoundland*
N. Guin. – *New Guinea, Terr. of,*
N.H. – *New Hampshire*
Nic. – *Nicaragua*
Nig. – *Nigeria*
N.J. – *New Jersey*
N. Mex. – *New Mexico*
Nor. – *Norway*
Northants. – *Northamptonshire*
Northumb. – *Northumberland*
Notts. – *Nottinghamshire*
N.S. – *Nova Scotia*
N.S.W. – *New South Wales*
N.Y. – *New York*
N.Z. – *New Zealand*
O. – *Oasis, Ouadi*
Oc. – *Ocean*
O.F.S. – *Orange Free State*
Okla. – *Oklahoma*
Ont. – *Ontario*
Oreg. – *Oregon*
Os. (Russ.) – *Ostrov (Island)*
Oz. (Russ.) – *Ozero (Lake)*
P. – *Paso, Pass, Passo*
Pa. – *Pennsylvania*
Pac. – *Pacific*
Pak. – *Pakistan*
Pan. – *Panama*
Par. – *Paraguay*
Pass. – *Passage*
P.E.I. – *Prince Edward Island*
Pen. – *Peninsula*
Phil. – *Philippines*
Pk. – *Peak, Park*
Pl. – *Plain, Planina*
Plat. – *Plateau*
Pol. – *Poland*

Port. – *Portugal, Portuguese*
Prét. – *Préfecture*
P. Rico – *Puerto Rico*
Prom. – *Promontory*
Prot. – *Protectorate*
Prov. – *Province, Provincial*
Pt. – *Point, Port*
Pta. – *Punta (Point)*
Pte. – *Pointe (Point)*
Pto. – *Porto, Puerto (Port)*
Que. – *Quebec*
Queens. – *Queensland*
R. – *River, Rio*
Ra. – *Range*
Raj. – *Rajasthan*
Ras. – *Ranges*
Rd. – *Road*
Reg. – *Region*
Rep. – *Republic*
Res. – *Reserve, Reservoir*
Rf. – *Reef*
Rhod. – *Rhodesia*
R.I. – *Rhode Island*
Rks. – *Rocks*
Rosc. – *Roscommon*
R.S.F.S.R. – *Russian Soviet Federal Socialist Republic*
Rum. – *Rumania*
S. – *Sea, South*
Sa. – *Sierra, Serra*
Sab. – *Sabah*
Sal. – *El Salvador*
Salop. – *Shropshire*
Sar. – *Sarawak*
Sard. – *Sardinia*
Sask. – *Saskatchewan*
S. Afr. – *Rep. of South Africa*
S. Austral. – *South Australia*
S.C. – *South Carolina*
Scot. – *Scotland*
S.D. – *South Dakota*
Sd. – *Sound*
Sen. – *Senegal*
Si. Arab. – *Saudi Arabia*
S. Leone – *Sierra Leone*
Sp., Span. – *Spain, Spanish*
S.S.R. – *Soviet Socialist Republic*
st. – *State*
S. – *San*
St. – *Saint*
Sta. – *Santa*
Ste. – *Sainte*
Sto. – *Santo*
Staffs. – *Staffordshire*
Stn. – *Station*
Str. – *Strait*
Sud. – *Sudan*

Sun. (Malay) – *Sungei (River)*
Sur. – *Suriname(e)*
Swazi. – *Swaziland*
Swed. – *Sweden*
Switz. – *Switzerland*
Tanz. – *Tanzania*
Tas. – *Tasmania*
Tenn. – *Tennessee*
Terr. – *Territory*
Tex. – *Texas*
Thai. – *Thailand*
Tipp. – *Tipperary*
tn. – *Town*
Trans. – *Transvaal*
Tr. States – *Trucial States*
Tun. – *Tunisia*
Tur. – *Turkey*
U.A.R. – *United Arab Republic*
Ugan. – *Uganda*
Ukr. – *Ukraine*
U.K. – *United Kingdom of Great Britain and Northern Ireland*
Ut. P. – *Uttar Pradesh*
Urug. – *Uruguay*
U.S.A. – *United States of America*
U.S.S.R. – *Union of Soviet Socialist Republics*
Va. – *Virginia*
Val. – *Valley*
Vdkhr. (Russ.) – *Vodokhranilishche (Reservoir)*
Ven. – *Venezuela*
Vic. – *Victoria*
Viet. – *Vietnam*
Vil. – *Village, Vilayet*
Vol. – *Volcano*
Vt. – *Vermont*
W. – *West, Wadi, Wady*
War. – *Warwickshire*
Wash. – *Washington*
W. I. – *West Indies*
Wick. – *Wicklow*
Wilts. – *Wiltshire*
Wind. Is. – *Windward Islands*
Wis. – *Wisconsin*
Worcs. – *Worcestershire*
W. A. – *Western Australia*
W. Va. – *West Virginia*
Wyo. – *Wyoming*
Yorks. – *Yorkshire*
Y.-slav. – *Yugoslavia*
Zam. – *Zambia*

HHF

* Incorporated within the region of Grampian
* Incorporated within the new Northern Province

Ajua INDEX Almodôvar

MAP
84 Ajua, Ghana 4 50N 1 55W
64 Ak Dağ, Turkey 36 30N 30 0E
85 Akaba, Togo 8 10N 1 2E
82 Akabli, Algeria 26 49N 1 31E
87 Akaki Beseka, Ethiopia 8 55N 38 45E
87 Akala, Sudan 15 39N 36 13E
101 Akaroa, N.Z. 43 49S 172 59E
95 Akaroa Harb., N.Z. 43 54S 172 59E
86 Akasha, Sudan 21 10N 30 32E
74 Akashi, Japan 34 45N 135 0E
82 Akbou, Algeria 36 31N 4 31E
85 Akegbe, Nigeria 6 17N 7 28E
73 Akelamo, Indonesia 1 35N 129 40E
47 Akershus Fylke ♦, Norway 60 10N 11 15E
70 Akeru, R., India 17 25N 80 0E
45 Akhaïa ♦, Greece 38 5N 21 45E
57 Akhalkalaki, U.S.S.R. 41 27N 43 25E
57 Akhaltsikhe, U.S.S.R. 41 40N 43 0E
45 Akharnai, Greece 38 5N 23 44E
45 Akhelóös, R., Greece 39 5N 21 25E
45 Akhendriá, Greece 34 58N 25 16E
44 Akhéron, R., Greece 39 31N 20 29E
64 Akhisar, Turkey 38 56N 27 48E
45 Akhladhókambos, Gr. 37 31N 22 35E
86 Akhmîm, Egypt 26 31N 31 47E
43 Akhtopol, Bulgaria 42 6N 27 56E
57 Akhtubinsk (Petropavlovskiy), U.S.S.R. 48 27N 46 7E
57 Akhty, U.S.S.R. 41 30N 47 45E
54 Akhtyrka, U.S.S.R. 50 25N 35 0E
106 Akimiski I., Canada 52 50N 81 30W
56 Akimovka, U.S.S.R. 46 44N 35 0E
45 Akincilar, Turkey 37 57N 27 25E
98 Akinum, Terr. of New Guinea 6 15S 149 30E
49 Akirkeby, Denmark 55 4N 14 55E
74 Akita, Japan 39 45N 140 0E
74 Akita-ken ♦, Japan 39 40N 140 30E
84 Akjoujt, Mauritania 19 45N 14 15W
82 Akka, Morocco 29 28N 8 9W
62 'Akko, Israel 32 35N 35 4E
58 Akkol, U.S.S.R. 43 36N 70 45E
45 Akköy, Turkey 37 30N 27 18E
85 Aklampa, Dahomey 8 15N 2 10E
104 Aklavik, Canada 68 25N 135 0W
82 Aknoul, Morocco 34 40N 3 55W
85 Ako, Nigeria 10 19N 10 48E
87 Akobo, R., Ethiopia 7 10N 34 25E
68 Akola, India 20 42N 77 2E
85 Akonolinga, Cameroon 3 50N 12 18E
87 Akordat, Ethiopia 15 30N 37 40E
85 Akosombo Dam, Ghana 6 20N 0 5E
68 Akot, India 21 10N 77 10E
87 Akot, Sudan 6 31N 30 9E
105 Akpatok I., Canada 60 30N 68 0W
50 Akranes, Iceland 64 19N 22 6W
47 Akrehamn, Norway 59 15N 5 10E
85 Akreïjit, Mauritania 18 19N 9 11W
45 Akritas Venétiko, Akra, Greece 36 43N 21 54E
116 Akron, Colo., U.S.A. 40 13N 103 15W
112 Akron, Ohio, U.S.A. 41 7N 81 31W
44 Akrotiri, Akra, Greece 40 26N 25 27W
66 Aksai Chih, Kashmir 35 30N 79 50E
64 Aksaray, Turkey 38 25N 34 2E
58 Aksarka, U.S.S.R. 66 31N 67 50E
64 Aksehir, Turkey 38 18N 31 30E
59 Aksenovo Zilovskoye, U.S.S.R. 53 20N 117 40E
75 Aksu, China 41 4N 80 5E
87 Aksum, Ethiopia 14 5N 38 40E
58 Aktogay, U.S.S.R. 46 57N 79 40E
53 Aktyubinsk, U.S.S.R. 50 10N 57 3E
85 Aku, Nigeria 6 40N 7 18E
85 Akure, Nigeria 7 15N 5 5E
50 Akureyri, Iceland 65 40N 18 6W
57 Akusha, U.S.S.R. 42 18N 47 30E
67 Akyab, Burma 20 15N 92 45E
83 Al Abyār, Libya 32 9N 20 29E
63 Al Ain, Saudi Arabia 19 35N 54 40E
64 Al Amadiyah, Iraq 37 5N 43 30E
64 Al Amarah, Iraq 31 55N 47 15E
64 Al Aqabah, Jordan 29 37N 35 0E
65 Al Ashkhara, Oman 21 50N 59 30E
83 Al 'Azīzīyah, Libya 32 30N 13 1E
64 Al Badi, Si. Arabia 22 0N 46 35E
62 Al Barah, Jordan 31 55N 35 12E
83 Al Barkāt, Libya 24 56N 10 14E
64 Al Basrah, Iraq 30 30N 47 55E
81 Al Bayḍā, Libya 32 30N 21 40E
83 Al Bu'ayrāt, Libya 31 24N 15 44E
62 Al Buqay'ah, Jordan 32 15N 35 30E
64 Al Diwāniyah, Iraq 32 0N 45 0E
64 Al Fallujah, Iraq 33 20N 43 55E
64 Al Faw, Iraq 30 0N 48 30E
64 Al Hadhtgam, Iraq 34 0N 41 13E
64 Al Hamad, Si. Arabia 31 30N 39 30E
64 Al Hamar, Si. Arabia 22 23N 46 6E
64 Al Hariq, Saudi Arabia 23 29N 46 27E
64 Al Hasakah, Syria 36 35N 40 45E
64 Al Hauta, S. Yemen 16 5N 48 20E
64 Al Hayy, Iraq 32 5N 46 5E
64 Al Hillah, Iraq 32 30N 44 25E
64 Al Hillah, Saudi Arabia 23 35N 46 50E
64 Al Hilwah, Saudi Arabia 23 24N 46 48E
64 Al Hina, Iraq 32 0N 44 25E
64 Al Hindiya, Iraq 32 30N 44 10E
82 Al Hoceima, Morocco 35 15N 3 58W
83 Al Hufrah, Awbārī, Libya 25 32N 14 1E
83 Al Hufrah, Misrātah, Libya 29 5N 18 3E
64 Al Hufuf, Si. Arabia 25 25N 49 45E
83 Al Husayyāt, Libya 30 24N 20 37E
62 Al Husn, Jordan 32 29N 35 6E
83 Al Irq, Libya 29 5N 21 35E
63 Al Ittihad = Madinat al Shaab, S. Yemen 12 50N 45 0E
64 Al Jahrah, Kuwait 29 25N 47 40E
31 Al Jalamid, Si. Arabia 31 20N 39 45E
81 Al Jarzirah, Libya 26 10N 42 25E
81 Al Jawf, Libya 24 10N 23 24E
63 Al Jazir, Oman 18 30N 56 31E
64 Al Jubail, Si. Arabia 27 0N 49 50E
63 Al Juwara, Oman 19 0N 57 13E
65 Al Khābūrah, Oman 23 57N 57 5E
62 Al Khalih, Jordan 31 32N 35 6E
83 Al Khums (Homs), Libya 32 40N 14 17E
64 Al Kut, Iraq 32 30N 46 0E
64 Al Kuwayt, Kuwait 29 20N 48 0E
64 Al Ladhiqiyah, Syria 35 30N 35 45E
86 Al Lith, Saudi Arabia 20 9N 40 15E
64 Al Madīnah, Saudi Arabia 24 35N 39 52E
62 Al-Mafraq, Jordan 32 17N 36 14E
64 Al Majma'ah, Saudi Arabia 25 57N 45 22E
65 Al Manamah, Bahrain 26 10N 50 30E
81 Al Marj, Libya 32 25N 20 30E
63 Al Masīrah, Oman 20 25N 58 50E
64 Al Mawsil, Iraq 36 15N 43 5E
64 Al Miqdaldiyah, Iraq 34 0N 45 0E
64 Al Mubarraz, Saudi Arabia 25 30N 49 40E
65 Al Muharraq, Bahrain 26 15N 50 40E
64 Al Musayyib, Iraq 32 40N 44 25E
64 Al Muwaylih, Saudi Arabia 27 40N 35 30E
83 Al Qaddāhīyah, Libya 31 15N 15 9E
64 Al Qamishli, Turkey 37 10N 41 10E
83 Al Qaryah ash Sharqīyah, Libya 30 28N 13 40E
83 Al Qasabāt, Libya 32 39N 14 1E
64 Al Qatif, Saudi Arabia 26 35N 50 0E
83 Al Qatrun, Libya 24 56N 15 3E
64 Al Quaisumah, Si. Arabia 28 10N 46 20E
62 Al Quds, Israel/Jordan 31 47N 35 10E
86 Al Qunfidha, Si. Arabia 19 3N 41 4E
65 Al Quraiyat, Oman 23 17N 58 53E
64 Al Qurnah, Iraq 31 1N 47 25E
64 Al 'Ula, Saudi Arabia 26 35N 38 0E
83 Al Uqaylah, Libya 30 12N 19 10E
64 Al Uqayr, Saudi Arabia 25 40N 50 15E
64 Al' Uwayqiyah, Si. Arabia 30 30N 42 10E
64 Al 'Uyūn, Saudi Arabia 26 30N 43 50E
86 Al Wajh, Si. Arabia 26 10N 36 30E
65 Al Wakrah, Qatar 25 10N 51 40E
64 Al Warīah, Si. Arabia 27 50N 47 30E
83 Al Wātīyah, Libya 32 28N 11 57E
38 Ala, Italy 45 46N 11 0E
48 Ala, Sweden 61 13N 17 9E
75 Ala Shan, China 40 0N 104 0E
115 Alabama, R., U.S.A. 31 30N 87 35W
115 Alabama ♦, U.S.A. 31 0N 87 0W
45 Alaçati, Turkey 38 16N 26 23E
30 Alaejos, Spain 41 18N 5 13W
38 Alagna Valsésia, Italy 45 51N 7 56E
127 Alagoa Grande, Brazil 7 3S 35 35W
127 Alagoas ♦, Brazil 9 0S 36 0W
127 Alagoinhas, Brazil 12 0S 38 20W
32 Alagón, Spain 41 46N 1 12W
30 Alagón, R., Spain 39 50N 6 50W
72 Alahanpandjang, Indon. 1 10S 100 45E
121 Alajuela, Costa Rica 10 2N 84 8W
93 Alakamisy, Malag. 21 19S 47 14E
52 Alakurtti, Finland 67 0N 30 30E
86 Alam Ajaib, Egypt 25 55N 27 14E
31 Alameda, Spain 37 12N 4 39W
119 Alameda, N. Mex., U.S.A. 35 10N 106 43W
118 Alameda, S.D., U.S.A. 43 2N 112 30W
120 Alamitos, Sierra de los, Mexico 26 30N 1 8W
119 Alamo, U.S.A. 37 21N 115 10W
119 Alamogordo, U.S.A. 32 59N 106 0W
120 Alamos, Mexico 27 0N 109 0W
119 Alamosa, U.S.A. 37 30N 106 0W
51 Aland, Finland 60 15N 20 0E
70 Aland, India 17 36N 76 35E
31 Alandroal, Portugal 38 41N 7 24W
31 Alange, Presa de, Spain 38 45N 6 18W
84 Alangouassou, Ivory C. 7 30N 4 34W
31 Alanis, Spain 38 3N 5 43W
64 Alanya, Turkey 36 38N 32 0E
93 Alaotra, L., Malag. 17 30S 48 30E
58 Alapayevsk, U.S.S.R. 57 55N 62 0E
32 Alar del Rey, Spain 42 38N 4 20W
30 Alaraz, Spain 40 45N 5 17W
53 Alaşehir, Turkey 38 23N 28 30E
76 Alashanchih, China 38 58N 105 14E
104 Alaska ♦, U.S.A. 65 0N 150 0W
104 Alaska, G. of, Pac. Oc. 58 0N 145 0W
104 Alaska Pen., Alaska 56 0N 160 0W
104 Alaska Range, Alaska 62 50N 151 0W
38 Alássio, Italy 44 1N 8 10E
40 Alatri, Italy 41 44N 13 21E
55 Alatyr, U.S.S.R. 54 45N 46 35E
55 Alatyr, R., U.S.S.R. 54 45N 45 30E
126 Alausi, Ecuador 2 0S 78 50W
118 Alava, C., U.S.A. 48 10N 124 40W
32 Alava ♦, Spain 42 48N 2 28W
57 Alaverdi, U.S.S.R. 41 2N 44 37E
99 Alawoona, Australia 34 45S 140 30E
32 Alayor, Spain 39 57N 4 8E
57 Alazan, R., U.S.S.R. 41 25N 46 35E
38 Alba, Italy 44 41N 8 1E
46 Alba ♦, Rumania 46 10N 23 30E
46 Alba-Iulia, Rumania 46 8N 23 39E
46 Albac, Rumania 46 28N 23 1E
33 Albacete, Spain 39 0N 1 50W
33 Albacete ♦, Spain 38 50N 2 0W
100 Albacutya L., Australia 35 45S 141 58E
33 Albalada, Spain 38 51N 0 31W
32 Albalate de las Nogueras, Spain 40 22N 2 18W
32 Albalate del Arzobispo, Spain 41 6N 0 31W
44 Albania ■, Europe 41 0N 20 0E
40 Albano Laziale, Italy 41 44N 12 40E
96 Albany, Australia 35 1S 117 58E
115 Albany, Ga., U.S.A. 31 40N 84 10W
116 Albany, Minn., U.S.A. 45 37N 94 38W
113 Albany, N.Y., U.S.A. 42 40N 73 47W
118 Albany, Oreg., U.S.A. 44 41N 123 0W
117 Albany, Tex., U.S.A. 32 45N 99 20W
106 Albany, R., Canada 51 30N 87 0W
124 Albardón, Argentina 31 20S 68 30W
32 Albarracín, Spain 40 25N 1 26W
32 Albarracín, Sierra de 40 30N 1 30W
98 Albatross B., Australia 12 45S 141 30E
39 Albegna, R., Italy 42 40N 11 28E
115 Albemarle, U.S.A. 35 27N 80 15W
115 Albemarle Sd., U.S.A. 36 0N 76 30W
38 Albenga, Italy 44 3N 8 12E
30 Alberche, R., Spain 40 10N 4 30W
124 Alberdi, Paraguay 26 14S 58 20W
32 Alberes, Mts., Spain 42 28N 2 56W
96 Alberga, R., Australia 26 50S 133 40E
33 Alberique, Spain 39 7N 0 31W
108 Alberni, Canada 49 20N 124 50W
24 Albersdorf, Germany 54 8N 9 19E
100 Albert, Australia 32 45S 147 31E
107 Albert, Canada 45 51N 64 38W
19 Albert, France 50 0N 2 38E
108 Albert Canyon, Canada 51 0N 121 55E
*90 Albert, L., Zaïre 1 30N 31 0E
99 Albert L., S. Australia 35 30S 139 10E
118 Albert L., U.S.A. 42 40N 120 8W
116 Albert Lea, U.S.A. 43 32N 93 20W
90 Albert Nile, R., Uganda 3 16N 31 38E
108 Alberta ♦, Canada 54 40N 115 0W
92 Albertinia, S. Africa 34 11S 21 34E
27 Albertirsa, Hungary 47 14N 19 37E
107 Alberton, Canada 46 50N 64 0W
100 Alberton, Australia 38 36S 146 37E
90 Albertville = Kalemie, Zaïre 5 55S 29 9E
21 Albertville, France 45 40N 6 22E
65 Alberz, Reshteh-Ye Kūkhā-Ye, Iran 36 0N 52 0E
20 Albi, France 43 56N 2 9E
116 Albia, U.S.A. 41 0N 92 50W
127 Albina, Surinam 5 37N 54 15W
92 Albina, Pta., Angola 15 52S 11 44E
38 Albino, Italy 45 47N 9 48E
118 Albion, Idaho, U.S.A. 42 21N 113 37W
114 Albion, Mich., U.S.A. 42 15N 84 45W
116 Albion, Nebr., U.S.A. 41 47N 98 0W
112 Albion, Pa., U.S.A. 41 53N 80 21W
32 Albocácer, Spain 40 21N 0 1E
49 Alböke, Sweden 56 57N 16 47E
30 Alborán, I., Spain 35 57N 3 0W
33 Alborea, Spain 39 17N 1 24W
49 Ålborg, Denmark 57 2N 9 54E
49 Ålborg Bugt, Denmark 56 50N 10 35E
31 Albox, Spain 37 23N 2 8W
108 Albreda, Canada 52 35N 119 10W
31 Albufeira, Portugal 37 5N 8 15W
25 Albula, R., Switzerland 46 28N 9 38E
33 Albuñol, Spain 36 48N 3 11W
119 Albuquerque, U.S.A. 35 5N 106 47W
113 Alburg, U.S.A. 44 58N 73 19W
41 Alburno, Mte., Italy 40 32N 15 20E
31 Alburquerque, Spain 39 15N 7 1W
100 Albury, Australia 36 0S 146 50E
48 Alby, Sweden 62 30N 15 28E
49 Albæk, Denmark 57 36N 10 25E
49 Albæk Bugt, Denmark 57 36N 10 40E
31 Alcácer do Sal, Portugal 38 22N 8 33W
31 Alcáçovas, Portugal 38 23N 8 9W
32 Alcalá de Chisvert, Sp. 40 19N 0 13E
31 Alcalá de Guadaira, Sp. 37 20N 5 50W
32 Alcalá de Henares, Sp. 40 28N 3 22W
31 Alcalá de los Gazules, Spain 36 29N 5 43W
31 Alcalá la Real, Spain 37 27N 3 57W
40 Alcamo, Italy 37 59N 12 55E
32 Alcanadre, Spain 42 24N 2 7W
32 Alcanadre, R., Spain 41 43N 0 12W
32 Alcanar, Spain 40 33N 0 28E
31 Alcanena, Portugal 39 27N 8 40W
31 Alcanede, Portugal 39 25N 8 49W
31 Alcañices, Spain 41 41N 6 21W
32 Alcañiz, Spain 41 2N 0 8W
127 Alcântara, Brazil 2 20S 44 30W
31 Alcántara, Spain 39 41N 6 57W
33 Alcantarilla, Spain 37 59N 1 12W
31 Alcaracejos, Spain 38 24N 4 58E
33 Alcaraz, Spain 38 40N 2 29W
33 Alcaraz, Sierra de, Spain 38 40N 2 20W
31 Alcaudete, Spain 37 35N 4 5W
33 Alcázar de San Juan, Sp. 39 24N 3 12W
33 Alcira, Spain 39 9N 0 30W
115 Alcoa, U.S.A. 35 50N 84 0W
31 Alcobaça, Portugal 39 32N 9 0W
32 Alcobendas, Spain 40 32N 3 38W
32 Alcolea del Pinar, Spain 41 2N 2 28W
32 Alcora, Spain 40 5N 0 14W
31 Alcoutim, Portugal 37 25N 7 28W
118 Alcova, U.S.A. 42 37N 106 52W
33 Alcoy, Spain 38 43N 0 30W
32 Alcubierre, Sierra de, Spain 41 45N 0 22W
33 Alcublas, Spain 39 48N 0 43W
32 Alcudia, Spain 39 51N 3 9E
32 Alcudia, Bahía de, Spain 39 47N 3 15E
31 Alcudia, Sierra de la, Sp. 38 34N 4 30W
3 Aldabra Is., Br. Indian Oc. Terr. 9 22S 46 28E
59 Aldan, U.S.S.R. 58 40N 125 30E
59 Aldan, R., U.S.S.R. 62 30N 135 10E
13 Aldeburgh, England 52 9N 1 35E
31 Aldeia Nova, Portugal 37 55N 7 24W
47 Alden I., Norway 61 19N 4 45E
118 Alder, U.S.A. 45 27N 112 3W

* Renamed L. Mobutu Sese Seko

18 Alderney, I., Chan. Is. 49 42N 2 12W
13 Aldershot, England 51 15N 0 43W
108 Aldersyde, Canada 50 40N 113 53W
116 Aledo, U.S.A. 41 10N 90 50W
87 Alefa, Ethiopia 11 55N 36 55E
125 Alegre, Brazil 20 50S 41 30W
125 Alegrete, Brazil 29 40S 56 0W
58 Aleisk, U.S.S.R. 52 40N 83 0E
95 Alejandro Selkirk, I., S. Pacific 33 50S 80 15W
53 Aleksandriya, U.S.S.R. 50 45N 26 22E
56 Aleksandriya, U.S.S.R. 48 42N 33 3E
57 Aleksandriyskaya, U.S.S.R. 43 59N 47 0E
55 Aleksandrov, U.S.S.R. 56 23N 38 44E
55 Aleksandrov Gay., U.S.S.R. 50 15N 48 35E
42 Aleksandrovac, Y.-slav 44 28N 21 13E
56 Aleksandrovka, U.S.S.R. 48 55N 32 20E
43 Aleksandrovo, Bulgaria 43 14N 24 51E
59 Aleksandrovsk-Sakhaliniskiy, U.S.S.R. 50 50N 142 20E
59 Aleksandrovskiy Zavod, U.S.S.R. 50 40N 117 50E
58 Aleksandrovskoye, U.S.S.R. 60 35N 77 50E
28 Aleksandrów Kujawski, Poland 52 53N 18 43E
28 Aleksandrów Łódski, Poland 51 49N 19 17E
55 Alekseyevka, U.S.S.R. 50 43N 38 40E
55 Aleksin, U.S.S.R. 54 31N 37 9E
42 Aleksinac, Yugoslavia 43 31N 21 42E
124 Alemania, Argentina 25 40S 65 30W
47 Alen, Norway 62 49N 11 17E
18 Alençon, France 48 27N 0 4E
110 Alenuihaha Chan., Hawaiian Is. 20 25N 156 0W
98 Alenquer, Brazil 1 56S 54 46W
64 Aleppo, Syria 36 10N 37 15E
108 Alert B., Canada 50 30N 127 35W
21 Alès, France 44 9N 4 5E
46 Aleşd, Rumania 47 3N 22 22E
38 Alessándria, Italy 44 54N 8 37E
49 Ålestrup, Denmark 56 42N 9 29E
47 Ålesund, Norway 62 28N 6 12E
87 Alet, Sudan 8 14N 29 2E
20 Alet-les-Bains, France 43 0N 2 14E
104 Aleutian Is., Pac. Oc. 52 0N 175 0W
116 Alexander, U.S.A. 47 51N 103 40W
104 Alexander Arch., Alaska 57 0N 135 0W
92 Alexander B., S. Africa 28 36S 16 33E
5 Alexander I., Antarc. 69 0S 70 0W
115 Alexander City, U.S.A. 32 58N 85 57W
100 Alexandra, Australia 37 8S 145 40E
101 Alexandra, N.Z. 45 14S 169 25E
75 Alexandretta = Iskenderun, Turkey 36 32N 36 10E
108 Alexandria, B.C., Can 52 35N 122 20W
106 Alexandria, Ont., Can. 45 19N 74 38W
86 Alexandria = El Iskandarîya, Egypt 31 0N 30 0E
46 Alexandria, Rumania 43 57N 25 24E
92 Alexandria, S. Africa 33 38S 26 28E
114 Alexandria, Ind., U.S.A. 40 18N 85 40W
117 Alexandria, La., U.S.A. 31 20N 92 30W
116 Alexandria, Minn., U.S.A. 45 50N 95 20W
116 Alexandria, S.D., U.S.A. 43 40N 97 45W
114 Alexandria, Va., U.S.A. 38 47N 77 1W
113 Alexandria Bay, U.S.A. 44 20N 75 52W
99 Alexandrina L., Australia 35 30S 139 15E
44 Alexandroúpolis, Gr. 40 50N 25 54E
108 Alexis Creek, Canada 52 0N 123 20W
32 Alfambra, Spain 40 33N 1 5W
30 Alfândega da Fé, Port. 41 20N 6 59W
32 Alfaro, Spain 42 10N 1 50W
43 Alfatar, Bulgaria 43 59N 27 13E
24 Alfeld, Germany 52 0N 9 49E
125 Alfenas, Brazil 21 40S 44 0W
45 Alfiós, R., Greece 37 36N 21 54E
39 Alfonsine, Italy 44 30N 12 1E
113 Alfred, Me., U.S.A. 43 28N 70 40W
112 Alfred, N.Y., U.S.A. 42 15N 77 45W
12 Alfreton, England 53 6N 1 22W
48 Alfta, Sweden 61 21N 16 4E
50 Alftanes, Iceland 64 29N 22 10W
112 Alganac, U.S.A. 42 36N 82 34W
31 Algar, Spain 36 40N 5 39W
47 Algård, Norway 58 46N 5 53E
31 Algarinejo, Spain 37 19N 4 9W
31 Algarve, Portugal 37 15N 8 10W
31 Algeciras, Spain 36 9N 5 28W
33 Algemesi, Spain 39 11N 0 27W
82 Alger, Algeria 36 42N 3 8E
82 Algeria ■, Africa 35 10N 3 11E
40 Alghero, Italy 40 34N 8 20E
82 Algiers = Alger, Algeria 36 42N 3 8E
92 Algoabaai, S. Africa 33 50S 25 45E
31 Algodanales, Spain 36 54N 5 24W
30 Algodor, R., Spain 39 51N 3 48W
114 Algoma, Mich., U.S.A. 44 35N 87 27W
118 Algoma, Oreg., U.S.A. 42 25N 121 54W
106 Algonquin Park, Can. 45 35N 78 35W
33 Alhama de Almería, Sp. 36 57N 2 34W
32 Alhama de Aragón, Sp. 41 18N 1 54W
31 Alhama de Granada, Sp. 37 0N 3 59W
33 Alhama de Murcia, Sp. 37 51N 1 25W
33 Alhambra, Spain 38 54N 3 4W
119 Alhambra, U.S.A. 34 0N 118 10W
31 Alhaurín el Grande, Sp. 36 39N 4 41W
82 Alhucemas = Al-Hoceïma, Morocco 35 8N 3 58W
57 Ali Bayramly, U.S.S.R. 39 43N 48 52E
64 Ali al Gharbi, Iraq 32 30N 46 45E
87 Ali Sabieh, Fr. Terr. Afars & Issas 11 10N 42 44E
40 Alia, Italy 37 47N 13 42E
65 Aliabad, Iran 28 10N 57 35E
32 Aliaga, Spain 40 40N 0 42W
44 Aliakmon, R., Greece 40 10N 22 0E
70 Alibag, India 18 38N 72 56E
87 Alibo, Ethiopia 9 52N 37 5E
42 Alibunar, Yugoslavia 45 5N 20 57E
33 Alicante, Spain 38 23N 0 30W
33 Alicante ♦, Spain 38 30N 0 37W
92 Alice, S. Africa 32 48S 26 55E
117 Alice, U.S.A. 27 47N 98 1W
41 Alice, Punta dell', Italy 39 23N 17 10E
98 Alice, R., Australia 23 50S 145 0E
108 Alice Arm, Canada 55 29N 129 23W
96 Alice Springs, Australia 23 36S 133 53E
92 Alicedale, S. Africa 33 15S 26 4E
115 Aliceville, U.S.A. 33 9N 88 10W
41 Alicudi, Italy 38 33N 14 20E
109 Alida, Canada 49 25N 101 55W
68 Aligarh, Raj., India 25 55N 76 15E
68 Aligarh, Ut. P., India 27 55N 78 10E
64 Aligudarz, Iran 33 25N 49 45E
30 Alijó, Portugal 41 16N 7 27W
41 Alimena, Italy 37 42N 14 4E
45 Alimnia, Greece 36 16N 27 43E
67 Aling Kangri, Range, China 31 45N 84 45E
49 Alingaabro, Denmark 56 56N 10 32E
49 Alingsås, Sweden 57 56N 12 31E
69 Alipore, India 22 32N 88 24E
68 Alipur, Pakistan 29 25N 70 55E
69 Alipur Duar, India 26 30N 89 35E
112 Aliquippa, U.S.A. 40 38N 80 18W
30 Aliste, R., Spain 41 48N 6 14W
45 Alivérion, Greece 38 24N 24 2E
92 Aliwal North, S. Africa 30 45S 26 45E
31 Aljezur, Portugal 37 18N 8 49W
31 Aljustrel, Portugal 37 55N 8 10W
85 Alkamari, Niger 13 27N 11 10E
63 Alkhalaf, Oman 20 30N 58 13E
16 Alkmaar, Netherlands 52 37N 4 45E
119 All American Canal, U.S.A. 32 45N 115 0W
85 Allada, Dahomey 6 41N 2 9E
68 Allah Dad, Pakistan 25 38N 67 34E
69 Allahabad, India 25 25N 81 58E
59 Allakh Yun, U.S.S.R. 60 50N 137 5E
82 Allal Razi, Morocco 34 30N 6 39W
20 Allanche, France 45 14N 2 57E
71 Allanmyo, Burma 19 16N 95 17E
92 Allanridge, S. Africa 27 45S 26 40E
100 Allansford, Australia 38 26S 142 39E
106 Allanwater, Canada 50 14N 90 10W
86 Allaqi, Wadi, Egypt 22 15N 134 55E
107 Allard Lake, Canada 50 40N 63 10W
30 Allariz, Spain 42 11N 7 50W
20 Allassac, France 45 15N 1 29E
114 Allegan, U.S.A. 42 32N 85 52W
112 Allegany, U.S.A. 41 30N 78 30W
114 Allegheny Mts., U.S.A. 38 0N 80 0W
112 Allegheny Res., U.S.A. 42 0N 78 55W
112 Allegheny, R., U.S.A. 41 14N 79 50W
20 Allègre, France 45 12N 3 41E
15 Allen, Bog of, Ireland 53 15N 7 0W
15 Allen L., Ireland 54 30N 8 5W
62 Allenby (Hussein) Bridge, Jordan 31 53N 35 33E
120 Allende, Mexico 28 20N 100 50W
113 Allentown, U.S.A. 40 36N 75 30W
26 Allentsteig, Austria 48 41N 15 20E
70 Alleppey, India 9 30N 76 28E
49 Allerød, Denmark 55 54N 12 19E
21 Allevard, France 45 24N 6 5E
116 Alliance, Nebr., U.S.A. 42 10N 102 50W
112 Alliance, Ohio, U.S.A. 40 53N 81 7W
19 Allier, R., France 46 57N 3 4E
20 Allier ♦, France 46 25N 3 0E
98 Alligator Creek, Mackay, Australia 21 20S 149 12E
98 Alligator Creek, Townsville, Australia 19 20S 146 55E
49 Allingåbro, Denmark 56 28N 10 20E
49 Allinge, Denmark 55 17N 14 50E
112 Alliston, Canada 44 15N 79 55W
14 Alloa, Scotland 56 7N 3 49W
21 Allos, France 44 15N 6 38E
107 Alma, Canada 48 35N 71 40W
116 Alma, Kans., U.S.A. 39 1N 96 22W
114 Alma, Mich., U.S.A. 43 25N 84 40W
116 Alma, Nebr., U.S.A. 40 10N 99 25W
116 Alma, Wis., U.S.A. 44 19N 91 54W
58 Alma Ata, U.S.S.R. 43 20N 76 50E
31 Almada, Portugal 38 40N 9 9W
98 Almaden, Australia 17 22S 144 40E
31 Almadén, Spain 38 49N 4 52W
96 Almadeus, L., Australia 24 45S 131 0E
31 Almagro, Spain 38 50N 3 45W
118 Almanor, L., U.S.A. 40 15N 121 11W
33 Almansa, Spain 38 51N 1 5W
30 Almanza, Spain 42 39N 5 3W
30 Almanzor, Pico de, Spain 40 15N 5 18W
33 Almanzora, R., Spain 37 22N 2 21W
46 Almaş, Mţii, Rum. 44 49N 22 12E
32 Almazán, Spain 41 30N 2 30W
32 Almazora, Spain 39 57N 0 3W
127 Almeirim, Brazil 1 10S 52 0W
31 Almeirim, Portugal 39 12N 8 37W
16 Almelo, Netherlands 52 22N 6 42E
32 Almenar, Spain 41 43N 2 12W
32 Almenara, Spain 39 46N 0 14W
33 Almenara, Sierra de, Spain 37 34N 1 32W
31 Almendralejo, Spain 38 41N 6 26W
33 Almería, Spain 36 52N 2 32W
33 Almería, G. de, Spain 36 41N 2 28W
33 Almería ♦, Spain 37 20N 2 20W
49 Almhult, Sweden 56 32N 14 10E
121 Almirante, Panama 9 10N 82 30W
45 Almiropótamos, Greece 38 16N 24 11E
45 Almirós, Greece 39 11N 22 45E
31 Almodôvar, Portugal 37 31N 8 2W

Almodóvar INDEX Ankober

MAP
31 Almodóvar del Campo, Spain 38 43N 4 10W
31 Almogia, Spain 36 50N 4 32W
31 Almonaster la Real, Sp. 37 52N 6 48W
112 Almont, U.S.A. 42 53N 83 2W
113 Almonte, Canada 45 15N 76 15W
31 Almonte, R., Spain 39 41N 6 12W
69 Almora, India 29 38N 79 4E
33 Almoradi, Spain 38 7N 0 46W
30 Almorox, Spain 40 14N 4 24W
31 Almuñécar, Spain 36 43N 3 41W
49 Almvik, Sweden 57 49N 16 30E
82 Alnif, Morocco 31 10N 5 8W
85 Almoustarat, Mali 17 35N 0 8E
48 Alnön I., Sweden 62 26N 17 33E
12 Alnwick, England 55 25N 1 42W
90 Aloi, Uganda 2 16N 33 10E
109 Alonsa, Canada 50 50N 99 0W
73 Alor, I., Indonesia 8 15S 124 30E
71 Alor Setar, Malaysia 6 7N 100 22E
31 Alora, Spain 36 49N 4 46W
31 Alosno, Spain 37 33N 7 7W
82 Alougoum, Morocco 30 17N 6 56W
30 Alpedrinha, Portugal 40 6N 7 27W
114 Alpena, U.S.A. 45 6N 83 24W
21 Alpes-Maritimes ♦, France 43 55N 7 10E
21 Alpes-de-Haute-Provence ♦, Fr. 44 8N 6 10E
25 Alpes Valaisannes, Switzerland 46 4N 7 30E
98 Alpha, Australia 23 45S 46 30E
38 Alpi Apuan, Italy 44 7N 10 14E
19 Alpi Craie, Italy 45 40N 7 0E
25 Alpi Lepontine, Italy 46 22N 8 27E
38 Alpi Orobie, Italy 46 7N 10 0E
25 Alpi Retiche, Switzerland 46 45N 10 0E
31 Alpiarca, Portugal 39 15N 8 35W
119 Alpine, Ariz., U.S.A. 33 57N 109 4W
117 Alpine, Tex., U.S.A. 30 35N 103 35W
22 Alps, Europe 47 0N 8 0E
49 Alrö, Denmark 55 52N 10 5E
49 Als, Aalborg, Denmark 56 46N 10 18E
19 Alsace, France 48 15N 7 25E
32 Alsasua, Spain 42 54N 2 10W
49 Alseda, Sweden 57 27N 15 20E
48 Alsen, Sweden 63 23N 13 56E
24 Alsfeld, Germany 50 44N 9 19E
27 Alsónémedi, Hungary 47 34N 19 15E
50 Alsten, Norway 65 58N 12 40E
32 Alta, Sierra, Spain 40 31N 1 30W
124 Alta Gracia, Argentina 31 40S 64 30W
108 Alta Lake, Canada 50 10N 123 0W
50 Altaelva, Norway 69 46N 23 45E
126 Altagracia, Venezuela 10 45N 71 30W
75 Altai, China 48 6N 87 2E
75 Altai = Aerhatai Shan, Mongolia 46 40N 92 45E
115 Altamaha, R., U.S.A. 31 50N 82 0W
127 Altamira, Brazil 3 0S 52 50W
126 Altamira, Colombia 2 3N 75 47W
124 Altamira, Chile 25 47S 69 51W
30 Altamira, Cuevas de, Spain 43 20N 4 5W
113 Altamont, U.S.A. 42 43N 74 3W
41 Altamura, Italy 40 50N 16 33E
76 Altanbulag, Mongolia 50 16N 106 30E
120 Altar, Mexico 30 40N 111 50W
120 Altata, Mexico 24 30N 108 0W
114 Altavista, U.S.A. 37 9N 79 22W
25 Altdorf, Switzerland 46 52N 8 36E
33 Altea, Spain 38 38N 0 2W
24 Altenberg, Germany 50 46N 13 47E
24 Altenbruch, Germany 53 48N 8 44E
24 Altenburg, Germany 50 59N 12 28E
24 Altenkirchen, Germany 50 41N 7 38E
26 Altenmarkt, Austria 47 43N 14 39E
31 Alter do Chão, Portugal 39 12N 7 40W
19 Altkirch, France 47 37N 7 15E
38 Alto Adige = Trentino-Alto Adige, Italy 46 5N 11 0E
127 Alto Araguaia, Brazil 17 15S 53 20W
91 Alto Chindio, Mozam. 16 19S 35 25E
120 Alto Cuchumatanes, Guatemala 15 30N 91 30W
124 Alto del Inca, Chile 24 10S 68 10W
91 Alto Ligonha, Mozam. 15 30S 38 11E
91 Alto Molocue, Mozam 15 50S 37 35E
125 Alto Paraná, R., Brazil 25 0S 54 35W
125 Alto Uruguai, R., Brazil 24 0S 53 30W
112 Alton, Canada 43 54N 80 5W
116 Alton, U.S.A. 38 55N 90 5W
99 Alton Downs, Australia 26 12S 138 58E
100 Altona, Australia 37 50S 145 40E
24 Altona, Germany 53 32N 9 56E
113 Altoona, U.S.A. 40 32N 78 24W
38 Altopáscio, Italy 43 50N 10 40E
25 Altstätten, Switzerland 47 22N 9 33E
64 Altun Kopru, Iraq 35 46N 44 10E
118 Alturas, U.S.A. 41 36N 120 37W
117 Altus, U.S.A. 34 30N 99 25W
75 Altyn Tagh, China 39 0N 90 0E
57 Alucra, Turkey 40 22N 38 47E
54 Aluksöne, U.S.S.R. 57 24N 27 3E
63 Alula, Somali Rep. 11 50N 50 45E
56 Alupka, U.S.S.R. 44 23N 34 2E
56 Alushta, U.S.S.R. 44 40N 34 25E
73 Alusi, Indonesia 7 35S 131 40E
32 Alustante, Spain 40 36N 1 40W
117 Alva, U.S.A. 36 50N 98 50W
30 Alvaiázere, Portugal 39 49N 8 23W
49 Alvangen, Sweden 58 0N 12 7E
120 Alvarado, Mexico 18 40N 95 50W
117 Alvarado, U.S.A. 32 25N 97 15W
49 Alvastra, Sweden 58 20N 14 44E
47 Alvdal, Norway 62 6N 10 37E
124 Alvear, Argentina 29 5S 57 40W
31 Alverca, Portugal 38 56N 9 1W
49 Alvesta, Sweden 56 54N 14 35E

MAP
48 Alvho, Sweden 61 30N 14 45E
100 Alvie, Austral. 38 15N 143 30E
117 Alvin, U.S.A. 29 23N 95 12W
112 Alvinston, Canada 42 50N 81 53W
31 Alvito, Portugal 38 15N 8 0W
48 Alvros, Sweden 62 3N 14 40E
49 Älvsborgs län ♦, Sweden 58 30N 12 30E
50 Alvsby, Sweden 65 42N 20 52E
49 Alvsered, Sweden 57 14N 12 51E
68 Alwar, India 27 38N 76 34E
70 Alwaye, India 10 8N 76 24E
97 Alyangula, Australia 13 55S 136 30E
59 Alyaskitovyy, U.S.S.R. 64 45N 141 30E
57 Alyata, U.S.S.R. 39 58N 49 25E
116 Alzada, U.S.A. 45 3N 104 22W
38 Alzano Lombardo, Italy 45 44N 9 43E
25 Alzey, France 49 48N 8 4E
81 Am-Dam, Chad 12 40N 20 35E
81 Am Djeress, Chad 16 15N 22 50E
81 Am Guereda, Chad 12 53N 21 14E
81 Am Timan, Chad 11 0N 20 10E
88 Am-Zoer, Chad 14 13N 21 23E
96 Amadeus, L., Australia 24 54S 131 0E
87 Amadi, Sudan 5 29N 30 25E
90 Amadi, Zaïre 3 40N 26 40E
64 Amadia, Iraq 37 6N 43 30E
105 Amadjuak, Canada 64 0N 72 50W
105 Amadjuak L., Canada 65 0N 71 0W
31 Amadora, Portugal 38 45N 9 13E
112 Amadore, U.S.A. 43 12N 82 36E
126 Amaga, Colombia 6 3N 75 42W
74 Amagasaki, Japan 34 42N 135 20E
49 Amager, Denmark 55 37N 12 35E
85 Amagunze, Nigeria 6 20N 7 40W
73 Amahai, Indonesia 3 2S 128 15E
74 Amakusa-Shotō, Japan 32 15N 130 10E
48 Åmål, Sweden 59 2N 12 40E
70 Amalapuram, India 16 35N 81 55E
126 Amalfi, Colombia 6 55N 75 4W
41 Amalfi, Italy 40 39N 14 34E
45 Amaliás, Greece 37 47N 21 22E
68 Amalner, India 21 5N 75 5E
77 Amami-guntō, Japan 28 0N 129 0E
39 Amandola, Italy 42 59N 13 21E
85 Amanfrom, Ghana 7 20N 0 25E
58 Amangeldy, U.S.S.R. 50 10N 65 10E
41 Amantea, Italy 39 8N 16 3E
127 Amapá, Brazil 2 5N 50 50W
127 Amapá ♦, Braz. 1 40N 52 0W
73 Amar, Indonesia 4 44S 131 40E
87 Amar Gedid, Sudan 14 27N 25 13E
64 Amara, Iraq 31 57N 47 12E
87 Amara, Sudan 10 25N 34 10E
127 Amarante, Brazil 6 14S 42 50W
30 Amarante, Portugal 41 16N 8 5W
109 Amaranth, Canada 50 36N 98 43W
68 Amaravati, India 20 55N 77 45E
70 Amaravati, R., India 10 50N 77 42E
31 Amareleja, Portugal 38 12N 7 13W
127 Amargosa, Brazil 13 2S 39 36W
117 Amarillo, U.S.A. 35 14N 101 46W
39 Amaro, Mte., Italy 42 5N 14 6E
69 Amarpur, Bihar, India 25 5N 87 0E
67 Amarpur, Tripura, India 23 30N 91 45E
64 Amasra, Turkey 41 45N 32 30E
85 Amassama, Nigeria 5 1N 6 2E
64 Amasya, Turkey 40 40N 35 50E
93 Amatikulu, S. Africa 29 3S 31 33E
120 Amatitlán, Guatemala 14 29N 90 38W
39 Amatrice, Italy 42 38N 13 16E
127 Amazon, R., S. America 2 0S 53 30W
126 Amazonas ♦, Brazil 4 20S 64 0W
126 Amazonas ♦, Colombia 1 0S 72 0W
126 Amazonas ♦, Ven. 3 30N 66 0W
127 Amazonas, R., S. America 2 0S 53 30W
70 Ambad, India 19 38N 75 50E
93 Ambahakily, Malag. 21 36S 43 41E
68 Ambala, India 30 23N 76 56E
70 Ambalangoda, Sri Lanka 6 15N 80 5E
70 Ambalapuzha, India 9 25N 76 25E
93 Ambalavao, Malagasy Rep. 21 50S 46 56E
88 Ambam, Cameroon 2 20N 11 15E
93 Ambanifilao, Malag. 12 48S 49 47E
93 Ambanja, Malagasy Rep. 13 40S 48 27E
93 Ambararata, Malag. 13 41S 48 27E
59 Ambarchik, U.S.S.R. 69 40N 162 20E
93 Ambarijeby, Malag. 14 56S 47 41E
70 Ambarnath, India 19 12N 73 22E
93 Ambaro, B. d', Malag. 13 23S 48 38E
70 Ambasamudram, India 8 43N 77 25E
126 Ambato, Ecuador 1 5S 78 42W
124 Ambato, Sierra de, Arg. 28 25N 66 10W
93 Ambato-Boeni, Malag. 16 28S 46 43E
93 Ambatolampy, Malag. 20 39S 47 35E
93 Ambatondrazaka, Malagasy Rep. 17 55S 48 28E
93 Ambatosoratra, Malag. 17 37S 48 31E
93 Ambenja, Malagasy Rep. 15 17S 46 58E
73 Ambeno, Timor (Port) 9 20S 124 30E
25 Amberg, Germany 49 25N 11 52E
120 Ambergris Cay, British Honduras 18 0N 88 0W
21 Ambérieu-en-Bugey, France 45 57N 5 20E
101 Amberley, N.Z. 43 9S 172 44E
20 Ambert, France 45 33N 3 44E
93 Ambevongo, Malagasy Rep. 15 25S 42 26E
93 Ambia, Malagasy Rep. 16 11S 45 33E
84 Ambidédi, Mali 14 35N 11 47W
69 Ambikapur, India 23 15N 83 15E
86 Ambikol, Sudan 21 20N 30 50E
93 Ambinanindrano, Malag. 20 5S 48 23E
49 Ambjörnarp, Sweden 57 25N 13 17E
12 Ambleside, Eng. 54 26N 2 58W
87 Ambo, Begemdir & Simen, Ethiopia 12 20N 37 30E
87 Ambo, Shewa, Ethiopia 0N 37 48E

MAP
126 Ambo, Peru 10 5S 76 10W
93 Ambodifototra, Malag. 16 59S 49 52E
93 Ambodilazana, Malag. 18 6S 49 10E
93 Ambohimahasoa, Malag. 21 7S 47 13E
93 Ambohimanga du Sud, Malag. 20 52S 47 36E
73 Ambon, Indonesia 3 35S 128 20E
93 Ambongao, Cones d', Malag. 17 0S 45 0E
90 Amboseli L., Kenya 2 40S 37 10E
93 Ambositra, Malagasy Rep. 20 31S 47 25E
119 Amboy, Calif., U.S.A. 34 33N 115 51W
113 Amboy, N.J., U.S.A. 40 31N 74 18W
93 Ambre, C. d', Malag. 11 57S 49 17E
112 Ambridge, U.S.A. 40 36N 80 15W
88 Ambriz, Angola 7 48S 13 8E
88 Ambrizete, Angola 7 10S 12 52E
70 Ambut, India 12 48N 78 43E
99 Amby, Australia 26 30S 148 11E
58 Amderma, U.S.S.R. 69 45N 61 30E
120 Ameca, Mexico 20 30N 104 0W
120 Ameca, R., Mexico 20 30N 104 0W
120 Amecameca, Mexico 19 10N 98 57W
16 Ameland, Netherlands 53 27N 5 45E
39 Amelia, Italy 42 34N 12 25E
20 Amèlie-les-Bains-Palalda, France 42 29N 2 41E
59 Amen, U.S.S.R. 68 45N 180 0E
41 Amendolara, Italy 39 58N 16 34E
118 American Falls, U.S.A. 42 46N 112 56W
118 American Falls Res., U.S.A. 43 0N 112 50W
5 American Highland, Antarctica 73 0S 75 0E
101 American Samoa, Pacific Ocean 14 20S 170 40W
125 Americana, Brazil 22 45S 47 20W
115 Americus, U.S.A. 32 0N 84 10W
16 Amersfoort, Neth. 52 9N 5 23E
93 Amersfoort, S. Africa 26 59S 29 53E
116 Ames, U.S.A. 42 0N 93 40W
113 Amesbury, U.S.A. 42 50N 70 52W
109 Amesdale, Canada 50 2N 92 55W
106 Ameson, Canada 49 50N 84 35W
45 Amfiklia, Greece 38 38N 22 35E
45 Amfilokhia, Greece 38 52N 21 9E
44 Amfipolis, Greece 40 48N 23 52E
45 Amfissa, Greece 38 32N 22 22E
59 Amga, R., U.S.S.R. 61 0N 132 0E
59 Amgu, U.S.S.R. 45 45N 137 15E
67 Amherst, Burma 16 2N 97 20E
107 Amherst, Canada 45 48N 64 8W
113 Amherst, Mass., U.S.A. 42 21N 72 30W
112 Amherst, Ohio, U.S.A. 41 23N 82 15W
117 Amherst, Tex., U.S.A. 34 0N 102 24W
113 Amherst, I., Can. 44 8N 76 45W
39 Amiata Mte., Italy 42 54N 11 40E
19 Amiens, France 49 54N 2 16E
45 Amigdhalokefáli, Gr. 35 23N 23 30E
44 Amindaion, Greece 40 42N 21 42E
3 Amirante Is., Ind. Oc. 6 0S 53 0E
109 Amisk L., Canada 54 35N 102 15W
117 Amite, U.S.A. 30 47N 90 31W
47 Amli, Norway 58 45N 8 32E
12 Amlwch, Wales 53 24N 4 21W
87 Amm Adam, Sudan 16 20N 36 1E
62 Amman, Jordan 32 0N 35 52E
48 Ammerån, Sweden 63 9N 16 13E
25 Ammersee, Ger. 48 0N 11 7E
48 Ammerån, Sweden 63 9N 16 13E
62 Ammi'ad, Israel 32 55N 35 32E
64 Ammókhostos, Cyprus 35 8N 33 55E
75 Amne Machin Shan, China 34 25N 99 40E
19 Amnéville, France 49 16N 6 9E
32 Amorebieta, Spain 43 13N 2 44W
45 Amorgós, Greece 36 50N 25 57E
31 Amory, U.S.A. 33 59N 88 30W
106 Amos, Canada 48 35N 78 5W
47 Amot, Norway 59 35N 8 0E
47 Amotsdal, Norway 59 37N 8 26E
82 Amour, Djebel, Algeria 33 42N 1 37E
77 Amoy = Hsiamen, China 24 25N 118 4E
93 Ampanihy, Malagasy Rep. 24 40S 44 45E
93 Amparihy Est., Malag. 23 57S 47 20E
93 Ampasindava, B. d', Malag. 13 40S 48 15E
93 Ampasindava, Presqu'ile d', Malag. 13 42S 47 55W
85 Amper, Nigeria 9 25N 9 40E
82 Ampère, Algeria 35 44N 5 27E
93 Ampombiantambo, Malag. 12 42S 48 57E
32 Amposta, Spain 40 43N 0 34E
93 Ampotaka, Malag. 25 3S 44 41E
93 Ampoza, Malagasy Rep. 22 20S 44 44E
62 Amqa, Israel 32 59N 35 10E
107 Amqui, Canada 48 28N 67 27W
68 Amraoti, India 20 55N 77 45E
68 Amreli, India 21 35N 71 17E
82 Amrenene el Kasba, Algeria 22 10N 0 30E
68 Amritsar, India 31 35N 74 57E
68 Amroha, India 28 53N 78 30E
24 Amrum, Germany 54 37N 8 21E
83 Amsel, Algeria 22 47N 5 29E
16 Amsterdam, Netherlands 52 23N 4 54E
113 Amsterdam, U.S.A. 42 58N 74 10W
3 Amsterdam, I., Ind. Oc. 37 30S 77 30E
26 Amstetten, Austria 48 7N 14 51E
58 Amu Darya, R., U.S.S.R. 37 50N 65 0E
126 Amuay, Venezuela 11 50N 70 10W
4 Amund Ringnes I., Can. 78 0N 97 0W
104 Amundsen Gulf, Canada 70 30N 123 0W
5 Amundsen Sea, Antarc. 72 0S 115 0W
48 Amungen, Sweden 61 10N 15 40E

MAP
72 Amuntai, Indonesia 2 28S 115 25E
59 Amur, R., U.S.S.R. 53 30N 122 30E
73 Amurang, Indonesia 1 5N 124 40E
101 Amuri Pass, N.Z. 42 31S 172 11E
32 Amurrio, Spain 43 3N 3 0W
59 Amurzet, U.S.S.R. 47 50N 131 5E
30 Amusco, Spain 42 10N 4 28W
45 Amvrakikós Kólpos, Greece 39 0N 27 55E
57 Amvrosiyvka, U.S.S.R. 47 43N 38 30E
82 Amzeglouf, Algeria 26 50N 0 1E
64 An Nafud, Arabia 28 15N 41 0E
64 An Najaf, Iraq 32 3N 44 15E
62 An-Nāqūrah, Lebanon 33 7N 35 8E
64 An Nasiriyah, Iraq 31 0N 46 15E
71 An Nhon (Binh Dinh), S. Vietnam 13 55N 109 7E
64 An Nu'ayriyah, Si. Arab. 27 30N 48 30E
83 An Nawfaliyah, Libya 30 54N 17 58E
15 An 'Uaimh, Ire. 53 39N 6 40W
100 Ana Branch, R., Australia 32 20S 143 0E
62 Anabta, Jordan 32 19N 35 7E
47 Ana-Sira, Norway 58 17N 6 25E
126 Anaco, Venezuela 9 27N 64 28W
118 Anaconda, U.S.A. 46 7N 113 0W
118 Anacortes, U.S.A. 48 30N 122 40W
117 Anadarko, U.S.A. 35 4N 98 15W
30 Anadia, Portugal 40 26N 8 27W
64 Anadolu, Turkey 38 0N 39 0E
59 Anadyr, U.S.S.R. 64 35N 177 20E
59 Anadyr, R., U.S.S.R. 66 50N 171 0E
59 Anadyrskiy Zaliv, U.S.S.R. 64 0N 180 0E
45 Anáfi, Greece 36 22N 25 48E
45 Anafópoulo, Greece 36 17N 25 50E
40 Anagni, Italy 41 44N 13 8E
108 Anahim Lake, Canada 52 28N 125 18W
120 Anáhuac, Mexico 27 14N 100 9W
64 Anah, Iraq 34 25N 42 0E
70 Anai Mudi, Mt., India 10 12N 77 20E
70 Anaimalai Hills, India 10 20N 76 40E
98 Anakie, Australia 23 32S 147 45E
57 Anaklia, U.S.S.R. 42 22N 41 35E
93 Analalava, Malagasy Rep. 14 35S 48 0E
93 Analapasy, Malagasy Rep. 25 11S 46 40E
85 Anam, Nigeria 6 19N 6 41E
68 Anambar, R., Pakistan 30 10N 68 50E
72 Anambas, Kepulauan, Indonesia 3 20N 106 30E
116 Anamoose, U.S.A. 47 55N 100 7W
116 Anamosa, U.S.A. 42 7N 91 28W
64 Anamur, Turkey 36 8N 32 58E
74 Anan, Japan 33 54N 134 40E
68 Anand, India 22 32N 72 59E
69 Anandpur, India 21 16N 86 13E
45 Anánes, Greece 36 33N 24 9E
70 Anantapur, India 14 39N 77 42E
66 Anantnag, Kashmir 33 45N 75 10E
56 Ananyev, U.S.S.R. 47 44N 29 57E
56 Anapa, U.S.S.R. 44 55N 37 25E
127 Anápolis, Brazil 16 15S 48 50W
65 Anar, Iran 30 55N 55 13E
65 Anarak, Iran 33 25N 53 40E
47 Ana-Sira, Norway 58 17N 6 22E
64 Anatolia = Anadolu, Turkey 38 0N 29 0E
118 Anatone, U.S.A. 46 9N 117 4W
124 Añatuya, Argentina 28 20S 62 50W
81 Anaye, Niger 19 15N 12 50E
18 Ancenis, France 47 21N 1 10W
104 Anchorage, Alaska 61 10N 149 50W
30 Ancião, Portugal 39 56N 8 27W
126 Ancohuma, Nevada, Bolivia 16 0S 68 50W
120 Ancon, Pan. Canal Zone 8 57N 79 33W
126 Ancón, Peru 11 50S 77 10W
39 Ancona, Italy 43 37N 13 30E
128 Ancud, Chile 42 0S 73 50W
128 Ancud, G. de, Chile 42 0S 73 0W
124 Andacolla, Argentina 37 10S 70 42W
124 Andacollo, Chile 30 15S 71 10W
124 Andalgalá, Argentina 27 40S 66 30W
47 Andalsnes, Norway 62 35N 7 43E
31 Andalucia, Spain 37 35N 5 0W
31 Andalusia, Reg., Spain 37 35N 5 0W
31 Andalusia = Andalucia, Spain 37 35N 5 0W
115 Andalusia, U.S.A. 31 51N 86 30W
71 Andaman Is., India 12 30N 92 30E
71 Andaman Sea, Ind. Oc. 13 0N 96 0E
71 Andaman Str., Andaman Islands, India 12 15N 92 20E
92 Andara, S.W. Africa 18 2S 21 9E
19 Andelot, France 46 51N 5 56E
16 Andenne, Belgium 50 30N 5 5E
85 Andéranboukane, Mali 15 26N 3 2E
25 Andermatt, Switzerland 46 38N 8 35E
24 Andernach, Germany 50 24N 7 25E
20 Andernos, France 44 44N 1 6W
49 Anderslöv, Sweden 55 26N 13 19E
100 Anderson, Australia 38 3S 145 25E
118 Anderson, Calif., U.S.A. 40 30N 122 19W
114 Anderson, Ind., U.S.A. 40 5N 85 40W
117 Anderson, Mo., U.S.A. 36 43N 94 29W
115 Anderson, S.C., U.S.A. 34 32N 82 40W
93 Anderson, Mt., S. Africa 25 5S 30 42E
104 Anderson, R., Canada 69 0N 127 0W
49 Anderstorp, Sweden 57 19N 13 39E
126 Andes, mts., S. America 20 0S 68 0W
50 Andfjorden, Norway 69 10N 16 20E
69 Andhra, L., India 18 30N 73 32E
70 Andhra Pradesh ♦, India 15 0N 80 0E
45 Andikíthira, Greece 35 52N 23 15E
45 Andimilos, Greece 36 47N 24 12E
45 Andíparos, Greece 37 0N 25 3E
45 Andipaxoi, Greece 39 9N 20 13E
45 Andipsara, Greece 39 30N 25 29E

MAP
58 Andizhan, U.S.S.R. 41 10N 72 0E
65 Andkhui, Afghanistan 36 52N 65 8E
100 Ando, Austral. 36 43S 149 16E
93 Andohararo, Malag. 22 58S 43 45E
70 Andol, India 17 51N 78 4E
32 Andorra ■, Europe 42 30N 1 30E
32 Andorra La Vella, Andorra 42 31N 1 32E
13 Andover, Eng. 51 13N 1 29W
112 Andover, N.Y., U.S.A. 42 11N 77 48W
112 Andover, Ohio, U.S.A. 41 35N 80 35W
93 Andrahary, Mt., Malag. 13 37S 49 17E
32 Andraitx, Sp. 39 35N 2 25E
93 Andramasina, Malag. 19 11S 47 35E
93 Andrano-Velona, Malag. 18 10S 46 52E
93 Andranopasy, Malag. 21 17S 43 44E
104 Andreanof Is., Alaska 51 0N 178 0W
54 Andreapol, U.S.S.R. 56 40N 32 17E
28 Andrespol, Poland 51 45N 19 34E
115 Andrews, S.C., U.S.A. 33 29N 79 30W
117 Andrews, Tex., U.S.A. 32 18N 102 33W
41 Andria, Italy 41 13N 16 17E
41 Andrian, Italy 46 30N 11 13E
93 Andriba, Malagasy Rep. 17 30S 46 58E
42 Andrijevica, Y.-slav. 42 45N 19 48E
45 Andritsaina, Greece 37 29N 21 52E
93 Androka, Malagasy Rep. 24 58S 44 2E
121 Andros I., Bahama Is. 24 30N 78 0W
45 Andros, Greece 37 50N 24 50E
27 Andrychów, Poland 49 51N 19 18E
31 Andújar, Spain 38 3N 4 5W
88 Andulo, Angola 11 25S 16 45E
89 Aneby, Sweden 57 48N 14 49E
85 Anécho, Togo 6 12N 1 34E
121 Anegada I., Virgin Is. 18 45N 64 20W
82 Anergane, Morocco 31 4N 7 14W
32 Aneto, Pico de, Sp. 42 37N 0 40E
83 Anfeg, Algeria 22 29N 5 58E
71 Ang Thong, Thailand 14 35N 100 31E
59 Anga, U.S.S.R. 60 35N 132 0E
76 Angangki, China 47 9N 123 48E
59 Angara, R., U.S.S.R. 58 30N 97 0E
59 Angarsk, U.S.S.R. 52 30N 104 0E
99 Angaston, Australia 34 30S 139 8E
48 Ange, Sweden 62 31N 15 35E
48 Angebo, Sweden 61 58N 16 22E
120 Angel de la Guarda, I., Mexico 29 30N 113 30W
49 Angelholm, Sweden 56 15N 12 58E
118 Angels Camp, U.S.A. 38 8N 120 30W
48 Angelsberg, Sweden 59 57N 15 58E
67 Angenong, China 31 57N 94 10E
87 Anger, R., Ethiopia 9 30N 36 35E
87 Angereb, Ethiopia 13 11N 37 7E
87 Angereb, R., Ethiopia 14 0N 36 0E
48 Angermanalven, Sweden 62 40N 18 0E
24 Angermünde, Germany 53 1N 14 0E
113 Angers, Canada 45 31N 75 30W
18 Angers, France 47 30N 0 35W
19 Angerville, France 48 19N 2 0E
50 Angesån, Sweden 66 50N 22 15E
39 Anghiari, Italy 43 32N 12 3E
109 Angikuni L., Canada 62 10N 99 40W
72 Angkor, Khmer Rep. 13 22N 103 50E
32 Anglès, Spain 41 57N 2 38E
12 Anglesey, I., Wales 53 17N 4 20W
•12 Anglesey ♦, Wales 53 17N 4 20W
20 Anglet, France 43 29N 1 31W
117 Angleton, U.S.A. 29 12N 95 23W
19 Anglure, France 48 35N 3 50E
4 Angmagssalik, Green. 65 40N 37 20W
90 Ango, Zaïre 4 10N 26 5E
91 Angoche, I., Mozam. 16 20S 39 50E
124 Angol, Chile 37 56S 72 45W
89 Angola ■, Africa 12 0S 18 0E
114 Angola, Ind., U.S.A. 41 40N 85 0W
112 Angola, N.Y., U.S.A. 42 38N 79 2W
98 Angoram, New Guinea 4 4S 144 4E
20 Angoulême, France 45 39N 0 10E
20 Angoumois, Fr. 45 30N 0 25E
58 Angran, U.S.S.R. 80 59N 69 3E
125 Angra dos Reis, Brazil 23 0S 44 10W
92 Angra-Juntas, S.W. Afr. 27 39S 15 31E
90 Angu, Zaïre 3 25N 24 28E
121 Anguilla, I., Leeward Is. 18 14N 63 5W
† 14 Angus ♦, Scot. 56 45N 2 55W
14 Angus, Braes of, Scotland 56 51N 3 0W
77 Anhwa, China 28 18N 111 25E
77 Ani, China 28 50N 115 29E
45 Anidhros, Greece 36 38N 25 43E
85 Anié, Togo 7 42N 1 8E
119 Animas, U.S.A. 31 58N 108 58W
119 Animas Pk., U.S.A. 31 33N 108 56W
49 Animskog, Sweden 58 53N 12 35E
71 Anin, Burma 15 36N 97 50E
93 Anivorano, Malag. 18 44S 48 58E
68 Anjangaon, India 21 10N 77 20E
68 Anjar, India 23 6N 70 10E
77 Anjen, China 26 42N 113 19E
73 Anjer-Lor, Indonesia 6 6S 105 56E
93 Anjiabé, Malag. 12 7S 49 20E
70 Anjidiv I., India 14 40N 74 10E
18 Anjou, France 47 20N 0 15W
93 Anjozorobe, Malagasy Rep. 18 22S 47 52E
76 Anju, Korea 39 40N 125 45E
85 Anka, Nigeria 12 13N 5 58E
77 Ankang, China 32 38N 109 5E
64 Ankara, Turkey 40 0N 32 54E
93 Ankaramena, Malag. 21 57S 46 39E
93 Ankaboa, Malag. 22 18S 44 31E
93 Ankazobé, Malagasy Rep. 18 20S 47 10E
93 Ankazotokana, Malag. 21 20S 48 9E
77 Anki, China 25 1N 118 4E
77 Anking, China 30 34N 117 1E
93 Ankisabé, Malag. 19 17S 46 29E
48 Anklesvar, India 21 38N 73 3E
87 Ankober, Ethiopia 9 35N 39 40E

• Incorporated within the county of Gwynedd
† Incorporated within the region of Tayside

* Incorporated within the new Southern Province
* Renamed Pagalu

† Renamed Angoche
†† In April 1973 districts replaced counties in N. Ireland

* Incorporated within the region of Strathclyde

* In April 1973 districts replaced counties in N. Ireland

Arrecife INDEX Áyios

MAP
86 Arrecife, Canary Is. 28 59N 13 40W
124 Arrecifes, Argentina 34 06S 60 9W
18 Arrée, Mts. d', France 48 26N 3 55W
120 Arriaga, Mexico 21 55N 101 23W
49 Arrild, Denmark 55 8N 8 58E
18 Arromanches-les- Bains, France 49 20N 0 38W
31 Arronches, Portugal 39 8N 7 16W
18 Arrou, France 48 6N 1 8E
118 Arrow Rock Res., U.S.A. 43 45N 115 50W
108 Arrowhead, Canada 50 40N 117 55W
101 Arrowtown, N.Z. 44 57S 168 50E
31 Arroyo de la Luz, Spain 39 30N 6 38W
119 Arroyo Grande, U.S.A. 35 9N 120 32W
49 Ars, Denmark 56 48N 9 30E
20 Ars, France 46 13N 1 30W
19 Ars-sur-Moselle, France 49 5N 6 4E
109 Arsenault L., Canada 55 5N 108 50W
76 Arshan, China 46 59N 120 0E
39 Arsiero, Italy 45 49N 11 22E
70 Arsikere, India 13 15N 76 15E
55 Arsk, U.S.S.R. 56 10N 49 50E
48 Arskogen, Sweden 62 8N 17 20E
45 Arta, Greece 39 8N 21 2E
32 Artá, Spain 39 40N 3 20E
44 Arta ♦, Greece 39 15N 26 0E
120 Arteaga, Mexico 18 50N 102 20W
30 Arteijo, Spain 43 19N 8 29W
57 Artem, Os., U.S.S.R. 40 28N 50 20E
84 Artémou, Mauritania 15 38N 12 16W
56 Artemovsk, U.S.S.R. 48 35N 37 55E
57 Artemovski, U.S.S.R. 54 45N 93 35E
19 Artenay, France 48 5N 1 50E
24 Artern, Germany 51 22N 11 18E
32 Artesa de Segre, Spain 41 54N 1 3E
92 Artesia, Botswana 24 2S 26 19E
117 Artesia, U.S.A. 32 55N 104 25W
117 Artesia Wells, U.S.A. 28 17N 99 18W
116 Artesian, U.S.A. 44 2N 97 54W
20 Arthez-de-Béarn, France 43 29N 0 38W
84 Arthington, Liberia 6 35N 10 45W
101 Arthur's Pass, N.Z. 42 54S 171 35E
124 Artigas, Uruguay 30 20S 56 30W
57 Artik, U.S.S.R. 40 38N 44 50E
19 Artois, France 50 20N 2 30E
45 Artotina, Greece 38 42N 22 2E
76 Arts Bogd Uul, mts., Mongolia 44 40N 102 20E
64 Artvin, Turkey 41 14N 41 44E
73 Aru, Kepulauan, Indonesia 6 0S 134 30E
90 Arua, Uganda 3 1N 30 58E
127 Aruanã, Brazil 15 0S 51 10W
121 Aruba I., Neth. W. Ind. 12 30N 70 0W
20 Arudy, France 43 7N 0 28W
100 Arumpo, Australia 33 48S 142 55E
69 Arun, R., Nepal 27 30N 87 15E
70 Aruppukottai, India 9 31N 78 8E
90 Arusha, Tanzania 3 20S 36 40E
90 Arusha ♦, Tanz. 4 0S 36 30E
90 Arusha Chini, Tanz. 3 32S 37 20E
87 Arusi ♦, Ethiopia 7 45N 39 00E
70 Aruvi, Aru, Sri Lanka 8 48N 79 53E
90 Aruwimi, R., Zaïre 1 30N 25 0E
118 Arvada, U.S.A. 44 43N 106 6W
70 Arvaklu, Sri Lanka 8 20N 79 58E
76 Arvayheer, Mongolia 46 15N 102 45E
21 Arve, R., France 46 11N 6 8E
68 Arvi, India 20 59N 78 16E
107 Arvida, Canada 48 16N 71 14W
50 Arvidsjaur, Sweden 65 35N 19 10E
48 Arvika, Sweden 59 40N 12 36E
44 Aryiaradhes, Greece 39 27N 19 58E
58 Arys, U.S.S.R. 42 20N 68 30E
40 Arzachena, Italy 41 5N 9 27E
55 Arzamas, U.S.S.R. 55 27N 43 55E
82 Arzew, Algeria 35 50N 0 23W
57 Arzgir, U.S.S.R. 45 18N 44 23E
39 Arzignano, Italy 45 30N 11 20E
26 Aš, Czechoslovakia 50 13N 12 12E
62 As Salt, Jordan 32 2N 35 43E
64 As Samawah, Iraq 31 15N 45 15E
62 As-Samū, Jordan 31 24N 35 4E
64 As Sulaimānīyah, Iraq 35 35N 45 29E
83 As Sultān, Libya 31 4N 17 8E
65 As Suwaih, Oman 22 10N 59 33E
64 As Suwayda, Syria 32 40N 36 30E
64 As Suwayrah, Iraq 32 55N 45 0E
92 Asab, S.W. Africa 25 30S 18 0E
85 Asaba, Nigeria 6 12N 6 38E
64 Asadabad, Iran 34 50N 48 10E
84 Asafo, Ghana 6 20N 2 40W
74 Asahigawa, Japan 43 45N 142 30E
87 Asale, L., Ethiopia 14 0N 40 20E
74 Asama, Japan 33 0N 140 0E
85 Asamankese, Ghana 5 50N 0 40W
84 Asankrangwa, Ghana 5 45N 2 30W
69 Asansol, India 23 40N 87 1E
48 Asarna, Sweden 62 40N 14 20E
87 Asbe Teferi, Ethiopia 9 4N 40 49E
92 Asbesberge, S. Africa 29 0S 23 0E
107 Asbestos, Canada 45 47N 71 58W
113 Asbury Park, U.S.A. 40 15N 74 1W
120 Ascensión, B. de la, Mex. 20 20N 87 20W
7 Ascension, I., Atlantic Oc. 8 0S 14 15W
25 Aschach, Germany 48 23N 14 0E
25 Aschaffenburg, Ger. 49 58N 9 8E
24 Aschendorf, Germany 53 2N 7 22E
24 Aschersleben, Germany 51 45N 11 28E
39 Asciano, Italy 43 14N 11 32E
39 Ascoli Piceno, Italy 42 51N 13 34E
41 Ascoli Satriano, Italy 41 11N 15 32E
126 Ascope, Peru 7 46S 79 8W
124 Ascotán, Chile 21 45S 68 17W
87 Aseb, Ethiopia 13 0N 42 40E
49 Aseda, Sweden 57 10N 15 20E
82 Asedjrad, Algeria 24 51N 1 29E
MAP
87 Aselle, Ethiopia 8 0N 39 0E
43 Asenovgrad, Bulgaria 42 1N 24 51E
47 Aseral, Norway 58 37N 7 25E
19 Asfeld, France 49 27N 4 5E
86 Asfûn el Matâ'na, Eg. 25 26N 32 30E
47 Asgardstrand, Norway 59 22N 10 27E
119 Ash Fork, U.S.A. 35 14N 112 32W
117 Ash Grove, U.S.A. 37 21N 93 36W
64 Ash Shām, Bādiyat, Asia 31 30N 40 0E
64 Ash Shāmīyah, Iraq 31 55N 44 35E
64 Ash Shatrah, Iraq 31 30N 46 10E
62 Ash Shuna, Jordan 32 32N 35 34E
86 Ashaira, Saudi Arabia 21 40N 40 40E
85 Ashanti, Ghana 7 30N 2 0W
115 Ashburn, U.S.A. 31 42N 83 40W
101 Ashburton, N.Z. 43 53S 171 48E
96 Ashburton, R., Australia 22 5S 115 0E
101 Ashburton, R., New Zealand 44 2S 171 50E
12 Ashby-de-la-Zouch, England 52 45N 1 29W
108 Ashcroft, Canada 50 40N 121 20W
62 Ashdod Yam, Israel 31 49N 34 35E
62 Ashdot Ya'aqov, Israel 32 39N 35 35E
115 Asheboro, U.S.A. 35 43N 79 46W
117 Asherton, U.S.A. 28 25N 99 43W
115 Asheville, U.S.A. 35 39N 82 30W
106 Asheweig, R., Canada 54 0N 88 0W
13 Ashford, England 51 8N 0 53E
99 Ashford, Australia 29 15S 151 3E
118 Ashford, U.S.A. 46 45N 122 2W
74 Ashikaga, Japan 36 28N 139 29E
74 Ashizuri-Zaki, Japan 32 35N 132 50E
58 Ashkhabad, U.S.S.R. 38 0N 57 50E
117 Ashland, Kans., U.S.A. 37 13N 99 43W
114 Ashland, Ky., U.S.A. 38 25N 82 40W
107 Ashland, Me., U.S.A. 46 34N 68 26W
118 Ashland, Mont., U.S.A. 45 41N 106 12W
116 Ashland, Nebr., U.S.A. 41 5N 96 27W
112 Ashland, Ohio, U.S.A. 40 52N 82 20W
118 Ashland, Oreg., U.S.A. 42 10N 122 38W
113 Ashland, Pa., U.S.A. 40 45N 76 22W
114 Ashland, Va., U.S.A. 37 46N 77 30W
116 Ashland, Wis., U.S.A. 46 40N 90 52W
116 Ashley, N.D., U.S.A. 46 3N 99 23W
113 Ashley, Pa., U.S.A. 41 12N 75 55W
108 Ashmont, Canada 54 7N 111 29W
96 Ashmore Reef, Australia 12 14S 123 05E
86 Ashmûn, Egypt 30 18N 30 55E
62 Ashquelon, Israel 31 42N 34 55E
112 Ashtabula, U.S.A. 41 52N 80 50W
70 Ashti, India 18 50N 75 15E
92 Ashton, S. Africa 33 50S 20 5E
118 Ashton, U.S.A. 44 6N 111 30W
12 Ashton-u.-Lyme, England 53 30N 2 8E
107 Ashuanipi, L., Canada 52 30N 66 10E
77 Ashun, China 25 10N 106 0E
60 Asia, cont. 45 0N 75 0E
73 Asia, Kepulauan, Indonesia 1 0N 131 13E
39 Asiago, Italy 45 52N 11 30E
82 Asilah, Morocco 35 29N 6 0W
40 Asinara, Italy 41 5N 8 15E
40 Asinara, G. dell', Italy 41 0N 8 30E
40 Asinara I., Italy 41 5N 8 15E
58 Asino, U.S.S.R. 57 0N 86 0E
63 Asir, Si. Arabia 18 40N 42 30E
63 Asir, Ras, Somali Rep. 11 55N 51 0E
70 Aska, India 19 37N 84 42E
47 Asker, Norway 59 50N 10 26E
49 Askersund, Sweden 58 53N 14 55E
47 Askim, Norway 59 35N 11 10E
49 Askloster, Sweden 57 13N 12 11E
86 Asl, Egypt 29 33N 32 44E
65 Asmar, Afghanistan 35 10N 71 27E
87 Asmera (Asmara), Ethiopia 15 19N 38 55E
49 Asnaes, Denmark 55 40N 11 0E
49 Asnen, Sweden 56 35N 15 45E
47 Asnes, Norway 60 37N 11 59E
82 Asni, Morocco 31 17N 7 58W
49 Asnaes, Denmark 55 49N 11 31E
49 Asnaes, Halvö, Denmark 55 40N 11 0E
74 Aso, Japan 33 0N 130 42E
90 Asoa, Zaïre 4 35N 25 48E
39 Asola, Italy 45 12N 10 25E
34 Asotin, U.S.A. 46 14N 117 2W
33 Aspe, Spain 38 20N 0 40W
119 Aspen, U.S.A. 39 12N 106 56W
117 Aspermont, U.S.A. 33 11N 100 15W
101 Aspiring, Mt., N.Z. 44 23S 168 46E
21 Aspres, France 44 32N 5 44E
68 Aspur, India 23 58N 74 7E
82 Assa, Morocco 28 35N 9 6W
84 Assaba, Massif de l', Mauritania 16 10N 11 45W
67 Assam ♦, India 25 45N 92 30E
85 Assamakka, Niger 19 21N 5 38E
16 Asse, Belgium 50 54N 4 6E
83 Assekrem, Algeria 23 16N 5 49E
40 Assémini, Italy 39 18N 9 0E
16 Assen, Netherlands 53 0N 6 35E
49 Assens, Odense, Den. 56 41N 10 3E
49 Assens, Randers, Den. 55 16N 9 55E
109 Assiniboia, Canada 49 40N 106 0W
109 Assiniboine, R., Canada 49 45N 99 0W
106 Assinica L., Canada 50 30N 75 20W
84 Assinie, Ivory Coast 5 9N 3 17W
125 Assis, Brazil 22 40S 50 20W
39 Assisi, Italy 43 4N 12 36E
45 Assos, Greece 38 22N 20 33E
12 Assynt, Scot. 58 25N 5 10W
14 Assynt, L., Scot. 58 25N 5 10W
45 Astakidha, Greece 35 53N 26 50E
20 Astaffort, France 44 4N 0 40E
53 Astara, U.S.S.R. 38 30N 48 50E
38 Asti, Italy 44 54N 8 11E
30 Astillero, Spain 43 24N 3 49W
45 Astipálaia, Greece 36 32N 26 22E
105 Aston C., Canada 70 10N 67 40W
MAP
30 Astorga, Spain 42 29N 6 8W
118 Astoria, U.S.A. 46 16N 123 50W
49 Astorp, Sweden 56 6N 12 55E
57 Astrakhan, U.S.S.R. 46 25N 48 5E
30 Astudillo, Spain 42 12N 4 22W
30 Asturias, Spain 43 15N 6 0W
124 Asunción, Paraguay 25 21S 57 30W
49 Asunden, Sweden 57 47N 13 18E
87 Asutri, Sudan 15 25N 35 45E
90 Aswa, R., Uganda 2 30N 33 5E
86 Aswad, Rasal, Si. Arab. 21 20N 39 0E
86 Aswân, Egypt 24 4N 32 57E
86 Aswân High Dam = Sadd el Aali, Egypt 24 5N 32 54E
86 Asyût, Egypt 27 11N 31 4E
86 Asyûti, Wadi, Egypt 27 18N 31 20E
27 Aszód, Hungary 47 39N 19 28E
64 At Tafilah, Jordan 30 45N 35 30E
86 At Ta'if, Saudi Arabia 21 5N 40 27E
124 Atacama, Arg. 25 40S 67 40W
124 Atacama ♦, Chile 27 30S 70 0W
128 Atacama, Desierto de, Chile 24 0S 69 20W
124 Atacama, Salar de, Chile 24 0S 68 20W
126 Ataco, Colombia 3 35N 75 23W
83 Atakor, Algeria 23 27N 5 31E
85 Atakpamé, Togoland 7 31N 1 13E
78 Atalaia, Brazil 9 25S 36 0W
45 Atalándi, Greece 38 39N 22 58E
126 Atalaya, Peru 10 45S 73 50W
74 Atami, Japan 35 0N 139 55E
80 Atar, Mauritania 20 30N 13 5W
59 Atara, U.S.S.R. 63 10N 129 10E
82 Ataram, Erg d', Algeria 23 57N 2 0E
31 Atarfe, Spain 37 13N 3 40W
119 Atascadero, U.S.A. 35 32N 120 44W
58 Atasu, U.S.S.R. 48 30N 71 0E
73 Atauro, Port. Timor 8 10S 125 30E
86 Atbara, Sudan 17 42N 33 59E
86 Atbara, R., Sudan 17 40N 33 56E
117 Atchafalaya B., U.S.A. 29 30N 91 20W
116 Atchison, U.S.A. 39 40N 95 0W
85 Atebubu, Ghana 7 47N 1 0W
32 Ateca, Spain 41 20N 1 49W
39 Aterno, R., Italy 42 18N 13 45E
38 Atesine, Alpi, Italy 46 55N 11 30E
39 Atessa, Italy 42 5N 14 27E
16 Ath, Belgium 50 38N 3 47E
64 Ath Thamami, Si. Arab. 27 45N 35 30E
108 Athabasca, Canada 54 45N 113 20W
109 Athabasca L., Canada 59 10N 109 30W
108 Athabasca, R., Canada 55 50N 112 40W
15 Athboy, Ireland 53 37N 6 55W
15 Athenry, Ireland 53 18N 8 45W
113 Athens, Canada 44 39N 75 55W
45 Athens = Athínai, Greece 37 58N 23 46E
115 Athens, Ala., U.S.A. 34 49N 86 58W
115 Athens, Ga., U.S.A. 33 56N 83 24W
113 Athens, N.Y., U.S.A. 42 15N 73 48W
114 Athens, Ohio, U.S.A. 39 52N 82 6W
113 Athens, Pa., U.S.A. 41 57N 76 36W
115 Athens, Tenn., U.S.A. 35 45N 84 38W
117 Athens, Tex., U.S.A. 32 11N 95 48W
112 Atherly, Canada 44 37N 79 20W
98 Atherton, Australia 17 17S 145 30E
85 Athiéme, Dahomey 6 37N 1 40E
45 Athínai, Greece 37 58N 23 46E
15 Athlone, Ireland 53 26N 7 57W
70 Athni, India 16 44N 75 6E
14 Atholl, Forest of, Scotland 56 51N 1 0W
107 Atholville, Canada 48 5N 67 5W
44 Athos, Mts., Greece 40 9N 24 22E
15 Athy, Ireland 53 0N 7 0W
87 Ati, Sudan 13 5N 29 2E
90 Atiak, Uganda 3 12N 32 2E
126 Atico, Peru 16 14S 73 40W
32 Atienza, Spain 41 12N 2 52W
106 Atikokan, Canada 48 40N 91 40W
107 Atikonak L., Canada 53 45N 64 30W
72 Atjeh ♦, Indon. 4 50N 96 0E
59 Atka, U.S.S.R. 60 50N 151 48E
55 Atkarsk, U.S.S.R. 51 55N 45 2E
116 Atkinson, U.S.A. 42 35N 98 59W
115 Atlanta, Ga., U.S.A. 33 50N 84 24W
117 Atlanta, Tex., U.S.A. 33 7N 94 8W
116 Atlantic, U.S.A. 41 25N 95 0W
114 Atlantic City, U.S.A. 39 25N 74 25W
6 Atlantic Ocean 0 0 20 0W
126 Atlántico ♦, Colombia 10 45N 75 0W
78 Atlas, Great, Mts., Afr. 33 0N 5 0W
104 Atlin, Canada 59 31N 133 41W
62 Atlit, Israel 32 42N 34 56E
47 Atlöy, Norway 61 21N 4 58E
70 Atmakur, India 14 37N 79 40E
115 Atmore, U.S.A. 31 2N 87 30W
108 Atnarko, Canada 52 25N 126 0W
117 Atoka, U.S.A. 34 22N 96 10W
45 Atokos, Greece 38 28N 20 49E
120 Atotonilco el Alto, Mexico 20 20N 98 40W
31 Atouguia, Portugal 39 20N 9 20W
49 Atrafors, Sweden 57 02N 12 40E
65 Atrak, R., Iran 37 50N 57 0E
49 Atran, Sweden 57 07N 12 55E
68 Atrauli, India 28 2N 78 20E
126 Atrato, R., Colombia 74 0N 77 0W
39 Atri, Italy 42 35N 14 0E
86 Atsbi, Ethiopia 13 52N 39 50E
115 Attalla, U.S.A. 34 2N 86 5W
106 Attawapiskat, Can. 53 0N 82 30W
106 Attawapiskat, L., Can. 52 20N 88 0W
106 Attawapiskat, R., Canada 53 0N 82 30W
24 Attendorn, Germany 51 8N 7 54E
26 Attersee, Austria 47 55N 13 31E
114 Attica, U.S.A. 40 20N 87 15W
19 Attichy, France 49 25N 3 3E
19 Attigny, France 49 28N 4 35E
107 Attikamagen L., Can. 54 54N 66 25W
MAP
45 Attiki ♦, Greece 38 10N 23 40E
62 Attil, Jordan 32 23N 35 4E
113 Attleboro, U.S.A. 41 56N 71 18W
66 Attock, Pakistan 33 52N 72 20E
71 Attopeu, Laos 14 56N 106 50E
70 Attur, India 11 35N 78 30E
75 Atunze = Tehtsin, China 28 45N 98 58E
49 Atvidaberg, Sweden 58 12N 16 0E
119 Atwater, U.S.A. 37 21N 120 37W
112 Atwood, Canada 43 42N 81 2W
116 Atwood, U.S.A. 39 52N 101 3W
114 Au Sable, R., U.S.A. 44 39N 84 10W
21 Aubagne, France 43 17N 5 37E
73 Aubarede Pt., Phil. 17 15N 122 20E
19 Aube ♦, France 48 15N 4 0E
21 Aubenas, France 44 37N 4 24E
19 Aubenton, France 49 50N 4 12E
19 Aubigny-sur-Nère, Fr. 47 30N 2 24E
20 Aubin, France 44 33N 2 15E
20 Aubrac, Mts. d', Fr. 44 38N 2 58E
115 Auburn, Ala., U.S.A. 32 37N 85 30W
118 Auburn, Calif., U.S.A. 38 50N 121 10W
114 Auburn, Ind., U.S.A. 41 20N 85 0W
116 Auburn, Nebr., U.S.A. 40 25N 95 50W
113 Auburn, N.Y., U.S.A. 42 57N 76 39W
115 Auburndale, U.S.A. 28 5N 81 45W
20 Aubusson, France 45 57N 2 11E
20 Auch, France 43 39N 0 36E
19 Auchel, France 50 30N 2 29E
85 Auchi, Nigeria 7 6N 6 13E
101 Auckland, N.Z. 36 52S 174 46E
101 Auckland ♦, N.Z. 37 0S 175 0E
101 Auckland Is., New Zealand 51 0S 166 0E
20 Aude, dépt., France 43 8N 2 28E
20 Aude, R., France 44 13N 3 15E
20 Aude ♦, France 43 8N 2 28E
106 Auden, Canada 50 17N 87 54W
18 Auderville, France 49 43N 1 57W
18 Audierne, France 48 1N 4 34W
19 Audincourt, France 47 30N 6 50E
87 Audo Ra., Ethiopia 6 20N 41 50E
116 Audubon, U.S.A. 41 43N 94 56W
24 Aue, Germany 50 34N 12 43E
24 Auerbach, Germany 50 30N 12 25E
18 Auffay, France 49 43N 1 07E
99 Augathella, Australia 26 2S 146 29E
92 Augrabies Falls, S. Afr. 28 35S 20 20E
25 Augsburg, Germany 48 22N 10 54E
41 Augusta, Italy 37 14N 15 12E
117 Augusta, Ark., U.S.A. 35 17N 91 25W
115 Augusta, Ga., U.S.A. 33 29N 81 59W
117 Augusta, Kans., U.S.A. 37 40N 97 0W
107 Augusta, Me., U.S.A. 44 20N 69 46E
118 Augusta, Mont., U.S.A. 47 30N 112 29W
116 Augusta, Wis., U.S.A. 44 41N 91 8W
49 Augustenborg, Den. 54 57N 9 53E
117 Augustine, U.S.A. 31 30N 94 37W
28 Augustów, Poland 53 51N 23 00E
96 Augustus, Mt., Australia 24 14S 116 48E
98 Augustus Downs, Australia 18 35S 139 55E
87 Aukan, Ethiopia 15 29N 40 50E
38 Aula, Italy 44 12N 9 57E
20 Aulnay, France 46 2N 0 22W
18 Aulne, R., France 48 17N 4 16W
116 Ault, U.S.A. 40 40N 104 42W
18 Ault-Onival, France 50 5N 1 29E
20 Aulus-les-Bains, Fr. 42 49N 1 19E
19 Aumale, France 49 46N 1 46E
20 Aumont-Aubrac, Fr. 44 43N 3 17E
85 Auna, Nigeria 10 9N 4 42E
70 Aundh, India 17 33N 74 23E
20 Aunis, France 46 0N 0 50W
73 Auponhia, Indonesia 1 58S 125 27E
21 Aups, France 43 37N 6 15E
47 Aurahorten, Mt., Nor. 59 15N 6 53E
69 Auraiya, India 26 28N 79 33E
69 Aurangabad, Bihar, India 24 45N 84 18E
70 Aurangabad, Maharashtra, India 19 50N 75 23E
18 Auray, France 47 40N 3 0W
83 Aures (Awras), Algeria 35 8N 6 30E
24 Aurich, Germany 53 28N 7 30E
47 Aurlandsvangen, Norway 60 55N 7 12E
20 Aurillac, France 44 55N 2 26E
39 Auronza, Italy 46 33N 12 27E
112 Aurora, Canada 44 0N 72 30E
92 Aurora, S. Africa 32 40S 18 29E
116 Aurora, Colo., U.S.A. 39 44N 104 55W
114 Aurora, Ill., U.S.A. 41 42N 88 20W
117 Aurora, Mo., U.S.A. 36 58N 93 42W
116 Aurora, Nebr., U.S.A. 40 55N 98 0W
112 Aurora, Ohio, U.S.A. 41 21N 81 20W
47 Aurskog, Norway 59 55N 11 26E
92 Aus, S.W. Africa 26 35S 16 12E
47 Austad, Norway 58 58N 7 37E
27 Austerlitz = Slavikov, Cz. 49 10N 16 52E
47 Austevoll, Norway 60 5N 5 13E
116 Austin, Minn., U.S.A. 43 37N 92 59W
118 Austin, Nev., U.S.A. 39 30N 117 1W
112 Austin, Pa., U.S.A. 41 40N 78 7W
117 Austin, Tex., U.S.A. 30 20N 97 45W
96 Austin, L., Australia 27 40S 118 0E
98 Austral Downs, Austral. 20 32S 137 33E
97 Australia ■, Oceania 23 0S 135 0E
100 Australian Alps, Australia 36 30S 148 8E
100 Australian Cap. Terr., Australia 35 15S 149 8E
5 Australian Dependency, Antarctica 73 0S 90 0E
26 Austria ■, Europe 47 0N 14 0E
50 Austvagöy, Norway 68 20N 14 40E
20 Auterive, France 43 21N 1 29E
19 Authie, R., France 50 22N 1 38E
120 Autlan, Mexico 19 40N 104 30W
19 Autun, France 46 58N 4 17E
MAP
20 Auvergne, France 45 20N 3 0E
19 Auxerre, France 47 48N 3 32E
19 Auxi-le-Château, Fr. 50 15N 2 8E
19 Auxonne, France 47 10N 5 20E
20 Auzances, France 46 2N 2 30E
47 Avaldsnes, Norway 59 21N 5 20E
19 Avallon, France 47 30N 3 53E
107 Avalon Pen., Canada 47 0N 53 20W
117 Avalon Res., U.S.A. 32 30N 104 30W
70 Avanigadda, India 16 0N 80 56E
125 Avaré, Brazil 23 4S 48 58W
44 Avas, Greece 40 57N 25 56E
64 Aveh, Iran 35 40N 49 15E
127 Aveiro, Brazil 3 10S 55 5W
30 Aveiro, Port. 40 37N 8 38W
30 Aveiro ♦, Portugal 40 40N 8 35W
124 Avellaneda, Argentina 34 50S 58 10W
41 Avellino, Italy 40 54N 14 46E
47 Averöya, Norway 63 0N 7 35E
41 Aversa, Italy 40 58N 14 11E
118 Avery, U.S.A. 47 22N 115 56W
126 Aves, Islas de, Venezuela 12 0N 67 40W
19 Avesnes-sur-Helpe, Fr. 50 8N 3 55E
48 Avesta, Sweden 60 9N 16 10E
20 Aveyron ♦, France 44 22N 2 45E
39 Avezzano, Italy 42 2N 13 24E
45 Avgó, Greece 35 33N 25 37E
124 Aviá Terai, Argentina 26 45S 60 50W
39 Aviano, Italy 46 3N 12 35E
41 Avigliano, Basilicata, Italy 40 44N 15 41E
38 Avigliano, Piemonte, Italy 45 7N 7 13E
21 Avignon, France 43 57N 4 50E
30 Avila, Spain 40 39N 4 43W
30 Avila ♦, Spain 40 30N 5 0W
30 Avila, Sierra de, Spain 40 40N 5 0W
30 Avilés, Spain 43 35N 5 57W
45 Avionárion, Greece 38 31N 24 8E
39 Avisio, R., Italy 46 14N 11 18E
31 Aviz, Portugal 39 4N 7 53W
19 Avize, France 48 59N 4 0E
100 Avoca, Australia 37 5S 143 20E
112 Avoca, U.S.A. 42 24N 77 25W
100 Avoca, R., Australia 35 50S 143 30E
15 Avoca, R., Ireland 52 48N 6 10W
108 Avola, Canada 51 45N 119 30W
41 Avola, Italy 36 56N 15 7E
112 Avon, N.Y., U.S.A. 43 0N 77 42W
116 Avon, S.D., U.S.A. 43 0N 98 3W
13 Avon, R., Hants., England 50 57N 1 45W
13 Avon, R., Worcs., England 52 8N 1 53W
98 Avon Downs, Australia 19 58S 137 25E
99 Avon Is., Pacific Ocean 19 37S 158 17E
112 Avon Lake, U.S.A. 41 28N 82 3W
91 Avondale, Rhodesia 17 43S 30 58E
106 Avonlea, Canada 50 0N 105 0W
113 Avonmore, Canada 45 11N 74 57W
13 Avonmouth, England 51 30N 2 42W
18 Avranches, France 48 40N 1 20W
46 Avrig, Rumania 45 43N 24 21E
20 Avrillé, Vendée, France 46 28N 1 28W
42 Avtovac, Y.-slav 43 9N 18 35E
87 Awag el Baqar, Sudan 10 10N 33 10E
65 Awali, Bahrain 26 0N 50 30E
70 Awarja, R., India 18 0N 76 15E
62 Awarta, Jordan 32 10N 35 17E
87 Awasa, L., Ethiopia 7 0N 38 30E
87 Awash, Ethiopia 9 1N 40 10E
87 Awash, R., Ethiopia 11 30N 42 0E
84 Awaso, Ghana 6 15N 2 22W
101 Awatere, R., N.Z. 41 55S 173 35E
83 Awbari, Libya 26 46N 12 57E
14 Awe, L., Scotland 56 15N 5 15W
87 Aweil, Sudan 8 42N 27 20E
85 Awgu, Nigeria 6 4N 7 24E
81 Awjilah, Libya 29 8N 21 7E
4 Axel Heiberg I., Can. 80 0N 90 0W
49 Axelfors, Sweden 57 26N 13 7E
84 Axim, Ghana 4 51N 2 15W
46 Axintele, Rumania 44 37N 26 47E
44 Axiós, R., Greece 40 57N 22 35E
48 Axmarsbruk, Sweden 61 3N 17 10E
13 Axminster, England 50 47N 3 1W
24 Axstedt, Germany 53 26N 8 43E
49 Axvall, Sweden 58 23N 13 34E
19 Ay, France 49 3N 4 0E
126 Ayabaca, Peru 4 40S 79 53W
74 Ayabe, Japan 35 20N 135 20E
124 Ayacucho, Argentina 37 5S 58 20W
126 Ayacucho, Peru 13 0S 74 0W
58 Ayaguz, U.S.S.R. 48 10N 80 0E
70 Ayakudi, India 10 57N 77 6E
31 Ayamonte, Spain 37 12N 7 24W
59 Ayan, U.S.S.R. 56 30N 138 16E
56 Ayancık, Turkey 41 57N 34 18E
126 Ayapel, Colombia 8 19N 75 9W
126 Ayapel, Sa. de, Colombia 7 45N 75 30W
56 Ayaş, Turkey 40 10N 32 14E
126 Ayaviri, Peru 14 50S 70 35W
45 Aydın, Turkey 37 52N 27 55E
85 Ayenngré, Togo 8 40N 1 1E
71 Ayerítam, Malaysia 5 24N 100 15E
113 Ayers Cliff, Canada 45 10N 72 3W
96 Ayers Rock, Australia 25 23S 131 5E
44 Ayia, Greece 39 43N 22 45E
45 Ayia Anna, Greece 38 52N 23 24E
45 Ayia Marina, Kasos, Gr. 35 27N 26 53E
45 Ayia Marina, Leros, Gr. 37 11N 26 48E
44 Ayia Paraskevi, Greece 39 14N 26 16E
45 Ayia Rouméli, Greece 35 14N 22 58E
45 Ayiássos, Greece 39 5N 26 23E
45 Ayios Andréas, Greece 37 21N 22 45E
44 Ayios Evstrátios, Gr. 39 34N 24 58E
45 Ayios Ioánnis, Akra, Greece 35 20N 25 40E

---

* Incorporated within the region of Grampian
    * Renamed Mobayi
    * Renamed Vadodara
    * Renamed Banjul
    † Renamed Moba

* Incorporated within the region of Borders
* Renamed Bight of Bonny

* Renamed Ras Nouadhibou

* Incorporated within the
county of Powys

* Renamed Belize
† Renamed Bharuch

* Renamed Bandar Seri Begawan

* Incorporated within the new Eastern Province

** Incorporated within the new Western Province

* Incorporated within the region of Strathclyde

* Incorporated within the
  county of Gwynedd
† Incorporated within the
  region of Highland

* Renamed Cambodia in January 1976

Chhatarpur INDEX Clewiston

MAP
69 Chhatarpur, India 24 55N 79 43E
68 Chhindwara, India 22 2N 78 59E
71 Chhlong, Kg., Khmer Rep. 12 11N 106 2E
71 Chi, Nam, Thailand 15 40N 104 20E
77 Chiai, Taiwan 23 29N 120 25E
71 Chiang Mai, Thailand 18 55N 98 55E
89 Chianje, Angola 15 35S 13 40E
120 Chiapas ♦, Mexico 17 0N 92 45W
41 Chiaramonte Gulfi, It. 37 1N 14 41E
39 Chiaravalle, Italy 38 41N 16 24E
41 Chiaravalle Centrale, It. 38 41N 16 25E
38 Chiari, Italy 45 31N 9 55E
38 Chiávari, Italy 44 20N 9 20E
38 Chiavenna, Italy 46 18N 9 23E
74 Chiba, Japan 35 30N 140 7E
74 Chiba-ken ♦, Japan 35 30N 140 20E
93 Chibabava, Mozambique 20 25S 33 35E
89 Chibemba, Angola 15 48S 14 8E
106 Chibougamau, Canada 49 56N 74 24W
106 Chibougamau L., Can. 49 50N 74 20W
106 Chibougamau, R., Can. 49 50N 75 40W
85 Chibuk, Nigeria 10 52N 12 50E
93 Chibuto, Mozambique 24 40S 33 33E
70 Chicacole = Strikakulam, India 18 14N 84 4E
114 Chicago, U.S.A. 41 45N 87 40W
114 Chicago Heights, U.S.A. 41 29N 87 37W
114 Chicago North, U.S.A. 42 20N 87 50W
104 Chichagof I., Alaska 58 0N 136 0W
82 Chichaoua, Morocco 31 32N 8 44W
13 Chichester, Eng. 50 50N 0 47W
74 Chichibu, Japan 36 5N 139 10E
76 Chichirin, China 50 35N 123 45E
126 Chichiriviche, Ven. 10 56N 68 16W
76 Chichow, China 38 30N 115 25E
117 Chickasha, U.S.A. 35 0N 98 0W
31 Chiclana de la Frontera, Spain 36 26N 6 9W
126 Chiclayo, Peru 6 42S 79 50W
118 Chico, U.S.A. 39 45N 121 54W
118 Chico, R., Chubut, Argentina 44 0S 67 0W
128 Chico, R., Santa Cruz, Argentina 49 30S 69 30W
119 Chicoma Pk., U.S.A. 36 8N 106 40W
93 Chicomo, Mozambique 24 31S 34 6E
113 Chicopee, U.S.A. 42 6N 72 37W
107 Chicoutimi, Canada 48 28N 71 5W
70 Chidambaram, India 11 20N 79 45E
93 Chidenguele, Mozam. 24 55S 34 2E
105 Chidley C., Canada 60 30N 64 15W
112 Chiefs Pt., Canada 44 42N 81 18W
25 Chiemsee, Germany 47 53N 12 27E
71 Chiengmai, Thailand 18 55N 98 55E
39 Chienti, R., Italy 43 15N 13 40E
38 Chieri, Italy 45 0N 7 50E
38 Chiese, R., Italy 45 45N 10 35E
39 Chieti, Italy 42 22N 14 10E
107 Chignecto B., Canada 45 33N 64 50W
126 Chigorodó, Colombia 7 41N 76 42W
124 Chiguana, Bolivia 21 0S 67 50W
76 Chihfeng, China 42 18N 118 57E
77 Chihing, China 25 2N 113 45E
77 Chihkiang, Hunan, China 27 21N 109 45E
77 Chihkiang, Hupei, China 30 25N 111 30E
77 Chihkin, China 26 30N 105 45E
76 Chihli, G. of (Po Hai), China 38 30N 119 0E
77 Chihsien (Weihwei), China 35 29N 114 1E
120 Chihuahua, Mexico 28 40N 106 3W
120 Chihuahua ♦, Mexico 28 40N 106 3W
58 Chiili, U.S.S.R. 44 10N 66 55E
91 Chikawawa, Malawi 16 2S 34 50E
70 Chik Ballapur, India 13 25N 77 45E
68 Chikhli, India 20 20N 76 18E
70 Chikmagalur, India 13 15N 75 45E
70 Chikodi, India 16 26N 74 38E
91 Chikonde, Zambia 12 16S 31 38E
91 Chilanga, Zambia 15 33S 28 16E
120 Chilapa, Mexico 17 40N 99 20W
66 Chilas, Kashmir 35 25N 74 5E
99 Childers, Australia 25 15S 152 17E
117 Childress, U.S.A. 34 30N 100 50W
128 Chile ■, S. Amer. 35 0S 71 15W
124 Chilecito, Argentina 29 0S 67 40W
126 Chilete, Peru 7 10S 78 50W
69 Chilka L., India 19 40N 85 25E
108 Chilko L., Canada 51 20N 124 10W
98 Chillagoe, Australia 17 14S 144 33E
124 Chillán, Chile 36 40S 72 10W
116 Chillicothe, Ill., U.S.A. 40 55N 89 32W
116 Chillicothe, Mo., U.S.A. 39 45N 93 30W
114 Chillicothe, Ohio, U.S.A. 39 53N 82 58W
100 Chillingollah, Australia 35 16S 143 3E
108 Chilliwack, Canada 49 10N 122 0W
68 Chilo, India 27 12N 73 32E
93 Chiloane, I., Mozam. 20 40S 34 55E
128 Chiloé, I. de, Chile 42 50S 73 45W
120 Chilpancingo, Mexico 17 30N 99 40W
100 Chiltern, Australia 36 10S 146 36E
13 Chiltern Hills, Eng. 51 44N 0 42W
114 Chilton, U.S.A. 44 1N 88 12W
88 Chiluage, Angola 9 15S 21 42E
91 Chilubula, Zambia 10 14S 30 51E
91 Chilumba, Malawi 10 28S 34 12E
77 Chilung, Taiwan 25 3N 121 45E
91 Chilwa, L. (Shirwa), Malawi 15 15S 35 40E
118 Chimacum, U.S.A. 48 1N 122 53W
75 Chimai, China 33 35N 102 10E
16 Chimay, Belgium 50 3N 4 20E
58 Chimbay, U.S.S.R. 42 57N 59 47E
126 Chimborazo, Ec. 1 20S 78 55W
126 Chimbote, Peru 9 0S 78 35W
126 Chimichaguá, Col. 9 15N 73 49W
46 Chimishliya, U.S.S.R. 46 34N 28 44E
58 Chimkent, U.S.S.R. 42 40N 69 25E
91 Chimpembe, Zambia 9 31S 29 33E
67 Chin, Burma 22 0N 93 0E
77 Chin Chai, China 31 58N 115 59E
75 China ■, Asia 30 0N 110 0E
120 China, Mexico 25 40N 99 20W
126 Chinacota, Colombia 7 37N 72 36W
121 Chinandega, Nicaragua 12 30N 87 0W
117 Chinati Pk., U.S.A. 30 0N 104 25W
126 Chincha Alta, Peru 13 20S 76 0W
99 Chinchilla, Australia 26 45S 150 38E
33 Chinchilla de Monte Aragón, Spain 38 53N 1 40W
32 Chinchón, Spain 40 9N 3 26W
76 Chinchow, China 41 10N 121 2E
114 Chincoteague, U.S.A. 37 58N 75 21W
91 Chinde, Mozambique 18 45S 36 30E
67 Chindwin, R., Burma 22 30N 95 0E
77 Ching Ho, R., China 34 20N 109 0E
91 Chinga, Mozambique 15 13S 38 35E
75 Chinghai ♦, China 36 0N 97 0E
70 Chingleput, India 12 42N 79 58E
91 Chingola, Zambia 12 31S 27 53E
91 Chingole, Malawi 13 4S 34 17E
89 Chinguar, Angola 12 18S 16 45E
80 Chinguetti, Mauritania 20 25N 12 15W
93 Chingune, Mozambique 20 33S 35 0E
76 Chinhae, S. Korea 35 9N 128 40E
93 Chinhanguanine, Mozam. 25 21S 32 30E
68 Chiniot, Pakistan 31 45N 73 0E
77 Chinkiang, China 32 2N 119 29E
119 Chinle, U.S.A. 36 14N 109 38W
77 Chinmu Chiao, China 18 10N 109 35E
70 Chinnamanur, India 9 50N 77 16E
76 Chinnampo, N. Korea 38 52N 125 28E
70 Chinnur, India 18 57N 79 43E
119 Chino Valley, U.S.A. 34 54N 112 28W
18 Chinon, France 47 10N 0 15E
109 Chinook, Canada 51 28N 110 59W
118 Chinook, U.S.A. 48 35N 109 19W
69 Chinsura, India 22 53N 88 27E
70 Chintamani, India 13 26N 78 3E
76 Chinwangtao, China 40 0N 119 31E
39 Chióggia, Italy 45 13N 12 15E
45 Chios = Khios, Greece 38 27N 26 9E
108 Chip Lake, Canada 53 35N 115 35W
91 Chipata (Ft. Jameson), Zambia 13 38S 32 28E
91 Chipinga, Rhodesia 20 13S 32 36E
31 Chipiona, Spain 36 44N 6 26W
115 Chipley, U.S.A. 30 45N 85 32W
70 Chiplun, India 17 31N 73 34E
107 Chipman, Canada 46 6N 65 53W
91 Chipoka, Malawi 13 57S 34 28E
42 Chiporovtsi, Bulgaria 43 24N 22 52E
112 Chippawa, Canada 43 5N 79 10W
13 Chippenham, Eng. 51 27N 2 7W
116 Chippewa, R., U.S.A. 44 45N 91 55W
116 Chippewa Falls, U.S.A. 44 55N 91 22W
126 Chiquian, Peru 10 10S 77 0W
120 Chiquimula, Guatemala 14 51N 89 37W
126 Chiquinquirá, Col. 5 37N 73 50W
57 Chir, R., U.S.S.R. 48 45N 42 10E
70 Chirala, India 15 50N 80 20E
91 Chiramba, Mozambique 16 55S 34 39E
65 Chiras, Afghanistan 35 14N 65 40E
68 Chirawa, India 28 14N 75 42E
70 Chirayinkil, India 8 41N 76 49E
58 Chirchik, U.S.S.R. 81 58N 69 15E
81 Chirfa, Niger 20 55N 12 14E
119 Chiricahua Pk., U.S.A. 31 53N 109 14W
121 Chiriquí, Golfo de, Panama 8 0N 82 10W
121 Chiriquí, Lago de, Pan. 9 10N 82 0W
121 Chiriquí, Vol., Panama 8 55N 82 35W
91 Chirivira Falls, Rhod. 21 10S 32 12E
46 Chirnogi, Rumania 44 7N 26 32E
91 Chiromo, Malawi 16 30S 35 7E
43 Chirpan, Bulgaria 42 10N 25 19E
91 Chisamba, Zambia 14 55S 28 20E
77 Chishan, Taiwan 22 44N 120 31E
91 Chisimba Falls, Zambia 10 12S 30 56E
42 Chisineu Cris, Rumania 46 32N 21 37E
38 Chisone, R., Italy 45 0N 7 5E
117 Chisos Mts., U.S.A. 29 20N 103 15W
68 Chistian Mandi, W. Pak. 29 50N 72 55E
55 Chistopol, U.S.S.R. 55 25N 50 38E
126 Chita, Colombia 6 11N 72 28W
59 Chita, U.S.S.R. 52 0N 113 25E
70 Chitapur, India 17 10N 76 50E
89 Chitembo, Angola 13 30S 16 50E
91 Chitipa, Malawi 9 41S 33 19E
89 Chitokoloki, Zambia 13 43S 23 4E
68 Chitorgarh, India 24 52N 74 43E
70 Chitrakot, India 19 20N 81 40E
66 Chitral, Pakistan 35 50N 71 56E
70 Chitravati, R., India 14 30N 78 0E
121 Chitré, Panama 7 59N 80 27W
67 Chittagong, Bangladesh 22 19N 91 55E
67 Chittagong ♦, Bangladesh 24 5N 91 25E
70 Chittoor, India 13 15N 79 5E
70 Chittur, India 10 40N 76 45E
87 Chitu, Ethiopia 8 38N 37 58E
39 Chiusi, Italy 43 1N 11 58E
33 Chiva, Spain 39 27N 0 41W
38 Chivasso, Italy 45 10N 7 52E
124 Chivilcoy, Argentina 35 0S 60 0W
91 Chiwanda, Tanzania 11 23S 34 55E
91 Chiwefwe, Zambia 13 37S 29 31E
91 Chizera, Zambia 13 10S 25 0E
52 Chkolov, U.S.S.R. 52 0N 55 5E
55 Chkolovsk, U.S.S.R. 56 50N 43 10E
26 Chlumec, Cz. 50 9N 15 29E
28 Chmielnik, Poland 50 37N 20 43E
76 Choahsien, China 37 48N 114 46E
90 Choba, Kenya 2 30N 38 5E
92 Chobe, R., Botswana 18 10S 24 10E
92 Chobe National Park, Botswana 21 30S 25 0E
85 Chobol, Nigeria 11 53N 13 1E
28 Chocianów, Poland 51 35N 15 33E
28 Chociwel, Poland 53 29N 15 21E
126 Chocó ♦, Colombia 6 0N 77 0W
126 Chocontá, Colombia 5 9N 73 41W
28 Chodaków, Poland 52 16N 20 18E
70 Chodavaram, India 17 40N 82 50E
28 Chodecz, Poland 52 56N 19 2E
28 Chodziez, Poland 52 58N 17 0E
128 Choele Choel, Arg. 39 11S 65 40W
19 Choisy-le-Roi, France 48 45N 2 24E
120 Choix, Mexico 26 40N 108 10W
28 Chojna, Poland 52 58N 14 25E
28 Chojnice, Poland 53 42N 17 40E
28 Chojnów, Poland 51 25N 15 58E
87 Choke Mts., Ethiopia 11 18N 37 15E
59 Chokurdakh, U.S.S.R. 70 38N 147 55E
18 Cholet, France 47 4N 0 52W
121 Choluteca, Honduras 13 20N 87 14W
91 Choma, Zambia 16 48S 26 59E
87 Chomen Swamp, Ethiopia 9 20N 37 10E
68 Chomu, India 27 15N 75 40E
26 Chomutov, Cz. 50 28N 13 23E
76 Chŏnan, S. Korea 36 48N 127 9E
71 Chonburi, Thailand 13 21N 101 1E
126 Chone, Ecuador 0 40S 80 0W
76 Chŏngjin, N. Korea 41 47N 129 50E
76 Chŏngju, S. Korea 36 39N 127 27E
76 Chŏnju, S. Korea 35 50N 127 4E
128 Chonos, Arch. de los, Chile 45 0S 75 0W
68 Chopda, India 21 20N 75 15E
12 Chopim, R., Brazil 25 35S 53 5W
83 Chormet el Melah, Libya 30 11N 16 29E
124 Chorolque, Cerro, Bolivia 20 59S 66 5W
28 Choroszcz, Poland 53 10N 22 59E
54 Chortkov, U.S.S.R. 49 2N 25 46E
69 Chorul Tso, China 32 30N 82 30E
76 Chŏrwŏn, S. Korea 38 15N 127 10E
28 Chorzele, Poland 53 15N 21 2E
28 Chorzów, Poland 50 18N 19 0E
124 Chos-Malal, Argentina 37 15S 70 5W
74 Choshi, Japan 35 45N 140 45E
28 Choszczno, Poland 53 7N 15 25E
118 Choteau, U.S.A. 47 50N 112 10W
68 Chotila, India 22 30N 71 15E
166 Choum, Mauritania 21 15N 16 45E
77 Chow Hu, China 31 35N 117 30E
119 Chowchilla, U.S.A. 37 11N 120 12W
76 Choybalsan, Mongolia 48 3N 114 28E
76 Choyr, Mongolia 46 24N 108 30E
13 Christchurch, Eng. 50 44N 1 47W
101 Christchurch, N.Z. 43 33S 172 47E
112 Christian, I., Canada 44 50N 80 39W
92 Christiana, S. Africa 27 52S 25 8E
49 Christiansfeld, Denmark 55 21N 9 29E
49 Christiansö, I., Den. 55 19N 15 12E
121 Christiansted, Virgin Is. 17 45N 64 42W
92 Christiana, S. Africa 27 52S 25 8E
95 Christmas I., Pac. Oc. 1 58N 157 27W
26 Chrudim, Cz. 49 58N 15 43E
27 Chrzanów, Poland 50 10N 19 21E
91 Chtimba, Malawi 10 35S 34 13E
58 Chu, U.S.S.R. 43 36N 73 42E
71 Chu, R., N. Vietnam 19 50N 105 20E
108 Chu Chua, Canada 51 30N 120 10W
77 Chu Kiang, China 22 15N 113 45E
77 Chuanchow, China 24 57N 118 31E
77 Chuanhsien, China 25 50N 111 12E
74 Chūbu, Japan 36 45N 137 0E
128 Chubut, R., Argentina 43 0S 70 0W
77 Chuchow (Lishui), China 28 30N 119 50E
77 Chuchow, China 27 56N 113 3E
54 Chudovo, U.S.S.R. 59 10N 31 30E
54 Chudskoye, Oz., U.S.S.R. 58 13N 27 30E
74 Chugoku, Japan 35 0N 133 0E
74 Chūgoku-Sanchi, Japan 35 0N 133 0E
56 Chuguyev, U.S.S.R. 49 55N 36 45E
116 Chugwater, U.S.A. 41 48N 104 47W
76 Chuho = Shangchih, China 45 10N 127 59E
76 Chuhsien, Chekiang, China 28 57N 118 58E
77 Chuhsien, Shantung, China 35 31N 118 45E
77 Chuhsien, Szechwan, China 30 51N 107 1E
71 Chukai, Malaysia 4 13N 103 25E
55 Chukhloma, U.S.S.R. 58 45N 42 40E
77 Chuki, Chekiang, China 29 30N 120 4E
77 Chuki, Hupei, China 32 26N 110 0E
59 Chukotskiy Khrebet, U.S.S.R. 68 0N 175 0E
59 Chukotskiy, Mys, U.S.S.R. 66 10N 169 3E
59 Chukotskoye More, U.S.S.R. 68 0N 175 0W
119 Chula Vista, U.S.A. 33 44N 117 8W
126 Chulucanas, Peru 5 0S 80 0W
77 Chumatien, China 33 0N 114 4E
124 Chumbicha, Argentina 29 0S 66 10W
43 Chumerna, Bulg. 42 45N 25 55E
59 Chumikan, U.S.S.R. 54 40N 135 10E
71 Chumphon, Thailand 10 35N 99 14E
91 Chumuare, Mozam. 14 31S 31 50E
76 Chunchŏn, S. Korea 37 58N 127 44E
91 Chunga, Zambia 15 0S 26 2E
77 Chungan, China 27 45N 118 0E
77 Chunghsien, China 30 17N 108 4E
77 Chungking, China 29 30N 106 30E
77 Chungsiang, China 31 14N 112 42E
67 Chungtien, China 27 51N 99 42E
68 Chunian, Pakistan 31 10N 74 0E
91 Chunya, Tanzania 8 30S 33 27E
90 Chunya ♦, Tanzania 7 48S 33 0E
126 Chuquibamba, Peru 15 47N 72 44W
124 Chuquicamata, Chile 22 15S 69 0W
124 Chuquisaca ♦, Bol. 23 30S 63 30W
25 Chur, Switzerland 46 52N 9 32E
67 Churachandpur, India 24 20N 93 40E
108 Church House, Canada 50 20N 125 10W
109 Churchill, Canada 58 45N 94 5W
109 Churchill L., Canada 56 0N 108 20W
108 Churchill Pk., Canada 58 10N 125 10W
107 Churchill Falls, Canada 53 32N 64 26W
109 Churchill, R., Man., Canada 57 5N 96 30W
107 Churchill, R., Newf., Canada 53 15N 63 0W
68 Churu, India 28 20N 75 0E
126 Churuguaro, Venezuela 10 49N 69 32W
77 Chusan, China 30 0N 122 20E
66 Chushul, Kashmir 33 40N 78 40E
77 Chusnan, China 32 14N 110 30E
52 Chusovoy, U.S.S.R. 58 15N 57 40E
77 Chuting, China 27 28N 113 1E
55 Chuvash A.S.S.R.♦, U.S.S.R. 55 30N 48 0E
76 Chwangho, China 39 41N 123 2E
42 Ciacovu, Rumania 45 35N 21 10E
114 Cicero, U.S.A. 41 48N 87 48W
32 Cidacos, R., Spain 42 15N 2 10W
56 Cide, Turkey 41 40N 32 50E
28 Ciechanów, Poland 52 52N 20 38E
28 Ciechocinek, Poland 52 53N 18 45E
121 Ciego de Avila, Cuba 21 50N 78 50W
126 Ciénaga, Colombia 11 1N 74 15W
126 Ciénaga de Oro, Col. 8 53N 75 37W
121 Cienfuegos, Cuba 22 10N 80 30W
28 Cieplice Slaskie Zdrój, Poland 50 50N 15 40E
20 Cierp, France 42 55N 0 40E
30 Cies, Islas, Spain 42 12N 8 55W
27 Cieszyn, Poland 49 45N 18 35E
33 Cieza, Spain 38 17N 1 23W
32 Cifuentes, Spain 40 47N 2 37W
71 Ciha Pa., N. Vietnam 22 20N 103 47E
31 Cijara, Pantano de, Spain 39 18N 4 52W
57 Cıldır, Turkey 41 10N 43 20E
64 Cilician Gates P., Tur. 37 20N 34 52E
64 Cilician Taurus, Tur. 36 40N 34 0E
46 Cilnicu, Rumania 44 54N 23 4E
117 Cimarron, Kans., U.S.A. 37 50N 100 20W
117 Cimarron, N. Mex., U.S.A. 36 30N 104 52W
117 Cimarron, R., U.S.A. 37 10N 102 10W
46 Cimpia Turzii, Rumania 46 34N 23 53E
46 Cimpina, Rumania 45 10N 25 45E
46 Cimpulung, Argeş, Rumania 45 17N 25 3E
46 Cimpulung, Suceava, Rumania 47 32N 25 30E
43 Cimpuri, Rumania 46 0N 26 50E
32 Cinca, R., Spain 42 20N 0 9E
42 Cincer, Y.-slav. 43 55N 17 5E
115 Cinch, R., U.S.A. 36 0N 84 15W
114 Cincinnati, U.S.A. 39 10N 84 26W
16 Ciney, Belgium 50 18N 5 5E
39 Cinigiano, Italy 42 53N 11 23E
39 Cinogli, Italy 43 23N 13 10E
21 Cinto, Mt., Corsica 42 24N 8 54E
46 Ciorani, Rumania 44 45N 26 25E
39 Ciovo, Yugoslavia 43 30N 16 17E
104 Circle, Alaska, U.S.A. 65 50N 144 10W
116 Circle, Montana, U.S.A. 47 26N 105 35W
114 Circleville, Ohio, U.S.A. 39 35N 82 57W
119 Circleville, Utah, U.S.A. 38 12N 112 24W
13 Cirencester, Eng. 51 43N 1 59W
46 Cireşu, Rumania 44 47N 22 31E
19 Cirey-sur-Vezouze, France 48 35N 6 57E
38 Ciriè, Italy 45 14N 7 35E
41 Cirò, Italy 39 23N 17 3E
117 Cisco, U.S.A. 32 25N 99 0W
46 Cislău, Rumania 45 14N 26 33E
27 Cisna, Poland 49 12N 22 20E
126 Cisneros, Colombia 6 33N 75 4W
46 Cisnădie, Rumania 45 42N 24 9E
40 Cisterna di Latina, It. 41 35N 12 50E
41 Cisternino, Italy 40 45N 17 26E
57 Citeli-Ckaro, U.S.S.R. 41 33N 46 0E
92 Citrusdal, S. Africa 32 35S 19 0E
39 Città della Pieve, Italy 42 57N 12 0E
39 Città di Castello, Italy 43 27N 12 14E
39 Città Sant' Angelo, It. 42 32N 14 5E
39 Cittadella, Italy 45 39N 11 48E
39 Cittaducale, Italy 42 24N 12 58E
41 Cittanova, Italy 38 22N 16 0E
46 Ciuca, mt., Rumania 45 31N 25 56E
120 Ciudad Acuña, Mexico 29 20N 101 10W
120 Ciudad Altamirano, Mexico 18 20N 100 40W
126 Ciudad Bolivar, Ven. 8 5N 63 30W
120 Ciudad Camargo, Mex. 27 41N 105 10W
120 Ciudad Delicias = Delicias, Mexico 28 10N 105 30W
120 Ciudad de Valles, Mex. 22 0N 98 30W
120 Ciudad del Carmen, Mex. 18 20N 97 50W
120 Ciudad Guerrero, Mex. 28 33N 107 28W
120 Ciudad Juárez, Mexico 31 40N 106 28W
120 Ciudad Madero, Mexico 22 19N 97 50W
120 Ciudad Mante, Mexico 22 50N 99 0W
120 Ciudad Obregón, Mex. 27 28N 109 59W
126 Ciudad Piar, Venezuela 7 27N 63 19W
31 Ciudad Real, Spain 38 59N 3 55W
31 Ciudad Real ♦, Spain 38 50N 4 0W
30 Ciudad Rodrigo, Spain 40 35N 6 32W
121 Ciudad Trujillo = Sto. Domingo, Dom. Rep. 18 30N 70 0W
120 Ciudad Victoria, Mex. 23 41N 99 9W
32 Ciudadela, Spain 40 0N 3 50E
46 Ciulnita, Rumania 44 26N 27 22E
56 Civa, B., Turkey 41 20N 36 40E
39 Cividale del Friuli, It. 46 6N 13 25E
39 Civita Castellana, Italy 42 18N 12 24E
39 Civitanova Marche, It. 43 18N 13 41E
39 Civitavécchia, Italy 42 6N 11 46E
39 Civitella del Tronto, It. 42 48N 13 40E
20 Civray, France 46 10N 0 17E
64 Civril, Turkey 38 20N 29 55E
40 Cixerri, R., Sardinia 39 45N 8 40E
64 Cizre, Turkey 37 19N 42 10E
*14 Clackmannan ♦, Scotland 56 10N 3 47W
13 Clacton-on-Sea, England 51 47N 1 10E
108 Claire L., Canada 58 30N 112 0W
117 Clairemont, U.S.A. 33 9N 100 44W
112 Clairton, U.S.A. 40 18N 79 54W
21 Clairvaux-les-Laes, France 46 35N 5 45E
19 Clamecy, France 47 28N 3 30E
115 Clanton, U.S.A. 32 48N 86 36W
92 Clanwilliam, S. Africa 32 11S 18 52E
15 Clara, Ireland 53 20N 7 38W
100 Clare, Australia 33 20S 143 50E
114 Clare, U.S.A. 43 47N 84 45W
15 Clare I., Ireland 53 48N 10 0W
15 Clare, R., Ireland 53 20N 9 0W
113 Claremont, U.S.A. 43 23N 72 20W
117 Claremore, U.S.A. 36 20N 95 20W
15 Claremorris, Ireland 53 45N 9 0W
5 Clarence I., Antarctica 61 30S 53 50W
128 Clarence, I., Chile 54 0S 72 0W
97 Clarence, R., Auatralia 29 25S 153 22E
101 Clarence R., N.Z. 42 17S 173 15E
109 Clarence Str., Alaska 55 40N 132 10W
96 Clarence Str., Australia 12 0S 131 0E
117 Clarendon, Ark., U.S.A. 34 41N 91 20W
117 Clarendon, Tex., U.S.A. 34 58N 100 54W
107 Clarenville, Canada 48 10N 54 1W
108 Claresholm, Canada 50 0N 113 45W
5 Clarie Coast, Antarctica 67 0S 135 0E
116 Clarinda, U.S.A. 40 45N 95 0W
116 Clarion, Ohio, U.S.A. 42 41N 93 46W
112 Clarion, Pa., U.S.A. 41 12N 79 22W
112 Clarion, R., U.S.A. 41 19N 79 10W
116 Clark, U.S.A. 44 55N 97 45W
112 Clark Pt., Canada 44 4N 81 45W
118 Clark Fork, U.S.A. 48 9N 116 9W
118 Clark Fork, R., U.S.A. 48 0N 115 40W
115 Clark Res., U.S.A. 33 45N 82 20W
119 Clarkdale, U.S.A. 34 53N 112 3W
98 Clarke Ra., Australia 20 45S 148 20E
107 Clarke City, Canada 50 12N 66 38W
100 Clarkefield, Australia 37 30S 44 40E
107 Clarkes Harbour, Can. 43 25N 65 38W
118 Clarks Fork, R., U.S.A. 45 0N 109 30W
113 Clarks Summit, U.S.A. 41 31N 75 44W
114 Clarksburg, U.S.A. 39 18N 80 21W
117 Clarksdale, U.S.A. 34 12N 90 33W
118 Clarkston, U.S.A. 46 28N 117 2W
117 Clarksville, Ark., U.S.A. 35 29N 93 27W
115 Clarksville, Tenn., U.S.A. 36 32N 87 20W
117 Clarksville, Tex., U.S.A. 33 37N 94 59W
118 Clatskanie, U.S.A. 46 9N 123 12W
117 Claude, U.S.A. 35 8N 101 22W
73 Claveria, Philippines 18 37N 121 15E
116 Clay Center, U.S.A. 39 27N 97 9W
119 Claypool, U.S.A. 33 27N 110 55W
112 Claysville, U.S.A. 40 5N 80 25W
118 Clayton, Idaho, U.S.A. 44 12N 114 31W
117 Clayton, N. Mex., U.S.A. 36 30N 103 10W
118 Cle Elum, U.S.A. 47 15N 120 57W
15 Clear C., Ireland 51 26N 9 30W
15 Clear I., Ireland 51 26N 9 30W
118 Clear Lake, Calif., U.S.A. 39 5N 122 54W
116 Clear Lake, S.D., U.S.A. 44 48N 96 41W
118 Clear Lake, Wash., U.S.A. 48 27N 122 15W
118 Clear Lake Res., U.S.A. 41 55N 121 10W
114 Clearfield, Pa., U.S.A. 41 0N 78 27W
118 Clearfield, Utah, U.S.A. 41 10N 112 0W
118 Clearmont, U.S.A. 44 43N 106 29W
108 Clearwater, Canada 51 38N 120 2W
115 Clearwater, U.S.A. 27 58N 82 45W
106 Clearwater L., Canada 56 10N 75 0W
118 Clearwater, Mts., U.S.A. 46 20N 115 30W
109 Clearwater, R., Canada 56 40N 109 30W
109 Clearwater Prov. Park, Canada 54 0N 101 0W
117 Cleburne, U.S.A. 32 18N 97 25W
12 Cleethorpes, Eng. 53 33N 0 2W
13 Cleeve Cloud, Eng. 51 56N 2 0W
13 Cleeve Hill, Eng. 51 54N 2 0W
21 Clelles, France 44 50N 5 38E
5 Clerks Rocks, Falkland Is. Dependencies 56 0S 36 30W
98 Clermont, Australia 22 46S 147 38E
19 Clermont, France 49 22N 2 24E
19 Clermont-en-Argonne, France 49 5N 5 4E
20 Clermont-Ferrand, Fr. 45 46N 3 4E
20 Clermont-l'Hérault, France 43 38N 3 26E
19 Clerval, France 47 25N 6 30E
19 Cléry-Saint-André, France 47 50N 1 46E
38 Cles, Italy 46 21N 11 4E
99 Cleveland, Australia 27 31S 153 3E
12 Cleveland, England 54 29N 1 0W
117 Cleveland, Miss., U.S.A. 33 43N 90 43W
112 Cleveland, Ohio, U.S.A. 41 28N 81 43W
117 Cleveland, Okla., U.S.A. 36 21N 96 33W
115 Cleveland, Tenn., U.S.A. 35 9N 84 52W
117 Cleveland, Tex., U.S.A. 30 18N 95 0W
98 Cleveland, C., Australia 19 11S 147 1E
99 Cleveland, Mt., Austral. 41 25S 145 23E
112 Cleveland Heights, U.S.A. 41 32N 81 30W
125 Clevelândia, Brazil 26 24S 52 23W
15 Clew Bay, Ireland 53 54N 9 50W
115 Clewiston, U.S.A. 26 44N 80 50W

* Incorporated within the region of Central

Córdoba INDEX Czempiń

MAP
120 Córdoba, Vera Cruz, Mexico 18 50N 97 0W
31 Córdoba, Spain 37 50N 4 50W
124 Córdoba ♦, Arg. 31 22S 64 15W
126 Córdoba ♦, Colombia 8 20N 75 40W
31 Córdoba ♦, Spain 38 5N 5 0W
124 Córdoba, Sierra de, Arg. 31 10S 64 25W
73 Cordon, Philippines 16 42N 121 32E
115 Cordova, Ala., U.S.A. 33 45N 87 12W
104 Cordova, Alaska, U.S.A. 60 36N 145 45W
32 Corella, Spain 42 7N 1 48W
98 Corfield, Australia 21 40S 143 21E
44 Corfu = Kerkira, Greece 39 38N 19 50E
30 Corgo, Spain 42 56N 7 25W
40 Cori, Italy 41 39N 12 53E
30 Coria, Spain 40 0N 6 33W
100 Coricudgy, Mt., Austral. 32 51S 150 24E
41 Corigliano Cálabro, It. 39 36N 16 31E
99 Corinna, Australia 41 35S 145 10E
45 Corinth = Korinthos, Greece 37 56N 22 55E
115 Corinth, Miss., U.S.A. 34 54N 88 30W
113 Corinth, N.Y., U.S.A. 43 15N 73 50W
45 Corinth Canal, Greece 37 48N 23 0E
45 Corinth, G. of = Korinthiakós, Gr. 38 16N 22 30E
127 Corinto, Brazil 18 20S 44 30W
121 Corinto, Nicaragua 12 30N 87 10W
46 Corj ♦, Rumania 45 5N 23 25E
15 Cork, Ireland 51 54N 8 30W
15 Cork ♦, Ireland 51 50N 8 50W
15 Cork Harbour, Ireland 51 46N 8 16W
18 Corlay, France 48 20N 3 5W
40 Corleone, Italy 37 48N 13 16E
41 Corleto Perticara, Italy 40 23N 16 2E
43 Corlu, Turkey 41 11N 27 49E
39 Cormòns, Italy 45 58N 13 29E
109 Cormorant, Canada 54 5N 100 45W
121 Corn Is., Cent. Amer. 12 0N 83 0W
125 Cornélio Procópio, Braz. 23 7S 50 40W
116 Cornell, U.S.A. 45 10N 91 8W
107 Corner Brook, Canada 49 0N 58 0W
100 Corner Inlet, Australia 38 40S 146 30E
38 Corniglio, Italy 44 29N 10 5E
117 Corning, Ark., U.S.A. 36 27N 90 34W
118 Corning, Calif., U.S.A. 39 56N 122 9W
116 Corning, Iowa, U.S.A. 40 57N 94 40W
112 Corning, N.Y., U.S.A. 42 10N 77 3W
106 Cornwall, Canada 45 5N 74 45W
13 Cornwall ♦, Eng. 50 26N 4 40W
4 Cornwallis I., Canada 75 0N 95 0W
126 Coro, Venezuela 11 25N 69 41W
127 Coroatá, Brazil 4 20S 44 0W
126 Corocoro, Bolivia 17 15S 69 19W
126 Coroico, Bolivia 16 0S 67 50W
101 Coromandel, N.Z. 36 45S 175 31E
70 Coromandel Coast, India 12 30N 81 0E
109 Coromorant, L., Canada 54 20N 100 50W
119 Corona, Calif., U.S.A. 33 49N 117 36W
119 Corona, N. Mex., U.S.A. 34 15N 105 32W
119 Coronado, U.S.A. 32 45N 117 9W
121 Coronado, Bahía de, Costa Rica 9 0N 83 40W
104 Coronation Gulf, Can. 68 0N 114 0W
5 Coronation I., Antarc. 60 45S 46 0W
124 Coronda, Argentina 31 58S 60 56W
124 Coronel, Chile 37 0S 73 10W
128 Coronel Dorrego, Arg. 38 40S 61 10W
128 Coronel Oviedo, Par. 25 24S 56 30W
124 Coronel Pringles, Arg. 38 0S 61 30W
124 Coronel Suárez, Arg. 37 30S 62 0W
124 Coronel Vidal, Arg. 37 28S 57 45W
127 Coronie, Surinam 5 55N 56 25W
44 Corovoda, Albania 40 31N 20 14E
100 Corowa, Australia 35 58S 146 21E
120 Corozal, Brit. Hond. 18 30N 88 30W
126 Corozal, Colombia 9 19N 75 18W
120 Corozal, Pan. Can. Zone 8 59N 79 34W
21 Corps, France 44 50N 5 56E
125 Corpus, Argentina 27 10S 55 30W
117 Corpus Christi, U.S.A. 27 50N 97 28W
117 Corpus Christi L., U.S.A. 28 5N 97 54W
126 Corque, Bolivia 18 10S 67 50W
32 Corral de Almaguer, Sp. 39 45N 3 10W
38 Corrégio, Italy 44 46N 10 47E
93 Correntes, C. das, Mozambique 24 6S 35 34E
20 Corrèze ♦, France 45 20N 1 45E
15 Corrib, L., Ireland 53 25N 9 10W
124 Corrientes, Argentina 27 30S 58 45W
126 Corrientes, C., Colombia 5 30N 77 34W
121 Corrientes, C., Cuba 21 43N 84 30W
126 Corrientes, R. Colombia 3 15S 75 58W
124 Corrientes ♦, Argentina 28 0S 57 0W
117 Corrigan, U.S.A. 31 0N 94 48W
112 Corry, U.S.A. 41 55N 79 39W
100 Corryong, Australia 36 12S 147 53E
21 Corse, C., Corsica 43 1N 9 25E
21 Corse, I, Mediterranean Sea 42 0N 9 0E
* 21 Corse ♦, France 42 0N 9 0E
21 Corsica = Corse, Mediterranean Sea 42 0N 9 0E
117 Corsicana, U.S.A. 32 5N 96 30W
21 Corté, France 42 19N 9 11E
31 Corte do Pinto, Port. 37 42N 7 29W
31 Cortegana, Spain 37 52N 6 49W
119 Cortez, U.S.A. 37 24N 108 35W
39 Cortina d'Ampezzo, It. 46 32N 12 9E
113 Cortland, U.S.A. 42 35N 76 11W
39 Cortona, Italy 43 16N 12 0E
31 Coruche, Portugal 38 57N 8 30W
64 Çorum, Turkey 40 30N 35 5E
127 Corumbá, Goias, Brazil 16 0S 48 50W
126 Corumbá, Mato Grosso, Brazil 19 0S 57 30W
30 Coruña ♦, Spain 43 0N 8 37E
46 Corund, Rumania 46 30N 25 13E

* *Divided into two new départements Haute-Corse and Corse-du-Sud.*

30 Corunna = La Coruña, Spain 43 20N 8 25W
127 Coruripe, Brazil 10 5S 36 10W
118 Corvallis, U.S.A. 44 36N 123 15W
106 Corvette, L., Canada 53 25N 73 55W
116 Corydon, U.S.A. 40 42N 93 22W
120 Cosamaloapán, Mexico 18 23N 95 50W
41 Cosenza, Italy 39 17N 16 14E
46 Coşereni, Rumania 44 38N 26 35E
112 Coshocton, U.S.A. 40 17N 81 51W
19 Cosne-s.-Loire, France 47 24N 2 54E
30 Cospeito, Spain 43 12N 7 34W
124 Cosquin, Argentina 31 15S 64 30W
38 Cossato, Italy 45 34N 8 10E
18 Cossé-le-Vivien, France 47 57N 0 54W
33 Costa Blanca, Sp. 38 25N 0 10W
32 Costa Brava, Spain 41 30N 3 0E
31 Costa del Sol, Sp. 36 30N 4 30W
32 Costa Dorada, Spain 40 45N 1 15E
121 Costa Rica ■, Central America 10 0N 84 0W
40 Costa Smeralda, Sardinia 41 5N 9 35E
38 Costigliole d'Asti, Italy 44 48N 8 11E
119 Costilla, U.S.A. 37 0N 105 30W
46 Coştiui, Rumania 47 53N 24 2E
24 Coswig, Germany 51 52N 12 31E
73 Cotabato, Philippines 7 14N 124 15E
124 Cotagaita, Bolivia 20 45S 65 30W
21 Côte d'Azur, Fr. 43 25N 6 50E
19 Côte d'Or, Fr. 47 10N 4 50E
19 Côte d'Or ♦, France 47 30N 4 50E
116 Coteau des Prairies, U.S.A. 44 30N 97 0W
110 Coteau du Missouri, Plat. du, U.S.A. 47 0N 101 0W
113 Coteau Sta., Canada 45 17N 74 14W
18 Cotentin, France 49 30N 1 30W
19 Côtes de Meuse, France 49 15N 5 22E
18 Côtes-du-Nord ♦, France 48 25N 2 40W
32 Cotiella, Spain 42 31N 0 19E
42 Cotina, R., Yugoslavia 43 36N 19 9E
85 Cotonou, Dahomey 6 20N 2 25E
126 Cotopaxi, Vol., Ecuador 0 30S 78 30W
41 Cotronei, Italy 39 9N 16 27E
13 Cotswold Hills, England 51 42N 2 10W
118 Cottage Grove, U.S.A. 43 48N 123 2W
24 Cottbus, Germany 51 44N 14 20E
24 Cottbus ♦, E. Ger. 51 43N 13 30E
108 Cottonwood, Canada 53 5N 121 50E
119 Cottonwood, U.S.A. 34 48N 112 1W
20 Coubre, Pte. de la, Fr. 45 42N 1 15W
19 Couches, France 46 53N 4 30E
31 Couço, Portugal 38 59N 8 17W
112 Coudersport, U.S.A. 41 45N 78 1W
18 Couëron, France 47 13N 1 44W
18 Coueson, R., France 48 20N 1 15W
20 Couhé-Vérac, France 46 18N 0 12E
20 Coulanges, Deux Sèvres, France 46 58N 0 35W
19 Coulanges, Yonne, Fr. 47 30N 3 30E
118 Coulee City, U.S.A. 47 44N 119 12W
5 Coulman I., Antarctica 73 35S 170 0E
19 Coulommiers, France 48 50N 3 3E
107 Coulonge, R., Canada 46 50N 77 20W
104 Council, Alaska, U.S.A. 64 55N 163 45W
116 Council Bluffs, U.S.A. 41 20N 95 50W
116 Council Grove, U.S.A. 38 41N 96 30W
126 Courantyne, R., S. Amer. 5 0N 57 45W
20 Courçon, France 46 15N 0 50W
21 Cours, France 46 7N 4 19E
20 Coursan, France 43 14N 3 4E
18 Courseulles, France 49 20N 0 29W
117 Courshatta, U.S.A. 32 3N 93 20W
108 Courtenay, Canada 49 45N 125 0W
16 Courtrai = Kortrijk, Belgium 50 50N 3 17E
112 Courtright, Canada 42 48N 82 55W
18 Courville, France 48 28N 1 15E
18 Coutances, France 49 3N 1 28W
18 Couterne, France 48 30N 0 25W
20 Coutras, France 45 3N 0 8W
32 Covarrubias, Spain 42 4N 3 31W
46 Covasna, Rumania 45 50N 26 10E
46 Covasna ♦, Rumania 45 50N 26 0E
13 Coventry, Eng. 52 25N 1 31W
109 Coventry L., Canada 61 15N 106 15W
30 Covilhã, Portugal 40 17N 7 31W
115 Covington, Ga., U.S.A. 33 36N 83 50W
114 Covington, Ky., U.S.A. 39 5N 84 30W
117 Covington, Okla., U.S.A. 36 21N 97 36W
117 Covington, Tenn., U.S.A. 35 34N 89 39W
98 Cowal Cr. Settlement, Australia 10 30S 142 16E
100 Cowal L., Australia 33 40S 147 25E
109 Cowan, Canada 52 5N 100 45W
96 Cowan L., Australia 31 45S 121 45E
100 Cowangie, Australia 35 12S 141 26E
113 Cowansville, Canada 45 14N 72 46W
99 Cowarie, Australia 27 45S 138 15E
14 Cowdenbeath, Scot. 56 7N 3 20W
99 Cowell, Australia 33 38S 136 40E
13 Cowes, England 50 45N 1 18W
100 Cowra, Austral. 33 49S 148 42E
127 Coxim, Brazil 18 30S 54 55W
67 Cox's Bazar, Bangladesh 21 25N 92 3E
107 Cox's Cove, Canada 49 7N 58 5W
120 Coyuca de Benítez, Mex. 17 1N 100 8W
120 Coyuca de Catalán, Mex. 18 58N 100 41W
116 Cozad, U.S.A. 40 55N 99 57W
38 Cozie, Alpi, It./Fr. 44 50N 6 59E
120 Cozumel, Isla de, Mex. 20 30N 86 40W
100 Craboon, Australia 32 3S 149 30E
99 Cracow, Australia 25 14S 150 24E
92 Cradock, S. Afr. 32 8S 25 36E
112 Crafton, U.S.A. 40 25N 80 4W
118 Craig, U.S.A. 40 32N 107 44W
15 Craigavon = Portadown, N. Ire. 54 27N 6 26W
91 Craigmore, Rhodesia 20 28S 32 30E
25 Crailsheim, Germany 49 7N 10 5E
46 Craiova, Rumania 44 21N 23 48E
98 Cramsie, Australia 23 20S 144 15E
109 Cranberry Portage, Can. 54 36N 101 22W
99 Cranbrook, Australia 42 0S 148 5E
108 Cranbrook, Canada 49 30N 115 55W
116 Crandon, U.S.A. 45 32N 88 52W
118 Crane, Oregon, U.S.A. 43 21N 118 39W
117 Crane, Texas, U.S.A. 31 26N 102 27W
113 Cranston, U.S.A. 41 47N 71 27W
18 Craon, France 47 50N 0 58W
19 Craonne, France 49 27N 3 46E
46 Crasna, Rumania 46 32N 27 51E
46 Crasna, R., Rumania 47 44N 27 35E
118 Crater Lake, U.S.A. 42 55N 122 3W
127 Cratéus, Brazil 5 10S 40 50W
41 Crati, R., Italy 39 41N 16 30E
127 Crato, Brazil 7 10S 39 25W
31 Crato, Portugal 39 16N 7 39W
21 Crau, France 43 32N 4 40E
116 Crawford, U.S.A. 42 40N 103 25W
114 Crawfordsville, U.S.A. 40 2N 86 51W
13 Crawley, England 51 7N 0 10W
118 Crazy Mts., U.S.A. 46 14N 110 30W
19 Crécy-en-Brie, France 48 50N 2 53E
19 Crécy-en-Ponthieu, Fr. 50 15N 1 53E
19 Crécy-sur-Serre, France 49 40N 3 32E
112 Crediton, Canada 43 19N 81 33W
14 Cree, R., Scotland 55 3N 4 35W
109 Cree L., Canada 57 30N 107 0W
119 Creede, U.S.A. 37 56N 106 59W
120 Creel, Mexico 27 45N 107 38W
116 Creighton, U.S.A. 42 30N 97 52W
19 Creil, France 49 15N 2 34E
38 Crema, Italy 45 21N 9 40E
38 Cremona, Italy 45 8N 10 2E
42 Crepaja, Yugoslavia 45 1N 20 38E
19 Crépy, France 49 37N 3 32E
19 Crépy-en-Valois, France 49 14N 2 54E
39 Cres, Yugoslavia 44 58N 14 25E
116 Cresbard, U.S.A. 45 13N 98 57W
117 Crescent, Okla., U.S.A. 35 38N 97 36W
118 Crescent, Oreg., U.S.A. 43 30N 121 37W
118 Crescent City, U.S.A. 41 45N 124 12W
38 Crescentino, Italy 45 11N 8 7E
39 Crespino, Italy 44 59N 11 51E
106 Cressman, Canada 47 40N 72 55W
100 Cressy, Australia 38 10S 143 38E
21 Crest, France 44 44N 5 2E
119 Crested Butte, U.S.A. 38 57N 107 0W
112 Crestline, U.S.A. 40 50N 82 45W
108 Creston, Canada 49 10N 116 40W
116 Creston, Iowa, U.S.A. 41 0N 94 20W
118 Creston, Wash., U.S.A. 47 47N 118 36W
118 Creston, Wyo., U.S.A. 41 46N 107 50W
119 Crestone, U.S.A. 35 2N 106 0W
115 Crestview, U.S.A. 30 45N 86 35W
100 Creswick, Australia 37 19S 143 50E
45 Crete = Kriti, Greece 35 15N 25 0E
116 Crete, U.S.A. 40 38N 96 58W
45 Crete, Sea of, Greece 26 0N 25 0E
32 Creus, C., Spain 42 20N 3 19E
20 Creuse, R., France 47 0N 0 34E
20 Creuse ♦, France 46 0N 2 0E
24 Creuzburg, Germany 51 3N 10 15E
39 Crevalcore, Italy 44 41N 11 10E
19 Crèvecäur-le-Grand, Fr. 49 37N 2 5E
33 Crevillente, Spain 38 12N 0 48W
12 Crewe, England 53 6N 2 28W
100 Crib Point, Australia 38 15S 145 11E
14 Crieff, Scotland 56 22N 3 50W
39 Crikvenica, Yugoslavia 45 11N 14 40E
108 Crillon, Mt., Canada 58 39N 137 14W
56 Crimea = Krymskaya, U.S.S.R. 45 0N 34 0E
24 Crimmitschau, Germany 50 48N 12 23E
14 Crinan, Scot. 56 6N 5 34W
46 Cristeşti, Rumania 47 15N 26 33E
120 Cristóbal, Pan. Can. Zone 9 10N 80 0W
42 Crişul Alb, R., Rum 46 25N 21 40E
46 Crişul Negru, R., Rum 46 38N 22 26E
46 Crişul Repede, R., Rum. 47 20N 22 25E
24 Crivitz, Germany 53 35N 11 39E
42 Crna Gora ♦, Y.-slav. 42 40N 19 20E
42 Crna Trava, Yugoslavia 42 49N 22 19E
42 Crni Drim, R., Y.-slav. 41 17N 20 40E
42 Crni Timok, R., Y.-slav. 43 53N 22 0E
42 Crnoljeva Planina, Yugoslavia 42 20N 21 0E
39 Črnomeij, Yugoslavia 45 33N 15 10E
15 Croagh Patrick, mt., Ire. 53 46N 9 40W
39 Croatia = Hrvatska, Y.-slav. 45 20N 16 0E
72 Crocker, Barisan, Sabah 5 0N 116 30E
117 Crockett, U.S.A. 31 20N 95 30W
96 Crocodile Is., Australia 11 43S 135 8E
20 Crocq, France 45 52N 2 21E
18 Croisic, Pte. du., Fr. 47 19N 2 31W
112 Croker, C., Canada 44 57N 80 59W
96 Croker, I., Australia 11 12N 132 32E
109 Cromarty, Canada 58 5N 94 10W
14 Cromarty, Scot. 57 40N 4 2W
12 Cromer, England 52 56N 1 18E
101 Cromwell, N.Z. 45 3S 169 14E
19 Cronat, France 46 43N 3 40E
100 Cronulla, Australia 34 3S 151 8E
121 Crooked I., Bahamas 22 50N 74 10W
118 Crooked, R., U.S.A. 44 30N 121 0W
116 Crookston, Minn., U.S.A. 47 50N 96 40W
116 Crookston, Nebr., U.S.A. 42 56N 100 45W
114 Crooksville, U.S.A. 39 45N 82 8W
100 Crookwell, Australia 34 28S 149 24E
116 Crosby, Minn., U.S.A. 46 28N 93 57W
112 Crosby, Pa., U.S.A. 41 45N 78 23W
117 Crosbyton, U.S.A. 33 37N 101 12W
85 Cross, R, Nigeria 4 46N 8 20E
115 Cross City, U.S.A. 29 35N 83 5W
12 Cross Fell, Eng. 54 44N 2 29W
117 Cross Plains, U.S.A. 32 8N 99 7W
104 Cross Sound, U.S.A. 58 20N 136 30W
117 Crossett, U.S.A. 33 10N 91 57W
108 Crossfield, Canada 51 25N 114 0W
15 Crosshaven, Ireland 51 48N 8 19W
113 Croton-on-Hudson, U.S.A. 41 19N 73 55W
41 Crotone, Italy 39 5N 17 6E
118 Crow Agency, U.S.A. 45 40N 107 30W
15 Crow Hd., Ireland 51 34N 10 9W
100 Crowdy Hd., Australia 31 48S 152 44E
117 Crowell, U.S.A. 33 59N 99 45W
100 Crowes, Australia 38 43S 143 24E
117 Crowley, U.S.A. 30 15N 92 20W
114 Crown Point, U.S.A. 41 24N 87 23W
99 Crow's Nest, Australia 27 14S 152 2E
108 Crowsnest P., Canada 49 40N 114 40W
98 Croydon, Australia 18 15S 142 14E
13 Croydon, Eng. 51 18N 0 5W
3 Crozet, Ile, Indian Ocean 46 27S 52 0E
18 Crozon, France 48 15N 4 30W
126 Cruces, Pta., Colombia 6 39N 77 32W
98 Crummer Peaks, Territory of Papua 6 40S 144 0E
121 Cruz, C., Cuba 19 50N 77 50W
124 Cruz del Eje, Argentina 30 45S 64 50W
125 Cruzeiro, Brazil 22 50S 45 0W
126 Cruzeiro do Sul, Brazil 7 35S 72 35W
28 Cryfow Sl., Poland 51 2N 15 24E
116 Crystal City, Mo., U.S.A. 38 15N 90 23W
117 Crystal City, Tex., U.S.A. 28 40N 99 50W
114 Crystal Falls, U.S.A. 46 9N 88 11W
115 Crystal River, U.S.A. 28 54N 82 35W
117 Crystal Springs, U.S.A. 31 59N 90 25W
27 Csongrád, Hungary 46 43N 20 12E
27 Csongrád ♦, Hungary 46 32N 20 15E
27 Csorna, Hungary 47 38N 17 18E
27 Csurgo, Hungary 46 16N 17 9E
64 Ctesiphon, Iraq 33 9N 44 35E
71 Cu Lao Hon, S. Vietnam 10 22N 109 12E
91 Cuácua, R., Mozam. 18 0S 36 0E
92 Cuamato, Angola 17 2S 15 7E
91 Cuamba = Nova Preixo, Mozam. 14 45S 36 22E
92 Cuando, Angola 16 25S 22 2E
89 Cuando, R., Angola 14 0S 19 30E
92 Cuando Cubango ♦, Angola 16 25S 20 0E
92 Cuangar, Angola 17 28S 14 40E
88 Cuango, Angola 6 15S 16 35E
121 Cuba ■, W. Indies 22 0N 79 0W
31 Cuba, Portugal 38 10N 7 54W
119 Cuba, N. Mex., U.S.A. 36 0N 107 0W
112 Cuba, N.Y., U.S.A. 42 12N 78 18W
92 Cubango, R., Africa 16 15S 17 45E
89 Cuchi, Angola 14 37S 17 10E
27 Cucurpe, Mexico 30 20N 110 43W
126 Cucurrupi, Colombia 4 23N 76 56W
126 Cucuta, Colombia 7 54N 72 31W
114 Cudahy, U.S.A. 42 54N 87 50W
46 Cudalbi, Rumania 45 46N 27 41E
70 Cuddalore, India 11 46N 79 45E
70 Cuddapah, India 14 30N 78 47E
100 Cudgewa, Australia 36 10S 147 42E
30 Cudillero, Spain 43 33N 6 9W
96 Cue, Australia 27 20S 117 55E
30 Cuéllar, Spain 41 23N 4 21E
126 Cuenca, Ecuador 2 50S 79 9W
32 Cuenca, Spain 40 5N 2 10W
32 Cuenca ♦, Spain 40 0N 2 0W
32 Cuenca, Serranía de, Spain 39 55N 1 50W
32 Cuerda del Pozo, Pantano de la, So. 41 51N 2 44W
120 Cuernavaca, Mexico 18 50N 99 20W
117 Cuero, U.S.A. 29 5N 97 17W
21 Cuers, France 43 14N 6 5E
117 Cuervo, U.S.A. 35 5N 104 25W
30 Cuevas de Altamira, Spain 43 20N 4 5W
33 Cuevas del Almanzora, Spain 37 18N 1 58W
126 Cuevo, Bolivia 20 25N 63 30W
46 Cugir, Rumania 43 48N 23 25E
87 Cugno, Ethiopia 6 14N 42 31E
126 Cuhimbre, Colombia 0 10S 75 23W
127 Cuiabá, Brazil 15 30S 56 0W
127 Cuiabá, R., Brazil 16 50S 56 30W
126 Cuidad Bolivia, Ven. 8 21N 70 34W
14 Cuillin Hills, Scot. 57 14N 6 15W
14 Cuillin Sd., Scot. 57 4N 6 20W
89 Cuima, Angola 13 0S 15 45E
21 Cuiseaux, France 46 30N 5 22E
92 Cuito, R., Angola 16 50S 19 30E
46 Cujmir, Rumania 44 13N 22 57E
20 Culan, France 46 34N 2 20E
116 Culbertson, U.S.A. 48 9N 104 30W
100 Culcairn, Australia 35 41S 147 3E
30 Culebra, Sierra de la, Sp. 41 55N 6 20W
100 Culgoa, Australia 35 44S 143 6E
120 Culiacán, Mexico 24 50N 107 40W
73 Culion, I., Philippine. 11 54N 120 1E
33 Cúllar de Baza, Spain 37 35N 2 34W
100 Cullarin Ra., Australia 34 30S 149 20E
14 Cullen, Scotland 57 45N 2 50W
98 Cullen Pt., Australia 11 50S 141 47E
33 Cullera, Spain 39 9N 0 17W
115 Cullman, U.S.A. 34 13N 86 50W
14 Culloden Moor, Scotland 57 29N 4 7W
21 Culoz, France 45 47N 5 46E
114 Culpeper, U.S.A. 38 29N 77 59W
127 Culuene, R., Brazil 12 15S 53 10W
96 Culver, Pt., Australia 32 54S 124 43E
101 Culverden, N.Z. 42 47S 172 49E
45 Cumali, Turkey 36 42N 27 28E
126 Cumaná, Venezuela 10 30N 64 5W
108 Cumberland, B.C., Can. 49 40N 125 0W
113 Cumberland, Que., Can. 45 30N 75 24W
114 Cumberland, Md., U.S.A. 39 40N 78 43W
116 Cumberland, Wis., U.S.A. 45 32N 92 3W
115 Cumberland I., U.S.A. 30 52N 81 30W
98 Cumberland Is., Australia 20 45S 149 25E
105 Cumberland Pen., Can. 67 0N 65 0W
115 Cumberland Plat., U.S.A. 36 0N 84 30W
115 Cumberland, R., U.S.A. 36 15N 87 0W
105 Cumberland Sd., Can. 65 30N 66 0W
* 12 Cumberland ♦, England 54 44N 2 55W
99 Cumborah, Australia 29 40S 147 45E
31 Cumbres Mayores, Sp. 38 4N 6 39W
12 Cumbrian Mts., Eng. 54 30N 3 0W
70 Cumbum, India 15 40N 79 10E
24 Cummerower See, Ger. 53 47N 12 52E
100 Cumnock, Australia 32 59S 148 46E
127 Cumuruxatiba, Brazil 17 6S 39 13W
126 Cuñaré, Colombia 0 49N 72 32W
126 Cundinamarca ♦, Col. 5 0N 74 0W
92 Cunene, R., Angola 17 0S 15 0E
38 Cúneo, Italy 44 23N 7 31E
33 Cunillera, I., Sp. 38 59N 1 13E
20 Cunlhat, France 45 38N 3 32E
99 Cunnamulla, Australia 28 2S 145 38E
38 Cuorgnè, Italy 45 23N 7 39E
109 Cupar, Canada 51 0N 104 10W
14 Cupar, Scotland 56 20N 3 0W
126 Cupica, Colombia 6 50N 77 30W
126 Cupica, Golfo de, Colombia 6 25N 77 30W
42 Cuprija, Yugoslavia 34 57N 21 26E
121 Curaçao, I., Neth. W.I. 12 10N 69 0W
124 Curanilahue, Chile 37 29S 73 28W
126 Curaray, R., Peru 1 30S 75 30W
126 Curatabaca, Venezuela 6 19N 62 51W
126 Curbarado, Colombia 7 3N 76 54W
124 Curepto, Chile 35 8S 72 1W
126 Curiapo, Venezuela 8 33N 61 5W
124 Curicó, Chile 34 55S 71 20W
124 Curicó ♦, Chile 34 50S 71 15W
126 Curiplaya, Colombia 0 16N 74 52W
125 Curitiba, Brazil 25 20S 49 10W
100 Curlwaa, Australia 34 2S 141 59E
92 Curoca Norte, Angola 16 15S 12 58E
100 Currabubula, Australia 31 16S 150 44E
99 Curracunya, Australia 28 29S 144 9E
127 Currais Novos, Brazil 6 13S 36 30W
127 Curralinho, Brazil 1 35S 49 30W
118 Currant, U.S.A. 38 51N 115 32W
99 Currawilla, Australia 25 10S 141 20E
117 Current, R., U.S.A. 37 15N 91 10W
118 Currie, U.S.A. 40 16N 114 45W
93 Currie, Mt., S. Africa 30 29S 29 21E
115 Currituck Sd., U.S.A. 36 20N 75 50W
100 Currockbilly Mt., Australia 35 25S 150 0E
46 Curtea-de-Argeş, Rum. 45 12N 24 42E
30 Curtis, Spain 43 7N 8 4W
116 Curtis, U.S.A. 40 41N 100 32W
98 Curtis, I., Australia 23 40S 151 15E
127 Curuapanema, R., Brazil 7 0S 54 30W
127 Curuçá, Brazil 0 35S 47 50W
125 Curuguaty, Paraguay 24 19S 55 49W
126 Curupira, Serra, Ven.-Braz. 1 25N 64 30W
120 Curundu, Pan. Can. Zone 8 59N 79 38W
127 Cururupu, Brazil 1 50S 44 50W
124 Curuzú Cuatiá, Arg. 29 50S 58 5W
127 Curvelo, Brazil 18 45S 44 27W
100 Curyo, Australia 35 53S 142 54E
120 Cusihuiriáchic, Mexico 28 10N 106 50W
83 Cussabat, Libya 32 39N 14 1E
20 Cusset, France 46 8N 3 28E
116 Custer, U.S.A. 43 45N 103 38W
118 Cut Bank, U.S.A. 48 40N 112 15W
115 Cuthbert, U.S.A. 31 47N 84 47W
41 Cutro, Italy 39 1N 16 58E
99 Cuttaburra R., Austral. 29 10S 145 0E
69 Cuttack, India 20 25N 85 57E
96 Cuvier, C., Australia 23 14S 113 22E
101 Cuvier I., N.Z. 36 27S 175 50E
24 Cuxhaven, Germany 53 51N 8 41E
126 Cuyabeno, Ecuador 0 16S 75 53W
112 Cuyahoga, R., U.S.A. 41 20N 81 35W
112 Cuyahoga Falls, U.S.A. 41 8N 81 30W
73 Cuyo, Philippines 10 50N 121 5E
127 Cuyuni, R., Guyana 7 0N 59 30W
126 Cuzco, Peru 13 32S 72 0W
126 Cuzco, Mt., Bolivia 20 0S 66 50W
42 Cvrsnica, Mt., Y.-slav. 43 36N 17 35E
90 Cyangugu, Rwanda 2 29S 28 54E
28 Cybinka, Poland 52 12N 14 46E
45 Cyclades = Kikladhes, Greece 37 20N 24 30E
99 Cygnet, Australia 43 8S 147 1E
114 Cynthiana, U.S.A. 38 23N 84 10W
109 Cypress Hills, Canada 49 40N 109 30W
64 Cyprus ■, E. Medit. Sea 35 0N 33 0E
81 Cyrenaica ♦, Libya 27 0N 20 0E
81 Cyrene, Libya 32 39N 21 18E
28 Czaplinek, Poland 53 34N 16 14E
28 Czarna Białostocka, Poland 53 27N 23 11E
28 Czarna Woda, Poland 53 51N 18 7E
28 Czarne, Poland 53 42N 16 58E
28 Czarnków, Poland 52 55N 16 38E
27 Czechoslovakia ■, Europe 49 0N 17 0E
27 Czechowice- Dziedzke, Poland 49 54N 18 59E
28 Czeladz, Poland 50 16N 19 2E
28 Czempiń, Poland 52 9N 16 33E

* *Incorporated within the county of Cumbria*

* Renamed Benin

* Incorporated within the county of Clwyd

* Renamed L. Idi Amin Dada

* Renamed Tuvalu

Fairweather, Mt. INDEX Foligno

MAP
104 Fairweather, Mt., Alaska 58 55N 137 45W
16 Faith, U.S.A. 45 2N 102 4W
65 Faizabad, Afghanistan 37 7N 70 33E
69 Faizabad, India 26 45N 82 10E
68 Faizpur, India 21 14N 75 49E
121 Fajardo, P. Rico 18 20N 65 39W
73 Fakfak, Indonesia 3 0S 132 15E
127 Fakiya, Bulgaria 42 10N 27 4E
84 Fakobli, Ivory Coast 7 23N 7 23W
49 Fakse, Denmark 55 15N 12 8E
49 Fakse B., Denmark 55 11N 12 15E
49 Fakse Ladeplads, Den. 55 16N 12 9E
18 Falaise, France 48 54N 0 12W
44 Falakrón Oros, Greece 41 15N 23 58E
67 Falam, Burma 23 0N 93 45E
32 Falces, Spain 42 24N 1 48W
46 Fălciu, Rumania 46 17N 28 7E
82 Falcon, C., Algeria 35 50N 0 50W
126 Falcón ♦, Venezuela 11 0N 69 50W
117 Falcón Dam, U.S.A. 26 50N 99 20W
39 Falconara Marittima, It. 43 37N 13 23E
112 Falconer, U.S.A. 42 7N 79 13W
84 Faléa, Mali 12 16N 11 17W
56 Faleshty, U.S.S.R. 47 32N 27 44E
117 Falfurrias, U.S.A. 27 8N 98 8W
108 Falher, Canada 55 50N 117 15W
112 Falkenberg, Canada 45 9N 79 21W
24 Falkenberg, Germany 51 34N 13 13E
49 Falkenberg, Sweden 56 54N 12 30E
24 Falkensee, Germany 52 35N 13 6E
24 Falkenstein, Germany 50 27N 12 24E
14 Falkirk, Scot. 56 0N 3 47W
128 Falkland Is., S. Atlantic 51 30S 59 0W
5 Falkland Is. Dep., S. Oc. 57 0S 40 0W
128 Falkland Sd., Falk. Is. 52 0S 60 0W
45 Falkonéra, Greece 36 50N 23 52E
49 Falköping, Sweden 58 12N 13 33E
119 Fall Brook, U.S.A. 33 25N 117 12W
113 Fall River, U.S.A. 41 45N 71 5W
118 Fall River Mills, U.S.A. 41 1N 121 30W
42 Fallon, Mont., U.S.A. 46 52N 105 8W
118 Fallon, Nev., U.S.A. 39 31N 118 51W
116 Falls City, Nebr., U.S.A. 40 0N 95 40W
118 Falls City, Oreg., U.S.A. 44 54N 123 29W
112 Falls Creek, U.S.A. 41 8N 78 49W
85 Falmey, Niger 12 36N 2 51E
121 Falmouth, Jamaica 18 30N 77 40W
13 Falmouth, Eng. 50 9N 5 5W
114 Falmouth, U.S.A. 38 40N 84 20W
13 Falmouth B., Eng. 50 7N 5 3E
92 False B., S. Afr. 34 15S 18 40E
70 False Divi Pt., India 15 35N 80 50E
32 Falset, Spain 41 7N 0 50E
49 Falster, Denmark 54 45N 11 55E
49 Falsterbo, Sweden 55 23N 12 50E
49 Falsterbokanalen, Sweden 55 25N 12 56E
46 Fălticeni, Rumania 47 21N 26 20W
62 Faluja, Israel 31 48N 31 37E
48 Falun, Sweden 60 37N 15 37E
64 Famagusta = Ammókhostos, Greece 35 8N 33 55E
87 Famaka, Sudan 11 24N 34 52E
124 Famatina, Sierra, de, Argentina 29 5S 68 0W
93 Fampotabe, Malag. 15 56S 50 8E
44 Fan i Madh, R., Alb. 41 56N 20 16E
84 Fana, Mali 13 0N 6 56W
47 Fana, Norway 60 16N 5 20E
93 Fanambana, Malagasy Rep. 13 34S 50 0E
44 Fanárion, Greece 39 50N 21 47E
77 Fancheng, China 32 1N 118 13E
93 Fandriana, Malagasy Republic 20 14S 47 21E
14 Fannich, L., Scot. 57 40N 5 0W
98 Fanning, Australia 19 56S 146 30E
95 Fanning I., Pac. Oc. 3 51N 159 22W
108 Fanny Bay, Canada 49 27N 124 58W
39 Fano, Italy 43 50N 13 0E
49 Fanö, I., Denmark 55 25N 8 25E
108 Fanshaw, Alaska 57 11N 133 30W
49 Fanö, Denmark 55 25N 8 25E
64 Fao (Al Fâw), Iraq 30 0N 48 30E
68 Faqirwali, Pakistan 29 27N 73 0E
39 Fara in Sabina, Italy 42 13N 12 44E
6 Faraday Seamount Group, N. Atlantic Oc. 50 0N 27 0W
90 Faradje, Zaïre 3 50N 29 45E
93 Farafangana, Malagasy Republic 22 49S 47 50E
86 Farâfra, El Wâhât el-, Egypt 27 15N 28 20E
65 Farah, Afghanistan 32 20N 62 7E
93 Farahalana, Malag. 14 26S 50 10E
86 Faraid, Gebel, Egypt 23 33N 35 19E
84 Faramana, Upper Volta 11 56N 4 45W
84 Faranah, Guinea 10 3N 10 45W
63 Farasān, Jazā'ir, Red Sea 16 45N 41 55E
63 Farasan Kebir, Saudi Arabia 16 40N 42 0E
93 Faratsiho, Malag. 19 24S 46 57E
33 Fardes, R., Spain 37 25N 3 10W
13 Fareham, Eng. 50 52N 1 11W
4 Farewell C. = Farvel, K., Greenland 59 48N 43 55W
101 Farewell, C., N.Z. 40 29S 172 43E
126 Farfán, Ecuador 0 16N 76 41W
116 Fargo, U.S.A. 47 0N 97 0W
62 Faria, R., Jordan 32 12N 35 27E
116 Faribault, U.S.A. 44 15N 93 19W
68 Faridkot, India 30 44N 74 45E
69 Faridpur, Bangladesh 23 36N 89 53E
69 Faridpur, India 18 14N 79 34E
48 Farila, Sweden 61 48N 15 50E
84 Farim, Port. Guinea 12 27N 15 17W
65 Fariman, Iran 35 40N 60 0E
99 Farina, South Australia 30 3S 138 15E
48 Faringe, Sweden 59 55N 18 7E
49 Färjestaden, Sweden 56 38N 16 25E
45 Farmakonisi, Greece 37 17N 27 8E
117 Farmerville, U.S.A. 32 48N 92 23W
113 Farmington, N.H., U.S.A. 43 25N 71 7W
119 Farmington, N. Mex., U.S.A. 36 45N 108 28W
118 Farmington, Utah, U.S.A. 41 0N 111 58W
113 Farmington, R., U.S.A. 42 0N 73 5W
114 Farmville, U.S.A. 37 19N 78 22W
13 Farnborough, Eng. 51 17N 0 46W
12 Farne Is., Eng. 55 38N 1 37W
113 Farnham, Canada 45 20N 72 55W
108 Farnham, Mt., Canada 45 20N 72 55W
127 Faro, Brazil 2 0S 56 45W
31 Faro, Port. 37 2N 7 55W
31 Faro ♦, Portugal 37 12N 8 10W
8 Faroe Is., N. Atl. Oc. 62 0N 7 0W
96 Farquhar, C., Australia 23 38S 113 36E
65 Farrashband, Iran 28 57N 52 5E
112 Farrell, U.S.A. 41 13N 80 29W
99 Farrell Flat, Austral. 33 48S 138 48E
69 Farrukhabad, India 27 30N 79 32E
65 Fars ♦, Iran 29 30N 55 0E
44 Fársala, Greece 39 17N 22 23E
49 Farsö, Denmark 56 48N 9 20E
49 Farstrup, Denmark 56 59N 9 28E
47 Farsund, Norway 58 5N 6 55E
49 Farsö, Denmark 56 46N 9 19E
125 Fartura, Serra da, Brazil 26 21S 52 52W
85 Faru, Nigeria 12 48N 6 12E
49 Farum, Denmark 55 49N 12 21E
65 Farur, Iran 26 20N 54 30E
4 Farvel, Kap, Greenland 59 48N 43 55W
117 Farwell, U.S.A. 34 25N 103 0W
65 Fasa, Iran 29 0N 53 32E
41 Fasano, Italy 40 50N 17 20E
87 Fashoda, Sudan 9 50N 32 2E
53 Faskari, Nigeria 11 42N 6 58E
15 Fastnet Rock, Ireland 51 22N 9 37W
54 Fastov, U.S.S.R. 50 7N 29 57E
69 Fatehgarh, India 27 25N 79 35E
68 Fatehpur, Raj., India 28 0N 75 4E
69 Fatehpur, Ut. P., India 27 8N 81 7E
77 Fati, China 23 10N 113 10E
84 Fatick, Senegal 14 19N 16 27W
31 Fátima, Portugal 39 37N 8 39W
77 Fatkeng, China 23 58N 113 29E
84 Fatoya, Guinea 11 37N 9 10W
77 Fatshan, China 23 0N 113 4E
19 Faucilles, Monts, France 48 5N 5 50E
116 Faulkton, U.S.A. 45 4N 99 8W
19 Faulquemont, France 49 3N 6 36E
19 Fauquembergues, Fr. 50 36N 2 5E
46 Făurel, Rumania 45 6N 27 19E
92 Fauresmith, S. Africa 29 44S 25 17E
50 Fauske, Norway 67 17N 15 25E
93 Faux-Cap, Malag. 25 33S 45 32E
40 Favara, Italy 37 19N 13 39E
40 Favignana, Italy 37 56N 12 18E
21 Favone, France 41 47N 9 26E
106 Favourable Lake, Can. 52 40N 93 0W
106 Fawn, R., Canada 54 20N 89 0W
50 Faxaflói, Iceland 64 29N 23 0W
48 Faxälven, Sweden 63 13N 17 13E
81 Faya = Largeau, Chad 17 58N 19 6E
21 Fayence, France 43 38N 6 42E
115 Fayette, Ala., U.S.A. 33 40N 87 50W
116 Fayette, Mo., U.S.A. 39 10N 92 40W
117 Fayetteville, Ark., U.S.A. 36 0N 94 5W
115 Fayetteville, N.C., U.S.A. 35 0N 78 58W
115 Fayetteville, Tenn., U.S.A. 35 0N 86 30W
32 Fayón, Spain 41 15N 0 20E
68 Fazilka, India 30 27N 74 2E
68 Fazilpur, Pakistan 29 18N 70 29E
80 F'Derik, Mauritania 22 40N 12 45W
15 Feale, R., Ireland 52 26N 9 28W
115 Fear, C., U.S.A. 33 45N 78 0W
118 Feather, R., U.S.A. 39 30N 121 20W
101 Featherston, N.Z. 41 6S 175 20E
91 Featherstone, Rhodesia 18 42S 30 55E
100 Feathertop, Mt., Australia 36 53S 147 7E
18 Fécamp, France 49 45N 0 22E
82 Fedala = Mohammedia, Morocco 33 44N 7 21W
124 Federación, Argentina 31 0S 57 55W
83 Fedjadj, Chott el, Tunisia 33 52N 9 14E
47 Fedje, Norway 60 47N 4 43E
56 Fedorovka, U.S.S.R. 47 4N 35 18E
27 Fehergyarmat, Hungary 48 0N 22 30E
24 Fehmarn, Germany 54 26N 11 10E
49 Fehmarn Baelt, Den. 54 35N 11 20E
101 Feilding, New Zealand 40 13S 175 35E
41 Feira, Zambia 15 35S 30 16E
27 Fejér ♦, Hungary 47 9N 18 30E
49 Fejö, Denmark 54 55N 11 30E
33 Felanitx, Spain 39 27N 3 7E
26 Feldbach, Austria 46 57N 15 52E
24 Feldberg, Germany 53 20N 13 26E
25 Feldberg, mt., Germany 47 51N 7 58E
26 Feldkirch, Austria 47 15N 9 37E
26 Feldkirchen, Austria 46 44N 14 6E
87 Felhit, Ethiopia 16 40N 38 1E
120 Felipe Carrillo Puerto, Mexico 19 38N 88 3W
13 Felixstowe, Eng. 51 58N 1 22W
20 Felletin, France 45 53N 2 11E
87 Fellit, Ethiopia 16 40N 38 1E
39 Feltre, Italy 46 1N 11 55E
49 Femö, Denmark 54 58N 11 53E
47 Femunden, Norway 62 10N 11 53E
76 Fen Ho, R., China 35 25N 110 30E
112 Fenelon Falls, Canada 44 31N 78 43W
93 Fénérive, Malagasy Rep. 17 22S 49 25E
87 Fenerwa, Ethiopia 13 5N 39 3E
44 Fengári, Greece 40 25N 25 32E
76 Fengcheng, Heilungkiang, China 45 41N 128 54E
77 Fengcheng, Kiangsi, China 28 2N 115 46E
76 Fengcheng, Liaoning, China 40 28N 124 4E
76 Fengfeng, China 36 40N 114 24E
77 Fenghsien, China 33 56N 106 41E
77 Fenghwa, China 29 37N 121 29E
77 Fengkieh (Kweichow), China 31 0N 109 33E
77 Fenglo, China 31 30N 112 29E
77 Fengsiang, China 34 27N 107 30E
77 Fengsin, China 28 41N 115 11E
77 Fengtu, China 29 58N 107 59E
77 Fengy, China 23 48N 106 50E
77 Fengyuan, Taiwan 24 10N 120 45E
98 Feni Is., Terr. of New Guinea 4 5S 153 25E
116 Fennimore, U.S.A. 42 58N 90 41W
69 Fenny, Bengladesh 22 55N 91 32E
93 Fenoarivo, Malagasy Rep. 18 26S 46 34E
21 Feno, C. de, Corsica 41 58N 8 33E
12 Fens, The, Eng. 52 45N 0 2E
109 Fenton, Canada 53 0N 105 35W
114 Fenton, U.S.A. 42 47N 83 42W
76 Fenyang, China 37 19N 111 46E
56 Feodosiya, U.S.S.R. 45 2N 35 28E
83 Fer, C. de, Algeria 37 3N 7 10E
65 Ferdows, Iran 33 58N 58 2E
19 Fère-Champenoise, Fr. 48 45N 4 0E
19 Fère-en-Tardenois, Fr. 49 10N 3 30E
40 Ferentino, Italy 41 42N 13 14E
63 Ferfer, Somali Rep. 5 18N 45 20E
58 Fergana, U.S.S.R. 40 50N 71 50E
106 Fergus, Canada 43 43N 80 24W
116 Fergus Falls, U.S.A. 46 25N 96 0W
106 Ferguson, Canada 47 50N 73 30W
98 Fergusson I., Papua 9 30S 150 40E
83 Fériana, Tunisia 34 59N 8 33E
42 Feričanci, Yugoslavia 45 32N 18 0E
83 Ferkane, Algeria 34 37N 7 26E
84 Ferkéssédougou, Ivory Coast 9 35N 5 6W
106 Ferland, Canada 50 19N 88 27W
26 Ferlach, Austria 46 32N 14 18E
84 Ferlo, Vallée du, Senegal 15 15N 14 15W
* 15 Fermanagh ♦, N. Ireland 54 21N 7 40W
39 Fermo, Italy 43 10N 13 42E
30 Fermoselle, Spain 41 19N 6 27W
15 Fermoy, Ireland 52 4N 8 18W
31 Fernan Núñez, Spain 37 40N 4 44W
124 Fernández, Argentina 27 55S 63 50W
115 Fernandina, U.S.A. 30 40N 81 30W
127 Fernando de Noronha, I., Brazil 4 0S 33 10W
127 Fernando de Noronha ♦, Brazil 4 0S 33 10W
† 79 Fernando Póo, I., Africa 3 30N 8 40E
118 Ferndale, Calif., U.S.A. 40 37N 124 12W
118 Ferndale, Wash., U.S.A. 48 51N 122 41W
108 Fernie, Canada 49 30N 115 5W
98 Fernlees, Australia 23 55S 148 10E
118 Fernley, U.S.A. 39 42N 119 20W
70 Feroke, India 11 9N 75 46E
68 Ferozepore, India 30 55N 74 40E
44 Férrai, Greece 40 53N 26 10E
41 Ferrandina, Italy 40 30N 16 28E
39 Ferrara, Italy 44 50N 11 36E
40 Ferrato, C., Sardinia 39 18N 9 39E
31 Ferreira do Alentejo, Portugal 38 4N 8 6W
126 Ferreñafe, Peru 6 35S 79 50W
19 Ferrette, France 47 30N 7 20E
117 Ferriday, U.S.A. 31 35N 91 33W
38 Ferriete, Italy 44 40N 9 30E
19 Ferrières, France 48 5N 2 48E
30 Ferrol, Spain 43 29N 8 15W
118 Ferron, U.S.A. 39 3N 111 3W
40 Fertília, Italy 40 37N 8 13E
116 Fertile, U.S.A. 47 37N 96 18W
27 Fertöszentmiklos, Hung. 47 35N 16 53E
82 Fès, Morocco 34 0N 5 0W
88 Feshi, Zaïre 6 0S 18 10E
116 Fessenden, U.S.A. 47 42N 99 44W
47 Fet, Norway 59 57N 11 12E
46 Fetești, Rumania 44 22N 27 51E
64 Fethiye, Turkey 36 36N 29 10E
14 Fetlar, I., Scot. 60 36N 0 52W
21 Feurs, France 45 45N 4 13E
12 Ffestiniog, Wales 52 58N 3 56W
124 Fiambalá, Argentina 27 45S 67 37W
93 Fianarantsoa ♦, Malag. 19 30S 47 0E
81 Fianga, Cameroon 9 55N 15 20E
42 Fibiș, Rumania 45 57N 21 26E
107 Fichot, I., Canada 51 12N 55 40W
25 Fichtelgebirge, Ger. 50 10N 12 0E
93 Ficksburg, S. Africa 28 51S 27 53E
38 Fidenza, Italy 44 51N 10 3E
93 Fierenana, Ethiopia 18 29S 48 24E
44 Fiéri, Albania 40 43N 19 33E
14 Fife ♦, Scot. 56 13N 3 2W
14 Fife Ness, Scot. 56 17N 2 35W
87 Fifth Cataract, Sudan 18 15N 33 50E
20 Figeac, France 44 37N 2 2E
49 Figline Valdarno, Italy 43 37N 11 28E
91 Figtree, Rhodesia 20 22S 28 20E
30 Figueira da Foz, Port. 40 7N 8 54W
30 Figueiró dos Vinhos, Portugal 39 55N 8 16W
32 Figueras, Spain 42 18N 2 58E
82 Figuig, Morocco 32 5N 1 11W
93 Fihaonana, Malag. 18 36S 47 12E
93 Fiherenana, R., Malag. 22 50S 44 0E
101 Fiji ■, Pacific Ocean 17 20S 179 0E
101 Fiji Is., Pacific Ocean 17 20S 179 0E

* In April 1973 districts replaced counties in N. Ireland
† Renamed Macias Nguema Biyoga

62 Fik, Syria 32 46N 35 41E
85 Fika, Nigeria 11 15N 11 13E
33 Filabres, Sierra de los, Spain 37 13N 2 20W
39 Filadélfia, Italy 38 47N 16 17E
27 Fil'akovo, Cz. 48 17N 19 50E
5 Filchner Ice Shelf, Antarctica 78 0S 60 0W
118 Filer, U.S.A. 42 30N 114 35W
12 Filey, England 54 13N 0 18W
46 Filiaşi, Rumania 44 32N 23 31E
44 Filiátes, Greece 39 38N 20 16E
45 Filiatrá, Greece 37 9N 21 35E
41 Filicudi, I., Italy 38 35N 14 33E
48 Filipstad, Sweden 59 43N 14 9E
25 Filisur, Switzerland 46 41N 9 40E
44 Filitouri, R., Greece 41 15N 25 40E
109 Fillmore, Canada 49 50N 103 25W
119 Fillmore, U.S.A. 34 23N 118 58W
39 Filottrano, Italy 43 28N 13 20E
56 Filyos, Turkey 41 34N 32 4E
64 Filyos çayi, Turkey 41 35N 32 10E
38 Finale Ligure, Italy 44 10N 8 21E
39 Finale nell'Emilia, It. 44 50N 11 18E
33 Fiñana, Spain 37 10N 2 50W
113 Finch, Canada 45 10N 75 5W
14 Findhorn, R., Scot. 57 30N 3 45W
114 Findlay, U.S.A. 41 0N 83 41W
109 Finger L., Canada 53 15N 93 35W
91 Fingoè, Mozambique 15 12S 31 50E
64 Finike, Turkey 36 21N 30 10E
18 Finistère ♦, France 48 20N 4 0W
30 Finisterre, Spain 42 54N 9 16W
30 Finisterre, C., Spain 42 50N 9 19W
52 Finland ■, Europe 70 0N 27 0E
52 Finland, G. of, Europe 60 0N 26 0E
100 Finley, Australia 35 50S 145 40E
116 Finley, U.S.A. 47 35N 97 50W
15 Finn, R., Ire. 54 50N 7 55W
50 Finnmark fylke ♦, Norway 69 30N 25 0E
98 Finschhafen, N.E. New Guinea 6 33S 147 48E
47 Finse, Norway 60 36N 7 30E
49 Finspång, Sweden 58 45N 15 43E
48 Finsta, Sweden 59 45N 18 34E
25 Finsteraarhorn, Switzerland 46 31N 8 10E
24 Finsterwalde, Germany 51 37N 13 42E
96 Finucanel, Australia 20 19S 118 30E
39 Fiora, R., Italy 42 25N 11 35E
38 Fiorenzuola d'Arda, It. 44 56N 9 54E
62 Fiq, Syria 32 46N 35 41E
106 Fire River, Canada 48 47N 83 36W
109 Firedrake L., Canada 61 25N 104 40W
39 Firenze, Italy 43 47N 11 15E
84 Firkessédougou, Ivory C. 9 35N 5 6W
20 Firmi, France 44 32N 2 19E
21 Firminy, France 45 23N 4 18E
65 Firoz Kohi, Afghanistan 34 45N 63 0E
68 Firozabad, India 27 10N 78 25E
86 First Cataract, Egypt 24 1N 32 51E
65 Fīrūzābād, Iran 28 52N 52 35E
65 Firuzkuh, Iran 35 50N 52 40E
92 Fish, R., S.W. Africa 27 40S 17 30E
100 Fish Creek, Australia 38 43S 146 7E
13 Fishguard, Wales 51 59N 4 59W
109 Fishing L., Canada 52 10N 95 30W
84 Fishtown, Liberia 4 24N 7 45E
47 Fiskum, Norway 59 42N 9 46E
19 Fismes, France 49 20N 3 40E
47 Fister, Norway 59 10N 6 5E
113 Fitchburg, U.S.A. 42 35N 71 47W
32 Fitero, Spain 42 4N 1 52W
47 Fitjar, Norway 59 55N 5 17E
88 Fitri, L., Chad 12 50N 17 28E
115 Fitzgerald, U.S.A. 31 45N 83 10W
106 Fitzpatrick, Canada 47 29N 72 46W
128 Fitz Roy, Argentina 47 10S 67 0W
98 Fitzroy, R., Queens., Austral. 23 10S 150 10E
96 Fitzroy, R., W.A., Austral. 17 30S 124 0E
96 Fitzroy Crossing, Australia 18 9S 125 38E
112 Fitzwilliam I., Canada 45 30N 81 45W
39 Fiume = Rijeka, Yugoslavia 45 20N 14 21E
41 Fiumefreddo Brúzio, It. 39 14N 16 4E
90 Fizi, Zaïre 4 17S 28 55E
47 Fjaera, Nor. 59 52N 6 22E
47 Fjaere, Nor. 58 23N 8 36E
49 Fjellerup, Denmark 56 29N 10 34E
49 Fjerritslev, Denmark 57 5N 9 15E
47 Fjaera, Norway 59 52N 6 23E
82 Fkih ben Salah, Mor. 32 45N 6 45W
47 Fla, Buskerud, Norway 60 25N 9 26E
47 Flå, Sör Tröndelag, Nor. 63 13N 10 18E
116 Flagler, U.S.A. 39 20N 103 4W
119 Flagstaff, U.S.A. 35 10N 111 40W
108 Flagstone, Canada 49 4N 115 10W
106 Flaherty, I., Canada 56 0N 79 55W
116 Flambeau, R., U.S.A. 45 40N 90 50W
12 Flamborough Hd., England 54 8N 0 4W
118 Flaming Gorge Dam, U.S.A. 40 50N 109 25W
118 Flaming Gorge L., U.S.A. 41 15N 109 30W
73 Flamingo, Teluk, Indonesia 5 30S 138 0E
16 Flanders = Flandres, Belgium 51 10N 3 15E
16 Flandre Occidental ♦, Belgium 51 0N 3 0E
16 Flandre Orientale ♦, Belgium 51 0N 4 0E
16 Flandres, Plaines des, Belg. 51 10N 3 15E
116 Flandreau, U.S.A. 44 5N 96 38W
14 Flannan Is., Scot. 58 9N 7 52W
49 Flaren L., Sweden 57 2N 14 5E
50 Flåsjön, Sweden 64 5N 15 50E
117 Flat River, U.S.A. 37 50N 90 30W
50 Flatey, Barðastrandarsýsla, Iceland 66 10N 17 52W
50 Flatey, Suður-þingeyjarsýsla, Iceland 65 22N 22 56W
118 Flathead L., U.S.A. 47 50N 114 0W
98 Flattery, C., Australia 14 58S 145 21E
118 Flattery, C., U.S.A. 48 21N 124 31W
19 Flavy-le-Martel, Fr. 49 43N 3 12E
116 Flaxton, U.S.A. 48 52N 102 24W
12 Fleetwood, Eng. 53 55N 3 1W
47 Flekkefjord, Norway 58 18N 6 39E
112 Flemington, U.S.A. 41 7N 77 28W
49 Flensburg Fjord, W. Germany 54 50N 9 40E
24 Flensburg, Germany 54 46N 9 28E
18 Flers, France 48 47N 0 33W
47 Flesberg, Norway 59 51N 9 22E
112 Flesherton, Canada 44 15N 80 34W
13 Fletton, Eng. 52 34N 0 13W
20 Fleurance, France 43 52N 0 40E
25 Fleurier, Switzerland 46 54N 6 35E
48 Flickerbäcken, Sweden 61 47N 12 34E
109 Flin Flon, Canada 54 50N 102 0W
96 Flinders B., Austral. 34 19S 115 9E
99 Flinders I., Australia 40 0S 148 0E
99 Flinders Ranges, Austral. 31 30S 138 30E
98 Flinders, R., Australia 20 0S 141 35E
12 Flint, Wales 53 15N 3 7W
114 Flint, U.S.A. 43 0N 83 40W
95 Flint, I., Pacific Ocean 11 26S 151 48W
115 Flint, R., U.S.A. 31 20N 84 10W
* 12 Flint ♦, Wales 53 15N 3 12W
99 Flinton, Australia 27 55S 149 32E
49 Fliseryd, Sweden 57 6N 16 15E
32 Flix, Spain 41 14N 0 32E
19 Flixecourt, France 50 0N 2 5E
48 Floda, Kopparbergs, Sweden 60 30N 14 53E
12 Flodden, England 55 37N 2 8W
116 Floodwood, U.S.A. 46 55N 92 55W
47 Flora, Norway 63 27N 11 22E
47 Flora, Sogn & Fjordane, Norway 61 35N 5 1E
114 Flora, U.S.A. 38 40N 88 30W
20 Florac, France 44 20N 3 37E
115 Florala, U.S.A. 31 0N 86 20W
39 Florence = Firenze, Italy 43 47N 11 15E
115 Florence, Ala., U.S.A. 34 50N 87 50W
119 Florence, Ariz., U.S.A. 33 0N 111 25W
116 Florence, Colo., U.S.A. 38 26N 105 0W
118 Florence, Oreg., U.S.A. 44 0N 124 3W
115 Florence, S.C., U.S.A. 34 5N 79 50W
16 Florennes, Belgium 50 15N 4 35E
20 Florensac, France 43 23N 3 28E
16 Florenville, Belgium 49 40N 5 19E
8 Flores, Azores 39 13N 31 13W
120 Flores, Guatemala 16 50N 89 40W
108 Flores I., Canada 49 20N 126 10W
73 Flores, I., Indonesia 8 35S 121 0E
72 Flores Sea, Indonesia 6 30S 124 0E
117 Floresville, U.S.A. 29 10N 98 10W
127 Floriano, Brazil 6 50S 43 0W
125 Florianópolis, Brazil 27 30S 48 30W
121 Florida, Cuba 21 32N 78 14W
125 Florida, Uruguay 34 7S 56 10W
115 Florida ♦, U.S.A. 28 30N 82 0W
121 Florida B., U.S.A. 25 0N 81 20W
121 Florida Keys, U.S.A. 25 0N 80 40W
121 Florida, Strait of, U.S.A. 25 0N 80 0W
41 Floridia, Italy 37 6N 15 9E
27 Floridsdorf, Austria 48 15N 16 25E
44 Flórina, Greece 40 48N 21 26E
44 Flórina ♦, Greece 40 45N 21 20E
47 Florö, Norway 61 35N 5 1E
47 Flosta, Norway 58 32N 8 56E
48 Florningen, Sweden 61 50N 12 16E
113 Flower Sta., Canada 45 10N 76 42W
107 Flower's Cove, Canada 51 14N 56 46W
117 Floydada, U.S.A. 33 58N 101 18W
73 Fluk, Indonesia 1 42S 127 38E
32 Flumen, R., Spain 41 50N 0 25W
40 Flumendosa, R., Italy 39 30N 9 25E
40 Fluminimaggiore, Italy 39 25N 8 30E
16 Flushing = Vlissingen, Netherlands 51 26N 3 34E
32 Fluviá, R., Spain 42 12N 3 7E
98 Fly, R., Papua 7 50S 141 20E
47 Flå, Norway 63 12N 10 20E
109 Foam Lake, Canada 51 40N 103 15W
42 Foča, Yugoslavia 43 31N 18 47E
46 Focsani, Rumania 45 41N 27 15E
98 Fofo Fofo, T. of Papua 8 9S 147 6E
82 Foggaret el Arab, Alg. 27 3N 2 59E
82 Foggaret ez Zoua, Alg. 27 20N 3 0E
41 Fóggia, Italy 41 28N 15 31E
85 Foggo, Nigeria 11 21N 9 57E
39 Foglia, R., Italy 43 50N 12 32E
107 Fogo I., Canada 49 40N 54 5W
26 Fohnsdorf, Austria 47 12N 14 40E
24 Föhr, Germany 54 40N 8 30E
31 Foia, Cerro da, Port. 37 19N 8 10W
20 Foix, France 42 58N 1 38E
42 Fojnica, Yugoslavia 43 59N 17 51E
54 Fokino, U.S.S.R. 53 30N 34 10E
45 Fokis ♦, Greece 38 30N 22 15E
47 Fokstua, Norway 62 8N 9 16E
50 Folda, Nord-Tröndelag, Norway 64 41N 10 50E
50 Folda, Nordland, Norway 67 38N 14 50E
27 Földeák, Hungary 46 19N 20 30E
92 Foley, U.S.A. 30 25N 87 40W
106 Foleyet, Canada 48 15N 82 25W
47 Folgefonni, Norway 60 23N 6 34E
39 Foligno, Italy 42 58N 12 40E

* Incorporated within the county of Clwyd

Fülöpszállás INDEX Georgetown

MAP
27 Fülöpszállás, Hungary 46 49N 19 16E
16 Fulton, Mo., U.S.A. 38 50N 91 55W
113 Fulton, N.Y., U.S.A. 43 20N 76 22W
48 Fuluälven, Sweden 61 18N 13 4E
48 Fulufjället, Sweden 61 32N 12 41E
27 Fülüpszállás, Hungary 46 49N 19 16E
19 Fumay, France 50 0N 4 40E
85 Fumbusi, Ghana 10 25N 1 20W
20 Fumel, France 44 30N 0 58E
74 Funabashi, Japan 35 45N 140 0E
94 Funafuti, I., Pac. Oc. 8 30S 179 0E
80 Funchal, Madeira 32 45N 16 55W
126 Fundación, Colombia 10 31N 74 11W
30 Fundão, Portugal 40 8N 7 30W
91 Fundu, Zambia 14 58S 30 14E
107 Fundy, B. of, Canada 45 0N 66 0W
126 Funes, Colombia 1 0N 77 28W
77 Fungchun, China 23 27N 111 30E
77 Funing, China 23 45N 105 30E
77 Funiu Shan, China 33 40N 112 30E
84 Funsi, Ghana 10 21N 1 54W
85 Funtua, Nigeria 11 30N 7 18E
49 Fur, Denmark 56 50N 9 0E
64 Furat, Nahr al, Asia 33 30N 43 0E
55 Furmanov, U.S.S.R. 57 25N 41 3E
57 Furmanovo, U.S.S.R. 49 42N 49 25E
99 Furneaux Group, Australia 40 10S 147 50E
12 Furness, England 54 14N 3 8W
24 Fürstenau, Germany 52 32N 7 40E
26 Fürstenfeld, Austria 47 3N 16 3E
25 Fürstenfeldbruck, Ger. 48 10N 11 15E
24 Fürstenwalde, Ger. 52 20N 14 3E
25 Fürth, Germany 49 29N 11 0E
25 Fürth i. Wald, Ger. 49 19N 12 51E
25 Furtwangen, Germany 48 3N 8 14E
48 Furudal, Sweden 61 10N 15 11E
48 Furusund, Sweden 59 40N 18 55E
105 Fury and Hecla Str., Canada 69 40N 81 0W
47 Fusa, Norway 60 12N 5 37E
126 Fusagasugá, Colombia 4 21N 74 22W
41 Fuscaldo, Italy 39 25N 16 1E
74 Fuse, Japan 34 40N 135 37E
44 Fushë Arrëzi, Albania 42 4N 20 2E
76 Fushun, China 42 0N 123 59E
76 Fusin, China 42 12N 121 33E
25 Füssen, Germany 47 12N 121 33E
77 Fusui, China 22 35N 107 58E
77 Futing, China 27 15N 120 10E
77 Futsing, China 25 46N 119 29E
85 Futuk, Nigeria 9 45N 10 56E
86 Fuwa, Egypt 31 12N 30 33E
77 Fuyang Ho, China 38 14N 116 5E
76 Fuyuan, China 48 9N 134 3E
27 Füzesgyarmat, Hung. 47 6N 21 14E
75 Fyekundo = Yushu, China 33 6N 96 48E
49 Fyn, Denmark 55 20N 10 30E
14 Fyne, L., Scot. 56 0N 5 20W
49 Fyns Amt ♦, Denmark 55 15N 10 30E
49 Fynshav, Denmark 54 59N 9 59E
47 Fyresvatn, Norway 59 6N 8 10E
85 Gaanda, Nigeria 10 10N 12 27E
87 Gaba, Ethiopia 6 20N 35 7E
56 Gaba Tula, Kenya 0 20N 38 35E
63 Gabah, C., Somali Rep. 8 0N 50 0W
85 Gabarin, Nigeria 11 8N 10 27E
88 Gabela, Angola 11 0S 14 37E
92 Gaberones = Gaborone, Botswana 24 37S 25 57E
83 Gabès, Tunisia 33 53N 10 2E
83 Gabès, Golfe de, Tunisia 34 0N 10 30E
86 Gabgaba, W., Egypt 22 10N 33 5E
28 Gabin, Poland 52 23N 19 41E
100 Gabo I., Australia 37 33S 149 57E
88 Gabon ■, Africa 0 10S 10 0E
92 Gaborone, Botswana 24 37S 25 57E
113 Gabriels, U.S.A. 44 26N 74 12W
43 Gabrovo, Bulgaria 42 52N 25 27E
18 Gacé, France 48 49N 0 20E
65 Gach Saran, Iran 30 15N 50 45E
42 Gacko, Yugoslavia 43 10N 18 33E
85 Gada, Nigeria 13 38N 5 36E
70 Gadag, India 15 30N 75 45E
87 Gadamai, Sudan 17 11N 36 10E
68 Gadap, Pakistan 25 5N 67 28E
68 Gadarwara, India 22 50N 78 50E
50 Gäddede, Sweden 64 30N 14 15E
24 Gadebusch, Germany 53 41N 11 6E
87 Gadein, Sudan 8 10N 28 45E
68 Gadhada, India 22 0N 71 35E
33 Gádor, Sierra de, Spain 36 57N 2 45W
115 Gadsden, Ala., U.S.A. 34 1N 86 0W
119 Gadsden, Ariz., U.S.A. 32 35N 114 47W
70 Gadwal, India 16 10N 77 50E
46 Gäești, Rumania 44 48N 25 19E
40 Gaeta, Italy 41 12N 13 35E
40 Gaeta, G. di, Italy 41 0N 13 25E
115 Gaffney, U.S.A. 35 10N 81 31W
83 Gafsa, Tunisia 34 24N 8 51E
54 Gagarin (Gzhatsk), U.S.S.R. 55 30N 35 0E
107 Gagetown, Canada 45 46N 66 29W
55 Gagino, U.S.S.R. 55 15N 45 10E
41 Gagliano del Capo, It. 39 50N 18 23E
48 Gagnef, Sweden 60 36N 15 5E
84 Gagnoa, Ivory Coast 6 4N 5 55W
107 Gagnon, Canada 51 50N 68 5W
109 Gagnon, L., Canada 61 55N 110 40W
89 Gago Coutinho, Angola 14 18S 21 18E
57 Gagra, U.S.S.R. 43 20N 40 10E
20 Gah, France 43 12N 0 27W
90 Gahini, Rwanda 1 50S 30 30E
69 Gahmar, India 25 27N 83 55E
69 Gaibandha, Bangladesh 25 20N 89 36E
45 Gaïdhouronísi, Gr. 34 53N 25 41E
117 Gail, U.S.A. 32 48N 101 25W
26 Gail, R., Austria 46 37N 13 15E
20 Gaillac, Tarn, France 43 54N 1 54E

MAP
18 Gaillon, France 49 10N 1 20E
112 Gaines, U.S.A. 41 45N 77 35W
115 Gainesville, Fla., U.S.A. 29 38N 82 20W
115 Gainesville, Ga., U.S.A. 34 17N 83 47W
117 Gainesville, Mo., U.S.A. 36 35N 92 26W
117 Gainesville, Tex., U.S.A. 33 40N 97 10W
12 Gainsborough, England 53 23N 0 46W
14 Gairloch L., Scot. 57 43N 5 45W
42 Gaj, Yugoslavia 45 28N 17 3E
85 Gajale, Nigeria 11 25N 8 10E
85 Gajiram, Nigeria 12 29N 13 9E
70 Gal Oya Res., Sri Lanka 8 5N 80 55E
69 Galachipa, Bangladesh 22 8N 90 26E
85 Galadi, Nigeria 13 5N 6 20E
90 Galana, R., Kenya 3 0S 39 10E
89 Galangue, Angola 13 48S 16 3E
27 Galanta, Czechoslovakia 48 11N 17 45E
95 Galápagos, Is., Pac. Oc. 0 0 89 0W
71 Galas, R., Malaya 4 55N 101 57E
14 Galashiels, Scot. 55 37N 2 50W
45 Galatás, Greece 37 30N 23 26E
46 Galaţi, Rumania 45 27N 28 2E
46 Galaţi ♦, Rumania 45 45N 27 30E
41 Galatina, Italy 40 10N 18 10E
41 Galátone, Italy 40 8N 18 3E
115 Galax, U.S.A. 36 42N 80 57W
45 Galaxidhion, Greece 38 22N 22 23E
98 Galbraith, Australia 16 25S 141 30E
47 Galdhöpiggen, Nor 61 38N 8 18E
73 Galela, Indonesia 1 50N 127 55E
33 Galera, Spain 37 45N 2 33W
126 Galera, Pta. de la, Col. 10 48N 75 16W
116 Galesburg, U.S.A. 40 57N 90 23W
112 Galeton, U.S.A. 41 43N 77 40W
46 Galicea Mare, Rumania 44 4N 23 19E
55 Galich, R.S.F.S.R., U.S.S.R. 58 23N 42 18E
54 Galich, Uk., U.S.S.R. 49 10N 24 40E
43 Galiche, Bulgaria 43 34N 23 50E
30 Galicia, Spain 42 43N 8 0W
62 Galilee = Hagalil, Israel 32 53N 35 18E
112 Galion, U.S.A. 40 43N 82 48W
83 Galite, Is. de la, Tunisia 37 30N 8 59E
119 Galivro Mts., U.S.A. 32 40N 110 30W
38 Gallarate, Italy 45 40N 8 48E
115 Gallatin, U.S.A. 36 24N 86 27W
70 Galle, Sri Lanka 6 5N 80 10E
32 Gállego, R., Spain 42 23N 0 30W
128 Gallegos, R., Argentina 51 50S 71 0W
38 Galliate, Italy 45 27N 8 44E
126 Gallinas, Pta., Col. 12 28N 71 40W
41 Gallipoli, Italy 40 8N 18 0E
44 Gallipoli = Gelibolu, Turkey 40 28N 26 43E
114 Gallipolis, U.S.A. 38 50N 82 10W
112 Gallitzin, U.S.A. 40 28N 78 32W
50 Gallivare, Sweden 67 7N 20 32E
48 Gällö, Sweden 62 56N 15 15E
40 Gallo, C. di, Italy 38 13N 13 19E
32 Gallocanta, Laguna de, Spain 40 58N 1 30W
14 Galloway, Scotland 55 0N 4 25W
14 Galloway, Mull of, Scotland 54 38N 4 50W
119 Gallup, U.S.A. 35 30N 108 54W
32 Gallur, Spain 41 52N 1 19W
85 Galmi, Niger 13 58N 5 41E
62 Gal'on, Israel 31 38N 34 51E
100 Galong, Australia 34 37S 148 34E
* 106 Galt, Canada 43 21N 80 19W
48 Galtström, Sweden 62 10N 17 30E
26 Galtür, Austria 46 58N 10 11E
15 Galty Mts., Ireland 52 22N 8 10W
15 Galtymore, Mt., Ireland 52 22N 8 12W
73 Galumpang, Indonesia 2 32S 119 32E
116 Galva, U.S.A. 41 10N 90 0W
32 Galve de Sorbe, Spain 41 13N 3 10W
117 Galveston, U.S.A. 29 15N 94 48W
117 Galveston B., U.S.A. 29 30N 94 50W
124 Gálvez, Argentina 32 0S 61 20W
31 Gálvez, Spain 39 42N 4 16W
15 Galway, Ireland 53 16N 9 4W
15 Galway B., Ireland 53 10N 9 20W
15 Galway ♦, Ireland 53 16N 9 3W
43 Galyamo Konare, Bulg. 42 16N 24 33E
87 Gamare, L., Ethiopia 11 32N 41 40E
126 Gamarra, Colombia 8 20N 73 45W
85 Gamawa, Nigeria 12 10N 10 31E
85 Gambaga, Ghana 10 30N 0 28W
68 Gambat, Pakistan 27 17N 68 26E
87 Gambela, Ethiopia 8 14N 34 38E
85 Gambia, R., & ■ W. Africa 13 20N 15 45W
120 Gamboa, Panama Canal Zone 9 8N 79 42W
68 Gamboli, Pakistan 29 53N 68 24E
88 Gamboma, Congo (Fr.) 1 55S 15 52E
98 Gamboola, Australia 16 29S 143 43E
127 Gameleira, Brazil 7 50S 50 0W
119 Gamerco, U.S.A. 35 33N 108 56W
49 Gamleby, Sweden 57 54N 16 20W
127 Gammelgarn, Sweden 57 24N 18 49E
73 Gamsungi, Indonesia 0 20N 128 50E
61 Gan (Addu Atoll), Indian Ocean 0 10S 71 10E
62 Gan Shemu'el, Israel 32 28N 34 56E
62 Gan Yavne, Israel 31 48N 34 42E
119 Ganado, Ariz., U.S.A. 35 46N 109 41W
117 Ganado, Tex., U.S.A. 29 4N 96 31W
106 Gananoque, Canada 44 20N 76 10W
65 Ganaveh, Iran 29 35N 50 35E
69 Gandak, R., India 27 0N 84 8E
68 Gandava, Pakistan 28 32N 67 32E
107 Gander, Canada 49 1N 54 33W
107 Gander L., Canada 48 58N 54 45W
91 Ganderowe Falls, Rhod. 17 20S 29 10E
32 Gandesa, Spain 41 3N 0 26E
68 Gandhi Sagar, India 24 40N 75 40E
85 Gandi, Nigeria 12 55N 5 49E
33 Gandia, Spain 38 58N 0 9W
38 Gandino, Italy 45 50N 9 52E

* Renamed Cambridge

MAP
85 Gandole, Nigeria 8 28N 11 35E
73 Ganedidalem = Gani, Indon. 0 48S 128 14E
86 Ganetti, Sudan 18 0N 31 10E
69 Ganga, R., India 25 0N 88 0E
69 Ganga, Mouths of the, India 21 30N 90 0E
68 Ganganagar, India 29 56N 73 56E
68 Gangapur, India 26 32N 76 37E
85 Gangara, Niger 14 35N 8 40E
70 Gangavati, India 15 30N 76 36E
67 Gangaw, Burma 22 5N 94 15E
20 Ganges, France 43 56N 3 42E
69 Ganges = Ganga, R., India 25 0N 88 0E
46 Gangiova, Rumania 43 54N 23 50E
68 Gangoh, India 29 46N 77 18E
69 Gangtok, India 27 20N 88 40E
68 Ganj, India 27 45N 78 47E
20 Gannat, France 46 7N 3 11E
118 Gannett Pk., U.S.A. 43 15N 109 47W
116 Gannvalley, U.S.A. 44 3N 98 57W
27 Ganserdorf, Austria 48 20N 16 43E
84 Ganta (Gompa), Liberia 7 15N 8 59W
96 Gantheaume B., Australia 27 40S 114 10E
54 Gantsevichi, U.S.S.R. 52 42N 26 30E
57 Ganyushkino, U.S.S.R. 46 35N 49 20E
87 Ganzi, Sudan 4 30N 31 15E
85 Gao ♦, Mali 18 0N 1 0E
71 Gao Bang, N. Vietnam 22 37N 106 18E
84 Gaoua, Upper Volta 10 20N 3 8W
84 Gaoual, Guinea 11 45N 13 25W
82 Gaouz, Morocco 31 52N 4 20W
21 Gap, France 44 33N 6 5E
121 Garachiné, Panama 8 0N 78 12W
127 Garanhuns, Brazil 8 50S 36 30W
84 Garawe, Liberia 4 35N 8 0W
90 Garba Tula, Kenya 0 30N 38 32E
117 Garber, U.S.A. 36 30N 97 36W
118 Garberville, U.S.A. 40 11N 123 50W
46 Gârbovi, Rumania 44 47N 26 47E
21 Gard ♦, France 44 2N 4 10E
38 Garda, L. di, Italy 45 40N 10 40E
21 Gardanne, France 43 27N 5 27E
24 Gardelegen, Germany 52 32N 11 21E
117 Garden City, Kans., U.S.A. 38 0N 100 45W
117 Garden City, Tex., U.S.A. 31 52N 101 28W
65 Gardez, Afghanistan 33 31N 68 59E
45 Gardhiki, Greece 38 50N 21 55E
81 Gardian, Chad 15 45N 19 40E
106 Gardiner, Canada 49 19N 81 2W
118 Gardiner, Mont., U.S.A. 45 3N 110 53W
117 Gardiner, New Mexico, U.S.A. 36 55N 104 29W
113 Gardiners I., U.S.A. 41 4N 72 5W
113 Gardner, U.S.A. 42 35N 72 0W
118 Gardnerville, U.S.A. 38 59N 119 47W
63 Gardo, Somali Rep. 9 18N 49 20E
42 Garešnica, Y.-slav. 45 36N 16 56E
38 Garéssio, Italy 44 12N 8 1E
118 Garfield, Utah, U.S.A. 40 45N 112 15W
118 Garfield, Wash., U.S.A. 47 3N 117 8W
45 Gargaliánoi, Greece 37 4N 21 38E
20 Gargans, Mt., France 45 37N 1 39E
106 Gargantua, C., Canada 47 35N 85 0W
85 Gargoune, Mali 15 56N 0 13E
68 Garhshankar, India 31 13N 76 11E
108 Garibaldi, Canada 49 56N 123 15W
40 Garigliano, R., Italy 41 13N 13 44E
90 Garissa, Kenya 0 25S 39 40E
90 Garissa ♦, Kenya 0 20S 40 0E
85 Garkida, Nigeria 10 27N 12 36E
85 Garko, Nigeria 11 45N 8 53E
118 Garland, U.S.A. 41 47N 112 10W
38 Garlasco, Italy 45 11N 8 55E
58 Garm, U.S.S.R. 39 0N 70 20E
25 Garmisch- Partenkirchen, Germany 47 30N 11 5E
90 Garmo, Norway 61 51N 8 48E
65 Garmsar, Iran 35 20N 52 25E
116 Garner, U.S.A. 43 4N 93 37W
116 Garnett, U.S.A. 38 18N 95 12W
69 Garo Hills, India 25 30N 90 30E
63 Garoe, Somali Rep. 8 35N 48 40E
99 Garoke, Australia 36 45S 141 30E
32 Garona, R., Spain 42 55N 0 45E
20 Garonne, R., France 45 2N 0 36W
85 Garoua (Garwa), Cam. 9 19N 13 21E
24 Garrel, Germany 52 58N 7 59E
84 Garraway, Liberia 4 35N 8 0W
20 Garrigues, Fr. 43 40N 3 30E
118 Garrison, Mont., U.S.A. 46 37N 112 56W
116 Garrison, N.D., U.S.A. 31 50N 94 28W
117 Garrison, Tex., U.S.A. 47 39N 101 27W
116 Garrison Res., U.S.A. 47 30N 102 0W
31 Garrovillas, Spain 39 40N 6 33W
33 Garrucha, Spain 37 11N 1 49W
104 Garry L., Canada 65 40N 100 0W
14 Garry L., Scot., U.K. 57 5N 4 52W
14 Garry, R., Scot. 56 47N 4 0W
14 Garry, Glen, Scot. 57 3N 5 7W
106 Garson, Canada 50 5N 96 50W
20 Gartempe, R., France 46 47N 0 49E
87 Gartok, Sudan 5 35N 31 20E
75 Gartok, Tibet 31 59N 80 30E
24 Gartz, Ger. 54 17N 13 21E
85 Garu, Ghana 10 55N 0 20W
85 Garu, Nigeria 13 35N 5 25E
92 Garub, S.W. Africa 26 37S 16 0E
127 Garupá, Brazil 1 25S 51 35W
73 Garut, Indonesia 7 14S 107 53E
31 Garvão, Portugal 37 42N 8 21W
101 Garvie Mts., N.Z. 45 27S 169 59E
69 Garwa, India 24 11N 83 47E
28 Garwolin, Poland 51 55N 21 38E
114 Gary, U.S.A. 41 35N 87 20W
126 Garzón, Colombia 2 10N 75 40W

MAP
58 Gasan Kuli, U.S.S.R. 37 40N 54 20E
20 Gascogne, France 43 45N 0 20E
32 Gascogne, G. de, France-Spain 44 0N 2 0W
20 Gascony = Gascogne, France 43 45N 0 20E
32 Gascueña, Spain 40 18N 2 31W
87 Gash, W., Ethiopia 15 0N 37 15E
85 Gashaka, Nigeria 7 20N 11 29E
75 Gashiun Nor, China 42 20N 100 40E
85 Gashua, Nigeria 12 54N 11 0E
98 Gasmata, Terr. of New Guinea 6 15S 150 30E
107 Gaspé, Canada 48 52N 64 30W
107 Gaspé, C., Canada 48 48N 64 7W
107 Gaspé Pass., Canada 49 10N 64 0W
107 Gaspé Pen., Canada 48 45N 65 40W
107 Gaspesian Prov. Park, Can. 49 0N 66 45W
114 Gassaway, U.S.A. 38 42N 80 43W
38 Gássino Torinese, Italy 45 8N 7 50E
85 Gassol, Nigeria 8 34N 10 25E
115 Gastonia, U.S.A. 35 17N 81 10W
45 Gastoúni, Greece 37 51N 21 15E
44 Gastoúri, Greece 39 34N 19 54E
128 Gastre, Argentina 42 10S 69 15W
33 Gata, C. de, Spain 36 41N 2 13W
30 Gata, Sierra de, Spain 40 20N 6 20W
42 Gătaia, Rumania 45 26N 21 30E
54 Gatchina, U.S.S.R. 59 35N 30 0E
12 Gateshead, Eng. 54 57N 1 37W
117 Gatesville, U.S.A. 31 29N 97 45W
91 Gaths, Rhodesia 26 2S 30 32E
19 Gatinais, France 48 5N 2 40E
113 Gatineau, Canada 45 28N 75 40W
106 Gatineau, R., Canada 46 20N 76 0W
38 Gattinara, Italy 45 37N 8 22E
120 Gatun, Pan. Can. Zone 9 16N 79 55W
120 Gatun Dam, Pan. Can. 9 16N 79 55W
120 Gatun, L., Panama 9 7N 79 56W
120 Gatun Locks, Pan. Can. 9 16N 79 55W
31 Gaucín, Spain 36 31N 5 19W
109 Gauer L., Canada 57 10N 97 30W
67 Gauhati, India 26 5N 91 55E
54 Gauja, R., U.S.S.R. 57 10N 24 45E
47 Gaula, R., Norway 62 57N 11 0E
5 Gaussberg, Mt., Antarc. 66 45S 89 0E
47 Gausta, Norway 59 50N 8 37E
32 Gavá, Spain 41 18N 2 0E
20 Gavarnie, France 42 44N 0 3W
65 Gavater, Iran 25 10N 61 23E
45 Gavdhopoúla, Greece 34 56N 24 0E
45 Gávdhos, Greece 34 50N 24 5E
31 Gavião, Portugal 39 28N 7 50W
48 Gavle, Sweden 60 41N 17 13E
48 Gävleborgs Lan ♦, Sweden 61 20N 16 15E
38 Gavorrano, Italy 42 55N 10 55E
18 Gavray, France 49 55N 1 20W
55 Gavrilov Yam, U.S.S.R. 57 10N 39 37E
45 Gávrion, Greece 37 54N 24 44E
92 Gawachab, S.W. Afr. 27 4S 17 55E
68 Gawilgarh Hills, India 21 15N 76 45E
99 Gawler, Australia 34 30S 138 42E
96 Gawler Ranges, Australia 32 30S 135 45E
69 Gaya, India 24 47N 85 4E
85 Gaya, Niger 11 58N 3 28E
85 Gaya, Nigeria 11 57N 9 0E
114 Gaylord, U.S.A. 45 1N 84 35W
99 Gayndah, Australia 25 35S 151 39E
56 Gaysin, U.S.S.R. 48 57N 28 25E
56 Gayvoron, U.S.S.R. 48 22N 29 45E
62 Gaza, Egypt 31 30N 34 28E
93 Gaza ♦, Mozambique 23 10S 32 45E
62 Gaza Strip, Egypt 31 29N 34 25E
85 Gazaoua, Niger 13 32N 7 55E
98 Gazelle Pen., New Guin. 4 30S 152 0E
90 Gazi, Zaïre 1 3N 24 30E
64 Gaziantep, Turkey 37 6N 37 23E
84 Gbanga, Liberia 7 19N 9 13W
85 Gbekebo, Nigeria 6 26N 4 48E
85 Gboko, Nigeria 7 17N 9 4E
85 Gbongan, Nigeria 7 28N 4 20E
28 Gdansk, Pol. 54 22N 18 40E
28 Gdansk ♦, Poland 54 10N 18 30E
28 Gdanska, Zatoka, Poland 54 30N 19 20E
54 Gdov, U.S.S.R. 58 40N 27 55E
28 Gdynia, Poland 54 35N 18 33E
73 Gebe, I., Indonesia 0 5N 129 25E
86 Gebeit Mine, Sudan 21 3N 36 29E
87 Gecoa, Ethiopia 7 30N 35 18E
87 Gedaref, Sudan 14 2N 35 28E
62 Gedera, Israel 31 49N 34 46E
87 Gedo, Ethiopia 9 2N 37 25E
20 Gèdre, France 42 47N 0 2E
49 Gedser, Denmark 54 35N 11 55E
49 Gedser Odde, C., Den. 54 30N 12 5E
100 Geelong, Australia 38 2S 144 20E
16 Geeraardsbergen, Belg. 50 45N 3 53E
24 Geestenseth, Germany 53 31N 8 51E
24 Geesthacht, Germany 53 25N 10 20E
90 Geh, Iran 26 10N 60 0E
62 Geia, Israel 31 38N 34 37E
85 Geidam, Nigeria 12 57N 11 57E
24 Geilenkirchen, Germany 50 58N 6 8E
87 Geili, Sudan 16 1N 32 37E
47 Geilo, Norway 60 32N 8 14E
27 Geinica, Czechoslovakia 48 51N 20 55E
25 Geisingen, Germany 47 55N 8 37E
90 Geita, Tanz. 2 48S 32 12E
90 Geita ♦, Tanz. 2 50S 32 10E
87 Gel River, Sudan 7 5N 29 10E
87 Gel, R., Sudan 7 5N 29 10E
41 Gela, Golfo di, Italy 37 0N 14 8E
63 Geladi, Ethiopia 6 59N 46 30E
16 Gelderland ♦, Netherlands 52 5N 6 10E
24 Geldern, Germany 51 32N 6 18E
16 Geldrop, Netherlands 51 25N 5 32E

MAP
16 Geleen, Netherlands 50 57N 5 49E
84 Gelehun, Sierra Leone 8 10N 10 30W
56 Gelendzhik, U.S.S.R. 44 33N 38 17E
44 Gelibolu, Turkey 40 28N 26 43E
25 Gelnhausen, Germany 50 12N 9 12E
24 Gelsenkirchen, Ger. 51 30N 7 5E
24 Gelting, Germany 54 43N 9 53E
71 Gemas, Malaysia 2 37N 102 36E
16 Gembloux, Belgium 50 34N 4 43E
100 Gembrook, Australia 37 58S 145 37E
85 Gembu, Nigeria 8 58N 12 31E
88 Gemena, Zaïre 3 20N 19 40E
64 Gemerek, Turkey 39 15N 36 10E
92 Gemiston, S. Africa 26 15S 28 10E
64 Gemlik, Turkey 40 28N 29 13E
39 Gemona del Friuli, Italy 46 16N 13 7E
86 Gemsa, Egypt 27 39N 33 35E
87 Gemu-Gofa ♦, Ethiopia 5 40N 36 40E
25 Gemünden, Germany 50 3N 9 43E
87 Genale, Ethiopia 6 0N 39 30E
20 Gençay, France 46 23N 0 23E
16 Gendringen, Neth. 51 52N 6 21E
86 Geneina, Gebel, Egypt 29 2N 33 55E
124 General Acha, Arg. 37 20S 64 38W
124 Gen. Alvear, B. A., Arg. 36 0S 60 0W
124 Gen. Alvear, Mend., Arg. 35 0S 67 40W
124 General Artigas, Par. 26 52S 56 16W
124 General Belgrano, Arg. 36 0S 58 30W
124 General Cabrera, Arg. 32 53S 63 58W
124 General Guido, Arg. 36 40S 57 50W
124 Gen. Juan Madariaga, Argentina 37 0S 57 0W
124 General La Madrid, Arg. 37 30S 61 10W
73 General MacArthur, Phil. 11 18N 125 28E
124 General Martin Mignel de Güemes, Arg. 24 50S 65 0W
124 General Paz, Argentina 27 45S 57 36W
128 General Paz, L., Chile 44 0S 72 0W
124 General Pico, Argentina 35 45S 63 50W
124 General Pinedo, Arg. 27 15S 61 30W
124 General Pinto, Arg. 34 45S 61 50W
128 General Roca, Arg. 30 0S 67 40W
73 General Santos, Philippines 6 12N 125 14E
43 General Toshevo, Bulg. 43 42N 28 6E
124 General Viamonte, Arg. 35 1S 61 3W
124 General Villegas, Arg. 35 0S 63 0W
118 Genesee, Idaho, U.S.A. 46 31N 116 59W
112 Genesee, Mich., U.S.A. 43 7N 83 38W
112 Genesee, Pa., U.S.A. 42 0N 77 54W
112 Genesee, R., U.S.A. 41 35N 78 0W
116 Geneseo, Ill., U.S.A. 41 25N 90 10W
116 Geneseo, Kans., U.S.A. 38 32N 98 8W
112 Geneseo, N.Y., U.S.A. 42 49N 77 49W
25 Geneva = Genève, Switz. 46 12N 6 9E
115 Geneva, Ala., U.S.A. 31 2N 85 52W
116 Geneva, Nebr., U.S.A. 40 35N 97 35W
112 Geneva, N.Y., U.S.A. 42 53N 77 0W
112 Geneva, Ohio, U.S.A. 41 49N 80 58W
114 Geneva, L., U.S.A. 42 38N 88 30W
25 Geneva, L. = Léman, Le, Switz. 46 26N 6 30E
25 Genève, Switz. 46 12N 6 9E
25 Genève ♦, Switz. 46 10N 6 10E
25 Gengenbach, Germany 48 25N 8 0E
56 Genichesk, U.S.S.R. 46 12N 34 50E
31 Genil, R., Spain 37 12N 3 50W
21 Génissiat, Barrage de, France 46 1N 5 48E
16 Genk, Belgium 50 58N 5 32E
19 Genlis, France 47 15N 5 12E
16 Gennep, Netherlands 51 41N 5 59E
18 Gennes, France 47 20N 0 17W
38 Genoa = Génova, Italy 44 24N 8 57E
116 Genoa, Nebr., U.S.A. 41 31N 97 44W
113 Genoa, N.Y., U.S.A. 42 40N 76 32W
100 Genoa, Australia 37 28S 149 33E
100 Genoa, R., Australia 37 25S 149 30E
38 Génova, Italy 44 24N 8 56E
38 Génova, Golfo di, Italy 44 0N 9 0E
16 Gent, Belgium 51 2N 3 37E
73 Genteng, Indonesia 7 25S 106 23E
24 Genthin, Germany 52 24N 12 10E
96 Geographe B., Australia 33 30S 115 15E
96 Geographe Chan., Australia 24 30S 113 0E
57 Geokchay, U.S.S.R. 40 42N 47 43E
107 George, Canada 46 12N 62 32W
92 George, S. Afr. 33 58S 22 29E
100 George, L., New South Wales, Australia 35 10S 149 25E
90 George, L., Uganda 0 5N 30 10E
115 George, L., Fla., U.S.A. 29 15N 81 35W
113 George, L., N.Y., U.S.A. 43 30N 73 30W
105 George R. = Port Nouveau, Can. 58 30N 65 50W
101 George Sound, New Zealand 44 52S 167 25E
5 George V Coast, Antarc. 67 0S 148 0E
99 George Town, Australia 41 5S 148 55E
71 George Town = Pinang, Malaysia 5 25N 100 19E
71 George Town, W. Malaysia 5 25N 100 19E
117 George West, U.S.A. 28 18N 98 5W
98 Georgetown, Australia 18 17S 143 33E
106 Georgetown, Ont., Can. 43 40N 80 0W
107 Georgetown, P.E.I., Can. 46 13N 62 24W
84 Georgetown, Gambia 13 30N 14 47W
126 Georgetown, Guyana 6 50N 58 12W
118 Georgetown, Colo., U.S.A. 39 46N 105 49W
114 Georgetown, Ohio, U.S.A. 38 50N 83 50W
115 Georgetown, S.C., U.S.A. 33 22N 79 15W
117 Georgetown, Tex., U.S.A. 30 45N 98 10W

* Divided into three new counties;
West, Mid and South Glamorgan

MAP

83 Hammamet, Tunisia 36 24N 10 38E
83 Hammamet, G. de, Tunisia 36 10N 10 48E
48 Hammarö, I. Sweden 59 20N 13 30E
48 Hammarstrand, Sweden 63 7N 16 20E
49 Hammel, Denmark 56 16N 9 52E
25 Hammelburg, Germany 50 7N 9 54E
114 Hammonton, U.S.A. 39 40N 74 47W
49 Hammeren, Den. 55 18N 14 47E
50 Hammerfest, Norway 70 39N 23 41E
113 Hammond, Can. 45 26N 75 15W
114 Hammond, Ind., U.S.A. 41 40N 87 30W
117 Hammond, La., U.S.A. 30 32N 90 30W
49 Hamneda, Sweden 56 41N 13 51E
101 Hampden, N.Z. 45 18S 170 50E
13 Hampshire ♦, England 51 3N 1 20W
13 Hampshire Downs, England 51 10N 1 10W
117 Hampton, Ark., U.S.A. 33 35N 92 29W
116 Hampton, Iowa, U.S.A. 42 42N 93 12W
113 Hampton, N.H., U.S.A. 42 56N 70 48W
115 Hampton, S.C., U.S.A. 32 52N 81 2W
114 Hampton, Va., U.S.A. 37 4N 76 18W
96 Hampton Harbour, Australia 20 30S 116 30E
96 Hampton Tableland, Australia 32 0N 127 0E
64 Hamra, Saudi Arabia 24 2N 38 55E
48 Hamrange, Sweden 60 59N 17 5E
87 Hamrat esh Sheykh, Sudan 14 45N 27 55E
47 Hamre, Norway 60 33N 5 20E
65 Hamun Helmand, Iran 31 15N 61 15E
66 Hamun-i-Mashkel, Pak. 28 30N 63 0E
66 Hamun-i-Lora, Pakistan 29 38N 64 58E
77 Han K., Hupei, China 31 40N 112 20E
77 Han K., Kwangtung, China 23 45N 116 35E
86 Hanak, Saudi Arabia 25 32N 37 0E
90 Hanang, mt. Tanz. 4 30S 35 25E
25 Hanau, Germany 50 8N 8 56E
76 Hancheng, China 35 14N 110 22E
76 Hanchow Wan, China 35 0N 119 0E
116 Hancock, Mich., U.S.A. 47 10N 88 35W
116 Hancock, Minn., U.S.A. 45 26N 95 46W
113 Hancock, Pa., U.S.A. 41 57N 75 19W
74 Handa, Japan 34 53N 137 0E
63 Handa, Somali Rep. 10 37N 51 2E
48 Handen, Sweden 59 12N 18 12E
90 Handeni ♦, Tanz. 5 30S 38 0E
111 Handlová, Cz. 48 45N 18 35E
76 Handshur, China 39 28N 118 2E
86 Handub, Sudan 19 15N 37 25E
62 Hanegev, Israel 30 50N 35 0E
108 Haney, Canada 49 12N 122 40W
119 Hanford, U.S.A. 36 25N 119 45W
75 Hangayn Nuruu, Mongolia 48 0N 99 0E
77 Hangchow, China 30 12N 120 1E
77 Hangchow Wan, China 30 30N 121 30E
77 Hangchwang, China 34 34N 117 27E
49 Hanger, Sweden 57 6N 13 58E
92 Hangklip, K., S. Africa 34 26S 18 48E
51 Hangö (Hanko), Finland 59 59N 22 57E
76 Hanh, Mongolia 51 32N 100 35E
63 Hanish J., Red Sea 13 45N 42 46E
62 Hanita, Israel 33 5N 35 10E
116 Hankinson, U.S.A. 46 9N 96 58W
51 Hanko = Hangö, Finland 59 59N 22 57E
77 Hankow, China 30 32N 114 20E
119 Hanksville, U.S.A. 38 19N 110 45W
76 Hanku, China 39 16N 117 50E
101 Hanmer, New Zealand 42 32S 172 50E
96 Hann, Mt., Australia 15 50S 125 50E
108 Hanna, Canada 51 40N 112 0W
116 Hannaford, U.S.A. 47 23N 98 18W
116 Hannah, U.S.A. 49 0N 98 56W
5 Hannah B., Canada 51 20N 80 0W
100 Hannahs Bridge, Australia 31 55S 149 41E
116 Hannibal, U.S.A. 39 42N 91 22W
86 Hannik, Sudan 18 12N 32 20E
24 Hannover, Germany 52 23N 9 43E
49 Hanö, I. Sweden 56 2N 14 50E
49 Hanöbukten, Sweden 55 35N 14 30E
71 Hanoi, N. Vietnam 21 5N 105 55E
112 Hanover, Canada 44 9N 81 2W
92 Hanover, S. Africa 31 4S 24 29E
113 Hanover, N.H., U.S.A. 43 43N 72 17W
112 Hanover, Ohio, U.S.A. 40 5N 82 17W
114 Hanover, Pa., U.S.A. 39 46N 76 59W
24 Hanover = Hannover, Germany 52 23N 9 43E
128 Hanover, I., Chile 51 0S 74 50W
49 Hansholm, Denmark 57 8N 8 38E
68 Hansi, India 29 10N 75 57E
48 Hansjö, Sweden 61 10N 14 40E
49 Hansted, Denmark 57 8N 8 36E
76 Hantan, China 36 42N 114 30E
76 Hanuy Gol, Mongolia 48 20N 101 30E
100 Hanwood, Australia 34 26S 146 3E
76 Hanyang, China 30 32N 114 10E
49 Hanö, Sweden 56 0N 14 50E
49 Hanöbukten, Sweden 55 50N 14 30E
50 Haparanda, Sweden 65 52N 24 8E
117 Happy, U.S.A. 34 47N 101 50W
118 Happy Camp, U.S.A. 41 52N 123 30W
107 Happy Valley, Canada 53 15N 60 20W
68 Hapur, India 28 45N 77 45E
64 Haql, Saudi Arabia 29 10N 35 0E
73 Har, Indonesia 5 16S 133 14E
76 Har-Ayrag, Mongolia 45 47N 109 16E
62 Har Tuv, Israel 31 46N 35 0E
75 Har Us Nuur, Mongolia 48 0N 92 0E
62 Har Yehuda, Israel 31 35N 34 57E
76 Hara Narinula, (Lang Shan), China 41 30N 107 0E
64 Haradh, Saudi Arabia 24 15N 49 0E
63 Haradera, Somali Rep. 4 33N 47 38E

MAP

64 Haradh, Saudi Arabia 24 15N 49 0E
47 Haramsöya, Norway 62 39N 6 12E
64 Haran, Turkey 36 48N 39 0E
87 Harat, Ethiopia 16 5N 39 26E
81 Haraze, Chad 14 20N 19 12E
81 Haraze-Mangueigne, Cent. Afr. Rep. 7 22N 17 3E
76 Harbin, China 45 46N 126 51E
49 Harboör, Denmark 56 38N 8 10E
114 Harbor Beach, U.S.A. 43 50N 82 38W
114 Harbor Springs, U.S.A. 45 28N 85 0W
107 Harbour Breton, Can. 47 29N 55 50W
107 Harbour Deep, Canada 50 25N 56 30W
107 Harbour Grace, Canada 47 40N 53 22W
24 Harburg, Germany 53 27N 9 58E
98 Harcourt, Australia 24 17S 149 55E
68 Harda, India 22 27N 77 5E
47 Hardangerfjorden., Norway 60 15N 6 0E
47 Hardangerjökulen, Norway 60 30N 7 0E
47 Hardangervidda, Nor. 60 20N 7 20E
92 Hardap Dam, S.W. Afr. 24 32S 17 50E
16 Hardenberg, Neth. 52 34N 6 37E
118 Hardin, U.S.A. 45 50N 107 35W
93 Harding, S. Afr. 30 22S 29 55E
108 Hardisty, Canada 52 40N 111 25W
118 Hardman, U.S.A. 45 12N 119 49W
69 Hardoi, India 27 26N 80 15E
68 Hardwar, India⁴ 29 58N 78 16E
113 Hardwick, U.S.A. 44 30N 72 20W
117 Hardy, U.S.A. 36 20N 91 30W
128 Hardy, Pen., Chile 55 30S 68 20W
62 Hare Gilboa, Israel 32 31N 35 25E
62 Hare Meron, Israel 32 59N 35 24E
24 Haren, Germany 52 47N 7 18E
87 Harer, Ethiopia 9 20N 42 8E
87 Harer ♦, Ethiopia 7 12N 42 0E
87 Hareto, Ethiopia 9 23N 37 6E
18 Harfleur, France 49 30N 0 10E
63 Hargeisa, Somali Rep. 9 30N 44 2E
46 Hârghita Mţii, Rumania 46 25N 25 35E
46 Hârghita ♦, Rumania 46 25N 25 30E
48 Hargshamn, Sweden 60 12N 18 30E
65 Hari, R., Afghanistan 34 20N 64 30E
72 Hari, R., Indon. 1 0S 101 50E
82 Haricha, Hamada el, Mali 22 40N 3 15W
70 Harihar, India 14 32N 75 44E
34 Harim, J. al, Oman 26 0N 56 10E
69 Haringhata, R., Bangladesh 22 0N 89 58E
70 Haripad, India 9 14N 76 28E
65 Harīrūd, Iran 35 0N 61 0E
86 Harkat, Saudi Arabia 20 25N 39 40E
116 Harlan, Iowa, U.S.A. 41 37N 95 20W
115 Harlan, Tenn., U.S.A. 36 58N 83 20W
12 Harlech, Wales 52 52N 4 7W
118 Harlem, U.S.A. 48 29N 108 39W
16 Harlingen, Netherlands 53 11N 5 25E
117 Harlingen, U.S.A. 26 30N 97 50W
118 Harlowton, U.S.A. 46 30N 109 54W
48 Harmånger, Sweden 61 55N 17 20E
87 Harmil, Ethiopia 16 30N 40 10E
118 Harney Basin, U.S.A. 43 30N 119 0W
118 Harney L., U.S.A. 43 0N 119 0W
116 Harney Pk., U.S.A. 43 52N 103 33W
48 Härnön, I. Sweden 62 38N 18 0E
25 Harnösand, Sweden 62 38N 18 5E
32 Haro, Spain 42 35N 2 55W
49 Häroy, Denmark 55 13N 10 8E
107 Harp L., Canada 55 10N 61 40W
70 Harpenhalli, India 14 47N 76 2E
84 Harper, Liberia 4 25N 7 43E
49 Harplinge, Sweden 56 45N 12 45E
64 Harput, Turkey 38 48N 39 15E
64 Harrand, Pakistan 29 28N 70 3E
64 Harrat al Kishb, Saudi Arabia 22 30N 40 15E
64 Harrat al Umuirid, South Arabia 26 50N 38 0E
86 Harrat Khaibar, Saudi Arabia 25 45N 40 0E
86 Harrat Nawāṣif, Saudi Arabia 21 30N 42 0E
106 Harricanaw, R., Canada 50 30N 79 10W
115 Harriman, U.S.A. 36 0N 84 35W
107 Harrington Harb., Can. 50 31N 59 30W
14 Harris, Scot. 57 50N 6 55W
96 Harris L., Australia 31 10S 135 10E
14 Harris, Sd. of, Scotland 57 44N 7 6W
117 Harrisburg, Ill., U.S.A. 37 42N 88 30W
116 Harrisburg, Nebr., U.S.A. 41 36N 103 46W
118 Harrisburg, Oreg., U.S.A. 44 25N 123 10W
112 Harrisburg, Pa., U.S.A. 40 18N 76 52W
93 Harrismith, S. Africa 28 15S 29 8E
117 Harrison, Ark., U.S.A. 36 10N 93 4W
118 Harrison, Idaho, U.S.A. 47 30N 116 51W
116 Harrison, Nebr., U.S.A. 42 42N 103 52W
104 Harrison B., Alaska 70 25N 151 0W
112 Harrison, U.S.A. 38 28N 78 52W
92 Harrisonville, U.S.A. 38 45N 93 45W
106 Harriston, Canada 43 57N 80 53W
112 Harrisville, U.S.A. 44 40N 83 19W
13 Harrogate, Eng. 53 59N 1 32W
112 Harrow, Canada 42 2N 82 53W
13 Harrow, Eng. 51 35N 0 15W
24 Harsefeld, Germany 53 26N 9 31E
50 Harstad, Norway 68 48N 16 30E
114 Hart, U.S.A. 43 42N 86 21W
26 Hartberg, Austria 47 17N 15 58E
47 Harteigen, Mt., Norway 60 11N 7 5E
113 Hartford, Conn., U.S.A. 41 47N 72 41W
115 Hartford, Ky., U.S.A. 37 26N 86 50W
116 Hartford, S.D., U.S.A. 43 40N 96 58W
116 Hartford, Wis., U.S.A. 43 18N 88 25W
114 Hartford City, U.S.A. 40 22N 85 20W
107 Hartland, Canada 46 20N 67 32W

MAP

13 Hartland Pt., U.K. 51 2N 4 32W
12 Hartlepool, U.K. 54 42N 1 11W
91 Hartley, Rhodesia 18 10S 30 7E
108 Hartley Bay, Canada 46 4N 80 45W
92 Hartmannberge, S. Afr. 17 0S 13 0E
109 Hartney, Canada 49 30N 100 35W
115 Hartselle, U.S.A. 34 25N 86 55W
117 Hartshorne, U.S.A. 34 51N 95 30W
115 Hartsville, U.S.A. 34 23N 80 2W
115 Hartwell, U.S.A. 34 21N 82 52W
68 Harunabad, Pakistan 29 35N 73 2E
70 Harur, India 12 3N 78 29E
64 Harvard, Mt., U.S.A. 39 0N 106 5W
114 Harvey, Ill., U.S.A. 41 40N 87 40W
116 Harvey, N.D., U.S.A. 47 50N 99 58W
13 Harwich, Eng. 51 56N 1 18E
112 Harwood, Canada 44 7N 78 11W
68 Haryana ♦, India 29 0N 76 10E
24 Harz, Germany 51 40N 10 40E
24 Harzgerode, Germany 51 38N 11 8E
64 Hasa, Si. Arabia 26 0N 49 0E
87 Hasaheisa, Sudan 14 25N 33 20E
86 Hasani, Saudi Arabia 25 0N 37 8E
68 Hasanpur, India 28 51N 78 9E
62 Hasharon, Israel 32 12N 34 49E
62 Hashefela, Israel 31 30N 34 43E
48 Hasjö, Sweden 63 2N 16 20E
117 Haskell, Kans., U.S.A. 35 51N 95 40W
117 Haskell, Tex., U.S.A. 33 10N 99 45W
25 Haslach, Germany 48 16N 8 7E
49 Hasle, Denmark 55 11N 14 44E
49 Haslev, Denmark 55 18N 11 57E
43 Hasparren, France 43 24N 1 18W
64 Hassan, India 13 0N 76 5E
16 Hasselt, Belgium 50 56N 5 21E
82 Hassene, Ad., Algeria 21 0N 4 0E
25 Hassfurt, Germany 50 2N 10 30E
83 Hassi Berrekrem, Alg. 33 45N 5 16E
83 Hassi Daoula, Algeria 33 4N 5 38E
82 Hassi el Biod, Algeria 28 30N 6 0E
82 Hassi Inifel, Algeria 29 50N 3 41E
83 Hassi Marroket, Algeria 30 10N 3 0E
50 Hassi el Heïda, Algeria 29 50N 0 14W
82 Hassi Messaoud, Alg. 31 43N 6 8E
83 Hassi Rhénami, Alg. 31 57N 5 58E
124 Hassi Taguenza, Algeria 29 8N 0 23W
82 Hassi Zerzour, Morocco 30 51N 3 56W
49 Hässleby, Sweden 57 37N 15 30E
56 Hässleholmen, Sweden 56 9N 13 45E
112 Hastings, Canada 44 18N 77 56W
13 Hastings, Eng. 50 51N 0 36E
101 Hastings, New Zealand 39 39S 176 52E
114 Hastings, Mich., U.S.A. 42 40N 85 20W
116 Hastings, Minn., U.S.A. 44 41N 92 51W
116 Hastings, Nebr., U.S.A. 40 34N 98 22W
112 Hastings, Pa., U.S.A. 40 40N 78 45W
99 Hastings Ra., Australia 31 15S 152 14E
49 Hästveda, Sweden 56 16N 13 55E
71 Hat Nhao, Laos 14 46N 106 32E
119 Hatch, U.S.A. 32 45N 107 8W
96 Hatches Cr., Australia 20 56S 135 12E
46 Haţeg, Rumania 45 36N 22 55E
46 Haţeg, Mţii, Rumania 45 25N 23 0E
100 Hatfield Post Office, Australia 33 54N 143 49E
75 Hatgal, Mongolia 50 40N 100 0E
68 Hathras, India 27 36N 78 6E
126 Hato de Corozal, Col. 6 11N 71 45W
100 Hattah, Australia 34 48N 142 17E
115 Hatteras, C., U.S.A. 35 10N 75 30W
117 Hattiesburg, U.S.A. 31 20N 89 20W
109 Hatton, Canada 50 2N 109 50W
107 Hatton Pt., Canada 49 8N 61 40W
73 Hatvan, Hungary 47 40N 19 45E
71 Hau Bon (Cheo Reo), S. Vietnam 13 25N 108 28E
120 Hauchinango, Mexico 20 12N 97 45W
47 Haug, Norway 60 23N 10 26E
47 Haugastöl, Norway 60 30N 7 50E
47 Haugesund, Norway 59 23N 5 13E
47 Haukelisaeter, Norway 59 51N 7 9E
63 Haura, South Yemen 13 50N 47 35E
101 Hauraki Gulf, N.Z. 36 35S 175 5E
26 Hausruck, Austria 48 6N 13 30E
82 Haut Atlas, Morocco 32 0N 7 0W
19 Haut-Rhin ♦, France 48 0N 7 15E
90 Haut Zaïre ♦, Zaïre 2 20N 26 0E
64 Hauta Oasis, Si. Arab. 23 40N 47 0E
64 Hautah, Wahât al, Si. Arab. 23 40N 47 0E
20 Haute-Garonne ♦, France 43 28N 1 0E
20 Haute-Loire ♦, Fr. 45 5N 3 50E
19 Haute-Marne ♦, Fr. 48 10N 5 20E
19 Haute-Saône ♦, Fr. 47 45N 6 10E
21 Haute-Savoie ♦, France 46 0N 6 20E
20 Haute-Vienne ♦, Fr. 45 50N 1 10E
107 Hauterive, Canada 49 10N 68 25W
21 Hautes-Alpes ♦, Fr. 44 42N 6 20E
20 Hautes-Pyrénées ♦, France 43 0N 0 10E
112 Hauteurs de Gâtine, France 46 35N 0 45W
21 Hauteville-Lompnes, France 45 59N 5 35E
19 Hautmont, France 50 15N 3 55E
19 Hauts-de-Seine ♦, Fr. 48 52N 2 15E
121 Havana, Cuba 23 8N 82 22W
121 Havana = La Habana, Cuba 23 8N 82 22W
116 Havana, U.S.A. 40 19N 90 3W
46 Havârna, Rumania 48 22N 26 37E
49 Havdhem, Sweden 57 10N 18 20E
16 Havelange, Belgium 50 23N 5 15E
106 Havelock, N.B., Can. 46 2N 65 24W
107 Havelock, Ont., Canada 44 26N 77 53W
101 Havelock, New Zealand 41 17S 173 48E
71 Havelock I., Andaman I. 11 55N 93 2E

MAP

13 Haverfordwest, Wales 51 48N 4 59W
113 Haverhill, U.S.A. 42 50N 71 2W
14 Haveri, India 14 53N 75 24E
13 Havering, Eng. 51 33N 0 20E
113 Haverstraw, U.S.A. 41 12N 73 58W
49 Håverund, Sweden 58 50N 12 28E
19 Havlíckuv Brod, Cz. 49 36N 15 33E
49 Havnby, Denmark 55 5N 8 34E
118 Havre, U.S.A. 48 40N 109 34W
107 Havre-Aubert, Canada 47 12N 62 0W
107 Havre St. Pierre, Can. 50 18N 63 33W
64 Havza, Turkey 41 0N 35 35E
115 Haw, R., U.S.A. 35 36N 79 3W
110 Hawaii ♦, U.S.A. 20 30N 157 0W
110 Hawaii I., Hawaii 20 0N 155 0W
110 Hawaiian Is., Pac. Oc. 20 30N 156 0W
109 Hawarden, Canada 51 25N 106 30W
116 Hawarden, U.S.A. 43 2N 96 28W
101 Hawea Lake, N.Z. 44 28S 169 19E
14 Hawick, Scotland 55 25N 2 48W
101 Hawke B., N.Z. 39 25N 177 20E
99 Hawker, Australia 31 59S 138 22E
101 Hawke's Bay ♦, N.Z. 39 45S 176 35E
101 Hawke's Harbour, Can. 53 2N 55 50W
106 Hawkesbury, Canada 45 35N 74 40W
108 Hawkesbury I., Canada 53 37N 129 3W
115 Hawkinsville, U.S.A. 32 17N 83 30W
99 Hawkwood, Australia 25 45S 150 50E
116 Hawley, U.S.A. 46 58N 96 20W
118 Hawthorne, U.S.A. 38 31N 118 47W
87 Hawzen, Ethiopia 13 58N 39 28E
116 Haxtun, U.S.A. 40 40N 102 39W
99 Hay, Australia 34 30S 144 51E
13 Hay, Wales 52 4N 3 9W
108 Hay Lakes, Canada 53 12N 113 2W
108 Hay River, Canada 60 50N 115 50W
116 Hay Springs, U.S.A. 42 40N 102 38W
20 Hayange, France 49 20N 6 2E
119 Hayden, Ariz., U.S.A. 33 2N 110 54W
118 Hayden, Wyo., U.S.A. 40 30N 107 22W
98 Haydon, Australia 18 0S 141 30E
116 Hayes, U.S.A. 44 22N 101 1W
109 Hayes, R., Canada 56 0N 93 0W
4 Hayes Pen., Greenland 75 30N 65 0W
117 Haymana, Turkey 39 30N 32 35E
117 Haynesville, U.S.A. 33 0N 93 7W
116 Hays, U.S.A. 38 55N 99 25W
13 Hayward's Heath, England 51 0N 0 5W
114 Hazard, Ky., U.S.A. 37 18N 83 10W
69 Hazaribagh, India 23 58N 85 26E
69 Hazaribagh Rd., India 24 12N 85 57E
18 Hazebrouck, France 50 42N 2 31E
117 Hazelhurst, U.S.A. 31 50N 82 35W
108 Hazelton, Canada 55 20N 127 42W
116 Hazelton, N.D., U.S.A. 46 30N 100 15W
113 Hazleton, Pa., U.S.A. 40 58N 76 0W
65 Hazrat Immam, Afghan. 37 15N 68 50E
119 Hazen, Nev., U.S.A. 39 37N 119 2W
65 Head of Bight, Australia 31 30S 131 25E
91 Headlands, Rhodesia 18 15S 32 2E
118 Healdsburg, U.S.A. 38 33N 122 51W
117 Healdton, U.S.A. 34 16N 97 31W
100 Healesville, Australia 37 35S 145 30E
13 Heanor, Eng. 53 1N 1 20W
3 Heard I., Southern Oc. 53 0S 74 0E
106 Hearst, Canada 49 40N 83 41W
116 Heart, R., U.S.A. 46 40N 101 30W
107 Heart's Content, Can. 47 54N 53 27W
98 Heathcote, Australia 36 58S 144 43E
117 Heavener, U.S.A. 34 54N 94 36W
117 Hebbronville, U.S.A. 27 20N 98 40W
117 Heber Springs, U.S.A. 35 29N 91 39W
118 Hebgen, L., U.S.A. 44 50N 111 15W
105 Hebron, Canada 58 10N 62 50W
62 Hebron (Al Khalil), Jordan 31 32N 35 6E
116 Hebron, N.D., U.S.A. 46 56N 102 2W
49 Heby, Sweden 59 56N 16 53E
108 Hecate Str., Canada 53 10N 130 30W
25 Hechingen, Germany 48 20N 8 58E
116 Hecla, U.S.A. 45 56N 98 8W
109 Hecla I., Canada 51 10N 96 50W
47 Heddal, Norway 59 36N 9 20E
48 Hede, Jämtland, Sweden 62 23N 13 30E
48 Hedemora, Sweden 60 18N 15 58E
47 Hedmark fylke ♦, Nor. 61 17N 11 40E
47 Hedrum, Norway 59 7N 10 5E
16 Heemstede, Netherlands 52 22N 4 37E
16 Heerde, Netherlands 52 24N 6 2E
16 Heerenveen, Neth. 52 57N 5 55E
16 Heerlen, Netherlands 50 55N 6 0E
73 Hegyalja, Mts., Hun. 48 25N 21 25E
24 Heide, Germany 54 10N 9 7E
25 Heidelberg, Germany 49 23N 8 41E
92 Heidelberg, C. Prov., S. Africa 34 6S 20 59E
93 Heidelberg, Trans., S. Africa 26 30S 28 23E
25 Heidenheim, Germany 48 40N 10 10E
93 Heilbron, S. Afr. 27 16S 27 59E
26 Heiligenblut, Austria 47 2N 12 51E
24 Heiligenhafen, Germany 54 21N 10 58E
24 Heiligenstadt, Germany 51 22N 10 9E
76 Heilungkiang ♦, China 48 30N 129 0E
47 Heim, Norway 63 26N 9 5E
51 Heinola, Finland 61 13N 26 24E
71 Heinze Is., Burma 14 25N 97 45E
47 Heistad, Norway 59 35N 9 40E
64 Hejaz = Hijâz, Si. Arab. 26 0N 37 30E

MAP

64 Hekimhan, Turkey 38 50N 38 0E
50 Hekla, Iceland 63 56N 19 35W
34 Hel, Poland 54 38N 18 50E
48 Helagsfjället, Swed. 62 54N 12 25E
31 Helechosa, Spain 39 22N 4 53W
117 Helena, Ark., U.S.A. 34 30N 90 35W
118 Helena, Mont., U.S.A. 46 40N 112 0W
100 Helensburgh, Australia 34 11S 151 1E
14 Helensburgh, Scot. 56 0N 4 44W
101 Helensville, N.Z. 36 41S 174 29E
62 Helets, Israel 31 36N 34 39E
49 Helgasjön, Sweden 57 0N 14 50E
50 Helgeland, Nor. 66 20N 13 30E
47 Helgeroa, Norway 59 0N 9 45E
24 Helgoland, I., Germany 54 10N 7 51E
48 Helgum, Sweden 63 25N 16 50E
24 Heligoland = Helgoland, Germany 54 10N 7 51E
86 Heliopolis, Egypt 30 6N 31 17E
93 Hell-Ville, Malag. 13 25S 48 16E
49 Hellebaek, Denmark 56 4N 12 32E
47 Helleland, Norway 58 33N 6 7E
16 Hellendoorn, Neth. 52 24N 6 27E
16 Hellevoetsluis, Neth. 51 50N 4 8E
5 Hellick Kenyon Plateau, Antarctica 82 0S 110 0W
33 Hellín, Spain 38 31N 1 40W
49 Hellum, Denmark 57 16N 10 10E
65 Helmand, R., Afghan. 34 0N 67 0E
16 Helmond, Netherlands 51 29N 5 41E
14 Helmsdale, Scot. 58 7N 3 40W
14 Helmsdale, R., Scot. 58 10N 3 50W
24 Helmstedt, Germany 52 16N 11 0E
49 Helnaes, Denmark 55 9N 10 0E
118 Helper, U.S.A. 39 44N 110 56W
49 Helsinge, Denmark 56 2N 12 12E
49 Helsingör, Denmark 56 2N 12 35E
51 Helsinki (Helsingfors), Finland 60 15N 25 3E
86 Helwân, Egypt 29 50N 31 20E
47 Hem, Norway 59 26N 10 0E
70 Hemavati, R., India 12 50N 76 0E
119 Hemet, U.S.A. 33 45N 116 59W
116 Hemingford, U.S.A. 42 21N 103 44W
117 Hemphill, U.S.A. 31 21N 93 49W
49 Hemse, Sweden 57 15N 18 22E
48 Hemsö, I., Sweden 62 43N 18 5E
48 Hemsön, Sweden 62 42N 18 5E
32 Henares, R., Spain 40 55N 3 0W
20 Hendaye, France 43 23N 1 47W
124 Henderson, Argentina 36 18S 61 43W
115 Henderson, Ky., U.S.A. 37 50N 87 38W
119 Henderson, Nev., U.S.A. 36 2N 115 0W
115 Henderson, Pa., U.S.A. 35 25N 88 40W
117 Henderson, Tex., U.S.A. 32 5N 94 49W
115 Hendersonville, U.S.A. 35 21N 82 28W
99 Hendon, Australia 28 5S 151 50E
46 Hendorf, Rumania 46 4N 24 5E
16 Hengelo, Netherlands 52 15N 6 48E
77 Henghsien, China 22 36N 109 16E
77 Hengshan, China 27 10N 112 45E
77 Hengyang, China 26 57N 112 28E
**19 Hénin-Liétard, France 50 25N 2 58E
114 Henlopen C., U.S.A. 38 48N 75 5W
48 Hennan, L., Sweden 62 3N 15 55E
49 Henne, Denmark 55 44N 8 11E
18 Hennebont, France 47 49N 3 19W
92 Hennenman, S. Africa 27 59S 27 1E
117 Hennessy, U.S.A. 36 8N 97 53W
24 Hennigsdorf, Germany 52 38N 13 13E
109 Henribourg, Canada 53 25N 105 38W
19 Henrichemont, France 47 20N 2 21E
117 Henrietta, U.S.A. 33 50N 98 15W
106 Henrietta Maria C., Can. 55 10N 82 30W
117 Henry, U.S.A. 41 5N 89 20W
117 Henryetta, U.S.A. 35 2N 96 0W
112 Hensall, Canada 43 27N 81 32W
76 Hentiyn Nuruu, Mongolia 48 30N 108 30E
100 Henty, Australia 35 30N 147 0E
67 Henzada, Burma 17 38N 95 35E
118 Heppner, U.S.A. 45 27N 119 34W
112 Hepworth, Canada 44 40N 81 10W
47 Herad, Vest-Agder, Norway 58 8N 6 47E
50 Héraðsflói, Iceland 65 42N 14 12W
50 Héraðsvötn, Iceland 65 25N 19 5W
65 Herât, Afghanistan 34 20N 62 7E
20 Hérault, R., France 43 34N 3 15E
20 Hérault ♦, France 43 34N 3 32E
109 Herbert, Canada 50 30N 107 10W
98 Herbert Downs, Australia 23 0S 139 11E
98 Herberton, Australia 17 28S 145 25E
18 Herbignac, France 47 27N 2 18W
24 Herborn, Germany 50 40N 8 19E
25 Herby, Poland 50 45N 18 50E
42 Hercegnovi, Y.-slav. 42 30N 18 33E
42 Hercegovina ♦, Yugoslavia 43 20N 18 0E
50 Herðubreið, Iceland 65 11N 16 21W
47 Heröya, Norway 60 34N 4 56E
13 Hereford, Eng. 52 4N 2 42W
117 Hereford, U.S.A. 34 50N 102 28W
• 13 Hereford ♦, Eng. 52 4N 2 43W
47 Herefoss, Norway 58 32N 8 32E
16 Herentals, Belgium 51 12N 4 51E
49 Herfölge, Denmark 55 26N 12 9E
49 Herföringe, Denmark 56 12N 9 40E
47 Héricourt, France 47 32N 6 55E
25 Herisau, Switzerland 47 22N 9 17E
20 Hérisson, France 46 32N 2 42E
113 Herkimer, U.S.A. 43 0N 74 59W
†26 Hermagor, Austria 46 38N 13 23E
116 Herman, U.S.A. 45 51N 96 8W

* Incorporated within the county
  of Hereford and Worcester
† Renamed Hermagor-Pressegger-See
** Renamed Hénin-Beaumont

31

Hermann INDEX Howick

MAP
116 Hermann, U.S.A. 38 40N 91 25W
24 Hermannsburg, Ger. 52 49N 10 6E
92 Hermanus, S. Africa 34 27S 19 12E
20 Herment, France 45 45N 2 24E
100 Hermidale, Australia 31 30S 146 42E
118 Hermiston, U.S.A. 45 50N 119 16W
101 Hermitage, N.Z. 43 44S 170 5E
107 Hermitage B., Canada 47 33N 56 10W
128 Hermite, Is., Chile 55 50S 68 0W
120 Hermosillo, Mexico 29 10N 111 0W
27 Hernad, R., Hungary 48 20N 21 15E
125 Hernandarias, Paraguay 25 20S 54 40W
124 Hernando, Argentina 32 28S 64 50W
117 Hernando, U.S.A. 34 50N 89 59W
24 Herne, Germany 51 33N 7 12E
13 Herne Bay, Eng. 51 22N 1 8E
49 Herning, Denmark 56 8N 8 58E
120 Heroica Nogales, Mexico 31 14N 110 56W
106 Heron Bay, Canada 48 40N 85 25W
47 Heröy, Norway 62 18N 5 45E
116 Herreid, U.S.A. 45 53N 100 5W
31 Herrera, Spain 39 12N 5 3W
31 Herrera de Alcántar, Spain 39 39N 7 25W
30 Herrera de Pisuerga, Sp. 42 35N 4 20W
31 Herrera del Duque, Sp. 39 10N 5 3W
99 Herrick, Tasmania 41 5S 147 55E
117 Herrin, U.S.A. 37 50N 89 0W
49 Herrljunga, Sweden 58 5N 13 1E
25 Hersbruck, Germany 49 30N 11 25E
47 Hersvik, Norway 61 10N 4 53E
13 Hertford, Eng. 51 47N 0 4W
13 Hertford ♦, Eng. 51 51N 0 5W
16 's Hertogenbosch, Neth. 51 42N 5 18E
92 Hertzogville, S. Africa 28 9S 25 30E
30 Hervás, Sapin 40 16N 5 52W
97 Hervey Bay, Australia 25 0S 153 0E
95 Hervey Is., Pac. O. 19 30S 159 0W
106 Hervey Junc., Canada 46 50N 72 29W
24 Herzberg, Cottbus, Ger. 51 40N 13 13E
24 Herzberg, Niedersachsen, Ger. 51 38N 10 20E
62 Herzliyya, Israel 32 10N 34 50E
26 Herzogenburg, Austria 48 17N 15 41E
19 Hesdin, France 50 21N 2 0E
24 Hesel, Germany 53 18N 7 36E
47 Heskestad, Norway 58 28N 6 22E
112 Hespeler, Canada 43 28N 80 19W
24 Hesse = Hessen, Germany 50 57N 9 20E
24 Hessen ♦, Germany 50 57N 9 20E
116 Hettinger, U.S.A. 46 8N 102 38W
24 Hettstedt, Germany 51 39N 11 30E
18 Hève, C. de la, France 49 30N 0 5E
27 Heves ♦, Hungary 47 50N 20 0E
62 Hevron, N., Isr.-Jord. 31 28N 34 52E
92 Hex River, S. Africa 33 30S 19 35E
12 Hexham, Eng. 54 58N 2 7W
100 Heyfield, Australia 37 59S 146 47E
12 Heysham, Eng. 54 5N 2 53W
100 Heywood, Australia 38 8S 141 37E
116 Hiawatha, Kans., U.S.A. 39 55N 95 33W
118 Hiawatha, Utah, U.S.A. 39 37N 111 1W
116 Hibbing, U.S.A. 47 30N 93 0W
117 Hickman, U.S.A. 36 35N 89 8W
115 Hickory, U.S.A. 35 46N 81 17W
113 Hicksville, U.S.A. 40 46N 73 30W
46 Hida-Gawa, Rumania 47 10N 23 9E
74 Hida-Sammyaku, Japan 36 30N 137 40E
120 Hidalgo ♦, Mexico 20 30N 99 10W
120 Hidalgo del Parral, Mex. 26 10N 104 50W
24 Hiddensee, Germany 54 30N 13 6E
26 Hieflau, Austria 47 36N 14 46E
32 Hiendelaencina, Spain 41 5N 3 0W
80 Hierro I., Can. I. 27 57N 17 56E
77 Hifung, China 22 59N 115 17E
117 Higgins, U.S.A. 36 9N 100 1W
115 Higgs I. L., U.S.A. 36 20N 78 30W
107 High I., Canada 56 40N 61 10W
82 High Atlas = Haut Atlas, N. Afr. 32 30N 5 0W
117 High Island, U.S.A. 29 32N 94 22W
115 High Point, U.S.A. 35 57N 79 58W
108 High Prairie, Canada 55 30N 116 30W
108 High River, Canada 50 30N 113 50W
115 High Springs, U.S.A. 29 50N 82 40W
93 High Veld = Hoëveld, S. Africa 26 30S 30 0E
13 High Wycombe, England 51 37N 0 45W
98 Highbank, New Zealand 47 34S 171 45E
114 Highland Pk., Ill., U.S.A. 42 10N 87 50W
112 Highland Pk., Mich., U.S.A. 42 25N 83 6W
116 Highmore, U.S.A. 44 35N 99 26W
119 Higley, U.S.A. 33 27N 111 46W
126 Higuerote, Venezuela 7 24N 62 3W
54 Hiiumaa, U.S.S.R. 58 50N 22 45E
32 Híjar, Spain 41 10N 0 27W
64 Hijāz, Saudi Arabia 26 0N 37 30E
119 Hiko, U.S.A. 37 30N 115 13W
74 Hikone, Japan 35 15N 136 10E
101 Hikurangi, New Zealand 37 54S 178 5E
101 Hikurangi, Mt., N.Z. 37 55S 178 4E
25 Hildburghhausen, Ger. 50 24N 10 43E
24 Hildesheim, Germany 52 9N 9 55E
118 Hill City, Idaho, U.S.A. 43 20N 115 2W
116 Hill City, Kans., U.S.A. 39 25N 99 51W
116 Hill City, Minn., U.S.A. 46 57N 93 35W
116 Hill City, S.D., U.S.A. 43 58N 103 35W
109 Hill Island L., Canada 60 30N 109 50W
64 Hilla, Iraq 32 30N 44 27E
64 Hilla, Saudi Arabia 23 35N 46 50E
49 Hillared, Sweden 57 37N 13 10E
49 Hilleröd, Denmark 55 56N 12 19E
49 Hillerstorp, Sweden 57 20N 13 52E
49 Hilleröd, Denmark 55 56N 12 19E
13 Hillingdon, Eng. 51 33N 0 29W
114 Hillman, U.S.A. 45 5N 83 52W
MAP
109 Hillmond, Canada 53 26N 109 41W
116 Hillsboro, Kans., U.S.A. 38 28N 97 10W
119 Hillsboro, N. Mex., U.S.A. 33 0N 107 35W
116 Hillsboro, N.D., U.S.A. 47 23N 97 9W
113 Hillsboro, N.H., U.S.A. 43 8N 71 56W
119 Hillsboro, N. Mex., U.S.A. 33 0N 107 35W
118 Hillsboro, Oreg., U.S.A. 45 31N 123 0W
117 Hillsboro, Tex., U.S.A. 32 0N 97 10W
114 Hillsdale, Mich., U.S.A. 41 55N 84 40W
113 Hillsdale, N.Y., U.S.A. 42 11N 73 30W
106 Hillsport, Canada 49 27N 85 34W
100 Hillston, Australia 33 30S 145 31E
110 Hilo, Hawaii 19 44N 155 5W
73 Hilonghilong, mt., Phil. 9 10N 125 45E
112 Hilton, U.S.A. 43 16N 77 48W
16 Hilversum, Netherlands 52 14N 5 10E
68 Himachal Pradesh ♦, India 31 30N 77 0E
67 Himalaya, Asia 29 0N 84 0E
44 Himara, Albania 40 8N 19 43E
74 Himeji, Japan 34 50N 134 40E
74 Himi, Japan 36 50N 137 0E
49 Himmerland, Den. 56 45N 9 30E
64 Hims = Homs, Syria 34 40N 36 45E
72 Hinako, Kepulauan, Indonesia 0 50N 97 20E
98 Hinchinbrook I., Australia 18 20S 146 15E
13 Hinckley, Eng. 52 33N 1 21W
118 Hinckley, U.S.A. 39 18N 112 41W
49 Hindås, Sweden 57 42N 12 29E
68 Hindaun, India 26 44N 77 5E
90 Hinde Rapids (Hells Gate), Congo 5 25S 27 3E
100 Hindmarsh L., Austral. 35 50S 141 55E
69 Hindol, India 20 40N 85 10E
49 Hindsholm, Den. 55 30N 10 40E
68 Hindu Bagh, Pakistan 30 56N 67 57E
65 Hindu Kush, Asia 36 0N 71 0E
70 Hindupur, India 13 49N 77 32E
49 Hindås, Sweden 57 42N 12 27E
108 Hines Creek, Canada 56 20N 118 40W
77 Hingan, China 25 39N 110 43E
68 Hinganghat, India 20 30N 78 59E
118 Hingham, U.S.A. 48 40N 110 29W
77 Hingi, China 25 4N 105 2E
77 Hingkwo, China 26 15N 115 13E
77 Hingning, China 24 2N 115 55E
66 Hingol, R., Pakistan 25 30N 65 30E
70 Hingoli, India 19 41N 77 15E
4 Hinlopen Strait, Spitsbergen 79 30N 19 0E
4 Hinlopenstretet, Svalbard 79 35N 18 40E
85 Hinna, Nigeria 10 25N 11 28E
50 Hinnöy, Norway 68 40N 16 28E
74 Hi-no-misaki, Japan 35 28N 132 45E
31 Hinojosa del Duque, Spain 38 30N 5 17W
118 Hinsdale, U.S.A. 48 26N 107 2W
25 Hinterrhein, R., Switz. 46 40N 9 25W
108 Hinton, Canada 53 26N 117 28W
114 Hinton, U.S.A. 37 40N 80 51W
16 Hippolytushoef, Neth. 52 54N 4 58E
69 Hirakud, India 21 32N 83 51E
69 Hirakud Dam, India 21 32N 83 45E
74 Hiratsuka, Japan 35 40N 139 36E
83 Hirhafok, Algeria 23 49N 5 45E
46 Hirlău, Rumania 47 23N 27 0E
74 Hirosaki, Japan 40 34N 140 28E
74 Hiroshima, Japan 34 30N 132 30E
74 Hiroshima-ken ♦, Japan 34 50N 133 0E
49 Hirsoholmene, Den. 57 30N 10 36E
19 Hirson, France 49 55N 4 4E
46 Hîrşova, Rumania 44 40N 27 59E
49 Hirtshals, Denmark 57 36N 9 57E
47 Hisoy, Norway 58 26N 8 44E
68 Hissar, India 29 12N 75 45E
74 Hitachi, Japan 16 40N 140 35E
74 Hita, Japan 33 42N 130 52E
13 Hitchin, Eng. 51 57N 0 16W
74 Hitoyoshi, Japan 32 13N 130 45E
47 Hitra, Norway 63 30N 8 45E
24 Hitzacker, Germany 53 9N 11 1E
76 Hiungyao, China 40 10N 122 9E
109 Hjalmer L., Canada 61 35N 109 15W
48 Hjälmare Kanal, Swed. 59 20N 15 59E
48 Hjälmaren, Sweden 59 18N 15 40E
47 Hjartdal, Norway 59 37N 8 41E
49 Hjärtsäter, Sweden 58 35N 12 3E
47 Hjerkinn, Norway 62 13N 9 33E
49 Hjerpsted, Denmark 55 2N 8 39E
49 Hjo, Sweden 58 22N 4 17E
49 Hjörring, Denmark 57 29N 9 59E
49 Hjorted, Sweden 57 37N 16 19E
49 Hjortkvarn, Sweden 58 54N 15 26E
48 Hjälmare kanal, Sweden 59 24N 15 56E
48 Hjälmaren, Sweden 59 15N 15 45E
49 Hjörring, Denmark 57 28N 10 0E
26 Hlinsko, Czechoslovakia 49 45N 15 54E
27 Hlohovec, Cz. 48 26N 17 49E
85 Ho, Ghana 6 37N 0 27E
71 Hoa Binh, Vietnam 20 52N 105 12E
71 Hoa Da (Phan Ri), S. Vietnam 11 16N 108 40E
108 Hoadley, Canada 52 45N 114 30W
71 Hoai Nhon (Bon Son), S. Vietnam 14 28N 103 37E
105 Hoare B., Canada 65 30N 62 30W
99 Hobart, Tasmania 42 50S 147 21E
117 Hobart, U.S.A. 35 0N 99 5W
117 Hobbs, U.S.A. 32 40N 103 3W
49 Hobjaerg, Denmark 56 19N 9 32E
126 Hobo, Colombia 2 35N 75 30W
16 Hoboken, Belgium 51 11N 4 21E
113 Hoboken, U.S.A. 40 45N 74 4W
49 Hobro, Denmark 56 39N 9 46E
49 Hoburg C., Sweden 56 54N 18 8E
49 Hoburgen, Sweden 56 55N 18 7E
MAP
117 Hochatown, U.S.A. 34 11N 94 39W
77 Hochih, China 24 43N 107 43E
25 Höchst, Germany 50 6N 8 33E
77 Hochwan, China 30 0N 106 15E
25 Hockenheim, Germany 49 18N 8 33E
49 Hodde, Denmark 55 42N 8 39E
63 Hodeïda, Yemen 14 50N 43 0E
109 Hodgson, Canada 51 20N 97 40W
27 Hódmezövásárhely, Hungary 46 28N 20 22E
82 Hodna, Chott el, Algeria 35 30N 5 0E
27 Hodonin, Cz. 48 50N 17 0E
49 Hodsager, Denmark 56 19N 8 51E
18 Hoëdic, I., France 47 21N 2 52W
16 Hoek van Holland, Netherlands 52 0N 4 7E
93 Hoëveld, South Africa 26 30S 30 0E
25 Hof, Germany 50 18N 11 55E
50 Hof, Suður-Múlisýsla, Iceland 64 33N 14 40W
77 Hofei, China 31 52N 117 15E
77 Hofeng, China 29 55N 110 5E
24 Hofgeismar, Germany 51 29N 9 23E
48 Hofors, Sweden 60 35N 16 15E
50 Hofsjökull, Iceland 64 49N 18 48W
50 Hofsós, Iceland 65 53N 19 26W
74 Hofu, Japan 34 0N 130 30E
64 Hofuf, Saudi Arabia 25 20N 49 40E
47 Hög-Gia, Mt., Norway 62 23N 10 7E
49 Höganäs, Sweden 56 13N 12 34E
115 Hogansville, U.S.A. 33 14N 84 50W
118 Hogeland, U.S.A. 48 50N 108 29W
49 Högen, Sweden 61 47N 14 11E
70 Hogenaki Falls, India 12 6N 77 50E
48 Högfors, Örebro, Swed. 59 58N 15 3E
48 Högfors, Västmanlands, Sweden 60 2N 16 3E
83 Hoggar = Ahaggar, Algeria 23 0N 6 30E
49 Högsäter, Sweden 58 38N 12 5E
49 Högsby, Sweden 57 10N 16 1E
48 Högsjö, Sweden 59 4N 15 44E
26 Hohe Rhön, Ger. 50 24N 9 58E
26 Hohe Tauern, Austria 47 11N 12 40E
27 Hohenau, Austria 48 36N 16 55E
26 Hohenems, Austria 47 22N 9 42E
24 Hohenstein Ernstthal, Germany 50 48N 12 43E
115 Hohenwald, U.S.A. 35 35N 87 30W
24 Hohenwestedt, Ger. 54 6N 9 40E
85 Hohoe, Ghana 7 8N 0 32E
76 Hohpi, China 35 59N 114 13E
72 Hôi An, S. Vietnam 15 30N 108 19E
71 Hoi Xuan, N. Vietnam 20 25N 105 9E
90 Hoima, Uganda 1 25N 31 20E
77 Hoiping, China 22 30N 112 12E
116 Hoisington, U.S.A. 38 33N 98 50W
49 Höjer, Denmark 54 58N 8 42E
49 Hok, Sweden 57 31N 14 16E
76 Hokang, China 47 36N 130 28E
49 Hokensås, Sweden 58 0N 14 5E
49 Hökerum, Sweden 57 51N 13 16E
101 Hokianga Harbour, N.Z. 35 31S 173 22E
101 Hokitika, New Zealand 42 42S 171 0E
74 Hokkaidō, Japan 43 30N 143 0E
47 Hokksund, Norway 59 44N 9 59E
71 Hokow, China 22 39N 103 57E
87 Hol-Hol., Fr. Terr. of the Afars £ Issas 11 20N 42 50E
76 Holan Shan, China 38 40N 105 50E
49 Holbaek, Denmark 55 43N 11 43E
100 Holbrook, Australia 35 42S 147 18E
119 Holbrook, U.S.A. 35 0N 110 0W
49 Holbaek, Denmark 55 43N 11 43E
108 Holden, Canada 53 13N 112 11W
118 Holden Fillmore, U.S.A. 39 0N 112 26W
117 Holdenville, U.S.A. 35 5N 96 25W
12 Holderness, Eng. 53 45N 0 5W
109 Holdrege, U.S.A. 40 25N 99 30W
47 Hole, Norway 60 6N 10 12E
70 Hole-Narsipur, India 12 48N 76 16E
27 Holešov, Czechoslovakia 49 20N 17 35E
121 Holguin, Cuba 20 50N 76 20W
27 Holič, Czechoslovakia 48 49N 17 10E
87 Holla, Mt., Ethiopia 7 5N 36 35E
26 Hollabrunn, Austria 48 34N 16 5E
92 Hollams Bird I., South-West Africa 24 40S 14 30E
12 Holland, England 52 50N 0 10W
114 Holland, U.S.A. 42 47N 86 0W
112 Holland Landing, Can. 44 7N 79 30W
73 Hollandia = Djajapura, Indonesia 2 28S 140 38E
92 Hollands Bird I., South-West Africa 24 40S 14 30E
47 Höllen, Norway 58 6N 7 49E
112 Hollidaysburg, U.S.A. 40 26N 78 25W
117 Hollis, U.S.A. 34 45N 99 55W
119 Hollister, Calif., U.S.A. 37 55N 121 30W
118 Hollister, Idaho, U.S.A. 42 21N 114 36W
116 Holly, U.S.A. 38 7N 102 7W
115 Holly Hill, U.S.A. 29 15N 81 3W
117 Holly Springs, U.S.A. 34 45N 89 25W
110 Hollywood, Calif., U.S.A. 34 7N 118 25W
115 Hollywood, Fla., U.S.A. 26 0N 80 9W
48 Holm, Sweden 62 40N 16 40E
104 Holman Island, Canada 71 0N 118 0W
50 Hólmavik, Iceland 65 42N 21 40W
47 Holmedal, Fjordane, Norway 61 22N 5 11E
47 Holmedal, Hordaland, Norway 59 46N 5 50E
48 Holmegil, Norway 59 10N 11 44E
47 Holmestrand, Norway 59 31N 10 14E
47 Holmsbu, Norway 59 32N 10 27E
48 Holmsjön, Sweden 62 26N 15 20E
48 Holmsjön, Sweden 62 42N 16 30E
49 Holmsland Klit, Den. 56 0N 8 5E
50 Holmsund, Sweden 63 41N 20 20E
MAP
48 Hölö, Sweden 59 3N 17 36E
46 Holod, Rumania 46 49N 22 8E
62 Holon, Israel 32 2N 34 47E
98 Holroyd, R., Australia 14 0S 141 0E
47 Holsen, Norway 61 25N 6 8E
49 Holstebro, Denmark 56 22N 8 37E
50 Holt, Iceland 63 33N 19 48W
49 Holte, Denmark 55 50N 12 29E
107 Holton Harbour, Can. 54 31N 57 12W
119 Holtville, U.S.A. 32 50N 115 27W
47 Holum, Norway 58 6N 7 32E
16 Holwerd, Netherlands 53 22N 5 54E
12 Holy I., Eng. 55 42N 1 48W
12 Holy I., Wales 53 17N 4 37W
12 Holyhead, Wales 53 18N 4 38W
12 Holyhead B., Wales 53 20N 4 35W
113 Holyoke, Mass., U.S.A. 42 14N 72 37W
116 Holyoke, Nebr., U.S.A. 40 39N 102 18W
107 Holyrood, Canada 47 27N 53 8W
24 Holzminden, Germany 51 49N 9 31E
90 Homa Bay, Kenya 0 36S 34 22E
90 Homa Bay ♦, Kenya 0 50S 34 30E
67 Homalin, Burma 24 55N 95 0E
24 Homberg, Hessen, Ger. 51 2N 9 20E
85 Hombori, Mali 15 20N 1 38W
25 Homburg, Ger. 49 19N 7 21E
105 Home B., Canada 68 40N 67 0W
98 Home Hill, Australia 19 43S 147 25E
118 Homedale, U.S.A. 43 42N 116 59W
104 Homer, Alaska, U.S.A. 59 40N 151 35W
117 Homer, La., U.S.A. 32 50N 93 4W
98 Homestead, Australia 20 20S 145 40E
115 Homestead, Fla., U.S.A. 25 29N 80 27W
112 Homestead, Idaho, U.S.A. 45 3N 116 58W
117 Hominy, U.S.A. 36 26N 96 24W
70 Homnabad, India 17 45N 77 5E
93 Homoine, Mozambique 23 55S 35 8E
46 Homorod, Rumania 46 5N 25 15E
83 Homs (Al Khums), Libya 32 40N 14 17E
64 Homs (Hims), Syria 34 40N 36 45E
71 Hon Chong, S. Vietnam 10 16N 104 38E
25 Honan ♦, China 33 50N 113 15E
126 Honda, Colombia 5 12N 74 45W
117 Hondo, U.S.A. 29 22N 99 6W
121 Honduras ■, Central America 14 40N 86 30W
120 Honduras, Golfo de, Central America 16 50N 87 0W
47 Hönefoss, Norway 60 10N 10 12E
113 Honesdale, U.S.A. 41 34N 75 17W
118 Honey L., U.S.A. 40 13N 120 14W
18 Honfleur, France 49 25N 0 13E
49 Höng, Denmark 55 30N 11 14E
71 Hong, N. Vietnam 22 0N 104 0E
71 Hongha, R., N. Vietnam 22 0N 104 0E
77 Hong Kong ■, China 22 11N 114 14E
77 Honghai B., China 22 45N 115 15E
86 Honkoráb, Ras, Egypt 24 35N 35 10E
110 Honolulu, Hawaii 21 19N 157 52W
74 Honshu, Japan 36 0N 138 0E
32 Hontoria del Pinar, Sp. 41 50N 3 10W
118 Hood Mt., U.S.A. 45 15N 122 0W
96 Hood, Pt., Australia 34 19S 119 03E
118 Hood River, U.S.A. 45 45N 121 37W
118 Hoodsport, U.S.A. 47 30N 123 7W
24 Hooge, Germany 54 31N 8 36E
16 Hoogeveen, Neth. 52 44N 6 30E
16 Hoogezand, Neth. 53 11N 6 45E
69 Hooghly, R., India 21 59N 88 10E
15 Hook Hd., Ireland 52 8N 6 57W
98 Hook I., Australia 20 4S 149 0E
16 Hook of Holland = Hoek v. Holland, Neth. 52 0N 4 7E
117 Hooker, U.S.A. 36 55N 101 10W
114 Hoopeston, U.S.A. 40 30N 87 40W
92 Hoopstad, S. Africa 27 50S 25 55E
49 Höör, Sweden 55 55N 13 33E
16 Hoorn, Netherlands 52 38N 5 4E
113 Hoosick Falls, U.S.A. 42 54N 73 21W
119 Hoover Dam, U.S.A. 36 0N 114 45W
112 Hooversville, U.S.A. 40 8N 78 57W
113 Hop Bottom, U.S.A. 41 41N 75 47W
57 Hopā, Turkey 41 28N 41 30E
117 Hope, Ark., U.S.A. 33 40N 93 30W
116 Hope, N.D., U.S.A. 47 21N 97 42W
5 Hope Bay, Ant. 65 0S 55 0W
104 Hope Pt., Alaska 68 20N 166 50W
115 Hope Town, Bahama Is. 26 30N 76 30W
107 Hopedale, Canada 55 27N 60 22W
92 Hopefield, S. Africa 33 3S 18 22E
120 Hopelchén, Mexico 19 46N 89 50W
47 Hopen, Möre og Romsdal, Norway 63 27N 8 2E
100 Hopetoun, Vic., Australia 35 48S 142 25E
96 Hopetoun, W. Austral., Australia 33 54S 120 6E
92 Hopetown, S. Africa 29 34S 24 3E
77 Hoping, China 24 31N 115 2E
116 Hopkins, U.S.A. 40 31N 94 45W
100 Hopkins, R., Australia 37 55S 142 40E
115 Hopkinsville, U.S.A. 36 52N 87 26W
118 Hopland, U.S.A. 39 0N 123 0W
77 Hoppo, China 21 32N 109 6E
49 Hoptrup, Denmark 55 11N 9 28E
118 Hoquiam, U.S.A. 47 0N 123 55W
26 Horazdovice, Cz. 49 19N 13 42E
49 Hörby, Sweden 55 50N 13 44E
32 Horcajo de Santiago, Sp. 39 50N 3 1W
47 Hordaland fylke ♦, Nor. 60 25N 6 15E
96 Hordern Hills, Australia 20 40S 130 20E
63 Hordio, Somali Rep. 10 36N 51 8E
46 Horezu, Rumania 45 6N 24 0E
25 Horgen, Switzerland 47 15N 8 35E
42 Horgoš, Yugoslavia 46 10N 20 0E
26 Horice, Czechoslovakia 50 21N 15 39E
5 Horlick Mts., Ant. 84 0S 102 0W
65 Hormoz, Iran 27 35N 55 0E
MAP
65 Hormuz, I., Iran 27 8N 56 28E
65 Hormuz Str., Persian G. 26 30N 56 30E
26 Horn, Austria 48 39N 15 40E
50 Horn, Isafjarðarsýsla, Iceland 66 28N 22 28W
50 Horn, Suður-Múlasýsla, Iceland 65 10N 13 31W
128 Horn, Cape = Hornos, C. de, Chile 55 50S 67 30W
15 Horn Head, Ireland 55 13N 8 0W
115 Horn, I., U.S.A. 30 17N 88 40W
108 Horn Mts., Canada 62 0N 119 0W
64 Horna Fd., Iceland 64 18N 15 15W
31 Hornachuelos, Spain 37 50N 5 14W
50 Hornavan, Sweden 66 15N 17 30E
49 Hornbaek, Frederiksborg, Denmark 56 5N 12 26E
117 Hornbeck, U.S.A. 31 22N 93 20W
118 Hornbrook, U.S.A. 41 58N 122 37W
24 Hornburg, Germany 52 2N 10 36E
49 Hornbaek, Frederiksborg, Denmark 56 6N 12 27E
49 Hornbaek, Viborg, Denmark 56 28N 9 58E
12 Horncastle, Eng. 53 13N 0 8W
48 Horndal, Sweden 60 18N 16 23E
106 Horne Payne, Canada 49 14N 84 48W
112 Hornell, U.S.A. 42 23N 77 41W
47 Hornindal, Norway 61 58N 6 30E
47 Hornnes, Norway 58 34N 7 45E
128 Hornos, Cabo de, Chile 55 50S 67 30E
19 Hornoy, France 49 50N 1 54E
48 Hornsberg, Jamtland, Sweden 63 14N 14 40E
48 Hornsberg, Kronobergs, Sweden 56 37N 13 47E
100 Hornsby, Australia 33 42S 151 2E
12 Hornsea, England 53 55N 0 10W
48 Hornslandet Pen., Swed. 61 35N 17 37E
49 Hornslet, Denmark 56 18N 10 19E
24 Hörnum, Germany 54 44N 8 18E
74 Horoshiri Dake, Japan 42 40N 142 40E
26 Horovice, Cz. 49 48N 13 53E
124 Horqueta, Paraguay 23 15S 56 55W
49 Horred, Sweden 57 22N 12 28E
116 Horse Cr., U.S.A. 41 33N 104 45W
107 Horse Is., Canada 50 15N 55 50W
100 Horse Lake, Australia 32 4S 142 5E
49 Horsens, Denmark 55 52N 9 51E
49 Horsens Fjord, Denmark 55 50N 10 0E
119 Horseshoe Dam, U.S.A. 33 45N 111 35W
13 Horsham, Eng. 51 4N 0 20W
26 Horsovsky Tyn, Cz. 49 31N 12 58E
47 Horten, Norway 59 25N 10 32E
27 Hortobágy, R., Hung. 47 30N 21 6E
116 Horton, U.S.A. 39 42N 95 30W
49 Hörviken, Sweden 56 2N 14 44E
106 Horwood, L., Canada 48 01N 82 55W
87 Hosaina, Ethiopia 7 30N 37 47E
70 Hosdurga, India 13 40N 76 17E
72 Hose, Pegunungan, Malaysia 2 5N 114 6E
68 Hoshangabad, India 22 45N 77 45E
68 Hoshiarpur, India 31 30N 75 58E
116 Hosmer, U.S.A. 45 36N 99 29W
70 Hospet, India 15 15N 76 20E
32 Hospitalet de Llobregat, Spain 41 21N 2 6E
128 Hoste, I., Chile 55 0S 69 0W
20 Hostens, France 44 30N 0 40W
71 Hot, Thailand 18 8N 98 29E
118 Hot Creek Ra., U.S.A. 39 0N 116 0W
117 Hot Springs, Ark, USA. 34 30N 93 0W
116 Hot Springs, S.D., USA. 43 25N 103 30W
92 Hotazel, S. Africa 27 17S 23 00E
119 Hotchkiss, U.S.A. 38 55N 107 47W
75 Hotien (Khotan), China 37 6N 79 59E
50 Hoting, Sweden 64 8N 16 15E
44 Hotolishti, Albania 41 10N 20 25E
92 Hottentotsbaai, S. W. Africa 26 8S 14 59E
18 Houat, I., France 47 24N 2 58W
119 Houck, U.S.A. 35 15N 109 15W
19 Houdan, France 48 48N 1 35E
16 Houffalize, Belgium 50 8N 5 48E
116 Houghton, U.S.A. 47 9N 88 39W
116 Houghton L., U.S.A. 44 20N 84 40W
12 Houghton-le-Spring, England 54 51N 1 28W
101 Houhora, N.Z. 34 49S 173 9E
107 Houlton, U.S.A. 46 5N 68 0W
117 Houma, U.S.A. 29 35N 90 50W
83 Houmt Souk = Djerba, Tunisia 33 53N 10 37E
84 Houndé, Upper Volta 11 34N 3 31W
108 Houston, Canada 54 25N 126 30W
117 Houston, Mo., U.S.A. 37 20N 92 0W
117 Houston, Tex., U.S.A. 29 50N 95 20W
96 Houtman Abrolhos, Australia 28 43S 113 48E
49 Hova, Sweden 58 53N 14 14E
47 Hövag, Norway 58 10N 8 15E
75 Hovd (Jargalant), Mongolia 48 2N 91 37E
47 Hovden, Aust-Agder, Norway 59 33N 7 22E
13 Hove, England 50 50N 0 10W
49 Hovmantorp, Sweden 56 47N 15 7E
76 Hövsgöl Nuur, Mongolia 51 0N 100 30E
48 Hovsta, Sweden 59 22N 15 15E
87 Howakil, Ethiopia 15 10N 40 16E
87 Howar, W., (Shau) Sud. 17 0N 25 30E
99 Howard, Australia 25 16S 152 32E
117 Howard, Kans., U.S.A. 37 30N 96 16W
112 Howard, Penn., U.S.A. 41 0N 77 40W
116 Howard, S.D., U.S.A. 44 2N 97 30W
118 Howe, U.S.A. 43 48N 113 0W
100 Howe, C., Australia 37 30S 150 0E
114 Howell, U.S.A. 42 38N 84 0W
113 Howick, Canada 45 10N 73 53W

* Incorporated within the
  county of Cambridge

  * Renamed Kapchagai
  † Renamed Gökçeada
  ** Renamed Dalnerechensk

Inderborskly INDEX Jandaq

MAP
57 Inderborskly, U.S.S.R. 48 30N 51 42E
61 India ■, Asia 20 0N 80 0E
119 India, U.S.A. 33 46N 116 15W
108 Indian Cabin, Canada 59 50N 117 12W
109 Indian Head, Canada 50 30N 103 35W
107 Indian House L., Can. 56 30N 64 30W
3 Indian Ocean 5 0S 75 0E
112 Indiana, U.S.A. 40 38N 79 9W
114 Indiana ♦, U.S.A. 40 0N 86 0W
114 Indianapolis, U.S.A. 39 42N 86 10W
116 Indianola, Iowa, U.S.A. 41 20N 93 38W
117 Indianola, Miss., U.S.A. 33 27N 90 40W
52 Indiga, U.S.S.R. 67 50N 48 50E
59 Indigirka, R., U.S.S.R. 69 0N 147 0E
42 Indija, Yugoslavia 45 6N 20 7E
72 Indonesia ■, Asia 5 0S 115 0E
68 Indore, India 22 42N 75 53E
73 Indramaju, Indonesia 6 21S 108 20E
73 Indramaju, Tg., Indonesia 6 20S 108 20E
70 Indravati, R., India 19 0N 81 15E
18 Indre, R., France 47 2N 1 8E
19 Indre ♦, France 47 12N 1 39E
18 Indre-et-Loire ♦, France 47 12N 0 40E
47 Indre Söndeled, Norway 58 46N 9 5E
68 Indus, R., Pakistan 28 40N 70 10E
64 Inebolu, Turkey 41 55N 33 40E
42 Ineu, Rumania 46 26N 21 51E
92 Infante, Kaap, S. Afr. 34 27S 20 51E
33 Infantes, Spain 38 43N 3 1W
30 Infiesto, Spain 43 21N 5 21W
85 In-Gall, Mali 16 51N 7 1E
100 Ingebyra, Australia 36 39S 148 31E
88 Ingende, Zaïre 0 12S 18 57E
124 Ingenio Santa Ana, Arg. 27 25S 65 40W
112 Ingersoll, Canada 43 4N 80 55W
49 Ingesvang, Denmark 56 10N 9 20E
98 Ingham, Australia 18 43S 146 10E
12 Ingleborough, mt., England 54 11N 2 23W
100 Inglega, Australia 31 20S 147 50E
100 Inglewood, Australia 36 29S 143 53E
99 Inglewood, Australia 28 25S 151 8E
101 Inglewood, New Zealand 39 9S 174 14E
119 Inglewood, U.S.A. 33 58N 118 27W
50 Ingólfshöfði, Iceland 63 48N 16 39W
25 Ingolstadt, Germany 48 45N 11 26W
118 Ingomar, U.S.A. 46 43N 107 37E
107 Ingonish, Canada 46 42N 60 18E
84 Ingore, Port. Guinea 12 24N 15 48W
56 Ingul, R., U.S.S.R 47 30N 32 15E
56 Ingulec, U.S.S.R. 47 42N 33 4E
56 Ingulets, R., U.S.S.R. 47 20N 33 20E
57 Inguri, R., U.S.S.R. 42 58N 42 17E
93 Inhaca, I., Mozambique 26 1S 32 57E
93 Inhafenga, Mozambique 20 36S 33 47E
93 Inhambane ♦, Mozambique 22 30S 34 20E
91 Inhamitanga, Mozam. 18 26S 35 0E
93 Inharrime, Mozambique 24 30S 35 0E
93 Inharrime, R., Mozambique 24 30S 35 0E
91 Inhassoro, Mozambique 21 50S 35 15E
33 Iniesta, Spain 39 27N 1 45W
77 Ining, Kwangsi-Chuang, China 25 8N 109 57E
75 Ining (Kuldja), Sinkiang-Uigur, China 43 57N 81 20E
126 Inírida, R., Colombia 3 0N 68 40W
15 Inishbofin I., Ireland 53 35N 10 12W
15 Inishowen, Pen., Ire. 55 14N 7 15W
99 Injune, Australia 25 46S 148 32E
2 Inklin, Can. 58 50N 132 30W
108 Inklin, R., Can. 58 50N 132 20W
118 Inkom, U.S.A. 42 51N 112 7W
13 Inkpen Beacon, Eng. 51 22N 1 28W
67 Inle Aing, Burma 20 30N 96 58E
25 Inn, R., Austria 47 15N 10 55E
99 Innamincka, Australia 27 44S 140 46E
14 Inner Hebrides, Is., U.K. 58 0N 7 0W
14 Inner Sound, Skye, Scotland 57 30N 5 55W
76 Inner Mongolia ♦, China 44 50N 117 40E
112 Innerkip, Canada 43 12N 80 41W
106 Innetalling I., Canada 55 50N 79 5W
98 Innisfail, Australia 17 33S 146 5E
108 Innisfail, Canada 52 0N 114 0W
26 Innsbruck, Austria 47 16N 11 23E
126 Inosu, Colombia 12 22N 71 38W
28 Inowrocław, Poland 52 50N 18 20E
126 Inquisive, Bolivia 16 50S 66 45W
67 Insein, Burma 16 46N 96 18E
46 Insurăţei, Rumania 44 50N 27 40E
124 Intendente Alvear, Arg. 35 12S 63 32W
116 Interior, U.S.A. 43 46N 101 59W
25 Interlaken, Switzerland 46 41N 7 50E
116 International Falls, U.S.A. 48 30N 93 25W
71 Interview I., India 12 55N 92 42E
71 Inthanon, Mt., Thailand 18 35N 98 29E
124 Intiyaco, Argentina 28 50S 60 0W
128 Inútil, B., Chile 53 30S 70 15W
14 Inverbervie, Scot. 56 50N 2 17W
101 Invercargill, N.Z. 46 24S 168 24E
99 Inverell, Australia 29 48S 151 36E
14 Invergordon, Scot. 57 41N 4 10W
108 Invermere, Canada 50 51N 116 9W
107 Inverness, Canada 46 15N 61 19W
14 Inverness, Scotland 57 29N 4 12W
115 Inverness, U.S.A. 28 50N 82 20W
*14 Inverness ♦, Scotland 57 6N 4 40W
14 Inverurie, Scot. 57 15N 2 21W
96 Investigator Group, Australia 34 45S 134 20E
99 Investigator Str., Australia 35 30S 137 0E
112 Invona, U.S.A. 40 46N 78 35W
91 Inyanga, Rhodesia 18 12S 32 40E
91 Inyangani, mt., Rhod. 18 20S 32 20E

Incorporated with the region of Highland

MAP
91 Inyantue, Rhodesia 18 30S 26 40E
91 Inyazura, Rhodesia 18 40S 31 40E
119 Inyo Range, U.S.A. 37 0N 118 0W
119 Inyokern, U.S.A. 35 37N 117 54W
55 Inza, U.S.S.R. 53 55N 46 25E
55 Inzhavino, U.S.S.R. 52 22N 42 23E
44 Ioánnina (Janinà) ♦, Gr. 39 39N 20 57E
117 Iola, U.S.A. 38 0N 95 20W
46 Ion Corvin, Rumania 44 7N 27 50E
14 Iona I., Scot. 56 20N 6 25W
54 Ionava, U.S.S.R. 55 8N 24 12E
118 Ione, Calif., U.S.A. 38 20N 121 0W
118 Ione, Wash., U.S.A. 48 44N 117 29W
114 Ionia, U.S.A. 42 59N 85 7W
35 Ionian Sea, Europe 37 30N 17 30E
45 Iónioi Nísoi, Greece 38 40N 20 8E
54 Ioniškis, U.S.S.R. 56 13N 23 35E
57 Iori, R., U.S.S.R. 41 12N 46 10E
45 Ios, I., Greece 36 41N 25 20E
116 Iowa ♦, U.S.A. 42 18N 93 30W
116 Iowa City, U.S.A. 41 40N 91 35W
116 Iowa Falls, U.S.A. 42 30N 93 15W
90 Ipala, Tanzania 4 30S 33 5E
127 Ipameri, Brazil 17 44S 48 9W
45 Ipáti, Greece 38 52N 22 14E
57 Ipatovo, U.S.S.R. 45 45N 42 50E
27 Ipel, R., Europe 48 10N 19 35E
126 Ipiales, Colombia 0 50N 77 37W
75 Ipin, China 28 48N 104 33E
44 Ipiros ♦, Greece 39 30N 20 30E
126 Ipixuna, Brazil 7 00S 71 30W
71 Ipoh, Malaysia 4 26N 101 4E
81 Ippy, Cent. Afr. Rep. 6 5N 21 7E
44 Ipsala, Turkey 40 55N 26 23E
44 Ipsárion Oros, Gr. 40 40N 24 40E
99 Ipswich, Australia 27 38S 152 37E
13 Ipswich, Eng. 52 4N 1 9E
113 Ipswich, N.H., U.S.A. 42 40N 70 50W
116 Ipswich, S.D., U.S.A. 45 28N 99 20W
127 Ipu, Brazil 4 23S 40 44W
72 Ipuh, Indonesia 2 58S 101 8E
54 Iput, R., U.S.S.R. 53 0N 32 10E
126 Iquique, Chile 20 19S 70 5W
126 Iquitos, Peru 3 45S 73 10W
127 Iracoubo, French Guiana 5 30N 53 10W
45 Iráklia, I., Greece 36 50N 25 28E
45 Iráklion, Greece 35 20N 25 12E
45 Iráklion ♦, Greece 35 10N 25 10E
125 Irala, Paraguay 25 55S 54 35W
90 Iramba ♦, Tanzania 4 30S 34 30E
65 Iran ■, Asia 33 0N 53 0E
72 Iran, Pegunungan, Malaysia 2 20N 114 50E
70 Iranamadu Tank, Sri Lanka 9 23N 80 29E
65 Iranshahr, Iran 27 75N 60 40E
126 Irapa, Venezuela 10 34N 62 35W
120 Irapuato, Mexico 20 40N 101 40W
64 Iraq ■, Asia 33 0N 44 0E
82 Irarrar, W., Mali 20 10N 1 30E
125 Irati, Brazil 25 25S 50 38W
62 Irbid, Jordan 32 35N 35 48E
88 Irebu, Zaïre 0 40S 17 55E
32 Iregua, R., Spain 42 22N 2 24E
15 Ireland's Eye, Ireland 53 25N 6 4W
85 Irele, Nigeria 7 40N 5 40E
76 Irentala Steppe, China 43 45N 112 15E
59 Iret, U.S.S.R. 60 10N 154 5E
55 Irgiz, Bol., U.S.S.R. 52 10N 49 10E
83 Irharharene, Algeria 27 37N 7 30E
83 Irharrhar, O., Algeria 27 30N 6 0E
*73 Irian Barat ♦, Indonesia 4 0S 137 0E
88 Iriba, Chad 15 7N 22 15E
84 Irié, Guinea 8 15N 9 10W
90 Iringa, Tanzania 7 48S 35 43E
90 Iringa ♦, Tanz. 7 48S 35 43E
91 Iringa ♦, Tanz. 9 0S 35 0E
70 Irinjalakuda, India 10 21N 76 14E
77 Iriomote, Japan 24 25N 123 58E
15 Irish Republic ■, Europe 53 0N 8 0E
59 Irkutsk, U.S.S.R. 52 10N 104 20E
64 Irmak, Turkey 39 58N 33 25E
18 Iroise, France 48 15N 4 45W
99 Iron Baron, Australia 33 3S 137 11E
46 Iron Gate = Porţile de Fier, Rum. 44 42N 22 30E
99 Iron Knob, Australia 32 46S 137 8E
114 Iron Mountain, U.S.A. 45 49N 88 4W
114 Iron River, U.S.A. 46 6N 88 40W
13 Ironbridge, Eng. 52 38N 2 29W
112 Irondale, Canada 44 51N 78 30W
92 Ironhurst, Australia 18 0S 143 35E
92 Ironstone Kopje, Mt., Botswana 25 17S 24 5E
117 Ironton, Mo., U.S.A. 37 40N 90 40W
114 Ironton, Ohio, U.S.A. 38 35N 82 40W
114 Ironwood, U.S.A. 46 30N 90 10W
106 Iroquois Falls, Canada 48 40N 80 40W
54 Irpen, U.S.S.R. 50 30N 30 8E
67 Irrawaddy = Erawadi Myit, Burma 19 30N 95 15E
76 Irshih, China 47 8N 119 57E
41 Irsina, Italy 40 45N 16 15E
58 Irtysh, R., U.S.S.R. 53 36N 75 30E
90 Irumu, Zaïre 1 32N 29 53E
32 Irún, Spain 43 20N 1 52W
32 Irurzun, Spain 42 55N 1 50W
14 Irvine, Scotland 55 37N 4 40W
114 Irvine, U.S.A. 37 42N 83 58W
14 Irvine, R., Scotland 55 35N 4 40W
15 Irvinstown, N. Ire. 54 28N 7 38W
100 Irymple, Australia 34 14S 142 8E
85 Isa, Nigeria 13 14N 6 24E
98 Isaac. R., Australia 21 30S 148 30E
116 Isabel, U.S.A. 45 27N 101 22W
121 Isabela, Cord., Nic. 13 30N 85 25W
50 Isafjarðardjúp, Iceland 66 10N 23 0W
50 Isafjörður, Iceland 66 5N 23 9W
68 Isagarh, India 24 48N 77 51E

Renamed Irian Jaya

MAP
90 Isaka, Tanzania 3 56S 32 59E
88 Isangi, Zaïre 0 52N 24 10E
39 Isarco, R., Italy 46 30N 11 35E
45 Isari, Greece 37 22N 22 0E
19 Isbergues, France 50 36N 2 24E
46 Isbiceni, Rumania 43 45N 24 40E
40 Ischia, I., Italy 40 45N 13 51E
126 Iscuandé, Colombia 2 28N 77 59W
49 Isefjord, Denmark 55 53N 11 50E
38 Iseo, Italy 45 40N 10 3E
90 Iseramagazi, Tanz. 4 37S 32 10E
20 Isère, R., France 45 15N 5 30E
21 Isère ♦, France 45 15N 5 40E
24 Iserlohn, Germany 51 22N 7 40E
41 Isérnia, Italy 41 35N 14 12E
74 Ise-Wan, Japan 34 45N 136 45E
85 Iseyin, Nigeria 8 0N 3 36E
63 Isha Baidoa, Somali Rep. 3 8N 43 30E
76 Ishan, China 24 30N 108 41E
85 Ishara, Nigeria 6 40N 3 40E
77 Ishigaki, Japan 24 26N 124 10E
74 Ishikari-Wan, Japan 43 20N 141 20E
74 Ishikawa-ken ♦, Japan 36 30N 136 30E
58 Ishim, U.S.S.R. 56 10N 69 18E
58 Ishim, R., U.S.S.R. 57 45N 71 10E
74 Ishinomaki, Japan 38 32N 141 20E
65 Ishkashim, Afghanistan 36 30N 71 40E
66 Ishkuman, Kashmir 36 40N 73 50E
44 Ishmi, Albania 41 33N 19 34E
114 Ishpeming, U.S.A. 46 30N 87 40W
85 Ishua, Nigeria 7 15N 5 50E
56 Işik, Turkey 40 40N 32 35E
58 Isil Kul, U.S.S.R. 54 55N 71 16E
20 Isili, Italy 39 45N 9 6E
90 Isiolo, Kenya 0 24N 37 33E
93 Isipingo, S. Afr. 30 00S 30 57E
93 Isipingo Beach, S. Afr. 30 00S 30 57E
90 Isiro, Zaïre 2 53N 27 58E
98 Isisford, Australia 24 15S 144 21E
64 Iskenderun, Turkey 36 32N 36 10E
56 Iskilip, Turkey 40 50N 34 20E
43 Iskyr, R., Bulgaria 43 35N 24 20E
14 Isla, R., Scotland 56 44N 3 20W
31 Isla Cristina, Spain 37 13N 7 17W
66 Islamabad, Pakistan 33 40N 73 0E
68 Islamkot, Pakistan 24 42N 70 13E
70 Islampur, India 17 2N 72 9E
106 Island Falls, Canada 49 35N 81 20W
107 Island Falls, U.S.A. 46 0N 68 25W
109 Island L., Canada 53 40N 94 30W
113 Island Pond, U.S.A. 44 50N 71 50W
107 Islands, B. of, Canada 49 11N 58 15W
101 Islands, B. of, N.Z. 35 20S 174 20E
14 Islay, I., Scotland 55 46N 6 10W
14 Islay Sound, Scotland 55 45N 6 5W
107 Isle aux Morts, Canada 47 35N 59 0W
116 Isle Royale, U.S.A. 48 0N 88 50W
119 Isleta, U.S.A. 34 58N 106 46W
56 Ismail, U.S.S.R. 45 22N 28 46E
86 Ismâ'ilya, Egypt 30 37N 32 18E
116 Ismay, U.S.A. 46 33N 104 44W
86 Isna, Egypt 25 17N 32 30E
40 Isola del Liri, Italy 41 39N 13 32E
38 Isola della Scala, Italy 45 16N 11 0E
41 Isola di Capo Rizzuto, Italy 38 56N 17 5E
64 Isparta, Turkey 37 47N 30 30E
43 Isperikh, Bulgaria 43 43N 26 50E
41 Ispica, Sicily, Italy 36 47N 14 53E
57 Ispir, Turkey 40 40N 40 50E
62 Israel ■, Asia 32 0N 34 50E
84 Issia, Ivory Coast 6 33N 6 33W
20 Issoire, France 45 32N 3 15E
19 Issoudun, France 46 57N 2 0E
19 Is-sur-Tille, France 47 30N 5 10E
58 Issyk-Kul, U.S.S.R. 42 30N 77 30E
64 Istanbul, Turkey 41 0N 29 0E
126 Istiaia, Greece 38 57N 23 10E
126 Istmina, Colombia 5 10N 76 39W
42 Istok, Yugoslavia 42 45N 20 24E
115 Istokpoga, L., U.S.A. 27 22N 81 14W
55 Istra, U.S.S.R. 55 55N 36 50E
39 Istra, Yugoslavia 45 10N 14 0E
43 Istranca Dağlari, Turkey 41 48N 27 30E
21 Istres, France 43 31N 4 59E
127 Itabaiana, Paraíba, Brazil 7 18S 35 19W
127 Itaberaba, Brazil 12 32S 40 18W
127 Itabira, Brazil 19 37S 43 13W
127 Itabuna, Brazil 14 48S 39 16W
127 Itaete, Brazil 13 0S 41 5W
127 Itaituba, Brazil 4 10S 55 50W
127 Itajaí, Brazil 27 0S 48 45W
125 Itajubá, Brazil 22 24S 45 30W
91 Itaka, Tanzania 8 50S 32 49E
36 Italy ■, Europe 42 0N 13 0E
127 Itambe, mt., Brazil 18 30S 43 15W
93 Itampolo, Malag. 24 41S 43 57E
85 Itanhaém, Brazil 24 9S 46 47W
127 Itapecuru, R., Brazil 3 20S 44 15W
127 Itaperuna, Brazil 21 10S 42 0W
125 Itapetininga, Brazil 23 36S 48 7W
125 Itapeva, Brazil 23 59S 48 59W
127 Itapicuru, R., Bahia, Brazil 10 50S 38 40W
127 Itapicuru, R., Maranhão, Brazil 5 40S 44 30W
125 Itapuá ♦, Paraguay 26 40S 55 40W
125 Itaquari, Brazil 20 12S 40 25W
125 Itaquatiana, Brazil 2 58S 58 30W
124 Itaqui, Brazil 29 0S 56 30W
125 Itararé, Brazil 24 6S 49 23W
68 Itarsi, India 22 36N 77 51E
126 Itatuba, Brazil 5 40S 63 20W
77 Itbayat I., Philippines 20 45N 121 50E
13 Itchen, R., Eng. 50 57N 1 20W
45 Itéa, Greece 38 25N 22 25E
45 Ithaca = Itháki, Greece 38 25N 20 43E
113 Ithaca, U.S.A. 42 25N 76 30W
45 Itháki, Greece 38 25N 20 43E

MAP
45 Itháki, I., Greece 38 25N 20 40E
74 Ito, Japan 34 58N 139 5E
77 Itoman, Okinawa 26 7N 127 40E
126 Itonamas, R., Bolivia 13 0S 64 25W
86 Itsa, Egypt 29 15N 30 40E
40 Ittiri, Italy 40 38N 8 32E
125 Itu, Brazil 23 10S 47 15W
85 Itu, Nigeria 5 10N 7 58E
127 Ituaçu, Brazil 13 50S 41 18W
126 Ituango, Colombia 7 4N 75 45W
127 Ituiutaba, Brazil 19 0S 49 25W
127 Itumbiara, Brazil 18 20S 49 10W
91 Itunge Port, Tanz. 9 40S 33 55E
124 Iturbe, Argentina 23 0S 65 25W
90 Ituri, R., Zaïre 1 45N 26 45E
59 Iturup, Ostrov, U.S.S.R. 45 0N 148 0E
124 Ituyuro, R., Argentina 22 40S 63 50W
24 Itzehoe, Germany 53 56N 9 31E
50 Ivalo, Finland 68 38N 27 35E
50 Ivalojoki, Finland 68 30N 27 0E
44 Ivanaj, Albania 42 17N 19 25E
100 Ivanhoe, Australia 32 56S 144 20E
109 Ivanhoe L., Canada 60 25N 106 30W
39 Ivanió Grad, Yugoslavia 45 41N 16 25E
42 Ivanjica, Yugoslavia 43 35N 20 12E
39 Ivanjscie, Y.-slav. 46 12N 16 13E
55 Ivankovskoye Vdkhr., U.S.S.R. 56 48N 36 55E
54 Ivano-Frankovsk, (Stanislav), U.S.S.R. 49 0N 24 40E
55 Ivanovo, R.S.F.S.R., U.S.S.R. 57 5N 41 0E
54 Ivanovo, White Russia, U.S.S.R. 52 7N 25 29E
93 Ivato, Malagasy Rep. 20 37S 47 10E
43 Ivaylovgrad, Bulgaria 41 32N 26 8E
125 Ivinheima, R., Brazil 21 48S 54 15W
33 Iviza = Ibiza, Spain 39 0N 1 30E
93 Ivohibe, Malagasy Rep. 22 31S 46 57E
84 Ivory Coast ■, Afr. 7 30N 5 0W
49 Ivösjön, Sweden 56 8N 14 25E
38 Ivrea, Italy 45 30N 7 52E
105 Ivugivik, (N.D. d'Ivugivic), Canada 62 18N 77 50W
72 Iwahig, Philippines 8 35N 117 32E
74 Iwakuni, Japan 34 15N 132 8E
74 Iwata, Japan 34 49N 137 59E
74 Iwate-ken ♦, Japan 39 30N 141 30E
85 Iwo, Nigeria 7 39N 4 9E
27 Iwonicz-Zdroj, Poland 49 37N 21 47E
126 Ixiamas, Bolivia 13 50S 68 5W
93 Ixopo, South Africa 30 11S 30 5E
120 Ixtepec, Mexico 16 40N 95 10W
120 Ixtlán de Juárez, Mexico 17 23N 96 28W
120 Ixtlán del Rio, Mexico 21 5N 104 28W
77 Iyang, China 28 40N 112 20E
120 Izabal, L., Guatemala 15 30N 89 10W
120 Izamal, Mexico 20 56N 89 1W
28 Izbica Kujawski, Poland 52 25N 18 30E
57 Izberbash, U.S.S.R. 42 35N 47 45E
16 Izegem, Belgium 50 55N 3 12E
43 Izgrev, Bulgaria 43 36N 26 58E
52 Izhevsk, U.S.S.R. 56 50N 53 0E
56 Izmail, U.S.S.R. 45 22N 28 46E
56 Izmir (Smyrna), Turkey 38 25N 27 8E
64 Izmit, Turkey 40 45N 29 50E
31 Iznajar, Spain 37 15N 4 19W
33 Iznalloz, Spain 37 24N 3 30W
39 Izola, Yugoslavia 45 32N 13 39E
74 Izumisano, Japan 34 40N 135 43E
74 Izumo, Japan 35 20N 132 55E
54 Izyaslav, U.S.S.R. 50 5N 25 50E
56 Izyum, U.S.S.R. 49 12N 37 28E
87 Jaba, Ethiopia 6 20N 35 7E
62 Jaba', Jordan 32 20N 35 13E
62 Jabaliya, Egypt 31 32N 34 27E
33 Jabalón, R., Spain 38 45N 3 35W
69 Jabalpur, India 23 9N 79 58E
64 Jablah, Syria 35 20N 36 0E
39 Jablanac, Yugoslavia 44 42N 14 56E
26 Jablonec, Cz. 50 43N 15 10E
27 Jablonica, Cz. 48 37N 17 26E
28 Jablonowo, Poland 53 23N 19 10E
125 Jaboticabal, Brazil 21 15S 48 17W
42 Jabukovac, Yugoslavia 44 22N 22 21E
126 Jaburu, Brazil 4 0S 66 25W
32 Jaca, Spain 42 35N 0 33W
125 Jacarei, Brazil 23 20S 46 0W
125 Jacarèzinho, Brazil 23 5S 50 0W
124 Jáchal, Argentina 30 5S 69 0W
26 Jáchymov, Cz. 50 22N 12 55E
107 Jack Lane B., Canada 55 45N 60 35W
106 Jackfish, Canada 48 45N 87 0W
107 Jackman, U.S.A. 45 35N 70 17W
117 Jacksboro, U.S.A. 33 14N 98 15W
99 Jackson, Australia 26 40S 149 30E
115 Jackson, Ala., U.S.A. 31 32N 87 53W
117 Jackson, Calif., U.S.A. 37 25N 89 42W
118 Jackson, Ill., U.S.A. 38 25N 120 47W
114 Jackson, Ky., U.S.A. 37 35N 83 22W
114 Jackson, Mich., U.S.A. 42 18N 84 25W
116 Jackson, Minn., U.S.A. 43 35N 95 30W
117 Jackson, Miss., U.S.A. 32 20N 90 10W
114 Jackson, Ohio, U.S.A. 39 0N 82 40W
115 Jackson, Tenn., U.S.A. 35 40N 88 50W
118 Jackson, Wyo., U.S.A. 43 30N 110 49W
108 Jackson Bay, Can. 50 32N 125 57W
101 Jackson Bay, N.Z. 43 58S 168 42E
118 Jackson, L., U.S.A. 43 55N 110 40W
101 Jacksons, New Zealand 42 46N 171 32E
115 Jacksonville, Ala., U.S.A. 33 49N 85 45W
115 Jacksonville, Fla., U.S.A. 30 15N 81 38W
116 Jacksonville, Ill., U.S.A. 39 42N 90 15W
115 Jacksonville, N.C., U.S.A. 34 50N 77 29W
118 Jacksonville, Oreg., U.S.A. 42 13N 122 56W
117 Jacksonville, Tex., U.S.A. 31 58N 95 12W

MAP
115 Jacksonville Beach, U.S.A. 30 19N 81 26W
121 Jacmel, Haiti 18 20N 72 40W
119 Jacob Lake, U.S.A. 36 45N 112 12W
68 Jacobabad, Pakistan 28 20N 68 29E
46 Jacobeni, Rumania 47 25N 25 20E
127 Jacobina, Brazil 11 11S 40 30W
62 Jacob's Well, Jordan 32 13N 35 13E
107 Jacques Cartier, Mt., Canada 48 57N 66 0W
107 Jacques Cartier Pass, Canada 49 50N 62 30W
84 Jacqueville, Ivory Coast 5 12N 4 25W
127 Jacuipe, R., Brazil 12 30S 39 5W
24 Jade, Germany 53 22N 8 14E
24 Jadebusen, B., Ger. 53 30N 8 15E
91 Jadotville = Likasi, Zaïre 10 55S 26 48E
42 Jadovnik, Y.-slav. 43 20N 19 45E
32 Jadraque, Spain 40 55N 2 55W
83 Jādū, Libya 32 0N 12 0E
126 Jaén, Peru 5 25S 78 40W
31 Jaén, Spain 37 44N 3 43W
31 Jaén ♦, Spain 37 50N 3 30W
82 Jafène, Sahara 20 35N 5 30W
62 Jaffa = Tel Aviv-Yafo, Israel 32 4N 34 48E
99 Jaffa C., Australia 36 49S 139 38E
70 Jaffna, Sri Lanka 9 45N 80 2E
68 Jagadhri, India 30 10N 77 20E
69 Jagadishpur, India 25 30N 84 21E
70 Jagdalpur, India 19 3N 82 6E
92 Jagersfontein, S. Afr. 29 44S 25 27E
81 Jaghbub, Libya 29 42N 24 38E
25 Jagst, R., Germany 49 13N 10 0E
70 Jagtial, India 18 50N 79 0E
125 Jaguariaíva, Brazil 24 10S 49 50W
127 Jaguaribe, R., Brazil 6 0S 38 35W
121 Jaguey, Cuba 22 35N 81 7W
100 Jagungal, Mount, Australia 36 12S 148 28W
70 Jagtial, India 18 50N 79 0E
68 Jahangirabad, India 28 19N 78 4E
64 Jahrom, Iran 28 30N 53 31E
69 Jainti, India 26 45N 89 40E
68 Jaipur, India 26 54N 72 52E
65 Jajarm, Iran 37 5N 56 20E
42 Jajce, Yugoslavia 44 19N 17 17E
85 Jajere, Nigeria 11 58N 10 25E
69 Jajpur, India 20 53N 86 22E
50 Jakobstad (Pietarsaari), Finland 63 40N 22 43E
42 Jakupica, Y.-slav. 41 45N 21 22E
117 Jal, U.S.A. 32 8N 103 8W
65 Jala, Iran 27 30N 62 40E
65 Jalalabad, Afghanistan 34 30N 70 29E
69 Jalalabad, India 26 41N 79 42E
68 Jalalpur Jattan, Pakistan 32 38N 74 19E
120 Jalapa, Guatemala 14 45N 89 59W
120 Jalapa, Mexico 19 30N 96 50W
64 Jalas, Jabal al, Saudi Arabia 27 30N 36 30E
69 Jalaun, India 26 8N 79 25E
69 Jaleswar, Nepal 26 38N 85 48E
68 Jalgaon, Mad. P., India 21 2N 76 31E
68 Jalgaon, Maharashtra, India 21 0N 75 42E
85 Jalingo, Nigeria 8 55N 11 25E
120 Jalisco ♦, Mexico 20 0N 104 0W
30 Jallas, R., Spain 42 57N 9 0W
100 Jallumba, Austral. 36 55N 141 57E
70 Jalna, India 19 48N 75 57E
32 Jalón, R., Spain 41 20N 1 40W
120 Jalpa, Mexico 21 38N 102 58W
69 Jalpaiguri, India 26 32N 88 46E
65 Jalq, Iran 27 35N 62 33E
94 Jaluit I., Pacific Ocean 6 0N 169 30E
85 Jamaari, Nigeria 11 44N 9 53E
121 Jamaica, I. ■, W. Indies 18 10N 77 30W
69 Jamalpur, Bangladesh 24 52N 90 2E
69 Jamalpur, India 25 18N 86 28E
69 Jamalpurganj, India 23 2N 88 1E
127 Jamanxim, R., Brazil 6 30S 55 50W
73 Jambe, Indonesia 1 15S 132 10E
68 Jambusar, India 22 3N 72 51E
73 Jamdena, I., Indonesia 7 45S 131 20E
106 James B., Canada 53 30N 80 30W
116 James, R., U.S.A. 44 50N 98 0W
96 James Ras., Australia 24 10N 132 0E
5 James Ross I., Br. Antarctic Terr. 66 58S 50 49W
92 Jamestown, S. Africa 31 6S 26 45E
99 Jamestown, Australia 33 10S 138 32E
114 Jamestown, Ky., U.S.A. 37 0N 85 5W
116 Jamestown, N.D., USA 47 0N 98 30W
116 Jamestown, N.Y., USA 42 5N 79 18W
112 Jamestown, Penn., U.S.A. 41 22N 80 27W
115 Jamestown, Tenn., U.S.A. 36 25N 85 0W
70 Jamkhandi, India 16 30N 75 15E
62 Jamma'in, Jordan 32 8N 35 12E
70 Jammalamadugu, India 14 51N 78 25E
49 Jammerbugt, Den. 57 15N 9 20E
68 Jammu, Jammu & Kashmir 32 46N 75 57E
66 Jammu & Kashmir ♦, India 34 25N 77 0W
68 Jamnagar, India 22 30N 70 0E
68 Jamner, India 20 45N 75 45E
68 Jampur, Pakistan 29 39N 70 32E
66 Jamrud, Pakistan 34 2N 71 24E
69 Jamshedpur, India 22 44N 86 20E
69 Jamtara, India 23 59N 86 41E
48 Jämtlands län ♦, Swed. 62 40N 13 50E
92 Jan Kemp, S. Africa 27 55S 24 51E
4 Jan Mayen Is., Arctic Ocean 71 0N 11 0W
66 Jand, Pakistan 33 30N 72 0E
64 Jandaq, Iran 34 3N 54 22E

* Renamed Mambilima Falls

Kala INDEX Kastlösa

MAP
85 Kala, Cameroon 12 2N 14 40E
70 Kala Oya., Sri Lanka 8 15N 80 0E
83 Kalaa-Kebira, Tunisia 35 59N 10 32E
68 Kalabagh, Pakistan 33 0N 71 28E
44 Kalabáka, Greece 39 42N 21 39E
89 Kalabo, Zambia 14 58S 22 33E
55 Kalach, U.S.S.R. 50 22N 41 0E
67 Kaladan, R., Burma 21 30N 92 45E
112 Kaladar, Canada 44 37N 77 5W
92 Kalahari, Des., Africa 24 0S 22 0E
92 Kalahari Gemsbok Nat. Pk., S. Afr. 26 0S 20 30E
70 Kalahasti, India 13 45N 79 44E
44 Kalaja e Turrës, Albania 41 10N 19 28E
93 Kalakamati, Bots. 20 40S 27 25E
59 Kalakan, U.S.S.R. 55 15N 116 45E
90 Kalama, Zaïre 2 52S 28 35E
118 Kalama, U.S.A. 46 0N 122 55W
44 Kalamariá, Greece 40 33N 22 55E
45 Kalamata, Greece 37 3N 22 10E
114 Kalamazoo, U.S.A. 42 20N 85 35W
114 Kalamazoo, R., U.S.A. 42 40N 86 0W
70 Kalamb, India 18 3N 74 48E
91 Kalambo Falls, Tanz. 8 37S 31 35E
45 Kálamos, Greece 38 37N 20 59E
45 Kálamos, I., Greece 38 37N 20 55E
45 Kalamoti, Greece 38 15N 26 4E
73 Kalao, I., Indonesia 7 21S 121 0E
73 Kalaotoa, I., Indonesia 7 20S 121 50E
48 Kälarne, Sweden 62 59N 16 8E
27 Kalárovo, Cz. 47 54N 18 0E
71 Kalasin, Thailand 16 26N 103 30E
66 Kalat, Pakistan 29 8N 66 31E
65 Kalat-i-Ghilzai, Afghan 32 15N 66 58E
45 Kálathos (Calato), Greece 36 9N 28 8E
57 Kalaus, R., U.S.S.R. 45 40N 43 30E
45 Kalávrita, Greece 38 3N 22 8E
84 Kalba, Ghana 9 30N 2 42W
47 Kaldhovd, Norway 60 5N 8 20E
56 Kalecik, Turkey 40 4N 33 26E
67 Kalegauk Kyun, Burma 15 33N 97 35E
90 Kalehe, Zaïre 2 6S 28 50E
90 Kalema, Tanzania 1 12S 31 55E
28 Kalety, Poland 50 35N 18 52E
67 Kalewa, Burma 23 15N 94 20E
50 Kálfafellsstaður, Iceland 64 11N 15 53W
96 Kalgoorlie, Australia 30 40S 121 22E
43 Kaliakra, Nos, Bulgaria 43 21N 28 30E
72 Kalianda, Indonesia 5 50S 105 45E
73 Kalioo, Philippines 11 43N 122 22E
90 Kalima, Zaïre 2 33S 26 32E
72 Kalimantan Barat ♦, Indonesia 0 0 110 30E
72 Kalimantan Selatan ♦, Indonesia 2 30S 115 30E
72 Kalimantan Tengah ♦, Indonesia 2 0S 113 30E
72 Kalimantan Timor ♦, Indonesia 1 30N 116 30E
45 Kálimnos, I., Greece 37 0N 27 0E
69 Kalimpong, India 27 4N 88 35E
70 Kalinadi, R., India 14 50N 74 20E
55 Kalinin, U.S.S.R. 56 55N 35 55E
54 Kaliningrad, U.S.S.R. 54 42N 20 32E
57 Kalinino, U.S.S.R. 45 12N 38 59E
54 Kalinkovichi, U.S.S.R. 52 12N 29 20E
42 Kalinovik, Yugoslavia 43 31N 18 29E
43 Kalipetrovo (Starčevo), Bulg. 44 5N 27 14E
90 Kaliro, Uganda 0 56N 33 30E
44 Kalirrákhi, Greece 40 40N 24 35E
118 Kalispell, U.S.A. 48 10N 114 22W
28 Kalisz, Poland 51 45N 18 8E
28 Kalisz Pom, Poland 53 17N 15 55E
90 Kaliua, Tanzania 5 5S 31 48E
70 Kaliveli Tank, India 12 5N 79 50E
50 Kalix R., Sweden 67 0N 22 0E
68 Kalka, India 30 56N 76 57E
114 Kalkaska, U.S.A. 0 44N 85 9W
92 Kalkfeld, S.W. Afr. 20 57S 16 14E
92 Kalkfontein, Botswana 22 4S 20 57E
92 Kalkfontein Dam, South Africa 29 30S 24 15E
92 Kalkrand, S.W. Africa 24 1S 17 35E
48 Kall L., Sweden 63 35N 13 10E
70 Kallakurichi, India 11 44N 79 1E
49 Källandsö, Sweden 58 40N 13 5E
49 Källby, Sweden 58 30N 13 8E
60 Kallia, Jordan 31 46N 35 30E
70 Kallidaikurichi, India 8 38N 77 31E
49 Kallinge, Sweden 56 15N 15 18E
45 Kallithéa, Greece 37 5N 23 41E
44 Kallmeti, Albania 41 51N 19 41E
45 Kallonís Kólpos, Greece 39 10N 26 10E
49 Kalltorp, Sweden 58 23N 13 20E
85 Kalmalo, Nigeria 13 40N 5 20E
49 Kalmar, Kalmar, Sweden 56 40N 16 20E
49 Kalmar län ♦, Swed. 57 25N 16 15E
49 Kalmar sund, Sweden 56 40N 16 25E
57 Kalmyk A.S.S.R. ♦, U.S.S.R. 46 5N 46 1E
57 Kalmykovo, U.S.S.R. 49 0N 51 35E
69 Kalna, India 23 13N 88 25E
98 Kalo, Terr. of Papua 10 0S 147 42E
27 Kalocsa, Hungary 46 32N 19 0E
43 Kalofer, Bulgaria 42 37N 24 59E
68 Kalol, Gujarat, India 23 15N 72 33E
68 Kalol, Gujarat, India 22 37N 73 31E
91 Kalola, Zaïre 10 0S 28 0E
45 Kalolimnos, Greece 37 4N 27 8E
91 Kalomo, Zambia 17 0S 26 30E
45 Kaloneròn, Greece 37 20N 21 38E
69 Kalpi, India 26 8N 79 47E
70 Kalrayan Hills, India 11 45N 78 40E
70 Kalsubai, Mt., India 17 35N 73 45E
85 Kaltungo, Nigeria 9 48N 11 19E
68 Kalu, Pakistan 25 5N 67 39E
55 Kaluga, U.S.S.R. 54 35N 36 10E
91 Kalulushi, Zambia 12 50S 28 3E

MAP
49 Kalundborg, Denmark 55 41N 11 5E
54 Kalush, U.S.S.R. 42 9N 24 12E
28 Kałuszyn, Poland 52 13N 21 52E
70 Kalutara, Sri Lanka 6 35N 80 0E
27 Kalwaria, Poland 49 53N 19 41E
68 Kalyan, India 20 30N 74 3E
70 Kalyani, India 17 53N 76 59E
55 Kalyazin, U.S.S.R. 57 15N 37 45E
71 Kam Keut, Laos 18 20N 104 48E
90 Kama, Zaïre 3 30S 27 5E
52 Kama, R., U.S.S.R. 60 0N 53 0E
90 Kamachumu, Tanz. 1 37S 31 37E
74 Kamaishi, Japan 39 20N 142 0E
68 Kamalia, Pakistan 30 44N 72 42E
90 Kamango, Zaïre 0 40N 29 52E
91 Kamapanda, Zambia 12 5S 24 0E
63 Kamaran, Red Sea 15 28N 42 35E
91 Kamativi, Rhodesia 18 15S 0 27E
85 Kamba, Nigeria 11 50N 3 45E
70 Kambam, India 9 45N 77 16E
68 Kambar, Pakistan 27 37N 68 1E
84 Kambia, Sierra Leone 9 3N 12 53W
91 Kambolé, Zambia 8 47S 30 48E
91 Kambove, Zaïre 10 51S 26 33E
59 Kamchatka, P-ov., U.S.S.R. 57 0N 160 0E
98 Kamde, Indonesia 8 0S 140 58E
58 Kamen, U.S.S.R. 53 50N 81 30E
54 Kamen Kashirskiy, U.S.S.R. 51 39N 24 56E
42 Kamenica, Yugoslavia 44 25N 19 40E
26 Kàmenice, Cz. 49 18N 15 2E
39 Kamenjak, Rt., Yugoslavia 44 47N 13 55E
52 Kamenka, R.S.F.S.R., U.S.S.R. 65 58N 44 0E
55 Kamenka, R.S.F.S.R., U.S.S.R. 50 47N 39 20E
54 Kamenka Bugskaya, U.S.S.R. 50 8N 24 16E
56 Kamenka Dneprovskaya, U.S.S.R. 47 29N 34 14E
58 Kamensk, U.S.S.R. 56 25N 62 45E
57 Kamensk Shakhtinskiy, U.S.S.R. 48 23N 40 20E
55 Kamenskiy, U.S.S.R. 50 48N 45 25E
59 Kamenskoye, U.S.S.R. 62 45N 165 30E
43 Kamenyak, Bulgaria 43 24N 26 57E
24 Kamenz, Germany 51 17N 14 7E
44 Kami, Albania 42 17N 20 18E
118 Kamiah, U.S.A. 46 12N 116 2W
28 Kamien Krajenskie, Poland 53 32N 17 32E
28 Kamien Pomorski, Poland 53 57N 14 43E
28 Kamiensk, Poland 51 12N 19 29E
45 Kamilonision, Greece 35 50N 26 15E
109 Kamilukuak, L., Can. 62 40N 100 0W
91 Kamina, Zaïre 8 45S 25 0E
109 Kaminak L., Canada 62 0N 95 0W
90 Kamituga Mungombe, Zaïre 3 2S 28 10E
108 Kamloops, Canada 50 40N 120 20W
68 Kamoke, Pakistan 32 4N 74 4E
88 Kamono, Congo (Fr.) 3 10S 13 20E
26 Kamp, R., Austria 48 35N 15 26E
72 Kampa, Indonesia 1 42S 105 24E
90 Kampala, Uganda 0 20N 32 30E
71 Kampar, W. Malaysia 4 18N 101 9E
72 Kampar, S., Indonesia 0 30N 102 0E
16 Kampen, Netherlands 52 33N 5 53E
91 Kampolombo, L., Zam. 11 30S 29 35E
71 Kampong Sedili Besar, Malaysia 1 57N 104 8E
71 Kampot, Khmer Rep. 10 36N 104 10E
68 Kamptee, India 21 9N 79 19E
84 Kampti, Upper Volta 10 7N 3 25W
73 Kamrau, Teluk, Indonesia 3 30S 133 45E
109 Kamsack, Canada 51 35N 101 50W
55 Kamskove Ustye, U.S.S.R. 55 10N 49 20E
52 Kamskoye Vdkhr., U.S.S.R. 58 0N 56 0E
55 Kamyshin, U.S.S.R. 50 10N 45 30E
57 Kamyzyak, U.S.S.R. 46 4N 48 10E
106 Kanaaupscow, Canada 54 0N 76 40W
119 Kanab, U.S.A. 37 3N 112 29W
119 Kanab Creek, U.S.A. 37 0N 112 40W
74 Kanagawa-ken ♦, Japan 35 20N 139 20E
70 Kanakapura, India 12 33N 77 28E
44 Kanália, Greece 39 30N 22 53E
88 Kananga, Zaïre 5 55S 22 18E
119 Kanarraville, U.S.A. 37 34N 113 12W
55 Kanash, U.S.S.R. 55 48N 47 32E
114 Kanawha, R., U.S.A. 39 40N 82 0W
86 Kanayis, Ras el, Egypt 31 30N 28 5E
74 Kanazawa, Japan 36 30N 136 38E
71 Kanchanaburi, Thailand 14 8N 99 31E
69 Kanchenjunga, Mt., Nep. 27 50N 88 10E
70 Kanchipuram (Conjeeveram), India 12 52N 79 45E
77 Kanchow, China 25 58N 114 55E
76 Kanchwan, China 36 29N 109 24E
28 Kanózuga, Poland 49 58N 22 25E
88 Kanda Kanda, Zaïre 6 52S 23 48E
*53 Kandagach, U.S.S.R. 49 20N 57 15E
65 Kandahar, Afghanistan 31 32N 65 30E
52 Kandalaksha, U.S.S.R. 67 9N 32 30E
52 Kandalakshkiyzaliv, U.S.S.R. 66 0N 35 0E
72 Kandangan, Indonesia 2 50S 115 20E
73 Kandanghaur, Indonesia 6 21S 108 6E
45 Kandanos, Greece 35 19N 23 44E
85 Kandé, Togo 9 57N 1 53E
91 Kandewu, Zambia 14 1S 26 16E
45 Kandhila, Greece 37 46N 22 22E
68 Kandhkot, Pakistan 28 16N 69 8E
68 Kandhla, India 29 18N 77 19E
85 Kandi, Dahomey 11 7N 2 55E

* Renamed Oktabrsk

MAP
69 Kandi, India 23 58N 88 5E
91 Kandinduna, Zam. 13 58S 24 19E
64 Kandira, Turkey 41 5N 30 10E
68 Kandla, India 23 0N 70 10E
100 Kandos, Australia 32 45S 149 58E
66 Kandrach, Pakistan 25 30N 65 30E
69 Kandukur, India 15 12N 79 57E
70 Kandy, Sri Lanka 7 18N 80 43E
112 Kane, U.S.A. 41 39N 78 53W
4 Kane Bassin, Greenland 79 30N 68 0W
84 Kanel, Senegal 13 18N 14 35W
77 Kanen, China 18 46N 108 33E
57 Kanevskaya, U.S.S.R. 46 3N 39 3E
39 Kanfanar, Yugoslavia 45 7N 13 50E
65 Kang, Afghanistan 30 55N 61 55E
84 Kangaba, Mali 11 56N 8 25W
71 Kangar, Malaysia 6 27N 100 12E
99 Kangaroo I., Austral. 35 45S 137 0E
98 Kangaroo Mts., Austral. 23 25S 142 0E
100 Kangaroo Flat, Austral. 36 45S 144 20E
64 Kangavar, Iran 34 40N 48 0E
72 Kangean, Kepulauan, Indonesia 6 55S 115 23E
4 Kangerdlugsuaé, Greenland 68 10N 32 20W
76 Kangnŭng, S. Korea 37 45N 128 59E
88 Kango, Gabon 0 11N 10 5E
77 Kangshan, Taiwan 22 43N 120 14E
69 Kangtissu Shan, Tibet 31 0N 82 0E
67 Kangto, Mt., India 27 50N 92 35E
70 Kanhangad, India 12 21N 74 58E
70 Kanheri, India 19 13N 72 50E
67 Kani, China 29 25N 95 25E
84 Kani, Ivory Coast 8 29N 6 36W
90 Kaniama, Zaïre 7 30S 24 12E
107 Kaniapiskau L., Can. 53 52N 69 20W
107 Kaniapiskau, R., Can. 55 15N 68 40E
52 Kanin, P-ov., U.S.S.R. 68 0N 45 0E
52 Kanin Nos, Mys, U.S.S.R. 68 45N 43 20E
44 Kanina, Albania 40 23N 19 30E
100 Kaniva, Australia 36 22S 141 18E
42 Kanjiza, Yugoslavia 46 3N 20 4E
114 Kankakee, U.S.A. 41 6N 87 50W
114 Kankakee, R., U.S.A. 41 13N 87 0W
84 Kankan, Guinea 10 30N 9 15W
59 Kankunskiy, U.S.S.R. 57 37N 126 8E
115 Kannapolis, U.S.A. 35 32N 80 37W
69 Kannauj, India 27 3N 79 26E
85 Kano, Nigeria 12 2N 8 30E
84 Kanoroba, Ivory Coast 9 7N 6 8W
72 Kanowit, Malaysia 2 14N 112 20E
96 Kanowna, Australia 30 32S 121 31E
74 Kanoya, Japan 31 25N 130 50E
74 Kantō-sammyaku, mts., Japan 36 0N 138 30E
67 Kanpetlet, Burma 21 10N 93 59E
69 Kanpur, India 26 35N 80 20E
116 Kansas, R., U.S.A. 39 15N 96 20W
116 Kansas ♦, U.S.A. 38 40N 98 0W
116 Kansas City, Kans., U.S.A. 39 0N 94 40W
116 Kansas City, Mo., U.S.A. 39 3N 94 30W
91 Kansenia, Zaïre 10 20S 26 0E
59 Kansk, U.S.S.R. 56 20N 95 37E
76 Kansu ♦, China 35 30N 104 30E
85 Kantché, Niger 13 31N 8 30E
57 Kantemirovka, U.S.S.R. 49 43N 39 55E
75 Kantse, China 31 30N 100 29E
15 Kanturk, Ire. 52 10N 8 55W
74 Kanuma, Japan 36 44N 139 42E
92 Kanus, S.W. Africa 27 50S 18 39E
92 Kanye, Botswana 25 0S 25 28E
92 Kanyu, Botswana 20 7S 24 37E
77 Kanyu, China 34 56N 119 8E
91 Kanzene, Zaïre 10 30S 25 12E
90 Kanzi, Ras, Tanzania 7 1S 39 33E
77 Kaoan, China 28 20N 115 17E
77 Kaohsiung, Taiwan 22 35N 120 16E
92 Kaokoveld, S. Afr. 19 0S 13 0E
84 Kaolack, Senegal 14 5N 16 8W
76 Kaomi, China 36 25N 119 45E
77 Kaoyu Hu, China 32 50N 119 10E
68 Kapadvanj, India 23 5N 73 0E
88 Kapanga, Zaïre 8 30S 22 40E
57 Kapanovka, U.S.S.R. 47 28N 46 50E
91 Kapata, Zambia 14 16S 26 15E
45 Kapello, Akra, Gr. 36 9N 23 3E
91 Kapema, Zaïre 10 45S 28 22E
26 Kapfenberg, Austria 47 26N 15 18E
91 Kapiri Mposhi, Zam. 13 59S 28 43E
106 Kapiskau, Canada 52 50N 82 1W
106 Kapiskau, R., Canada 52 20N 83 40W
72 Kapit, Malaysia 2 0N 113 5E
101 Kapiti I., N.Z. 40 50S 174 56E
26 Kaplice, Czechoslovakia 48 42N 14 30E
87 Kapoeta, Sudan 4 50N 33 35E
27 Kápolnásnyék, Hung. 47 16N 18 41E
27 Kapos, R., Hungary 46 30N 18 20E
27 Kaposvár, Hungary 46 25N 17 47E
73 Kapotjol, Indonesia 2 0S 130 9E
24 Kappeln, Germany 54 37N 9 56E
92 Kapps, S.W. Africa 22 32S 17 18E
39 Kaprije, Y.-slavia 43 42N 15 43E
54 Kapsukas, U.S.S.R. 54 33N 23 19E
72 Kapuas, R., Indonesia 0 20N 111 40E
72 Kapuas Hulu, Pegunungan, Malaysia 1 30N 113 30E
91 Kapuka, Zambia 10 30S 32 55E
91 Kapulo, Zaïre 8 18S 29 15E
99 Kapunda, Australia 34 20S 138 56E
101 Kapuni, New Zealand 39 29S 174 08E
68 Kapurthala, India 31 23N 75 25E
106 Kapuskasing, Canada 49 25N 82 30W
106 Kapuskasing, R., Can. 49 0N 82 50W
57 Kapustin Yar, U.S.S.R. 48 37N 45 40E
99 Kaputar, Mt., Austral. 30 15S 150 10E
90 Kaputir, Kenya 2 5N 35 28E
27 Kapuvár, Hungary 47 36N 17 1E

MAP
45 Kara, Turkey 38 29N 26 19E
58 Kara, U.S.S.R. 69 10N 65 25E
45 Kara, I., Turkey 36 58N 27 30E
58 Kara Bogaz Gol, Zaliv, U.S.S.R. 41 0N 53 30E
45 Kara Burun, Turkey 38 41N 26 28E
58 Kara Kalpak A.S.S.R. ♦, U.S.S.R. 43 0N 60 0E
75 Kara Nor, China 38 45N 98 0E
58 Kara Sea, U.S.S.R. 75 0N 70 0E
86 Kara, Wadi, Si. Arab. 20 40N 42 0E
56 Karabük, Turkey 41 10N 32 30E
44 Karaburuni, Albania 40 25N 19 20E
58 Karabutak, U.S.S.R. 50 0N 60 45E
57 Karachala, U.S.S.R. 39 45N 48 53E
57 Karachayevsk, U.S.S.R. 43 50N 42 0E
54 Karachev, U.S.S.R. 53 10N 35 5E
100 Karachi, Australia 36 58S 148 45E
68 Karachi, Pakistan 24 53N 67 0E
70 Karad, India 17 15N 74 10E
64 Karadeniz Boğazı, Turkey 41 10N 29 5E
64 Karadeniz Dağlari, Turkey 41 30N 35 0E
85 Karaga, Ghana 9 58N 0 28W
58 Karagajly, U.S.S.R. 49 26N 76 0E
58 Karaganda, U.S.S.R. 49 50N 73 0E
59 Karaginskiy, Ostrov, U.S.S.R. 58 45N 164 0E
90 Karagwe ♦, Tanz. 1 15S 30 45E
70 Karaikal, India 10 59N 79 50E
70 Karaikkudi, India 10 0N 78 45E
70 Karaitivu I., Sri Lanka 9 45N 79 52E
65 Karaj, Iran 35 4N 51 0E
44 Karajë, Albania 41 11N 19 33E
62 Karak, Jordan 31 14N 35 40E
58 Karakas, U.S.S.R. 48 20N 83 30E
73 Karakitang, Indon. 3 14N 125 28E
92 Karakobis, Bots. 22 3S 20 37E
66 Karakoram, Kashmir 35 20N 76 0E
66 Karakoram Pass, Kashmir 35 20N 78 0E
76 Karakorum, Mongolia 47 30N 102 20E
59 Karakum, Peski, U.S.S.R. 39 30N 60 0E
59 Karalon, U.S.S.R. 57 5N 115 50E
75 Karamai, China 45 57N 84 30E
64 Karaman, Turkey 37 14N 33 13E
72 Karambu, Indonesia 3 53S 116 6E
101 Karamea Bight, N.Z. 41 22S 171 40E
90 Karamoja ♦, Uganda 3 0N 34 15E
68 Karamsad, India 22 35N 72 50E
73 Karanganjar, Indonesia 7 38S 109 37E
68 Karanja, India 20 29N 77 31E
56 Karaşar, Turkey 40 21N 31 55E
92 Karasburg, S.W. Africa 28 0S 18 44E
58 Karasino, U.S.S.R. 66 50N 86 50E
58 Karasuk, U.S.S.R. 53 44N 78 2E
90 Karasuk ♦, Kenya 2 12N 35 15E
58 Karatau, U.S.S.R. 43 10N 70 28E
70 Karativu, I., Sri Lanka 8 22N 79 52E
62 Karatiya, Israel 31 39N 34 43E
74 Karatsu, Japan 33 30N 130 0E
68 Karauli, India 26 30N 77 4E
44 Karavasta, Albania 40 53N 19 28E
88 Karawa, Zaïre 3 18N 20 17E
26 Karawanken, Eur. 46 30N 14 40E
58 Karazhal, U.S.S.R. 48 2N 70 49E
64 Karbala, Iraq 32 47N 44 3E
48 Kärböle, Sweden 61 59N 15 22E
27 Karcag, Hungary 47 19N 21 1E
49 Kärda, Sweden 57 10N 13 49E
42 Kardeljevo, Y.-slavia 43 2N 17 27E
45 Kardhámila, Greece 38 35N 26 5E
44 Kardhítsa, Greece 39 23N 21 54E
44 Kardhítsa ♦, Greece 39 15N 21 50E
54 Kärdla, U.S.S.R. 58 50N 22 40E
92 Kareeberg, S. Afr. 30 50S 22 0E
86 Kareima, Sudan 18 30N 31 49E
52 Karelian A.S.S.R. ♦, U.S.S.R. 65 30N 32 30E
90 Karema, Tanzania 6 49S 30 24E
71 Karen, Andaman Is. 12 49N 92 53E
64 Karganrud, Iran 37 55N 49 0E
58 Kargasok, U.S.S.R. 59 3N 80 53E
58 Kargat, U.S.S.R. 55 10N 80 15E
56 Kargı, Turkey 41 11N 34 30E
66 Kargil, Kashmir 23 32N 76 12E
66 Kargil, Kashmir 34 32N 76 12E
28 Kargowa, Poland 52 5N 15 51E
85 Karguéri, Niger 13 36N 10 30E
45 Kariai, Greece 40 14N 24 19E
91 Kariba, Rhodesia 16 28S 28 36E
91 Kariba Gorge, Zambia 16 30S 28 35E
91 Kariba Lake, Rhodesia 16 40S 28 25E
92 Karibib, S.W. Africa 21 0S 15 56E
70 Karikal, India 10 59N 79 50E
64 Karikkale, Turkey 39 55N 33 30E
72 Karimata, Kepulauan, Indon. 1 40S 109 0E
72 Karimata, Selat, Indon. 2 0S 108 20E
70 Karimnagar, India 18 26N 79 10E
72 Karimundjawa, Kepulauan, Indon. 5 50S 110 30E
63 Karin, Somali Rep. 10 50N 45 52E
45 Káristos, Greece 38 1N 24 29E
74 Kariya, Japan 34 58N 137 1E
70 Karkal, India 13 15N 74 56E
98 Karkar I., New Guinea 4 40S 146 0E
56 Karkinitskiy Zaliv, U.S.S.R. 45 36N 32 35E
62 Karkur, Israel 32 29N 34 57E
86 Karkur Tohl, Egypt 22 5N 25 5E
54 Karl Libknekht, U.S.S.R. 51 40N 35 45E
24 Karl-Marx-Stadt, Ger. 50 50N 12 55E
24 Karl-Marx-Stadt ♦, Germany 50 45N 13 0E
44 Karla, L = Voiviis, Limni, Greece 39 35N 22 45E
28 Karlino, Poland 54 3N 15 53E

MAP
39 Karlobag, Y.-slavia 44 32N 15 5E
39 Karlovac, Y.-slavia 45 31N 15 36E
56 Karlovka, U.S.S.R. 49 29N 35 8E
26 Karlovy Vary, Cz. 50 13N 12 51E
49 Karlsborg, Östergötland, Sweden 58 33N 14 33E
49 Karlshamn, Sweden 56 10N 14 51E
48 Karlskoga, Sweden 59 22N 14 33E
49 Karlskrona, Sweden 56 10N 15 35E
25 Karlsruhe, Germany 49 3N 8 23E
48 Karlstad, Sweden 59 23N 13 30E
116 Karlstad, U.S.A. 48 38N 96 30W
47 Karmöy, Norway 59 15N 5 15E
68 Karnal, India 29 42N 77 2E
69 Karnali, R., Nepal 29 0N 82 0E
71 Karnaphuli Res., Bangladesh 22 40N 92 20E
117 Karnes City, U.S.A. 28 53N 97 53W
84 Karni, Ghana 10 45N 2 40W
26 Karnische Alpen, Europe 46 36N 13 0E
43 Karnobat, Bulgaria 42 40N 27 0E
26 Kârnten ♦, Austria 46 52N 13 30E
84 Karo, Upper Volta 12 16N 2 22W
91 Karoi, Rhodesia 16 48S 29 45E
91 Karonga, Malawi 9 57S 33 55E
99 Karoonda, Australia 35 1S 139 59E
45 Karos, Is., Greece 36 54N 25 40E
44 Karousâdhes, Greece 39 47N 19 45E
49 Karpalund, Sweden 56 4N 14 5E
45 Karpathos, I., Greece 35 37N 27 10E
45 Kárpathos, Stenón, Greece 36 0N 27 30E
52 Karpogory, U.S.S.R. 63 59N 44 27E
49 Karrebaek, Denmark 55 12N 11 39E
64 Kars, Turkey 40 40N 43 5E
58 Karsakpay, U.S.S.R. 47 55N 66 40E
57 Karsha, U.S.S.R. 49 45N 51 35E
58 Karshi, U.S.S.R. 39 0N 65 55E
55 Karsun, U.S.S.R. 54 14N 46 57E
44 Kartál Óros, Gr. 41 15N 25 13E
58 Kartaly, U.S.S.R. 53 10N 60 50E
68 Kartapur, India 31 27N 75 32E
112 Karthaus, U.S.A. 41 8N 78 9W
28 Kartuzy, Poland 54 22N 18 10E
73 Karufa, Indonesia 3 50S 133 20E
98 Karumba, Australia 17 31S 140 50E
90 Karumo, Tanzania 2 25S 32 50E
90 Karumwa, Tanzania 3 12S 32 38E
90 Karungu, Kenya 0 50S 34 10E
49 Karup, Denmark 56 19N 9 10E
70 Karur, India 10 59N 78 2E
27 Karviná, Cz. 49 53N 18 25E
69 Karwi, India 25 12N 80 57E
71 Kas Kong, Khmer Rep. 11 27N 102 12E
91 Kasache, Malawi 13 25S 34 20E
88 Kasai, R., Zaïre 8 20S 22 0E
90 Kasai Oriental ♦, Zaïre 5 0S 24 30E
91 Kasai Occidental ♦, Zaïre 6 30S 22 30E
91 Kasaji, Zaïre 10 25S 23 27E
91 Kasama, Zambia 10 16S 31 9E
92 Kasane, S.W. Afr. 17 34S 24 50E
91 Kasanga, Tanzania 8 30S 31 10E
88 Kasangulu, Zaïre 4 15S 15 15E
70 Kasaragod, India 12 30N 74 58E
109 Kasba L., Canada 60 20N 102 10W
82 Kasba Tadla, Morocco 32 36N 6 17W
65 Kaschmar, Iran 35 16N 58 26E
49 Kaseberga, Sweden 55 24N 14 8E
91 Kasempa, Zambia 13 30S 25 44E
91 Kasenga, Zaïre 10 20S 28 45E
90 Kasese, Uganda 0 13N 30 3E
91 Kasewa, Zambia 14 28S 28 53E
68 Kasganj, India 27 48N 78 42E
106 Kashabowie, Canada 48 40N 90 26W
65 Kashan, Iran 34 5N 51 30E
75 Kashgar, China 39 46N 75 52E
91 Kashimbo, Zaïre 11 12S 26 19E
55 Kashin, U.S.S.R. 57 20N 37 36E
77 Kashing, China 30 45N 120 41E
70 Kashipur, Orissa, India 19 16N 83 3E
68 Kashipur, Ut. P., India 29 15N 79 0E
55 Kashira, U.S.S.R. 54 45N 38 10E
66 Kashmir ♦, Asia 32 44N 74 54E
68 Kashmor, Pakistan 28 28N 69 32E
55 Kashpirovka, U.S.S.R. 53 0N 48 30E
67 Kashum Tso, Tibet 34 45N 86 0E
55 Kasimov, U.S.S.R. 54 55N 41 20E
90 Kasing,e Zaïre 6 15S 26 58E
116 Kaskaskia, R., U.S.A. 38 40N 89 12W
50 Kaskinen (Kaskö), Finland 62 22N 21 15E
50 Kaskö (Kaskinen), Finland 62 22N 21 15E
108 Kaslo, Canada 49 55N 117 0W
91 Kasonawedjo, Indon. 1 50S 137 41E
90 Kasongo, Zaïre 4 30S 26 33E
88 Kasongo Lunda, Zaïre 6 35S 17 0E
45 Kásos, I., Greece 35 20N 26 55E
45 Kásos, Stenón, Greece 35 30N 26 30E
57 Kaspi, U.S.S.R. 41 54N 44 17E
43 Kaspichan, Bulgaria 43 18N 27 8E
57 Kaspiyskiy, U.S.S.R. 45 22N 47 23E
57 Kaspiyskiy, U.S.S.R. 45 22N 47 23E
57 Kaspiysk, U.S.S.R. 42 45N 47 40E
87 Kassab ed Doleib, Sud. 13 30N 33 35E
86 Kassaba, Egypt 22 40N 29 55E
87 Kassâla, Sudan 15 23N 36 26E
87 Kassāla ♦, Sudan 15 20N 36 26E
44 Kassandra, Greece 40 0N 23 30E
24 Kassel, Germany 51 19N 9 32E
86 Kassinger, Sudan 18 46N 31 51E
54 Kassiopi, Gr. 39 48N 19 55E
73 Kassue, Indonesia 6 58S 139 21E
64 Kastamonu, Turkey 41 25N 33 43E
39 Kastav, Y.-slavia 45 22N 14 20E
45 Kastélli, Greece 35 29N 23 38E
45 Kastéllion, Gr. 35 12N 25 20E
45 Kastellou, Akra, Gr. 35 30N 27 15E
49 Kastlösa, Sweden 56 26N 16 25E

* Renamed Shaba
† Renamed Winam Gulf

Kiangshan INDEX Koko

MAP
77 Kiangshan, China 28 51N 118 38E
77 Kiangsi ♦, China 27 20N 115 40E
77 Kiangsu ♦, China 33 0N 119 50E
77 Kiangyin, China 31 51N 120 0E
77 Kiangyu, China 31 41N 104 26E
93 Kianja, Malagasy Rep. 20 18S 47 8E
76 Kiaochow Wan., China 36 10N 120 15E
76 Kiaohsien, China 36 20N 120 0E
90 Kibanga Port, Uganda 0 10S 32 58E
88 Kibangou, Congo 3 18S 12 22E
90 Kibara, Tanzania 2 8S 33 30E
90 Kibara, Mts., Zaïre 8 25S 27 10E
90 Kibombo, Zaïre 3 57S 25 53E
90 Kibondo, Tanzania 3 35S 30 45E
90 Kibondo ♦, Tanz. 4 0S 30 55E
90 Kibumbu, Burundi 3 32S 29 45E
90 Kibungu, Rwanda 2 10S 30 32E
90 Kibuye, Burundi 3 39S 29 59E
90 Kibuye, Rwanda 2 3S 29 21E
90 Kibwesa, Tanzania 6 30S 29 58E
49 Kibaek, Denmark 56 2N 8 51E
42 Kičevo, Yugoslavia 41 34N 20 59E
59 Kichiga, U.S.S.R. 59 50N 163 5E
77 Kichow, China 30 0N 115 30E
100 Kickabil, Australia 31 50S 148 30E
108 Kicking Horse Pass, Canada 51 27N 116 25W
85 Kidal, Mali 17 50N 1 22E
13 Kidderminster, England 52 24N 2 13W
90 Kidete, Tanzania 6 40S 30 40E
90 Kidete, Tanzania 6 25S 37 17E
84 Kidira, Senegal 14 28N 12 13W
101 Kidnappers, C., New Zealand 39 38S 117 5E
98 Kidston, Australia 18 52S 144 8E
90 Kidugalle, Tanzania 6 49S 38 15E
24 Kiel, Germany 54 16N 10 8E
24 Kiel Canal = Nord-Ostee-Kanal, Germany 54 15N 9 40E
28 Kielce, Poland 50 58N 20 42E
28 Kielce ♦, Poland 51 0N 20 40E
24 Kieler Bucht, Germany 54 30N 10 30E
67 Kienchwan, China 26 30N 99 45E
91 Kienge, Zaïre 10 30S 27 30E
77 Kienhinghsien, China 26 50N 116 50E
77 Kienko, China 31 50N 105 30E
77 Kienning, China 27 4N 118 21E
77 Kienow, China 27 0N 118 16E
75 Kienshui, China 23 57N 102 45E
77 Kiensi, China 26 58N 106 0E
77 Kienteh, China 29 30N 119 28E
77 Kienyang, Fukien, China 27 30N 118 0E
77 Kienyang, Hunan, China 27 10N 109 50E
85 Kiessé, Niger 13 29N 4 1E
54 Kiev = Kiyev, U.S.S.R. 50 30N 30 28E
84 Kiffa, Mauritania 16 50N 11 15W
45 Kifisiá, Greece 38 4N 23 49E
45 Kifissós ♦, Greece 38 30N 23 0E
64 Kifri, Iraq 34 45N 45 0E
90 Kigali, Rwanda 1 5S 30 4E
90 Kigarama, Tanzania 1 1S 31 50E
*90 Kigezi ♦, Uganda 0 45S 29 50E
90 Kigoma ♦, Tanz. 4 50S 30 30E
90 Kigoma-Ujiji, Tanz. 5 30S 30 0E
90 Kigomasha, Ras, Tanz. 4 58S 38 58E
99 Kihee, Australia 27 30S 142 25E
74 Kii-Suido, Japan 33 40N 135 0E
77 Kikiang, China 28 58N 106 44E
42 Kikinda, Yugoslavia 45 50N 20 30E
45 Kikládhes, Is., Greece 37 20N 24 30E
45 Kikládhes ♦, Greece 37 0N 25 0E
98 Kikori, Papua 7 13S 144 15E
98 Kikori, R., Papua 7 5S 144 0E
88 Kikwit, Zaïre 5 5S 18 45E
48 Kil, Sweden 59 30N 13 20E
48 Kilafors, Sweden 61 14N 16 36E
70 Kilakarai, India 9 12N 78 47E
110 Kilauea Crater, Hawaii 19 24N 155 17W
99 Kilcoy, Australia 26 59S 152 30E
15 Kildare, Ireland 53 10N 6 50W
15 Kildare ♦, Ireland 53 10N 6 50W
90 Kilembe, Uganda 0 15N 30 3E
117 Kilgore, U.S.A. 32 22N 94 40W
66 Kilian Qurghan, China 36 52N 78 3E
90 Kilifi, Kenya 3 40S 39 48E
90 Kilifi ♦, Kenya 3 30S 39 40E
90 Kilimanjaro, Mt., Tanz. 3 7S 37 20E
90 Kilimanjaro ♦, Tanz. 4 50S 37 45E
90 Kilindini, Kenya 4 4S 39 40E
64 Kilis, Turkey 36 50N 37 10E
56 Kiliya, U.S.S.R. 45 28N 29 16E
15 Kilkee, Ireland 52 41N 9 40W
15 Kilkenny, Ireland 52 40N 7 17W
15 Kilkenny ♦, Ireland 52 35N 7 15W
15 Kilkieran B., Ireland 53 18N 9 45W
44 Kilkis, Greece 40 58N 22 57E
44 Kilkis ♦, Greece 41 5N 22 50E
15 Killala, Ireland 54 13N 9 12W
15 Killala B., Ireland 54 20N 9 12W
15 Killaloe, Ireland 52 48N 8 28W
112 Killaloe Sta., Canada 45 34N 77 25W
99 Killarney, Australia 28 19S 152 14E
106 Killarney, Man., Can. 49 10N 99 40W
109 Killarney, Ont., Can. 45 55N 81 30W
15 Killarney, Ireland 52 2N 9 30W
15 Killarney, L's. of, Ire. 52 0N 9 30W
15 Killary Harb., Ireland 53 38N 9 52W
112 Killbuck, U.S.A. 40 29N 81 58W
109 Killdeer, Canada 49 6N 106 22W
116 Killdeer, U.S.A. 47 26N 102 48W
117 Killeen, U.S.A. 31 7N 97 45W
14 Killiecrankie P., Scotland 56 44N 3 46W
47 Killingdal, Norway 62 47N 11 26E
45 Killini, Greece 37 55N 21 8E
45 Killini, Mts., Greece 37 54N 22 25E
15 Killybegs, Ireland 54 38N 8 26W
100 Kilmany, Austral. 38 8S 146 55E
14 Kilmarnock, Scot. 55 36N 4 30W
55 Kilmez, R., U.S.S.R. 56 58N 51 10E

* *Incorporated within the new Southern Province*

91 Kilondo, Tanzania 9 45S 34 20E
90 Kilosa, Tanzania 6 48S 37 0E
15 Kilrush, Ireland 52 39N 9 30W
48 Kilsmo, Sweden 59 6N 15 35E
91 Kilwa ♦, Tanzania 9 0S 39 0E
91 Kilwa Kisiwani, Tanz. 8 58S 39 32E
91 Kilwa Kivinje, Tanz. 8 45S 39 25E
91 Kilwa Masoko, Tanz. 8 55S 39 30E
117 Kim, U.S.A. 37 18N 103 20W
90 Kimamba, Tanzania 6 45S 37 10E
96 Kimba, Australia 33 8S 136 23E
116 Kimball, Nebr., U.S.A. 41 17N 103 20W
116 Kimball, S.D., U.S.A. 43 47N 98 57W
98 Kimbe B., Terr. of New Guinea 5 3S 150 45E
96 Kimberley, Australia 16 20S 127 0E
108 Kimberley, Canada 49 40N 116 10W
92 Kimberley, S. Africa 28 43S 24 46E
118 Kimberly, U.S.A. 42 33N 114 25W
45 Kimi, Greece 38 38N 24 6E
45 Kimolos, Greece 36 48N 24 37E
45 Kimolos, I., Greece 36 48N 24 35E
55 Kimovsk, U.S.S.R. 54 0N 38 29E
84 Kimparana, Mali 12 48N 5 0W
55 Kimry, U.S.S.R. 56 55N 37 15E
108 Kimsquit, Canada 52 45N 127 5W
48 Kimstad, Sweden 58 35N 15 58E
72 Kinabalu, mt., Sabah, E. Malaysia 6 0N 116 0E
45 Kinaros, I., Greece 36 59N 26 15E
109 Kincaid, Canada 49 40N 107 0W
106 Kincardine, Canada 44 10N 81 40W
*14 Kincardine ♦, Scot. 56 56N 2 28W
109 Kindersley, Canada 51 30N 109 10W
84 Kindia, Guinea 10 0N 12 52W
90 Kindu, Zaïre 2 55S 25 50E
55 Kinel, U.S.S.R. 53 15N 50 40E
55 Kineshma, U.S.S.R. 57 30N 42 5E
90 Kinesi, Tanzania 1 25S 33 50E
119 King City, U.S.A. 36 11N 121 8W
4 King Frederick VI Land, Greenland 63 0N 43 0W
4 King Frederick VIII Land, Greenland 77 30N 25 0W
128 King George B., Falk. Is. 51 30S 60 30W
5 King George I., Antarctica 60 0S 60 0W
105 King George Is., Can. 53 40N 80 30W
96 King George Sd., Australia 35 5S 118 0E
71 King I. = Kadah Kyun, Burma 12 30N 98 20E
99 King I., Australia 39 40S 144 0E
96 King Leopold Ranges, Australia 17 20S 124 20E
96 King Sd., Australia 16 50S 123 20E
104 King William I., Can. 69 0N 98 0W
92 King William's Town, S. Africa 32 51S 27 22E
99 Kingaroy, Australia 26 32S 151 51E
117 Kingfisher, U.S.A. 35 50N 97 55W
54 Kingisepp, U.S.S.R. 59 25N 28 40E
54 Kingisepp (Kuressaare), U.S.S.R. 58 15N 22 15E
75 Kingku, China 23 49N 100 30E
119 Kingman, Ariz., U.S.A. 35 12N 114 2W
117 Kingman, Kans., U.S.A. 37 41N 96 9W
77 Kingmen, China 31 10N 112 15E
77 Kingning, China 27 55N 119 30E
4 Kings B., Spitzbergen 78 0N 15 0E
119 Kings, R., U.S.A. 36 57N 119 0W
119 Kings Canyon National Park, U.S.A. 37 0N 118 45W
12 King's Lynn, England 52 45N 0 25E
115 Kings Mt., U.S.A. 35 13N 81 20W
118 King's Peak, U.S.A. 40 46N 110 27W
115 Kingsport, U.S.A. 36 33N 82 36W
119 Kingsburg, U.S.A. 36 35N 119 36W
99 Kingscote, Australia 35 33S 137 31E
15 Kingscourt, Ireland 53 55N 6 48W
116 Kingsley, U.S.A. 42 37N 95 58W
116 Kingsley Dam, U.S.A. 41 20N 101 40W
106 Kingston, Canada 44 20N 76 30W
121 Kingston, Jamaica 18 0N 76 50W
101 Kingston, N.Z. 45 20S 168 43E
113 Kingston, N.Y., U.S.A. 41 55N 74 0W
113 Kingston, Pa., U.S.A. 41 19N 75 58W
113 Kingston, R.I., U.S.A. 41 29N 71 30W
99 Kingston South East, Australia 36 51S 139 55E
121 Kingstown, St. Vincent 13 10N 61 10W
115 Kingstree, U.S.A. 33 40N 79 48W
106 Kingsville, Canada 42 3N 82 45W
117 Kingsville, U.S.A. 27 30N 97 53W
77 Kingtehchen (Fowliang), China 29 8N 117 21E
67 Kingtung, China 24 30N 100 50E
14 Kingussie, Scot. 57 4N 4 2W
76 Kinhsien, China 36 6N 107 49E
77 Kinhwa, China 29 5N 119 32E
88 Kinkala, Congo 4 18S 14 49E
101 Kinleith, New Zealand 38 20S 175 56E
101 Kinloch, New Zealand 44 51S 168 20E
77 Kinmen (Quemoy) Is., china 24 25N 118 24E
112 Kinmount, Canada 44 45N 78 40W
47 Kinn, Norway 61 34N 4 45E
48 Kinna, Sweden 57 32N 12 42E
14 Kinnaird's Hd., Scotland 57 40N 2 0W
48 Kinnared, Sweden 57 2N 13 7E
62 Kinneret, Israel 32 44N 35 34E
62 Kinneret, Yam, Israel 32 45N 35 35E
49 Kinneviken, B., Sweden 58 38N 18 20E
87 Kinoni, Cent. Afr. Rep. 5 40N 26 10E
90 Kinoni, Uganda 0 41S 30 28E
71 Kinping, China 22 56N 103 15E
14 Kinross, Scotland 56 13N 3 25W
†14 Kinross ♦, Scotland 56 13N 3 25W
15 Kinsale, Ire. 51 42N 8 31W

* *Incorporated within the region of Grampian*
† *Incorporated within the region of Tayside*

15 Kinsale Harbour, Ire. 51 40N 8 30W
15 Kinsale Old Hd., Ire. 51 37N 8 32W
47 Kinsarvik, Norway 60 22N 6 43E
75 Kinsha (Yangtze), China 32 30N 98 30E
88 Kinshasa, Zaïre 4 20S 15 15E
117 Kinsley, U.S.A. 37 57N 99 30W
115 Kinston, U.S.A. 35 18N 77 35W
85 Kintampo, Ghana 8 5N 1 41W
72 Kintap, Indonesia 3 51S 115 13E
14 Kintyre, pen., Scot. 55 30N 5 35W
14 Kintyre, Mull of, Scotland 55 17N 5 4W
108 Kinuso, Canada 55 25N 115 25W
90 Kinyangiri, Tanzania 4 35S 34 37E
112 Kinzua, U.S.A. 41 52N 78 58W
112 Kinzua Dam, U.S.A. 41 53N 79 0W
45 Kióni, Greece 38 27N 20 41E
106 Kiosk, Canada 46 6N 78 53W
117 Kiowa, Kans., U.S.A. 37 3N 98 30W
117 Kiowa, Okla., U.S.A. 34 45N 95 50W
90 Kipanga, Tanzania 6 15S 35 20E
45 Kiparissia, Greece 37 15N 21 40E
45 Kiparissiakós Kólpos, Greece 37 25N 21 25E
106 Kipawa Res. Prov. Park, Canada 47 0N 78 30W
91 Kipengere Ra., Tanz. 9 12S 34 15E
90 Kipili, Tanzania 7 28S 30 32E
90 Kipini, Kenya 2 30S 40 32E
15 Kippure, Mt., Ireland 53 11N 6 23W
91 Kipushi, Zaïre 11 48S 27 12E
88 Kir, Zaïre 1 29S 19 25E
70 Kirandul, India 18 33N 81 10E
68 Kiratpur, India 29 32N 78 12E
24 Kirchhain, Germany 50 49N 8 54E
25 Kirchheim Bolanden, Germany 49 40N 8 0E
27 Kirchschlag, Austria 47 30N 16 19E
25 Kirchheim, Germany 48 38N 9 20E
59 Kirensk, U.S.S.R. 57 50N 107 55E
58 Kirgiz S.S.R. ♦, U.S.S.R. 42 0N 75 0E
53 Kirgiziya Steppe, U.S.S.R. 50 0N 55 0E
55 Kirillov, U.S.S.R. 59 51N 38 14E
76 Kirin, China 43 58N 126 31E
76 Kirin ♦, China 43 50N 125 45E
70 Kirindi, R., Sri Lanka 6 15N 81 20E
54 Kirishi, U.S.S.R. 51 28N 31 59E
98 Kiriwina Is. = Trobriand Is., Solomon Sea 8 40S 151 0E
98 Kirk River, Australia 20 0S 146 38E
14 Kirkcaldy, Scot. 56 7N 3 10W
14 Kirkcudbright, Scotland 54 50N 4 3W
49 Kirkeby, Denmark 55 7N 8 33E
70 Kirkee, India 18 34N 73 56E
47 Kirkenaer, Norway 60 27N 12 3E
50 Kirkenes, Norway 69 40N 30 5E
14 Kirkintilloch, Scot. 55 57N 4 10W
50 Kirkjubaejarklaustur, Iceland 63 47N 18 4W
119 Kirkland, Ariz., U.S.A. 34 29N 112 46W
118 Kirkland, Wash., U.S.A. 47 40N 122 10W
106 Kirkland Lake, Canada 48 15N 80 0W
43 Kirklareli, Turkey 41 44N 27 15E
116 Kirksville, U.S.A. 40 8N 92 35W
64 Kirkuk, Iraq 35 30N 44 21E
14 Kirkwall, Scot. 58 59N 2 59W
92 Kirkwood, S. Africa 33 22S 25 15E
70 Kirlampudi, India 17 12N 82 12E
25 Kirn, Germany 49 46N 7 29E
45 Kirov, R.S.F.S.R., U.S.S.R. 58 35N 49 40E
55 Kirov, R.S.F.S.R., U.S.S.R. 54 3N 34 12E
57 Kirovabad, U.S.S.R. 40 45N 46 10E
57 Kirovakan, U.S.S.R. 41 0N 44 0E
55 Kirovo-Chepetsk, U.S.S.R. 58 28N 50 0E
56 Kirovograd, U.S.S.R. 48 35N 32 20E
52 Kirovsk, R.S.F.S.R., U.S.S.R. 67 48N 33 50E
57 Kirovsk, Ukraine, U.S.S.R. 48 35N 38 30E
57 Kirovski, U.S.S.R. 45 51N 48 11E
59 Kirovskiy, U.S.S.R. 54 31N 155 42E
109 Kirriemuir, Canada 51 56N 110 20W
55 Kirsanov, U.S.S.R. 52 35N 42 40E
64 Kirşehir, Turkey 39 14N 34 5E
92 Kirstonia, S. Africa 25 30S 23 45E
85 Kirtachi, Niger 12 52N 2 30E
66 Kirthar Range, Pakistan 27 0N 67 0E
50 Kiruna, Sweden 67 52N 20 15E
73 Kiruru, Indonesia 3 55S 134 55E
55 Kiryu, U.S.S.R. 55 5N 46 45E
74 Kiryu, Japan 36 25N 139 20E
55 Kirzhach, U.S.S.R. 56 12N 38 50E
49 Kisa, Sweden 58 0N 15 39E
90 Kisaga, Tanzania 4 30S 34 23E
45 Kisámou, Kólpos, Greece 35 30N 23 38E
90 Kisanga, Zaïre 2 30N 26 35E
90 Kisangani, Zaïre 0 35N 25 15E
73 Kisar, I., Indonesia 8 5S 127 10E
72 Kisaran, Indonesia 2 47N 99 29E
74 Kisaratzu, Japan 35 25N 139 59E
90 Kisarawe, Tanzania 6 53S 39 0E
90 Kisarawe ♦, Tanz. 7 3S 39 0E
27 Kisbér, Hungary 47 30N 18 0E
58 Kiselevsk, U.S.S.R. 54 5N 86 6E
69 Kishanganj, India 26 3N 88 14E
68 Kishangarh, India 27 50N 70 30E
85 Kishi, Nigeria 9 1N 3 45E
56 Kishinev, U.S.S.R. 47 0N 28 50E
56 Kishinoi, U.S.S.R. 47 1N 28 50E
74 Kishiwada, Japan 34 50N 135 25E
62 Kishon, Israel 32 33N 35 12E
69 Kishorganj, Bangladesh 24 26N 90 40E
77 Kishow, China 28 16N 109 47E
66 Kishtwar, Kashmir 33 20N 75 48E
MAP
76 Kisi, China 45 21N 131 0E
90 Kisii, Kenya 0 40S 34 45E
90 Kisii ♦, Kenya 0 40S 34 45E
57 Kisır, Dağ, Turkey 41 0N 43 5E
90 Kisizi, Uganda 1 0S 29 58E
104 Kiska I., Alaska 52 0N 177 30E
27 Kiskomárom = Zalakomár, Hung. 46 33N 17 10E
27 Kiskörös, Hungary 46 37N 19 20E
27 Kiskundorozsma, Hung. 46 16N 20 5E
27 Kiskunfelegyháza, Hungary 46 42N 19 53E
27 Kiskunhalas, Hungary 46 28N 19 37E
27 Kiskunmajsa, Hungary 46 30N 19 48E
57 Kislovodsk, U.S.S.R. 43 50N 42 45E
79 Kismayu, Somali Rep. 0 20S 42 30E
74 Kisogawa, Japan 35 20N 137 0E
90 Kisoro, Uganda 1 17S 29 48E
27 Kispest, Hungary 47 27N 19 9E
84 Kissidougou, Guinea 9 5N 10 0W
115 Kissimmee, U.S.A. 28 18N 81 22W
115 Kissimmee, R., U.S.A. 27 20N 81 0W
39 Kistanje, Yugoslavia 43 58N 15 55E
27 Kisterenye, Hungary 48 3N 19 50E
27 Kisújszállás, Hungary 47 12N 20 50E
90 Kisumu, Kenya 0 3S 34 45E
27 Kisvárda, Hungary 48 14N 22 4E
90 Kiswani, Tanzania 4 5S 37 57E
90 Kiswere, Tanz. 9 27S 39 30E
116 Kit Carson, U.S.A. 38 48N 102 45W
84 Kita, Mali 13 5N 9 25W
75 Kitai, China 44 0N 89 27E
74 Kitaibaraki, Japan 36 50N 140 45E
74 Kitakami-Gawa, Japan 39 30N 141 15E
74 Kitakyūshū, Japan 33 50N 130 50E
90 Kitale, Kenya 1 0N 35 12E
90 Kitangiri, L., Tanzania 4 5S 34 20E
91 Kitaya, Tanzania 10 38S 40 8E
106 Kitchener, Canada 43 30N 80 30W
106 Kitchigami, R., Canada 50 35N 78 5W
90 Kitega = Citega, Burundi 3 30S 29 58E
90 Kitgum Matidi, Uganda 3 17N 32 52E
45 Kithira, Greece 36 9N 23 0E
45 Kithira, I., Greece 36 15N 23 0E
45 Kithnos, Greece 37 26N 24 27E
45 Kithnos, I., Greece 37 25N 24 25E
108 Kitimat, Canada 53 55N 129 0W
91 Kitiyab, Sudan 17 13N 33 35E
44 Kitros, Greece 40 22N 22 34E
112 Kittanning, U.S.A. 40 49N 79 30W
113 Kittatinny Mts., U.S.A. 41 0N 75 0W
113 Kittery, U.S.A. 43 7N 70 42W
90 Kitui, Kenya 1 17S 38 0E
90 Kitui ♦, Kenya 1 30S 38 25E
91 Kitwe, Zambia 12 54S 28 7E
77 Kityang, China 23 30N 116 29E
26 Kitzbühel, Austria 47 27N 12 24E
25 Kitzingen, Germany 49 44N 10 9E
75 Kiuchuan, China 39 51N 98 30E
77 Kiukiang, China 29 37N 116 2E
77 Kiungchow, China 19 57N 110 17E
77 Kiungchow Haihsia, China 20 40N 110 0E
68 Kivarli, India 24 33N 72 46E
44 Kivotós, Greece 40 13N 21 26E
90 Kivu, L., Zaïre 1 48S 29 0E
90 Kivu ♦, Zaïre 3 10S 27 0E
77 Kiyuanshan, China 28 6N 117 46E
77 Kiyang, China 26 36N 111 42E
54 Kiyev, U.S.S.R. 50 30N 30 28E
54 Kiyevskoye Vdkhr., U.S.S.R. 51 0N 30 0E
52 Kizel, U.S.S.R. 59 0N 57 0E
90 Kiziguru, Rwanda 1 46S 30 23E
56 Kızılcahaman, Turkey 40 30N 32 30E
57 Kızılırmak, Turkey 39 15N 36 0E
58 Kizil Kiya, U.S.S.R. 40 20N 72 35E
90 Kizimkazi, Tanzania 6 28S 39 30E
57 Kizlyar, U.S.S.R. 43 51N 46 40E
58 Kizyl-Arvat, U.S.S.R. 38 58N 56 15E
49 Kjellerup, Denmark 56 17N 9 25E
72 Klabat, Teluk, Indonesia 1 30S 105 40E
42 Kladanj, Yugoslavia 44 14N 18 42E
42 Kladnica, Yugoslavia 43 23N 20 2E
26 Kladno, Czechoslovakia 50 10N 14 7E
42 Kladovo, Yugoslavia 44 36N 22 33E
26 Klagenfurt, Austria 46 38N 14 20E
54 Klaipeda, U.S.S.R. 55 43N 21 10E
49 Klagerup, Sweden 55 36N 13 17E
49 Klagshamn, Sweden 55 32N 12 53E
49 Klagstorp, Sweden 55 22N 13 23E
49 Klakring, Denmark 55 42N 9 59E
118 Klamath Falls, U.S.A. 42 20N 121 50W
118 Klamath Mts., U.S.A. 41 20N 123 0W
118 Klamath, R., U.S.A. 41 40N 123 30W
71 Klang = Kelang, Mal. 3 1N 101 33E
39 Klanjec, Yugoslavia 46 3N 15 45E
48 Klarälven, Sweden 60 32N 13 15E
73 Klaten, Indonesia 7 43S 110 36E
26 Klatovy, Cz. 49 23N 13 18E
108 Klawak, Alaska 55 35N 133 0W
92 Klawer, S. Afr. 31 44S 18 36E
28 Kłecko, Poland 52 38N 17 25E
28 Kleczew, Poland 52 22N 18 9E
108 Kleena Kleene, Can. 52 0N 124 50W
118 Klein, U.S.A. 46 26N 108 31W
92 Klein-Karas, S.W. Afr. 27 33S 18 7E
92 Klein Karoo, S. Africa 33 45S 21 30E
39 Klekovača, mt., Y.-slav. 44 25N 16 32E
108 Klemtu, Canada 52 35N 128 55W
27 Klenovec, Cz. 48 36N 19 54E
42 Klenovec, Yugoslavia 31 32N 20 49E
47 Klepp Norway 59 48N 5 36E
92 Klerksdorp, S. Africa 26 51S 26 38E
54 Kletnya, U.S.S.R. 53 30N 33 2E
54 Kletsk, U.S.S.R. 53 5N 26 45E
57 Kletskiy, U.S.S.R. 49 20N 43 0E
24 Kleve, Germany 51 46N 6 10E
118 Klickitat, U.S.A. 45 50N 12 10W
MAP
54 Klimovichi, U.S.S.R. 53 36N 32 0E
55 Klin, U.S.S.R. 56 28N 36 48E
49 Klinte, Denmark 53 35N 10 12E
49 Klintehamn, Sweden 57 22N 18 12E
54 Klintsey, U.S.S.R. 52 50N 32 10E
92 Klipplaat, S. Africa 33 0S 24 22E
43 Klisura, Bulgaria 42 40N 24 28E
49 Klitmöller, Denmark 57 3N 8 30E
42 Kljajićevo, Yugoslavia 45 45N 19 17E
39 Ključ, Yugoslavia 44 32N 16 48E
28 Kłobuck, Poland 50 55N 19 5E
28 Kłodawa, Poland 53 16N 18 52E
28 Kłodzko, Poland 50 28N 16 38E
104 Klondike, Canada 64 0N 139 40W
44 Klosi, Albania 41 28N 26 10E
27 Klosterneuburg, Austria 48 18N 16 19E
25 Klosters, Switzerland 46 52N 9 52E
48 Kloten, Sweden 59 54N 15 19E
24 Klötze, Germany 52 38N 11 9E
85 Klouto, Togoland 6 57N 0 44E
49 Klovborg, Denmark 55 56N 9 30E
48 Klövsjöfj, mt., Sweden 62 36N 13 57E
104 Kluane, L., Canada 61 25N 138 50W
71 Kluang, Malaysia 1 59N 103 20E
28 Kluczbork, Poland 50 58N 18 12E
57 Klyuchevskaya, Guba, U.S.S.R. 55 50N 160 30E
24 Klötze, Germany 52 38N 11 9E
54 Kmelnitski, U.S.S.R. 49 23N 27 0E
12 Knaresborough, England 54 1N 1 29W
43 Knezha, Bulgaria 43 30N 23 56E
42 Knic, Yugoslavia 43 53N 20 45E
13 Knighton, Wales 52 21N 3 2W
118 Knight's Landing, USA 38 50N 121 49W
39 Knin, Yugoslavia 44 1N 16 17E
26 Knittelfeld, Austria 47 13N 14 51E
42 Knjazevac, Yugoslavia 43 35N 22 18E
96 Knob, C., Australia 34 32S 119 16E
15 Knockmealdown Mts., Ireland 52 16N 8 0W
16 Knokke, Belgium 51 20N 3 17E
100 Knowsley, Australia 36 50S 144 35E
114 Knox, U.S.A. 41 18N 86 36W
117 Knox City, U.S.A. 33 26N 99 38W
5 Knox Coast, Antarctica 66 30S 108 0E
116 Knoxville, Iowa, U.S.A. 41 20N 93 5W
115 Knoxville, Pa., U.S.A. 41 57N 77 26W
115 Knoxville, Tenn., U.S.A. 35 58N 83 57W
28 Knurów, Poland 50 13N 18 38E
47 Knutshö, Norway 62 18N 9 41E
92 Knysna, S. Afr. 34 2S 23 2E
28 Knyszyn, Poland 53 20N 22 56E
71 Ko Chang, Thailand 12 0N 102 20E
71 Ko Kut, Thailand 11 40N 102 32E
71 Ko Phangan, Thai. 9 45N 100 10E
71 Ko Phra Thong, Thai. 9 6N 98 15E
71 Ko Samui, Thailand 9 30N 100 0E
105 Koartac (Notre Dame de Koartac), Canada 61 5N 69 36E
73 Koba, Aru, Indon. 6 37S 134 37E
72 Koba, Bangka, Indon. 2 26S 106 14E
39 Kobarid, Yugoslavia 46 15N 13 30E
74 Kobayashi, Japan 31 56N 130 59E
74 Kōbe, Japan 34 45N 135 10E
56 Kobelyaki, U.S.S.R. 49 11N 34 9E
49 København, Denmark 55 41N 12 34E
25 Koblenz, Germany 50 21N 7 36E
87 Kobo, Ethiopia 12 2N 39 56E
54 Kobrin, U.S.S.R. 52 15N 24 22E
73 Kobroor, Kepulauan, Indonesia 6 10S 134 30E
57 Kobuleti, U.S.S.R. 41 55N 41 45E
28 Kobylin, Poland 51 43N 17 12E
28 Kobyłka, Poland 52 21N 21 10E
55 Kobylkino, U.S.S.R. 54 8N 43 46E
54 Kobylnik, U.S.S.R. 54 58N 26 39E
42 Kočani, Yugoslavia 41 55N 22 25E
45 Koçarli, Turkey 37 45N 27 43E
42 Koceljevo, Yugoslavia 44 28N 19 50E
125 Kočevje, Yugoslavia 45 39N 14 50E
69 Kochas, India 25 15N 83 56E
74 Kōchi, Japan 33 30N 133 35E
74 Kochi-ken ♦, Japan 33 40N 133 30E
70 Kodaikanai, India 10 13N 77 32E
70 Koddiyar Bay, Sri Lanka 8 33N 81 15E
104 Kodiak I., U.S.A. 57 30N 152 45W
71 Kodiang, Malaysia 6 21N 100 18E
68 Kodinar, India 20 46N 70 46E
57 Kodori, R., U.S.S.R. 43 0N 41 40E
89 Koes, S.W. Africa 26 0S 19 15E
100 Koetong, Australia 36 10S 147 30E
5 Köflach, Austria 47 4N 15 4E
85 Koforidua, Ghana 6 3N 0 17W
74 Kōfu, Japan 35 40N 138 30E
99 Kogan, Australia 27 2S 150 40E
85 Kogin Baba, Nigeria 7 55N 11 35E
64 Kogizman, Turkey 40 5N 43 10E
85 Kogon, Guinea 11 20N 14 32W
65 Koh-i-Bab, mts., Afghanistan 34 30N 67 0E
66 Kohat, Pakistan 33 40N 71 29E
67 Kohima, India 25 35N 94 10E
5 Kohler Ra., Antarctica 77 0N 110 0W
54 Kohtla-Järve, U.S.S.R. 59 20N 27 20E
73 Kojabuti, Indonesia 2 36S 140 37E
27 Kojetin, Czechoslovakia 49 21N 17 20E
86 Koka, Sudan 20 5N 30 35E
58 Kokand, U.S.S.R. 40 30N 70 58E
73 Kokas, Indonesia 2 42S 132 26E
27 Kokava, Czechoslovakia 48 35N 19 50E
58 Kokchetav, U.S.S.R. 53 20N 69 10E
51 Kokemäenjoki = Kumo älv, Finland 61 32N 21 44E
55 Kokhma, U.S.S.R. 56 55N 41 18E
75 Kokiu, China 23 30N 103 0E
50 Kokkola (Gamlakarleby), Finland 63 50N 23 8E
85 Koko, Mid-Western, Nigeria 6 5N 5 28E
85 Koko, North-Western, Nigeria 11 28N 4 29E

Koko Kyunzu INDEX Krško

MAP
71 Koko Kyunzu, Burma 14 10N 93 25E
67 Koko Shili, China 35 20N 91 0E
98 Kokoda, Papua 9 0S 148 0E
84 Kokolopozo, Ivory Coast 5 8N 6 5W
70 Kokomo, U.S.A. 40 30N 86 6W
75 Koko-Nor, China 37 0N 100 0E
98 Kokopo, New Guinea 4 23S 152 15E
85 Kokoro, Niger 14 12N 0 55E
105 Koksoak, R., Canada 54 5N 64 10W
59 Kokuora, U.S.S.R. 71 35N 144 50E
52 Kola, U.S.S.R. 68 45N 33 8E
73 Kola, I., Indonesia 5 35S 134 30E
52 Kola Pen. = Kolskiy P-ov., U.S.S.R. 67 30N 38 0E
73 Kolagede, Indonesia 7 54S 110 26E
84 Kolahun, Liberia 8 15N 10 4W
73 Kolaka, Indonesia 4 3S 121 46E
70 Kolar, India 13 12N 78 15E
70 Kolar Gold Fields, India 12 58N 78 16E
43 Kolarovgrad, Bulgaria 43 27N 26 42E
27 Kolarovo, Cz. 47 56N 18 0E
42 Kolašin, Yugoslavia 42 50N 19 31E
49 Kolby, Denmark 55 49N 10 33E
49 Kolby Kas, Denmark 55 48N 10 32E
55 Kolchugino, U.S.S.R. 56 17N 39 22E
84 Kolda, Senegal 12 55N 14 50W
4 Koldewey I., Greenland 77 0N 18 0W
49 Kolding, Denmark 55 30N 9 29E
82 Koléa, Algeria 36 38N 2 46E
73 Kolepom, I. = Dolak, I., Indon. 8 0S 138 30E
48 Kölfors, Sweden 62 9N 16 30E
52 Kolguyev, Ostrov, U.S.S.R. 69 20N 48 30E
70 Kolhapur, India 16 43N 74 15E
84 Kolia, Ivory Coast 9 46N 6 28W
26 Kolin, Czechoslovakia 50 2N 15 9E
49 Kolind, Denmark 56 21N 10 34E
24 Kölleda, Germany 51 11N 11 14E
70 Kollegal, India 12 9N 77 9E
70 Kolleru L., India 16 40N 81 10E
92 Kolmanskop, S.W. Afr. 26 45S 15 14E
24 Köln, Ger. 50 56N 9 58E
28 Kolno, Poland 53 25N 21 25E
28 Kolo, Poland 52 14N 18 40E
28 Kołobrzeg, Poland 54 10N 15 35E
55 Kologriv, U.S.S.R. 58 48N 44 25E
84 Kolokani, Mali 13 35N 7 45W
55 Kolomna, U.S.S.R. 55 8N 38 45E
56 Kolomyya, U.S.S.R. 48 31N 25 2E
73 Kolonodale, Indonesia 2 3S 121 25E
84 Kolondiéba, Mali 11 5N 6 54W
67 Kolosib, India 24 15N 92 45E
58 Kolpashevo, U.S.S.R. 58 20N 83 5E
54 Kolpino, U.S.S.R. 59 44N 30 39E
55 Kolpny, U.S.S.R. 52 12N 37 10E
52 Kolskiy Poluostrov, U.S.S.R. 67 30N 38 0E
52 Kolskiy Zaliv, U.S.S.R. 69 23N 34 0E
42 Kolubara, R., Y-slav. 44 35N 20 15E
28 Kolumna, Poland 51 36N 19 14E
28 Koluszki, Poland 51 45N 19 46E
55 Kolyberovo, U.S.S.R. 55 15N 38 40E
59 Kolyma, R., U.S.S.R. 64 40N 153 0E
59 Kolymskoye, Okhotsko, U.S.S.R. 63 0N 157 0E
86 Kôm Ombo, Egypt 24 25N 32 52E
59 Komandorskiye Ostrava, U.S.S.R. 55 0N 167 0E
27 Komárno, Cz. 47 49N 18 5E
27 Komárom, Hungary 47 43N 18 7E
27 Komárom ♦, Hungary 47 35N 18 20E
54 Komarovo, U.S.S.R. 58 38N 33 40E
85 Kombissiri, Upper Volta 12 4N 1 20W
84 Kombori, Upper Volta 13 26N 3 56W
45 Kombóti, Greece 39 6N 21 5E
39 Komen, Yugoslavia 45 49N 13 45E
85 Komenda, Ghana 5 4N 1 28W
52 Komi, A.S.S.R. ♦, U.S.S.R. 64 0N 55 0E
39 Komiza, Yugoslavia 43 3N 16 11E
27 Komló, Hungary 46 15N 18 16E
70 Kommamur Canal, India 16 0N 80 25E
57 Kommunarsk, U.S.S.R. 48 30N 38 45E
65 Kommunizma, U.S.S.R. 38 40N 72 20E
47 Komnes, Norway 59 30N 9 55E
73 Komodo, Indonesia 8 37S 119 20E
84 Komoé, Ivory Coast 5 12N 3 44W
73 Komoran, Pulau, Indonesia 8 18S 138 45E
28 Komorze, Poland 62 8N 17 38E
44 Komotini, Greece 41 9N 25 26E
71 Kompong Cham, Khmer Rep. 11 54N 105 30E
71 Kompong Chhnang, Khmer Rep. 12 20N 104 35E
71 Kompong Som, Khmer Rep. 11 3N 103 41E
71 Kompong Speu, Khmer Rep. 11 26N 104 32E
71 Kompong Thom, Khmer Rep. 12 35N 104 51E
56 Komrat, U.S.S.R. 46 18N 28 40E
92 Komsberge, S. Afr. 32 40S 20 45E
59 Komsomoleto, Ostrov, U.S.S.R. 80 30N 95 0E
59 Komsomolsk, U.S.S.R. 50 30N 137 0E
58 Komsomolskiy, U.S.S.R. 53 30N 49 40E
85 Kona, Niger 13 33N 8 3E
85 Kona, Nigeria 8 58N 11 15E
55 Konakovo, U.S.S.R. 56 52N 36 45E
67 Konam Dzong, China 29 5N 93 0E
117 Konawa, U.S.A. 34 59N 96 46W
70 Kondagaon, India 19 35N 81 35E
90 Konde, Tanzania 4 57S 39 45E
44 Kondiá, Greece 39 52N 25 10E
90 Kondoa, Tanz. 4 55S 35 50E
59 Kondratyevo, U.S.S.R. 57 30N 98 30E
85 Konduga, Nigeria 11 35N 13 26E
84 Kong, Ivory Coast 8 54N 4 36W
MAP
71 Kong Koh, Cambodia 11 20N 103 0E
4 Kong Christian IX.s Land, Greenland 68 0N 36 0W
4 Kong Christian X.s Land, Greenland 74 0N 29 0W
4 Kong Frederik VI.s Kyst, Greenland 63 0N 43 0W
4 Kong Frederik VIII.s Land, Greenland 78 30N 26 0W
4 Kong Oscar Fjord, Greenland 72 20N 24 0W
49 Konga, Sweden 56 30N 15 6E
49 Kongea, Denmark 55 24N 8 39E
67 Konglu, Burma 27 13N 97 57E
77 Kongmoon, China 22 35N 113 1E
90 Kongolo, Zaïre 5 22S 27 0E
85 Kongoussi, Upper Volta 13 19N 1 32W
47 Kongsberg, Norway 59 39N 9 39E
47 Kongsvinger, Norway 60 12N 12 2E
47 Kongsvoll, Norway 62 20N 9 36E
91 Koni, Zaïre 10 40S 27 11E
91 Koni, Mts., Zaïre 10 36S 27 10E
28 Koniecpol, Poland 50 46N 19 40E
54 Königsberg = Kaliningrad, U.S.S.R. 54 42N 20 32E
24 Königslutter, Germany 52 14N 10 50E
24 Königswusterhausen, Germany 52 19N 13 38E
28 Konin, Poland 52 12N 18 15E
44 Konispol, Albania 39 42N 20 10E
44 Kónitsa, Greece 40 5N 20 48E
39 Konjice, Yugoslavia 43 42N 18 0E
85 Konkoure, R., Guinea 10 30N 13 40W
24 Könnern, Germany 51 40N 11 45E
70 Konnur, India 16 14N 74 49E
84 Kono, S. Leone 8 30N 11 5W
56 Konoğlu, Turkey 40 35N 31 50E
85 Konongo, Ghana 6 40N 1 15W
52 Konosha, U.S.S.R. 61 0N 40 5E
54 Konotop, U.S.S.R. 51 12N 33 7E
56 Konskaya, R., U.S.S.R. 47 30N 35 0E
28 Konskie, Poland 51 15N 20 23E
47 Konsmo, Norway 58 16N 7 23E
56 Konstantinovka, U.S.S.R. 48 32N 37 39E
55 Konstantinovski, R.S.F.S.R., U.S.S.R. 57 45N 39 35E
57 Konstantinovski, R.S.F.S.R., U.S.S.R. 47 33N 41 10E
28 Konstantynów Łódzki, Poland 51 45N 19 20E
25 Konstanz, Germany 47 39N 9 10E
85 Kontagora, Nigeria 10 23N 5 27E
71 Kontum, S. Vietnam 14 24N 108 0E
64 Konya, Turkey 37 52N 32 35E
25 Konz Karthaus, Ger. 49 41N 6 36E
4 Koog, Netherlands 52 27N 4 49E
96 Koolan I., Australia 16 0S 123 45E
100 Kooloonong, Austral. 34 48S 143 10E
100 Koondrook, Austral. 35 33S 144 8E
100 Koorakee, Australia 34 27S 142 56E
100 Koorawatha, Australia 34 2S 148 33E
118 Kooskia, U.S.A. 46 9N 115 59W
109 Koostatak, Canada 51 26N 97 26W
118 Kooteaai R., U.S.A. 48 30N 115 30W
109 Kootenay L., Canada 49 30N 117 0W
100 Koo-wee-rup, Australia 38 13S 145 28E
42 Kopaonik, mts., Y.-slav. 43 10N 21 0E
70 Kopargaon, India 19 51N 74 28E
50 Kópavogur, Iceland 64 6N 21 55W
39 Koper, Yugoslavia 45 31N 13 44E
47 Kopervik, Norway 59 17N 5 17E
58 Kopeysk, U.S.S.R. 54 55N 61 31E
48 Köping, Sweden 59 31N 16 3E
39 Kopiste, Yugoslavia 42 48N 16 42E
44 Kopliku, Albania 42 15N 19 25E
49 Köpmanholmen, Sweden 63 10N 18 35E
49 Köpmannebro, Sweden 58 45N 12 30E
70 Koppal, India 15 23N 76 5E
47 Koppang, Norway 61 34N 11 3E
65 Koppeh Dāgh, Asia 38 0N 58 0E
47 Kopperå, Norway 63 24N 11 52E
47 Kopperå, Norway 63 24N 11 50E
48 Koppom, Sweden 59 43N 12 10E
43 Koprivlen, Bulgaria 41 36N 23 53E
39 Koprivnica, Yugoslavia 46 12N 16 45E
43 Koprivshtitsa, Bulgaria 42 40N 24 19E
54 Kopychintsy, U.S.S.R. 49 7N 25 58E
44 Korakiána, Greece 39 42N 19 45E
42 Korab, mt., Yugoslavia 41 44N 20 40E
70 Koraput, India 18 50N 82 40E
69 Korba, India 22 20N 82 45E
24 Korbach, Germany 51 17N 8 50E
44 Korça, Albania 40 37N 20 50E
44 Korca ♦, Albania 40 40N 20 50E
39 Korcula, Y.-slav. 42 57N 17 8E
39 Korcula, I., Y.-slav. 42 57N 17 0E
39 Korčulanski Kanal, Yugoslavia 43 3N 16 40E
64 Kordestān ♦, Iran 36 0N 47 0E
87 Kordofân, Reg., Sudan 13 0N 29 0E
70 Koregaon, India 17 40N 74 10E
54 Korenevo, U.S.S.R. 51 27N 34 55E
57 Korenovsk, U.S.S.R. 45 12N 39 22E
54 Korets, U.S.S.R. 50 40N 27 5E
86 Korgus, Sudan 19 16N 33 48E
84 Korhogo, Ivory Coast 9 29N 5 28W
84 Koribundu, Sierra Leone 7 41N 11 46W
99 Koridina, Australia 29 42S 143 25E
73 Korim, Indonesia 0 58S 136 10E
45 Korinthia ♦, Greece 37 50N 22 35E
45 Korinthiakós Kólpos, Greece 38 16N 22 30E
45 Kórinthos, Greece 37 56N 22 55E
84 Korioume, Mali 16 35N 3 0W
74 Kōriyama, Japan 37 10N 140 18E
75 Korla, China 41 45N 86 4E
27 Körmend, Hungary 47 5N 16 35E
39 Kornat, I., Yugoslavia 43 50N 15 20E
56 Korneshty, U.S.S.R. 47 21N 28 1E
27 Korneuburg, Austria 48 20N 16 20E
MAP
49 Korning, Denmark 56 30N 9 44E
47 Kornsjö, Norway 58 57N 11 39E
47 Kornstad, Norway 62 59N 7 27E
84 Koro, Ivory Coast 8 32N 7 30W
84 Koro, Mali 14 1N 2 58W
101 Koro, I., Fiji 17 19S 179 23E
55 Korocha, U.S.S.R. 50 55N 37 30E
100 Koroit, Australia 38 18S 142 24E
45 Koróni, Greece 36 48N 21 57E
44 Korónia, Limni, Greece 40 47N 23 37E
45 Koronis, Greece 37 12N 25 35E
28 Koronowo, Poland 53 19N 17 55E
73 Koror, Palaru Is. 7 20N 134 28E
27 Körös, R., Hungary 46 45N 20 20E
27 Korostarcsa, Hungary 46 53N 21 3E
54 Korosten, U.S.S.R. 50 57N 28 25E
55 Korotoyak, U.S.S.R. 51 1N 39 2E
93 Korraraika, B. de, Malag. 17 45S 43 57E
59 Korsakov, U.S.S.R. 46 30N 142 42E
47 Korshavn, Norway 58 2N 7 0E
59 Korshunovo, U.S.S.R. 58 37N 110 10E
49 Korsör, Denmark 55 20N 11 9E
28 Korsze, Poland 54 11N 21 9E
86 Korti, Sudan 18 0N 31 40E
16 Kortrijk, Belgium 50 50N 3 17E
100 Korumburra, Australia 38 26S 145 50E
68 Korwai, India 24 7N 78 5E
59 Koryakskiy Khrebet, U.S.S.R. 61 0N 171 0E
45 Kos, Greece 36 52N 27 19E
45 Kos, I., Greece 36 50N 27 15E
87 Kosa, Ethiopia 7 50N 36 50E
55 Kosaya Gora, U.S.S.R. 54 10N 37 30E
53 Koschagy, U.S.S.R. 46 40N 54 0E
28 Kościan, Poland 52 5N 16 40E
28 Kościerzyna, Poland 54 8N 17 59E
117 Kosciusko, U.S.A. 33 3N 89 34W
108 Kosciusko, I., Alaska 56 0N 133 40W
100 Kosciusko, Mt., Austral. 36 27S 148 16E
27 Kösély, R., Hungary 47 25N 21 30E
70 Kosgi, India 16 58N 77 43E
86 Kosha, Sudan 20 50N 30 30E
68 Kosi, India 27 48N 77 29E
27 Košice, Czechoslovakia 48 42N 21 15E
93 Kosi-meer, S. Africa 27 0S 32 50E
42 Kosjeric, Yugoslavia 44 0N 19 55E
52 Koslan, U.S.S.R. 63 28N 48 52E
76 Kosŏnf, N. Korea 38 40N 128 22E
42 Kosovo-Metohija = Metahiska, Y.-slav. 42 30N 21 0E
42 Kosovska-Mitrovica, Yugoslavia 42 54N 20 52E
84 Kosso, Ivory Coast 5 3N 5 47W
39 Kostajnica, Yugoslavia 45 17N 16 30E
39 Kostanjevica, Y.-slav. 45 51N 15 27E
27 Kostelec, Cz. 50 14N 16 35E
43 Kostenets, Bulgaria 42 15N 23 52E
92 Koster, S. Afr. 25 52S 26 54E
87 Kôsti, Sudan 13 8N 32 43E
42 Kostolac, Yugoslavia 44 43N 21 15E
55 Kostroma, U.S.S.R. 57 50N 41 58E
55 Kostromskoye Vdkhr., U.S.S.R. 57 52N 40 49E
28 Kostrzyn, Poland 52 24N 17 14E
54 Kostyukovichi, U.S.S.R. 53 10N 32 4E
28 Koszalin, Poland 54 12N 16 8E
28 Koszalin ♦, Poland 54 10N 16 10E
27 Kőszeg, Hungary 47 23N 16 33E
68 Kot Adu, Pakistan 30 30N 71 0E
68 Kot Moman, Pakistan 32 13N 73 0E
68 Kota, India 25 14N 75 49E
71 Kota Baharu, Malaysia 6 7N 102 14E
72 Kota Kinabalu, Malaysia 6 0N 116 12E
91 Kota-Kota = Khota Kota, Malawi 12 55S 34 15E
71 Kota Tinggi, Malaysia 1 44N 103 53E
72 Kotaagung, Indonesia 5 38S 104 29E
72 Kotabaru, Indonesia 3 20S 116 20E
72 Kotabumi, Indonesia 4 49S 104 46E
73 Kotamobagu, Indonesia 0 57N 124 31E
72 Kotawaringin, Indon. 2 28S 111 27E
43 Kotel, Bulgaria 42 52N 26 26E
55 Kotelnich, U.S.S.R. 58 20N 48 10E
57 Kotelnikovo, U.S.S.R. 47 45N 43 15E
59 Kotelnyy, Ostrov, U.S.S.R. 75 10N 139 0E
70 Kothagudam, India 17 30N 80 40E
70 Kothapet, India 19 21N 79 28E
24 Köthen, Germany 51 44N 11 59E
69 Kothi, India 24 45N 80 40E
68 Kotiro, Pakistan 26 17N 67 13E
51 Kotka, Finland 60 30N 26 28E
52 Kotlas, U.S.S.R. 61 15N 47 0E
43 Kotlenska Planina, Bulgaria 42 56N 26 30E
66 Kotli, Kashmir 33 30N 73 55E
85 Kotonkoro, Nigeria 11 3N 5 58E
42 Kotor, Yugoslavia 42 25N 18 47E
42 Kotor Varoš, Y.-slav. 44 38N 17 22E
39 Kotoriba, Yugoslavia 46 37N 16 48E
55 Kotovo, U.S.S.R. 50 22N 44 45E
56 Kotovsk, U.S.S.R. 47 55N 29 35E
68 Kotputli, India 27 43N 76 12E
68 Kotri, Pakistan 25 22N 68 22E
45 Kótronas, Greece 36 38N 22 29E
*26 Kötschach, Austria 46 41N 13 1E
70 Kottayam, India 9 35N 76 33E
70 Kottur, India 10 34N 76 56E
59 Kotuy, R., U.S.S.R. 70 30N 103 0E
104 Kotzebue, Alaska 66 50N 162 40W
88 Kouango, Cent. Afr. Rep. 5 0N 20 10E
84 Koudougou, Upper Volta 12 10N 2 20W
45 Koufonisi, I., Ger. 34 56N 26 8E
45 Koufonisia, I., Greece 36 57N 25 35E
92 Kougaberge, S. Africa 33 48S 24 20E
84 Kouibli, Ivory Coast 7 15N 7 14W
88 Kouilou, R., Congo 4 10S 12 5E
MAP
88 Kouki, Cent. Afr. Rep. 7 22N 17 3E
88 Koula Moutou, Gabon 1 15S 12 25E
71 Koulen, Khmer Rep. 13 50N 104 40E
84 Koulikoro, Mali 12 40N 7 50W
98 Koumala, Australia 21 38S 149 15E
84 Koumankoun, Mali 11 58N 6 6W
84 Koumbia, Guinea 11 54N 13 40W
84 Koumbia, Upper Volta 11 10N 3 50W
84 Koumboum, Guinea 10 25N 13 0W
84 Koumpenntoum, Senegal 13 59N 14 34W
81 Koumra, Chad 8 50N 17 35E
84 Koundara, Guinea 12 29N 13 18W
58 Koumradskiy, U.S.S.R. 47 20N 75 0E
117 Kountze, U.S.A. 30 20N 94 22W
85 Koupéla, Upper Volta 12 11N 0 21E
83 Kourizo, Passe de, Chad 22 28N 15 27E
84 Kouroussa, Guinea 10 45N 9 45W
84 Koussané, Mali 14 53N 11 14W
84 Koutiala, Mali 12 25N 5 35W
84 Kouto, Ivory Coast 9 53N 6 25W
85 Kouvé, Togo 6 25N 0 59E
42 Kovačica, Yugoslavia 45 5N 20 38E
54 Kovel, U.S.S.R. 51 10N 25 0E
105 Kovik, Canada 61 40N 77 40W
70 Kovilpatti, India 9 10N 77 50E
42 Kovin, Yugoslavia 44 44N 20 59E
55 Kovrov, U.S.S.R. 56 25N 41 25E
70 Kovur, Andhra Pradesh, India 17 3N 81 39E
70 Kovur, Andhra Pradesh, India 14 30N 80 1E
28 Kowal, Poland 52 32N 19 7E
28 Kowalewo Pomorskie, Pol. 53 10N 18 52E
106 Kowkash, Canada 50 20N 87 20W
77 Kowloon, Hong Kong 22 20N 114 15E
72 Koyan, Pegunungan, Malaysia 3 15N 114 30E
77 Koyiu, China 23 2N 112 28E
104 Koyukuk, R., Alaska 65 45N 156 30W
56 Koyulhisar, Turkey 40 20N 37 52E
77 Koza, Okinawa 26 20N 127 47E
64 Kozan, Turkey 37 35N 35 50E
45 Kozáni, Greece 40 19N 21 47E
45 Kozáni ♦, Greece 40 18N 21 45E
39 Kozara, Mts., Y.-slavia 45 0N 17 0E
39 Kozarac, Yugoslavia 44 58N 16 48E
54 Kozelsk, U.S.S.R. 54 2N 35 38E
70 Kozhikode = Calicut, India 11 15N 75 43E
52 Kozhva, U.S.S.R. 65 10N 57 0E
28 Koziegłowy, Poland 50 37N 19 8E
39 Kozje, Yugoslavia 46 5N 15 35E
28 Kozle, Poland 50 20N 18 8E
43 Kozlodui, Bulgaria 43 45N 23 42E
43 Kozlovets, Bulgaria 43 30N 25 20E
28 Kozmin, Poland 51 48N 17 27E
28 Kożuchów, Poland 51 45N 15 31E
85 Kpabia, Ghana 9 10N 0 20W
85 Kpandae, Ghana 8 30N 0 2W
85 Kpandu, Ghana 7 2N 0 18E
85 Kpessi, Togo 8 4N 1 16E
71 Kra, Kho Khot, Thailand 10 15N 99 30E
71 Kra Buri, Thailand 10 22N 98 46E
71 Kra, Isthmus of = Kra, Kho Khot, Thai. 10 15N 99 30E
73 Kragan, Indonesia 6 43S 111 38E
47 Kragerö, Norway 58 52N 9 25E
42 Kragujevac, Y.-slavia 44 2N 20 56E
28 Krajenka, Poland 53 18N 16 59E
72 Krakatau = Rakata, Pulau, Indonesia 6 10S 105 20E
27 Kraków, Pol. 50 4N 19 57E
27 Kraków ♦, Pol. 49 45N 20 0E
73 Kraksaan, Indonesia 7 43S 113 23E
49 Kraksmala, Sweden 57 2N 15 20E
47 Kråkstad, Norway 59 40N 10 50E
27 Králiky, Czechoslovakia 50 6N 16 45E
42 Kraljevo, Yugoslavia 43 44N 20 41E
26 Kralovice, Cz. 49 59N 13 29E
27 Královsky Chlmec, Cz. 48 27N 22 0E
26 Kralupy, Czechoslovakia 50 13N 14 20E
56 Kramatorsk, U.S.S.R. 48 50N 37 30E
119 Kramer, U.S.A. 35 0N 117 38W
48 Kramfors, Sweden 62 55N 17 48E
82 Kramis, C., Algeria 36 26N 0 45E
48 Krangede, Sweden 63 9N 16 10E
44 Kraniá, Greece 39 53N 21 18E
45 Kranidhion, Greece 37 20N 23 10E
39 Kranj, Yugoslavia 46 16N 14 22E
39 Kranjska Gora, Y.-slav. 46 29N 13 48E
92 Kranzberg, S.W. Afr. 21 59S 15 37E
39 Krapina, Yugoslavia 46 10N 15 52E
39 Krapina, R., Yugoslavia 46 0N 15 55E
55 Krapivna, U.S.S.R. 53 58N 37 10E
28 Krapkowice, Poland 50 29N 17 56E
59 Kraskino, U.S.S.R. 42 44N 130 48E
54 Krāslāva, U.S.S.R. 55 52N 27 12E
26 Kraslice, Czechoslovakia 50 19N 12 31E
55 Krasnaya Gorbatka, U.S.S.R. 55 52N 41 45E
57 Kras Polyana, U.S.S.R. 43 40N 40 25E
28 Kraśnik, Poland 50 55N 22 5E
28 Krasnik Fabryezny, Pol. 50 58N 22 11E
56 Krasnoarmeisk, U.S.S.R. 48 18N 37 11E
57 Krasnoarmeysk, R.S.F.S.R., U.S.S.R. 48 30N 44 25E
55 Krasnoarmeysk, R.S.F.S.R., U.S.S.R. 50 32N 45 50E
57 Krasnodar, U.S.S.R. 45 5N 38 50E
57 Krasnodonetskaya, U.S.S.R. 48 5N 40 50E
55 Krasnogorskiy, U.S.S.R. 56 10N 48 28E
56 Krasnog Dardeiskoye, U.S.S.R. 45 32N 34 16E
56 Krasnograd, U.S.S.R. 49 27N 35 27E
57 Krasnogvardeyskoye, U.S.S.R. 45 52N 41 33E
52 Krasnokamsk, U.S.S.R. 58 0N 56 0E
MAP
54 Krasnokutsk, U.S.S.R. 50 10N 34 50E
56 Krasnoperekopsk, U.S.S.R. 46 0N 33 54E
58 Krasnoselkupsk, U.S.S.R. 65 20N 82 10E
55 Krasnoslobodsk, Mordovian ASSR, U.S.S.R. 54 30N 43 45E
57 Krasnoslobodsk, R.S.F.S.R., U.S.S.R. 48 42N 44 33E
58 Krasnoturinsk, U.S.S.R. 59 39N 60 1E
52 Krasnoufimsk, U.S.S.R. 56 30N 57 37E
58 Krasnouralsk, U.S.S.R. 58 0N 60 0E
53 Krasnovodsk, U.S.S.R. 40 0N 52 52E
59 Krasnoyarsk, U.S.S.R. 56 8N 93 0E
57 Krasnoye, Kal., U.S.S.R. 46 16N 45 0E
55 Krasnoye, R.S.F.S.R., U.S.S.R. 59 15N 47 40E
54 Krasnoye, Ukr., U.S.S.R. 49 56N 24 42E
55 Krasnozavodsk, U.S.S.R. 56 38N 38 16E
56 Krasny Liman, U.S.S.R. 48 58N 37 50E
57 Krasny Sulin, U.S.S.R. 47 52N 40 8E
28 Krasnystaw, Poland 50 57N 23 5E
54 Krasnyy, U.S.S.R. 49 56N 24 42E
55 Krasnyy Kholm, U.S.S.R. 58 10N 37 10E
55 Krasnyy Kut, U.S.S.R. 50 50N 47 0E
57 Krasnyy Luch, U.S.S.R. 48 13N 39 0E
57 Krasnyy Yar, Kal., U.S.S.R. 46 43N 48 23E
55 Krasnyy Yar, R.S.F.S.R., U.S.S.R. 50 42N 44 45E
55 Krasnyy Yar, R.S.F.S.R., U.S.S.R. 53 30N 50 30E
56 Krasnyyoskolskoye, Vdkhr, U.S.S.R. 49 30N 37 30E
27 Kraszna, R., Hungary 48 0N 22 20E
71 Kratie, Khmer Rep. 12 32N 106 10E
42 Kratovo, Yugoslavia 42 6N 22 10E
71 Kravanh, Phnom, Khmer Rep. 12 15N 103 5E
73 Krawang, Indonesia 6 19N 107 18E
24 Krefeld, Germany 51 20N 6 22E
45 Kremaston, Limni, Greece 38 52N 21 30E
56 Kremenchug, U.S.S.R. 49 5N 33 25E
56 Kremenchugskeye Vdkhr., U.S.S.R. 49 20N 32 30E
56 Kremenets, U.S.S.R. 50 8N 25 43E
42 Kremenica, Yugoslavia 40 55N 21 25E
56 Kremennaya, U.S.S.R. 49 1N 38 10E
43 Kremikovtsi, Bulgaria 42 46N 23 28E
24 Kremmen, Germany 52 45N 13 1E
118 Kremmling, U.S.A. 40 10N 106 30W
27 Kremnica, Cz. 48 45N 18 50E
26 Krems, Austria 48 25N 15 36E
26 Kremsmünster, Austria 48 3N 14 8E
54 Kretinga, U.S.S.R. 55 53N 21 15E
82 Krettamia, Algeria 28 47N 3 27W
54 Krettsy, U.S.S.R. 58 15N 32 30E
85 Kribi, Cameroon 2 57N 9 56E
46 Krichem, Bulgaria 46 16N 24 28E
54 Krichev, U.S.S.R. 53 45N 31 50E
43 Krichim, Bulgaria 42 8N 24 32E
39 Krim, mt., Y.-slavia 45 53N 14 30E
45 Krionéri, Greece 38 20N 21 35E
70 Krishna, R., India 16 30N 77 0E
70 Krishnagiri, India 12 32N 78 16E
69 Krishnanagar, India 23 24N 88 33E
70 Krishnaraja Sagara, India 12 20N 76 30E
49 Kristianopel, Sweden 56 12N 16 0E
47 Kristiansand, Norway 58 9N 8 1E
49 Kristianstad, Sweden 56 2N 14 9E
47 Kristiansund, Norway 63 7N 7 45E
50 Kristiinankaupunki, Fin. 62 16N 21 21E
48 Kristinehamn, Sweden 59 18N 14 13E
50 Kristinestad, Finland 62 16N 21 21E
45 Kriti, I., Greece 35 15N 25 0E
45 Kritsá, Greece 35 10N 25 41E
42 Kriva, R., Y.-slavia 42 12N 22 18E
42 Kriva Palanka, Y.-slav. 42 11N 22 19E
42 Krivaja, R., Y.-slavia 44 15N 18 22E
42 Krivelj, Yugoslavia 44 8N 22 5E
56 Krivoy Rog, U.S.S.R. 47 51N 33 20E
39 Krizevci, Yugoslavia 46 3N 16 32E
39 Krk, Yugoslavia 45 5N 14 56E
39 Krk, I., Yugoslavia 45 10N 14 55E
39 Krka, R., Yugoslavia 45 50N 15 30E
26 Krkonoše, Cz. 50 50N 16 10E
27 Krnov, Czechoslovakia 50 5N 17 40E
28 Krobia, Poland 51 47N 16 59E
26 Kročehlavy, Cz. 50 8N 14 9E
71 Kroeng Krai, Thailand 14 55N 98 30E
28 Krokawo, Poland 54 47N 18 9E
45 Krokeai, Greece 36 53N 22 32E
47 Kroken, Telemark, Norway 58 57N 9 8E
47 Kroken, Sweden 59 2N 11 23E
48 Krokom, Sweden 63 20N 14 30E
54 Krolevets, U.S.S.R. 51 35N 33 20E
27 Kromeriz, Cz. 49 18N 17 21E
27 Krompachy, Cz. 48 54N 20 52E
54 Kromy, U.S.S.R. 52 40N 35 48E
49 Kronobergs län ♦, Swed. 56 45N 14 30E
5 Kronprins Harald Kyst, Antarctica 70 0S 35 1E
5 Kronprins Olav Kyst, Antarctica 69 0S 42 0E
5 Kronprinsesse Märtha Kyst, Antarctica 73 30S 10 0W
54 Kronshtadt, U.S.S.R. 60 5N 29 35E
24 Kröpelin, Germany 54 4N 11 48E
57 Kropotkin, U.S.S.R. 58 50N 115 10E
24 Kropp, Germany 54 24N 9 32E
27 Kroscienko, Poland 49 29N 20 25E
28 Krośniewice, Poland 52 15N 19 11E
27 Krosno, Poland 49 35N 21 56E
28 Krosno Odrz, Poland 52 3N 15 7E
28 Krotoszyn, Poland 51 42N 17 23E
44 Krraba, Albania 41 13N 20 0E
39 Krško, Y.-slavia 45 57N 15 30E

* *Renamed Kötschach-Mauthern*

Krstača INDEX La Serena

MAP
42 Krstača, mt., Y.-slavia 42 57N 20 8E
93 Kruger Nat. Pk., S. Afr. 24 0s 31 40E
93 Krugersdorp, S. Africa 26 5s 27 46E
72 Krui, Indonesia 5 10s 104 0E
92 Kruidfontein, S. Africa 32 48s 21 59E
92 Kruis, Kaap, S.W. Africa 21 55s 13 57E
44 Kruja, Albania 41 32N 19 46E
54 Krulevshchina, U.S.S.R. 55 5N 27 45E
44 Kruma, Albania 42 37N 20 28E
43 Krumovgrad, Bulgaria 41 29N 25 38E
71 Krung Thep, Thailand 13 45N 100 35E
42 Krupanj, Yugoslavia 44 25N 19 22E
27 Krupina, Cz. 48 22N 19 5E
27 Krupinica, R., Cz. 48 15N 19 5E
42 Kruševac, Yugoslavia 43 35N 21 28E
42 Kruševo, Yugoslavia 41 23N 21 19E
28 Kruszwica, Poland 52 40N 18 20E
108 Kruzof I., Alaska 57 10N 135 40W
48 Krylbo, Sweden 60 7N 16 15E
56 Krymsk Abinsk, U.S.S.R. 44 50N 38 0E
56 Krymskaya, U.S.S.R. 45 0N 34 0E
27 Krynica, Poland 49 25N 20 57E
28 Krynica Morska, Poland 54 23N 19 28E
28 Krynki, Poland 53 17N 23 43E
46 Kryulyany, U.S.S.R. 47 12N 29 9E
28 Krzepice, Poland 50 58N 18 50E
27 Krzeszowice, Poland 50 8N 19 37E
28 Krzywin, Poland 51 58N 16 50E
28 Krzyz, Poland 52 52N 16 0E
24 Kröpelin, Germany 54 4N 11 48E
47 Krakstad, Norway 59 39N 10 55E
48 Krångede, Sweden 63 9N 16 6E
82 Ksabi, Algeria 29 8N 0 58W
82 Ksabi, Morocco 32 51N 4 13W
82 Ksar Chellala, Algeria 35 13N 2 19E
82 Ksar el Boukhari, Algeria 35 51N 2 52E
82 Ksar el Kebir, Morocco 35 0N 6 0W
82 Ksar es Souk, Morocco 31 58N 4 20W
83 Ksar Rhilane, Tunisia 33 0N 9 39E
82 Ksiba, Morocco 32 46N 6 0W
82 Ksour, Mts. des, Algeria 32 45N 0 30W
55 Kstova, U.S.S.R. 56 12N 44 13E
72 Kuala, Indonesia 2 46N 105 47E
71 Kuala Belait, Brunei 4 45N 114 25E
71 Kuala Dungun, Malay. 4 46N 103 25E
71 Kuala Kangsar, Malay. 4 49N 100 57E
71 Kuala Kerai, Malay. 5 32N 102 12E
71 Kuala Kubu Bahru, Malaysia 3 35N 101 38E
71 Kuala Lipis, Malaysia 4 22N 102 5E
71 Kuala Lumpur, Malay. 3 9N 101 41E
71 Kuala Pilah, Malaysia 2 45N 102 14E
71 Kuala Sedili, Malaysia 1 57N 104 8E
71 Kuala Selangor, Malay. 3 20N 101 15E
72 Kualakapuas, Indonesia 2 55s 114 20E
72 Kualakurun, Indonesia 1 10s 113 50E
72 Kualapembuang, Indon. 3 14s 112 38E
73 Kuandang, Indonesia 0 56N 123 1E
71 Kuantan, Malaysia 3 49N 103 20E
87 Kuaram, Ethiopia 12 25N 39 30E
57 Kuba, U.S.S.R. 41 21N 48 32E
66 Kubak, Iran 27 10N 63 10E
56 Kuban, R., U.S.S.R. 45 5N 38 0E
55 Kubenskoye, Oz., U.S.S.R. 59 40N 39 25E
57 Kuberle, U.S.S.R. 47 0N 42 20E
43 Kubrat, Bulgaria 43 49N 26 31E
42 Kučevo, Yugoslavia 44 30N 21 40E
75 Kucha, China 41 50N 82 30E
68 Kuchaman, India 27 13N 74 47E
25 Kuchenspitze, Aust. 47 3N 10 14E
72 Kuching, Malaysia 1 33N 110 25E
44 Kuçove = Qytet Stalin, Albania 40 47N 19 57E
44 Küçükkuyu, Turkey 39 35N 26 27E
70 Kudalier, R., India 18 20N 78 40E
72 Kudat, Malay. 6 55N 116 55E
100 Kudgee, Australia 32 43s 141 38E
70 Kudremukh, Mt., India 13 15N 75 20E
73 Kudus, Indonesia 6 48s 110 51E
81 Kufra, El Wâhât el, Libya 24 17N 23 15E
62 Kufrinja, Jordan 32 20N 35 41E
26 Kufstein, Austria 47 35N 12 11E
106 Kugong, I., Canada 56 25N 80 0W
65 Kūhak, Iran 27 12N 63 10E
65 Kūh-e-Alijuq, Iran 31 30N 51 41E
65 Kūh-e-Hazaran, Iran 29 35N 57 20E
65 Kūh-e-Jebel Barez, Iran 29 0N 58 0E
65 Kūh-e-Sorkh, Iran 35 30N 58 45E
65 Kūh-e-Taftan, Iran 28 40N 61 0E
65 Kūhha-ye-Bashakerd, Iran 26 45N 59 0E
65 Kūhha-ye Sabalān, Iran 38 15N 47 45E
26 Kuhnsdorf, Austria 46 37N 14 38E
65 Kuhpayeh, Iran 32 44N 52 20E
89 Kuiseb, R., S.W. Africa 23 40s 15 30E
108 Kuiu I., Alaska 56 40N 134 15W
42 Kukavica, mt., Y.-slav. 42 48N 21 57E
85 Kukawa, Nigeria 12 58N 13 27E
44 Kukësi, Albania 42 5N 20 20E
44 Kukësi ♦, Albania 42 25N 20 15E
87 Kukko, Ethiopia 8 26N 41 35E
55 Kukmar, U.S.S.R. 56 15N 50 45E
55 Kukvidze, U.S.S.R. 50 40N 43 15E
42 Kula, Bulgaria 43 52N 22 36E
42 Kula, Yugoslavia 45 37N 19 32E
71 Kulai, Malaysia 1 44N 103 35E
90 Kulal, Mt., Kenya 2 42N 36 57E
57 Kulaly, O., U.S.S.R. 45 0N 50 0E
70 Kulasekharapattanam, India 8 20N 78 0E
54 Kuldiga, U.S.S.R. 56 58N 21 59E
75 Kuldja = Ining, China 44 0N 81 0E
87 Kuldu, Sudan 12 50N 28 30E
55 Kulebaki, U.S.S.R. 55 22N 42 25E
39 Kulen Vakuf, Yugoslavia 44 35N 16 2E

MAP
57 Kuli, U.S.S.R. 42 2N 46 12E
116 Kulm, U.S.A. 46 22N 98 58W
58 Kulsary, U.S.S.R. 46 59N 54 1E
57 Kultay, U.S.S.R. 45 5N 51 40E
69 Kulti, India 23 43N 86 50E
98 Kulumadau, Papua 9 15s 152 50E
58 Kulunda, U.S.S.R. 52 45N 79 15E
100 Kulwin, Australia 35 0s 142 42E
58 Kulyab, U.S.S.R. 37 55N 69 50E
75 Kum Darya, China 41 0N 89 0E
58 Kum Tekei, U.S.S.R. 43 10N 79 30E
57 Kuma, R., U.S.S.R. 44 55N 45 57E
85 Kumaganum, Nigeria 13 8N 10 38E
72 Kumai, Indonesia 2 52s 111 45E
74 Kumamoto, Japan 32 45N 130 45E
74 Kumamoto-ken ♦, Japan 32 30N 130 40E
42 Kumanovo, Yugoslavia 42 9N 21 42E
101 Kumara, New Zealand 42 37s 171 12E
84 Kumasi, Ghana 6 41N 1 38W
85 Kumba, Cameroon 4 36N 9 24E
70 Kumbakonam, India 10 58N 79 25E
99 Kumbarilla, Australia 27 15s 150 55E
85 Kumbo, Cameroon 6 15N 10 36E
70 Kumbukkan Oya, Sri Lanka 6 35N 81 40E
77 Kume-guntō, Japan 26 8N 126 45E
55 Kumeny, U.S.S.R. 58 10N 49 47E
90 Kumi, Uganda 1 30N 33 58E
44 Kumkale, Turkey 40 30N 26 13E
48 Kumla, Örebro, Sweden 59 8N 15 10E
85 Kumo, Nigeria 10 1N 11 12E
70 Kumta, India 14 29N 74 32E
57 Kumtorkala, U.S.S.R. 43 2N 46 50E
57 Kumylzhenskaya, U.S.S.R. 49 51N 42 38E
27 Kunágota, Hungary 46 26N 21 3E
100 Kunama, Australia 35 35s 148 4E
59 Kunashir, Ostrov, U.S.S.R. 44 0N 146 0E
68 Kunch, India 26 0N 79 10E
54 Kunda, U.S.S.R. 59 30N 26 34E
98 Kundiawa, New Guinea 6 00s 145 00E
68 Kundla, India 21 21N 71 25E
65 Kunduz, Afghanistan 36 50N 68 50E
92 Kunene, R., S.W. Afr. 17 15s 13 40E
99 Kungala, Australia 29 58s 153 7E
49 Kungälv, Sweden 57 54N 12 0E
77 Kungan, China 30 0N 112 2E
76 Kungchuling, China 43 31N 124 58E
75 Kungho, China 36 28N 100 45E
58 Kungrad, U.S.S.R. 43 6N 58 54E
49 Kungsbacka, Sweden 57 30N 12 5E
52 Kungur, U.S.S.R. 57 20N 56 40E
98 Kungurri, Australia 21 3s 148 46E
77 Kungyifow, China 22 24N 112 41E
49 Kungälv, Sweden 57 53N 11 59E
27 Kunhegyes, Hungary 47 22N 20 36E
77 Kunhsien, China 32 30N 111 17E
73 Kuningan, Indonesia 6 59s 108 29E
67 Kunlong, Burma 23 20N 98 50E
75 Kunlun Shan, Asia 36 0N 86 30E
27 Kunmadaras, Hungary 47 28N 20 45E
75 Kunming, China 25 11N 102 37E
70 Kunnamkulam, India 10 38N 76 7E
76 Kunsan, S. Korea 35 59N 126 45E
77 Kunshan, China 31 16N 121 0E
27 Kunszentmárton, Hung. 46 50N 20 20E
96 Kununurra, Australia 15 40s 128 39E
98 Kunwararo, Australia 22 55s 150 7E
50 Kuopio, Fin. 62 53N 27 35E
50 Kuopion Lääni ♦, Finland 63 25N 27 10E
39 Kupa, R., Yugoslavia 45 30N 15 10E
73 Kupang, Indonesia 10 19s 123 39E
42 Kupres, Yugoslavia 44 1N 17 15E
56 Kupyansk, U.S.S.R. 49 45N 37 35E
56 Kupyansk-Uzlovoi, U.S.S.R. 49 52N 37 34E
57 Kura, R., U.S.S.R. 41 20N 46 15E
98 Kuranda, Australia 16 48s 145 35E
70 Kurandvad, India 16 45N 74 39E
74 Kurashiki, Japan 34 40N 133 50E
74 Kurayoshi, Japan 35 26N 133 50E
64 Kurdistan, reg., Asia 37 30N 42 0E
70 Kurduvadi, India 18 8N 75 29E
74 Kure, Japan 34 14N 132 32E
54 Kuressaare = Kingisepp, U.S.S.R. 58 15N 22 15E
58 Kurgaldzhino, U.S.S.R. 50 35N 70 20E
58 Kurgan, R.S.F.S.R., U.S.S.R. 55 30N 65 0E
59 Kurgan, R.S.F.S.R., U.S.S.R. 64 5N 172 50W
57 Kurganinsk, U.S.S.R. 44 50N 40 40E
63 Kuria Muria Is. = Khūryān Mūryān, Arab. 17 30N 55 58E
70 Kurichchi, India 11 36N 77 35E
98 Kuridala, Australia 21 16s 140 29E
59 Kurilsk, U.S.S.R. 45 14N 147 53E
59 Kurilskiye Ostrova, U.S.S.R. 45 0N 150 0E
92 Kuring Kuru, S.W. Afr. 17 42s 18 32E
86 Kurkur, Egypt 23 50N 32 0E
83 Kurkūrah, Libya 31 30N 20 1E
70 Kurla, India 19 5N 72 52E
55 Kurlovski, U.S.S.R. 55 25N 40 40E
87 Kurma, Sudan 13 55N 24 40E
87 Kurmuk, Sudan 10 33N 34 21E
100 Kurnell, Australia 34 2s 151 12E
70 Kurnool, India 15 45N 78 0E
55 Kurovskoye, U.S.S.R. 55 35N 38 55E
101 Kurow, New Zealand 44 4s 170 29E
100 Kurrajong, N.S.W., Australia 33 33s 150 42E
100 Kurri Kurri, Australia 32 50s 151 28E
54 Kuršenai, U.S.S.R. 56 1N 23 3E
69 Kurseong, India 26 56N 88 18E
55 Kursk, U.S.S.R. 51 42N 36 11E
42 Kuršumlija, Yugoslavia 43 9N 21 19E
42 Kuršumlijska Banja, Yugoslavia 43 3N 21 11E

MAP
64 Kurtalon, Turkey 37 55N 41 40E
87 Kuru (Chel), Bahr el, Sudan 8 10N 26 50E
92 Kuruman, S. Africa 27 28s 23 28E
74 Kurume, Japan 33 15N 130 30E
70 Kurunegala, Sri Lanka 7 30N 80 18E
59 Kurya, U.S.S.R. 61 15N 108 10E
45 Kuşadası, Turkey 37 52N 27 15E
45 Kuşadası Körfezi, Turkey 37 56N 27 0E
77 Kusagaki, Ryukyu Is. 30 54N 129 28E
108 Kusawa L., Canada 60 25N 136 20W
25 Kusel, Germany 49 31N 7 25E
76 Kushan, China 39 58N 123 30E
57 Kushchevskaya, U.S.S.R. 46 33N 39 35E
77 Kushin, China 32 12N 115 43E
74 Kushirogawa, Japan 43 0N 144 30E
65 Kushk, Afghanistan 34 55N 62 30E
58 Kushka, U.S.S.R. 35 20N 62 18E
69 Kushtia, Bangladesh 23 55N 89 5E
57 Kushum, R., U.S.S.R. 50 40N 50 20E
104 Kuskokwim Bay, Alaska 59 50N 162 56W
104 Kuskokwin, R., Alaska 61 48N 157 0W
87 Kussa, Ethiopia 4 9N 38 58E
58 Kustanai, U.S.S.R. 53 20N 63 45E
26 Kutá Horq, Cz. 49 57N 15 16E
57 Kutaisi, U.S.S.R. 42 19N 42 40E
72 Kutaradja = Banda Atjeh, Indonesia 5 35N 95 20E
72 Kutatjane, Indonesia 3 45N 97 50E
68 Kutch, G. of, India 22 50N 69 15E
68 Kutch, Rann of, India 24 0N 70 0E
39 Kutina, Yugoslavia 45 29N 16 48E
68 Kutiyana, India 21 36N 70 2E
42 Kutjevo, Yugoslavia 45 23N 17 55E
57 Kutkashen, U.S.S.R. 40 58N 47 47E
26 Kutá Hora, Cz. 49 57N 15 16E
28 Kutno, Poland 52 15N 19 23E
98 Kuttabul, Australia 21 5s 148 48E
87 Kutum, Sudan 14 20N 24 10E
27 Kúty, Czechoslovakia 48 40N 17 3E
54 Kuvshinovo, U.S.S.R. 57 2N 34 11E
64 Kuwait = Al Kuwayt, Kuwait 29 30N 47 30E
64 Kuwait ■, Arabia 29 30N 47 30E
76 Kuyang, China 41 8N 110 1E
55 Kuybyshev, R.S.F.S.R., U.S.S.R. 53 10N 50 15E
58 Kuybyshev, R.S.F.S.R., U.S.S.R. 55 27N 78 19E
56 Kuybyshevo, U.S.S.R. 47 25N 36 40E
55 Kuybyshevskoye Vdkhr., U.S.S.R. 55 2N 49 30E
52 Kuyto, Oz., U.S.S.R. 64 40N 31 0E
77 Kuyung, China 32 0N 119 8E
70 Kuzhithura, India 8 18N 77 11E
42 Kuzmin, Yugoslavia 45 2N 19 25E
55 Kuznetsk, U.S.S.R. 53 12N 46 40E
52 Kuzomen, U.S.S.R. 66 22N 36 50E
50 Kvaenangen, Norway 69 55N 21 15E
47 Kvam, Oppland, Norway 61 40N 9 42E
47 Kvamsöy, Norway 61 7N 6 28E
50 Kvarken, Finland 63 30N 21 0E
39 Kvarner, Yugoslavia 44 50N 14 10E
39 Kvarneric, Yugoslavia 44 43N 14 37E
48 Kvarnsveden, Sweden 60 32N 15 25E
48 Kvarntorp, Sweden 59 8N 15 17E
47 Kvås, Norway 58 16N 7 14E
47 Kvernes, Norway 63 1N 7 44E
49 Kvillsfors, Sweden 57 24N 15 29E
47 Kvina, R., Norway 58 43N 6 52E
47 Kvinesdal, Norway 58 18N 6 59E
47 Kviteseid, Norway 59 24N 8 29E
47 Kvås, Norway 58 16N 7 14E
92 Kwakhanai, Botswana 21 39s 21 16E
127 Kwakoegron, Surinam 5 25N 55 25W
90 Kwale ♦, Kenya 4 15s 39 10E
85 Kwale, Nigeria 6 18N 5 28E
88 Kwamouth, Zaïre 3 9s 16 20E
92 Kwando, R., Angola & Zam. 16 48s 22 45E
77 Kwangan, China 30 35N 106 40E
77 Kwangchow, China 23 10N 113 10E
77 Kwangchow Wan., China 21 0N 111 0E
76 Kwangju, S. Korea 35 9N 126 55E
75 Kwangnan, China 24 10N 105 0E
77 Kwangshui, China 31 45N 114 0E
77 Kwangsi-Chuang ♦, China 23 30N 108 55E
77 Kwangtseh, China 27 30N 117 25E
77 Kwangtsi, China 30 2N 115 46E
77 Kwangtung, China 23 35N 114 0E
77 Kwangyuan, China 32 30N 105 49E
75 Kwanhsien, China 30 59N 103 40E
92 Kwaraga, Botswana 20 26s 24 32E
73 Kwatisore, Indonesia 3 7s 139 59E
77 Kweichih, China 30 40N 117 30E
77 Kweichow = Fengkieh, China 31 0N 109 33E
77 Kweichow ♦, China 27 20N 107 0E
77 Kweihsien, China 22 59N 109 44E
77 Kweihwa = Mingki, China 26 10N 117 14E
77 Kweiki, China 28 10N 117 8E
77 Kweilin, China 25 16N 110 15E
77 Kweiping, China 23 12N 110 0E
77 Kweishun = Tsingsing, China 38 1N 114 4E
77 Kweitung, China 26 0N 113 35E
77 Kweiyang, Hunan, China 25 50N 112 25E
77 Kweiyang, Kweichow, China 26 30N 106 35E
28 Kwidzyn, Poland 54 5N 18 58E
96 Kwinana, Australia 32 15s 115 47E
90 Kwitaba, Burundi 3 56s 29 39E
77 Kwo Ho, China 33 20N 116 50E
77 Kwohwa, China 23 10N 107 0E
81 Kyabe, Chad 9 30N 19 0E

MAP
100 Kyabram, Australia 36 19s 145 4E
71 Kyaikto, Burma 17 20N 97 3E
59 Kyakhta, U.S.S.R. 50 30N 106 25E
67 Kyangin, Burma 18 20N 95 20E
75 Kyargas Nuur, Mongolia 49 0N 93 0E
67 Kyaring Nor, China 34 40N 97 20E
67 Kyaring Tso, Tibet 31 5N 88 25E
67 Kyaukpadaung, Burma 20 52N 95 8E
67 Kyaukpyu, Burma 19 28N 93 30E
67 Kyaukse, Burma 21 36N 96 10E
90 Kyegegwa, Uganda 0 30N 31 0E
67 Kyeikdon, Burma 16 3N 98 25E
90 Kyenjojo, Uganda 0 40N 30 37E
91 Kyle Dam, Rhodesia 20 15s 31 0E
14 Kyle of Lochalsh, Scotland 57 17N 5 43W
100 Kyneton, Australia 37 10s 144 29E
74 Kyō-ga-Saki, Japan 35 45N 135 15E
90 Kyoga, L., Uganda 1 35N 33 0E
99 Kyogle, Australia 28 40s 153 0E
76 Kyongju, S. Korea 35 50N 129 13E
67 Kyongpyaw, Burma 17 12N 95 10E
74 Kyōto, Japan 35 0N 135 45E
74 Kyōto-fu ♦, Japan 35 15N 135 30E
64 Kyrenia, Cyprus 35 20N 33 20E
24 Kyritz, Germany 52 57N 12 25E
48 Kyrkebyn, Sweden 59 18N 13 3E
47 Kyrping, Norway 59 45N 6 5E
59 Kystatyam, U.S.S.R. 67 20N 123 10E
59 Kytalktakh, U.S.S.R. 65 30N 123 40E
59 Kyulyunken, U.S.S.R. 64 10N 137 5E
67 Kyunhla, Burma 23 25N 95 15E
108 Kyuquot, Canada 50 3N 127 25W
57 Kyuquot Sd., Canada 50 0N 127 25W
57 Kyurdamir, U.S.S.R. 40 25N 48 3E
74 Kyushu, I., Japan 32 30N 131 0E
74 Kyūshū-Sanchi, Japan 32 45N 131 40E
42 Kyustendil, Bulgaria 42 25N 22 41E
59 Kyusyur, U.S.S.R. 70 39N 127 15E
100 Kywong, Australia 34 58s 146 44E
58 Kyzyl, U.S.S.R. 51 50N 94 30E
58 Kyzyl Kum, U.S.S.R. 42 0N 65 0E
58 Kyzyl Kum, Peski, U.S.S.R. 42 0N 65 0E
59 Kyzyl Rabot, U.S.S.R. 37 45N 74 55E
58 Kzyl-Orda, U.S.S.R. 44 50N 65 10E
31 La Albuera, Spain 38 45N 6 49W
32 La Alcarria, Spain 40 31N 2 45W
31 La Algaba, Spain 37 27N 6 1W
32 La Almarcha, Spain 39 41N 2 24W
32 La Almunia de Doña Godina, Spain 41 29N 1 23W
126 La Asunción, Ven. 11 2N 63 53W
32 La Baña, Punta de, Sp. 40 33N 0 40E
124 La Banda, Argentina 27 45s 64 10W
30 La Bañeza, Spain 42 17N 5 43W
120 La Barca, Mexico 20 20N 102 40W
118 La Barge, U.S.A. 41 12N 110 4W
19 La Bassée, France 50 31N 2 49E
20 La Bastide, France 44 35N 3 55E
18 La Baule, France 47 18N 2 23W
115 La Belle, U.S.A. 26 45N 81 22W
32 La Bisbal, Spain 41 58N 3 2E
126 La Blanquilla, Ven. 11 51N 64 37W
120 La Boca, Pan. Can. Zone 9 0N 79 30W
19 La Bresse, France 48 0N 6 53E
32 La Bureba, Spain 42 36N 3 24W
124 La Calera, Chile 32 50s 71 10W
31 La Campiña, Spain 37 45N 4 45W
30 La Cañiza, Spain 42 13N 8 16W
19 La Capelle, France 49 59N 3 50E
124 La Carlota, Argentina 33 30s 63 20W
31 La Carolina, Spain 38 17N 3 38W
20 La Cavalerie, France 44 0N 3 10E
121 La Ceiba, Honduras 15 40N 86 50W
20 La Chaise Dieu, France 45 20N 3 40E
18 La Chaize-le-Vicomté, France 46 40N 1 18W
19 La Chapelle-d'Angillon, France 47 21N 2 25E
18 La Chapelle Glain, Fr. 47 38N 1 11W
19 La Charité, France 47 10N 3 0E
18 La Chartre, France 47 42N 0 34E
18 La Châtaigneraie, France 46 38N 0 45W
20 La Châtre, France 46 35N 1 59E
25 La Chaux de Fonds, Switzerland 47 7N 6 50E
120 La Chorrera, Panama 8 50N 79 50W
21 La Ciotat, France 43 12N 5 36E
21 La Clayette, France 46 17N 4 19E
124 La Cocha, Argentina 27 50s 65 40W
*85 La Concepción, Eq. Guinea 3 28N 84 0E
120 La Concordia, Mexico 16 8N 92 38W
118 La Conner, U.S.A. 48 22N 122 27W
30 La Coruña, Spain 43 20N 8 25W
30 La Coruña ♦, Spain 43 10N 8 30W
30 La Corunne = La Coruña, Spain 43 20N 8 25W
21 La Côte-St. André, Fr. 45 24N 5 15E
20 La Courtine, France 45 43N 2 16E
20 La Crèche, France 46 23N 0 19W
108 La Crete, Canada 58 10N 116 29W
116 La Crosse, Kans., U.S.A. 38 33N 99 20W
116 La Crosse, Wis., U.S.A. 43 48N 91 13W
126 La Cruz, Colombia 1 35N 76 58W
120 La Cruz, Mexico 23 55N 106 54W
126 La Dorada, Colombia 5 30N 74 40W
124 La Esmeralda, Paraguay 22 16s 62 33W
124 La Esperanza, Jujuy, Arg. 24 9s 64 52W
126 La Esperanza, Bolivia 14 20s 62 0W
30 La Estrada, Spain 42 43N 8 27W
113 La Fargeville, U.S.A. 44 12N 75 58W
114 La Fayette, U.S.A. 40 22N 86 52W
19 La Fère, France 49 40N 3 20E
19 La Ferté, France 48 57N 3 6E
18 La Ferté Bernard, Fr. 48 10N 0 40E
18 La Ferté-Mace, France 48 35N 0 21W

MAP
19 La Ferté-St. Aubin, Fr. 47 42N 1 57E
18 La Ferté-Vidame, Fr. 48 37N 0 53E
18 La Flèche, France 47 42N 0 5W
115 La Folette, U.S.A. 36 23N 84 9W
30 La Fregeneda, Spain 40 58N 6 54W
126 La Fria, Venezuela 8 13N 72 15W
30 La Fuente de San Esteban, Spain 40 49N 6 15W
33 La Gineta, Spain 39 8N 2 1W
126 La Gloria, Colombia 8 37N 73 48W
126 La Gran Sabana, Ven. 5 30N 61 30W
21 La Grand 'Combe, France 44 13N 4 2E
21 La Grand Motte, France 48 35N 1 4E
118 La Grande, U.S.A. 45 15N 118 0W
96 La Grange, Australia 18 45s 121 43E
115 La Grange, Ga., U.S.A. 33 4N 85 0W
114 La Grange, Ky., U.S.A. 38 20N 85 20W
117 La Grange, Tex., U.S.A. 29 54N 96 52W
126 La Grita, Venezuela 8 8N 71 59W
126 La Guaira, Venezuela 10 36N 66 56W
126 La Guajira ♦, Col. 11 30N 72 30W
30 La Guardia, Spain 41 56N 8 52W
30 La Gudiña, Spain 42 4N 7 8W
18 La Guerche, France 47 57N 1 16W
19 La Guerche-sur-l'Aubois, France 46 58N 2 56E
121 La Habana, Cuba 23 8N 82 22W
116 La Harpe, U.S.A. 40 30N 91 0W
18 La Haye Descartes, Fr. 46 58N 0 42E
18 La Haye-du-Puits, Fr. 49 17N 1 33W
30 La Horra, Spain 41 44N 3 53W
126 La Isla, Colombia 6 51N 76 56W
119 La Jara, U.S.A. 37 16N 106 0W
32 La Junquera, Spain 42 25N 2 53E
117 La Junta, U.S.A. 38 0N 103 30W
124 La Ligua, Chile 32 30s 71 16W
31 La Linea de la Concepción, Sp. 36 15N 5 23W
109 La Loche L., Canada 56 40N 109 30W
21 La Londe, France 43 8N 6 14E
30 La Lora, Spain 42 45N 4 0W
16 La Louvière, Belgium 50 27N 4 10E
19 La Machine, France 46 54N 3 27E
40 La Maddalena, Italy 41 13N 9 25E
107 La Malbaie, Canada 47 40N 70 10W
33 La Mancha, dist., Spain 39 10N 2 54W
30 La Mariña, Spain 43 30N 7 40W
104 La Martre, L., Can. 63 0N 118 0W
104 La Martre, R., Canada 63 0N 118 0W
126 La Mesa, Colombia 4 38N 74 28W
119 La Mesa, Calif., U.S.A. 32 48N 117 5W
119 La Mesa, N. Mex., U.S.A. 32 6N 106 48W
32 La Mola, Cabo de, Sp. 39 53N 4 19E
18 La Mothe Archard, Fr. 46 37N 1 39W
21 La Motte, France 44 20N 6 3E
21 La Motte-Chalançon, Fr. 44 30N 5 21E
116 La Moure, U.S.A. 46 27N 98 17W
32 La Muela, Spain 41 36N 1 7W
21 La Mure, France 44 55N 5 48E
33 La Nao, Cabo de, Spain 38 44N 0 14E
21 La Napoule, France 43 31N 6 56E
124 La Negra, Chile 23 46s 70 18W
20 La Pacaudière, France 46 10N 3 50E
121 La Palma, Panama 8 15N 78 0W
31 La Palma, Spain 37 21N 6 38W
124 La Paloma, Chile 30 35s 71 0W
124 La Pampa ♦, Arg. 38 0s 66 0W
126 La Paragua, Venezuela 6 50N 63 20W
124 La Paz, Entre Rios, Arg. 30 50s 59 45W
124 La Paz, San Luis, Arg. 33 30s 67 20W
120 La Paz, Honduras 14 20N 87 47W
120 La Paz, Mexico 24 10N 110 20W
120 La Paz, Bide, Mexico 24 20N 110 40W
126 La Pedrera, Colombia 1 18s 69 43W
60 La Perouse Str., Japan 45 40N 142 0E
120 La Piedad, Mexico 20 20N 102 1W
118 La Pine, U.S.A. 40 53N 80 45W
116 La Plant, U.S.A. 45 11N 100 40W
124 La Plata, Argentina 35 0s 57 55W
124 La Plata, Rio de, S. Amer. 35 0s 56 40W
32 La Pobla de Lillet, Sp. 42 16N 1 59E
30 La Pola de Gordón, Sp. 42 51N 5 41W
114 La Porte, U.S.A. 41 40N 86 40W
32 La Puebla, Spain 39 50N 4 25W
31 La Puebla de los Infantes, Spain 37 47N 5 24W
30 La Puebla de Montalbán, Spain 39 52N 4 22W
33 La Puerta, Spain 38 22N 2 45W
124 La Quiaca, Argentina 22 5s 65 35W
31 La Rambla, Spain 37 37N 4 45W
106 La Reine, Canada 48 50N 79 30W
20 La Réole, France 44 35N 0 1W
124 La Rioja, Argentina 29 20s 67 0W
32 La 'rioja, Spain 42 20N 2 20W
124 La Rioja ♦, Arg. 29 30s 67 0W
30 La Robla, Spain 42 50N 5 41W
21 La Roche, France 46 4N 6 19E
18 La Roche Bernard, Fr. 47 32N 2 18W
20 La Roche-Canillac, Fr. 45 12N 1 57E
18 La Roche-sur-Yon, Fr. 46 40N 1 25W
20 La Rochefoucauld, Fr. 45 44N 0 24E
20 La Rochelle, France 46 10N 1 9W
33 La Roda, Spain 39 13N 2 15W
121 La Romana, Dom. Rep. 18 27N 68 57W
109 La Ronge, Canada 55 5N 105 20W
109 La Ronge L., Canada 55 10N 105 0W
33 La Sagra, Mt., Spain 38 0N 2 35W
126 La Salina, Venezuela 10 22N 71 27W
116 La Salle, U.S.A. 41 20N 89 5W
30 La Sanabria, Spain 42 0N 6 30W
106 La Sarre, Canada 48 45N 79 15W
107 La Scie, Canada 49 58N 55 36W
32 La Selva, Spain 42 0N 2 45E
124 La Serena, Chile 29 55s 71 10W
31 La Serena, Spain 38 45N 5 40W

* Renamed Ri-Aba

La Seyne-sur-Mer INDEX Laut, Kepulauan

MAP
21 La Seyne-sur-Mer, Fr. 43 7N 5 52E
41 La Sila, Mts., Italy 39 15N 16 35E
83 La Skhirra = Cekhira, Tunisia 34 20N 10 5E
33 La Solana, Spain 38 59N 3 14W
20 La Souterraine, France 46 15N 1 30E
38 La Spèzia, Italy 44 8N 9 50E
18 La Suze, France 47 54N 0 2E
126 La Tagua, Colombia 0 3N 74 40W
20 La Teste, France 44 34N 1 9W
21 La Tour-du-Pin, France 45 34N 5 27E
20 La Tranche, France 46 20N 1 26W
20 La Tremblade, France 45 46N 1 8W
106 La Tuque, Canada 47 30N 72 50W
128 La Unión, Chile 40 10S 73 0W
126 La Unión, Colombia 1 35N 77 5W
120 La Unión, Salvador 13 20N 87 50W
33 La Unión, Spain 37 38N 0 53W
126 La Unión, Venezuela 7 28N 67 53W
126 La Urbana, Venezuela 7 8N 66 56W
124 La Valdivia, Chile 34 43S 72 5W
30 La Vecilla, Spain 42 51N 5 27W
121 La Vega, Dom. Rep. 19 20N 70 30W
126 La Venturosa, Col. 6 8N 68 48W
126 La Victoria, Venezuela 10 14N 67 20W
21 La Voulte, France 44 49N 4 48E
31 La Zarza, Spain 37 42N 6 51W
27 Laa, Austria 48 43N 16 23E
24 Laage, Germany 53 55N 12 21E
100 Laanecoorie Res., Australia 36 52S 143 50E
24 Laasphe, Germany 50 56N 8 23E
57 Laba, R., U.S.S.R. 45 0N 40 30E
73 Labala, Indonesia 8 35S 123 32E
20 Labastide, France 43 28N 2 39E
20 Labastide-Murat, Fr. 44 39N 1 33E
85 Labbézenga, Mali 15 2N 0 48E
83 Labdah = Leptis Magna, Libya 32 40N 14 12E
84 Labé, Guinea 11 24N 12 16W
26 Labe, R., Czechoslovakia 50 3N 15 20E
27 Laberec, R., Cz. 21 57N 49 7E
108 Laberge, L., Canada 61 15N 135 0W
39 Labin, Yugoslavia 45 5N 14 8E
57 Labinsk, U.S.S.R. 44 40N 40 48W
71 Labis, Malaysia 2 22N 103 2E
28 Labiszyn, Poland 52 57N 17 54E
73 Laboa, Indonesia 8 6S 122 50E
24 Laboe, Germany 54 25N 10 13E
20 Labouheyre, France 44 13N 0 55W
124 Laboulaye, Argentina 34 10S 63 30W
105 Labrador, Canada 53 20N 61 0W
107 Labrador City, Canada 52 42N 67 0W
126 Labranzagrande, Col. 5 33N 72 34W
126 Lábrea, Brazil 7 15S 64 51W
20 Labrède, France 44 41N 0 32W
72 Labuan, I., Malaysia 5 15N 115 38W
73 Labuha, Indonesia 0 30S 127 30E
73 Labuhan, Indonesia 6 26S 105 50E
73 Labuhanbadjo, Indon. 8 28S 120 1E
72 Labuk, Telok, Malaysia 6 10N 117 50E
52 Labytnangi, U.S.S.R. 66 29N 66 40E
107 Lac Bouchette, Canada 48 16N 72 11W
116 Lac du Flambeau, U.S.A. 46 1N 89 51W
107 Lac Edouard, Canada 47 40N 72 16W
108 Lac la Biche, Canada 54 45N 111 50W
109 Lac Seul, Canada 50 28N 92 0W
20 Lacanau, Etang de, Fr. 44 58N 1 7W
20 Lacanau Médoc, France 44 59N 1 5W
31 Lacara, R., Spain 39 7N 6 25W
20 Lacauna, Mts. de, Fr. 43 43N 2 50E
20 Lacaune, France 43 43N 2 40E
60 Laccadive Is., Ind. Oc. 10 0N 72 30E
96 Lacepede Is., W. Austral. 16 55S 122 0E
91 Lacerdónia, Mozam. 18 3S 35 35E
106 Lachine, Canada 45 30N 73 40W
100 Lachlan, R., Australia 34 0S 144 45E
68 Lachmangarh, India 27 50N 75 4E
106 Lachute, Canada 45 39N 74 21E
112 Lackawanna, U.S.A. 42 49N 78 50W
113 Lacolle, Canada 45 6N 73 24W
108 Lacombe, Canada 52 30N 113 50W
113 Lacona, U.S.A. 43 37N 76 5W
40 Laconi, Italy 39 54N 9 4E
113 Laconia, U.S.A. 43 32N 71 30W
20 Lacq, France 43 25N 0 35W
118 Lacrosse, U.S.A. 46 51N 117 58W
66 Ladakh Ra., Kashmir 34 0N 78 0E
28 Ladek Zdrój, Poland 50 21N 16 51E
45 Ladhon, R., Greece 37 40N 21 50E
56 Lâdik, Turkey 40 57N 35 58E
92 Ladismith, S. Africa 33 28S 21 15E
65 Lādiz, Iran 28 55N 61 15E
68 Ladnun, India 27 38N 74 25E
52 Ladoga, L. = Ladozhskoye Oz., U.S.S.R. 61 15N 30 30E
19 Ladon, France 48 0N 2 30E
91 Lady Babbie, Rhodesia 18 30S 29 20E
106 Lady Beatrix L., Can. 5 20N 76 50W
92 Lady Grey, S. Africa 30 43S 27 13E
92 Ladybrand, S. Africa 29 9S 27 29E
108 Ladysmith, Canada 49 0N 124 0W
93 Ladysmith, S. Afr. 28 32S 29 46E
116 Ladysmith, U.S.A. 45 27N 91 4W
98 Lae, Terr. of N. Guin. 6 48S 146 53E
49 Laesö, Denmark 57 15N 10 53E
49 Laesö Rende, Den. 57 15N 10 50E
116 Lafayette, Colo., U.S.A. 40 0N 105 2W
115 Lafayette, Ga., U.S.A. 34 44N 85 15W
117 Lafayette, La., U.S.A. 30 18N 92 0W
115 Lafayette, Tenn., U.S.A. 36 35N 86 0W
106 Laferte, Canada 48 37N 78 48W
85 Lafia, Nigeria 8 30N 8 34E
85 Lafiagi, Nigeria 8 52N 5 20E
20 Laflèche, Canada 49 45N 106 40W
87 Lafon, Sudan 5 5N 32 29E
106 Laforest, Canada 47 4N 81 12W
48 Laforsen, Sweden 61 56N 15 3E

MAP
49 Lagan, Sweden 56 32N 12 58E
15 Lagan, R., N. Ire. 54 35N 5 55W
50 Lagarfljót, Iceland 65 40N 14 18W
125 Lagarto, Serra do, Brazil 23 0S 57 15W
24 Lage, Germany 52 0N 8 47E
30 Lage, Spain 43 13N 9 0W
47 Lågen, Norway 61 29N 10 2E
24 Lägerdorf, Germany 53 53N 9 35E
82 Laghouat, Algeria 33 50N 2 59E
57 Lagich, U.S.S.R. 40 50N 48 20E
21 Lagnieu, France 45 55N 5 20E
19 Lagny, France 48 52N 2 40E
41 Lago, Italy 39 9N 16 8E
31 Lagôa, Portugal 37 8N 8 27W
30 Lagoaça, Portugal 41 11N 6 44W
57 Lagodekhi, U.S.S.R. 41 50N 46 22E
41 Lagónegro, Italy 40 8N 15 45E
73 Lagonoy Gulf, Phil. 13 50N 123 50E
85 Lagos, Nigeria 6 25N 3 27E
31 Lagos, Portugal 37 5N 8 41W
120 Lagos de Moreno, Mex. 21 21N 101 55W
32 Laguardia, Spain 42 33N 2 35W
20 Laguépie, France 44 8N 1 57E
125 Laguna, Brazil 28 30S 48 50W
119 Laguna, U.S.A. 35 3N 107 28W
30 Laguna Antela, Spain 47 7N 7 40W
119 Laguna Beach, U.S.A. 33 31N 117 52W
119 Laguna Dam, U.S.A. 32 55N 114 30W
31 Laguna dela Janda, Spain 36 15N 5 45W
124 Laguna Limpia, Arg. 26 32S 59 45W
72 Laguna Madre, U.S.A. 27 0N 97 20W
124 Laguna Olmos, Arg. 33 25S 63 19W
39 Laguna Veneta, Italy 45 23N 12 25E
124 Lagunas, Chile 21 0S 69 45W
126 Lagunas, Peru 5 10S 75 35W
126 Lagunillas, Venzuela 10 8N 71 16W
76 Laha, China 48 9N 124 30E
73 Lahad Datu, Malaysia 5 0N 118 30E
69 Laharpur, India 27 43N 80 56E
72 Lahat, Indonesia 3 45S 103 30E
72 Lahewa, Indonesia 1 22N 97 12E
65 Lahijan, Iran 37 10N 50 6E
24 Lahn, R., Germany 50 52N 8 35E
49 Laholm, Sweden 56 30N 13 2E
49 Laholmsbukten, Sweden 56 30N 12 45E
118 Lahontan Res., U.S.A. 39 28N 118 58W
68 Lahore, Pakistan 31 32N 74 22E
68 Lahore ♦, Pakistan 31 55N 74 5E
25 Lahr, Germany 48 20N 7 52E
51 Lahti, Finland 60 58N 25 40E
81 Lai (Béhagle), Chad 9 25N 16 30E
71 Lai Chau, N. Vietnam 22 5N 103 3E
76 Laichow Wan, China 37 30N 119 30E
99 Laidley, Australia 27 39S 152 20E
77 Laifeng, China 29 30N 109 30E
18 Laigle, France 48 46N 0 38E
19 Laignes, France 47 50N 4 20E
20 L'Aiguillon, France 46 20N 1 16W
90 Laikipia ♦, Kenya 0 30N 36 30E
64 Laila, Saudi Arabia 22 10N 46 40E
126 Laillahue, Mt., Peru 17 0S 69 30W
92 Laingsburg, S. Africa 33 9S 20 52E
77 Laipin, China 23 45N 109 10E
14 Lairg, Scotland 58 1N 4 24W
72 Lais, Indonesia 3 35S 102 0E
76 Laiyang, China 37 0N 120 42E
125 Lajes, Sta. Catarina, Brazil 27 48S 50 20W
42 Lajkovac, Yugoslavia 44 27N 20 14E
27 Lajosmizse, Hungary 47 3N 19 32E
69 Laka Chih, Tibet 30 40N 81 10E
68 Lakaband, Pakistan 31 2N 69 15E
73 Lakar, Indonesia 8 15S 128 17E
116 Lake Andes, U.S.A. 43 10N 98 32W
114 Lake Anse, U.S.A. 46 42N 88 25W
117 Lake Arthur, U.S.A. 30 8N 92 40W
100 Lake Boga, Australia 35 26S 143 38E
100 Lake Cargelligo, Australia 33 15S 146 22E
117 Lake Charles, U.S.A. 31 10N 93 10W
119 Lake City, Colo, U.S.A. 38 3N 107 27W
115 Lake City, Fla., U.S.A. 30 10N 82 40W
116 Lake City, Iowa, U.S.A. 42 12N 94 42W
114 Lake City, Mich., U.S.A. 44 20N 85 10W
116 Lake City, Minn., U.S.A. 44 28N 92 21W
112 Lake City, Pa., U.S.A. 42 2N 80 20W
115 Lake City, S.C., U.S.A. 33 51N 79 44W
113 Lake George, U.S.A. 43 25N 73 36W
105 Lake Harbour, Canada 62 30N 69 50W
119 Lake Havasu City, U.S.A. 34 25N 114 20W
108 Lake Louise, Canada 51 30N 116 10W
119 Lake Mead Nat. Rec. Area, U.S.A. 36 20N 114 30W
116 Lake Mills, U.S.A. 43 23N 93 33W
98 Lake Nash, Australia 20 57S 138 0E
111 Lake of the Woods, Can. 49 0N 95 0W
117 Lake Providence, U.S.A. 32 49N 91 12W
106 Lake River, Canada 54 30N 82 30W
106 Lake Superior Prov. Park, Can. 47 45N 85 0W
106 Lake Traverse, Canada 45 56N 78 4W
100 Lake Tyers, Australia 37 52S 148 5E
100 Lake Victoria Res., Australia 34 0S 141 17E
117 Lake Village, U.S.A. 33 20N 91 19W
115 Lake Wales, U.S.A. 27 55N 81 32W
115 Lake Worth, U.S.A. 26 36N 80 3W
106 Lakefield, Canada 44 25N 78 16W
115 Lakeland, U.S.A. 28 0N 82 0W
101 Lakemba, I., Fiji 18 13S 178 47W
100 Lakes Entrance, Australia 37 50S 148 0E
119 Lakeside, Ariz., U.S.A. 34 12N 109 59W
116 Lakeside, Nebr., U.S.A. 42 5N 102 24W
114 Lakeview, N.Y., U.S.A. 42 43N 78 57W
118 Lakeview, Oreg., U.S.A. 42 15N 120 22W

MAP
113 Lakewood, N.J., U.S.A. 40 5N 74 13W
112 Lakewood, Ohio, U.S.A. 41 28N 81 50W
45 Lakhaniá, Gr. 35 58N 27 54E
45 Lákhi, Greece 35 24N 23 27E
69 Lakhimpur, India 27 14N 94 7E
68 Lakhpat, India 23 48N 68 47E
117 Lakin, U.S.A. 37 58N 101 18W
66 Lakki, Pakistan 32 38N 70 50E
45 Lakonia ♦, Greece 36 55N 22 30E
45 Lakonikós Kólpos, Greece 36 40N 22 40E
73 Lakor, I., Indonesia 8 15S 128 17E
84 Lakota, Ivory Coast 5 50N 5 30W
116 Lakota, U.S.A. 48 0N 98 22W
50 Laksefjorden, Norway 70 45N 26 50E
50 Lakselv, Norway 70 2N 24 56E
50 Lakselvbukt, Norway 69 26N 19 40E
69 Lakshmi Kantapur, India 22 5N 88 20E
67 Lala Ghat, India 24 30N 92 40E
68 Lala Musa, Pakistan 32 40N 73 57E
90 Lalago, Tanzania 3 28S 33 58E
91 Lalapanzi, Rhodesia 19 20S 30 15E
100 Lalbert, Australia 35 38S 143 20E
69 Lalganj, India 25 52N 85 13E
87 Lalibala, Ethiopia 12 8N 39 10E
30 Lalin, Spain 42 40N 8 5W
20 Lalinde, France 44 50N 0 44E
†68 Lalitpur, India 24 42N 78 28E
67 Lalitapur, India 26 36N 85 32E
85 Lama Kara, Togo 9 30N 1 15E
67 Lamaing, Burma 15 25N 97 53E
116 Lamar, Colo., U.S.A. 38 9N 102 35W
117 Lamar, Mo., U.S.A. 37 30N 94 20W
126 Lamas, Peru 6 28S 76 31W
21 Lamastre, France 44 59N 4 35E
76 Lamatientze, China 46 46N 124 46E
26 Lambach, Austria 48 6N 13 51E
18 Lamballe, France 48 29N 2 31W
88 Lambaréné, Gabon 0 20S 10 12E
15 Lambay I., Ireland 53 30N 6 0W
126 Lambayeque ♦, Peru 6 45S 80 0W
116 Lambert, U.S.A. 47 44N 104 39W
4 Lambert Land, Green. 79 12N 20 30W
25 Lambesc, France 43 39N 5 16E
71 Lambi Kyun, (Sullivan I.), Burma 10 50N 98 20E
45 Lámbia, Greece 37 52N 21 53E
38 Lambro, R., Italy 45 18N 9 20E
85 Lame, Nigeria 10 27N 9 12E
118 Lame Deer, U.S.A. 45 45N 106 40W
30 Lamego, Portugal 41 5N 7 52W
107 Lameque, Canada 47 45N 64 38W
99 Lameroo, Australia 35 19S 140 33E
117 Lamesa, U.S.A. 32 45N 101 57W
49 Lamhult, Sweden 57 12N 14 36E
45 Lamia, Greece 38 55N 22 41E
73 Lamitan, Philippines 6 40N 122 10E
14 Lammermuir Hills, Scotland 55 50N 24 0W
118 Lamoille, U.S.A. 40 47N 115 31W
73 Lamon Bay, Phil. 14 30N 122 20E
108 Lamont, Canada 53 40N 112 50W
126 Lampa, Peru 15 10S 70 30W
71 Lampang, Thailand 18 40N 98 53E
117 Lampasas, U.S.A. 31 5N 98 10W
18 Lampaul, France 48 28N 5 7W
120 Lampazos de Naranjo, Mexico 27 2N 100 32W
36 Lampedusa, I., Medit. 35 36N 12 40E
13 Lampeter, U.K. 52 6N 4 6W
83 Lampione, I., Medit. 35 33N 12 20E
109 Lampman, Canada 49 25N 102 50W
26 Lamprechtshausen, Austria 48 0N 12 58E
72 Lampung, Indonesia 1 48S 115 0E
90 Lamu, Kenya 2 10S 40 55E
119 Lamy, U.S.A. 35 30N 105 58W
61 Lan Tsan Kiang (Mekong), Asia 18 0N 104 15E
66 Lanak La, Kashmir 34 27N 79 32E
73 Lanao, L., Philippines 7 52N 124 15E
113 Lanark, Canada 44 59N 76 21W
14 Lanark, Scot. 55 40N 3 48W
*14 Lanark ♦, Scot. 55 37N 3 50W
14 Lancashire ♦, Eng. 53 40N 2 30W
107 Lancaster, N.B., Can. 45 17N 66 10W
113 Lancaster, Ont., Can. 45 10N 74 30W
12 Lancaster, Eng. 54 3N 2 48W
119 Lancaster, Calif., U.S.A. 34 47N 118 8W
114 Lancaster, Ky., U.S.A. 37 40N 84 40W
113 Lancaster, N.H., U.S.A. 44 27N 71 33W
112 Lancaster, N.Y., U.S.A. 42 53N 78 43W
113 Lancaster, Pa., U.S.A. 40 4N 76 19W
115 Lancaster, S.C., U.S.A. 34 45N 80 47W
116 Lancaster, Wis., U.S.A. 42 48N 90 43W
4 Lancaster Sd., Canada 74 0N 84 0W
100 Lancefield, Australia 37 18S 144 45E
76 Lanchow, China 36 4N 103 44E
39 Lanciano, Italy 42 15N 14 22E
27 Łancut, Poland 50 10N 22 20E
88 Landana, Angola 5 11S 12 5E
25 Landau, Germany 49 12N 8 7E
26 Landeck, Austria 47 9N 10 34E
118 Lander, U.S.A. 42 50N 108 49W
18 Landerneau, France 48 28N 4 17W
49 Landeryd, Sweden 57 7N 13 15E
20 Landes ♦, France 43 57N 0 48W
32 Landete, Spain 39 56N 1 25W
66 Landi Kotal, Pakistan 34 7N 71 6E
18 Landivisiau, France 48 31N 4 6W
25 Landquart, Switzerland 46 58N 9 32E
19 Landrecies, France 50 7N 3 40E
4 Land's End, Canada 76 10N 123 0W
13 Land's End, Eng. 50 4N 5 43W
25 Landsberg, Germany 48 3N 10 52E
49 Landsbro, Sweden 57 24N 14 56E
24 Landshut, W. Ger. 48 31N 12 10E
49 Landskrona, Sweden 56 53N 12 50E
49 Landvetter, Sweden 57 41N 12 17E
49 Lane, Sweden 58 25N 12 3E

MAP
113 Lanesboro, U.S.A. 41 57N 75 34W
115 Lanett, U.S.A. 33 0N 85 15W
72 Lang Suan, Thailand 9 57N 99 4E
49 Langaa, Den. 56 23N 9 51E
44 Langadhás, Greece 40 46N 23 2E
45 Langádhia, Greece 37 43N 22 1E
48 Langan, Sweden 63 20N 14 30E
69 Langchen Khambah (Sutlej), Tibet 31 25N 80 0E
77 Langchung (Paoning), China 31 30N 106 0E
116 Langdon, U.S.A. 48 47N 98 24W
20 Langeac, France 45 7N 3 29E
86 Langeb, R., Sudan 17 28N 36 50E
92 Langeberge, C. Province, S. Africa 33 55S 21 20E
92 Langeberge, C. Province, S. Africa 28 15S 22 33E
49 Langeland, Denmark 54 56N 10 48E
49 Langelands Baelt, Den. 54 55N 10 56E
25 Langen, Germany 53 36N 8 36E
24 Langeness, Germany 54 34N 8 35E
26 Langenlois, Austria 48 29N 15 40E
24 Langensalza, Germany 51 6N 10 40E
24 Langeoog, Germany 53 44N 7 33E
49 Langeskov, Denmark 55 22N 10 35E
47 Langesund, Norway 59 0N 9 45E
76 Langfeng, China 48 4N 121 10E
49 Langhem, Sweden 57 36N 13 14E
38 Langhirano, Italy 44 39N 10 16E
14 Langholm, Scot. 55 9N 2 59W
50 Langjökull, Iceland 64 39N 20 12W
71 Langkawi I., Malaysia 6 20N 99 45E
72 Langkon, Malaysia 6 30N 116 40E
106 Langlade, Canada 48 14N 76 10W
118 Langlois, U.S.A. 42 54N 124 26W
25 Langnau, Switzerland 46 56N 7 47E
*90 Lango ♦, Ugan. 1 57N 32 40E
20 Langogne, France 44 43N 3 50E
20 Langon, France 44 33N 0 16W
50 Langöya, Norway 68 45N 15 10E
19 Langres, France 47 52N 5 20E
19 Langres, Plateau de, Fr. 47 45N 5 20E
72 Langsa, Indonesia 4 30N 97 57E
48 Langsele, Sweden 63 11N 17 5E
48 Långshyttan, Sweden 60 27N 16 2E
71 Langson, N. Vietnam 21 52N 106 42E
117 Langtry, U.S.A. 29 50N 101 33W
20 Languedoc ♦, Fr. 43 58N 3 22E
50 Langöya, Norway 68 44N 14 45E
48 Lanna, Sweden 59 16N 14 56E
20 Lannemezan, France 43 8N 0 23E
98 Lannercost, Australia 18 35S 146 0E
18 Lannilis, France 48 35N 4 32W
18 Lannion, France 48 46N 3 29W
117 L'Annonciation, Can. 46 25N 74 55W
113 Lansdale, U.S.A. 40 14N 75 18W
100 Lansdowne, Australia 31 48S 152 30E
113 Lansdowne, Canada 44 25N 76 1W
106 Lansdowne House, Can. 52 5N 88 0W
107 L'Anse au Loup, Canada 51 32N 56 50W
113 Lansford, U.S.A. 40 48N 75 55W
114 Lansing, U.S.A. 42 47N 84 32W
21 Lanslebourg-Mont-Cenis, Fr. 45 17N 6 52E
67 Lantsien, China 32 4N 96 6E
73 Lantuna, Indonesia 8 19S 124 8E
124 Lanus, Argentina 34 44S 58 27W
40 Lanusei, Italy 39 53N 9 31E
80 Lanzarote, I., Islas Canarias 29 0N 13 40W
38 Lanzo Torinese, Italy 45 16N 7 29E
41 Lao, R., Italy 39 45N 15 45E
73 Laoag, Philippines 18 7N 120 34E
73 Laoang, Philippines 12 32N 125 8E
99 Laoha Ho, R., China 43 24N 120 39E
15 Laois ♦, Ireland 53 0N 7 20W
19 Laon, France 49 33N 3 35E
114 Laona, U.S.A. 45 32N 88 41W
71 Laos ■, Asia 17 45N 105 0E
125 Lapa, Brazil 25 46S 49 44W
20 Lapalisse, France 46 15N 3 44E
73 Laparan Cap, I., Phil. 6 0N 120 0E
114 Lapeer, U.S.A. 43 3N 83 20W
50 Lapland = Lappland, Eur. 68 7N 24 0E
113 Laporte, U.S.A. 41 27N 76 30W
42 Lapovo, Yugoslavia 44 10N 21 2E
50 Lappland, Europe 68 7N 24 0E
113 Laprairie, Canada 45 25N 73 30W
124 Laprida, Argentina 37 34S 60 45W
59 Laptev Sea, U.S.S.R. 76 0N 125 0E
118 Lapush, U.S.A. 47 56N 124 33W
46 Lăpusu, R., Rumania 47 25N 23 40E
39 L'Aquila, Italy 42 21N 13 24E
82 L'Arba, Algeria 36 40N 3 9E
65 Lar, Iran 27 40N 54 14E
126 Lara ♦, Venezuela 10 10N 69 50W
84 Larabanga, Ghana 9 16N 1 56W
30 Laracha, Spain 43 15N 8 35W
82 Larache, Morocco 35 10N 6 5W
21 Laragne-Montéglin, France 44 18N 5 49E
116 Laramie, U.S.A. 41 15N 105 29W
116 Laramie Mts., U.S.A. 42 0N 105 30W
125 Laranjeiras do Sul, Braz. 25 23S 52 23W
73 Larantuka, Indonesia 8 5S 122 55E
73 Larap, Philippines 14 18N 122 39E
73 Larat, I., Tanimbar, Is., Indonesia 7 0S 132 0E
21 L'Arbresle, France 45 50N 4 26E
49 Lärbro, Sweden 57 47N 18 50E
105 Larch, R., Canada 57 30N 71 0W
47 Lärdal, Norway 59 20N 8 25E
91 Larde, Mozambique 16 28S 39 43E
106 Larder Lake, Canada 48 5N 79 40W
45 Lárdhos, Akra, Greece 36 4N 28 10E
32 Laredo, Spain 43 26N 3 28W
117 Laredo, U.S.A. 27 34N 99 29W
81 Largeau (Faya), Chad 17 58N 19 6E

MAP
21 Largentière, France 44 34N 4 18E
14 Largs, Scotland 55 48N 4 51W
38 Lari, Italy 43 34N 10 35E
73 Lariang, Indonesia 1 35S 119 25E
116 Larimore, U.S.A. 47 55N 97 35W
41 Larino, Italy 41 48N 14 54E
44 Lárisa, Greece 39 38N 22 28E
44 Lárisa ♦, Greece 39 39N 22 24E
68 Larkana, Pakistan 27 32N 68 2E
47 Larkollen, Norway 59 20N 10 41E
64 Lárnax, Cyprus 35 0N 33 35E
15 Larne, N. Ireland 54 52N 5 50W
116 Larned, U.S.A. 38 15N 99 10W
20 Laroquebrou, France 44 58N 2 12E
96 Larrimah, Australia 15 35S 133 12E
5 Larsen Ice Shelf, Antarc. 67 0S 62 0W
85 Larteh, Ghana 5 50N 0 5W
90 Laru, Zaïre 2 54N 24 25E
47 Larvik, Norway 59 4N 10 0E
58 Laryak, U.S.S.R. 61 15N 80 0E
20 Larzac, Causse du, France 44 0N 3 17E
117 Las Animas, U.S.A. 38 8N 103 18W
63 Las Anod, Somali Rep. 8 26N 47 19E
33 Las Blancos, Spain 37 38N 0 49W
126 Las Bonitas, Venezuela 7 50N 65 40W
124 Las Brenãs, Arg. 27 5S 61 7W
31 Las Cabezas de San Juan, Spain 37 0N 5 58W
120 Las Cascadas, Panama Canal Zone 9 5N 79 41W
119 Las Cruces, U.S.A. 32 25N 106 50W
120 Las Delicias, Panama 9 27N 79 35W
124 Las Flores, Argentina 36 0S 59 0W
33 Las Huertas, Cabo de, Spain 38 22N 0 24W
63 Las Khoreh, Somali Rep. 11 4N 48 20E
128 Las Lajas, Argentina 38 30S 70 25W
126 Las Lajitas, Venezuela 6 55N 65 39W
124 Las Lomitas, Arg. 24 35S 60 50W
31 Las Marismas, Spain 37 5N 6 20W
126 Las Mercedes, Venezuela 9 7N 66 24W
31 Las Navas de la Concepción, Spain 37 56N 5 30W
31 Las Navas de Tolosa, Spain 38 18N 3 38W
124 Las Palmas, Argentina 27 8S 58 45W
80 Las Palmas, Can. Is. 28 10N 15 28W
80 Las Palmas ♦, Spain 28 10N 15 28W
128 Las Plumas, Argentina 43 40S 67 15W
124 Las Rosas, Argentina 32 30S 61 40W
121 Las Tablas, Panama 7 49N 80 14W
120 Las Tres Marías, Is., Mexico 20 12N 106 30W
124 Las Varillas, Argentina 32 0S 62 50W
119 Las Vegas, Nev., U.S.A. 36 10N 115 5W
119 Las Vegas, N.M., U.S.A. 35 35N 105 10W
125 Lascano, Uruguay 33 35S 54 18W
20 Lascaux, France 45 5N 1 10E
109 Lashburn, Canada 53 10N 109 40W
67 Lashio, Burma 23 0N 98 0E
68 Lashkar, India 26 10N 78 10E
28 Łasin, Poland 53 30N 19 2E
45 Lasithi ♦, Greece 35 5N 25 50E
28 Lask, Poland 51 34N 19 8E
39 Laško, Yugoslavia 46 10N 15 16E
18 Lassay, France 48 27N 0 30W
118 Lassen, Pk., U.S.A. 40 20N 121 0W
88 Lastoursville, Gabon 0 55S 12 38E
39 Lastovo, I., Y.-slavia 42 46N 16 55E
39 Lastovo, I., Y.-slav. 42 46N 16 55E
39 Lastovski Kanal, Y.-slav. 42 50N 17 0E
126 Latacunga, Ecuador 0 50S 78 35W
64 Latakia = Al Ladhiqiya, Syria 35 30N 35 45E
106 Latchford, Canada 47 20N 79 50W
41 Laterza, Italy 40 38N 16 47E
24 Lathen, Germany 52 51N 7 21E
41 Latiano, Italy 40 33N 17 43E
40 Latina, Italy 41 26N 12 53E
76 Lating, China 39 23N 118 55E
39 Latisana, Italy 45 47N 13 1E
39 Latium = Lazio, Italy 42 0N 12 30E
27 Latorica, R., Cz. 48 31N 22 0E
99 Latrobe, Tas., Austral. 41 14S 146 30E
100 Latrobe, Vic., Australia 38 8S 146 44E
112 Latrobe, U.S.A. 40 19N 79 21W
99 Latrobe, Mt., Australia 39 0S 146 23E
41 Latrónico, Italy 40 5N 16 0E
62 Latrun, Jordan 31 50N 34 58E
70 Latur, India 18 25N 76 40E
101 Lau (Eastern) Group, Fiji Is. 17 0S 178 30W
24 Lauchhammer, Germany 51 35N 13 40E
47 Laudal, Norway 58 15N 7 30E
24 Lauenburg, Germany 53 23N 10 33E
50 Laugarbakki, Iceland 65 20N 20 55W
33 Laujar, Spain 37 0N 2 54W
99 Launceston, Australia 41 24S 147 8E
13 Launceston, Eng. 50 38N 4 21W
15 Laune, R., Ireland 52 5N 9 40W
71 Launglon Bok, Burma 13 50N 97 54E
25 Laupheim, Germany 48 13N 9 53E
98 Laura, Australia 15 32S 144 32E
41 Laureana di Borrello, It. 38 28N 16 5E
117 Laurel, Miss., U.S.A. 31 50N 89 0W
118 Laurel, Mont., U.S.A. 45 46N 108 49W
14 Laurencekirk, Scot. 56 50N 2 30W
115 Laurens, U.S.A. 34 32N 82 2W
107 Laurentian Plat., Can. 51 30N 65 0W
41 Lauria, Italy 40 3N 15 50E
5 Laurie I., Antarctica 60 0S 46 0W
109 Laurie L., Canada 56 35N 101 50W
115 Laurinburg, U.S.A. 34 50N 79 25W
114 Laurium, U.S.A. 47 31N 88 36W
25 Lausanne, Switzerland 46 32N 6 38E
72 Laut, I., Indonesia 3 40S 116 10E
72 Laut, Kepulauan, Indonesia 4 45N 108 0E

* *Incorporated within the region of Strathclyde*
† *Renamed Patan*

* *Incorporated within the new Northern Province*

Laut Ketjil, Kepulauan INDEX Limbourg

MAP
72 Laut Ketjil, Kepulauan, Indonesia 4 45S 115 40E
24 Lauterbach, Germany 50 39N 9 23E
25 Lauterecken, Germany 49 38N 7 35E
101 Lautoka, Fiji Is. 17 37S 177 27E
107 Lauzon, Canada 46 48N 71 4W
118 Lava Hot Springs, U.S.A. 42 38N 112 1W
30 Lavadores, Spain 42 14N 8 41W
38 Lavagna, Italy 44 18N 9 22E
18 Laval, France 48 4N 0 48W
124 Lavalle, Argentina 32 45S 68 30W
44 Lâvara, Greece 41 19N 26 22E
20 Lavardac, France 44 12N 0 20E
20 Lavaur, France 43 42N 1 49E
20 Lavaveix, France 46 5N 2 8E
20 Lavelanet, France 42 57N 1 51E
41 Lavello, Italy 41 4N 15 47E
106 Laverendrye Prov. Park, Canada 46 15N 17 15W
117 Laverne, U.S.A. 36 43N 99 58W
96 Laverton, Australia 28 44S 122 29E
62 Lavi, Israel 32 47N 35 25E
47 Lavik, Norway 61 6N 5 25E
45 Lávkos, Greece 39 9N 23 14E
30 Lavos, Portugal 40 6N 8 49W
31 Lavre, Portugal 38 46N 8 22W
59 Lavrentiya, U.S.S.R. 65 35N 171 0W
45 Lávrion, Greece 37 40N 24 4E
93 Lavumisa, Swaziland 27 20S 31 55E
72 Lawas, Malaysia 4 55N 115 40E
73 Lawele, Indonesia 5 16S 123 3E
98 Lawn Hill, Australia 18 36S 138 33E
67 Lawng Pit, Burma 26 45N 98 35E
84 Lawra, Ghana 10 39N 2 51W
101 Lawrence, New Zealand 45 55S 169 41E
116 Lawrence, Kans., U.S.A. 39 0N 95 10W
113 Lawrence, Mass., U.S.A. 42 40N 71 9W
114 Lawrenceburg, Indiana, U.S.A. 39 5N 84 50W
115 Lawrenceburg, Tenn., U.S.A. 35 12N 87 19W
115 Lawrenceville, U.S.A. 33 55N 83 59W
117 Lawton, U.S.A. 34 33N 98 25W
73 Lawu Mt., Indonesia 7 40S 111 13E
48 Laxa, Sweden 59 0N 14 37E
14 Laxford, L., Scot. 58 25N 5 10W
70 Laxmeshwar, India 15 9N 75 28E
118 Laytonville, U.S.A. 39 44N 123 29W
42 Lazarevac, Yugoslavia 44 23N 20 17E
39 Lazio ♦, It. 42 0N 12 30E
28 Łazy, Poland 50 27N 19 24E
20 Le Bacarès, France 42 47N 3 3E
21 Le Beausset, France 43 10N 5 46E
20 Le Blanc, France 46 37N 1 3E
20 Le Bleymard, France 44 30N 3 42E
18 Le Bourgneuf, France 48 10N 0 59W
20 Le Bouscat, France 44 53N 0 32W
107 Le Bouthillier, Canada 47 47N 64 55W
20 Le Bugue, France 44 55N 0 56E
20 Le Canourgue, France 44 26N 3 13E
19 Le Cateau, France 50 6N 3 30E
21 Le Châmbon, France 45 35N 4 26E
21 Le Chambon-Feugerolles, France 45 24N 4 18E
20 Le Château, France 45 52N 1 12W
20 Le Châtelet, Cher, Fr. 46 40N 2 20E
19 Le Châtelet, Seine et Marne, France 48 30N 2 47E
19 Le Chesne, France 49 30N 4 45E
21 Le Cheylard, France 44 55N 4 25E
18 Le Conquet, France 48 21N 4 46W
19 Le Creusot, France 46 50N 4 24E
18 Le Croisic, France 47 18N 2 30W
20 Le Donjon, France 46 22N 3 48E
20 Le Dorat, France 46 14N 1 5E
121 Le François, Martinique 14 38N 60 57W
18 Le Grand Fougeray, Fr. 47 44N 1 43W
18 Le Grand Pressigny, Fr. 46 55N 0 48E
18 Le Havre, France 49 30N 0 5E
21 Le Lavandou, France 43 8N 6 22E
25 Le Léman, Switzerland 46 30N 6 30E
18 Le Lion d'Angers, Fr. 47 38N 0 42W
25 Le Locle, Switzerland 47 3N 6 44E
18 Le Louroux Béconnais, France 47 30N 0 55W
21 Le Luc, France 43 23N 6 21E
40 Le Madonie, Mts., Italy 37 50N 13 50E
18 Le Mans, France 48 0N 0 10E
91 Le Marinel, Congo 10 25S 25 17E
116 Le Mars, U.S.A. 43 0N 96 0W
107 Le Mayne, L., Canada 57 5N 68 30W
18 Le Merlerault, France 48 41N 0 16E
20 Le Monastier, France 44 57N 4 0E
21 Le Monêtier-les-Bains, France 44 58N 6 30E
20 Le Mont-Dore, France 45 35N 2 50E
121 Le Moule, Guadeloupe 16 20N 61 22W
21 Le Muy, France 43 28N 6 34E
18 Le Palais, France 47 21N 3 10W
20 Le Perthus, France 42 30N 2 53E
18 Le Petit-Quevilly, Fr. 49 26N 1 0E
20 Le Puy, France 45 3N 3 52E
117 Le Roy, U.S.A. 38 8N 95 35W
20 Le Rozier, France 44 13N 3 12E
116 Le Sueur, U.S.A. 44 25N 93 52W
20 Le Teich, France 44 38N 0 59W
21 Le Teil, France 44 34N 4 41E
18 Le Teilleul, France 48 31N 0 52W
19 Le Thillot, France 47 52N 6 55E
19 Le Touquet, France 50 30N 1 36E
18 Le Tréport, France 50 3N 1 20E
19 Le Valdahon, France 47 8N 6 20E
20 Le Verdon, France 45 32N 1 5W
20 Le Vigan, France 43 59N 3 24E
13 Lea, R., Eng. 51 40N 0 3W
116 Lead, U.S.A. 44 20N 103 40W
109 Leader, Canada 50 50N 109 30W
14 Leadhills, Scot. 55 25N 3 47W
100 Leadville, Australia 32 1N 149 38E

MAP
119 Leadville, U.S.A. 39 17N 106 23W
105 Leaf, R., Canada 58 15N 71 0W
117 Leaf, R., U.S.A. 31 45N 89 20W
117 Leakey, U.S.A. 29 45N 99 45W
115 Leaksville, U.S.A. 36 30N 79 49W
89 Lealui, Zambia 15 10S 23 2E
106 Leamington, Canada 42 10N 82 30W
94 Leamington, New Zealand 37 55S 175 29E
13 Leamington, Eng. 52 18N 1 32W
118 Leamington, U.S.A. 39 37N 112 17W
125 Leandro Norte Alem, Arg. 27 34S 55 15W
46 Leaoto, Mt., Rumania 45 20N 25 20E
96 Learmonth, Australia 22 40S 114 10E
109 Leask, Canada 53 5N 106 45W
116 Leavenworth, Mo., USA 39 25N 95 0W
118 Leavenworth, Wash., U.S.A. 47 44N 120 37W
28 Łeba, Poland 54 45N 17 32E
73 Lebak, Philippines 6 32N 124 5E
42 Lebane, Yugoslavia 42 56N 21 44E
64 Lebanon ■, Asia 34 0N 36 0E
114 Lebanon, Ind., U.S.A. 40 3N 86 55W
116 Lebanon, Kans., U.S.A. 39 50N 98 35W
114 Lebanon, Ky., U.S.A. 37 35N 85 15W
117 Lebanon, Mo., U.S.A. 37 40N 92 40W
113 Lebanon, N.H., U.S.A. 43 38N 72 15W
118 Lebanon, Oreg., U.S.A. 44 31N 122 57W
113 Lebanon, Pa., U.S.A. 40 20N 76 28W
115 Lebanon, Tenn., U.S.A. 36 15N 86 20W
119 Lebec, U.S.A. 34 36N 118 59W
54 Lebedin, U.S.S.R. 50 35N 34 30E
55 Lebedyan, U.S.S.R. 53 0N 39 10E
93 Lebomboberge, S. Afr. 24 30S 32 0E
28 Lebork, Poland 54 33N 17 46E
31 Lebrija, Spain 36 53N 6 5W
124 Lebu, Chile 37 40S 73 47W
41 Lecce, Italy 40 20N 18 10E
38 Lecco, Italy 45 50N 9 27E
38 Lecco, L. di., Italy 45 51N 9 22E
32 Lécera, Spain 41 13N 0 43W
26 Lech, Austria 47 13N 10 9E
26 Lech, R., Germany 47 19N 10 27E
26 Lechtaler Alpen, Aust. 47 15N 10 30E
20 Lectoure, France 43 56N 0 38E
28 Łęczyca, Poland 52 5N 19 45E
13 Ledbury, Eng. 52 3N 2 25W
26 Ledec, Czechoslovakia 49 41N 15 18E
30 Ledesma, Spain 41 6N 5 59W
108 Leduc, Canada 53 20N 113 30W
28 Ledyczek, Poland 53 33N 16 59E
113 Lee, Mass., U.S.A. 42 17N 73 18W
118 Lee, Nev., U.S.A. 40 35N 115 36W
15 Lee, R., Ireland 51 51N 9 2W
116 Leech L., U.S.A. 47 15N 94 23W
117 Leedey, U.S.A. 35 53N 99 24W
12 Leeds, Eng. 53 48N 1 34W
115 Leeds, U.S.A. 33 32N 86 30W
12 Leek, England 53 7N 2 2W
24 Leer, Germany 53 13N 7 29E
115 Leesburg, U.S.A. 28 47N 81 52W
117 Leesville, U.S.A. 31 12N 93 15W
100 Leeton, Australia 34 23S 146 23E
112 Leetonia, U.S.A. 40 53N 80 45W
16 Leeuwarden, Neth. 53 15N 5 48E
96 Leeuwin, C., Australia 34 20S 115 9E
121 Leeward Is., W. Indies 16 30N 63 30W
117 Lefors, U.S.A. 35 30N 100 50W
96 Lefroy, L., Australia 31 21S 121 40E
108 Legal, Canada 53 55N 113 45W
73 Legazpi, Philippines 13 10N 123 46E
38 Leghorn = Livorno, Italy 43 32N 10 18E
91 Legion, Rhodesia 21 25S 28 30E
28 Legionowo, Poland 52 25N 20 50E
39 Legnago, Italy 45 10N 11 19E
38 Legnano, Italy 45 35N 8 55E
28 Legnica, Poland 51 12N 16 10E
39 Legrad, Yugoslavia 46 17N 16 51E
99 Legume, Australia 28 20S 152 12E
66 Leh, India 34 15N 77 35E
118 Lehi, U.S.A. 40 20N 112 0W
113 Lehighton, U.S.A. 40 50N 75 44W
46 Lehliu, Rumania 44 29N 26 20E
24 Lehrte, Germany 52 22N 9 58E
92 Lehututu, Botswana 23 54S 21 55E
68 Leiah, Pakistan 30 58N 70 58E
26 Leibnitz, Austria 46 47N 15 34E
13 Leicester, Eng. 52 39N 1 9W
13 Leicester ♦, England 52 40N 1 10W
98 Leichhardt Ra., Austral. 20 46S 147 40E
98 Leichhardt, R., Australia 17 50S 139 49E
77 Leichow = Haihang, China 20 55N 110 3E
77 Leichow Pantao, China 20 30N 110 0E
16 Leiden, Netherlands 52 9N 4 30E
16 Leie, R., Belgium 51 2N 3 45E
100 Leigh, R., Australia 37 50S 144 0E
99 Leigh Creek, Australia 30 28S 138 24E
15 Leinster, Mt., Ireland 52 38N 6 47W
24 Leipzig, Germany 51 20N 12 23E
24 Leipzig ♦, E. Ger. 51 20N 12 30E
31 Leiria, Portugal 39 46N 8 53W
31 Leiria ♦, Portugal 39 46N 8 53W
77 Leishan, China 25 55N 108 15E
14 Leith, Scotland 55 59N 3 10W
13 Leith Hill, Eng. 51 10N 0 23W
27 Leitha, R., Aust.-Hung. 47 57N 17 5E
15 Leitrim, Ireland 54 0N 8 5W
15 Leitrim ♦, Ire. 54 8N 8 0W
77 Leiyang, China 26 27N 112 50E
32 Leiza, Spain 43 5N 1 55W
44 Lekáni, Greece 41 10N 24 35E
45 Lekhainá, Greece 37 57N 21 16E
35 Leknice, Poland 51 34N 14 45E
73 Leksula, Indonesia 3 46S 126 31E
117 Leland, U.S.A. 33 25N 90 52W
128 Leleque, Argentina 42 15S 71 0W
16 Lelystad, Netherlands 52 30N 5 25E

MAP
85 Lema, Nigeria 12 58N 4 13E
87 Lemagrut, bg., Ethiopia 3 9S 35 22E
25 Léman, Lac, Switzerland 46 26N 6 30E
90 Lemera, Zaïre 3 0S 28 55E
73 Lemery, Philippines 13 58N 120 56E
64 Lemesós, Cyprus 34 42N 33 1E
24 Lemgo, Germany 52 2N 8 52E
118 Lemhi Ra., U.S.A. 44 30N 113 30W
116 Lemmon, U.S.A. 45 59N 102 10W
119 Lemoore, U.S.A. 36 23N 119 54W
20 Lempdes, France 45 22N 3 17E
49 Lemvig, Denmark 56 33N 8 20E
59 Lena, R., U.S.S.R. 64 30N 127 0E
18 Lencloître, France 46 50N 0 20E
39 Lendinara, Italy 45 4N 11 37E
24 Lengerich, Germany 52 12N 7 50E
71 Lenggong, Malaysia 5 17N 100 57E
27 Lengyeltóti, Hungary 46 40N 17 40E
49 Lenhovda, Sweden 57 0N 15 16E
87 Lenia, Ethiopia 4 10N 37 25E
57 Lenin, U.S.S.R. 48 20N 40 56E
58 Leninabad, U.S.S.R. 40 10N 69 40E
57 Leninakan, U.S.S.R. 41 0N 42 50E
54 Leningrad, U.S.S.R. 59 55N 30 20E
58 Leninogorsk, U.S.S.R. 50 20N 83 30E
57 Leninsk, U.S.S.R. 56 38N 46 10E
58 Leninsk-Kuznetskiy, U.S.S.R. 55 10N 86 10E
55 Leninskaya, U.S.S.R. 56 7N 44 29E
55 Leninskoye, R.S.F.S.R., U.S.S.R. 58 23N 47 3E
59 Leninskoye, R.S.F.S.R., U.S.S.R. 47 56N 132 38E
25 Lenk, Switzerland 46 27N 7 28E
53 Lenkoran, U.S.S.R. 39 45N 48 50E
73 Lenmalu, Indonesia 1 58S 130 0E
113 Lennoxville, Canada 45 23N 71 53W
38 Leno, Italy 45 24N 10 14E
115 Lenoir, U.S.A. 35 55N 81 36W
115 Lenoir City, U.S.A. 35 40N 84 20W
116 Lenora, U.S.A. 39 39N 100 1W
113 Lenox, U.S.A. 42 20N 73 18W
19 Lens, France 50 26N 2 50E
59 Lensk (Mukhtuya), U.S.S.R. 60 48N 114 55E
56 Lenskoye, U.S.S.R. 45 3N 34 1E
41 Lentini, Italy 37 18N 15 0E
24 Lenzen, Germany 53 6N 11 26E
84 Léo, Upper Volta 11 3N 2 2W
26 Leoben, Austria 47 22N 15 5E
116 Leola, U.S.A. 45 47N 98 58W
13 Leominster, Eng. 52 15N 2 43W
116 Leon, U.S.A. 40 40N 93 40W
20 Léon, France 43 53N 1 18W
120 León, Mexico 21 7N 101 30W
121 León, Nicaragua 12 20N 86 51W
30 León, Spain 42 38N 5 34W
30 León ♦, Spain 42 40N 5 55W
30 León, Montañas de, Spain 42 30N 6 18W
96 Leonara, Australia 28 47S 121 15E
114 Leonardtown, U.S.A. 38 19N 76 39W
41 Leonforte, Italy 37 39N 14 22E
100 Leongatha, Australia 38 30S 145 58E
45 Leonidhion, Greece 37 9N 22 52E
*88 Léopold II, Lac, Zaïre 2 0S 18 0E
125 Leopoldina, Brazil 21 28S 42 40W
16 Leopoldsburg, Belgium 51 7N 5 13E
88 Léopoldville = Kinshasa, Zaïre 4 20S 15 15E
116 Leoti, U.S.A. 38 31N 101 19W
109 Leoville, Canada 53 39N 107 33W
92 Lépa, L. do, Angola 17 0S 19 0E
31 Lepe, Spain 37 15N 7 12W
54 Lepel, U.S.S.R. 54 50N 28 40E
59 Lepikha, U.S.S.R. 64 45N 125 55E
92 Lépo, L. do, Angola 17 0S 19 0E
38 Lepontine Alps, Italy 46 22N 8 27E
27 Lepsény, Hungary 47 0N 18 15E
83 Leptis Magna, Libya 32 40N 14 12E
32 Lequeitio, Spain 43 20N 2 32W
48 Lerbäck, Sweden 58 56N 15 2E
40 Lercara Friddi, It. 37 42N 13 36E
88 Léré, Chad 9 39N 14 13E
85 Leré, Nigeria 10 22N 8 31E
93 Leribe, Lesotho 28 51S 28 3E
38 Lérici, Italy 44 4N 9 48E
32 Lérida, Spain 41 37N 0 39E
32 Lérida ♦, Spain 42 6N 1 0E
30 Lerma, Spain 42 0N 3 47W
45 Léros, I., Greece 37 10N 26 50E
19 Lérouville, France 48 50N 5 30E
14 Lerwick, Scotland 60 10N 1 10W
46 Les, Rumania 46 58N 21 50E
21 Les Abrets, France 45 32N 5 35E
18 Les Andelys, France 49 15N 1 25E
21 Les Baux, France 43 45N 4 51E
121 Les Cayes, Haiti 18 15N 73 46W
21 Les Echelles, France 45 27N 5 45E
18 Les Essarts, France 46 47N 1 12W
107 Les Etroits, Canada 47 24N 68 54W
18 Les Herbiers, France 46 52N 1 0W
20 Les Landes, Fr. 44 20N 1 0W
18 Les Ponts-de Cé, France 47 25N 0 30W
20 Les Sables-D'Olonne, Fr. 46 30N 1 45W
21 Les Saintes Maries, Fr. 43 27N 4 25E
21 Les Vans, France 44 26N 4 9E
45 Lesbos, I. = Lésvos, Greece 39 0N 26 20E
39 Lésina, L. di, Italy 41 45N 15 25E
47 Lesja, Norway 62 7N 8 51E
47 Lesjaverk, Norway 62 12N 8 34E
27 Lesko, Poland 49 30N 22 23E
5 Leskov, I., Falkland Is. Dependencies 56 0S 28 0W
44 Leskovic, Albania 40 10N 20 34E
42 Leskovika, Y.-slavia 43 0N 21 58E
117 Leslie, U.S.A. 35 50N 92 35W
28 Lesna, Poland 51 0N 15 15E
18 Lesneven, France 48 35N 4 20W

MAP
42 Lesniča, Yugoslavia 44 39N 19 20E
*52 Lesnoi, U.S.S.R. 66 50N 34 20E
54 Lesnoye, U.S.S.R. 58 15N 35 31E
93 Lesotho ■, Africa 29 40S 28 0E
59 Lesozavodsk, U.S.S.R. 45 30N 133 20E
20 Lesparre-Médoc, France 45 18N 0 57W
18 Lessay, France 49 14N 1 30W
16 Lesse, R., Belgium 50 15N 4 54E
121 Lesser Antilles, W. Ind. 12 30N 61 0W
108 Lesser Slave L., Can. 55 30N 115 10W
16 Lessines, Belgium 50 42N 3 50E
109 Lestock, Canada 51 25N 104 0W
92 Lesuma, Botswana 17 58S 25 12E
45 Lésvos, I., Greece 39 0N 26 20E
28 Leszno, Poland 51 50N 16 30E
13 Letchworth, Eng. 51 58N 0 13W
46 Letea, Ostrov, Rum. 45 18N 29 20E
100 Lethbridge, Australia 37 58S 144 6E
108 Lethbridge, Canada 49 45N 112 45W
73 Leti, Indonesia 8 10S 127 40E
73 Leti, Kepulauan, Indonesia 8 10S 128 0E
92 Letiahau, R., Botswana 21 40S 23 30E
126 Leticia, Colombia 4 0S 70 0W
92 Lethlhakeng, Botswana 24 0S 24 59E
67 Letpadan, Burma 17 45N 96 0E
67 Letpan, Burma 19 28N 93 52E
71 Letsôk-aw-Kyun (Domel I.), Burma 11 30N 98 25E
100 Lette, Austral. 34 3S 143 4E
15 Letterkenny, Ireland 54 57N 7 42W
46 Leu, Rumania 44 10N 24 0E
20 Leucate, France 42 56N 3 3E
25 Leuk, Switzerland 46 19N 7 37E
72 Leuser, G., Indonesia 4 0N 96 51E
25 Leutkirch, Germany 47 49N 10 1E
16 Leuven (Louvain), Belg. 50 52N 4 42E
16 Leuze, Hainaut, Belg. 50 36N 3 37E
16 Leuze, Namur, Belg. 50 33N 4 54E
55 Lev Tolstoy, U.S.S.R. 53 13N 39 29E
45 Levádhia, Greece 38 27N 22 54E
118 Levan, U.S.A. 39 37N 111 32W
44 Levan-Samari, Albania 40 40N 19 28E
50 Levanger, Norway 63 45N 11 19E
43 Levani, Bulgaria 43 8N 24 42E
38 Lévanto, Italy 44 10N 9 37E
40 Levanzo, I., Italy 38 0N 12 19E
117 Levelland, U.S.A. 33 38N 102 17W
14 Leven, Scotland 56 12N 3 0W
93 Leven, Banc du, Malag. 12 30S 47 45E
14 Leven, L., Scot. 56 12N 3 22W
21 Levens, France 43 50N 7 12E
96 Leveque C., Australia 16 20S 123 0E
40 Leverano, Italy 40 16N 18 0E
24 Leverkusen, Germany 51 2N 6 59E
19 Levet, France 46 56N 2 22E
27 Levice, Czechoslovakia 48 13N 18 35E
5 Levick, Mt., Antarctica 75 0S 164 0E
39 Levico, Italy 46 0N 11 18E
19 Levier, France 46 58N 6 8E
101 Levin, New Zealand 40 37S 175 18E
107 Levis, Canada 46 48N 71 9W
45 Levitha, I., Greece 37 0N 26 28E
113 Levittown, U.S.A. 40 10N 74 51W
43 Levka, Bulgaria 41 52N 26 15E
45 Lévka, Mt., Gr. 35 18N 24 3E
45 Levkás, Greece 38 48N 20 43E
45 Levkás, I., Greece 38 40N 20 43E
44 Levkimmi, Greece 39 25N 20 3E
64 Levkôsia, Cyprus 35 10N 33 25E
27 Levoča, Czechoslovakia 48 59N 20 35E
19 Levroux, France 47 0N 1 38E
43 Levski, Bulgaria 43 21N 25 10E
43 Levskigrad, Bulgaria 42 38N 24 47E
116 Lewellen, U.S.A. 41 22N 102 5W
13 Lewes, England 50 53N 0 2E
114 Lewes, U.S.A. 38 45N 75 8W
104 Lewes, R., Canada 60 30N 134 20W
28 Lewin Brzeski, Poland 50 45N 17 37E
14 Lewis, Butt of, Scotland 58 30N 6 12W
14 Lewis, I., Scot. 58 10N 6 40W
118 Lewis, R., U.S.A. 46 0N 113 15W
112 Lewisburg, Pa., U.S.A. 40 57N 76 57W
115 Lewisburg, Tenn., USA 35 29N 86 46W
107 Lewisporte, Canada 49 15N 55 3W
118 Lewiston, Idaho, U.S.A. 45 58N 117 0W
118 Lewiston, Utah, U.S.A. 42 0N 111 56W
118 Lewistown, Mont., USA 47 0N 109 25W
112 Lewistown, Pa., U.S.A. 40 37N 77 33W
116 Lexington, Ill., U.S.A. 40 37N 88 47W
114 Lexington, Ky., U.S.A. 38 6N 84 30W
117 Lexington, Miss., U.S.A. 33 8N 90 2W
116 Lexington, Mo., U.S.A. 39 7N 93 55W
116 Lexington, Nebr., U.S.A. 40 48N 99 45W
115 Lexington, N.C., U.S.A. 35 50N 80 13W
112 Lexington, Ohio, U.S.A. 40 39N 82 35W
118 Lexington, Oreg., U.S.A. 45 29N 119 46W
115 Lexington, Tenn., USA 35 38N 88 25W
73 Leyte, I., Philippines 11 0N 125 0E
20 Lezay, France 46 17N 0 0E
44 Lezha, Albania 41 47N 19 42E
20 Lézignan-Corbières, Fr. 43 13N 2 43E
20 Lezoux, France 45 49N 3 21E
54 Lgov, U.S.S.R. 51 42N 35 10E
67 Lhariguo, China 30 29N 93 4E
75 Lhasa, China 29 50N 91 3E
75 Lhatse Dzong, China 29 10N 87 45E
72 Lhokseumawe, Indon. 5 20N 97 10E
20 L'Hospitalet, France 44 23N 1 26E
67 Lhuntse Dzong, China 28 25N 92 20E
50 Li, Finland 65 20N 25 20E
45 Liádhoi, I., Greece 36 50N 26 11E
73 Liang Liang, Philippines 5 58N 121 30E
73 Lianga, Philippines 8 38N 126 6E
72 Liangpran, Gunong, Indon. 1 0N 114 23E
76 Liao Ho, R., China 41 0N 121 55E
76 Liaocheng, China 41 35N 122 45E
76 Liaoning ♦, China 41 40N 122 30E

MAP
76 Liaotung, China 40 10N 123 0E
76 Liaotung Wan, China 40 0N 120 45E
76 Liaoyang, China 41 15N 123 10E
76 Liaoyüan, China 42 55N 125 10E
44 Liapádhes, Greece 39 42N 19 40E
108 Liard, R., Canada 61 20N 122 30W
54 Libau = Liepaja, U.S.S.R. 56 30N 21 0E
118 Libby, U.S.A. 48 20N 115 10W
88 Libenge, Zaïre 3 40N 18 55E
117 Liberal, Kans., U. S. A. 37 4N 101 0W
117 Liberal, Mo., U.S.A. 37 35N 94 30W
26 Liberec, Czechoslovakia 50 47N 15 7E
121 Liberia, Costa Rica 10 40N 85 30W
84 Liberia ■, West Africa 6 30N 9 30W
126 Libertad, Venezuela 8 20N 69 37W
116 Liberty, Mo., U.S.A. 39 15N 94 24W
113 Liberty, N.Y., U.S.A. 41 48N 74 45W
117 Liberty, Tex., U.S.A. 30 5N 94 50W
27 Libiaz, Poland 50 7N 19 21E
78 Lîbîya, Sahrâ', N. Africa 27 35N 25 0E
44 Libohava, Albania 40 3N 20 10E
20 Libourne, France 44 55N 0 14W
16 Libramont, Belgium 49 55N 5 23E
44 Librazhdi, Albania 41 12N 20 22E
88 Libreville, Gabon 0 25N 9 26E
81 Libya ■, N. Africa 28 30N 17 30E
86 Libyan Plateau = Ed-Déffa, Egypt 30 40N 26 30E
124 Licantén, Chile 34 55S 72 0W
40 Licata, Italy 37 6N 13 55E
12 Lichfield, Eng. 52 40N 1 50W
92 Lichtenburg, S. Africa 26 8S 26 8E
25 Lichtenfels, Germany 50 7N 11 4E
41 Licosa, Punta, Italy 40 15N 14 53E
119 Lida, U.S.A. 37 30N 117 30W
54 Lida, U.S.S.R. 53 53N 25 15E
49 Lidhult, Sweden 56 50N 13 27E
49 Lidingö, Sweden 59 22N 18 8E
49 Lidköping, Sweden 58 31N 13 14E
39 Lido, Italy 45 25N 12 23E
85 Lido, Niger 12 54N 3 44E
40 Lido di Ostia, Italy 41 44N 12 14E
28 Lidzbark, Poland 53 15N 19 49E
28 Lidzbark Warminski, Poland 54 7N 20 34E
24 Liebenwalde, Germany 52 51N 13 23E
24 Lieberose, Germany 51 59N 14 18E
42 Liebling, Rumania 45 36N 21 20E
25 Liechtenstein ■, Europe 47 8N 9 35E
16 Liège, Belgium 50 38N 5 35E
16 Liège ♦, Belgium 50 32N 5 35E
28 Liegnitz = Legnica, Poland 51 12N 16 10E
90 Lienart, Zaïre 3 3N 25 31E
90 Lienartville, Zaïre 3 3N 25 31E
77 Lienhua, China 26 58N 113 59E
77 Lienyang, China 26 11N 119 30E
26 Lienz, Austria 46 50N 12 46E
54 Liepāja, U.S.S.R. 56 30N 21 0E
16 Lier, Belgium 51 7N 4 34E
76 Lieshankwan, China 40 56N 124 51E
46 Liesta, Rumania 45 38N 27 34E
19 Lievin, France 50 24N 2 47E
106 Lievre, R., Canada 45 40N 75 40W
26 Liezen, Austria 47 34N 14 15E
15 Liffey, R., Ireland 53 21N 6 20W
15 Lifford, Ireland 54 50N 7 30W
18 Liffré, Fr. 48 12N 1 30W
47 Lifjell, Norway 59 27N 8 45E
99 Lightning Ridge, Australia 29 22S 148 0E
39 Lignano, Italy 45 42N 13 8E
19 Ligny-er-Barrois, Fr. 48 36N 5 20E
19 Ligny-le-Château, France 47 54N 3 45E
45 Ligourion, Greece 37 37N 23 2E
38 Liguria ♦, Italy 44 30N 9 0E
38 Ligurian Sea, Italy 43 20N 9 0E
98 Lihir Group, Terr. of New Guin. 3 0S 152 35E
110 Lihue, Hawaii 21 59N 159 24W
67 Lihwa, China 30 4N 100 18E
91 Likasi, Zaïre 10 55S 26 48E
88 Likati, Zaïre 3 20N 24 0E
54 Likhoslavl, U.S.S.R. 57 12N 35 30E
57 Likhovski, U.S.S.R. 48 10N 40 10E
75 Likiang, China 26 50N 100 15E
91 Likoma I., Malawi 12 3S 34 45E
91 Likumburu, Tanzania 9 43S 35 8E
77 Liling, China 27 47N 113 30E
19 Lille, France 50 38N 3 3E
49 Lille Baelt, Denmark 55 30N 9 45E
18 Lillebonne, France 49 30N 0 32E
47 Lillehammer, Norway 61 8N 10 30E
19 Lillers, France 50 35N 2 28E
47 Lillesand, Norway 58 15N 8 23E
47 Lilleström, Norway 59 58N 11 5E
32 Lillo, Spain 39 45N 3 20W
91 Lilongwe, Malawi 14 0S 33 48E
73 Liloy, Philippines 8 4N 122 39E
100 Lilydale, Australia 37 43S 145 29E
42 Lim, R., Yugoslavia 43 0N 19 40E
100 Lima, Australia 36 44S 146 10E
73 Lima, Indonesia 3 37S 128 4E
126 Lima, Peru 12 0S 77 0W
48 Lima, Sweden 60 55N 13 20E
118 Lima, Mont., U.S.A. 44 41N 112 38W
114 Lima, Ohio, U.S.A. 40 42N 84 5W
30 Lima, R., Portugal 41 50N 8 18W
113 Limages, Canada 45 20N 75 16W
85 Liman Katagum, Nigeria 10 4N 9 49E
27 Limanowa, Poland 49 42N 20 22E
64 Limassol = Lemesós, Cyprus 34 42N 33 1E
128 Limay, R., Argentina 39 40S 69 45W
124 Limay Mahuida, Arg. 37 10S 66 45W
72 Limbang, Brunei 4 42N 115 6E
40 Limbara Monti, Italy 40 50N 9 10E
68 Limbdi, India 22 34N 71 51E
16 Limbourg ♦, Belg. 51 2N 5 25E

* Renamed L. Mai-Ndombe

* Renamed Umba

* In April 1973 districts replaced counties in N. Ireland

Madagali INDEX Manchester Depot

MAP
85 Madagali, Nigeria 10 56N 13 33E
93 Madagascar, I., Africa 20 0S 47 0E
84 Madam, Ivory Coast 7 58N 3 32W
83 Madama, Niger 22 0N 14 0E
107 Madame I., Canada 45 30N 60 58W
70 Madanapalle, India 13 33N 78 34E
98 Madang, N.E. New Guin. 5 0S 145 46E
85 Madaoua, Niger 14 5N 6 27E
85 Madara, Nigeria 11 45N 10 35E
69 Madaripur, Bangladesh 23 2N 90 15E
67 Madauk, Burma 17 56N 96 52E
112 Madawaska, Canada 45 30N 77 55W
112 Madawaska, R., Canada 45 20N 77 30W
67 Madaya, Burma 22 20N 96 10E
87 Madbar, Sudan 6 17N 30 45E
40 Maddalena, I., Italy 41 15N 9 23E
41 Maddaloni, Italy 41 4N 14 23E
120 Madden Dam, Panama Canal Zone 9 13N 79 37W
120 Madden Lake, Panama Canal Zone 9 20N 79 37W
87 Madebele, Ethiopia 12 30N 41 10E
80 Madeira, Is., Atlan. Oc. 32 50N 17 0W
126 Madeira, R., Brazil 5 30S 61 20W
91 Madenda, Malawi 13 42S 35 1W
119 Madera, U.S.A. 37 0N 120 1W
70 Madha, India 18 0N 75 55E
69 Madhubani, India 26 21N 86 7E
90 Madhupur, India 24 18N 86 37E
68 Madhya Pradesh ♦, India 21 50N 81 0E
*90 Madi ♦, Uganda 3 0N 32 0E
90 Madi Opei, Uganda 3 47N 33 5E
117 Madill, U.S.A. 34 5N 96 49W
88 Madimba, Zaïre 5 0S 15 0E
91 Madimba, Mozambique 4 58S 15 6E
63 Madinat al Shaab, S. Yemen 12 50N 45 0E
88 Madingou, Congo 4 10S 13 33E
93 Madirovalo, Malag. 16 26S 46 32E
115 Madison, Fla., U.S.A. 30 29N 83 26W
114 Madison, Ind., U.S.A. 38 42N 85 20W
116 Madison, Nebr., U.S.A. 41 53N 97 25W
112 Madison, Ohio, U.S.A. 41 45N 81 4W
116 Madison, S.D., U.S.A. 44 0N 97 8W
116 Madison, Wis., U.S.A. 43 5N 89 25W
118 Madison, R., U.S.A. 45 0N 111 48W
116 Madison City, U.S.A. 43 5N 93 10W
118 Madison Junc., U.S.A. 44 42N 110 56W
114 Madisonville, U.S.A. 37 42N 87 30W
92 Madista, Botswana 21 15S 25 6E
73 Madiun, Indonesia 7 38S 111 32E
73 Madjalengka, Indonesia 6 55S 108 14E
73 Madjene, Indonesia 3 27S 118 57E
87 Madol, Sudan 9 3N 27 45E
54 Madona, U.S.S.R. 56 53N 26 5E
64 Madraqa, Saudi Arabia 21 57N 40 0E
70 Madras, India 13 8N 80 19E
70 Madras = Tamil Nadu ♦, India 11 0N 77 0E
118 Madras, U.S.A. 44 40N 121 10W
117 Madre L., U.S.A. 26 30N 90 20W
120 Madre, Laguna, Mexico 25 0N 97 30W
120 Madre, Sierra, Mexico 16 0N 93 0W
73 Madre, Sierra, Phil. 17 0N 122 0E
128 Madre de Dios, I., Chile 50 20N 75 10W
126 Madre de Dios, R., Bol. 11 30S 67 30W
120 Madre del Sur, Sierra, Mexico 17 30N 100 0W
120 Madre Occidental, Sierra, Mexico 27 0N 107 0W
120 Madre Oriental, Sierra, Mexico 25 0N 100 0W
68 Madri, India 24 16N 73 32E
30 Madrid, Spain 40 25N 3 45W
30 Madrid ♦, Spain 40 30N 3 45W
31 Madridejos, Spain 39 28N 3 33W
30 Madrigal de las Altas Torres, Sp. 41 5N 5 0W
31 Madrona, Sierra, Spain 38 27N 4 16W
31 Madroñera, Spain 39 26N 5 42W
87 Madu, Sudan 14 37N 26 4E
73 Madura, I., Indonesia 7 0S 113 20E
73 Madura, Selat, Indonesia 7 30S 113 20E
70 Madurai, India 9 55N 78 10E
70 Madurantakam, India 12 30N 79 50E
70 Maduru Oya, Sri Lanka 7 40N 81 7E
57 Madzhalis, U.S.S.R. 42 9N 47 47E
71 Mae Hong Son, Thai. 19 16N 98 8E
71 Mae Sot, Thailand 16 43N 98 34E
32 Maella, Spain 41 8N 0 7E
46 Mâeruş, Rumania 45 53N 25 31E
13 Maesteg, Wales 51 36N 3 40W
121 Maestra, Sierra, Cuba 20 15N 77 0W
32 Maestrazgo, Mts. del, Spain 40 30N 0 25W
83 Mafan, Libya 25 56N 14 56E
109 Mafeking, Canada 52 40N 101 10W
92 Mafeking, S. Africa 25 50S 25 38E
84 Maféré, Ivory Coast 5 30N 3 2W
92 Mafeteng, Lesotho 29 51S 27 15E
100 Maffra, Australia 37 53S 146 58E
90 Mafia I., Tanzania 7 45S 39 50E
125 Mafra, Brazil 26 10S 50 0W
31 Mafra, Portugal 38 55N 9 20W
127 Mafrense, Brazil 8 10S 41 10W
91 Mafungabusi Plateau, Rhodesia 18 30S 29 8E
59 Magadan, U.S.S.R. 59 30N 151 0E
90 Magadi, Kenya 1 54S 36 19E
90 Magadi, L., Kenya 1 54S 36 19E
93 Magaliesburg, S. Africa 26 1S 27 32E
128 Magallanes, Estrecho de, Chile 52 30S 75 0W
126 Magangue, Colombia 9 14N 74 45W
85 Magaria, Niger 13 4N 9 5W
84 Magburaka, Sierra Leone 8 47N 12 0W
62 Magdal, Israel 32 51N 35 30E
107 Magdalen Is., Canada 47 30N 61 40W
124 Magdalena, Argentina 35 5S 57 30W
126 Magdalena, Bolivia 13 13S 63 57W
120 Magdalena, Mexico 30 50N 112 0W
119 Magdalena, U.S.A. 34 10N 107 20W
120 Magdalena, B., Mexico 24 30N 112 10W
126 Magdalena ♦, Col. 10 0N 74 0W
120 Magdalena, I., Mexico 24 40N 112 15W
120 Magdalena, Llano de la, Mexico 25 0N 111 30W
72 Magdalena, mt., Malaysia 4 25N 117 55E
126 Magdalena, R., Col. 8 30N 74 0W
120 Magdalena, R., Mex. 30 50N 112 0W
24 Magdeburg, Germany 52 8N 11 36E
24 Magdeburg ♦, E. Germany 52 20N 11 40E
62 Magdiel, Israel 32 10N 34 54E
87 Magdub, Sudan 13 42N 25 5E
117 Magee, U.S.A. 31 53N 89 45W
15 Magee, I., N.Ire. U.K. 54 48N 5 44W
73 Magelang, Indonesia 7 29S 110 13E
128 Magellan's Str = Magallanes, Est de, Chile 52 30S 75 0W
38 Magenta, Italy 45 28N 8 53E
25 Maggia, R., Switzerland 46 18N 8 36E
38 Maggiorasca, Mt., Italy 44 33N 9 29E
38 Maggiore, L., Italy 46 0N 8 35E
84 Maghama, Mauritania 15 32N 12 57W
62 Maghar, Israel 32 54N 35 24E
82 Maghnia, Algeria 34 50N 1 43W
39 Magione, Italy 43 10N 12 12E
42 Maglaj, Yugoslavia 44 33N 18 7E
39 Magliano in Toscana, It. 42 36N 11 18E
41 Máglie, Italy 40 8N 18 17E
86 Magna, Saudi Arabia 28 25N 34 46E
20 Magnac-Laval, France 46 13N 1 11E
4 Magnetic Pole, 1965(North), Canada 75 0N 101 0W
5 Magnetic Pole, 1965, (South), Antarctica 66 30S 139 30E
45 Magnisia ♦, Greece 39 24N 22 46E
52 Magnitogorsk, U.S.S.R. 53 20N 59 0E
117 Magnolia, Ark., U.S.A. 33 18N 93 12W
117 Magnolia, Miss., U.S.A. 31 8N 90 28W
47 Magnor, Norway 59 56N 12 15E
19 Magny-en-Vexin, France 49 9N 1 47E
91 Magoé, Mozambique 15 45S 31 42E
107 Magog, Canada 45 18N 72 9W
90 Magoro, Uganda 1 45N 34 12E
91 Magoye, Zambia 16 1S 27 30E
107 Magpie L., Canada 51 0N 64 40W
108 Magrath, Canada 49 25N 112 50W
33 Magro, R., Spain 39 20N 0 45W
87 Magrur, W., Sudan 16 5N 26 30E
127 Maguarinho, C., Brazil 0 15S 48 30W
109 Maguse L., Canada 61 35N 95 20W
109 Maguse, R., Canada 61 20N 94 25W
67 Magwe, Burma 20 10N 95 0E
64 Mahabad, Iran 36 50N 45 45E
69 Mahabharat Lekh, Nepal 28 30N 82 0E
93 Mahabo, Malag. 20 23S 44 40E
70 Mahad, India 18 6N 73 29E
68 Mahadeo Hills, India 22 20N 78 30E
70 Mahadeopur, India 18 48N 80 0E
90 Mahagi, Zaïre 2 20N 31 0E
93 Mahajamba, B. de la, Malag. 15 24S 47 5E
93 Mahajamba, R., Malag. 17 0S 47 30E
68 Mahajan, India 28 48N 73 56E
93 Mahajilo, R., Malag. 19 30S 46 0E
72 Mahakam, R., Indonesia 1 0N 114 40E
92 Mahalapye, Botswana 23 1S 26 51E
86 Mahalla el Kubra, Egypt 31 10N 31 0E
64 Mahallat, Iran 33 55N 50 30E
69 Mahanadi R., India 20 33N 85 0E
93 Mahanoro, Malagasy Republic 19 54S 48 48E
113 Mahanoy City, U.S.A. 40 48N 76 10W
66 Maharashtra ♦, India 19 30N 75 30E
83 Maharès, Tunisia 34 32N 10 29E
90 Mahari Mts., Tanzania 6 20S 30 0E
93 Mahasolo, Malag. 19 7S 46 22E
70 Mahaweli Ganga, Sri Lanka 8 0N 81 10E
70 Mahboobabad, India 17 42N 80 2E
70 Mahbubnagar, India 16 45N 77 59E
64 Mahd Dhahab, Si. Arab. 25 55N 45 30E
83 Mahdia, Tunisia 35 28N 11 0E
70 Mahé, India 11 42N 75 34E
70 Mahendra Giri, mt., India 8 20N 77 30E
91 Mahenge, Tanzania 8 45S 36 35E
101 Maheno, New Zealand 45 10S 170 50E
101 Mahia Pen., N.Z. 39 9S 177 55E
82 Mahirijah, Morocco 34 0N 3 16W
87 Mahmiya, Sudan 17 5N 33 50E
68 Mahmud Kot, Pakistan 30 16N 71 0E
46 Mahmudia, Rumania 45 5N 29 5E
116 Mahnomen, U.S.A. 47 22N 95 57W
69 Mahoba, India 25 15N 79 55E
32 Mahón, Spain 39 50N 4 18E
85 Mahuta, Nigeria 11 32N 4 58E
68 Mahuva, India 25 7N 71 46E
19 Maîche, France 47 16N 6 48E
127 Maicuru, R., Brazil 1 0S 54 30W
41 Máida, Italy 38 51N 16 21E
13 Maidenhead, Eng. 51 31N 0 42W
87 Maidi, Yemen 16 20N 42 45E
109 Maidstone, Canada 53 5N 109 20W
13 Maidstone, Eng. 51 16N 0 31E
85 Maiduguri, Nigeria 12 0N 13 20E
19 Maignelay, France 49 32N 2 30E
126 Maigualida, Sierra, Ven. 5 30N 65 10W
69 Maijdi, Bangladesh 22 48N 91 10E
69 Maikala Ra., India 22 0N 81 0E
19 Mailly-le-Camp, France 48 41N 4 12E
68 Mailsi, Pakistan 29 48N 72 15E
65 Maimana, Afghanistan 35 53N 64 38E
25 Main, R., Germany 50 13N 11 0E
15 Main, R., N. Ire. 54 49N 6 20W
99 Main Barrier Ra., Australia 31 10S 141 20E
112 Main Channel, Canada 45 22N 81 45W
98 Main Coast Ra., Australia 16 22S 145 10E
25 Mainburg, Germany 48 37N 11 49E
70 Maindargi, India 17 33N 74 21E
18 Maine, France 48 0N 0 0E
15 Maine, R., Ireland 52 10N 9 40W
107 Maine ♦, U.S.A. 45 20N 69 0W
18 Maine-et-Loire ♦, France 47 31N 0 30W
85 Maïne-Soroa, Niger 13 13N 12 2E
67 Maingkwan, Burma 26 15N 96 45E
73 Mainit, L., Philippines 9 31N 125 30E
14 Mainland, I., Orkneys, Scot. 59 0N 3 10W
14 Mainland, I., Shetlands, Scotland 60 15N 1 22W
68 Mainpuri, India 27 18N 79 4E
19 Maintenon, France 48 35N 1 35E
93 Maintirano, Malagasy Republic 18 3S 44 1E
25 Mainz, Germany 50 0N 8 17E
124 Maipú, Argentina 37 0S 58 0W
126 Maipures, Colombia 5 11N 67 49W
126 Maiquetia, Venezuela 10 36N 66 57W
38 Maira, R., Italy 44 29N 7 15E
67 Mairabari, India 26 30N 92 30E
121 Maisi, C., Cuba 20 10N 74 10W
19 Maisse, France 48 24N 2 21E
100 Maitland, N.S.W., Australia 32 44S 151 36E
99 Maitland, S. Australia, Australia 34 23S 137 40E
112 Maitland, R., Canada 43 45N 81 33W
85 Maiyema, Nigeria 12 5N 4 25E
74 Maizuru, Japan 35 25N 135 22E
126 Majagual, Colombia 8 33N 74 38W
62 Majd el Kurum, Israel 32 56N 35 15E
44 Maj'-e-Cikës, Albania 40 14N 19 33E
42 Majevica Planina, Yugoslavia 44 45N 18 50E
87 Maji, Ethiopia 6 20N 35 30E
64 Majma'a, Saudi Arabia 25 57N 45 22E
32 Majorca, I. = Mallorca, I., Spain 39 30N 3 0E
73 Maju, I., Indonesia 1 30N 126 30E
93 Majunga ♦, Malagasy Rep. 17 0S 47 0E
84 Maka, Senegal 13 40N 14 10W
85 Makak, Cameroon 3 36N 11 0E
73 Makale, Indonesia 3 6S 119 51E
90 Makamba, Burundi 4 8S 29 49E
106 Makamik, Canada 48 45N 79 0W
88 Makari, Cameroon 12 35N 14 28E
92 Makarikari = Makgadikgadi, Bots. 20 40S 25 45E
59 Makarovo, U.S.S.R. 57 40N 107 45E
42 Makarska, Yugoslavia 43 20N 17 2E
55 Makaryev, U.S.S.R. 57 52N 43 50E
*73 Makasar, Indonesia 5 10S 119 20E
73 Makasar, Selat, Indonesia 1 0S 118 20E
58 Makat, U.S.S.R. 47 39N 53 19E
93 Makaw, Zaïre 3 29S 18 22E
44 Makedhonia ♦, Greece 40 39N 22 0E
42 Makedonija ♦, Y.-slavia 41 53N 21 40E
84 Makeni, Sierra Leone 8 55N 12 5W
56 Makeyevka, U.S.S.R. 48 0N 38 0E
92 Makgadikgadi, Botswana 20 40S 25 45E
92 Makgadikari Salt Pans, Botswana 20 40S 25 45E
92 Makgobistad, S. Africa 25 45S 25 12E
57 Makhachkala, U.S.S.R. 43 0N 47 15E
57 Makharadze, U.S.S.R. 41 55N 42 2E
43 Makhlata, Bulgaria 43 26N 24 17E
73 Makian, I., Indonesia 0 12N 127 20E
94 Makin, I., Pacific Ocean 3 30N 174 0E
58 Makinsk, U.S.S.R. 52 37N 70 26E
86 Makkah, Saudi Arabia 21 30N 39 54E
107 Makkovik, Canada 55 0N 59 10W
59 Maklakovo, U.S.S.R. 58 16N 92 29E
27 Makó, Hungary 46 14N 20 33E
88 Makokou, Gabon 0 40N 12 50E
90 Makongo, Zaïre 3 15N 26 17E
90 Makoro, Zaïre 3 10N 29 59E
88 Makoua, Congo 0 5S 15 50E
27 Maków Podhal, Poland 49 43N 19 45E
45 Makrá, I., Greece 36 15N 25 54E
65 Makran, Iran & Pakistan 26 13N 61 30E
66 Makran Coast Range, Pakistan 25 40N 4 0E
68 Makrana, India 27 2N 74 46E
44 Mákri, Greece 40 52N 25 40E
58 Maksimkin Yar, U.S.S.R. 58 58N 86 50E
83 Maktar, Tunisia 35 48N 9 12E
64 Maku, Iran 39 15N 44 31E
92 Makumbe, Botswana 20 15S 24 26E
88 Makumbi, Zaïre 5 50S 20 43E
92 Makunda, Botswana 22 30S 20 7E
74 Makurazaki, Japan 31 15N 130 20E
92 Makwassie, S. Africa 27 17S 26 0E
44 Mal i Gribës, Albania 40 17N 9 45E
44 Mal i Nemërçkës, Alb. 40 15N 20 15E
44 Mal i Tomorit, Albania 40 42N 20 11E
15 Mal B., Ireland 52 50N 9 30W
39 Mala Kapela, Y.-slavia 44 45N 15 30E
73 Malabang, Philippines 7 36N 124 3E
70 Malabar Coast, India 11 0N 75 0E
71 Malacca = Melaka, Malaysia 2 15N 102 15E
72 Malacca, Str. of, Indon. 3 0N 101 0E
27 Malacky, Cz. 48 27N 17 0E
118 Malad City, U.S.A. 41 10N 112 20E
33 Maladetta, Mt., Europe 42 40N 0 30E
87 Malafaburi, Ethiopia 10 37N 40 30E
126 Málaga, Colombia 6 42N 72 44W
31 Málaga, Spain 36 43N 4 23W
31 Málaga ♦, Spain 36 38N 4 58W
117 Malaga, U.S.A. 32 12N 104 2W
90 Malagarasi, Tanzania 5 5S 30 50E
90 Malagarasi, R., Tanz. 3 50S 30 30E
*93 Malagasy Rep. ■, Africa 19 0S 46 0E
31 Malagón, Spain 39 11N 3 52W
31 Malagón, R., Spain 37 40N 7 20W
93 Malaimbandy, Malag. 20 20S 45 36E
87 Malakâl, Sudan 9 33N 31 50E
66 Malakand, Pakistan 34 40N 71 55E
117 Malakoff, U.S.A. 32 10N 95 55W
108 Malakwa, Canada 50 55N 118 50W
59 Malamyzh, U.S.S.R. 50 0N 136 50E
73 Malang, Indonesia 7 59S 112 35E
88 Malanje, Angola 9 30S 16 17E
48 Mälaren, Sweden 59 30N 17 10E
124 Malargüe, Argentina 35 40S 69 30W
106 Malartic, Canada 48 9N 78 9W
64 Malatya, Turkey 38 25N 38 20E
91 Malawi ■, Africa 13 0S 34 0E
91 Malawi, L. (Lago Niassa), Africa 12 30S 34 30E
71 Malaya ♦, S.E. Asia 4 0N 102 0E
56 Malaya Belözerka, U.S.S.R. 47 12N 34 56E
54 Malaya Vishera, USSR 58 55N 32 25E
73 Malaybalay, Philippines 8 5N 125 15E
64 Malayer, Iran 28 22N 56 38E
72 Malaysia ■, S.E. Asia 5 0N 110 0E
64 Malazgirt, Turkey 39 10N 42 33E
98 Malbon, Australia 21 5S 140 17E
28 Malbork, Poland 54 3N 19 10E
87 Malca Dube, Ethiopia 6 40N 41 52E
24 Malchin, Germany 53 43N 12 44E
24 Malchow, Germany 53 29N 12 25E
96 Malcolm, Australia 28 51S 121 25E
28 Malczyce, Poland 51 14N 16 29E
16 Maldegem, Belgium 51 14N 3 26E
113 Malden, Mass., U.S.A. 42 26N 71 5W
117 Malden, Mo., U.S.A. 36 35N 90 0W
60 Maldive Is. ■, Indian Oc. 2 0N 73 0W
100 Maldon, Australia 37 0S 144 6E
125 Maldonado, Uruguay 35 0S 55 0W
120 Maldonado, Punta, Mex. 16 19N 98 35W
38 Malé, Italy 46 20N 10 55E
27 Malé Karpaty, Cz. 48 30N 17 20E
45 Malea, Akra, Greece 36 28N 23 7E
68 Malegaon, India 20 30N 74 30E
91 Malei, Mozambique 17 12S 36 58E
87 Malek, Sudan 6 2N 11 38E
90 Malela, Zaïre 4 22S 26 8E
91 Malenge, Zambia 12 40S 26 42E
49 Målerås, Sweden 56 54N 15 34E
68 Malerkotla, India 30 32N 75 58E
45 Males, Greece 35 6N 25 35E
19 Malesherbes, France 48 15N 2 24E
42 Maleske Planina, Y.-slav.-Bulg. 41 38N 23 7E
18 Malestroit, France 47 49N 2 25W
41 Malfa, Italy 38 35N 14 50E
57 Malgobek, U.S.S.R. 43 30N 44 52E
50 Malgomaj L., Sweden 64 40N 16 30E
32 Malgrat, Spain 41 39N 2 46E
118 Malheur L., U.S.A. 43 19N 118 42W
118 Malheur, R., U.S.A. 43 55N 117 55W
84 Mali, Guinea 12 10N 12 20W
85 Mali ■, Africa 15 0N 10 0W
42 Mali Kanal, Y.-slavia 45 36N 19 24E
67 Mali, R., Burma 26 20N 97 40E
44 Mal-i-Gjalicës së Lumës, Alb. 42 2N 20 25E
39 Mali Kvarner, Yugoslavia 44 50N 14 10E
71 Mali Kyun, I., Burma 13 0N 98 20E
62 Malih, Nahr al, Jordan 32 20N 35 29E
73 Malik, Indonesia 0 39S 123 16E
73 Malili, Indonesia 2 42S 121 23E
70 Malimba, Mts., Zaïre 7 30S 29 30E
54 Malin, U.S.S.R. 50 46N 29 15E
15 Malin Hd., Ireland 55 18N 7 16W
72 Malinau, Indonesia 3 35N 116 30E
90 Malindi, Kenya 3 12S 40 5E
73 Maling, Mt., Indonesia 1 0N 121 0E
73 Malingping, Indonesia 6 45S 106 2E
91 Malinyi, Tanzania 8 56S 36 0E
44 Maliqi, Albania 40 45N 20 48E
73 Malita, Philippines 6 19N 125 39E
70 Malkapur, Maharashtra, India 20 53N 76 17E
70 Malkapur, Maharashtra, India 16 57N 74 0W
28 Małkinia Grn., Poland 52 42N 21 58E
43 Malko Turnovo, Bulg. 41 59N 27 31E
100 Mallacoota, Australia 37 40S 149 40E
100 Mallacoota Inlet, Australia 37 40S 149 40E
62 Mallaha, Israel 33 6N 35 35E
14 Mallaig, Scotland 57 0N 5 50W
69 Mallawan, India 27 4N 80 12E
86 Mallawi, Egypt 27 44N 30 44E
100 Mallee, Australia 35 10S 142 20E
21 Mallemort, France 43 44N 5 11E
38 Málles Venosta, Italy 46 42N 10 32E
45 Mállia, Greece 35 17N 25 27E
32 Mallorca, I., Spain 39 30N 3 0E
113 Mallorytown, Canada 44 29N 75 53W
49 Malmbäck, Sweden 57 34N 14 28E
50 Malmberget, Sweden 67 11N 20 40E
16 Malmédy, Belgium 50 25N 6 2E
92 Malmesbury, S. Africa 33 28S 18 41E
49 Malmö, Sweden 55 36N 12 59E
49 Malmöhus län ♦, Sweden 55 45N 13 25E
49 Malmslätt, Sweden 58 27N 15 33E
15 Malmyzh Mozhga, U.S.S.R. 56 35N 50 30E
49 Malmöhus län ♦, Sweden 55 45N 13 30E
46 Malnaş, Rumania 46 2N 25 49E
43 Malo Konare, Bulgaria 42 12N 24 24E
55 Maloarkhangelsk, U.S.S.R. 52 28N 36 30E
73 Malolos, Philippines 14 50N 21 2E
91 Malombe L., Malawi 14 40S 35 15E
43 Malomir, Bulgaria 42 16N 26 30E
113 Malone, U.S.A. 44 50N 74 19W
43 Malorad, Bulgaria 43 28N 23 41E
54 Malorita, U.S.S.R. 51 41N 24 3E
55 Maloyaroslovets, USSR 55 2N 36 20E
52 Malozemelskaya Tundra, U.S.S.R. 67 0N 50 0E
31 Malpartida, Spain 39 26N 6 30W
126 Malpelo I., Colombia 4 3N 80 35W
30 Malpica, Spain 43 19N 8 50W
70 Malprabha, R., India 15 40N 74 50E
118 Malta, Idaho, U.S.A. 42 15N 113 50W
118 Malta, Mont., U.S.A. 48 20N 107 55W
36 Malta ■, Europe 35 50N 14 30E
40 Malta Channel, Medit. 36 40N 14 0E
112 Malton, Canada 43 41N 79 38W
12 Malton, England 54 9N 0 48W
73 Maluku, Kepulauan, Indonesia 3 0S 128 0E
73 Maluku ♦, Indonesia 3 0S 128 0E
85 Malumfashi, Nigeria 11 48N 7 39E
48 Malung, Sweden 60 42N 13 44E
70 Malvalli, India 12 28N 77 8E
70 Malvan, India 16 2N 73 30E
13 Malvern, Eng. 52 7N 2 19W
117 Malvern, Ark., U.S.A. 34 22N 92 50W
112 Malvern, Ohio, U.S.A. 40 31N 31 12W
13 Malvern Hills, Eng. 52 0N 2 19W
93 Malvérnia, Mozambique 22 6S 31 42E
47 Malvik, Norway 63 25N 10 40E
126 Malvinas Is. = Falkland Is., S. Atl. Oc. 51 30S 59 0W
90 Malya, Tanzania 3 5S 33 38E
59 Mama, U.S.S.R. 58 18N 112 54E
55 Mamadysh, U.S.S.R. 55 44N 51 23E
46 Mamaia, Rumania 44 18N 28 37E
127 Mamanguape, Brazil 6 50S 35 4W
73 Mamasa, Indonesia 2 55S 119 20E
90 Mambasa, Zaïre 1 22N 29 3E
73 Mamberamo, R., Indon. 2 0S 137 50E
91 Mambirima, Zaïre 11 25S 27 33E
90 Mambo, Tanzania 4 52S 38 22E
90 Mambrui, Kenya 3 5S 40 5E
18 Mamers, France 48 21N 0 22E
85 Mamfe, Cameroon 5 50N 9 15E
106 Mammamattawa, Canada 50 25N 84 23W
41 Mámmola, Italy 38 23N 16 13E
119 Mammoth, U.S.A. 32 46N 110 43W
77 Mamoi, China 26 0N 119 25E
127 Mamoré, R., Bolivia 9 55S 65 20W
84 Mamou, Guinea 10 15N 12 0W
84 Mampatá, Port. Guinea 11 54N 14 53W
72 Mampawah, Indonesia 0 30N 109 5E
85 Mampong, Ghana 7 6N 1 26W
73 Mamudju, Indonesia 2 50S 118 50E
84 Man, Ivory Coast 7 30N 7 40W
12 Man, I. of, U.K. 54 15N 4 30W
70 Man, R., India 17 20N 75 0E
67 Man Na, Burma 23 27N 97 19E
127 Mana, Fr. Guina 5 45N 53 55W
72 Mana, Indonesia 4 25S 102 55E
87 Mana, R., Ethiopia 6 20N 40 41E
47 Måna, R., Norway 59 55N 8 50E
70 Manaar, Gulf of, Asia 8 30N 79 0E
126 Manacacías, R., Col. 4 23N 72 4W
126 Manacapuru, Brazil 3 10S 60 50W
32 Manacor, Spain 39 32N 3 12E
73 Manado, Indonesia 1 40N 124 45E
121 Managua, Nicaragua 12 0N 86 20W
121 Managua, L., Nicaragua 12 20N 86 30W
94 Manaia, New Zealand 39 33S 174 8E
93 Manakana, Malagasy Rep. 13 45S 50 4E
93 Manakara, Malagasy Republic 22 8S 48 1E
98 Manam I., Terr. of New Guinea 4 5S 145 5E
93 Manamah, Bahrain I. 26 11N 50 35E
93 Manambaho, R., Malag. 17 35S 44 45E
93 Manambato, Malagasy Rep. 13 43S 49 7E
93 Manambolo, R., Malag. 19 20S 45 0E
93 Manambolosy, Malag. 16 2S 49 40E
93 Mananara, Malagasy Republic 16 10S 49 30E
93 Mananara, R., Malag. 23 25S 48 10E
93 Mananjary, Malagasy Republic 21 13S 48 20E
93 Manantenina, Malag. 24 17S 47 19E
101 Manapouri, N.Z. 45 34S 167 39E
101 Manapouri, L., N.Z. 45 32S 167 32E
70 Manar, R., India 18 50N 77 20E
75 Manasalowo Chih, China 30 45N 81 20E
65 Manasir, Si. Arabia 24 30N 51 10E
69 Manaslu, Mt., Nepal 28 33N 84 33E
113 Manasquan, U.S.A. 40 7N 74 3W
75 Manass, China 44 20N 86 21E
119 Manassa, U.S.A. 37 12N 105 58W
67 Manaung Kyun, Burma 18 45N 93 40E
126 Manaus, Brazil 3 0S 60 0W
73 Manay, Philippines 7 17N 126 33E
114 Mancelona, U.S.A. 44 54N 85 5W
31 Mancha Real, Spain 37 48N 3 39W
18 Manche ♦, France 49 10N 1 20W
12 Manchester, Eng. 53 30N 2 15W
113 Manchester, Conn., U.S.A. 41 47N 72 30W
115 Manchester, Ga., U.S.A. 32 53N 84 32W
116 Manchester, Iowa, U.S.A. 42 28N 91 27W
114 Manchester, Ky., U.S.A. 37 10N 83 45W
113 Manchester, N.H., USA 42 58N 71 29W
112 Manchester, N.Y., USA 42 56N 77 16W
113 Manchester Depot, U.S.A. 43 10N 73 5W

* *Incorporated within the new Nile district*

* *Renamed Ujung Pandang*

* *Renamed Madagascar*

* Incorporated within the county of Gwynedd

* Incorporated within the regions of Lothian and Borders

MAP
77 Mintsing, China 26 8N 118 57E
118 Minturn, U.S.A. 39 45N 106 25W
40 Minturno, Italy 41 15N 13 43E
86 Minûf, Egypt 30 26N 30 52E
59 Minusinsk, U.S.S.R. 53 50N 91 20E
67 Minutang, India 28 15N 96 30E
88 Minvoul, Gabon 2 9N 12 8E
75 Minya Konka, mt., China 29 36N 101 50E
100 Minyip, Australia 36 29s 142 36E
42 Mionica, Yugoslavia 44 14N 20 6E
73 Mios Num, I., Indon. 1 30s 135 10E
107 Miquelon, St. Pierre et. ♦, N. Amer. 47 8N 56 24W
57 Mir-Bashir, U.S.S.R. 40 11N 46 58E
39 Mira, Italy 45 26N 12 9E
30 Mira, Portugal 40 26N 8 44W
31 Mira, R., Portugal 37 30N 8 30W
41 Mirabella Eclano, Italy 41 3N 14 59E
120 Miraflores Locks, Panama Canal Zone 8 59N 79 36W
70 Miraj, India 16 50N 74 45E
124 Miramar, Argentina 38 15s 57 50W
93 Miramar, Mozambique 23 50s 35 35E
21 Miramas, France 43 33N 4 59E
20 Mirambeau, France 45 23N 0 35W
107 Miramichi B., Canada 47 15N 65 0w
20 Miramont-de-Guyenne, France 44 37N 0 21E
127 Miranda, Brazil 20 10s 56 15W
126 Miranda ♦, Venezuela 10 15s 66 25W
32 Miranda de Ebro, Spain 42 41N 2 57W
30 Miranda do Corvo, Spain 40 6N 8 20W
30 Miranda do Douro, Port. 41 30N 6 16W
30 Miranda do Ebro, Spain 41 30N 6 16W
117 Mirando City, U.S.A. 27 28N 98 59W
38 Mirandola, Italy 44 53N 11 2E
125 Mirandópolis, Brazil 21 9s 51 6w
91 Mirango, Malawi 13 32s 34 58E
98 Mirani, Australia 21 12s 148 59E
39 Mirano, Italy 45 29N 12 6E
29 Miraporvos, I., Bahama Is. 22 9N 74 30W
125 Mirassol, Brazil 20 46s 49 28W
100 Mirboo, Australia 38 15s 146 7E
86 Mirear, I., Egypt 23 15N 35 41E
19 Mirebeau, Côte d'Or, Fr. 47 25N 5 20E
18 Mirebeau, Vienne, Fr. 46 49N 0 10E
19 Mirecourt, France 48 20N 6 10E
65 Mirfa, Trucial Oman 24 0N 53 24E
54 Mirgorod, U.S.S.R. 49 58N 33 50E
72 Miri, Malaysia 4 18N 114 0E
98 Miriam Vale, Australia 24 20s 151 39E
125 Mirim, Brazil 32 40s 52 58W
125 Mirim, Lagoa, Brazil/Urug. 32 45s 52 50W
126 Mirimire, Venezuela 11 10N 68 43W
5 Mirny, Antarctica 66 0s 95 0E
59 Mirnyy, U.S.S.R. 62 33N 113 53E
100 Mirool, Australia 34 24s 147 5E
28 Mirosławiec, Poland 53 20N 16 5E
68 Mirpur Bibiwari, Pak. 28 33N 67 44E
68 Mirpur Khas, Pakistan 25 30N 69 0E
68 Mirpur Sakro, Pakistan 24 33N 67 41E
108 Mirror, Canada 52 30N 113 0W
28 Mirsk, Poland 50 58N 15 23E
76 Miryang, S. Korea 35 34N 128 42E
57 Mirzaani, U.S.S.R. 41 24N 46 5E
69 Mirzapur, India 25 10N 82 45E
17 Miscou I., Canada 47 57N 64 31W
64 Mish'ab, Ra'as al, Saudi Arabia 28 15N 48 43E
76 Mishan, China 45 31N 132 2E
114 Mishawaka, U.S.A. 41 40N 86 8w
86 Mishbih, Gebel, Egypt 22 48N 34 38E
74 Mishima, Japan 35 10N 138 52E
62 Mishmar Aiyalon, Isr. 31 52N 34 57E
62 Mishmar Ha' Emeq, Israel 32 37N 35 7E
62 Mishmar Ha Negev, Israel 31 32N 34 48E
62 Mishmar Ha Yarden, Israel 33 0N 35 56E
40 Misilmeri, Italy 38 3N 13 25E
98 Misima I., Papua 10 40s 152 50E
125 Misiones ♦, Arg. 27 0s 55 0w
124 Misiones ♦, Paraguay 27 0s 56 0w
65 Miskin, Oman 23 44N 56 52E
121 Miskitos, Cayos, Nicaragua 14 26N 82 50W
27 Miskolc, Hungary 48 7N 20 50E
90 Misoke, Zaïre 0 42s 28 2E
73 Misoöl, I., Indonesia 2 0s 130 0E
83 Misrâtah, Libya 32 18N 15 3E
106 Missanabie, Canada 48 20N 84 6w
82 Misserghin, Algeria 35 44N 0 49W
106 Missinaibi L., Canada 48 14N 83 15W
106 Missinaibi, R., Canada 50 30N 82 40W
116 Mission, S.D., U.S.A. 43 21N 100 36W
117 Mission, Tex., U.S.A. 26 15N 98 30W
108 Mission City, Canada 49 10N 122 15W
106 Missisa L., Canada 52 20N 85 7w
113 Mississippi L., Canada 45 5N 76 12W
117 Mississippi ♦, U.S.A. 33 0N 90 0w
117 Mississippi R., U.S.A. 35 30N 90 0w
73 Mississippi Sd., U.S.A. 30 25N 89 0W
117 Mississippi ♦, U.S.A. 33 0N 90 0w
118 Missoula, U.S.A. 47 0N 114 0w
116 Missouri, R., U.S.A. 40 20N 95 40W
116 Missouri, Little, R., U.S.A. 46 0N 111 55E
116 Missouri ♦, U.S.A. 38 25N 92 30W
109 Mistake B., Canada 62 8N 93 0w
106 Mistassini L., Canada 51 0N 73 40W
107 Mistastin L., Canada 55 58N 63 40W
27 Mistelbach, Austria 48 34N 16 34E
40 Misterbianco, Italy 37 32N 15 0E
41 Mistretta, Italy 37 56N 14 20E

MAP
86 Mit Ghamr, Egypt 30 42N 31 12E
87 Mitatib, Sudan 15 59N 36 12E
99 Mitchell, Australia 26 29s 147 58E
112 Mitchell, Canada 43 29N 81 21W
114 Mitchell, Ind., U.S.A. 38 42N 86 25W
116 Mitchell, Nebr., U.S.A. 41 58N 103 45W
118 Mitchell, Oreg., U.S.A. 44 31N 120 8w
116 Mitchell, S.D., U.S.A. 43 40N 98 0w
115 Mitchell, Mt., U.S.A. 35 40N 82 20w
98 Mitchell, R., Australia 37 20s 147 0E
15 Mitchelstown, Ireland 52 16N 8 18W
68 Mitha Tiwana, Pakistan 32 13N 72 6E
44 Mithimna, Greece 39 20N 26 12E
100 Mitiamo, Australia 36 19s 144 14E
101 Mitiaro, I., Cook Is. 19 49s 157 43W
45 Mitilini, Greece 39 6N 26 35E
44 Mitilini = Lesvos, Greece 39 0N 26 20E
45 Mitilinii, Greece 37 42N 26 56E
74 Mito, Japan 36 20N 140 30E
94 Mitre Pk., N.Z. 44 35s 167 45E
93 Mitsinjo, Malagasy Republic 16 1s 45 52E
87 Mitsiwa, Ethiopia 15 35N 39 25E
87 Mitsiwa Channel, Ethiopia 15 30N 40 0E
100 Mitta Mitta, Australia 36 45s 147 36E
100 Mitta Mitta, R., Australia 36 45s 147 36E
126 Mitú, Colombia 1 8N 70 3w
126 Mituas, Colombia 3 52N 68 49w
90 Mitumba, Tanzania 7 8s 31 2E
90 Mitumba, Chaîne des, Zaïre 10 0s 26 20E
91 Mitwaba, Zaïre 8 2N 27 17E
90 Mityana, Uganda 0 23N 32 2E
88 Mitzick, Gabon 0 45N 11 40E
57 Mius, R., U.S.S.R. 47 30N 39 0E
74 Miyagi-Ken ♦, Japan 38 15N 140 45E
86 Miyah, W. el, Egypt 25 10N 33 30E
74 Miyake-Jima, Japan 34 0N 139 30E
74 Miyako, Japan 39 40N 141 75E
77 Miyako-rettō, Japan 24 47N 125 20E
74 Miyakonojo, Japan 31 32N 131 5E
74 Miyazaki, Japan 31 56N 131 30E
74 Miyazaki-ken ♦, Japan 32 0N 131 30E
74 Miyazu, Japan 35 35N 135 10E
64 Miyet, Bahr el, Jordan-Israel 31 30N 35 30E
76 Miyun, China 40 25N 116 50E
79 Mizamis = Ozamiz, Philippines 8 15N 123 50E
83 Mizdah, Libya 31 30N 13 0E
15 Mizen Hd., Cork, Ire. 51 27N 9 50W
15 Mizen Hd., Wick., Ire. 52 52N 6 4w
46 Mizil, Rumania 44 59N 26 29E
49 Mjöbäck, Sweden 57 28N 12 53E
49 Mjölby, Sweden 58 20N 15 10E
47 Mjömna, Norway 60 55N 4 55E
49 Mjörn, Sweden 57 55N 12 25E
47 Mjøsa, R., Sweden 60 40N 11 0E
90 Mkata, Tanzania 5 45s 38 20E
90 Mkokotoni, Tanz. 5 55s 39 15E
90 Mkomazi, Tanzania 4 40s 38 7E
90 Mkulwe, Tanzania 8 37s 32 20E
90 Mkumbi, Ras, Tanzania 7 38s 39 55E
91 Mkushi, Zambia 14 25s 29 15E
91 Mkushi River, Zambia 13 40s 29 30E
93 Mkuze, R., S. Afr. 27 45s 32 30E
90 Mkwaya, Tanzania 6 17s 35 40E
26 Mladá Boleslav, Cz. 50 27N 14 53E
42 Mladenovac, Y.-slav. 44 28N 20 44E
90 Mlala Hills, Tanzania 6 50s 31 40E
42 Mlange, Malawi 16 2s 35 33E
42 Mlava, R., Yugoslavia 44 35N 21 18E
28 Mława, Poland 53 9N 20 25E
39 Mliniste, Yugoslavia 44 13N 16 50E
42 Mljet, I., Yugoslavia 42 43N 17 30E
28 Mlynary, Poland 54 12N 19 46E
85 Mme, Cameroon 6 18N 10 14E
47 Mo, Hordaland, Norway 60 49N 5 48E
50 Mo, Nordland, Norway 66 19N 14 7E
47 Mo, Telemark, Norway 59 28N 7 50E
48 Mo, Gävleborg, Sweden 61 19N 16 47E
73 Moa, I., Indonesia 8 0s 128 0E
84 Moa, R., Sierra Leone 7 0N 11 40W
119 Moab, U.S.A. 38 40N 109 35W
88 Moabi, Gabon 2 24s 10 59E
101 Moala, I., Fiji 18 36s 179 53E
99 Moalla Park, Australia 29 42s 143 3E
100 Moama, Australia 36 3s 144 45E
100 Moamba, Mozambique 25 34s 32 16E
30 Moaña, Spain 42 18N 8 43W
88 Moanda, Gabon 1 28s 13 21E
119 Moapo, U.S.A. 36 45s 114 43W
88 Mobaye, Cent. Afr. Rep. 4 25N 21 5E
116 Moberley, U.S.A. 39 25N 92 25W
106 Mobert, Canada 48 41N 85 40W
115 Mobile, U.S.A. 30 41N 88 3w
115 Mobile, B., U.S.A. 30 30N 88 0w
115 Mobile, Pt., U.S.A. 30 15N 88 0w
49 Moborg, Denmark 56 25N 8 28E
116 Mobridge, U.S.A. 45 40N 100 28W
91 Mocabe Kasari, Zaïre 9 58s 26 12E
91 Moçambique, Mozam. 15 3s 40 42E
91 Moçambique ♦, Mozam. 14 45s 38 30E
91 Moçambique ♦, Ang. 20 43s 21 50E
92 Mochiara Grove, Bots. 20 43s 21 50E
92 Mochudi, Botswana 24 27s 26 7E
91 Mocimboa da Praia, Mozam. 11 25s 40 20E
46 Mociu, Rumania 46 46N 24 3E
49 Möckeln, Sweden 56 40N 14 15E
118 Moclips, U.S.A. 47 29N 124 10w
126 Mocoa, Colombia 1 15N 76 45W

MAP
125 Mococa, Brazil 21 28s 47 0w
120 Mocorito, Mexico 25 20N 108 0w
91 Mocuba, Mozambique 16 54s 37 25E
21 Modane, France 45 12N 6 40E
92 Modasa, India 23 30N 73 21E
92 Modder, R., S. Africa 28 50s 24 50E
92 Modderrivier, S. Africa 29 2s 24 38E
38 Módena, Italy 44 39N 10 55E
119 Modena, U.S.A. 37 55N 113 56W
119 Modesto, U.S.A. 37 43N 121 0w
41 Módica, Italy 36 52N 14 45E
73 Modjokerto, Indonesia 7 29s 112 25E
28 Modlin, Poland 52 24N 20 41E
28 Mödling, Austria 48 5N 16 17E
87 Modo, Sudan 5 31N 30 33E
27 Modra, Czechoslovakia 48 19N 17 20E
42 Modrica, Yugoslavia 44 57N 18 17E
100 Moe, Australia 38 12s 146 19E
92 Moebase, Mozambique 17 3s 38 41E
71 Moei, R., Thailand 17 25N 98 10E
18 Moëlan-s-Mer, France 47 49N 3 38W
127 Moengo, Surinam 5 45N 54 20W
14 Moffat, Scot. 55 20N 3 27W
68 Moga, India 30 48N 75 8E
63 Mogadiscio = Mogadishu, Somali Rep. 2 2N 45 25E
63 Mogadishu, Somali Rep. 2 2N 45 25E
82 Mogador = Essaouira, Morocco 31 32N 9 42W
30 Mogadouro, Portugal 41 22N 6 47w
74 Mogami-gawa, R., Japan 38 45N 140 0E
67 Mogaung, Burma 25 20N 97 0E
49 Mögeltönder, Denmark 54 57N 8 48E
33 Mogente, Spain 38 52N 0 45W
87 Mogho, Ethiopia 4 54N 40 16E
125 Mogi das Cruzes, Brazil 23 45s 46 20W
125 Mogi-Guaçu, R., Brazil 20 53s 48 10W
125 Mogi Mirim, Brazil 22 20s 47 0w
28 Mogielnica, Poland 51 42N 20 41E
54 Mogilev, U.S.S.R. 53 55N 30 18E
56 Mogilev Podolskiy, U.S.S.R. 48 20N 27 40E
100 Mogilla, Australia 36 1s 149 38E
28 Mogilno, Poland 52 39N 17 55E
89 Moginqual, Mozambique 15 35s 40 25E
39 Mogliano Veneto, Italy 45 33N 12 15E
59 Mogocha, U.S.S.R. 53 40N 119 50E
73 Mogoi, Indonesia 1 55s 133 10E
67 Mogók, Burma 23 0N 96 40E
119 Mogollon, U.S.A. 33 25N 108 55W
119 Mogollon Mesa, U.S.A. 43 40N 111 0W
31 Moguer, Spain 37 15N 6 52w
27 Mohács, Hungary 45 58N 18 41E
116 Mohall, U.S.A. 48 46N 101 30W
65 Mohammadabad, Iran 37 30N 59 5E
82 Mohammedia, Morocco 33 44N 7 21W
119 Mohave Desert, U.S.A. 35 0N 117 30W
119 Mohawk, U.S.A. 32 45N 113 50W
49 Moheda, Sweden 57 1N 14 35E
108 Mohémbo, Botswana 18 15s 21 43E
24 Möhne, R., Germany 51 29N 8 10E
76 Moho, China 53 15N 122 27E
49 Moholm, Sweden 58 37N 14 5E
90 Mohoro, Tanzania 8 6s 39 8E
87 Moia, Sudan 5 3N 28 2E
70 Moinabad, India 17 44N 77 16E
58 Mointy, U.S.S.R. 47 40N 73 45E
44 Moirais, Greece 35 4N 24 56E
21 Moirans, France 45 20N 5 33E
21 Moirans-en-Montagne, France 46 26N 5 43E
54 Moisákula, U.S.S.R. 58 3N 24 38E
107 Moisie, Canada 50 7N 66 1w
20 Moissac, France 44 7N 1 5E
74 Moita, Portugal 38 38N 8 58W
126 Moitaco, Venezuela 8 1N 64 21W
30 Mojácar, Spain 37 6N 1 55W
30 Mojados, Spain 41 26N 4 40w
119 Mojave, U.S.A. 35 8N 118 8W
119 Mojave Desert, U.S.A. 35 0N 117 30W
87 Mojjio, Ethiopia 8 35N 39 5E
126 Mojo, Bolivia 21 48s 65 33w
87 Mojo, Ethiopia 8 35N 39 5E
73 Mojo, I., Indonesia 8 10s 117 40E
101 Mokai, New Zealand 38 32s 175 56E
91 Mokambo, Zaïre 12 25s 28 20E
69 Mokameh, India 25 24N 85 55E
101 Mokau, New Zealand 38 42s 174 39E
72 Mokha, Yemen 13 18N 43 15E
45 Mokhós, Greece 35 16N 25 27E
92 Mokhotlong, Les. 29 22s 29 2E
82 Mokněine, Tunisia 35 35N 10 58E
67 Mokokchung, India 26 15N 94 30E
77 Mokpo, S. Korea 34 50N 126 30E
43 Mokra Gora, Yugoslavia 42 50N 20 30E
43 Mokren, Bulgaria 42 52N 26 30E
39 Mokronog, Yugoslavia 45 57N 15 9E
55 Moksha, R., U.S.S.R. 54 45N 43 40E
55 Mokshan, U.S.S.R. 52 25N 44 35E
84 Mokta Spera, Mauritania 16 38N 9 6w
67 Moktama Kwe, Burma 15 40N 96 30E
16 Mol, Belgium 51 11N 5 5E
31 Mola, C. de la, Spain 39 53N 4 20E
41 Mola di Bari, Italy 41 3N 17 5E
47 Moland, Norway 59 11N 8 40E
45 Moláoi, Greece 36 49N 22 56E
42 Molat, I., Yugoslavia 44 15N 14 50E
58 Molchanovo, U.S.S.R. 57 40N 83 50E
12 Mold, Wales 53 10N 3 10w
27 Moldava nad Bodvou, Czechoslovakia 48 38N 21 0E
46 Moldavia = Moldova, Rumania 46 30N 27 0E
56 Moldavian S.S.R.♦, U.S.S.R. 47 0N 28 0E
47 Molde, Norway 62 45N 7 9E
46 Moldova, Rumania 46 30N 27 0E

MAP
42 Moldova Nouă, Rum. 44 45N 21 41E
43 Moldoveanu, mt., Rumania 45 36N 24 45E
41 Molfetta, Italy 41 12N 16 35E
32 Molina de Aragón, Sp. 40 46N 1 52W
41 Moline, Italy 41 30N 90 30W
38 Molinella, Italy 44 38N 11 40E
90 Moliro, Zaïre 8 12s 30 30E
39 Molise ♦, Italy 41 45N 14 30E
41 Moliterno, Italy 40 14N 15 50E
49 Mölle, Sweden 56 17N 12 31E
43 Molledo, Spain 43 8N 4 6w
126 Mollendo, Peru 17 0s 72 0w
31 Mollerusa, Spain 41 37N 0 54E
31 Mollina, Spain 37 8N 4 38w
24 Möllin, Germany 53 37N 10 41E
49 Mollösund, Sweden 58 4N 11 30E
49 Mölndal, Sweden 57 40N 12 3E
56 Molochansk, U.S.S.R. 47 15N 35 23E
56 Molochaya, R., U.S.S.R. 47 0N 35 30E
54 Molodechno, U.S.S.R. 54 20N 26 50E
110 Molokai, I., U.S.A. 21 8N 157 0w
89 Molopo, R., Botswana 28 30s 20 12E
55 Molotov, Mys, U.S.S.R. 81 0N 95 0E
19 Molsheim, France 48 33N 7 29E
92 Molteno, S. Afr. 31 22s 26 22E
73 Molu, I., Indonesia 6 45s 131 40E
73 Molucca Sea, Indonesia 4 0s 124 0E
73 Moluccas = Maluku, Is., Indonesia 1 0s 127 0E
92 Molusi, Botswana 20 21s 24 29E
54 Molvotitsy, U.S.S.R. 57 21N 32 24E
90 Moma, Zaïre 1 35s 23 52E
91 Moma, Mozambique 16 47s 39 4E
92 Momba, S.W. Africa 18 7s 21 41E
90 Mombasa, Kenya 4 2s 39 43E
43 Momchilgrad, Bulgaria 41 33N 25 23E
90 Momi, Zaïre 1 42s 27 0E
126 Mompós, Colombia 9 14N 74 26w
49 Møn, Denmark 54 57N 12 15E
67 Mön, R., Burma 20 25N 94 30E
121 Mona, I., Puerto Rico 18 5N 67 54w
121 Mona Passage, W. Ind. 18 0N 67 40w
14 Monach, Is., Scot. 57 32N 7 40w
14 Monaco ■, Europe 43 46N 7 23E
14 Monadhliath Mts., Scotland 57 10N 4 4w
15 Monaghan, Ireland 54 15N 6 58W
15 Monaghan ♦, Ireland 54 10N 7 0E
117 Monahans, U.S.A. 31 35N 102 50W
108 Monapo, Mozambique 14 50s 40 12E
108 Monarch Mt., Canada 51 55N 125 57w
100 Monaro Ra., Australia 36 20s 149 0E
82 Monastir, Tunisia 35 50N 10 49E
54 Monastyriska, U.S.S.R. 49 8N 25 14E
32 Moncada, Spain 39 30N 0 24W
38 Moncalieri, Italy 45 0N 7 40E
38 Moncalvo, Italy 45 3N 8 15E
30 Monção, Portugal 42 4N 8 27w
31 Moncarapacho, Port. 37 5N 7 46w
32 Moncayo, Mt., Spain 41 48N 1 50W
24 Mönchen-Gladbach, Ger. 51 12N 6 23E
30 Monchique, Portugal 37 19N 8 38w
120 Monclova, Mexico 26 50N 101 30w
18 Moncontour, France 48 22N 2 38W
18 Moncoutant, France 46 43N 0 36W
107 Moncton, Canada 46 7N 64 51w
30 Mondego, Cabo, Port. 40 11N 8 54w
30 Mondego, R., Portugal 40 28N 8 0w
73 Mondeodo, Indonesia 3 21s 122 9E
39 Mondolfo, Italy 43 45N 13 8E
30 Mondoñedo, Spain 43 25N 7 23E
38 Mondovi, Italy 44 23N 7 56E
114 Mondovi, U.S.A. 44 37N 91 40w
21 Mondragon, France 44 13N 4 44E
45 Monemvasia, Greece 36 41N 23 3E
112 Monessen, U.S.A. 40 9N 79 50w
30 Monesterio, Spain 38 6N 6 15w
21 Monestier-de- Clermont, France 44 55N 5 38E
106 Monet, Canada 48 10N 75 40w
117 Monett, U.S.A. 36 55N 93 56w
39 Monfalcone, Italy 45 49N 13 32E
20 Monflanquin, France 44 32N 0 47E
30 Monforte, Portugal 39 6N 7 25w
30 Monforte de Lemos, Spain 42 31N 7 33w
71 Mong Cai, N. Vietnam 21 27N 107 54E
67 Möng Hsu, Burma 21 54N 98 30E
67 Möng Kung, Burma 20 29N 97 52E
71 Möng Lang, Burma 20 29N 97 52E
67 Möng Nai, Burma 20 32N 97 55E
67 Möng Pawk, Burma 22 4N 99 16E
67 Möng Ton, Burma 20 25N 98 45E
67 Möng Wa, Burma 21 26N 100 27E
67 Möng Yai, Burma 22 21N 98 3E
87 Mongalla, Sudan 5 8N 31 55E
69 Monghyr, India 25 23N 86 30E
68 Mongla, Pakistan 22 8N 89 35E
81 Mongo, Chad 12 14N 18 43E
75 Mongolia ■, Asia 47 0N 103 0E
76 Mongolia, Inner, ♦, China 44 35N 117 0E
85 Mongonu, Nigeria 12 40N 13 32E
88 Mongororo, Chad 12 22N 22 26E
88 Mongoumba, Cen. Afr. 3 33N 18 40E
71 Mongpang, China 24 25N 100 25E
89 Mongu, Zambia 15 16s 23 12E

MAP
82 Môngua, Angola 16 43s 15 20E
21 Monistair-St.-Loire, France 45 17N 4 11E
20 Monistrol-sur-Loire, Fr. 45 17N 4 11E
109 Monk, Canada 47 7N 69 59w
91 Monkey Bay, Malawi 14 7s 35 1E
28 Mońki, Poland 53 23N 22 48E
98 Monkira, Australia 24 46s 140 30E
88 Monkoto, Zaïre 1 38s 20 35E
13 Monmouth 51 48N 2 43w
116 Monmouth, U.S.A. 40 50N 90 40w
13 Monmouth ♦, Wales 51 34N 3 5w
121 Mono, L., U.S.A. 38 0N 119 0w
121 Mono, Punta del, Nic. 12 0N 83 30w
112 Monongahela, U.S.A. 40 12N 79 56w
41 Monópoli, Italy 40 57N 17 18E
27 Monor, Hungary 47 21N 19 27E
33 Monóvar, Spain 38 28N 0 53W
95 Monowai, N.Z. 45 53s 167 25E
95 Monowai, L., N.Z. 45 53s 167 25E
32 Monreal del Campo, Sp. 40 47N 1 20E
40 Monreale, Italy 38 6N 13 16E
117 Monroe, La., U.S.A. 32 32N 92 4w
114 Monroe, Mich., U.S.A. 41 55N 83 26w
113 Monroe, N.Y., U.S.A. 41 19N 74 11w
115 Monroe, N.C., U.S.A. 35 2N 80 37w
119 Monroe, Utah, U.S.A. 38 45N 111 39w
116 Monroe, Wis., U.S.A. 42 38N 89 40w
116 Monroe City, U.S.A. 39 40N 91 40w
115 Monroeville, U.S.A. 31 33N 87 15w
84 Monrovia, Liberia 6 18N 10 47w
119 Monrovia, U.S.A. 34 7N 118 1w
16 Mons, Belgium 50 27N 3 58E
49 Möns Klint, Den. 54 57N 12 33E
31 Monsaraz, Portugal 38 28N 7 22w
73 Monse, Indonesia 4 0s 123 10E
20 Monségur, France 44 38N 0 4E
39 Monselice, Italy 43 13N 11 45E
20 Mont-de-Marsin, France 43 54N 0 31w
19 Mont d'Or, Tunnel, Fr. 46 45N 6 18E
107 Mont Joli, Canada 48 37N 68 10w
106 Mont Laurier, Canada 46 35N 75 30w
107 Mont Louis, France 42 31N 2 6E
18 Mont St. Michel, France 48 40N 1 30w
106 Mont Tremblant Prov. Park, Canada 46 30N 74 30w
24 Montabaur, Germany 50 26N 7 49E
39 Montagnana, Italy 45 13N 11 29E
92 Montagu, S. Africa 33 45s 20 8E
120 Montagu, I., Falk. Is. 58 30s 26 15w
118 Montague, Calif., U.S.A. 41 47N 122 30w
113 Montague, Mass., U.S.A. 42 31N 72 33w
120 Montague, I., Mexico 31 40N 114 56w
21 Montaigu, France 46 59N 1 18w
20 Montalbán, Spain 40 50N 0 45w
41 Montalbano di Elicona, Italy 38 1N 15 0E
41 Montalbano Iónico, It. 40 17N 16 33E
32 Montalbo, Spain 39 53N 2 42w
39 Montalcino, Italy 43 4N 11 30E
30 Montalegre, Portugal 41 49N 7 47w
41 Montalto di Castro, Italy 42 20N 11 36E
41 Montalto Uffugo, Italy 39 25N 16 9E
30 Montamarta, Spain 41 39N 5 49w
126 Montana ♦, Peru 6 0s 73 0w
118 Montana ♦, U.S.A. 47 0N 110 0w
30 Montañas de Léon, Sp. 42 30N 6 20w
30 Montánchez, Spain 39 15N 6 8w
126 Montañita, Colombia 1 30N 75 28w
19 Montargis, France 48 0N 2 43E
20 Montauban, France 44 0N 1 21E
113 Montauk, U.S.A. 41 3N 71 57w
93 Mont-aux-Sources, S. Africa 28 44s 28 52E
19 Montbard, France 47 38N 4 20E
19 Montbéliard, France 47 31N 6 48E
31 Montblanch, Spain 41 23N 1 4E
21 Montbrison, France 45 36N 4 3E
21 Montceau-les-Mines, Fr. 46 40N 4 23E
19 Montchanin, Fr. 46 47N 4 30E
113 Montclair, U.S.A. 40 53N 74 49w
19 Montcornet, France 49 40N 4 0E
20 Mont-de-Marsan, Fr. 43 54N 0 31w
127 Monte Alegre, Brazil 2 0s 54 0w
96 Monte Bello Is., W. Australia 20 30s 115 45E
21 Monte Carlo, Monaco 43 46N 7 23E
124 Monte Caseros, Arg. 30 10s 57 50w
8 Monte Comán, Arg. 34 40s 68 0w
126 Monte Líbano, Col. 8 5N 75 29w
30 Monte Redondo, Port. 39 53N 8 50w
40 Monte San Giuliano, It. 38 1N 12 35E
39 Monte San Savino, It. 43 20N 11 42E
41 Monte Sant' Angelo, It. 41 42N 15 59E
41 Monte Santo, C. di, It. 40 5N 9 42E
119 Monte Visto, U.S.A. 37 40N 106 8w
124 Monteagudo, Argentina 27 14s 54 8w
106 Montebello, Canada 45 40N 74 55w
39 Montebelluna, Italy 45 47N 12 3E
18 Montebourg, France 49 30N 1 20w
39 Montecastrilli, Italy 42 40N 12 30E
124 Montecristi, Ecuador 1 0s 80 40w
40 Montecristo, I., Italy 42 20N 10 20E
41 Montefiascone, Italy 42 31N 12 2E
32 Montéglin, France 44 13N 5 50E
121 Montego B., Jamaica 18 30N 78 0w
39 Montegranaro, Italy 43 13N 13 38E
33 Montejicar, Spain 37 33N 3 30w
71 Montekomu Hu, China 34 40N 89 0E
126 Montelíbano, Colombia 8 5N 75 29w

Montélimar INDEX Mpraeso

MAP
21 Montélimar, France 44 33N 4 45E
41 Montella, Italy 40 50N 15 0E
31 Montellano, Spain 36 59N 5 36W
116 Montello, U.S.A. 43 49N 89 21W
38 Montelupo Florentino, Italy 43 44N 11 2E
31 Montemór-o-Novo, Port. 38 40N 8 12W
30 Montemór-o-Velho, Portugal 40 11N 8 40W
120 Montemorelos, Mexico 25 11N 99 42W
20 Montendre, France 45 16N 0 26W
125 Montenegro, Brazil 29 39S 51 29W
42 Montenegro ♦, 'Y.-slav. 42 40N 19 20E
39 Montenero di Bisaccia, Italy 42 0N 14 47E
91 Montepuez, Mozam. 13 8S 38 59E
91 Montepuez, R., Mozam. 12 40S 40 15E
39 Montepulciano, Italy 43 5N 11 46E
39 Montereale, Italy 42 31N 13 13E
19 Montereau, France 48 22N 2 57E
119 Monterey, U.S.A. 36 35N 121 57W
126 Montería, Colombia 8 46N 75 53W
124 Monteros, Argentina 27 11S 65 30W
39 Monterotondo, Italy 42 3N 12 36E
120 Monterrey, Mexico 25 40N 100 30W
127 Montes Claros, Brazil 16 30S 43 50W
31 Montes de Toledo, Sp. 39 35N 4 30W
118 Montesano, U.S.A. 47 0N 123 39W
41 Montesárchio, Italy 41 5N 14 37E
41 Montescaglioso, Italy 40 34N 16 40E
39 Montesilvano, Italy 42 30N 14 8E
39 Montevarchi, Italy 43 30N 11 32E
88 Monteverde, Angola 8 45S 16 45E
125 Montevideo, Uruguay 34 50S 56 11W
116 Montezuma, U.S.A. 41 32N 92 35W
21 Montfaucon, Haute-Loire, France 45 11N 4 20E
19 Montfaucon, Meuse, Fr. 49 16N 5 8E
19 Montfort-l'Amaury, Fr. 48 47N 1 49E
18 Montfort-sur-Meu, Fr. 48 8N 1 58W
21 Montgenèvre, France 44 56N 6 42E
68 Montgomery, Wales 52 34N 3 9W
115 Montgomery, Ala., U.S.A. 32 20N 86 20W
114 Montgomery, W. Va., U.S.A. 38 9N 81 21W
68 Montgomery = Sahiwal, Pakistan 30 45N 73 8E
*13 Montgomery ♦, Wales 52 34N 3 9W
20 Montguyon, France 45 12N 0 12W
25 Monthey, Switzerland 46 15N 6 56E
40 Monti del Gennargentu, Sardinia 40 0N 9 15E
41 Monti Iblei, Italy 37 15N 14 45E
41 Monti Nébrodi, It. 37 48N 14 20E
41 Monti Peloritani, It. 38 2N 15 15E
38 Monticelli d'Ongina, It. 45 3N 9 56E
117 Monticello, Ark., U.S.A. 33 40N 91 48W
115 Monticello, Fla., U.S.A. 30 35N 83 50W
114 Monticello, Ind., U.S.A. 40 40N 86 45W
116 Monticello, Iowa, U.S.A. 42 18N 91 18W
115 Monticello, Ky., U.S.A. 36 52N 84 50W
116 Monticello, Minn., U.S.A. 45 17N 93 52W
117 Monticello, Miss., U.S.A. 31 35N 90 8W
113 Monticello, N.Y., U.S.A. 41 37N 74 42W
119 Monticello, Utah, U.S.A. 37 55N 109 27W
38 Montichiari, Italy 45 28N 10 29E
19 Montieri, France 48 30N 4 45E
20 Montignac, France 45 4N 1 10E
19 Montigny-les- Metz, Fr. 49 7N 6 10E
19 Montigny-sur- Aube, Fr. 47 57N 4 45E
31 Montijo, Spain 38 52N 6 39W
31 Montijo, Presa de, Sp. 38 55N 6 26W
31 Montilla, Spain 37 36N 4 40W
116 Montivideo, U.S.A. 44 55N 95 40W
19 Montlhéry, France 48 39N 2 15E
20 Montluçon, France 46 22N 2 36E
107 Montmagny, Canada 46 58N 70 34W
27 Montmarault, France 46 11N 2 54E
109 Montmartre, Canada 50 20N 103 15W
19 Montmédy, France 49 30N 5 20E
21 Montmélian, France 45 30N 6 4E
19 Montmirail, France 48 51N 3 30E
20 Montmoreau-St.-Cybard, France 45 23N 0 8E
107 Montmorency, Canada 46 53N 71 11W
20 Montmorillon, France 46 26N 0 50E
19 Montmort, France 48 55N 3 49E
98 Monto, Australia 24 52S 151 12E
39 Montório al Vomano, It. 42 35N 13 38E
31 Montoro, Spain 38 1N 4 27W
112 Montour Falls, U.S.A. 42 20N 76 51W
118 Montpelier, Idaho, U.S.A. 42 15N 111 29W
114 Montpelier, Ohio, U.S.A. 41 34N 84 40W
113 Montpelier, Vt., U.S.A. 44 15N 72 38W
20 Montpellier, France 43 37N 3 52E
20 Montpezat-de-Quercy, France 44 15N 1 30E
20 Montpon-Ménestrol, France 45 2N 0 11E
106 Montréal, Canada 45 31N 73 34W
20 Montréal, France 43 13N 2 8E
109 Montreal L., Canada 54 20N 105 45W
20 Montredon- Labessonnié, France 43 45N 2 18E
20 Montréjeau, France 43 6N 0 35E
18 Montrésor, France 47 10N 1 10E
19 Montreuil, France 50 27N 1 45E
18 Montreuil-Bellay, Fr. 47 8N 0 9W
25 Montreux, Switzerland 46 26N 6 55E
18 Montrésor, France 47 10N 1 10E
18 Montrevault, France 47 17N 1 2W
21 Montrevel-en-Bresse, France 46 21N 5 8E
18 Montrichard, France 47 20N 1 10E
14 Montrose, Scot. 56 43N 2 28W
119 Montrose, Col., U.S.A. 38 30N 107 52W
113 Montrose, Pa., U.S.A. 41 50N 75 55W

* *Incorporated within the county of Powys*

MAP
107 Monts, Pte des, Canada 49 27N 67 12W
20 Montsalvy, France 44 41N 2 30E
32 Montsant, Sierra de, Spain 41 17N 0 1E
19 Montsauche, France 47 13N 4 0E
32 Montsech, Sierra del, Spain 42 0N 0 45E
32 Montseny, Spain 42 29N 1 2E
121 Montserrat, I., W.I. 16 40N 62 10W
32 Montserrat, mt., Spain 41 36N 1 49E
30 Montuenga, Spain 41 3N 4 38W
32 Montuiri, Spain 39 34N 2 59E
88 Monveda, Zaïre 2 52N 21 30E
67 Mônywa, Burma 22 7N 95 11E
38 Monza, Italy 45 35N 9 15E
91 Monze, Zambia 16 17S 27 29E
66 Monze, C., Pakistan 24 47N 66 37E
32 Monzón, Spain 41 52N 0 10E
99 Moolawatana, Australia 29 55S 139 45E
106 Moonbeam, Canada 49 20N 82 10W
100 Moondarra, Australia 38 2S 146 30E
99 Moonie, Australia 27 37S 150 17E
99 Moonie, R., Australia 29 0S 148 30E
99 Moonta, Australia 34 6S 137 32E
99 Mooraberree, Australia 25 13S 140 54E
116 Moorcroft, U.S.A. 44 17N 104 58W
96 Moore, L., Australia 29 30S 117 30E
114 Moorefield, U.S.A. 39 5N 78 59W
113 Moores Res., U.S.A. 44 45N 71 50W
115 Mooresville, U.S.A. 35 36N 80 45W
14 Moorfoot Hills, Scotland 55 44N 3 8W
116 Moorhead, U.S.A. 47 0N 97 0W
100 Moorland, Australia 31 46S 152 38E
100 Mooroopna, Australia 36 25S 145 22E
92 Moorreesburg, S. Africa 33 6S 18 38E
25 Moosburg, Germany 48 28N 11 57E
106 Moose, R., Canada 51 20N 81 15W
106 Moose Factory, Canada 52 20N 80 40W
109 Moose Jaw, Canada 50 30N 105 30W
116 Moose Lake, U.S.A. 46 27N 92 48W
106 Moose River, Can. 51 10N 81 47W
107 Moosehead L., U.S.A. 45 40N 69 40W
109 Moosomin, Canada 50 9N 101 40W
106 Moosonee, Canada 51 25N 80 51W
113 Moosup, U.S.A. 41 44N 71 52W
92 Mopipi, Botswana 21 6S 24 55E
87 Mopoi, Central Africa 5 6N 26 54E
99 Moppin, Australia 29 12S 146 45E
84 Mopti, Mali 14 30N 4 0W
87 Moqatta, Sudan 14 38N 35 50E
126 Moquegua, Peru 17 15S 70 46W
27 Mór, Hungary 47 25N 18 12E
31 Móra, Portugal 38 55N 8 10W
48 Mora, Sweden 61 2N 14 38E
116 Mora, Minn., U.S.A. 45 52N 93 19W
119 Mora, N. Mex., U.S.A. 35 58N 105 21W
32 Mora de Ebro, Spain 41 6N 0 38E
32 Mora la Nueva, Spain 41 7N 0 39E
32 Mora de Rubielos, Spain 40 15N 0 45W
42 Morača, R., Y.-slavia 42 40N 19 20E
68 Moradabad, India 28 50N 78 50E
89 Morafenobe, Malagasy Rep. 17 50S 44 53E
28 Morag, Poland 53 55N 19 56E
33 Moral de Calatrava, Sp. 38 51N 3 33W
30 Moraleja, Spain 40 6N 6 43W
126 Morales, Colombia 2 45N 76 38W
117 Moran, Kans., U.S.A. 37 53N 94 35W
118 Moran, Wyo., U.S.A. 43 53N 110 37W
41 Morano Cálabro, Italy 39 51N 16 8E
121 Morant Pt., Jamaica 17 55N 76 12W
14 Morar L., Scot. 56 57N 5 40W
33 Moratalla, Spain 38 14N 1 49W
70 Moratuwa, Sri Lanka 6 45N 79 55E
27 Morava, R., Cz. 49 50N 16 50E
27 Moravia = Země, Cz. 49 7N 15 57E
116 Moravia, U.S.A. 40 50N 92 50W
26 Moravian Hts. = Ceskemoravská V., Cz. 49 30N 15 40E
42 Moravica, R., Y.-slavia 43 40N 20 8E
27 Moravice, R., Cz. 49 50N 17 43E
42 Moravita, Rumania 45 17N 21 14E
27 Moravská Ostrava, Cz. 49 50N 18 20E
27 Moravska Trebová, Cz. 49 45N 16 40E
26 Moravské Budějovice, Czechoslovakia 49 4N 15 49E
126 Morawhanna, Guyana 8 30N 59 40W
*14 Moray ♦, Scot. 57 32N 3 25W
14 Moray Firth, Scot. 57 50N 3 30W
25 Morbach, Germany 49 48N 7 7E
38 Morbegno, Italy 46 8N 9 34E
18 Morbihan ♦, Fr. 47 55N 3 0W
20 Morcenx, France 44 0N 0 55W
18 Mordelles, France 48 5N 1 52W
109 Morden, Canada 49 15N 98 10W
100 Mordialloc, Australia 38 1S 145 6E
55 Mordovian S.S.R.♦, U.S.S.R. 54 20N 44 30E
55 Mordovo, U.S.S.R. 52 13N 40 50E
14 Mordvinske A S S R, U.S.S.R. 54 20N 44 30E
14 More L., Scot. 58 18N 4 52W
47 Möre og Romsdal ♦, Norway 63 0N 9 0E
45 Morea, Greece 37 45N 22 10E
116 Moreau, R., U.S.A. 45 15N 102 45W
12 Morecambe, Eng. 54 5N 2 52W
12 Morecambe B., Eng. 54 7N 3 0W
99 Moree, Australia 29 28S 149 48E
114 Morehead, U.S.A. 38 12N 83 22W
115 Morehead City, U.S.A. 34 46N 76 44W
126 Moreira, Brazil 0 34S 63 26W
120 Morelia, Mexico 19 40N 101 11W
98 Morella, Australia 23 0S 143 47E
32 Morella, Spain 40 35N 0 2E
120 Morelos ♦, Mexico 18 40N 99 10W
31 Morena, Sierra, Spain 38 20N 4 0W
119 Morenci, U.S.A. 33 7N 109 20W
46 Moreni, Rumania 44 59N 25 36E
115 Mores, I., Bahama Is. 26 15N 77 35W

* *Incorporated within the regions of Grampian and Highland*

MAP
108 Moresby I., Canada 52 30N 131 40W
21 Morestel, France 45 40N 5 28E
19 Moret, France 48 22N 2 48E
99 Moreton, I., Australia 27 10S 153 10E
98 Moreton Telegraph Office, Australia 12 22S 142 30E
19 Moreuil, France 49 46N 2 30E
21 Morez, France 46 31N 6 2E
99 Morgan, Australia 34 0S 139 35E
118 Morgan, U.S.A. 41 3N 111 44W
117 Morgan City, U.S.A. 29 40N 91 15W
114 Morganfield, U.S.A. 37 40N 87 55W
115 Morganton, U.S.A. 35 46N 81 48W
114 Morgantown, U.S.A. 39 39N 75 58W
99 Morganville, Australia 25 10S 152 0E
18 Morgat, France 48 15N 4 32E
93 Morgenzon, S. Africa 26 45S 29 36E
25 Morges, Switzerland 46 31N 6 29E
19 Morhange, France 48 55N 6 38E
38 Mori, Italy 45 51N 10 59E
119 Moriarty, U.S.A. 35 3N 106 2W
108 Morice L., Canada 53 50N 127 40W
126 Morichal, Colombia 2 10N 70 34W
126 Morichal Largo, R., Ven. 8 55N 63 0W
85 Moriki, Nigeria 12 52N 6 30E
108 Morinville, Canada 53 49N 113 41W
74 Morioka, Japan 39 45N 141 8E
14 Moriston, Glen, Scot. 57 10N 5 0W
14 Moriston, R., Scot. 57 10N 5 0W
100 Morkalla, Australia 34 18S 141 4E
20 Morlaàs, France 43 21N 0 18W
18 Morlaix, France 48 36N 3 52W
41 Mormanno, Italy 39 53N 15 59E
19 Mormant, France 48 37N 2 52E
99 Morney, Australia 25 22S 141 23E
100 Mornington, Australia 38 15S 145 5E
98 Mornington I., Australia 16 30S 139 30E
128 Mornington, I., Chile 49 50S 75 30W
45 Mórnos, R., Greece 38 30N 22 0E
87 Moro, Sudan 10 50N 30 9E
73 Moro G., Philippines 6 30N 123 0E
98 Morobe, Terr. of New Guinea 7 49S 147 38E
82 Morocco ■, N. Afr. 32 0N 5 50W
126 Morococha, Peru 11 40S 76 5W
90 Morogoro, Tanzania 6 50S 37 40E
120 Moroleón, Mexico 20 8N 101 32W
93 Morombé, Malagasy Rep. 21 45S 43 22E
124 Moron, Argentina 34 39S 58 37W
121 Morón, Cuba 22 0N 78 30W
32 Morón de Almazán, Sp. 41 29N 2 27W
31 Morón de la Frontera, Spain 37 6N 5 28W
93 Morondava, Malagasy Rep. 20 17S 44 17E
84 Morondo, Ivory Coast 8 57N 6 47W
84 Moronou, Ivory Coast 6 16N 4 59W
73 Morotai, I., Indonesia 2 10N 128 30E
90 Moroto Summit, Mt., Kenya 2 30N 34 43E
43 Morozov (Bratan), mt., Bulgaria 42 30N 25 10E
57 Morozovsk, U.S.S.R. 48 25N 41 50E
100 Morpeth, Australia 32 44S 151 39E
12 Morpeth, Eng. 55 11N 1 41W
117 Morrilton, U.S.A. 35 10N 92 45W
127 Morrinhos, Minas Gerais, Braz. 17 45S 49 10W
121 Morrinsville, N.Z. 37 40S 175 32E
109 Morris, Canada 49 25N 97 30W
114 Morris, Ill., U.S.A. 41 20N 88 20W
116 Morris, Minn., U.S.A. 45 33N 95 56W
106 Morrisburg, Canada 44 55N 75 7W
116 Morrison, U.S.A. 41 47N 90 0W
119 Morristown, Ariz., U.S.A. 33 54N 112 45W
113 Morristown, N.J., U.S.A. 40 48N 74 30W
116 Morristown, S.D., U.S.A. 45 57N 101 44W
115 Morristown, Tenn., U.S.A. 36 18N 83 20W
124 Morro, Pta., Chile 27 6S 71 0W
119 Morro Bay, U.S.A. 35 27N 120 54W
121 Morrosquillo, Golfo de, Colombia 9 35N 75 40W
49 Morrum, Sweden 56 12N 14 45E
49 Mors, Denmark 56 50N 8 45E
55 Morshank, U.S.S.R. 53 28N 41 50E
48 Mörsil, Sweden 63 19N 13 40E
20 Mortagne, Charente Maritime, France 45 28N 0 49W
18 Mortagne, Orne, France 48 30N 0 32E
18 Mortagne, Vendée, Fr. 46 59N 0 57W
19 Mortagne, R., France 48 30N 6 30E
18 Mortain, France 48 40N 0 57W
38 Mortara, Italy 45 15N 8 43E
19 Morteau, France 47 3N 6 35E
124 Morteros, Argentina 30 50S 62 0W
100 Mortlake, Australia 38 5S 142 50E
117 Morton, Tex., U.S.A. 33 39N 102 49W
118 Morton, Wash., U.S.A. 46 42N 122 11W
100 Morundah, Australia 34 57S 146 19E
100 Moruya, Australia 35 58N 150 3E
19 Morvan, Mts. du, Fr. 47 5N 4 0E
99 Morven, Australia 26 22S 147 5E
14 Morvern, Scot. 56 38N 5 44W
68 Morvi, India 22 25N 72 5E
28 Moryń, Poland 52 51N 14 22E
54 Mosalsk, U.S.S.R. 54 30N 34 55E
25 Mosbach, Germany 49 21N 9 9E
39 Mošćenice, Y.-slavia 45 17N 14 16E
39 Mosciano Sant' Angelo, Italy 42 42N 13 52E
118 Moscow, U.S.A. 46 45N 116 59W
55 Moscow = Moskva, U.S.S.R. 55 45N 37 35E
25 Mosel, R., Germany 49 48N 6 45E
16 Moselle, R., Lux. 49 42N 6 30E
19 Moselle ♦, France 48 59N 6 33E

MAP
118 Moses Lake, U.S.A. 47 16N 119 17W
101 Mosgiel, N.Z. 45 53S 170 21E
90 Moshi, Tanzania 3 22S 37 18E
90 Moshi ♦, Tanzania 3 22S 37 18E
92 Moshupa, Botswana 24 46S 25 29E
28 Mósina, Poland 52 15N 16 50E
50 Mosjöen, Norway 65 51N 13 12E
50 Moskenesöya, Norway 67 58N 13 0E
50 Moskenstraumen, Nor. 67 47N 13 0E
55 Moskva, U.S.S.R. 55 45N 37 35E
55 Moskva, R., U.S.S.R. 55 5N 38 51E
39 Moslavačka Gora, Yugoslavia 45 40N 16 37E
92 Mosomane (Artesia), Botswana 24 2S 26 19E
27 Mosonmagyaróvár, Hungary 47 52N 17 18E
*27 Mosonszentjános, Hung. 47 47N 17 11E
42 Mošorin, Yugoslavia 45 19N 20 4E
56 Mospina, U.S.S.R. 47 52N 38 6E
126 Mosquera, Colombia 2 35N 78 30W
117 Mosquero, U.S.A. 35 48N 103 57W
32 Mosqueruela, Spain 40 21N 0 27W
121 Mosquitos, Golfo de los, Pan. 9 15N 81 10W
47 Moss, Norway 59 27N 10 40E
100 Moss Vale, Australia 34 32S 150 25E
88 Mossaka, Congo 1 15S 16 45E
89 Mossâmedes, Angola 15 7S 12 11E
109 Mossbank, Canada 50 0N 106 0W
101 Mossburn, N.Z. 45 41S 168 15E
92 Mosselbaai, S. Africa 34 11S 22 8E
88 Mossendjo, Congo 2 55S 12 42E
100 Mossgiel, Australi 33 15S 144 30E
98 Mossman, Australia 16 21S 145 15E
127 Mossoró, Brazil 5 10S 37 15W
91 Mossuril, Mozambique 14 58S 40 42E
26 Most, Czechoslovakia 50 31N 13 38E
42 Mostar, Yugoslavia 43 22N 17 50E
125 Mostardas, Brazil 31 2S 50 51W
83 Mostefa, Rass, Tunisia 36 55N 11 3E
47 Mosteröy, Norway 59 5N 5 37E
54 Mostiska, U.S.S.R. 49 48N 23 4E
54 Mosty, U.S.S.R. 53 27N 24 38E
64 Mosul = Al Mawsil, Iraq 36 20N 43 5E
77 Mosun, China 23 35N 109 30E
47 Mosvatn, L., Norway 59 52N 8 5E
32 Mota del Cuervo, Spain 39 30N 2 52W
30 Mota del Marqués, Sp. 41 38N 5 11W
49 Motala, Sweden 58 32N 15 1E
14 Motherwell, Scot. 55 48N 4 0W
69 Motihari, India 26 37N 85 1E
32 Motilla del Palancar, Spain 39 34N 1 55W
39 Motnik, Yugoslavia 46 14N 14 54E
126 Motocurunya, Ven. 4 24N 64 5W
120 Motozintea de Mendoza, Mexico 15 21N 92 14W
39 Motovun, Yugoslavia 45 20N 13 50E
33 Motril, Spain 36 44N 3 37W
46 Motru, R., Rumania 44 44N 22 59E
116 Mott, U.S.A. 46 25N 102 14W
41 Mottola, Italy 40 38N 17 0E
101 Motueka, N.Z. 41 7S 173 1E
120 Motul, Mexico 21 0N 89 20W
44 Moúdhros, Greece 39 50N 25 18E
84 Moudjéria, Mauritania 17 50N 12 15W
25 Moudon, Switzerland 46 40N 6 49E
88 Mouila, Gabon 1 50S 11 0E
100 Moulamein, Australia 35 3S 144 1E
100 Moulamein Cr., Australia 35 6S 144 3E
20 Moulins, France 46 35N 3 19E
67 Moulmein = Maulamyaing, Burma 16 30N 97 40E
82 Moulouya, O., Morocco 35 8N 2 22W
117 Moulton, U.S.A. 29 35N 97 8W
115 Moultrie, U.S.A. 31 11N 83 47W
115 Moultrie, L., U.S.A. 33 25N 80 10W
116 Mound City, Mo., U.S.A. 40 2N 95 25W
116 Mound City, S.D., U.S.A. 45 46N 100 3W
45 Moúnda, Akra, Greece 38 5N 27 45E
81 Moundou, Chad 8 40N 16 10E
112 Moundsville, U.S.A. 39 53N 80 43W
115 Mount Airy, U.S.A. 36 31N 80 37W
112 Mount Albert, Canada 44 10N 79 20W
118 Mount Angel, U.S.A. 45 4N 122 46W
96 Mount Barker, W.A., Australia 34 38S 117 40E
98 Mount Buckley, Australia 20 6S 148 0E
114 Mount Carmel, Ill., U.S.A. 38 20N 87 48W
113 Mount Carmel, Pa., U.S.A. 40 46N 76 25W
112 Mount Clemens, U.S.A. 42 35N 82 50W
98 Mount Coolon, Austral. 21 25S 147 25E
107 Mount Desert I., U.S.A. 44 25N 68 25W
115 Mount Dora, U.S.A. 28 49N 81 32W
98 Mount Douglas, Austral. 21 35S 146 50E
96 Mount Enid, Australia 21 42S 116 26E
100 Mount Evelyn, Austral. 37 45S 145 29W
106 Mount Forest, Canada 43 59N 80 43W
98 Mount Fox, Australia 18 45S 145 45E
93 Mount Frere, S. Africa 30 51S 29 0E
99 Mount Gambier, Australia 37 38S 140 44E
98 Mount Garnet, Austral. 17 37S 145 6E
114 Mount Hope, U.S.A. 37 52N 81 9W
116 Mount Horeb, U.S.A. 43 0N 89 42W
100 Mount Hotham, Austral. 37 2S 146 52E
98 Mount Isa, Australia 20 42S 139 26E
113 Mount Joy, U.S.A. 40 6N 76 30W
66 Mount Lavinia, Sri Lanka 6 50N 79 50E
99 Mount Lofty Ranges, Australia 35 0S 138 0E

* *Renamed Jánossomorja*

MAP
96 Mount Magnet, Australia 28 2S 117 47E
101 Mount Maunganui, N.Z. 37 40S 176 14E
98 Mount Molloy, Austral. 16 32S 145 20E
98 Mount Morgan, Australia 23 40S 150 25E
112 Mount Morris, Mich., USA 43 8N 83 42W
112 Mount Morris, N.Y., USA 42 43N 77 50W
98 Mount Mulligan, Australia 16 45S 144 47E
96 Mount Nicholas, Australia 22 54S 120 27E
98 Mount Oxide, Australia 19 30S 139 29E
99 Mount Perry, Australia 25 13S 151 42E
116 Mount Pleasant, Iowa, USA 41 0N 91 35W
114 Mount Pleasant, Mich., USA 43 38N 84 46W
112 Mount Pleasant, Pa., USA 40 9N 79 31W
115 Mount Pleasant, S.C., USA 32 45N 79 48W
115 Mount Pleasant, Tenn., USA 35 31N 87 11W
117 Mount Pleasant, Tex., USA 33 5N 95 0W
118 Mount Pleasant, Ut., USA 39 40N 111 29W
113 Mount Pocono, U.S.A. 41 8N 75 21W
118 Mount Rainier Nat. Park., U.S.A. 46 50N 121 20W
108 Mount Robson, Canada 52 56N 119 15W
118 Mount Shasta, U.S.A. 41 20N 122 18W
100 Mount Singleton, Australia 32 30S 151 3E
116 Mount Sterling, Ill., U.S.A. 40 0N 90 40W
116 Mount Sterling, Ky., U.S.A. 38 0N 84 0W
98 Mount Surprise, Australia 18 10S 144 17E
96 Mount Tom Price, Australia 22 50S 117 40E
112 Mount Union, U.S.A. 40 22N 77 51W
116 Mount Vernon, Ind., U.S.A. 38 17N 88 57W
113 Mount Vernon, N.Y., USA 40 57N 73 49W
114 Mount Vernon, Ohio, USA 40 20N 82 30W
118 Mount Vernon, Wash., USA 48 27N 122 18W
96 Mount Whaleback, Australia 24 38S 113 33E
118 Mountain City, Nev., U.S.A. 41 54N 116 0W
115 Mountain City, Tenn., U.S.A. 36 30N 81 50W
117 Mountain Grove, U.S.A. 37 5N 92 20W
117 Mountain Home, Ark., U.S.A. 36 20N 92 25W
118 Mountain Home, Idaho, U.S.A. 43 11N 115 45W
116 Mountain Iron, U.S.A. 47 30N 92 87W
108 Mountain Park., Canada 52 50N 117 15W
117 Mountain View, Ark., U.S.A. 35 52N 92 10W
119 Mountain View, Calif., U.S.A. 37 26N 122 5W
119 Mountainair, U.S.A. 34 35N 106 15W
15 Mountmellick, Ireland 53 7N 7 20W
15 Mountnorris, N. Ireland 54 15N 6 29W
126 Moura, Brazil 1 25S 61 45W
31 Moura, Portugal 38 7N 7 30W
98 Moura, Australia 24 35S 149 58E
31 Mourão, Portugal 38 22N 7 22W
81 Mourdi, Depression du, Chad 18 10N 23 0E
84 Mourdiah, Mali 14 35N 7 25W
20 Mourenx, France 43 23N 0 36W
85 Mouri, Ghana 5 6N 1 14W
98 Mourilyan, Australia 17 35S 146 10E
19 Mourmelon-le-Grand, Fr. 49 8N 4 22E
15 Mourne Mts., N. Ire. 54 10N 6 0W
15 Mourne, R., N. Ireland 54 45N 7 25W
83 Mourzouq, Libya 25 53N 14 10W
16 Mouscron, Belgium 50 45N 3 12E
81 Moussoro, Chad 13 50N 16 35E
19 Mouthe, France 46 44N 6 12E
25 Moutier, Switzerland 47 16N 7 21E
21 Moutiers, France 45 29N 6 31E
73 Moutong, Indonesia 0 28N 121 13E
19 Mouy, France 49 18N 2 20E
82 Mouydir, Algeria 25 20N 4 15E
44 Mouzáki, Greece 39 25N 21 37E
15 Moville, Ireland 55 11N 7 3W
77 Mowming, China 21 50N 110 32E
15 Moy, R., Ireland 54 5N 8 50W
87 Moyale, Ethiopia 3 34N 39 4E
90 Moyale, Kenya 3 30N 39 0E
84 Moyamba, Sierra Leone 8 15N 12 30W
108 Moyie, Canada 49 17N 115 50W
126 Moyobamba, Peru 6 0S 77 0W
62 Moza, Israel 31 48N 35 8E
93 Mozambique ■, Africa 19 0S 35 0E
89 Mozambique = Moçambique, Mozambique 15 3S 40 42E
93 Mozambique Chan. Africa 20 0S 39 0E
57 Mozdok, U.S.S.R. 43 45N 44 48E
55 Mozhaisk, U.S.S.R. 55 30N 36 2E
39 Mozirje, Yugoslavia 46 22N 14 58E
90 Mozua, Zaïre 3 57N 24 2E
54 Mozyr, U.S.S.R. 52 0N 29 15E
90 Mpanda, Tanzania 6 23S 31 40E
90 Mpanda ♦, Tanzania 6 23S 31 40E
84 Mpésoba, Mali 12 31N 5 39W
91 Mpika, Zambia 11 51S 31 25E
85 Mpraeso, Ghana 6 50N 0 50W

Mpulungy INDEX Nambucca Heads

MAP
91 Mpulungy, Zambia 8 51S 31 5E
28 Mragowo, Poland 53 57N 21 18E
42 Mramor, Yugoslavia 43 20N 21 45E
82 Mrhaïer, Algeria 33 55N 5 58E
82 Mrimina, Morocco 29 50N 7 9W
42 Mrkonjić Grad, Y.-slav. 44 26N 17 4E
39 Mrkopalj, Yugoslavia 45 21N 14 52E
28 Mrocza, Poland 53 16N 17 35E
83 Msa, Oueden, Alg. 32 35N 5 20E
83 Msaken, Tunisia 35 49N 10 33E
91 M'Salu, R., Mozam. 12 25S 39 15E
91 Msambansovu, mt., Rhodesia 15 50S 30 3E
82 M'sila, Algeria 35 46N 4 30E
54 Msta, R., U.S.S.R. 58 30N 33 30E
54 Mstislavl, U.S.S.R. 54 0N 31 50E
27 Mszana Dolna, Poland 49 41N 20 5E
28 Mszczonów, Poland 51 58N 20 33E
91 Mtama, Tanzania 10 17S 39 21E
91 Mtilikwe, R., Rhodesia 21 0S 31 12E
55 Mtsensk, U.S.S.R. 53 25N 36 30E
57 Mtskheta, U.S.S.R. 41 52N 44 45E
91 Mtwara ♦, Tanzania 9 40S 38 30E
91 Mtwara-Mikindani, Tanzania 10 20S 40 20E
71 Mu, R., Burma 23 0N 95 20E
127 Muaná, Brazil 1 25S 49 15W
71 Muang Chiang Rai, Thailand 19 52N 99 50E
71 Muang Kalasin, Thai. 16 26N 103 30E
71 Muang Lampang, Thai. 18 16N 99 32E
71 Muang Lamphun, Thai. 18 40N 98 53E
71 Muang Nan, Thailand 18 52N 100 42E
71 Muang Phetchabun, Thai. 16 23N 101 12E
71 Muang Phichit, Thai. 16 29N 100 21E
71 Muang Ubon, Thai. 15 15N 104 50E
71 Muang Yasothon, Thai. 15 50N 104 10E
71 Muar = Bandar Maharani, Malaysia 2 3N 102 34E
71 Muar, R., Malaysia 2 15N 102 48E
72 Muarabungo, Indonesia 1 40S 101 10E
72 Muaradjuloi, Indonesia 0 12S 114 3E
72 Muaraenim, Indonesia 3 40S 103 50E
72 Muarakaman, Indon. 0 2S 116 45E
72 Muaratebo, Indonesia 1 30S 102 26E
72 Muaratembesi, Indon. 1 42S 103 2E
72 Muaratewe, Indonesia 0 50S 115 0E
64 Mubairik, Saudi Arabia 23 22N 39 8E
69 Mubarakpur, India 26 12N 83 24E
90 Mubende, Uganda 0 33N 31 22E
90 Mubende ♦, Ugan. 0 55N 31 0E
126 Mucajai, Serra do, Braz. 2 23N 61 10W
24 Mücheln, Germany 51 18N 11 49E
91 Muchinga Mts., Zambia 11 30S 31 30E
55 Muchkapskiy, U.S.S.R. 51 52N 42 28E
14 Muck, I., Scot. 56 50N 6 15W
99 Muckadilla, Australia 26 32S 148 36E
93 Mucubela, Mozambique 16 53S 37 49E
127 Mucugê, Brazil 13 5S 37 49E
127 Mucuri, Brazil 18 0S 40 0W
118 Mud L., U.S.A. 40 15N 120 15W
64 Mudanya, Turkey 40 25N 28 50E
119 Muddy, R., U.S.A. 38 30N 110 55W
100 Mudgee, Australia 32 32S 149 31E
64 Mudhnib, Saudi Arabia 25 50N 44 18E
91 Muecate, Mozambique 14 55S 39 34E
91 Muêda, Mozambique 11 36S 39 28E
91 Mufulira, Zambia 12 32S 28 15E
90 Mufumbiro Range, Ugan. 1 25S 29 30E
30 Mugardos, Spain 43 27N 8 15W
31 Muge, Portugal 39 3N 8 40W
31 Muge, R., Portugal 39 15N 8 18W
39 Múggia, Italy 45 36N 13 47E
30 Mugia, Spain 43 3N 9 17W
90 Mugila, Mts., Zaïre 7 0S 28 50E
64 Muğla, Turkey 37 15N 28 28E
43 Müglizh, Bulgaria 42 37N 25 32E
69 Mugu, Nepal 29 45N 82 30E
86 Muhammad Qol, Sudan 20 53N 37 9E
86 Muhammad Râs, Egypt 27 50N 34 0E
69 Muhammadabad, India 26 4N 83 25E
62 Muharraqa = Sa'ad, Israel 31 28N 34 33E
90 Muhesi, R., Tanzania 6 40S 35 5E
25 Mühldorf, Germany 48 14N 12 23E
24 Mühlhausen, Germany 51 12N 10 29E
5 Mühlig-Hofmann-fjella, Antarctica 72 30S 5 0E
90 Muhutwe, Tanzania 1 35S 31 45E
71 Mui Bai Bung, S. Vietnam 8 35N 104 42E
71 Mui Ron, N. Vietnam 18 7N 106 27E
15 Muine Bheag, Ireland 52 42N 6 59W
30 Muiños, Spain 41 58N 7 59W
87 Muja, Ethiopia 12 2N 39 30E
62 Mujeidil, Israel 32 41N 35 14E
54 Mukachevo, U.S.S.R. 48 27N 22 45E
72 Mukah, Malaysia 2 55N 112 5E
63 Mukalla, South Yemen 14 33N 49 2E
86 Mukawwa, Geziret, Egypt 23 55N 35 53E
76 Mukden = Shenyang, China 41 35N 123 30E
63 Mukeiras, Yemen 13 59N 45 52E
63 Mukha, Yemen 13 18N 43 15E
55 Mukhtolovo, U.S.S.R. 55 29N 43 15E
91 Mukombwe, Zambia 15 48S 26 32E
72 Mukomuko, Indonesia 2 20S 101 10E
90 Mukomwenze, Zaïre 6 49S 27 15E
68 Muktsar, India 30 30N 74 30E
65 Mukur, Afghanistan 32 50N 67 50E
91 Mukwela, Zambia 17 0S 26 40E
33 Mula, Spain 38 3N 1 33W
70 Mula, R., India 19 16N 74 20E
73 Mulanay, Philippines 13 30N 122 30E
90 Mulange, Zaïre 3 40S 27 10E
121 Mulatas, Arch. de las, Panama 6 51N 78 31W

MAP
124 Mulchén, Chile 37 45S 72 20W
24 Mulde, R., Germany 50 55N 12 42E
116 Mule Creek, U.S.A. 43 19N 104 8W
90 Muleba, Tanzania 1 50S 31 37E
117 Muleshoe, U.S.A. 34 17N 102 42W
107 Mulgrave, Canada 45 38N 61 31W
98 Mulgrave I., Australia 10 5S 142 0E
33 Mulhacén, Spain 37 4N 3 20W
24 Mülheim, Germany 51 26N 6 53W
19 Mulhouse, France 47 40N 7 20E
67 Muli, China 28 21N 100 40E
14 Mull I., Scotland 56 27N 6 0W
14 Mull, Sound of, Scotland 56 30N 5 50W
70 Mullaitivu, Sri Lanka 9 15N 80 55E
116 Mullen, U.S.A. 42 5N 101 0W
100 Mullengudgery, Australia 31 43S 147 29E
114 Mullens, U.S.A. 37 34N 81 22W
72 Muller, Pegunungan, Indon. 0 30N 113 30E
98 Muller Ra., N.E. New Guinea 5 30S 143 0E
15 Mullet Pen., Ireland 54 10N 10 2W
96 Mullewa, Australia 28 29S 115 30E
24 Mullheim, Germany 47 48N 7 37E
117 Mullin, U.S.A. 31 33N 98 38W
15 Mullingar, Ireland 53 31N 7 20W
115 Mullins, U.S.A. 34 12N 79 15W
100 Mullion Creek, Australia 33 9S 148 7E
49 Mullsjö, Sweden 57 56N 13 55E
99 Mullumbimby, Australia 28 30S 153 30E
91 Mulobezi, Zambia 16 45S 25 7E
92 Mulonga Plain, Botswana 23 12S 23 30E
70 Mulshi L., India 18 30N 73 20E
68 Multai, India 21 39N 78 15E
68 Multan, Pakistan 30 15N 71 30E
68 Multan ♦, Pakistan 30 29N 72 29E
48 Multrå, Sweden 63 10N 17 24E
91 Mulumbe, Mts. Zaïre 8 40S 27 30E
91 Mulungushi Dam, Zam. 14 48S 28 48E
117 Mulvane, U.S.A. 37 30N 97 15W
86 Mulwad, Sudan 18 45N 30 39E
100 Mulwala, Australia 35 59S 146 0E
57 Mumra, U.S.S.R. 45 45N 47 41E
71 Mun, Nam, Thailand 15 17N 103 0E
73 Muna, I., Indonesia 5 0S 122 30E
25 Münchberg, Germany 50 11N 11 48E
24 Müncheberg, Germany 52 30N 14 9E
25 München, Germany 48 8N 11 33E
108 Muncho Lake, Canada 58 44N 125 50W
114 Muncie, U.S.A. 40 10N 85 20W
70 Mundakayam, India 9 30N 76 32E
108 Mundare, Canada 53 35N 112 30W
117 Munday, U.S.A. 33 26N 99 39W
24 Münden, Germany 51 25N 9 42E
33 Mundo, R., Spain 38 30N 2 15W
127 Mundo Novo, Brazil 11 50S 40 29W
68 Mundra, India 22 54N 69 26E
33 Munera, Spain 39 2N 2 29W
70 Muneru, R., India 16 45N 80 3E
98 Mungana, Australia 17 8S 144 27E
68 Mungaoli, India 24 24N 78 7E
41 Mungari, Mozambique 17 12S 33 42E
99 Mungindi, Australia 28 58S 149 1E
25 Munich = München, Germany 48 8N 11 35E
114 Munising, U.S.A. 46 25N 86 39W
89 Munhango, Angola 12 10S 18 38E
86 Munjiye, Saudi Arabia 18 47N 41 20W
49 Munka-Ljungby, Swed. 56 16N 12 58E
49 Munkedal, Sweden 58 28N 11 40E
48 Munkfors, Sweden 59 50N 13 30E
128 Muñoz Gamero, Pen., Chile 52 30S 73 5E
99 Munro, Australia 25 30S 142 45E
109 Munroe L., Canada 59 0N 98 40W
19 Munster, France 48 2N 7 8E
24 Münster, Niedersachsen, Germany 52 59N 10 5E
24 Münster, Nordrhein-Westfalen, Germany 51 58N 7 37E
15 Munster ♦, Ire. 52 20N 8 40W
46 Muntelui Mare, Rumania 46 30N 23 12E
72 Muntok, Indonesia 2 5S 105 10E
58 Munyak, U.S.S.R. 43 35N 59 30E
71 Muon Pak Beng, Laos 19 51N 101 4E
71 Muong La, Laos 20 52N 102 5E
71 Muong Ngoi, Laos 20 41N 102 39E
71 Muong Sing, Laos 21 12N 101 12E
71 Muong Soui, Laos 19 32N 102 47E
50 Muonio, Finland 67 57N 23 40E
50 Muonio, Sweden 67 57N 23 40E
50 Muonio älv, Sweden 67 48N 23 25E
89 Mupa, Angola 16 5S 15 50E
65 Muqab, Trucial Oman 23 0N 53 0E
87 Muqaddam, Wadi, Sud. 17 0N 32 0E
26 Mur, R., Austria 47 7N 13 55E
18 Mur-de-Bretagne, Fr. 48 12N 3 0W
39 Mura, R., Yugoslavia 46 37N 16 9E
128 Murallón, Cuerro, Chile 49 55S 73 30W
90 Muranda, Rwanda 1 52S 29 20E
90 Murangá (Ft. Hall), Kenya 0 45S 37 9E
55 Murashi, U.S.S.R. 59 30N 49 0E
20 Murat, France 45 7N 2 53E
26 Murau, Austria 47 6N 14 10E
40 Muravera, Italy 39 25N 9 35E
30 Murça, Portugal 41 24N 7 28W
100 Murchison, Australia 36 39S 145 14E
96 Murchison, R., Australia 27 30S 114 0E
• 90 Murchison Falls, Uganda 2 15N 31 38E
91 Murchison Rapids, Malawi 15 55S 34 35E
33 Murcia, Spain 38 2N 1 10W
33 Murcia ♦, Spain 37 50N 1 30W
116 Murdo, U.S.A. 43 56N 100 43W
46 Mureş ♦, Rumania 46 45N 24 40E
46 Mureşul, Rumania 46 0N 22 0E
20 Muret, France 43 30N 1 20E

* *Renamed Kabarega Falls*

MAP
115 Murfreesboro, U.S.A. 35 50N 86 21W
58 Murgab, U.S.S.R. 38 10N 73 59E
46 Murgeni, Rumania 46 12N 28 1E
99 Murgon, Australia 26 15S 151 54E
125 Muriaé, Brazil 21 8S 42 23W
30 Murias de Paredes, Spain 45 52N 6 19W
91 Muriel Mine, Rhodesia 17 14S 30 40E
73 Muris, Indonesia 2 23S 140 5E
24 Murits see, Germany 53 25N 12 40E
73 Murjo Mt., Indonesia 6 36S 110 53E
90 Murka, Kenya 3 27S 38 0E
52 Murmansk, U.S.S.R. 68 57N 33 10E
25 Murnau, Germany 47 40N 11 11E
21 Muro, Corsica 42 34N 8 54E
32 Muro, Spain 39 45N 3 3E
21 Muro, C. di, Corsica 41 44N 8 37E
41 Muro Lucano, Italy 40 45N 15 30E
55 Murom, U.S.S.R. 55 35N 42 3E
74 Muroran, Japan 42 25N 141 0E
30 Muros, Spain 42 45N 9 5W
30 Muros y de Noya, Ria de, Spain 42 45N 9 0W
74 Muroto-Misaki, Japan 33 15N 134 10E
118 Murphy, U.S.A. 43 11N 116 33W
117 Murphysboro, U.S.A. 37 50N 89 20W
86 Murrat, Sudan 18 51N 29 33E
115 Murray, Ky., U.S.A. 36 40N 88 20W
118 Murray, Utah, U.S.A. 40 41N 111 58W
99 Murray Br., Australia 35 6S 139 14E
107 Murray Harb., Canada 46 0N 62 28W
115 Murray, L., U.S.A. 34 8N 81 30W
99 Murray, R., Australia 35 50S 147 40E
92 Murraysburg, S. Africa 31 58S 23 47E
100 Murrayville, Australia 35 20S 140 16E
66 Murree, Pakistan 33 56N 73 28E
100 Murringo, Australia 34 16S 148 32E
99 Murrumbidgee, R., Australia 34 30S 145 30E
100 Murrumburrah, Australia 34 30S 148 15E
100 Murrurundi, Australia 31 42S 150 51E
86 Murshid, Sudan 21 40N 31 10E
69 Murshidabad, India 24 11N 88 19E
39 Murska Sobota, Y.-slavia 46 39N 16 12E
68 Murtazapur, India 20 40N 77 25E
100 Murtoa, Australia 36 29S 142 29E
30 Murtosa, Portugal 40 44N 8 40W
87 Muru, Sudan 6 36N 29 16E
90 Murungu, Tanzania 4 12S 31 10E
69 Murwara, India 23 46N 80 28E
99 Murwillumbah, Australia 28 18S 153 27E
26 Mürz, R., Austria 47 30N 15 25E
26 Mürzzuschlag, Austria 47 36N 15 41E
64 Mus, Turkey 38 45N 41 30E
86 Musa, Gebel (Sinai), Egypt 28 32N 33 59E
66 Musa Qala (Musa Kala), Afghanistan 32 20N 64 50E
68 Musaffargarh, Pakistan 30 10N 71 10E
86 Musairik, Wadi, Saudi Arabia 19 30N 43 10E
68 Musakhel, Pakistan 30 29N 69 52E
72 Musala, I., Indonesia 1 41N 98 28E
43 Musalla, mt., Bulgaria 42 13N 23 37E
76 Musan, N. Korea 42 12N 129 12E
91 Musangu, Zaïre 10 28S 23 55E
90 Musasa, Tanzania 3 25S 31 30E
65 Muscat = Masqat, Oman 23 37N 58 36E
63 Muscat & Oman ■, Arabia 23 0N 58 0E
116 Muscatine, U.S.A. 41 25N 91 5W
30 Musel, Spain 43 34N 5 42W
91 Musetula, Zambia 14 28S 24 1E
96 Musgrave Ras., Austral. 26 0S 132 0E
88 Mushie, Zaïre 2 56S 17 4E
85 Mushin, Nigeria 6 32N 3 21E
70 Musi, R., India 17 10N 79 25E
72 Musi, R., Indonesia 2 55S 103 40E
114 Muskegon, U.S.A. 43 15N 86 17W
114 Muskegon, R., U.S.A. 43 25N 86 0W
114 Muskegon Hts., U.S.A. 43 12N 86 17W
117 Muskogee, U.S.A. 35 50N 95 25W
86 Musmar, Sudan 18 6N 35 40E
91 Musofu, Zambia 13 30S 29 0E
90 Musoma, Tanzania 1 30S 33 48E
90 Musoma ♦, Tanz. 1 50S 34 30E
107 Musquaro, L., Canada 50 42N 61 5W
107 Musquodoboit Harbour, Canada 44 50N 63 9W
14 Musselburgh, Scot. 55 57N 3 3W
118 Musselshell, R., U.S.A. 46 30N 108 15W
20 Mussidan, France 45 2N 0 22E
40 Mussomeli, Italy 37 35N 13 43E
68 Mussoorie, India 30 27N 78 6E
92 Mussuco, Angola 17 2S 19 3E
64 Mustafa Kemalpasa, Turkey 40 3N 28 25E
64 Mustajidda, S. Arabia 26 30N 41 50E
69 Mustang, Nepal 29 10N 83 55E
83 Mustapha, C., Tunisia 36 55N 11 3E
128 Musters, L., Argentina 45 20S 69 25W
100 Muswellbrook, Australia 32 16S 150 56E
27 Muszyna, Poland 49 22N 20 55E
86 Mût, Egypt 25 28N 28 58E
64 Mut, Turkey 36 40N 33 28E
76 Mutan Kiang, China 46 18N 129 31E
93 Mutanda, Mozambique 21 0S 33 34E
91 Mutanda, Zambia 12 15S 26 13E
68 Mutankiang, China 44 35N 129 30E
126 Mutis, Colombia 1 4N 77 25W
91 Mutshatsha, Zaïre 10 35S 24 20E
98 Muttaburra, Australia 22 38S 144 29E
107 Mutton Bay, Canada 50 50N 59 2W
91 Mutuáli, Mozambique 14 55S 37 0E
70 Muvatupusha, India 9 53N 76 35E
64 Muwaih, Saudi Arabia 22 35N 41 32E
88 Muxima, Angola 9 25S 13 52E
59 Muya, U.S.S.R. 56 27N 115 39E
90 Muyaga, Burundi 3 14S 30 33E

MAP
66 Muzaffarabad, Kashmir 34 25N 73 30E
68 Muzaffargarh, Pakistan 30 5N 71 14E
68 Muzaffarnagar, India 29 26N 77 40E
69 Muzaffarpur, India 26 7N 85 32E
62 Muzeiri'a, Israel 32 3N 34 53E
58 Muzhi, U.S.S.R. 65 25N 64 40E
18 Muzillac, France 47 35N 2 30W
126 Muzo, Colombia 5 32N 74 6W
108 Muzon C., Alaska 54 40N 132 40W
75 Muztagh P., China 36 30N 87 22E
87 Mvôlô, Sudan 6 10N 29 53E
90 Mwadui, Tanzania 3 35S 33 40E
91 Mwandi Mission, Zam. 17 30S 24 51E
90 Mwango, Zaïre 6 48S 24 12E
90 Mwanza, Malawi 16 58S 24 28E
90 Mwanza, Tanzania 2 30S 32 58E
90 Mwanza, Katanga, Zaïre 7 55S 26 43E
91 Mwanza, Kwango, Zaïre 5 29S 17 43E
90 Mwanza ♦, Tanzania 2 30S 32 30E
90 Mwaya, Tanzania 9 32S 33 55E
15 Mweelrea, Mt., Ireland 53 37N 9 48W
88 Mweka, Zaïre 4 50S 21 40E
90 Mwenga, Zaïre 3 1S 28 21E
91 Mwepo, Zaïre 11 50S 26 10E
91 Mweru, L., Zambia 9 0S 29 0E
91 Mweza Range, Rhod. 21 0S 30 0E
91 Mwimbi, Tanzania 8 38S 31 39E
91 Mwinilunga, Zambia 11 43S 24 25E
91 Mwinilunga, Mt., Zambia 11 43S 24 25E
71 My Tho, S. Vietnam 10 29N 106 23E
82 Mya, O., Algeria 30 46N 4 44E
88 Myadhi, Gabon 1 16N 13 10E
100 Myall L., Australia 32 30S 152 25E
100 Myall, R., Australia 32 30S 152 25E
67 Myanaung, Burma 18 25N 95 10E
67 Myaungmya, Burma 16 30N 95 0E
113 Myerstown, U.S.A. 40 22N 76 18W
71 Myingyan, Burma 21 30N 95 30E
67 Myitkyina, Burma 25 30N 97 26E
27 Myjava, Czechoslovakia 48 41N 17 37E
69 Mymensingh = Nasirabad, E. Pak. 24 42N 90 30E
116 Myndmere, U.S.A. 46 23N 97 7W
71 Myogi, Burma 21 24N 96 28E
47 Myrdal, Norway 60 43N 7 10E
50 Mýrdalsjökull, Iceland 63 40N 19 6W
115 Myrtle Beach, U.S.A. 33 43N 78 50W
118 Myrtle Creek, U.S.A. 43 0N 123 19W
118 Myrtle Point, U.S.A. 43 0N 124 4W
100 Myrtleford, Australia 36 34S 146 44E
47 Mysen, Norway 59 33N 11 20E
27 Myslenice, Poland 49 51N 19 57E
28 Myslibórz, Poland 52 55N 14 50E
27 Mysłowice, Poland 50 15N 19 12E
68 Mysore, India 12 17N 76 41E
• 70 Mysore ♦, India 13 15N 77 0E
113 Mystic, U.S.A. 41 21N 71 58W
28 Myszków, Poland 50 45N 19 22E
55 Mytishchi, U.S.S.R. 57 50N 37 50E
118 Myton, U.S.A. 40 10N 110 2W
50 Mývatn, Iceland 65 36N 17 0W
26 Mže, R., Czechoslovakia 49 47N 12 50E
91 Mzimba, Malawi 11 48S 33 33E
91 Mzuzu, Malawi 11 30S 33 55E
87 Na'am, Sudan 9 42N 28 27E
62 Na'an, Israel 31 53N 34 52E
51 Naantali, Finland 60 29N 22 2E
15 Naas, Ireland 53 12N 6 40W
92 Nababeep, S. Africa 29 36S 17 46E
69 Nabadwip, India 23 34N 88 20E
73 Nabas, Philippines 11 47N 122 6E
83 Nabeul, Tunisia 36 30N 10 51E
68 Nabha, India 30 26N 76 14E
62 Nabi Rubin, Israel 31 56N 34 44E
73 Nabire, Indonesia 3 15S 136 27E
68 Nabisar, Pakistan 25 8N 69 40E
90 Nabiswera, Uganda 1 27N 32 15E
93 Naboomspruit, S. Africa 24 32S 28 40E
86 Nabq, Egypt 28 5N 29 23E
62 Nābulus, Jordan 32 14N 35 15E
91 Nabúri, Mozambique 16 53S 38 59E
91 Nacala-Velha, Mozambique 14 32S 40 34E
91 Nacaroa, Mozambique 14 22S 39 56E
118 Naches, U.S.A. 46 48N 120 49W
77 Nachi, China 28 50N 105 25E
91 Nachingwea, Tanzania 10 49S 38 49E
91 Nachingwea ♦, Tanz. 9 20S 38 0E
68 Nachna, India 27 34N 71 41E
27 Náchod, Czechoslovakia 50 25N 16 8E
48 Nacka, Sweden 59 17N 18 12E
99 Nackara, S. Australia 32 48S 139 12E
119 Naco, U.S.A. 31 24N 109 58W
117 Nacogdoches, U.S.A. 31 33N 95 30W
120 Nacozari, Mexico 30 30N 109 50W
86 Nadi, Sudan 18 40N 33 41E
68 Nadiad, India 22 41N 72 56E
42 Nădlac, Rumania 46 10N 20 50E
82 Nador, Morocco 35 14N 2 58W
65 Nadushan, Iran 32 2N 53 35E
54 Nadvornaya, U.S.S.R. 48 40N 24 35E
58 Nadym, U.S.S.R. 63 35N 72 42E
58 Nadym, R., U.S.S.R. 65 30N 73 0E
47 Naerbö, Norway 58 40N 5 39E
49 Naestved, Denmark 55 13N 11 44E
85 Nafada, Nigeria 11 8N 11 20E
64 Naft Shāh, Iran 34 0N 45 30E
64 Nafūd ad Dahy, Saudi Arabia 22 0N 45 0E
83 Nafūsah, Jabal, Libya 32 12N 12 30E
86 Nag 'Hammâdi, Egypt 26 2N 32 18E
77 Naga, Ryukyu Is. 26 34N 127 43E
73 Naga, Philippines 13 38N 123 15E
82 Naga, Kreb en, Sahara 24 12N 6 0W
106 Nagagami, R., Canada 49 40N 84 40W
68 Nagar Parkar, Pakistan 24 28N 70 46E
67 Nagaland ♦, India 26 0N 94 30E

* *Renamed Karnataka*

MAP
100 Nagambie, Australia 36 47S 145 10E
74 Nagano, Japan 36 40N 138 10E
74 Nagano-ken ♦, Japan 36 15N 138 0E
70 Nagappattinam, India 10 46N 79 51E
70 Nagari Hills, India 15 30N 79 45E
70 Nagarjuna Sagar, India 16 35N 79 17E
74 Nagasaki, Japan 32 47N 129 50E
74 Nagasaki-ken ♦, Japan 32 50N 129 40E
74 Nagashima, Japan 34 15N 136 15E
68 Nagaur, India 27 15N 73 45E
69 Nagbhir, India 20 34N 79 42E
67 Nagchu Dzong, China 31 22N 91 54E
70 Nagercoil, India 8 12N 77 33E
68 Nagina, India 29 30N 78 30E
65 Nagineh, Iran 34 20N 57 15E
77 Nago, Okinawa 26 36N 128 0E
25 Nagold, Ger. 48 38N 8 40E
98 Nagoorin, Australia 24 17S 151 15E
55 Nagorsk, U.S.S.R. 59 18N 50 48E
90 Nagorum, Kenya 4 1N 34 33E
74 Nagoya, Japan 35 10N 136 50E
68 Nagpur, India 21 8N 79 10E
67 Nagrong, Tibet 32 46N 84 16E
27 Nagyatád, Hungary 46 14N 17 22E
27 Nagyecsed, Hungary 47 53N 22 24E
27 Nagykanizsa, Hungary 46 28N 17 0E
27 Nagykörös, Hungary 46 55N 19 48E
27 Nagyléta, Hungary 47 23N 21 55E
77 Naha, Okinawa 26 12N 127 40E
62 Nahalal, Israel 32 41N 35 12E
108 Nahanni Butte, Canada 61 5N 123 30W
62 Naharayim, Israel 32 28N 35 33E
62 Nahariyya, Israel 33 1N 35 5E
64 Nahavand, Iran 34 10N 48 30E
25 Nahe, R., Germany 49 48N 7 33E
62 Nahf, Israel 32 56N 35 18E
86 Nahîya, Wadi, Egypt 27 37N 32 0E
86 Nahud, Saudi Arabia 18 12N 41 40E
46 Naiapu, Rumania 44 12N 25 47E
109 Naicam, Canada 52 30N 104 30W
63 Na'i Fah, Saudi Arabia 19 59N 50 46E
25 Naila, Germany 50 19N 11 43E
107 Nain, Canada 56 34N 61 40W
65 Na'in, Iran 32 54N 53 0E
69 Naini Tal, India 29 23N 79 30E
18 Naintré, France 46 46N 0 29E
73 Naira, I., Indonesia 4 28S 130 0E
14 Nairn, Scotland 57 35N 3 54W
• 14 Nairn ♦, Scot. 57 28N 3 52W
90 Nairobi, Kenya 1 17S 36 48E
52 Naistenyarvi, U.S.S.R. 62 25N 32 27E
90 Naivasha, Kenya 0 40S 36 30E
90 Naivasha ♦, Kenya 0 40S 36 30E
90 Naivasha L., Kenya 0 48S 36 20E
20 Najac, France 44 14N 1 58E
65 Najafābad, Iran 32 40N 51 15E
64 Najd, Saudi Arabia 26 30N 42 0E
32 Nájera, Spain 42 26N 2 48W
32 Najerilla, R., Spain 42 15N 2 45W
68 Najibabad, India 29 40N 78 20E
90 Nakalagba, Zaïre 2 50N 27 58E
74 Nakamura, Japan 33 0N 133 0E
74 Nakano Shima, Jap. 29 50N 130 0E
87 Nakfa, Ethiopia 16 40N 38 25E
53 Nakhichevan, A.S.S.R. ♦, U.S.S.R. 39 14N 45 30E
86 Nakhl, Egypt 29 55N 33 43E
64 Nakhl Mubarak, Saudi Arabia 24 10N 38 10E
59 Nakhodka, U.S.S.R. 43 10N 132 45E
71 Nakhon Phanom, Thai. 17 23N 104 43E
71 Nakhon Ratchasima (Khorat), Thailand 14 59N 102 12E
71 Nakhon Sawan, Thai. 15 35N 100 10E
71 Nakhon Si Thammarat, Thailand 8 29N 100 0E
71 Nakhon Sawan, Thai. 15 35N 100 10E
106 Nakina, Canada 50 10N 86 40W
28 Nakło n. Noteoja, Poland 53 9N 17 38E
68 Nakodar, India 31 8N 75 31E
91 Nakomis, U.S.A. 39 19N 89 19W
49 Nakskov, Denmark 54 50N 11 8E
48 Näkten, Sweden 62 48N 14 38E
76 Naktong-gang, S. Korea 35 7N 128 57E
68 Nakur, India 30 2N 77 32E
90 Nakuru, Kenya 0 15S 35 5E
90 Nakuru ♦, Kenya 0 15S 35 5E
90 Nakuru, L., Kenya 0 23S 36 5E
108 Nakusp, Canada 50 20N 117 45W
66 Nal, R., Pakistan 27 0N 65 50E
76 Nalayh, Mongolia 47 43N 107 22E
57 Nalchik, U.S.S.R. 43 30N 43 33E
48 Nälden, Sweden 63 21N 14 14E
48 Nälsjön, Sweden 63 25N 14 15E
85 Nalerigu, Ghana 10 35N 0 25W
70 Nalgonda, India 17 6N 79 15E
69 Nalharti, India 24 17N 87 52E
70 Nallamala Hills, India 15 30N 78 50E
30 Nalon, R., Spain 43 35N 6 10W
83 Nālūt, Libya 31 54N 11 0E
71 Nam Dinh, N. Vietnam 20 25N 106 5E
71 Nam Phong, Thailand 16 42N 102 52E
71 Nam-Phun, South Vietnam 10 30N 106 0E
71 Nam Tha, Laos 20 58N 101 30E
75 Nam Tso, China 30 40N 90 30E
77 Nama, China 23 45N 108 1E
70 Namakkal, India 11 13N 78 13E
77 Naman, China 25 0N 118 30E
58 Namangan, U.S.S.R. 41 30N 71 30E
91 Namapa, Mozambique 13 43S 39 50E
92 Namaqualand, S. Africa 30 0S 18 0E
90 Namasagali, Uganda 1 2N 33 0E
98 Namatanai, Terr. of New Guinea 4 35S 152 30E
84 Nambala, Mali 14 1N 5 58W
73 Namber, Indonesia 1 2S 134 57E
99 Nambour, Australia 26 38S 152 49E
99 Nambucca Heads, Australia 30 40S 152 48E

* *Incorporated within the region of Highland*

Namcha Barwa INDEX Nevrokop

MAP
75 Namcha Barwa, China 29 30N 95 10E
69 Namche Bazar, Nepal 27 51N 86 47E
91 Namecund, Mozambique 14 54S 37 37E
72 Nameh, Indonesia 2 34N 116 21E
91 Nameponda, Mozam. 15 50S 39 50E
27 Náměšt nad Oslavou, Czechoslovakia 49 12N 16 10E
27 Námestovo, Cz. 49 24N 19 25E
91 Nametil, Mozambique 15 40S 39 15E
92 Namib Des. = Namib-Woestyn, S.W. Africa 22 30S 15 0W
92 Namib-Woestyn, S.W. Africa 22 30S 15 0W
92 Namibia = South West Africa 22 0S 18 9E
69 Namja Pass, Nepal 30 0N 82 25E
73 Namlea, Indonesia 3 10S 127 5E
77 Namoa tao, China 23 30N 117 0E
99 Namoi, R., Australia 30 16S 149 15E
82 Namous, O., Algeria 30 44N 0 18W
118 Nampa, U.S.A. 43 40N 116 40W
91 Nampula, Mozambique 15 6S 39 7E
73 Namrole, Indonesia 3 46S 126 46E
50 Namsen, Norway 64 27N 11 42E
67 Namtu, Burma 23 5N 97 28E
91 Namtumbo, Tanz. 10 30S 36 4E
108 Namu, Canada 51 45N 127 50W
16 Namur, Belgium 50 27N 4 52E
16 Namur ♦, Belgium 50 17N 5 0E
92 Namutoni, S.W. Africa 18 49S 16 55E
91 Namwala, Zambia 15 44S 26 30E
28 Namyslow, Poland 51 6N 17 42E
77 Namyung, China 25 15N 114 5E
75 Nan shan, China 38 0N 98 0E
46 Nana, Rumania 44 17N 26 34E
83 Nânâ, W., Libya 30 0N 15 24E
74 Nanaimo, Canada 49 10N 124 0W
99 Nanango, Australia 26 40S 152 0E
74 Nanao, Japan 37 0N 137 0E
77 Nanchang, Hupei, China 31 50N 111 50E
77 Nanchang, Kiangsi, China 28 34N 115 48E
77 Nancheng, Kiangsi, China 27 30N 116 28E
77 Nancheng = Hanchung, China 33 10N 107 2E
77 Nanchung, China 30 47N 105 59E
77 Nanchwan, China 29 10N 107 15E
19 Nancy, France 48 42N 6 12E
69 Nanda Devi, Mt., India 30 30N 80 30E
70 Nander, India 19 10N 77 20E
101 Nandi, Fiji Is. 17 25S 176 50E
90 Nandi ♦, Kenya 0 15N 35 0E
70 Nandikotkur, India 15 52N 78 18E
68 Nandura, India 20 52N 76 25E
68 Nandurbar, India 21 20N 74 15E
70 Nandyal, India 15 30N 78 30E
85 Nanga Eboko, Cameroon 4 41N 12 22E
66 Nanga Parbat, mt., Kashmir 35 10N 74 35E
91 Nangade, Mozambique 11 5S 39 36E
72 Nangapinoh, Indonesia 0 20S 111 14E
72 Nangatajap, Indonesia 1 32S 110 34E
90 Nangeya Mts., Uganda 3 30N 33 30E
77 Nangfeng, China 27 10N 116 20E
19 Nangis, France 48 33N 3 0E
85 Nangodi, Ghana 10 58N 0 42W
84 Nangola, Mali 12 41N 6 35W
66 Nangrahar ♦, Afghan. 34 20N 70 0E
70 Nanjangud, India 12 6N 76 43E
91 Nanjeko, Zambia 5 31S 23 30E
91 Nanjirinji, Tanz. 9 41S 39 5E
68 Nankana Sahib, Pakistan 31 27N 73 38E
77 Nankang, China 25 42N 114 35E
77 Nankiang, China 32 20N 106 50E
77 Nanking, China 32 10N 118 50E
96 Nannine, Australia 26 51S 118 18E
77 Nanning, China 22 51N 108 18E
69 Nanpara, India 27 52N 81 33E
77 Nanping, Fukien, China 26 45N 118 5E
77 Nanping, Szechwan, China 33 20N 103 56E
77 Nanpu, China 31 17N 105 59E
91 Nanripe, Mozambique 13 52S 38 52E
74 Nansei-Shotō, Japan 29 0N 129 0E
4 Nansen Sd., Canada 81 0N 91 0W
90 Nansio, Tanzania 2 3S 33 4E
20 Nant, France 44 1N 3 18E
77 Nantan, China 25 0N 107 35E
59 Nantay, U.S.S.R. 62 43N 129 37E
18 Nantes, France 47 12N 1 33W
19 Nanteuil-le-Haudouin, France 49 9N 2 48E
20 Nantiat, France 46 1N 1 11E
113 Nanticoke, U.S.A. 41 12N 76 1W
108 Nanton, Canada 50 20N 113 50W
77 Nantou, Taiwan 23 57N 120 35E
21 Nantua, France 46 10N 5 35E
111 Nantucket I., U.S.A. 41 16N 70 3W
77 Nantung, China 32 0N 120 50E
77 Nanyang, China 33 2N 112 35E
90 Nanyuki, Kenya 0 2N 37 4E
33 Nao, C. de la, Spain 38 44N 0 14E
107 Naococane L., Canada 52 50N 70 45W
74 Naoetsu, Japan 37 12N 138 10E
69 Naogaon, Bangladesh 24 52N 88 52E
44 Náousa, Greece 40 42N 22 9E
73 Napabalana, Indonesia 4 42S 127 43E
106 Napanee, Canada 44 15N 77 0W
113 Napanoch, U.S.A. 41 44N 74 2W
84 Napiéolédougou, Ivory Coast 9 18N 5 35W
101 Napier, New Zealand 39 30S 176 56E
94 Napier, S. Afr. 34 30S 19 54E
41 Naples = Napoli, Italy 40 50N 14 5E
115 Naples, Fla., U.S.A. 26 10N 81 45W
112 Naples, N.Y., U.S.A. 42 35N 77 25W
41 Naples, Gulf of, Italy 40 40N 14 10E
126 Napo, R., Peru 3 5S 73 0W
MAP
126 Napo ♦, Ecuador 0 30S 77 0W
116 Napoleon, N. Dak., U.S.A. 46 32N 99 49W
114 Napoleon, Ohio, U.S.A. 41 24N 84 7W
41 Nápoli, Italy 40 50N 14 5E
41 Nápoli, G. di, Italy 40 40N 14 10E
90 Napopo, Zaïre 4 15N 28 0E
99 Nappa Merrie, Australia 27 7N 141 7E
86 Naqâda, Egypt 25 53N 32 42E
84 Nara, Mali 15 25N 7 20W
74 Nara, Japan 34 40N 135 49E
68 Nara, Canal, Pakistan 26 0N 69 20E
117 Nara Visa, U.S.A. 35 39N 103 10W
99 Naracoorte, Austral. 36 50S 140 44E
100 Naradhan, Australia 33 34S 146 17E
74 Nara-ken ♦, Japan 34 30N 136 0E
70 Narasapur, India 16 26N 81 50E
70 Narasaropet, India 16 14N 80 4E
71 Narathiwat, Thailand 6 40N 101 55E
69 Narayanganj, Bangladesh 23 31N 90 33E
70 Narayanpet, India 16 45N 77 30E
20 Narbonne, France 43 11N 3 0E
30 Narcea, R., Spain 43 15N 6 30W
41 Nardò, Italy 40 10N 18 0E
68 Nari, R., Pakistan 29 10N 67 50E
65 Narin, Afghanistan 36 5N 69 0E
93 Narinda, B. de, Malag. 14 55S 47 30E
126 Narino ♦, Colombia 1 30N 78 0W
68 Narmada, R., India 22 40N 77 30E
68 Narnaul, India 28 5N 76 11E
39 Narni, Italy 42 30N 12 30E
84 Naro, Ghana 10 22N 2 27W
40 Naro, Italy 37 18N 13 48E
55 Naro Fominsk, U.S.S.R. 55 23N 36 32E
52 Narodnaya, G., U.S.S.R. 65 5N 60 0E
90 Narok, Kenya 1 20S 33 30E
90 Narok ♦, Kenya 1 20S 33 30E
30 Narón, Spain 43 32N 8 9W
100 Narooma, Australia 36 14S 150 4E
68 Narowal, Pakistan 32 6N 74 52E
99 Narrabri, Australia 30 19S 149 46E
99 Narran, R., Australia 29 20S 147 30E
100 Narrandera, Australia 34 42S 146 31E
100 Narriah, Australia 33 56S 146 43E
96 Narrogin, Australia 32 58S 117 14E
100 Narromine, Australia 32 12S 148 12E
70 Narsampet, India 17 57N 79 58E
68 Narsinghpur, India 22 54N 79 14E
54 Narva, U.S.S.R. 59 10N 28 5E
54 Narva, R., U.S.S.R. 59 10N 27 50E
50 Narvik, Norway 68 28N 17 26E
54 Narvskoye Vdkhr., U.S.S.R. 59 10N 28 5E
68 Narwana, India 29 39N 76 6E
52 Naryan-Mar, U.S.S.R. 68 0N 53 0E
99 Naryilco, Australia 28 37S 141 53E
58 Narym, U.S.S.R. 59 0N 81 58E
58 Narymskoye, U.S.S.R. 49 10N 84 15E
58 Naryn, U.S.S.R. 41 30N 76 10E
50 Nasa, Norway 66 29N 15 23E
85 Nasarawa, Nigeria 8 32N 7 41E
46 Năsăud, Rumania 47 19N 24 29E
77 Naseby, Eng., U.K. 52 24N 0 59W
101 Naseby, New Zealand 45 1S 170 10E
86 Naser, Buheirat en, Egypt 23 0N 32 30E
116 Nashua, Iowa, U.S.A. 42 55N 92 34W
118 Nashua, Mont., U.S.A. 48 10N 106 25W
113 Nashua, N.H., U.S.A. 42 50N 71 25W
117 Nashville, Ark., U.S.A. 33 56N 93 50W
115 Nashville, Ga., U.S.A. 31 13N 83 15W
115 Nashville, Tenn., U.S.A. 36 12N 86 46W
42 Našice, Yugoslavia 45 32N 18 4E
28 Nasielsk, Poland 52 35N 20 50E
68 Nasik, India 20 2N 73 50E
69 Nasirabad, Bangladesh 24 42N 90 30E
68 Nasirabad, India 26 15N 74 45E
68 Nasirabad, Pakistan 28 25N 68 25E
41 Naso, Italy 38 8N 14 46E
65 Nasratabad, Iran 29 55N 59 53E
121 Nassau, Bahamas 25 0N 77 30W
113 Nassau, U.S.A. 42 30N 73 34W
128 Nassau, Bahía, Chile 55 20S 68 0W
86 Nasser City = Kôm Ombo, Egypt 24 25N 32 52E
86 Nasser, L., = Naser, Buheirat en, Eg. 23 0N 32 30E
84 Nassian, Ivory Coast 7 58N 2 57W
49 Nässjö, Sweden 57 38N 14 45E
106 Nastopoka Is., Canada 57 0N 77 0W
49 Näsum, Sweden 56 10N 14 29E
48 Näsviken, Sweden 61 46N 16 52E
77 Nata, China 19 37N 109 17E
64 Nata, Saudi Arabia 27 15N 48 35E
92 Nata, Botswana 20 7S 26 4E
126 Natagaima, Colombia 3 37N 75 6W
127 Natal, Brazil 5 47S 35 13W
72 Natal, Indonesia 0 35N 99 0E
93 Natal ♦, S. Africa 28 30S 30 30E
42 Natalinci, Yugoslavia 44 15N 20 49E
65 Natanz, Iran 33 30N 51 55E
107 Natashquan, Canada 50 14N 61 46W
107 Natashquan Pt., Can. 50 8N 61 40W
107 Natashquan, R., Canada 51 48N 62 0W
117 Natchez, U.S.A. 31 35N 91 25W
117 Natchitoches, U.S.A. 31 47N 93 4W
99 Nathalia, Australia 36 1S 145 7E
68 Nathdwara, India 24 55N 73 50E
113 Natick, U.S.A. 42 16N 71 19W
65 Natih, Muscat & Oman 22 25N 56 30E
100 Natimuk, Australia 36 35S 141 59E
119 National City, U.S.A. 32 45N 117 7W
109 National Mills, Canada 52 52N 101 40W
85 Natitingou, Dahomey 10 20N 1 26E
71 Natkyizin, Burma 14 57N 97 59E
116 Natoma, U.S.A. 39 14N 99 0W
90 Natron L., Tanzania 2 20S 36 0E
112 Natrona, U.S.A. 40 39N 79 43W
86 Natrûn, W. el., Egypt 30 25N 30 0E
72 Natuna Besar, Kepulauan, Indonesia 4 0N 108 0E
MAP
72 Natuna Selatan, Kepulauan, Indonesia 3 0N 109 55E
113 Natural Bridge, U.S.A. 44 5N 75 30W
99 Naturaliste C., Tas., Australia 40 50S 148 15E
96 Naturaliste, C., W. Australia, Australia 33 32S 115 0E
96 Naturaliste Channel, Australia 25 20S 113 0E
20 Naucelle, France 44 13N 2 20E
26 Nauders, Austria 46 54N 10 30E
24 Nauen, Germany 52 36N 12 52E
113 Naugatuck, U.S.A. 41 28N 73 4W
54 Naujoji Vilnia, U.S.S.R. 54 48N 25 27E
24 Naumburg, Germany 51 10N 11 48E
92 Nau-Nau, Botswana 18 57S 21 4E
94 Nauru I., Pacific Ocean 0 25N 166 0E
126 Nauta, Peru 4 20S 73 35W
120 Nautla, Mexico 20 20N 96 50W
30 Nava del Rey, Spain 41 22N 5 6W
30 Navacerrada, Puerto de, Spain 40 47N 4 0W
30 Navahermosa, Spain 39 41N 4 28W
30 Navalcarnero, Spain 40 17N 4 5W
30 Navalmoral de la Mata, Spain 39 52N 5 16W
31 Navalvillar de Pela, Sp. 39 9N 5 24W
15 Navan = An Uaimh 53 39N 6 40W
128 Navarino, I., Chile 55 0S 67 30W
32 Navarra ♦, Spain 42 40N 1 40W
20 Navarre, France 43 15N 1 20E
112 Navarre, U.S.A. 40 43N 81 31W
20 Navarreux, France 43 20N 0 47W
117 Navasota, U.S.A. 30 20N 96 5W
121 Navassa I., W.I. 18 30N 75 0W
38 Nave, Italy 45 35N 10 17E
14 Naver, R., Scot. 58 24N 4 10W
30 Navia, Spain 43 24N 6 42W
30 Navia, R., Spain 43 15N 6 50W
30 Navia de Suarna, Spain 42 58N 6 59W
124 Navidad, Chile 33 57S 71 50W
54 Navlya, U.S.S.R. 52 53N 34 15E
58 Navoi, U.S.S.R. 40 9N 65 22E
120 Navojoa, Mexico 27 0N 109 30W
52 Navolok, U.S.S.R. 62 33N 39 57E
45 Návpaktos, Greece 38 23N 21 42E
45 Návplion, Greece 37 33N 22 50E
85 Navrongo, Ghana 10 57N 0 58W
68 Navsari, India 20 57N 72 59E
68 Nawa Kot, Pakistan 28 21N 71 24E
69 Nawabganj, Bareilly, U.P., India 28 32N 79 40E
69 Nawabganj, Bara Banki, U.P., India 26 56N 81 14E
69 Nawabganj, Bangladesh 24 35N 81 14E
68 Nawabshah, Pakistan 26 15N 68 25E
69 Nawada, India 24 50N 85 25E
69 Nawakot, Nepal 28 0N 85 10E
68 Nawalgarh, India 27 50N 75 15E
69 Nawapara, India 20 52N 82 33E
87 Nawāsīf, Harrat, Si. Arabia 21 20N 42 10E
86 Nawi, Sudan 18 32N 13 50E
45 Náxos, Greece 37 8N 25 25E
45 Náxos, I., Greece 37 5N 25 30E
20 Nay, France 43 10N 0 18W
65 Nay Band, Iran 27 20N 52 40E
126 Naya, Colombia 3 13N 77 22W
126 Naya, R., Colombia 3 13N 77 22W
59 Nayakhan, U.S.S.R. 62 10N 159 0E
120 Nayarit ♦, Mexico 22 0N 105 0W
84 Nayé, Senegal 14 28N 12 12W
128 Nazaré, Brazil 13 0S 39 0W
31 Nazaré, Portugal 39 36N 9 4W
127 Nazaré da Mata, Brazil 7 44S 35 14W
62 Nazareth, Israel 32 42N 35 17E
120 Nazas, Mexico 25 10N 104 0W
120 Nazas, R., Mexico 25 20N 104 4W
13 Naze, The, Eng. 51 43N 1 19E
87 Nazeret, Ethiopia 8 45N 39 15E
67 Nazir Hat, Bangladesh 22 35N 91 55E
108 Nazko, Canada 52 50N 123 25W
93 Nchacoongo, Mozam. 24 20S 35 9E
91 Nchanga, Zambia 12 30S 27 49E
91 Ncheu, Malawi 14 50S 34 37E
84 Nchira, Ghana 12 54N 2 0W
90 Ndala, Tanzania 4 45S 33 23E
85 Ndali, Dahomey 9 50N 2 46E
90 Ndareda, Tanzania 4 12S 35 30E
81 Ndélé, Cent. Afr. Rep. 8 25N 20 36E
88 Ndendeé, Gabon 2 29S 10 46E
84 N' Dioum, Senegal 16 31N 14 39W
88 Ndjolé, Gabon 0 10S 10 45E
91 Ndola, Zambia 13 0S 28 34E
90 Ndoto Mts., Kenya 2 0N 37 0E
84 Ndrhamcha, Sebkra de, Mauritania 18 30N 15 55W
90 Nduguti, Tanzania 4 18S 34 41E
47 Nea, Norway 63 15N 11 0E
45 Néa Epidhavros, Greece 37 40N 33 7E
45 Néa Filippiás, Greece 39 12N 20 53W
44 Néa Kallikrátia, Greece 40 21N 23 1E
44 Néa Vissi, Greece 41 34N 26 33E
15 Neagh, Lough, Northern Ireland 54 35N 6 25W
118 Neah Bay, U.S.A. 48 19N 124 29W
96 Neales, R., Australia 28 0S 136 0E
91 Neamarrói, Mozam. 15 58S 36 50E
46 Neamţ ♦, Rumania 47 0N 26 20E
44 Neápolis, Kozan, Greece 40 20N 21 24E
45 Neápolis, Kriti, Greece 35 15N 25 36E
45 Neápolis, Lakonia, Gr. 36 27N 23 8E
104 Near Is., Alaska 53 0N 172 0W
13 Neath, Wales 51 39N 3 49W
85 Nebbou, Upper Volta 11 9N 1 51W
55 Nebolchy, U.S.S.R. 59 12N 32 58E
116 Nebraska ♦, U.S.A. 41 30N 100 0W
116 Nebraska City, U.S.A. 40 40N 95 52W
116 Necedah, U.S.A. 44 2N 90 7W
108 Nechako, R., Canada 53 30N 125 0W
117 Neches, R., U.S.A. 31 80N 94 20W
25 Neckar, R., Germany 48 43N 9 15E
MAP
124 Necochea, Argentina 38 30S 58 50W
39 Nedelišće, Yugoslavia 46 23N 16 22E
47 Nederlandsöy I., Nor. 62 20N 5 35E
45 Nedha, R., Greece 37 25N 21 45E
82 Nedroma, Algeria 35 1N 1 45W
47 Nedstrand, Norway 59 21N 5 49E
119 Needles, U.S.A. 34 50N 114 35W
124 Neembucú ♦, Paraguay 27 0S 58 0W
68 Neemuch (Nimach), India 24 30N 74 50E
114 Neenah, U.S.A. 44 10N 88 30W
109 Neepawa, Canada 50 20N 99 30W
83 Nefta, Tunisia 33 53N 7 58E
82 Neftah Sidi Boubekeur, Algeria 35 1N 0 4E
57 Neftegorsk, U.S.S.R. 44 25N 39 45E
53 Neftyannye Kamni, U.S.S.R. 40 20N 50 55E
70 Negapatam = Nagappattinam, India 10 46N 79 38E
114 Negaunee, U.S.A. 46 30N 87 36W
62 Negba, Israel 31 40N 34 41E
87 Negele, Ethiopia 5 20N 39 30E
71 Negeri Sembilan ♦, Malaysia 2 50N 102 10E
62 Negev = Hanegev, Israel 30 50N 35 0E
46 Negoiu, Rumania 45 48N 24 32E
70 Negombo, Sri Lanka 7 12N 79 50E
42 Negotin, Makedonija, Yugoslavia 41 29N 22 9E
42 Negotin, Srbija, Y.-slav. 44 16N 22 37E
30 Negra, Peña, Spain 42 11N 6 30W
73 Negra Pt., Philippines 18 40N 120 50E
30 Negreira, Spain 42 54N 8 45W
46 Negreşti, Rumania 46 50N 27 30E
83 Négrine, Algeria 34 30N 7 30E
82 Negro, C., Morocco 35 40N 5 11W
128 Negro, R., Argentina 40 0S 64 0W
126 Negro, R., Brazil 0 25S 64 0W
125 Negro, R., Uruguay 32 30S 55 30W
73 Negros, I., Philippines 10 0N 123 0E
46 Negru Vodă, Rumania 43 47N 28 21E
65 Nehbandan, Iran 31 35N 60 5E
24 Neheim, Germany 51 27N 7 58E
46 Nehoiaşu, Rumania 45 24N 26 20E
109 Neidpath, Canada 50 12N 107 20W
118 Neihart, U.S.A. 47 0N 110 52W
77 Neikiang, China 29 35N 105 10E
100 Neilrex, Australia 31 38S 149 25E
100 Neila Gaari Post Office, Australia 31 15S 142 48E
118 Neilton, U.S.A. 47 24N 123 59W
30 Neira de Justá, Spain 42 53N 7 14W
24 Neisse, R., Pol.-Ger. 51 0N 15 0E
126 Neiva, Colombia 2 56N 75 18W
109 Nejanilini, L., Canada 59 30N 97 30W
64 Nejd = Wajd, Si. Arabia 26 30N 42 0E
87 Nejo, Ethiopia 9 30N 35 28E
87 Nekemte, Ethiopia 9 4N 36 30E
86 Nêkheb, Egypt 25 10N 33 0E
49 Neksö, Denmark 55 4N 15 8E
30 Nelas, Portugal 40 32N 7 52W
47 Nelaug, Norway 58 39N 8 40E
98 Nelia, Austral. 20 39S 142 12E
54 Nelidovo, U.S.S.R. 56 13N 32 49E
116 Neligh, U.S.A. 42 11N 98 2W
59 Nelkan, U.S.S.R. 57 50N 136 15E
70 Nellikuppam, India 11 46N 79 43E
70 Nellore, India 14 27N 79 59E
59 Nelma, U.S.S.R. 47 30N 139 0E
100 Nelson, Australia 38 3S 141 2E
108 Nelson, Canada 49 30N 117 20W
12 Nelson, England 53 50N 2 14W
101 Nelson, New Zealand 41 18S 173 16E
119 Nelson, Ariz., U.S.A. 35 35N 113 24W
119 Nelson, Nev., U.S.A. 35 46N 114 55W
100 Nelson, C., Austral. 38 14S 141 33E
128 Nelson, Estrecho, Chile 51 30S 75 0W
109 Nelson, R., Canada 55 30N 96 50W
101 Nelson ♦, N.Z. 42 11S 172 15E
100 Nelson Bay, Australia 32 43S 152 9E
108 Nelson Forks, Canada 59 30N 124 0W
109 Nelson House, Canada 55 50N 99 0W
90 Nelspruit, S. Afr. 25 29S 30 59E
84 Néma, Mauritania 16 40N 7 15W
54 Neman (Nemunas), R., U.S.S.R. 53 30N 25 10E
45 Neméa, Greece 57 49N 22 40E
106 Nemegos, Canada 47 40N 83 15W
46 Nemira, Mt., Rumania 46 17N 26 19E
106 Nemiscam, Canada 49 30N 111 15W
19 Nemours, France 48 16N 2 40E
54 Nemunas, R., U.S.S.R. 55 25N 21 10E
74 Nemuro, Japan 43 20N 145 35E
74 Nemuro-Kaikyō, Japan 43 30N 145 30E
59 Nemuy, U.S.S.R. 55 40N 135 55E
15 Nenagh, Ireland 52 52N 8 11W
12 Nene, R., England 52 38N 0 7E
91 Neno, Malawi 15 25S 34 40E
73 Nenusa, Kepulauan, Indonesia 4 45N 127 1E
117 Neodesha, U.S.A. 37 30N 95 37W
44 Néon Petritsi, Greece 41 16N 23 15E
117 Neosho, U.S.A. 36 56N 94 28W
117 Neosho, R., U.S.A. 35 59N 95 10W
69 Nepal ■, Asia 28 0N 84 30E
69 Nepalganj, Nepal 28 0N 81 40E
118 Nephi, U.S.A. 39 43N 111 52W
15 Nephin, Mt., Ireland 54 1N 9 21W
26 Nepomuk, Cz. 49 29N 13 35E
113 Neptune City, U.S.A. 40 13N 74 4W
42 Néra, R., Rumania 44 52N 21 45E
20 Nérac, France 44 19N 0 20E
59 Nerchinsk, U.S.S.R. 52 0N 116 39E
59 Nerchinskiy Zavod, U.S.S.R. 51 10N 119 30E
46 Nereju, Rumania 45 43N 26 43E
55 Nerekhta, U.S.S.R. 57 26N 40 38E
MAP
107 Neret L., Canada 54 40N 71 0W
42 Neretva, R., Yugoslavia 43 30N 17 50E
42 Neretvanski, Yugoslavia 43 7N 17 10E
55 Neri, R., U.S.S.R. 56 30N 40 30E
54 Neringa, U.S.S.R. 55 21N 21 5E
31 Nerja, Spain 36 43N 3 55W
45 Nerokoúrou, Gr. 35 29N 24 3E
33 Nerpio, Spain 38 11N 2 16W
31 Nerva, Spain 37 42N 6 30W
50 Nes, Iceland 65 53N 17 24W
62 Nes Ziyyona, Israel 31 56N 34 48W
47 Nesbyen, Norway 60 34N 9 6E
43 Nesebyr, Bulgaria 42 41N 27 46E
47 Nesflaten, Norway 59 38N 6 48E
50 Neskaupstaður, Iceland 65 9N 13 42W
47 Nesland, Norway 59 31N 7 59E
47 Neslandsvatn, Norway 58 57N 9 10E
19 Nesle, France 49 45N 2 53E
47 Nesodden, Norway 59 48N 10 40E
14 Ness, Loch, Scot. 57 15N 4 30W
50 Nesseby, Norway 70 9N 28 51E
44 Nestórion Óros, Gr. 40 24N 20 55E
44 Néstos, R., Greece 41 20N 24 35E
47 Nesttun, Norway 60 19N 5 21E
54 Nesvizh, U.S.S.R. 53 14N 26 38E
62 Netanya, Israel 32 20N 34 51E
16 Nethe, R., Belgium 51 5N 4 55E
100 Netherby, Austral. 36 8S 141 40E
98 Netherdale, Australia 21 10S 148 33E
16 Netherlands ■, Eur. 52 0N 5 30E
127 Netherlands Guiana = Surinam, S. Amer. 4 0N 56 0W
41 Neto, R., Italy 39 10N 16 58E
69 Netrakong, Bangladesh 24 53N 90 47E
19 Nettancourt, France 48 51N 4 57E
105 Nettilling L., Canada 66 30N 71 0W
40 Nettuno, Italy 41 29N 12 40E
120 Netzahualcoyotl, Presa, Mexico 17 10N 93 30W
25 Neu-Isenburg, Germany 50 3N 8 42E
25 Neu Ulm, Germany 48 23N 10 2E
24 Neubrandenburg, E. Ger. 53 33N 13 17E
24 Neubrandenburg Burg ♦, E. Germany 53 30N 13 20E
24 Neubukow, Germany 54 1N 11 40E
25 Neuburg, Germany 48 43N 11 11E
25 Neuchâtel, Switz. 47 0N 6 55E
25 Neuchâtel ♦, Switzerland 47 0N 6 55E
25 Neuchâtel, Lac de, Switz. 46 53N 6 50E
26 Neudau, Austria 47 11N 16 6E
24 Neuenhaus, Germany 52 30N 6 55E
19 Neuf-Brisach, France 48 0N 7 30E
16 Neufchâteau, Belgium 49 50N 5 25E
19 Neufchâteau, France 48 21N 5 40E
19 Neufchâtel, France 49 43N 1 30E
19 Neufchâtel-sur-Aisne, France 49 26N 4 0E
24 Neuhaus, Ger. 53 16N 10 54E
19 Neuilly-St. Front, Fr. 49 10N 3 15E
25 Neukalen, Germany 53 49N 12 48E
25 Neumarkt, Germany 49 16N 11 28E
24 Neumünster, Germany 54 4N 9 58E
19 Neung-sur-Beuvron, France 47 30N 1 50E
26 Neunkirchen, Austria 47 43N 16 4E
25 Neunkirchen, Germany 49 23N 7 6E
128 Neuquén, Argentina 38 0S 68 0E
124 Neuquén ♦, Argentina 38 0S 69 50W
24 Neuruppin, Germany 52 56N 12 48E
115 Neuse, R., U.S.A. 35 5N 77 40W
27 Neusiedl, Austria 47 57N 16 50E
27 Neusiedler See, Aust. 47 50N 16 47E
24 Neuss, Germany 51 12N 6 39E
20 Neussargues, France 45 9N 2 59E
25 Neustadt, Bay., Ger. 49 42N 12 10E
25 Neustadt, Bay., Ger. 48 48N 11 47E
25 Neustadt, Bay., Ger. 50 23N 11 0E
25 Neustadt, Bay., Ger. 49 34N 10 37E
24 Neustadt, Gera, Ger. 50 45N 11 43E
24 Neustadt, Hessen, Ger. 50 51N 9 9E
24 Neustadt, Niedersachsen, Ger. 52 30N 9 30E
24 Neustadt, Potsdam, Ger. 52 50N 12 27E
25 Neustadt, Rhld-Pfz., Ger. 49 21N 8 10E
24 Neustadt, S.-Holst., Ger. 54 6N 10 49E
24 Neustrelitz, Germany 53 22N 13 4E
20 Neuvic, France 45 23N 2 16E
19 Neuville, France 45 52N 4 51E
19 Neuville-aux-Bois, Fr. 48 4N 2 3E
20 Neuvy-St.-Sépulchure, France 46 35N 1 48E
19 Neuvy-sur-Barangeon, France 47 20N 2 15E
24 Neuwerk, I., Germany 53 55N 8 30E
24 Neuwied, Germany 50 26N 7 29E
52 Neva, R., U.S.S.R. 59 50N 30 30E
117 Nevada, U.S.A. 37 20N 94 40W
118 Nevada ♦, U.S.A. 39 20N 117 0W
33 Nevada, Sierra, Spain 37 3N 3 15W
118 Nevada, Sierra, U.S.A. 39 0N 120 30W
118 Nevada City, U.S.A. 39 20N 121 0W
126 Nevada de Sta. Marta, Sa., Colombia 10 55N 73 50W
124 Nevado, Cerro, Argentina 35 30S 68 20W
120 Nevado de Colima, Mt., Mexico 19 35N 103 45W
62 Nevallat, Israel 31 59N 34 57E
59 Nevanka, U.S.S.R. 56 45N 98 55E
70 Nevasa, India 19 34N 75 0E
54 Nevel, U.S.S.R. 56 0N 29 55E
19 Nevers, France 47 0N 3 9E
100 Nevertire, Australia 31 50S 147 44E
109 Neville, Canada 49 58N 107 39W
57 Nevinnomyssk, U.S.S.R. 44 40N 42 0E
121 Nevis I., Leeward Is. 17 0N 62 30W
47 Nevlunghavn, Norway 58 58N 9 53E
43 Nevrokop, Bulgaria 41 43N 23 46E

* Incorporated in Papua New Guinea

Norfolk INDEX Obbia

MAP
12 Norfolk ♦, Eng. 52 39N 1 0E
116 Norfolk, Nebr., U.S.A. 42 3N 97 25W
113 Norfolk, N.Y., U.S.A. 44 47N 75 1W
114 Norfolk, Va., U.S.A. 36 52N 76 15W
94 Norfolk I., Pacific Ocean 28 58S 168 3E
117 Norfork Res., U.S.A. 36 25N 92 0W
59 Norilsk, U.S.S.R. 69 20N 88 0E
99 Norley, Australia 27 45S 143 48E
116 Normal, U.S.A. 40 30N 89 0W
117 Norman, U.S.A. 35 12N 97 30W
98 Norman, R., Australia 19 15S 142 10E
104 Norman Wells, Canada 65 40N 126 45W
98 Normanby I., Papua 9 55S 151 0E
98 Normanby, R., Australia 14 23S 144 10E
18 Normandie, France 48 45N 0 10E
18 Normandie, Collines de, France 48 55N 0 45W
106 Normandin, Canada 48 49N 72 31W
18 Normandy = Normandie, France 48 45N 0 10E
98 Normanton, Australia 17 40S 141 10E
128 Norquinco, Argentina 41 51S 70 55W
49 Norrahammar, Sweden 57 43N 14 7E
49 Nörre Aby, Denmark 55 27N 9 52E
49 Nörre Nebel, Denmark 55 47N 8 17E
49 Nörresundby, Denmark 57 5N 9 52E
118 Norris, U.S.A. 45 40N 111 48W
113 Norristown, U.S.A. 40 9N 75 15W
49 Norrköping, Sweden 58 37N 16 11E
48 Norrtälje, Sweden 59 46N 18 42E
96 Norseman, Australia 32 8S 121 43E
49 Norsholm, Sweden 58 31N 15 59E
50 Norsjö, Sweden 64 53N 19 30E
59 Norsk, U.S.S.R. 52 30N 130 0E
126 Norte de Santander ♦, Col. 8 0N 73 0W
5 North C., Antarctica 71 0N 166 0E
107 North C., Canada 47 2N 60 20W
101 North C., New Zealand 34 23S 173 4E
4 North C., Spitsbergen 80 40N 20 0E
90 North I., Kenya 4 5N 36 5E
94 North I., New Zealand 38 0S 175 0E
113 North Adams, U.S.A. 42 42N 73 6W
71 North Andaman I., India 13 15N 92 40E
6 North Atlantic Ocean 30 0N 50 0W
109 North Battleford, Can. 52 50N 108 10W
106 North Bay, Can. 46 20N 79 30W
106 North Belcher Is., Can. 56 30N 79 0W
108 North Bend, Canada 49 50N 121 35W
118 North Bend, Oreg., U.S.A. 43 28N 124 7W
112 North Bend, Pa., U.S.A. 41 20N 77 42W
14 North Berwick, Scotland 56 4N 2 44W
113 North Berwick, U.S.A. 43 18N 70 43W
117 North Canadian, R., U.S.A. 36 48N 103 0W
106 North Caribou L., Can. 52 50N 90 50W
115 North Carolina ♦, U.S.A. 35 30N 80 0W
14 North Channel, Br. Is. 55 0N 5 30W
106 North Channel, North America 46 0N 83 0W
114 North Chicago, U.S.A. 42 19N 87 50W
116 North Dakota ♦, U.S.A. 47 30N 100 0W
13 North Downs, England 51 17N 0 30W
112 North East, U.S.A. 42 17N 79 50W
67 North East Frontier Agency ♦, India 28 0N 95 0E
4 N.E. Land, Spitsbergen 80 0N 24 0E
†98 N.E. New Guinea, Terr. of ♦, N. Guin. 5 30S 144 30E
90 North Eastern ♦, Kenya 1 30N 40 0E
14 North Esk, R., Scotland 56 54N 2 45W
9 North European Plain, £ 55 0N 25 0E
13 N. Foreland, Pt., England 51 22N 1 28E
24 N. Frisian Is. = Nordfr'sche Inseln, Ger 54 50N 8 20E
90 North Horr, Kenya 3 20N 37 8E
108 North Kamloops, Can. 50 40N 120 25W
112 North Kingsville, U.S.A. 41 53N 80 42W
109 North Knife L., Canada 58 0N 97 0W
69 North Koel, R., India 23 50N 84 5E
76 North Korea ■, Asia 40 0N 127 0E
67 N. Lakhimpur, India 27 15N 94 10E
119 N. Las Vegas, U.S.A. 36 15N 115 6W
90 North Mara ♦, Tanzania 1 20S 34 20E
14 North Minch, Scot. 58 5N 5 55W
57 North Ossetian A.S.S.R. ♦, U.S.S.R. 43 30N 44 30E
119 North Palisade, U.S.A. 37 6N 118 32W
116 North Platte, U.S.A. 41 10N 100 50W
118 North Platte, R., U.S.A. 42 50N 106 50W
107 North Pt., Canada 47 5N 65 0W
4 North Pole, Arctic Reg. 90 0N 0 0E
118 North Powder, U.S.A. 45 2N 117 59W
•12 North Riding ♦, Eng. 54 22N 1 30W
14 North Ronaldsay, I., Scotland 59 20N 2 30W
8 North Sea, N. W. Europe 56 0N 4 0E
45 North Sporades = Voriai Sporádhes 39 0N 24 10E
99 North Stradbroke I., Australia 27 30S 153 34E
107 North Sydney, Canada 46 12N 60 21W
56 N. Taranaki Bt., N.Z. 38 45S 174 20E
112 N. Tonawanda, U.S.A. 43 5N 78 50W
113 North Troy, U.S.A. 44 59N 72 24W
119 N. Truchas Pk., U.S.A. 36 0N 105 30W
106 North Twin I., Canada 53 20N 80 0W
12 North Tyne, R., Eng. 55 12N 2 30W
14 North Uist I., Scotland 57 40N 7 15W
108 North Vancouver, Can. 49 25N 123 20W
108 North Vermilion, Can. 58 25N 116 0W
114 North Vernon, U.S.A. 39 0N 85 35W
•• 71 North Vietnam ■, Asia 22 0N 105 0E
100 North Village, Bermuda 32 15N 64 45W
12 North Walsham, England 52 49N 1 22E
96 N.W. Basin, Austral. 25 45S 115 0E
96 North West C., Australia 21 45S 114 9E
14 North West Highlands, Scot. 57 35N 5 2W
121 N.W. Providence Chan., W. Indies 26 0N 78 0W
107 North West River, Can. 53 30N 60 10W
104 Northwest Terr., Can. 65 0N 100 0W
91 North Western ♦, Zam. 13 30S 25 30E
12 North York Moors, England 54 25N 0 50W
12 Northallerton, Eng. 54 20N 1 26W
96 Northam, Australia 31 35S 116 42W
92 Northam, S. Africa 24 55S 27 15E
96 Northampton, Australia 28 21S 114 33E
13 Northampton, England 52 14N 0 54W
113 Northampton, Mass., U.S.A. 42 22N 72 39W
113 Northampton, Pa., U.S.A. 40 38N 75 24W
96 Northampton, Australia 28 21S 114 33E
13 Northampton ♦, England 52 16N 0 55W
98 Northampton Downs, Austral. 24 35S 145 48E
113 Northbridge, U.S.A. 42 12N 71 40W
121 Northeast Providence Channel, W. Indies 26 0N 76 0W
24 Northeim, Germany 51 42N 10 0E
91 Northern ♦, Malawi 11 0S 34 0E
86 Northern ♦, Sudan 19 0N 31 0E
91 Northern ♦, Zam. 10 30S 31 0E
70 Northern Circars, India 17 30N 82 30E
101 Northern Group, Cook Is. 10 00S 160 00W
15 Northern Ireland ♦, U.K. 54 45N 7 0W
106 Northern Lights L., Can. 49 15N 90 45W
84 Northern Province ♦, • Sierra Leone 9 0S 11 30W
96 Northern Territory ♦, Australia 16 0S 133 0E
116 Northfield, U.S.A. 44 37N 93 10W
116 Northome, U.S.A. 47 53N 94 15W
115 Northport, Ala., U.S.A. 33 15N 87 35W
114 Northport, Mich., U.S.A. 45 8N 85 39W
118 Northport, Wash., U.S.A. 48 57N 117 56W
12 Northumberland ♦, England 55 12N 2 0W
98 Northumberland Is., Austral. 21 45S 150 20E
107 Northumberland Str., Canada 46 20N 64 0W
12 Northwich, Eng. 53 16N 2 30W
116 Northwood, Iowa, U.S.A. 43 27N 93 12W
116 Northwood, N.D., U.S.A. 47 44N 97 30W
91 Norton, Rhodesia 17 52S 30 40E
116 Norton, U.S.A. 39 50N 100 0W
104 Norton Sd., Alaska 64 0N 165 0W
24 Nortorf, Germany 54 14N 10 47E
113 Norwalk, Conn., U.S.A. 41 9N 73 25W
112 Norwalk, Ohio, U.S.A. 41 13N 82 38W
50 Norway ■, Eur. 67 0N 11 0E
114 Norway, U.S.A. 45 46N 87 57W
109 Norway House, Canada 53 55N 98 50W
5 Norwegian Dependency, Antarctica 66 0N 15 0E
6 Norwegian Sea, North Atlantic Ocean 66 0N 1 0E
112 Norwich, Canada 43 1N 80 39W
12 Norwich, England 52 38N 1 17E
113 Norwich, Conn., U.S.A. 41 33N 72 5W
113 Norwich, N.Y., U.S.A. 42 32N 75 30W
112 Norwood, Canada 44 25N 77 59W
113 Norwood, U.S.A. 42 10N 71 10W
74 Noshiro, R., Japan 40 15N 140 15E
58 Nosok, U.S.S.R. 70 10N 82 20E
54 Nosovka, U.S.S.R. 50 50N 31 30E
65 Nosratābād, Iran 29 55N 60 0E
14 Noss Hd., Scot. 58 29N 3 4W
49 Nossebro, Sweden 58 12N 12 43E
92 Nossob, S.W. Africa 22 15S 17 48E
92 Nossob, R., Africa 25 15S 20 30E
109 Notigi Dam, Canada 56 35N 99 0W
108 Notikewin, Canada 56 55N 117 50W
45 Notios Evvoïkós Kólpos, Greece 38 20N 24 0E
77 Notituchow, China 24 25N 107 20E
41 Noto, Italy 36 52N 15 4E
41 Noto, G. di, Italy 36 50N 15 10E
47 Notodden, Norway 59 35N 9 17E
74 Noto-Hanto, Japan 37 0N 137 0E
107 Notre Dame, Canada 46 18N 64 46W
109 Notre Dame B., Canada 49 45N 55 30W
105 Notre Dame de Koartac, Canada 60 55N 69 40W
105 Notre Dame d'Ivugivic, Canada 62 20N 78 0W
107 Nottaway, R., Canada 50 50N 78 20W
47 Nötteröy, Norway 59 14N 10 24E
12 Nottingham, England 52 57N 1 10W
12 Nottingham ♦, England 53 10N 1 0W
114 Nottoway, R., U.S.A. 37 0N 77 45W
92 Notwani, R., Botswana 24 14S 26 20E
80 Nouadhibou, Mauritania 21 0N 17 0W
84 Nouakchott, Mauritania 18 20N 15 50W
94 Nouméa, New Caledonia 22 17S 166 30E
92 Noupoort, S. Africa 31 10S 24 57E
106 Nouveau Comptoir (Paint Hills), Canada 53 2N 78 55W
94 Nouvelle Calédonie, Pacific Ocean 21 0S 165 0E
19 Nouzonville, France 49 48N 4 44E
57 Novaleksandrovskaya, U.S.S.R. 45 29N 41 17E
55 Nova-Annenskiy, U.S.S.R. 50 32N 42 39E
27 Nová Bana, Cz. 48 28N 18 39E
26 Nova Bystrice, Cz. 49 2N 15 8E
88 Nova Chaves, Angola 10 50S 21 15E
127 Nova Cruz, Brazil 6 28S 35 25W
125 Nova Esperança, Brazil 23 8S 52 13W
125 Nova Friburgo, Brazil 22 10S 42 30W
88 Nova Gaia, Angola 10 10S 17 35E
42 Nova Gradiška, Y.-slav. 45 17N 17 28E
125 Nova Iguaçu, Brazil 22 45S 43 28W
127 Nova Iorque, Brazil 7 0S 44 5W
84 Nova Lamego, Portuguese Guinea 12 19N 14 11W
125 Nova Lima, Brazil 19 59S 43 51W
89 Nova Lisboa, Angola 12 42S 15 54E
91 Nova Lusitânia, Mozam. 19 50S 34 34E
93 Nova Mambone, Mozambique 21 0S 35 3E
39 Nova Mesto, Y.-slavia 45 47N 15 12E
26 Nova Paka, Cz. 50 29N 15 30E
73 Nova Sagres = Tutuaia, Port. Timor 8 25S 127 15E
107 Nova Scotia ♦, Canada 45 10N 63 0W
93 Nova Sofala, Mozam. 20 7S 34 48E
42 Nova Varoš, Y.-slavia 43 29N 19 48E
127 Nova Venécia, Brazil 18 45S 40 24W
43 Nova Zagora, Bulgaria 42 32N 25 59E
46 Novaci, Rumania 45 10N 23 42E
42 Novaci, Yugoslavia 41 5N 21 29E
127 Novalorque, Brazil 6 48S 44 0W
38 Novara, Italy 45 27N 8 36E
56 Novaya Kakhovka, U.S.S.R. 46 42N 33 27E
52 Novaya Ladoga, U.S.S.R. 60 7N 32 16E
58 Novaya Lyalya, U.S.S.R. 58 50N 60 35E
59 Novaya Sibir, O., U.S.S.R. 75 10N 150 0E
58 Novaya Zemlya, U.S.S.R. 75 0N 56 0E
27 Nové Mésto, Cz. 49 33N 16 7E
33 Novelda, Spain 38 24N 0 45W
38 Novellara, Italy 44 50N 10 43E
39 Noventa Vicentina, It. 45 18N 11 30E
54 Novgorod, U.S.S.R. 58 30N 31 25E
54 Novgorod Severskiy, U.S.S.R. 52 2N 33 10E
54 Novgorod Volynski, U.S.S.R. 50 38N 27 47E
42 Novi Bečej., Y.-slavia 45 36N 20 10E
39 Novi Grad, Y.-slavia 45 19N 13 33E
42 Novi Knezeva, Y.-slav. 46 4N 20 8E
43 Novi Krichim, Bulgaria 42 22N 24 31E
38 Novi Lígure, Italy 44 45N 8 47E
43 Novi-Pazar, Bulgaria 43 25N 27 15E
42 Novi Pazar, Yugoslavia 43 12N 20 28E
42 Novi Sad, Yugoslavia 45 18N 19 52E
39 Novi Vinodolski, Y.-slavia 45 10N 14 48E
39 Novigrad, Yugoslavia 44 10N 15 32E
58 Novoataysk, U.S.S.R. 53 30N 84 0E
91 Novo Freixo, Mozambique 14 49S 36 30E
125 Nôvo Hamburgo, Braz. 29 37S 51 7W
88 Novo Redondo, Angola 11 10S 13 48E
42 Novo Selo, Bulgaria 44 11N 22 47E
55 Novo-Zavidovskiy, U.S.S.R. 56 32N 36 29E
56 Novoazovsk, U.S.S.R. 47 15N 38 4E
54 Novobelitsa, U.S.S.R. 52 27N 31 2E
57 Novobogatinskoye, U.S.S.R. 47 26N 51 17E
57 Novocherkassk, U.S.S.R. 47 27N 40 5E
55 Novodevichye, U.S.S.R. 53 37N 48 58E
54 Novograd Volynskiy, U.S.S.R. 50 40N 27 35E
54 Novogrudok, U.S.S.R. 53 40N 25 50E
57 Novokayakent, U.S.S.R. 42 45N 42 52E
58 Novokazalinsk, U.S.S.R. 45 40N 61 40E
55 Novokhopersk, U.S.S.R. 51 5N 41 50E
58 Novokuznetsk, U.S.S.R. 54 0N 87 10E
56 Novomirgorod, U.S.S.R. 48 57N 31 33E
55 Novomoskovsk, R.S.F.S.R., U.S.S.R. 54 5N 38 15E
55 Novomoskovsk, Ukrainian S.S.R., U.S.S.R. 48 33N 35 17E
54 Novopolotsk, U.S.S.R. 55 38N 28 37E
56 Novorossiysk, U.S.S.R. 44 43N 37 52E
55 Novorzhev, U.S.S.R. 57 3N 29 25E
56 Novoselitsa, U.S.S.R. 48 14N 26 15E
57 Novoshakhtinsk, U.S.S.R. 47 39N 39 58E
58 Novosibirsk, U.S.S.R. 55 0N 83 5E
59 Novosibirskiye Ostrava, U.S.S.R. 75 0N 140 0E
55 Novosil, U.S.S.R. 52 58N 36 58E
54 Novosokolniki, U.S.S.R. 56 33N 28 42E
52 Novotroitsk, U.S.S.R. 51 10N 58 15E
55 Novotulskiy, U.S.S.R. 54 10N 37 36E
56 Novoukrainka, U.S.S.R. 46 25N 31 30E
55 Novouzensk, U.S.S.R. 50 32N 48 17E
54 Novovolynsk, U.S.S.R. 50 45N 24 4E
55 Novovyatsk, U.S.S.R. 58 24N 49 45E
54 Novozybkov, U.S.S.R. 52 30N 32 0E
42 Novska, Yugoslavia 45 19N 17 0E
56 Novy Bug, U.S.S.R. 47 34N 34 29E
26 Novy Bydzov, Cz. 50 14N 15 29E
28 Novy Dwór, Poland 52 26N 20 44E
27 Novy Jicin, Cz. 49 15N 18 0E
55 Novyy Oskol, U.S.S.R. 50 44N 37 55E
58 Novyy Port, U.S.S.R. 67 40N 72 30E
46 Novyye Aneny, U.S.S.R. 46 51N 29 13E
65 Now Shahr, Iran 36 40N 51 40E
28 Nowa Deba, Poland 50 26N 21 41E
28 Nowa Skalmierzyce, Poland 51 43N 18 0E
100 Nowa Nowa, Australia 37 44S 148 3E
28 Nowa Sól, Poland 51 48N 15 44E
28 Nowe, Poland 53 41N 18 44E
28 Mowe Miasteczko, Poland 51 42N 15 42E
28 Nowe Miasto, Łódz, Pol. 52 38N 20 34E
28 Nowe Miasto, Lubowskie, Poland 53 27N 19 33E
28 Nowe Warpno, Poland 53 42N 14 18E
100 Nowendoc, Australia 31 32S 151 44E
67 Nowgong, India 26 20N 92 50E
100 Nowingi, Australia 34 33S 142 15E
28 Nowogard, Poland 53 41N 15 10E
28 Nowogród, Poland 53 14N 21 53E
100 Nowra, Australia 34 53S 150 35E
66 Nowshera, Pakistan 34 0N 71 55E
28 Nowy Dwór, Białystok, Poland 53 40N 23 0E
28 Nowy Dwór, Warszawa, Poland 52 27N 20 44E
28 Nowy Korczyn, Poland 50 19N 20 48E
27 Nowy Sacz, Poland 49 40N 20 41E
28 Nowy Staw, Poland 54 13N 19 2E
27 Nowy Targ, Poland 49 30N 20 2E
28 Nowy Tomyśl, Poland 52 19N 16 10E
113 Noxen, U.S.A. 41 25N 76 4E
118 Noxon, U.S.A. 48 0N 115 54W
30 Noya, Spain 42 48N 8 53W
18 Noyant, France 47 30N 0 6E
18 Noyers, France 47 40N 4 0E
108 Noyes, I., Alaska 55 30N 133 40W
19 Noyon, France 49 34N 3 0E
89 Nriquinha, Angola 16 0S 21 25E
82 Nsa, O. en, Algeria 32 23N 5 20E
91 Nsanje, Malawi 16 55S 35 12E
85 Nsawam, Ghana 5 50N 0 24W
91 Nsomba, Zambia 10 45S 29 59E
85 Nsukka, Nigeria 7 0N 7 50E
91 Nuanetsi, R., Rhodesia 21 10S 31 20E
85 Nuatja, Togo 7 0N 1 10E
87 Nuba Mts. = Nubāh, Jibālan, Sudan 12 0N 31 0E
87 Nubāh, Jibālan, Sudan 12 0N 31 0E
86 Nûbîya, Es Sahrâ En, Sudan 21 30N 33 30E
124 Ñuble ♦, Chile 37 0S 72 0W
73 Nuboai, Indonesia 2 10S 136 30E
126 Nudo Ausangate, Mt., Peru 13 45S 71 10W
126 Nudo de Vilcanota, Peru 14 30S 70 0W
65 Nudushan, Iran 32 2N 53 20E
117 Nueces, R., U.S.A. 28 18N 98 39W
109 Nueltin L., Canada 60 0N 100 0W
126 Nueva Antioquia, Col. 6 5N 69 26W
126 Nueva Esparta ♦, Ven. 11 0N 64 0W
121 Nueva Gerona, Cuba 21 53N 82 49W
128 Nueva Imperial, Chile 38 45S 72 58W
124 Nueva Palmira, Urug. 33 52S 58 20W
120 Nueva Rosita, Mexico 28 0N 101 20W
120 Nueva San Salvador, Salvador 13 40N 89 25W
124 Nuéve de Julio, Arg. 35 30S 61 0W
121 Nuevitas, Cuba 21 30N 77 20W
128 Nuevo, Golfo, Argentina 43 0S 64 30W
120 Nuevo Laredo, Mexico 27 30N 99 40W
120 Nuevo León ♦, Mex. 25 0N 100 0W
126 Nuevo Rocafuerte, Ecuador 0 55S 76 50W
101 Nugget Pt., N.Z. 46 27S 169 50E
86 Nugrus Gebel, Egypt 24 58N 39 34E
101 Nuhaka, New Zealand 39 3S 177 45E
73 Nuhurowa, I., Indon. 5 30S 132 45E
19 Nuits, France 47 10N 4 56E
19 Nuits-St.-Georges, Fr. 47 10N 4 56E
86 Nukheila (Merga), Sudan 19 1N 26 21E
58 Nukus, U.S.S.R. 42 20N 59 40E
32 Nules, Spain 39 51N 0 9W
100 Nulla Nulla, Australia 33 47S 141 28E
96 Nullagine, Australia 21 53S 120 6E
96 Nullarbor Plain, Austral. 31 20S 128 0E
85 Numan, Nigeria 9 29N 12 3E
87 Numatinna, W., Sudan 6 38N 27 15E
74 Numazu, Japan 35 7N 138 51E
73 Numfoor, I., Indonesia 1 0S 134 50E
51 Nummi, Finland 60 24N 23 54E
100 Numurkah, Australia 36 0S 145 26E
83 Nuna, W., Libya 29 37N 15 14E
107 Nunaksaluk, I., Canada 55 40N 60 12W
13 Nuneaton, England 52 32N 1 29W
13 Nungan, China 44 29N 125 10E
91 Nungo, Mozambique 13 23S 37 43E
90 Nungwe, Tanzania 2 48S 32 2E
104 Nunivak I., Alaska 60 0N 166 0W
76 Nunkiang, China 49 11N 125 12E
66 Nunkun, Mt., Kashmir 33 57N 76 8E
16 Nunspeet, Netherlands 52 21N 5 45E
40 Nuoro, Italy 40 20N 9 20E
83 Nuqayy, Jabal, Libya 23 11N 19 30E
126 Nuqui, Colombia 5 42N 77 17W
100 Nurcoung, Australia 36 45S 141 42E
38 Nure, R., Italy 44 40N 9 32E
25 Nuremburg = Nürnberg, Germany 49 26N 11 5E
99 Nuriootpa, Australia 34 27S 139 0E
55 Nurlat, U.S.S.R. 54 29N 50 45E
25 Nürnberg, Germany 49 26N 11 5E
40 Nurri, Sardinia 39 43N 9 13E
70 Nurzvid, India 16 47N 80 53E
73 Nusa Barung, Indonesia 8 22S 113 20E
73 Nusa Kambangan, Indonesia 7 47S 109 0E
72 Nusa Tenggara ♦, Indon. 7 30S 117 0E
72 Nusa Tenggara Barat, Indon. 8 50S 117 30E
73 Nusa Tenggara Timur, Indon 9 30S 122 0E
66 Nushki, Pakistan 29 35N 65 65E
105 Nutak, Canada 57 30N 61 59W
86 Nuwaiba, Egypt 28 58N 34 40E
69 Nuwakot, Nepal 28 10N 83 55E
70 Nuwara Eliya, Sri Lanka 6 58N 80 55E
92 Nuwefontein, S.W. Afr. 28 1S 19 6E
92 Nuweveldberge, S. Africa 32 10S 21 45E
96 Nuyts, Pt., Australia 35 4S 116 38E
84 Nyaake (Webo), Liberia 4 52N 7 37W
96 Nyabing, Australia 33 30S 118 7E
113 Nyack, U.S.A. 41 5N 73 57W
48 Nyadal, Sweden 62 48N 17 59E
58 Nyagyn, U.S.S.R. 62 8N 63 36E
100 Nyah, Australia 35 12S 143 25E
100 Nyah West, Australia 35 11S 143 21E
90 Nyahanga, Tanz. 2 20S 33 37E
90 Nyahua, Tanzania 5 25S 33 23E
90 Nyakanazi, Tanzania 3 2S 31 10E
90 Nyakasu, Burundi 3 58S 30 6E
85 Nyakrom, Ghana 5 40N 0 50W
87 Nyâlâ, Sudan 12 2N 24 58E
91 Nyamandhlovu, Rhod. 19 55S 28 16E
90 Nyambiti, Tanzania 2 48S 33 27E
90 Nyamwaga, Tanz. 1 27S 34 33E
90 Nyandekwa, Tanz. 3 57S 32 32E
92 Nyangana, S.W. Africa 18 0S 20 40E
90 Nyanguge, Tanz. 2 30S 33 12E
91 Nyangwena, Zambia 15 18S 28 45E
91 Nyanji, Zambia 14 25S 31 46E
85 Nyankpala, Ghana 9 21N 0 58W
90 Nyanza, Burundi 4 21S 29 36E
90 Nyanza, Rwanda 2 20S 29 42E
90 Nyanza ♦, Kenya 0 10S 34 15E
91 Nyasa, L. = Malawi, L., E. Africa 12 0S 34 30E
71 Nyaunglebin, Burma 17 52N 96 42E
91 Nyazwidzi, R., Rhod. 19 35S 32 0E
49 Nyborg, Denmark 55 18N 10 47E
49 Nybro, Sweden 56 44N 15 55E
58 Nyda, U.S.S.R. 66 40N 73 10E
67 Nyenchen Tanglha Shan, China 30 30N 95 0E
90 Nyeri, Kenya 0 23S 36 56E
90 Nyeri ♦, Kenya 0 25S 56 55E
87 Nyerol, Sudan 8 41N 32 1E
48 Nyhem, Sweden 62 54N 15 37E
87 Nyiel, Sudan 6 9N 31 4E
91 Nyika Plat., Malawi 10 30S 36 0E
91 Nyilumba, Tanz. 10 30S 40 22E
84 Nyinahin, Ghana 6 43N 2 3W
27 Nyirbátor, Hungary 47 49N 22 9E
27 Nyíregyháza, Hungary 48 0N 21 47E
50 Nykarleby (Uusikaarlepyy), Finland 63 32N 22 31E
49 Nykøbing, Falster, Denmark 54 56N 11 52E
49 Nykøbing, Mors, Denmark 56 48N 8 51E
49 Nykøbing, Sjaelland, Denmark 55 55N 11 40E
49 Nykøbing, Tisted, Den. 56 49N 8 50E
49 Nyköping, Sweden 58 45N 17 0E
48 Nykroppa, Sweden 59 37N 14 18E
48 Nykvarn, Sweden 59 11N 17 25E
48 Nyland, Sweden 63 1N 17 45E
93 Nylstroom, S. Africa 24 42S 28 22E
26 Nymburk, Cz. 50 10N 15 1E
49 Nymindegab, Denmark 55 50N 8 12E
48 Nynäshamn, Sweden 58 54N 17 57E
100 Nyngan, Australia 31 30S 147 8E
25 Nyon, Switzerland 46 23N 6 14E
21 Nyons, France 44 22N 5 10E
100 Nyora, Australia 38 20S 145 41E
49 Nyord, Denmark 55 4N 12 13E
28 Nysa, Poland 50 40N 17 22E
24 Nysa, R., Pol.-Ger. 51 0N 15 0E
118 Nyssa, U.S.A. 43 56N 117 2W
49 Nysted, Denmark 54 40N 11 44E
90 Nyunzu, Zaïre 5 57S 27 58E
59 Nyurba, U.S.S.R. 63 17N 118 20E
90 Nzega, Tanzania 4 10S 33 12E
90 Nzega ♦, Tanz. 4 10S 33 10E
84 N'Zérékore, Guinea 7 49N 8 48W
91 Nzilo, Chutes de, Zaïre 10 18S 25 27E
90 Nzubuka, Tanzania 4 45S 32 50E
74 O-shima, Japan 34 45N 139 25E
116 Oacoma, U.S.A. 43 50N 99 26W
116 Oahe, U.S.A. 44 33N 100 29W
116 Oahe Dam, U.S.A. 44 28N 100 25W
116 Oahe Res, U.S.A. 45 30N 100 15W
110 Oahu I., Hawaii 21 30N 158 0W
118 Oak Creek, U.S.A. 40 15N 106 59W
118 Oak Harb., U.S.A. 48 20N 122 38W
109 Oak Lake, Canada 49 45N 100 45W
114 Oak Park, U.S.A. 41 55N 87 45W
115 Oak Ridge, U.S.A. 36 1N 84 5W
99 Oakbank, Australia 33 0S 140 20E
119 Oakdale, Calif., U.S.A. 37 49N 120 56W
117 Oakdale, La., U.S.A. 30 50N 92 38W
12 Oakengates, Eng. 52 42N 2 29W
116 Oakes, U.S.A. 46 14N 98 4W
118 Oakesdale, U.S.A. 47 11N 117 9W
99 Oakey, Austral. 27 25S 151 43E
12 Oakham, Eng. 52 40N 0 43W
114 Oakhill, U.S.A. 38 0N 81 7W
118 Oakland, U.S.A. 37 50N 122 18W
114 Oakland City, U.S.A. 38 20N 87 20W
100 Oaklands, Australia 35 34S 146 10E
100 Oakleigh, Austral. 37 54S 145 6E
118 Oakley, U.S.A. 42 14N 113 55W
118 Oakridge, U.S.A. 43 47N 122 31W
117 Oakwood, U.S.A. 31 35N 95 47W
46 Oancea, Rumania 45 4N 28 7E
5 Oates Coast, Antarctica 69 0S 160 0E
119 Oatman, U.S.A. 35 1N 114 19W
120 Oaxaca, Mexico 17 2N 96 40W
120 Oaxaca ♦, Mexico 17 0N 97 0W
58 Ob, R., U.S.S.R. 62 40N 66 0E
106 Oba, Canada 49 4N 84 7W
85 Obala, Cameroon 4 9N 11 32E
101 Oban, New Zealand 46 55S 168 10E
14 Oban, Scotland 56 25N 5 30W
106 Obatogamau L., Can. 49 34N 74 26W
63 Obbia, Somali Rep. 5 25N 48 30E

* *Incorporated within the county of North Yorkshire*
† *Incorporated in Papua New Guinea*
** *Now part of Vietnam*

Incorporated in Papua New Guinea

Pearl INDEX Pindiga

MAP
117 Pearl, R., U.S.A. 31 50N 90 0W
117 Pearsall, U.S.A. 28 55N 99 8W
108 Pearse I., Canada 54 9N 130 4W
4 Peary Land, Greenland 82 40N 33 0W
117 Pease, R., U.S.A. 34 18N 100 15W
91 Pebane, Mozambique 17 10S 38 8E
126 Pebas, Peru 3 10S 71 55W
42 Peć, Yugoslavia 42 40N 20 17E
38 Péccioli, Italy 43 32N 10 43E
46 Pechea, Rumania 45 36N 27 49E
56 Pechenezhin, U.S.S.R. 48 30N 24 48E
52 Pechenga, U.S.S.R. 69 30N 31 25E
55 Pechnezhskoye Vdkhr., U.S.S.R. 50 0N 36 50E
52 Pechora, R., U.S.S.R. 62 30N 56 30E
52 Pechorskaya Guba, U.S.S.R. 68 40N 54 0E
54 Pechory, U.S.S.R. 57 48N 27 40E
42 Pecica, Rumania 46 10N 21 3E
42 Pečka, Yugoslavia 44 18N 19 33E
40 Pécora, C., Italy 39 28N 8 23E
117 Pecos, U.S.A. 31 25N 103 35W
117 Pecos, R., U.S.A. 31 22N 102 30W
27 Pécs, Hungary 46 5N 18 15E
70 Peddapalli, India 18 40N 79 24E
70 Peddapuram, India 17 6N 82 5E
70 Peddavagu, R., India 16 33N 79 8E
84 Pedembu, Sierra Leone 8 7N 10 48W
72 Pedjantan, I., Indonesia 0 5S 106 15E
126 Pedreg, Venezuela 9 48N 68 30W
127 Pedreiras, Brazil 4 32S 44 40W
127 Pedro Afonso, Brazil 9 0S 48 10W
126 Pedro Chico, Colombia 1 4N 70 25W
124 Pedro de Valdivia, Chile 22 33S 69 38W
125 Pedro Juan Caballero, Paraguay 22 30S 55 40W
120 Pedro Miguel Locks, Panama Canal Zone 9 1N 79 36W
33 Pedro Muñoz, Spain 39 25N 2 56W
30 Pedrógão Grande, Port. 39 55N 8 0W
99 Peebinga, S. Australia 34 52S 140 57E
14 Peebles, Scotland 55 40N 3 12W
† 14 Peebles ♦, Scot. 55 37N 3 4W
113 Peekshill, U.S.A. 41 18N 73 57W
12 Peel, I. of Man 54 14N 4 40W
104 Peel, R., Canada 67 0N 135 0W
24 Peene, R., Germany 53 53N 13 53E
99 Peera Peera Poolanna L. South Australia 26 30S 138 0E
101 Pegasus Bay, N.Z. 43 20S 173 10E
26 Peggau, Austria 47 12N 15 21E
33 Pego, Spain 38 51N 0 8W
67 Pegu, Burma 17 20N 96 29E
67 Pegu Yoma, mts., Burma 19 0N 96 0E
77 Peh K., China 24 20N 113 20E
76 Pehan, China 48 17N 120 31E
42 Pehčevo, Yugoslavia 41 41N 23 3E
77 Pehpei, China 29 44N 106 29E
124 Pehuajó, Argentina 36 0S 62 0W
124 Peine, Chile 23 45S 68 8W
24 Peine, Germany 52 19N 10 12E
76 Peiping, China 39 50N 116 20E
25 Peissenberg, Germany 47 48N 11 4E
24 Peitz, Germany 51 50N 14 23E
127 Peixe, Brazil 12 0S 48 40W
42 Pek, R., Yugoslavia 44 58N 21 55E
73 Pekalongan, Indonesia 6 53S 109 40E
71 Pekan, W. Malaysia 3 30N 103 25E
116 Pekin, U.S.A. 40 35N 89 40W
76 Peking = Peiping, China 39 50N 116 20E
73 Pelabuhanratu, Indon. 7 0S 106 32E
73 Pelabuhan Ratu, Teluk, Indonesia 7 5S 106 30E
44 Pélagos, I., Greece 39 17N 24 4E
39 Pelagruza, Is., Y.-slavia 42 24N 16 15E
72 Pelaihari, Indonesia 3 55S 114 45E
28 Pelczyce, Poland 53 3N 15 16E
46 Peleaga, mt., Rumania 45 22N 22 55E
106 Pelee I., Canada 41 40N 82 40W
121 Pelée, Mt., Martinique 14 40N 61 0W
90 Pelekech, mt., Kenya 3 52N 35 8E
73 Peleng, I., Indonesia 1 20S 123 30E
115 Pelham, U.S.A. 31 5N 84 6W
26 Pelhřimov, Cz. 49 24N 15 12E
109 Pelican Narrows, Can. 55 12N 102 55W
108 Pelican Portage, Can. 55 51N 113 0W
109 Pelican Rapids, Canada 52 38N 100 42W
121 Peligre, L. de, Haiti 19 1N 71 58W
116 Pella, U.S.A. 41 20N 93 0W
44 Pélla ♦, Greece 40 52N 22 0E
41 Pellaro, Italy 38 1N 15 40E
24 Pellworm, I., Germany 54 30N 8 40E
104 Pelly L., Canada 66 0N 102 0W
104 Pelly, R., Canada 62 15N 133 30W
105 Pelly Bay, Canada 68 0N 89 50W
45 Peloponnese = Pelóponnisos, Gr. 37 10N 22 0E
45 Pelopónnisos, Greece 37 10N 22 0E
41 Peloro, C., Italy 38 15N 15 40E
101 Pelorus Sound, N.Z. 40 59S 173 59E
125 Pelotas, Brazil 31 42S 52 23W
43 Pel'ovo, Bulgaria 43 26N 24 17E
21 Pelvoux, Massif de, Fr. 44 52N 6 20E
73 Pemalang, Indonesia 6 53S 109 23E
72 Pematang, I., Indonesia 2 50N 96 55E
72 Pematang Siantar, Indonesia 2 57N 99 5E
91 Pemba, Zambia 16 30S 27 28E
90 Pemba Channel, Tanz. 5 0S 39 37E
90 Pemba, I., Tanz. 5 0S 39 45E
96 Pemberton, Austral. 34 30S 116 0E
108 Pemberton, Canada 50 25N 122 50W
114 Pembine, U.S.A. 45 38N 87 59W
106 Pembroke, Canada 45 50N 77 15W
‡ 101 Pembroke, New Zealand 44 33S 169 9E
13 Pembroke, Wales 51 41N 4 57W
115 Pembroke, U.S.A. 32 5N 81 32W
• 13 Pembroke ♦, Wales 51 40N 5 0W
113 Pen Argyl, U.S.A. 40 52N 75 17E
12 Pen-y-Ghent, mt., Eng. 54 10N 2 15W
32 Peña, Sierra de la, Spain 42 32N 0 45W
30 Peña de Francia, Sierra de, Spain 40 32N 6 10W
32 Peña Roya, mt., Spain 40 24N 0 40W
30 Peñafiel, Portugal 41 12N 8 17W
30 Peñafliet, Spain 41 35N 4 7W
31 Peñaflor, Sp. 37 43N 5 21W
30 Peñalara, Pico, Spain 40 51N 3 57W
30 Penamacôr, Portugal 40 10N 7 10W
71 Penang = Pinang, Malaysia 5 25N 100 15E
125 Penápolis, Brazil 21 30S 50 0W
30 Peñaranda de Bracamonte, Spain 40 53N 5 13W
100 Penarie, Austral. 34 30S 143 35E
31 Peñarroya- Pueblonuevo, Spain 38 19N 5 16W
126 Peñas, Pta., Ven. 11 17N 70 28W
30 Peñas, C. de, Spain 43 42N 5 52W
128 Peñas, G. de, Chile 47 0S 75 0W
33 Peñas de San Pedro, Sp. 38 44N 2 0W
118 Pend Oreille, L., U.S.A. 48 0N 116 30W
118 Pend Oreille, R., U.S.A. 48 30N 117 8W
44 Pendálofon, Greece 40 14N 21 12E
45 Pendelikón, Gr. 38 5N 23 53E
118 Pendleton, U.S.A. 45 35N 118 50W
97 Penedo, Brazil 10 15S 36 36W
106 Penetanguishene, Can. 44 50N 79 55W
73 Pengalengan, Indon. 7 9S 107 30E
77 Pengan, China 31 0N 106 18E
77 Pengchia Yu (Agincourt) Is., Taiwan 25 4N 122 2E
90 Penge, Kasai, Congo 5 30S 24 33E
90 Penge, Kivu, Congo 4 27S 28 25E
77 Penghu (Pescadores), Taiwan 23 34N 119 30E
76 Penglai (Tengchowfu), China 37 50N 120 50E
77 Pengpu, China 33 0N 117 25E
77 Pengshui, China 29 20N 108 15E
99 Penguin, Austral. 41 8S 146 6E
91 Penhalonga, Rhodesia 18 52S 32 40E
31 Peniche, Portugal 39 19N 9 22W
72 Penida, I., Indonesia 8 45S 115 30E
32 Peñiscola, Spain 40 22N 0 24E
76 Penki, China 41 20N 132 50E
18 Penmarch, France 47 49N 4 21W
18 Penmarch, Pte. de, Fr. 47 48N 4 22W
112 Penn Yan, U.S.A. 42 39N 77 7W
39 Pennabilli, Italy 43 50N 12 17E
39 Penne, Italy 42 28N 13 56E
70 Penner, R., India 14 50N 78 20E
12 Pennines, Eng. 54 50N 2 20W
39 Pennino, Mte., Italy 43 6N 12 54E
114 Pennsylvania ♦, U.S.A. 40 50N 78 0W
108 Penny, Canada 53 58N 121 1W
55 Peno, U.S.S.R. 57 2N 32 33E
100 Penola, Australia 37 12S 140 51E
96 Penong, Australia 31 59S 133 5E
95 Penrhyn Is., Pac. Oc. 9 0S 150 30W
12 Penrith, England 54 40N 2 45W
100 Penrith, Austral. 33 43S 150 38E
115 Pensacola, U.S.A. 30 30N 87 10W
5 Pensacola Mts., Antarc. 84 0S 40 0W
100 Penshurst, Austral. 37 49S 142 20W
108 Penticton, Canada 49 30N 119 30W
98 Pentland, Australia 20 32S 145 25E
14 Pentland Firth, Scot. 58 43N 3 10W
14 Pentland Hills, Scotland 55 48N 3 25W
70 Penukonda, India 14 5N 77 38E
55 Penza, U.S.S.R. 53 15N 45 5E
13 Penzance, Eng. 50 7N 5 32W
25 Penzberg, Germany 47 46N 11 23E
59 Penzhinskaya Guba, U.S.S.R. 61 30N 163 0E
24 Penzlin, Germany 53 32N 13 6E
119 Peoria, Ariz., U.S.A. 33 40N 112 15W
116 Peoria, Ill., U.S.A. 40 40N 89 40W
118 Pepperwood, U.S.A. 40 23N 124 0W
44 Peqini, Albania 41 4N 19 44E
62 Pequ'in, Israel 32 58N 35 20E
72 Perabumilih, Indonesia 3 27S 104 15E
126 Peraitepuy, Ven. 4 59N 60 54W
71 Peraki, R., W. Malaysia 5 10N 101 4E
45 Perakhóra, Greece 38 2N 22 56E
32 Perales de Alfambra, Sp. 40 38N 1 0W
30 Perales del Puerto, Sp. 40 10N 6 40W
32 Peralta, Spain 42 21N 1 49W
45 Pérama, Greece 34 55N 24 22E
42 Perast, Yugoslavia 42 31N 8 47E
18 Perche, France 48 31N 1 1E
18 Perche, Collines de la, Fr. 42 30N 2 5E
18 Percy, France 48 55N 1 11W
98 Percy Is., Australia 21 39S 150 16E
98 Percyville, Australia 19 2S 143 45E
32 Perdido, Mt., Spain 42 40N 0 50E
100 Perekerton, Australia 34 53S 143 49E
126 Pereira, Colombia 4 49N 75 43W
92 Pereire de Eça, Angola 16 48S 15 50E
54 Pereslavi-Zelesskiy, U.S.S.R. 56 45N 38 58E
54 Pereyaslav-Khmelnitskiy, U.S.S.R. 50 3N 31 28E
26 Perg, Austria 48 15N 14 38E
124 Pergamino, Argentina 33 52S 60 30W
39 Pergine Valsugano, It. 46 4N 11 15E
39 Pérgola, Italy 43 35N 12 50E
116 Perham, U.S.A. 46 36N 95 36W
71 Perhentian, Kepulauan, W. Malaysia 5 54N 102 42E
42 Periam, Rumania 46 2N 20 59E
107 Peribonca, L., Canada 50 1N 71 0W
124 Perico, Argentina 24 20S 65 5W
120 Pericos, Mexico 25 3N 107 42W
18 Périers, France 49 11N 1 25W
20 Périgord, France 45 0N 0 40E
20 Périgueux, France 45 10N 0 42E
126 Perija, Sierra de, Col. 9 30N 73 3W
63 Perim, I., Red Sea 12 39N 43 25E
127 Periperi, Serra do, Brazil 14 50S 40 30W
45 Peristera, I., Greece 39 15N 23 58E
70 Periyakulam, India 10 5N 77 30E
70 Periyar, L., India 9 25N 77 10E
70 Periyar, R., India 10 15N 78 10E
73 Perkam, Tg., Indonesia 1 35S 137 50E
39 Perkovió, Yugoslavia 43 41N 16 10E
121 Perlas, Arch. de las, Panama 8 41N 79 7W
121 Perlas, Punta de, Nic. 11 30N 83 30W
127 Perleberg, Germany 53 5N 11 50E
55 Perlevka, U.S.S.R. 51 56N 38 57E
42 Perlez, Yugoslavia 45 11N 20 22E
71 Perlis ♦, W. Malaysia 6 30N 100 15E
52 Perm (Molotov), U.S.S.R. 58 0N 57 10E
44 Përmeti, Albania 40 15N 20 21E
127 Pernambuco = Recife, Brazil 8 0S 35 0W
127 Pernambuco ♦, Braz. 8 0S 37 0W
19 Péronne, France 49 55N 2 57E
38 Perosa Argentina, Italy 44 57N 7 11E
108 Perow, Canada 54 35N 126 10W
20 Perpignan, France 42 42N 2 53E
18 Perros-Guirec, France 48 49N 3 28W
115 Perry, Fla., U.S.A. 30 9N 83 10W
115 Perry, Ga., U.S.A. 32 25N 83 41W
116 Perry, Iowa, U.S.A. 41 48N 94 5W
115 Perry, Maine, U.S.A. 44 59N 67 20W
112 Perry, N.Y., U.S.A. 42 44N 77 59W
117 Perry, Okla., U.S.A. 36 20N 97 20W
117 Perryton, U.S.A. 36 28N 100 48W
117 Perryville, Mo., U.S.A. 37 42N 89 50W
48 Persberg, Sweden 59 47N 14 15E
65 Persepolis, Iran 29 55N 52 50E
65 Persia = Iran, Asia 35 0N 50 0E
65 Persian Gulf, Asia 27 0N 50 0E
49 Perstorp, Sweden 56 10N 13 25E
96 Perth, Australia 31 57S 115 52E
106 Perth, N.B., Canada 46 43N 67 42W
114 Perth, Ont., Canada 44 55N 76 20W
14 Perth, Scotland 56 24N 3 27W
113 Perth, U.S.A. 40 33N 74 36W
• 14 Perth ♦, Scot. 56 30N 4 0W
21 Pertuis, France 43 42N 5 30E
20 Pertuis Breton, France 46 17N 1 25W
20 Pertuis d'Antioche, Fr. 46 6N 1 20W
116 Peru, Ill., U.S.A. 41 18N 89 12W
114 Peru, Ind., U.S.A. 40 42N 86 0W
126 Peru ■, S. America 8 0S 75 0W
39 Perúgia, Italy 43 6N 12 24E
39 Perušić, Yugoslavia 44 40N 15 22E
55 Pervomayskiy, U.S.S.R. 53 20N 40 10E
58 Pervouralsk, U.S.S.R. 56 55N 60 0E
39 Pésaro, Italy 43 55N 12 53E
77 Pescadores = Penghu, Taiwan 23 34N 119 30E
39 Pescara, Italy 42 28N 14 13E
57 Peschanokopskoye, U.S.S.R. 46 14N 41 4E
55 Peski, U.S.S.R. 51 14N 42 12E
39 Pescina, Abruzzi, Italy 42 0N 13 39E
38 Pescina, Toscana, Italy 43 54N 10 40E
66 Peshawar, Pakistan 34 2N 71 37E
44 Peshkopia, Albania 41 41N 20 25E
43 Peshtera, Bulgaria 42 2N 24 18E
114 Peshtigo, U.S.A. 45 4N 87 46W
55 Peskovka, U.S.S.R. 59 9N 52 28E
55 Peski, U.S.S.R. 51 14N 42 12E
30 Pêso da Régua, Port. 41 10N 7 47W
127 Pesqueira, Brazil 8 20S 36 42W
20 Pessac, France 44 48N 0 37W
27 Pest ♦, Hungary 47 29N 19 5E
54 Pestovo, U.S.S.R. 58 33N 35 18E
55 Pestravka, U.S.S.R. 52 28N 49 57E
45 Péta, Greece 39 10N 21 2E
62 Petah Tiqwa, Israel 32 6N 34 53E
45 Petalidhion, Khóra, Greece 36 57N 21 55E
71 Petaling Jaya, Malaysia 3 4N 101 42E
118 Petaluma, U.S.A. 38 13N 122 45W
16 Petange, Luxembourg 49 33N 5 55E
126 Petare, Venezuela 10 29N 66 49W
120 Petatlán, Mexico 17 31N 101 16W
91 Petauke, Zambia 14 14S 31 12E
106 Petawawa, Canada 45 54N 77 17W
5 Peter 1st, I., S. Oc. 69 0S 91 0W
109 Peter Pond L., Canada 56 0N 109 0W
106 Peterbell, Canada 48 36N 83 21W
113 Peterboro, U.S.A. 42 55N 71 59W
112 Peterborough, Canada 44 20N 78 20W
13 Peterborough, Eng. 52 35N 0 14W
99 Peterborough, Austral. 33 0S 138 45E
14 Peterhead, Scot. 57 30N 1 49W
109 Petersburg, Alas., U.S.A. 56 50N 133 0W
114 Petersburg, Ind., U.S.A. 38 30N 87 15W
114 Petersburg, Va., U.S.A. 37 17N 77 26W
114 Petersburg, W. Va., U.S.A. 38 59N 79 10W
98 Petford, Australia 17 20S 144 50E
41 Petília Policastro, It. 39 7N 16 48E
115 Petit Bois I., U.S.A. 30 16N 88 25W
107 Petit Cap, Canada 48 58N 63 58W
121 Petit Goâve, Haiti 18 27N 72 51W
107 Petitcodiac, Canada 45 57N 65 11W
107 Petite Saguenay, Can. 47 59N 70 1W
107 Petitsikapau, L., Can. 54 50N 66 30W
68 Petlad, India 22 30N 72 45E
120 Peto, Mexico 20 10N 89 0W
101 Petone, New Zealand 41 13S 174 53E
114 Petoskey, U.S.A. 45 21N 84 55W
62 Petra, Jordan 30 20N 35 22E
32 Petra, Spain 39 37N 3 6E
4 Petra, Ostrova, U.S.S.R. 76 15N 118 30E
41 Petralia, Italy 37 49N 14 4E
33 Petrel, Spain 38 30N 0 46W
43 Petrich, Bulgaria 41 24N 23 13E
39 Petrijanec, Yugoslavia 46 23N 16 17E
54 Petrikov, U.S.S.R. 52 11N 28 29E
46 Petrila, Rumania 45 29N 23 29E
39 Petrinja, Yugoslavia 45 28N 16 18E
127 Petrolândia, Brazil 9 5S 38 20W
106 Petrolia, Canada 42 54N 82 9W
127 Petrolina, Brazil 9 24S 40 30W
58 Petropavlovsk, U.S.S.R. 55 0N 69 0E
59 Petropavlovsk-Kamchatskiy, U.S.S.R. 53 16N 159 0E
127 Petrópolis, Brazil 22 33S 43 9W
46 Petroşani, Rumania 45 28N 23 20E
39 Petrova Gora, Y.-slav. 45 15N 15 45E
42 Petrovac, Yugoslavia 42 13N 18 57E
42 Petrovaradin, Y.-slav. 45 16N 19 55E
55 Petrovsk, Saratov, U.S.S.R. 52 22N 45 19E
59 Petrovsk-Zabaykalskiy, U.S.S.R. 51 26N 108 30E
57 Petrovskoye, U.S.S.R. 45 25N 42 58E
52 Petrozavodsk, U.S.S.R. 61 41N 34 20E
93 Petrus Steyn, S. Africa 27 38S 28 8E
92 Petrusburg, S. Africa 29 4S 25 26E
124 Peumo, Chile 34 21S 71 19W
72 Peureulak, Indonesia 4 48N 97 45E
59 Pevek, U.S.S.R. 69 15N 171 0E
38 Peveragno, Italy 44 20N 7 37E
20 Peyrehorade, France 43 34N 1 7W
21 Peyruis, France 44 1N 5 56E
20 Pézenas, France 43 28N 3 24E
27 Pezinok, Czechoslovakia 48 17N 17 17E
25 Pfaffenhofen, Germany 48 31N 11 31E
25 Pfarrkirchen, Germany 48 25N 12 57E
25 Pforzheim, Germany 48 53N 8 43E
25 Pfungstadt, Germany 49 47N 8 36E
92 Phala, Botswana 23 45S 26 50E
68 Phalodi, India 27 12N 72 24E
19 Phalsbourg, France 48 46N 7 15E
71 Phan Rang, S. Vietnam 11 40N 109 9E
71 Phan Thiet, S. Vietnam 11 1N 108 9E
71 Phangnga, Thailand 8 28N 98 30E
69 Pharenda, India 27 5N 83 17E
75 Pharo Dzong, China 27 45N 89 14E
71 Phatthalung, Thailand 7 39N 100 6E
112 Phelps, N.Y., U.S.A. 42 57N 77 5W
116 Phelps, Wis., U.S.A. 46 2N 89 2W
115 Phenix City, U.S.A. 32 30N 85 0W
71 Phetchabun, Thailand 16 25N 101 8E
71 Phetchaburi, Thailand 13 1N 99 55E
71 Phichai, Thailand 17 22N 100 10E
117 Philadelphia, Miss., U.S.A. 32 47N 89 5W
113 Philadelphia, N.Y., U.S.A. 44 9N 75 40W
114 Philadelphia, Pa., U.S.A. 40 0N 75 10W
116 Philip, U.S.A. 44 4N 101 42W
83 Philippe Thomas, Tun. 34 21N 8 28E
16 Philippeville, Belgium 50 12N 4 33E
98 Philippi L., Australia 24 20S 138 55E
73 Philippines ■, Asia 12 0N 123 0E
92 Philippolis, S. Afr. 30 15S 25 16E
43 Philippopolis = Plovdiv, Bulgaria 42 8N 24 44E
118 Philipsburg, Mont., USA 46 20N 113 21W
112 Philipsburg, Pa., U.S.A. 40 53N 78 10W
92 Philipstown, S Africa 30 28S 24 30E
100 Phillip I., Austral. 38 20S 145 15E
117 Phillips, Texas, U.S.A. 35 48N 101 17W
116 Phillips, Wis., U.S.A. 45 41N 90 22W
116 Phillipsburg, Kans., U.S.A. 39 48N 99 20W
113 Phillipsburg, Penn., U.S.A. 40 43N 75 12W
99 Phillott, Australia 27 53S 145 50E
113 Philmont, U.S.A. 42 14N 73 37W
118 Philomath, U.S.A. 44 28N 123 21W
71 Phitsanulok, Thailand 16 50N 100 12E
71 Phnom Penh, Khmer Rep. 11 33N 104 55E
71 Phnom Thbeng, Khmer Rep. 13 50N 104 56E
119 Phoenix, Ariz., U.S.A. 33 30N 112 10W
113 Phoenix, N.Y., U.S.A. 43 13N 76 18W
95 Phoenix Is., Pac. Oc. 3 30S 172 0W
113 Phoenixville, U.S.A. 40 12N 75 29W
71 Phong Saly, Laos 21 42N 102 9E
67 Phongdo, China 30 14N 91 14E
71 Phra Chedi Sam Ong, Thailand 15 16N 98 23E
71 Phra Nakhon Si Ayutthaya, Thailand 14 25N 100 30E
71 Phrae, Thailand 18 7N 100 9E
71 Phrao, Thailand 19 23N 99 15E
71 Phu Doan, N. Vietnam 21 40N 105 10E
71 Phu Loi, Laos 20 14N 103 14E
71 Phu Ly (Ha Nam), N. Vietnam 20 35N 105 50E
71 Phu Qui, Vietnam 19 20N 105 20E
71 Phuket, Thailand 8 0N 98 28E
68 Phulera (Phalera), India 26 52N 75 16E
71 Phuoc Le (Baria), S. Vietnam 10 39N 107 19E
77 Pi Ho, China 32 0N 116 20E
98 Piabia, Austral. 25 12S 152 45E
38 Piacenza, Italy 45 2N 9 42E
38 Piádena, Italy 45 8N 10 22E
98 Pialba, Australia 25 20S 152 45E
99 Pian Cr., Austral. 30 0S 149 0E
39 Pianella, Italy 42 24N 14 5E
100 Piangil, Australia 43 25S 35 5E
39 Pianoro, Italy 44 20N 11 20E
39 Pianosa, I., Puglia, Italy 42 12N 15 44E
38 Pianosa, I., Toscana, Italy 42 36N 10 4E
109 Piapot, Canada 49 59N 109 8W
31 Pias, Portugal 38 1N 7 29W
28 Piaseczno, Poland 52 5N 21 2E
28 Piastow, Poland 52 12N 20 48E
46 Piatra, Rum. 43 51N 25 9E
46 Piatra Neamţ, Rum. 46 56N 26 21E
127 Piauí ♦, Brazil 7 0S 43 0W
39 Piave, R., Italy 45 50N 13 9E
41 Piazza Armerina, Italy 37 21N 14 20E
87 Pibor, Sudan 6 52N 33 0E
87 Pibor Post, Sudan 6 47N 33 3E
126 Pica, Chile 20 35S 69 25W
19 Picard, Plaine de, France 50 0N 2 0E
19 Picardie, France 50 0N 2 15E
19 Picardy = Picardie, France 50 0N 2 15E
117 Picayune, U.S.A. 30 40N 89 40W
91 Piccadilly, Zambia 14 0S 29 30E
41 Picerno, Italy 40 40N 15 37E
77 Pichieh, China 27 20N 105 20E
124 Pichilemu, Chile 34 22S 72 9W
126 Pichincha, vol., Ec. 0 10S 78 30W
106 Pickerel L., Canada 48 40N 91 25W
106 Pickle Crow, Canada 51 30N 90 0W
8 Pico, Azores 38 28N 28 18W
128 Pico Truncado, Arg. 46 40S 68 10W
30 Picos Ancares, Sierra de, Spain 42 51N 6 52W
19 Picquigny, France 49 56N 2 10E
100 Picton, Austral. 34 12S 150 34E
106 Picton, Canada 44 1N 77 9W
101 Picton, New Zealand 41 18S 174 3E
107 Pictou, Canada 45 41N 62 42W
108 Picture Butte, Canada 49 55N 112 45W
128 Picún-Leufú, Arg. 39 30S 69 5W
70 Pidurutalagala, mt., Sri Lanka 7 10N 80 50E
126 Piedecuesta, Col. 6 59N 73 3W
38 Piedicavallo, Italy 45 41N 7 57E
38 Piedmont = Piemonte, Italy 45 0N 7 30E
115 Piedmont, U.S.A. 33 55N 85 39W
115 Piedmont Plat., U.S.A. 34 0N 81 30W
41 Piedmonte d'Alife, Italy 41 22N 14 22E
32 Piedra, R., Spain 41 10N 1 45W
31 Piedrabuena, Spain 39 0N 4 10W
30 Piedrahita, Spain 40 28N 5 23W
126 Piedras, R. de las, Peru 11 40S 70 50W
119 Piedras Blancas Pt., U.S.A. 35 45N 121 18W
120 Piedras Negras, Mexico 28 35N 100 35W
50 Pieksämäki, Finland 62 18N 27 10E
38 Piemonte, Italy 45 0N 7 30E
21 Piena, Corsica 42 15N 8 34E
28 Pieńsk, Poland 51 16N 15 2E
118 Pierce, U.S.A. 46 46N 115 53W
113 Piercefield, U.S.A. 44 13N 74 35W
44 Piería ♦, Greece 40 13N 22 25E
19 Pierre, France 46 54N 5 13E
116 Pierre, U.S.A. 44 23N 100 20W
38 Pierrefeu, France 43 8N 6 9E
19 Pierrefonds, France 49 20N 3 0E
19 Pierrefontaine, France 47 14N 6 32E
20 Pierrefort, France 44 55N 2 50E
21 Pierrelatte, France 44 23N 4 43E
28 Pieszyce, Poland 50 43N 16 33E
111 Piešťany, Cz. 48 35N 17 50E
27 Piesting, R., Austria 48 0N 16 19E
93 Piet Retief, S. Africa 27 1S 30 50E
50 Pietarsaari, Finland 63 41N 22 40E
93 Pietermaritzburg, South Africa 29 35S 30 25E
93 Pietersburg, S. Africa 23 54S 29 25E
41 Pietraperzia, Italy 37 26N 14 8E
38 Pietrasanta, Italy 43 57N 10 12E
46 Pietrosu, mt., Rumania 47 12N 25 8E
46 Pietrosul, mt., Rumania 47 35N 24 43E
39 Pieve di Cadore, Italy 46 25N 12 22E
41 Pieve di Teco, Italy 44 3N 7 54E
38 Pievepélago, Italy 44 12N 10 35E
45 Pigadia, Greece 35 30N 27 12E
44 Pigadhitsa, Greece 39 59N 21 23E
70 Pigeon I., India 14 2N 74 20E
106 Pigeon, R., Canada 48 1N 89 42W
117 Piggott, U.S.A. 36 20N 90 10W
38 Pigna, Italy 43 57N 7 40E
124 Pigüé, Argentina 37 36S 62 25W
69 Pihani, India 27 36N 80 15E
54 Pikalevo, U.S.S.R. 59 37N 34 0E
116 Pikes Peak, U.S.A. 38 50N 105 10W
92 Pikeberg, S. Africa 32 54S 18 42E
114 Pikeville, U.S.A. 37 30N 82 30W
109 Pikwitonei, Canada 55 35N 97 11W
28 Piła, Poland 53 10N 16 48E
33 Pila, mte., Spain 38 16N 1 11W
44 Pilaia, Greece 40 32N 22 59E
68 Pilani, India 28 22N 75 33E
124 Pilar, Paraguay 26 50S 58 10W
73 Pilas, I., Philippines 6 39N 121 37E
96 Pilbara, Australia 21 14S 118 19E
124 Pilcomayo, R., Par. 25 21S 57 42W
45 Pili, Greece 36 50N 27 15E
69 Pilibhit, India 28 40N 79 50E
44 Pilion, mt. Greece 39 27N 23 7E
27 Pilis, Hungary 47 17N 19 35E
27 Pilisvörösvár, Hung. 47 38N 18 56E
68 Pilkhawa, India 28 43N 77 42E
45 Pilos, Greece 36 55N 21 42E
109 Pilot Mound, Canada 49 15N 99 0W
117 Pilot Point, U.S.A. 33 26N 97 0W
118 Pilot Rock, U.S.A. 45 30N 118 58W
26 Pilsen = Pilzen, Czech. 49 45N 13 22E
39 Pilštanj, Yugoslavia 46 8N 15 39E
27 Pilzno, Poland 50 0N 21 16E
99 Pimba, Australia 31 18S 136 46E
126 Pimenta Bueno, Brazil 11 35S 61 10W
126 Pimentel, Peru 6 45S 79 55W
32 Pina, Spain 41 29N 0 33W
71 Pinang, I., W. Malaysia 5 25N 100 15E
121 Pinar del Rio, Cuba 22 26N 83 40W
105 Pinawa, Canada 50 15N 95 50W
107 Pince C., Canada 46 38N 53 45W
108 Pincher Creek, Canada 49 30N 113 35W
116 Pinckneyville, U.S.A. 38 5N 89 20W
68 Pind Dadan Khan, Pakistan 32 55N 73 47E
85 Pindiga, Nigeria 9 58N 10 53E

* Incorporated within the county of Dyfed
† Incorporated within the region of Borders
‡ Renamed Wanaka

* Incorporated within the regions of Tayside and Central

Port Blair INDEX Puebla de Don Fadrique

MAP
71 Port Blair, Andaman Is. 11 40N 92 30E
107 Port Blandford, Canada 48 30N 53 50W
117 Port Bolivar, U.S.A. 29 20N 94 40W
32 Port Bou, Spain 42 25N 3 9E
84 Port Bouet, Ivory C. 5 16N 4 57W
97 Port Bradshaw, Austral. 12 30S 137 0E
106 Port Burwell, Canada 42 40N 80 48W
69 Port Canning, India 22 17N 88 48E
107 Port Cartier, Canada 50 10N 66 50W
101 Port Chalmers, N.Z. 45 49S 170 30E
113 Port Chester, U.S.A. 41 0N 73 41W
108 Port Clements, Canada 53 40N 132 10W
98 Port Clinton, Australia 22 30S 150 46E
114 Port Clinton, U.S.A. 41 30N 83 0W
106 Port Colborne, Canada 42 50N 79 10W
108 Port Coquitlam, Can. 49 20N 122 45W
112 Port Credit, Canada 43 34N 79 35W
98 Port Curtis, Australia 24 0S 151 34E
112 Port Dalhousie, Canada 43 13N 79 17W
128 Port Darwin, Falk. Is. 51 50S 59 0W
99 Port Davey, Australia 43 16S 145 55E
38 Port-de-Bouce, Fr. 43 19N 4 58E
121 Port de Paix, Haiti 19 50N 72 50W
71 Port Dickson, Malaysia 2 30N 101 49E
98 Port Douglas, Australia 16 30S 145 30E
112 Port Dover, Canada 42 45N 80 10W
108 Port Edward, Canada 54 12N 130 10W
112 Port Elgin, Canada 44 25N 81 25W
92 Port Elizabeth, S. Afr. 33 58S 25 40E
99 Port Elliott, Austral. 35 32S 138 41E
12 Port Erin, I. of M. 54 5N 4 45W
80 Port Étienne = Nouadhibou, Mauritania 21 0N 17 0W
100 Port Fairy, Australia 38 13S 142 14E
86 Port Fouâd = Bûr Fuad, Egypt 31 15N 32 20E
88 Port Francqui, Congo 4 17S 20 47E
88 Port-Gentil, Gabon 0 47S 8 40E
117 Port Gibson, U.S.A. 31 57N 91 0W
14 Port Glasgow, Scot. 55 57N 4 40W
96 Port Gregory, Australia 27 40S 114 0E
85 Port Harcourt, Nigeria 4 40N 7 10E
108 Port Hardy, Canada 50 41N 127 30W
105 Port Harrison, Canada 58 25N 78 15W
107 Port Hawkesbury, Can. 45 36N 61 22W
96 Port Hedland, Austral. 20 25S 118 35E
113 Port Henry, U.S.A. 44 0N 73 30W
107 Port Hood, Canada 46 0N 61 32W
106 Port Hope, Canada 44 0N 78 20W
114 Port Huron, U.S.A. 43 0N 82 28W
117 Port Isabel, U.S.A. 26 12N 97 9W
100 Port Jackson, Australia 33 53S 151 12E
113 Port Jefferson, U.S.A. 40 58N 73 5W
113 Port Jervis, U.S.A. 41 22N 74 42W
18 Port Joinville, France 46 45N 2 23W
126 Port Kaituma, Guyana 8 3N 59 58W
57 Port Katon, U.S.S.R. 46 27N 38 56E
71 Port Kelang, Malaysia 3 0N 101 23E
100 Port Kembla, Australia 34 29S 150 56E
20 Port La Nouvelle, France 43 1N 3 3E
15 Port Laoise, Ireland 53 2N 7 20W
117 Port Lavaca, U.S.A. 28 38N 96 38W
96 Port Lincoln, Austral. 34 42S 135 52E
84 Port Loko, Sierra Leone 8 48N 12 46W
18 Port Louis, France 47 42N 3 22W
82 Port Lyautey = Kenitra, Morocco 34 15N 6 40W
99 Port Macquarie, Austral. 31 25S 152 54E
107 Port Maitland, N.S., Canada 44 0N 66 2W
112 Port Maitland, Ont., Can. 42 53N 79 35W
108 Port Mellon, Canada 49 32N 123 31W
107 Port Menier, Canada 49 51N 64 15W
98 Port Moresby, Papua 9 24S 147 8E
107 Port Mouton, Canada 43 58N 64 50W
98 Port Musgrave, Austral. 11 55S 141 50E
18 Port Navalo, France 47 34N 2 54W
109 Port Nelson, Canada 57 5N 92 56W
92 Port Nolloth, S. Africa 29 17S 16 52E
105 Port Nouveau-Quebec (George R.), Canada 58 30N 65 50W
117 Port O'Connor, U.S.A. 28 26N 96 24W
121 Port of Spain, Trinidad 10 40N 61 20W
118 Port Orchard, U.S.A. 47 31N 122 47W
118 Port Oxford, U.S.A. 42 45N 124 28W
96 Port Patterson, Austral. 12 40S 130 30E
101 Port Pegasus, N.Z. 47 12S 167 41E
112 Port Perry, Canada 44 6N 78 56W
100 Port Phillip B., Austral. 38 0S 145 0E
99 Port Pirie, Australia 33 10S 137 58E
113 Port Pleasant, U.S.A. 40 5N 74 4W
* 104 Port Radium, Canada 66 10N 117 40W
108 Port Renfrew, Canada 48 30N 124 20W
112 Port Rowan, Canada 42 40N 80 30W
112 Port Ryerse, Canada 42 47N 80 15W
86 Port Safaga = Bûr Safâga, Egypt 26 43N 33 57E
86 Port Said = Bûr Sa'îd, Egypt 31 16N 32 18E
115 Port St. Joe, U.S.A. 29 49N 85 20W
† 93 Port St. Johns, S. Africa 31 38S 29 33E
21 Port-St. Louis, France 43 23N 4 50E
93 Port St. Louis, Malag. 13 7S 48 48E
107 Port St. Servain, Can. 51 21N 58 0W
112 Port Sanilac, U.S.A. 43 26N 82 33W
107 Port Saunders, Canada 50 40N 57 18W
112 Port Severn, Canada 44 47N 79 43W
93 Port Shepstone, S. Afr. 30 44S 30 28E
108 Port Simpson, Canada 54 30N 130 20W
106 Port Stanley, Canada 42 40N 81 10W
100 Port Stephens, Austral. 32 38S 152 12E
86 Port Sudan = Bôr Sôdân, Sudan 19 32N 37 9E
13 Port Talbot, Wales 51 35N 3 48W
86 Port Taufiq = Bôr Taufiq, Egypt 29 54N 32 32E
118 Port Townsend, U.S.A. 48 0N 122 50W
20 Port-Vendres, France 42 32N 3 8E

MAP
114 Port Washington, U.S.A. 43 25N 87 52W
71 Port Weld, Malaysia 4 50N 100 38E
126 Portachuelo, Bolivia 17 10S 63 20W
15 Portadown (Craigaven), N. Ire. 54 27N 6 26W
107 Portage, Canada 46 40N 64 5W
116 Portage, U.S.A. 43 31N 89 25W
109 Portage la Prairie, Can. 49 58N 98 18W
108 Portage Mt. Dam, Canada 56 0N 122 0W
117 Portageville, U.S.A. 36 25N 89 40W
31 Portalegre, Portugal 39 19N 7 25W
31 Portalegre ♦, Portugal 39 20N 7 40W
117 Portales, U.S.A. 34 12N 103 25W
15 Portarlington, Ireland 53 10N 7 10W
31 Portel, Portugal 38 19N 7 41W
92 Porterville, S. Africa 33 0S 18 57E
119 Porterville, U.S.A. 36 5N 119 0W
20 Portet, France 43 34N 0 11W
118 Porthill, U.S.A. 49 0N 116 30W
46 Portile de Fier, Rumania-Y.-slav. 44 42N 22 30E
31 Portimão, Port. 37 8N 8 32W
100 Portland, N.S.W., Austral. 33 13S 149 59E
100 Portland, Victoria, Australia 38 15S 141 45E
113 Portland, Canada 44 42N 76 11W
113 Portland, Conn., U.S.A. 41 34N 72 39W
107 Portland, Me., U.S.A. 43 40N 70 15W
114 Portland, Mich., U.S.A. 42 52N 84 58W
118 Portland, Oreg., U.S.A. 45 35N 122 40W
100 Portland B., Australia 38 15S 141 45E
13 Portland Bill, Eng. 50 31N 2 27W
99 Portland, C., Australia 40 46S 148 0E
94 Portland I., N.Z. 39 20S 177 51E
94 Portland, I. of, England 50 32N 2 25W
105 Portland Prom., Can. 59 0N 78 0W
107 Portneuf, Canada 46 43N 71 55W
30 Pôrto, Portugal 41 8N 8 40W
21 Porto, G. de, Corsica 42 17N 8 34E
30 Pôrto ♦, Portugal 41 8N 8 20W
125 Pôrto Alegre, Rio Grande do Sul, Braz. 30 5S 51 3W
127 Pôrto Alegre, Mato Grosso, Brazil 21 40S 53 30W
92 Porto Alexandre, Angola 15 55S 11 55E
88 Porto Amboim, Angola 10 50S 13 50E
*91 Porto Amelia, Mozam. 12 58S 40 30E
38 Porto Argentera, Italy 44 15N 7 27E
38 Porto Azzurro, Italy 42 46N 10 24E
40 Porto Botte, Italy 39 3N 8 33E
39 Porto Civitanova, Italy 43 19N 13 44E
127 Pôrto de Moz, Brazil 1 41S 52 22W
40 Porto Empédocie, Sicily 37 18N 13 30E
126 Pôrto Esperança, Brazil 19 37S 57 29W
127 Pôrto Franco, Brazil 6 20S 47 24W
39 Porto Garibaldi, Italy 44 41N 12 14E
44 Pôrto Lago, Greece 41 1N 25 6E
125 Pôrto Mendes, Brazil 24 30S 54 15W
126 Pôrto Murtinho, Brazil 21 45S 57 55W
127 Pôrto Nacional, Brazil 10 40S 48 30W
85 Porto Novo, Dahomey 6 23N 2 42E
70 Porto Novo, India 11 30N 79 38E
39 Porto Recanati, Italy 43 26N 13 40E
125 Pôrto São José, Brazil 22 43S 53 10W
39 Porto San Giorgio, Italy 43 11N 13 49E
44 Porto San Stéfano, It. 42 26N 11 6E
80 Porto Santo, I., Madeira 33 45N 16 25W
125 Pôrto São José, Brazil 22 43S 53 10W
127 Pôrto Seguro, Brazil 16 26S 39 5W
39 Porto Tolle, Italy 44 57N 12 20E
40 Porto Tórres, Italy 40 50N 8 23E
125 Pôrto União, Brazil 26 10S 51 10W
126 Pôrto Válter, Brazil 8 5S 72 40W
126 Pôrto Velho, Brazil 8 46S 63 54W
121 Portobelo, Panama 9 35N 79 42W
38 Portoferráio, Italy 42 50N 10 20E
39 Portogruaro, Italy 45 47N 12 50E
118 Portola, U.S.A. 39 49N 120 28W
39 Portomaggiore, Italy 44 41N 11 47E
40 Portoscuso, Italy 39 12N 8 22E
38 Portovénere, Italy 44 2N 9 50E
126 Portoviejo, Ecuador 1 0S 80 20W
14 Portpatrick, Scot. 54 50N 5 7W
14 Portree, Scot. 57 25N 6 11W
15 Portrush, N. Ire. 55 13N 6 40W
18 Portsall, France 48 37N 4 45W
113 Portsmouth, Canada 44 14N 76 34W
13 Portsmouth, Eng. 50 48N 1 6W
113 Portsmouth, N.H., U.S.A. 43 5N 70 45W
114 Portsmouth, Ohio, U.S.A. 38 45N 83 0W
113 Portsmouth, R.I., U.S.A. 41 35N 71 44W
114 Portsmouth, Va., U.S.A. 36 50N 76 20W
50 Porttipahta, Finland 68 5N 26 30E
30 Portugal ■, Europe 40 0N 7 0W
32 Portugalete, Spain 43 19N 3 4W
88 Portugalia, Angola 7 23S 20 48E
126 Portuguesa ♦, Venezuela 9 10N 69 15W
† 84 Portuguese Guinea ■, West Africa 12 0N 15 0W
** 73 Portuguese Timor ■, E. Indies 8 0S 126 30E
15 Portumna, Ireland 53 5N 8 12W
112 Portville, U.S.A. 42 3N 78 21W
128 Porvenir, Chile 53 10S 70 30W
51 Porvoo, Finland 60 24N 25 40E
31 Porzuna, Spain 39 9N 4 9W
40 Posada, R., Italy 40 40N 9 35E
31 Posadas, Spain 37 47N 5 11W
25 Poschiavo, Switzerland 46 19N 10 4E
77 Poseh, China 23 50N 106 0E
32 Posets, mt., Spain 42 39N 0 25E
44 Posidhio, Akra, Gr. 39 57N 23 30E
43 Poski Trûmbesh, Bulg. 43 20N 25 38E
28 Poslek, Poland 54 3N 19 41E
73 Poso, Indonesia 1 20S 120 55E
73 Poso, D., Indonesia 1 20S 120 55E

MAP
124 Poso Colorado, Paraguay 23 30S 58 45W
127 Posse, Brazil 14 4S 46 18W
5 Possession I., Antarctica 72 4S 172 0E
24 Pössneck, Germany 50 42N 11 34E
117 Post, U.S.A. 33 13N 101 21W
118 Post Falls, U.S.A. 47 50N 116 59W
54 Postavy, U.S.S.R. 55 4N 26 58E
106 Poste de la Baleine, Canada 55 20N 77 40E
82 Poste Maurice Cortier (Bidon 5), Algeria 22 14N 1 2E
73 Postiljon, Kepulauan, Indonesia 6 30S 118 50E
92 Postmasburg, S. Africa 28 18S 23 5E
39 Postojna, Yugoslavia 45 46N 14 12E
45 Potamós, Greece 39 38N 19 53E
92 Potchefstroom, S. Afr. 26 41S 27 7E
46 Potcoava, Rumania 44 30N 24 39E
117 Poteau, U.S.A. 35 5N 94 37W
117 Poteet, U.S.A. 29 4N 98 35W
46 Poteiu, Lacul, Rum. 43 44N 24 20E
41 Potenza, Italy 40 40N 15 50E
39 Potenza Picena, Italy 43 22N 13 37E
101 Poteriteri, L., N.Z. 46 5S 167 10E
30 Potes, Spain 43 15N 4 42W
93 Potgietersrus, S. Africa 24 10S 29 3E
57 Poti, U.S.S.R. 42 10N 41 38E
85 Potiskum, Nigeria 11 39N 11 2E
46 Potlogi, Rumania 44 34N 25 34E
114 Potomac, R., U.S.A. 39 40N 78 25W
126 Potosi, Bolivia 19 38S 65 50W
126 Potosi ♦, Bolivia 20 31S 67 0W
124 Potrerillos, Chile 26 20S 69 30W
124 Potros, Cerro del, Chile 28 32S 69 0W
24 Potsdam, Germany 52 23N 13 4E
113 Potsdam, U.S.A. 44 40N 74 59W
24 Potsdam ♦, E. Ger. 52 40N 12 50E
116 Potter, U.S.A. 41 15N 103 20W
86 Pottery Hill = Abu Ballas, Egypt 24 26N 27 36E
113 Pottstown, U.S.A. 40 17N 75 40W
113 Pottsville, U.S.A. 40 39N 76 12W
18 Pouancé, France 47 44N 1 10W
108 Pouce Coupé, Canada 55 40N 120 10W
113 Poughkeepsie, U.S.A. 41 40N 73 57W
19 Pouilly, France 47 18N 2 57E
15 Poulaphouca Res., Ire. 53 8N 6 30W
18 Pouldu, le, France 47 41N 3 36W
118 Poulsbo, U.S.A. 47 45N 122 45W
127 Pouso Alegre, Mato Grosso, Brazil 11 55S 57 0W
125 Pouso Alegre, Minas Gerais, Brazil 22 14S 45 57W
20 Pouzages, France 46 40N 0 50W
50 Povenets, U.S.S.R. 62 50N 34 50E
101 Poverty Bay, N.Z. 38 43S 178 2E
30 Póvoa de Lanhosa, Port. 41 33N 8 15W
30 Póvoa de Varzim, Port. 41 25N 8 46W
55 Povorino, U.S.S.R. 51 12N 42 28E
106 Powassan, Canada 46 5N 79 25W
116 Powder, R., U.S.A. 46 47N 105 12W
118 Powell, U.S.A. 44 45N 108 45W
96 Powell Creek, Austral. 18 6S 133 46E
108 Powell River, Canada 49 48N 125 20W
114 Powers, Mich., U.S.A. 45 40N 87 32W
118 Powers, Oreg., U.S.A. 42 53N 124 2W
116 Powers Lake, U.S.A. 48 37N 102 38W
77 Poyang Hu, China 29 10N 116 10E
59 Poyarkovo, U.S.S.R. 49 36N 128 41E
27 Poysdorf, Austria 48 40N 16 37E
32 Poza de la Sal, Spain 42 35N 3 31W
120 Poza Rica, Mexico 20 33N 97 27W
42 Požarevac, Yugoslavia 44 35N 21 18E
42 Požega, Yugoslavia 45 21N 17 41E
28 Poznań, Poland 52 25N 17 0E
28 Poznań ♦, Poland 52 30N 18 0E
33 Pozo Alcón, Sp. 37 42N 2 56W
126 Pozo Almonte, Chile 20 10S 69 50W
31 Pozoblanco, Spain 38 23N 4 51W
125 Pozzallo, Italy 36 44N 15 40E
85 Pra, R., Ghana 5 30N 1 38W
28 Prabuty, Poland 53 47N 19 15E
42 Prača, Yugoslavia 43 47N 18 43E
26 Prachatice, Cz. 49 1N 14 0E
71 Prachin Buri, Thailand 14 0N 101 25E
72 Prachuap Khiri Khan, Thailand 11 49N 99 48E
20 Pradelles, France 44 46N 3 52E
126 Pradera, Colombia 3 25N 76 15W
20 Prades, France 42 38N 2 23E
127 Prado, Brazil 17 20S 39 13W
31 Prado del Rey, Spain 36 48N 5 33W
49 Praestö, Denmark 55 8N 12 2E
49 Prasto Amt ♦, Denmark 51 15N 12 0E
39 Pragersko, Yugoslavia 46 27N 15 42E
26 Prague = Praha, Cz. 50 5N 14 22E
26 Praha, Cz. 50 5N 14 22E
20 Prahecq, France 46 19N 0 26W
70 Prahita, R., India 19 0N 79 55E
46 Prahova, Reg., Rumania 44 50N 25 50E
46 Prahova, R., Rumania 44 50N 25 50E
46 Prahova ♦, Rumania 45 10N 26 0E
42 Prahovo, Yugoslavia 44 18N 22 39E
46 Praid, Rumania 46 32N 25 10E
126 Prainha, Amazonas, Braz. 7 10S 60 30W
127 Prainha, Pará, Brazil 1 45S 53 30W
98 Prairie, Australia 20 50S 144 35E
117 Prairie, R., U.S.A. 34 45N 101 15W
118 Prairie City, U.S.A. 45 27N 118 44W
116 Prairie du Chien, U.S.A. 43 1N 91 9W
72 Praja, Indonesia 8 39S 116 27E
28 Prajeczno, Poland 51 10N 19 0E
44 Pramánda, Greece 39 32N 21 8E
85 Prang, Ghana 8 1N 0 56W
72 Prapat, Indonesia 2 41N 98 58E
127 Prappia, Brazil 10 15S 37 1W
28 Praszka, Poland 51 32N 18 31E
127 Prata, Minas Gerais, Brazil 19 25S 49 0W

MAP
127 Prata, Pará, Brazil 1 10S 47 35W
40 Prática di Mare, Italy 41 40N 12 26E
38 Prato, Italy 43 53N 11 5E
39 Prátola Poligna, Italy 42 7N 13 51E
39 Pratovécchio, Italy 43 44N 11 43E
20 Prats-de-Molló, France 42 25N 2 27E
117 Pratt, U.S.A. 37 40N 98 45W
115 Prattville, U.S.A. 32 30N 86 28W
70 Pravara, R., India 19 30N 74 28E
55 Pravdinsk, U.S.S.R. 56 29N 43 28E
30 Pravia, Spain 43 30N 6 12W
73 Pre Pare, Indonesia 3 59S 119 45E
38 Pré St. Didier, Italy 45 45N 7 0E
124 Precordillera, Argentina 30 0S 69 1W
39 Predáppio, Italy 44 7N 11 58E
39 Predazzo, Italy 46 19N 11 37E
42 Predejane, Yugoslavia 42 51N 22 9E
109 Preeceville, Canada 52 0N 102 50W
18 Pré-en-Pail, France 48 28N 0 12W
18 Préfailles, France 47 9N 2 11W
126 Pregonero, Venezuela 8 1N 71 46W
39 Pregrada, Yugoslavia 46 11N 15 45E
39 Preko, Yugoslavia 44 7N 15 14E
39 Prelog, Yugoslavia 46 18N 16 32E
100 Premer, Austral. 31 29S 149 56E
96 Premier Downs, Australia 30 30S 126 30E
117 Premont, U.S.A. 27 19N 91 8W
39 Premuda, I., Yugoslavia 44 20N 14 36E
42 Prenj, mt., Yugoslavia 43 33N 17 53E
44 Prenjasi, Albania 41 6N 20 32E
116 Prentice, U.S.A. 45 31N 90 19W
24 Prenzlau, Germany 53 19N 13 51E
44 Prepansko Jezero, Yugoslavia 40 45N 21 0E
67 Preparis I., Burma 14 55N 93 45E
71 Preparis North Channel, Andaman Islands 15 12N 93 40E
71 Preparis South Channel, Andaman Islands 14 36N 93 40E
27 Prerov, Czechoslovakia 49 28N 17 27E
106 Prescott, Canada 44 45N 75 30W
119 Prescott, Ariz., U.S.A. 34 35N 112 30W
117 Prescott, Ark., U.S.A. 33 49N 93 22W
101 Preservation Inlet, N.Z. 46 8S 166 35E
42 Preševo, Yugoslavia 42 19N 21 39E
116 Presho, U.S.A. 43 56N 100 4W
41 Presicce, Italy 39 53N 18 13E
124 Presidencia de la Plaza, Argentina 27 0S 60 0W
124 Presidencia Roque Sáenz Peña, Arg. 26 45S 60 30W
124 Presidente Jayes ♦, Paraguay 24 0S 59 0W
126 Presidente Hermes, Brazil 11 0S 61 55W
125 Presidente Prudente, Brazil 22 5S 51 25W
124 Presidente Rogue Saena Peña, Arg. 34 33S 58 30W
117 Presidio, U.S.A. 29 30N 104 20W
43 Preslav, Bulgaria 43 10N 26 52E
43 Prespa, mt., Bulgaria 41 44N 25 0E
107 Presque Isle, U.S.A. 46 40N 68 0W
84 Prestea, Ghana 5 22N 2 7W
13 Presteigne, Wales 52 17N 3 0W
26 Preštice, Czechoslovakia 49 34N 13 20E
112 Preston, Canada 43 25N 80 20W
12 Preston, England 53 46N 2 42W
118 Preston, Idaho, U.S.A. 42 0N 112 0W
116 Preston, Minn., U.S.A. 43 39N 92 3W
118 Preston, Nev., U.S.A. 38 59N 115 2W
14 Prestonpans, Scot. 55 58N 3 0W
14 Prestwick, Scot. 55 30N 4 38W
93 Pretoria, S. Afr. 25 44S 28 12E
45 Préveza, Greece 38 57N 20 47E
44 Préveza ♦, Greece 39 20N 20 40E
71 Prey-Veng, Khmer Rep. 11 35N 105 29E
56 Priazovskoye, U.S.S.R. 46 22N 35 28E
4 Pribilof Is., Bering Sea 56 0N 170 0W
42 Priboj, Yugoslavia 43 35N 19 32E
26 Pribram, Cz. 49 41N 14 2E
118 Price, U.S.A. 39 40N 110 48W
57 Prichalnaya, U.S.S.R. 48 57N 44 33E
32 Priego, Spain 40 38N 2 21W
31 Priego de Córdoba, Sp. 37 27N 4 12W
54 Priekule, U.S.S.R. 37 27N 21 45E
92 Prieska, S. Afr. 29 40S 22 42E
118 Priest L., U.S.A. 48 30N 116 55W
118 Priest River, U.S.A. 48 11N 117 0W
27 Prievidza, Cz. 48 46N 18 36E
39 Prijedor, Yugoslavia 44 58N 16 41E
42 Prijepolje, Yugoslavia 43 27N 19 40E
42 Prilep, Yugoslavia 41 21N 21 37E
54 Priluki, U.S.S.R. 50 30N 32 15E
43 Primorsko, Bulgaria 42 15N 27 44E
56 Primorsko-Akhtarsk, U.S.S.R. 46 2N 38 10E
109 Primrose L., Canada 54 55N 109 40W
108 Prince Albert, Canada 53 15N 105 50W
104 Prince Albert Pen., Can. 72 0N 116 0W
4 Prince Alfred C., Can. 74 0N 124 0W
105 Prince Charles I., Can. 68 0N 76 0W
3 Prince Edward Is., Indian Oc. 45 15S 39 0E
107 Prince Edward I. ♦., Canada 44 2N 77 20W
108 Prince George, Canada 53 50N 122 50W
104 Prince of Wales, I., Alaska 53 50N 131 30W
98 Prince of Wales I., Austral. 10 35S 142 0E
4 Prince Patrick I., Can. 77 0N 120 0W
4 Prince Regent Inlet, Can. 73 0N 90 0W
108 Prince Rupert, Canada 54 20N 130 20W
98 Princess Charlotte B., Australia 14 15S 144 0E
108 Princess Royal I., Can. 53 0N 128 40W
108 Princeton, Can. 49 27N 120 30W

MAP
116 Princeton, Ill., U.S.A. 41 25N 89 25W
114 Princeton, Ind., U.S.A. 38 20N 87 35W
114 Princeton, Ky., U.S.A. 37 6N 87 55W
116 Princeton, Mo., U.S.A. 40 23N 93 35W
113 Princeton, N.J., U.S.A. 40 18N 74 40W
114 Princeton, W. Va., U.S.A. 37 21N 81 8W
78 Principe, I. de, Gulf of Guinea 1 37N 7 27E
126 Principe da Beira, Brazil 12 20S 64 30W
118 Prineville, U.S.A. 44 17N 120 57W
92 Prins Albert, S. Africa 33 12S 22 2E
5 Prins Harald Kyst, Ant. 70 0S 35 1E
121 Prinzapolca, Nicaragua 13 20N 83 35W
30 Prior, C., Spain 43 34N 8 17W
54 Pripet Marshes = Polesye, U.S.S.R. 52 0N 28 10E
54 Pripet, R. = Pripyat, R., U.S.S.R. 51 30N 30 0E
54 Pripyat, R., U.S.S.R. 51 30N 30 0E
46 Prislop, Pasul, Rumania 47 37N 25 15E
55 Pristen, Italy 41 47N 12 40E
42 Priština, Yugoslavia 42 40N 21 13E
115 Pritchard, U.S.A. 30 47N 88 5W
24 Pritzwalk, Germany 53 10N 12 11E
21 Privas, France 44 45N 4 37E
40 Priverno, Italy 41 29N 13 10E
55 Privolzhsk, U.S.S.R. 57 9N 14 9E
55 Privolzhskaya Vozvyshennest, U.S.S.R. 51 0N 46 0E
55 Privolzhskiy, U.S.S.R. 51 25N 46 3E
55 Privolzhye, U.S.S.R. 52 52N 48 33E
57 Privutnoye, U.S.S.R. 47 12N 43 30E
42 Prizren, Yugoslavia 42 13N 20 45E
40 Prizzi, Italy 37 44N 13 24E
42 Prnjavor, Yugoslavia 44 52N 17 43E
73 Probolinggo, Indonesia 7 46S 113 13E
28 Prochowice, Poland 51 17N 16 20E
40 Procida, I., Italy 40 46N 14 0E
70 Proddatur, India 14 45N 78 30E
31 Proença-a-Nova, Port. 37 45N 7 54W
120 Progreso, Mex. 21 20N 89 40W
57 Prokhladnyy, U.S.S.R. 43 50N 44 2E
44 Prokletije, Alb. 42 30N 19 45E
58 Prokopyevsk, U.S.S.R. 54 0N 87 3E
42 Prokuplje, Yugoslavia 43 16N 21 36E
57 Proletarskaya, U.S.S.R. 46 42N 41 50E
67 Prome, Burma 18 45N 95 30E
21 Propriano, Corsica 41 41N 8 52E
98 Proserpine, Australia 20 21S 148 36E
118 Prosser, U.S.A. 46 11N 119 52W
27 Prostějov, Cz. 49 30N 17 9E
28 Prostki, Poland 53 45N 22 25E
99 Proston, Australia 26 14S 151 32E
27 Proszowice, Poland 50 13N 20 16E
117 Protection, U.S.A. 37 16N 99 30W
45 Próti, I., Greece 37 5N 21 32E
43 Provadija, Bulgaria 43 12N 27 30E
21 Provence, Fr. 43 40N 5 46E
114 Providence, Ky., U.S.A. 37 25N 87 46W
113 Providence, R.I., U.S.A. 41 41N 71 15W
106 Providence Bay, Can. 45 41N 82 15W
87 Providence C., N.Z. 45 59S 166 29E
119 Providence Mts., U.S.A. 35 0N 115 30W
126 Providencia, Ecuador 0 28S 76 28W
121 Providencia, I. de, Colombia 13 25N 81 26W
59 Provideniya, U.S.S.R. 64 23N 173 18W
71 Province Wellesley, Malaysia 5 15N 100 20E
114 Provincetown, U.S.A. 42 5N 70 11W
19 Provins, France 48 33N 3 15E
118 Provo, U.S.A. 40 16N 111 37W
109 Provost, Canada 52 25N 110 20W
42 Prozor, Yugoslavia 43 50N 17 34E
96 Prudhoe Bay, Australia 21 30S 149 30W
98 Prudhoe I., Australia 21 23S 149 45E
4 Prudhoe Land, Green. 78 1N 65 0W
28 Prudnik, Poland 50 20N 17 38E
25 Prüm, Germany 50 14N 6 22E
28 Pruszcz, Poland 54 17N 19 40E
28 Pruszków, Poland 52 9N 20 49E
46 Prut, R., Rumania 46 3N 28 10E
39 Prvić, I., Yugoslavia 44 55N 14 47E
5 Prydz B., Antarctica 69 0S 74 0E
117 Pryor, U.S.A. 36 17N 95 20W
28 Przasnysz, Poland 53 2N 20 45E
28 Przedbórz, Poland 51 6N 19 53E
28 Przedecz, Poland 52 20N 18 53E
27 Przemysl, Poland 49 50N 22 45E
27 Przeworsk, Poland 50 6N 22 32E
28 Przewóz, Poland 51 28N 14 57E
58 Przhevalsk, U.S.S.R. 42 30N 78 20E
28 Przysucha, Poland 51 22N 20 38E
45 Psakhná, Greece 38 34N 23 35E
45 Psarà, I., Greece 38 37N 25 38E
45 Psathoúra, I., Greece 39 30N 24 12E
56 Psel, R., U.S.S.R. 49 25N 33 50E
45 Pserimos, I., Greece 36 56N 27 12E
54 Pskov, U.S.S.R. 57 50N 28 25E
42 Psunj, mt., Yugoslavia 45 25N 17 19E
27 Pszczyna, Poland 49 59N 18 58E
45 Pteleón, Greece 39 3N 22 57E
54 Ptich, R., U.S.S.R. 52 30N 28 45E
44 Ptolemais, Greece 40 30N 21 43E
39 Ptuj, Yugoslavia 46 28N 15 50E
39 Ptujska Gora, Y.-slav. 46 23N 15 47E
124 Puán, Argentina 37 30S 63 0W
107 Pubnico, Canada 43 47N 65 50W
126 Pucallpa, Peru 8 25S 74 30W
77 Pucheng, China 28 0N 118 30E
46 Pucheni, Rumania 45 12N 25 17E
77 Puchi, China 29 42N 113 54E
39 Pucisce, Yugoslavia 43 22N 16 43E
28 Puck, Poland 54 45N 18 23E
70 Pudukkottai, India 10 28N 78 47E
120 Puebla, Mexico 19 0N 98 10W
120 Puebla ♦, Mexico 18 30N 98 0W
31 Puebla de Alcocer, Sp. 38 59N 5 14W
33 Puebla de Don Fadrique, Spain 37 58N 2 25W

* Renamed Echo Bay
† Renamed Umzimvuba

* Renamed Pemba
† Renamed Guinea-Bissau
** Annexed by Indonesia

Incorporated within the region of Strathclyde

Rovigo INDEX St. Jerone

MAP
39 Rovigo, Italy 45 4N 11 48E
46 Rovinari, Rumania 46 56N 23 10E
39 Rovinj, Yugoslavia 45 18N 13 40E
126 Rovira, Colombia 4 15N 75 20W
54 Rovno, U.S.S.R. 50 40N 26 10E
55 Rovnoye, U.S.S.R. 50 52N 46 3E
91 Rovuma, R., Mozambique 11 30S 36 10E
100 Rowes, Australia 36 59S 149 12E
96 Rowley Shoals, Australia 17 40S 119 20E
119 Rowood, U.S.A. 32 18N 112 54W
84 Roxa, Port. Guinea 11 15N 15 45W
73 Roxas, Philippines 11 36N 122 49E
115 Roxboro, U.S.A. 36 24N 78 59W
98 Roxborough Downs, Australia 22 20S 138 45E
101 Roxburgh, New Zealand 45 33S 169 19E
14 Roxburgh, Scotland 55 34N 2 30W
• 14 Roxburgh ♦, Scotland 55 30N 2 30W
49 Roxen, Sweden 58 30N 15 40E
118 Roy, U.S.A. 47 17N 109 0W
32 Roya, Peña, Sp. 40 25N 0 40W
114 Royal Oak, U.S.A. 42 30N 83 5W
20 Royan, France 45 37N 1 2W
19 Roye, France 47 40N 6 31E
47 Röyken, Norway 59 45N 10 23E
42 Rozaj, Yugoslavia 42 50N 20 15E
28 Rozan, Poland 52 52N 21 25E
54 Rozdol, U.S.S.R. 49 30N 24 1E
27 Roznava, Cz. 48 37N 20 35E
19 Rozoy, France 48 40N 2 56E
19 Rozoy-sur-Serre, Fr. 49 40N 4 8E
28 Rozwadów, Poland 50 37N 22 2E
44 Rrësheni, Albania 41 47N 19 49E
42 Rtanj, mt., Yugoslavia 43 45N 21 50W
82 Rtem, Oued el, Alg. 33 40N 5 34E
55 Rtishchevo, U.S.S.R. 52 35N 43 50E
30 Rúa, Spain 42 24N 7 6W
92 Ruacaná, S.W. Afr. 17 20S 14 12E
101 Ruahine Ra., N.Z. 39 55S 176 2E
101 Ruapehu, New Zealand 39 17S 175 35E
101 Ruapuke I., N.Z. 46 46S 168 31E
83 Ruâus, W., Libya 30 14N 15 0E
90 Rubeho, mts., Tanzania 6 50S 36 25E
56 Rubezhnoye, U.S.S.R. 49 6N 38 25E
39 Rubicone, R., Italy 44 0N 12 20E
84 Rubino, Ivory Coast 6 4N 4 18W
126 Rubio, Venezuela 7 43N 72 22W
90 Rubona, Uganda 0 29N 30 9E
58 Rubtsovsk, U.S.S.R. 51 30N 80 50E
118 Ruby L., U.S.A. 40 10N 115 28W
118 Ruby Mts., U.S.A. 40 30N 115 30W
98 Rubyvale, Australia 23 25S 147 45E
54 Rucava, U.S.S.R. 56 9N 20 32E
28 Ruciane-Nida, Poland 53 40N 21 32E
47 Rud, Buskerud, Norway 60 1N 10 1E
49 Ruda, Sweden 57 6N 16 7E
27 Ruda Slaska, Poland 50 16N 18 50E
65 Rudbar, Afghanistan 30 0N 62 30E
24 Ruden, I., E. Germany 54 13N 13 47E
24 Rüdersdorf, Germany 52 28N 13 48E
91 Rudewa, Tanzania 10 7S 34 47E
14 Rudh a'Mhail, C., Scotland 55 55N 6 25W
49 Rudköbing, Denmark 54 56N 10 41E
28 Rudna, Poland 51 30N 16 17E
52 Rudnichny, U.S.S.R. 59 40N 52 20E
43 Rudnik, Bulgaria 42 36N 27 30E
43 Rudnik, Yugoslavia 44 7N 20 35E
43 Rudnik, mt., Yugoslavia 44 7N 20 35E
59 Rudnogorsk, U.S.S.R. 57 15N 103 42E
54 Rudnya, U.S.S.R. 54 55N 31 13E
58 Rudnyy, U.S.S.R. 52 57N 63 7E
42 Rudo, Yugoslavia 43 41N 19 23E
75 Rudok, China 33 30N 79 40E
† 90 Rudolf, L., Kenya 4 10N 36 10E
24 Rudolstadt, Germany 50 44N 11 20E
43 Rudozem, Bulgaria 41 29N 24 51E
114 Rudyard, U.S.A. 46 14N 84 35E
19 Rue, France 50 15N 1 40E
20 Ruelle, France 45 41N 0 14E
87 Rufa'a, Sudan 14 44N 33 32E
20 Ruffec Charente, Fr. 46 2N 0 12W
87 Rufi, Sudan 5 58N 30 18E
124 Rufino, Argentina 34 20S 62 50W
84 Rufisque, Senegal 14 40N 17 15W
91 Rufunsa, Zambia 15 4S 29 34E
13 Rugby, England 52 23N 1 16W
116 Rugby, U.S.A. 48 21N 100 0W
24 Rügen, I., Germany 54 22N 13 25E
90 Rugezi, Tanzania 2 6S 33 18E
18 Rugles, France 48 50N 0 40E
62 Ruhama, Israel 31 31N 34 43E
90 Ruhengeri, Rwanda 1 30S 29 36E
24 Ruhla, Germany 50 53N 10 21E
24 Ruhland, Germany 51 27N 13 52E
24 Ruhr, R., Germany 51 25N 7 15E
91 Ruhuhu, R., Tanzania 10 15S 34 55E
117 Ruidosa, U.S.A. 29 59N 104 39W
119 Ruidoso, U.S.A. 33 19N 105 39W
42 Ruj, mt., Bulgaria 42 52N 22 42E
42 Rujen, mt., Yugoslavia 42 9N 22 30E
68 Ruk, Pakistan 27 50N 68 42E
90 Rukwa L., Tanzania 7 50S 32 10E
96 Rum Jungle, Australia 13 1S 131 0E
42 Ruma, Yugoslavia 45 8N 19 50E
64 Rumah, Saudi Arabia 25 35N 47 10E
35 Rumania ■, Europe 46 0N 25 0E
87 Rumbek, Sudan 6 54N 29 37E
26 Rumburk, Cz. 50 57N 14 32E
113 Rumford, U.S.A. 44 30N 70 30W
28 Rumia, Poland 54 37N 18 25E
21 Rumilly, France 45 53N 5 56E
90 Rumonge, Burundi 3 59S 29 26E
108 Rumsey, Canada 51 51N 112 48W
98 Rumula, Australia 16 28S 145 20E
90 Rumuruti, Kenya 0 17N 36 32E
101 Runanga, N.Z. 42 25S 171 15E
101 Runaway, C., N.Z. 37 32S 178 2E
12 Runcorn, England 53 20N 2 44W

* Incorporated within the region of Borders
† Renamed L. Turkana

MAP
90 Rungwa, Tanzania 6 55S 33 32E
90 Rungwa, R., Tanzania 7 15S 33 10E
91 Rungwe, Tanz. 9 11S 33 32E
91 Rungwe ♦, Tanz. 9 25S 33 32E
85 Runka, Nigeria 12 28N 7 20E
48 Runn, Sweden 60 30N 15 40E
100 Runton Ra., Austral. 23 35S 123 15E
67 Rupa, India 27 15N 92 30E
100 Rupanyup, Australia 36 39S 14 39E
68 Rupar, India 31 2N 76 38E
72 Rupat, I., Indonesia 1 45N 101 40E
106 Rupert House = Fort Rupert, Canada 51 30N 78 40W
106 Rupert, R., Canada 51 20N 77 30W
69 Rupsa, Bangladesh 21 44N 87 20E
127 Rupununi, R., Guyana 3 30N 59 30W
67 Ruquka Gie La, China 31 35N 97 55E
126 Rurrenabaque, Bolivia 14 30S 67 32W
32 Rus, R., Spain 39 30N 2 30W
91 Rusambo, Rhodesia 16 30S 32 4E
43 Ruschuk = Ruse, Bulg. 43 48N 25 59E
43 Ruse, Bulg. 43 48N 25 59E
46 Rusetu, Rumania 44 57N 27 14E
13 Rushden, Eng. 52 17N 0 37W
116 Rushford, U.S.A. 43 48N 91 46W
116 Rushville, Ill., U.S.A. 40 6N 90 35W
114 Rushville, Ind., U.S.A. 39 38N 85 22W
116 Rushville, Nebr., U.S.A. 42 43N 102 35W
49 Rusken, Sweden 57 15N 14 20E
113 Russell, Que., Canada 45 16N 75 21W
116 Russell, U.S.A. 38 56N 98 55W
69 Russellkonda, India 19 57N 84 42E
115 Russellville, Ala., U.S.A. 34 30N 87 44W
117 Russellville, Ark., U.S.A. 35 15N 93 0W
115 Russellville, Ky., U.S.A. 36 50N 86 50W
39 Russi, Italy 44 21N 12 1E
59 Russian S.F.S.R. ♦, U.S.S.R. 62 0N 105 0E
4 Russkoye Ustie, U.S.S.R. 71 0N 149 0E
27 Rust, Austria 47 49N 16 42E
57 Rustavi, U.S.S.R. 40 45N 44 30E
92 Rustenburg, S. Africa 25 41S 27 14E
117 Ruston, U.S.A. 32 30N 92 40W
90 Rutana, Burundi 3 55S 30 0E
64 Rutba, Iraq 33 4N 40 15E
31 Rute, Spain 37 19N 4 29W
73 Ruteng, Indonesia 8 26S 120 30E
112 Ruth, Mich., U.S.A. 43 42N 82 45W
118 Ruth, Nev., U.S.A. 39 15N 115 1W
14 Rutherglen, Australia 36 5S 146 29E
14 Rutherglen, Scot. 55 50N 4 11W
41 Rutigliano, Italy 41 1N 17 0E
113 Rutland, U.S.A. 43 38N 73 0W
• 13 Rutland ♦, Eng. 52 38N 0 40W
71 Rutland I., Andaman Is. 11 25N 92 40E
109 Rutledge L., Canada 16 58N 110 58W
90 Rutshuru, Zaïre 1 13S 29 25E
16 Ruurlo, Netherlands 52 5N 6 24E
41 Ruvo di Púglia, Italy 41 7N 16 27E
90 Ruvu, Tanzania 6 49S 38 43E
90 Ruvu, R., Tanzania 7 25S 38 15E
91 Ruvuma, R., Tanzania 11 30S 36 10E
91 Ruvuma ♦, Tanz. 11 0S 36 30E
64 Ruwaidha, Si. Arabia 23 40N 44 40E
64 Ruwandiz, Iraq 36 40N 44 32E
90 Ruwenzori Mts., Africa 0 30N 29 55E
90 Ruyigi, Burundi 3 29S 30 15E
55 Ruzayevka, U.S.S.R. 54 10N 45 0E
43 Ruzhevo Konare, Bulg. 42 23N 24 46E
27 Ruzomberok, Cz. 49 3N 19 17E
90 Rwanda ■, Africa 2 0S 30 0E
56 Ryaberg, Sweden 56 47N 13 15E
43 Ryakhovo, Bulgaria 44 0N 26 18E
14 Ryan, L., Scot. 55 0N 5 2W
55 Ryazan, U.S.S.R. 54 50N 39 40E
55 Ryazhsk, U.S.S.R. 53 45N 40 3E
58 Rybache, U.S.S.R. 46 40N 81 20E
52 Rybachi Poluostrov, U.S.S.R. 69 43N 32 0E
55 Rybinsk (Shcherbakov), U.S.S.R. 58 5N 38 50E
55 Rybinsk Vdkhr., U.S.S.R. 58 30N 38 0E
27 Rybnik, Poland 50 6N 18 32E
56 Rybnitsa, U.S.S.R. 47 45N 29 0E
28 Rychwał, Poland 52 4N 18 10E
49 Ryd, Sweden 56 27N 14 42E
13 Ryde, England 50 44N 1 9W
49 Rydö, Sweden 56 58N 13 10E
49 Rydsnäs, Sweden 57 47N 15 9E
27 Rydułtowy, Poland 50 4N 18 23E
28 Rydzyna, Poland 51 47N 16 39E
49 Rye, Denmark 56 5N 9 45E
13 Rye, Eng. 50 57N 0 46E
12 Rye, R., Eng. 54 12N 0 53W
118 Rye Patch Res., U.S.A. 40 45N 118 20W
118 Ryegate, U.S.A. 46 21N 109 27W
58 Rylsk, U.S.S.R. 51 30N 34 51E
100 Rylstone, Austral. 32 46S 149 58E
27 Rymanów, Poland 49 35N 21 51E
28 Ryn, Poland 53 57N 21 34E
49 Ryningsnäs, Sweden 57 17N 15 58E
28 Rypin, Poland 53 3N 19 32E
77 Ryūkyū-rettō, Asia 26 0N 127 0E
28 Rzepin, Poland 52 20N 14 49E
27 Rzeszów, Poland 50 5N 21 58E
27 Rzeszów ♦, Poland 50 0N 22 0E
54 Rzhev, U.S.S.R. 56 20N 34 20E
71 Sa Dec, S. Vietnam 10 20N 105 46E
62 Sa'ad (Muharraga), Isr. 31 28N 34 33E
65 Sa'ādatabād, Iran 30 10N 53 5E
24 Saale, R., Germany 51 25N 11 56E
24 Saaler Bodden, Ger. 54 20N 12 25E
24 Saalfeld, Germany 50 39N 11 21E
26 Saalfelden, Austria 47 26N 12 51E
25 Saane, R., Switzerland 46 23N 7 18E
25 Saanen, Switzerland 46 29N 7 15E
19 Saar (Sarre), ♦, Ger. 49 20N 6 45E
25 Saarbrücken, Germany 49 15N 6 58E
25 Saarburg, Germany 49 36N 6 32E

• Incorporated within the county of Leicester

MAP
54 Saaremaa, U.S.S.R. 58 30N 22 30E
95 Saarland, Germany 49 20N 0 75E
25 Saarlouis, Germany 49 19N 6 45E
121 Saba I., Leeward Is. 17 30N 63 10W
42 Sabac, Yugoslavia 44 48N 19 42E
32 Sabadell, Spain 41 28N 2 7E
72 Sabagalel, Indonesia 1 36S 98 40E
72 Sabah ♦, Malaysia 6 0N 117 0E
71 Sabak, Malaysia 3 46N 100 58E
121 Sábana de la Mar, Dom. Rep. 19 7N 69 40W
126 Sábanalarga, Colombia 10 38N 74 55W
72 Sabang, O., Indonesia 5 50N 95 15E
127 Sabará, Brazil 19 55S 43 55W
73 Sabarania, Indonesia 2 5S 138 18E
70 Sabari, R., India 18 0N 81 25E
62 Sabastiya, Jordan 32 17N 35 12E
113 Sabattis, U.S.A. 44 6N 74 40W
40 Sabaudia, Italy 41 17N 13 2E
87 Sabderat, Ethiopia 15 26N 36 42E
83 Sabhah, Libya 27 9N 14 29E
93 Sabie, S. Africa 25 4S 30 48E
120 Sabinal, Mexico 30 50N 107 25W
117 Sabinal, U.S.A. 29 20N 99 27W
33 Sabinal, Punta del, Sp. 36 43N 2 44W
120 Sabinas, Mexico 27 50N 101 10W
120 Sabinas Hidalgo, Mex. 26 40N 100 10W
117 Sabine, U.S.A. 29 42N 93 54W
117 Sabine, R., U.S.A. 31 30N 93 35W
36 Sabine, Monti, Italy 42 15N 12 50E
27 Sabinov, Czechoslovakia 49 6N 21 5E
57 Sabirabad, U.S.S.R. 40 0N 48 30E
83 Sabkhat Tawurgha, Lib. 31 48N 15 30E
73 Sablayan, Philippines 12 5N 120 50E
18 Sable, France 47 50N 0 21W
107 Sable C., Canada 43 29N 65 38W
111 Sable, C., U.S.A. 25 5N 81 0W
107 Sable I., Canada 44 0N 60 0W
20 Sables-d'Olonne, les, France 46 30N 1 45W
30 Sabor, R., Portugal 41 16N 7 10W
84 Sabou, Upper Volta 12 1N 2 28W
83 Sabrātah, Libya 32 47N 12 29E
5 Sabrina Coast, Antarc. 67 0S 120 0E
77 Sabtang I., Philippines 20 15N 121 30E
30 Sabugal, Portugal 40 20N 7 5W
49 Saeby, Denmark 57 21N 10 30E
65 Sabzevar, Iran 36 15N 57 40E
65 Sabzvaran, Iran 28 45N 57 50E
116 Sac City, U.S.A. 42 26N 95 0W
32 Sacedón, Spain 40 29N 2 41W
106 Sachigo, L., Canada 53 50N 92 12W
57 Sachkhere, U.S.S.R. 42 25N 43 28E
39 Sacile, Italy 45 58N 16 7E
113 Sackett's Harbor, U.S.A. 43 56N 72 38W
25 Säckingen, W. Germany 47 34N 7 56E
114 Saco, Me., U.S.A. 43 30N 70 27W
118 Saco, Mont., U.S.A. 48 28N 107 19W
118 Sacramento, U.S.A. 38 39N 121 30E
119 Sacramento Mts., U.S.A. 32 30N 105 30W
118 Sacramento, R., U.S.A. 39 30N 122 0W
33 Sacratif, Cabo, Spain 36 42N 3 28W
46 Săcueni, Rumania 47 20N 22 5E
100 Sada, Spain 43 22N 8 15W
32 Sadaba, Spain 2 19N 1 12W
71 Sadao, Thailand 6 38N 100 26E
70 Sadasivpet, India 17 38N 77 50E
86 Sadd el Aali, Egypt 24 5N 32 54E
85 Sade, Nigeria 11 22N 10 45E
92 Sadiba, Botswana 18 53S 23 1E
91 Sadimi, Zaïre 9 25S 23 32E
31 Sado, R., Portugal 38 10N 8 22W
74 Sado, Shima, Japan 38 15N 138 30E
67 Sadon, Burma 25 28N 98 0E
57 Sadon, U.S.S.R. 42 52N 43 58E
68 Sadri, India 24 28N 74 30E
112 Saegerstown, U.S.A. 80 10N 41 42W
32 Saelices, Spain 39 55N 2 49W
86 Safâga, Egypt 26 42N 34 0E
86 Safaha, Saudi Arabia 26 25N 39 0E
64 Safaniya, Saudi Arabia 28 5N 48 42E
27 Safárikovo, Cz. 48 25N 20 20E
65 Safed Koh, Mts., Afghan. 34 15N 64 0E
48 Säffle, Sweden 59 8N 12 55E
35 Safford, U.S.A. 32 54N 109 52W
13 Saffron Walden, England 52 2N 0 15E
62 Safi, Jordan 31 2N 35 28E
82 Safi, Morocco 32 18N 9 14W
18 Safiah, Israel 31 27N 34 46E
54 Safonovo, U.S.S.R. 65 40N 47 50E
56 Safranbolu, Turkey 41 15N 32 34E
113 Sag Harbor, U.S.A. 40 59N 72 17W
73 Saga, Indonesia 2 40S 132 55E
74 Saga-ken ♦, Japan 33 15N 130 20E
67 Sagaing, Burma 22 0N 96 0E
84 Sagala, Mali 14 9N 6 38W
68 Sagar, India 23 50N 78 50E
70 Sagara, India 14 14N 75 6E
90 Sagara, L., Tanz. 5 20S 31 0E
48 Sågen, Sweden 60 17N 14 10E
114 Saginaw, U.S.A. 43 26N 83 55W
75 Sagil, Mongolia 50 15N 91 15E
21 Sagleipie, Liberia 45 25N 7 0E
105 Saglouc (Sugluk), Canada 62 30N 74 15W
21 Sagone, France 42 7N 8 42E
21 Sagone, G. de, Fr. 42 4N 8 40E
31 Sagres, Portugal 37 0N 8 58W
121 Sagua la Grande, Cuba 22 50N 80 10W
119 Saguache, U.S.A. 38 10N 106 4W
107 Saguenay, R., Canada 48 22N 70 30W
32 Sagunto, Spain 39 42N 0 18W
47 Sagåg, Norway 59 46N 5 25E
86 Sahaba, Sudan 18 57N 30 25E
126 Sahagún, Colombia 8 57N 75 27W
30 Sahagún, Spain 42 18N 5 2W
62 Saham, Jordan 32 42N 35 46E
82 Sahara, Africa 23 0N 5 0W
82 Saharien Atlas, Algeria 34 9N 3 29E

MAP
68 Saharanpur, India 29 58N 77 33E
82 Saharien Atlas, Algeria 34 9N 3 29E
68 Sahaswan, India 28 5N 78 45E
93 Sahasinaka, Malag. 21 49S 47 49E
68 Sahaswan, India 28 5N 78 45E
84 Sahel, Canal du, Mali 14 20N 6 0W
69 Sahibganj, India 25 12N 87 55E
68 Sahiwal, Pakistan 30 45N 73 8E
62 Sahl Arraba, Jordan 37 26N 35 12E
120 Sahuaripa, Mexico 29 30N 109 0W
119 Sahuarita, U.S.A. 31 58N 110 59W
120 Sahuayo, Mexico 20 4N 102 43W
27 Sahy, Czechoslovakia 48 4N 18 55E
81 Sa'id Bundas, Sudan 8 24N 24 48E
65 Sa'idabad, Iran 29 30N 55 45E
82 Saïda, Algeria 34 50N 0 11E
70 Saidapet, India 13 0N 80 15E
66 Saidu, Pakistan 34 50N 72 15E
65 Saighan, Afghanistan 35 10N 67 55E
20 Saignes, France 45 20N 2 31E
63 Saihut, S. Yemen 15 12N 51 10E
• 71 Saigon, S. Vietnam 10 58N 106 40E
65 Saih-al-Malih, Oman 23 37N 58 31E
63 Saihut, S. Yemen 15 12N 51 10E
74 Saijō, Japan 34 0N 133 5E
74 Saiki, Japan 32 35N 131 50E
67 Saikhoa Ghat, India 27 50N 95 40E
74 Saiki, Japan 32 35N 131 50E
21 Saillans, France 44 42N 5 12E
73 Sailolof, Indonesia 1 7S 130 46E
52 Saimaa, L., Finland 61 15N 28 15E
14 St., Abbs Head, Scotland 55 55N 2 10W
26 St. Aegyd, Austria 47 52N 15 33E
20 St. Affrique, France 43 57N 2 53E
18 St.-Aignan, France 47 16N 1 22E
98 St. Albans, Australia 24 43S 139 56E
107 St. Albans, Canada 47 51N 55 50W
13 St. Albans, Eng. 51 44N 0 19W
113 St. Albans, Vt., U.S.A. 44 49N 73 7W
114 St. Albans, W. Va., U.S.A. 38 21N 81 50W
13 St. Albans Head, England 50 34N 2 3W
108 St. Albert, Canada 53 37N 113 40W
19 St. Amand, France 50 25N 3 6E
20 St.-Amand-Mont- Rond, France 46 43N 2 30E
19 St.-Amarin, France 47 54N 7 0E
21 St.-Amour, France 46 26N 5 21E
26 St. Andrä, Austria 46 46N 14 50E
18 St. André de l'Eure, Fr. 48 54N 1 16E
20 St.-André-de- Cubzac, France 44 59N 0 26W
21 St. André-les-Alpes, Fr. 43 58N 6 30E
93 St. André, C., Malag. 16 11S 44 27E
107 St. Andrews, Canada 47 45N 59 15W
101 St. Andrews, Scot. 56 20N 2 48W
113 St. Anicet, Canada 45 9N 74 23W
107 St. Ann B., Canada 46 22N 60 25W
18 St. Anne, U.K. 49 43N 2 11W
118 St. Anthony, U.S.A. 44 0N 111 49W
20 St.-Antonin-Noble- Val, France 44 10N 1 45E
100 St. Arnaud, Australia 36 32S 143 16E
107 St. Arthur, Canada 47 32N 67 28W
12 St. Asaph, Wales 53 15N 3 27W
20 St. Astier, France 45 8N 0 31E
18 St.-Aubin-du- Cormier, France 48 15N 1 26W
107 St. Augustin, Canada 51 19N 58 48W
93 St. Augustin, Malag. 23 33S 43 46E
115 St. Augustine, U.S.A. 29 52N 81 20W
13 St. Austell, Eng. 50 20N 4 48W
19 St. Avoed, France 49 7N 6 40E
121 St. Barthélemy, I., W.I. 17 50N 62 50W
12 St. Bee's Hd., Eng. 54 30N 3 38E
20 St.-Benoît-du-Sault, France 46 26N 1 24E
25 St. Bernard, Col du Grand, Fr.-Switz. 45 53N 7 11E
109 St. Boniface, Canada 49 50N 97 10W
21 St. Bonnet, France 44 40N 6 5E
18 St.-Brévin-les-Pins, France 47 14N 2 10W
18 St.-Brice-en-Coglès, France 48 25N 1 22W
107 St. Bride's, Canada 46 56N 54 10W
13 St. Bride's B., Wales 51 48N 5 15W
18 St.-Brieuc, France 48 30N 2 46W
18 St.-Cast, France 48 37N 2 18W
106 St. Catharines, Canada 43 10N 79 15W
115 St. Catherine's I., U.S.A. 31 35N 81 10W
13 St. Catherine's Pt., U.K. 50 34N 1 18W
20 St.-Céré, France 44 51N 1 54E
25 St. Cergue, Switzerland 46 27N 6 10E
20 St. Cernin, France 45 5N 2 25E
21 St.-Chamond, France 45 28N 4 31E
114 St. Charles, Ill., U.S.A. 41 55N 88 21W
116 St. Charles, Mo., U.S.A. 38 46N 90 30W
20 St.-Chély-d'Apcher, France 44 48N 3 17E
20 St.-Chinian, France 43 25N 2 56E
121 St. Christopher (St. Kitts), Leeward Is. 17 20N 62 40W
20 St.-Ciers-sur- Gironde, France 45 17N 0 37W
112 St. Clair, Mich, U.S.A. 42 47N 82 27W
113 St. Clair, Pa., U.S.A. 40 42N 76 12W
112 St. Clair, L., Canada 42 30N 82 45W
112 St. Clair, R., N. Amer. 42 40N 82 25W
112 St. Clairsville, U.S.A. 40 5N 80 53W
20 St.-Claud, France 45 54N 0 28E
21 St.-Claude, France 46 22N 5 52E
115 St. Cloud, Fla., U.S.A. 28 15N 81 15W
116 St. Cloud, Minn., U.S.A. 45 30N 94 11W
107 St. Coeur de Marie, Can. 48 39N 71 43W
116 St. Croix, R., U.S.A. 45 20N 92 50W
116 St. Croix Falls, U.S.A. 45 18N 92 22W
20 St. Cyprien, France 43 37N 3 0E

• Renamed Phanh Bho Ho Chi Minh

MAP
21 St.-Cyr, France 43 11N 5 43E
13 St. David's, Wales 51 54N 5 16W
13 St. David's Head, Wales 51 54N 5 16W
19 St.-Denis, France 48 56N 2 22E
18 St.-Denis-d'Orques, France 48 2N 0 17W
19 St.-Dié, France 48 17N 6 56E
19 St. Dizier, France 48 40N 5 0E
21 St.-Egrève, France 45 14N 5 41E
104 St. Elias, Mt., Alaska 60 20N 141 59W
20 St. Eloy, France 46 10N 2 51E
20 St. Emilon, France 44 53N 0 9W
21 St. Étienne, Fr. 45 27N 4 22E
21 St.-Étienne-de- Tinée, France 44 16N 6 56E
113 St. Eugene, Canada 45 30N 74 28W
106 St. Félicien, Canada 48 40N 72 25W
107 St. Fintan's, Canada 48 10N 58 50W
21 St.-Florent, France 42 41N 9 18E
19 St.-Florent-sur- Cher, France 46 59N 2 15E
19 St.-Florentin, France 48 0N 3 45E
20 St.-Flour, France 45 2N 3 6E
21 St.-Fons, France 45 42N 4 52E
116 St. Francis, U.S.A. 39 48N 101 47W
92 St. Francis, C., S. Africa 34 14S 24 49E
113 St. Francis L., Canada 45 10N 74 20W
117 St. Francis, R., U.S.A. 32 25N 90 36W
18 St.-Fulgent, France 46 50N 1 10W
106 St. Gabriel de Brandon, Canada 46 17N 73 24W
20 St.-Guadens, France 43 6N 0 44E
18 St.-Gaultier, France 46 39N 1 26E
21 St.-Gengoux-le- National, France 46 37N 4 40E
20 St.-Geniez-d'Olt, France 44 27N 2 58E
99 St. George, Australia 28 1S 148 41E
121 St. George, Bermuda 32 24N 64 42W
107 St. George, Canada 45 11N 66 57W
115 St. George, S.C., U.S.A. 33 13N 80 37W
119 St. George, Utah, U.S.A. 37 10N 113 35W
98 St. George, Austral. 28 2S 148 35E
107 St. George, C., Canada 48 30N 59 16W
115 St. George, C., U.S.A. 29 36N 85 2W
100 St. George Hd., Australia 35 11S 150 45E
109 St. George West, Can. 50 33N 96 7W
107 St. George's, Canada 48 26N 58 31W
107 St. Georges, Canada 46 8N 70 40W
106 St. Georges, Canada 46 42N 72 35W
16 St.-Georges, Belgium 50 37N 4 20E
127 St.-Georges, Fr. Gui. 4 0N 52 0W
121 St. George's, Grenada 12 5N 61 43W
110 St. George's Channel, U.K. 52 0N 6 0W
20 St. Georges, France 45 36N 1 0W
19 St. Germain, France 48 53N 2 5E
20 St.-Germain-de- Calberte, France 44 13N 3 48E
20 St.-Germain-des- Fossés, France 46 12N 3 26E
19 St.-Germain-du- Plain, France 46 42N 4 58E
21 St.-Germain-Laval, France 45 50N 4 1E
20 St.-Germain- Lembron, France 45 27N 3 14E
21 St. Gervais, Haute Savoie, France 45 53N 6 42E
20 St. Gervais, Puy de Dôme, France 46 4N 2 50E
18 St.-Gildas, Pte. de, Fr. 47 8N 2 14W
21 St.-Gilles, Gard, France 43 40N 4 26E
18 St. Gilles Croix-de- Vie, France 46 41N 1 55W
20 St.-Girons, Ariège, France 42 59N 1 8E
48 St. Gla, L., Sweden 59 35N 12 30E
25 St. Goar, Germany 50 31N 7 43E
25 St. Gotthard P. = San Gottardo, Switz. 46 33N 8 33E
49 St. Heddinge, Denmark 55 9N 12 26E
7 St. Helena, I., Atl. Oc. 15 55S 5 44W
34 St. Helena, U.S.A. 38 29N 122 30W
92 St. Helenabaai, S. Africa 32 40S 18 10E
12 St. Helens, England 53 28N 2 44W
118 St. Helens, U.S.A. 45 55N 122 50W
18 St. Helier, U.K. 49 11N 2 6W
18 St. Hilaire, France 48 35N 1 7W
19 St. Hippolyte, France 47 20N 6 50E
20 St. Hippolyte-du- Fort, France 43 58N 3 52E
19 St.-Honoré, France 46 54N 3 50E
16 St.-Hubert, Belgium 50 2N 5 23E
106 St. Hyacinthe, Canada 45 40N 72 58W
114 St. Ignace, U.S.A. 45 53N 84 43W
106 St. Ignace I., Canada 48 45N 88 0W
118 St. Ignatius, U.S.A. 47 25N 114 2W
25 St.-Imier, Switzerland 47 9N 6 58E
13 St. Ives, Cornwall, England 50 13N 5 29W
13 St. Ives, Hunts., England 52 20N 0 5W
18 St.-James, France 48 31N 1 20W
116 St. James, U.S.A. 43 57N 94 40W
108 St. James C., Canada 51 55N 131 0W
106 St. Jean, Canada 45 20N 73 50W
109 St. Jean Baptiste, Can. 49 15N 97 20W
88 St. Jean, C., Eq. Guinea 1 5N 9 20E
20 St.-Jean-de-Luz, France 43 23N 1 39W
21 St.-Jean-de- Maurienne, France 45 16N 6 28E
18 St.-Jean-de-Monts, France 46 47N 2 4W
20 St. Jean-du-Gard, Fr. 47 7N 3 52E
21 St.-Jean-en-Royans, France 45 1N 5 18E
107 St. Jean-Port-Joli, Can. 47 15N 70 13W
107 St. Jerome, L. St. John, Can. 48 26N 71 53W
106 St. Jerone, Canada 45 55N 74 0W

St. John INDEX San Clemente

MAP
107 St. John, Canada 45 20N 66 8W
117 St. John, Kans., U.S.A. 37 59N 98 45W
116 St. John, N.D., U.S.A. 48 58N 99 40W
77 St. John I., China 21 45N 112 45E
107 St. John L., Canada 48 40N 72 0W
107 St. John, R., Canada 46 30N 67 40W
107 St. John's, Canada 47 35N 52 40W
119 St. Johns, Ariz., U.S.A. 34 31N 109 26W
114 St. Johns, Mich., U.S.A. 43 0N 84 38W
115 St. Johns, R., U.S.A. 30 20N 81 30W
113 St. Johnsbury, U.S.A. 44 25N 72 1W
113 St. Johnsville, U.S.A. 43 0N 74 43W
117 St. Joseph, La., U.S.A. 31 55N 91 15W
116 St. Joseph, Mo., U.S.A. 39 40N 94 50W
106 St. Joseph I., Canada 46 12N 83 58W
106 St. Joseph L., Canada 51 10N 90 50W
114 St. Joseph, R., U.S.A. 42 0N 85 30W
114 St. Joseph's, U.S.A. 42 5N 86 30W
106 St. Jovite, Canada 46 8N 74 38W
20 St. Juéry, France 43 55N 2 42E
21 St. Julien, France 46 8N 6 5E
21 St.-Julien- Chapteuil, France 45 2N 4 4E
19 St.-Julien-de-Sault, France 48 2N 3 18E
20 St.-Junien, France 45 53N 0 55E
19 St.-Just-en- Chaussée, France 49 30N 2 25E
20 St.-Just-en- Chevalet, France 45 55N 3 50E
20 St.-Justin, France 43 59N 0 14W
49 St. Karlsö, I., Sweden 57 17N 17 58E
101 St. Kilda, New Zealand 45 53S 170 31E
121 St. Kitts, I., Leeward Is. 17 20N 62 40W
109 St. Laurent, Canada 50 25N 97 58W
21 St. Laurent, Fr. 46 35N 5 56E
21 St.-Laurent-du-Pont, France 45 23N 5 45E
98 St. Lawrence, Australia 22 16S 149 31E
107 St. Lawrence, Canada 46 54N 55 23W
107 St. Lawrence, Gulf of, Canada 48 25N 62 0W
107 St. Lawrence, Canada 46 54N 55 23W
98 St. Lawrence, Australia 22 16S 149 31E
104 St. Lawrence, I., U.S.A. 63 0N 170 0W
107 St. Lawrence, R., Canada 49 30N 66 0W
107 St. Leonard, Canada 47 12N 67 58W
20 St.-Léonard-de- Noblat, France 45 49N 1 29E
106 St. Lin, Canada 45 44N 73 46W
18 St.-Lô, France 49 7N 1 5W
84 St. Louis, Senegal 16 8N 16 27W
114 St. Louis, Mich., U.S.A. 43 27N 84 38W
116 St. Louis, Mo., U.S.A. 38 40N 90 20W
116 St. Louis R., U.S.A. 47 15N 92 45W
19 St.-Loup-sur- Semouse, France 47 53N 6 16E
93 St. Lucia, C., S. Africa 28 32S 32 29E
121 St. Lucia I., Wind. Is. 14 0N 60 50W
93 St. Lucia, Lake, S. Afr. 28 5S 32 30E
121 St. Maarten, I., Leeward Is. 18 0N 63 5W
20 St.-Maixent-l'École, France 46 24N 0 12W
18 St.-Malo, France 48 39N 2 1W
18 St. Malo, G. de, France 48 50N 2 30W
21 St. Mandrier, France 43 4N 5 56E
121 St. Marc, Haiti 19 10N 72 50W
21 St.-Marcellin, France 45 9N 5 20E
18 St. Marcouf, Is., France 49 30N 1 10W
118 St. Maries, U.S.A. 47 17N 116 34W
19 St. Martin, France 50 42N 1 38E
121 St. Martin, I., Leeward Is. 18 0N 63 0W
109 St. Martin L., Canada 51 40N 98 30W
21 St. Martin-Tende-Vésubie, Fr. 44 4N 7 15E
107 St. Martins, Canada 45 22N 65 38W
117 St. Martinsville, U.S.A. 30 10N 91 50W
20 St.-Martory, France 43 9N 0 56E
107 St. Mary B., Canada 46 50N 53 50W
84 St. Mary C., Gambia 13 24N 13 10E
70 St. Mary Is., India 13 20N 74 35E
99 St. Mary's, Australia 41 32S 148 11E
107 St. Mary's, Newf., Canada 46 56N 53 34W
112 St. Mary's, Ont., Canada 43 20N 81 10W
114 St. Mary's, Ohio, U.S.A. 40 33N 84 20W
112 St. Mary's, Pa., U.S.A. 41 30N 78 33W
107 St. Mary's, Bay, Canada 46 56N 53 45W
107 St. Mary's, C., Canada 46 50N 54 12W
13 St. Mary's I., U.K. 49 55N 6 17W
99 St. Mary's Pk., Australia 31 30S 138 33E
18 St.-Mathieu, Pte. de, France 48 20N 4 45W
21 St. Matthew's I. = Zadetkyi Kyun, Burma 10 0N 98 25E
19 St.-Maur-des- Fosses, France 48 48N 2 30E
106 St. Maurice R., Canada 47 20N 72 50W
20 St.-Médard-de- Guizières, France 45 1N 0 4W
18 St.-Méen-le-Grand, France 48 11N 2 12W
119 St. Michaels, U.S.A. 35 45N 109 5W
13 St. Michael's Mt., England 50 7N 5 30W
21 St. Michel, Fr. 45 15N 6 29E
19 St. Mihiel, France 48 54N 5 30E
18 St.-Nazaire, France 47 17N 2 12W
13 St. Neots, Eng. 52 14N 0 16W
19 St.-Nicholas-de- Port, France 48 38N 6 18E
112 St. Ola Sta., Canada 44 50N 77 38W
49 St. Olaf, Sweden 55 40N 14 12E
19 St.-Omer, France 50 45N 2 15E
19 St. Ouen, France 48 50N 2 20E
107 St. Pacome, Canada 47 24N 69 58W
20 St.-Palais, France 45 40N 1 8W
107 St. Pamphile, Canada 46 58N 69 48W
20 St.-Pardoux-la- Rivière, France 45 29N 0 45E
107 St. Pascal, Canada 47 32N 69 48W
109 St. Paul, Canada 51 34N 57 47W
20 St. Paul, France 43 44N 1 3W
116 St. Paul, Minn., U.S.A. 44 54N 93 5W
116 St. Paul, Nebr., U.S.A. 41 15N 98 30W
6 St. Paul, I., Atlantic Oc. 0 50N 31 40W
107 St. Paul, I., Canada 47 12N 60 9W
3 St. Paul I., Ind. Oc. 30 40S 77 34E
20 St. Paul-de- Fenouillet, France 42 50N 2 28E
107 St. Paul's B., Canada 49 48N 57 58W
21 St.-Peray, France 44 57N 4 50E
18 St.-Père-en-Retz, France 47 11N 2 2W
116 St. Peter, U.S.A. 44 15N 93 57W
18 St. Peter Port, Channel Is. 49 27N 2 31W
107 St. Peters, N.S., Can. 45 40N 60 53W
107 St. Peters, P.E.I., Can. 46 20N 62 25W
115 St. Petersburg, U.S.A. 27 45N 82 40W
18 St.-Philbert-de-Grand-Lieu, France 47 2N 1 39W
20 St.-Pierre-d'Oleron, France 45 57N 1 19W
18 St.-Pierre-Eglise, France 49 40N 1 24W
18 St.-Pierre-en-Port, France 49 48N 0 30E
18 St. Pierre-sur-Dives, Fr. 49 2N 0 1W
107 St. Pierre Miquelon ♦, N. Amer. 46 49N 56 15W
19 St. Pol, France 50 21N 2 20E
18 St.-Pol-de-Léon, France 48 41N 4 0W
19 St.-Pol-sur-Mer, France 51 1N 2 20E
20 St. Pons, France 43 30N 2 45E
19 St.-Pourçain-sur- Sioule, France 46 18N 3 18E
19 St.-Quentin, France 49 50N 3 16E
21 St. Rambert-d'Albon, Fr. 45 17N 1 35E
21 St.-Raphaël, France 43 25N 6 46E
118 St. Regis, Mont., U.S.A. 47 20N 115 3W
113 St. Regis, N.Y., U.S.A. 44 39N 74 34W
21 St.-Rémy-de- Provence, France 43 48N 4 50E
18 St.-Renan, France 48 26N 4 37W
18 St.-Saëns, France 49 41N 1 16E
19 St.-Sauveur-en- Puisaye, France 47 37N 3 12E
18 St.-Sauveur-le- Vicomte, France 49 23N 1 32W
20 St. Savin, France 46 34N 0 50E
20 St.-Savinien, France 45 53N 0 42W
93 St. Sebastien, C., Malag. 12 26S 48 44E
19 St.-Seine-l'Abbaye, France 47 26N 4 47E
20 St. Sernin, France 43 54N 2 35E
18 St.-Servan-sur-Mer, France 48 38N 2 0E
18 St.-Sever-Calvados, France 48 50N 1 3W
107 St. Simeon, Canada 47 51N 69 54W
107 St. Stephen, Canada 45 16N 67 17W
20 St.-Sulpice, France 43 46N 1 41E
20 St.-Sulpice- Laurière, France 46 3N 1 29E
18 St.-Thegonnec, France 48 31N 3 57W
106 St. Thomas, Canada 42 45N 81 10W
106 St. Tite, Canada 46 45N 72 40W
16 St. Troud, Belgium 50 48N 5 10E
21 St. Tropez, France 43 17N 6 38E
18 St.-Vaast-la-Hougue, France 49 35N 1 17W
19 St. Valéry, France 50 10N 1 38E
18 St.-Valéry-en-Caux, France 49 52N 0 43E
21 St.-Vallier, Drôme, France 45 11N 4 50E
21 St.-Vallier-de- Thiey, France 43 42N 6 51E
18 St.-Varent, France 46 53N 0 13W
6 St. Vincent, C., Verde Is. 18 0N 26 1W
89 St. Vincent C., Malag. 21 58S 43 20E
31 St. Vincent, C. = São Vincente, Port. 37 0N 9 0W
99 St. Vincent, G., Austral. 35 0S 138 0E
121 St. Vincent, I., Wind. Is. 13 10N 61 10W
20 St. Vincent-de- Tyrosse, France 43 39N 1 18W
20 St.-Yrieux-la- Perche, France 45 31N 1 12E
18 Ste.-Adresse, France 49 31N 0 5E
107 Ste. Anne de Beaupré, Canada 47 2N 70 58W
107 Ste. Anne de Portneuf, Canada 48 38N 69 8W
19 Ste. Benoîte, France 49 47N 3 30E
107 Ste. Cecile, Canada 47 56N 64 34W
19 Ste.-Croix, Switzerland 46 49N 6 34W
20 Ste.-Foy-la-Grande, France 44 50N 0 13E
116 Ste. Genevieve, U.S.A. 37 59N 90 2W
107 Ste. Germaine, Canada 46 24N 70 24W
20 Ste.-Hermine, France 46 32N 1 4W
20 Ste.-Livrade-sur-Lot, France 44 24N 0 36E
121 Ste. Marie, Martinique 14 48N 61 1W
93 Ste. Marie, C., Malag. 25 36S 45 8E
93 Ste. Marie, I., Malag. 16 50S 49 55E
19 Ste.-Marie-aux- Mines, France 48 10N 7 12E
107 Ste. Marie de la Madeleine, Canada 46 26N 71 0W
18 Ste.-Maure-de- Touraine, France 47 7N 0 37E
21 Ste.-Maxime, France 43 19N 6 39E
19 Ste.-Menehould, France 49 5N 4 54E
18 Ste.-Mère-Eglise, France 49 24N 1 19W
121 Ste. Rose, Guadaloupe 16 20N 61 45W
109 Ste. Rose du lac, Can. 51 10N 99 30W
124 Ste. Teresa, Argentina 33 33S 60 54W
20 Saintes, France 45 45N 0 37W
20 Saintonge, Fr. 45 40N 0 50W
67 Sairang, India 23 50N 92 45E
74 Saitama-ken ♦, Japan 36 25N 137 0E
126 Sajama, Nevada, Bolivia 18 0S 68 55W
91 Sajan, Yugoslavia 45 50N 20 58E
27 Sajószentpéter, Hung. 48 12N 20 44E
66 Saka Ilkalat, Pakistan 27 20N 64 7E
74 Sakai, Japan 34 30N 135 30E
74 Sakai Shimane, Japan 35 30N 133 25E
74 Sakaimachi, Japan 35 30N 133 15E
74 Sakaide, Japan 34 32N 133 50E
64 Sakaka, Saudi Arabia 30 0N 40 8E
106 Sakami, L., Canada 53 10N 77 0W
82 Sâkâne, 'Erg i-n, Mali 20 30N 1 30W
91 Sakania, Zaïre 12 43S 28 30E
98 Sakar, I., Terr. of New Guinea 5 30S 148 0E
56 Sakarya, R., Turkey 40 5N 31 0E
74 Sakata, Japan 38 55N 139 56E
93 Sakeny, R., Malag. 20 0S 45 25E
85 Sakété, Dahomey 6 40N 2 32E
59 Sakhalin, Ostrov, U.S.S.R. 51 0N 143 0E
69 Sakhi Gopal, India 19 58N 85 50E
62 Sakhnin, Israel 32 52N 35 12E
56 Saki, U.S.S.R. 45 16N 33 34E
49 Sakiai, U.S.S.R. 54 59N 23 0E
77 Sakishima-guntō, Japan 24 30N 124 0E
28 Sakołow Małopolski, Poland 50 10N 22 9E
71 Sakon Nakhon, Thailand 17 0N 104 0E
68 Sakrand, Pakistan 26 10N 68 15E
68 Sakri, India 21 2N 74 40E
49 Sakskōbing, Denmark 54 49N 11 39E
51 Säkylä, Finland 61 4N 22 20E
57 Sal, R., U.S.S.R. 47 25N 42 20E
27 Sal'a, Czechoslovakia 48 10N 17 50E
48 Sala, Sweden 59 58N 16 35E
48 Sala Consilina, Italy 40 23N 15 35E
95 Sala-y-Gomez, I., Pacific Ocean 26 28S 105 28W
124 Saladas, Argentina 28 15S 58 40W
124 Saladillo, Argentina 35 40S 59 55W
124 Salado, R., Buenos Aires, Argentina 35 40S 58 10W
124 Salado R., Santa Fe, Argentina 27 0S 63 40W
85 Salaga, Ghana 8 31N 0 31W
46 Sălaj ♦, Rumania 47 15N 23 0E
73 Salajar, I., Indonesia 6 15S 120 30E
84 Salala, Liberia 6 42N 10 7W
86 Salala, Sudan 21 17N 36 16E
63 Salalah, Oman 16 56N 53 59E
62 Salama, Israel 32 3N 34 48E
124 Salamanca, Chile 32 0S 71 25W
30 Salamanca, Spain 40 58N 5 39W
112 Salamanca, U.S.A. 42 10N 78 42W
30 Salamanca ♦, Spain 40 57N 5 40W
98 Salamaua, Terr. of New Guinea 7 10S 147 0E
126 Salamina, Colombia 5 25N 75 29W
45 Salamis, Greece 37 56N 23 30E
128 Salar de Atacama, Chile 23 30S 68 25W
126 Salar de Uyuni, Bolivia 20 30S 67 45W
46 Salard, Rumania 47 12N 22 3E
30 Salas, Spain 43 25N 6 15W
32 Salas de los Infantes, Sp. 42 2N 3 17W
76 Salatu, Mongolia 44 25N 107 58E
126 Salaverry, Peru 8 15S 79 0W
90 Salawe, Tanzania 3 17S 32 56E
32 Salazar, R., Spain 42 45N 1 8W
48 Salbohed, Sweden 59 55N 16 22E
19 Salbris, France 47 25N 2 3E
46 Salcia, Rumania 43 56N 24 55E
30 Saldaña, Spain 42 32N 4 48W
92 Saldanha, S. Afr. 33 0S 17 58E
92 Saldanhabaai, S. Africa 33 6S 18 0E
54 Saldus, U.S.S.R. 56 45N 22 37E
100 Sale, Australia 38 7S 147 0E
12 Sale, England 53 26N 2 19W
82 Salé, Morocco 34 3N 6 48W
85 Saléa-koira, Mali 16 54N 0 46W
73 Salebabu, Indonesia 3 45N 125 55E
65 Salehabad, Iran 35 40N 61 2E
58 Salekhard, U.S.S.R. 66 30N 66 25E
70 Salem, India 11 40N 78 11E
114 Salem, Ind., U.S.A. 38 38N 86 0W
113 Salem, Mass., U.S.A. 42 29N 70 53W
117 Salem, Mo., U.S.A. 37 40N 91 30W
114 Salem, N.J., U.S.A. 39 34N 75 29W
112 Salem, Ohio, U.S.A. 40 52N 80 50W
118 Salem, Oreg., U.S.A. 45 0N 123 0W
114 Salem, Va., U.S.A. 37 19N 80 8W
72 Salembu, Kepulauan, Indonesia 5 35S 114 30E
40 Salemi, Italy 37 49N 12 47E
21 Salernes, France 43 34N 6 15E
41 Salerno, Italy 40 40N 14 44E
41 Salerno, G. di, Italy 40 35N 14 45E
62 Salfit, Jordan 32 5N 35 11E
12 Salford, England 53 30N 2 17W
56 Salgir, R., U.S.S.R. 45 30N 34 30E
27 Salgótarján, Hungary 48 5N 19 47E
20 Salies-de-Béarn, France 43 28N 0 56W
116 Salina, U.S.A. 38 50N 97 40W
41 Salina, I., Italy 38 35N 14 50E
120 Salina Cruz, Mexico 16 10N 95 10W
127 Salinas, Brazil 16 20S 42 10W
124 Salinas, Chile 23 31S 69 29W
126 Salinas, Ecuador 2 10S 80 50W
121 Salinas, B. de, Nicaragua 11 4N 85 45W
33 Salinas, Cabo de, Spain 39 16N 3 4E
124 Salinas, Pampa de las, Arg. 31 58S 66 42W
119 Salinas, R., U.S.A. 36 10N 121 10W
124 Salinas Ambargasta, Arg. 29 0S 65 30W
120 Salinas (de Hidalgo), Mexico 22 30N 101 40W
124 Salinas Grandes, Arg. 30 0S 65 0W
116 Saline, R., U.S.A. 39 10N 99 5W
127 Salinópolis, Brazil 0 40S 47 20W
19 Salines-les-Bains, France 46 58N 5 52E
31 Salir, Portugal 37 14N 8 2W
13 Salisbury, Eng. 51 4N 1 48W
91 Salisbury, Rhodesia 17 50S 31 2E
114 Salisbury, Md., U.S.A. 38 20N 75 38W
115 Salisbury, N.C., U.S.A. 35 42N 80 29W
13 Salisbury Plain, England 51 13N 2 0W
46 Săliște, Rumania 45 45N 23 56E
85 Salka, Nigeria 10 20N 4 58E
32 Sallent, Spain 41 49N 1 54E
20 Salles-Curan, France 44 11N 2 48E
49 Salling, Denmark 56 40N 8 55E
117 Sallisaw, U.S.A. 35 26N 94 45W
86 Sallom Junc., Sudan 19 23N 37 6E
32 Salmerón, Spain 40 33N 2 29W
108 Salmo, Canada 49 10N 117 20W
118 Salmon, U.S.A. 45 12N 113 56W
118 Salmon, R., U.S.A. 46 0N 116 30W
108 Salmon Arm, Canada 50 40N 119 15W
118 Salmon Falls, U.S.A. 42 55N 114 59W
107 Salmon Res., Canada 48 05N 56 00W
118 Salmon River Mts., U.S.A. 45 0N 114 30W
51 Salo, Finland 60 22N 23 3E
38 Saló, Italy 45 37N 10 32E
31 Salobreña, Spain 36 44N 3 35W
119 Salome, U.S.A. 33 51N 113 37W
21 Salon-de-Provence, France 43 39N 5 6E
44 Salonica = Thessaloníki, Greece 40 38N 22 58E
46 Salonta, Rumania 46 49N 21 42E
31 Salor, R., Spain 39 39N 7 3W
32 Salou, Cabo, Spain 41 3N 1 10E
124 Salsacate, Argentina 31 20S 65 5W
48 Salsaker, Sweden 62 59N 18 20E
20 Salses, France 42 50N 2 55E
66 Salsette I., India 19 5N 72 50E
57 Salsk, U.S.S.R. 46 28N 41 30E
41 Salso, R., Italy 37 6N 13 55E
38 Salsomaggiore, Italy 44 48N 9 59E
62 Salt, Jordan 32 2N 35 43E
119 Salt, R., U.S.A. 33 50N 110 25W
68 Salt Range, Pakistan 32 30N 72 25E
99 Salt Creek Telegraph Office, S. Australia 36 0S 139 35E
117 Salt Fork R., U.S.A. 37 25N 98 40W
118 Salt Lake City, U.S.A. 40 45N 111 58W
49 Salta, Argentina 24 47S 65 25W
124 Salta ♦, Argentina 24 48S 65 30W
14 Saltcoats, Scot. 55 38N 4 47W
15 Saltee Is., Ireland 52 7N 6 37W
50 Saltfjorden, Norway 67 15N 14 20E
49 Saltholm, Denmark 55 38N 12 43E
50 Salthólmavik, Iceland 65 24N 21 57W
120 Saltillo, Mexico 25 30N 100 57W
124 Salto, Argentina 34 20S 60 15W
124 Salto ♦, Uruguay 31 20S 57 59W
124 Salto Augusto, falls, Brazil 8 30S 58 0W
119 Salton Sea, U.S.A. 33 20N 116 0W
85 Saltpond, Ghana 5 15N 1 3W
49 Saltsjöbaden, Sweden 59 15N 18 20E
108 Saltspring, Canada 48 54N 123 37W
115 Salula, R., U.S.A. 34 12N 81 45W
86 Salûm, Egypt 31 31N 25 7E
86 Salûm, Khâlig el, Egypt 31 30N 25 9E
70 Salur, India 18 27N 83 18E
38 Saluzzo, Italy 44 39N 7 29E
127 Salvador, Brazil 13 0S 38 30W
109 Salvador, Canada 52 20N 109 25W
120 Salvador ■, Central America 13 50N 89 0W
117 Salvador, L., U.S.A. 29 46N 90 16W
31 Salvaterra de Magos, Portugal 39 1N 8 47W
30 Sálvora, Isla, Spain 42 30N 8 58W
65 Salwa, Qatar 24 45N 50 55E
67 Salween, R. = Thanlwin Myit, Burma 20 0N 98 0E
26 Salza, R., Austria 47 43N 15 0E
26 Salzach, R., Austria 47 15N 12 25E
26 Salzburg, Austria 47 48N 13 2E
24 Salzgitter, Germany 52 2N 10 22E
24 Salzwedel, Germany 52 50N 11 11E
68 Sam Neua, Laos 20 29N 104 0E
71 Sam Ngao, Thailand 17 18N 99 0E
117 Sam Rayburn Res., U.S.A. 31 15N 94 20W
58 Sama, U.S.S.R. 60 10N 60 15E
30 Sama de Langreo, Sp. 43 18N 5 40W
73 Samak, Indonesia 4 40S 122 26E
73 Samales Group, Phil. 6 0N 122 0E
70 Samalkot, India 17 3N 82 13E
86 Samâlût, Egypt 28 20N 30 42E
68 Samana, India 30 10N 76 13E
126 Samanco, Peru 9 10S 78 30W
91 Samanga, Tanzania 8 20S 39 13E
90 Samangwa, Zaïre 4 23S 24 10E
73 Samar, I., Philippines 12 0N 125 0E
56 Samara, R., U.S.S.R. 52 30N 53 0E
98 Samarai, Terr. of Papua 10 32S 150 35E
62 Samaria = Shomron, Jordan 32 15N 35 13E
58 Samarkand, U.S.S.R. 39 40N 67 0E
64 Samarra, Iraq 34 16N 43 55E
69 Samastipur, India 25 50N 85 50E
90 Samba, Zaïre 4 38S 26 22E
93 Sambaina, Malag. 19 37S 47 8E
41 Sambiase, Italy 38 58N 16 16E
69 Sambalpur, India 21 28N 83 58E
72 Sambas, S., Indonesia 1 20N 109 20E
93 Sambava, Malagasy Rep. 14 16S 50 10E
91 Sambawizi, Rhodesia 18 24S 26 13E
68 Sambhal, India 28 35N 78 37E
68 Sambhar, India 26 52N 11 16E
38 Sambonifacio, Italy 45 24N 11 16E
71 Samoor, Khmer Rep. 12 46N 106 0E
54 Sambor, U.S.S.R. 49 30N 23 10E
124 Samoorombón, Bahía, Argentina 36 5S 57 20W
16 Samore, R., Belg.-Fr. 50 27N 4 52E
40 Sambuca, Italy 37 39N 13 6E
90 Samburu ♦, Kenya 1 10N 37 0E
92 Sambusu, S.W. Afr. 17 55S 19 21E
90 Same, Tanzania 4 2S 37 38E
19 Samer, France 50 38N 1 44E
91 Samfya, Zambia 11 16S 29 31E
45 Sámi, Greece 38 15N 20 39E
86 Samna, Saudi Arabia 25 12N 37 17E
47 Samnager, Norway 60 23N 5 39E
83 Samnu, Libya 27 15N 14 55E
124 Samo Alto, Chile 30 22S 71 0W
2 Samoan Is., Pac. Ocean 14 0S 171 0W
39 Samobor, Yugoslavia 45 47N 15 44E
21 Samoëns, France 46 5N 6 45E
84 Samorogouan, Upper Volta 11 21N 4 57W
30 Samos, Spain 42 44N 7 20W
42 Samoš, Yugoslavia 45 13N 20 49E
45 Sámos, I., Greece 37 45N 26 50E
72 Samosir, P., Indonesia 2 35N 98 50E
72 Samosir Balige, Indon. 2 20N 98 50E
44 Samothráki, Greece 40 28N 25 38E
44 Samothráki, I., Greece 40 25N 25 40E
84 Sampa, Ghana 8 0N 2 36W
124 Sampacho, Argentina 33 20S 64 50W
73 Sampang, Indonesia 7 11S 113 13E
32 Samper de Calanda, Sp. 41 11N 04 2W
72 Sampit, Indonesia 2 20S 113 0E
72 Sampit, Teluk, Indonesia 3 10S 113 20E
64 Samra, Saudi Arabia 25 35N 41 0E
84 Samreboi, Ghana 5 34N 7 28E
77 Samshui, China 23 7N 112 58E
49 Samsö, Denmark 55 50N 10 35E
49 Samsö Baelt, Denmark 55 45N 10 45E
64 Samsun, Turkey 41 15N 36 15E
45 Samsun Daği, Tur. 37 45N 27 10E
57 Samtredia, U.S.S.R. 42 7N 42 24E
57 Samur, R., U.S.S.R. 41 30N 48 0E
91 Samusole, Zaïre 10 2S 24 0E
71 Samut Prakan, Thailand 13 32N 100 40E
71 Samut Sakhon, Thai. 13 31N 100 20E
71 Samut Songkhram (Mekong), Thailand 13 24N 100 1E
68 Samwari, Pakistan 28 5N 66 46E
67 Samyo La, China 29 55N 84 46E
84 San, Mali 13 15N 4 45W
27 San, R., Poland 50 25N 22 20E
30 San Adrián, C. de, Sp. 43 21N 8 50W
30 San Adrián, G. de, Sp. 43 21N 8 50W
126 San Agustin, Colombia 1 53N 76 16W
73 San Agustin, C., Phil. 6 20N 126 13E
124 San Agustin de Valle Fértil, Arg. 30 35S 67 30W
95 San Ambrosio, I., Pac. Oc. 26 35S 79 30W
118 San Andreas, U.S.A. 38 17N 120 39W
121 San Andrés, I. de, Caribbean 12 42N 81 46W
119 San Andres Mts., U.S.A. 33 0N 106 45W
120 San Andrés Tuxtla, Mex. 18 30N 95 20W
79 San Angelo, U.S.A. 31 30N 100 30W
124 San Antonio, Chile 33 40S 71 40W
119 San Antonio, N. Mex., U.S.A. 33 58N 106 57W
117 San Antonio, Tex., U.S.A. 29 30N 98 30W
126 San Antonio, Venezuela 3 30N 66 44W
124 San Antonio, C., Arg. 36 15S 56 40W
121 San Antonio, C., Cuba 21 50N 84 57W
33 San Antonio, C. de, Sp. 38 48N 0 12E
117 San Antonio, R., U.S.A. 28 30N 97 14W
33 San Antonio Abad, Sp. 38 59N 1 19E
126 San Antonio de Caparo, Ven. 7 35N 71 27W
121 San Antonio de los Baños, Cuba 22 54N 82 31W
124 San Antonio de los Cobres, Arg. 24 16S 66 2W
128 San Antonio Oeste, Arg. 40 40S 65 0W
38 San Benedetto, Italy 45 2N 10 57E
39 San Benedetto del Tronto, Italy 42 57N 13 52E
117 San Benito, U.S.A. 26 5N 97 32W
119 San Bernardino, U.S.A. 34 7N 117 18W
124 San Bernardo, Chile 33 40S 70 50W
126 San Bernardo, I. de, Col. 9 45N 75 50W
120 San Blas, Mex. 26 10N 108 40W
115 San Blas, C., U.S.A. 29 40N 85 25W
121 San Blas, Cord. de, Pan. 9 15N 78 30W
126 San Borja, Bolivia 15 0S 67 12W
124 San Carlos, Argentina 33 50S 69 0W
76 San Carlos, Chile 36 25S 72 0W
•85 San Carlos, Eq. Guinea 3 29N 8 33E
120 San Carlos, Mexico 29 0N 101 10W
121 San Carlos, Nicaragua 11 12N 84 50W
73 San Carlos, Philippines 10 29N 123 25E
125 San Carlos, Uruguay 34 46S 54 58W
119 San Carlos, U.S.A. 33 24N 110 27W
126 San Carlos, Amazonas, Venezuela 1 55N 67 4W
126 San Carlos, Cojedes, Venezuela 9 40N 68 36W
119 San Carlos L., U.S.A. 33 20N 110 10W
128 San Carlos de Bariloche, Argentina 41 10S 71 25W
32 San Carlos de la Rápita, Spain 40 37N 0 35E
126 San Carlos del Zulia, Ven. 9 1N 71 55W
40 San Cataldo, Italy 37 30N 13 58E
32 San Celoni, Spain 41 42N 2 30E
124 San Clemente, Chile 35 30S 71 39W
33 San Clemente, Spain 39 24N 2 25W
119 San Clemente, U.S.A. 33 29N 117 45W

• *Renamed Butuku-Luba*

San Clemente I. INDEX Santa Paula

MAP
119 San Clemente I., U.S.A. 33 0N 118 30W
39 San Constanzo, Italy 43 46N 13 5E
124 San Cristóbal, Argentina 30 20S 61 10W
126 San Cristóbal, Ven. 7 46N 72 14W
120 San Cristóbal de las Casas, Mexico 16 50N 92 33W
38 San Damiano d'Asti, It. 44 51N 8 4E
39 San Daniel del Friuli, It. 46 10N 13 0E
41 San Demétrio Corone, It. 39 34N 16 22E
119 San Diego, Calif., U.S.A. 32 50N 117 10W
117 San Diego, Tex., U.S.A. 27 47N 98 15W
128 San Diego, C., Arg. 54 40S 65 10W
39 San Doná di Piave, It. 45 38N 12 34E
39 San Elpídio a Mare, It. 43 16N 13 41E
124 San Estanislao, Paraguay 24 39S 56 26W
32 San Esteban de Gormaz, Spain 41 34N 3 13W
38 San Felice sul Panaro, Italy 44 51N 11 9E
124 San Felipe, Chile 32 43S 70 50W
126 San Felipe, Venezuela 10 20N 68 44W
32 San Feliu de Guixols, Sp. 41 45N 3 1E
32 San Feliu de Llobregat, Spain 41 23N 2 2E
126 San Félix, Venezuela 8 20N 62 35W
95 San Felix, I., lac. Oc. 26 30S 80 0W
124 San Fernando, Chile 34 30S 71 0W
120 San Fernando, Mexico 30 0N 115 10W
73 San Fernando, Luzon, Phil. 15 5N 120 37E
73 San Fernando, Luzon, Phil. 16 40N 120 23E
31 San Fernando, Spain 36 22N 6 17W
121 San Fernando, Trinidad 10 20N 61 30W
119 San Fernando, U.S.A. 34 15N 118 29W
42 San Fernando, Ven. 8 0N 67 30W
120 San Fernando, R., Mex. 25 0N 99 0W
126 San Fernando de Apure, Ven. 7 54N 67 28W
126 San Fernando de Atabapo, Venezuela 4 3N 67 42W
41 San Fernando di Puglia, Italy 41 18N 16 5E
124 San Francisco, Córdoba, Arg. 31 30S 62 5W
124 San Francisco, San Luis, Arg. 32 45S 66 10W
119 San Francisco, U.S.A. 37 35N 122 30W
124 San Francisco, Paso de, Arg.-Chile 35 40S 70 24W
119 San Francisco, R., U.S.A. 33 30N 109 0W
121 San Francisco de Macoris, Dom. Rep. 19 19N 70 15W
124 San Francisco del Monte de Oro, Arg. 32 36S 66 8W
120 San Francisco del Oro, Mexico 26 52N 105 50W
33 San Francisco Javier, Sp. 38 40N 1 25E
126 San Francisco Solano, Pta., Col. 6 18N 77 29W
117 San Francisville, U.S.A. 30 48N 91 22W
41 San Fratello, Italy 38 1N 14 33E
126 San Gabriel, Ecuador 0 36N 77 49W
40 San Gavino Monreale, It. 39 33N 8 47E
126 San Gil, Colombia 6 33N 73 8W
38 San Gimignano, Italy 43 28N 11 3E
39 San Giórgio di Nogaro, Italy 45 50N 13 13E
41 San Giórgio Iónico, It. 40 27N 17 23E
38 San Giovanni Bianco, It 45 52N 9 40E
41 San Giovanni in Fiore, Italy 39 16N 16 42E
39 San Giovanni in Persiceto, Italy 44 39N 11 12E
41 San Giovanni Rotondo, Italy 41 41N 15 42E
39 San Giovanni Valdarno, It. 43 32N 11 30E
38 San Giuliano Terme, It. 43 45N 10 26E
25 San Gottardo, Paso del, Switz. 46 33N 8 33E
125 San Gregorio, Uruguay 32 37S 55 40W
40 San Guiseppe Iato, It. 37 37N 13 11E
126 San Ignacio, Bolivia 16 20S 60 55W
124 San Ignacio, Paraguay 26 52S 57 3W
73 San Ildefonso, C., Phil. 16 0N 122 10E
124 San Isidro, Argentina 34 29S 58 31W
126 San Jacinto, Col. 9 50N 75 8W
125 San Javier, Misiones, Argentina 27 55S 55 5W
124 San Javier, Santa Fe, Argentina 30 40S 59 55W
126 San Javier, Santa Cruz, Bolivia 16 18S 62 30W
124 San Javier, Chile 35 40S 71 45W
33 San Javier, Spain 37 49N 0 50W
126 San Jerónimo, Sa. de, Col. 8 0N 75 50W
126 San Joaquin, Venezuela 10 16N 67 47W
119 San Joaquin R., U.S.A. 37 0N 120 0W
124 San Jorge, Argentina 31 54S 61 50W
120 San Jorge, Bahía de, Mexico 31 20N 113 20W
128 San Jorge, Golfo de, Argentina 46 0S 66 0W
32 San Jorge, G. de, Spain 40 50N 0 55W
126 San José, Bolivia 17 45S 60 50W
120 San José, Guatemala 14 0N 90 50W
73 San Jose, Luzon, Philippines 15 45N 120 55E
73 San Jose, Mindoro, Philippines 10 50N 122 5E
33 San José, Spain 38 55N 1 18E
119 San Jose, Calif., U.S.A. 37 20N 122 0W
117 San Jose, N. Mex., U.S.A. 35 26N 105 30W
124 San José de Feliciano, Argentina 30 26S 58 46W
124 San José de Jáchal, Arg. 30 5S 69 0W
124 San José de Mayo, Urug. 34 27S 56 27W
126 San José de Ocuné, Col. 4 15N 70 20W
120 San José del Cabo, Mex. 23 0N 109 50W
126 San José del Guaviare, Col. 2 35N 72 38W
124 San Juan, Argentina 31 30S 68 30W
126 San Juan, Antioquia, Colombia 8 46N 76 32W
126 San Juan, Meta, Colombia 3 26N 73 50W
121 San Juan, Dom. Rep. 18 49N 71 12W
120 San Juan, Coahuila, Mex. 29 34N 101 53W
120 San Juan, Jalisco, Mex. 21 20N 102 50W
120 San Juan, Querétaro, Mex. 20 25N 100 0W
73 San Juan, Philippines 8 35N 126 20E
119 San Juan Mts., U.S.A. 38 30N 108 30W
120 San Juan, Presa de, Mexico 17 45N 95 15W
124 San Juan, R., Argentina 32 20S 67 25W
126 San Juan, R., Colombia 4 0N 77 20W
121 San Juan, R., Nicaragua 11 0N 84 30W
119 San Juan, R., U.S.A. 37 20N 110 20W
124 San Juan ♦, Arg. 31 9S 69 0W
33 San Juan Bautista, Sp. 39 5N 1 31E
124 San Juan Bautista, Par. 26 37S 57 6W
119 San Juan Capistrano, U.S.A. 33 29N 117 46W
126 San Juan de los Cayos, Ven. 11 10N 68 25W
126 San Juan de los Morros, Venezuela 9 55N 67 21W
121 San Juan de Norte, B. de, Nicaragua 11 30N 83 40W
31 San Juan del Puerto, Sp. 37 20N 6 50W
121 San Juan del Sur, Nic. 11 20N 86 0W
128 San Julián, Argentina 49 15S 68 0W
32 San Just, Sierra de, Spain 40 45N 0 41W
124 San Justo, Argentina 30 55S 60 30W
120 San Lázaro, Sa. de, Mex. 23 25N 110 0W
119 San Leandro, U.S.A. 37 40N 122 6W
32 San Leonardo, Spain 41 51N 3 5W
124 San Lorenzo, Argentina 32 45S 60 45W
126 San Lorenzo, Ecuador 1 15N 78 50W
124 San Lorenzo, Paraguay 25 20S 57 32W
126 San Lorenzo, Venezuela 9 47N 71 4W
126 San Lorenzo, I., Peru 12 20S 77 35W
128 San Lorenzo, Mt., Arg. 47 40S 72 20W
32 San Lorenzo de la Parilla, Spain 39 51N 2 22W
32 San Lorenzo de Morunys, Spain 42 8N 1 35E
126 San Lucas, Bolivia 20 5S 65 0W
120 San Lucas, C. de, Mexico 22 50N 110 0W
41 San Lucido, Italy 39 18N 16 3E
124 San Luis, Argentina 33 20S 66 20W
119 San Luis, U.S.A. 37 14N 105 26W
126 San Luis, Venezuela 11 7N 69 42W
120 San Luis Río Colorado, Mexico 32 29N 114 48W
126 Sao Marcelino, Braz. 1 0N 67 12W
41 San Marco Argentano, It. 39 34N 16 8E
41 San Marco dei Cavoti, It. 41 20N 14 50E
41 San Marco in Lámis, It. 41 43N 15 38E
120 San Marcos, Guatemala 14 59N 91 52W
117 San Marcos, U.S.A. 29 53N 98 0W
39 San Marino, San Marino 43 56N 12 25E
39 San Marino ■, Europe 43 56N 12 25E
124 San Martín, Argentina 33 5S 68 28W
126 San Martín, Colombia 3 42N 73 42W
128 San Martín, L., Arg. 48 50S 72 50W
30 San Martín de Valdeiglesias, Spain 40 21N 4 24W
38 San Martino de Calvi, It. 45 57N 9 41E
32 San Mateo, Spain 40 28N 0 10E
119 San Mateo, U.S.A. 37 32N 122 25W
126 San Matías, Bolivia 16 25S 58 20W
128 San Matías, Golfo de, Argentina 41 30S 64 0W
120 San Miguel, Salvador 13 30N 88 12W
33 San Miguel, Spain 39 3N 1 26E
126 San Miguel, Venezuela 9 40N 65 11W
126 San Miguel, R., Bolivia 16 0S 62 45W
126 San Miguel, R., Ec./Col. 0 25N 76 30W
33 San Miguel de Salinas, Sp. 37 59N 0 47W
124 San Miguel de Tucumán, Arg. 26 50S 65 20W
124 San Miguel del Monte, Arg. 35 23S 58 50W
38 San Miniato, Italy 43 40N 10 50E
73 San Narcisco, Phil. 15 2N 120 3E
124 San Nicolás de los Arroyas, Argentina 33 17S 60 10W
110 San Nicolas I., U.S.A. 33 16N 119 30W
126 San Onofre, Colombia 9 44N 75 32W
124 San Pablo, Bolivia 21 43S 66 38W
126 San Pablo, Colombia 5 27N 70 56W
41 San Paolo di Civitate, It. 41 44N 15 16E
125 San Pedro, Buenos Aires, Argentina 33 43S 59 45W
124 San Pedro, Jujuy, Argentina 24 12S 64 55W
124 San Pedro, Chile 21 58S 68 30W
126 San Pedro, Colombia 4 56N 71 53W
121 San Pedro, Dom. Rep. 18 30N 69 18W
84 San Pedro, Ivory Coast 4 50N 6 33W
124 San Pedro, Pta., Chile 25 30S 70 38W
120 San Pedro, R., Chihuahua, Mexico 28 20N 106 10W
119 San Pedro, R., U.S.A. 32 45N 110 35W
31 San Pedro, Sierra de, Spain 39 18N 6 40W
124 San Pedro ♦, Paraguay 24 0S 57 0W
126 San Pedro de Arimena, Col. 4 37N 71 42W
124 San Pedro de Atacama, Chile 22 55S 68 15W
124 San Pedro de Jujuy, Paraguay 24 12S 64 55W
120 San Pedro de las Colonias, Mexico 25 50N 102 59W
126 San Pedro de Lloc, Peru 7 15S 79 28W
125 San Pedro del Paraná, Paraguay 26 43S 56 13W
33 San Pedro del Pinatar, Spain 37 50N 0 50W
120 San Pedro Mártir, Sierra, Mexico 31 0N 115 30W
120 San Pedro Mixtepec, Mexico 16 2N 97 0W
120 San Pedro Ocampo, Mex. 24 52N 101 40W
120 San Pedro Sula, Hond. 15 30N 88 0W
40 San Pietro, I., Italy 39 9N 8 17E
41 San Pietro Vernotico, It. 40 28N 18 0E
73 San Quintín, Philippines 16 1N 120 56E
124 San Rafael, Argentina 34 40S 68 30W
126 San Rafael, Colombia 6 2N 69 45W
118 San Rafael, Calif., U.S.A. 38 0N 122 40W
119 San Rafael, N. Mex., U.S.A. 35 6N 107 58W
126 San Rafael, Venezuela 10 42N 71 46W
124 San Ramón de la Nueva Orán, Arg. 23 10S 64 20W
38 San Remo, Italy 43 48N 7 47E
126 San Román, C., Ven. 12 12N 70 0W
124 San Roque, Argentina 28 15S 58 45W
31 San Roque, Spain 36 17N 5 21W
124 San Rosendo, Chile 37 10S 72 50W
117 San Saba, U.S.A. 31 12N 98 45W
120 San Salvador, Salvador 13 40N 89 20W
121 San Salvador (Watlings) I., Bahamas 24 0N 74 40W
124 San Salvador de Jujuy, Arg. 23 30S 65 40W
128 San Sebastián, Arg. 53 10S 68 30W
32 San Sebastián, Spain 43 17N 1 58W
126 San Sebastián, Ven. 9 57N 67 11W
39 San Serverino, Italy 43 13N 13 10E
39 San Severo, Italy 41 41N 15 23E
119 San Simon, U.S.A. 32 14N 109 16W
39 San Stéfano di Cadore, It. 46 34N 12 33E
128 San Valentin, Mte., Chile 46 30S 73 30W
31 San Vicente de Alcántara, Spain 39 22N 7 8W
30 San Vicente de la Barquera, Spain 43 30N 4 29W
126 San Vicente del Caguán, Col. 2 7N 74 46W
65 San Vicenzo, Italy 43 9N 10 32E
40 San Vito, C., Italy 38 11N 12 41E
39 San Vito al Tagliamento, Italy 45 55N 12 50E
39 San Vito Chietino, Italy 42 19N 14 27E
41 San Vito dei Normanni, Italy 40 40N 17 40E
126 San Yanaro, Colombia 2 47N 69 42W
117 San Ygnacio, U.S.A. 27 6N 92 24W
119 San Ysidro, U.S.A. 32 33N 117 5W
63 San'a, Yemen 15 27N 44 12E
39 Sana, R., Yugoslavia 44 40N 16 43E
84 Sanaba, Upper Volta 12 25N 3 47W
86 Sanâfir, Saudi Arabia 27 49N 34 37E
73 Sanana, Indonesia 2 5S 125 50E
68 Sanand, India 22 59N 72 25E
64 Sanandaj, Iran 35 25N 47 7E
21 Sanary, France 43 7N 5 48E
68 Sanawad, India 22 11N 76 5E
19 Sancergues, France 47 10N 2 54E
19 Sancerre, France 47 20N 2 50E
77 Sancha Ho, China 26 20N 105 30E
68 Sanchor, India 24 52N 71 49E
73 Sanco, Pt., Philippines 8 15N 126 24E
19 Sancoins, France 46 47N 2 55E
121 Sancti-Spiritus, Cuba 21 52N 79 33W
93 Sand, R., S. Afr. 22 25S 30 5E
106 Sand Lake, Canada 47 46N 84 31W
117 Sand Springs, U.S.A. 36 12N 96 5W
86 Sandah, Saudi Arabia 20 35N 39 32E
72 Sandai, Indonesia 1 15S 110 31E
72 Sandakan, Malaysia 5 53N 118 10E
71 Sandan, Khmer Rep. 12 46N 106 0E
43 Sandanski, Bulgaria 41 35N 23 16E
84 Sandaré, Mali 14 40N 10 15W
14 Sanday I., Scotland 59 15N 2 30W
47 Sande, Möre og Romsdal, Norway 62 15N 5 27E
47 Sande, Sogn og Fjordane, Norway 61 20N 5 47E
47 Sandefjord, Norway 59 10N 10 15E
47 Sandeid, Norway 59 33N 5 52E
119 Sanders, U.S.A. 35 12N 109 25W
117 Sanderson, U.S.A. 30 5N 102 30W
50 Sandfell, Iceland 63 57N 16 48W
99 Sandgate, Australia 27 19S 152 53E
49 Sandhammaren, C., Sweden 55 23N 14 14E
126 Sandía, Peru 14 10S 69 30W
64 Sandikli, Turkey 38 30N 30 20E
47 Sandnes, Norway 58 50N 5 45E
88 Sandoa, Zaïre 9 48S 23 0E
28 Sandomierz, Poland 50 40N 21 43E
126 Sandona, Colombia 1 17N 77 28W
67 Sandoway, Burma 18 20N 94 30E
118 Sandpoint, U.S.A. 48 20N 116 40W
12 Sandringham, Eng. 52 50N 0 30E
48 Sandslån, Sweden 63 2N 17 49E
96 Sandstone, W. Australia 28 0S 119 15E
112 Sandusky, Mich., U.S.A. 43 26N 82 50W
112 Sandusky, Ohio, U.S.A. 41 25N 82 40W
92 Sandvels, S. Afr. 32 0S 18 15E
49 Sandvig, Denmark 55 18N 14 48E
48 Sandvig, Sweden 55 32N 14 47E
47 Sandvika, Akershus, Norway 59 54N 10 29E
48 Sandviken, Sweden 60 38N 16 46E
107 Sandwich B., Canada 53 40N 57 15W
92 Sandwich B., S. Afr. 23 25S 14 20E
5 Sandwich Group, Falkland Is. Dep. 57 0S 27 0W
67 Sandwip Chan., Bangladesh 22 35N 91 35E
99 Sandy C., Australia 24 41S 153 8E
106 Sandy L., Canada 52 10N 94 30W
106 Sandy Lake, Canada 53 0N 93 0W
118 Sandy Cr., R., U.S.A. 42 20N 109 30W
100 Sandy Hollow, Austral. 32 36S 150 15E
113 Sandy Hook, U.S.A. 40 22N 74 0W
115 Sanford, Fla., U.S.A. 28 45N 81 20W
113 Sanford, Me., U.S.A. 43 28N 70 47W
115 Sanford, N.C., U.S.A. 35 30N 79 10W
104 Sanford Mt., Alas. 62 30N 143 0W
96 Sanford, R., Australia 27 22S 115 53E
91 Sanga, Mozam. 12 22S 35 21E
88 Sanga, R., Congo 1 0N 16 30E
59 Sanga Tolon, U.S.S.R. 61 50N 149 40E
70 Sangamner, India 19 30N 74 15E
59 Sangar, U.S.S.R. 63 55N 127 31E
72 Sangasanga, Indonesia 0 29S 117 13E
67 Sangchen La, China 31 30N 84 40E
77 Sangchih, China 29 25N 109 30E
90 Sange, Zaïre 6 58S 84 40E
73 Sangeang, I., Indonesia 8 12S 119 6E
119 Sanger, U.S.A. 36 47N 119 35W
24 Sangerhausen, Germany 51 28N 11 18E
72 Sanggau, Indonesia 0 5N 110 30E
73 Sangihe, Kep., Indonesia 3 0N 126 0E
73 Sangihe, P., Indonesia 3 45N 125 30E
72 Sangkapura, Indonesia 5 52S 112 40E
72 Sangkulirang, Indonesia 1 0N 118 0E
70 Sangli, India 16 55N 74 33E
85 Sangmélina, Cameroon 2 57N 12 1E
33 Sangonera, R., Spain 37 39N 2 0W
117 Sangre de Cristo Mts., U.S.A. 37 0N 105 0W
39 Sangro, R., Italy 42 10N 14 30E
75 Sangsang, China 29 30N 86 0E
108 Sangudo, Canada 53 50N 115 0W
32 Sangüesa, Spain 42 37N 1 17W
21 Sanguinaires, I., France 41 51N 8 36E
84 Sanhala, Ivory Coast 10 3N 6 51W
116 Sanish, U.S.A. 48 0N 102 30W
90 Sanje, Uganda 0 49S 31 30E
70 Sankaranayinarkovil, India 9 10N 77 35E
70 Sankeshwar, India 16 23N 74 23E
88 Sankiang, China 25 39N 109 30E
26 Sankt Andra, Austria 46 46N 14 50E
25 Sankt Blasien, Germany 47 47N 8 7E
25 Sankt Gallen, Switzerland 47 26N 9 22E
25 Sankt Gallen ♦, Switzerland 47 25N 9 22E
25 Sankt Ingbert, Germany 49 16N 7 6E
26 Sankt Johann, Austria 47 22N 13 12E
25 Sankt Moritz, Switzerland 46 30N 9 50E
49 Sankt Olof, Sweden 55 37N 14 8E
26 Sankt Pölten, Austria 48 12N 15 38E
26 Sankt Valentin, Austria 48 11N 14 33E
26 Sankt Veit, Austria 46 54N 14 22E
25 Sankt Wendel, Germany 49 27N 7 9E
26 Sankt Wolfgang, Austria 47 43N 13 27E
31 Sanlúcar de Barrameda, Sp. 37 26N 6 18W
31 Sanlucár la Mayor, Sp. 37 26N 6 18W
40 Sanluri, Italy 39 35N 8 55E
46 Sanmártin, Rumania 46 19N 25 58E
77 Sanmen Wan, China 29 10N 121 45E
77 Sanmenhsia, China 34 46N 111 30E
92 Sannaspos, S. Afr. 29 6S 26 34E
41 Sannicandro Gargánico, Italy 41 50N 15 34E
42 Sânnicolaul-Maré, Rum. 46 5N 20 39E
47 Sannidal, Norway 58 55N 9 15E
92 Sannieshof, S. Africa 26 30S 25 47E
27 Sanok, Poland 49 35N 22 10E
84 Sanokwelle, Liberia 7 19N 8 38W
99 Sanpah, Australia 30 32S 141 12E
14 Sanquhar, Scot. 55 21N 3 56W
84 Sansanding Dam, Mali 13 37N 6 0W
85 Sansanné- Mango, Togo 10 20N 0 30E
39 Sansepolcro, Italy 43 34N 12 8E
39 Sanski Most, Yugoslavia 44 46N 16 40E
41 Sant' Ágata de Gati, It. 41 6N 14 30E
41 Sant' Ágata di Militello, Italy 38 2N 14 40E
126 Santa Ana, El Beni, Bolivia 13 50S 65 40W
126 Santa Ana, Ecuador 1 10S 80 20W
120 Santa Ana, Mexico 30 31N 111 8W
120 Santa Ana, Salvador 14 0N 89 40W
119 Santa Ana, U.S.A. 33 48N 117 55W
38 Sant' Angelo Lodigiano, Italy 45 14N 9 25E
40 Sant' Antíoco, Italy 39 2N 8 30E
40 Sant' Antíoco, I., Italy 39 2N 8 30E
39 Sant' Arcángelo di Romagna, Italy 44 4N 12 26E
126 Santa Bárbara, Colombia 5 53N 75 35W
127 Santa Bárbara, Brazil 16 0S 59 0W
120 Santa Bárbara, Mexico 26 48N 105 50W
32 Santa Bárbara, Spain 40 42N 0 29E
119 Santa Barbara, U.S.A. 34 25N 119 40W
126 Santa Bárbara, Venezuela 7 47N 71 10W
33 Santa Bárbara, Mt., Sp. 37 23N 2 50W
119 Santa Barbara Is., U.S.A. 33 31N 119 0W
126 Santa Catalina, Colombia 10 36N 75 17W
119 Santa Catalina, G. of, U.S.A. 33 0N 118 0W
119 Santa Catalina, I., U.S.A. 33 20N 118 30W
125 Santa Catarina, I. de, Braz. 27 30S 48 40W
125 Santa Catarina ♦, Brazil 27 25S 48 30W
41 Santa Caterina, Italy 37 37N 14 1E
125 Santa Cecília, Brazil 26 56S 50 27W
121 Santa Clara, Cuba 22 20N 80 0W
119 Santa Clara, Calif., U.S.A. 37 21N 122 0W
119 Santa Clara, Utah, U.S.A. 37 10N 113 38W
125 Santa Clara de Olimar, Uruguay 32 50S 54 54W
126 Santa Clotilde, Peru 2 25S 73 45W
32 Santa Coloma de Farnés, Spain 41 50N 2 39E
32 Santa Coloma de Gramanet, Spain 41 27N 2 13E
30 Santa Comba, Spain 43 2N 8 49W
41 Santa Croce Camerina, It. 36 50N 14 30E
128 Santa Cruz, Argentina 50 0S 68 50W
124 Santa Cruz, Chile 34 38S 71 27W
121 Santa Cruz, Costa Rica 10 15N 85 41W
80 Santa Cruz, Canary Is. 28 29N 16 26W
73 Santa Cruz, Philippines 14 20N 121 30E
119 Santa Cruz, Calif., U.S.A. 36 55N 122 10W
119 Santa Cruz, N. Mexico, U.S.A. 35 59N 106 1W
110 Santa Cruz I., U.S.A. 34 0N 119 45W
128 Santa Cruz, R., Arg. 50 10S 70 0W
126 Santa Cruz ♦, Bolivia 17 43S 63 10W
33 Santa Cruz de Mudela, Sp. 38 39N 3 28W
48 Santa Cruz de Tenerife ♦, Spain 28 10N 17 20W
30 Santa Cruz del Retamar, Spain 40 8N 4 14W
121 Santa Cruz del Sur, Cuba 20 50N 78 0W
125 Santa Cruz do Rio Pardo, Brazil 22 54S 49 37W
125 Santa Cruz do Sul, Braz. 29 42S 52 25W
124 Santa Elena, Argentina 30 58S 59 47W
121 Santa Elena, Costa Rica 10 54N 85 56W
126 Santa Elena, Ecuador 2 16S 80 52W
20 Santa Enimie, France 44 24N 3 26E
41 Sant' Eufémia, Golfo di, Italy 38 50N 16 10E
33 Santa Eulalia, Spain 40 34N 1 20W
124 Santa Fe, Argentina 31 35S 60 41W
31 Santa Fe, Spain 37 11N 3 43W
119 Santa Fe, U.S.A. 35 40N 106 0W
127 Santa Filomena, Brazil 9 0S 45 50W
41 Santa Groce di Magliano, Italy 41 43N 14 59E
128 Santa Inés, I., Chile 54 0S 73 0W
31 Santa Inés, Mt., Spain 38 32N 5 37W
124 Santa Isabel, Arg. 36 10S 67 0W
•85 Santa Isabel, Eq. Guinea 3 45N 8 50E
85 Santa Isabel, Pico, Eq. Guinea 4 43N 8 49E
124 Santa Lucía, Corrientes, Argentina 28 58S 59 5W
124 Santa Lucía, San Juan, Argentina 31 30S 68 45W
33 Santa Lucia, Spain 37 35N 0 58W
125 Santa Lucía, Uruguay 34 27S 56 24W
119 Santa Lucia Range, U.S.A. 36 0N 121 30W
124 Santa Margarita, Arg. 38 18S 61 35W
120 Santa Margarita, I., Mex. 24 30N 112 0W
38 Santa Margherita, Italy 44 20N 9 11E
124 Santa María, Argentina 26 40S 66 0W
125 Santa Maria, Brazil 29 40S 53 40W
41 Santa Maria, Italy 41 3N 14 29E
120 Santa María, Mexico 27 40N 114 40W
32 Santa María, Spain 39 39N 2 45E
119 Santa Maria, U.S.A. 34 58N 120 29W
91 Santa Maria, Zambia 11 5S 29 58E
120 Santa María, Bahía de, Mexico 25 10N 108 40W
31 Santa María, Cabo de, Portugal 36 39N 7 53W
127 Santa Maria da Vitória, Brazil 13 24S 44 12W
120 Santa María del Oro, Mexico 25 30N 105 20W
41 Santa Maria di Leuca, C., Italy 39 48N 18 20E
30 Santa María la Real de Nieva, Sp. 41 4N 4 24W
126 Santa Marta, Colombia 11 15N 74 13W
31 Santa Marta, Spain 38 37N 6 39W
110 Santa Marta, Sierra Nevada de, Colombia 10 55N 73 50W
30 Santa Marta, Ría de, Sp. 43 44N 7 45W
125 Santa Marta Grande, C., Brazil 28 43S 48 50W
119 Santa Monica, U.S.A. 34 0N 118 30W
118 Santa Napa, U.S.A. 38 28N 122 45W
31 Santa Olalla, Huelva, Sp. 37 54N 6 14W
30 Santa Olalla, Toledo, Sp. 40 2N 4 25W
41 Sant' Onofrio, Italy 38 42N 16 10E
119 Santa Paula, U.S.A. 34 20N 119 2W

* Renamed Rey Malabo

Sebkra Azzel INDEX Shelby

MAP
82 Sebkra Azzel Mati, Alg. 26 10N 0 43E
82 Sebkra Mekerghene, Alg. 26 21N 1 30E
82 Sebou, Oued, Morocco 34 16N 6 40W
115 Sebring, Fla., U.S.A. 27 36N 81 47W
112 Sebring, Ohio, U.S.A. 40 55N 81 2W
112 Sebringville, Canada 43 25N 81 4W
82 Sebta = Ceuta, Morocco 35 52N 5 26W
72 Sebuku, I., Indonesia 3 30S 116 25E
72 Sebuku, Teluk, Sabah 4 0N 118 10E
42 Sečanj, Yugoslavia 45 25N 20 47E
38 Secchia, R., Italy 44 30N 10 40E
108 Sechelt, Canada 49 25N 123 42W
126 Sechura, Desierto de, Peru 6 0S 80 30W
19 Seclin, France 50 33N 3 2E
18 Secondigny, France 46 37N 0 26W
27 Sečovce, Cz. 48 42N 21 40E
101 Secretary I., N.Z. 45 15S 166 56E
70 Secunderabad, India 17 28N 78 30E
31 Seda, R., Portugal 39 6N 7 53W
116 Sedalia, U.S.A. 38 40N 93 18W
19 Sedan, France 49 43N 4 57E
99 Sedan, Australia 34 35S 139 29E
117 Sedan, U.S.A. 37 10N 96 11W
32 Sedano, Spain 42 43N 3 49W
101 Seddon, New Zealand 41 40S 174 7E
101 Seddonville, N.Z. 41 33S 172 1E
62 Sede Ya'aqov, Israel 32 43N 35 7E
92 Sederberg, Mt., S. Afr. 32 22S 19 7E
108 Sedgewick, Canada 52 48N 111 41W
84 Sedhiou, Senegal 12 50N 15 30W
39 Sedico, Italy 46 8N 12 6E
26 Sedičany, Cz. 49 40N 14 25E
43 Sedinenie, Bulgaria 42 16N 24 33E
109 Sedley, Canada 50 10N 104 0W
62 Sedom, Israel 31 5N 35 20E
58 Sedova, Pik, U.S.S.R. 73 20N 55 10E
83 Sédrata, Algeria 36 7N 7 31E
118 Sedro Woolley, U.S.A. 48 30N 122 15W
54 Seduva, U.S.S.R. 55 45N 23 45E
27 Sedziszów Małapolski, Poland 50 5N 21 45E
24 Seebad Ahlbeck, Germany 53 56N 14 10E
26 Seefeld, Germany 51 53N 13 17E
24 Seehausen, Germany 52 52N 11 43E
92 Seeheim, S.W. Africa 26 32S 17 52E
92 Seekoe, R., S. Afr. 30 34S 24 45E
24 Seelaw, Germany 52 32N 14 22E
18 Sées, France 48 38N 0 10E
24 Seesen, Germany 51 53N 10 10E
84 Sefadu, Sierra Leone 8 35N 10 58W
84 Séfeto, Mali 14 8N 9 49W
82 Sefrou, Morocco 33 52N 4 52W
84 Sefwi Bekwai, Ghana 6 10N 2 25W
58 Seg-ozero, U.S.S.R. 63 0N 33 10E
71 Segamat, Malaysia 2 30N 102 50E
46 Segarcea, Rumania 44 6N 23 43E
84 Segbwema, Sierra Leone 8 0N 11 0W
73 Seget, Indonesia 1 24S 130 58E
82 Seggueur, O., Algeria 32 4N 2 4E
87 Segid, Saudi Arabia 16 55N 42 0E
20 Segonzac, France 45 36N 0 14W
32 Segorbe, Spain 39 50N 0 30W
84 Ségou, Mali 13 30N 6 10W
30 Segovia, Spain 40 57N 4 10W
30 Segovia ♦, SPain 40 55N 4 10W
18 Segré, France 47 40N 0 52W
32 Segre, R., Spain 41 40N 0 43E
84 Ségéla, Ivory Coast 7 55N 6 40W
117 Segundo, U.S.A. 37 12N 104 50W
124 Segundo, R., Argentina 30 53S 62 44W
33 Segura, R., Spain 38 9N 0 40W
33 Segura, Sierra de, Spain 38 5N 2 45W
68 Sehore, India 23 10N 77 5E
68 Sehwan, Pakistan 26 28N 67 53E
46 Seica Mare, Rumania 46 1N 24 7E
117 Seiling, U.S.A. 36 10N 99 5W
21 Seille, R., France 46 31N 4 57E
18 Seine, R., France 49 28N 0 15E
19 Seine ♦, France 49 0N 3 0E
19 Seine-et-Marne ♦, France 48 45N 3 0E
18 Seine- Maritime ♦, France 49 40N 1 0E
19 Seine-Saint-Denis ♦, France 48 58N 2 24E
46 Seini, Rumania 47 44N 23 21E
65 Seistan, Iran 30 50N 61 0E
86 Seiyala, Egypt 22 57N 32 41E
126 Sejal, Colombia 2 45N 68 0W
49 Sejerby, Denmark 55 54N 11 10E
49 Sejerö, Denmark 55 54N 11 15E
49 Sejerö Bugt, Denmark 55 53N 11 9E
87 Seka, Ethiopia 8 10N 36 52E
72 Sekaju, Indonesia 2 58S 103 58E
90 Seke, Tanzania 3 20S 33 31E
90 Sekenke, Tanz. 4 18S 34 11E
77 Sekibi-shō, Japan 25 45N 124 35E
118 Sekiu, U.S.A. 48 30N 124 29W
82 Sekkane, Erg in, Mali 20 30N 1 30W
84 Sekondi, Ghana 5 2N 1 48W
92 Sekuma, Botswana 24 36S 23 57E
87 Sela Dingay, Ethiopia 9 58N 39 32E
118 Selah, U.S.A. 46 44N 120 30W
71 Selama, Malaysia 5 12N 100 42E
71 Selangor ♦, Malaysia 3 20N 101 30E
40 Selargius, Sardinia 39 14N 9 14E
73 Selaru, I., Indonesia 8 18S 131 0E
72 Selat Bangka, Indonesia 2 30S 105 30E
72 Seletan, Tg., Indon. 4 10S 114 40E
25 Selb, Germany 50 9N 12 9E
116 Selby, England 53 47N 1 5W
116 Selby, U.S.A. 45 34N 99 55W
39 Selce, Yugoslavia 43 20N 16 50E
116 Selden, U.S.A. 39 24N 100 39W
41 Sele, R., Italy 40 27N 15 0E
76 Selenga, R. = Selenge Mörön, Mongolia 49 25N 103 45E
76 Selenge, Mongolia 49 25N 103 59E
76 Selenge Mörön, Mongolia 52 16N 106 16E
44 Selenica, Albania 40 33N 19 39E
24 Selenter See, Germany 54 19N 10 26E
19 Selestat, France 48 10N 7 26E
48 Selet, Sweden 63 15N 15 45E
46 Seletin, Rumania 47 50N 25 12E
42 Selevac, Yugoslavia 44 44N 20 52E
116 Selfridge, U.S.A. 46 3N 100 57W
84 Sélibaby, Mauritania 15 20N 12 15W
54 Seliger, Oz., U.S.S.R. 57 15N 33 0E
119 Seligman, U.S.A. 35 17N 112 56W
90 Selim, Cen. Africa 5 31N 23 48E
57 Selim, Turkey 40 15N 42 58E
86 Selima, El Wâhât el, Sudan 21 28N 29 31E
92 Selinda Spillway, Bots. 18 35S 23 10E
45 Selinoús, Greece 37 35N 21 37E
69 Selipuk Gompa, Tibet 31 23N 82 49E
54 Selizharovo, U.S.S.R. 57 1N 33 17E
47 Selje, Norway 62 3N 5 22E
47 Seljord, Norway 59 30N 8 40E
109 Selkirk, Canada 50 10N 97 20W
14 Selkirk, Scotland 55 33N 2 50W
*14 Selkirk ♦, Scotland 55 30N 3 0W
108 Selkirk Mts., Canada 51 0N 117 10W
19 Selles-sur-Cher, France 47 16N 1 33E
19 Sellières, France 46 50N 5 32E
119 Sells, U.S.A. 31 57N 111 57W
27 Sellye, Hungary 45 52N 17 51E
115 Selma, Ala., U.S.A. 32 30N 87 0W
119 Selma, Calif., U.S.A. 36 39N 119 39W
115 Selma, N.C., U.S.A. 35 32N 78 15W
115 Selmer, U.S.A. 35 9N 88 36W
44 Sélo, Oros, Greece 41 10N 126 0E
19 Selongey, France 47 36N 5 10E
91 Selowandoma Falls, Rhod. 21 15S 31 50E
73 Selpele, Indonesia 0 1S 130 5E
13 Selsey Bill, Eng. 50 44N 0 47W
19 Seltz, France 48 48N 8 4E
73 Selu, I., Indonesia 7 26S 130 55E
91 Selukwe, Rhodesia 19 40S 30 0E
18 Sélune, R., France 48 38N 1 22W
124 Selva, Argentina 29 50S 62 0W
32 Selva, Spain 41 13N 1 8E
126 Selvas, Brazil 6 30S 67 0W
98 Selwyn, Australia 21 30S 140 29E
109 Selwyn L., Canada 60 0N 104 30W
98 Selwyn Ra., Australia 21 10S 140 0E
44 Semani, R., Albania 40 45N 19 50E
73 Semarang, Indonesia 7 0S 110 26E
90 Sembabule, Ugan. 0 4S 31 25E
87 Semeih, Sudan 12 43N 30 53E
55 Semenov, U.S.S.R. 56 43N 44 30E
56 Semenovka, U.S.S.R. 49 37N 33 2E
73 Semeru, Mt., Indonesia 8 4S 113 3E
84 Sémi, Senegal 15 4N 13 41W
55 Semiluki, U.S.S.R. 51 41N 39 10E
118 Seminoe Res., U.S.A. 42 0N 107 0W
117 Seminole, Okla., U.S.A. 35 15N 96 45W
117 Seminole, Tex., U.S.A. 32 41N 102 38W
58 Semiozernoye, U.S.S.R. 52 35N 64 0E
58 Semipalatinsk, U.S.S.R. 50 30N 80 10E
73 Semirara Is., Phil. 12 0N 121 20E
72 Semitau, Indonesia 0 29N 111 57E
58 Semiyarskoye, U.S.S.R. 50 55N 78 30E
26 Semmering Pass., Aust. 47 41N 15 45E
65 Semnan, Iran 35 55N 53 25E
65 Semnan ♦, Iran 36 0N 54 0E
16 Semois, R., Belgium 49 53N 4 44E
73 Semporna, Malaysia 4 30N 118 33E
72 Semuda, Indonesia 2 51S 112 58E
19 Semur-en-Auxois, Fr. 47 30N 4 20E
71 Sen, R., Khmer Rep. 13 45N 105 12E
126 Sena Madureira, Brazil 9 5S 68 45W
127 Senador Pompeu, Brazil 5 40S 39 20W
71 Senai, Malaysia 1 38N 103 38E
72 Senaja, Malaysia 6 49S 117 2E
92 Senanga, Zambia 16 2S 23 14E
117 Senatobia, U.S.A. 34 38N 89 57W
87 Sendafa, Ethiopia 9 11N 39 3E
74 Sendai, Kagoshima, Jap. 31 50N 130 20E
74 Sendai, Miyagi, Japan 38 15N 141 0E
70 Sendamangalam, India 11 17N 78 17E
92 Sendeling's Drift, S.W. Afr. 28 12S 16 52E
24 Sendenhorst, Germany 51 50N 7 49E
68 Sendurjana, India 21 32N 78 24E
72 Senduruhan, Indonesia 1 0S 110 46E
27 Senec, Czechoslovakia 48 12N 17 23E
118 Seneca, Oreg., U.S.A. 44 10N 119 2W
115 Seneca, S.C., U.S.A. 34 43N 82 59W
112 Seneca L., U.S.A. 42 40N 76 58W
112 Seneca Falls, U.S.A. 42 55N 76 50W
84 Senegal ■, W. Africa 14 30N 14 30W
84 Senegal, R., W. Africa 16 30N 15 30W
93 Senekal, S. Afr. 28 18S 27 36E
24 Senftenberg, Germany 51 30N 13 51E
91 Senga Hill, Zam. 9 19S 31 11E
68 Senge Khambab (Indus), R., Pak. 28 40N 70 10E
55 Sengiley, U.S.S.R. 53 58N 48 54E
91 Sengwa, R., Rhod. 17 10S 28 15E
127 Senhor-do-Bonfim, Braz. 10 30S 40 10W
27 Senica, Czechoslovakia 48 41N 17 25E
39 Senigállia, Italy 43 42N 13 12E
39 Senio, R., Italy 44 18N 11 47E
39 Senj, Yugoslavia 45 0N 14 58E
50 Senja, Norway 69 25N 17 20E
50 Senja I., Norway 69 15N 17 30E
77 Senkaku-guntō, Japan 25 50N 123 30E
19 Senlis, France 49 13N 2 35E
71 Senmonorom, Khmer Rep. 12 50N 107 15E
87 Sennar, Sudan 13 30N 33 35E
106 Senneterre, Canada 48 25N 77 15W
54 Senno, U.S.S.R. 54 45N 29 58E
40 Sennori, Italy 40 49N 8 36E

* *Incorporated within the region of Borders*

18 Senonches, France 48 34N 1 2E
40 Senorbì, Italy 39 33N 9 8E
39 Senozeče, Yugoslavia 45 43N 14 3E
19 Sens, France 48 11N 3 15E
42 Senta, Yugoslavia 45 55N 20 3E
20 Sentein, France 42 53N 0 58E
90 Senteny, Zaïre 5 17S 25 42E
119 Sentinel, U.S.A. 32 56N 113 13W
71 North Sentinel, I., Andaman Is. 11 35N 92 15E
71 South Sentinel, I., Andaman Is. 11 1N 92 16E
73 Sentolo, Indonesia 7 55S 110 13E
85 Senya Beraku, Ghana 5 28N 0 31W
32 Seo de Urgel, Spain 42 22N 1 23E
68 Seohara, India 29 15N 78 33E
69 Seoni, India 22 5N 79 30E
69 Seorinayan, India 21 45N 82 34E
107 Separation Point, Can. 53 40N 57 16W
98 Sepik, R., Terr. of New Guinea 4 5S 143 0E
28 Sepólno Krajenskie, Poland 53 26N 17 30E
71 Sepone, Laos 16 45N 106 13E
92 Sepopa, Botswana 18 49S 22 12E
28 Sepopol, Poland 54 16N 21 2E
107 Sept Iles, Canada 50 13N 66 22W
43 Septemvri, Bulgaria 42 13N 24 6E
98 Septimus, Australia 21 20S 148 35E
30 Sepúlveda, Spain 41 18N 3 45W
30 Sequeros, Spain 40 31N 6 2W
118 Sequim, U.S.A. 48 3N 123 9W
119 Sequoia Nat. Park, U.S.A. 36 20N 118 30W
57 Serafimovich, U.S.S.R. 49 30N 42 50E
16 Seraing, Belgium 50 35N 5 32E
73 Seram, I., Indonesia 3 10S 129 0E
69 Serampore, India 22 44N 88 30E
73 Serang, Indonesia 6 8S 106 10E
72 Serasan, I., Indonesia 2 29N 109 4E
38 Seravezza, Italy 43 59N 10 13E
42 Serbia = Srbija, Y.-slav. 43 30N 21 0E
46 Sercaia, Rumania 45 49N 25 9E
87 Serdo, Ethiopia 11 56N 41 14E
55 Serdobsk, U.S.S.R. 52 28N 44 10E
54 Seredka, U.S.S.R. 58 12N 28 3E
38 Seregno, Italy 45 40N 9 12E
71 Seremban, Malaysia 2 43N 101 53E
90 Serengeti Plain, Tanz. 2 40S 35 0E
55 Sergach, U.S.S.R. 55 30N 45 30E
32 Serge, R., Spain 42 5N 1 21E
55 Sergievsk, U.S.S.R. 54 0N 51 10E
72 Seria, Brunei 4 37N 114 30E
72 Serian, Malaysia 1 10N 110 40E
38 Seriate, Italy 45 42N 9 43E
19 Sérifontaine, France 49 20N 1 45E
45 Sérifos, I., Greece 37 9N 24 30E
20 Sérignan, France 43 17N 3 17E
64 Serik, Turkey 36 55N 31 10E
19 Sermaize-les-Bains, Fr. 48 47N 4 54E
73 Sermata, I., Indonesia 8 15S 128 50E
39 Sérmide, Italy 45 0N 11 17E
84 Sero, Mali 14 42N 10 59W
33 Serón, Spain 37 20N 2 29W
32 Serós, Spain 41 27N 0 24E
58 Serov, U.S.S.R. 59 40N 60 20E
92 Serowe, Botswana 22 25S 26 43E
31 Serpa, Portugal 37 57N 7 38E
89 Serpa Pinto, Angola 14 48S 17 52E
40 Serpeddi, Punta, Italy 39 19N 9 28E
40 Serpentara, Italy 39 8N 9 38E
126 Serpent's Mouth, Trinidad 10 0N 61 30W
33 Serpis, R., Spain 38 45N 0 21W
55 Serpukhov, U.S.S.R. 54 55N 37 28E
89 Sa. da Canastra, Brazil 19 30S 46 5W
41 Serra Capriola, Italy 41 47N 15 12E
50 Serra do Salitre, Brazil 19 6S 46 41W
30 Serradilla, Spain 39 50N 6 9W
44 Sérrai ♦, Greece 41 5N 23 37E
40 Serramanna, Sard. 39 26N 8 56E
32 Serrania de Cuenca, Sp. 40 10N 1 50W
83 Serrat, C., Tunisia 37 14N 9 10E
21 Serres, France 44 26N 5 43E
124 Serrezuela, Argentina 30 40S 65 20W
127 Serrinha, Brazil 11 39S 39 0W
41 Sersale, Italy 39 1N 16 44E
30 Sertã, Portugal 39 48N 8 6W
127 Sertânia, Brazil 8 5S 37 20W
127 Sertão, Brazil 10 0S 40 20W
73 Serua, P., Indonesia 6 18S 130 1E
73 Serui, Indonesia 1 45S 136 10E
92 Serule, Botswana 21 57S 27 11E
44 Sérvia, Greece 40 9N 21 58E
100 Serviceton, Austral. 36 25S 141 55E
72 Sesajap Lama, Indon. 3 32N 117 11E
90 Sese Is., Uganda 0 30S 32 30E
73 Sesepe, Indonesia 1 30S 127 59E
92 Sesfontein, S. Africa 19 7S 13 39E
92 Sesheke, Zambia 17 29S 24 13E
38 Sesia, R., Italy 45 35N 8 23E
31 Sesimbra, Portugal 38 28N 9 20W
40 Sessa Aurunca, Italy 41 14N 13 55E
76 Sessy, China 42 40N 110 30E
32 Sestao, Spain 43 18N 3 0W
38 Sesto S. Giovanni, Italy 45 32N 9 14E
38 Sestri Levante, Italy 44 17N 9 22E
38 Sestrières, Italy 44 58N 6 56E
39 Sestrunj, I., Y.-slav. 44 10N 15 0E
40 Sestu, Sardinia 39 18N 9 6E
20 Sète, France 43 25N 3 42E
127 Sete Lagoas, Brazil 19 27S 44 16W
82 Sétif, Algeria 36 9N 5 26E
74 Setonaikai, Japan 34 10N 133 10E
82 Settat, Morocco 33 0N 7 40W
88 Setté Cama, Gabon 2 32S 9 57E
38 Séttimo Tor, Italy 45 9N 7 46E
12 Settle, England 54 5N 2 18W
115 Settlement Pt., Bahamas 26 40N 79 0W
38 Setto Calende, Italy 45 44N 8 37E
31 Setúbal, Portugal 38 30N 8 58W
31 Setúbal, B. de, Port. 38 40N 8 56W
31 Setúbal ♦, Portugal 38 25N 8 35W
106 Seul L., Canada 50 25N 92 30W
72 Seulimeum, Indonesia 5 27N 95 15E
56 Sevastopol, U.S.S.R. 44 35N 33 30E
31 Sever, R., Sp. -Port. 39 40N 7 32W
20 Sévérac-le-Chateau, Fr. 44 20N 3 5E
106 Severn, R., Canada 44 52N 79 30W
13 Severn, R., Eng. 52 35N 2 38W
59 Severnaya Zemlya, U.S.S.R. 79 0N 100 0E
52 Severnyye Uvaly, U.S.S.R. 58 0N 48 0E
59 Severo-Kurilsk, U.S.S.R. 50 40N 156 8E
57 Severodonetsk, U.S.S.R. 48 50N 38 30E
52 Severodvinsk, U.S.S.R. 64 27N 39 58E
27 Severomoravsky ♦, Czechoslovakia 49 38N 17 40E
119 Sevier, U.S.A. 38 39N 112 11W
118 Sevier L., U.S.A. 39 0N 113 20W
119 Sevier, R., U.S.A. 39 10N 112 50W
126 Sevilla, Colombia 4 16N 75 57W
31 Sevilla, Spain 37 23N 6 0W
31 Sevilla ♦, Spain 37 0N 6 0W
31 Seville = Sevilla, Spain 37 23N 6 0W
39 Sevnica, Yugoslavia 46 2N 15 19E
54 Sevsk, U.S.S.R. 52 10N 34 30E
104 Seward, U.S.A. 60 0N 149 40W
104 Seward Pen., Alaska 65 0N 164 0W
128 Sewell, Chile 34 10S 70 45W
73 Sewer, Indonesia 5 46S 134 40E
112 Sewickley, U.S.A. 40 33N 80 12W
3 Seychelles, Is., Indian Ocean 5 0S 56 0E
50 Seyðisfjörður, Iceland 65 16N 14 0W
54 Seym, R., U.S.S.R. 51 45N 35 0E
59 Seymchan, U.S.S.R. 62 40N 152 30E
13 Seymour, Austral. 36 58S 145 10E
113 Seymour, Conn., U.S.A. 41 23N 73 5W
114 Seymour, Ind., U.S.A. 39 0N 85 50W
117 Seymour, Tex., U.S.A. 33 35N 99 18W
114 Seymour, Wis., U.S.A. 44 30N 88 20W
21 Seyne, France 44 21N 6 22E
39 Sezana, Yugoslavia 45 43N 13 41E
19 Sézanne, France 48 40N 3 40E
40 Sezze, Italy 41 30N 13 3E
83 Sfax, Tunisia 34 49N 10 48E
46 Sfântu Gheorghe, Rum. 45 52N 25 48E
16 's-Gravendeel, Neth. 51 47N 4 37E
16 's-Gravenhage, Neth. 52 7N 4 17E
67 Shaba Gamba, Tibet, China 32 8N 88 55E
91 Shabani, Rhodesia 20 17S 30 2E
43 Shabla, Bulgaria 43 31N 28 32E
107 Shabogama L., Canada 48 40N 77 0W
90 Shabunda, Zaïre 2 40S 27 16E
5 Shackleton, Antarctica 78 30S 36 1W
5 Shackleton Inlet, Ant. 83 0S 160 0E
86 Shaddad, Saudi Arabia 21 25N 40 2E
86 Shadwân, Egypt 27 30N 34 0E
85 Shaffa, Nigeria 10 30N 12 6E
119 Shafter, U.S.A. 35 32N 119 14W
13 Shaftesbury, Eng. 51 0N 2 12W
85 Shagamu, Nigeria 6 51N 3 39E
68 Shah Bunder, Pakistan 24 13N 67 50E
70 Shahabad, And. P., India 17 10N 78 11E
68 Shahabad, Raj., India 25 15N 77 11E
68 Shahabad, Punjab, India 30 10N 76 55E
69 Shahabad, Uttar Pradesh, India 27 36N 79 56E
65 Shāhābād, Iran 37 40N 56 50E
68 Shahada, India 21 33N 74 30E
70 Shahapur, India 15 50N 74 34E
64 Shāhbād, Iran 34 10N 46 30E
76 Shahcheng, China 40 18N 115 27E
65 Shahdād, Iran 30 30N 57 40E
68 Shahdadkot, Pakistan 27 50N 67 55E
68 Shahddpur, Pakistan 25 55N 68 35E
69 Shahganj, India 26 3N 82 44E
81 Shahhat (Cyrene), Libya 32 40N 21 35E
65 Shāhī, Iran 36 30N 52 55E
69 Shahjahanpur, India 27 54N 79 57E
77 Shaho, China 28 29N 113 2E
70 Shahpur, Mysore, India 16 40N 76 48E
68 Shahpur, Mad. P., India 22 12N 77 58E
64 Shahpur, Iran 38 12N 44 45E
68 Shahpur, Pakistan 28 46N 68 27E
69 Shahpura, India 23 10N 80 45E
65 Shahr Kord, Iran 32 15N 50 55E
65 Shahr-e Babak, Iran 30 10N 55 20E
64 Shahraban, Iraq 34 0N 45 0E
65 Shahreza, Iran 32 0N 51 55E
68 Shahrig, Pakistan 30 15N 67 40E
65 Shahriza, Iran 32 0N 51 50E
65 Shahrud, Iran 36 30N 55 0E
65 Shahrukh, Iran 33 50N 60 10E
65 Shahsavar, Iran 36 45N 51 12E
77 Shahsien, China 26 25N 117 50E
87 Shaibâra, Saudi Arabia 25 26N 36 47E
65 Shaikhabad, Afghan. 34 0N 68 45E
68 Shajapur, India 23 20N 76 15E
68 Shakargarh, Pakistan 32 17N 75 43E
92 Shakawe, Botswana 18 28S 21 49E
57 Shakhty, U.S.S.R. 47 40N 40 10E
55 Shakhunya, U.S.S.R. 57 40N 47 0E
85 Shaki, Nigeria 8 41N 3 21E
116 Shakopee, U.S.A. 44 45N 93 30W
87 Shala Lake, Ethiopia 7 30N 38 30E
112 Shallow Lake, Canada 44 37N 81 6W
77 Shalu, Taiwan 24 24N 120 26E
65 Sham, J. ash, Oman 23 10N 57 5E
85 Shama, Ghana 5 1N 1 42W
64 Shamar, Jabal, Si. Arabia 27 40N 41 0E
87 Shambe, Sudan 7 2N 30 46E
87 Shambu, Ethiopia 9 32N 37 3E
69 Shamgong Dzong, Bhutan 27 19N 90 35E
68 Shamil, India 29 32N 77 18E
65 Shamil, Iran 27 30N 56 55E
57 Shamkhor, U.S.S.R. 40 56N 46 0E
75 Shamo (Gobi), Asia 44 0N 111 0E
87 Shamo, L., Ethiopia 5 45N 37 30E
113 Shamokin, U.S.A. 40 47N 76 33W
117 Shamrock, U.S.A. 35 15N 100 15W
67 Shan ♦, Burma 21 30N 98 30E
87 Shanan, R., Ethiopia 8 0N 40 20E
85 Shanga, Nigeria 9 1N 5 2E
91 Shangalowe, Zaïre 10 50S 26 30E
91 Shangani, Rhod. 19 1S 28 51E
91 Shangani, R., Rhod. 18 35S 27 45E
77 Shangch'eng, China 31 44N 115 22E
76 Shangchih, (Chuho), China 45 10N 127 59E
77 Shangchwan Shan, China 21 35N 112 45E
77 Shanghai, China 31 10N 121 25E
77 Shanghsien, China 33 30N 109 58E
77 Shangjao, China 28 25N 117 57E
77 Shangkao, China 28 16N 114 50E
77 Shangkiu, China 34 28N 115 42E
77 Shangshui, China 33 42N 115 4E
77 Shangsze, China 22 0N 107 45E
76 Shangtu, China 41 31N 113 35E
77 Shangyu, China 25 59N 114 29E
76 Shanh, Mongolia 47 5N 103 5E
85 Shani, Nigeria 10 14N 12 2E
118 Shaniko, U.S.A. 45 0N 120 15W
4 Shannon, Greenland 75 10N 18 30W
101 Shannon, N.Z. 40 33S 175 25E
4 Shannon I., Greenland 75 0N 18 0W
15 Shannon, R., Ireland 53 10N 8 10W
59 Shantar, Ostrov Bolshoi, U.S.S.R. 55 9N 137 40E
77 Shantow (Swatow), China 23 25N 116 40E
77 Shanyang, China 33 39N 110 2E
77 Shaohsing, China 30 0N 120 32E
77 Shaowu, China 27 25N 117 30E
77 Shaoyang, China 27 10N 111 30E
14 Shapinsay I., Scot. 59 2N 2 50W
64 Shaqra, Saudi Arabia 25 15N 45 16E
87 Sharafa (Ogr), Sudan 11 59N 27 7E
70 Sharavati, R., India 14 32N 74 0E
113 Sharbot Lake, Canada 44 47N 76 41W
65 Sharhjui, Afghanistan 32 30N 67 22E
64 Shari, Saudi Arabia 27 20N 43 45E
76 Sharin Gol, Mongolia 49 12N 106 27E
65 Sharjah, Trucial States 25 23N 55 26E
96 Shark B., Australia 25 15S 133 20E
86 Sharm el Sheikh, Egypt 27 53N 34 15E
112 Sharon, U.S.A. 41 18N 80 30W
62 Sharon, Plain of = Hasharon, Israel 32 12N 34 49E
106 Sharpe, L., Canada 54 10N 93 21W
112 Sharpsburg, U.S.A. 40 30N 79 56W
112 Sharpsville, U.S.A. 41 16N 80 28W
55 Sharya, U.S.S.R. 58 12N 45 40E
87 Shasha, Ethiopia 6 29N 35 59E
87 Shashemene, Ethiopia 7 13N 38 33E
91 Shashi, R., Rhod. & Botswana 21 40S 28 40E
77 Shasi, China 30 16N 112 20E
118 Shasta, Mt., U.S.A. 41 45N 122 0W
118 Shasta Res., U.S.A. 40 50N 122 15W
55 Shatsk, U.S.S.R. 54 0N 41 45E
117 Shattuck, U.S.A. 36 17N 99 55W
57 Shaumyani, U.S.S.R. 41 13N 44 45E
109 Shaunavon, Canada 49 35N 108 40W
98 Shaw I., Australia 20 30S 149 10E
96 Shaw, R., Australia 20 30S 119 15E
75 Shawan, China 44 34N 85 48E
112 Shawanaga, Canada 45 31N 80 14W
114 Shawano, U.S.A. 44 45N 88 38W
106 Shawinigan, Can. 46 35N 72 50W
117 Shawnee, U.S.A. 35 15N 97 0W
67 Shaziz, China 33 10N 82 43E
55 Shchëkino, U.S.S.R. 54 1N 37 28E
55 Shcherbakov = Rybinsk, U.S.S.R. 58 5N 38 50E
55 Shchigri, U.S.S.R. 51 55N 36 58E
54 Schors, U.S.S.R. 51 48N 31 56E
58 Shchuchinsk, U.S.S.R. 52 56N 70 12E
55 Shchurovo, U.S.S.R. 55 0N 38 51E
55 Shebekino, U.S.S.R. 50 28N 37 0E
87 Shebele, Wabi, Ethiopia 2 0N 44 0E
114 Sheboygan, U.S.A. 43 46N 87 45W
62 Shechem, Jordan 32 13N 35 21E
107 Shediac, Canada 46 14N 64 32W
15 Sheelin Lough, Ireland 53 48N 7 20W
15 Sheep Haven, Ireland 55 12N 7 55W
13 Sheerness, Eng. 51 26N 0 47E
107 Sheet Harbour, Canada 44 56N 62 31W
62 Shefar'am, Israel 32 48N 35 10E
62 Shefeiya, Israel 32 35N 34 58E
12 Sheffield, Eng. 53 23N 1 28W
12 Sheffield, New Zealand 43 23S 172 2E
115 Sheffield, Ala., U.S.A. 34 45N 87 42W
113 Sheffield, Mass., U.S.A. 42 6N 73 23W
112 Sheffield, Pa., U.S.A. 41 42N 79 3W
117 Sheffield, Tex., U.S.A. 30 42N 101 49W
68 Shegaon, India 20 48N 76 59E
87 Shehojele, Ethiopia 10 40N 35 27E
69 Sheikhpura, India 25 9N 85 53E
87 Shek Hasan, Ethiopia 13 5N 35 58E
69 Shekar Dzong, China 28 45N 87 0E
68 Shekhupura, Pakistan 31 42N 73 58E
57 Sheki, U.S.S.R. 41 10N 47 5E
77 Shekki, China 22 30N 113 15E
77 Sheklung, China 23 5N 113 55E
55 Sheksna, R., U.S.S.R. 59 30N 38 30E
106 Shelburne, Ont., Canada 44 4N 80 15W
107 Shelburne, N.S., Canada 43 47N 65 20W
113 Shelburne, U.S.A. 44 23N 73 15W
99 Shelburne B., Australia 11 50S 143 0E
113 Shelburne Falls, U.S.A. 42 36N 72 45W
114 Shelby, Mich., U.S.A. 43 34N 86 27W
118 Shelby, Mont., U.S.A. 48 30N 111 59W
115 Shelby, N.C., U.S.A. 35 18N 81 34W
112 Shelby, Ohio, U.S.A. 40 52N 82 40W

* Renamed Salop

* Now an administrative subdivision of India

* Renamed Bié

70

Sour el Ghozlane INDEX Stour, R.

MAP
83 Sour el Ghozlane, Alg. 36 10N 3 45E
93 Sources, Mt. aux, Les. 28 45S 28 50E
127 Soure, Brazil 0 35S 48 30W
30 Soure, Portugal 40 4N 8 38W
107 Souris, Canada 49 40N 100 20W
116 Souris, R., U.S.A. 48 35N 101 29W
45 Soúrpi, Greece 39 6N 22 54E
82 Sous, R., Morocco 30 31N 9 27W
127 Sousa, Brazil 6 45S 38 10W
127 Sousel, Brazil 2 38S 52 29W
31 Sousel, Portugal 38 57N 7 40W
82 Souss, O., Morocco 30 23N 8 24W
83 Sousse, Tunisia 35 50N 10 38E
20 Soustons, France 43 45N 1 19W
107 South Pt., Canada 49 6N 62 11W
89 South Africa, Rep. of, ■, Afr. 30 0S 25 0E
122 South America, cont. 10 0S 60 0W
96 South Australia ♦, Australia 32 0S 139 0E
119 South Baldy, Mt., U.S.A. 34 6N 107 27W
114 South Bend, Indiana, U.S.A. 41 38N 86 20W
118 South Bend, Wash., U.S.A. 46 44N 123 52W
113 South Berwick, U.S.A. 43 15N 70 47W
98 South Blackwater, Australia 24 00S 148 35E
115 South Boston, U.S.A. 36 42N 78 58W
107 South Branch, U.S.A. 44 30N 83 55W
115 South Carolina ♦, U.S.A. 33 45N 81 0W
114 South Charleston, U.S.A. 38 20N 81 40W
77 South China Sea, Asia 20 0N 115 0E
116 South Dakota ♦, U.S.A. 45 0N 100 0W
13 South Downs, Eng. 50 53N 0 10W
99 South East Cape, Australia 43 39S 146 50E
14 South Esk, R., Scot. 56 44N 2 40W
13 South Foreland, Eng. 51 7N 1 23E
118 South Fork, R., U.S.A. 47 54N 113 15W
120 South Gamboa, Panama Canal Zone 9 4N 79 40W
5 South Georgia, Falk. Is. Dep. 54 30S 37 0W
114 South Haven, U.S.A. 42 22N 86 20W
109 South Henik, L., Can. 61 30N 98 0W
90 South Horr, Kenya 2 12N 36 56E
90 South I., Kenya 2 35N 36 35E
101 South Invercargill, N.Z. 46 26N 168 23E
90 South Island, L. Rudolf, Kenya 2 40N 26 25E
76 South Korea ■, Asia 36 0N 128 0E
5 South Magnetic Pole (1965) 66 30S 139 30E
114 South Milwaukee, U.S.A. 42 50N 87 52W
5 South Orkney Is., Falk. Is. Dep. 63 0S 45 0W
118 South Pass, U.S.A. 42 20N 108 58W
96 South Passage, Australia 26 07S 113 09E
115 South Pines, U.S.A. 35 10N 79 25W
116 South Platte, R., U.S.A. 40 50N 102 45W
5 South Pole, Antarctica 90 0S 0 0E
106 South Porcupine, Can. 48 30N 81 12W
14 South Ronaldsay I., Scotland 58 46N 2 58W
7 S. Sandwich Is., Falk. Is. Dep. 57 0S 27 0W
109 South Saskatchewan, R., Canada 51 0N 109 0W
5 South Shetland Is., Ant. 62 0S 59 0W
12 South Shields, Eng. 54 59N 1 26W
116 South Sioux City, U.S.A. 42 30N 96 30W
101 South Taranaki Bight, N.Z. 39 40S 174 5E
106 South Twin I., Canada 53 0N 79 50W
12 South Tyne, R., England 54 46N 2 25W
14 South Uist, I., Scot. 57 10N 7 10W
48 South Ulvön, I., Swed. 63 0N 18 45E
•71 South Vietnam ■, Asia 11 0N 108 40E
101 South West Cape, N.Z. 47 16S 167 31E
92 South West Africa ■, South Africa 22 0S 18 9E
63 South Yemen ■, Asia 15 0N 48 0E
106 Southampton, Canada 44 30N 81 25W
13 Southampton, Eng. 50 54N 1 23W
113 Southampton, U.S.A. 40 54N 72 22W
105 Southampton I., Can. 64 30N 84 0W
101 Southbridge, N.Z. 43 48S 172 16E
113 Southbridge, U.S.A. 42 4N 72 2W
109 Southend, Canada 56 28N 103 14W
13 Southend-on-Sea, England 51 32N 0 43E
91 Southern ♦, Malawi 15 0S 35 0E
84 Southern ♦, Sierra Leone 8 0N 12 30E
101 Southern Alps, N.Z. 43 41S 170 11E
96 Southern Cross, Austral. 31 12S 119 15E
109 Southern Indian Lake, Canada 57 0N 99 0W
5 Southern Ocean 62 0S 160 0W
91 Southern ♦, Zambia 16 20S 26 20E
14 Southern Uplands, Scotland 55 30N 4 0W
113 Southington, U.S.A. 41 37N 72 53W
113 Southold, U.S.A. 41 4N 72 26W
99 Southport, Australia 28 0S 153 25E
12 Southport, Eng. 53 38N 3 1W
115 Southport, U.S.A. 33 55N 78 0W
13 Southwold, Eng. 52 19N 1 41E
93 Soutpansberge, S. Africa 23 0S 29 30E
20 Souvigny, France 46 33N 3 10E
46 Sovata, Rumania 46 35N 25 3E
54 Sovetsk, Lithuania, U.S.S.R. 55 6N 21 50E
55 Sovetsk, R.S.F.S.R., U.S.S.R. 57 38N 48 53E

* Now part of Vietnam

MAP
59 Sovetskaya Gavan, U.S.S.R. 48 50N 140 0E
39 Sovicille, Italy 43 16N 11 12E
42 Sovra, Yugoslavia 42 44N 17 34E
74 Sōya-Misaki, Japan 45 30N 142 0E
54 Sozh, R., U.S.S.R. 53 50N 31 50E
43 Sozopol, Bulgaria 42 23N 27 42E
16 Spa, Belgium 50 29N 5 53E
29 Spain ■, Europe 40 0N 5 0W
12 Spalding, England 52 47N 0 9W
116 Spalding, U.S.A. 41 45N 98 27W
49 Spandet, Denmark 55 15N 8 54E
48 Spånga, Sweden 59 23N 17 55E
49 Spångenäs, Sweden 57 36N 16 7E
47 Spangereid, Norway 58 3N 7 9E
112 Spangler, U.S.A. 40 39N 78 48W
107 Spaniard's Bay, Canada 47 38N 53 20W
106 Spanish, Canada 46 12N 82 20W
118 Spanish Fork, U.S.A. 40 10N 111 37W
•80 Spanish Sahara ♦, Africa 25 0N 13 0W
121 Spanish Town, Jamaica 18 0N 77 20W
118 Sparks, U.S.A. 39 30N 119 45W
45 Sparta = Spárti, Greece 37 5N 22 25E
115 Sparta, Ga., U.S.A. 33 18N 82 59W
116 Sparta, Wis., U.S.A. 43 55N 91 10W
112 Spartanburg, Pa., U.S.A. 41 48N 79 43W
115 Spartanburg, S.C., U.S.A. 35 0N 82 0W
82 Spartel, C., Morocco 35 47N 5 56W
45 Spárti, Greece 37 5N 22 25E
41 Spartivento, C., Calabria, Italy 37 56N 16 4E
41 Spartivento, C., Sard., It. 38 52N 8 50E
54 Spas-Demensk, U.S.S.R. 54 20N 34 0E
55 Spas-Klepiki, U.S.S.R. 54 34N 40 2E
59 Spassk-Dalniy, U.S.S.R. 44 40N 132 40E
55 Spassk-Ryazanskiy, U.S.S.R. 54 30N 40 25E
45 Spatha Akra., Greece 35 42N 23 43E
116 Spearfish, U.S.A. 44 32N 103 52W
117 Spearman, U.S.A. 36 15N 101 10W
100 Speed, Australia 35 21S 142 27E
90 Speke Gulf, L. Victoria 2 20S 32 50E
104 Spenard, Alaska 61 5N 149 50W
118 Spencer, Idaho, U.S.A. 44 18N 112 8W
116 Spencer, Iowa, U.S.A. 43 5N 95 3W
116 Spencer, Nebr., U.S.A. 42 52N 98 43W
113 Spencer, N.Y., U.S.A. 42 14N 76 13W
114 Spencer, W. Va., U.S.A. 38 47N 81 24W
104 Spencer B., Canada 69 30N 94 0W
92 Spencer B., S.W. Afr. 25 30S 14 47E
99 Spencer, C., Austral. 35 20S 136 45E
99 Spencer G., Austral. 34 30S 137 0E
113 Spencerville, Canada 44 51N 75 34W
101 Spenser Mts., N.Z. 42 15S 172 45E
45 Sperkhiós, R., Greece 38 57N 22 3E
15 Sperrin Mts., U.K. 54 50N 7 0W
25 Spessart, Germany 50 0N 9 20E
45 Spetsai, Greece 37 16N 23 9E
45 Spétsai, I., Greece 37 15N 23 10E
14 Spey, R., Scotland 57 26N 4 30W
25 Speyer, Germany 49 19N 8 26E
17 Speyer, R., Germany 49 18N 7 52E
38 Spezia (La Spezia), Italy 44 7N 9 49E
41 Spezzano Albanese, It. 39 41N 16 19E
24 Spiekeroog, I., Germany 53 45N 7 42E
39 Spielfeld, Austria 46 43N 15 38E
25 Spiez, Switzerland 46 40N 7 40E
45 Spili, Greece 35 13N 24 31E
39 Spilimbergo, Italy 46 7N 12 53E
108 Spillimacheen, Canada 51 6N 117 0W
65 Spin Baldak, Afghan. 31 3N 66 16E
41 Spinazzola, Italy 40 58N 16 5E
19 Spincourt, France 49 20N 5 39E
47 Spind, Norway 58 6N 6 53E
46 Spineni, Rumania 44 43N 24 37E
118 Spirit Lake, U.S.A. 47 56N 116 56W
108 Spirit River, Canada 55 45N 119 0W
109 Spiritwood, Canada 53 24N 107 33W
27 Spišská Nová Ves, Cz. 48 58N 20 34E
27 Spišské Podhradie, Cz. 49 0N 20 48E
26 Spittal, Austria 46 48N 13 31E
4 Spitzbergen (Svalbard), Norway 78 0N 17 0E
39 Split, Yugoslavia 43 31N 16 26E
109 Split L., Canada 56 15N 96 0W
39 Splitski Kan, Y.-slavia 43 31N 16 20E
25 Splügen Pass, Switz. 46 30N 9 20E
117 Spofford, U.S.A. 29 10N 100 27W
118 Spokane, U.S.A. 47 45N 117 25W
47 Sponvika, Norway 59 7N 11 15E
116 Spooner, U.S.A. 45 49N 91 51W
45 Sporádhes, Greece 37 0N 27 0E
58 Sporyy Navolok, M., U.S.S.R. 75 50N 68 40E
106 Spragge, Canada 46 15N 82 40W
118 Sprague, U.S.A. 47 25N 117 59W
118 Sprague River, U.S.A. 42 49N 121 31W
•72 Spratly, I., S. China Sea 8 20N 112 0E
118 Spray, U.S.A. 44 56N 119 46W
24 Spree, R., Germany 52 23N 13 52E
119 Spring Mts., U.S.A. 36 20N 115 43W
118 Spring City, U.S.A. 39 31N 111 28W
116 Spring Valley, Minn., U.S.A. 43 40N 92 30W
113 Spring Valley, N.Y., U.S.A. 41 7N 74 4W
92 Springbok, S. Africa 29 42S 17 54E
101 Springburn, N.Z. 43 40S 171 32E
107 Springdale, Canada 49 30N 56 6W
117 Springdale, Ark., U.S.A. 36 10N 94 5W
118 Springdale, Wash., U.S.A. 48 1N 117 50W
24 Springe, Germany 52 12N 9 35E
119 Springerville, U.S.A. 34 10N 109 16W
112 Springfield, Canada 42 52N 80 57W
101 Springfield, N.Z. 43 19S 171 56E
117 Springfield, Colo., U.S.A. 37 26N 102 40W

* Annexed by Morocco and Mauritania

MAP
116 Springfield, Ill., U.S.A. 39 58N 89 40W
113 Springfield, Mass., U.S.A. 42 8N 72 37W
117 Springfield, Mo., U.S.A. 37 15N 93 20W
114 Springfield, Ohio, U.S.A. 39 50N 83 48W
118 Springfield, Oreg., U.S.A. 44 2N 123 0W
115 Springfield, Tenn., U.S.A. 36 35N 86 55W
113 Springfield, Vt., U.S.A. 43 20N 72 30W
92 Springfontein, S. Africa 30 15S 25 40E
107 Springhill, Canada 45 40N 64 4W
108 Springhouse, Canada 51 56N 122 7W
100 Springhurst, Australia 36 12S 146 24E
93 Springs, S. Afr. 26 13S 28 25E
98 Springsure, Australia 24 8S 148 6E
113 Springvale, U.S.A. 43 28N 70 48W
112 Springville, N.Y., U.S.A. 42 31N 78 41W
118 Springville, Utah, U.S.A. 40 14N 111 35W
109 Springwater, Canada 51 58N 108 23W
112 Spruce-Creek, U.S.A. 40 36N 78 9W
117 Spur, U.S.A. 33 28N 100 50W
12 Spurn Hd., Eng. 53 34N 0 8W
42 Spuz, Yugoslavia 42 32N 19 10E
108 Spuzzum, Canada 49 37N 121 23W
47 Spydeberg, Norway 59 37N 11 4E
108 Squamish, Canada 49 45N 123 10W
107 Square Islands, Canada 52 47N 55 47W
41 Squillace, Golfo di, Italy 38 43N 16 35E
41 Squinzano, Italy 40 27N 18 1E
73 Sragen, Indonesia 7 28S 110 59E
42 Srbac, Yugoslavia 45 7N 17 30E
42 Srbija ♦, Y.-slavia 43 30N 21 0E
42 Srbobran, Yugoslavia 45 32N 19 48E
71 Sre Umbell, Khmer Rep. 11 8N 103 46E
42 Srebrnica, Yugoslavia 44 10N 19 18E
59 Sredinyy Khrebet, U.S.S.R. 57 0N 160 0E
39 Središce, Yugoslavia 46 24N 16 17E
43 Sredna Gora, Bulg. 42 40N 25 0E
59 Sredne Tambovskoye, U.S.S.R. 50 55N 137 45E
59 Srednekolymsk, U.S.S.R. 67 20N 154 40E
59 Srednevilyuysk, U.S.S.R. 63 50N 123 5E
43 Sredni Rodopi, Rum. 41 40N 24 45E
28 Srem, Poland 52 6N 17 2E
59 Sretensk, U.S.S.R. 52 10N 117 40E
70 Sri Lanka ■, S. Asia 7 30N 80 50E
70 Sriharikota, I., India 13 40N 81 30E
70 Srikakulam, India 18 14N 84 4E
66 Srinagar, Kashmir 34 12N 74 50E
69 Sripur, Bangladesh 24 14N 90 30E
70 Srirangam, India 10 54N 78 42E
70 Srirangapatnam, India 12 26N 76 43E
70 Śrivilliputtur, India 9 31N 77 40E
28 Środa Slaska, Poland 51 10N 16 35E
28 Środa Wlkp., Poland 52 15N 17 19E
42 Srpska Crnja, Y.-slav. 45 38N 20 44E
42 Srpska Itabej, Y.-slav. 45 35N 20 44E
24 Stade, Germany 53 35N 9 31E
50 Staðarhólskirkja, Iceland 65 23N 21 58W
49 Stadil, Denmark 56 12N 8 12E
48 Städjan, Sweden 61 56N 12 30E
47 Stadlandet, Norway 62 10N 5 10E
48 Stadsforsen, Swed. 63 0N 16 45E
24 Stadthagen, Germany 52 20N 9 14E
24 Stadtlohn, Germany 51 59N 6 52E
24 Stadtroda, E. Germany 50 51N 11 44E
50 Stafafell, Iceland 64 25N 14 52W
12 Staffa, I., Scot. 56 26N 6 21W
14 Stafford, England 52 49N 2 9W
12 Stafford ♦, Eng. 52 53N 2 10W
117 Stafford, U.S.A. 38 0N 98 35W
113 Stafford Springs, U.S.A. 41 58N 72 20W
40 Stagnone, I., Italy 37 50N 12 28E
13 Staines, England 51 26N 0 30W
26 Stainz, Austria 46 53N 15 17E
49 Stakkroge, Denmark 55 53N 8 51E
42 Stalač, Yugoslavia 43 43N 21 28E
57 Stalingrad = Volgograd, U.S.S.R. 48 40N 44 25E
57 Staliniri = Iskhinvali, U.S.S.R. 42 14N 44 1E
56 Stalino = Donetsky, U.S.S.R. 48 0N 37 45E
55 Stalinogorsk = Novomoskovsk, U.S.S.R. 54 5N 38 15E
28 Stalowa Wola, Poland 50 34N 22 3E
12 Stalybridge, Eng. 53 29N 2 2W
98 Stamford, Australia 21 15S 143 46E
13 Stamford, Eng. 52 39N 0 29W
113 Stamford, Conn., U.S.A. 41 5N 73 30W
117 Stamford, Tex., U.S.A. 32 58N 99 50W
117 Stamps, U.S.A. 33 22N 93 30W
116 Stanberry, U.S.A. 40 12N 94 32W
93 Standerton, S. Africa 26 55S 29 13E
114 Standish, U.S.A. 43 58N 83 57W
118 Stanford, U.S.A. 47 11N 110 10W
47 Stange Hedmark, Norway 60 43N 11 11E
93 Stanger, S. Africa 29 18S 31 21E
27 Stanišic, Yugoslavia 45 53N 19 12E
54 Stanislav = Ivano-Frankovsk, U.S.S.R. 49 0N 24 40E
42 Stanke Dimitrov, Bulg. 42 27N 23 9E
99 Stanley, Australia 40 46S 145 19E
107 Stanley, N.B., Canada 46 20N 66 50W
109 Stanley, Sask., Canada 55 20N 104 40W
118 Stanley, U.S.A. 44 10N 114 59W
128 Stanley, Falkland Is. 51 40S 58 0W
118 Stanley, Idaho, U.S.A. 44 10N 114 59W
116 Stanley, N.D., U.S.A. 48 20N 102 23W
112 Stanley, N.Y., U.S.A. 42 48N 77 6W
116 Stanley, Wis., U.S.A. 44 57N 91 0W
•90 Stanley, Chutes, Congo 0 12N 25 25E
70 Stanley Res., India 11 50N 77 40E
90 Stanleyville = Kisangani, Zaïre 0 35N 25 15E
120 Stann Creek, Br. Hond. 17 0N 88 20W

* Renamed Chutes Boyoma

MAP
59 Stanovoy Khrebet, U.S.S.R 55 0N 130 0E
99 Stanthorpe, Australia 28 36S 151 59E
104 Stanton, Canada 69 45N 128 52W
117 Stanton, U.S.A. 32 8N 101 45W
116 Stapleton, U.S.A. 41 30N 100 31W
28 Staporkow, Poland 51 9N 20 31E
109 Star City, Canada 52 55N 104 20W
57 Stara-minskaya, U.S.S.R. 46 33N 39 0E
42 Stara Moravica, Y.-slav. 45 50N 19 30E
42 Stara Pazova, Y.-slavia 45 0N 20 10E
43 Stara Planina, Bulgaria 43 15N 23 0E
43 Stara Zagora, Bulgaria 42 26N 25 39E
28 Starachowice- Wierzbnik, Poland 51 3N 21 2E
54 Staraya Russa, U.S.S.R. 57 58N 31 10E
95 Starbuck I., Pac. Oc. 5 37S 155 55W
24 Stargard, Germany 53 29N 13 19E
28 Stargard Szczecinski, Pol. 53 20N 15 0E
42 Stari Bar, Yugoslavia 42 7N 19 13E
39 Stari Trg., Y.-slavia 45 29N 15 7E
54 Staritsa, U.S.S.R. 56 33N 35 0E
115 Starke, U.S.A. 30 0N 82 10W
117 Starkville, Colo., U.S.A. 37 10N 104 31W
115 Starkville, Miss., U.S.A. 33 26N 88 48W
25 Starnberg, Germany 48 0N 11 20E
25 Starnberger See, Ger. 48 0N 11 0E
57 Starobelsk, U.S.S.R. 49 27N 39 0E
54 Starodub, U.S.S.R. 52 30N 32 50E
28 Starogard, Poland 53 55N 18 30E
13 Start Pt., Scotland 59 17N 2 25W
27 Stary Sacz, Poland 49 33N 30 26E
57 Staryy Biryuzyak, U.S.S.R. 44 46N 46 50E
59 Staryy Kheydzhan, U.S.S.R. 60 0N 144 50E
56 Staryy Krym, U.S.S.R. 44 48N 35 8E
55 Staryy Oskol, U.S.S.R. 51 12N 37 55E
24 Stassfurt, Germany 51 51N 11 34E
112 State College, U.S.A. 40 47N 77 49W
128 Staten, I. = Los Estados, I. de, Arg. 54 40S 64 0W
113 Staten I., U.S.A. 40 35N 74 10W
115 Statesboro, U.S.A. 32 26N 81 46W
115 Statesville, U.S.A. 35 48N 80 51W
47 Stathelle, Norway 59 3N 9 41E
116 Staunton, Ill., U.S.A. 39 0N 89 49W
114 Staunton, Va., U.S.A. 38 7N 79 4W
117 Stavanger, Norway 58 57N 5 40E
16 Stavelot, Belgium 50 23N 5 55E
47 Stavern, Norway 59 0N 10 1E
47 Stavfjord, Norway 61 30N 5 0E
16 Stavoren, Netherlands 52 53N 5 21E
48 Stavre, Sweden 62 51N 15 19E
57 Stavropol, U.S.S.R. 45 5N 42 0E
44 Stavroúpolis, Greece 41 12N 24 45E
49 Stavsjö, Sweden 58 42N 16 30E
100 Stawell, Australia 36 58S 142 47E
28 Stawiszyn, Poland 51 56N 18 4E
112 Stayner, Canada 44 25N 80 5W
118 Steamboat Springs, U.S.A. 40 30N 106 58W
28 Stebark, Poland 53 30N 20 10E
44 Stebleva, Albania 41 18N 20 33E
116 Steele, U.S.A. 46 56N 99 52W
112 Steelton, U.S.A. 40 17N 76 50W
117 Steelville, U.S.A. 37 57N 91 21W
108 Steen River, Canada 59 40N 117 12W
19 Steenvoorde, France 50 48N 2 33E
96 Steep Pt., Australia 26 08S 113 8E
109 Steep Rock, Can. 51 30N 98 40W
106 Steep Rock Lake, Can. 48 50N 91 38W
46 Stefănesti, Rumania 47 44N 27 15E
87 Stefanie L. = Chew Bahir, Ethiopia 4 40N 30 50E
46 Stefănesti, Rumania 47 44N 27 15E
49 Stege, Denamrk 55 0N 12 18E
42 Steierdorf Anina, Rum. 45 6N 21 51E
26 Steiermark ♦, Austria 47 26N 15 0E
25 Steigerwald, West Germany 49 45N 10 30E
109 Steinbach, Canada 49 32N 96 40W
16 Steinfort, Luxembourg 49 39N 5 55E
24 Steinheim, Germany 51 50N 9 6E
50 Steinkjer, Norway 63 59N 11 31E
92 Stella Land, S. Africa 26 45S 24 50E
92 Stellenbosch, S. Africa 33 58S 18 50E
47 Stemshaug, Norway 63 19N 8 44E
24 Stendal, Germany 52 36N 11 50E
49 Stenmagle, Denmark 55 49N 11 39E
50 Stensele, Sweden 65 3N 17 8E
49 Stenstorp, Sweden 58 17N 13 45E
49 Stenungsund, Sweden 58 6N 11 50E
53 Stepanakert, U.S.S.R. 40 0N 46 25E
116 Stephan, U.S.A. 48 30N 96 53W
100 Stephens Creek, Austral. 31 50S 141 30E
107 Stephenville, Canada 48 31N 58 30W
117 Stephenville, U.S.A. 32 12N 98 12W
28 Stepnica, Poland 53 38N 14 36E
57 Stepnoi = Elista, U.S.S.R. 46 25N 44 17E
45 Stereáellas, Greece 38 55N 22 0E
92 Sterkstroom, S. Africa 31 32S 26 32E
4 Sterlego, Mys, U.S.S.R. 80 30N 90 0E
116 Sterling, Colo., U.S.A. 40 40N 103 15W
116 Sterling, Ill., U.S.A. 41 45N 89 45W
116 Sterling, Kans., U.S.A. 38 17N 98 13W
117 Sterling City, U.S.A. 31 50N 100 59W
112 Sterling Run, U.S.A. 41 25N 78 12W
52 Sterlitamak, U.S.S.R. 53 40N 56 0E
24 Sternberg, Germany 53 42N 11 48E
27 Sternberk, Cz. 49 45N 17 15E
28 Stettin = Szczecin, Poland 53 27N 14 27E
24 Stettiner Haff, Germany 53 50N 14 25E
108 Stettler, Canada 52 25N 112 40W
112 Steubenville, U.S.A. 40 21N 80 39W
116 Stevens Port, U.S.A. 44 32N 89 34W
96 Stevenson, R., Australia 46 15S 134 10E

MAP
49 Stevns Klint, Den. 55 17N 12 28E
128 Stewart, I., Chile 54 50S 71 30W
101 Stewart I., N.Z. 46 58S 167 54E
107 Stewiacke, Canada 45 9N 63 22W
92 Steynsburg, S. Africa 31 15S 25 49E
26 Steyr, Austria 48 3N 14 25E
26 Steyr, R., Austria 48 57N 14 15E
92 Steytlerville, S. Africa 33 17S 24 19E
39 Stia, Italy 43 48N 11 41E
117 Stigler, U.S.A. 35 19N 95 6W
41 Stigliano, Italy 40 24N 16 13E
49 Stigsnaes, Denmark 55 13N 11 18E
49 Stigtomta, Sweden 58 47N 16 48E
104 Stikine Mts., Canada 59 30N 129 30W
104 Stikine, R., Canada 58 0N 131 0W
92 Stilfontein, S. Africa 26 50S 26 50E
45 Stilis, Greece 38 55N 22 37E
116 Stillwater, Minn., U.S.A. 45 3N 92 47W
113 Stillwater, N.Y., U.S.A. 42 55N 73 41W
117 Stillwater, Okla., U.S.A. 36 5N 97 3W
118 Stillwater Mts., U.S.A. 39 45N 118 6W
117 Stilwell, U.S.A. 35 52N 94 36W
45 Stimfalias, L., Greece 37 51N 22 27E
106 Stimson, Canada 48 58N 80 30W
42 Stip, Yugoslavia 41 42N 22 10E
45 Stira, Greece 38 9N 24 14E
19 Stiring Wendel, France 49 12N 6 57E
96 Stirling, Australia 17 12S 141 35E
108 Stirling, Canada 49 30N 112 30W
14 Stirling, Scotland 56 17N 3 57W
•14 Stirling ♦, Scot. 56 3N 4 10W
113 Stittsville, Canada 45 15N 75 58W
49 Stjärneborg, Sweden 57 53N 14 45E
48 Stjarnsfors, Sweden 60 2N 13 45E
47 Stjördalshalsen, Nor. 63 29N 10 51E
49 Stockaryd, Sweden 57 19N 14 36E
27 Stockerau, Austria 48 24N 16 12E
118 Stockett, U.S.A. 47 23N 111 7W
48 Stockholm, Sweden 59 20N 18 3E
48 Stockholms län ♦, Sweden 59 30N 18 20E
100 Stockinbingal, Austral. 34 30S 147 53E
12 Stockport, Eng. 53 25N 2 11W
100 Stockton, Australia 32 56S 151 47E
118 Stockton, Calif., U.S.A. 38 0N 121 20W
116 Stockton, Kans., U.S.A. 39 30N 99 20W
117 Stockton, Mo., U.S.A. 37 40N 93 48W
12 Stockton-on-Tees, England 54 34N 1 20W
48 Stockvik, Sweden 62 17N 17 23E
28 Stoczek Łukowski, Poland 51 58N 22 22E
48 Stode, Sweden 62 28N 16 35E
42 Stogovo, mts., Y.-slavia 41 31N 20 38E
12 Stoke-on-Trent, England 53 1N 2 11W
106 Stokes Bay, Canada 45 0N 81 22W
47 Stokke, Norway 59 13N 10 17E
47 Stokken, Norway 58 31N 8 53E
50 Stokksnes, Iceland 64 14N 14 58W
42 Stolac, Yugoslavia 43 8N 17 59E
24 Stolberg, E. Germany 51 33N 11 0E
24 Stolberg, W. Germany 50 48N 6 13E
55 Stolbovaya, R.S.F.S.R., U.S.S.R. 55 10N 37 32E
59 Stolbovaya, R.S.F.S.R., U.S.S.R. 64 50N 153 50E
54 Stolbtsy, U.S.S.R. 53 22N 26 43E
54 Stolin, U.S.S.R. 51 53N 26 50E
46 Stolnici, Rumania 44 31N 24 48E
42 Ston, Yugoslavia 42 51N 17 43E
106 Stonecliffe, Canada 46 13N 77 56W
14 Stonehaven, Scot. 56 58N 2 11W
13 Stonehenge, Eng. 51 9N 1 45W
109 Stonewall, Canada 50 10N 96 50W
47 Stongfjord, Norway 61 28N 14 0E
112 Stony L., Canada 44 35N 78 15W
109 Stony Rapids, Canada 59 15N 105 55W
28 Stopnica, Poland 50 27N 20 57E
47 Stor Elvdal, Norway 61 30N 11 1E
24 Stora Borge Fjell, Mt., Norway 65 12N 14 0E
48 Stora Gla, Sweden 59 30N 12 30E
49 Stora Karlsö, Sweden 57 17N 17 59E
50 Stora Lulevatten, Swed. 67 10N 19 30E
50 Stora Sjöfallet, Sweden 67 29N 18 40E
50 Storavan, Sweden 65 45N 18 10E
47 Stord Leirvik, I., Nor. 59 48N 5 27E
49 Store Baelt, Den. 55 20N 11 0E
100 Store Creek, Australia 32 54S 149 6E
49 Store Heddinge, Denmark 55 18N 12 23E
47 Storen, Norway 63 3N 10 18E
47 Storfjorden, Möre og Romsdal, Norway 62 7N 6 34E
47 Storfjorden, Möre og Romsdal, Norway 62 25N 6 30E
99 Storm B., Austral. 43 10S 147 30E
116 Storm Lake, U.S.A. 42 35N 95 5W
92 Stormsrivier, S. Africa 33 59S 23 52E
14 Stornoway, Scot. 58 12N 6 23W
56 Storozhinets, U.S.S.R. 48 14S 25 45E
48 Storsjö, Sweden 62 49N 13 5E
47 Storsjöen, Hedmark, Norway 60 20N 11 40E
47 Storsjöen, Hedmark, Norway 61 30N 11 14E
48 Storsjön, Gavleborg, Sweden 60 35N 16 45E
48 Storsjön, Jämtland, Sweden 62 50N 13 8E
49 Storstroms Amt ♦, Denmark 49 50N 11 45E
50 Storuman, Sweden 65 5N 17 10E
48 Storvätteshagna, Mt., Sweden 62 6N 12 30E
48 Storvik, Sweden 60 35N 16 33E
109 Stoughton, Canada 49 40N 103 0W
13 Stour, R., Dorset, England 50 48N 2 7W
13 Stour, R., Kent, Eng. 51 15N 0 57E

* Incorporated within the regions of Central and Strathclyde

* Renamed Ambartsevo
* United to form the county of Suffolk
* Incorporated with the region of Highland
72

* *Incorporated within the new Eastern Province*
† *Renamed Dalnegorsk*

* Renamed Nyahururu
† Renamed Mbanza Ngungu

Tone gawa INDEX Tsingsi

MAP
74 Tone gawa, Japan 36 15N 139 30E
101 Tonga Is. ■, Pacific Ocean 20 0S 173 0W
101 Tonga Trench, Pac. Oc. 18 0S 175 0W
93 Tongaat, S. Afr. 29 33S 31 9E
93 Tongaland, S. Afr. 27 0S 32 0E
101 Tongatapu I., Tonga I. 21 10S 174 0W
16 Tongeren, Belgium 50 47N 5 28E
71 Tongking = Bac-Phan, North Vietnam 21 30N 105 0E
71 Tongking, G. of, Asia 20 0N 108 0E
93 Tongobory, Malagasy Rep. 23 32S 44 20E
124 Tongoy, Chile 30 25S 71 40W
16 Tongres = Tongeren, Belg. 50 47N 5 28E
118 Tongue, R., U.S.A. 48 30N 106 30W
87 Tonj, Sudan 7 20N 28 44E
68 Tonk, India 26 6N 75 54E
117 Tonkawa, U.S.A. 36 44N 67 22W
71 Tonlé Sap, Cambodia 13 0N 104 0E
20 Tonnay-Charente, Fr. 45 56N 0 55W
20 Tonneins, France 44 24N 0 20E
19 Tonnerre, France 47 51N 3 59E
24 Tönning, Germany 54 18N 8 57E
119 Tonopah, U.S.A. 38 4N 117 12W
47 Tonsberg, Norway 59 19N 10 25E
47 Tonstad, Norway 58 40N 6 45E
35 Tonto Basin, U.S.A. 33 58N 111 15W
118 Tooele, U.S.A. 40 30N 112 20W
99 Toompine, Australia 27 15S 144 19E
100 Toongi, Austral. 32 28S 148 30E
98 Toonpan, Australia 19 28S 146 48E
59 Toora-Khem, U.S.S.R. 52 28N 96 9E
99 Toowong, Australia 27 30S 152 58E
99 Toowoomba, Austral. 27 32S 151 56E
52 Top Ozero, U.S.S.R. 65 35N 32 0E
46 Topalu, Rumania 44 31N 28 3E
116 Topeka, U.S.A. 39 3N 95 40W
58 Topki, U.S.S.R. 55 25N 85 20E
27 Topla, R., Cz. 49 0N 21 36E
108 Topley, Canada 54 32N 126 5W
42 Toplica, R., Yugoslavia 43 15N 21 30E
46 Toplița, Rumania 46 55N 25 27E
124 Topocalma, Pta., Chile 34 10S 72 2W
119 Topock, U.S.A. 34 46N 114 29W
42 Topola, Yugoslavia 44 17N 20 32E
27 Topol'čany, Cz. 48 35N 18 12E
57 Topoli, U.S.S.R. 47 59N 51 45E
43 Topolnitsa, R., Bulg. 42 21N 24 0E
120 Topolobampo, Mexico 25 40N 109 10W
43 Topolovgrad, Bulgaria 42 5N 26 20E
42 Topolvăț Mare, Rum. 45 46N 21 41E
118 Toppenish, U.S.A. 46 27N 120 16W
39 Topusko, Yugoslavia 45 18N 15 59E
96 Tor Bay, Australia 35 5S 117 50E
32 Torá, Spain 41 49N 1 25E
87 Tora Kit, Sudan 11 2N 32 30E
126 Torata, Peru 17 3S 70 1W
65 Torbat-e Heydarīyeh, Iran 35 15N 59 12E
65 Torbat-e Jām, Iran 35 8N 60 35E
107 Torbay, Canada 47 40N 52 42W
13 Torbay, U.K. 50 26N 3 31W
100 Torbreck Mt., Austral. 37 10S 145 57E
54 Torchin, U.S.S.R. 50 45N 25 0E
47 Tordal, Norway 59 10N 8 45E
30 Tordesillas, Spain 41 30N 5 0W
30 Tordoya, Spain 43 6N 8 36W
50 Töre, Sweden 65 55N 22 40E
49 Töreboda, Sweden 58 41N 14 7E
50 Torfajökull, Iceland 63 54N 19 0W
24 Torgau, Germany 51 32N 13 0E
24 Torgelow, Germany 53 40N 13 59E
16 Torhout, Belgium 51 5N 3 7E
87 Tori, Ethiopia 7 53N 33 35E
18 Torigni-sur-Vire, France 49 3N 0 58W
32 Torija, Spain 40 44N 3 2W
120 Torin, Mexico 27 33N 110 5W
30 Toriñana, C., Spain 43 3N 9 17W
38 Torino, Italy 45 4N 7 40E
87 Torit, Sudan 4 20N 32 55E
54 Torkovichi, U.S.S.R. 58 51N 30 50E
42 Tormac, Rumania 45 30N 21 30E
107 Tormentine, Canada 46 6N 63 46W
30 Tormes, R., Spain 41 7N 6 0W
108 Tornado Mt., Canada 49 55N 114 40W
49 Tornby, Denmark 57 32N 9 56E
50 Torne älv, Sweden 65 50N 24 12E
50 Torneträsk, Sweden 68 24N 19 15E
50 Torneå = Tornio, Finland 65 50N 24 12E
50 Tornio, Finland 65 50N 24 12E
50 Tornionjoki, Finland 65 50N 24 12E
124 Tornquist, Argentina 38 0S 62 15W
30 Toro, Spain 41 35N 5 24W
49 Torö, Sweden 58 48N 17 50E
120 Toro, Pta., Panama Canal Zone 9 22N 79 57W
* 90 Toro ♦, Uganda 0 20N 30 15E
124 Toro, Cerro del, Chile 29 0S 69 50W
27 Törökszentmiklós, Hungary 47 11N 20 27E
44 Toronátos Kólpos, Greece 40 5N 23 30E
100 Toronto, Austral. 33 0S 151 30E
106 Toronto, Canada 43 39N 79 20W
112 Toronto, U.S.A. 40 27N 80 36W
120 Toronto, L., Mexico 27 40N 105 30W
54 Toropets, U.S.S.R. 56 30N 31 40E
90 Tororo, Uganda 0 45N 34 12E
64 Toros Dağlari, Turkey 37 0N 35 0E
48 Torpshammar, Sweden 62 29N 16 20E
100 Torquay, Australia 38 20S 144 19E
13 Torquay, U.K. 50 27N 3 31W
30 Torquemada, Spain 42 2N 4 19W
31 Torralba de Calatrava, Spain 39 1N 3 44W
31 Torrão, Portugal 38 16N 8 11W
40 Torre Annunziata, Italy 40 45N 14 26E

* *Incorporated within the new Western Province*

30 Tôrre de Moncorvo, Port. 41 12N 7 8W
41 Torre del Greco, Italy 40 47N 14 22E
31 Torre del Mar, Spain 36 44N 4 6W
38 Torre Pellice, Italy 44 49N 7 13E
32 Torreblanca, Spain 40 14N 0 12E
31 Torrecampo, Spain 38 29N 4 41W
32 Torrecilla en Cameros, Spain 42 15N 2 38W
32 Torredembarra, Spain 41 9N 1 24W
31 Torredonjimeno, Spain 37 46N 3 57W
30 Torrejoncillo, Spain 39 54N 6 28W
32 Torrelaguna, Spain 40 50N 3 38W
30 Torrelavega, Spain 43 20N 4 5W
41 Torremaggiore, Italy 41 42N 15 17E
31 Torremolinos, Spain 36 38N 4 30W
98 Torrens Creek, Austral. 20 48S 145 3E
99 Torrens, L., S. Austral. 31 0S 137 45E
33 Torrente, Spain 39 27N 0 28W
33 Torrenueva, Spain 38 38N 3 22W
120 Torreón, Mexico 25 33N 103 25W
33 Torreperogil, Spain 38 2N 3 17W
30 Torres, Spain 41 6N 5 0W
31 Tôrres Novas, Portugal 39 27N 8 33W
98 Torres Strait, Austral. 10 20S 142 0E
31 Torres Vedras, Portugal 39 5N 9 15W
33 Torrevieja, Spain 37 59N 0 42W
119 Torrey, U.S.A. 38 12N 111 30W
13 Torridge, R., Eng. 50 57N 4 10W
14 Torridon, L., Scot. 57 35N 5 50W
30 Torrijos, Spain 39 59N 4 18W
49 Törring, Denmark 55 52N 9 29E
113 Torrington, Conn., U.S.A. 41 50N 73 9W
116 Torrington, Wyo., U.S.A. 42 5N 104 8W
32 Torroella de Montgri, Spain 42 2N 3 8E
100 Torrowangee, Australia 31 22S 141 30E
31 Torrox, Spain 36 46N 3 57W
49 Torsås, Sweden 56 24N 16 0E
48 Torsby, Sweden 60 7N 13 0E
48 Torsjok, U.S.S.R. 57 5N 34 55E
49 Torsö, Sweden 58 48N 13 45E
30 Tórtoles de Esgueva, Sp. 41 49N 4 2W
38 Tortona, Italy 44 53N 8 54E
39 Tortoreto, Italy 42 50N 13 55E
41 Tortorici, Italy 38 2N 14 48E
32 Tortosa, Spain 40 49N 0 31E
32 Tortosa C., Spain 40 41N 0 52E
30 Tortosendo, Portugal 40 15N 7 31W
121 Tortue, I. de la, Haiti 20 5N 72 57W
121 Tortuga, Isla la, Venezuela 11 8N 67 2W
65 Torud, Iran 35 25N 55 5E
28 Toruń, Poland 53 0N 18 39E
49 Torup, Sweden 56 57N 13 5E
47 Torvastad, Norway 59 23N 5 15E
15 Tory I., Ireland 55 17N 8 12W
112 Tory Hill, Canada 44 56N 78 18W
27 Torysa, R., Cz. 48 50N 21 15E
54 Torzhok, U.S.S.R. 57 5N 34 55E
74 Tosa-Wan, Japan 33 15N 133 30E
38 Toscana, Italy 43 30N 11 5E
54 Tosno, U.S.S.R. 59 30N 30 58E
32 Tossa, Spain 41 43N 2 56E
124 Tostado, Argentina 29 15S 61 50W
24 Tostedt, Germany 53 17N 9 42E
28 Toszek, Poland 50 27N 18 32E
47 Totak, Norway 59 40N 7 45E
33 Totana, Spain 37 45N 1 30W
47 Toten, Norway 60 37N 10 53E
92 Toteng, Botswana 20 22S 22 58E
55 Totma, U.S.S.R. 60 0N 42 40E
120 Totonicapán, Guat. 14 50N 91 20W
112 Tottenham, Australia 32 15S 147 15E
112 Tottenham, Canada 44 2N 79 48W
74 Tottori, Japan 35 30N 134 15E
74 Tottori-ken ♦, Japan 35 30N 134 12E
82 Touat, Algeria 27 30N 0 30E
84 Touba, Ivory Coast 8 15N 7 40W
82 Toubkal, Djebel, Morocco 31 0N 8 0W
19 Toucy, France 47 44N 3 15E
84 Tougan, Upper Volta 13 11N 2 58W
83 Touggourt, Algeria 33 10N 6 0E
84 Tougué, Guinea 11 25N 11 50W
83 Toukmatine, Algeria 24 49N 7 11E
19 Toul, France 48 40N 5 53E
21 Toulon, France 43 10N 5 55E
20 Toulouse, France 43 37N 1 27E
83 Toummo, Niger 22 45N 14 8E
83 Toummo Dhoba, Niger 22 30N 14 31E
84 Toumodi, Ivory Coast 6 32N 5 4W
82 Tounassine, Hamada, Algeria 28 48N 5 0W
67 Toungoo, Burma 19 0N 96 30E
18 Touques, R., France 49 22N 0 8E
18 Touraine, France 47 20N 0 30E
19 Tourcoing, France 50 42N 3 10E
85 Tourcoingbam, Upper Volta 13 23N 1 33W
16 Tournai, Belgium 50 35N 3 25E
19 Tournan-en-Brie, France 48 44N 2 46E
20 Tournay, France 43 13N 0 13E
21 Tournon, France 45 4N 4 50E
18 Tournon-St.-Martin, France 46 45N 0 58E
21 Tournus, France 46 35N 4 54E
18 Tours, France 47 22N 0 40E
83 Touside, Pic, Chad 21 1N 16 18E
92 Touwsrivier, S. Africa 33 20S 20 0E
126 Tovar, Venezuela 8 20N 71 46W
55 Tovarkovskiy, U.S.S.R. 53 40N 38 5E
47 Tovdal, Norway 58 47N 8 10E
47 Tovdalselva, Nor. 58 20N 8 16E
100 Towamba, Australia 37 6S 149 55E
113 Towanda, U.S.A. 41 46N 76 30W
116 Tower, U.S.A. 47 49N 92 17W
116 Towner, U.S.A. 48 25N 100 26W
118 Townsend, U.S.A. 46 25N 111 32W
100 Townsend Mt., Austral. 36 25S 148 16E
98 Townshend, C., Australia 22 18S 150 30E
98 Townshend, I., Australia 22 16S 150 31E
98 Townsville, Australia 19 15S 146 45E
100 Towong, Australia 36 8S 147 59E
77 Towshan, China 22 5N 112 50E
114 Towson, U.S.A. 39 26N 76 34W
73 Towuti, D, Indonesia 2 40S 121 30E
117 Toyah, U.S.A. 31 20N 103 48W
117 Toyahvale, U.S.A. 30 58N 103 45W
74 Toyama, Japan 36 40N 137 15E
74 Toyama-ken ♦, Japan 36 45N 137 30E
74 Toyama-Wan, Japan 37 0N 137 30E
74 Toyohashi, Japan 34 45N 137 25E
74 Toyokawa, Japan 34 48N 137 27E
74 Toyonaka, Japan 34 50N 135 28E
74 Toyooka, Japan 35 35N 134 55E
83 Tozeur, Tunisia 33 56N 8 8E
30 Trabancos, R., Spain 41 0N 5 3E
64 Trabzon, Turkey 41 0N 39 45E
107 Tracadie, Canada 47 30N 64 55W
119 Tracy, Calif., U.S.A. 37 46N 121 27W
116 Tracy, Minn., U.S.A. 44 12N 95 3W
38 Tradate, Italy 45 43N 8 54E
75 Tradom, China 30 0N 83 59E
100 Trafalgar, Australia 38 14S 146 12E
31 Trafalgar, C., Spain 36 10N 6 2W
83 Traghan, Libya 26 0N 14 30E
100 Tragowel, Austral. 35 51S 143 59E
46 Traian, Rumania 45 2N 28 15E
108 Trail, Canada 49 5N 117 40W
15 Tralee, Ireland 52 16N 9 42W
15 Tralee B., Ireland 52 17N 9 55W
15 Tramore, Ireland 52 10N 7 10W
71 Tran Ninh, Cao Nguyen, Laos 19 30N 103 10E
49 Tranås, Sweden 58 3N 14 59E
124 Trancas, Argentina 26 20S 65 20W
30 Trancoso, Portugal 40 49N 7 21W
49 Tranebjerg, Denmark 55 51N 10 36E
49 Tranemo, Sweden 57 30N 13 20E
71 Trang, Thailand 7 33N 99 38E
93 Trangahy, Malagasy Rep. 19 7S 44 43E
73 Trangan, I., Indonesia 6 40S 134 20E
100 Trangie, Austral. 32 4S 148 0E
48 Trångsviken, Sweden 63 19N 14 0E
41 Trani, Italy 41 17N 16 24E
93 Tranoroa, Malag. 24 42S 45 4E
70 Tranquebar, India 11 1N 79 54E
125 Tranqueras, Uruguay 31 8S 56 0W
90 Trans Nzoia ♦, Kenya 1 0N 35 0E
109 Transcona, Canada 49 50N 97 0W
46 Transilvania, Rum. 46 19N 25 0E
93 Transkei ♦, S. Afr. 32 15S 28 15E
49 Träslöv, Sweden 57 8N 12 21E
48 Transtrand, Sweden 61 6N 13 20E
92 Transvaal ♦, S. Africa 25 0S 29 0E
46 Transylvania = Transilvania, Rum. 46 19N 25 0E
46 Transylvanian Alps, Rumania 45 30N 25 0E
49 Tranås, Sweden 55 37N 13 59E
40 Trápani, Italy 38 1N 12 30E
118 Trappe Peak, Mt., U.S.A. 45 56N 114 29W
100 Traralgon, Austral. 38 6S 146 31E
49 Traryd, Sweden 56 35N 13 45E
84 Trarza ♦, Mauritania 17 30N 15 0W
39 Trasacco, Italy 41 58N 13 30E
46 Trăscău, Muntii, Rumania 46 14N 23 14E
39 Trasimeno, L., Italy 43 10N 12 5E
71 Trat, Thailand 12 14N 102 33E
26 Traun, Austria 48 14N 14 15E
25 Traun-see, Austria 47 48N 13 45E
25 Traunstein, Germany 47 52N 12 40E
49 Trävad, Sweden 58 15N 13 5E
24 Travemünde, Germany 53 58N 10 52E
101 Travers, Mt., N.Z. 42 1S 172 45E
114 Traverse City, U.S.A. 44 45N 85 39W
5 Traverse I., Falk. Is. Dep. 48 0S 28 0E
42 Travnik, Yugoslavia 44 17N 17 39E
109 Traynor, Canada 52 20N 108 32W
30 Trazo, Spain 43 0N 8 30W
39 Trbovlje, Yugoslavia 46 12N 15 5E
38 Trebbia, R., Italy 44 52N 9 30E
24 Trebel, R., Germany 54 0N 12 50E
42 Trebinje, Yugoslavia 42 44N 18 22E
41 Trebisacce, Italy 39 52N 16 32E
42 Trebišnica, R., Y.-slavia 42 47N 18 8E
27 Trebišov, Cz. 48 38N 21 41E
42 Trebižat, Yugoslavia 43 15N 17 30E
26 Třebon, Czechoslovakia 48 59N 14 48E
31 Trebujena, Spain 36 52N 6 11W
38 Trecate, Italy 45 29N 8 42E
13 Tredegar, U.K. 51 47N 3 16W
18 Trégastel-Plage, France 48 49N 3 31W
39 Tregnago, Italy 45 31N 11 10E
97 Tregosse Is., Australia 17 40S 150 50E
18 Tréguier, France 48 47N 3 16W
109 Treherne, Canada 49 39N 98 41W
39 Tréia, Italy 43 30N 13 20E
20 Treignac, France 45 32N 1 48E
125 Treinta y Tres, Uruguay 33 10S 54 50W
25 Treis, Germany 50 9N 7 19E
92 Trekveld, S. Africa 30 35S 19 45E
49 Trelde Naes, Den. 55 38N 9 53E
128 Trelew, Argentina 43 10S 65 20W
20 Trélissac, France 45 11N 0 47E
49 Trelleborg, Sweden 55 20N 13 10E
19 Trélon, France 50 5N 4 6E
117 Trementina, U.S.A. 35 27N 105 30W
39 Tremiti, I., Italy 42 8N 15 30E
118 Tremonton, U.S.A. 41 45N 112 10W
32 Tremp, Spain 42 10N 0 52E
114 Trenary, U.S.A. 46 12N 86 59W
27 Trenčín, Czechoslovakia 48 52N 18 4E
73 Trenggalek, Indonesia 8 5S 111 44E
124 Trenque Lauquen, Arg. 36 0S 62 45W
12 Trent, R., Eng. 53 33N 0 44W
38 Trentino-Alto Adige ♦, Italy 46 5N 11 0E
38 Trento, Italy 46 5N 11 8E
106 Trenton, Canada 44 10N 77 40W
116 Trenton, Mo., U.S.A. 40 5N 93 37W
116 Trenton, Nebr., U.S.A. 40 14N 101 4W
113 Trenton, N.J., U.S.A. 40 15N 74 41W
117 Trenton, Tenn., U.S.A. 35 58N 88 57W
107 Trepassey, Canada 46 43N 53 25W
24 Treptow, Germany 53 42N 13 15E
41 Trepuzzi, Italy 40 26N 18 4E
124 Tres Arroyos, Argentina 38 20S 60 20W
125 Três Corações, Brazil 21 30S 45 30W
82 Tres Fourches, C. de, Mor. 35 26N 3 0W
127 Três Lagoas, Brazil 20 50S 51 50W
128 Tres Montes, C., Chile 47 0S 75 35W
125 Tres Pontas, Brazil 21 23S 45 29W
124 Tres Puentes, Chile 27 50S 70 15W
128 Tres Puntas, C., Arg. 47 0S 66 0W
125 Tres Rios, Brazil 22 20S 43 30W
42 Treska, R., Yugoslavia 41 45N 21 11E
42 Treskavika Planina, Yugoslavia 43 40N 18 20E
32 Trespaderne, Spain 42 47N 3 24W
21 Trets, France 43 27N 5 41E
25 Treuchtlingen, Ger. 48 58N 10 55E
24 Treuenbrietzen, Ger. 52 6N 12 51E
38 Treviglio, Italy 45 31N 9 35E
30 Trevinca, Peña, Spain 42 15N 6 46W
39 Treviso, Italy 45 40N 12 15E
21 Trévoux, France 45 57N 4 47E
24 Treysa, West Germany 50 55N 9 11E
42 Trgovište, Yugoslavia 42 20N 22 10E
99 Triabunna, Australia 42 28S 148 0E
45 Triánda, Greece 36 25N 28 10E
71 Triang, Malaysia 3 13N 102 27E
19 Triaucourt-en-Argonne, France 48 59N 5 2E
24 Tribsees, Germany 54 4N 12 46E
98 Tribulation, C., Australia 16 10S 145 50E
116 Tribune, U.S.A. 38 30N 101 45W
41 Tricárico, Italy 40 37N 16 9E
41 Tricase, Italy 39 56N 18 20E
70 Trichinopoly = Tiruchchirappalli, India 10 45N 78 45E
70 Trichur, India 10 30N 76 18E
100 Trida, Austral. 33 2S 144 57E
25 Trier, Germany 49 45N 6 37E
39 Trieste, Italy 45 39N 13 45E
39 Trieste, G. di, Italy 45 37N 13 40E
41 Triggiano, Italy 41 4N 16 58E
39 Triglav, Y.-slavia 46 30N 13 45E
39 Trigno, R., Italy 41 55N 14 37E
31 Trigueros, Spain 37 24N 6 50W
45 Trikeri, Greece 39 6N 23 5E
45 Trikhonis, Límni, Gr. 38 34N 21 30E
44 Trikkala, Greece 39 34N 21 47E
44 Trikkala ♦, Greece 39 41N 21 30E
73 Trikora, G., Indonesia 4 11S 138 0E
39 Trilj, Yugoslavia 43 38N 16 42E
32 Trillo, Spain 40 42N 2 35W
15 Trim, Ireland 53 34N 6 48W
70 Trincomalee, Sri Lanka 8 38N 81 15E
7 Trindade, I., Southern Atlantic Ocean 20 20S 29 50W
126 Trinidad, Bolivia 14 54S 64 50W
126 Trinidad, Colombia 5 25N 71 40W
121 Trinidad, Cuba 21 40N 80 0W
117 Trinidad, U.S.A. 37 15N 104 30W
124 Trinidad, Uruguay 33 30S 56 50W
128 Trinidad, I., Argentina 39 10S 62 0W
121 Trinidad & Tobago ■, West Indies 10 30N 61 20W
41 Trinitápoli, Italy 41 22N 16 5E
107 Trinity, Canada 48 22N 53 29W
117 Trinity, U.S.A. 30 50N 95 20W
98 Trinity B., Australia 16 30S 146 0E
107 Trinity B., Canada 48 20N 53 10W
117 Trinity Mts., U.S.A. 40 20N 118 50W
117 Trinity R., U.S.A. 30 30N 95 0W
38 Trino, Italy 45 10N 8 18E
115 Trion, U.S.A. 34 35N 85 18W
41 Trionto C., Italy 39 38N 16 47E
38 Triora, Italy 44 0N 7 46E
83 Tripoli = Tarābulus, Libya 32 49N 13 7E
45 Tripolis, Greece 37 31N 22 25E
116 Tripp, U.S.A. 43 16N 97 58W
67 Tripura ♦, India 24 0N 92 0E
24 Trischen, I., W. Ger. 54 3N 8 32E
7 Tristan da Cunha, I., Atlantic Ocean 37 6S 12 20W
70 Trivandrum, India 8 31N 77 0E
41 Trivento, Italy 41 48N 14 31E
27 Trnava, Czechoslovakia 48 23N 17 35E
98 Trobriand, Papua 8 40S 15 10E
108 Trochu, Canada 51 50N 113 20W
106 Trodely I., Canada 52 20N 79 20W
39 Trogir, Yugoslavia 43 32N 16 15E
39 Troglav, mt., Y.-slavia 43 56N 16 36E
47 Trögstad, Norway 59 37N 11 16E
41 Tróia, Italy 41 22N 15 19E
106 Troilus, L., Canada 50 50N 74 35W
41 Troina, Italy 37 47N 14 34E
107 Trois Pistoles, Canada 48 5N 69 10W
106 Trois Rivières, Canada 46 25N 72 40W
58 Troitsk, U.S.S.R. 54 10N 61 35E
52 Troitsko-Pechorsk, U.S.S.R. 62 40N 56 10E
49 Trollhättan, Sweden 58 17N 12 20E
47 Trollheimen, Nor. 62 46N 9 1E
47 Tromöy, Norway 58 28N 8 53E
50 Troms fylke ♦, Norway 68 56N 19 0E
50 Tromsö, Norway 69 40N 18 56E
128 Tronador, Mt., Arg. 41 53S 71 0W
50 Tröndelag, N. ♦, Nor. 65 0N 12 0E
47 Tröndelag, S. ♦, Nor. 62 0N 10 0E
47 Trondheim, Norway 63 25N 10 25E
50 Trondheimsfjorden, Nor. 63 35N 10 30E
49 Trönninge, Sweden 56 38N 12 59E
48 Trönö, Sweden 61 22N 16 54E
39 Tronto, R., Italy 42 50N 13 46E
92 Troodos, mt., Cyprus 34 58N 32 55E
41 Tropea, Italy 38 40N 15 53E
119 Tropic, U.S.A. 37 44N 112 4W
44 Tropoja, Albania 42 23N 20 10E
14 Trossachs, The, Scotland 56 14N 4 24W
15 Trostan Mt., N. Ireland 55 4N 6 10W
25 Trostberg, Germany 48 2N 12 33E
117 Troup, U.S.A. 32 10N 95 3W
108 Trout L., N.W. Terr., Canada 60 40N 121 40W
109 Trout L., Ont., Canada 51 20N 93 15W
118 Trout Peak, Mt., U.S.A. 44 37N 109 30W
18 Trouville, France 49 21N 0 5E
13 Trowbridge, Eng. 51 18N 2 12W
64 Troy, Turkey 39 55N 26 20E
115 Troy, Alabama, U.S.A. 31 50N 85 58W
116 Troy, Kans., U.S.A. 39 47N 95 2W
116 Troy, Mo., U.S.A. 38 56N 90 59W
118 Troy, Montana, U.S.A. 48 30N 115 58W
113 Troy, N.Y., U.S.A. 42 45N 73 39W
114 Troy, Ohio, U.S.A. 40 0N 84 10W
112 Troy, Tur. 39 55N 26 20E
43 Troyan, Bulgaria 42 57N 24 43E
19 Troyes, France 48 19N 4 3E
42 Trpanj, Yugoslavia 43 1N 17 15E
27 Trstena, Czechoslovakia 49 21N 19 37E
42 Trstenik, Yugoslavia 43 36N 21 0E
54 Trubchevsk, U.S.S.R. 52 33N 33 47E
65 Trucial States ■, Asia 24 0N 54 30E
118 Truckee, U.S.A. 39 29N 120 12W
126 Trujillo, Colombia 4 10N 76 19W
121 Trujillo, Honduras 16 0N 86 0W
126 Trujillo, Peru 8 0S 79 0W
31 Trujillo, Spain 39 28N 5 55W
117 Trujillo, U.S.A. 35 34N 104 44W
126 Trujillo, Venezuela 9 22N 70 26W
95 Truk Is., U.S. Pac. Is. Trust Terr. 7 25N 151 46E
117 Trumann, U.S.A. 35 42N 90 32W
119 Trumbull, Mt., U.S.A. 36 25N 113 32W
42 Trŭn, Bulgaria 42 51N 22 38E
18 Trun, France 48 50N 0 2E
100 Trundle, Austral. 32 52S 147 35E
107 Truro, Canada 45 21N 63 14E
13 Truro, England 50 17N 5 2W
49 Trustrup, Denmark 56 20N 10 46E
119 Truth or Consequences, U.S.A. 33 9N 107 16W
26 Trutnov, Cz. 50 37N 15 54E
20 Truyère, R., France 44 38N 2 34E
43 Tryavna, Bulgaria 42 54N 25 25E
115 Tryon, U.S.A. 35 15N 82 16W
112 Tryonville, U.S.A. 41 42N 79 48W
28 Trzciarka, Poland 53 3N 16 25E
28 Trzciel, Poland 52 23N 15 50E
28 Trzcinsko-Zdroj, Poland 52 58N 14 35E
28 Trzeblatów, Poland 54 3N 15 18E
27 Trzebinia, Poland 50 11N 19 30E
28 Trzebiez, Poland 53 38N 14 31E
28 Trzebnica, Poland 51 20N 17 1E
28 Trzemeszno, Poland 52 33N 17 48E
39 Tržič, Yugoslavia 46 22N 14 18E
50 Trölladyngja, Iceland 64 54N 17 15W
62 Tsafriya, Israel 31 59N 34 51E
76 Tsagaan-Oür, Mongolia 50 20N 105 3E
75 Tsaidam, China 37 0N 95 0E
44 Tsamandás, Greece 39 46N 20 21E
67 Tsana Dzong, China 28 0N 91 55E
67 Tsanga, China 30 43N 100 32E
75 Tsangpo, China 29 40N 89 0E
77 Tsaohsien, China 34 50N 115 45E
93 Tsaratanana, Malg. 16 47S 47 39E
93 Tsaratanana, Mt. de, Malag. 14 0S 49 0E
43 Tsarevo = Michurin, Bulgaria 42 9N 27 51E
75 Tsaring Nor, China 35 0N 97 0E
44 Tsaritsáni, Greece 39 53N 15 14E
92 Tsau, Botswana 20 8S 22 29E
92 Tsaukaib, S.W. Afr. 26 37S 15 39E
56 Tsebrikovo, U.S.S.R. 47 9N 30 10E
58 Tselinograd, U.S.S.R. 51 10N 71 30E
53 Tskhinali, U.S.S.R. 42 22N 43 52E
77 Tsenkung, China 27 3N 108 40E
76 Tsetserling, Mongolia 47 29N 101 10E
75 Tsetserleg, Mongolia 47 36N 101 32E
92 Tshabong, Botswana 26 2S 22 29E
88 Tshela, Zaïre 5 4S 13 0E
93 Tshesebe, Botswana 20 43S 27 32E
90 Tshibeke, Zaïre 2 40S 28 35E
90 Tshibinda, Zaïre 2 23S 28 30E
88 Tshikapa, Zaïre 6 17S 21 0E
90 Tshilenge, Zaïre 6 12S 23 40E
91 Tshinsenda, Congo 12 15N 28 0E
93 Tshombe, Malagasy Rep. 25 18S 45 29E
92 Tshwane, Botswana 22 24S 22 1E
76 Tsian, China 41 12N 126 5E
77 Tsiaotso, China 35 11N 113 37E
92 Tsigara, Botswana 20 22S 25 54E
87 Tsilmamo, Ethiopia 6 1N 35 10E
57 Tsimlyansk, U.S.S.R. 47 45N 42 0E
57 Tsimlyanskoye Vdkhr., U.S.S.R. 48 0N 43 0E
77 Tsinan, China 36 41N 116 59E
92 Tsineng, S. Africa 27 05S 23 05E
44 Tsinga, mt., Greece 41 23N 24 44E
75 Tsinghai, China 35 10N 96 0E
77 Tsinghsien, China 26 30N 109 30E
77 Tsingkiang, China 27 50N 114 38E
77 Tsingliu, China 26 0N 116 50E
77 Tsingshih, China 29 43N 112 13E
76 Tsingshuiho, China 39 56N 111 55E
77 Tsingsi (Kweishun), China 23 6N 106 25E

Tsingsi INDEX Umm al Aranib

MAP
76 Tsingsi, China 38 1N 114 4E
76 Tsingtung Hu, China 37 34N 105 40E
76 Tsingyuan, China 37 43N 104 35E
77 Tsingyun, China 23 45N 112 55E
77 Tsining, China 35 30N 116 35E
93 Tsinjomitondraka, Malag. 15 40S 47 8E
93 Tsiroanomandidy, Malag. 18 46S 46 2E
76 Tsitsihar, China 47 20N 124 0E
55 Tsivilsk, U.S.S.R. 55 50N 47 25E
93 Tsivory, Malagasy Rep. 24 4S 46 5E
57 Tskhinali, U.S.S.R. 42 14N 44 1E
92 Tsodilo Hill, Botswana 18 49S 21 43E
67 Tsona Dzong, China 28 0N 91 55E
74 Tsu, Japan 34 45N 136 25E
74 Tsuchiura, Japan 36 12N 140 15E
74 Tsugaru-Kaikyo, Japan 41 30N 140 30E
76 Tsuiluan, China 47 58N 28 27E
92 Tsumeb, S.W. Africa 19 9S 17 44E
92 Tsumis, S.W. Africa 23 39S 17 29E
77 Tsungfa, China 23 35N 113 35E
77 Tsungming Tao, China 31 40N 121 40E
77 Tsungtso, China 22 26N 107 34E
77 Tsunyi, China 27 40N 107 0E
74 Tsuruga, Japan 35 35N 136 0E
74 Tsushima, Japan 34 20N 129 20E
74 Tsushima-kaikyō, Japan 34 20N 130 0E
74 Tsuyama, Japan 35 0N 134 0E
56 Tsvetkovo, U.S.S.R. 49 15N 31 33E
93 Tswana ♦, S. Africa 24 0S 27 50E
71 Tu, R., Burma 22 50N 97 15E
31 Tua, R., Portugal 41 19N 7 15W
73 Tual, Indonesia 5 30S 132 50E
15 Tuam, Ireland 53 30N 8 50W
95 Tuamotu Arch = Touamotou, Pac. Oc. 17 0S 144 0W
73 Tuao, Philippines 17 47S 121 30E
57 Tuapse, U.S.S.R. 44 5N 39 10E
101 Tuatapere, N.Z. 48 7S 167 43E
119 Tuba City, U.S.A. 36 8N 111 12W
119 Tubac, U.S.A. 31 45N 111 2W
95 Tubai Is. = Toubouai, Iles, Pac. Oc. 25 0S 150 0W
72 Tuban, Indonesia 6 57S 112 4E
125 Tubarão, Brazil 28 30S 49 0W
62 Tubas, Jordan 32 20N 35 22E
72 Tubau, Malaysia 3 10N 113 40E
86 Tubayq, Jabal at, Jordan 29 30N 27 30E
24 Tübingen, Germany 48 31N 9 4E
86 Tubja, W., Si.-Arabia 25 27N 38 55E
81 Tubruq, (Tobruk), Libya 32 7N 23 55E
126 Tucacas, Venezuela 10 48N 68 19W
77 Tuchang, China 29 15N 116 15E
28 Tuchola, Poland 53 33N 17 52E
27 Tuchów, Poland 49 54N 21 1E
121 Tucker's Town, Bermuda 32 19N 64 43W
119 Tucson, U.S.A. 32 14N 110 59W
124 Tucumán, Argentina 26 50S 65 20W
124 Tucumán ♦, Arg. 26 48S 66 2W
117 Tucumcari, U.S.A. 35 12N 103 45W
126 Tucupido, Venezuela 9 17N 65 47W
126 Tucupita, Venezuela 9 14N 62 3W
126 Tucuracas, Colombia 11 45N 72 22W
28 Tuczno, Poland 53 13N 16 10E
32 Tudela, Spain 42 4N 1 39W
30 Tudela de Duero, Spain 41 37N 4 39W
107 Tudor, Lac, Canada 55 50N 65 0W
46 Tudora, Rumania 47 31N 26 45E
30 Tuella, R., Portugal 41 50N 7 10W
99 Tuen, Austral. 28 33S 145 37E
98 Tufi, Terr. of Papua 9 3S 149 16E
73 Tuguegarao, Philippines 17 35N 121 42E
59 Tugur, U.S.S.R. 53 50N 136 45E
92 Tugwa, Angola 17 27S 18 33E
77 Tuhshan, China 25 40N 107 30E
73 Tukangbesi, Kepulauan, Indonesia 6 0S 124 0E
106 Tukarak I., Canada 56 15N 78 10W
84 Tukobo, Ghana 5 1N 2 47W
83 Tūkrah, Libya 32 30N 20 37E
87 Tuku, mt., Ethiopia 9 10N 36 43E
54 Tukums, U.S.S.R. 57 2N 23 3E
91 Tukuyu, Tanzania 9 17S 33 35E
120 Tula, Hidalgo, Mexico 20 0N 99 20W
120 Tula, Tamaulipas, Mex. 23 0N 99 40W
85 Tula, Nigeria 9 51N 11 27E
55 Tula, U.S.S.R. 54 13N 37 32E
65 Tulak, Afghanistan 33 55N 63 40E
75 Tulan, China 37 24N 98 1E
119 Tulare, U.S.A. 36 15N 119 26W
119 Tulare Lake, U.S.A. 36 0N 119 53W
119 Tularosa, U.S.A. 33 4N 106 1W
92 Tulbagh, S. Africa 33 16S 19 6E
126 Tulcán, Ecuador 0 48N 77 43W
46 Tulcea, Rumania 45 13N 28 46E
46 Tulcea ♦, Rumania 45 0N 29 0E
56 Tulchin, U.S.S.R. 48 41N 28 55E
93 Tuléar, Malagasy Rep. 23 21S 43 40E
93 Tuléar ♦, Malag. 21 0S 45 0E
109 Tulemalu L., Canada 62 50N 100 0W
46 Tulghes, Rumania 4 58N 25 45E
73 Tuli, Indonesia 1 24S 122 26E
91 Tuli, Rhodesia 21 58S 29 13E
62 Tulkarm, Jordan 32 19N 35 10E
117 Tulla, U.S.A. 34 35N 101 44W
115 Tullahoma, U.S.A. 35 23N 86 12W
100 Tullamore, Australia 32 39S 147 36E
15 Tullamore, Ireland 53 17N 7 30W
20 Tulle, France 45 16N 0 47E
100 Tullibigeal, Australia 34 19S 146 20E
21 Tullins, France 45 18N 5 29E
26 Tulln, Austria 48 20N 16 4E
15 Tullow, Ireland 52 48N 6 45W
87 Tullus, Sudan 11 7N 24 40E
98 Tully, Austral. 17 30S 141 0E
81 Tulmaythah, Libya 32 40N 20 55E
98 Tulmur, Australia 22 40S 142 20E
46 Tulnici, Rumania 45 51N 26 38E
43 Tulovo, Bulgaria 42 33N 25 32E
117 Tulsa, U.S.A. 36 10N 96 0W
108 Tulsequah, Canada 58 39N 133 35W
MAP
87 Tulu Milki, Ethiopia 9 55N 38 14E
87 Tulu Welel, Mt., Ethiopia 8 56N 35 30E
126 Tulua, Colombia 4 6N 76 11W
59 Tulun, U.S.S.R. 54 40N 100 10E
73 Tulungagung, Indon. 8 5S 111 54E
73 Tum, Indonesia 3 28S 130 21E
55 Tuma, U.S.S.R. 55 10N 40 30E
121 Tuma, R., Nicaragua 13 18N 84 50W
126 Tumaco, Colombia 1 50N 78 45W
126 Tumatumari, Guyana 5 20N 58 55W
48 Tumba, Sweden 59 12N 17 48E
88 Tumba, L., Zaïre 0 50S 18 0E
100 Tumbarumba, Australia 35 44S 148 0E
124 Tumbaya, Argentina 23 50S 65 20W
126 Tumbes, Peru 3 30S 80 20W
91 Tumbwa, Zaïre 11 25S 27 15E
96 Tumby B., S. Australia 34 21S 136 8E
76 Tumen K., China 42 30N 130 0E
126 Tumeremo, Venezuela 7 18N 61 30W
70 Tumkur, India 13 18N 77 12E
49 Tumleberg, Sweden 58 16N 12 52E
14 Tummel L., Scot. 56 43N 3 55W
66 Tump, Pakistan 26 7N 62 16E
71 Tumpat, Malaysia 6 11N 102 10E
69 Tumsar, India 21 26N 79 45E
84 Tumu, Ghana 10 56N 1 56E
127 Tumucumaque, Serra de, Brazil 2 0N 55 0W
100 Tumut, Austral. 35 16S 148 13E
118 Tumwater, U.S.A. 47 0N 122 58W
121 Tunas de Zaza, Cuba 21 39N 79 34W
99 Tunbridge, Australia 42 5S 147 28E
13 Tunbridge Wells, England 51 7N 0 16E
100 Tuncurry, Australia 32 9S 152 29E
91 Tunduru, Tanzania 11 0S 37 25E
91 Tunduru ♦, Tanz. 11 5S 37 22E
43 Tundzha, R., Bulgaria 42 0N 26 35E
47 Tune, Norway 59 16N 11 2E
59 Tung-Pei, China 44 0N 126 0E
77 Tung-Shan, China 23 40N 117 25E
67 Tunga La, India-China 29 0N 94 14E
70 Tunga, R., India 13 42N 75 20E
70 Tungabhadra Dam, India 15 21N 76 23E
70 Tungabhadra, R., India 15 30N 77 0E
77 Tungcheng, China 31 0N 117 3E
76 Tungfanghsien, (Paso), China 18 50N 108 33E
76 Tunghwa, China 41 46N 126 0E
77 Tungien, China 27 45N 109 3E
77 Tungjen, China 27 40N 109 10E
77 Tungkang, Taiwan 22 18N 120 29E
76 Tungkiang, Heilungkiang, China 47 40N 132 30E
77 Tungkiang, Szechwan, China 31 55N 107 30E
77 Tungkun, China 23 0N 113 45E
77 Tungkwan, China 37 50N 116 35E
77 Tungkwan, China 34 40N 110 10E
120 Tungla, Nicaragua 13 24N 84 15W
77 Tunglan, China 24 30N 107 23E
76 Tungliao, China 43 42N 122 11E
77 Tungliu, China 31 0N 117 54E
77 Tunglu, China 29 50N 119 35E
50 Tungnafellsjökull, Iceland 64 45N 17 55W
76 Tungping, China 35 50N 116 20E
67 Tungpu, China 31 42N 98 19E
77 Tungshan, Fukien, China 23 40N 17 31E
77 Tungshan, Hupeh, China 29 36N 114 28E
108 Tungsten, Canada 61 52N 128 01W
118 Tungsten, U.S.A. 40 50N 118 10W
77 Tungtao, China 26 15N 109 25E
77 Tungting Hu, China 29 15N 112 30E
77 Tungtze, China 27 59N 106 56E
60 Tunguska, Nizhmaya, R., U.S.S.R. 64 0N 95 0E
59 Tunguska, Podkammenaya, R., U.S.S.R. 61 0N 98 0E
77 Tungyang, China 29 12N 120 12E
76 Tunhwa, China 43 27N 128 16E
75 Tunhwang, China 40 5N 94 46E
70 Tuni, India 17 22N 82 43E
126 Tunia, Colombia 2 41N 76 31W
117 Tunica, U.S.A. 34 43N 90 23W
83 Tunis, Tunisia 36 50N 10 11E
83 Tunis, Golfe de, Tunisia 37 0N 10 30E
83 Tunisia ■, Africa 33 30N 9 10E
126 Tunja, Colombia 5 40N 73 25W
113 Tunkhannock, U.S.A. 41 32N 75 56W
77 Tunki, China 29 44N 118 4E
76 Tunliu, China 36 15N 112 54E
50 Tunnsjöen, Norway 64 45N 13 25E
49 Tuno I., Denmark 55 58N 10 27E
107 Tunungayualuk I., Can. 56 0N 61 0W
124 Tunuyán, Argentina 33 55S 69 0W
124 Tunuyán, R., Argentina 33 33S 67 30W
119 Tuolumne, U.S.A. 37 59N 120 16W
59 Tuoy-Khaya, U.S.S.R. 62 32N 111 18E
125 Tupã, Brazil 21 57S 50 28W
126 Tuparro, R., Col. 5 0N 68 40W
115 Tupelo, U.S.A. 34 15N 88 42W
59 Tupik, U.S.S.R. 54 26N 119 57E
126 Tupinambaranas, I., Brazil 3 0S 58 0W
124 Tupiza, Bolivia 21 30S 65 40W
113 Tupper L., U.S.A. 44 18N 74 30W
124 Tupungato, Cerro, Arg.-Chile 33 15S 69 50W
126 Túquerres, Colombia 1 5N 77 37W
62 Tur, Jordan 31 47N 35 14E
69 Tura, India 25 30N 90 16E
59 Tura, U.S.S.R. 64 20N 99 30E
86 Turaba, W., Si. Arabia 21 15N 41 32E
126 Turagua, Serrania, Ven. 7 20N 64 35W
70 Turaiyur, India 11 9N 78 38E
65 Tūrān, Iran 35 45N 56 50E
59 Turan, U.S.S.R. 51 38N 101 40E
48 Tureburg, Sweden 59 30N 17 58E
30 Turégano, Spain 41 9N 4 1W
MAP
28 Turek, Poland 52 3N 18 30E
126 Turen, Venezuela 9 17N 69 6W
75 Turfan, China 43 6N 89 24E
75 Turfan Depression, China 43 0N 88 0E
43 Turgovishte, Bulgaria 43 17N 26 38E
64 Turgutlu, Turkey 38 30N 27 48E
56 Turhal, Turkey 40 24N 36 19E
32 Turia, R., Spain 39 43N 1 0W
127 Turiaçú, Brazil 1 40S 45 28W
127 Turiaçú, R., Brazil 3 0S 46 0W
27 Turiec, R., Cz. 48 52N 18 30E
38 Turin (Torino), Italy 45 3N 7 40E
108 Turin Taber, Canada 49 47N 112 24W
54 Turka, U.S.S.R. 49 10N 23 0E
90 Turkana ♦, Kenya 3 0N 35 30E
58 Turkestan, U.S.S.R. 43 10N 68 10E
27 Túrkeve, Hungary 47 6N 20 44E
64 Turkey ■, Europe & Asia 39 0N 36 0E
55 Turki, U.S.S.R. 52 0N 43 15E
58 Turkmenistan (Turkmen S.S.R.), U.S.S.R. 39 0N 59 0E
121 Turks Is., West Indies 21 20N 71 20W
121 Turks Island Passage, West Indies 21 30N 71 20W
51 Turku (Abo), Finland 60 27N 22 14E
51 Turku-Pori ♦, Fin. 2 30N 35 20E
90 Turkwell, R., Kenya 60 27N 22 15E
119 Turlock, U.S.A. 37 30N 120 55W
101 Turnagain, C., N.Z. 40 28S 176 38E
109 Turnberry, Canada 53 25N 101 45W
120 Turneffe Is., Br. Hond. 17 20N 87 50W
118 Turner, U.S.A. 48 52N 108 25W
108 Turner Valley, Canada 50 40N 114 30W
113 Turners Falls, U.S.A. 42 36N 72 34W
16 Turnhout, Belgium 51 19N 4 57E
26 Türnitz, Austria 47 55N 15 29E
109 Turnor L., Canada 56 35N 108 50W
26 Turnov, Czechoslovakia 50 34N 15 10E
43 Turnovo, Bulgaria 43 5N 25 41E
43 Turnovo ♦, Bulg. 43 4N 25 39E
46 Turnu Măgurele, Rum. 43 46N 24 56E
46 Turnu Roşu Pasul, Rum. 45 33N 24 17E
46 Turnu-Severin, Rum. 44 39N 22 41E
49 Turö, Denmark 55 2N 10 40E
117 Turon, U.S.A. 37 48N 98 27W
14 Turriff, Scot. 57 32N 2 28W
55 Tursha, U.S.S.R. 56 50N 47 45E
41 Tursi, Italy 40 15N 16 27E
98 Turtle Hd. I., Austral. 10 50S 142 37E
116 Turtle L., N.D., U.S.A. 47 30N 100 55W
116 Turtle L., Wis., U.S.A. 45 22N 92 10W
109 Turtleford, Canada 53 30N 108 50W
64 Turubah, Saudi Arabia 28 20N 43 15E
59 Turukhansk, U.S.S.R. 65 50N 87 50E
51 Turun ja Porin lääni ♦, Finland 60 27N 22 15E
27 Turzovka, Cz. 49 25N 18 41E
115 Tuscaloosa, U.S.A. 33 13N 87 31W
39 Tuscánia, Italy 42 25N 11 53E
38 Tuscany = Toscana, Italy 43 28N 11 15E
15 Tuscar Rock, Ire. 52 10N 6 15W
114 Tuscola, Ill., U.S.A. 39 48N 88 15W
117 Tuscola, Tex., U.S.A. 32 15N 99 48W
115 Tuscumbia, U.S.A. 34 42N 87 42W
55 Tushino, U.S.S.R. 55 44N 37 29E
115 Tuskegee, U.S.A. 32 24N 85 39W
47 Tustna, Norway 63 10N 8 5E
28 Tuszyn, Poland 51 36N 19 33E
49 Tutaryd, Sweden 56 54N 13 59E
70 Tuticorin, India 8 50N 78 12E
42 Tutin, Yugoslavia 43 0N 20 20E
127 Tutóia, Brazil 2 45S 42 20W
72 Tutong, Brunei 4 47N 114 34E
46 Tutova, R., Rumania 46 20N 27 30E
43 Tutrakan, Bulgaria 44 2N 26 40E
25 Tuttlingen, Germany 47 59N 8 50E
73 Tutuaia, Portuguese Timor 8 25S 127 15E
101 Tutuila, I., Amer. Samoa 14 19S 170 50W
76 Tuul Gol, R., Mongolia 48 30N 104 25E
59 Tuva, A.S.S.R. ♦, U.S.S.R. 51 30N 95 0E
120 Tuxpan, Mexico 20 50N 97 30W
120 Tuxtla Gutiérrez, Mex. 16 50N 93 10W
30 Tuy, Spain 42 3N 8 39W
71 Tuy Hoa, S. Vietnam 13 5N 109 17E
71 Tuyen Hoa, S. Vietnam 17 55N 106 3E
77 Tuyun, China 26 15N 107 32E
64 Tuz Gölü, Turkey 38 45N 33 30E
64 Tuz Khurmatli, Iraq 34 52N 44 41E
64 Tuz Khurmatu, Iraq 34 50N 44 45E
42 Tuzla, Yugoslavia 44 34N 18 41E
57 Tuzlov, R., U.S.S.R. 47 28N 39 45E
49 Tvååker, Sweden 57 4N 12 25E
49 Tvaersted, Denmark 57 36N 10 12E
49 Tvarskog, Sweden 56 34N 16 0E
49 Tved, Denmark 56 12N 10 25E
47 Tvedestrand, Norway 58 38N 8 58E
47 Tvelt, Norway 60 30N 7 11E
47 Tveitsund, Norway 59 2N 8 31E
43 Tvyrditsa, Bulgaria 42 42N 25 53E
28 Twardogóra, Poland 51 23N 17 28E
112 Tweed, Canada 44 30N 77 20W
12 Tweed, R., Scot. 55 42N 2 10W
108 Tweedsmuir Prov. Park, Canada 53 10N 126 20W
15 Twelve Pins, Ire. 53 32N 9 50W
119 Twentynine Palms, U.S.A. 34 10N 116 4W
107 Twillingate, Canada 49 42N 54 45W
118 Twin Bridges, U.S.A. 45 33N 112 23W
118 Twin Falls, U.S.A. 42 30N 114 30W
116 Twin Valley, U.S.A. 47 18N 96 15W
118 Twisp, U.S.A. 48 21N 120 5W
24 Twistringen, Germany 52 48N 8 38E
116 Two Harbors, U.S.A. 47 6N 91 30W
MAP
114 Two Rivers, U.S.A. 44 10N 87 31W
98 Two Tree, Australia 18 25S 140 3E
100 Twofold B., Australia 37 8S 149 59E
87 Twong, Sudan 5 18N 28 29E
49 Ty, Denmark 56 27N 8 32E
49 Tyborön, Denmark 56 42N 8 12E
27 Tychy, Poland 50 9N 18 59E
27 Tyczyn, Poland 49 58N 22 2E
28 Tykocin, Poland 53 13N 22 46E
47 Tyldal, Norway 62 8N 10 48E
116 Tyler, Minn., U.S.A. 44 18N 96 15W
117 Tyler, Tex., U.S.A. 44 18N 96 15W
47 Tylldal, Norway 62 7N 10 45E
49 Tylösand, Sweden 56 33N 12 40E
26 Týn nad Vltavou, Cz. 49 13N 14 26E
59 Tyndinskiy, U.S.S.R. 55 10N 124 43E
12 Tyne, R., Eng. 54 58N 1 56W
12 Tynemouth, Eng. 55 1N 1 27W
47 Tynset, Norway 62 17N 10 47E
62 Tyre = Sūr, Lebanon 33 19N 35 16E
100 Tyrell Creek, Australia 35 22S 143 0E
100 Tyrell L., Austral. 35 22S 143 0E
100 Tyrendarra, Australia 38 12S 141 50E
47 Tyrifjorden, Nor. 60 2N 10 8E
49 Tyringe, Sweden 56 9N 13 35E
47 Tyristrand, Norway 60 5N 10 5E
76 Tyrma, U.S.S.R. 50 0N 132 2E
57 Tyrnyauz, U.S.S.R. 43 21N 42 45E
26 Tyrol = Tirol, Austria 46 50N 11 20E
*15 Tyrone ♦, N. Ire. 54 40N 7 15W
112 Tyrone, U.S.A. 40 39N 78 10W
34 Tyrrhenian Sea, Europe 40 0N 12 30E
50 Tysfjörden, Norway 68 10N 16 10E
47 Tysnes, Norway 60 1N 5 30E
47 Tyssedal, Norway 60 7N 6 35E
49 Tystberga, Sweden 58 51N 17 15E
54 Tysmenitsa, U.S.S.R. 48 58N 24 50E
58 Tyumen, U.S.S.R. 57 0N 65 18E
47 Tyvoll, Norway 62 43N 11 21E
13 Tywi, R., Wales 52 2N 3 53W
93 Tzaneen, S. Afr. 23 47S 30 9E
77 Tzechung, China 29 47N 104 50E
62 Tzefa, Israel 31 7N 35 12E
77 Tzeki, China 27 40N 117 5E
77 Tzekung, China 29 25N 104 30E
77 Tzekwei, China 31 0N 110 46E
76 Tzepo, China 36 28N 117 58E
45 Tzermiadhes Neapolis, Greece 35 11N 25 29E
77 Tzetung, China 31 31N 105 1E
44 Tzoumérka, Óros, Greece 39 30N 21 26E
67 Tzuchien, China 27 43N 98 34E
77 Tzuyang, China 35 44N 116 51E
82 Uad Erni, O., Spanish Sahara 26 30N 9 30W
126 Uainambi, Colombia 1 43N 69 51W
63 Uarsciek, Somali Rep. 2 28N 45 55E
126 Uasadi-jidi, Sierra, Ven. 4 54N 65 18W
90 Uasin ♦, Kenya 0 30N 35 20E
62 Uassem, Syria 32 59N 36 2E
73 Uato-Udo, Port Timor 4 3S 126 6E
126 Uatumã, R., Brazil 1 30S 59 25W
126 Uaupés, Brazil 0 8S 67 5W
42 Ub, Yugoslavia 44 28N 20 6E
125 Ubá, Brazil 21 0S 43 0W
126 Ubaté, Colombia 5 19N 73 49W
68 Ubauro, Pakistan 28 15N 69 45E
74 Ube, Japan 34 6N 131 20E
33 Ubeda, Spain 38 3N 3 23W
127 Uberaba, Brazil 19 50S 47 55W
127 Uberlândia, Brazil 19 0S 48 20W
85 Ubiaja, Nigeria 6 41N 6 22E
93 Ubombo, S. Africa 27 31S 32 4E
71 Ubon Ratchathani, Thailand 15 15N 104 50E
90 Ubondo, Zaïre 0 55S 25 42E
54 Ubort, R., U.S.S.R. 51 45N 28 30E
31 Ubrique, Spain 36 41N 5 27W
90 Ubundi, Zaïre 0 22S 25 30E
126 Ucayali, R., Peru 6 0S 75 0W
109 Uchi Lake, Canada 51 10N 92 40W
74 Uchiura-Wan, Japan 42 25N 140 40E
24 Uchte, Germany 52 29N 8 52E
24 Uckerath, W. Germany 50 44N 7 22E
108 Ucluelet, Canada 48 57N 125 32W
46 Ucuriş, Rumania 46 41N 21 58E
59 Uda, R., U.S.S.R. 54 42N 135 14E
68 Udaipur, India 24 36N 73 44E
69 Udaipur Garhi, Nepal 27 0N 86 35E
70 Udamalpet, India 10 35N 77 15E
39 Udbina, Yugoslavia 44 31N 15 47E
48 Uddeholm, Sweden 60 1N 13 38E
49 Uddevalla, Sweden 58 21N 11 55E
50 Uddjaur, Sweden 65 55N 17 50E
70 Udgir, India 18 25N 77 5E
68 Udhampur, Kashmir 33 0N 75 5E
85 Udi, Nigeria 6 23N 7 21E
39 Údine, Italy 46 5N 13 10E
39 Údine ♦, Italy 46 3N 13 13E
70 Udipi, India 13 25N 74 42E
52 Udmurt, A.S.S.R. ♦, U.S.S.R. 57 30N 52 30E
71 Udon Thani, Thailand 17 29N 102 46E
85 Udubo, Nigeria 11 52N 10 35E
43 Udvoj Balken, Bulgaria 42 50N 26 50E
91 Udzungwa Range, Tanz. 11 15S 35 10E
24 Ueckermünde, Ger. 53 45N 14 1E
74 Ueda, Japan 36 30N 138 10E
4 Uedineniya, O., U.S.S.R. 78 0N 85 0E
59 Uelen, U.S.S.R. 66 10N 170 0W
24 Uelzen, Germany 53 0N 10 33E
88 Uere, R., Zaïre 3 45N 24 45E
52 Ufa, U.S.S.R. 54 45N 55 55E
52 Ufa, R., U.S.S.R. 56 30N 58 10E
90 Ugalla, R., Tanzania 6 0S 32 0E
92 Ugamas, S.W. Africa 28 0S 19 41E
90 Uganda ■, E. Africa 2 0N 32 0E
41 Ugento, Italy 39 55N 18 10E
85 Ugep, Nigeria 5 53N 8 2E
MAP
93 Ugie, S. Africa 31 10S 28 13E
33 Ugijar, Spain 36 58N 3 7W
21 Ugine, France 45 45N 6 25E
86 Ugla, Saudi Arabia 25 40N 37 42E
55 Uglich, U.S.S.R. 57 33N 38 13E
39 Ugljane, Yugoslavia 43 35N 16 46E
54 Ugra, R., U.S.S.R. 54 45N 35 30E
43 Ugurchin, Bulgaria 43 6N 24 26E
27 Uh, R., Czechoslovakia 48 40N 22 0E
27 Uherske Hradiště, Cz. 49 4N 17 30E
27 Uhersky Brod, Cz. 49 1N 17 40E
112 Uhrichsville, U.S.A. 40 23N 81 22W
88 Uige ♦, Angola 7 0S 15 30E
76 Uiji, North Korea 40 15N 124 35E
118 Uinta Mts., U.S.A. 40 45N 110 30W
92 Uitenhage, S. Africa 33 40S 25 28E
16 Uithuizen, Netherlands 53 24N 6 41E
82 Ujda = Oujda, Morocco 34 45N 2 0W
27 Ujfehértó, Hungary 47 49N 21 41E
68 Ujhani, India 28 0N 79 6E
77 Uji-guntō, Japan 31 15N 129 25E
68 Ujjain, India 23 9N 75 43E
27 Újpest, Hungary 47 22N 19 6E
27 Ujszász, Hungary 47 19N 20 7E
59 Uka, U.S.S.R. 57 50N 162 0E
90 Ukara I., Tanzania 1 44S 33 0E
85 Ukehe, Nigeria 6 40N 7 24E
90 Ukerewe Is., Tanzania 2 0S 33 0E
90 Ukerewe ♦, Tanzania 2 0S 32 30E
55 Ukholovo, U.S.S.R. 54 47N 40 30E
67 Ukhrul, India 25 10N 94 25E
52 Ukhta, U.S.S.R. 63 55N 54 0E
118 Ukiah, U.S.A. 39 10N 123 9W
54 Ukmerge, U.S.S.R. 55 15N 24 45E
56 Ukraine S.S.R. ♦, U.S.S.R. 48 0N 35 0E
92 Ukwi, Botswana 23 29S 20 30E
76 Ulaanbaatar, Mongolia 47 54N 106 52E
75 Ulaangom, Mongolia 50 0N 92 10E
91 Ulamba, Zaïre 9 3S 23 38E
76 Ulan-Bator = Ulaanbaatar, Mongolia 47 54N 106 52E
59 Ulan Ude, U.S.S.R. 52 0N 107 30E
91 Ulanga ♦, Tanzania 8 40S 36 50E
76 Ulanhot, China 46 5N 122 1E
28 Ulanów, Poland 50 30N 22 16E
90 Ulaya, Shinyanga, Tanzania 4 25S 33 30E
90 Ulaya, Morogoro, Tanzania 7 3S 36 55E
42 Ulcinj, Yugoslavia 41 58N 19 10E
92 Ulco, S. Africa 28 21S 24 15E
76 Uldz Gol, Mongolia 49 30N 114 0E
47 Ulefoss, Norway 59 17N 9 16E
44 Ulëza, Albania 41 46N 19 57E
49 Ulfborg, Denmark 56 16N 8 20E
70 Ulhasnagar, India 19 15N 73 10E
42 Uljma, Yugoslavia 45 2N 21 10E
30 Ulla, R., Spain 42 45N 8 30W
100 Ulladulla, Australia 35 21S 150 29E
48 Ullånger, Sweden 62 58N 18 16E
14 Ullapool, Scot. 57 54N 5 10W
49 Ullared, Sweden 57 8N 12 42E
32 Ulldecona, Spain 40 36N 0 20E
12 Ullswater, L., Eng. 54 35N 2 52W
76 Ullung Do, S. Korea 37 30N 130 30E
48 Ullvättern, L., Sweden 59 30N 14 21E
25 Ulm, Germany 48 23N 10 0E
100 Ulmarra, Australia 29 31S 153 6E
46 Ulmeni, Rumania 45 4N 46 40E
46 Ulmu, Rumania 44 16N 27 0E
49 Ulricehamn, Sweden 57 46N 13 26E
47 Ulsberg, Norway 62 45N 9 59E
47 Ulsfeinvik, Norway 62 21N 5 53E
15 Ulster ♦, N. Ire. 54 45N 6 30W
43 Ulstrem, Bulgaria 42 1N 26 27E
100 Ultima, Australia 35 22S 143 18E
69 Ulubaria, India 22 31N 88 4E
67 Ulugh Muztagh, China 36 40N 87 30E
90 Uluguru Mts., Tanzania 7 15S 37 30E
12 Ulverston, Eng. 54 13N 3 7W
99 Ulverstone, Australia 41 11S 146 11E
47 Ulvik, Norway 60 35N 6 54E
49 Ulvo, Sweden 56 40N 14 37E
59 Ulya, U.S.S.R. 59 10N 142 0E
55 Ulyanovsk, U.S.S.R. 54 25N 48 25E
75 Ulyasutay, (Javhlant), Mongolia 47 56N 97 28E
117 Ulysses, U.S.A. 37 39N 101 25W
62 Um Qeis, Jordan 32 40N 35 41E
39 Umag, Yugoslavia 45 26N 13 31E
126 Umala, Bolivia 17 25S 68 5W
56 Uman, U.S.S.R. 48 40N 30 12E
4 Umánaé, Greenland 70 40N 52 10W
2 Umánaé Fjord, Greenland 70 40N 52 0W
70 Umarkhed, India 19 37N 77 38E
68 Umarkot, Pakistan 25 15N 69 40E
118 Umatilla, U.S.A. 45 58N 119 17W
39 Umbertide, Italy 43 18N 12 20E
98 Umboi I., Terr. of New Guinea 5 59S 148 0E
101 Umbrella Mts., N.Z. 45 35S 169 5E
39 Umbria ♦, Italy 42 53N 12 30E
50 Ume, R., Sweden 64 45N 18 30E
50 Umeå, Sweden 63 45N 20 20E
73 Umera, Indonesia 0 12S 129 30E
91 Umfuli, R., Rhodesia 17 50S 29 40E
91 Umgusa, Rhodesia 19 29S 27 52E
42 Umka, Yugoslavia 44 40N 20 19E
93 Umkomaas, S. Africa 30 13S 30 48E
65 Umm al Qaiwain, Trucial States 25 30N 55 35E
87 Umm Arda, Sudan 15 17N 32 31E
65 Umm az Zamul, Muscat & Oman 22 35N 55 18E
87 Umm Bel, Sudan 13 35N 28 0E
87 Umm Digulgulaya, Sud. 10 28N 24 58E
87 Umm Dubban, Sudan 15 23N 32 52E
83 Umm al Aranib, Libya 26 10N 14 54E

* In April 1973 districts replaced counties in N. Ireland

Varteig INDEX Villalón de Campos

MAP
47 Varteig, Norway 59 23N 11 12E
64 Varto, Turkey 39 10N 41 28E
49 Vartofta, Sweden 58 6N 13 40E
42 Varvarin, Yugoslavia 43 43N 21 20E
65 Varzaneh, Iran 32 25N 52 40E
38 Varzi, Italy 44 50N 9 12E
38 Varzo, Italy 46 12N 8 15E
19 Varzy, France 47 22N 3 20E
27 Vas ♦, Hungary 47 10N 16 55E
27 Vásárosnamény, Hung. 48 9N 22 19E
49 Väsby, Sweden 56 13N 12 37E
31 Vascão, R., Portugal 37 44N 8 15W
46 Vaşcău, Rumania 46 28N 22 30E
32 Vascongadas, Sp. 42 50N 2 45W
48 Väse, Sweden 59 23N 13 52E
65 Vasht = Khāsh, Iran 28 20N 61 6E
43 Vasil Levski, Bulgaria 43 23N 25 26E
54 Vasilevichi, U.S.S.R. 52 15N 29 50E
45 Vasilikón, Greece 38 25N 23 40E
54 Vasilkov, U.S.S.R. 50 7N 30 28E
46 Vaslui, Rumania 46 38N 27 42E
47 Vaslui ♦, Rumania 46 30N 27 30E
48 Väsman, Sweden 60 9N 15 5E
109 Vassar, Canada 49 10N 95 55W
114 Vassar, U.S.A. 43 23N 83 33W
48 Vast Silen, L., Sweden 59 15N 12 15E
49 Västerås, Sweden 59 37N 16 38E
50 Västerbottens län ♦, Swed. 64 58N 18 0E
48 Västerdalälven, Swed. 60 50N 13 25E
48 Västernorrlands län ♦, Sweden 63 30N 17 40E
49 Västervik, Sweden 57 43N 16 43E
48 Västmanland ♦, Swed. 59 55N 16 30E
39 Vasto, Italy 42 8N 14 40E
27 Vasvár, Hungary 47 3N 16 47E
19 Vatan, France 47 4N 1 50E
45 Vathi, Greece 37 46N 27 1E
45 Váthia, Greece 36 29N 22 29E
39 Vatican City, Italy 41 54N 12 27E
42 Vatin, Yugoslavia 45 12N 21 20E
50 Vatnajökull, Ice. 64 30N 16 48W
47 Vatne, Norway 62 33N 6 38E
50 Vatneyri, Iceland 65 35N 24 0W
47 Vatnås, Norway 59 58N 9 37E
101 Vatoa, I., Fiji 19 50S 178 13W
93 Vatoloha, Mt., Malag. 17 52S 47 48E
93 Vatomandry, Malag. 19 20S 48 59E
46 Vatra-Dornei, Rum. 47 22N 25 22E
47 Vats, Norway 59 29N 5 45E
49 Vättern, L., Sweden 58 25N 14 30E
21 Vaucluse ♦, France 44 3N 5 10E
19 Vaucouleurs, France 48 37N 5 40E
25 Vaud ♦, Switzerland 46 35N 6 30E
119 Vaughan, U.S.A. 34 37N 105 12W
118 Vaughn, U.S.A. 47 37N 111 36W
126 Vaupés, R., Colombia 1 0N 71 0W
126 Vaupés ♦, Colombia 1 0N 71 0W
21 Vauvert, France 43 42N 4 17E
108 Vauxhall, Canada 50 5N 112 9W
101 Vavău, I., Tonga 18 36S 174 0W
19 Vavincourt, France 48 49N 5 12E
84 Vavoua, Ivory Coast 7 23N 6 29W
48 Vaxholm, Sweden 59 25N 18 20E
49 Växjö, Sweden 56 52N 14 50E
58 Vaygach, Ostrov, U.S.S.R. 70 0N 60 0E
127 Vaza Barris, R., Brazil 10 0S 37 30W
24 Vechta, Germany 52 47N 8 18E
16 Vechte, R., Netherlands 52 34N 6 6E
27 Vecsés, Hungary 47 26N 19 19E
70 Vedaraniam, India 10 25N 79 50E
49 Vedbaek, Denmark 55 50N 12 33E
49 Veddige, Sweden 57 17N 12 20E
46 Vedea, R., Rumania 44 0N 25 20E
124 Vedia, Argentina 34 30S 61 31W
33 Vedra, Isla del, Spain 38 52N 1 12E
13 Veendam, Netherlands 53 5N 6 52E
16 Veenendaal, Neth. 52 2N 5 34E
50 Vefsna, Norway 65 48N 13 10E
50 Vega, Norway 65 40N 11 55E
117 Vega, U.S.A. 35 18N 102 26W
50 Vega Fd., Norway 65 37N 12 0E
30 Vegadeo, Spain 43 27N 7 4W
24 Vegesack, Germany 53 10N 8 38E
50 Vegfjorden, Norway 65 37N 12 0E
49 Veggerby, Denmark 56 54N 9 39E
47 Veggli, Norway 60 3N 9 9E
16 Veghel, Netherlands 51 37N 5 32E
44 Vegorritis, Limni, Gr. 40 45N 21 45E
108 Vegreville, Canada 53 30N 112 5W
47 Vegusdal, Norway 58 32N 8 10E
39 Veii, Italy 42 0N 12 24E
124 Veinticino de Mayo, Arg. 38 0S 67 40W
49 Vejen, Denmark 55 30N 9 9E
31 Vejer de la Frontera, Spain 36 15N 5 59W
49 Vejle, Denmark 55 43N 9 30E
49 Vejle Amt ♦, Den. 55 2N 11 22E
49 Vejle Fjord, Denmark 55 40N 9 50E
49 Vejlo, Denmark 55 10N 11 45E
39 Vela Luka, Yugoslavia 42 59N 16 44E
70 Velanai I., Sri Lanka 9 45N 79 45E
119 Velarde, U.S.A. 36 11N 106 1W
117 Velasco, U.S.A. 29 0N 95 20W
124 Velasco, Sierra de., Arg. 29 20S 67 10W
20 Velay, Mts. du, France 45 0N 3 40E
92 Velddrif, S. Africa 32 42S 18 11E
39 Velebit Planina, Y.-slav. 44 50N 15 20E
39 Velebitski Kanal, Yugoslavia 44 45N 14 55E
43 Veleka, R., Bulgaria 42 4N 27 30E
39 Velenje, Yugoslavia 46 23N 15 8E
45 Velestinon, Greece 39 23N 22 43E
126 Vélez, Colombia 6 1N 73 41W
42 Velez, mt., Yugoslavia 43 19N 18 2E
31 Vélez Blanco, Spain 37 41N 2 5W
31 Vélez Málaga, Spain 36 48N 4 5W
33 Vélez Rubio, Spain 37 41N 2 5W

MAP
127 Velhas, R., Brazil 17 13S 44 49W
42 Velika, Yugoslavia 45 27N 17 40E
39 Velika Goricá, Y.-slavia 45 44N 16 5E
39 Velika Kapela, Y.-slav. 45 10N 15 5E
39 Velika Kladuša, Y.-slav. 45 11N 15 48E
42 Velika Morava, R., Yugoslavia 44 30N 21 9E
42 Velika Plana, Y.-slavia 44 20N 21 1E
54 Velikaya, R., U.S.S.R. 56 40N 28 40E
27 Veliké Kapušany, Cz. 48 34N 22 5E
39 Velike Lašče, Y.-slavia 45 49N 14 45E
44 Veliki Backa Kanal, Yugoslavia 45 45N 19 15E
42 Veliki Jastrebac, Yugoslavia 43 25N 21 30E
52 Veliki Ustyug, U.S.S.R. 60 47N 46 20E
54 Velikiye Luki, U.S.S.R. 56 25N 30 32E
43 Veliko Turnovo, Bulgaria 43 5N 25 41E
70 Velikonda Range, India 14 45N 79 10E
55 Velikoye, Oz., U.S.S.R. 55 15N 40 0E
43 Velingrad, Bulgaria 42 4N 23 58E
39 Velino, Mt., Italy 42 10N 13 20E
54 Velizh, U.S.S.R. 55 30N 31 11E
27 Velké Karlovice, Cz. 49 20N 18 17E
26 Velke Mezirici, Cz. 49 21N 16 1E
27 Velký ostrov Zitný, Cz. 48 5N 17 20E
70 Vellar, R., India 11 30N 79 36E
40 Velletri, Italy 41 43N 12 43E
49 Velling, Denmark 56 2N 8 20E
49 Vellinge, Sweden 55 29N 13 0E
50 Vellir, Iceland 65 55N 18 28W
70 Vellore, India 12 57N 79 10E
16 Velsen, Netherlands 52 27N 4 40E
52 Velsk, U.S.S.R. 61 10N 42 5E
24 Velten, Germany 52 40N 13 11E
116 Velva, U.S.A. 48 6N 100 56W
44 Velvendós, Greece 40 15N 22 6E
49 Vem, Denmark 56 21N 8 21E
70 Vembanad Lake, India 9 36N 76 15E
47 Veme, Norway 60 14N 10 7E
49 Ven, Sweden 55 55N 12 45E
49 Vena, Sweden 57 31N 16 0E
120 Venado, Mexico 22 50N 101 10W
124 Venado Tuerto, Arg. 33 50S 62 0W
41 Venafro, Italy 41 28N 14 3E
19 Venarey, France 47 32N 4 26E
38 Venaria, Italy 45 12N 7 39E
42 Venčane, Yugoslavia 44 24N 20 28E
21 Vence, France 43 43N 7 6E
31 Vendas Novas, Portugal 38 39N 8 27W
18 Vendée, France 46 50N 1 35W
18 Vendée, Collines de, France 46 35N 0 45W
18 Vendée, R., France 46 30N 0 45W
20 Vendée ♦, France 46 40N 1 20W
19 Vendeuvres, France 48 14N 4 27E
19 Vendôme, France 47 47N 1 3E
32 Vendrell, Spain 41 10N 1 30E
57 Vendsyssel, Den. 57 22N 10 0E
39 Veneta, Laguna, Italy 45 19N 12 13E
39 Véneto ♦, Italy 45 30N 12 0E
55 Venev, U.S.S.R. 54 22N 38 17E
39 Venézia, Italy 45 27N 12 20E
39 Venézia, Golfo di, Italy 45 20N 13 0E
126 Venezuela ■, S. Amer. 8 0N 65 0W
126 Venezuela, Golfo de, Ven. 11 30N 71 0W
70 Vengurla, India 15 53N 73 45E
70 Vengurla Rocks, India 15 50N 73 22E
39 Venice = Venézia, Italy 45 27N 12 20E
21 Vénissieux, France 45 43N 4 53E
48 Venjansjön, Sweden 60 58N 14 2E
70 Venkatagiri, India 14 0N 79 35E
70 Venkatapuram, India 18 20N 80 30E
16 Venlo, Netherlands 51 22N 6 11E
47 Vennesla, Norway 58 15N 8 0E
49 Venö, Is., Denmark 56 33N 8 38E
16 Venraij, Netherlands 51 31N 6 0E
31 Venta de Cardeña, Sp. 38 16N 4 20W
30 Venta de San Rafael, Spain 40 42N 4 12W
120 Ventana, Punta de la, Mexico 24 4N 109 48W
92 Ventersburg, S. Africa 28 7S 27 9E
38 Ventimíglia, Italy 43 50N 7 39E
13 Ventnor, Eng. 50 35N 1 12W
40 Ventotene, I., Italy 40 48N 13 25E
54 Ventspils, U.S.S.R. 57 25N 21 32E
126 Ventuari, R., Venezuela 5 20N 66 0W
119 Ventura, U.S.A. 34 16N 119 25W
47 Veoy, Norway 62 45N 7 30E
47 Veoy Is., Norway 62 45N 7 30E
124 Vera, Argentina 29 30S 60 20W
33 Vera, Spain 37 15N 1 15W
120 Veracruz, Mexico 19 10N 96 10W
120 Veracruz ♦, Mexico 19 0N 96 15W
68 Veraval, India 20 53N 70 27E
38 Verbánia, Italy 45 50N 8 55E
41 Verbicaro, Italy 39 46N 15 54E
38 Vercelli, Italy 45 19N 8 25E
128 Verde, R., Argentina 41 55S 66 0W
120 Verde, R., Veracruz, Mexico 21 10N 102 50W
124 Verde, R., Paraguay 23 9S 57 37W
44 Verdhikoúsa, Greece 39 47N 21 59E
30 Veriña, Spain 43 32N 5 43W
116 Verdigre, U.S.A. 42 38N 98 0W
19 Verdun, France 49 12N 5 24E
19 Verdun-sur-le Doubs, Fr. 46 54N 5 0E
93 Vereeniging, S. Africa 26 38S 27 57E
32 Vergara, Spain 43 9N 2 28W
38 Vergato, Italy 44 18N 11 8E
113 Vergennes, U.S.A. 44 9N 73 15W
20 Vergt, France 45 2N 0 43E
30 Verín, Spain 41 57N 7 27W
30 Veriña, Spain 43 32N 5 43W
55 Verkhnedvinsk, U.S.S.R. 55 45N 27 58E
59 Verkhneye Kalinino, U.S.S.R. 60 0N 108 15E

MAP
57 Verkhniy Baskunchak, U.S.S.R. 48 5N 46 50E
55 Verkhovye, U.S.S.R. 52 55N 37 15E
59 Verkhoyansk, U.S.S.R. 67 50N 133 50E
59 Verkhoyanskiy Khrebet, U.S.S.R. 66 0N 129 0E
109 Verlo, Canada 50 25N 108 35W
47 Verma, Norway 62 21N 8 3E
19 Vermenton, France 47 40N 3 42E
109 Vermilion, Canada 53 20N 110 50W
109 Vermilion Bay, Canada 49 50N 93 20W
117 Vermilion, B., U.S.A. 29 45N 91 55W
116 Vermillion, U.S.A. 42 50N 96 56W
118 Vernal, U.S.A. 40 28N 109 35W
106 Verner, Canada 46 25N 80 8W
18 Verneuil, France 48 45N 0 56E
108 Vernon, Canada 50 20N 119 15W
18 Vernon, France 49 5N 1 30E
117 Vernon, U.S.A. 34 0N 99 15W
115 Vero Beach, U.S.A. 27 39N 80 23W
44 Véroia, Greece 40 34N 22 18E
38 Verolanuova, Italy 45 20N 10 5E
40 Véroli, Italy 41 43N 13 24E
38 Verona, Italy 45 27N 11 0E
59 Veropol, U.S.S.R. 66 0N 168 0E
19 Versailles, France 48 48N 2 8E
84 Vert, C., Senegal 14 45N 17 30W
18 Vertou, France 47 10N 1 28W
19 Vertus, France 48 54N 4 0E
93 Verulam, S. Afr. 29 38S 31 2E
16 Verviers, Belgium 50 37N 5 52E
19 Vervins, France 49 50N 3 53E
109 Verwood, Canada 49 30N 105 40W
39 Verzej, Yugoslavia 46 34N 16 13E
26 Veselí nad Luznicí, Cz. 49 12N 14 15E
43 Veselie, Bulgaria 42 18N 27 38E
57 Veselovskoye Vdkhr., U.S.S.R. 47 0N 41 0E
57 Veselyy Res., U.S.S.R. 47 0N 41 0E
57 Veshenskaya, U.S.S.R. 49 35N 41 44E
19 Vesle, R., France 49 17N 3 50E
19 Vesoul, France 60 40N 6 11E
49 Vessigebro, Sweden 56 58N 12 40E
47 Vest-Agder fylke ♦, Norway 58 30N 7 15E
47 Vest Fjorden, Norway 68 0N 15 0E
47 Vestby, Norway 59 37N 10 45E
49 Vester Hassing, Den. 57 4N 10 8E
50 Vestfjorden, Norway 67 55N 14 0E
47 Vestfold fylke ♦, Norway 59 15N 10 0E
49 Vestjaellands Amt ♦, Denmark 55 30N 11 20E
50 Vestmannaeyjar, Ice. 63 27N 20 15W
47 Vestmarka, Norway 59 56N 11 59E
47 Vestnes, Norway 62 39N 7 5E
38 Vestone, Italy 45 43N 10 25E
4 Vestspitsbergen, Svalbard 78 40N 17 0E
50 Vestvågöy, Norway 68 18N 13 50E
41 Vesuvio, Italy 40 50N 14 22E
27 Veszprém, Hungary 47 8N 17 57E
27 Veszprém ♦, Hungary 47 5N 17 55E
27 Vésztő, Hungary 46 55N 21 16E
70 Vetapalam, India 15 47N 80 18E
49 Vetlanda, Sweden 57 24N 15 3E
55 Vetluga, U.S.S.R. 57 53N 45 45E
55 Vetluzhskiy, U.S.S.R. 57 17N 45 12E
43 Vetovo, Bulgaria 43 42N 26 16E
39 Vetralia, Italy 42 20N 12 2E
43 Vetren, Bulgaria 42 15N 24 3E
39 Vettore, Mte., Italy 44 38N 7 5E
16 Veurne, Belgium 51 5N 2 40E
25 Vevey, Switzerland 46 28N 6 51E
44 Vévi, Greece 40 47N 21 38E
64 Veys, Iran 31 30N 49 0E
19 Vézelise, France 48 30N 6 5E
43 Vezhen, mt., Bulgaria 42 50N 24 20E
126 Viacha, Bolivia 16 30S 68 5W
38 Viadana, Italy 44 55N 10 30E
127 Viana, Brazil 3 0S 44 40W
32 Viana, Spain 42 31N 2 22W
30 Viana do Castelo, Port. 41 42N 8 50W
30 Vianna do Castelo ♦, Portugal 41 50N 8 30W
127 Vianópolis, Brazil 16 40S 48 35W
30 Viar, R., Spain 37 45N 5 54W
38 Viaréggio, Italy 43 52N 10 13E
109 Vibank, Canada 50 25N 104 0W
30 Vibey, R., Spain 42 21N 7 15E
41 Vibo Valéntia, Italy 38 40N 16 5E
49 Viborg, Denmark 56 27N 9 23E
49 Viborg Amt ♦, Den. 56 30N 9 20E
20 Vic Fézensac, France 43 47N 0 19E
20 Vic-en-Bigorre, France 43 24N 0 3E
39 Vicenza, Italy 45 32N 11 31E
32 Vich, Spain 41 58N 2 19E
126 Vichada ♦, Col. 5 0N 69 30W
55 Vichuga, U.S.S.R. 57 25N 41 55E
20 Vichy, France 46 9N 3 26E
114 Vicksburg, Mich., U.S.A. 42 10N 85 30W
117 Vicksburg, Miss., U.S.A. 32 22N 90 56W
39 Vico, L. di, Italy 42 20N 12 10E
127 Viçosa, Min. Ger., Brazil 20 45S 42 53W
127 Viçosa, Pernambuco, Brazil 9 28S 36 14W
20 Vic-sur-Cère, France 44 59N 2 38E
19 Vic-sur-Seille, France 48 45N 6 33E
116 Victor, Col., U.S.A. 38 43N 105 7W
112 Victor, N.Y., U.S.A. 42 58N 77 24W
99 Victor Harbour, Austral. 35 30S 138 37E
124 Victoria, Argentina 32 40S 60 10W
98 Victoria, Australia 21 16S 149 3E
85 Victoria, Cameroon 4 1N 9 10E
108 Victoria, Canada 48 30N 123 25W
128 Victoria, Chile 38 13S 72 20W
77 Victoria, Hong Kong 22 25N 114 15E
72 Victoria, Malaysia 5 20N 115 20E
117 Victoria, Tex., U.S.A. 28 50N 97 0W
116 Victoria, Va., U.S.A. 38 52N 99 8W
104 Victoria I., Canada 71 0N 11 0W

MAP
90 Victoria, L., E. Africa 1 0S 33 0E
100 Victoria, L., Australia 38 0S 147 35E
98 Victoria, Mt., Territory of New Guinea 8 40S 147 20E
96 Victoria, R., Australia 15 30S 131 0E
100 Victoria ♦, Australia 37 0S 144 0E
91 Victoria ♦, Rhodesia 21 0S 31 30E
109 Victoria Beach, Canada 50 45N 96 32W
121 Victoria de las Tunas, Cuba 20 58N 76 59W
91 Victoria Falls, Rhodesia 17 58S 25 45E
106 Victoria Harbour, Canada 44 45N 79 45W
5 Victoria Ld., Antarctica 75 0S 160 0E
90 Victoria Nile R., Uganda 2 25N 31 50E
107 Victoria Res., Canada 48 20N 57 27W
96 Victoria R. Downs, Austral. 16 30S 131 20E
67 Victoria Taungdeik, Burma 21 15N 93 55E
92 Victoria West, S. Africa 31 25S 23 4E
107 Victoriaville, Canada 46 4N 71 56W
124 Victorica, Argentina 36 20S 65 30W
126 Victorino, Venezuela 2 48N 67 50W
124 Vicuña, Chile 30 0S 70 50W
124 Vicuña Mackenna, Arg. 33 53S 64 25W
115 Vidalia, U.S.A. 32 13N 82 25W
21 Vidauban, France 43 25N 6 27E
47 Videlv, R., Norway 58 50N 8 32E
31 Vidigueira, Portugal 38 12N 7 48W
30 Vidio, Cabo, Spain 43 35N 6 14W
68 Vidisha (Bhilsa), India 23 28N 77 53E
49 Vidöstern, Sweden 57 5N 14 0E
46 Vidra, Rumania 45 56N 26 55E
42 Viduša, mts., Y.-slavia 42 55N 18 21E
54 Vidzy, U.S.S.R. 54 40N 26 37E
128 Viedma, Argentina 40 50S 63 0W
128 Viedma, L., Argentina 49 30S 72 30W
30 Vieira, Portugal 41 38N 8 8W
32 Viella, Spain 42 43N 0 44E
71 Vien Pou Kha, Laos 20 45N 101 5E
24 Vienenburg, W. Ger. 51 57N 10 35E
27 Vienna = Wien, Austria 48 12N 16 22E
117 Vienna, U.S.A. 37 29N 88 54W
21 Vienne, France 45 31N 4 53E
18 Vienne, R., France 47 5N 0 30E
20 Vienne ♦, France 45 53N 0 42E
71 Vientiane, Laos 18 7N 102 35E
24 Viersen, Germany 51 15N 6 23E
25 Vierwaldstättersee, Switzerland 47 0N 8 30E
19 Vierzon, France 47 13N 2 5E
20 Vieux-Boucau-les- Bains, France 43 48N 1 23W
21 Vif, France 45 5N 5 41E
73 Vigan, Philippines 17 35N 120 28E
38 Vigevano, Italy 45 18N 8 50E
127 Vigia, Brazil 0 50S 48 5W
19 Vignacourt, France 50 1N 2 15E
20 Vignemale, Pic du, Fr. 42 47N 0 10W
19 Vigneulles, France 48 59N 5 40E
38 Vignola, Italy 44 29N 11 0E
30 Vigo, Spain 42 12N 8 41W
30 Vigo, Ria de, Spain 42 15N 8 45W
18 Vihiers, France 47 10N 0 30W
70 Vijayadurg, India 16 30N 73 25E
70 Vijayawada (Bezwada), India 16 31N 80 39E
47 Vikedal, Norway 59 30N 5 55E
49 Viken, sjö, Skaraborgs, Sweden 58 40N 14 20E
49 Viken, L., Sweden 58 40N 10 2E
47 Vikersund, Norway 59 58N 10 2E
108 Viking, Canada 53 7N 111 50W
50 Vikna, Norway 64 52N 10 57E
70 Vikramasingapuram, India 8 40N 76 47E
48 Viksjö, Sweden 62 45N 17 26E
58 Vikulovo, U.S.S.R. 56 50N 70 40E
93 Vila Alferes Chamusca, Mozam. 24 27S 33 0E
89 Vila Arriaga, Angola 14 35S 13 30E
126 Vila Bittencourt, Brazil 1 20S 69 20W
† 91 Vila Cabral, Mozam. 13 13S 35 11E
91 Vila Caldas Xavier, Mozambique 14 28S 33 0E
91 Vila Coutinho, Mozam. 14 37S 34 19E
91 Vila da Maganja, Mozambique 17 18S 37 30E
89 Vila da Ponte, Angola 14 35S 16 40E
89 Vila de Aljustrel, Ang. 13 30S 19 45E
* 93 Vila de João Belo, Mozambique 25 6S 33 31E
73 Vila de Liquica, Portuguese Timor 8 40S 125 20E
31 Vila de Rei, Portugal 39 41N 8 9W
91 Vila de Sena, Mozam. 17 25S 35 0E
30 Vila do Bispo, Portugal 37 5N 8 53W
30 Vila do Conde, Portugal 41 21N 8 45W
91 Vila Fontes Velha, Mozam. 17 51S 35 24E
31 Vila Franca de Xira, Portugal 38 57N 8 59W
91 Vila Gamito, Mozam. 14 12S 33 0E
89 Vila General Machado, Angola 11 58S 17 22E
93 Vila Gomes da Costa, Mozambique 24 20S 33 37E
** 88 Vila Henrique de Carvalho, Angola 9 40S 20 12E
91 Vila Junqueiro, Mozam. 15 25S 36 58E
91 Vila Luiza, Mozam. 25 45S 32 35E
†† 89 Vila Luso, Angola 11 53S 19 55E
91 Vila Machado, Mozam. 19 15S 34 14E
88 Vila Marechal Carmona, Angola 7 30S 14 40E
89 Vila Mariano Machado, Angola 13 3S 14 35E
91 Vila Moatize, Mozambique 16 11S 33 40E

MAP
91 Vila Mouzinho, Mozam. 14 48S 34 25E
126 Vila Murtinho, Brazil 10 20S 65 20W
30 Vila Nova de Fozcôa, Port. 41 5N 7 9W
31 Vila Nova de Ourém, Portugal 39 40N 8 35W
30 Vila Novo de Gaia, Port. 41 4N 8 40W
89 Vila Nova do Seles, Angola 11 35S 14 22E
89 Vila Paiva Couceiro, Angola 14 37S 14 40E
91 Vila Paiva de Andrada, Mozam. 18 37S 34 2E
† 91 Vila Pery, Mozambique 19 4S 33 30E
30 Vila Pouca de Aguiar, Portugal 41 30N 7 38W
30 Vila Real, Portugal 41 17N 7 48W
31 Vila Real de Santo Antonio, Portugal 37 10N 7 28W
89 Vila Robert Williams, Angola 12 46S 15 30E
88 Vila Salazar, Angola 9 12S 14 48E
73 Vila Salazar, Port. Timor 5 25S 123 50E
89 Vila Teixeira da Silva, Angola 12 10S 15 50E
91 Vila Vasco da Gama, Mozambique 14 54S 32 14E
88 Vila Verissimo Sarmento, Angola 8 15S 20 50E
31 Vila Viçosa, Portugal 38 45N 7 27W
30 Vilaboa, Spain 42 21N 8 39W
18 Vilaine, R., France 47 35N 2 10W
93 Vilanculos, Mozam. 22 1S 35 17E
30 Vilar Formosa, Portugal 40 38N 6 45W
30 Vilareal ♦, Portugal 41 36N 7 35W
54 Vileyka, U.S.S.R. 54 30N 27 0E
50 Vilhelmina, Sweden 64 35N 16 39E
126 Vilhena, Brazil 12 30S 60 0W
59 Viliga, U.S.S.R. 60 2N 156 56E
54 Viliya, R., U.S.S.R. 54 57N 24 35E
54 Viljandi, U.S.S.R. 58 28N 25 30E
124 Villa Abecia, Bolivia 21 0S 68 18W
120 Villa Ahumada, Mexico 30 30N 106 40W
124 Villa Ana, Argentina 28 28S 59 40W
124 Villa Angela, Argentina 27 34S 60 45W
126 Villa Bella, Bolivia 10 25S 65 30W
80 Villa Bens (Tarfaya), Morocco 27 55N 12 55W
124 Villa Cañás, Argentina 34 0S 61 35W
* 80 Villa Cisneros, Spanish Sahara 23 50N 15 53W
* 80 Villa Cisneros ♦, Span. Sahara 25 0N 13 30W
124 Villa Colón, Argentina 31 38S 68 20W
124 Villa Constitución, Arg. 33 15S 60 20W
126 Villa de Cura, Ven. 10 2N 67 29W
124 Villa de María, Arg. 30 0S 63 43W
124 Villa de Rosario, Par. 24 30S 57 35W
124 Villa Dolores, Argentina 31 58S 65 15W
124 Villa Franca, Paraguay 26 14S 58 20W
124 Villa Guillermina, Arg. 28 15S 59 29W
124 Villa Hayes, Paraguay 25 0S 57 20W
124 Villa Iris, Argentina 38 12S 63 12W
121 Villa Julia Molina, Dominican Republic 19 5N 69 45W
120 Villa Madero, Mexico 24 28N 104 10W
124 Villa María, Argentina 32 20S 63 10W
124 Villa Mazán, Arg. 28 40S 66 30W
124 Villa Mentes, Bolivia 21 10S 63 30W
38 Villa Minozzo, Italy 44 21N 10 30E
124 Villa Montes, Bolivia 21 10S 63 30W
124 Villa Ocampo, Argentina 28 30S 59 20W
124 Villa Ojo de Agua, Argentina 29 30S 63 44W
124 Villa San Agustín, Arg. 30 35S 67 30W
41 Villa San Giovanni, It. 38 13N 15 38E
124 Villa San José, Argentina 32 12S 58 15W
124 Villa San Martín, Arg. 28 9S 64 9W
39 Villa Santina, Italy 46 25N 12 55E
30 Villablino, Spain 42 57N 6 19W
63 Villabruzzi, Somali Rep. 3 3N 45 18E
30 Villacampo, Pontano de, Spain 41 31N 6 0W
32 Villacañas, Spain 39 38N 3 20W
32 Villacarlos, Spain 39 53N 4 17E
32 Villacarriedo, Spain 43 14N 3 48W
33 Villacarrillo, Spain 38 7N 3 3W
30 Villacastín, Spain 40 46N 4 25W
26 Villach, Austria 46 37N 13 51E
40 Villaciaro, Italy 39 27N 8 45E
30 Villada, Spain 42 15N 4 59W
30 Villadiego, Spain 42 31N 4 1W
38 Villadossóla, Italy 46 4N 8 16E
32 Villafeliche, Spain 41 10N 1 30W
32 Villafranca, Spain 42 17N 1 46W
31 Villafranca de los Barros, Spain 38 35N 6 18W
33 Villafranca de los Caballeros, Spain 39 26N 3 21W
30 Villafranca del Bierzo, Spain 42 38N 6 50W
32 Villafranca del Cid, Sp. 40 26N 0 16W
32 Villafranca del Panadés, Spain 41 21N 1 40E
38 Villafranca di Verona, Italy 45 20N 10 51E
30 Villagarcía de Arosa, Spain 42 34N 8 46W
124 Villaguay, Argentina 32 0S 58 45W
31 Villaharta, Spain 38 9N 4 54W
120 Villahermosa, Mexico 17 45N 92 50W
33 Villahermosa, Spain 38 46N 2 52W
18 Villaines-la-Juhel, Fr. 48 21N 0 20W
33 Villajoyosa, Spain 38 30N 0 12W
30 Villalba, Spain 40 36N 3 59W
30 Villalba de Guardo, Sp. 42 42N 4 49W
30 Villalón de Campos, Sp. 42 5N 5 4W

* Renamed Xai-Xai
† Renamed Lichinga
** Renamed Lunda
†† Renamed Moxico

* Renamed Dakhla
† Renamed Chimoio

Wairoa INDEX Westbrook

MAP
101 Wairoa, New Zealand 39 3S 177 25E
101 Waitaki, R., N.Z. 44 23S 169 55E
101 Waitara, New Zealand 38 59S 174 15E
118 Waitsburg, U.S.A. 46 15N 118 10W
101 Waiuku, New Zealand 37 15S 174 45E
73 Wajabula Rau, Indon. 2 29N 128 17E
74 Wajima, Japan 37 30N 137 0E
90 Wajir, Kenya 1 42N 40 20E
90 Wajir ♦, Kenya 1 42N 40 20E
74 Wakamatsu, Japan 33 50N 130 45E
74 Wakasa-Wan, Japan 34 45N 135 30E
101 Wakatipu, L., N.Z. 45 5S 168 33E
74 Wakayama, Japan 34 15N 135 15E
74 Wakayama-ken ♦, Jap. 33 50N 135 30E
115 Wake Forest, U.S.A. 35 58N 78 30W
94 Wake I., Pacific Ocean 19 18N 166 36E
12 Wakefield, Eng. 53 41N 1 31W
101 Wakefield, N.Z. 41 24S 173 5E
113 Wakefield, Mass., U.S.A. 42 30N 71 3W
116 Wakefield, Mich., U.S.A. 46 28N 89 53W
71 Wakema, Burma 16 40N 95 18E
65 Wakhan ♦, Afghan. 37 0N 73 0E
74 Wakkanai, Japan 45 28N 141 35E
93 Wakkerstroom, S. Afr. 27 24S 30 10E
106 Wako, Canada 49 50N 91 22W
100 Wakool, R., Australia 32 25S 144 15E
73 Wakre, Indonesia 0 30S 131 5E
107 Wakuach L., Canada 55 20N 67 10W
46 Walachia ♦, Rum. 44 40N 25 0E
91 Walamba, Zambia 13 30S 28 42E
28 Wałbrzych, Poland 50 45N 16 18E
99 Walcha, Australia 30 55S 151 31E
16 Walcheren, I., Neth. 51 30N 3 35E
118 Walcott, U.S.A. 41 50N 106 55W
28 Walcz, Poland 53 17N 16 27E
25 Wald, Switzerland 47 17N 8 56E
24 Waldbröl, Germany 50 52N 7 36E
24 Waldeck, Germany 51 12N 9 4E
118 Walden, Colo., U.S.A. 40 47N 106 20W
113 Walden, N.Y., U.S.A. 41 32N 74 13W
118 Waldport, U.S.A. 44 30N 124 2W
109 Waldron, Canada 50 53N 102 35W
117 Waldron, U.S.A. 34 52N 94 4W
25 Waldshut, Germany 47 37N 8 12E
87 Waldya, Ethiopia 11 50N 39 34E
84 Walembele, Ghana 10 30N 1 14W
13 Wales ♦, U.K. 52 30N 3 30W
85 Walewale, Ghana 10 21N 0 50W
99 Walgett, Australia 30 0S 148 5E
100 Walhalla, Australia 37 50S 146 25E
87 Waliso, Ethiopia 8 33N 38 1E
116 Walker, U.S.A. 47 4N 94 35W
107 Walker L., Canada 50 20N 67 11W
118 Walker L., U.S.A. 38 56N 118 46W
98 Walkerston, Australia 21 11S 149 8E
112 Walkerton, Canada 44 10N 81 10W
116 Wall, U.S.A. 44 0N 102 14W
118 Walla Walla, U.S.A. 46 3N 118 25W
98 Wallabadah, Australia 17 57S 142 15E
112 Wallace, Canada 45 12N 78 9W
118 Wallace, Idaho, U.S.A. 47 30N 116 0W
116 Wallace, Nebr., U.S.A. 40 51N 101 12W
115 Wallace, N.C., U.S.A. 34 50N 77 59W
106 Wallaceburg, Canada 42 40N 82 30W
46 Wallachia = Valahia, Rumania 44 35N 25 0E
99 Wallal, Australia 26 32S 146 7E
99 Wallangarra, Australia 28 56S 151 58E
99 Wallaroo, Australia 33 55S 137 33E
12 Wallasey, Eng. 53 26S 3 2W
25 Walldurn, Germany 49 34N 9 23E
100 Wallerawang, Australia 33 25S 150 4E
113 Wallingford, Eng. 51 36N 1 7W
113 Wallingford, U.S.A. 43 27N 72 58W
100 Wallis, L., Australia 32 15S 152 28E
118 Wallowa, U.S.A. 45 40N 117 35W
118 Wallowa, Mts., U.S.A. 45 20N 117 30W
12 Wallsend, England 54 59N 1 30W
100 Wallsend, Australia 32 55S 151 40E
118 Wallula, U.S.A. 46 3N 118 59W
99 Wallumbilla, Australia 26 33S 149 9E
92 Walmer, S. Africa 33 57S 25 35E
109 Walmsley, L., Canada 63 25N 109 0W
12 Walney, Isle of, England 54 5N 3 15W
117 Walnut Ridge, U.S.A. 36 7N 90 58W
100 Walpeup, Australia 35 10S 142 2E
13 Walsall, England 52 36N 1 59W
117 Walsenburg, U.S.A. 37 42N 104 45W
98 Walsh, Australia 16 40S 144 0E
117 Walsh, U.S.A. 37 28N 102 15W
24 Walsrode, Germany 52 51N 9 37E
70 Waltair, India 17 44N 83 23E
115 Walterboro, U.S.A. 32 53N 80 40W
117 Walters, U.S.A. 34 25N 98 20W
24 Waltershausen, Ger. 50 53N 10 33E
106 Waltham, Canada 45 57N 76 57W
113 Waltham, U.S.A. 42 22N 71 12W
118 Waltman, U.S.A. 43 8N 107 15W
113 Walton, U.S.A. 42 12N 75 9W
7 Walvis Ridge, South Atlantic Ocean 30 0S 3 0E
92 Walvisbaai, S. Africa 23 0S 14 28E
90 Wamaza, Zaïre 4 12S 27 2E
90 Wamba, Kenya 0 58N 37 19E
85 Wamba, Nigeria 8 58N 8 34E
90 Wamba, Zaïre 2 10N 27 57E
100 Wamberra, Australia 33 52S 142 21E
116 Wamego, U.S.A. 39 14N 96 22W
73 Wamena, Indonesia 3 58S 138 50E
67 Wampo, China 31 30N 86 38E
113 Wampsville, U.S.A. 43 4N 75 42W
73 Wamsasi, Indonesia 3 27S 126 7E
76 Wan Ta Shan, China 46 20N 132 20E
68 Wana, Pakistan 32 20N 69 32E
101 Wanaka L., N.Z. 44 33S 169 7E
77 Wanan, China 26 25N 114 50E
73 Wanapiri, Indonesia 4 30S 135 50E
106 Wanapitei, Canada 46 30N 80 45W
106 Wanapitei L., Canada 46 45N 80 40W
99 Wanbi, S. Australia 34 46S 140 21E

MAP
76 Wanchuan, China 40 53N 114 32E
91 Wanderer, Rhodesia 19 36S 30 1E
70 Wandiwash, India 12 30N 79 30E
99 Wandoan, Australia 26 5S 149 55E
87 Wang Kai (Ghâbat el Arab), Sudan 9 3N 29 23E
71 Wang Saphung, Thailand 17 29N 101 33E
90 Wanga, Zaïre 2 58N 29 12E
73 Wangal, Indonesia 6 8S 134 9E
100 Wanganella, Australia 35 6S 144 49E
101 Wanganui, N.Z. 39 35S 175 3E
100 Wangaratta, Australia 36 20S 146 7E
76 Wangching, China 43 15N 129 37E
24 Wangerooge I., Ger. 53 47N 7 52E
90 Wangi, Kenya 1 58S 40 58E
73 Wangiwangi, I., Indonesia 5 22S 123 37E
77 Wangkiang, China 30 6N 116 45E
77 Wanhsien, Szechwan, China 30 50N 108 30E
76 Wanhsien, Kansu, China 36 45N 107 24E
68 Wankaner, India 22 42N 71 0E
92 Wanki Nat. Park, Rhodesia 19 0S 26 30E
91 Wankie, Rhod. 18 18S 26 30E
91 Wankie ♦, Rhod. 18 18S 26 30E
109 Wanless, Canada 54 11N 101 21W
77 Wanning, China 18 45N 110 28E
100 Wannon, R., Australia 37 40S 141 53E
77 Wantsai, China 28 5N 114 22E
77 Wanyüan, China 32 4N 108 5E
83 Wanzarīk, Libya 27 3N 13 30E
114 Wapakoneta, U.S.A. 40 35N 84 10W
118 Wapato, U.S.A. 46 30N 120 25W
106 Wapikopa L., Canada 42 50N 88 10W
106 Wapiti, R., Canada 55 5N 119 0W
113 Wappingers Fs., U.S.A. 41 35N 73 56W
116 Wapsipinicon, R., U.S.A. 42 10N 91 30W
63 Warandab, Ethiopia 7 20N 44 2E
100 Waranga Res., Austral. 36 38S 145 4E
70 Warangal, India 17 58N 79 45E
99 Waratah, Austral. 41 30S 145 30E
100 Waratah B., Australia 38 45S 146 8E
24 Warburg, Germany 51 29N 9 10E
100 Warburton, Australia 37 41S 145 42E
101 Warburton, R., Austral. 27 30S 138 30E
101 Ward, New Zealand 41 49S 174 11E
108 Ward Cove, Alas. 55 25N 132 10W
93 Warden, S. Afr. 27 50S 29 0E
68 Wardha, India 20 45N 78 39E
108 Wardlow, Canada 50 56N 111 31W
99 Wardoan, Australia 25 59S 149 59E
108 Ware, Canada 57 26N 125 41W
113 Ware, U.S.A. 42 16N 72 15W
113 Wareham, U.S.A. 41 45N 70 44W
24 Waren, Germany 53 30N 12 41E
24 Warendorf, Germany 51 57N 8 0E
99 Warialda, Australia 29 29S 150 33E
73 Warkopi, Indonesia 1 12S 134 9E
101 Warkworth, Eng. 55 22N 1 38W
13 Warley, Eng. 52 30N 2 0W
118 Warm Springs, Mont., U.S.A. 46 11N 112 56W
119 Warm Springs, Nev., U.S.A. 38 16N 116 32W
109 Warman, Canada 52 25N 106 30W
92 Warmbad, S.W. Africa 28 25S 18 42E
92 Warmbad, S.W. Afr. 19 14S 13 51E
93 Warmbad, S. Africa 24 51S 28 19E
19 Warmeriville, France 49 20N 4 13E
100 Warnambool, Australia 38 12S 142 31E
98 Warnambool Downs, Australia 22 50S 142 45E
100 Warncoort, Australia 38 30S 143 45E
24 Warnemünde, Germany 54 9N 12 5E
118 Warner Range, Mts., U.S.A. 41 30S 120 20W
115 Warner Robins, U.S.A. 32 41N 83 36W
24 Warnow, R., Germany 54 0N 12 9E
70 Warora, India 20 14N 79 1E
100 Waracknabeal, Austral. 36 9S 142 26E
100 Warragul, Australia 38 1S 145 57E
87 Warrayelu, Ethiopia 10 40N 39 28E
98 Warrego Ra., Australia 25 15S 146 0E
99 Warrego, R., Australia 26 30S 146 0E
100 Warren, Austral. 31 42S 147 51E
117 Warren, Ark., U.S.A. 33 35N 92 3W
112 Warren, Ohio, U.S.A. 41 18N 80 52W
112 Warren, Pa., U.S.A. 41 52N 79 10W
113 Warren, R.I., U.S.A. 41 43N 71 19W
15 Warrenpoint, Northern Ireland 54 7N 6 15W
109 Warrens Landing, Can. 53 40N 98 0W
116 Warrensburg, U.S.A. 38 45N 93 45W
92 Warrenton, S. Africa 28 9S 24 47E
118 Warrenton, U.S.A. 46 11N 123 59W
99 Warrenville, Australia 25 48S 147 22E
85 Warri, Nigeria 5 30N 5 41E
96 Warrina, Australia 28 12S 135 50E
12 Warrington, Eng. 53 25N 2 38W
115 Warrington, U.S.A. 30 22N 87 16W
116 Warroad, U.S.A. 49 0N 95 20W
28 Warsaw = Warszawa, Poland 52 13N 21 0E
114 Warsaw, Ind., U.S.A. 41 14N 85 50W
112 Warsaw, N.Y., U.S.A. 42 46N 78 10W
114 Warsaw, Ohio, U.S.A. 40 20N 82 0W
28 Warszawa, Poland 52 13N 21 0E
28 Warszawa ♦, Poland 52 35N 21 0E
24 Warstein, Germany 51 26N 8 20E
28 Warta, Poland 51 43N 18 38E
28 Warta, R., Poland 52 40N 16 10E
73 Waru, Indonesia 3 30S 130 36E
68 Warud, India 21 30N 78 16E
99 Warwick, Australia 28 10S 152 1E
13 Warwick, Eng. 52 17N 1 36W
13 Warwick ♦, Eng. 52 20N 1 30W
113 Warwick, U.S.A. 41 43N 71 25W
108 Wasa, Canada 49 45N 115 50W
112 Wasaga Beach, Canada 44 31N 80 0W

MAP
118 Wasatch, Mt., Ra., U.S.A. 40 30N 111 15W
93 Wasbank, S. Afr. 28 15S 30 9E
119 Wasco, Calif., U.S.A. 35 37N 119 16W
118 Wasco, Oreg., U.S.A. 45 45N 120 46W
116 Waseca, U.S.A. 44 3N 93 31W
12 Wash, The, Eng. 52 58N 0 20W
112 Washago, Canada 44 46N 79 21W
116 Washburn, N.D., U.S.A. 47 23N 101 0W
116 Washburn, Wis., U.S.A. 46 38N 90 55W
114 Washington, D.C., U.S.A. 38 52N 77 0W
115 Washington, Ga., U.S.A. 33 45N 82 45W
114 Washington, Ind., U.S.A. 38 40N 87 8W
116 Washington, Iowa, U.S.A. 41 20N 91 45W
116 Washington, Miss., U.S.A. 38 35N 91 20W
115 Washington, N.C., U.S.A. 35 35N 77 1W
113 Washington, N.J., U.S.A. 40 45N 74 59W
114 Washington, Ohio, U.S.A. 39 34N 83 26W
112 Washington, Pa., U.S.A. 40 10N 80 20W
119 Washington, Utah, U.S.A. 37 10N 113 30W
118 Washington ♦, U.S.A. 47 45N 120 30W
114 Washington Court House, U.S.A. 39 34N 83 26W
95 Washington I., Pac. Oc. 4 43N 160 25W
114 Washington I., U.S.A. 45 24N 86 54W
113 Washington Mt., U.S.A. 44 15N 71 18W
73 Wasian, Indonesia 1 47S 133 19E
28 Wasilków, Poland 53 12N 23 13E
73 Wasior, Indonesia 2 43S 134 30E
109 Waskaiowaka, L., Can. 56 35N 96 40W
86 Wasm, Saudi Arabia 18 2N 41 32E
16 Wassenaar, Netherlands 52 8N 4 24E
25 Wasserburg, Germany 48 4N 12 15E
19 Wassy, France 48 30N 4 58E
106 Waswanipi L., Canada 49 35N 76 40W
73 Watampone, Indonesia 4 29S 120 25E
73 Watawaha, P., Indon. 6 30S 122 20E
117 Water Valley, U.S.A. 34 9N 89 38W
93 Waterberg, S. Africa 24 14S 28 0E
92 Waterberg, S.W. Africa 20 30S 17 18E
92 Waterberg, mt., S. W. Afr. 20 26S 17 13E
113 Waterbury, Conn., U.S.A. 41 32N 73 0W
113 Waterbury, Vt., U.S.A. 44 22N 72 44W
109 Waterbury, L., Canada 58 16N 105 0W
112 Waterdown, Canada 43 21N 79 53W
112 Waterford, Canada 42 58N 80 20W
92 Waterford, S. Afr. 33 6S 25 0E
15 Waterford ♦, Ireland 51 10N 7 40W
15 Waterford Harb., Ire. 52 10N 6 58W
109 Waterhen L., Canada 52 10N 99 40W
16 Waterloo, Belgium 50 43N 4 25E
113 Waterloo, Que., Canada 45 22N 72 32W
106 Waterloo, Ont., Canada 43 30N 80 32W
84 Waterloo, Sierra Leone 8 26N 13 8W
116 Waterloo, Ill., U.S.A. 38 22N 90 6W
116 Waterloo, Iowa, U.S.A. 42 27N 92 20W
112 Waterloo, N.Y., U.S.A. 42 54N 76 53W
112 Waterpoint, U.S.A. 43 19N 78 15W
116 Watermeet, U.S.A. 46 15N 89 12W
113 Watertown, Conn., U.S.A. 41 36N 73 7W
113 Watertown, N.Y., U.S.A. 43 58N 75 57W
116 Watertown, S.D., U.S.A. 44 57N 97 5W
116 Watertown, Wis., U.S.A. 43 15N 88 45W
93 Waterval-Boven, Africa 25 40S 30 18E
113 Waterville, Canada 45 17N 71 53W
107 Waterville, Me., U.S.A. 44 35N 69 40W
113 Waterville, N.Y., U.S.A. 42 56N 75 23W
112 Waterville, Pa., U.S.A. 41 19N 77 21W
118 Waterville, Wash., USA 47 45N 120 1W
113 Watervliet, U.S.A. 42 46N 73 43W
73 Wates, Indonesia 7 53S 110 6E
112 Watford, Canada 42 58N 81 52W
13 Watford, England 51 38N 0 23W
116 Watford City, U.S.A. 47 50N 103 23W
112 Watkins Glen, U.S.A. 42 25N 76 55W
117 Watonga, U.S.A. 35 51N 98 24W
109 Watrous, Canada 51 40N 105 25W
117 Watrous, U.S.A. 35 50N 104 55W
90 Watsa, Zaïre 3 4N 29 30E
114 Watseka, U.S.A. 40 45N 87 45W
96 Watson, Australia 30 19S 131 41E
109 Watson, Canada 52 10N 104 30W
104 Watson Lake, Canada 60 12N 129 0W
119 Watsonville, U.S.A. 37 58N 121 49W
100 Wattle Hill, Australia 38 42S 143 17E
25 Wattwil, Switzerland 47 18N 9 6E
73 Watubela, Kepulauan, Indonesia 4 28S 131 54E
98 Wau, New Guinea 7 25S 146 42E
112 Waubamik, Canada 45 29N 80 3W
116 Waubay, U.S.A. 45 42N 97 17W
100 Waubra, Australia 37 21S 143 39E
115 Wauchula, U.S.A. 27 35N 81 50W
109 Waugh, Canada 49 40N 95 20W
114 Waukegan, U.S.A. 42 22N 87 54W
114 Waukesha, U.S.A. 43 0N 88 15W
116 Waukon, U.S.A. 43 14N 91 33W
116 Wauneta, U.S.A. 40 27N 101 25W
116 Waupaca, U.S.A. 44 22N 89 8W
116 Waupun, U.S.A. 43 38N 88 44W
117 Waurika, U.S.A. 34 12N 98 0W
116 Wausau, U.S.A. 44 57N 89 40W
116 Wautoma, U.S.A. 44 3N 89 20W
114 Wauwatosa, U.S.A. 43 6N 87 59W
96 Wave Hill, Australia 17 32N 131 0E
13 Waveney, R., Eng. 52 24N 1 20E
101 Waverley, N.Z. 39 46S 174 37E
116 Waverly, Iowa, U.S.A. 42 40N 92 30W
113 Waverly, N.Y., U.S.A. 42 0N 76 33W
16 Wavre, Belgium 50 43N 4 38E
87 Wâw, Sudan 7 45N 28 1E

MAP
83 Waw an Namus, Libya 24 24N 18 11E
85 Wawa, Nigeria 9 54N 4 27E
86 Wawa, Sudan 20 30N 30 22E
109 Wawanesa, Canada 49 30N 99 40W
117 Waxahachie, U.S.A. 32 22N 96 53W
25 Waxweiler, Germany 50 6N 6 22E
100 Way Way, Australia 33 30S 151 18E
99 Wayatinah, Australia 42 15S 146 15E
115 Waycross, U.S.A. 31 12N 82 25W
87 Wayi, Sudan 5 8N 30 10E
116 Wayne, Mich., U.S.A. 42 16N 97 0W
114 Wayne, W. Va., U.S.A. 38 15N 82 27W
115 Waynesboro, Miss., U.S.A. 31 40N 88 39W
114 Waynesboro, Pa., U.S.A. 39 46N 77 32W
114 Waynesboro, Va., U.S.A. 38 4N 78 57W
114 Waynesburg, U.S.A. 39 54N 80 12W
115 Waynesville, U.S.A. 35 31N 83 0W
117 Waynoka, U.S.A. 36 38N 98 53W
83 Wāzin, Libya 31 58N 10 51E
65 Wazirabad, Afghanistan 36 44N 66 47E
68 Wazirabad, Pakistan 32 30N 74 8E
72 We, Indonesia 6 3N 95 56E
13 Weald, The, Eng. 51 7N 0 9E
12 Wear, R., Eng. 54 44N 1 58W
117 Weatherford, Okla., U.S.A. 35 30N 98 45W
117 Weatherford, Tex., U.S.A. 32 45N 97 48W
117 Webb City, U.S.A. 37 9N 94 30W
87 Webera, Bale, Ethiopia 6 29N 40 33E
87 Webera, Shewa, Ethiopia 9 40N 39 0E
113 Webster, Mass., U.S.A. 42 4N 71 54W
112 Webster, N.Y., U.S.A. 43 11N 77 27W
116 Webster, S.D., U.S.A. 45 24N 97 33W
116 Webster, Wis., U.S.A. 45 53N 92 25W
116 Webster City, U.S.A. 42 30N 93 50W
116 Webster Green, U.S.A. 38 38N 90 20W
114 Webster Springs, U.S.A. 38 30N 80 25W
28 Wecliniec, Poland 51 18N 15 10E
73 Weda, Indonesia 0 30N 127 50E
73 Weda, Teluk, Indonesia 0 30N 127 50E
128 Weddell I., Falk. Is. 51 50S 61 0W
5 Weddell Sea, Antarctica 72 30S 40 0W
100 Wedderburn, Australia 36 20S 143 33E
96 Wedge I., Australia 30 50S 115 11E
91 Wedza, Rhodesia 18 40S 31 33E
100 Wee Elwah, Australia 32 56S 145 20E
99 Wee Waa, Australia 30 11S 149 26E
118 Weed, U.S.A. 41 29N 122 22W
113 Weedsport, U.S.A. 43 3N 76 35W
112 Weedville, U.S.A. 41 17N 78 28W
99 Weemelah, Australia 39 0S 149 15E
93 Weenen, S. Afr. 28 48S 30 7E
24 Weener, Germany 53 10N 7 23E
16 Weert, Netherlands 51 15N 5 43E
100 Weetallba, Australia 32 37S 149 41E
27 Wegierska-Gorka, Poland 49 36N 19 7E
28 Wegorzewo, Poland 54 13N 21 43E
28 Wegroów, Poland 52 24N 22 0E
77 Wei Ho, China 35 45N 114 30E
77 Weichow Tao, China 21 0N 109 1E
24 Weida, Ger. 50 47N 12 3E
25 Weiden, Germany 49 40N 12 10E
76 Weifang, China 36 47N 119 10E
76 Weihai, China 37 30N 122 10E
24 Weilburg, Germany 50 28N 8 17E
25 Weilheim, Germany 47 50N 11 9E
24 Weimar, Germany 51 0N 11 20E
27 Weiner Neustadt, Aust. 47 50N 16 15E
25 Weingarten, Germany 47 49N 9 39E
25 Weinheim, Germany 49 33N 8 40E
98 Weipa, Austral. 12 24S 142 0E
109 Weir River, Canada 57 0N 94 10W
112 Weirton, U.S.A. 40 22N 80 35W
118 Weiser, U.S.A. 44 10N 117 0W
67 Wei-si, China 27 18N 99 18E
25 Weissenburg, Germany 49 2N 10 58E
24 Weissenfels, Germany 51 11N 11 58E
24 Weisswasser, Germany 51 30N 14 36E
26 Weitra, Austria 48 41N 14 54E
76 Weiyüan, China 35 10N 104 10E
26 Weiz, Austria 47 13N 15 39E
28 Wejherowo, Poland 54 35N 18 12E
109 Wekusko, Canada 54 45N 99 45W
109 Wekusko L., Canada 54 40N 99 50W
109 Welby, Canada 50 33N 101 29W
114 Welch, U.S.A. 37 29N 81 36W
98 Welcome, Australia 15 20S 144 40E
87 Welega ♦, Ethiopia 9 25N 34 20E
87 Welkite, Ethiopia 8 15N 37 42E
92 Welkom, S. Afr. 28 0S 26 50E
106 Welland, Canada 43 0N 79 10W
12 Welland, R., Eng. 52 43N 0 10W
98 Wellesley Is., Australia 17 20S 139 30E
16 Wellin, Belgium 50 5N 5 6E
13 Wellingborough, England 52 18N 0 41W
100 Wellington, N.S.W., Austral. 32 30S 149 0E
106 Wellington, Canada 43 57N 77 20W
12 Wellington (Telford), England 52 42N 2 31W
101 Wellington, N.Z. 41 19S 174 46E
92 Wellington, S. Africa 33 38S 18 57E
116 Wellington, Col., U.S.A. 40 43N 105 0W
117 Wellington, Kans., U.S.A. 37 15N 97 25W
118 Wellington, Nev., U.S.A. 38 47N 119 28W
112 Wellington, Ohio, U.S.A. 41 9N 82 12W
117 Wellington, Okla., U.S.A. 34 55N 100 13W
101 Wellington, dist., N.Z. 40 8S 175 36E
128 Wellington, I., Chile 49 30S 75 0W
100 Wellington, L., Austral. 38 5S 147 22E
12 Wells, Norfolk, Eng. 52 57N 0 51E
13 Wells, Somerset, Eng. 51 12N 2 39W
113 Wells, Me., U.S.A. 43 18N 70 35W
113 Wells, Minn., U.S.A. 43 44N 93 45W
118 Wells, Nev., U.S.A. 41 8N 115 0W
108 Wells Gray Prov. Park, Canada 52 30N 120 0W

MAP
96 Wells L., Australia 26 44S 123 15E
113 Wells River, U.S.A. 44 9N 72 4W
112 Wellsboro, U.S.A. 41 46N 77 20W
112 Wellsburg, U.S.A. 40 15N 80 36W
116 Wellsville, Mo., U.S.A. 39 4N 91 30W
112 Wellsville, N.Y., U.S.A. 42 9N 77 53W
112 Wellsville, Ohio, U.S.A. 40 36N 80 40W
118 Wellsville, Utah, U.S.A. 41 35N 111 59W
119 Wellton, U.S.A. 32 46N 114 6W
87 Welmel, W., Ethiopia 6 0N 40 20E
87 Welo ♦, Ethiopia 11 50N 39 48E
26 Wels, Austria 48 9N 14 1E
100 Welshpool, Australia 38 42S 146 26E
13 Welshpool, Wales 52 40N 3 9W
63 Welwel, Ethiopia 7 5N 45 25E
92 Welwitschia, S.W. Afr. 20 16S 14 59E
109 Welwyn, Canada 50 20N 101 30W
12 Wem, England 52 52N 2 45W
90 Wembere, R., Tanzania 4 45S 34 0E
118 Wenatchee, U.S.A. 47 30N 120 17W
77 Wenchang, China 19 45N 110 50E
84 Wenchi, Ghana 7 46N 2 8W
77 Wenchow, China 28 0N 120 35E
118 Wendell, U.S.A. 42 50N 114 51W
73 Wendesi, Indonesia 2 30S 134 10E
87 Wendo, Ethiopia 6 40N 38 27E
118 Wendover, U.S.A. 40 49N 114 1W
90 Wenge, Zaïre 0 3N 24 0E
76 Wengteng, China 37 15N 122 10E
98 Wenlock, R., Australia 12 15S 142 0E
75 Wensu, China 41 6N 80 3E
76 Wenteng, China 37 10N 122 0E
100 Wentworth, Australia 34 2S 141 54E
73 Wenut, Indonesia 3 11S 133 19E
118 Weott, U.S.A. 40 19N 123 56W
92 Wepener, S. Afr. 29 42S 27 3E
24 Werdau, Germany 50 45N 12 20E
92 Werda, Botswana 25 24S 23 15E
63 Werder, Ethiopia 6 58N 45 1E
24 Werder, Germany 52 23N 12 56E
24 Werdohl, Germany 51 15N 7 47E
73 Weri, Indonesia 3 10S 132 30E
24 Werne, Germany 51 38N 7 38E
24 Wernigerode, Germany 51 49N 0 45E
100 Werribee, Austral. 37 54S 144 40E
100 Werrimull, Austral. 34 22S 143 30E
100 Werris Creek, Australia 31 18S 150 38E
73 Wersar, Indonesia 1 30S 131 55E
25 Wertheim, Germany 49 44N 9 32E
24 Wesel, Germany 51 39N 6 34E
24 Weser, R., Germany 53 33N 8 30E
73 Wesiri, Indonesia 7 30S 126 30E
107 Wesleyville, Canada 49 8N 53 36W
112 Wesleyville, U.S.A. 42 9N 80 1W
97 Wessel Is., Australia 11 10S 136 45E
24 Wesselburen, Germany 54 11N 8 53E
116 Wessington, U.S.A. 44 30N 98 40W
116 Wessington Springs, U.S.A. 44 10N 98 35W
117 West, U.S.A. 31 50N 97 5W
107 West B., Canada 45 53N 82 8W
117 West, B., U.S.A. 29 5N 89 27W
114 West Bend, U.S.A. 43 25N 88 10W
69 West Bengal ♦, India 25 0N 90 0E
114 West Branch, U.S.A. 44 16N 84 13W
13 West Bromwich, England 52 32N 2 1W
113 West Chazy, U.S.A. 44 49N 73 28W
114 West Chester, U.S.A. 39 58N 75 36W
117 West Columbia, U.S.A. 29 10N 95 38W
116 West Des Moines, U.S.A. 41 30N 93 45W
128 West Falkland Island, Falkland Islands 51 30S 60 0W
116 West Frankfort, U.S.A. 37 56N 89 0W
95 West Harbour, N.Z. 45 51S 170 33E
113 West Hartford, U.S.A. 41 45N 72 45W
113 West Haven, U.S.A. 41 18N 72 57W
117 West Helena, U.S.A. 34 30N 90 40W
116 West Indies, Atlantic Ocean 15 0N 70 0W
90 West Lake ♦, Tanzania 2 5S 31 20E
† 14 West Lothian ♦, Scot. 55 55N 3 35W
112 West Lorne, Canada 42 37N 81 41W
91 West Lunga, R., Zam. 12 35S 24 45E
94 West Malling, Eng. 51 16N 0 25E
117 West Memphis, U.S.A. 35 5N 90 3W
‡ 90 West Mengo ♦, Uganda 0 15N 32 15E
117 West Monroe, U.S.A. 32 32N 92 7W
112 West Newton, U.S.A. 40 14N 79 46W
91 West Nicholson, Rhod. 21 2S 29 20E
66 West Pakistan ■, Asia 27 0N 67 0W
115 West Palm Beach, U.S.A. 26 44N 80 3W
71 West Paris, U.S.A. 44 18N 70 30W
113 West Pittston, U.S.A. 41 19N 75 49W
117 West Plains, U.S.A. 36 45N 91 50W
107 West Point, Canada 49 55N 64 30W
121 West Point, Jamaica 18 14N 78 30W
115 West Point, Ga., U.S.A. 32 54N 85 10W
115 West Point, Miss., U.S.A. 33 36N 88 38W
116 West Point, Nebr., U.S.A. 41 50N 96 43W
114 West Point, Va., U.S.A. 37 35N 76 47W
90 West Pokot ♦, Kenya 1 30N 35 40E
* 12 West Riding ♦, England 53 50N 1 30W
16 West Schelde = Westerschelde, Neth. 51 25N 4 0E
16 West Schelde = Westerschelde, Neth. 51 23N 3 50E
4 West Spitsbergen, Spitsbergen 78 40N 17 0E
16 West-Terschelling, Neth. 53 22N 5 13E
114 West Virginia ♦, U.S.A. 39 0N 18 0W
100 West Wyalong, Austral. 33 56S 147 10E
118 West Yellowstone, U.S.A. 44 47N 111 4W
108 Westbank, Canada 49 50N 119 25W
114 Westbrook, Maine, U.S.A. 48 40N 70 22W

* *Incorporated within the counties of North, West and South Yorkshire*
† *Incorporated within the region of Lothian*
‡ *Incorporated within the new N. Buganda Province*

Westbrook INDEX Wrightson, Mt.

MAP
117 Westbrook, Tex., U.S.A. 32 25N 101 0W
99 Westbury, Australia 41 30S 146 51E
100 Westby, Australia 35 30S 147 24E
116 Westby, U.S.A. 48 52N 104 3W
24 Westerland, Germany 54 51N 8 20E
96 Western Australia ♦, Australia 25 0S 118 0E
107 Western Bay, Canada 46 50N 52 30W
24 Western Germany ■, Europe 50 0N 8 0E
70 Western Ghatis, mts., India 15 30N 74 30E
90 Western ♦, Kenya 0 30N 34 30E
91 Western ♦, Zambia 13 15N 27 30E
101 Western Samoa ■, Pacific Ocean 14 0S 172 0W
114 Westernport, U.S.A. 30 30N 79 5W
16 Westerschelde, R., Neth. 51 25N 4 0E
24 Westerstede, Germany 51 15N 7 55E
24 Westerwald, mts., Ger. 50 39N 8 0E
113 Westfield, Mass., U.S.A. 42 9N 72 49W
112 Westfield, N.Y., U.S.A. 42 20N 79 38W
112 Westfield, Pa., U.S.A. 41 54N 77 32W
116 Westhope, U.S.A. 48 55N 101 0W
101 Westland ♦, N.Z. 43 33S 169 59E
101 Westland Bight, N.Z. 42 55S 170 5E
108 Westlock, Canada 54 20N 113 55W
15 Westmeath, co., Ire. 53 30N 7 30W
114 Westminster, U.S.A. 39 34S 77 1W
•12 Westmorland ♦, Eng. 54 28N 2 40W
72 Weston, Malaysia 5 10N 115 35E
118 Weston, Oreg., U.S.A. 45 50N 118 30W
114 Weston, W. Va., U.S.A. 39 3N 80 29W
106 Weston I., Canada 52 30N 79 50W
13 Weston-super-Mare, England 51 20N 2 59W
113 Westport, Canada 44 38N 76 28W
15 Westport, Ireland 53 44N 9 31W
101 Westport, N.Z. 41 46S 171 37E
118 Westport, U.S.A. 46 48N 124 4W
14 Westray I., Scot. 59 18N 3 0W
106 Westree, Canada 47 26N 81 34W
108 Westview, Canada 49 50N 124 31W
114 Westville, Ill., U.S.A. 40 3N 87 36W
117 Westville, Okla., U.S.A. 36 0N 94 33W
118 Westwood, U.S.A. 40 26N 121 0W
73 Wetar, I., Indonesia 7 30S 126 30E
108 Wetaskiwin, Canada 52 55N 113 24W
16 Wetteren, Belgium 51 0N 3 53E
100 Wetupoa, Australia 35 16S 143 46E
24 Wetzlar, Germany 50 33N 8 30E
98 Wewak, N. Guinea 3 29S 143 28E
117 Wewaka, U.S.A. 35 10N 96 35W
15 Wexford, Ireland 52 20N 6 28W
15 Wexford Harb., Ireland 52 20N 6 25W
109 Weyburn, Canada 49 40N 103 50W
26 Weyer, Austria 47 51N 14 40E
106 Weymont, Canada 47 50N 73 50W
107 Weymouth, Canada 44 30N 66 1W
13 Weymouth, Eng. 50 36N 2 28W
113 Weymouth, U.S.A. 42 13N 70 53W
98 Weymouth, C., Australia 12 37S 143 27E
101 Whakatane, N.Z. 37 57S 177 1E
105 Whale, R., Canada 57 40N 67 0W
104 Whale Cove, Canada 62 10N 93 0W
5 Whales, B. of Antarc. 78 0S 165 0W
14 Whalsay I., Scot. 60 22N 1 0W
77 Whampoa, China 23 5N 113 20E
101 Whangamomona, N.Z. 39 8S 174 44E
101 Whangarei, N.Z. 35 43S 174 21E
101 Whangarei Harbour, N.Z. 35 45S 174 28E
101 Whangaroa Harbour, N.Z. 35 4S 173 46E
12 Wharfe, R., Eng. 53 55N 1 30W
113 Wharton, N.J., U.S.A. 40 53N 74 36W
112 Wharton, Pa., U.S.A. 41 31N 78 1W
117 Wharton, Tex., U.S.A. 29 20N 96 6W
99 Whayjonta, Australia 29 40S 142 35E
116 Wheatland, U.S.A. 42 4N 105 58W
112 Wheatley, Canada 42 7N 82 29W
116 Wheaton, U.S.A. 45 50N 96 29W
118 Wheeler, Oreg., U.S.A. 45 45N 123 57W
117 Wheeler, Tex., U.S.A. 35 29N 100 15W
118 Wheeler Peak, Mt., U.S.A. 38 57N 114 15W
112 Wheeling, U.S.A. 40 2N 80 41W
12 Whernside, Mt., England 54 14N 2 24W
96 Whidbey Is., S. Austral. 34 30S 135 3E
108 Whiskey Gap, Canada 49 0N 113 3W
109 Whiskey Jack, L., Canada 58 25N 101 55W
115 Whistler, U.S.A. 30 50N 88 10W
112 Whitby, Canada 43 50N 78 50W
12 Whitby, England 54 29N 0 37W
95 Whitcombe, Mt., New Zealand 43 12S 171 0E
95 Whitcombe, P., New Zealand 43 12S 171 0E
107 White B., Canada 50 0N 56 35W
101 White I., N.Z. 37 30S 177 13E
113 White I., Canada 45 17N 76 35W
117 White L., U.S.A. 29 45N 92 30W
119 White Mts., Calif., U.S.A. 37 30N 118 6W
113 White, Mts., N.H., U.S.A. 44 15N 71 15W
117 White, R., Ark., U.S.A. 36 28N 93 55W
118 White, R., Colo., U.S.A. 40 8N 108 52W
114 White, R., Ind., U.S.A. 39 25N 86 30W
116 White, R., S.D., U.S.A. 43 10N 102 52W
107 White Bear Res., Canada 48 10N 57 05W
118 White Bird, U.S.A. 45 46N 116 21W
114 White Butte, U.S.A. 46 23N 103 25W
116 White City, U.S.A. 38 50N 96 45W
99 White Cliffs, Australia 30 50S 143 10E
101 White Cliffs, N.Z. 43 26S 171 55E
117 White Deer, U.S.A. 35 30N 101 8W
116 White Hall, U.S.A. 39 25N 90 27W

* Incorporated within the county of Cumbria

MAP
113 White Haven, U.S.A. 41 3N 75 47W
13 Whitehorse, Vale of, Eng. 51 37N 1 30W
87 White Nile = Nil el Abyad, Bahr, Sudan 9 30N 31 40E
87 White Nile Dam, Sudan 15 24N 32 30E
106 White Otter L., Canada 49 5N 91 55W
108 White Pass, Canada 59 40N 135 3W
84 White Plains, Liberia 6 28N 10 40W
113 White Plains, U.S.A. 41 2N 73 44W
106 White River, Canada 48 35N 85 20W
93 White River, S. Africa 25 20S 31 00E
116 White River, U.S.A. 43 48N 100 5W
113 White River Junc., U.S.A. 43 38N 72 20W
54 White Russia = Byelorussia, SSR, USSR 53 30N 27 0E
52 White Sea = Beloye More, U.S.S.R. 66 30N 38 0E
118 White Sulphur Springs, Mont., U.S.A. 46 35N 111 0W
118 White Sulphur Springs, W. Va., U.S.A. 37 50N 80 16W
85 White Volta, R., (Volta Blanche), Ghana 10 0N 1 0W
108 Whitecourt, Canada 54 10N 115 45W
117 Whiteface, U.S.A. 33 35N 102 40W
113 Whitefield, U.S.A. 44 23N 71 37W
118 Whitefish, U.S.A. 48 25N 114 22W
109 Whitefish L., Canada 62 35N 107 20W
114 Whitefish Pt., U.S.A. 46 45N 85 0W
107 Whitegull, L., Canada 55 30N 64 40W
114 Whitehall, Mich., U.S.A. 43 21N 86 20W
118 Whitehall, Mont., U.S.A. 45 52N 112 4W
113 Whitehall, N.Y., U.S.A. 43 32N 73 28W
116 Whitehall, Wis., U.S.A. 44 20N 91 19W
12 Whitehaven, Eng. 54 33N 3 35W
104 Whitehorse, Canada 60 45N 135 10W
13 Whitehorse, Vale of, Eng. 51 37N 1 30W
98 Whiteman Ra., Territory of New Guinea 5 54S 149 56E
109 Whitemouth, Canada 50 0N 96 10W
108 Whitesail, L., Canada 53 35N 127 45W
113 Whitesboro, N.Y., U.S.A. 43 8N 75 20W
117 Whitesboro, Tex., U.S.A. 33 40N 96 58W
116 Whitetail, U.S.A. 48 54N 105 15W
115 Whiteville, U.S.A. 34 20N 78 40W
114 Whitewater, U.S.A. 42 50N 88 45W
119 Whitewater Baldy, Mt., U.S.A. 33 20N 108 44W
106 Whitewater L., Canada 50 50N 89 10W
98 Whitewood, Australia 21 28S 143 30E
109 Whitewood, Canada 50 20N 102 20W
100 Whitfield, Austral. 36 42S 146 24E
14 Whithorn, Scot. 54 55N 4 25W
101 Whitianga, N.Z. 36 47S 175 41E
113 Whitman, U.S.A. 42 4N 70 55W
115 Whitmire, U.S.A. 34 33N 81 40W
112 Whitney, Canada 45 31N 78 14W
119 Whitney, Mt., U.S.A. 36 35N 118 14W
113 Whitney Pt., U.S.A. 42 19N 75 59W
13 Whitstable, Eng. 51 21N 1 2E
98 Whitsunday I., Austral. 20 15S 149 4E
104 Whittier, Alaska 60 46N 148 48W
107 Whittle, C., Canada 50 11N 60 8W
100 Whittlesea, Australia 37 27S 145 9E
100 Whitton, Australia 34 30S 146 6E
115 Whitwell, U.S.A. 35 15N 85 30W
109 Wholdaia L., Canada 60 40N 104 20W
99 Whyalla, S. Australia 33 2S 137 30E
112 Wiarton, Canada 44 50N 81 10W
84 Wiawso, Ghana 6 10N 2 25W
28 Wiazow, Poland 50 50N 17 10E
116 Wibaux, U.S.A. 47 0N 104 13W
117 Wichita, U.S.A. 37 40N 97 29W
117 Wichita Falls, U.S.A. 33 57N 98 30W
14 Wick, Scotland 58 26N 3 5W
119 Wickenburg, U.S.A. 33 58N 112 45W
117 Wickett, U.S.A. 31 37N 102 58W
112 Wickliffe, U.S.A. 41 46N 81 29W
15 Wicklow, Ireland 53 0N 6 2W
15 Wicklow ♦, Ireland 52 59N 6 25W
15 Wicklow Hd., Ireland 52 59N 6 3W
28 Widawa, Poland 51 27N 18 51E
98 Wide B., Territory of New Guinea 4 52S 152 0E
12 Widnes, England 53 22N 2 44W
24 Wiek, Germany 54 37N 13 17E
28 Wielbark, Poland 53 24N 20 55E
28 Wieleń, Poland 52 53N 16 9E
27 Wieliczka, Poland 50 0N 20 5E
28 Wielun, Poland 51 15N 18 40E
27 Wien, Austria 48 12N 16 22E
27 Wiener Neustadt, Aust. 47 49N 16 16E
28 Wieprz, R., Koszalin, Poland 54 26N 16 35E
28 Wieprz, R., Lublin, Pol. 51 15N 22 50E
16 Wierden, Netherlands 52 22N 6 35E
28 Wieruszów, Poland 51 19N 18 9E
25 Wiesbaden, Germany 50 7N 8 17E
25 Wiesental, Germany 49 15N 8 30E
12 Wigan, England 53 33N 2 38W
116 Wiggins, Colo., U.S.A. 40 16N 104 3W
117 Wiggins, Miss., U.S.A. 30 53N 89 9W
•13 Wight, I. of, Eng. 50 40N 1 20W
14 Wigtown, Scot. 54 52N 4 27W
†14 Wigtown ♦, Scot. 54 53N 4 45W
14 Wigtown B., Scot. 54 46N 4 15W
25 Wil, Switzerland 47 28N 9 3E
27 Wilamowice, Poland 49 55N 19 9E
116 Wilber, U.S.A. 40 34N 96 59W
112 Wilberforce, Canada 45 0N 78 15W
117 Wilburton, U.S.A. 34 55N 95 15W
100 Wilcannia, Australia 31 30S 143 26E
112 Wilcox, U.S.A. 41 34N 78 43W
24 Wildbad, Germany 48 44N 8 32E
24 Wildeshausen, Germany 52 54N 8 25E
26 Wildon, Austria 46 52N 15 31E

* Created a county, separate from Hampshire

† Incorporated within the region of Dumfries & Galloway

MAP
116 Wildrose, U.S.A. 48 36N 103 17W
26 Wildspitze, Austria 46 53N 10 53E
114 Wildwood, U.S.A. 39 5N 74 46W
98 Wilhelm Mt., North East New Guinea 5 57S 145 0E
24 Wilhelm-Pieck-Stadt Guben, Ger. 51 59N 14 48E
5 Wilhelm II Coast, Antarctica 67 0S 90 0E
127 Wilhelmina, Mt., Surinam 3 50N 56 30W
26 Wilhelmsburg, Austria 48 6N 15 36E
24 Wilhelmsburg, Germany 53 28N 10 1E
24 Wilhelmshaven, Ger. 53 30N 8 9E
92 Wilhelmstal, S.W. Afr. 21 58S 16 21E
5 Wilkes Land, Antarc 69 0S 120 0E
113 Wilkes-Barre, U.S.A. 41 15N 75 52W
115 Wilkesboro, U.S.A. 36 10N 81 9W
109 Wilkie, Canada 52 27N 108 42W
112 Wilkinsburg, U.S.A. 40 26N 79 50W
118 Willamina, U.S.A. 45 9N 123 32W
118 Willapa, B., U.S.A. 46 44N 124 0W
119 Willard, N.M., U.S.A. 34 35N 106 1W
118 Willard, Utah, U.S.A. 41 28N 112 1W
98 Willaumez Pen., Territory of New Guinea 5 3S 150 3E
119 Willcox, U.S.A. 32 13N 109 53W
121 Willemstad, Curacao 12 5N 69 0W
100 William Mt., Australia 37 11S 142 33E
119 Williams, U.S.A. 35 16N 112 11W
108 Williams Lake, Canada 52 20N 122 10W
115 Williamsburg, Ky., U.S.A. 36 45N 84 10W
112 Williamsburg, Pa., U.S.A. 40 27N 78 14W
114 Williamsburg, Va., U.S.A. 37 17N 76 44W
112 Williamson, N.Y., U.S.A. 43 14N 77 15W
114 Williamson, W. Va., U.S.A. 37 46N 82 17W
112 Williamsport, U.S.A. 41 18N 77 1W
115 Williamston, U.S.A. 35 50N 77 5W
100 Williamstown, Austral. 37 46S 144 58E
113 Williamstown, Mass., U.S.A. 42 41N 73 12W
113 Williamstown, N.Y., U.S.A. 43 25N 75 54W
117 Williamsville, U.S.A. 37 0N 90 33W
113 Willimantic, U.S.A. 41 45N 72 12W
92 Williston, S. Africa 31 20S 20 53E
115 Williston, Fla, U.S.A. 29 25N 82 28W
116 Williston, N.D., U.S.A. 48 10N 103 35W
118 Willits, U.S.A. 39 28N 123 17W
116 Willmar, U.S.A. 45 5N 95 0W
112 Willoughby, U.S.A. 41 38N 81 26W
109 Willow Bunch, Canada 49 20N 105 35W
116 Willow Lake, U.S.A. 44 40N 97 40W
108 Willow River, Canada 54 6N 122 28W
117 Willow Springs, U.S.A. 37 0N 92 0W
100 Willow Tree, Australia 31 40S 150 45E
92 Willowmore, S. Africa 33 15S 23 30E
98 Willows, Australia 23 45S 147 25E
118 Willows, U.S.A. 39 30N 122 10W
117 Wills Pt., U.S.A. 32 42N 95 57W
99 Willunga, Australia 35 15S 138 30E
114 Wilmete, U.S.A. 42 6N 87 44W
114 Wilmington, Del., U.S.A. 39 45N 75 32W
114 Wilmington, Ill., U.S.A. 41 19N 88 10W
115 Wilmington, N.C., U.S.A. 34 14N 77 54W
114 Wilmington, Ohio, U.S.A. 39 29N 83 46W
118 Wilsall, U.S.A. 45 59N 110 4W
115 Wilson, U.S.A. 35 44N 77 54W
119 Wilson, Mt., U.S.A. 37 55N 105 3W
100 Wilson's Prom., Austral. 39 5S 146 28E
24 Wilster, Germany 53 55N 9 23E
116 Wilton, U.S.A. 47 12N 100 53W
13 Wiltshire ♦, Egn. 51 20N 2 0W
16 Wiltz, Luxembourg 49 57N 5 55E
96 Wiluna, Australia 26 40S 120 25E
19 Wimereux, France 50 45N 1 37E
100 Wimmera, Austral. 36 30S 142 0E
100 Wimmera, R., Australia 36 48S 142 50E
92 Winburg, S. Afr. 28 30S 27 2E
113 Winch, U.S.A. 42 26N 71 9W
100 Winchelsea, Australia 38 10S 144 1E
113 Winchendon, U.S.A. 42 40N 72 3W
13 Winchester, Eng. 51 4N 1 19W
113 Winchester, Conn., U.S.A. 41 53N 73 9W
118 Winchester, Idaho, U.S.A. 46 11N 116 32W
114 Winchester, Ind., U.S.A. 40 10N 84 56W
114 Winchester, Ky., U.S.A. 38 0N 84 8W
113 Winchester, N.H., U.S.A. 42 47N 72 22W
115 Winchester, Tenn., U.S.A. 35 11N 86 8W
114 Winchester, Va., U.S.A. 39 14N 78 8W
118 Wind, R., U.S.A. 43 30N 109 30W
118 Wind River Range, Mts., U.S.A. 43 0N 109 30W
112 Windber, U.S.A. 40 14N 78 50W
115 Winder, U.S.A. 34 0N 83 40W
99 Windera, Australia 26 17S 151 51E
12 Windermere, Eng. 54 24N 2 56W
108 Windfall, Canada 54 12N 116 25W
92 Windhoek, S.W. Africa 22 35S 17 4E
26 Windischgarsten, Aust. 47 42N 14 21E
116 Windom, U.S.A. 43 48N 95 3W
99 Windorah, Australia 25 24S 142 36E
119 Window Rock, U.S.A. 35 47N 109 4W
13 Windrush, R., Eng. 51 48N 1 35W
100 Windsor, Austral. 33 34S 150 44E
107 Windsor, N.S., Canada 44 59N 64 5W
106 Windsor, Ont., Canada 42 25N 83 0W
13 Windsor, England 51 28N 0 36W
116 Windsor, Col., U.S.A. 40 33N 104 55W

MAP
113 Windsor, Conn., U.S.A. 41 50N 72 40W
116 Windsor, Miss., U.S.A. 38 32N 93 31W
113 Windsor, N.Y., U.S.A. 42 5N 75 37W
113 Windsor, Vt., U.S.A. 43 30N 72 25W
92 Windsorton, S. Africa 28 16S 24 44E
121 Windward Is., W. Ind. 13 0N 63 0W
121 Windward Passage, Caribbean 20 0N 74 0W
109 Winefred L., Canada 55 30N 110 30W
87 Winejok, Sudan 9 1N 27 30E
117 Winfield, U.S.A. 37 15N 97 0W
100 Wingen Mt., Australia 31 50S 150 58E
100 Wingham, Australia 31 48S 152 22E
106 Wingham, Canada 43 55N 81 25W
118 Winifred, U.S.A. 47 30N 109 28W
106 Winisk, Canada 55 20N 85 15W
106 Winisk L., Canada 52 55N 87 40W
106 Winisk, R., Canada 54 40N 87 0W
117 Wink, U.S.A. 31 49N 103 9W
109 Winkler, Canada 49 15N 98 0W
26 Winklern, Austria 46 52N 12 52E
85 Winneba, Ghana 5 25N 0 36W
116 Winnebago, U.S.A. 43 43N 94 8W
114 Winnebago L., U.S.A. 44 0N 88 20W
118 Winnemucca, U.S.A. 41 0N 117 45W
118 Winnemucca, L., U.S.A. 40 25N 19 21W
116 Winner, U.S.A. 43 23N 99 52W
114 Winnetka, U.S.A. 42 8N 87 46W
118 Winnett, U.S.A. 47 2N 108 28W
117 Winnfield, U.S.A. 31 57N 92 38W
116 Winnibigoshish L., U.S.A. 47 25N 94 12W
109 Winnipeg, Canada 49 50N 97 15W
109 Winnipeg, L., Canada 52 30N 98 0W
109 Winnipeg, R., Canada 50 25N 95 30W
109 Winnipeg Beach, Can. 50 30N 96 58W
109 Winnipegosis, Canada 52 40N 100 0W
109 Winnipegosis L., Can. 52 40N 100 0W
117 Winnsboro, Lou, U.S.A. 32 10N 91 41W
115 Winnsboro, S.C., U.S.A. 34 23N 81 5W
116 Winnsboro, Tex., U.S.A. 32 56N 95 15W
107 Winokapau, L., Canada 53 15N 62 50W
117 Winona, Miss., U.S.A. 33 30N 89 42W
116 Winona, Wis., U.S.A. 44 2N 91 45W
113 Winooski, U.S.A. 44 31N 73 11W
16 Winschoten, Neth. 53 9N 7 3E
24 Winsen, Germany 52 40N 9 54E
24 Winsen, Ger. 53 20N 10 11E
119 Winslow, U.S.A. 35 2N 110 41W
113 Winstead, U.S.A. 41 55N 73 5W
115 Winston-Salem, U.S.A. 36 7N 80 15W
115 Winter Garden, U.S.A. 28 33N 81 35W
115 Winter Haven, U.S.A. 28 0N 81 42W
115 Winter Park, U.S.A. 28 34N 81 19W
24 Winterberg, Germany 51 12N 8 30E
117 Winters, U.S.A. 31 58N 99 58W
116 Winterset, U.S.A. 41 18N 94 0W
112 Wintersville, U.S.A. 40 23N 80 38W
16 Winterswijk, Neth. 51 58N 6 43E
25 Winterthur, Switzerland 47 30N 8 44E
116 Winthorp, U.S.A. 44 31N 94 25W
118 Winthrop, U.S.A. 48 27N 120 6W
98 Winton, Australia 22 21S 143 0E
101 Winton, New Zealand 46 8S 168 20E
115 Winton, N.C., U.S.A. 36 25N 76 58W
113 Winton, Pa., U.S.A. 41 27N 75 33W
12 Wirral, Eng. 53 25N 3 0W
12 Wisbech, England 52 39N 0 10E
116 Wisconsin ♦, U.S.A. 44 30N 90 0W
116 Wisconsin, R., U.S.A. 45 25N 89 45W
116 Wisconsin Dells, U.S.A. 43 38N 89 45W
116 Wisconsin Rapids, U.S.A. 44 25N 89 50W
14 Wishaw, Scot. 55 46N 3 55W
116 Wishek, U.S.A. 46 20N 99 35W
27 Wisła, Poland 49 38N 18 53E
28 Wisła, R., Poland 53 38N 18 47E
28 Wiślany, Zalew, Poland-U.S.S.R. 54 20N 19 50E
27 Wisłok, R., Poland 50 7N 22 25E
27 Wisłoka, R., Poland 49 50N 21 28E
24 Wismar, Germany 53 53N 11 23E
24 Wismar B., Germany 54 0N 11 15E
116 Wisner, U.S.A. 42 0N 96 46W
19 Wissant, France 50 52N 1 40E
19 Wissembourg, France 48 57N 7 57E
93 Witbank, S. Afr. 25 51S 29 14E
117 Witchita, U.S.A. 37 40N 97 22W
92 Witdraai, S. Africa 26 58S 20 48E
12 Witham, R., Eng. 53 3N 0 8W
12 Withernsea, Eng. 53 43N 0 2W
28 Witkowo, Poland 52 26N 17 45E
13 Witney, England 51 47N 1 29W
28 Witnica, Poland 52 41N 14 55E
92 Witnossob, R., S.W. Africa 23 0S 18 40E
24 Wittdün, Germany 54 38N 8 23E
24 Witten, Germany 51 26N 7 19E
24 Wittenberg, Germany 51 51N 12 39E
24 Wittenberge, Germany 53 0N 11 44E
24 Wittenburg, Germany 53 30N 11 4E
96 Wittenoom, Australia 22 15S 118 20E
24 Wittingen, Germany 52 43N 10 43E
25 Wittlich, Germany 50 0N 6 54E
24 Wittmund, Germany 53 39N 7 35E
24 Wittow, Germany 54 37N 13 21E
24 Wittstock, Germany 53 10N 12 30E
24 Witzenhausen, Ger. 51 20N 9 50E
87 Wiyeb, W., Ethiopia 7 15N 40 15E
28 Władysławowo, Poland 52 6N 18 28E
28 Wlen, Poland 51 0N 15 39E
73 Wlingi, Indonesia 8 5S 112 25E
28 Włocławek, Poland 52 40N 19 3E
28 Włodawa, Poland 51 33N 23 31E
28 Włoszczowa, Poland 50 50N 19 55E
113 Woburn, U.S.A. 42 31N 71 7W
100 Wodonga, Austral. 36 5S 146 50E
27 Wodzisław Sl., Poland 50 1N 18 26E
19 Woerth, France 48 57N 7 45E
19 Woevre, France 49 15N 5 45E

MAP
73 Wokam, I., Indonesia 5 45S 134 28E
108 Woking, Canada 55 35N 118 50W
28 Wolbrom, Poland 50 24N 19 45E
24 Woldegk, Germany 53 27N 13 35E
118 Wolf Creek, U.S.A. 47 1N 112 2W
116 Wolf Point, U.S.A. 48 6N 105 40W
113 Wolfe I., Canada 44 7N 76 27W
24 Wolfenbüttel, Germany 52 10N 10 33E
108 Wolfenden, Canada 52 0N 119 25W
98 Wolfram, Australia 17 6S 145 0E
26 Wolfsberg, Austria 46 50N 14 52E
24 Wolfsburg, Germany 52 27N 10 49E
24 Wolgast, Germany 54 3N 13 46E
25 Wolhusen, Switzerland 47 4N 8 4E
28 Wolin, Poland 53 40N 14 37E
128 Wollaston, Islas, Chile 55 40S 67 30W
109 Wollaston L., Canada 58 20N 103 30W
104 Wollaston Pen., Can. 69 30N 113 0W
100 Wollondilly, R., Austral. 34 0S 150 27E
100 Wollongong, Australia 34 25S 150 54E
92 Wolmaransstad, S. Afr. 27 12S 26 13E
24 Wolmirstedt, Germany 52 15N 11 35E
28 Wołomin, Poland 52 19N 21 15E
28 Wołow, Poland 51 20N 16 38E
99 Wolseley, Australia 36 14S 140 58E
109 Wolseley, Canada 50 25N 103 15W
92 Wolseley, S. Africa 33 26S 19 7E
4 Wolstenholme Sound, Greenland 74 30N 75 0W
28 Wolsztyn, Poland 52 8N 16 5E
13 Wolverhampton, England 52 35N 2 6W
87 Wombera, Ethiopia 10 45N 35 49E
100 Won Wron, Australia 38 23S 146 45E
99 Wondai, Australia 26 20S 151 49E
91 Wonder Gorge, Zam. 14 40S 29 0E
100 Wongalorroo L., Australia 31 35S 144 2E
76 Wŏnjui, South Korea 37 30N 127 59E
73 Wonosari, Indonesia 7 38S 110 36E
76 Wŏnsan, North Korea 39 11N 127 27E
100 Wonthaggi, Australia 38 29S 145 31E
109 Wood, Mt., Canada 49 13N 106 13W
108 Wood Buffalo Pk., Can. 59 30N 113 0W
116 Wood Lake, U.S.A. 42 38N 100 14W
112 Woodbridge, Canada 43 48N 79 35W
100 Woodend, Austral. 37 20N 144 33E
118 Woodland, U.S.A. 38 40N 121 50W
98 Woodlark I., Territory of Papua 9 1S 148 0E
108 Woodpecker, Canada 53 30N 122 40W
109 Woodridge, Canada 49 20N 96 20W
96 Woodroffe, Mt., Australia 26 20S 131 45E
119 Woodruff, Ariz., U.S.A. 34 51N 110 1W
118 Woodruff, Utah, U.S.A. 41 30N 111 4W
100 Woodside, Australia 38 28S 146 53E
96 Woods, L., Australia 17 50S 133 30E
107 Woods, L., Canada 54 30N 65 0W
109 Woods, Lake of the, Canada-U.S.A. 49 30N 94 30W
100 Woodside, Australia 38 28S 146 53E
98 Woodstock, Australia 19 22S 142 45E
107 Woodstock, N.B., Can. 46 11N 67 37W
106 Woodstock, Ont., Can. 43 10N 80 45W
13 Woodstock, Eng. 51 51N 1 20W
116 Woodstock, Ill., U.S.A. 42 17N 88 30W
65 Woodstock, N.H., U.S.A. 43 59N 71 41W
113 Woodstock, Vt., U.S.A. 43 37N 72 31W
113 Woodsville, U.S.A. 44 10N 72 0W
101 Woodville, N.Z. 40 20S 175 53E
117 Woodville, U.S.A. 30 45N 94 25W
117 Woodward, U.S.A. 36 24N 99 28W
100 Woolamai, C., Austral. 38 30S 145 23E
100 Woomargama, Austral. 35 45S 147 15E
99 Woombye, Australia 26 40S 152 55E
100 Woomelang, Australia 35 37S 142 40E
99 Woomera, Australia 31 9S 136 56E
100 Woonona, Australia 34 32S 150 49E
113 Woonsocker, U.S.A. 42 0N 71 30W
116 Woonsockett, U.S.A. 44 5N 98 15W
96 Wooramel, R., Austral. 25 30S 114 30E
100 Woorinen, Australia 35 14S 143 27E
99 Wooroorooka, Austral. 29 0S 145 41E
112 Wooster, U.S.A. 40 38N 81 55W
13 Worcester, Eng. 52 12N 2 12W
113 Worcester, Mass., U.S.A. 42 14N 71 49W
113 Worcester, N.Y., U.S.A. 42 35N 74 45W
•13 Worcestershire ♦, Eng. 52 13N 2 10W
26 Wörgl, Austria 47 29N 12 3E
85 Worikambo, Ghana 10 43N 0 1W
12 Workington, Eng. 54 39N 3 34W
12 Worksop, Eng. 53 19N 1 9W
16 Workum, Netherlands 52 59N 5 26E
118 Worland, U.S.A. 44 0N 107 59W
19 Wormhoudt, France 50 52N 2 28E
25 Worms, Germany 49 37N 8 21E
117 Wortham, U.S.A. 31 48N 96 27W
26 Wörther See, Aust. 46 37N 14 19E
13 Worthing, Eng. 50 49N 0 21W
116 Worthington, U.S.A. 43 35N 95 30W
73 Wosi, Indonesia 0 15S 128 0E
87 Wota (Shoa Ghimirra), Ethiopia 7 4N 35 51E
83 Wour, Chad. 21 14N 16 0E
73 Wowoni, I., Indonesia 4 5S 123 5E
28 Woźniki, Poland 50 36N 19 2E
104 Wrangell, Alaska 56 30N 132 25W
14 Wrath, C., Scot. 58 38N 5 0W
116 Wray, U.S.A. 40 8N 102 18W
12 Wrekin, The, Mt., England 52 41N 2 35W
115 Wrens, U.S.A. 33 13N 82 23W
12 Wrexham, Wales 53 5N 3 0W
24 Wriezen, Germany 52 43N 14 9E
108 Wright, Canada 51 45N 121 30W
73 Wright, Philippines 11 42N 125 2E
107 Wright, Mt., Canada 52 40N 67 25W
119 Wrightson, Mt., U.S.A. 31 49N 110 56W

* Incorporated within the county of Hereford and Worcester

The following are new or considerably enlarged counties in England and Wales and new regions in Scotland created by the Local Government Act 1972. In Northern Ireland 26 new districts were created. The co-ordinates will help to locate these new areas on the maps on pages 12-13, 14 and 15.